FINANCIAL STATEMENT ANALYSIS

EDITED BY

Ray Ball
S. P. Kothari

*William E. Simon Graduate School
of Business Administration
University of Rochester*

McGRAW-HILL, INC.
New York   St. Louis   San Francisco
Auckland   Bogotá   Caracas   Lisbon   London
Madrid   Mexico City   Milan   Montreal   New Delhi
San Juan   Singapore   Sydney   Tokyo   Toronto

McGraw-Hill Series in Advanced Topics in Finance and Accounting

CONSULTING EDITORS
Ray Ball
Clifford W. Smith, Jr.

Ball and Kothari: Financial Statement Analysis
Ball and Smith: The Economics of Accounting Policy Choice
Chew: The New Corporate Finance: Where Theory Meets Practice
James and Smith: Studies in Financial Institutions: Commercial Banks
James and Smith: Studies in Financial Institutions: Nonbank Intermediaries
Schwert and Smith: Empirical Research in Capital Markets
Smith: The Modern Theory of Corporate Finance

FINANCIAL STATEMENT ANALYSIS

Copyright © 1994 by McGraw-Hill, Inc. All rights reserved. Printed in the United States of America. Except as permitted under the United States Copyright Act of 1976, no part of this publication may be reproduced or distributed in any form or by any means, or stored in a data base or retrieval system, without the prior written permission of the publisher.

 This book is printed on recycled, acid-free paper containing 10% postconsumer waste.

2 3 4 5 6 7 8 9 0 DOH DOH 9 0 9 8 7 6 5 4

ISBN 0-07-004645-X

The editors were Kenneth A. MacLeod and Peitr Bohen;
the production supervisor was Elizabeth J. Strange.
The cover was designed by Karen K. Quigley.
R. R. Donnelley & Sons Company was printer and binder.

Library of Congress Cataloging-in-Publication Data

Financial statement analysis / edited by Ray Ball, S. P. Kothari.
    p.   cm. — (McGraw-Hill series in advanced topics in finance and accounting)
    Includes bibliographical references.
    ISBN 0-07-004645-X
    1. Investment analysis.   2. Financial statements.   3. Rate of return.   4. Corporations—Valuation.   I. Ball, Ray, (date).
II. Kothari. S. P.   III. Series.
HG4529.F56   1994
657'.3—dc20   93-40433

CONTENTS

INTRODUCTION vii
ACKNOWLEDGMENTS ix

I FINANCIAL STATEMENT INFORMATION AND STOCK PRICES   1

AGGREGATE ACCOUNTING EARNINGS CAN EXPLAIN MOST OF SECURITY
RETURNS: THE CASE OF LONG RETURN INTERVALS   10
Peter D. Easton, Trevor S. Harris, and James A. Ohlson

INFORMATION IN PRICES ABOUT FUTURE EARNINGS: IMPLICATIONS FOR
EARNINGS RESPONSE COEFFICIENTS   34
S. P. Kothari and Richard G. Sloan

EARNINGS RELEASES, ANOMALIES, AND THE BEHAVIOR OF SECURITY
RETURNS   63
George Foster, Chris Olsen, and Terry Shevlin

ASSOCIATION BETWEEN ACCOUNTING PERFORMANCE MEASURES AND
STOCK PRICES: A TEST OF THE LIFE CYCLE HYPOTHESIS   93
Joseph H. Anthony and K. Ramesh

INFORMATION TRANSFERS   118
Katherine Schipper

EVIDENCE THAT STOCK PRICES DO NOT FULLY REFLECT THE IMPLICATIONS
OF CURRENT EARNINGS FOR FUTURE EARNINGS   129
Victor L. Bernard and Jacob K. Thomas

	FINANCIAL STATEMENT ANALYSIS AND THE PREDICTION OF STOCK RETURNS Jane A. Ou and Steven H. Penman	165
	THE EARNINGS-PRICE ANOMALY Ray Ball	200
II	**ACCRUALS, CASH FLOWS, AND ALTERNATIVE ACCOUNTING METHODS**	227
	THE INCREMENTAL INFORMATION CONTENT OF CASH-FLOW COMPONENTS Joshua Livnat and Paul Zarowin	231
	ON ASSESSING A FIRM'S CASH GENERATING ABILITY Ray G. Stephens and Vijay Govindarajan	253
	EVIDENCE ON THE CHOICE OF INVENTORY ACCOUNTING METHODS: LIFO VERSUS FIFO Nicholas Dopuch and Morton Pincus	269
	RESTATING FINANCIAL STATEMENTS FOR ALTERNATIVE GAAPS: IS IT WORTH THE EFFORT? James P. Dawson, Peter M. Neupert, and Clyde P. Stickney	301
	HOW WELL DO STATEMENT NO. 33 EARNINGS EXPLAIN STOCK RETURNS? William H. Beaver and Stephen G. Ryan	310
	THE MARKET VALUATION IMPLICATIONS OF NET PERIODIC PENSION COST COMPONENTS Mary E. Barth, William H. Beaver, and Wayne R. Landsman	316
III	**FORECASTING EARNINGS AND INVESTMENT PERFORMANCE USING FINANCIAL STATEMENT INFORMATION**	353
	SOME TIME SERIES PROPERTIES OF ACCOUNTING INCOME Ray Ball and Ross Watts	358
	FURTHER EVIDENCE OF THE TIME SERIES PROPERTIES OF ACCOUNTING INCOME LeRoy D. Brooks and Dale A. Buckmaster	377
	THE INFORMATION CONTENT OF NONEARNINGS ACCOUNTING NUMBERS AS EARNINGS PREDICTORS Jane A. Ou	392
	AN EVALUATION OF ALTERNATIVE PROXIES FOR THE MARKET'S ASSESSMENT OF UNEXPECTED EARNINGS Lawrence D. Brown, Robert L. Hagerman, Paul A. Griffin, and Mark E. Zmijewski	412
	ANALYSTS' USE OF INFORMATION ABOUT PERMANENT AND TRANSITORY EARNINGS COMPONENTS IN FORECASTING ANNUAL EPS Ashiq Ali, April Klein, and James Rosenfeld	447

THE EFFECT OF VALUE LINE INVESTMENT SURVEY RANK CHANGES ON
COMMON STOCK PRICES 465
Scott E. Stickel

IV FINANCIAL STATEMENT INFORMATION IN DEBT AND EQUITY RISK ASSESSMENT 487

THE EFFECT OF BOND RATING AGENCY ANNOUNCEMENTS ON BOND AND
STOCK PRICES 492
John R. M. Hand, Robert W. Holthausen, and Richard W. Leftwich

FINANCIAL RATIOS AND THE PROBABILISTIC PREDICTION OF BANKRUPTCY 512
James A. Ohlson

PREDICTING BANKRUPTCY: THE VALUE LINE RELATIVE FINANCIAL STRENGTH
SYSTEM VS. THE ZETA BANKRUPTCY CLASSIFICATION APPROACH 535
Edward I. Altman and Joseph Spivack

PREDICTION OF BETA FROM INVESTMENT FUNDAMENTALS: PART ONE 544
Barr Rosenberg and James Guy

PREDICTION OF BETA FROM INVESTMENT FUNDAMENTALS: PART TWO 558
Barr Rosenberg and James Guy

WHAT DETERMINES PRICE-EARNINGS RATIOS? 567
William H. Beaver and Dale Morse

ON THE ASSOCIATION BETWEEN OPERATING LEVERAGE AND RISK 579
Baruch Lev

ECONOMIC DETERMINANTS OF THE RELATION BETWEEN EARNINGS
CHANGES AND STOCK RETURNS 594
Ray Ball, S. P. Kothari, and Ross L. Watts

THE CROSS-SECTION OF EXPECTED STOCK RETURNS 611
Eugene F. Fama and Kenneth R. French

V FINANCIAL STATEMENT INFORMATION AND CORPORATE CONTROL 651

THE EVALUATION OF AN ACQUISITION TARGET 655
Stewart Myers

PREDICTING TAKEOVER TARGETS: A METHODOLOGICAL AND EMPIRICAL
ANALYSIS 663
Krishna G. Palepu

THE EFFECTS OF MANAGEMENT BUYOUTS ON OPERATING PERFORMANCE
AND VALUE 695
Steven N. Kaplan

CAMPEAU'S ACQUISITION OF FEDERATED: VALUE DESTROYED OR VALUE ADDED? 733
Steven N. Kaplan

CONSEQUENCES OF LEVERAGED BUYOUTS 755
Krishna G. Palepu

REFERENCES 771

INTRODUCTION

This collection brings together thirty-four previously published articles on financial statement analysis. We have included several literature survey articles and have provided an introduction to each topic area. These put the individual articles into perspective and provide exposure to a literature that is much wider than can be contained in one collection.

To be selected for inclusion, an article had to satisfy three criteria:

1. *Results are of use in financial statement analysis:* the article provides insights that are of value in the practice of financial analysis.
2. *Approach is empirical:* the article presents data on financial statements and/or how they are used in any of a variety of settings.
3. *There is some underlying theory:* the results are based at least in part on some underlying structure (however loose or formal) that allows readers to generalize and thus to use the results in their own settings.

The articles in this collection, and the criteria used to select them, reflect the revolutionary changes that have occurred in our knowledge of financial statements, and in their use, over the past twenty-five years. During that period, financial statement analysis has been transformed from a largely *ad hoc* field, rife with untested and often illogical conjectures, into a comparatively sophisticated discipline. It has been transformed by a wide range of closely related developments, including:

- Revolutionary changes in the theory of financial markets
- The now-widespread use of empirical methods to test theory
- The availability of many large, inexpensive, and accessible financial databases, containing both financial statement and financial market information, for both practitioner and academic use

- A breathtaking reduction in the computing costs of analyzing financial databases
- An explosion in the number of business school graduates trained in sophisticated methods of financial statement analysis
- The rapid growth in assets managed by financial institutions that are equipped with well-staffed, well-funded, professional research facilities

The future generation of financial analysts now must be trained to at least understand the types of empirical analyses contained in this literature. While it is designed primarily for courses on financial statement analysis, the collection also will be useful in capital markets, investments, and security analysis courses and in accounting theory or other research-level courses in accounting. It can be used in conjunction with cases or with texts that cover more of the mechanical and institutional aspects of financial statement analysis.

The articles are organized into five parts. The first part covers the relation between financial statement information and the stock market, which is where financial statement information is most widely and actively used. Emphasis is placed on reported earnings information, due in turn to the emphasis on earnings by financial analysts and to its primary role in determining value in the long term. The part contains six contemporary contributions and two survey articles. The second part introduces cash flows and accounting accruals, which are the two major components of reported earnings. It then includes four articles on alternative methods of accounting and their effects on analyzing financial statements. The third part covers earnings forecasting, including: statistical time series models that use only past earnings to forecast future earnings; models that use information in financial statements, other than earnings, to forecast earnings; properties of professional financial analysts' earnings forecasts; and the performance of the Value Line Investment Survey. The fourth part introduces the analysis of risk, from the perspectives of both lenders and stockholders. The studies here investigate the determinants of investment risk (and P/E ratios) in the stock market and the determinants of risk (and bankruptcy) in the bond market. The final part focuses on the role of financial statement analysis in the more unusual context of corporate control contests, including predicting acquisition targets, management buyouts, and leveraged buyouts.

Because the part themes are not mutually exclusive, the organization we have chosen is unlikely to be optimal for all courses of study. We therefore recommend that instructors experiment with the order in which the articles are prescribed. Each part begins with an introduction that places the part in perspective and briefly describes the articles contained in it. In each part's introduction, references to articles reproduced in this collection are set in **bold**. Other references are to sources that are listed at the end of the collection.

The original publication of the articles was approximately evenly distributed between accounting and finance journals. These include *Accounting Horizons, The Accounting Review, Financial Analysts Journal, Journal of Accounting and Economics, Journal of Accounting Research, Journal of Finance, Journal of Financial and Quantitative Analysis, Journal of Financial Economics,* and *Midland Corporate Finance Journal.* We acknowledge the cooperation of all the authors and publishers represented in the collection and our indebtedness to many authors who have contributed to a vibrant literature but whose work we have not been able to include. We also gratefully acknowledge the encouragement and support of Kenneth MacLeod at McGraw-Hill and the professional secretarial assistance of Jane Muellner.

Ray Ball
S. P. Kothari

ACKNOWLEDGMENTS

The editors wish to thank the following authors for permission to reprint their articles:

Professor Ashiq Ali, Stern School of Business, New York University
Professor Edward I. Altman, Stern School of Business, New York University
Professor Joseph H. Anthony, Eli Broad Graduate School of Management, Michigan State University
Professor Mary E. Barth, Graduate School of Business Administration, Harvard University
Professor William H. Beaver, Graduate School of Business, Stanford University
Professor Victor L. Bernard, School of Business Administration, The University of Michigan
Professor Leroy D. Brooks, College of Business Administration, University of S. Carolina
Professor Lawrence D. Brown, School of Management, SUNY Buffalo
Professor Dale A. Buckmaster, College of Business & Economics, University of Delaware
Mr. James P. Dawson, Manager, Teradyne, Inc., Waltham, MA
Professor Nicholas Dopuch, Olin School of Business, Washington University
Professor Roland E. Dukes, School of Business Administration, University of Washington
Professor Peter D. Easton, Graduate School of Business, University of Chicago
Professor Eugene F. Fama, Graduate School of Business, University of Chicago
Professor George J. Foster, Graduate School of Business, Stanford University
Professor Kenneth R. French, Graduate School of Business, University of Chicago
Professor Vijay Govindarajan, Amos Tuck School of Business, Dartmouth College
Professor Paul A. Griffin, Graduate School of Management, University of California-Davis
Professor Robert L. Hagerman, School of Management, SUNY Buffalo
Professor John R.M. Hand, Kenan-Flagler Graduate School of Business, University of North Carolina
Professor Trevor S. Harris, Graduate School of Business, Columbia University

Professor Robert W. Holthausen, Wharton School, University of Pennsylvania
Professor Steven Kaplan, Graduate School of Business, University of Chicago
Professor April Klein, Stern School of Business, New York University
Professor Wayne R. Landsman, Graduate School of Management, University of Southern California
Professor Richard Leftwich, Graduate School of Business, University of Chicago
Professor Baruch Lev, Haas School of Business, University of California-Berkeley
Professor Joshua Livnat, Stern School of Business, New York University
Professor Dale C. Morse, College of Business Administration, University of Oregon
Professor Stewart C. Myers, Sloan School of Management, Massachusetts Institute of Technology
Mr. Peter M. Neupert, Senior Director, Microsoft Corporation
Professor James A. Ohlson, Graduate School of Business, Columbia University
Professor J. Christian Olsen, College of Business Administration, University of Texas at Austin
Professor Jane Ou, Leavey School of Business and Administration, Santa Clara University
Professor Krishna G. Palepu, Graduate School of Business Administration, Harvard University
Professor Stephen H. Penman, Haas School of Business, University of California at Berkeley
Professor Morton P. K. Pincus, Olin School of Business, Washington University
Professor Krishnamoorthy Ramesh, Kellogg Graduate School of Management, Northwestern University
Mr. Barr Rosenberg, Barr Rosenberg Investment Management
Professor James Rosenfeld, School of Business Administration, Emory University
Professor Stephen G. Ryan, Stern School of Business, New York University
Professor Katherine Schipper, Graduate School of Business, University of Chicago
Professor Terrence J. Shevlin, School of Business Administration, University of Washington
Professor Richard G. Sloan, Wharton School, University of Pennsylvania
Mr. Joseph Spivack, Analyst, Arnold Bernhard Company, Inc.
Professor Ray G. Stephens, College of Business Administration, Kent State University
Professor Scott E. Stickel, School of Business, LaSalle University
Professor Clyde P. Stickney, Amos Tuck School of Business Administration, Dartmouth College
Professor Jacob K. Thomas, Graduate School of Business, Columbia University
Professor Ross L. Watts, William E. Simon Graduate School of Business, University of Rochester
Professor Paul Zarowin, Stern School of Business, New York University
Professor Mark E. Zmijewski, Graduate School of Business, University of Chicago

The editors wish to acknowledge the sources of the articles reprinted in this volume:

American Accounting Association:
Foster, George, Chris Olsen, and Terry Shevlin, "Earnings Releases, Anomalies, and the Behavior of Security Returns," *The Accounting Review,* 59, (1984), pp. 574-603.
Schipper, Katherine, "Information Transfers," *Accounting Horizons,* December, (1990), pp. 97-107.

Stephens, Ray G. and Vijay Govindarajan, "On Assessing a Firm's Cash Generating Ability, *The Accounting Review,* 65, (1990), pp. 242-257.

Ali, Ashiq, April Klein, and James Rosenfeld, "Analysts' Use of Information About Permanent and Transitory Earnings Components in Forecasting Annual EPS," *The Accounting Review,* 67, (1992), pp. 183-198.

Ball, Ray, S. P. Kothari, and Ross L. Watts, "Economic Determinants of the Relation Between Earnings Changes and Stock Returns," *The Accounting Review,* 68, (1993), pp. 622-638.

American Finance Association

Ball, Ray and Ross L. Watts, "Some Time Series Properties of Accounting Income," *Journal of Finance,* 27, (1972), pp. 663-681.

Brooks, Leroy D. and Dale A. Buckmaster, "Further Evidence of the Time Series Properties of Accounting Income," *Journal of Finance,* 31, (1976), pp. 1359-1373.

Hand, John R.M., Robert W. Holthausen, and Richard W. Leftwich, "The Effect of Bond Rating Agency Announcements on Bond and Stock Prices," *Journal of Finance,* 47 (1986), pp. 733-752.

Fama, Eugene F. and Kenneth R. French, "The Cross-section of Expected Returns," *Journal of Finance,* 47, (1992), pp. 427-465.

Association for Investment Management and Research

Rosenberg, Barr and James Guy, "Prediction of Beta From Investment Fundamentals: Part I," *Financial Analysts Journal,* May-June, (1976), pp. 60-72.

Rosenberg, Barr and James Guy, "Prediction of Beta From Investment Fundamentals: Part II," *Financial Analysts Journal,* July-August, (1976), pp. 62-70.

Beaver, William H. and Dale Morse, "What Determines Price-earnings Ratios?," *Financial Analysts Journal,* July-August, (1978), pp. 65-76.

Altman, Edward I. and Joseph Spivack, "Predicting Bankruptcy: The Value Line Relative Financial Strength System vs. the ZETA Bankruptcy Classification Approach," *Financial Analysts Journal,* November-December, (1983), pp. 60-67.

Dawson, James P., Peter M. Neupert, and Clyde P. Stickney, "Restating Financial Statements for Alternative GAAPs: Is It Worth the Effort?," *Financial Analysts Journal,* November-December, (1980), pp. 38-46.

Beaver, William H. and Stephen G. Ryan, "How Well Do Statement No. 33 Earnings Explain Stock Returns," *Financial Analysts Journal,* September-October, (1985), pp. 66-71.

Institute of Professional Accounting

Ohlson, James A., "Financial Ratios and the Probabilistic Prediction of Bankruptcy," *Journal of Accounting Research,* 18, (1980), pp. 109-131.

Dopuch, Nicholas and Morton Pincus, "Evidence on the Choice of Inventory Accounting Methods: LIFO Versus FIFO," *Journal of Accounting Research,* 26, (1988), 28-59.

Ou, Jane, "The Information Content of Nonearnings Numbers as Earnings Predictors," *Journal of Accounting Research,* 28, (1990), pp. 144-163.

North Holland Publishing Co.:

Stickel, Scott E., "The Effect of Value Line Investment Survey Rank Changes on Common Stock Prices," *Journal of Financial Economics,* 14, (1985), pp. 121-143.

Palepu, Krishna, "Predicting Takeover Targets: A Methodological and Empirical Analysis," *Journal of Accounting & Economics,* 8, (1986), pp. 3-35.

Brown, Larry D., Paul A. Griffin, Robert L. Hagerman, and Mark E. Zmijewski, "An Evaluation of Alternative Proxies for the Market's Assessment of Unexpected Earnings," *Journal of Accounting & Economics,* 9, (1987), pp. 159-193.

Kaplan, Steven N., "The Effects of Management Buyouts on Operations and Value," *Journal of Financial Economics,* 24, (1989), pp. 217-254.

Ou, Jane and Steven H. Penman, "Financial Statement Analysis and the Prediction of Stock Returns," *Journal of Accounting & Economics,* 11, (1989), pp. 295-329.

Livnat, Joshua and Paul Zarowin, "The Incremental Information Content of Cash-flow Components," *Journal of Accounting & Economics,* 13, (1990), pp. 25-46.

Kaplan, Steven N., "Campeau's Acquisition of Federated: Value Destroyed or Added?," *Journal of Financial Economics,* 25, (1989), pp. 191-212.

Palepu, Krishna, "Consequences of Leveraged Buyouts," *Journal of Financial Economics,* 27, (1990), pp. 247-262.

Bernard, Victor L. and Jacob K. Thomas, "Evidence that Stock Prices Do Not Fully Reflect Implications of Current Earnings for Future Earnings," *Journal of Accounting & Economics,* 13, (1990), pp. 305-340.

Barth, Mary E., William H. Beaver, and Wayne Landsman, "The Market Valuation Implications of Net Periodic Pension Cost Components," *Journal of Accounting & Economics,* 15, (1992), pp. 27-62.

Easton, Peter D., Trevor S. Harris, and James A. Ohlson, "Accounting Earnings Can Explain Most of Security Returns: The Case of Long Event Windows," *Journal of Accounting & Economics,* 15, (1992), pp. 119-142.

Kothari, S. P. and Richard G. Sloan, "Information in Prices About Future Earnings: Implications for Earnings Response Coefficients," *Journal of Accounting & Economics,* 15, (1992), pp. 143-171.

Anthony, Joseph H. and K. Ramesh, "Association Between Accounting Performance Measures and Stock Prices: A Test of the Life Cycle Hypothesis," *Journal of Accounting & Economics,* 15, (1992), pp. 203-227.

Ball, Ray, "The Earnings-price Anomaly," *Journal of Accounting & Economics,* 15, (1992), pp. 319-345.

Stern Stewart Management Services, Inc.:
Myers, Stewart, "The Evaluation of an Acquisition Target," *Midland Corporate Finance Journal,* 4, Winter, (1983), pp. 39-46.

University of Washington School of Business Administration
Lev, Baruch, "On the Association Between Operating Leverage and Risk," *Journal of Financial and Quantitative Analysis,* 9, (1974), pp. 627-641.

I

FINANCIAL STATEMENT INFORMATION AND STOCK PRICES

1 Easton, Peter D., Trevor S. Harris, and James A. Ohlson, "Aggregate Accounting Earnings Can Explain Most of Security Returns: The Case of Long Return Intervals," *Journal of Accounting and Economics,* 15 (1992), pp. 119–142.
2 Kothari, S.P., and Richard G. Sloan, "Information in Prices about Future Earnings: Implications for Earnings Response Coefficients," *Journal of Accounting and Economics,* 15 (1992), pp. 143–171.
3 Foster, George, Chris Olsen, and Terry Shevlin, "Earnings Releases, Anomalies, and the Behavior of Security Returns," *The Accounting Review,* 59 (1984), pp. 574–603.
4 Anthony, Joseph H., and K. Ramesh, "Association between Accounting Performance Measures and Stock Prices: A Test of the Life Cycle Hypothesis," *Journal of Accounting and Economics,* 15 (1992), pp. 203–227.
5 Schipper, Katherine, "Information Transfers," *Accounting Horizons,* December 1990, pp. 97–107.
6 Bernard, Victor L., and Jacob K. Thomas, "Evidence that Stock Prices Do Not Fully Reflect Implications of Current Earnings for Future Earnings," *Journal of Accounting and Economics,* 13 (1990), pp. 305–340.
7 Ou, Jane A., and Steven H. Penman, "Financial Statement Analysis and the Prediction of Stock Returns," *Journal of Accounting and Economics,* 11 (1989), pp. 295–329.
8 Ball, Ray, "The Earnings-Price Anomaly," *Journal of Accounting and Economics,* 15 (1992), pp. 319–345.

The first part deals with evidence on the relation between financial statement information and stock prices. We begin with the stock market because this is where financial statement information is most widely and actively used. Not surprisingly, it is one of the most thoroughly researched areas in financial statement analysis. Use of financial statement information in the credit and long-term debt markets is deferred to Part IV.

Emphasis on Earnings Information
The majority of the research in this area deals with the relation between earnings and stock prices. This also is not surprising, because earnings is the single most important

item in contemporary financial statements. Earnings literally is "the bottom line." Over the lifetime of a corporation, essentially all of the events influencing the value created in it are ultimately captured in its earnings. This is because, as a matter of law, over the corporation's lifetime all the distributions it makes to its stockholders either are dividends paid out of earnings or are capital distributions (i.e., returns of contributed capital). Essentially all the added value, over and above the capital contributed by stockholders, is therefore reflected in lifetime earnings, by construction.[1] Thus, in the long term, there is a fundamental linkage in law between earnings, dividends, returns to stockholders, and the performance of the corporation and its managers.

In the short term, the connection between earnings and returns to stockholders is not as precise, due to difficulties in calculating earnings over short intervals (e.g., calculating depreciation, accounts receivable, and revenues). Earnings calculation problems arise because many of these calculations require estimation. For example, calculating labor costs requires an estimate of future outlays for vacations, pensions, or health care benefits that employees earn as a result of their current work. Calculating revenues to include credit sales requires an estimate of the proportion of credit sales that ultimately will not be collected. As students of even introductory accounting know, all accruals are a matter of timing, because over the life of a corporation, its aggregate earnings is determined by the difference between the cash invested in it and the cash withdrawn from it. Accruals are made because investors are not prepared to wait until the end of the corporation's life for information about its performance. As Keynes once said, "in the long run we are all dead." But because it is expensive and perhaps even impossible to implement a perfect system of accrual accounting, however defined, short-term accounting earnings necessarily is an imperfect measure of value to the investor.

Despite imperfections, the evidence shows that short-term (that is, quarterly and annual) earnings is an important determinant of stock prices, for several interrelated reasons. First, while short-term earnings is by no means a perfect measure, it does reflect some (though certainly not all) of the contemporary actions influencing a corporation's value, as the studies in this part reveal. Second, the methods of accrual accounting that have evolved over centuries into Generally Accepted Accounting Procedures (GAAP) in the U.S., and into its equivalents in other countries, constitute a relatively refined and successful system for producing useful information about the firm. This topic is covered in the second part. Third, current earnings is a relatively good predictor of future earnings, and hence short-term earnings is more closely tied to long-term value than it would otherwise be (the evidence of this is contained in Part III). Fourth, even in the short term there is a tie between dividends and earnings, arising from legal constraints on the distribution of contributed capital which essentially limit dividends to current and past retained earnings. For all these interrelated reasons, the importance of earnings (and earnings forecasts) in financial statement analysis is easy to understand.

Early Studies of Earnings and Prices
The seminal research showing the existence of a relation between earnings and stock prices was done by Ball and Brown (1968). They studied the average firm's response to

---
[1] The exception is events that influence the timing of cash flows. As **Easton, Harris, and Ohlson (1992)** show clearly, neither law nor accounting incorporates discounting in the same fashion as valuation. For example, the action of deferring a capital expenditure (and its cash flows) for one year will influence present value, but not lifetime earnings.

annual earnings. They reported the following summary graph, which depicts the typical movement of firms' stock prices over the year before, and the half year after, the firms announce their earnings. Firms with increases in earnings are shown separately from firms with decreases.

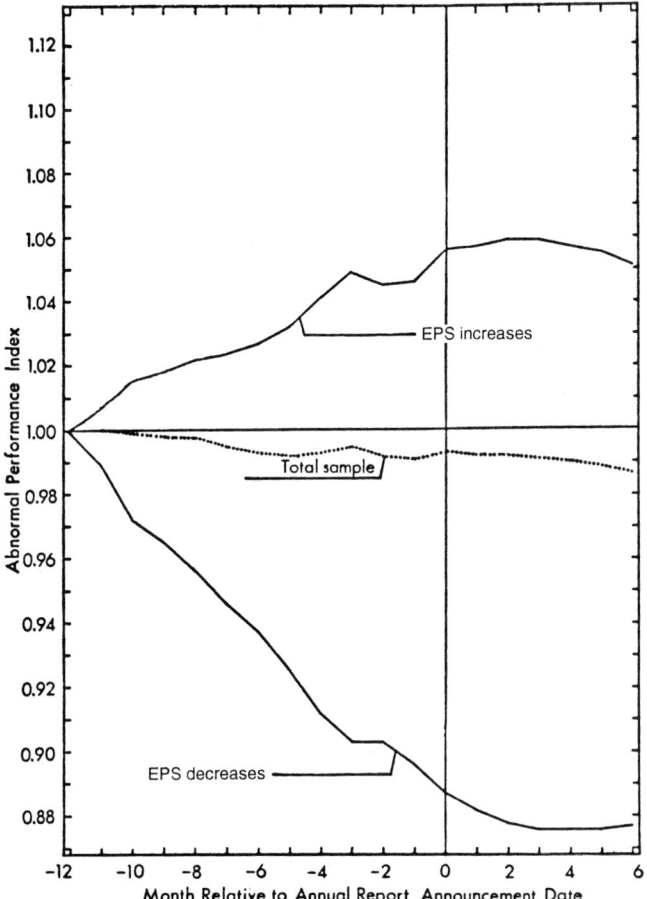

Relation between annual earnings and stock prices
(Firms categorized by sign of annual earnings change)

Source: After Ball and Brown (1968)

Earnings is defined here as earnings per share (EPS). Time, as it is depicted on the graph, is defined relative to the time of the earnings announcement, and has become known as "event time." Thus, the month of the announcement is described as month 0, and can be different points in calendar time for different firms (depending on how long they take to announce their earnings). Six months before the announcement is denoted by -6, three months after is +3, and so on. The announcement is made some time into the next fiscal year because earnings here is the full-year figure and also because there are delays in preparing and auditing the accounts.[2] Prices are scaled by the stock price one year before the announcement, so the relative price at month -12 always is 1.00. Price movements are calculated after controlling for movements in the average stock in the entire market (i.e., the "index"), which means that on the graph the market index tracks the horizontal axis over time (i.e., always has a value of 1.00). Thus, 0.96 represents a return that is 4 percent below the return on the index. The index averaged approximately 10 percent over the period studied. The sample is 261 firms making over 2,000 annual earnings announcements during 1957–1965.

The graph reveals four major features of the relation between earnings and stock prices:

1. *Comovement in earnings and stock prices.* The average firm with increased (decreased) earnings also has increased (decreased) stock prices during the year, relative to the market as a whole. Thus, at least some of the information flowing into stock prices during the year is captured in the annual earnings number released after the end of the year.

2. *Anticipation and timeliness.* Throughout the year covered by the earnings report, stock prices move in anticipation of its contents. By the time it is released, the earnings report is largely anticipated, so it is not a very timely information release. Anticipatory price movements are due to announcements of quarterly earnings, managers' earnings forecasts, analysts' forecasts, earnings announcements of other firms, news about sales or expenses, rumors, insider trades, etc. (Many subsequent studies have traced these information sources down more closely.)

3. *Reaction at time of announcement.* Earnings information is not completely anticipated, however, so prices typically react in the same direction as the earnings news, at the time of its release. (Subsequent studies of transaction-by-transaction data have confirmed this more closely.)

4. *Efficiency and anomaly.* Most of the price reaction is completed immediately after earnings are announced. There is little delay in the reaction, so there is little opportunity to earn abnormal returns from the market systematically erring in its response to the announcement. This is known as market "efficiency" [see Fama (1991) for a review]. On the other hand, there is some evidence of inefficiency in the graph because prices continue to "drift" after the earnings are announced, suggesting some opportunity to profit from a slow reaction.

The basic results in Ball and Brown (1968) have been replicated and extended in a wide range of studies. These include studies of earnings announcements in more than ten countries; studies of different time periods; studies of quarterly earnings [commencing with Jones and Litzenberger (1970) and Brown and Kennelly (1972)] as well as studies of annual earnings that have been aggregated for up to ten years [**Easton, Harris, and Ohlson (1992)**]; and studies of stock price movements over intervals ranging from the minutes sur-

[2] In addition, managers might delay the earnings announcement, either to delay bad news [Givoly and Palmon (1982), Chambers and Penman (1984)] or to avoid strategic disclosure to competitors, suppliers, or customers [Verrecchia (1983)]. Note that the announcement date here is the date of the first official earnings announcement, which precedes the date of the mailing of the annual report by at least several weeks.

rounding earnings announcements [Patell and Wolfson (1984)] to as much as ten years [**Easton, Harris, and Ohlson (1992)**].

Foster, Olsen, and Shevlin (1984) describe price behavior around the announcement of quarterly earnings. Panels A and B of their Figure 1 summarize the data well. Each line represents the average percentage movement in stock prices (after controlling for the market index, which therefore always tracks zero) for 10 percent of the companies, grouped together on the basis of their quarterly earnings performance. The top line represents price movements of those 10 percent of all companies that reported the top quarterly earnings outcomes. The next line is the second 10 percent of earnings performers, and so on down to the last line, which represents the group of the 10 percent biggest earnings losers during the quarter. The figure shows price movements over sixty trading days before and after the earnings announcement, which is approximately three months, or one quarter, on either side.

The relation between earnings and prices is made very clear in this figure. Focussing for the moment on the sixty days up to and including the announcement, the price movements of the ten portfolios are perfectly ranked with their earnings performances. This is true throughout the quarter, with the differences in price becoming more exaggerated over time as a variety of information about the companies' fortunes reaches the market. Similar results are reported in many studies, including Beaver, Clarke, and Wright (1979), the extensive and careful study of almost 100,000 quarterly earnings announcements by Bernard and Thomas (1989), and their follow-up study, **Bernard and Thomas (1990)**.

Effect of Widening the Investment Horizon
Easton, Harris, and Ohlson (1992) and **Kothari and Sloan (1992)** independently investigate the relation between annual earnings and prices over intervals greater than one year. They do so in subtly different ways and thus produce different (though generally consistent) results. These studies provide further insight into the timeliness of earnings as an information medium, as questioned by Ball and Brown (1968).

Easton, Harris, and **Ohlson (1992)** aggregate both earnings and investment outcomes over periods of up to ten years to investigate the relation between earnings and prices. They show that over increasingly long intervals, the contemporary relation between aggregated earnings and stock prices grows stronger. The return-earnings association over shorter intervals (e.g., one quarter or one year) is low because some economic events that cause revisions in the market's expectations about future earnings are not captured in current earnings or some past economic events are reflected in current earnings. Over longer intervals, however, the impact of a greater fraction of economic events is captured in earnings, thereby yielding a stronger contemporaneous correspondence between longer-interval returns and earnings. To the financial analyst, the implication is that long-term earnings essentially is the game; earnings essentially is the ultimate source of value created in the firm.

Kothari and Sloan (1992) make use of the additional idea that prices lead earnings. This is an implication of stock market efficiency, and thus assumes away the anomalous "post-announcement drift" described above (see also the discussion below). This assumption, when combined with the idea that earnings essentially is the ultimate source of value created, implies that problems in calculating accrual earnings are strictly a matter of timeliness. Ball and Brown (1968) show that prices lead annual earnings during the year.

Beaver, Lambert, and Morse (1980) investigate this idea further, and show that prices lead annual earnings by at least two years. Kothari and Sloan show anticipation of annual earnings over as much as four years before it is announced. In addition, they show that the magnitude of the four-year price change in anticipation of earnings is consistent with this period's capturing essentially all the price response. They estimate an average "earnings response coefficient" of 5.45 over four years.[3] To the financial analyst, the implication is that forecasting earnings four years ahead is about as far as is feasible. A stronger implication is of interest. Since essentially all the information about value created that is in price must ultimately be captured in earnings (i.e., ignoring "discounting" effects), if price leads earnings by no more than four years, then it follows that essentially all the information in price is captured in earnings within four years. To the financial analyst, the implication is that four-year-ahead earnings generally is the game.

These papers provide useful insights into the nature of accounting earnings and the relation between accounting earnings and stock prices. Several factors are relevant when comparing their results. First, the market for accounting information has settled on reporting quarterly and annual earnings.[4] For example, shareholders and creditors receive quarterly earnings. Management compensation typically is based on annual earnings. Covenants in long-term debt contracts typically are written in terms of the annual numbers. Thus, the informativeness of quarterly or annual numbers is what is relevant to users, and aggregating accounting earnings over periods longer than one year fundamentally distorts the informativeness of the reported numbers. This is because over longer periods the estimation problems of accrual accounting (such as estimating depreciation or cost of goods sold) constitute a lower proportion of the variability in earnings. These problems are relatively constant over intervals of increasing length, but earnings (and earnings variability) becomes larger over longer intervals. Thus, the noise in earnings declines relative to the signal in earnings as the interval over which earnings is calculated increases. Artificial aggregation of earnings, over intervals longer than those reported, artificially distorts the signal-to-noise ratio in the reported numbers, which can be misleading.

Second, aggregation of earnings over longer intervals is likely to make the data more consistent with the assumption of linearity in the relation between earnings and price. Black and Scholes (1973) demonstrate that stock prices incorporate a component that is the value of the right to put losses in excess of contributed capital to holders of the firm's debt. This implies a nonlinear relation between earnings and stock prices. For example, consider firms with negative earnings but positive stock prices (discussed further in the introduction to Part III). Beaver, Clarke, and Wright (1979) show that the price-earnings relation is in fact nonlinear, and subsequent research confirms this finding. However, as the aggregation interval increases, the option component of stock price seems likely to reduce in comparative importance.

Market Use of Information: Some Extensions

The studies surveyed above investigate the relation between price and earnings for the average firm. Several subsequent studies investigate systematic differences among firms. They are of interest for two reasons. First, they tend to show that the stock market uses

---

[3] Interpretation of the magnitude of this coefficient is deferred until the introduction to Part III.

[4] Quarterly earnings is not reported in some countries. The minimum frequency, then, is either annual or semiannual.

information in relatively sophisticated ways. Second, to the financial analyst they offer assistance in assessing the full implications of an earnings announcement or forecast.

Anthony and Ramesh (1992) investigate how the market reaction to information varies across firms as a function of the point at which the firm and its products are positioned on its growth cycle. They show that announcements of sales growth or of new capital expenditures elicit declining stock price response as the firm's strategy ages. The different significance of earnings in mature firms, relative to firms that are in the early phase of their growth cycle, is of interest to analysts and shows that the market is not "fixated" on the reported numbers. This is one of several studies showing that the typical market reaction to an average firm's financial statement information disguises systematic differences among firms.

Schipper (1990) surveys the literature on information transfers, which was initiated by Foster (1981). The idea behind this literature is that the information released by one firm can have implications for the values of other firms, particularly since Brown and Ball (1967) show that the earnings of a firm are correlated with those in the same industry and with an index of economywide earnings. These articles show that the stock market can use information in subtle ways.

The Earnings "Anomalies" Studies
A series of articles investigate what have come to be known as "anomalies" in the stock market reaction to earnings. The anomalous behavior is that there are predictable, systematic stock price movements *after* earnings are announced. One type of anomaly is the "post-announcement drift" in stock prices. This first showed up in Ball and Brown (1968), and has been carefully studied by many authors. Panels A and B of Figure 1 in **Foster, Olsen, and Shevlin (1984)** show this drift very clearly. In the graphs, the average price reaction to earnings that are announced on day 0 keeps on going during the following sixty trading days (approximately one quarter). This appears to contradict the efficient market hypothesis, since it implies that relatively commonplace knowledge of firms' quarterly earnings allows one to make abnormally high profits over an extended period.[5]

Bernard and Thomas (1990) conduct a careful investigation of almost 100,000 quarterly earnings announcements. They simulate the performance of a portfolio that invests with equal weights in each of the top decile of earnings-performing stocks after they announce earnings each quarter, and sells short each of the bottom-decile earnings stocks. They estimate that such a portfolio would have earned +4.19 percent average abnormal return over the sixty trading days (approximately one quarter) following the earnings announcement, and +7.74 percent over 180 trading days (approximately three quarters). There is essentially no "drift" after day 180. Bernard and Thomas also replicate and extend the study of Rendleman, Jones, and Latané (1987), who hypothesize that the post-announcement "drift" is due in part to the stock market's not fully understanding that changes in quarterly earnings are correlated over time. Bernard and Thomas report evidence that a substantial component of the "drift" occurs at the announcement of the following four quarters' earnings. They simulate a portfolio that invests on the basis of the sign of the deseasonalized change in EPS. The portfolio earns estimated abnormal returns of +1.32 percent, +0.70 percent, +0.04 percent and -0.66 percent, at the time of the following four

---

[5] Recall that in this graph returns are calculated after controlling for the return on the "market index," which tracks zero on the graph. It is in this sense that the returns in the graph are "abnormal."

quarters' earnings announcements (the t-statistics are +14.63, +8.46, +0.45 and -7.86, respectively). The market appears to be unaware that due to the serial correlation in quarterly earnings changes, the current quarter's change in EPS helps in predicting the next four quarters' EPS figures.

Ou and Penman (1989) study the usefulness of a wide variety of financial statement information in predicting future earnings. The variables they find to be particularly useful include return on assets, return on equity, change in return on equity, debt/equity ratio, percent change in dividend per share, and percent change in inventories. They develop a model that uses these variables to predict changes in annual EPS one year ahead, and under the assumption that the market is unaware of the predictive value of the variables, they develop an investment strategy to exploit the model. Thus, they simulate an investment strategy that takes long positions in the 45.3 percent of all stocks with the highest predicted probability of an earnings increase and short positions in the lowest 10.8 percent of all stocks. The strategy earns +8.3 percent estimated abnormal return in the first year after the EPS predictions are made (this is the year covered by the EPS forecast), +6.2 percent in the second year, and +6.3 percent in the third year. Ou and Penman interpret this evidence as supporting the view that:

> Firms' ("fundamental") values are indicated by information in financial statements. Stock prices deviate at times from these values and only slowly gravitate towards the fundamental values. Thus, analysis of published financial statements can discover values that are not reflected in stock prices.

Ball (1992) provides a summary of the research on earnings anomalies. A variety of evidence and explanations is canvassed. The conclusions are mixed. Some evidence clearly indicates that one can earn abnormal returns from using publicly available information (an apparent violation of the efficient markets hypothesis), whereas other evidence suggests not.

Financial Statement Analysis and Stock Market Efficiency
One widely misunderstood issue is whether stock market efficiency is consistent with the analysis of financial statements. At a superficial level, the very idea of market efficiency seems to imply that analyzing any publicly available information is futile, since it is already impounded in prices. This type of reasoning has led some commentators to conclude that financial statement analysis and stock market efficiency are fundamentally inconsistent. The reasoning is flawed.

At its most basic level, the efficient markets hypothesis simply says that the world of investments is fiercely competitive. Economists reason that in any competitive activity, there are only competitive levels of expected return to be obtained at the margin (i.e., to new entrants). While some of the incumbents can be inframarginal and thus can earn above-competitive returns, the competitive force of new entry bids away any high expected returns from new entry. The stock market is perhaps the paradigm example of a large, open-entry market, so this type of competitive-economics reasoning has a lot going for it in that context. Financial statement analysis certainly is a competitive game, so the theory of market efficiency should be compatible with it. Thus, simple competitive-economic logic suggests that after all the dust is settled, there should be only competitive expected returns from financial statement analysis.

That is not to say that financial statement analysis is useless, for at least two reasons. First, there is the important difference between the average player and the marginal entrant. Elimination of above-competitive expected returns at the margin does not imply their absence for inframarginal players. It can be difficult to break into the automobile market, but the incumbents can be making economic rents. Second, financial statement analysis is an economically costly productive activity and, in a competitive world, presumably offers rewards (that is, competitive expected returns) consistent with costs — just like other productive activities.

In relation to the second point, an important factor to consider is the cost involved in using financial statement information, including the cost of acquiring it and the cost of analyzing (or processing) it. Consider an item of information that is "public" in the sense that it is approximately costless for investors to use (i.e., to acquire and process). An example of such information might be the most recent quarter's EPS, which is approximately costless to acquire because it is placed in the public domain at the time of its announcement and subsequently is made available on a range of databases. If the manner in which it is processed is approximately costless, then in a competitive market there will be approximately zero expected return from doing so. Simple investment strategies based on public information that is costless to process can expect to earn only the normal competitive return from investing in securities, but can expect approximately no additional return from using the information in choosing investments. Simple financial statement analysis, involving information acquisition and processing that is easy for many other investors to duplicate, can expect to earn commensurably low (or zero) returns. In contrast, costly sophisticated financial statement analysis that is difficult to duplicate can expect a competitive reward, and this is entirely consistent with the notion of competitive stock markets. The skepticism in **Ball (1992)**, concerning the enormous estimated profitability of financial statement analysis in **Ou and Penman (1989),** is not based on the profitability *per se,* but on the simplicity and generic nature of the analysis. Digging for gold is a tough, competitive business; it is not a simple matter of picking it up off the street.

The financial analysis industry is large and robust, and its practitioners presumably remain in it because they earn competitive returns or greater. And due to the intensely competitive nature of their behavior, they help make the stock market efficient.

Aggregate accounting earnings can explain most of security returns

The case of long return intervals*

Peter D. Easton
Macquarie University, Sydney, Australia 2109

Trevor S. Harris and James A. Ohlson
Columbia University, New York City, NY 10027, USA

Received December 1989, final version received December 1991

The paper analyzes the contemporaneous association between market returns and earnings for long return intervals. The research design exploits two fundamental accounting attributes: (i) earnings aggregate over periods, and (ii) expanding the interval over which earnings are determined, is likely to reduce 'measurement errors' in (aggregate) earnings. These concepts lead to the level of (aggregate) earnings as a natural earnings variable for explaining security returns. We hypothesize that the longer the interval over which earnings are aggregated, the higher the cross-sectional correlation between earnings and returns. The empirical findings support this hypothesis.

1. Introduction and summary

The focus of this paper is on the association between market returns and accounting earnings with a particular emphasis on the increase in the strength of this association as the time period for calculation of returns and earnings increases.

The empirical analyses are developed from two fundamental attributes of the accounting process that have received little attention in the literature to date: (i) earnings aggregate over time, and (ii) 'errors' in aggregate earnings are likely to become relatively less important for longer periods of aggregation. The use of

---

*The authors wish to thank the participants of workshops at the Australian Graduate School of Management, Auckland, University of California, Berkeley, Drexel, Duke, Iowa, Macquarie, Michigan, Monash, Purdue, Queensland, Southern California, Stanford, Texas, and Washington for valuable comments. Special thanks are due D. Shores and Bob Bowen. The last two authors received partial funding from the Faculty Research Fund, Columbia Business School.

0165-4101/92/$05.00 © 1992—Elsevier Science Publishers B.V. All rights reserved

these two ideas in an analysis of returns–earnings associations suggests (aggregate) earnings – that is, the earnings 'level' – as a natural explanatory variable of returns. Previous research has generally used earnings changes as the explanatory variable, frequently as a measure of unexpected earnings.

Virtually all research designs within the literature that consider how accounting earnings explain security returns use return intervals from a few days up to one year. The one-year return period was introduced by Ball and Brown (1968), presumably because it aligns with the period covered in an annual report. This, and subsequent studies, using annual return windows examine the extent to which earnings of the reporting period reflect the information used by the market in forming prices during that period. The justification for using shorter windows is that they reduce the effects of confounding information. These studies seek evidence concerning the market's response to the actual release of earnings data. Although the issues underlying the annual and shorter return interval studies differ, the results of both forms of empirical analysis have been similarly 'disappointing' in the sense of unimpressive correlations between returns and (unexpected) earnings. For one-year as well as short (for example, two- to three-day) windows, the R^2s rarely exceed 10%. Bernard (1989) and Lev (1989) note that these empirical findings are robust across alternative econometric specifications and estimation procedures, and that the source of the problem is thus unlikely to be econometric in nature.[1] The pervasive low explanatory power is of concern for at least two reasons. First, Lev (1989) suggests that the research casts serious doubt on the value relevance of earnings as currently prepared. Second, for researchers interested in understanding the returns–earnings relation, progress in empirical analysis of regression coefficients is hampered by low explanatory power.

The literature provides several explanations for both the poor returns–earnings associations and why the estimated earnings' coefficients generally seem implausibly small [Easton and Zmijewski (1989, 1991)]. Although the various explanations naturally interrelate, distinctions are relevant because they affect motivations for improvements in research designs. Three streams of thought of how to improve estimation of returns–earnings relations can be identified. The first and most traditional approach deals with the earnings expectation model. This issue is discussed in detail in Brown et al. (1987). The second approach views accounting earnings as a measure of 'true' or 'ungarbled' earnings plus an error. This idea, initiated by Beaver, Lambert, and Morse (1980), has led to an errors-in-variables analysis of returns–earnings relations. [See Beaver, Lambert, and Ryan (1989) and Collins and Kothari (1989).] The third approach allows for 'imperfect' earnings because not all value-relevant events observed by the market will be recognized as (part of) earnings during the return period, and conversely, earnings include the effects of events observed by the market prior to

---

[1] Roll (1988) also comments on the inability of financial models to explain returns.

the return period. Ou and Penman (1989a, b) reduce the effects of such events by introducing financial data other than earnings. These additional variables thus control for the value-relevant events not recognized in the earnings of the return period under consideration.

The approach in this paper minimizes the effects of these three problems by focusing on fundamental attributes of accounting. Since we use the level of earnings as the explanatory variable for returns, measurement of earnings expectations is unnecessary. Most value-relevant events occurring during a specific time interval should be part of the concurrent earnings, provided that the interval is sufficiently long: since earnings aggregate over time periods, it makes no difference in which subperiod of the interval under consideration the value-relevant events are recognized as earnings. In other words, of concern are only two kinds of 'errors': (i) value-relevant events occurring during the return interval which are recognized in earnings of subsequent periods, and (ii) value-relevant events occurring prior to the return interval which are recognized in earnings during the interval. But, for long intervals, the two error sources should be relatively unimportant compared to the effects due to value-relevant events 'correctly' recognized during the interval. A simple theoretical benchmark is a firm whose life (creation to liquidation) matches the event window perfectly, in which case no 'errors' are present in (life-time) earnings.

The empirical evaluation of this broadly outlined hypothesis concerning the returns–earnings relation yields impressive and consistent results. For a ten-year return period the market and earnings variables have an R^2 of approximately 63%. As expected, for a five-year return interval the R^2s are smaller – the R^2s average 33% – and for two- and one-year return periods the R^2s decrease even further (the R^2s average 15% and 5%, respectively). Additional analyses across variables, models, and correlation metrics support the hypothesis that the expansion of the return period reduces 'errors' in earnings.

Lev (1989) anticipates the thrust of the empirical results of this study. He reports that correlations between earnings and returns are indeed higher for longer return periods. In this study we develop and motivate the concepts and framework that support the conclusion. We also provide extensive analysis of the variables required to evaluate the returns–earnings relation over long return horizons.

Even though the empirical findings may seem somewhat obvious, several conceptual subtleties must be considered. The idea of (almost) perfect correlations for (sufficiently) long return intervals cannot be developed without careful consideration as to how the earnings variable is constructed and related theoretically to the returns variable. 'Mechanical' extensions of conventional approaches used for one-year return intervals may be unworkable or conceptually deficient for longer periods. To deal with these problems the research design in this paper views earnings as a measure of value changes, consistent with Hicksian income theory [Hicks (1939)]. The constructed earnings and returns variables relate perfectly in a certainty setting, regardless of the return interval and the dividend policy. We retain this Hicksian framework under uncertainty and (essentially) use aggregate earnings over the period as an explanatory variable for value changes. Thus, in contrast to the conventional approach, our model does not adjust current earnings for prior-period earnings to measure unexpected earnings. Complementary empirical analysis shows that the conventional earnings change variable has much less explanatory power than the simple earnings variable, at least for long return intervals.

No published theoretical research has demonstrated why returns and earnings should be almost perfectly correlated for (sufficiently) long return intervals. This paper shows that a perfect correlation can be anticipated if prior restrictions are imposed on the behavior of goodwill (that is, market value minus book value). However, the analysis is limited because it does not flow from more primitive assumptions about the attributes of the underlying accounting model that measures earnings. Given the lack of an insightful theory, we cannot claim that the empirical findings reported in this paper are obvious.

2. Concepts and the specification of variables

We posit that the market return variable is a function of an aggregate earnings (levels) variable. We define the two variables and then develop a model that reflects the intuition behind the hypothesized relation.

We use the following notation to develop a model that relates a firm's earnings to its market performance for a general return interval, $(0, T)$:

P_t = the firm's market value at date t,
d_t = dividends paid at date t,
$R_t = (P_t + d_t - P_{t-1})/P_{t-1}$ = market return for the $(t-1, t)$ period,
x_t = earnings for the $(t-1, t)$ time period, and
R_F = one plus the risk-free rate of return.

The dates run from $t = 1$ to $t = T$. A firm subscript j has been omitted to simplify the notation. The firm-specific variables are on an adjusted per-share basis to make them comparable across dates. Without substantive loss of generality, it is assumed that the term structure of interest rates is flat and nonstochastic.

The dependent variable must measure the firm's market performance. This poses no problems for an interval $(t, t + 1)$, provided that no dividends are paid between these two dates (generally ruled out by assumption). The firm's market performance, or return, is then determined by R_{t+1}. Extending this concept to a $(0, T)$ interval requires an assumption concerning the use of the dividends paid at dates $t = 1, \ldots, T - 1$. This study assumes that these dividends are invested in the risk-free asset. In that case the market return (dependent variable) is

$$y_T^1 \equiv [P_T + FVS(d_1, \ldots, d_T) - P_0]/P_0,$$

where

$$FVS(d_1, \ldots, d_T) \equiv d_1(R_F^{T-1}) + d_2(R_F^{T-2}) + \cdots + d_{T-1}(R_F) + d_T$$

$$\equiv FVS_T.$$

FV in FVS denotes future value and the S denotes a stock of value. Hence, FVS_T is the total amount an investor can withdraw at date T due to the payment and subsequent investment of dividends in the risk-free asset, and $(P_T + FVS_T)$ represents the total amount that can be withdrawn at date T. By relating this quantity to the initial market price (P_0) one obtains the market return variable y_T^1. (The variable can be generalized to allow for a nonflat and stochastic term structure. We will return to this matter.)

The construction of the independent (earnings) variable requires an adjustment for dividends to make it consistent with the dependent (market return) variable y_T^1. The earnings variable consists of two parts, aggregate earnings over $(0, T)$ *and* the earnings due to the presumed investment of the dividends in the risk-free asset:

$$z_T^1 \equiv [AX_T + FVF(d_1, \ldots, d_T)]/P_0,$$

where

$$AX_T \equiv \sum_{t=1}^{T} x_t,$$

and

$$FVF(d_1, \ldots, d_T) \equiv d_1(R_F^{T-1} - 1) + d_2(R_F^{T-2} - 1)$$
$$+ \cdots + d_{T-1}(R_F - 1) \equiv FVF_T.$$

FVF_T represents the earnings due to investment of dividends, FV still denotes future value, and an F has been appended to FV to indicate the (earnings) flow concept. $(AX_T + FVF_T)$ is the earnings that would have been earned by the firm had it not paid any dividends and instead retained this cash to invest in the risk-free asset.[2]

---

[2]The definition of the earnings variable z_T^1 suggests why we are using returns variable y_T^1 rather than $\prod_{t=1}^{T} R_t - 1$. Had we used the latter variable, consistency would require that we assume dividends to be invested in treasury stock rather than the risk-free asset. But the treasury stock approach introduces accounting complexities since we must account for the (hypothetical) effects of treasury stock on earnings. Also, it is unclear whether or not the 'standard' treasury stock method should be used rather than an 'asset' method based on market valuation.

The use of aggregate earnings, AX_T, is a central feature of the earnings variable, z_T^1. Intertemporal earnings aggregation is, of course, intrinsic, and standard financial accounting embeds this attribute. (For example, four quarterly earnings add up to annual earnings, and so forth.)[3] The aggregation attribute of earnings has important implications. The variable AX_T measures the outcome of a firm's economic activity (that is, value-relevant events) in terms of generally accepted accounting practice (GAAP). Though firms vary in their choice of GAAP revenue–expense rules, the argument that AX_T should be relatively insensitive to such choices for large T seems quite reasonable. For example, aggregate cost of goods sold under FIFO and LIFO are unlikely to differ materially for, say, a ten-year interval. This aspect of GAAP and aggregation is a special case of the more general idea that 'most' value-relevant events occurring during $(0, T)$ should be part of earnings for that period. Further, the intertemporal aggregation property of earnings makes it irrelevant in which subperiod of $(0, T)$ the value-relevant events are recognized as earnings. Of course, in reality the abstract notion of value-relevant events and their explicit accounting recognition cannot be observed separately. But this differentiation plays no role as long as, to an increasing degree, accounting earnings incorporate the events implicit in the change in market value as the return interval (T) lengthens.

The idea of (an almost) perfect correlation between y_T^1 and z_T^1 as $T \to \infty$ can be developed more formally. Define the difference between the market value of equity at date t and the book value of equity at date t, BV_t, as 'goodwill' g_t.[4] Thus,

$$P_T - P_0 = \{BV_T - BV_0\} + \{g_T - g_0\}.$$

But in general,

$$BV_t - BV_{t-1} = x_t - d_t.$$

This 'comprehensive income' or 'clean surplus' relation implies

$$\{BV_T - BV_0\} = \sum_{t=1}^{T} x_t - \sum_{t=1}^{T} d_t = AX_T - \{FVS_T - FVF_T\}.$$

---

[3]By contrast, any discounting or time value of earnings concept destroys the intertemporal aggregation property by placing weights on the subperiods' earnings. But no economic meaning can be generally attached to calculations such as $R_F^{-1} x_1 + \cdots + R_F^{-T} x_T$. This claim is independent of any notions of 'errors' in accounting earnings. Dividends alone permit discounting (as in FVS_T and FVF_T), and the discounting of realized (or expected) earnings achieves validity only in highly restrictive circumstances such as when earnings equal dividends at all dates.

[4]The concept of date t goodwill refers to unrecorded goodwill, that is, $goodwill_t \equiv g_t \equiv P_t - BV_t$. It is not recorded ('accounting') goodwill.

Combining the relations yields

$$\{P_T - P_0\}/P_0 + FVS_T/P_0 = \{AX_T + FVF_T\}/P_0 + \Delta g_T/P_0,$$

which reduces to

$$y_T^1 = z_T^1 + g_T^*,$$

where

$$g_T^* \equiv \Delta g_T/P_0.$$

Within this framework the *change* in goodwill captures the 'measurement error' in (aggregate) earnings, and, for long return intervals, we hypothesize that the variation in the earnings variable overwhelms the variation in the earnings' 'error' variable (g_T^*). Specifically, the correlation between y_T^1 and z_T^1 approaches one if the variance of g_T^* divided by the variance of z_T^1 approaches zero as $T \to \infty$. This conclusion is valid even if g_T^* correlates with z_T^1 or if g_T^* has a nonzero mean.[5]

The basic cross-sectional regression model is expressed as

[M1] $\quad y_{Tj}^1 = \alpha_T^1 + \beta_T^1 z_{Tj}^1 + \varepsilon_{Tj}^1,$

where j denotes firm j and ε_{Tj}^1 captures omitted factors. The subscript T emphasizes that the regression coefficients may depend on the return interval. The basic empirical analysis evaluates the hypothesis that the R^2 for M1 increases as T increases. Less attention will be paid to the behavior of $\hat{\beta}_T^1$. Note, however, that the previous paragraph suggests that $\hat{\beta}_T^1 = 1$ serves as a useful theoretical benchmark in the following sense: a dollar of additional earnings yields a dollar of additional value. In the above extreme case, the result obtains if the market

---

[5]The proof of a perfect asymptotic correlation is as follows. Let $R^2(y_T^1, z_T^1)$ denote the R^2 obtained by regressing y_T^1 on z_T^1. Note next that $R^2(y_T^1, z_T^1) = R^2(z_T^1, y_T^1)$. Further,

$$\min_{\alpha, \beta} E(\tilde{z}_T^1 - \alpha - \beta \tilde{y}_T^1)^2 \leq \text{var}(\tilde{g}_T^*),$$

since $\alpha = -E(\tilde{g}_T^*)$ and $\beta = 1$ imply that

$$E(\tilde{z}_T^1 - \alpha - \beta \tilde{y}_T^1)^2 = \text{var}(-\tilde{g}_T^*) = \text{var}(\tilde{g}_T^*).$$

The result now follows since

$$1 - R^2(y_T^1, z_T^1) = \left[\min_{\alpha, \beta} E(\tilde{z}_T^1 - \alpha - \beta \tilde{y}_T^1)^2\right] \Big/ \text{var}(\tilde{z}_T^1)$$

$$\leq \text{var}(\tilde{g}_T^*)/\text{var}(\tilde{z}_T^1) \to 0 \quad \text{as} \quad T \to \infty.$$

value equals the book value so that $y^1_{Tj} = z^1_{Tj}$. More generally, $\hat{\beta}^1_T = 1$ if and only if $\text{cov}[\tilde{z}^1_T, \tilde{g}^*_T] = 0$. While this might be a reasonable approximation, we do not imply that we test or presume such a valuation relation. Similarly, the argument for an increase in R^2 as T increases does not require that $\hat{\beta}^1_T$ equals, or approaches, one.[6]

Since the literature, as reviewed in Bernard (1989) and Lev (1989), generally uses unexpected earnings as the independent variable in explaining abnormal returns it may seem surprising that model M1 has been developed without any reference to expected and unexpected earnings. Although an expected earnings framework is not necessary for the reasoning leading up to model M1, we next consider how M1 can be made consistent with an (un)expected earnings analysis.

Suppose we view P_{0j} as a function of the market's anticipation of firm j's expected earnings for the next T years. In colloquial terms, the scenario emanates from the basic idea that 'the market buys earnings'. Thus assume that

[E1] $\quad P_{0j} \times \psi_T = \text{E}[A\tilde{X}_{Tj} + F\tilde{V}F_{Tj} | \text{information available at } t = 0]$,

for some constant ψ_T which does not depend on j. The future expected earnings (adjusted for expected dividends) determine the current price, and one interprets ψ_T^{-1} as the market's required expected earnings 'multiplier factor'.[7] It follows immediately that $(z^1_{Tj} - \psi_T)$ measures the price-normalized unexpected earnings, but to regress y^1_{Tj} on $(z^1_{Tj} - \psi_T)$ rather than z^1_{Tj} serves no useful purpose. The effect of adjusting z^1_{Tj} for price-normalized expected earnings (ψ_T) would be reflected only in the regression's estimated intercept, while the estimated slope coefficient and the R^2 remain unaffected. This sharp but simple conclusion obtains because firm j's expected earnings determines P_{0j} up to a scale factor which is presumed not to vary across firms. Thus, we note further that the model E1 (and M1) differs from the standard approach which estimates expected earnings as a function of earnings realizations from prior periods. (We will return to this issue in section 6.)

Conceivably, the descriptive validity of model E1 may improve with an increase in the return interval. That is, ψ_T depends less on information at date

---

[6]Note that the certainty theory of income implies no variation in z^1_T across 'firms', so this theory does not *per se* predict β^1_T. The parameters α^1_T and β^1_T are nonunique under certainty, and one can only infer that α^1_T and β^1_T satisfy $R^T_F - 1 = y^1_T = \alpha^1_T + \beta^1_T z^1_T = \alpha^1_T + \beta^1_T(R^T_F - 1)$.

[7]Ohlson (1988, 1991) discusses the model E1 and its relation to the valuation model based on the present value of expected dividends. Ohlson (1991) also shows that if ψ_T does not depend on the information at $t = 0$, then in a world of risk neutrality $\psi_T = R^T_F - 1$, provided that two Modigliani and Miller (1961) concepts apply: (i) $\partial P_0/\partial d_0 = -1$ and (ii) $\partial \text{E}[\tilde{A}X_T + F\tilde{V}F_T | \text{information at date } t = 0]/\partial d_0 = -(R^T_F - 1)$.

$t = 0$ as T increases, and this claim would seem to be reasonable unless the market is myopic in its expectations. It follows that the problems associated with earnings expectation models, traditionally a matter of great concern, can be reduced in settings with long return intervals.

The above analysis poses no problems provided that the price multiplier ψ_T is identical for all firms entering into the sample. This presumption can, of course, be questioned. At the very least it may be hypothesized that a firm's *ex ante* risk influences the multiplier, that is, ψ_T is relatively large (small) for firms with more (less) risky earnings–dividends streams. In such a case model E1, as applied to M1, would lead to a misspecification. Furthermore, the misspecification may become more pronounced for longer return intervals since the value of ψ_T increases exponentially with time (see footnote 7). It follows that the increase in R^2 as the return interval increases potentially depends on the lack of a risk adjustment in the estimated regression models. The direction and degree of influence of this issue is unclear to us. Attempts to analytically model the implications of any misspecification have been unsuccessful.

The empirical analysis considers the above risk adjustment problem by controlling for beta risk. That is, we include an estimate of beta as an additional explanatory variable in the regression model M1. If the inclusion of this variable leaves the estimated regression model substantively intact, then one can reasonably conclude that the possibility of differential capitalization parameters ψ_T has not confounded our interpretations of the results.

3. The role of dividends and interest rates

One issue arising from M1 relates to the effect of dividends on the empirical results. This aspect of the model suggests a potentially contrived correlation analysis because the two regression variables y^1_{Tj} and z^1_{Tj} include their respective dividend components FVS_{Tj} and FVF_{Tj}. The relative effect of these dividend components is more likely to be significant for long return intervals, in which case it is arguably neither surprising nor interesting to find that the correlations between y^1_{Tj} and z^1_{Tj} increase as the return interval increases. It turns out that the issue is of no empirical concern given the relatively low variation in dividends for the intervals and sample used in this study. The variability of z^1_{Tj} is virtually unaffected by the inclusion of FVF_{Tj} even for the longest return period (ten years). The same is true for y^1_{Tj} and the FVS_{Tj} component. Nevertheless, to ensure that FVS_{Tj} and FVF_{Tj} do not significantly influence the correlations we also consider the following two modifications of model M1.

First,

[M2] $y^2_{Tj} = \alpha^2_T + \beta^2_T z^2_{Tj} + \varepsilon^2_{Tj},$

where

$$y^2_{Tj} \equiv (y^1_{Tj} - \hat{\beta}^1_T FVF_{Tj}/P_{0j}),$$

$$z^2_{Tj} \equiv \hat{\beta}^1_T AX_{Tj}/P_{0j} = \hat{\beta}^1_T z^1_T - \hat{\beta}^1_T FVF_{Tj}/P_{0j},$$

and

$\hat{\beta}^1_T$ is estimated from M1.

This modification removes the effect of dividends from the right-hand side in M1 (FVF_{Tj}) to the left-hand side [that is, $y^2_{Tj} \equiv (P_{Tj} + FVS_{Tj} - \hat{\beta}^1_T FVF_{Tj} - P_{0j})/P_{0j}$]. Regardless of the values of $\hat{\beta}^1_T$, the estimated parameter $\hat{\beta}^2_T$ should be close to one if the R^2 is independent of the dividends.

Second,

[M3] $y^3_{Tj} = \alpha^3_T + \beta^3_T z^3_{Tj} + \varepsilon^3_{Tj},$

where

$$y^3_{Tj} \equiv \left(P_{Tj} + \sum_{t=1}^{T} d_{tj} - P_{0j}\right) \bigg/ P_{0j},$$

$$z^3_{Tj} \equiv AX_{Tj}/P_{0j}.$$

This model has a particularly simple interpretation: Accounting earnings, AX_{Tj}, explain economic earnings, $P_{Tj} + \sum_{t=1}^{T} d_{tj} - P_{0j}$, where both variables are normalized by P_{0j} in the regression.

A second issue concerns the use of interest rates as inputs in model M1 (and M2). In theory the term structure of interest rates at the various dividend payment dates should be used. However, as the previous paragraph notes, the two dividend terms (FVS_{Tj} and FVF_{Tj}) are relatively unimportant empirically, so we use a simplified procedure. In correlating the two variables in the various models we assume a flat term structure and try different values for R_F. These range from 1.05 to 1.20. The results remain virtually unchanged across specifications for R_F, and thus it is implausible that the use of the actual term structure would have changed any conclusions. The general insensitivity to interest rates also becomes apparent from examination of model M3. This model assumes no discounting or compounding of the dividend stream ($R_F = 1.00$). Since models M1, M2, and M3 yield essentially the same correlations, it is apparent that the choice of interest rate in the calculation of the dependent and independent variables does not affect the conclusions. As reported in section 5, the three models differ little empirically for the return intervals with which we are concerned.

4. Data and sample selection

The samples consist of firms for which annual earnings per share, dividends, and adjustment factors are available on the 1987 version of the Compustat Annual Industrial File, and prices and adjustment factors are available on the Center for Research in Security Prices Daily Master files. In constructing samples we have to balance two conflicting objectives: (i) to have a long return interval, which requires earnings and dividend data for each year within the interval, and (ii) to have a large number of observations. We impose the constraint that the earnings–dividends variables must be available for at least ten consecutive years and we use ten years as the maximum return interval.

The contemporaneous correlation analysis requires that the return interval aligns with the earnings disclosure dates. Each return calculation uses both an end (P_{Tj}) and a beginning (P_{0j}) of period price for any prespecified interval $(0, T)$. We set P_{Tj} equal to the price on the first trading day three months after the fiscal year end of the last year of earnings used in the calculation of aggregate earnings. This procedure should ensure that the price P_{Tj} fully reflects fiscal period $(T-1, T)$ earnings. To attain symmetry, we set P_{0j} equal to the price on the first trading day three months after the beginning of the fiscal year of the first year used in the calculation of aggregate earnings. Since the longest return interval is ten years, a firm must have ten consecutive years of P_{Tj} and P_{0j} and at least a ten-year history of earnings and dividends to be included in the sample.

Panel A of table 1 reports the number of firms satisfying the data requirements for ten-year return intervals beginning with 1968–1977 and ending with 1977–1986. Note that any given firm becomes part of several ten-year intervals if the data history exceeds ten years.

To minimize problems associated with interdependence in observations, each firm contributes only one observation for a sample. We must also consider the selection of a ten-year event return interval for each firm entering into a sample. Several different schemes were implemented. These include a sample in which each firm contributes its earliest possible ten-year period. Similarly, in another sample each firm contributes its latest possible ten-year period. In each of these cases the firms have very similar calendar time intervals, that is, the sample displays time clustering. To alleviate any potential effects due to time clustering, we also selected return intervals using a random selection procedure. Panel B of table 1 shows the number of observations contributed by each return interval for five different selection procedures. In all instances the substance of the results remains the same. Thus we only report the results for one sample, the 'random selection' sample.[8] Table 2 provides some summary statistics for this case.

---

[8] We do not wish to imply that time clustering is inappropriate, nor that the random sample is in some sense preferable to the other samples.

Table 1

Summary of numbers of sample observations.

Sample[a]	1968–77	1969–78	1970–79	1971–80	1972–81	1973–82	1974–83	1975–84	1976–85	1977–86	Total
Full	706	790	905	1007	1074	1146	1182	1203	1236	1203	10452
					Panel A[b]						
					Panel B[c]						
Random	70	88	106	121	122	123	143	172	160	188	1293
Earliest forward	706	87	119	106	70	75	40	26	35	28	1293
Middle forward	—	—	—	—	—	1146	40	27	35	28	1276
Middle backward	3	4	4	3	1074	—	—	—	—	—	1088
Latest backward	3	4	4	3	3	4	5	3	61	1203	1293

[a]Samples include firms for which returns, earnings, and dividend data are available on the Compustat and CRSP tapes for each of ten consecutive years.
[b]Full = total number of observations for each ten-year period.
[c]Random = random selection of observations. Earliest forward = earliest observation for each firm for which ten years of data exists. Middle forward = earliest observations after 1972 for each firm for which ten years of data exists. Middle backward = observation beginning 1972 for each firm or the previous observation for which ten years of data exists. Latest backward = latest observation for each firm for which ten years of data exists.

Table 2

Descriptive statistics for the primary variables used for the ten-year return interval for the random selection sample ($N = 1293$).

Variable[a]	1st quartile	Median	3rd quartile	Mean	SD[b]	Correlations				
						AX_{Tj}	AD_{Tj}	FVS_{Tj}	FVF_{Tj}
PD_{Tj}	0.027	0.971	2.935	2.646	5.215	0.731	0.335	0.296	0.216
AX_{Tj}	0.720	1.286	2.250	1.751	2.578		0.422	0.391	0.324
AD_{Tj}	0.161	0.381	0.645	0.456	0.404			0.996	0.964
FVS_{Tj}	0.245	0.611	1.027	0.708	0.612				0.985
FVF_{Tj}	0.085	0.220	0.376	0.252	0.213				

[a] PD_{Tj} = price plus dividends at time T ($T = 10$) minus price at the beginning of the return period ($P_{T-10j} = P_{0j}$) and then divided by P_{0j}, for firm j. AX_{Tj} = sum of earnings over the period $T - 9$ to T, divided by P_{0j}, for firm j. AD_{Tj} = sum of dividends over the period $T - 9$ to $T - 1$, divided by P_{0j}, for firm j. FVS_{Tj} = future value of dividends paid over the period $T - 9$ to $T - 1$, using an interest rate of 10% (that is $R_F = 1.1$), divided by P_{0j}, for firm j. $FVF_{Tj} = FVS_{Tj} - AD_{Tj}$, divided by P_{0j}, for firm j.
[b] SD = standard deviation.

5. Basic correlation results

5.1. Ten-year return interval

Table 3 provides estimation results for model M1 using the random selection sample when $T = 10$ and $R_F = 1.1$. The R^2 is 63%, which is obviously much larger than the R^2 typically obtained for one-year return intervals (see below). We also consider two alternative association metrics. First, the Spearman rank correlation between $z^1_{T=10,j}$ and $y^1_{T=10,j}$ which is 83%. Second, $y^1_{T=10,j}$ and $z^1_{T=10,j}$ are partitioned into 'high' and 'low' values by using the respective medians as cut-off points, with the resulting binary variables having 84% concordant pairs.

Table 3

Estimation results for the ten-year return period for the random selection sample ($N = 1289$, $R_F = 1.10$); numbers in parentheses are t-statistics.

Model[a]	$\hat{\alpha}_T$	$\hat{\beta}_T$	$\bar{R}^2$	Spearman correlation	Concordant pairs (high–low)
M1	−0.128 (−1.1)	1.659 (46.8)	0.63	0.83	84%
M2	−0.137 (−1.3)	1.003 (45.6)	0.62	0.80	81%
M3	−0.130 (−1.2)	1.665 (45.6)	0.62	0.81	81%

[a]M1: $y^1_{Tj} = \alpha^1_T + \beta^1_T z^1_{Tj} + \varepsilon^1_{Tj}$

$y^1_{Tj} \equiv [P_{Tj} + d_{1j}(R_F^{T-1}) + d_{2j}(R_F^{T-2}) + \cdots + d_{T-1,j}(R_F) + d_{Tj} - P_{0j}]/P_{0j}$

$z^1_{Tj} \equiv \left\{ \sum_{t=1}^{T} x_{tj} + [d_{1j}(R_F^{T-1} - 1) + d_{2j}(R_F^{T-2} - 1) + \cdots + d_{T-1,j}(R_F - 1)] \right\} / P_{0j}$

M2: $y^2_{Tj} = \alpha^2_T + \beta^2_T z^2_{Tj} + \varepsilon^2_{Tj}$

$y^2_{Tj} \equiv y^1_{Tj} - \{\hat{\beta}^1_T[d_{1j}(R_F^{T-1} - 1) + \cdots + d_{T-1,j}(R_F - 1)]/P_{0j}\}$

$z^2_{Tj} \equiv \hat{\beta}^1_T \left(\sum_{t=1}^{T} x_{tj} \right) / P_{0j}$

M3: $y^3_{Tj} = \alpha^3_T + \beta^3_T z^3_{Tj} + \varepsilon^3_{Tj}$

$y^3_{Tj} \equiv \left(P_{Tj} + \sum_{t=1}^{T} d_{tj} - P_{0j} \right) / P_{0j}$

$z^3_{Tj} \equiv \sum_{t=1}^{T} x_{tj}/P_{0j}$

where P_{tj} = price at time t for firm j, x_{tj} = earnings per share at time t for firm j, d_{tj} = dividends per share at time t for firm j, $R_F = 1 +$ risk-free rate.

As reported in table 3, the correlations associated with models M2 and M3 are less than those of M1, but only by a small margin. M2 and M3 have R^2s of 62%. Examination of the two other correlation metrics leads to the same conclusion. The results reject the notion that FVS_T and FVF_T are of any empirical importance in the evaluation of correlations.

We tried various values for R_F in M1 and M2. The range was 1.05 and 1.20. This has no substantive effect on the results. Similarly, the inclusion of estimated betas in the regression had no material effect on the results. We estimated betas using monthly returns over the ten-year intervals (120 observations) for each firm.[9] While the coefficient associated with the beta variable is positive and statistically significant (t-statistic = 5.4), the R^2 changes only by one percentage point (that is, 64% rather than 63%). Moreover, the estimated betas are essentially uncorrelated with the earnings variable, so that the estimated coefficient (and t-statistic) for the earnings variable ($\hat{\beta}_T^1$) is unchanged at 1.66 (46.9). We also considered the regression model M1 after partitioning the sample into quartiles of estimated betas. There was little effect on the coefficients or R^2. Overall, we conclude that beta estimated over the ten-year period of the return interval does not affect the measured relation between aggregate earnings and returns over this interval.

5.2. Five-, two-, and one-year return intervals

The results for the shorter return intervals substantiate the hypothesis of a decrease in correlations as the length of the return interval shortens. Panel A of table 4 shows the correlations for model M1 for five-year return intervals. (Because M2 and M3 have virtually identical results as M1, these are not presented.) Two five-year samples were obtained by partitioning the ten-year sample into an 'early' and a 'late' subperiod. The R^2s are, respectively, 38% and 28%. The related Spearman rank correlations are 76% and 70%, and the concordant pairs are 80% and 76%. In sum, for each of the three correlation metrics, the five-year return interval correlations are clearly less than those of the ten-year return interval.

For the five samples of two-year return intervals, the correlations decline even further, as shown in panel B of table 4. The R^2s average 15%, with a maximum

---

[9]The choice of a beta estimation period was limited by data availability. Thus, we could not use ten years of monthly returns prior to the start of each ten-year interval without severely limiting the sample. Moreover, the lack of any effect once (in-sample) beta is included as an additional variable in M1 suggests that a search for alternative estimates is unwarranted. Nevertheless, we did consider beta estimates based (separately) on both equal- and value-weighted market returns but this did not affect the results. Handa, Kothari, and Wasley (1989) show that estimates of beta using monthly returns have more measurement error than estimates using annual returns, but data limitations restrict our ability to use annual returns. (We are grateful to the editor for pointing this issue out to us.) Also, the results are sufficiently robust that such an estimation is unlikely to have any significant effect.

of 18% and a minimum of 14%. Since the maximum R^2 for the two-year return interval (18%) is more than a third less than the minimum R^2 for the five-year return interval (28%), there is no question that the decline in correlations is statistically significant. The Spearman rank correlations and concordant pairs metrics produce a similar conclusion.

Finally, panel C of table 4 shows the results for the one-year return periods. The average R^2 is 6%, and the average Spearman rank correlation is 39%. Even a cursory examination of the numbers indicates a significant decline in correlations for one-year intervals as compared to two-year intervals.

The results of this section corroborate the hypothesis that earnings and returns associations increase as the return interval expands.[10] A reasonable approximation of the results may be obtained via the formula: $R^2 = 6\%$ times the number of years in the return interval.

Table 4

Estimation results from model M1[a] for the five-, two-, and one-year return periods for the random selection sample ($R_F = 1.10$); numbers in parentheses are t-statistics.

Subperiod	$\hat{\alpha}_T$	$\hat{\beta}_T$	$\bar{R}^2$	Spearman correlation	Concordant pairs (high–low)	N
		Panel A: Five-year return period				
2 (late)	0.486 (7.2)	1.340 (22.3)	0.28	0.70	76%	1291
1 (early)	−0.231 (−3.9)	1.559 (28.4)	0.38	0.76	80%	1291
		Panel B: Two-year return period				
5 (latest)	0.309 (14.3)	0.767 (14.4)	0.14	0.51	68%	1290
4	0.308 (14.4)	0.704 (14.9)	0.14	0.49	67%	1292
3	0.125 (4.6)	1.066 (16.4)	0.17	0.56	70%	1292
2	0.146 (6.4)	0.812 (14.6)	0.14	0.57	71%	1292
1 (earliest)	0.060 (2.7)	0.935 (16.9)	0.18	0.58	71%	1293

[10] As an additional specification check we constrained $\hat{\beta}_T^1$ to be one and, as expected, the ratio $\text{var}(g_T^*)/\text{var}(\tilde{y}_T^1)$ monotonically declined as the return interval increased. In addition all tests were performed with and without outliers and there is no effect on the quality of the results. For example, in the case of model M1 reported in table 3, for the ten-year return interval when all 1293 observations are used the R^2 is 0.56 and the coefficient $\hat{\beta}_T^1$ is 1.81.

Table 4 (continued)

Subperiod	$\hat{\alpha}_T$	$\hat{\beta}_T$	$\bar{R}^2$	Spearman correlation	Concordant pairs (high–low)	N
Panel C: One-year return period						
10 (latest)	0.178 (14.6)	0.292 (7.2)	0.04	0.35	61%	1291
9	0.206 (13.9)	0.453 (6.7)	0.03	0.36	63%	1290
8	0.182 (13.2)	0.448 (8.6)	0.05	0.38	64%	1293
7	0.184 (12.4)	0.510 (8.2)	0.05	0.32	61%	1293
6	0.126 (7.7)	0.824 (10.7)	0.08	0.40	64%	1290
5	0.078 (5.8)	0.587 (9.5)	0.06	0.43	65%	1291
4	0.121 (8.4)	0.686 (10.8)	0.08	0.43	66%	1293
3	0.065 (5.6)	0.440 (9.2)	0.06	0.41	64%	1293
2	0.060 (4.6)	0.554 (10.7)	0.08	0.40	65%	1293
1 (earliest)	0.063 (5.0)	0.539 (10.1)	0.07	0.45	64%	1293

[a] M1: $y^1_{Tj} = \alpha^1_T + \beta^1_T z^1_{Tj} + \varepsilon^1_{Tj}$

$y^1_{Tj} \equiv [P_{Tj} + d_{1j}(R_F^{T-1}) + d_{2j}(R_F^{T-2}) + \cdots + d_{T-1,j}(R_F) + d_{Tj} - P_{0j}]/P_{0j}$

$z^1_{Tj} \equiv \left\{ \sum_{t=1}^{T} x_{tj} + [d_{1j}(R_F^{T-1} - 1) + d_{2j}(R_F^{T-2} - 1) + \cdots + d_{T-1,j}(R_F - 1)] \right\} / P_{0j}$

where P_{tj} = price at time t for firm j, x_{tj} = earnings per share at time t for firm j, d_{tj} = dividends per share at time t for firm j, $R_F = 1$ + risk-free rate.

The next section evaluates the importance of earnings of the prior period in the regression. Then section 7 discusses the estimates of the coefficient ($\hat{\beta}^1_T$).

6. The relevance of earnings of the previous period

The analysis in section 2 demonstrates that model M1 may subsume concepts of expected earnings. The scheme depends on the assumption that the price deflator in the explanatory variable reflects the expected future earnings (adjusted for the effect of dividends). Thus, the model reduces to a simple and direct evaluation of whether 'the market buys earnings'. This earnings expectation framework differs from the traditional one which includes earnings of the previous period in the modeling of future expected earnings. For annual return intervals the (unexpected) earnings variable is frequently defined as the change in earnings divided by initial price, that is, $(x_t - x_{t-1})/P_{t-1}$. The relevance of this variable is based on the idea that the earnings of the previous period, x_{t-1}, contribute to the explanation of returns. The popularity of the earnings change variable in the extant literature motivates our consideration of this as an additional explanatory variable for returns.

The discussion in section 2 can be cast in a rigorous framework such that the returns variable (y_T^1) and the earnings level variable (z_T^1) will correlate perfectly as $T \to \infty$ in which case there is no role for change in earnings. Justification for inclusion of an earnings change variable for other return periods requires an argument relating g_{Tj}^* to Δz_{Tj}^1. For example, earnings changes may be correlated with the 'error' in earnings levels for shorter return intervals.

Of course, in the final analysis, the relative importance of the earnings change and z_{Tj}^1 variables is an empirical question. Hence we consider the regression

$$y_{Tj}^1 = \gamma_{1T} + \gamma_{2T} z_{Tj}^1 + \gamma_{3T} \Delta z_{Tj}^1 + \eta_{Tj},$$

where Δz_{Tj}^1 denotes the change in earnings compared to the previous period. The earnings of the previous period are aggregated over the number of years (T) as z_{Tj}^1, and both variables are normalized by P_{0j}.

We estimate the above regression to evaluate two hypotheses. First, we hypothesize that z_{Tj}^1 contributes more than Δz_{Tj}^1 in explaining y_{Tj}^1 for all three return periods: one year, two years, and five years. (Ten years are not examined since it would have required twenty consecutive years of data.) The relative t-statistics of $\hat{\gamma}_{2T}$ and $\hat{\gamma}_{3T}$ are used to determine the relative explanatory power of the two variables respectively.[11] Second, we hypothesize that the relative importance of z_{Tj}^1 compared to Δz_{Tj}^1 in explaining y_{Tj}^1 is more apparent for longer return intervals. The hypothesis is motivated by the simple fact that M1 has a lower R^2 for shorter return intervals. This in turn suggests greater misspecification in an implied earnings expectation model $P_{0j} = \psi_T^{-1} \, \mathrm{E}[A\tilde{X}_{Tj} + F\tilde{V}F_{Tj}|$ information available at $t = 0$]. This potential increased misspecification makes it more likely that an alternative earnings expectations model – that is the one implied by the inclusion of Δz_{Tj}^1 – adds significantly to the explanation of returns.

The empirical results support both hypotheses. Table 5 provides the t-statistics for $\hat{\gamma}_{2T}$ and $\hat{\gamma}_{3T}$ given the three interval lengths and various subperiods. For intervals of two years or longer, table 5 shows that $t(\hat{\gamma}_{2T}) > t(\hat{\gamma}_{3T})$ in *all* cases. For the one-year return interval, $t(\hat{\gamma}_{2T}) > t(\hat{\gamma}_{3T})$ in all but two of the

---

[11]This comparison is equivalent to the comparison of incremental R^2 and the comparison of univariate R^2.

Table 5

Summary of estimation results from regressions of the basic model[a] and the change in the independent variable.

($R_F = 1.10$)

Subperiod	$t(\hat{\gamma}_{2T})$	$t(\hat{\gamma}_{3T})$	$\bar{R}^2$	N
Panel A: Five-year return interval				
2	12.45	0.26	0.277	1291
Panel B: Two-year return interval				
5	13.10	−1.46	0.140	1291
4	9.17	1.69	0.139	1292
3	8.72	8.33	0.214	1292
2	9.67	2.65	0.145	1292
Average	10.17	2.80		
Panel C: One-year return interval				
10	2.95	3.71	0.047	1291
9	4.16	4.47	0.047	1290
8	6.87	1.54	0.054	1293
7	4.95	2.07	0.052	1293
6	7.03	4.54	0.095	1290
5	7.41	1.46	0.065	1291
4	7.59	1.81	0.084	1293
3	5.40	2.96	0.067	1293
2	6.60	2.82	0.086	1293
Average	5.30	2.54		

[a]Model: $y^1_{Tj} = \gamma_{1T} + \gamma_{2T} z^1_{Tj} + \gamma_{3T} \Delta z^1_{Tj} + \eta_{Tj}$

$y^1_{Tj} \equiv [P_{Tj} + d_{1j}(R_F^{T-1}) + d_{2j}(R_F^{T-2}) + \cdots + d_{T-1j}(R_F) + d_{Tj} - P_{0j}]/P_{0j}$

$z^1_{Tj} \equiv \left\{ \sum_{t=1}^{T} x_{tj} + [d_{1j}(R_F^{T-1} - 1) + d_{2j}(R_F^{T-2} - 1) + \cdots + d_{T-1j}(R_F - 1)] \right\} / P_{0j}$

$\Delta z^1_{Tj} = z^1_{Tj} - z^1_{Sj}$

$z^1_{Sj} = z^1_{Tj}$ for period S where S is the immediately preceding return period of length T

where P_{tj} = price at time t for firm j, x_{tj} = earnings per share at time t for firm j, d_{tj} = dividends per share at time t for firm j, $R_F = 1$ + risk-free rate.

ten cases. The evidence refutes any contention that Δz^1_{Tj} is as powerful as z^1_{Tj} in explaining the return variable.

The evidence supports the second hypothesis as well. The relative explanatory power of Δz^1_{Tj} as compared to z^1_{Tj} is better for the shorter return intervals. As table 5 shows, for the five-year return interval $t(\hat{\gamma}_{2T})$ is approximately forty-eight times greater than $t(\hat{\gamma}_{3T})$. For the two-year interval the average $t(\hat{\gamma}_{2T})$ is about four times greater than the average $t(\hat{\gamma}_{3T})$, and for the one-year return interval the ratio of the two averages differ by a factor of two.

The above results may depend on how prior-period earnings are used in the definition of the second explanatory variable. For example, for the (relatively) long five-year return interval it may be argued that a five-year history of prior-period earnings is excessive, and too long, to effectively estimate the subsequent five years of aggregate earnings. As a modification of the unexpected earnings model $\Delta z_{T=5j}^1$ we used the annual earnings prior to the return period multiplied by five as the expected earnings. An analogous scheme was applied for two-year return periods. We also tried alternative specifications without the dividends and various ways of constructing subsamples. The results remain basically unaffected in all cases and thus we do not report on these.

Both Easton and Harris (1991) and Ohlson and Shroff (1991) provide theoretical reasons as to why both earnings levels and earnings changes can be expected to be associated with returns over annual intervals. Easton and Harris (1991) have examined the competing explanatory powers of z_{Tj}^1 and Δz_{Tj}^1 for one-year return intervals. Their much more comprehensive work evaluates the explicit possibility of various confounding effects (such as market inefficiency) and alternative specifications of the dependent variable [e.g., abnormal (unexpected) returns]. Consistent with the findings reported here, a review of the Easton and Harris results leaves few doubts that the level variable (z_{Tj}^1) overall performs better than the change variable (Δz_{Tj}^1) in explaining measures of annual returns. Similar empirical conclusions are found in Ali and Zarowin (1991) and Ohlson and Shroff (1991) for annual total earnings after tax. The totality of the empirical evidence suggests earnings levels rather than earnings changes as an explanatory variable for returns for intervals of a year or longer.[12]

7. The behavior of the earnings coefficient ($\hat{\beta}_T^1$)

While observations concerning $\hat{\beta}_T^1$ are basically outside the scope of this paper, some discussion seems appropriate given the extensive literature on the slope coefficient from various returns and earnings metrics [for example, see Beaver, Lambert, and Morse (1980), Collins and Kothari (1989), and Easton and Zmijewski (1991)]. We believe that the approach of varying the return interval could potentially enhance an understanding of the mixed results that have been reported to date. (The literature frequently suggests that the estimated earnings coefficients are too small.)

We first note that $\hat{\beta}_T^1$ increases steadily with the length of the return interval. For a one-year interval the average $\hat{\beta}_{T=1}^1$ is 0.53, and for the ten-year interval the earnings coefficient is roughly three times as large ($\hat{\beta}_{T=10}^1 = 1.66$). Tables 3 and 4 show a clear monotonic increase in $\hat{\beta}_T^1$ as the interval increases. Unfortunately, we know of no easy and direct explanation as to why this pattern occurs.

---

[12] Warfield and Wild (1991) show that for quarterly earnings the earnings levels explain more of the cumulative abnormal return than do earnings changes (see their table 6).

Perhaps it could be argued that this pattern reflects an errors-in-variables phenomenon in earnings and/or in the implied earnings expectation model (E1). As discussed in section 5, accounting earnings is most likely to be a complete, or 'accurate', indicator of the effect of value-relevant events, or value changes, when the return interval is long. Similarly, the quality of the earnings expectation model may increase with T since T determines the market's horizon of earnings' anticipation. Both scenarios suggest that the variable z_{Tj}^1 is measured with less of an error for large T, and thus, $\hat{\beta}_T^1$ increases as T increases. But this informal argument requires careful analysis before the claim that the pattern is 'what should be expected' is warranted.

The hypothesis that $\hat{\beta}_T^1 \leq 1$ can be rejected for relatively long (five- and ten-year) return intervals. A dollar of earnings evidently is associated with *more* than a dollar of change in value for long return periods. Stated somewhat differently, the (P_0-normalized) change in goodwill, g_{Tj}^*, correlates positively with the (P_0-normalized) aggregate earnings variable z_{Tj}^1 for $T \geq 5$. [The conclusion follows since $g_{Tj}^* = y_{Tj}^1 - z_{Tj}^1$ and thus $\text{cov}(g_T^*, \tilde{z}_T^1) = \text{var}(\tilde{z}_T^1)(\hat{\beta}_T^1 - 1)$.] Why this strictly positive correlation occurs for long return intervals is unclear to us presently. An explanation requires a theory showing why large earnings realizations (relative to P_{0j}) lead to an increase in a firm's goodwill. Future research needs to address this issue.

8. Comparison with the portfolio concept of returns–earnings analysis

The relatively high R^2 for the ten-year return interval may suggest that the results are akin to those of Beaver, Clark, and Wright (1979) (BCW). BCW group firms into portfolios and correlate the portfolios' returns and unexpected earnings. This aggregation scheme leads to a dramatic improvement in correlations compared to those not using portfolios. Their results, and the logic behind their procedure, point toward the possibility of attaining (almost) perfect corrections if enough data were available. It is, therefore, pertinent to ask whether this study uses a similar idea in the sense that it relies on intertemporal rather than cross-sectional aggregation.

For several reasons, the aggregation concept used in this study has nothing substantive in common with the BCW portfolio aggregation concept. BCW construct their portfolios *conditional* on the realizations of the earnings variable. The aggregation performed on earnings in this research is *unconditional* on any realizations. We also note that the BCW procedure increases the R^2 for virtually any two variables, provided that the two variables have an approximately linear but imperfect population correlation. To claim that the BCW portfolio aggregation procedure improves correlations because it reduces the 'errors' in the earnings variable is arguably too simplistic. The aggregation applied in this study, by contrast, emanates from concepts inherent in the financial reporting model. The two aggregation schemes therefore differ in terms of procedure as well as in concept.

Of course, one may still hypothesize that the results are spurious because the high R^2 could be due to statistical effects of time aggregation in the two variables. To test this hypothesis we aggregated annual returns ($y^1_{T=1j} = R_{tj}$) and annual x_{tj}/P_{t-1j} over ten years, and correlated the two variables cross-sectionally. Specifically, consider the regression

$$\sum_{t=1}^{10} R_{tj} = \theta_1 + \theta_2 \sum_{t=1}^{10} (x_{tj}/P_{t-1j}) + \zeta_j.$$

Note that the two regression variables differ from $y^1_{T=10j}$ and $z^1_{T=10j}$, respectively, even when the dividend terms are disregarded. The M1 derives from accounting concepts, whereas the last regression derives from time aggregation.

The R^2 for the above model is 0.037. The result does not lend support to notions that simple aggregation of the price-normalized variables can improve the R^2. Indeed, we view earnings aggregation as the central accounting concept applied to achieve the relatively high correlation for the ten-year return interval.

9. Concluding remarks

This paper has shown that the correlation between earnings and returns improves with increases in the return interval, and that for a ten-year return period 'most' of the returns can be explained. While this finding has descriptive content, the more interesting aspect is the motivation for the empirical analysis. The idea of a correlation increase as the return interval increases stems from an application of accounting concepts. That is, earnings aggregate over periods, so that earnings are more likely to reflect the value-relevant events and their effect on value changes over longer periods. This framework naturally leads to the conclusion that investors 'buy earnings'.

We certainly do *not* wish to suggest that long return intervals are superior or more logical than shorter ones. Empirical research designs should be motivated by questions asked, and not by the magnitude of correlation measures. However, we note that 'high R^2 settings' often make it easier to conceptualize and test for the effects of variables potentially relevant in explaining the dependent variable. This point, combined with the behavior of the R^2 as the return interval increases, might be useful in some contexts of market-based accounting research; research designs using long (ten-year) return intervals may have a better chance of providing useful evidence for many empirical issues.

For example, one issue of interest concerns how various components of earnings contribute to explaining returns. Aggregate earnings AX_{Tj} may be decomposed into items, such as operating profit, depreciation, and tax expense. Regressions of market return (y_{Tj}) on these income statement components (normalized by P_{0j}) can be used to test whether aggregation applies for various return intervals, that is whether the coefficients for the various 'line items' are of the same magnitude and have the correct signs. We expect such an analysis to provide information about whether investors 'price' earnings components such as depreciation. Paton (1963) in his article on the 'cash flow' illusion argues that depreciation is basically no different from direct cash expense since all costs incurred must be allocated to some period. For long return intervals, no depreciation allocation issues arise provided that the useful life of the asset falls within the return interval. Thus, the long return interval can help initially to control for the accounting method, and then, as the interval is shortened, to facilitate evaluation of investor differentiation among alternative depreciation methods, in the spirit of Beaver and Dukes (1972, 1973).

At the very least this study suggests that researchers should be aware of the return period when deciding on a research design. The effects of the return interval on the returns–earnings relation are clearly significant, and long intervals seem to have some advantages compared to short intervals. This research also raises the possibility that studies in the extant literature could be reexamined because inferences and conclusions may depend on the return interval under consideration.[13]

References

Ali, A. and P. Zarowin, 1991, On the role of the earnings level variable in annual earnings–returns studies, Working paper (New York University, New York, NY).

Ball, R. and P. Brown, 1968, An empirical evaluation of accounting income numbers, Journal of Accounting Research 6, 159–178.

Beaver, W.H. and R.E. Dukes, 1972, Interperiod tax allocation, earnings expectations, and the behavior of security prices, The Accounting Review XLVI, 320–332.

Beaver, W.H. and R.E. Dukes, 1973, Delta-depreciation methods: Some empirical results, The Accounting Review XLVII, 549–569.

Beaver, W.H., R. Clarke, and W. Wright, 1979, Association between unsystematic security returns and the magnitude of the earnings forecast error, Journal of Accounting Research 17, 316–340.

Beaver, W.H., R.A. Lambert, and D. Morse, 1980, The information content of security prices, Journal of Accounting and Economics 2, 3–28.

Beaver, W.H., R.A. Lambert, and S.G. Ryan, 1989, The information content of security prices: A second look, Journal of Accounting and Economics 11, 139–158.

Bernard, V.L., 1989, Capital market research in accounting during the 1980s: A critical review, in: T.J. Frecka, ed., The state of accounting research as we enter the 1990's (University of Illinois, Urbana-Champaign, IL) 72–120.

Brown, L.D., R.L. Hagerman, P.A. Griffin, and M.E. Zmijewski, 1987, An evaluation of alternative proxies for the market's assessment of unexpected earnings, Journal of Accounting and Economics 9, 159–194.

---

[13]For example, U.S. firms provided replacement cost income data under ASR 190 and SFAS 33 for the seven years 1979 to 1985. Comparison of the explanatory power of historic cost and replacement cost income for returns over this period will provide indications of the extent to which replacement cost data provide a better or poorer summary of the events that affect the firm over the various return intervals. Haw and Lustgarten (1988) use this data and return intervals ranging from one to seven years to test hypotheses regarding ASR 190 and FAS 33.

Collins, D.W. and S.P. Kothari, 1989, An analysis of the intertemporal and cross-sectional determinants of earnings response coefficients, Journal of Accounting and Economics 11, 143–181.

Easton, P.D. and T.S. Harris, 1991, Earnings as an explanatory variable for returns, Journal of Accounting Research 29, 19–36.

Easton, P.D. and M.E. Zmijewski, 1989, Cross-sectional variation in the stock market response to accounting earnings announcements, Journal of Accounting and Economics 11, 117–141.

Easton, P.D. and M.E. Zmijewski, 1991, A conceptual and empirical comparison of coefficients relating stock return metrics and earnings metrics, Working paper (Macquarie University, Sydney).

Fama, E.F. and K.R. French, 1988, Dividend yields and expected stock returns, Journal of Financial Economics 22, 3–25.

Handa, P., S.P. Kothari, and C. Wasley, 1989, The relation between the return interval and betas: Implications for the size effect, Journal of Financial Economics 23, 79–100.

Haw, I. and S. Lustgarten, 1988, Evidence on income measurement properties of ASR no. 190 and SFAS no. 33 data, Journal of Accounting Research 26, 331–352.

Hicks, J.R., 1939, Value and capital (Oxford University Press, London).

Kormendi, R.C. and R. Lipe, 1987, Earnings innovations, earnings persistence, and stock returns, Journal of Business 60, 323–346.

Lev, B., 1989, On the usefulness of earnings: Lessons and directions from two decades of empirical research, Supplement of Journal of Accounting Research 27, 153–192.

Ohlson, J.A., 1988, Accounting earnings, book value, and dividends: The theory of the clean surplus equation (part I), Working paper (Columbia University, New York, NY).

Ohlson, J.A., 1990, A synthesis of security valuation theory and the role of dividends, cash flows, and earnings, Contemporary Accounting Research 6, 648–676.

Ohlson, J.A., 1991, The theory of value and earnings, and an introduction to the Ball-Brown analysis, Contemporary Accounting Research, forthcoming.

Ohlson, J.A. and P. Shroff, 1991, Changes vs. levels in earnings as explanatory variables for returns: Some theoretical considerations, Working paper (Columbia University, New York, NY).

Ou, J.A., 1990, The incremental information content of non-earnings accounting numbers as earnings predictions, Journal of Accounting Research 28, 144–163.

Ou, J.A. and S.H. Penman, 1989a, Financial statement analysis and the prediction of stock returns, Journal of Accounting and Economics 11, 295–330.

Ou, J.A. and S.H. Penman, 1989b, Accounting measurement, price–earnings ratios, and the information content of security prices, Supplement of Journal of Accounting Research 26, 111–144.

Paton, W.A., 1963, The 'cash-flow' illusion, The Accounting Review XXXVIII, 243–251.

Roll, R., 1988, R^2, Journal of Finance 43, 541–566.

Warfield, T.D. and J.J. Wild, 1991, Accounting measurement error and the pricing of interim earnings, Working paper (University of Wisconsin, Madison, WI).

Information in prices about future earnings

Implications for earnings response coefficients*

S.P. Kothari
University of Rochester, Rochester, NY 14627, USA

Richard G. Sloan
University of Pennsylvania, Philadelphia, PA 19104-6365, USA

Received April 1990, final version received February 1992

Stock return over a period reflects the market's revision in expectation of future earnings. Accounting earnings over the same period, however, have limited ability to reflect such revised expectations. Therefore, returns anticipate earnings changes and the earnings response coefficient from a regression of returns on contemporaneous earnings changes is biased toward zero. We reduce this bias by including leading-period returns in price–earnings regressions. The resulting estimated earnings response coefficient magnitudes suggest that the capital market, on average, views earnings changes to be largely permanent. This is consistent with the random walk time series property of annual earnings.

1. Introduction

Recently the relation between time series properties of earnings and earnings response coefficients [formally defined below in eq. (1)] has been a topic of considerable interest among accounting researchers [see, e.g., Kormendi and Lipe (1987), Collins and Kothari (1989), Easton and Zmijewski (1989)]. Since

---

*We acknowledge Celal Aksu, Andrew Alford, Vic Bernard, Fischer Black, Carol Frost, Dan Givoly, Paul Healy, Pat Hughes, Bob Lipe, Tom Lys, Jim Manegold, Krish Palepu, K. Ramesh, Doug Skinner, Charlie Wasley, Ross Watts, Peter Wilson, Jerry Zimmerman, Mark Zmijewski, workshop participants at the University of Arizona, Harvard University, Northwestern University, Ohio State University, University of Southern California, Temple University, Washington University at St. Louis, and especially an anonymous referee and Ray Ball (the editor) for many useful comments. S.P. Kothari acknowledges financial support from the Bradley Policy Research Center at the Simon School and the John M. Olin Foundation.

0165-4101/92/$05.00 © 1992—Elsevier Science Publishers B.V. All rights reserved

Journal of Accounting and Economics 15 (1992) 143–171. North-Holland

time series properties of annual earnings suggest that firms' earnings changes are largely permanent, the earnings response coefficient is predicted to be about $(1 + 1/r_i)$, where r_i is the expected rate of return on firm i's equity [Kormendi and Lipe (1987) and Collins and Kothari (1989)].[1] Earnings response coefficients reported in the literature, however, are considerably smaller than implied by the time series properties of earnings. For example, Penman's (1990, table 2) estimate using annual returns/earnings data is 0.894, whereas Kormendi and Lipe (1987, table 1) report a median coefficient of 2.5. Ali and Zarowin (1992), who control for the effect of serial correlation in earnings, report a median earnings response coefficient of 1.59. Use of analysts' earnings forecasts as better proxies for the market's expectation also yields coefficients of similar magnitudes [see, for example, Easton and Zmijewski (1989a,b) and Brown, Griffin, Hagerman, and Zmijewski (1987) who use *Value Line*'s quarterly earnings forecasts].

In this paper we resolve the apparent inconsistency between the time series behavior of annual earnings and the market's valuation of earnings changes, as reflected in an earnings response coefficient estimate, by using the information in stock prices about future earnings. By exploiting the earnings forecasts embedded in security prices, we obtain coefficients that are comparable to those implied by the time series properties of earnings.

One source of stock prices' predictive ability with respect to future earnings changes is that the information set reflected in the market's expectations, and thus in prices, is richer than that in the past time series of earnings. Price change over a period reflects revision in the market's expectation of future earnings as well as realized earnings over the period. In comparison, accounting earnings over a period primarily summarize: (i) the effect of sales transactions during a fiscal period that have generated cash or almost certainly will generate cash (e.g., cash sales and net change in receivables), (ii) the effect of past periods' activities (e.g., via depreciation expense and cost of goods sold), and (iii) cash outlays for investments generating uncertain future benefits (e.g., research and development and advertising expenses). Compared to stock prices, earnings thus have a limited ability to contemporaneously reflect the market's revised expectations of future cash flows. Such limited ability is attributable to the conservatism, objectivity, verifiability, and other conventions that underlie Generally Accepted Accounting Principles (GAAP). For example, earnings for a period are unlikely to reflect the *expected* net cash flow from a new growth opportunity facing the firm. Since, on average, the market's expectations eventually get reflected in earnings, price changes anticipate earnings changes, or prices lead

---

[1]Annual earnings changes exhibit a small degree of negative serial correlation [see, for example, Ball and Watts (1972, tables 3, 4), Brooks and Buckmaster (1980), and Ali and Zarowin (1992)]. For a typical firm, we therefore expect its earnings response coefficient to be somewhat smaller than $(1 + 1/r_i)$.

earnings.[2] This phenomenon has long been recognized in the literature. For evidence in the accounting literature, see Ball and Brown (1968), Beaver, Lambert, and Morst (1980), Brown, Foster, and Noreen (1985), Collins, Kothari, and Rayburn (1987), Freeman (1987), and Collins and Kothari (1989).

The effect of prices leading earnings on an earnings response coefficient, can be seen from the following commonly estimated regression:

$$R_{it} = \gamma_{0i} + \gamma_{1i} UE_{it} + \varepsilon_{it}, \tag{1}$$

where R_{it} is return in excess of its expected return for firm i measured over fiscal quarter or year t, UE_{it} is reported earnings minus a proxy for the market's expectation of earnings at the beginning of period t, scaled by price at the beginning of period t, γ_{0i} is the intercept, γ_{1i} is firm i's earnings response coefficient, and ε_{it} is a disturbance term. Consider estimating eq. (1) using annual returns and a time series expectation of annual earnings to obtain UE_{it}. The limitation of a time series expectation is that the market's expectation is based on a richer information set. Therefore, UE_{it} will be measured with error and the coefficient on UE_{it} will be biased towards zero. This is suggested by numerous researchers. For example, Watts and Zimmerman (1986, p. 55), in their discussion of the Beaver, Clarke, and Wright (1979) study, reason that earnings response coefficient estimates could be biased toward zero because 'stock price adjustment to some factors reflected in annual earnings may have occurred in previous years'.

To reduce the bias that arises because information in prices about future earnings is ignored, we include return over a leading period in R_{it}.[3] The average earnings response coefficient increases from 3.1 when annual, contemporaneous price–earnings regressions are estimated, to 6.0 when returns from the three previous years are also included in R_{it}. Compared to the previous research, which documents that return over one leading year is related to the annual earnings change [see, e.g., Beaver et al. (1980), Brown et al. (1985), and Collins and Kothari (1989)], we provide reliable evidence that returns measured over three leading years contain information about an annual earnings change. The increase in the average earnings response coefficient suggests leading-period

---

[2]We hasten to add that by 'prices lead earnings' we do not imply there is any 'error' in historical cost accounting earnings. While managers have incentives to 'manipulate' accruals [e.g., Healy (1985)], it is neither necessary nor do we rely on such 'manipulations' or 'error' to argue that returns anticipate earnings changes. Moreover, since accrual 'manipulations' do not have a first-order stock price effect, returns are unlikely to be useful in forecasting future earnings changes stemming from accrual 'manipulations'. The latter are probably helpful in forecasting future earnings changes on the basis of past earnings changes.

[3]Collins and Kothari (1989) also include leading-period returns in estimating price–earnings regressions. They measure return over a 15-month window that begins five (two) months earlier than the fiscal period t for the large (small) firms. We include up to three leading years' returns to more fully exploit the information in prices with respect to future earnings.

returns are as important as contemporaneous returns in terms of their sensitivity to annual earnings changes. Perhaps more importantly, the inference is that the capital market views earnings changes to be largely permanent, which is consistent with the annual earnings' time series properties.

We also report earnings response coefficients estimated using both returns and earnings measured over relatively long windows of up to four years [see also Easton, Harris, and Ohlson (1992) who focus on the explanatory power of price–earnings regressions]. While a longer window is expected to be more effective than a shorter one in reducing the bias stemming from earnings anticipation, a longer window is, *a priori*, unlikely to be as effective as including leading-period returns. Longer price–earnings measurement windows cannot fully incorporate earnings anticipation impounded in returns. Instead, longer windows reduce the proportion of the earnings change that has already been anticipated. This is supported by our results. Longer windows for both returns and earnings yield less biased earnings response coefficient estimates, but not to the same extent as when leading period returns are included.

Our empirical analysis using longer measurement windows for returns and earnings differs from Easton, Harris, and Ohlson (1992) in one important respect, We estimate time series, compared to their *cross-sectional* regressions; we focus on earnings response coefficient magnitudes whereas they evaluate the degree of price–earnings association. The degree of price–earnings association attributable to risk differences (and therefore expected return differences) in a *cross-section* is an increasing function of the return–earnings measurement interval. This clouds researchers' ability to unambiguously attribute any increase in the explanatory power of cross-sectional regressions to variation in unexpected earnings across firms. This issue is discussed more fully in section 4.2.

Section 2 provides the rationale for a relation between leading-period returns and earnings response coefficients. Data, sample selection, and descriptive statistics are provided in the third section. Section 4 presents empirical results. The earnings response coefficients' sensitivity to leading-period returns and to measurement intervals is documented in sections 4.1 and 4.2. Diagnostic tests' results are discussed in section 4.3. A summary and implications for other research are provided in section 5.

2. Implication of accounting principles for earnings response coefficients

In an efficient market, price changes reflect the revision in the market's expectation of future cash flows, whereas accounting earnings have only a limited ability in this respect. As a result, the market's expectation reflects a richer information set than a time series expectation. The primary reason for this is that conservatism, objectivity, verifiability, and other conventions that underlie GAAP limit accounting earnings' ability to contemporaneously reflect the market's revision in expectation of future net cash flows.

We illustrate this by considering the timing of the impact of several economic events on stock prices and current and expected future cash flows and earnings. Events such as long-term sales contracts (e.g., aircraft sales, shipbuilding) affect the market's expectation of future earnings and cash flows, and stock prices reflect these revised beliefs at the time the economic events become known. Neither earnings nor cash flows for the period, however, fully reflect their expected future cash flow implications. Around the time of new investments, stock prices reflect their net present values [e.g., McConnell and Muscarella (1985) and Chan, Martin, and Kensinger (1990)]. Earnings for the period in which capital investments are made are reduced by the depreciation charge, and cash inflows from the new investment are captured in future earnings only when revenues are generated. Thus, returns are expected to lead earnings changes. That is, price changes are expected to have some predictive power with respect to future earnings changes. This, however, does not imply that price changes represent a perfect forecast of future earnings changes.

Research and development investments are expensed in the period in which they are incurred, whereas the expected cash inflows from these investments are reflected only as and when they materialize in the future. Because prices reflect the present value of the expected net effect of the expenditures around the time of these investments [see Chan, Martin, and Kensinger (1990)], prices will lead earnings. Other examples of investments that are expensed in the period in which they are incurred include advertising, marketing, repair and maintenance, restructuring costs [e.g., Brickley and VanDrunen (1990)], and plant closing costs [Blackwell, Marr, and Spivey (1990)]. Finally, growth opportunities (i.e., opportunities to make positive net present value investments) facing a firm are reflected in stock prices, but are not generally reflected in earnings until they begin to generate revenues [e.g., Brealey and Myers (1988) and Ross, Westerfield, and Jaffe (1990)].[4] Thus, in the presence of growth opportunities, returns tend to anticipate future earnings changes.

One implication of prices leading earnings is that the market's expectation of earnings differs from a time series expectation. Since annual earnings are reasonably described as a random walk, information in the past earnings is not useful in predicting successive earnings changes. As of the beginning of a year, however, the market has typically anticipated some of the current period's earnings change. Therefore, in estimating the price–earnings relation either a timely and accurate proxy for the market's earnings expectation should be used, or information in leading-period returns should be exploited. In this study

---

[4]The generally observed large price run-up in a target firm's stock can also be viewed as a growth opportunity in that the bidder firm is expected to utilize the target firm's assets more efficiently and generate greater amounts of cash flows, that will be reflected in future earnings.

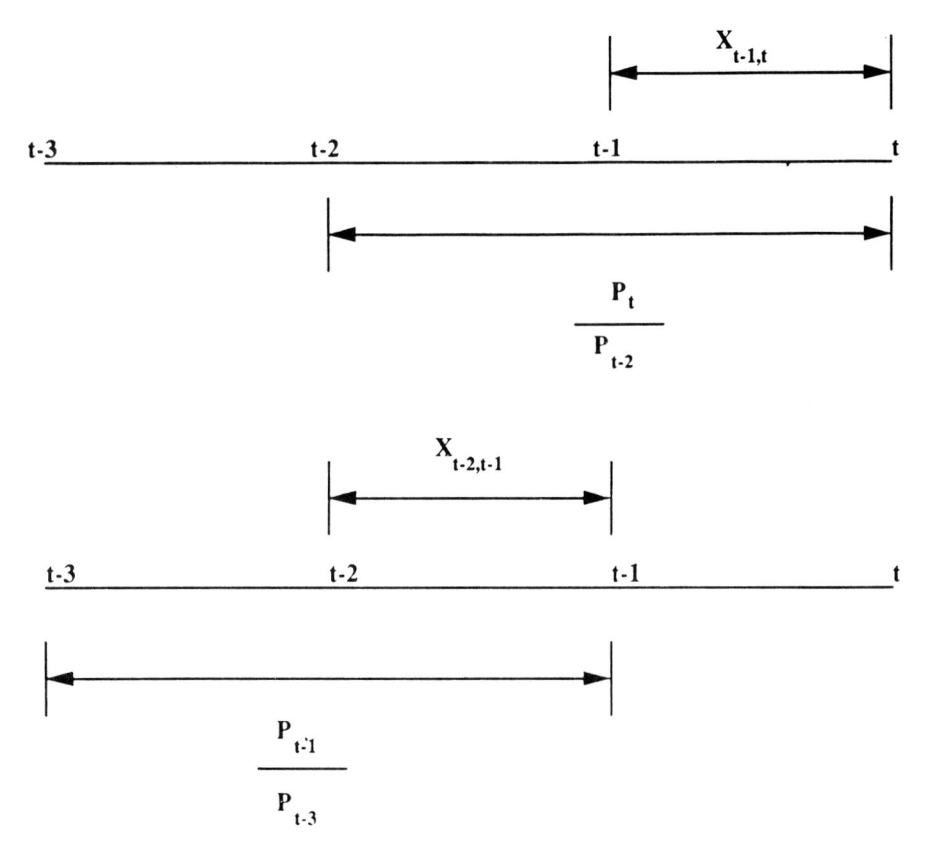

Fig. 1. Earnings and returns measurement intervals in lead–lag price–earnings regressions. Two-year buy-and-hold returns, inclusive of dividends, regressed on annual earnings deflated by price at the beginning of the return measurement interval. Return measurement interval consists of the contemporaneous and one leading year. Return observations are overlapping.

we include leading-period returns. We estimate the price–earnings relation using earnings measured over a given interval (e.g., one year), but with a return measurement interval that includes a leading time period (see fig. 1). We employ the earnings level, rather than change, deflated by price as the explanatory variable in the price–earnings regression, which is motivated by the random walk time series property of annual earnings [see Biddle and Seow (1990) and Ohlson (1991)], and the evidence in Easton and Harris (1991):

$$P_{it}/P_{it-\tau} = \gamma_{i0} + \gamma_{i1} X_{it}/P_{it-\tau} + \varepsilon_{it}, \qquad (2)$$

where X_{it} is accounting earnings over the period t, $P_{it}/P_{it-\tau}$ is one plus the buy-and-hold return, inclusive of dividends, over the period from the end of

$t - \tau$ to the end of t, and $\tau > 1$ so that leading-period returns are included in $P_{it}/P_{it-\tau}$. Thus, when $\tau = 3$, we regress overlapping three-year returns on the third year's annual earnings scaled by price at the beginning of the return holding period. As τ increases, it is more probable that the information reflected in X_{it} will be incorporated in the return over the period $t - \tau$ to t. Consequently, γ_{i1} is expected to approach its predicted value of $(1 + 1/r_i)$. Note that the multi-year return over the period $t - \tau$ to t reflects more information than that reflected in the one year's earnings, X_{it}. Since this 'extra' (uncorrelated) information resides in the dependent variable, it does not bias the estimated slope coefficient, although the R^2s will be less than one.[5]

It is important to determine whether the inclusion of leading-period returns spuriously increases the estimated earnings response coefficient. In an appendix we show that, *if* prices do not lead earnings and the dividend payout is zero, then the inclusion of leading-period returns to estimate the earnings response coefficient has no effect on the coefficient. Thus, the inclusion of leading-period returns is not helpful unless returns anticipate future earnings changes.

The appendix also examines the effect of a positive dividend payout policy. The estimated coefficient is biased upwards by the order of the firm's dividend yield, which is small compared to $(1 + 1/r_i)$. This bias arises because of an asymmetric effect of dividends on the dependent and independent variables. Specifically, earnings in the $X_{it}/P_{it-\tau}$ variable reflect earnings on the firm's initial equity investment and on the increase in investment over time through earnings retention. Thus, X_{it} does not reflect earnings on past dividend payments. The return variable, $P_{it}/P_{it-\tau}$, on the other hand, assumes dividends are reinvested. The result, as shown in the appendix, is that earnings response coefficient estimates are upwardly biased. Intuitively, the earnings yield is systematically biased downwards relative to the return-inclusive-of-dividend variable, which causes the bias. The bias increases in dividend yield and thus with the length of leading period. We report earnings response coefficients adjusted for this bias. The adjustment entails dividing the estimated earnings response coefficients by $(1 + \text{dividend yield})^{\tau-1}$, where we use the realized dividend yield of 3.9% per year on the CRSP equal-weighted portfolio from 1926–88 and $\tau - 1$ is the number of leading years included in the analysis. Since the bias is small relative to the magnitude of the predicted and estimated coefficient, we believe our adjustment is sufficient.

---

[5]We also considered a reverse regression of annual earnings on annual returns, in the spirit of Beaver, Lambert, and Ryan (1987), to estimate earnings response coefficients. Since prices lead earnings, the return variable contains information about the current year's earnings (the dependent variable in a reverse regression) as well as the future years' earnings. The presence of the latter type of information in the return variable means it measures the variable of interest (i.e., the component of return that is attributable to the current period's earnings information) with error. The estimated slope is therefore expected to be biased, much the same way as in the direct regression. See Lipe (1990, p. 64) and Beaver et al. (1987, pp. 150–151).

3. Data, sample selection, and descriptive statistics

3.1. Data

We use data from the Compustat Quarterly, Annual Industrial, and Annual Res earch tapes, and the Center for Research in Security Prices (CRSP) monthly tape. We use earnings data for 1979-88 from the quarterly tape for earnings measurement intervals shorter than one year and data for 1950-88 from the annual tapes when the earnings measurement interval is one year or longer.

We use monthly returns to calculate buy-and-hold returns *including* dividends over holding periods ranging from one quarter to four years. Returns are measured over intervals that end in the earnings fiscal quarter- or year-end. The effect of including earnings-announcement and post-earnings-announcement-period returns on earnings response coefficients is discussed in sections 4.2 and 4.3.

3.2. Sample selection and descriptive statistics

We include all firms that have at least five consecutive earnings and return observations available for the measurement interval of interest. We apply this critierion separately for each measurement interval. Thus, if the measurement inverval is one quarter, then earnings and return data for at least five consecutive quarters must be available. This enables us to estimate a time series regression separately for each firm.

Table 1 reports descriptive statistics for the earnings yield ($X_{t-\tau,t}/P_{t-\tau}$) and price relative ($P_t/P_{t-\tau}$) variables. $P_t/P_{t-\tau}$ is one plus the buy-and-hold return, inclusive of dividends, over the period $t - \tau$ to t. The descriptive statistics are reported for measurement intervals, τ, ranging from one to four years. For each measurement interval, the average earnings yield and price relative are calculated for each firm. Using these firm level data, sample mean, standard deviation, median, minimum, and maximum values are obtained. For $\tau = 1$ year, the average earnings yield for a sample of 2,721 firms is 6.1% and the median is 9.1%. The mean and median earnings yields for the four-year-interval sample of 2,319 firms are 13.2% and 12.7%. The mean as well as median earnings yields reported in table 1 increase monotonically with τ. One reason is that the earnings per share is deflated by $P_{t-\tau}$ which, on average, declines in τ. A second reason is that there is a survivorship bias that results in higher earnings yield samples as the measurement interval is increased. A survivorship bias also reduces the sample size from 2,721 for $\tau =$ one year to 2,319 for $\tau =$ four years.

Descriptive statistics for $P_t/P_{t-\tau}$ for the various measurement interval samples are reported in the bottom panel of table 1. The last row reports annualized mean values. The annualized mean price relatives measured over all intervals are almost identical. They range from 1.168 to 1.170. This means the average

Table 1

Descriptive statistics for earnings yield ($X_{t-\tau,t}/P_{t-\tau}$) and price relative ($P_t/P_{t-\tau}$) variables measured over intervals ranging from one to four years and data from 1950–88. Sample sizes are from 2,319 to 2,721 firms.[a,b]

	Measurement interval			
	1 year	2 years	3 years	4 years
	Earnings yield			
Mean	0.061	0.091	0.112	0.132
Std. deviation	0.156	0.121	0.131	0.143
Median	0.091	0.104	0.116	0.127
Minimum	−2.874	−2.072	−2.534	−2.020
Maximum	0.639	0.856	1.045	1.400
N	2,721	2,588	2,471	2,319
	Price relatives			
Mean	1.168	1.371	1.598	1.864
Std. deviation	0.139	0.310	0.543	0.788
Median	1.165	1.345	1.532	1.734
Minimum	0.527	0.288	0.102	0.221
Maximum	2.521	3.803	7.492	9.867
Annualized mean[c]	1.168	1.170	1.169	1.168

[a] Sample selection: Any firm that had earnings data on the Compustat Annual Industrial or the Compustat Annual Research tape and return data on the Center for Research in Security Prices monthly tape for five consecutive measurement interval periods during 1950–88 is included. Data for the longer than one-year measurement intervals contain overlapping periods because the measurement window is moved forward only one year at a time.

[b] Earnings yield $X_{t-\tau,t}/P_{t-\tau}$ = primary annual earnings per share before extraordinary items and discontinued operations for year t, divided by the price at the beginning of the return measurement interval. All earnings per share numbers and prices are adjusted for stock splits and stock dividends. Price relative $P_t/P_{t-\tau}$ = one plus the buy-and-hold return, inclusive of dividends, over the years $t - \tau$ to t.

[c] Annualized price relative is calculated as the geometric mean annual price relative for the particular measurement interval.

annual return on the sample firms is 16.8% to 17.0%. The sample firms' returns thus do not reveal any obvious survivorship bias problem as a function of the return measurement interval. The mean and median raw price relatives naturally increase with the measurement interval. The mean price relative increases from 1.168 for the one-year-interval sample to 1.864 for the four-year-interval sample.

4. Regression results

4.1. Leading-period returns' effect on earnings response coefficient estimates

To examine the effect of leading-period returns on the earnings response coefficient estimates, we estimate the model in eq. (2) for the sample firms. We focus on the effect of up to three leading years' returns (i.e., $\tau \leq 4$) for two reasons. First, with hindsight, there were only slight increases in the earnings response coefficients from adding more than three leading years' return. We discuss the results of adding up to nine leading years' return in the 'diagnostic tests' section of the paper, to enable the reader to judge the efficacy of adding more than three leading years' return. Second, as noted earlier, inclusion of leading-period returns induces a small upward bias in the estimated coefficients.

Table 2

Selected fractiles from the distribution of estimated parameters of firm-specific regressions of price relatives on earnings deflated by price. Earnings measurement interval is one year and price relatives are for the contemporaneous one year and for periods that also include leading years. Annual earnings data from 1950–88. Sample sizes from 2,319 to 2,721 firms.[a]

$$P_{it}/P_{it-\tau} = \gamma_{i0\tau} + \gamma_{i1\tau} X_{it}/P_{it-\tau} + \varepsilon_{it}^{b,c}$$

	$\tau = 1$	$\tau = 2$	$\tau = 3$	$\tau = 4$
Panel A: Intercept estimates			
Minimum	−1.31	−2.72	−6.59	−3.53
10th percentile	0.61	0.33	0.31	0.27
Median	0.96	0.85	0.89	0.97
90th percentile	1.18	1.30	1.46	1.67
Maximum	3.27	6.08	4.63	4.27
Mean	0.92	0.83	0.89	0.97
Std. error	0.0057	0.0089	0.0111	0.0136
N	2,721	2,588	2,471	2,319
Panel B: Coefficient on earnings			
Minimum	−21.01	−28.85	−20.09	−25.47
10th percentile	0.06	0.50	0.58	0.60
Median	1.89	3.94	4.30	4.42
90th percentile	5.78	9.57	10.12	11.19
Maximum	60.60	104.41	93.52	94.52
Mean	2.56	4.69	5.08	5.45
Std. error	0.0701	0.0966	0.1016	0.1198

[a] Sample selection: Any firm that has earnings data on the Compustat Annual Industrial or Research tape for five consecutive years during 1950–88 and return data for the earnings measurement years and the three leading years is included. The return observations contain overlapping periods when one or more years of leading-period returns are included.

[b] Earnings yield $X_t/P_{t-\tau}$ = primary annual earnings per share before extraordinary items and discontinued operations for year t, divided by the price at the beginning of the return measurement interval. All earnings per share numbers and prices are adjusted for stock splits and stock dividends. Price relative $P_t/P_{t-\tau}$ = one plus the buy-and-hold return, inclusive of dividends, over the years $t - \tau$ to t.

[c] The model is estimated by modeling the residuals from the ordinary least squares regressions as a first-order autoregressive process and then ordinary least squares parameters are reestimated using transformed variables. The estimated slope coefficients are deflated by $(1.039)^{\tau-1}$ to control for bias stemming from using dividend-reinvested returns.

While we provide an approximate correction for this bias, we also avoid adding unnecessary leading-period returns.

When we include leading-period returns (i.e., $\tau > 1$), we obtain overlapping return observations, as shown in fig. 1, and the regression errors become serially correlated (we discuss below an adjustment for serial correlation in errors). Under these conditions, ordinary least squares estimators are unbiased, but less efficient than generalized least squares estimates that take account of the autocorrelation [Maddala (1977, p. 281)]. We therefore transform the price–earnings variables by modelling residuals from the ordinary least squares regressions as a first-order, autoregressive process and then reestimate the price–earnings regression using the transformed variables. This two-step, full transform procedure is similar to the Cochrane and Orcutt (1949) procedure. We also estimate ordinary least squares regressions and regressions using nonoverlapping return data. The former are discussed in the 'diagnostic tests' section and the latter are discussed later in this section.

We report regression results in table 2, comparing the average estimated coefficient with its predicted value. By focusing on the average coefficient, we draw inferences about the price–earnings relation of the average security in our sample. The average coefficient is predicted to be $(1 + 1/r)$, where r is the average security's expected rate of return on equity.[6] We use the average realized annual return of 17.15% on the CRSP equal-weighted portfolio from 1926–88 as a proxy for the expected rate of return. We consider this to be a reasonable proxy for expected return on the sample firms because the average return on the sample firms, as reported in table 1, is close to the CRSP equal-weighted return over 1926–88 and the market model average beta for the sample using the CRSP equal-weighted portfolio is 1.01. For $r = 17.15\%$, the average earnings response coefficient is predicted to be 6.83.[7]

As our hypothesis predicts, the average earnings response coefficient increases as returns from leading years are included. The average earnings response coefficient from the annual contemporaneous regressions for 2,721 sample firms is 2.56. The median earnings response coefficient is 1.89, indicating that the

---

[6]Since $(1/N)\sum(1/r_i) \geq 1/r$, where N is the number of securities, r_i is the expected return on security i, and r is the average expected return for the securities, $(1 + 1/r)$ underestimates the predicted average coefficient. However, since expected return on equities is almost invariably greater than 8–10%, and for reasonable values of cross-sectional variance of the expected returns on equities, the bias in using $(1 + 1/r)$ as the predicted coefficient can be shown to be relatively small. Throughout in this paper we compare the estimated average earnings response coefficient against $(1 + 1/r)$.

[7]An alternative to using the CRSP realized rate of return as a proxy for r would be to use a proxy for the expected real rate of return on common stocks. If inflation is assumed to have no real effect on valuation, then the latter proxy would be consistent with the valuation model underlying the price–earnings relation. We, however, do not adjust the average realized rate of return on the CRSP equal-weighted portfolio for the average inflation rate of 3.2% over 1926–87 [Ibbotson and Sinquefield (1989)] because it is not obvious how inflation affects the price–earnings multiple. If we use a proxy for the expected real rate of return, then the predicted value of the earnings response coefficient is 8.17.

distribution is skewed to the right. More than 90% of the coefficient estimates are positive. As one, two, and three leading years' returns are added to the contemporaneous annual returns, the average earnings response coefficient increases to 4.69, 5.08, and 5.45 (a 113% increase). Taken together, leading-period returns are at least as important as contemporaneous returns in terms of their sensitivity with annual earnings. The median earnings response coefficients always are lower than the sample means, but they too increase substantially with the inclusion of leading-period returns. For example, when three leading years' return is included, the median earnings response coefficient is 4.42.

We next compare the estimated coefficients with their predicted values. The sample mean's standard error is affected by (i) cross-correlation among the coefficient estimates, (ii) variation in the 'true' coefficient magnitudes across firms, and (iii) cross-sectional variation in the degree to which stock prices lead earnings. Since the price–earnings regressions' errors are expected to be positively cross-correlated, the estimated standard errors will likely understate the 'true' standard error.[8] Cross-sectional variation in the firms' earnings response coefficients due to variation in their expected returns will also affect the estimated standard errors. Since we do not model individual firm's earnings response coefficients, this will tend to overstate standard errors. However, as seen from the 10th and 90th percentiles of their distribution in table 2, many firms' earnings response coefficient estimates appear to substantially deviate from their predicted values. We, therefore believe sampling variation in the coefficient estimates dominates the estimated standard errors. Cross-sectional variation in the degree to which prices lead earnings will also magnify the estimated standard errors, particularly when return over a short leading period is included. As τ is increased, virtually all the effect of earnings anticipation is incorporated in the price–earnings relation. Therefore, for $\tau = 4$, we expect cross-sectional variation in the degree to which prices lead earnings will have relatively little effect on the standard error.

The estimated average coefficient is closer, both in absolute terms and statistically, to the predicted value of 6.83 as the leading-period return is incorporated in the analysis. For all leading periods from one to three years, however, the estimated earnings response coefficient is at least two standard errors smaller than the predicted value of 6.83. For example, when three leading-year returns are included, the earnings response coefficient estimate is 5.45, with a standard error of 0.1198. The null hypothesis that the estimated average coefficient is equal to its predicted value of 6.83 is rejected at a p-value less than 0.01.

---

[8]We report below results of regressions that include the market return as an additional independent variable which controls the positive cross-sectional correlation among residuals. As a result, the estimated standard error of the cross-sectional average earnings response coefficient will be less biased.

We conjecture the earnings response coefficient estimates are smaller than their predicted counterparts for at least two reasons. First, the earnings announcement period is not included in calculating returns. For the results in table 2, we end the return measurement period with the firms' fiscal year-ends. If we reestimate firm-specific regressions using returns measured over periods ending three months after the fiscal year-end, the earnings response coefficients estimates are uniformly higher than those reported in table 2. The average earnings response coeffficient is 3.09 when no leading-period return is included and it is 6.04 when leading return over three years is included. Thus, once the three-month announcement period return is included, the average earnings response coefficient is closer to, but still reliably smaller than, its predicted value. Second, previous research by Ball and Watts (1972), Brooks and Buckmaster (1977), Ali and Zarowin (1992), among others, suggests that annual earnings exhibit a small degree of negative serial correlation, which means earnings response coefficients, on average, are predicted to be somewhat smaller than $(1 + 1/r)$.[9]

Overall, the results in this section are consistent with the hypothesis that price changes lead earnings changes, and on incorporating leading-period returns, the earnings response coefficient estimates are significantly closer to their predicted values.

4.2. Earnings response coefficient sensitivity to the price–earnings measurement window

This section reports results of estimating earnings response coefficients using a longer, contemporaneous window for both returns and earnings. The motivation is to assess the effectiveness of longer measurement windows in reducing bias in earnings response coefficient estimates. The fraction of information in earnings that is anticipated by the leading period's return is expected to decrease with the earnings measurement window. The bias in the estimated earnings response coefficients will therefore decline with the measurement window for earnings and returns. However, unless the window length equals the life of a firm, some earnings anticipation will persist. Consequently, longer measurement windows for both earnings and returns are unlikely to be as effective as including leading-period returns.

This analysis using longer contemporaneous price–earnings measurement window is similar to that of Easton et al. (1992), who also study multi-year earnings and returns. The focus of their analysis, however, is on the R^2s of *cross-sectional* price–earnings regressions. We estimate *time series* regressions

---

[9]Kormendi and Lipe (1991) argue that collectively the higher-order negative serial correlations imply earnings response coefficients' predicted value is about 30% less than that based on the random walk time series property of annual earnings [also see Kendall and Zarowin (1990) and Ramesh (1990)]. Since these estimates are derived for a sample of 118 firms surviving over a 40-year period, it is not obvious that they are the appropriate benchmark in our context.

and draw inferences from the average earnings response coefficient estimates for the following reason.

Expected-return variation through time for individual stocks is small compared to the expected-return variation across stocks, particularly when measurement intervals are long.[10] The effect of expected-return variation through time is that the estimated earnings response coefficient, on average, is approximately equal to $(1 + 1/r_{avg})$, where r_{avg} is the average expected return over the sample period. The reason for focussing on earnings response coefficients is that price–earnings regressions' explanatory power is affected by the expected-return variation and the problem is acute in a cross-sectional analysis. The proportion of cross-sectional variation in returns (the dependent variable in price–earnings regressions) attributable to risk differences is an increasing function of the measurement interval. Because the independent variable, $X_{t-\tau,t}/P_{t-\tau}$, in price–earnings regressions is a risk proxy [e.g., Ball (1978)], the *cross-sectional* association between returns and the $X_{t-\tau,t}/P_{t-\tau}$ variable is due to both unexpected earnings and risk differences. Variation due to unexpected earnings yield, on average, will tend to be a smaller fraction of the cross-sectional variation in $X_{t-\tau,t}/P_{t-\tau}$ when earnings are aggregated, i.e., as the measurement interval is increased. Variation due to expected earnings yield, on the other hand, will constitute an increasing fraction of the cross-sectional variation in $X_{t-\tau,t}/P_{t-\tau}$. Therefore the *cross-sectional* price–earnings association will also be due increasingly to cross-sectional differences in expected earnings yields. As noted above, variation in expected return (and therefore expected earnings yield) does not bias earnings response coefficient estimates.

We estimate the following time series model for each firm i:

$$P_{it}/P_{it-\tau} = \gamma_{i0\tau} + \gamma_{i1\tau} X_{it-\tau,t}/P_{it-\tau} + \varepsilon_{it}, \qquad (3)$$

where τ = one, two, or three quarters or one, two, three, or four years and $X_{it-\tau,t}$ = firm i's earnings from $t - \tau$ to t. When τ = two quarters, earnings for two quarters are summed, and when τ = two years, annual earnings for two years are summed.

In estimating (3), data availability requirements are more restrictive than using only annual earnings. As a result, sample sizes decline substantially with longer price–earnings measurement windows. To the extent expected rates of return differ across the samples, the estimated earnings response coefficients are not strictly comparable. Because the smaller samples at the longer measurement intervals are likely to consist of larger-sized firms with relatively low expected rates of return, *ceteris paribus*, their earnings response coefficients are expected

---

[10]Since expected returns are positively autocorrelated and mean reverting [e.g., Fama and French (1988) and Poterba and Summers (1988)], there is relatively less variation in expected returns through time over longer measurement intervals.

Table 3

Selected fractiles from the distribution of estimated parameters of firm-specific regressions of price relatives on contemporaneous earnings deflated by price. Earnings measurement interval ranging from one quarter to four years. One-, two-, and three-quarter price–earnings data are from 1979–88 and annual and longer-interval data are from 1950–88. Sample sizes are from 1,002 to 2,721 firms.[a]

$$P_{it}/P_{it-\tau} = \gamma_{i0\tau} + \gamma_{i1\tau} X_{it-\tau,t}/P_{it-\tau} + \varepsilon_{it}^{\,b,c}$$

	\multicolumn{7}{c}{Earnings measurement interval}
	1 qtr	2 qtrs	3 qtrs	1 year	2 years	3 years	4 years

Panel A: Intercept estimates

	1 qtr	2 qtrs	3 qtrs	1 year	2 years	3 years	4 years
Minimum	−0.21	−1.35	−0.81	−1.31	−3.79	−2.70	−2.92
10th percentile	0.82	0.67	0.55	0.61	0.32	0.14	0.03
Median	1.01	0.99	0.99	0.96	0.86	0.84	0.75
90th percentile	1.07	1.14	1.21	1.18	1.34	1.47	1.42
Maximum	1.60	1.44	2.02	3.27	5.17	3.56	3.16
Mean	0.97	0.94	0.93	0.92	0.84	0.82	0.74
Std. error	0.0032	0.0055	0.0076	0.0057	0.0102	0.0150	0.0203
N	1,948	1,660	1,536	2,721	2,045	1,535	1,002

Panel B: Annualized slope coefficient estimates[d]

	1 qtr	2 qtrs	3 qtrs	1 year	2 years	3 years	4 years
Minimum	−7.11	−11.29	−7.41	−21.01	−19.59	−33.58	−10.80
10th percentile	0.60	0.27	−0.06	0.06	−0.36	−0.95	−1.06
Median	1.03	1.39	1.80	1.89	3.53	3.96	4.15
90th percentile	3.17	5.29	7.43	5.78	9.31	11.52	11.79
Maximum	35.27	68.08	128.88	60.60	57.03	62.37	58.95
Mean	1.58	2.28	2.97	2.56	4.23	4.90	4.91
Std. error	0.0450	0.0879	0.1302	0.0701	0.1102	0.1702	0.2161

[a]For the one-, two-, and three-quarter interval price–earnings data, any firm that had earnings data on the Compustat quarterly tape and return data on the Center for Research in Security Prices monthly tape for five nonoverlapping measurement intervals during 1979–88 is included. For the annual and longer measurement intervals, the Compustat Annual Industrial and the Compustat Annual Research tapes are used from 1950–88.

[b]$X_{it-\tau,t}/P_{it-\tau}$ = primary earnings per share before extraordinary items and discontinued operations, summed over the relevant measurement interval τ and then divided by the price at the beginning of the earnings measurement interval. Price relative $P_t/P_{t-\tau}$ = one plus the buy-and-hold return, inclusive of dividends, over the interval $t-\tau$ to t. All earnings and price data are adjusted for stock splits, stock dividends, and dividend payments.

[c]The model is estimated by modeling the residuals from the ordinary least squares regressions as a first-order autoregressive process, and then ordinary least squares parameters are reestimated using transformed variables.

[d]Annualized slope coefficient = $[1 + \tau(\hat{\gamma}_{1\tau} - 1)]$, where $\hat{\gamma}_{1\tau}$ is the estimated coefficient from the regressions. The annualized slope coefficients are deflated by 1.039 to control for bias stemming from using dividend-reinvested returns.

to be larger. Any increase in earnings response coefficient estimates with the measurement interval is thus due to a better control for earnings anticipation as well as changing sample composition.

Table 3 reports the results of estimating (3) using price–earnings data measured over intervals ranging from one quarter to four years. We report annualized values of the earnings response coefficients. Assuming $\hat{\gamma}_{1\tau}$ is an estimate of $(1 + 1/r_\tau)$, where r_τ is the expected rate of return over a period of length τ (expressed as a fraction or multiple of one year), then $[1 + \tau(\hat{r}_{1\tau} - 1)]$ is the annualized coefficient estimate.

The average annualized $\hat{\gamma}_{1\tau}$ using quarterly price–earnings data is 1.58, which is small compared to the predicted earnings response coefficient of 6.83. When the measurement interval is two quarters, the earnings response coefficient is 2.28, which is an improvement over the estimate using quarterly data. The average coefficient increases to 2.56 at a one-year window and 4.91 when the measurement window is four years.[11] The medians for the corresponding measurement intervals are 1.89 and 4.15. Thus, the earnings response coefficients exhibit a substantial increase as a function of the measurement interval. The average coefficients at all measurement intervals are, however, reliably smaller than the predicted value of 6.83.

The results in table 3 are consistent with a reduced bias in earnings response coefficient estimates as one increases the earnings and return measurement interval. The results also suggest that a longer price–earnings window is not as effective as including the leading-period return because longer price–earnings mesurement windows do not fully incorporate earnings anticipation. This is seen from a comparison of the earnings response coefficients reported in table 3 with those in table 2. Specifically, the average earnings response coefficient estimates reported in table 2 are uniformly greater than those in table 3.

In summary, the results in this section suggest that increasing the price–earnings measurement window helps reduce bias in earnings response coefficient estimates, but is not as effective as including leading-period returns.

4.3. Diagnostic tests

4.3.1. Results using returns exclusive of dividends

The tests in this section assess whether the increase in the earnings response coefficient estimates as leading-period returns are included is spurious. As seen from the appendix, the earnings response coefficient is biased upwards by

---

[11]Somewhat surprisingly, the average coefficient for the three-quarter measurement interval is 2.97 which is greater than that for the annual measurement interval. This is due to a different sample and time period for the quarterly earnings data compared to the annual and longer-interval earnings data. The median earnings response coefficients, however, increase monotonically with the measurement interval.

a factor of $(1 + \text{dividend yield})^{\tau-1}$ and the bias arises because of the asymmetric effect of dividend payments on returns versus earnings. This bias should be reduced if returns exclusive of dividends are used. We therefore repeat the entire analysis using price relatives exclusive of dividends. If all firms' dividend payouts are 100%, then it is easy to show that using returns excluding dividends leads to an earnings response coefficient of $1/r$ [see e.g., Beaver, Lambert, and Morse (1980)]. For a less than 100% divided payout, they predicted earnings response coefficient is $(1 - \text{dividend payout} + 1/r)$. The estimated average coefficient using returns *excluding* dividends for none to three leading years are 2.41, 4.35, 4.57, and 4.74. These magnitudes are uniformly smaller than those reported above for the corresponding return measurement intervals in table 2, which range from 2.56 to 5.45. As expected, the estimates using returns exclusive of dividends are not smaller by one than those using with-dividends returns because firms' dividend payouts are less than 100%. The pattern of the earnings response coefficient estimates as a function of leading-period returns, however, is similar to that noted earlier.

We also estimate regressions by including up to nine leading years' returns. As more than three leading years' returns are included in the analysis, the average coefficient estimated using returns *exclusive* of dividends shows little systematic increase. It changes from 4.74 when three leading years' returns are included to 4.70 when six leading years' returns are included to 4.64 when nine leading years' returns are included. The corresponding medians are 3.75, 3.78, and 3.64. The average and median coefficients are thus largely insensitive to including additional leading-period returns.

When more than three leading years' returns *inclusive* of dividends are added, the coefficient increases from 5.45 to 6.13 to 6.83 as three, six, and nine leading years' returns are included. This means the coefficient, on average, increases by 3.8% per year beyond three leading years. While it is not obvious whether this small increase is a spurious one (because the sample size declines with additional leading-period returns), it is too small to explain the increase in the average coefficient from 2.56 when no leading-period return is included to 5.45 when three leading years' returns are included.[12]

We also assess whether the increase in the average coefficient is due to the changing sample composition as leading period returns are included in the analysis. We estimate earnings response coefficients for the subsample for which price–earnings data are available over all the return mesurement intervals. We obtain a sample of 1,669 firms. As none to three leading years' returns are included, the average coefficients for this sample are 2.52, 4.60, 4.88, and 5.07. These coefficient values are very similar to those reported in table 2 where the

---

[12]A portion of the increase in the earnings response coefficient estimates could arise if the same dividend yield is greater than the dividend yield for the CRSP equal-weighted portfolio that we use in our adjustment.

sample composition changes with the return measurement interval. Therefore, differences in the sample composition do not explain the increase in the average earnings response coefficient.

4.3.2. Pooled time-series and cross-sectional regression results

We discuss results of pooled time-series and cross-sectional regressions with none to three leading-years' returns included to provide a comparison with previous research [e.g., Collins and Kothari (1989)] and give an indication of the robustness of our findings against alternative specifications. The pooled regressions constrain the earnings response coefficient to be a cross-sectional constant. One obtains an unbiased, but statistically less precise estimate of the cross-sectional mean earnings response coefficient. In estimating the pooled regressions, we exclude 2% extreme observations because of their excessive influence on the estimated regression.[13]

When overlapping returns data are used, the earnings response coefficient increases from 1.25 (standard error = 0.018) for the contemporaneous regression to 4.89 (standard error = 0.041) when returns over three leading years (i.e., $\tau = 4$) are included. The corresponding numbers using strictly nonoverlapping data are 1.25 (standard error = 0.018) and 6.25 (standard error = 0.15). The difference in the estimated coefficients obtained using overlapping and nonoverlapping return data likely is due to a systematic difference in the two samples. A sample selection bias is introduced because, when nonoverlapping data are used and $\tau = 4$, only firms with a minimum of twenty years of continuous data are included. These firms are relatively large market value firms. Previous research suggests that expected returns and firm size are negatively correlated [e.g., Banz (1981), Foster, Olsen, and Shevlin (1984), and Handa, Kothari, and Wasley (1989)]. We therefore expect the larger, surviving firms' average earnings response coefficient to be larger. If the 11.8% realized return on the CRSP value-weighted index from 1926–88 was used as a proxy for r for this sample, then the predicted earnings response coefficient for this sample would be 9.48.

Overall, the pooled regressions yield coefficient estimates similar to the cross-sectional average coefficient from the firm-specific time-series regressions. The basic conclusion from both the analyses is that earnings response coefficient estimates substantially increase with the inclusion of leading-period returns and converge toward their predicted values.

---

[13]Since we report fractiles of the distribution of firm-specific coefficients, we do not exclude extreme observations in the analysis discussed earlier.

4.3.3. Results of including the market return in price–earnings regressions

We next report the results of estimating a model similar to (2) except that the return on the market is also included as an explanatory variable.[14] The motivation for including the market return variable is threefold: (i) The average cross-correlation among the residuals will be closer to zero when the market return is included as an independent variable. The standard error of the sample mean of the earnings response coefficients will then be less biased due to cross-sectional correlation, which will enable us to perform more reliable statistical significance tests of the average earnings response coefficient. (ii) If some of the price movement is not explained by the earnings variable, but is related to the market return, then potentially statistically more precise estimates of the earnings response coefficients are possible by including the market return variable [see Sloan (1993) for evidence]. The standard error of the average earnings response coefficient is therefore likely to decrease with the inclusion of the market return variable as an additional independent variable. (iii) Since many researchers use market- and risk-adjusted returns in estimating the earnings response coefficient [e.g., Kormendi and Lipe (1987)], our analysis facilitates comparison with their results.

Table 4 reports results of including $R_{mt-\tau,t}$ as an additional explanatory variable, where $R_{mt-\tau,t}$ is the CRSP equal-weighted return including dividends from $t-\tau$ to t, obtained by summing monthly returns over the period from $t-\tau$ to t. The results in table 4 are similar to those reported in table 2. The average earnings response coefficient increases from 1.96 when no leading-period return is included to 4.49 when the three-year leading return is included. The average and median earnings response coefficients are smaller than those in table 2 at all lengths of leading-period returns. The standard errors of the average earnings response coefficients are very similar to the corresponding standard errors reported in table 2.

The average coefficient on the market return, $\hat{\gamma}_{2\tau}$, is the estimated relative risk (beta) of the average stock in the sample. At first glance, it is puzzling to find the average security in our sample is considerably less risky than the market, especially when leading-period returns are included. For example, the average $\hat{\gamma}_{2\tau}$ is 0.92 for the annual contemporaneous regression and it is only 0.66 when three-year leading returns are included. It is likely that $\hat{\gamma}_{1\tau}$ and $\hat{\gamma}_{2\tau}$ are affected by

---

[14]An alternative approach would be to regress market and risk adjusted returns on correspondingly adjusted earnings. Our approach is econometrically preferable to the alternative two-stage approach which is likely to yield biased estimates [see Beaver (1987)]. Moreover, in the alternative two-stage approach the test period would be shorter than that examined here. The reason is that the two-stage approach entails estimating the market model parameters separately for the security-return-generating process and the earnings-generating process. This estimation will use up data over the initial few years from 1950 which then cannot be included in the test period.

Table 4

Selected fractiles from the distribution of estimated parameters of firm-specific regressions of price relatives on earnings deflated by price and market return including dividends. Earnings measurement interval is one year and price relatives are for the contemporaneous one year and for periods t that include leading years. Annual earnings data from 1950–88. Sample sizes from 2,319 to 2,721 firms.[a]

$$P_{it}/P_{it-\tau} = \gamma_{i0\tau} + \gamma_{i1\tau}X_{it}/P_{it-\tau} + \gamma_{i2\tau}R_{mt-\tau,t} + \varepsilon_{it}^{\,b,c}$$

	$\tau = 1$	$\tau = 2$	$\tau = 3$	$\tau = 4$
Panel A: Intercept estimates				
Minimum	−1.64	−2.87	−17.40	−9.60
10th percentile	0.56	0.31	0.11	−0.03
Median	0.86	0.71	0.65	0.60
90th percentile	1.06	1.04	1.32	1.18
Maximum	4.70	5.39	9.66	9.41
Mean	0.84	0.69	0.61	0.58
Std. error	0.0054	0.0083	0.0167	0.0146
N	2,721	2,588	2,471	2,319
Panel B: Coefficient on earnings				
Minimum	−31.61	−48.58	−28.23	−38.51
10th percentile	−0.09	0.22	0.27	0.22
Median	1.36	2.80	3.25	3.43
90th percentile	4.82	7.90	9.33	10.26
Maximum	60.55	100.16	91.52	81.90
Mean	1.96	3.59	4.31	4.49
Std. error	0.0662	0.0951	0.1095	0.1104
Panel C: Coefficient on the market return				
Minimum	−10.56	−7.23	−9.48	−4.93
10th percentile	0.25	0.13	−0.04	−0.05
Median	0.82	0.65	0.55	0.51
90th percentile	1.74	2.13	1.60	1.58
Maximum	8.15	5.58	24.34	10.62
Mean	0.92	0.75	0.68	0.66
Std. error	0.0151	0.0154	0.0222	0.0186

[a] Sample selection: Any firm that has earnings data on the Compustat Annual Industrial or Research tape for five consecutive years during 1950–88 and return data for the earnings measurement years and the three leading years is included. The return observations contain overlapping periods when one or more years of leading-period returns are included.

[b] Earnings yield $X_t/P_{t-\tau}$ = primary annual earnings per share before extraordinary items and discontinued operations for year t, divided by the price at the beginning of the return measurement interval. All earnings per share numbers and prices are adjusted for stock splits and stock dividends. Price relative $P_t/P_{t-\tau}$ = one plus the buy-and-hold return, inclusive of dividends, over the years $t - \tau$ to t. $R_{mt-\tau,t}$ = CRSP equal-weighted return including dividends over years $t - \tau$ to t.

[c] The model is estimated by modeling the residuals from the ordinary least squares regressions as a first-order autoregressive process and then ordinary least squares parameters are reestimated using transformed variables. The estimated slope coefficients are deflated by $(1.039)^{\tau-1}$ to control for bias stemming from using dividend-reinvested returns.

a positive correlation between the market return and the earnings variable, particularly when leading-period return is included. To verify that the sample firms' average beta risk is not unusually small, we reestimate firm-specific regressions without the earnings variable included as an independent variable. That is, we estimate the market model for each firm using annual returns. The average market model beta of the sample firms then is 1.01.

4.3.4. Sensitivity to alternative estimation procedures and statistical tests

This section assesses whether our inferences are sensitive to alternative estimation procedures and statistical tests. We estimate ordinary least squares coefficients without making an adjustment for autocorrelated errors. Since the ordinary least squares estimates are unbiased, the average coefficients should be similar to those reported earlier. The average coefficients when one to three leading years' returns are included are 4.67, 5.07, and 5.67.

Earlier in this section, we tested whether the average estimated coefficient equals its predicted value using a t-test. An alternative test is based on the sample distribution of the firm-specific estimated t-statistics. For each firm a t-statistic is calculated to test the null hypothesis that the firm's earnings response coefficient equals the predicted value of 6.83. By aggregating these t-statistics, we then calculate a Z-statistic to test the null hypothesis that the average estimated coefficient equals its predicted value of 6.83 [see, e.g., Healy, Kang, and Palepu (1987) for a description of this test]. This test weights each coefficient by the precision with which it is estimated, as compared to an equal weight in the t-test of the sample mean coefficient. The estimated Z-statistic also rejects the hypothesis that the estimated average coefficient equals its predicted value when none to three leading-year returns are included.

4.3.5. Effect of the post-earnings-announcement drift in abnormal returns

In this section we perform tests to incorporate the implications of the post-earnings-announcement drift in abnormal returns [see Bernard and Thomas (1989) for recent evidence] for earnings response coefficient estimates. We are motivated to perform this analysis by the previous, anomalous empirical evidence, rather than rational, economic reasoning. Under the maintained hypothesis of market efficiency, the Capital Asset Pricing Model, and constant expected rates of returns, future returns should not be related to the current period's earnings surprise. We estimate (2) with a three-year leading-period return, but also include return over approximately a nine-month period beyond the earnings announcement dates (i.e., one year beyond the fiscal year-end). The estimated average earnings response coefficient increases to 6.92 and the median to 5.56. Much of this increase occurs when return over the first three months following the earnings announcement is included in the analysis. This is consistent with Bernard and Thomas (1989), who report that the drift is pronounced over a three-month post-earnings-announcement period and virtually all of it occurs over a 180-trading-day period (i.e., about nine months).

5. Conclusions and implications

We examine the implications of returns anticipating future earnings changes for price–earnings relations. Returns tend to lead earnings changes because the historical cost accounting measurement process is not designed to fully reflect expectations of future net cash flows on a timely basis. As a result the commonly estimated price–earnings regression of contemporaneous annual returns on earnings changes is misspecified and the earnings response coefficient estimates are biased towards zero. We argue that including the leading-period return should ameliorate the missspecification and the estimated earnings response coefficients should increase.

Our empirical results are consistent with this prediction. We provide evidence that earnings response coefficient estimates are sensitive to the inclusion of leading-period returns. The coefficient more than doubles as leading-period returns are included in the price–earnings regression. The resulting average earnings response coefficient estimate is consistent with the previously documented time series properties of annual earnings. We also estimate price–earnings regressions using returns and earnings measured over longer contemporaneous windows. The results suggest that longer measurement intervals yield less biased estimates of earnings response coefficients, but this approach is not as effective as including the leading-period return. The reason is returns measured over longer intervals do not completely incorporate earnings anticipation, unless, of course, the measurement interval coincides with the life of a firm.

In this study we focus on earnings response coefficients estimated using returns measured over a fairly long interval (e.g., one quarter or longer). Some researchers estimate a short-window earnings response coefficient using two-day earnings-announcement period returns and a proxy for the market's earnings expectation at the start of the two-day return window. Even if accurate proxies for the market's earnings expectation were available, we expect the short-window coefficients to differ from the long-window ones because the nature of earnings information probably changes in event time. The two-day announcement period information is likely to include the effects of restructuring charges, accounting changes, plant closings, etc. which could be less persistent (i.e., nonrecurring) than information about earnings released in earlier time periods.

This study has several implications for related research. First, our findings have implications for the research seeking to explain cross-sectional variation in earnings response coefficients. The observed cross-sectional variation in earnings response coefficients, estimated using contemporaneous, annual measurement interval data, could stem from variation in the degree to which prices lead earnings as well as 'true' variation in earnings response coefficients (e.g., due to variation in earnings persistence and expected return). More meaningful inferences, therefore, are possible if the effects of these two sources of variation are isolated and controlled. A fruitful avenue for future research would be to explore cross-sectional differences in the degree to which prices lead earnings as a function of the nature of a firm's production, investment and financing policies as well as accounting method choices. Industry membership and a firm's life cycle phase could serve as instruments for these cross-firm differences. Recent evidence in Rao (1991), Anthony and Ramesh (1992), and Lang (1991) suggests that a firm's life cycle phase (e.g., a newly-public, growth firm versus a mature firm) affects the price–earnings relation and earnings response coefficients.

A second avenue for future research would be to examine whether the importance of leading-period returns is reduced by incorporating financial statement information in addition to earnings. Lev and Thiagarajan (1991) and Ou and Penman (1989) are recent examples of studies that document significant information content (i.e., association with returns) of financial statement data in addition to earnings. This suggests that conditioning earnings expectation on other balance sheet and income statement data items, footnote disclosures (e.g., information on loss contingencies), and finally 'management's outlook' type of information will be helpful in forecasting earnings changes. Focusing only on the earnings number is likely to overstate the degree to which returns anticipate the information in a firm's financial statements.

Finally, there has been considerable recent interest in identifying the reasons for the observed low contemporaneous price–earnings association documented in previous research using quarterly or annual earnings data [e.g., Lev (1989) and Easton et al. (1992)]. 'Low earnings quality' sometimes is offered as the primary reason [e.g., Lev (1989)]. Low earnings quality is generally claimed to be due to 'the impact of accounting techniques and occasionally management manipulation' [Lev (1989, p. 175)]. Evidence in this paper suggests that anticipation of future earnings changes impounded in returns is an important determinant of the price–earnings association that has been relatively unexplored. Moreover, we do not think that information impounded in security prices about future earnings changes is an indication of 'earnings quality' and/or 'deficiency' of historical cost measurement. In this regard, we emphasize that unless we understand the role of accounting earnings or financial statement information in the context of security markets, competing sources of information, and bondholder–shareholder or management–shareholder contracts, it would be premature to conclude that we should alter the accounting mesurement process to improve the contemporaneous price–earnings association.

Appendix

The objective is to assess whether the earnings response coefficient spuriously increases with the inclusion of leading-period return, by examining the effect of including leading-period return in the price–earnings regression when prices are *assumed not* to lead earnings. If, under this stylized setting, the earnings response coefficient estimate is unaffected by including return over the leading period, then concern that the observed increase in earnings response coefficient estimates is spurious is mitigated.

We begin with a stylized, constant price–earnings ratio model that can be obtained by assuming constant expected returns, earnings follow a random walk, and returns do not anticipate future earnings changes. The price–earnings relation then is given by (firm-specific subscript is suppressed):

$$P_t/P_{t-1} = \gamma_0 + \gamma_1 X_t/P_{t-1} + \varepsilon_t, \tag{A.1}$$

where P_t/P_{t-1} is return inclusive of dividends over period t, X_t/P_{t-1} is earnings over period t deflated by price at the end of period $t-1$, and $\gamma_1 = (1 + 1/r)$. We assess whether the slope coefficient is expected to differ from $(1 + 1/r)$ when (A.1) is modified to include leading-period returns in the dependent variable.

We initially assume firms do not pay dividends. Earnings through time thus reflect the effect of reinvesting all earnings in each period. The empirical analog of the price–earnings eq. (A.1) is estimated, then the earnings response coefficient estimate, $\hat{\gamma}_1$, is

$$\hat{\gamma}_1 = \mathrm{cov}(X_t/P_{t-1}, P_t/P_{t-1})\,\mathrm{var}(X_t/P_{t-1}) \tag{A.2}$$

and

$$\mathrm{E}(\hat{\gamma}_1) = (1 + 1/r),$$

which means a one-period, contemporaneous price–earnings regression yields an unbiased earnings response coefficient estimate.

On including leading periods' return, the price–earnings regression becomes

$$P_t/P_{t-\tau} = \gamma_0 + \gamma_1 X_t/P_{t-\tau} + \varepsilon_t, \tag{A.3}$$

where $\mathrm{E}(\hat{\gamma}_1) = (1 + 1/r)$ in the absence of any bias. The estimated coefficient from (A.2) is

$$\begin{aligned}
\hat{\gamma}_1 &= \mathrm{cov}(X_t/P_{t-\tau}, P_t/P_{t-\tau})/\mathrm{var}(X_t/P_{t-\tau}) \\
&= \frac{\mathrm{cov}[(X_t/P_{t-1})(P_{t-1}/P_{t-\tau}),\,(P_t/P_{t-1})(P_{t-1}/P_{t-\tau})]}{\mathrm{var}[(X_t/P_{t-1})(P_{t-1}/P_{t-\tau})]}.
\end{aligned} \tag{A.4}$$

Focusing on the numerator of (A.4), the covariance term is simplified by noting that (i) X_t/P_{t-1} and $P_{t-1}/P_{t-\tau}$ are uncorrelated because prices, by assumption, do not lead earnings, and (ii) price relatives are serially uncorrelated. Therefore, the covariance term is expanded as

$$E[(X_t/P_{t-1})(P_t/P_{t-1})]E[(P_{t-1}/P_{t-\tau})^2]$$
$$- E(X_t/P_{t-1})E(P_t/P_{t-1})[E(P_{t-1}/P_{t-\tau})]^2.$$

To simplify the above expression, we substitute:

$$E(X_t/P_{t-1}) = r,$$

$$E(P_t/P_{t-1}) = (1+r),$$

$$\mathrm{var}(P_t/P_{t-1}) = \sigma^2,$$

$$E[(P_t/P_{t-1})^2] = [\sigma^2 + (1+r)^2],$$

$$E[(P_t/P_{t-\tau})^2] = [\sigma^2 + (1+r)^2]^\tau.$$

After substituting and rearranging terms, we obtain

$$\mathrm{cov}[(X_t/P_{t-1})(P_{t-1}/P_{t-\tau}), (P_t/P_{t-1})(P_{t-1}/P_{t-\tau})]$$
$$= \mathrm{cov}[X_t/P_{t-1}, P_t/P_{t-1}] * \{[1 + r^2/\sigma^2][\sigma^2 + (1+r)^2]^{\tau-1}$$
$$- (r^2/\sigma^2)(1+r)^{2(\tau-1)}\}. \tag{A.5}$$

The denominator of (A.4) is simplified similarly to obtain

$$\mathrm{var}[(X_t/P_{t-1})(P_{t-1}/P_{t-\tau})]$$
$$= \mathrm{var}(X_t/P_{t-1}) * \{[1 + r^2/\sigma^2][\sigma^2 + (1+r)^2]^{\tau-1}$$
$$- (r^2/\sigma^2)(1+r)^{2(\tau-1)}\}. \tag{A.6}$$

The ratio of (A.5) to (A.6) yields the earnings response coefficient estimate whose expectation is

$$E(\hat{\gamma}_1) = E\{\mathrm{cov}[X_t/P_{t-1}, P_t/P_{t-1}]/\mathrm{var}(X_t/P_{t-1})\} = \gamma_1, \tag{A.7}$$

which means there is no bias introduced by including leading-period returns.

In the more realistic case of firms paying dividends, earnings through time represent earnings on the initial equity and earnings on the increase in equity through earnings retention (i.e., less than 100% dividend payout). The return variable, on the other hand, assumes dividends are reinvested and thus is unaffected by dividend payments (except for a small effect of the assumption with respect to the rate of return on reinvested dividends). Under these circumstances, the estimated coefficient is

$$\hat{\gamma}_1 = \text{cov}[X_t/P_{t-\tau}, P_t/P_{t-\tau}]/\text{var}(X_t/P_{t-\tau}). \quad (A.8)$$

Eq. (A.8) is simplified by decomposing with-dividend returns into capital appreciation and dividend yield as follows:

$$P_t/P_{t-\tau} \approx (p_t/p_{t-\tau})(1 + \text{dividend yield})^{\tau}, \quad (A.9)$$

where $p_t/p_{t-\tau}$ = buy-and-hold return exclusive of dividends (i.e., capital appreciation) and dividend yield = geometric average realized dividend yield over τ periods. Using (A.8) it is easy to see that $\hat{\gamma}_1$ is biased upwards because only the covariance is affected by the dividend yield, whereas the variance term in the denominator is the same as before. Specifically, if leading-period returns are not included, then

$$\hat{\gamma}_1 = \text{cov}(X_t/P_{t-1}, P_t/P_{t-1})/\text{var}(X_t/P_{t-1}), \quad (A.10)$$

and if leading-period returns are included, then

$$\hat{\gamma}_1 = \text{cov}(X_t/P_{t-\tau}, P_t/P_{t-\tau})/\text{var}(X_t/P_{t-\tau}) \quad (A.11)$$

$$= \frac{\text{cov}[(X_t/P_{t-1})(p_{t-1}/p_{t-\tau}), (P_t/P_{t-1})(p_{t-1}/p_{t-\tau})(1 + \text{dividend yield})^{\tau-1}]}{\text{var}[(X_t/P_{t-1}(p_{t-1}/p_{t-\tau})]}$$

Eq. (A.11) can be simplified to show that

$$E(\hat{\gamma}_1) = \gamma_1^*[1 + \text{dividend yield}]^{\tau-1}, \quad (A.12)$$

where dividend yield is the realized dividend yield over one period, which is assumed constant through time. Eq. (A.12) reveals that the earnings response coefficient estimate will be biased upwards and the bias is approximately equal to the compounded dividend yield over the leading-return period. We adjust the estimated earnings response coefficients for the bias stemming from using returns inclusive of dividends.

References

Albrecht, William, L. Lookabill, and James McKeown, 1977, The time series properties of annual earnings, Journal of Accounting Research, 226–244.

Ali, Ashiq and Paul Zarowin, 1992, Permanent versus transitory components of annual earnings and estimation error in earnings response coefficients, Journal of Accounting and Economics, this issue.

Anthony, Joseph H. and Krishnamoorthy Ramesh, 1992, Association between accounting performance measures and stock price: A test of the life cycle hypothesis, Journal of Accounting and Economics, this issue.

Ball, Raymond, 1978, Anomalies in reltionships between securities' yields and yield surrogates, Journal of Financial Economics 6, 103–126.

Ball, Raymond and Philip Brown, 1968, An empirical evaluation of accounting income numbers, Journal of Accounting Research, 159–178.

Ball, Raymond and Ross L. Watts, 1972, Some time series properties of accounting income, Journal of Finance 27, 663–682.

Banz, Rolf, 1981, The relationship between return and market value of common stock, Journal of Financial Economics 9, 3–18.

Beaver, William H., 1987, The properties of sequential regressions with multiple explanatory variables, The Accounting Review, 137–144.

Beaver, William H., 1989, Financial accounting: An accounting revolution (Prentice Hall, Englewood Cliffs, NJ).

Beaver, William H., Roger Clarke, and William Wright, 1979, The association between unsystematic security returns and the magnitude of earnings forecast errors, Journal of Accounting Research 17, 316–340.

Beaver, William H., Richard Lambert, and Dale Morse, 1980, The information content of security prices, Journal of Accounting and Economics 2, 3–28.

Beaver, William H., Richard Lambert, and Stephen Ryan, 1987, The information content of security prices: A second look, Journal of Accounting and Economics 9, 139–157.

Bernard, Victor L., 1987, Cross-sectional dependence and problems in inference in market-based accounting research, Journal of Accounting Research 25, 1–48.

Bernard, Victor L. and Jacob Thomas, 1989, Post-earnings-announcement drift: Delayed price response or risk premium, Supplement of Journal of Accounting Research, 1–36.

Biddle, Gary and Gim Seow, 1990, The estimation and determinants of association between returns and earnings: Evidence from cross-industry comparisons, Working paper (University of Washington, Seattle, WA).

Blackwell, David, M. Wayne Marr, and Michael F. Spivey, Plant-closing decisions and the market value of the firm, Journal of Financial Economics 26, 277–288.

Brealey, Richard and Stewart Myers, 1988, Principles of corporate finance (McGraw-Hill, New York, NY).

Brickley, James and Leonard VanDrunen, 1990, Internal corporate restructuring: An empirical analysis, Journal of Accounting and Economics 12, 251–280.

Brooks, L. and D. Buckmaster, 1980, First difference signals and accounting income time series properties, Journal of Business, Finance and Accounting, 437–454.

Brown, Larry, Paul Griffin, Robert Hagerman, and Mark Zmijewski, 1987, An evaluation of alternative proxies for the market's assessment of unexpected earnings, Journal of Accounting and Economics 9, 153–193.

Brown, Philip, George Foster, and Eric Noreen, 1985, Security analyst multi-year earnings forecasts and the capital market, Studies in accounting research no. 21 (American Accounting Association, Sarasota, FL).

Chan, Su Han, John Martin, and John Kensinger, 1990, Corporate research and development expenditures and share value, Journal of Financial Economics 26, 255–276.

Cochrane, D. and G. Orcutt, 1949, Application of least squares regressions to relationships containing autocorrelated error terms, Journal of the American Statistical Association, 32–61.

Collins, Daniel and S.P. Kothari, 1989, An analysis of the intertemporal and cross-sectional determinants of the earnings response coefficients, Journal of Accounting and Economics 11, 143–181.

Collins, Daniel, S.P. Kothari, and Judy Rayburn, 1987, Firm size and the information content of prices with respect to earnings, Journal of Accounting and Economics 9, 111–138.

Easton, Peter and Trevor Harris, 1991, Earnings as an explanatory variable for returns, Journal of Accounting Research 29, 19–36.

Easton, Peter and Mark Zmijewski, 1989a, Cross-sectional variation in the stock market response to the announcement of accounting earnings, Journal of Accounting and Economics 11, 117–141.

Easton, Peter and Mark Zmijewski, 1989b, On the estimation of earnings response coefficients, Working paper (University of Chicago, Chicago, IL).

Easton, Peter, Trevor Harris, and James Ohlson, 1992, Aggregate accounting earnings can explain most of security returns: The case of long return intervals, Journal of Accounting and Economics, this issue.

Fama, Eugene and Kenneth French, 1988, Permanent and temporary components of stock prices, Journal of Political Economy 96, 246–273.

Foster, George, Chris Olsen, and Terry Shevlin, 1984, Earnings releases, anomalies and the behavior of security returns, The Accounting Review, 574–603.

Freeman, Robert, 1987, The association between accounting earnings and security returns for large and small firms, Journal of Accounting and Economics 9, 195–228.

Handa, Puneet, S.P. Kothari, and Charles Wasley, 1989, The relation between the return interval and betas: Implications for the size effect, Journal of Financial Economics 23, 79–100.

Healy, Paul, 1985, The effect of bonus schemes on accounting decisions, Journal of Accounting and Economics 7, 85–107.

Healy, Paul, Sok-Hyon Kang, and Krishna Palepu, 1987, The effect of accounting procedure changes on CEO's cash salary and bonus compensation, Journal of Accounting and Economics 9, 7–34.

Ibbotson, Roger and Rex Sinquefield, 1989, Stocks, bonds, bills and inflation: Historical returns (1926–1987) (The Research Foundation of the Institute of Chartered Financial Analysts, Charlottesville, VA).

Kendall, C.S. and Paul Zarowin, 1990, Time series properties of earnings, earnings persistence and earnings response coefficients, Working paper (New York University, New York, NY).

Kormendi, Roger and Robert Lipe, 1987, Earnings innovations, earnings persistence and stock returns, Journal of Business 60, 323–345.

Kormendi, Roger and Robert Lipe, 1991, The implications of the higher-order properties of annual earnings for security valuation, Working paper (University of Michigan, Ann Arbor, MI).

Landsman, Wayne and Joseph Magliolo, 1988, Cross-sectional capital market research and model specification, The Accounting Review 64, 586–604.

Lang, Mark, 1991, Time-varying stock-price responses to earnings induced by uncertainty about the time-series properties of earnings, Working paper (Graduate School of Business, Stanford University, Stanford, CA).

Lev, Baruch, 1989, On the usefulness of earnings: Lessons and directions from two decades of empirical research, Supplement of Journal of Accounting Research, 153–192.

Lev, Baruch and S. Ramu Thiagarajan, 1991, Financial statement information, Working paper (University of California, Berkeley, CA).

Lipe, Robert, 1990, The relation between stock returns and accounting earnings given alternative information, The Accounting Review 65, 49–71.

Maddala, G.S., 1977, Econometrics (McGraw-Hill, New York, NY).

McConnell, John and Chris Muscarella, 1985, Corporate capital expenditure decisions and the market value of the firm, Journal of Financial Economics 14, 399–422.

Ohlson, James A., 1991, The theory and value of earnings and an introduction to the Ball-Brown analysis, Contemporary Accounting Research, 1–19.

Ou, Jane and Stephen H. Penman, 1989, Financial statement analysis and the prediction of stock returns, Journal of Accounting and Economics 11, 295–329.

Penman, Stephen H., 1990, Financial statement information and the pricing of earnings, Working paper (University of California, Berkeley, CA).

Poterba, James and Larry Summers, 1988, Mean reversion in stock prices: Evidence and implications, Journal of Financial Economics 22, 27–59.

Ramesh, Krishnamurthi, 1990, The existence of a unit root in earnings as a determinant of the price–earnings relation, Working paper (Michigan State University, East Lansing, MI).

Rao, Gita R., 1991, The relation between stock returns and earnings: A study of newly-public firms, Working paper (University of Illinois, Urbana-Champaign, IL).

Ross, Stephen A., Rudolf W. Westerfield, and Jeffrey F. Jaffe, 1990, Corporate finance (Richard D. Irwin, Homewood, IL).

Sloan, Richard, 1992, Accounting earnings and top executive compensation, Journal of Accounting and Economics, forthcoming.

Watts, Ross L. and Richard Leftwich, 1977, The time series of annual accounting earnings, Journal of Accounting and Research 15, 253–271.

Watts, Ross L. and Jerold L. Zimmerman, 1986, Positive accounting theory (Prentice-Hall, Englewood Cliffs, NJ).

Earnings Releases, Anomalies, and the Behavior of Security Returns

George Foster, Chris Olsen and Terry Shevlin

ABSTRACT: A common finding in the literature is that systematic post-announcement drifts in security returns are associated with the sign or magnitude of unexpected earnings changes. This paper examines proposed explanations for these drifts. The paper also documents that the systematic drifts in security returns are found for only a subset of earnings expectations models. For a class of expectations models based on the time series of reported quarterly earnings, variables coding (1) the sign and magnitude of the earnings forecast error and (2) firm size independently explain 81 percent and 61 percent, respectively, of the variation in post-announcement drifts. The joint explanatory power of (1) and (2) is 85 percent, indicating that the effect of these two variables is highly collinear. The drifts are a persistent phenomenon over the 1974 to 1981 period with no evidence of being concentrated in a specific subperiod. The properties of expectations models based on the time series of earnings are contrasted with earnings expectations models based on security returns. The latter exhibit no evidence of systematic post-announcement drift behavior. The expectations models based on security returns have the appealing property that the assignment of firms to unexpected earnings change portfolios better approximates the independence-over-time assumption. This property means that these models are less vulnerable to the "proxy effect" criticism that has been made of results previously reported in the literature. The results in this paper are based on a sample of over 56,000 observations covering the 1974 to 1981 time period.

1. Introduction

THE literature on market efficiency anomalies is both large in size and broad-based in terms of the topic areas covered.[1] One frequently cited anomaly relates to the behavior of security returns subsequent to earnings announcements by firms. Many studies have reported evidence that the sign and magnitude of security returns in the *post-earnings announcement period* are positively correlated with the sign and magnitude of the unexpected component of the earnings release. This finding is consistent with the speed of adjustment to information contained in earnings releases being gradual rather than instantaneous. Section 2 of this paper discusses the existing literature and competing explanations proposed for the

[1] Foster [1984] classifies evidence viewed as anomalous with respect to market efficiency into four cate-

This paper benefited from the comments of seminar participants at The Australian Graduate School of Management, Stanford University, U.C.L.A., University of Texas at Austin, University of Oregon, Rice University, and Washington University. Detailed comments from R. Ball, W. Beaver, R. Bowman, P. Brown, J. Demski, N. Dopuch, R. Leftwich, L. Marais, D. Morse, E. Noreen, J. Patell, M. Pincus, R. Roll, and two anonymous reviewers were much appreciated. The research was supported by the Stanford Program in Accounting.

George Foster is Associate Professor of Accounting, Stanford University, Chris Olsen is Assistant Professor of Accounting, The University of Texas at Austin, and Terry Shevlin is a Ph.D. candidate in Accounting, Stanford University.

Manuscript received August 1983.
Revision received January 1984.
Accepted March 1984.

post-announcement security return behavior. The research design facilitates the probing of at least four explanations—the misspecified asset pricing model explanation, the use of hindsight information explanation, the time-period explanation, and the information market explanation. Details of sample selection, expectations models, and residual estimation/significance testing appear in Sections 3, 4, and 5, respectively. Results examining the post-announcement drifts in security returns and explanations for those drifts are presented in Sections 6 and 7. These results are based on a sample of over 56,000 observations covering the 1974 to 1981 period. Summary comments on the findings and unresolved issues are made in Section 8.

The results reported in this paper are of interest in several areas. One area is the numerous information content studies on interim and annual earnings announcements, dividend announcements, acquisition and divestiture announcements, etc. These studies typically assume market efficiency and focus on short time periods surrounding the chosen announcement to measure its information content. A similar assumption appears in the many studies on the capital market effect of FASB and SEC accounting regulations. Results discussed in Section 2 are inconsistent with this market efficiency assumption and thus raise the possibility that some inferences drawn in prior information content and accounting regulation studies are incorrect. The results are also of interest to the investment community. Studies which conclude that systematic post-announcement drifts in security returns imply market inefficiencies have stressed this rationale for the research; e.g., Latane, Jones and Rieke [1974, p. 130] conclude that their results "evidence the potential value of quarterly data in selecting investment alternatives." The Value Line security ranking system includes a "quarterly earnings momentum" factor and an "earnings surprise" factor to exploit the post-announcement security return results reported in the literature.[2] The results in this paper provide insight into some of the factors that may explain the security return differences Eisenstadt [1980] reports for stocks differentially coded in the Value Line ranking system.

The most important result reported in this paper is that systematic post-announcement drifts in security returns are found for only a subset of the earnings expectations models examined. For two expectations models based on the past quarterly earnings series, post-announcement drifts are found over the 1974 to 1981 period. However, for two expectations models based on the security return series, post-announcement drifts are not found. The latter expectations models have the appealing property that they are less vulnerable to the "proxy effect" criticism that has been made of results previously reported in the literature.

---

gories: (a) evidence on the speed of adjustment of prices to information releases, (b) evidence on price adjustments associated with releases by information intermediaries, (c) evidence on pricing anomalies assuming complete and perfect markets, and (d) evidence relating to the behavior of the aggregate market over time.

[2] Eisenstadt [1980, pp. 3, 4] describes these two factors as follows:
- "*Quarterly Earnings Momentum* . . . . each stock's quarterly earnings change from the same quarter in the preceding year is graded as to whether the change is above average, average, or below. . . .
- *An Earnings Surprise Factor* . . . . takes into account the deviation between an analyst's earnings estimate for a particular quarter and the actual earnings report. Studies have indicated that where earnings surprises occur, sharp price movements tend to follow in the direction of the surprise."

2. Overview of Existing Literature

2.1 Research Results Reported in Literature

Research that documents post-earnings announcement drifts in security returns has been published in many studies. Two review papers—Ball [1978] and Joy and Jones [1979]—summarize at least eight studies reporting post-announcement drifts for unexpected good news or unexpected bad news observations. Several studies published subsequent to these review papers, using more refined methods and larger samples, have also reported similar results—e.g., Latane and Jones [1979], Bidwell and Riddle [1981], and Rendleman, Jones and Latane [1982]. The last cited study examined quarterly earnings announcements over the 1971–1980 period. Using a standardized unexpected earnings (SUE) measure, each observation was placed into one of ten SUE categories (category 1 = most negative ... category 10 = most positive). Summary results from Table 4 of this study are:

Standardized Unexpected Earnings Category	Cumulative Average Residual [Days −20 to −1]	Average Residual [Day 0]	Cumulative Average Residual [Days 1 to 90]	Average Beta
1 (Most Negative)	−8.7	−1.4	−4.0	1.02
2	−7.3	−1.0	−3.2	1.00
3	−5.6	−0.7	−3.3	0.97
4	−3.6	−0.2	−1.8	1.00
5	−1.1	0.1	−0.8	1.03
6	1.2	0.3	0.5	1.03
7	2.8	0.6	1.2	1.01
8	3.9	0.8	1.6	1.02
9	6.9	1.3	3.4	1.02
10 (Most Positive)	8.0	1.3	4.3	1.02

The authors concluded that their "results are remarkably consistent in suggesting that the market does not assimilate unexpectedly favorable or unfavorable quarterly earnings information by the day of earnings announcement" (p. 283).

A smaller set of studies has reported evidence of less significant or insignificant systematic drift behavior. Watts [1978] examined a sample of 73 firms over the 1962 to 1968 period and reported that "abnormal returns" were found in "the 1962–1965 period but not in the 1965–1968 period" (p. 148). Moreover, he argued that the "inefficiency [in the 1962–1965 period] is not substantial. Only those who can avoid some of the direct transaction costs can make abnormal returns after quarterly earnings announcements" (p. 146). Reinganum [1981] examined 566 firms over the 1975–1977 period and reported that "'abnormal' returns cannot be earned over the period studied by constructing portfolios on the basis of firms' standardized unexpected earnings" (p. 24).

2.2 Competing Explanations for Systematic Drifts

The set of explanations offered for the post-earnings announcement anomalies reported in many studies can be classified into (a) capital market inefficiency explanations, and (b) noncapital market inefficiency explanations.

A. *Capital Market Inefficiency Explanations.* The most frequently referenced explanation for the reported systematic drifts is market inefficiency. For instance, Brown [1978, p. 27] concludes his study thus:

> The most important results of this study are the findings relative to market efficiency. The excess returns from purchasing the qualifying securities at the time of publication of the EPS number substantially exceed transaction costs. The adjustment process, rather than being instantaneous, is lengthy (about 45 market days). Thus, with respect to this particular sample of securities, the market exhibited inefficiencies.

In a review of much of this literature, Joy and Jones [1979, p. 51] conclude "that, at least with respect to quarterly earnings announcements there have been marked inefficiencies."

The notion of market efficiency implicit in the anomalies literature appears to preclude a trading strategy yielding "abnormal returns" if it is based only on publicly available information. Following Fama [1976], let ϕ_t^A be the information set available to the capital market at time t and ϕ_t^M be the information set used by the market at time t in setting equilibrium prices. If the capital market is efficient with respect to ϕ_t^A, then equilibrium prices will be set "as if"

$$\phi_t^A = \phi_t^M. \qquad (1)$$

Tests of (1) typically have used the two-parameter model of Sharpe [1964] to give content to what is an "abnormal return":

$$E(\tilde{R}_{it}) = R_{ft} + \beta_i(E(\tilde{R}_{Mt}) - R_{ft}), \qquad (2)$$

where

R_{it} = return on ith security in period t,
R_{Mt} = return on the market portfolio in period t,
R_{ft} = return on a riskless asset in period t, and
β_{it} = the relative (systematic) risk of firm i in period t.

Market efficiency implies that:

$$f(\tilde{R}_{it}|\beta_{it}, E(\tilde{R}_{Mt}), R_{ft}, \phi_t^A)$$
$$= f(\tilde{R}_{it}|\beta_{it}, E(\tilde{R}_{Mt}), R_{ft}, \phi_t^M), \qquad (3)$$

where $f(\ )$ is a distribution function. Let

$$\tilde{u}_{i,t} = [\tilde{R}_{it}|\phi_t^M]$$
$$- [E(\tilde{R}_{it})|\beta_{it}, \tilde{R}_{Mt}, R_{ft}, \phi_t^A]. \qquad (4)$$

Assume zero information processing costs for data in ϕ_t^A and unbiased estimates of β_{it}, $\tilde{R}_{Mt}$ and R_{ft}. An implication of (1) and (2) is that $\tilde{u}_{i,t}$ in (4) should not behave in a systematic way that is related to an information cue that is already in ϕ_t^A.

Direct empirical tests of the above market efficiency notion do not appear possible; the left-hand side of (3) is an unobservable. Empirical tests concentrate on the descriptive validity of implications of the market efficiency notion. Assumptions typically made in these tests include:

(i) that the two-parameter asset pricing model in (2)—CAPM—is descriptively valid,
(ii) that unbiased estimates of $E(\tilde{R}_{it})$, β_{it}, $E(\tilde{R}_{Mt})$ and R_{ft} are used in the test,
(iii) that the specific information cue is part of ϕ_t^A, and
(iv) that the processing costs of using the information are zero.

Note that if one or more of these assumptions does not hold, conclusions drawn about market inefficiencies can be premature.

B. *Non-Capital Market Inefficiency Explanations.* This section outlines non-market inefficiency explanations for the systematic post-announcement drifts.

(i) *CAPM—An Inadequate Model of Asset Pricing.* This explanation asserts that some model other than the two-parameter model is descriptively valid. Ball [1978] summarizes the argument thus:

The hypothesis is that: (i) the two-parameter model, when applied to a portfolio of common stocks, misspecifies the process generating securities' yields in equilibrium; and (ii) earnings and dividend variables proxy for the underlying determinants of equilibrium yields. The implication is that the estimated post-announcement excess returns result from earnings and dividends proxying for omitted variables or other misspecification effects (p. 111).

Using a multi-factor model approach, Sharpe [1982] presents results that "call into question naive applications in which expected returns are assumed to be related only to estimates of future betas based on past patterns of returns" (p. 18). Factors reported to be significant by Sharpe include the alpha and beta from a market model regression of R_{it} against R_{Mt}, β_{it}, dividend yield, firm size, and a bond beta from a regression of R_{it} against a long-term government bond index. Several other papers also report results consistent with firm size being (or proxying for) an omitted variable in the CAPM—see Banz [1981], Reinganum [1981] and Keim [1983]. This paper examines the ability of the firm size variable to explain the post-earnings announcement drifts in security returns.

In addition to examining firm size as an omitted variable, the paper analyzes the "proxy" argument of Ball [1978], i.e., that the variables used to classify firms into earnings change categories proxy for variables omitted in the CAPM but priced by the capital market. Proxy effects are more likely with earnings expectations models that exhibit period by period dependencies in their classification of firms to earnings change categories. To illustrate, suppose a study examined the earnings releases of one large firm and one small firm over 20 quarters and ranked the two firms each quarter into a high and low earnings category. Pooling the 40 observations, 20 observations will be in the high earnings category and 20 will be in the low earnings category. Inferences about the market reaction to the two earnings classifications will be most reliable if the classification on earnings is independent of firm size. Under independence, both earnings categories would include approximately ten large-firm and ten small-firm observations randomly drawn from the 20 quarters. If, however, the earnings-change classification perfectly proxies for the firm-size classification, the high/low earnings category each would include all observations of the one firm-size category. In this context, the experiment cannot discriminate between firm size or earnings classification being the causal variable in a capital market reaction study. Section 4 of this paper reports data on period by period dependencies in the assignment of firms to earnings change categories for each of the expectations models used in the research.

(ii) *Biased Estimates of Parameters of Adopted Asset Pricing Model.* To illustrate this explanation, assume the CAPM is a descriptively valid model. To employ the CAPM in empirical research, estimates of β_{it}, R_{ft} and R_{Mt} are required. Let $\tilde{u}_{i,t}^T$ be the "true" abnormal return and $\tilde{u}_{i,t}^E$ be the "estimated" abnormal return. This explanation posits that

$$E(\tilde{u}_{i,t}^T|\phi_t^M) = E(\tilde{u}_{i,t}^T|\phi_t^A) = 0 \qquad (5)$$

in the post-announcement period, but that $\tilde{u}_{i,t}^E$ behaves in a systematic way due to estimation errors in β_{it}, R_{ft} or R_{Mt}. Given that many prior studies report positive $\tilde{u}_{i,t}^E$ for positive unexpected earnings changes and negative $\tilde{u}_{i,t}^E$ for negative unexpected earnings changes, the precise form that the estimation error would have to take would depend on the sign of the unexpected earnings change and the sign of $(\tilde{R}_{Mt} - R_{ft})$.[3]

Rendleman, Jones and Latane [1982] examine the importance of relative risk adjustments and conclude that "the typical SUE (standardized unexpected earnings) portfolio has a beta of approximately 1.0, and that risk adjustment procedures are not the critical issue here. One must look elsewhere for an explanation of these results" (p. 287). In Sections 6 and 7 of this paper abnormal returns are estimated via a companion portfolio technique that controls for beta (and other) differences across portfolios with different market capitalization characteristics.

iii) *Use of Hindsight Information in the Experiment.* One assumption made when testing market efficiency with respect to a specific information item is that the information is available to the market at the time it is used to classify securities differentially. In several studies, information appears to have been assumed available before it is publicly released; e.g., Jones and Litzenberger [1970] assume all interim releases to be available to the market within two months subsequent to the end of the fiscal quarter. This assumption is correct for many but not all firms—see Foster [1981, Table 2]. The effect of this violation of a "predictive experiment" design is to include as part of the post-announcement returns the announcement month effect of those firms releasing their interim report after the two-month post-fiscal year-end period. Typically this will result in the post-announcement returns for positive (negative) earnings change groups being overstated (understated). The research in this paper uses actual earnings announcement dates (as reported by Standard and Poor's) in an attempt to avoid this problem.

Another example of the use of hindsight information is in the Watts [1978] study. The 1962 to 1968 period first was used to choose the "best" time-series model to employ in the research. Then the same 1962 to 1968 period was used to examine the post-announcement drifts associated with the unexpected earnings increase and decrease classifications from the "best" time-series model. The research in this paper employs time-series models that are estimated using only data available at the time the earnings increase/decrease classifications are made.

A third example of the use of hindsight information is the classification of firms into portfolios based on information not available at the time a trading strategy is implemented. For example, a trading strategy based on the rank of each firm's earnings change is not implementable until the last firm in the sample has announced its earnings. A related problem is when observations are placed into portfolios each quarter and the mean aggregate results based on the mean of the individual quarter's (mean) results; this implicitly "assumes that the trader knows the distribution of standardized forecast errors at the time of the first earnings announcement in each calendar quarter" [Holthausen, 1983, p. 41]. Holthausen notes that the trading strategies in Watts [1978] and Rendleman, Jones and Latane [1982] suffer from this experimental defect. He reports that use of a ranking scheme based on publicly released information results in "the association between post earnings

---

[3] To illustrate, consider markets in which $(\tilde{R}_{Mt} - R_{ft}) < 0$. To explain the results in Rendleman, Jones and Latane [1982] would require β_{it} to be over-estimated for firms with positive SUE, but under-estimated for firms with negative SUE. In contrast, in markets in which $(\tilde{R}_{Mt} - R_{ft}) > 0$, β_{it} would have to be under-estimated for firms with positive SUE but over-estimated for firms with negative SUE.

announcement abnormal performance and the size of forecast errors [being] much weaker than those reported by Rendleman, Jones and Latane [1982]" (p. 56). The research in this paper uses cut-off points based on a ranking of the *previous* quarter's earnings forecast errors to assign firms into one of ten forecast error portfolios, and all observations in a given portfolio are weighted equally.[4]

A fourth example of the use of hindsight information is the survivorship bias encountered when the Compustat data base is employed. For instance, the 1982 Compustat quarterly tape includes the most recent 40 quarters of data for firms surviving in 1982. Firms that were publicly listed in 1973 but were delisted prior to 1982 are excluded from the 1982 tape. The effect of these exclusions is difficult to predict; e.g., the exclusion of bankrupt firms may impart an upward bias to the sample security returns whereas the exclusion of acquired firms may have the opposite effect. In the initial stage of this research project, a sample of 79 companies publicly listed in 1962 was selected. Earnings announcement dates for these firms over the 1963 to 1977 period were hand-collected. Of the 79 companies available in 1962, 55 were surviving in 1978. Results for the sample of 79 companies vis-a-vis the sample of 55 surviving companies were very similar, e.g., a policy of investing long in firms with actual earnings $>1.6*$ expected earnings and short in firms with actual earnings $<.6*$ expected earnings yielded a six-month post-announcement CAR of 2.02 percent for the 55 survived-firm sample vis-a-vis 2.10 percent for the 79-firm sample. The conclusion drawn was that survivorship was not an important explanation for the systematic post-announcement CAR drifts.[5] Subsequent to the collection of data for the above noted 79 companies, we became aware that the Compustat quarterly tape includes earnings announcement dates as well as reported earnings data. The results reported in this paper are for the 1982 Compustat sample. This sample choice is based both on (a) the above noted results on the minimal effect of survivorship bias and (b) the sizeable increase in sample size available with the Compustat tape.

(iv) *Time-Period Phenomenon.* This explanation has two variants. The first variant hypothesizes that the underlying process is one for which

$$E(\tilde{u}_{i,t}|\phi_t^A)=0 \qquad (6)$$

but that the time period examined is one in which the realizations of $\tilde{u}_{i,t}$ appear inconsistent with (6); this possibility exists especially when short time periods are examined. Beaver and Landsman [1981] illustrate how a process consistent with (6) holding over the 46-year period from 1932 to 1977 can show apparent systematic drifts in $\tilde{u}_{it}$ for (say) two- or three-year subperiods.

The second variant of this explanation is that in an early subperiod examined,

$$E(\tilde{u}_{i,t}|\phi_t^A)\neq 0, \qquad (7)$$

but that in a later subperiod learning occurs such that (6) holds. Watts [1978, p. 146] puts forward this argument in a study examining the 1962 to 1968 period:

> The observation of abnormal returns in the 1962–1965 period but not in the 1965–1968 period raises several possibilities. One is that the 1962–1965 abnormal returns are observed by chance. ... [Another possibility is] that the

---

[4] We are indebted to an anonymous reviewer of this paper and R. Holthausen for pointing out this class of experimental problems.

[5] Survivorship was also reported not to be an important factor in drawing inferences about the time series properties of reported earnings—see Ball and Watts [1979].

market was inefficient in the 1962–1965 period but learned over time. Discrimination among these alternative explanations requires estimation of abnormal returns outside the 1962–1968 period.

Results reported in Sections 6 and 7 of this paper are for the first quarter of 1974 to the fourth quarter of 1981 period. Results will be presented for all 32 quarters pooled as well as a breakdown of results on a subperiod basis. This relatively long time period was chosen to address better both variants of the time period explanation for the systematic post-announcement drifts in security returns.

(v) *Capital Market Efficient but Anomalies due to Attributes of Other Markets.* This explanation posits that the market for information could explain the pattern of post-announcement drifts—see Gonedes [1976]. The explanation has been offered only in a very general way, with no specific reference to earnings announcement-based anomalies. *A priori*, the costs of processing information about the magnitude of unexpected earnings changes appear minimal. Moreover, there are no obvious barriers to the entry of individual market participants employing the ranking procedures used in this and prior papers.

One variant of the information market explanation posits a link between the size of a company and the efficiency with which that stock is priced. For instance, the following comment was made in a brochure circulated by Equity Research Associates [undated], an investment company that focuses on so-called "junior companies":

> The larger and more visible a company, the more "perfect" its market is likely to be—"perfect" meaning that most of the likely factors affecting the price of its securities are presumably known to the market. Conversely, the smaller a company is, the less visible it is to the investing public and the more "imperfect" the market price for its shares is likely to be.

As applied to the post-earnings announcement drift anomaly, this argument would imply larger systematic drifts for smaller firms than for larger firms. In Section 7 of this paper, results are presented for different size partitions to probe this argument.

3. Sample Selection

The 1982 Compustat tape, covering 2,454 companies, was the initial data base examined. The first screen, requiring each company to have at least ten consecutive earnings observations, reduced the sample to 2,213 companies. The second screen required each company to have data on the CRSP daily tape. This further reduced the sample to 2,053 companies. Early versions of the quarterly Compustat tape were then used to build for each company (if available) a quarterly earnings file covering the second quarter of 1970 to the fourth quarter of the 1981 period.

The cumulative abnormal return (CAR) results reported in this paper cover the 1974 to 1981 period. The pre-1974 period is used in estimating univariate time-series models. In any one quarter, fewer than the maximum of 2,053 companies are available. Some observations are lost due to the Compustat tape not having a complete set of earnings announcement dates for each company. Other observations are lost for firms which were not publicly listed over the entire 1974–1981 period. The minimum number of observations in any one quarter is 1,495 while the maximum number is 1,978.

4. Models Used to Estimate Unexpected Earnings

Results will be presented for four

models of estimating unexpected earnings. Models 1 and 2 use quarterly earnings forecasts from the following univariate time-series model:

$$E(Q_{i,t}) = Q_{i,t-4} + \phi_i(Q_{i,t-1} - Q_{i,t-5}) + \delta_i \quad (8)$$

where $Q_{i,t}$ = quarterly earnings of the ith firm in period t. The ϕ_i and δ_i parameters are estimated using the most recent twenty quarters of data.[6]

Model 1

$$FE_i^1 = \frac{Q_{i,t} - E(Q_{i,t})}{|Q_{i,t}|} \quad (9)$$

Model 2

$$FE_i^2 = \frac{Q_{i,t} - E(Q_{i,t})}{\sigma[Q_{i,t} - E(Q_{i,t})]} \quad (10)$$

where FE_i = forecast error for firm i. Model 1 uses the absolute value of the series as the deflator while Model 2 uses the standard deviation of the forecast error.[7] The following time-series model was also examined in this research with no substantive change in the results reported in this paper for Models 1 and 2 using (8):

$$E(Q_{i,t}) = Q_{i,t-4} + \delta_i. \quad (11)$$

Foster [1977] also found that using a market association criterion, there was little difference between the results of (8) and (11).

Models 3 and 4 use security returns as the basis for estimating unexpected earnings. Model 3 focuses on the short-run market reaction to the earnings announcement:

Model 3

$$FE_i^3 = \frac{\sum_{t=-1}^{0} \tilde{u}_{i,t}}{\sigma(\tilde{u}_{i,t})} \quad (12)$$

where

$\sum_{t=-1}^{0} \tilde{u}_{i,t}$ = the cumulative two-day abnormal return in the day preceding and the day of the earnings announcement, and

$\sigma(\tilde{u}_{i,t})$ = the standard deviation of $\tilde{u}_{i,t}$ in the 250-trading-day period prior to the $[-1, 0]$ event time period being examined.

Model 4 focuses on a longer time frame to capture an anticipation period when some of the information embedded in the earnings release is impounded in security prices:

Model 4

$$FE_i^4 = \frac{\left(\sum_{t=-60}^{0} \tilde{u}_{i,t}\right)/61}{\sigma(\tilde{u}_{i,t})} \quad (13)$$

where

$\sum_{t=-60}^{0} \tilde{u}_{i,t}$ = the cumulative abnormal return in the 61-trading-day period up to and including the day of the earnings announcement, and

$\sigma(\tilde{u}_{i,t})$ = the standard deviation of $\tilde{u}_{i,t}$ in the 250-trading-day period prior to the $[-60, 0]$ event time period being examined.

Details of abnormal return estimation are provided in the next section of this paper. One motivation for using Models 3 and 4 is prior research documenting the broad information set impounded in security

---

[6] For the first five quarters of the 1974–1981 period, 15, 16, 17, 18, and 19 observations, respectively, are used to estimate ϕ_i and δ_i. The remaining 27 quarters use the most recent 20 quarters of data to estimate ϕ_i and δ_i. See Foster [1977] for further description of this model.

[7] Only forecast errors observed prior to the quarter examined are used to estimate the standard deviation of the forecast error. The maximum number of observations used to compute the standard deviation is 20.

TABLE 1

UNCONDITIONAL AND CONDITIONAL RELATIVE FREQUENCIES FOR MEMBERSHIP OF FORECAST ERROR PORTFOLIOS[a]

Forecast Error Portfolio	$\phi(\text{FEP}_t)$	$\phi(\text{FEP}_t\|\text{FEP}_{t-1})$	$\phi(\text{FEP}_t\|\text{FEP}_{t-2})$	$\phi(\text{FEP}_t\|\text{FEP}_{t-3})$	$\phi(\text{FEP}_t\|\text{FEP}_{t-4})$
A. Model 1[b]					
1	.101	.334	.245	.202	.109
2	.101	.192	.159	.134	.099
3	.100	.171	.146	.126	.099
4	.101	.189	.162	.140	.134
5	.096	.193	.171	.159	.166
6	.099	.197	.173	.163	.165
7	.100	.189	.152	.141	.132
8	.100	.192	.151	.124	.106
9	.101	.228	.166	.151	.101
10	.101	.372	.297	.266	.166
B. Model 2[c]					
1	.101	.270	.197	.149	.075
2	.098	.176	.143	.130	.096
3	.101	.147	.134	.115	.111
4	.102	.172	.153	.143	.151
5	.100	.155	.133	.130	.141
6	.098	.135	.114	.110	.114
7	.098	.133	.112	.101	.102
8	.099	.146	.124	.116	.098
9	.101	.186	.151	.129	.122
10	.103	.322	.248	.220	.197
C. Model 3[d]					
1	.100	.116	.106	.108	.116
2	.099	.102	.096	.099	.109
3	.100	.096	.097	.100	.105
4	.102	.099	.093	.106	.111
5	.099	.099	.097	.106	.100
6	.100	.105	.100	.103	.106
7	.101	.101	.105	.095	.105
8	.098	.106	.101	.103	.101
9	.099	.104	.106	.111	.106
10	.101	.114	.105	.109	.112
D. Model 4[e]					
1	.102	.156	.136	.163	.150
2	.097	.111	.104	.105	.104
3	.100	.101	.110	.101	.103
4	.098	.107	.100	.104	.103
5	.101	.099	.104	.099	.105
6	.102	.106	.102	.101	.102
7	.099	.107	.101	.108	.097
8	.098	.102	.101	.096	.099
9	.100	.109	.093	.100	.112
10	.103	.161	.116	.126	.118

[a] Forecast error portfolios 1 and 10 are formed using lowest and highest forecast error decile cut-offs, respectively.
[b] Model 1 forecast error $=(Q_{i,t}-E(Q_{i,t}))/\text{Abs}(Q_{i,t})$ where $E(Q_{i,t})=Q_{i,t-4}+\phi_i(Q_{i,t-1}-Q_{i,t-5})+\delta_i$.
[c] Model 2 forecast error $=(Q_{i,t}-E(Q_{i,t}))/\sigma(Q_{i,t}-E(Q_{i,t}))$ where $E(Q_{i,t})$ as in Model 1.
[d] Model 3 forecast error $=\sum_t \tilde{u}_{i,t}/\sigma(\tilde{u}_{i,t})$ where $\tilde{u}_{i,t}=\tilde{R}_{i,t}-\tilde{R}_{p,t}$; $t=-1$ to 0; $\tilde{R}_{p,t}$ = equally weighted mean daily return on the firm size decile that firm i falls into in the quarter examined; $\sigma(\tilde{u}_{i,t})$ = standard deviation of the residual return estimated over 250 trading days prior to the $[-1, 0]$ period.
[e] Model 4 forecast error $=((\sum_t \tilde{u}_{i,t})/61)/\sigma(\tilde{u}_{i,t})$ where $\tilde{u}_{i,t}=\tilde{R}_{i,t}-\tilde{R}_{p,t}$; $t=-60$ to 0; $\tilde{R}_{p,t}$ as in Model 3; $\sigma(\tilde{u}_{i,t})$ = standard deviation estimated over 250 trading days prior to the $[-60, 0]$ period.

prices—see Beaver, Lambert and Morse [1980] for the use of security price when forecasting earnings, Foster [1981] for the use of security price in identifying information transfers associated with earnings releases, and Patell and Wolfson [1982] for the use of security price in classifying earnings releases into "good news" and "bad news" categories.

The portfolio formation technique will be explained using FE_i^1. For each quarter from the fourth quarter of 1973 to the third quarter of 1981, all observations were ranked using the FE_i^1 for that quarter. Then the deciles of the distribution for each quarter were determined. These deciles were used as the cut-offs for assigning firms into one of ten forecast error portfolios in the quarter subsequent to that in which the cut-off points were determined. The same procedure independently was used with FE_i^2, FE_i^3 and FE_i^4.

Table 1 presents the unconditional and conditional relative frequencies of a firm being in portfolio j in quarter t:

$\phi(FEP_{j,t}) =$ unconditional relative frequency of a firm being in forecast error portfolio j (FEP_j) in period t, and

$\phi(FEP_{j,t}|FEP_{j,t-n}) =$ relative frequency of a firm being in FEP_j in period t, conditional upon being in FEP_j in period $t-n$.

If there is independence in period-by-period classification of firms to a specific FEP,

$$\phi(FEP_{j,t}) = \phi(FEP_{j,t}|FEP_{j,t-1})$$
$$= \ldots = \phi(FEP_{j,t}|FEP_{j,t-n}). \quad (14)$$

The two models that violate the independence assumption most are Models 1 and 2. For instance, using Model 2 the unconditional relative frequency of being in the most negative (positive) unexpected earnings portfolio is .101 (.103). However, conditional upon the firm being in $FEP_1^2(FEP_{10}^2)$ in period $t-1$, the probability of it also being in $FEP_1^2(FEP_{10}^2)$ in period t increases to .270 (.322). Results using Models 1 and 2 are more exposed than Models 3 and 4 to the "proxy bias" described in Section 2.2B(i) of this paper. Models 1 and 2 are similar to those used in prior studies reporting systematic drifts in security returns.

Table 2 presents the median values of FE_i^1, FE_i^2, FE_i^3 and FE_i^4 for observations in each of the ten forecast error portfolios of each model. The Spearman rank correlations between the median values of each model are:

	Spearman Rank Correlation Between					
Model Used To Form Portfolios	FE_i^1 and FE_i^2	FE_i^1 and FE_i^3	FE_i^1 and FE_i^4	FE_i^2 and FE_i^3	FE_i^2 and FE_i^4	FE_i^3 and FE_i^4
Model 1	.96	.93	.96	.99	1.00	.99
Model 2	1.00	1.00	1.00	1.00	1.00	1.00
Model 3	1.00	.99	.99	.99	.99	1.00
Model 4	1.00	1.00	1.00	1.00	1.00	1.00

The above correlations are all significant at the .01 level. They are consistent with each of the four models capturing related phenomena.

5. SECURITY RETURN ESTIMATION AND SIGNIFICANCE TESTING

Abnormal returns reported in Section 6 of this paper are computed as:

$$\tilde{u}_{i,t} = \tilde{R}_{i,t} - \tilde{R}_{p,t} \quad (15)$$

where

$\tilde{R}_{i,t}$ = return on security i in day t, and
$\tilde{R}_{p,t}$ = equally weighted mean return on the NYSE firm size decile that firm i is a member of in the quarter examined.

This companion portfolio approach assumes that all firms in a firm size decile are homogeneous but allows for heterogeneity across firm size deciles. Adopting the capital asset pricing model perspective of (2), it allows for relative risk differences across firm size deciles but assumes homogeneity within firm size deciles. One benefit of (15) is that it controls for the firm size effects in security returns noted in Banz [1981], Reinganum [1981], Sharpe [1982] and Keim [1983]. This benefit is especially important in Section 7 where the effect of firm size on the magnitude of the post-earnings announcement drifts in security returns is examined—see the Appendix of this paper for further discussion.

The firm size deciles used in (15) are constructed by ranking all firms on the NYSE at the start of each year and then computing the mean daily returns of each decile for the next 12 months. Table 3 presents the average daily return and relative risk estimates of the ten firm size deciles over the 1973–1981 period. The firm size effect on security returns reported previously in the literature is apparent over the 1973–1981 period; e.g., the mean return for the smallest decile is more than five times the mean

TABLE 2

MEDIAN VALUES OF ALTERNATIVE ERROR METRICS FOR FORECAST ERROR PORTFOLIOS[a]

Forecast Error Portfolio	Median[b] FE_i^1	Median[b] FE_i^2	Median[b] FE_i^3	Median[b] FE_i^4
Model 1				
1	−2.335	−1.445	−0.388	−0.038
2	−0.600	−0.994	−0.319	−0.032
3	−0.165	−0.458	−0.249	−0.022
4	−0.011	−0.028	−0.146	−0.014
5	0.066	0.353	−0.023	−0.005
6	0.126	0.784	0.069	0.006
7	0.192	1.108	0.163	0.010
8	0.286	1.355	0.216	0.020
9	0.459	1.399	0.264	0.025
10	1.233	1.158	0.152	0.019
Model 2				
1	−1.093	−2.244	−0.437	−0.045
2	−0.496	−0.907	−0.301	−0.031
3	−0.191	−0.363	−0.194	−0.020
4	−0.012	−0.030	−0.165	−0.008
5	0.084	0.200	−0.026	−0.003
6	0.157	0.467	0.040	0.003
7	0.206	0.775	0.110	0.009
8	0.243	1.182	0.184	0.014
9	0.282	1.803	0.245	0.022
10	0.343	3.151	0.318	0.030
Model 3				
1	−0.039	−0.098	−2.412	−0.041
2	0.038	0.097	−1.385	−0.022
3	0.071	0.208	−0.884	−0.013
4	0.080	0.254	−0.503	−0.009
5	0.079	0.235	−0.174	−0.007
6	0.095	0.310	0.120	−0.002
7	0.112	0.415	0.472	0.002
8	0.124	0.456	0.904	0.005
9	0.141	0.534	1.505	0.014
10	0.204	0.817	2.829	0.038
Model 4				
1	−0.027	−0.081	−0.504	−0.165
2	0.003	0.010	−0.316	−0.099
3	0.047	0.123	−0.203	−0.065
4	0.070	0.196	−0.079	−0.038
5	0.095	0.309	−0.044	−0.015
6	0.105	0.337	0.005	0.008
7	0.121	0.402	0.073	0.033
8	0.132	0.490	0.115	0.061
9	0.158	0.634	0.262	0.099
10	0.189	0.793	0.406	0.174

[a] Forecast error portfolios and models are noted in Table 1.
[b] The median of the sorted distribution of forecast errors based on portfolio membership as per the model in the far left column.

return of the largest decile. The relative risks of the ten deciles range from 1.11 to .92 using OLS and 1.16 to 0.83 using Scholes-Williams [1977] estimation techniques.

TABLE 3

NYSE FIRM SIZE DECILES: 1973–1981

Firm Size Decile	Average Daily Security Return	Average O.L.S. Beta[a]	Average Scholes-Williams [1977] Beta[a]
0–.1 (Smallest)	0.111%	1.11	1.16
.1–.2	0.084%	1.10	1.10
.2–.3	0.070%	1.07	1.06
.3–.4	0.063%	1.02	1.01
.4–.5	0.061%	1.00	0.98
.5–.6	0.053%	0.97	0.94
.6–.7	0.048%	0.96	0.93
.7–.8	0.046%	0.93	0.90
.8–.9	0.038%	0.92	0.88
.9–1.00 (Largest)	0.021%	0.92	0.83

[a] The beta is based on a separate regression using daily data for each year. The annual betas are averaged over the nine-year period.

Statistical significance of cumulative abnormal return (CAR) results is assessed by comparing the observed CAR with the empirical distribution of CAR's for the sample of firms. The empirical distribution is generated as follows:

1. Randomly select 8,000 firm/quarter combinations over the 1974 to 1981 period (out of a maximum of 65,696—2,053 firms × 32 quarters).
2. Select those observations satisfying the announcement date/security return availability requirements and compute the CAR for that sample over the time period in question. (This is equivalent to randomly assigning an observation to a specific earnings forecast error portfolio.) The typical sample size in Step 2 approximates that of each of the ten portfolios examined in Section 6.
3. Repeat Steps 1 and 2 1,000 times and then rank the sample CAR's from lowest to highest to obtain the empirical distribution of CAR's for the sample.

This significance test has several appealing properties vis-a-vis the use of the more conventional t tests or standardized t tests; e.g., it does *not* assume normality, it does *not* assume constant variance across securities or over time, and it does *not* assume cross-sectional independence in the residuals.[8]

In Section 7, firms are classified into one of five firm size quintiles each quarter and CAR results are presented for each quintile. Significance tests presented in Section 7 for the separate firm size quintiles are based on an empirical distribution generated over 200 independent trials for the specific firm size quintile being examined.

6. CAR RESULTS FOR ALL OBSERVATIONS

CAR results are presented in Table 4 for three time periods:

[−1, 0] = CAR for the trading day preceding and the trading day of the earnings announcement,

[−60, 0] = CAR from 61 trading days up to and including the day of the earnings announcement, and

[+1, +60] = CAR for the 60-trading-day period subsequent to the earnings announcement date.

All four models used to estimate unexpected earnings show a consistent pattern

---

[8] The assistance of E. Noreen in devising this significance test is gratefully acknowledged. L. Marais of The University of Chicago is conducting related research in this area.

TABLE 4

CUMULATIVE AVERAGE RESIDUALS FOR FORECAST ERROR PORTFOLIOS: ALL OBSERVATIONS POOLED[a]

Forecast Error Portfolio	Days [−1, 0]				Days [−60, 0]				Days [+1, +60]			
	Model 1	Model 2	Model 3	Model 4	Model 1	Model 2	Model 3	Model 4	Model 1	Model 2	Model 3	Model 4
1	−1.36*	−1.34*	−6.54*	−1.38*	−5.57*	−5.94*	−5.39*	−21.50*	−3.02*	−3.08*	0.04	0.17
2	−0.94*	−0.88*	−3.70*	−0.86*	−4.01*	−3.95*	−2.65*	−14.48*	−2.59*	−2.73*	0.40	0.47
3	−0.50*	−0.49*	−2.44*	−0.56*	−2.29*	−2.37*	−1.04*	−10.19*	−1.58*	−1.78*	0.06	0.42
4	−0.25*	−0.25*	−1.36*	−0.24*	−1.19*	−0.32*	−0.54*	−6.33*	−1.34*	−0.92*	−0.06	0.16
5	0.04	0.19	−0.50*	0.06	−0.18*	0.93	−0.25*	−2.55*	−0.48*	0.22	0.00	0.39
6	0.28	0.44*	0.34*	0.28	0.96*	1.51*	0.92*	1.41*	0.55*	0.79*	0.14	−0.02
7	0.54*	0.73*	1.24*	0.52*	1.71*	2.38*	1.12*	5.52*	1.31*	1.32*	−0.02	0.07
8	0.90*	0.81*	2.38*	0.80*	3.41*	2.75*	1.99*	9.99*	2.46*	1.70*	0.03	−0.13
9	1.40*	1.03*	3.91*	1.18*	5.35*	3.78*	3.10*	15.20*	3.22*	2.21*	0.13	0.12
10	1.44*	1.26*	8.16*	1.65*	5.83*	4.83*	6.50*	26.73*	2.93*	3.23*	0.11	−0.37

Significance Testing.
For Portfolio 1–5, * Indicates CAR < 1st Percentile of Sample Distribution of $R_i - R_{p'}$
For Portfolio 6–10, * Indicates CAR > 99th Percentile of Sample Distribution of $R_i - R_{p'}$.

[a] Forecast error portfolios and models are noted in Table 1. Residuals are calculated as $\hat{u}_{i,t} = R_{i,t} - \bar{R}_{p,t}$, where $\bar{R}_{p,t}$ = equally weighted mean daily return on the firm size decile that firm i falls into the quarter examined.

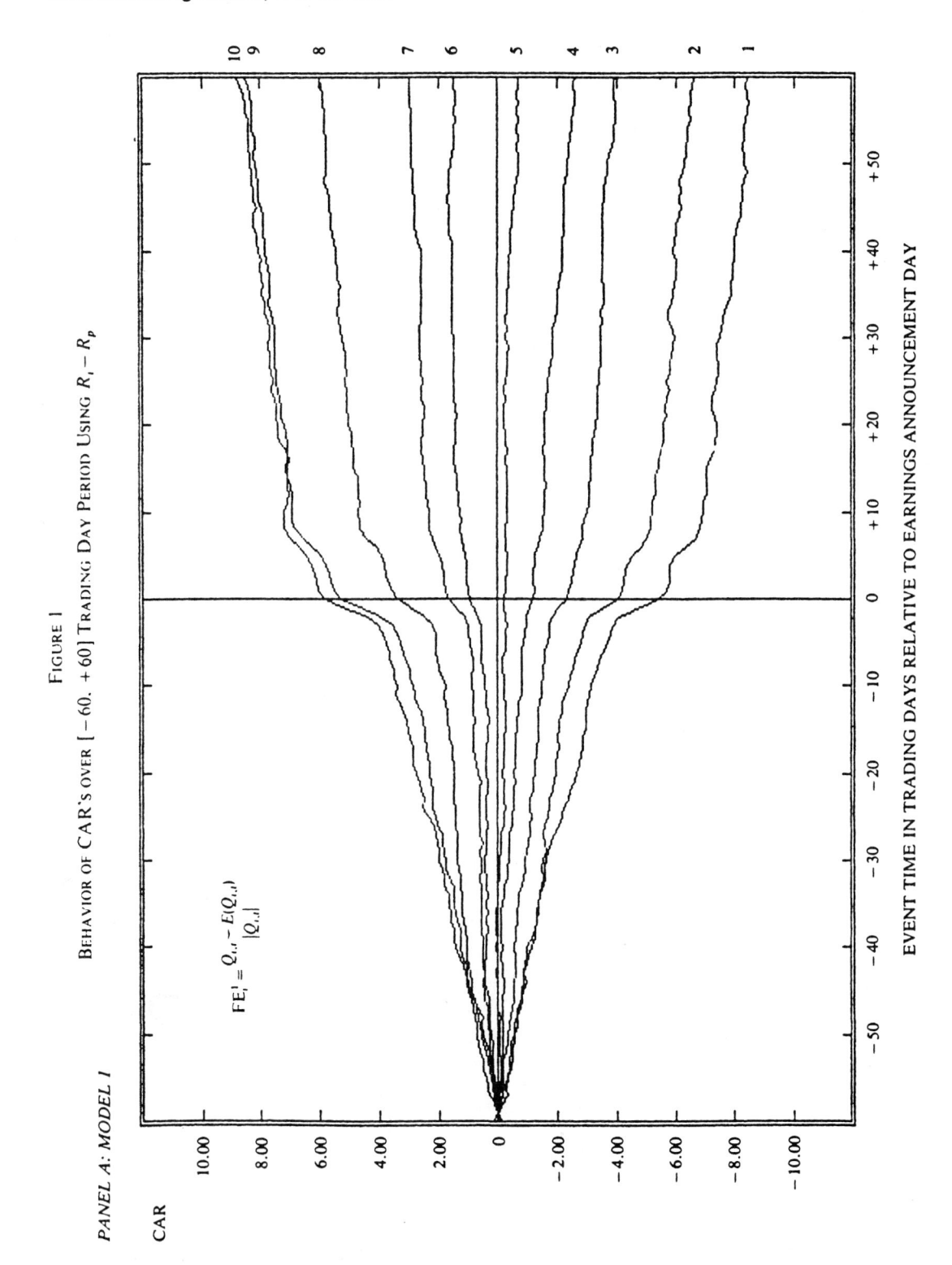

FIGURE 1
BEHAVIOR OF CAR's OVER [−60, +60] TRADING DAY PERIOD USING $R_i - R_p$

PANEL A: MODEL I

$$FE_{i,t}^1 = \frac{Q_{i,t} - E(Q_{i,t})}{|Q_{i,t}|}$$

EVENT TIME IN TRADING DAYS RELATIVE TO EARNINGS ANNOUNCEMENT DAY

FIGURE 1—(Continued)

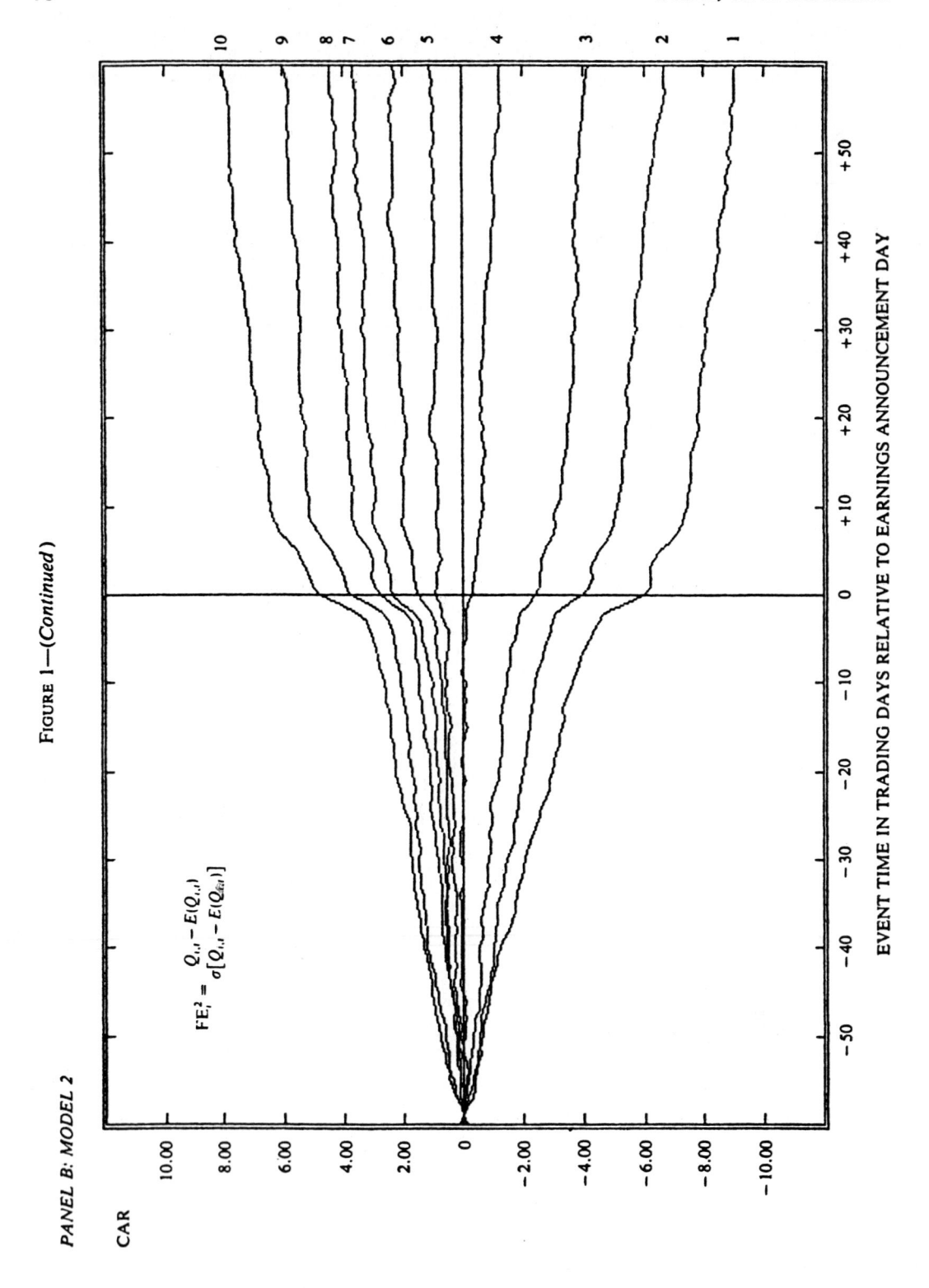

PANEL B: MODEL 2

$$FE_{i}^{2} = \frac{Q_{i,t} - E(Q_{i,t})}{\sigma[Q_{i,t} - E(Q_{i,t})]}$$

EVENT TIME IN TRADING DAYS RELATIVE TO EARNINGS ANNOUNCEMENT DAY

FIGURE 1—(Continued)

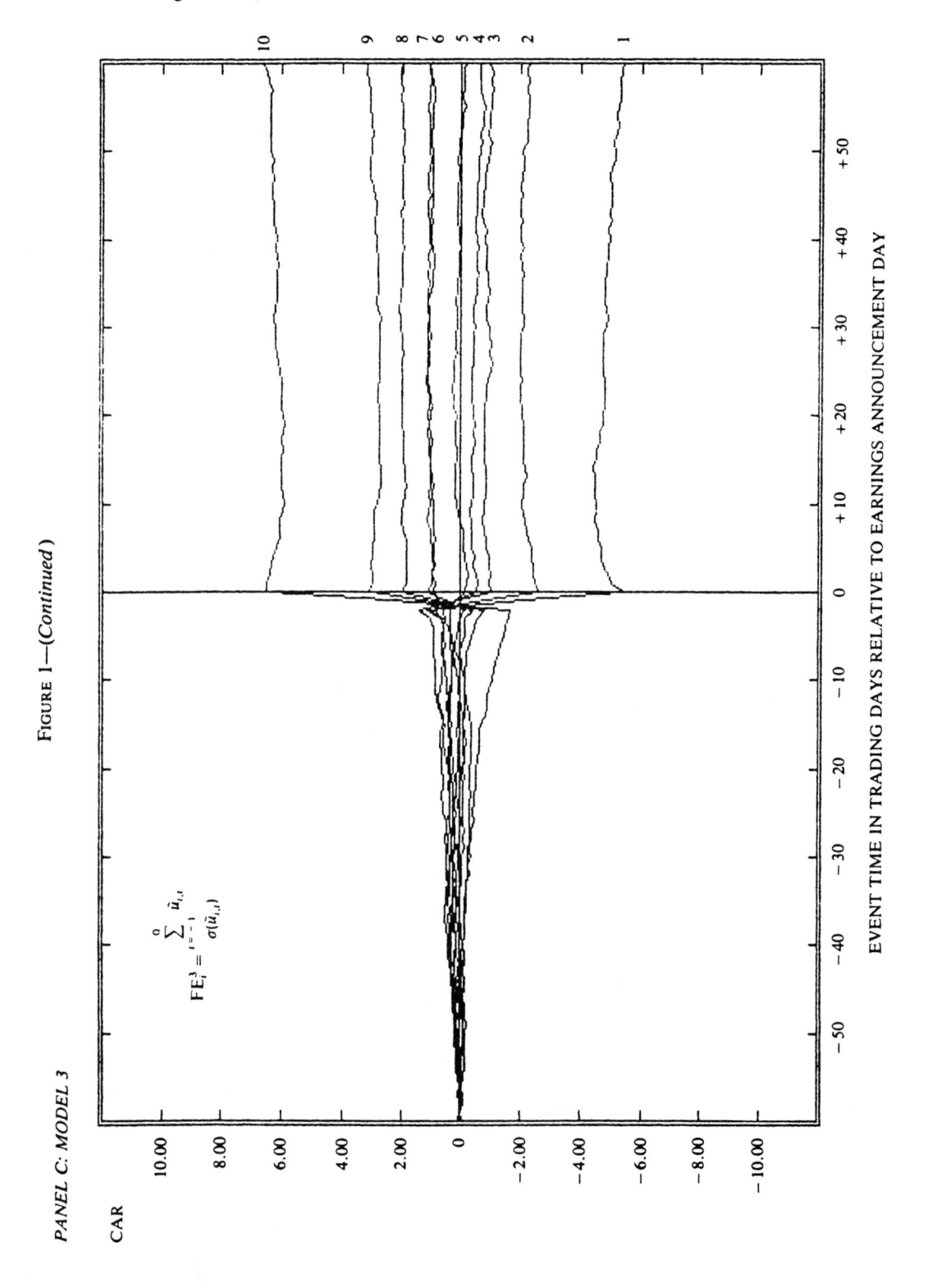

PANEL C: MODEL 3

$$FE_i^3 = \sum_{t=-1}^{0} \frac{\hat{u}_{i,t}}{\sigma(\hat{u}_{i,t})}$$

EVENT TIME IN TRADING DAYS RELATIVE TO EARNINGS ANNOUNCEMENT DAY

FIGURE 1—*(Continued)*

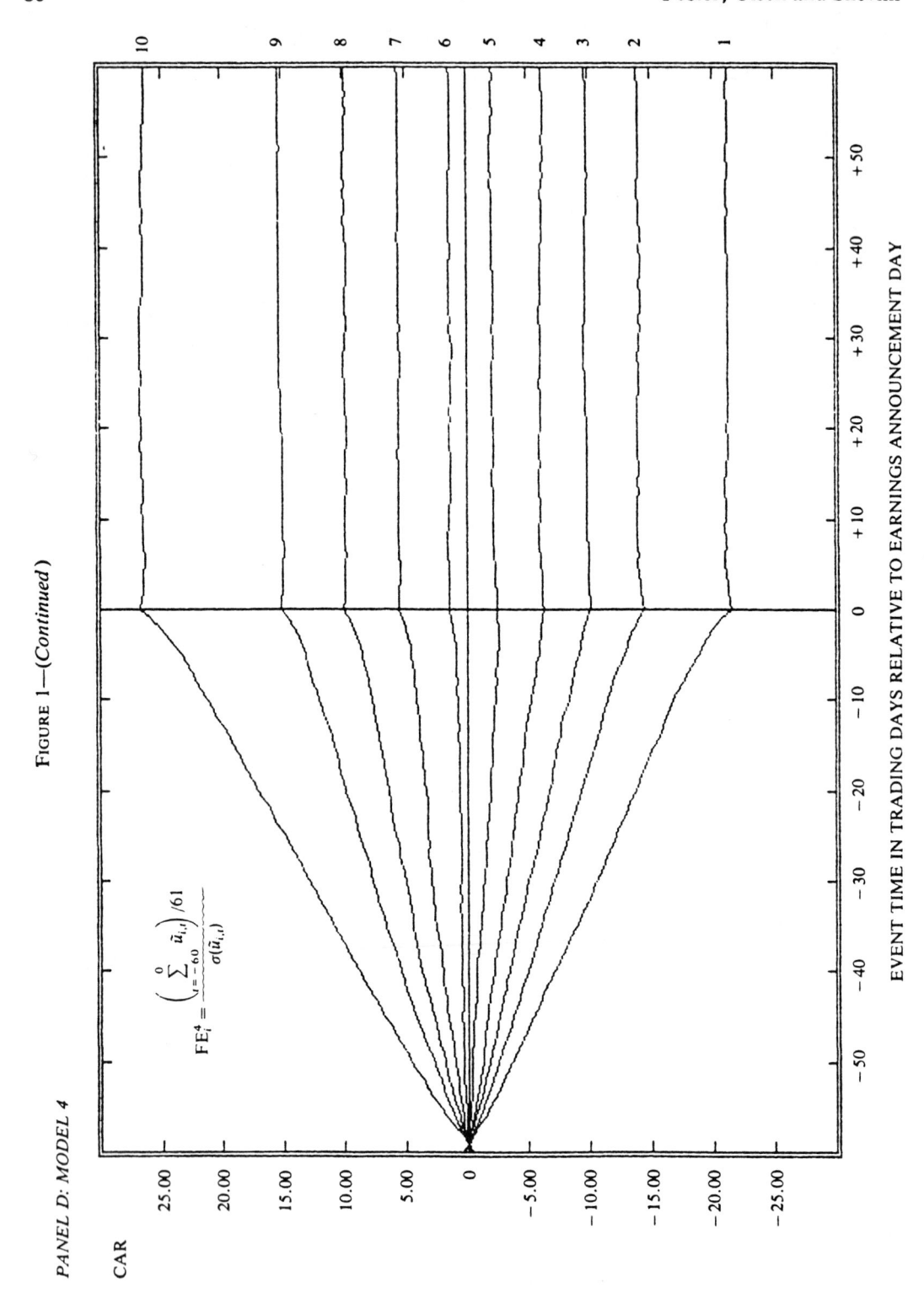

PANEL D: MODEL 4

$$FE_i^4 = \frac{\left(\sum_{t=-60}^{0} \bar{u}_{i,t}\right)/61}{\sigma(\bar{u}_{i,t})}$$

for [−1, 0], i.e., the sign and magnitude of the earnings forecast error is significantly associated with the sign and magnitude of the CAR for [−1, 0].[9]

The [−60, 0] and [+1, +60] time-periods focus on a longer time frame. Panels A, B, C, and D of Figure 1 present the CAR's of the ten forecast error portfolios for Models 1, 2, 3, and 4, respectively. Models 1 and 2 exhibit both pre-announcement and post-announcement drifts in the CAR which are associated with the sign and magnitude of the earnings forecast error. The post-announcement drift is the anomaly highlighted previously in the literature. For instance, the results in Panel B of Figure 1 and Table 4 for Model 2 imply that an investor could use a publicly available earnings release on day 1 to form one portfolio that has a −3.08 percent abnormal return (observations with ten percent most negative earnings forecast error) and another portfolio with an abnormal return of +3.23 percent (ten percent most positive earnings forecast error). Based on the empirical sampling distribution, these abnormal returns are significantly different from zero at, at least, the .01 level. Indeed, in none of the 1,000 trials used to compute the empirical sampling distribution were CAR's of −3.08 percent or +3.23 percent encountered for the [+1, +60] period. These results suggest that the hindsight biases found in prior studies (see Section 2B(iii) of this paper) do not explain the post-announcement systematic drifts in security returns reported in those studies.

Models 3 and 4 present a different pattern of results, with little evidence that portfolios with negative (positive) CAR's in [−1, 0] or [−60, 0], respectively, have negative (positive) CAR's in the subsequent [+1, +60] time period—see Panels C and D of Figure 1. Using the empirical sampling distribution, not one of ten portfolios for either Model 3 or Model 4 is significantly different from zero at the .01 level. Thus, the post-announcement drifts reported in the literature are observed for Models 1 and 2 but not for Models 3 and 4.[10]

The results in Table 4 are pooled over 32 quarters from the first quarter of 1974 (7401) to the last quarter of 1981 (8104). Table 5 presents results for [+1, +60] for three sub-periods: 7401 to 7602 (10 quarters), 7603 to 7804 (10 quarters) and 7901 to 8104 (12 quarters). Table 5 reports the number of quarters in each sub-period for which the CAR in [+1, +60] was negative. The previously noted association between the sign and magnitude of the forecast error and the CAR in [+1, +60] is found in each sub-period in Table 5 for Models 1 and 2 but not for Models 3 and 4. To further probe the time-period explanation for the models reporting post-announcement drifts in security returns, Figure 2 presents a histogram of the CAR's of Model 2 for [+1, +60] for each of the 32 quarters for the most extreme bad news portfolio (FEP_1) and the most extreme good news portfolio (FEP_{10}). (A similar pattern is observed for Model 1.) No discernible sub-period behavior is observed for either FEP_1 or FEP_{10}, with no evidence that the magnitude of the post-announcement drifts decreased over the 1974 to 1981 period. Based on the results in Table 5 and Figure 2, the time period explanation (see Section 2B(iv) of this paper) does not have support for being the source of the post-announcement drifts in security returns.

---

[9] This result for FEP_i^3 is by construction; firms were placed into the FEP_i^3 portfolios based on their security return behavior in [−1, 0].

[10] The results for Model 3 are consistent with those reported in Arbel and Jaggi [1982]. The results for Model 4 are consistent with those reported in Beaver and Landsman [1981]. While both these papers adopted an event-time format, neither used actual earnings announcement dates in determining day 0 (month 0) in their experiments.

TABLE 5

TIME PERIOD ANALYSIS OF CAR's OF FORECAST ERROR PORTFOLIOS[a] IN [+1, +60] EVENT TIME: FREQUENCY WITH WHICH QUARTERLY CAR NEGATIVE IN THREE NON-OVERLAPPING SUB-PERIODS

Forecast Error Portfolio	Model 1 7401–7602 10 Qtrs	Model 1 7603–7804 10 Qtrs	Model 1 7901–8104 12 Qtrs	Model 2 7401–7602 10 Qtrs	Model 2 7603–7804 10 Qtrs	Model 2 7901–8104 12 Qtrs	Model 3 7401–7602 10 Qtrs	Model 3 7603–7804 10 Qtrs	Model 3 7901–8104 12 Qtrs	Model 4 7401–7602 10 Qtrs	Model 4 7603–7804 10 Qtrs	Model 4 7901–8104 12 Qtrs
1	8	9	11	9	9	12	3	6	7	3	7	6
2	8	9	12	9	9	11	4	2	8	2	5	7
3	8	10	12	8	7	11	4	0	6	3	2	5
4	8	9	10	7	5	10	5	3	7	5	0	8
5	8	4	8	6	6	5	6	4	4	6	1	7
6	4	3	2	4	1	5	7	8	6	4	3	6
7	6	1	2	2	0	2	8	6	6	4	4	7
8	1	1	0	4	1	0	7	4	6	7	5	8
9	1	0	0	2	1	0	5	4	6	7	5	3
10	3	0	4	1	0	0	5	5	6	7	5	5

[a] Forecast error portfolios and models are noted in Table 1.

FIGURE 2
QUARTER BY QUARTER CAR's FOR [+1, +60] PERIOD USING MODEL 2:
1974 FIRST QUARTER TO 1981 FOURTH QUARTER

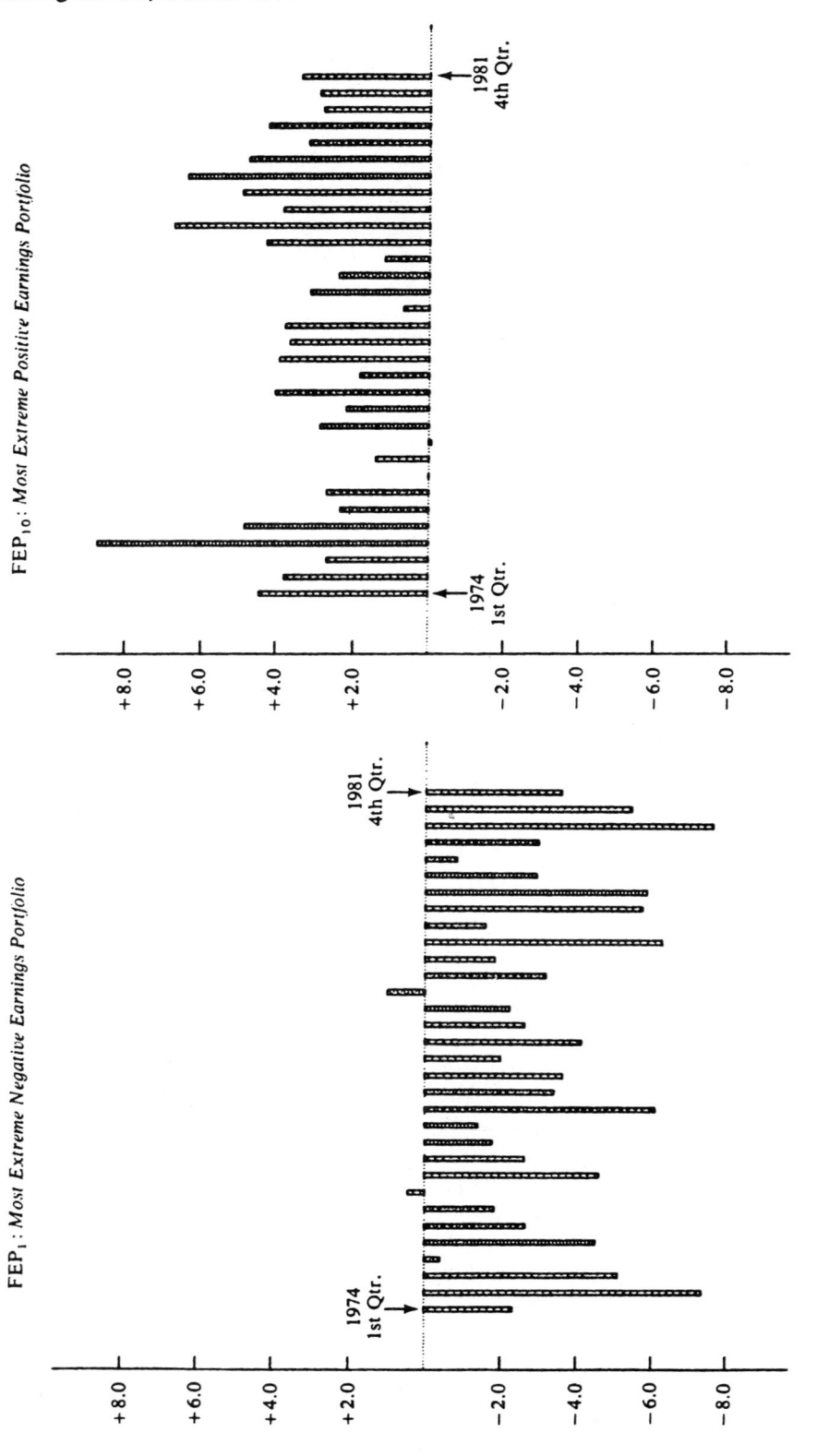

7. CAR Results for Firm Size Partitions

This section examines the ability of a firm size variable to explain the sign and magnitude of the post-announcement drifts. Each observation underlying Tables 4 and 5 was placed into one of five NYSE firm size quintiles based on the firm's market capitalization at the start of the year of each earnings announcement examined: I = smallest firm to .20 market capitalization decile, II = .20 decile to .40 decile, ... V = .80 decile to largest firm.

Table 6 presents results of each firm size quintile for Model 2 and Model 4. The inferences drawn from this table for the post-announcement drifts for Model 2(4) also apply to Model 1(3). Focusing on the $[+1, +60]$ trading-day period, there are significant post-announcement drifts (at the .01 level) across all five firm size quintiles for Model 2. The empirical distribution for each firm size quintile is based on 200 independent trials (see Section 5). The smallest firm size quintile has the most number (nine) of earnings forecast error portfolios with significant post-announcement drifts at the .01 level—the observed CAR in Table 6 for portfolios 1 (-3.34), 2 (-4.10), and 3 (-1.98) are less than the lowest on any of the 200 independent trials; the observed CAR for portfolios 6 (1.82), 7 (2.34), 8 (3.60), 9 (3.51), and 10 (5.00) exceed the highest on any of the 200 independent trials for this firm size quintile. The largest firm quintile has five of the ten forecast error portfolios exhibiting significant post-announcement drifts—the observed CAR for all five (1, 2, 3, 9, and 10) are on more extreme points of the distribution than observed on any of the 200 independent trials for this firm size quintile. The results for Model 4 over the $[+1, +60]$ period are in marked contrast to those reported for Model 2. Not one of the ten portfolios in any of the five size quintiles has significant post-announcement drifts using Model 4.

Using the data in Table 6, the following regression was run to probe the relative importance of the earnings forecast error variable and the firm size variable in explaining the sign and magnitude of CAR_j:

$$C\tilde{A}R_j = \hat{\alpha} + \hat{\beta}_1 \cdot F\tilde{E}P_j + \hat{\beta}_2 \cdot FSQ_j + \tilde{e}_j \quad (16)$$

where

CAR_j = the CAR of the jth portfolio,
FEP_j = a coding from 1 to 10 of the earnings forecast error of portfolio j, and
FSQ_j = a coding of the firm size quintile of portfolio j. For FEP_1 to FEP_5, the firm size quintiles (I–V) are each coded I(10), II(9), III(8), IV(7) and V(6). For FEP_6 to FEP_{10}, the firm size quintiles were each coded I(1), II(2), III(3), IV(4) and V(5). This coding is designed to test the hypothesis that the magnitudes of the drifts are a function of firm size, but that their sign is a function of whether the earnings are coded as "bad news" (portfolios 1–5) or "good news" (portfolios 6–10).

Results for Models 1 to 4 are presented in Table 7. Consider Model 2; the results across all three time periods in Table 7 are consistent. For instance, in the $[+1, +60]$ period, 81 percent of the variation in CAR_j is explained by a coding of the earnings forecast error portfolio—the positive coefficient on β_1 implies the more positive (negative) the magnitude of the earnings change, the more positive (negative) the magnitude of CAR_j in $[+1, +60]$. The firm size quintile variable explains 66 percent of the variation in CAR_j. The negative β_2

TABLE 6
CUMULATIVE AVERAGE RESIDUALS FOR FORECAST ERROR PORTFOLIOS:[a] BREAKDOWN INTO NYSE POPULATION FIRM SIZE QUINTILES[b]

Forecast Error Portfolio	Days [−1, 0]					Days [−60, 0]					Days [+1, +60]				
	I	II	III	IV	V	I	II	III	IV	V	I	II	III	IV	V
Model 2															
1	−1.83*	−1.49*	−1.04*	−0.71*	−0.81*	−7.26*	−7.29*	−5.44*	−5.07*	−3.43*	−3.34*	−4.12*	−2.56*	−2.91*	−1.87*
2	−1.07*	−1.29*	−0.54*	−0.41*	−0.71*	−4.83*	−5.25*	−2.92*	−2.91*	−2.20*	−4.10*	−2.32*	−1.44*	−1.90*	−1.40*
3	−0.50*	−0.67*	−0.44*	−0.51*	−0.26*	−3.26*	−1.95*	−2.58*	−2.31*	−1.05*	−1.98*	−1.58	−1.88*	−1.50	−1.52*
4	−0.09*	−0.43*	−0.43*	−0.34*	−0.31*	−0.50	−0.51	−0.21	−0.12	−0.16	−0.97*	−1.42	−0.93	−1.13	0.23
5	0.38	0.11	−0.01	0.01	0.05	1.98	0.79	0.42	−0.07	−0.38	1.45	−1.21	−0.14	−0.91	−0.63
6	0.81*	0.26	0.26	−0.02	0.20	2.60*	1.57	1.59*	0.22	0.74	1.82*	0.60	0.50	−0.51	−0.27
7	1.36*	0.68*	0.45*	0.26	0.19	4.14*	2.25*	1.39	1.41*	0.99	2.34*	1.60*	1.06	−0.35	0.79
8	1.41*	0.89*	0.63*	0.45*	0.36*	4.29*	3.92*	1.81*	1.55*	2.10*	3.60*	1.35*	1.41	1.11*	0.02
9	1.91*	1.00*	0.82*	0.65*	0.41*	6.50*	4.87*	3.39*	2.28*	2.13*	3.51*	2.88*	1.89*	1.16*	1.25*
10	2.58*	1.42*	1.06*	0.86*	0.50*	9.38*	6.35*	4.50*	3.74*	1.96*	5.00*	4.86*	2.83*	2.52*	1.73*
Model 4															
1	−1.97*	−1.74*	−1.21*	−0.87*	−0.88*	−28.68*	−24.43*	−20.75*	−19.10*	−16.66*	−0.40	−1.42	0.77	0.37	1.41
2	−1.23*	−1.10*	−0.66*	−0.50*	−0.32*	−19.71*	−15.18*	−13.66*	−11.72*	−9.57*	1.03	−0.59	0.19	0.36	0.63
3	−0.87*	−0.38*	−0.41*	−0.29*	−0.34*	−13.97*	−10.68*	−9.04*	−7.82*	−6.47*	0.53	0.83	0.46	0.17	−0.18
4	−0.40*	−0.22	0.00	−0.21*	−0.04	−8.87*	−6.32*	−5.55*	−4.74*	−3.80*	0.52	−0.92	0.62	−0.13	0.10
5	0.12	0.00	−0.11	0.20	−0.04	−3.62*	−2.37	−2.04*	−1.84*	−1.43*	1.12	0.64	−0.24	−0.64	−0.37
6	0.53	0.35	0.12	0.00	−0.10	2.01*	1.56	1.38	1.10	0.88	0.70	−0.33	−0.92	−0.42	−0.54
7	0.81*	0.32	0.56*	0.14	0.29	7.99*	5.59*	4.80*	4.12*	3.31*	0.51	−0.15	0.93	−0.81	−0.85
8	1.38*	0.62*	0.69*	0.29	0.24	14.92*	10.04*	8.54*	7.52*	6.14*	−0.22	−0.11	0.35	−0.35	−0.18
9	2.01*	0.95*	0.89*	0.79*	0.43*	22.57*	15.61*	13.63*	12.29*	9.49*	−0.19	0.87	0.59	−0.17	−0.03
10	2.72*	1.36*	1.19*	1.39*	0.99*	40.07*	28.36*	25.62*	22.00*	18.08*	−1.14	0.02	−0.48	0.05	0.09

Significance Testing
For Portfolios 1–5, * Indicates CAR <1st Percentile of Sample Distribution of $R_i − R_p$ for Firm Size Quintile.
For Portfolios 6–10, * Indicates CAR >99th Percentile of Sample Distribution of $R_i − R_p$ for Firm Size Quintile.
[a] Forecast error portfolios and models are noted in Table 1. Residuals are calculated as $\hat{u}_{i,t} = R_{i,t} − R_{p,t}$.
[b] Firm size quintiles I and V comprise the smallest and largest firms, respectively.

TABLE 7
REGRESSION STATISTICS FOR CAR_j AS DEPENDENT VARIABLE AND FEP_j AND FSQ_j AS INDEPENDENT VARIABLES[a]

	α	$t \cdot (\alpha)$	β_1	$t(\beta_1)$	β_2	$t(\beta_2)$	ADJ R^2
A. Model 1[b]							
$[-1, 0]$	−1.38	−17.23	0.27	20.96	—	—	.899
	1.37	9.13	—	—	−0.23	−9.49	.645
	−0.81	−4.28	0.23	12.53	−0.06	−3.28	.916
$[-60, 0]$	−6.30	−24.69	1.21	29.50	—	—	.947
	5.71	8.15	—	—	−0.97	−8.60	.598
	−5.14	−8.01	1.12	18.33	−0.12	−1.97	.950
$[+1, +60]$	−3.57	−14.22	0.65	16.20	—	—	.842
	3.31	9.46	—	—	−0.60	−10.56	.693
	−1.31	−2.39	0.48	9.11	−0.23	−4.44	.886
B. Model 2[b]							
$[-1, 0]$	−1.33	−10.82	0.26	13.32	—	—	.783
	1.47	9.65	—	—	−0.24	−9.98	.668
	−0.32	−1.15	0.18	6.94	−0.10	−3.92	.833
$[-60, 0]$	−5.71	−12.82	1.11	15.43	—	—	.829
	5.65	8.46	—	—	−0.96	−8.90	.615
	−3.01	−2.78	0.90	8.67	−0.28	−2.70	.849
$[+1, +60]$	−3.62	−12.65	0.67	14.48	—	—	.810
	3.38	8.85	—	—	−0.60	−9.83	.661
	−1.37	−2.08	0.49	7.82	−0.23	−3.70	.850
C. Model 3[b]							
$[-1, 0]$	−6.52	−15.29	1.21	17.57	—	—	.863
	5.50	7.20	—	—	−0.98	−7.95	.559
	−5.07	−4.65	1.09	10.50	−0.15	−1.44	.866
$[-60, 0]$	−4.90	−13.90	0.96	16.87	—	—	.853
	4.46	6.93	—	—	−0.74	−7.17	.507
	−4.46	−4.86	0.92	10.54	−0.04	−0.51	.850
$[+1, +60]$	0.08	0.58	−0.01	−0.22	—	—	.000
	0.04	0.28	—	—	0.01	0.12	.000
	0.11	0.29	−0.01	−0.20	−0.01	−0.08	.000
D. Model 4[b]							
$[-1, 0]$	−1.41	−11.73	0.28	14.28	—	—	.805
	1.45	8.63	—	—	−0.24	−8.99	.620
	−0.64	−2.21	0.22	7.82	−0.08	−2.89	.831
$[-60, 0]$	−25.32	−18.97	4.68	21.74	—	—	.906
	21.59	7.94	—	—	−3.85	−8.80	.609
	−18.22	−5.51	4.12	13.06	−0.73	−2.33	.914
$[+1, +60]$	0.30	1.60	−0.05	−1.55	—	—	.028
	−0.17	−0.87	—	—	−0.04	1.23	.010
	0.26	0.52	−0.04	−0.93	0.01	0.10	.008

[a] Regression equation $C\tilde{A}R_j = \hat{\alpha} + \hat{\beta}_1 \cdot F\tilde{E}P_j + \hat{\beta}_2 \cdot F\tilde{S}Q_j + \tilde{e}_j$, where FEP_j = forecast error portfolio, FSQ = firm size quintile (see text for coding).

[b] Models are noted in Table 1.

coefficient on FSQ_j implies that the smaller the firm size, the larger the absolute magnitude of CAR_j in the $[+1, +60]$ period, with portfolios 1–5 having negative drifts and portfolios 6–10 having positive drifts. The FEP_j and FSQ_j effects are collinear. Focusing still on the $[+1, +60]$ period for Model 2, the explanatory power of the two variables in a multiple regression is 85 percent; the incremental power of adding the FSQ_j variable to a regression already including the FEP_j variable is only four percent.

Consider the results in Table 7 for Models 3 and 4 over the $[+1, +60]$ period. Neither the FEP_j nor FSQ_j variables have any significant ability to explain CAR_j differences across the 50 portfolios used in each regression. The consistent result that emerges is that for both the pooled sample and the firm size quintiles, Models 3 and 4 do not provide any evidence of significant post-earnings announcement drifts in security returns.

8. Summary

The most important result in this paper is that the systematic post-announcement drifts in security returns reported in the literature are found for only a subset of earnings expectations models. Portfolios based on two price-based earnings expectations models exhibit no systematic post-announcement drifts in the $[+1, +60]$ trading day period. The price-based expectations models have the appealing property that the assignment of firms to unexpected earnings change portfolios better approximates the independence-over-time assumption than do models used previously. This property means that the abnormal returns reported for each earnings change portfolio are less likely to capture firm-specific variables priced by the capital market but not incorporated into abnormal return estimation.

Another important set of results in this paper relates to the class of earnings expectations models reporting systematic drifts in security returns in the $[+1, +60]$ period. These drifts persist throughout the entire 1974 to 1981 period and thus a sub-time-period explanation for their existence appears unlikely. Approximately 80 percent of the variation in cumulative abnormal returns of the ten earnings change portfolios in the $[+1, +60]$ time period can be explained by a coding of the sign and magnitude of the unexpected earnings change of each portfolio. The more positive (negative) the unexpected earnings change, the more positive (negative) the post-announcement abnormal returns. A coding based on firm size explained approximately 65 percent of the variation in the portfolio cumulative abnormal returns in the $[+1, +60]$ time period. The smaller the firm size, the larger the post-announcement cumulative abnormal return, with positive (negative) earnings change portfolios having positive (negative) cumulative abnormal returns. Although the smallest quintile of firms examined in this paper had the greatest number of portfolios with significant abnormal returns in the $[+1, +60]$ period, the two most extreme positive unexpected earnings portfolios and the two most extreme negative unexpected earnings portfolios had significant post-announcement drifts across all five firm size quintiles examined. The earnings magnitude effect and the firm size effect were collinear; together, they explained 85 percent of the variation across portfolios in their post-announcement security return behavior.

The results in this paper raise a major

unresolved issue: Why do systematic post-announcement drifts appear with Models 1 and 2 but not with Models 3 and 4? One possible avenue of research is to use univariate or multivariate time-series models based on the past earnings series that are better specified using a conventional time-series criterion—e.g., the Box-Jenkins Q statistic. Another avenue of research is to examine the characteristics of the observations Models 1 and 2 assign to different portfolios in an attempt to gain more insight into the proxy effect explanation for the systematic drifts. A third avenue is to focus on that subset of observations that make marked transitions over time in their membership of forecast error portfolios, e.g., to examine if observations that are in portfolio 1 in period t and portfolio 10 in $t+1$ exhibit the patterns reported for Models 1 and 10 for the forecast error portfolios that they are members of in that period. A fourth avenue is to examine how the earnings concept implicit in security price differs from the earnings concept implicit in a single quarter's (or year's) reported accounting earnings. This research involves issues such as the forecast time horizon used to price securities and the models used to forecast earnings over the (presumably) multi-year time horizon. Such research could facilitate understanding how earnings forecast error models based on quarterly or annual accounting data may classify securities differently than does the capital market when it revalues security prices at the time of earnings announcements.

Appendix

Abnormal Return Estimation

Rendleman, Jones and Latane [1982], in one of the most extensive studies on post-earnings announcement drifts in security returns, estimated abnormal returns using (17) in Section 5 of their paper:

$$\tilde{u}_{i,t} = \tilde{R}_{i,t} - \tilde{R}_{M,t} \qquad (17)$$

where

$R_{i,t}$ = return on security i in day t and
$R_{M,t}$ = equally weighted return on CRSP daily file (NYSE and ASE firms) in day t.

Table 8 presents results for the pooled sample previously reported in Table 4 of this paper when (17) is used to estimate abnormal returns.[11] Use of (17) does not change any of the inferences drawn previously in this paper as regards the pooled sample population.

However, when observations are placed into firm size quintiles, use of (17) will cause the earnings association results to be confounded with the effect that firm size (or related variables) has on security returns—see Banz [1981], Reinganum [1981], Sharpe [1982] and Keim [1983]. To illustrate, Table 9 presents results for earnings forecast Model 2 when (17) is used to estimate abnormal returns. Note, for instance, that in both the $[-60,0]$ and $[+1,+60]$ periods, firm size quintile V (.80 market capitalization decile to largest firm) has negative CAR's across all ten forecast error portfolios. Portfolio 10 (the ten percent with the most favorable unexpected increase in earnings using Model 2) has a CAR of -1.98 percent in $[-60,0]$ and -0.78 percent in $[+1, +60]$. This result arises from the firm

---

[11] For Models 3 and 4 in Table 8, (17) was used to estimate both the FE_i variable and the CAR. There was no change in the inferences drawn when (15) was used to estimate the CAR.

TABLE 8

CUMULATIVE AVERAGE RESIDUALS FOR FORECAST ERROR PORTFOLIOS:[a] ALL OBSERVATIONS POOLED WITH $R_i - R_m$ USED TO COMPUTE CAR

Forecast Error Portfolio	Days [−1,0] Model 1	Model 2	Model 3	Model 4	Days [−60,0] Model 1	Model 2	Model 3	Model 4	Days [+1,+60] Model 1	Model 2	Model 3	Model 4
1	−1.35*	−1.36*	−6.52*	−1.23*	−5.22*	−6.75*	−6.28*	−22.44*	−2.69*	−3.46*	−0.90*	−1.04*
2	−0.95*	−0.90*	−3.66*	−0.87*	−4.47*	−4.64*	−3.75*	−15.88*	−2.72*	−3.06*	−0.07	−0.76*
3	−0.52*	−0.52*	−2.48*	−0.64*	−3.52*	−2.98*	−1.67*	−11.94*	−2.31*	−2.08*	−0.20	0.08
4	−0.30*	−0.25*	−1.39*	−0.36*	−2.59*	−0.64	−1.30*	−8.27*	−2.16*	−1.00*	−0.56	0.11
5	−0.01*	0.18	−0.55*	0.00	−1.88*	0.57	−0.75	−4.28*	−1.51*	0.21	0.03	0.04
6	0.23	0.43*	0.27*	0.17	−0.76	0.95*	0.27*	−0.01	−0.42	0.69*	0.08	0.22
7	0.51*	0.71*	1.17*	0.43*	0.36*	1.53*	0.18*	4.56*	0.58*	0.87*	−0.52	0.37*
8	0.88*	0.79*	2.34*	0.80*	2.50*	1.60*	1.14*	9.67*	2.10*	1.01*	−0.24	−0.35
9	1.40*	1.00*	3.91*	1.18*	5.28*	2.75*	2.46*	15.67*	3.08*	1.59*	−0.46	−0.14
10	1.48*	1.20*	8.27*	1.75*	6.72*	3.38*	5.91*	28.72*	3.78*	2.32*	−0.33	−1.09

Significance Testing
For Portfolio 1–5, * Indicates CAR < 1st Percentile of Sample Distribution of $R_i - R_m$.
For Portfolio 6–10, * Indicates CAR > 99th Percentile of Sample Distribution of $R_i - R_m$.
[a] Forecast error portfolios and Models 1 and 2 are noted in Table 1. Models 3 and 4 are the same except $\hat{u}_{i,t} = \tilde{R}_{i,t} - \tilde{R}_{M,t}$, where $\tilde{R}_{M,t}$ = equally weighted market index.

TABLE 9

CUMULATIVE AVERAGE RESIDUALS FOR FORECAST ERROR PORTFOLIOS[a] OF MODEL 2 WITH $R_i - R_m$
USED TO COMPUTE CAR: BREAKDOWN INTO NYSE POPULATION FIRM SIZE QUINTILES[b]

Forecast Error Portfolio	Days [−1,0]					Days [−60,0]					Days [+1,+60]				
	I	II	III	IV	V	I	II	III	IV	V	I	II	III	IV	V
1	−1.78*	−1.49*	−1.08*	−0.81*	−0.94*	−5.51*	−7.92*	−6.83*	−7.46*	−8.06*	−2.10*	−4.74*	−3.85*	−4.37*	−4.62*
2	−1.03*	−1.32*	−0.56*	−0.48*	−0.85*	−3.11*	−5.93*	−4.30*	−5.57*	−6.66*	−2.85*	−2.95*	−2.41*	−3.28*	−4.27*
3	−0.45*	−0.71*	−0.50*	−0.60*	−0.38*	−1.47*	−2.60*	−4.05*	−4.74*	−5.40*	−0.88*	−2.12*	−2.89*	−2.88*	−4.64*
4	−0.03*	−0.44*	−0.47*	−0.41*	−0.39*	1.24	−1.20	−1.82	−2.39	−4.40	0.29*	−1.88	−1.90*	−2.81*	−2.34
5	0.43	0.10	−0.05	−0.06	−0.04	3.53	0.08	−0.86	−2.48	−4.60*	3.06	−1.84	−1.14	−2.53*	−3.32*
6	0.88*	0.25	0.22	−0.07	0.10	4.22*	0.78*	0.06	−2.24	−3.77	3.25*	0.11	−0.39	−1.93	−2.66
7	1.41*	0.68*	0.42*	0.20	0.07	5.85*	1.60*	−0.12	−0.99*	−3.44	3.69*	1.02*	0.21	−1.75	−1.77
8	1.44*	0.89*	0.58*	0.42*	0.25*	5.94*	3.27*	0.37*	−1.12	−2.39*	4.69*	0.78*	0.42	−0.26*	−2.43
9	1.95*	0.97*	0.78*	0.59*	0.32*	8.17*	4.06*	1.84*	−0.28*	−1.73*	4.88*	2.53*	0.93*	−0.06*	−1.41
10	2.62*	1.37*	1.01*	0.78*	0.39*	10.98*	5.58*	2.91*	1.13*	−1.98*	6.36*	4.26*	1.63*	1.16*	−0.78*

Significance Testing
For Portfolios 1–5, * Indicates CAR < 1st Percentile of Sample Distribution of $R_i - R_m$ for Firm Size Quintile.
For Portfolios 6–10, * Indicates CAR > 99th Percentile of Sample Distribution of $R_i - R_m$ for Firm Size Quintile.
[a] Forecast error portfolios and Models 1 and 2 are noted in Table 1. Models 3 and 4 are the same except $\tilde{u}_{i,t} = \tilde{R}_{i,t} - \bar{R}_{M,t}$, where $\bar{R}_{m,t}$ = equally weighted market index.
[b] Firm size quintiles I and V comprise the smallest and largest firms, respectively.

size effect on security returns being stronger in magnitude than the earnings forecast error effect for that portfolio. Note, however, that the significance test employed in this paper will take account of the firm size effect in generating the empirical distribution.[12]

ALTERNATIVE CUMULATION APPROACHES

The cumulative abnormal return (CAR) measures reported in this paper are calculated as:

$$CAR = \frac{1}{n} \sum_{i=1}^{N} \sum_{t=1}^{T} \tilde{u}_{i,t} \qquad (18)$$

Roll [1983] discusses three alternative approaches and notes differences in their underlying assumptions:

AR (Arithmetic)

$$= \left(\left[\frac{1}{N \cdot \tau} \sum_i \sum_t R_{it} \right]^{\tau} - 1 \right) \times 100 \qquad (19)$$

BH (Buy and Hold)

$$= \left(\frac{1}{N} \sum_i [\Pi_t R_{it}] - 1 \right) \times 100 \qquad (20)$$

RB (Rebalanced)

$$= \left(\Pi_i \left[\frac{1}{N} \sum_i R_{it} \right] - 1 \right) \times 100 \qquad (21)$$

where $R_{i,t} = 1 + \tilde{u}_{i,t}$.

A subset of the results was run using these three cumulation approaches with no change in the inferences previously drawn in this paper. For instance, results for forecast error portfolios 1 to 10 for Model 2 over the [+1, +60] period using (15) are:

Cumulation Approach	Forecast Error Portfolio									
	1	2	3	4	5	6	7	8	9	10
CAR	−3.08*	−2.73*	−1.78*	−0.92*	0.22	0.79*	1.32*	1.70*	2.21*	3.23*
AR	−3.00*	−2.63*	−1.75*	−0.91*	0.19	0.79*	1.27*	1.67*	2.22*	3.18*
BH	−4.71*	−4.10*	−3.32*	−2.50*	−1.49	−0.53*	0.16*	0.78*	1.37*	2.42*
RB	−3.00*	−2.63*	−1.75*	−0.91*	0.19	0.78*	1.27*	1.67*	2.22*	3.18*

For portfolios 1 to 5, * indicates that the CAR (AR, BH or RB) is less than the first percentile of the empirical distribution. For portfolios 6 to 10, * indicates the CAR (AR, BH, or RB) is greater than the 99th percentile of the empirical distribution. The empirical distributions are calculated over 1,000 trials. Separate distributions were generated for the CAR, AR, BH and RB cumulation approaches. Note that all four approaches indicate the same forecast error portfolios as having significant post-announcement drifts in security returns.

[12] Abnormal returns were also calculated using the market model, with α and β estimated using the 600 trading days prior to the [−60] trading day. Separate simulations were run to generate the empirical distribution of the CAR for each event time period examined. Portfolios 1 to 5 and 8 to 10 of Model 1 and 1 to 4 and 6 to 10 of Model 2 reported evidence of statistically significant abnormal returns in the [+1, +60] period. No portfolios for Model 3 or Model 4 had significant abnormal returns in the [+1, +60] period. Full results are available from the authors.

REFERENCES

Arbel, A. and B. Jaggi, "Market Information Assimilation Related to Extreme Daily Price Jumps," *Financial Analysts Journal* (November-December 1982), pp. 60-66.

Ball, R., "Anomalies in Relationships Between Securities' Yields and Yield-Surrogates," *Journal of Financial Economics* (June/September 1978), pp. 103-126.

———— and R. Watts, "Some Additional Evidence on Survival Biases," *The Journal of Finance* (March 1979), pp. 197-206.

Banz, R. W., "The Relationship Between Return and Market Value of Common Stocks," *Journal of Financial Economics* (March 1981), pp. 3-18.

Beaver, W., R. Lambert and D. Morse, "The Information Content of Security Prices," *Journal of Accounting and Economics* (March 1980), pp. 3-28.

———— and W. R. Landsman, "Note on the Behavior of Residual Security Returns for Winner and Loser Portfolios," *Journal of Accounting and Economics* (December 1981), pp. 233-241.

Bidwell, C. M. and J. R. Riddle, "Market Inefficiencies—Opportunities for Profits," *Journal of Accounting, Auditing and Finance* (Spring 1981), pp. 198-214.

Brown, S. L., "Earnings Changes, Stock Prices, and Market Efficiency," *The Journal of Finance* (March 1978), pp. 17-28.

Eisenstadt, S., "An Update on the Value Line Performance Rankings" (Value Line, 1980).

Fama, E. F., *Foundations of Finance* (Basic Books, 1976).

Foster, G., "Quarterly Accounting Data: Time-Series Properties and Predictive-Ability Results," THE ACCOUNTING REVIEW (January 1977), pp. 1-21.

————, "Intra-Industry Information Transfers Associated with Earnings Releases," *Journal of Accounting and Economics* (December 1981), pp. 201-232.

————, "Capital Market Efficiency: Definitions, Testing Issues and Anomalies," in M. J. Gaffikin (ed.), *Contemporary Accounting Thought* (Prentice-Hall, 1984), pp. 151-180.

Gonedes, N. J., "The Capital Market, The Market for Information, and External Accounting," *The Journal of Finance* (May 1976), pp. 611-630.

Holthausen, R. W., "Abnormal Returns Following Quarterly Earnings Announcements," *Proceedings of Seminar On the Analysis of Security Prices* (The University of Chicago, May 1983), pp. 37-59.

Jones, C. P. and R. H. Litzenberger, "Quarterly Earnings Reports and Intermediate Stock Price Trends," *The Journal of Finance* (March 1970), pp. 143-148.

Joy, O. M. and C. P. Jones, "Earnings Reports and Market Efficiencies: An Analysis of the Contrary Evidence," *The Journal of Financial Research* (Spring 1979), pp. 51-63.

Keim, D. B., "Size-Related Anomalies and Stock Return Seasonality: Further Empirical Evidence," *Journal of Financial Economics* (June 1983), pp. 13-32.

Latane, H. A., and C. P. Jones, "Standardized Unexpected Earnings—1971-1977," *The Journal of Finance* (June 1979), pp. 717-724.

————, ————, and R. D. Rieke, "Quarterly Earnings Reports and Subsequent Holding Period Returns," *Journal of Business Research* (April 1974), pp. 119-132.

Patell, J. M. and M. A. Wolfson, "Good News, Bad News, and the Intraday Timing of Corporate Disclosures," THE ACCOUNTING REVIEW (July 1982), pp. 509-527.

Reinganum, M. R., "Misspecification of Capital Asset Pricing: Empirical Anomalies Based on Earnings' Yields and Market Values," *Journal of Financial Economics* (March 1981), pp. 19-46.

Rendleman, R. J., C. P. Jones and H. A. Latane, "Empirical Anomalies Based on Unexpected Earnings and the Importance of Risk Adjustments," *Journal of Financial Economics* (November 1982), pp. 269-287.

Roll, R., "On Computing Mean Returns and the Small Firm Premium," *Journal of Financial Economics* (November 1983), pp. 371-386.

Scholes, M. and J. Williams, "Estimating Betas from Nonsynchronous Data," *Journal of Financial Economics* (December 1977), pp. 309-327.

Sharpe, W. F., "Capital Asset Prices: A Theory of Market Equilibrium under Conditions of Risk," *The Journal of Finance* (September 1964), pp. 425-442.

————, "Factors in New York Stock Exchange Security Returns, 1931-1979," *The Journal of Portfolio Management* (Summer 1982), pp. 5-19.

Watts, R. L., "Systematic 'Abnormal' Returns After Quarterly Earnings Announcements," *Journal of Financial Economics* (June/September 1978), pp. 127-150.

Association between accounting performance measures and stock prices

A test of the life cycle hypothesis*

Joseph H. Anthony
Michigan State University, East Lansing, MI 48824-1121, USA

K. Ramesh
Northwestern University, Evanston, IL 60201, USA

Received July 1988, final version received January 1992

This paper posits that stock market response to two accounting performance measures – sales growth and capital investment – is a function of firm life cycle stage. Firms are grouped into various life cycle portfolios using dividend payout, sales growth, and age. As predicted, the empirical results indicate a monotonic decline in the response coefficients of unexpected sales growth and unexpected capital investment from the growth to the stagnant stages. Additional analysis suggests that this relation is not driven by a firm size effect, risk differences, or measurement error in the proxies for performance measures.

1. Introduction

We investigate the implications of a life cycle theory of the firm for the stock market response to accounting performance measures. A sizeable literature (detailed below) suggests that (1) changes in sales growth and capital expenditure signal the strategic emphasis of the firm (e.g., capturing market share and increasing capital capacity versus cost trimming) and (2) the cost effectiveness of

---

*We are especially thankful for numerous comments and suggestions provided by an anonymous referee on earlier versions of this manuscript, and appreciate input from Ray Ball (the editor), Bob Capettini, Rajiv Dewan, S. P. Kothari, Bob Magee, Tom Prince, Gita Rao, Siva Nathan, S. Thiagarajan, Ross Watts; workshop participants at Rice, Maryland, and Cincinnati; and participants at the 1988 meeting of the American Accounting Association. The research support provided by the Department of Accounting of the Eli Broad Graduate School of Management of Michigan State University and the Accounting Research Center of the J.L. Kellogg Graduate School of Management of Northwestern University is gratefully acknowledged. We also acknowledge research assistance provided by Geoff Gurka.

0165-4101/92/$05.00 © 1992—Elsevier Science Publishers B.V. All rights reserved

a strategy is a function of life cycle stage. We predict and find empirically that stock market reactions to sales growth and capital expenditure are functions of life cycle stage.

Our argument is motivated by strategic prescriptions prevalent in the management, marketing, and economics literature, which originated with the Boston Consulting Group (1968) (hereafter BCG). BCG's underlying idea is that a firm maximizes revenue growth early in its life cycle, to create permanent cost or demand advantages over competitors, but in its mature stage market growth slows and investments are less rewarding [Porter (1980, p. 248)]. Economists rationalize this model in a variety of ways [Spence (1977, 1979, 1981), Karnani (1984), and Wernerfelt (1985)]. For example, Spence rationalizes early growth maximization through irreversibility of investment with a growth constraint, and early capacity maximization as a deterrent to potential entrants.

This reasoning suggests that performance measures differ across life cycle stages, which is evident in the management accounting literature [Richardson and Gordon (1980), Rappaport (1981), and National Association of Accountants (NAA) (1986)]. For example, NAA argues that '[a]t each stage of growth in an entity's life cycle, different measures of financial performance take on varying degrees of importance. Therefore, neither growth nor net income nor cash flows nor return on investment should be emphasized to the exclusion of other meaningful measures' (p. 13).

We use a market-based approach to test if stock market reactions to sales growth and capital expenditure are functions of life cycle stage. Specifically, we hypothesize that unexpected positive sales growth and capital expenditure are most (least) valued by the capital market during the firm's growth (stagnant) stage. We choose dividend payout, sales growth, and firm age as indicators of life cycle stage. We classify firm-years into life cycle groups, first using individual variables and then using a composite score obtained from all variables (univariate and multivariate groupings).

We test our hypotheses by regressing cumulative abnormal returns (CAR) on differenced earnings, capital expenditure, and sales growth variables, with slope dummies for various life cycle groups formed by the univariate and multivariate approaches. The results are consistent with our predictions. In the univariate groupings, the response coefficients of unexpected sales growth and unexpected capital expenditure are higher for low dividend payout (young/high sales growth) compared to high dividend payout (old/low sales growth) firms. The multivariate results indicate a monotonic decline both in the magnitude and statistical significance of the response coefficients from the growth to the stagnant groups. Directional t-tests of differential response coefficients also support our predictions. Taken together, the evidence suggests that the stock market reaction to performance measures is a function of life cycle stage.

Additional analyses suggest that differential response coefficients are not driven by a firm size effect or risk differences, and that differences in time-series properties of the performance measures do not systematically contribute to measurement error across life cycle groups. Overall, our results highlight the role of nonearnings data in explaining stock returns and suggest that strategic issues are important in performance evaluation.

The remainder of the paper is organized as follows. Section 2 develops the hypotheses. The sample selection procedure, life cycle descriptors, definition of the independent and dependent variables, and regression model are provided in section 3. Empirical results and alternative explanations are discussed in sections 4 and 5, respectively. Limitations and concluding remarks are provided in the final section.

2. Hypothesis development

The central idea in business strategy is to create a 'lasting' cost or demand advantage over competitors [BCG (1968)]. Cost advantages might include building capacity to achieve economies of scale, while demand advantages stem from building a large market share, either of which creates a barrier to entry. Life cycle theory suggests that appropriate growth and capital capacity strategies depend on the firm's life cycle stage. Early growth maximization is suggested in many business strategy texts [e.g., Porter (1980) and BCG (1968)]. Similarly, a firm can strategically position itself by creating capital capacity early in its life cycle. Thus, the benefit–cost ratio of acquiring market share and building capacity is highest in the firm's early life cycle stages.

Economists attempt to derive these prescriptions analytically. Spence (1977) shows that firms can deter entry by creating capacity and incurring significant capital expenditures early in the life cycle, making the product market unattractive to potential entrants. Spence (1979) further rationalizes early growth maximization through irreversibility of investments combined with a growth constraint. Spence shows that the individual firm invests rapidly until the present value of the net marginal profitability of capital is zero. Firms that can grow rapidly can make preemptive investments.

Demand- and supply-side learning are considered important by strategists in many industries. Spence (1981) argues that the learning curve creates entry barriers and protection from competition by creating cost advantages for those who achieve large market shares early in the life cycle. Even though cost advantages are only temporary, they significantly impact market share and profitability. Wernerfelt (1985) shows that in the presence of learning curves, declining price sensitivity, and declining growth rates, growth maximization early in the life cycle can be a means of profit maximization.

Since acquisition of market share and capital capacity are highly valued in early life cycle stages, it is reasonable to expect a higher stock price reaction to unexpected sales growth (or unexpected capital expenditure) in the early life cycle stages. This leads to the following research hypotheses (stated in alternative form):

(1) Unexpected positive sales growth is most (least) highly valued by the capital market during the growth (stagnant) stage.

(2) Unexpected positive capital expenditure is most (least) highly valued by the capital market during the growth (stagnant) stage.

Even though our hypotheses relate only to unexpected capital expenditures and sales growth, we also investigate the response to unexpected earnings, to mitigate omitted variables concerns. The association between earnings and stock prices is well documented in the accounting literature [e.g., Ball and Brown (1968) and Beaver (1968)]. Further, profitability measures are frequently referenced in the business strategy and management accounting literatures in the context of life cycle analysis [see Porter (1980) and NAA (1986)]. Unlike market share and capital capacity, there are no analytical models offering a directional relation between unexpected earnings and life cycle stage. Lacking adequate theoretical arguments, we develop no specific life cycle hypothesis with respect to unexpected earnings [see Rao (1989) for an investigation of the informativeness of earnings changes as a function of firm age].

3. Research design

3.1. Sample selection

Our initial sample includes 3,686 firms found on both the 1987 Compustat (Annual and Research) and CRSP tapes. We eliminate 740 utilities, insurance, and financial institutions. We exclude 1,037 firms not on the CRSP or Compustat tape for at least six years (explained in more detail below). We also eliminate 84 firms lacking sufficient data to estimate the market model parameters, leaving a potential sample of 1,825 firms with 14,258 firm-years of data.

We further restrict our analysis to those years for which life cycle data are available for at least 1,000 firms. This requirement is satisfied for the years 1976 to 1986. The year 1987 is excluded since our version of Compustat lacks necessary updated information. Additional restrictions are imposed by data requirements of the individual tests performed. Elimination due to specific missing data items (noted where appropriate) and deletion of outliers in the regression analyses cause sample size to vary from 11,768 to 13,882 firm-years across the various tests.[1]

---

[1]To mitigate the impact of outliers, we delet firm-years having extreme values ($\pm 300\%$) in independent variables.

Table 1

Expectations for firm-specific descriptors of life cycle stages.[a]

Life cycle stages	Life cycle descriptors			
	DP	SG	CEV	AGE
Growth	Low	High	High	Young
Mature	Medium	Medium	Medium	Adult
Stagnant	High	Low	Low	Old

[a]*DP*, *SG*, *CEV*, and *AGE* refer to dividend payout, sales growth, capital expenditure divided by value of the firm (market value of equity plus book value of long-term debt), and firm age, respectively.

3.2. Life cycle descriptors

We classify firms into life cycle stages using both univariate and multivariate ranking procedures. We use four classification variables: (1) annual dividend as a percentage of income (*DP*), (2) percent sales growth (*SG*), (3) capital expenditure as a percentage of total value of the firm (*CEV*), and (4) age of the firm (*AGE*).[2] We choose variables based on their frequent reference in the economics, management, and management accounting literature in similar contexts [e.g., Spence (1979, p. 1), Kotler (1980, table 12-1, p. 301), and NAA (1986, table 1, p. 10)]. Expectations regarding these life cycle descriptors are provided in table 1. The intuition is straightforward. Firms in early life cycle stages, on average, exhibit higher sales growth. Growth firms invest larger proportional amounts in plant and equipment, and have lower dividend payout ratios given their opportunity set of positive net present value projects. Younger firms are more likely to have new products.

We compute firm-specific financial variables to identify the life cycle stage from Compustat data as follows:

$$DP_t = (DIV_t/IBED_t) \times 100, \qquad (1)$$

$$SG_t = ((SALES_t - SALES_{t-1})/SALES_{t-1}) \times 100, \qquad (2)$$

$$CEV_t = (CE_t/VALUE_t) \times 100, \qquad (3)$$

[2]We thank the referee for suggesting firm age as a variable.

where (number in parentheses refers to the Compustat data item)

DIV_t = common dividends in year t (21),
$IBED_t$ = income before extraordinary items and discontinued operations in year t (18),
$SALES_t$ = net sales in year t (12),
CE_t = capital expenditure in year t (128), and
$VALUE_t$ = market value of equity plus book value of long-term debt at the end of year t.

The financial variables chosen as life cycle descriptors are directly related to firm risk, so firms sorted on these variables could have a differential response to performance measures, even without life cycle considerations. For example, prior research [Easton and Zmijewski (1989) and Collins and Kothari (1989)] demonstrates a relation between earnings response coefficients and risk, and a correlation between sales and earnings. To minimize the effect of possible correlation of risk with life cycle stage, we choose firm age as a nonfinancial life cycle descriptor, and we control for risk in our specification tests.

The three financial life cycle descriptors are calculated for each year for each sample firm. Then, for each firm-year, median values of the variables (denoted MDP, MSG, and MCEV) are computed using the prior five years' data. This requires at least six years of data availability for each firm. Information on the AGE variable is obtained from Moody's manuals. For each firm, we obtain the year in which the business was originally formed (denoted BYEAR).[3] AGE is computed as the difference between the current year and BYEAR for each firm-year.

We rank firms on each of the four life cycle descriptors (MDP, MSG, MCEV, and AGE)[4] and group them into various life cycle stages [Low, Medium, and High (Young, Adult, and Old for the AGE variable)] based on table 1. This approach is employed separately in each year to allow for temporal shifts in the life cycle stage of sample firms.

Once a firm-year is assigned to a group, it is given a score (growth = 1, mature = 2, and stagnant = 3). For example, a firm-year with a low SG (a candidate for the 'stagnant' stage) is given a score of three for the sales growth

---

[3]If the date of business formation is not available, then the year in which the firm was originally *incorporated* is considered the BYEAR. If two firms are merged, then for each firm, BYEAR is obtained, and the earlier of the two BYEAR's is considered the year of business formation for the new corporation. Missing information on BYEAR reduces the sample to 1,777 firms (13,466 firm years).

[4]The choice of median value for dividend payout reduces the problem of negative values for MDP. Only 68 firm-years are associated with negative MDP's. These are assigned to the 'High MDP' group. Tables 5 through 8 were replicated using median dividend yield (MDY), instead of MDP, as a life cycle descriptor. The results (not reported here) are qualitatively similar.

variable and a firm-year with a low DP (a candidate for the 'growth' stage) is given a score of one for the dividend payout variable.

In our multivariate analysis, we create five life cycle groups using MDP, MSG, and AGE as descriptors, based on a composite score obtained by summing the individual variable scores.[5] Although based on a simple summation, the composite score incorporates some interactions among the individual variables. For example, a low dividend payout could signal either high growth opportunities or cash flow problems. While a stagnant firm with cash flow problems would exhibit a low dividend payout, it is unlikely to rank high on the remaining variables, and thus should end up properly classified as a stagnant firm.[6]

When we use the composite scoring technique, 73.35% of firms remain in the same life cycle group compared to the prior year. The percentage decreases to 53.29% (44.09%) when comparing to three years (five years) before. A significant portion of this variability is due to shifts to adjacent groups. Compared with one (three/five) year(s) prior to the current year, 96.46% (88.77%/84.06%) of firms remain within one adjacent group.

3.3. Definition of independent and dependent variables

Three financial performance measures are used as independent variables:

(1) unexpected earnings $[\Delta IBED = (IBED_t - IBED_{t-1})/MVE_{t-1}]$,

(2) unexpected capital expenditures $[\Delta CE = (CE_t - CE_{t-1})/MVE_{t-1}]$,

(3) unexpected sales growth $[\Delta SG = SG_t - SG_{t-1}]$,[7]

where MVE_{t-1} is market value of equity at the end of time $t - 1$, and other variables are as already defined.

The dependent variable is the cumulative abnormal return (CAR) from the market model. The market model parameters are derived from OLS regression using returns from month -1 to month -60 (the estimation period), where month zero is the first month of the fiscal year. CAR is computed by cumulating

---

[5] MCEV is eliminated as a descriptor due to its low explanatory power. See sections 4.2 and 4.3 for additional detail.

[6] As the referee points out, future research which explicitly considers interaction terms for the life cycle measures or an alternative weighting scheme may provide additional insights. However, at present, we have no means of further weighting the interactions, other than an ad hoc approach.

[7] We adopt random walk expectation models for sales growth and capital expenditure. Future research might include financial analysts' forecasts (e.g., Value Line) as expectations proxies. We credit the referee for this suggestion.

Unexpected earnings and unexpected capital expenditure are scaled by MVE to mitigate the impact of cross-sectional differences in firm size. Scaling is not needed for unexpected sales growth, since this variable is based on a pure number.

abnormal returns from the fourth month of the relevant fiscal year to the third month following the end of the fiscal year.[8]

3.4. Regression model

We estimate the following regression model to test the life cycle hypotheses:

$$CAR = \sum_i D_i[\alpha_{0i} + \alpha_{1i}\Delta IBED + \alpha_{2i}\Delta CE + \alpha_{3i}\Delta SG] + \varepsilon. \tag{4}$$

D_i is a dummy variable which takes a value of zero or one and the summation is over the n life cycle categories (either three or five). In the univariate procedure, D_1 equals one when a firm-year is assigned to Low MDP (High MSG/High $MCEV$/Young) group, D_2 equals one when a firm-year is assigned to Medium MDP (Medium MSG/Medium $MCEV$/Adult) group, and D_3 equals one when a firm-year is assigned to High MDP (Low MSG/Low $MCEV$/Old) group. The life cycle hypotheses translate into restrictions on α_2 and α_3 across subsamples. For example, if the dummy variables correspond to levels of MDP, then we expect α_2 and α_3 of the Low MDP group to be greater than those of the High MDP group. The following statistical hypotheses (stated in alternative form) are tested:

$$H_1: \alpha_{j1} - \alpha_{j2} \geq 0, \quad j = 2,3,$$

$$H_2: \alpha_{j1} - \alpha_{j3} \geq 0, \quad j = 2,3,$$

$$H_3: \alpha_{j2} - \alpha_{j3} \geq 0, \quad j = 2,3$$

In the multivariate procedure, we assign firm-years to five life cycle groups [Growth (G), Growth/Mature (GM), Mature (M), Mature/Stagnant (MS), and Stagnant (S)] based on the composite score.[9] We expect α_2 and α_3 to monotonically decline from the Growth to Stagnant portfolios. In this procedure, D_1 takes a value of one when a firm-year belongs to the Growth group, whereas D_5 takes a value of one when a firm-year belongs to the Stagnant group. D_2 through

---

[8] The cumulation period is selected to cover the period between consecutive annual report release dates. Firms with as few as five data points in the estimation period are included. Of the 14,258 betas estimated, sixteen are estimated with less than twenty observations, and 14,066 betas are estimated with no missing observations.

[9] The range of the composite score depends on the number of grouping variables. For example, with three variables, the composite score ranges from three to nine. Firm-years are assigned to the five life cycle groups to yield an approximately equal number of observations in each group.

Table 2
Summary descriptive statistics.[a]

Variable[b]	Mean	Std. dev.	Quartiles 0.25	0.50	0.75
MROA	6.004	4.262	3.501	5.771	8.306
MDP	22.628	19.598	0.439	22.598	34.991
MSG	11.878	10.751	6.138	11.400	16.990
MCEV	10.373	6.785	5.455	8.950	13.618
MVALUE	663.440	2495.820	30.337	106.408	433.953
β	1.261	0.900	0.918	1.206	1.535
AGE	56.922	31.466	31.000	53.000	77.000

[a] Based on 13,882 firm-years, except for the *AGE* variable, where only 13,686 firm-years of data are available. All median variables are recalculated for each firm-year using the prior five years' data.

[b] *MROA* = median of income before extraordinary items and discontinued operations divided by market value of equity, expressed as a percentage;

MDP = median of common dividends divided by income before extraordinary items and discontinued operations, expressed as a percentage;

MSG = median annual percentage sales growth;

MCEV = median of capital expenditure divided by the market value of equity plus book value of long-term debt, expressed as a percentage;

MVALUE = median market value of equity plus book value of debt;

β = estimate of market model slope coefficient, using prior five years' data;

AGE = age of the firm, computed as the difference between the current year and the year in which the business was originally formed.

D_4 are dummy variables representing the middle three groups. We test the following statistical hypotheses (stated in alternative form):

$$H_4: \alpha_{j1} - \alpha_{j3} \geq 0, \quad j = 2,3,$$

$$H_5: \alpha_{j1} - \alpha_{j5} \geq 0, \quad j = 2,3,$$

$$H_6: \alpha_{j3} - \alpha_{j5} \geq 0, \quad j = 2,3.$$

Statistical testing is restricted to the Growth, Mature, and Stagnant groups to minimize the number of statistical comparisons.

4. Analysis of the results

4.1. Descriptive information

Table 2 provides descriptive information on the life cycle descriptors (*MDP*, *MSG*, *MCEV*, and *AGE*), median firm value (*MVALUE*), beta (β) of the sample firm-years, and median return on assets ($MROA$).[10] The mean of $MVALUE$ is driven by extreme outliers. Higher mean and median values for beta (i.e., greater than 1.00) are due to inclusion of many smaller AMEX firms and exclusion of utilities from the sample.

Table 3 provides median values for the same variables grouped by levels of the life cycle descriptors. For example, panel A of table 3 provides median values for three groups formed by levels of MDP. Therefore, in each panel, the monotonic increase in median values reported for one variable is by construction. Table 3 indicates the interrelations among the various performance measures and other firm characteristics. In general, observed relations among MDP, MSG, and AGE are consistent with our expectations, supporting their choice as life cycle descriptors. Specifically, there is a positive association between dividend payout and firm age, and a negative association between sales growth and firm age.

4.2. Industry-level life cycles information

We next investigate the reasonableness of our life cycle descriptors at the industry level. We use data on all firm-years to obtain industry median values (based on four-digit SIC codes) for each life cycle descriptor (denoted $IMDP$, $IMSG$, $IMCEV$, and $IMAGE$). We exclude industries with less than 40 firm-years of data. We rank industries and then consider the reasonableness of the classifications for the top and bottom 20 industries. The evidence (not presented) suggests that dividend payout, sales growth, and firm age are reasonable proxies for life cycle stage. The low dividend payout, high sales growth, and young industries include those generally considered 'growth' industries during the period studied (e.g., computers and semiconductors in the low dividend payout category; computers and hospitals in the high sales growth category; and semiconductors and consulting in the new industries category). However, one can point out 'inappropriate' classifications obtained using the individual life cycle descriptors.

Capital expenditure provides little insight on life cycle stage. There is a concentration of capital-intensive firms in the 'High $IMCEV$' category, many of which are not typically considered 'growth' industries. Inter-industry differences in $IMCEV$ appear more related to an industry's production function than to life cycle stage. Thus, $IMCEV$, in the univariate industry level analysis, proxies poorly for life cycle stage.

Combining the three proxies ($IMDP$, $IMSG$, and $IMAGE$) should reduce the probability of misclassification. To test this argument, we first rank industries

---

[10]Return on assets is defined as $IBED$ divided by total assets. Consistent with the presentation for the life cycle descriptors, we provide descriptive information on *median* values for total firm value and return on assets.

Table 3

Median values for alternative life cycle groups.[a,b]

Group	n	MROA	MDP	MSG	MCEV	MVALUE	β	AGE
Panel A: Median values for groups formed by levels of dividend payout (MDP)							
Low	4,292	3.332	0.000	10.140	9.182	36.474	1.471	34.0
Medium	4,668	6.637	21.625	13.640	9.157	124.640	1.246	50.0
High	4,922	6.521	39.535	10.201	8.615	269.163	1.019	72.0
Panel B: Median values for groups formed by levels of sales growth (MSG)							
Low	4,825	4.179	21.549	3.890	8.887	58.971	1.178	55.0
Medium	4,804	6.322	26.943	11.970	8.900	149.681	1.151	60.0
High	4,253	7.118	18.602	20.430	9.109	143.588	1.313	42.0
Panel C: Median values for groups formed by levels of capital expenditure (MCEV)							
Low	4,537	7.196	22.940	11.460	4.276	82.529	1.244	51.0
Medium	4,691	5.710	24.346	11.100	8.901	102.203	1.198	55.0
High	4,654	5.043	19.908	11.655	16.194	148.939	1.180	53.5
Panel D: Median values for groups formed by levels of firm age (AGE)							
Young	4,071	5.333	8.805	13.390	9.029	53.580	1.427	24.0
Adult	4,773	5.692	22.062	10.990	8.825	93.345	1.214	51.0
Old	4,842	6.226	32.406	10.680	8.937	241.231	1.064	84.0

[a]Based on 13,882 firm-years, except for the *AGE* variable, where only 13,686 firm-years of data are available. *n* refers to the number of firm-years of data available. All median variables are recalculated for each firm-year using the prior five years' data.

[b]MROA = median of income before extraordinary items and discontinued operations divided by market value of equity, expressed as a percentage;

MDP = median of common dividends divided by income before extraordinary items and discontinued operations, expressed as a percentage;

MSG = median annual percentage sales growth;

MCEV = median of capital expenditure divided by the market value of equity plus book value of long-term debt, expressed as a percentage;

MVALUE = median market value of equity plus book value of debt;

β = estimate of market model slope coefficient, using prior five years' data;

AGE = age of the firm, computed as the difference between the current year and the year in which the business was originally formed.

based on median values of each life cycle descriptor. Second, we obtain a combined rank by adding the univariate ranks.[11] Third, we resort industries on the combined rank. Table 4 provides the top and bottom 20 industries based on the combined rank, and indicates an improvement in classification when combining

---

[11]To make the combined rank meaningful, industries are ranked in ascending order of *IMDP*, *IMAGE*, and descending order of *IMSG*. Thus, industries with smaller combined rank are lower dividend payout, higher sales growth, and newer industries.

Table 4

List of industries sorted by median values of DP, SG, and AGE.

SIC code	Industry name	Firm-years[a]	IMDP	IMSG	IMAGE
	Low DP, High SG, and Young industries				
7372	Cmp program & software svcs	47	0.000	16.140	25.000
3679	Electronic components, nec	118	7.100	14.210	32.500
5945	Hobby, toy, and game shops	40	0.000	13.950	46.500
5065	Electronic parts & eq-whsl	102	7.360	12.560	31.000
3674	Semiconductor, related device	83	0.000	10.240	24.000
7011	Hotels, motels, tourist courts	67	9.750	11.580	25.000
1311	Crude petroleum & natural gas	397	9.980	12.630	32.000
3724	Aircraft engine, engine parts	44	7.190	11.110	30.500
8062	Gen med & surgical hospitals	46	21.830	22.460	20.500
4511	Air transportation, certified	161	0.000	13.110	49.000
3825	Elec meas & test instruments	90	11.240	11.790	31.000
8911	Engr, architect, survey svcs	134	18.910	14.060	34.000
5063	Elec apparatus & equip-whsl	45	15.270	12.670	36.000
3585	Air cond, heating, refrig eq	64	0.510	11.560	46.500
4210	Trucking, local, long distance	42	17.790	14.160	45.000
3990	Misc manufacturing industries	43	21.170	11.850	28.000
5331	Variety stores	166	14.170	11.350	42.000
3680	Electronic computing equip	92	10.610	13.460	53.500
5812	Eating places	124	14.770	11.050	40.500
4833	Television broadcasting	75	22.130	13.840	43.000
	High DP, Low SG, and Old industries				
5311	Department stores	142	33.110	9.020	69.000
3861	Photographic equip & suppl	58	42.230	9.690	68.000
2834	Pharmaceutical preparations	258	38.690	9.950	81.000
3530	Constr, mining, matl handle eq	47	30.080	7.650	65.000
2911	Petroleum refining	364	33.080	8.370	65.500
5051	Metals service centers-whsl	42	23.850	5.830	70.500
2211	Brd woven fabric mill, cotton	56	30.540	9.130	89.500
1600	Construction-not bldg constr	77	26.400	7.730	78.000
2030	Can, preserve fruit, vegetable	80	36.520	4.720	53.500
3290	Abrasive, asbestos, misc minrl	61	24.880	5.390	69.000
2040	Grain mill products	55	37.820	9.230	78.000
2080	Beverages	63	35.520	9.500	99.000
2200	Textile mill products	148	24.080	5.830	81.000
1000	Metal mining	53	32.400	5.360	61.000
3630	Household appliances	79	40.740	8.560	71.000
2421	Sawmills, planing mills, gen	40	46.990	7.870	67.500
2000	Food and kindred products	96	33.590	7.910	81.500
2840	Soap, detergent, toilet preps	42	44.610	9.010	140.500
2821	Plastics, resins, elastomers	44	36.550	6.080	77.500
2800	Chemicals & allied prods	152	36.980	7.820	92.000

[a] Firm-years represent the total number of observations available within the four-digit SIC code over the sample period.

information from the three life cycle descriptors. Most of the top 20 industries in the list are typically cited as 'growth' industries. Similarly, a substantial number in the bottom 20 are from industries where new product developments are more rare.

4.3. Differential response coefficients across life cycle descriptors

Table 5 provides the results of regressing CAR on accounting performance measures with slope dummies for groups formed by median levels of dividend payout, sales growth, capital expenditure, and firm age, respectively.[12] The test results for our differential response coefficient hypotheses are also presented.[13] We initially adopt the univariate classification procedure to investigate the contribution of each variable to the multivariate grouping scheme. In addition, since sales growth is used both in defining an independent variable and as a grouping variable (ΔSG and MSG, respectively), observed monotonicity in the slope coefficient of ΔSG may be attributed to spurious effects of the classification scheme. The univariate results demonstrate that the trend in the slope coefficient of ΔSG is generally consistent with our predictions, even when MSG is not used as a classification variable.

Results in panel A are consistent with our hypotheses. Slope coefficients of ΔCE and ΔSG decrease from the low to high dividend payout group. The slope coefficient of ΔCE, α_2, for the low MDP group is 0.081 (significant at the 0.01 level), whereas those of the other groups are insignificantly different from zero. In addition, α_2 of the low MDP group is significantly greater than those of the medium and high MDP groups at the 0.05 level. The slope coefficient of ΔSG, α_3, is 0.172 for the low MDP group which is more than twice that of 0.074 for the high MDP group. While α_3 is significantly different from zero for all three dividend payout groups, α_3 of the high MDP group is significantly smaller than those of the low and medium MDP groups. Overall, in four of six cases, we reject the null hypothesis.

Using sales growth as a grouping variable fails to support the capital capacity argument even though the results (see panel B) are consistent with the market share argument. There is a monotonic decline in α_3 from the high to the low MSG group, and α_3 of the high MSG group is more than twice that of the low MSG group. In addition, α_3 of the high MSG group is significantly greater than those of the lower MSG groups at the 0.01 level. With respect to the capital capacity argument, while α_2 of the high MSG group is greater than those of the

---

[12]Our outlier deletion rule is applied here and in all subsequent regression analyses. While having marginal impact on α_1 and α_2, the deletion rule significantly increases the magnitude and statistical significance of α_3 in all regressions. Regression sample size is reduced to 13,653 firm-years after deleting outliers.

[13]We test the significance of the slope coefficients (difference between the slope coefficients) using two-tailed (one-tailed) t-tests.

Table 5

Regression of CAR on differenced accounting performance measures with slope dummies for levels of life cycle descriptors.[a,b]

$$CAR = \sum_{i=1}^{3} D_i [\alpha_{0i} + \alpha_{1i} \Delta IBED + \alpha_{2i} \Delta CE + \alpha_{3i} \Delta SG] + \varepsilon$$

	Levels	n	α_0	α_1	α_2	α_3
Panel A: Slope dummies for levels of median dividend payout (MDP)						
MDP:	Low (L)	4122	−0.0176 (−3.099)***	0.4155 (24.215)***	0.0812 (3.481)***	0.1717 (9.919)***
	Medium (M)	4628	−0.0582 (−10.928)***	0.5595 (15.677)***	−0.0227 (−0.666)	0.1607 (7.276)***
	High (H)	4903	0.0012 (0.240)	0.5785 (13.713)***	−0.0123 (−0.260)	0.0741 (3.0·14)***
	L (−) M				0.1039 (2.514)***	0.0110 (0.391)
	L (−) H				0.0935 (1.773)**	0.0976 (3.247)***
	M (−) H				−0.0104 (−0.178)	0.0867 (2.622)***
Panel B: Slope dummies for levels of median sales growth (MSG)						
MSG:	High (H)	4154	−0.0882 (−15.497)***	0.6372 (17.130)***	0.0813 (2.775)***	0.1824 (9.094)***
	Medium (M)	4747	−0.0237 (−4.541)***	0.4984 (17.561)***	−0.0121 (−0.353)	0.0969 (3.950)***
	Low (L)	4752	0.0333 (6.324)***	0.3991 (21.307)***	0.0648 (2.216)**	0.0825˙ (4.430)***
	H (−) M				0.0933 (2.075)**	0.0856 (2.701)***
	H (−) L				0.0165 (0.398)	0.0999 (3.652)***
	M (−) L				−0.0769 (−1.710)	0.0144 (0.467)
Panel C: Slope dummies for levels of median capital expenditure (MCEV)						
MCEV:	High (H)	4569	−0.0013 (−0.242)	0.4226 (19.848)***	0.0305 (1.452)	0.1017 (4.691)***
	Medium (M)	4626	−0.0268 (−4.975)***	0.4615 (17.460)***	0.0751 (1.839)*	0.1807 (8.215)***
	Low (L)	4458	−0.0484 (−8.747)***	0.5322 (17.516)***	0.1003 (1.654)*	0.1583 (8.429)***

Table 5 (continued)

Levels	n	α_0	α_1	α_2	α_3
H (−) M				− 0.0446 (− 0.972)	− 0.0789 (− 2.557)
H (−) L				− 0.0698 (− 1.088)	− 0.0566 (− 1.972)
M (−) L				− 0.0252 (− 0.344)	0.0224 (0.775)

Panel D: Slope dummies for levels of firm age (AGE)

AGE:		n	α_0	α_1	α_2	α_3
	Young (N)	3981	− 0.0369 (− 6.402)***	0.5520 (22.431)***	0.0806 (2.796)***	0.2256 (11.529)***
	Adult (A)	4670	− 0.0233 (− 4.380)***	0.5480 (21.528)***	0.0133 (0.469)	0.0953 (4.663)***
	Old (O)	4815	− 0.0182 (− 3.498)***	0.2877 (10.772)***	0.0500 (1.134)	0.1202 (5.318)***
	N (−) A				0.0673 (1.664)**	0.1303 (4.602)***
	N (−) O				0.0306 (0.580)	0.1054 (3.526)***
	A (−) O				− 0.0367 (− 0.700)	− 0.0249 (− 0.815)

[a]The number in parentheses is the *t*-statistic. A *** (**/*) designates statistical significance at the 0.01 (0.05/0.10) level. The significance of the slope coefficients (difference between the slope coefficients) is tested using two-tailed (one-tailed) *t*-tests. The elimination of outliers reduces the sample size to 13,653 firm-years for these tests (13,466 firm-years for the *AGE* subsample). *n* refers to the number of firm-years of data available for each subsample. Firm-years are assigned to one of the three groups based on their relative cross-sectional ranking on the grouping variable. As in prior tables, median values are based on the prior five years' data.

[b]*MDP* = median of common dividends divided by income before extraordinary items and discontinued operations (*IBED*), expressed as a percentage;
MSG = median annual percentage sales growth;
MCEV = median of capital expenditure divided by the market value of equity plus book value of long-term debt, expressed as a percentage;
AGE = age of the firm, computed as the difference between the current year and the year in which the business was orginally formed;
CAR = sum of abnormal returns from the fourth month of the relevant fiscal year to the third month following the end of the fiscal year;
D_i = zero/one dummy variables proxying for the level of grouping variable;
ΔIBED = differenced *IBED* divided by prior-year market value of equity (*MVE*);
ΔCE = differenced capital expenditure divided by prior-year *MVE*;
ΔSG = change in percentage sales growth.

other groups, there is no monotonic decline in α_2 from the high to low MSG groups. In addition, while α_2 of the high MSG group is significantly greater than that of the medium MSG group, it is insignificantly different from that of the low MSG group. We reject the null hypothesis in three of six cases.

Grouping firms by level of capital expenditure (panel C) provides response coefficients inconsistent with our predictions on market share and capital capacity. There is a monotonic increase in α_2 from the high to the low $MCEV$ group, and α_3 does not provide any discernable pattern. $MCEV$ is excluded as a life cycle descriptor in subsequent analysis since understanding inter-industry differences in $MCEV$ (see section 4.2) requires knowledge of industry-level production functions, which is beyond the scope of this paper.[14]

Panel D of table 5 presents the results of regressing CAR on accounting performance measures for AGE subsamples. The results are consistent with our hypotheses. While the magnitude of response coefficients for ΔSG and ΔCE does not monotonically decrease from Young to Old firms, they are largest for the Young firms. In terms of hypothesis testing, while α_3 of Young firms is significantly greater than that of both Adult and Old firms, α_2 of Young firms is significantly greater than that of only Adult firms. Overall, the evidence suggests that the mean benefit–cost ratio of increased market share and capital capacity is a function of firm age, consistent with the life cycle theory.

4.4. Differential response coefficients across life cycle stages

Table 6 presents the results of regressing CAR on the accounting performance measures for each of the five life cycle groups formed using the composite score.[15] Results are consistent with our hypotheses. There is almost a monotonic decline in the slope coefficients of ΔCE and ΔSG from the Growth to Stagnant stages, and both α_2 and α_3 are insignificant for the Stagnant firms.

The test results of the differential response coefficient hypotheses also are presented in table 6. Five of the six t-tests reject the null hypothesis at the 0.05 level. Not only is α_3 of the Growth stage significantly greater than that of both the Mature and Stagnant stages, but α_3 of the Mature stage is also significantly greater than that of the Stagnant stage. While the Growth stage α_2 is greater than that of both the Mature and Stagnant stages, the Mature stage α_2 is insignificantly different from that of the Stagnant stage.

---

[14] Ex post we rationalize that a firm's total investment in resources would be closely related to life cycle stage. This requires a much broader measure of investment than simple capital expenditures. For example, a service industry invests heavily in human capital, which is not captured by our capital expenditure measure.

[15] Since the score for each variable ranges from one to three, the composite score ranges from three to nine. Firm-years with scores less than or equal to four (greater than or equal to eight) are assigned to the Growth (Stagnant) group. Firm-years with scores five, six, or seven are assigned to the three intermediate groups.

Table 6

Regression of CAR on differenced accounting performance measures with slope dummies for life cycle groups based on MDP, MSG, and AGE.[a,b]

$$CAR = \sum_{i=1}^{5} D_i[\alpha_{0i} + \alpha_{1i}\Delta IBED + \alpha_{2i}\Delta CE + \alpha_{3i}\Delta SG] + \varepsilon$$

Stage	n	α_0	α_1	α_2	α_3
Growth (G)	2420	−0.0942 (−12.656)***	0.5627 (16.513)***	0.1200 (3.536)***	0.2078 (8.473)***
Growth/Mature	2454	−0.0169 (−2.307)**	0.5637 (19.471)***	0.0342 (0.976)	0.1786 (7.149)***
Mature (M)	2599	−0.0217 (−3.066)***	0.4688 (15.484)***	0.0297 (0.766)	0.1365 (4.996)***
Mature/Stagnant	2666	−0.0158 (−2.269)**	0.2627 (8.170)***	0.0515 (0.971)	0.1279 (4.600)***
Stagnant (S)	3327	0.0113 (1.809)*	0.5185 (11.760)***	−0.0413 (−0.693)	−0.0022 (−0.072)
G(−)M				0.0903 (1.753)**	0.0713 (1.943)**
G(−)S				(0.1613 (2.351)***	0.2100 (5.352)***
M(−)S				0.0710 (0.998)	0.1387 (3.379)***

[a] The number in parentheses is the t-statistic. A *** (**/*) designates statistical significance at the 0.01 (0.05/0.10) level. The significance of the slope coefficients (difference between the slope coefficients) is tested using two-tailed (one-tailed) t-tests. Elimination of outliers and firms with missing AGE data reduces the sample size to 13,466 firm-years for these tests. n refers to the number of firm-years of data available for each subsample. Firm-years are assigned to one of the five life cycle groups based on a composite ranking on the grouping variables such that low (high) MDP, high (low) MSG, and young (old) AGE firms are in Growth (Stagnant) groups. As in prior tables, median values are based on the prior five years' data.

[b] MDP = median of common dividends divided by income before extraordinary items and discontinued operations ($IBED$), expressed as a percentage;
MSG = median annual percentage sales growth;
$MCEV$ = median of capital expenditure divided by the market value of equity plus book value of long-term debt, expressed as a percentage;
AGE = age of the firm, computed as the difference between the current year and the year in which the business was originally formed;
CAR = sum of abnormal returns from the fourth month of the relevant fiscal year to the third month following the end of the fiscal year;
D_i = zero/one dummy variables proxying for life cycle stage;
$\Delta IBED$ = differenced $IBED$ divided by prior-year market value of equity (MVE);
ΔCE = differenced capital expenditure divided by prior-year MVE;
ΔSG = change in percentage sales growth.

Table 7

Average slope coefficients from firm-specific regression of CAR on differenced accounting performance measures and results of aggregation tests.[a,b]

$$CAR = \alpha_0 + \alpha_1 \Delta IBED + \alpha_2 \Delta CE + \alpha_3 \Delta SG + \varepsilon$$

Stage	Firms	n	$\Delta IBED$ Average α_1 (Z-stat.)	ΔCE Average α_2 (Z-stat.)	ΔSG Average α_3 (Z-stat.)
Growth (G)	236	2351	1.3899 (15.042)***	0.1548 (1.673)*	0.1690 (3.982)***
Growth/Mature	223	2243	1.0772 (14.735)***	0.0066 (0.273)	0.0358 (0.779)
Mature (M)	226	2298	1.1662 (15.322)***	−0.0645 (−0.766)	0.0263 (0.560)
Mature/Stagnant	219	2296	1.0197 (14.612)***	−0.1161 (−1.431)	−0.0028 (−0.095)
Stagnant (S)	248	2580	0.7806 (8.451)***	−0.2752 (−2.634)***	−0.0419 (−0.945)
G(−)M				0.2193 (1.731)**	0.1427 (2.454)***
G(−)S				0.4300 (3.053)***	0.2109 (3.457)***
M(−)S				0.2107 (1.376)*	0.0682 (1.070)

[a]Average α's are weighted average means of firm-specific α's with weights inversely proportional to coefficient standard error. Computation of the standard normal Z-statistic assumes that firm-specific t-statistics are independent. A *** (**/*) designates statistical significance at the 0.01 (0.05/0.10) level. The significance of the average slope coefficients (difference between the average slope coefficients) is tested using two-tailed (one-tailed) tests. n refers to the number of firm-years of data available. Firm-years are assigned to one of the five life cycle groups based on a composite ranking on the grouping variables such that low (high) MDP, high (low) MSG, and young (old) AGE firms are in Growth (Stagnant) groups. As in prior tables, median values are based on the prior five years' data.

[b]MDP = median of common dividends divided by income before extraordinary items and discontinued operations ($IBED$), expressed as a percentage;
MSG = median annual percentage sales growth;
$MCEV$ = median of capital expenditure divided by the market value of equity plus book value of long-term debt, expressed as a percentage;
AGE = age of the firm, computed as the difference between the current year and the year in which the business was originally formed;
CAR = sum of abnormal returns from the fourth month of the relevant fiscal year to the third month following the end of the fiscal year;
$\Delta IBED$ = differenced $IBED$ divided by prior-year market value of equity (MVE);
ΔCE = differenced capital expenditure divided by prior-year MVE;
ΔSG = change in percentage sales growth.

4.5. Firm-specific response coefficients as a function of life cycle stage

In the analysis conducted so far, we classify firm-years into life cycle groups, and estimate the response coefficients based on all firm-years within each group. This approach assumes cross-sectional stability in the response coefficients. In the context of earnings, prior empirical evidence suggests systematic differences in response coefficients across firms [see Easton and Zmijewski (1989), Lipe (1986), Kormendi and Lipe (1987), and Collins and Kothari (1989)]. We adopt an alternative approach, estimating firm-specific response coefficients, to control for this possibility.

CAR is regressed on the three differenced performance measures ($\Delta IBED$, ΔCE, and ΔSG) to estimate firm-specific response coefficients. Median values of dividend payout, sales growth, and age for each firm are used to assign firms to portfolios. A modification of Christie's (1990) Z-statistic is used to test for significant differences between the average response coefficients of the groups.[16]

The multivariate results are presented in table 7. The average α_2 and α_3 monotonically decrease from the Growth to the Stagnant groups, and five of the six Z-tests of the differential response coefficients reject the null hypothesis at the 0.10 level. The firm-specific analysis reported in table 7 supports the conclusions from the pooled cross-sectional analysis reported in table 6.

5. Alternative explanations and additional evidence

This section discusses the results of specification checks conducted to investigate the principal alternative explanations of our results.[17]

5.1. Firm size effects

Table 3 indicates that firm size, defined by $MVALUE$, is positively associated with dividend payout and firm age, suggesting that the differential response coefficients could be due to size effects.[18] One would expect that more information is available on the activities of larger firms and that more individuals process and disseminate this information to a broader group of market agents. If prices of larger firms reflect reported earnings earlier, one might expect a similar information effect for capital expenditure and sales growth. In such a case, small

---

[16]The formulation for the modified Z-statistic is available from the authors.

[17]We briefly describe the additional specification tests performed and the results thereof. The results of the firm size tests (section 5.1) are presented in table 8 to give readers a flavor for the nature and results of the specification tests. All other results are omitted, but available from the authors on request.

[18]Similar effects have been documented by Freeman (1987) and Collins, Kothari, and Rayburn (1987). The impact of firm size is mitigated by the observed positive association between sales growth and firm size.

firms' response coefficients for $\varDelta CE$ and $\varDelta SG$ would be higher than those of large firms, and the larger response coefficients for the growth firms would be driven by the smaller growth firms.

To test this argument, we separately regress CAR on differenced performance measures for three size portfolios (defined by $MVALUE$), and report the response coefficients of $\varDelta CE$ and $\varDelta SG$ in panel A of table 8 (row 1). The decline in α_2 and α_3 from Small to Large firms is less pronounced than that obtained across life cycle groups. The observed monotonicity across size portfolios is not inconsistent with the life cycle theory since one would expect the growth (stagnant) firms to be smaller (larger) firms.

We run the life cycle regression separately for each size portfolio to separate the confounding effects. The slope coefficients in panel A (rows 2 to 4) indicate that, with one exception, α_2 and α_3 monotonically decline from the Growth to the Stagnant groups for all three size portfolios.[19] The magnitude of the response coefficients for the size portfolios is to some extent driven by the life cycle grouping. For example, while the magnitudes of α_2 and α_3 of the Small firms are driven by the Growth firms, those of the Large firms are driven by the Stagnant firms.

The results of t-tests of differences in response coefficients across stages (the $\varDelta \alpha_j$s) are presented in panel B of table 8. While all $\varDelta \alpha_2$s have the correct sign, only two differences are significant at the 0.10 level. Market share results are stronger. Eight $\varDelta \alpha_3$s have the correct sign, and six are statistically significant at the 0.10 level. Although observed differences in response coefficients are not driven by the size effect, the evidence is consistent with firm size acting as another proxy for life cycle stage. However, since we use proxies (e.g., firm size, dividend payout, sales growth, and firm age) for underlying economic characteristics, our tests cannot categorically distinguish between informational effects and life cycle effects without observing such characteristics.

5.2. Differential risk effects

Table 3 indicates that firm risk, defined by beta, has a negative association with dividend payout and firm age, suggesting that the observed monotonicity in response coefficients could be due to risk differences across life cycle groups. Unlike the size effect, no theory links the response coefficients of sales growth and capital expenditure to beta. While the dependent variable (CAR) is risk-adjusted, no such adjustment is made for the independent variables, which could spuriously contribute to differences in the response coefficients. For example, the larger response coefficients of the growth firms could be driven by the high beta firms.

---

[19]Qualitatively similar results are obtained when market value of equity is used as a proxy for firm size.

Table 8

Regression of CAR on differenced accounting performance measures with slope dummies for life cycle groups by levels of firm size.[a,b]

$$CAR = \sum_{i=1}^{5} D_i [\alpha_{0i} + \alpha_{1i} \Delta IBED + \alpha_{2i} \Delta CE + \alpha_{3i} \Delta SG] + \varepsilon$$

	Small firms				Medium firms				Large firms			
	n	α_2	α_3		n	α_2	α_3		n	α_2	α_3	

Panel A: Slope coefficients[c]

All firms	4090	0.0885	0.2111		4480	0.0422	0.1128		4896	−0.0091	0.0924	
Growth (G)	986	0.1865	0.2439		874	0.0742	0.1728		560	0.1053	0.2097	
Mature (M)	930	0.0748	0.1451		825	−0.0102	0.0045		844	0.0656	0.2477	
Stagnant (S)	568	0.0166	0.1134		941	−0.0384	−0.0350		1818	−0.0853	−0.0585	

Panel B: Results of t-tests of differential response coefficients[d]

G (−) M		0.1116	0.0988			0.0844	0.1683			0.0397	−0.0379	
		(1.112)	(1.499)*			(1.052)	(2.755)***			(0.427)	(−0.514)	
G (−) S		0.1699	0.1306			0.1126	0.2078			0.1906	0.2682	
		(1.249)	(1.562)*			(0.801)	(3.144)***			(1.939)**	(3.827)***	
M (−) S		0.0582	0.0318			0.0282	0.0395			0.1509	0.3062	
		(0.428)	(0.373)			(0.192)	(0.530)			(1.532)*	(5.290)***	

[a] Firm-years are assigned to one of the five life cycle groups based on a composite ranking procedure such that low (high) dividend payout, high (low) sales growth, and young (old) firms are in Growth (Stagnant) groups. Firm-years are assigned to one of the three size groups based on their relative cross-sectional ranking on market value of equity plus book value of long-term debt.

[b]
CAR = sum of abnormal returns from the fourth month of the relevant fiscal year to the third month following the end of the fiscal year;
D_i = zero/one dummy variables proxying for the life cycle stages;
$\Delta IBED$ = differenced $IBED$ divided by prior-year market value of equity (MVE);
ΔCE = differenced capital expenditure divided by prior-year MVE;
ΔSG = change in percentage sales growth.

[c] Elimination of outliers and firms with missing AGE data reduces the sample size to 13,466 firm-years for the multivariate tests. n refers to the number of firm-years in each size/stage combination.

[d] The number in parentheses is the t-statistic. A *** (**/*) designates statistical significance at the 0.01 (0.05/0.10) level, using one-tailed t-tests.

We conduct the life cycle regression separately for three risk portfolios (defined by level of beta). The results are qualitatively similar for all risk portfolios and indicate no discernible relation between risk and the response coefficients of ΔSG and ΔCE, suggesting that the differential response coefficients are not driven by risk differences across firms.

5.3. Differential information content of prices

Since we assume a random walk (RW) expectations model for our independent variables, it is reasonable to expect measurement error in the independent variables if that assumption is violated. It is well known that measurement error in independent variables yields inconsistent slope estimates [Schmidt (1976, pp. 105–115)]. The error in unexpected performance measures, using a RW assumption, may be related to the information content of prices [see Collins and Kothari (1989)]. If the amount of measurement error is a function of the life cycle descriptors, then differential response coefficients across stages could be driven by the measurement error. Since it is difficult to obtain better estimates of the market's expectations of CE_t and SG_t at the beginning of the CAR cumulation period (e.g., analysts' forecasts), an alternative is to begin the return cumulation period at a point such that CE_{t-1} and SG_{t-1} approximate the market's expectations. This approach, suggested by Collins and Kothari (1989), is adopted here by varying the return window. Specifically, we choose a two-year CAR (denoted $CAR2$) as an alternative dependent variable.[20]

The magnitude and statistical significance of α_2 from the $CAR2$ regression increases substantially for all life cycle groups, suggesting that CE_{t-1} may be a better proxy for CE_t at the beginning of the $CAR2$ cumulation period. Altering the CAR cumulation period changes none of our inferences with respect to the life cycle hypotheses.

5.4. Firm-specific time-series model for performance measures

In addition to changing the cumulation period, we estimate firm-specific time-series models for the performance measures to reduce measurement error in the estimation of unexpected values. Systematic differences in the time-series properties of the independent variables across life cycle stages could explain the monotonic decline in the response coefficients of ΔCE and ΔSG. To mitigate this concern, we estimate univariate AR(1) models (with an intercept) for $IBED_t$, CE_t (both deflated by MVE_{t-1}), and SG_t, and compute residuals from the time-series

---

[20]The cumulation period of $CAR2$ begins twelve months prior to the beginning of the CAR cumulation period. In measuring $CAR2$, β is estimated separately for each of the two one-year components of $CAR2$.

model.[21] The life cycle regression is replicated with time-series residuals replacing the differenced performance measures as independent variables. The results are consistent with those in table 6.

5.5. Industry-adjusted independent variables

The analysis so far conducted employs changes in sales growth and capital expenditure to proxy for changes in market share and capital capacity, respectively, which has obvious limitations. If a firm increases sales growth by 5% (i.e., positive ΔSG) when the industry increases sales growth by 10%, then the firm is losing market share. Similar arguments can be made for capital capacity. To mitigate this problem, we calculate unexpected values for the independent variables using industry medians as our expectation, rather than a random walk.[22] To investigate the relative role of industry-adjusted and differenced performance measures, we include both in a single regression model.

The results of this regression and t-tests of differential response coefficients indicate that differencing (industry adjustment) provides results more consistent with our theory for the sales growth (capital expenditure) variable.[23]

6. Limitations and concluding remarks

We test whether the stock market response to accounting performance measures is a function of the life cycle stage of a firm, hypothesizing that response coefficients of unexpected sales growth and unexpected capital expenditure decrease from the growth to the stagnant portfolios. We test our hypotheses, regressing market model abnormal returns on accounting performance

---

[21]The choice of an AR(1) model is influenced by the limited time-series observations available. The number of time-series observations ranges from 6 to 17 with a median of 15. An intercept is estimated to capture any potential mean reversions in the variables. The parameter estimates and the residuals are obtained using the same set of time-series observations. These results are available from the authors.

[22]We include all industry-years with at least three firms, which results in a total of 2,177 industry-years (with three to 61 firms) and a median (mean) of five (6.89) firms. However, the median firm in each industry-year is eliminated in the regressions since the unexpected value for that firm is zero by construction.

An alternative is to construct direct measures of market share for the sales and capital capacity variables. The validity of industry definition is much more crucial in computing market share compared to our industry adjustment. While a single outlier (or misclassification) could materially affect the market share numbers, it has no significant effect on the computation of industry medians.

[23]While unexpected change in market share (of sales or capital capacity) is the variable of interest, we use first-differenced and industry-adjusted sales growth/capital expenditures as two proxies. While the first proxy ignores the industry effects, the second fails to control for the expected portion of the change in market share. Therefore, in different settings, either of the two proxies could be a better measure of the unexpected change in market share. This could explain why differencing (industry adjustment) provides results more consistent with our theory for the sales growth (capital expenditure) variable. We thank the referee for this suggestion.

measures (earnings, sales growth, and capital expenditure), using pooled cross-sectional data for the various life cycle groups.

In the univariate analysis, the response coefficients of unexpected sales growth and unexpected capital expenditure are higher for low dividend payout (young/high sales growth) compared to high dividend payout (old/low sales growth) firms. For the multivariate procedure, the results indicate a nearly monotonic decline both in the magnitude and statistical significance of the response coefficients of unexpected sales growth and unexpected capital expenditure from the growth to the stagnant portfolios. Additional analysis suggests that this relation is not driven by a firm size effect, risk differences, differences in the time-series properties of performance measures across life cycle groups, or differential information content of prices with respect to performance measures.

Our inferences depend on the quality of our life cycle proxies and the absence of correlated omitted variables. While the descriptive analysis suggests that our descriptors are reasonable proxies for life cycle stage, they could proxy for other economic phenomena. The sample period (1970–86) might be systematically affected by macro economic factors (business cycles, political climate, international business environment, etc.) unrelated to life cycle stages. Our sample suffers from self-selection bias, since we do not have many start-up firms.

Overall, our results indicate a differential role of accounting performance measures across life cycle stages, and highlight the role of nonearnings data in explaining stock returns.

References

Ball, Ray and Philip Brown, 1968, An empirical evaluation of accounting income numbers, Journal of Accounting Research, 159–178.
Beaver, William H., 1968, The information content of annual earnings announcements, Supplement of Journal of Accounting Research, 67–92.
Boston Consulting Group, 1968, Perspectives on experience (BCG, Boston, MA).
Christie, Andrew A., 1990, Aggregation of test statistics: An evaluation of the evidence on contracting and size hypotheses, Journal of Accounting and Economics 12, 15–36.
Collins, Daniel W. and S.P. Kothari, 1989, An analysis of intertemporal and cross-sectional determinants of earnings response coefficients, Journal of Accounting and Economics 11, 143–181.
Collins, Daniel W., S.P. Kothari, and Judy Dawson Rayburn, 1987, Firm size and the information content of prices with respect to earnings, Journal of Accounting and Economics 9, 111–138.
Easton, Peter D. and Mark E. Zmijewski, 1989, Cross-sectional variation in the stock market response to the announcement of accounting earnings, Journal of Accounting and Economics 11, 117–141.
Freeman, Robert N., 1987, The association between accounting earnings and security returns for large and small firms, Journal of Accounting and Economics 9, 195–228.
Karnani, Aneel, 1984, The value of market share and the product life cycle: A game-theoretic model, Management Science 30, 696–712.
Kormendi, R. and Robert C. Lipe, 1987, Earnings innovations, earnings persistence, and stock returns, Journal of Business, July, 323–345.
Kotler, Philip, 1980, Marketing management (Prentice-Hall, Englewood Cliffs, NJ).

Lipe, Robert C., 1986, The information contained in the components of earnings, Supplement of Journal of Accounting Research, 37–64.
National Association of Accountants, 1986, Statements on management accounting, Statement no. 4D, Measuring entity performance, Jan. (NAA, Montvale, NJ).
Porter, M. E., 1980, Competitive strategy: Techniques for analyzing industries and competitors (Free Press, New York, NY).
Rao, Gita R., 1989, The relation between stock returns and earnings: A study of newly-public firms, Working paper (University of Rochester, Rochester, NY).
Rappaport, Alfred, 1981, Selecting strategies that create shareholder value, Harvard Business Review, May–June, 139–149.
Richardson, Peter R. and John R. M. Gordon, 1980, Measuring total manufacturing performance, Sloan Management Review, Winter, 47–58.
Schmidt, Peter, 1976, Econometrics (Marcel Dekker, New York, NY).
Spence, A. Michael, 1977, Entry, capacity, investment, and oligopolistic pricing, Bell Journal of Economics 8, 534–544.
Spence, A. Michael, 1979, Investment strategy and growth in a new market, Bell Journal of Economics 10, 1–19.
Spence, A. Michael, 1981, The learning curve and competition, Bell Journal of Economics 12, 49–70.
Wernerfelt, Birger, 1985, The dynamics of prices and market shares over the product life cycle, Management Science 31, 928–939.

COMMENTARY

Katherine Schipper
on

Information Transfers

INTRODUCTION

The purpose of this commentary is to explore some of the currently-accepted definitions and motivations used in empirical investigations of earnings information transfers, to comment on what is known about information transfers from existing research and to suggest some extensions.[1] My initial, casual, definition of information transfers is consistent with that used in much accounting research: information transfers occur if announcements made by one group of one or more firms contemporaneously affect the returns to shares of another group of one or more non-announcing firms.

The motivation for this commentary arises in part from a consideration of what, if anything, the study of information transfers might eventually contribute to accounting policy deliberations.[2] With this consideration in mind, the commentary is based on a two-part question: why study information transfers, and why focus on earnings-related information, as much prior research in accounting has done? Based on research to date, I believe the answers are not necessarily clear and compelling, regardless of whether we focus on the possibility of a strong before-the-fact policy motivation for information transfer research or whether we evaluate the question in terms of what has been learned. Current research, however, also suggests a number of ways the question of information transfers might be reconsidered, with the potential for generating useful insights.

Regardless of the nature and definitiveness of results obtained, many questions of interest to accounting researchers are ultimately if not immediately driven by issues which are inherently policy-oriented. The numerous investigations of share price and other effects of voluntary and mandatory accounting changes provide one example. In contrast, it is not straightforward to identify a class of accounting policy questions which turn on the existence or non-existence of earnings information transfers.[3] To put this another way, under the assumption that required earnings disclosures will continue, what accounting policy issues of any substance are directly affected if one firm's (mandatory) earnings announcement

---

[1] This commentary is not intended to provide a review of the literature related to information transfers. The papers discussed are chosen merely to illustrate points that may well appear in other published and unpublished research as well.

[2] Other, non-policy, motivations could also be used to support information transfer research. For example, one might attempt to incorporate information transfer effects into earnings expectation models. While motivations with no (or extremely indirect) policy implications are not the focus of this commentary, I will touch on them in some later sections.

[3] Although it seems difficult at best to make a direct connection between information transfers and accounting policy, two kinds of indirect connections may be possible. First, it may be possible to incorporate information transfer effects into discussions of questions associated with voluntary disclosures, or of adding to or reducing the set of mandated disclosures, as discussed later. In addition, it may be possible to incorporate information transfer effects into research designs for investigating some traditional questions with relatively direct policy connections; see note 4 for additional discussion.

I appreciate useful conversations with J. Richard Dietrich, Ronald Dye and Laurentius Marais, and comments on an earlier draft from Stephen Baginski, John Burton, J. Richard Dietrich, Ronald Dye, George Foster, Laurentius Marais, Chris Olsen, Grace Pownall, Linda Vincent, Gregory Waymire and John Wild.

affects—or does not affect—its competitor's stock price? The study of information transfers associated with earnings announcements lacks the immediate relevance for accounting policy inherent in much empirical accounting research on earnings information content and related issues (e.g., separating the incremental information content of accruals over cash flows, investigating earnings management).[4]

Because of the roundabout nature of potential links between the existence of information transfers associated with mandated disclosures (such as earnings announcements) and specific accounting policy questions, the examination of information transfers might usefully be motivated from the perspective of voluntary disclosures and the interaction of voluntary with mandatory disclosures. The interaction arises because of the potential for externalities.[5] Under this perspective, one might consider firms' voluntary disclosure decisions—perhaps the decision to release or not to release earnings forecasts— in light of results on whether firms receive information transfers because of mandated disclosures as well as an understanding of the nature and consequences of those information transfers.[6]

Suppose, for example, that the case can be made that voluntary disclosures either create information transfer effects themselves or affect the information transfers associated with mandatory disclosures, and that such direct and indirect information transfer effects are for all intents and purposes externalities.[7] Then it is possible to explore the possibility that such transfers lead to voluntary disclosures that are in some sense in need of regulation (for example, they might be suboptimal in terms of quantity or quality). Dye [1990] adopts an information-transfer-like approach in his analytical comparison of mandatory and voluntary disclosures in the presence of various kinds of inter-firm dependencies. His results illustrate the difficulty of making any general statements without (at a minimum) a precise specification of the nature of the interdependencies. Regardless of the results, however, a clear and full development of some policy perspective or question can provide a motivation for information transfer research.

It would be especially valuable to develop a strong disclosure-policy motivational foundation in this instance because it is not in general easy to motivate information transfer research by pointing to definitive results.[8] The empirical results obtained so far from such research have not been striking in the sense of uncovering a previously unknown source of substantial variation in stock prices. In fact,

---

[4] The policy relevance of research on the information content of accruals arises from arguments over whether accounting (in the form of GAAP) merely adds noise to cash flows; if so, there is a potential improvement in information content from restricting accruals. The policy relevance of research on earnings management arises from debates over whether managerial discretion in choosing accounting methods, estimates and some accruals is desirable. Although the connection is by no means immediate, it may be possible to tie some aspects of information transfer research to questions of accruals and managerial discretion. For example, one might ask if there are some accruals whose presence in the earnings figure enhances information transfers. Or one might investigate whether firms that use a uniform set of accounting methods exhibit more marked information transfers.

[5] Research which considers disclosure issues in the context of externalities includes R. Dye, "Mandatory Versus Voluntary Disclosures: The Cases of Financial and Real Externalities," *The Accounting Review* 65, 1990, pp. 1-24 and G. Foster, "Externalities and Financial Reporting," *Journal of Finance* XXXV, 1990, pp. 521-533.

[6] Adopting a related motivation, Pownall and Waymire investigate whether firms that never released an earnings forecast during their sample period (July 1969 to December 1973) receive larger earnings information transfers than do firms that released at least one earnings forecast during the same period. See G. Pownall and G. Waymire, "Voluntary Disclosure Choice and Earnings Information Transfer," *Journal of Accounting Research* 27 supplement, 1989, pp. 85-105.

[7] I am using "externalities" here to mean roughly "interdependencies that may affect resource allocations." For a contrasting view which emphasizes the importance of resource allocations, in particular, resource misallocations, see S. Baiman, "Discussion of 'Externalities and Financial Reporting'" *Journal of Finance* XXXV, 1990, pp. 534-535.

[8] This is particularly true for earnings-related announcements. In contrast, research which studies information transfers associated with non-earnings-related announcements in carefully structured settings has in some cases obtained fairly strong results. See, for example, D. Dranove and C. Olsen, "The Stock Price Effects of Anticipated Regulation: A Resolution of the Event Study 'Paradox' in the Drug Industry," working paper, July, 1990, University of Texas and University of Chicago. This paper is more fully discussed in section 2 below.

whatever effects have been found have been described as "second-order."[9] In contrast, if tests for earnings information transfers had systematically isolated material price effects, or resolved previously unexplained findings, the result would probably have inherent interest for researchers and financial analysts, even if there were no links at all to accounting policy.[10] Finally, the results to date have not been inconsistent with received wisdom, so there is no anomaly to explore, as there is, for example, in the case of post-earnings-announcement drifts in share returns.

The difficulty in invoking directly our usual policy-based motivations for accounting research and the absence of startling results suggest that it may be useful to reconsider our views about the objectives of information transfer research. In the remaining three sections, I will discuss existing motivations and definitions, offer some suggestions and interpretations, and summarize some of the existing findings and open issues.

EXISTING MOTIVATIONS FOR AND DEFINITIONS OF INFORMATION TRANSFERS

Questions of definition and motivation are in general comingled, so that the objective of the research (its motivation) and the way the concept of interest is defined are mutually determined. While a proliferation of definitions of information transfer is unlikely to be of much benefit, there may be some advantages to a reconsideration of the currently-used representations. In this section, I will first discuss alternative potential characterizations of information transfers and then consider the relation between these characterizations and the motivation issue.

Defining Information Transfers

The casual definition of information transfers stated earlier focusses on the existence of interdependencies among firms' share returns. In addition, much accounting research has further narrowed the focus to a concern with earnings and earnings-related disclosures. The definition as I have stated it is silent on the question of the effect on the announcing firm's share values, and it does not distinguish between mandatory and voluntary disclosures, or restrict the identities of announcing and non-announcing firms. But taken in the context of much existing empirical accounting research, there is an implicit restriction on the relations among firms, because the definition seems to arise from a notion of industry commonalities; for example, firms in the same industry face the same or similar states of the world, so each firm's announcement says something about state-of-the-world uncertainty for its competitors.[11]

Although economy effects are sometimes mentioned in this research, they are generally not the focus of the inquiry. In the context of the definition given earlier, economy effects imply that an announcement made by any firm in the same economy could affect any other firm's share returns, regardless of industry membership. Possibly researchers believe economy effects for a given firm are too attenuated to be captured by existing techniques, or possibly such effects are simply viewed as less interesting. Regardless of the reason, the typical treatment of economy effects is to take account of them using a market index of returns, and to focus on industry effects.

The casual definition given earlier refers

---

[9]One characterization is as follows: "What we seem to have learned so far is that EPS-determined information transfers are a second-order phenomenon...," p. 212 of P. Brown, "Invited Remarks: Ball and Brown [1968]" *Journal of Accounting Research* 27 supplement, 1989, pp. 202-217.

[10]Interest in large market-adjusted returns arises because, to the extent that such returns are associated with identifiable information events, they indicate that shareholder wealth, hence investment strategies and possibly the wealth of other stakeholders, will be affected by the events.

[11]For examples of contexts that stress industry commonalities as support for the view of information transfers that focusses on competitors' announcements, see G. Foster, "Intra-Industry Information Transfers Associated with Earnings Release," *Journal of Accounting and Economics* 3, 1981, pp. 201-232, section 2.1 and S. Baginski, "Intraindustry Information Transfers Associated with Management Forecasts of Earnings," *Journal of Accounting Research* 25, 1987, pp. 196-216, section 2.

to announcements made by firms, so it is more restrictive than might be inferred from a qualitative consideration of announcements reflecting industry commonalities. For example, the definition rules out announcements made by non-corporate entities, such as analysts or governmental agencies, as potential mechanisms of information transfer. Specifically, suppose that an analyst revises the forecast of GM's earnings materially—would we expect to see a return response from Ford and if we did, would this be an information transfer? Perhaps more important, does the analyst forecast setting suggest research questions which are as interesting and informative as those currently considered in information transfer research? To the extent the answer is yes, this example illustrates the potential gains in understanding, and the potential for generating interesting research, from reconsidering the definition of information transfers.

It is also possible to place information transfers, broadly construed, in the context of a widely-accepted conceptualization of asset pricing.[12] Expression (1) is a simple conceptualization of the evolution of all asset prices in an economy:

$$\underline{v}_t = h(I_t) \tag{1}$$

In expression (1), $\underline{v}$ is the vector of all asset prices, h is the function linking the information set I to asset prices, and observations are made at each time t. In this representation, the vector of asset prices is a function of the entire information set, so if the representation is empirically descriptive, then information transfers exist by definition, as long as the asset markets are informationally efficient.[13]

Clearly, the casual definition given earlier and its related restrictions in practice are special cases of the representation given in (1). The casual definition was chosen to suit the purpose at hand (documenting the presence of share price reactions of non-announcing firms at other firms' earnings announcements), but the disadvantage of creating new definitions, one for each purpose, is that we are left with a series of special cases. The advantage of a very general representation such as that in (1) is that it subsumes most applications of interest to accountants. For example, the framework for a conventional test for the information content of accounting earnings of a single firm A could be represented as: $v_A = h_A(I_{EA})$, where v_A represents firm A's stock price, h_A is the function linking stock price with information, and the information of interest is that portion of the total information set I which refers to firm A's earnings, I_{EA}. (I have dropped the time subscript for expositional convenience).

Note that under the representation given in (1), information transfers would not exist if some asset price v_j were a function only of the elements of I that referred specifically to j. Casual empiricism combined with previous research rejects this view as inconsistent with the fact that firms belong to a common world economy. Therefore, I argue that the non-existence of information transfers is a "straw man"—but this does not, of course, indicate anything about which of the myriad information transfers implied by (1) are of research interest to accountants. For example, when one firm in an industry receives a takeover offer embodying a large premium, the prices of other firms in that industry frequently increase—this is an information transfer with little or no relation to an accounting research question.

Regardless of the specific characteristics of information transfer settings selected for study, the representation given in (1) indicates

---

[12] This conceptualization of how asset prices evolve is consistent with current textbook treatments of asset pricing. See for, example, M. Harris, *Dynamic Economic Analysis,* New York: Oxford University Press, 1987, and J. Ingersoll, *Theory of Financial Decision Making,* Totawa, New Jersey: Rowman & Littlefield, 1987. It is also consistent with the informational perspective on accounting, which adopts the view that accounting numbers are potentially informative signals for asset pricing.

[13] Baiman [1990] provides this intuitive discussion: "To begin with, at equilibrium every commodity in the economy is interrelated with every other commodity. Thus, the price of shoes is related to the number of diesel engines produced. Therefore, saying that corporate financial reporting produces interdependencies... within the economy says very little" (p. 534).

that such research should adopt a multilateral approach to both information signals and estimation of effects. For example, the researcher might focus on various information signals as substitutes. Estimation of effects, on the other hand, requires simultaneous consideration of several firms linked by a common information structure which creates the information transfer setting. The multilateral approach required by information transfer research is immediately a contrast to much of mainstream accounting research, which often considers one signal at a time (e.g., each sample firm's announcement to adopt the LIFO method is considered independently) and several or many firms only as independent observations in a sample.[14]

Motivations For Information Transfer Research

The definition of information transfers used in much empirical accounting research focusses on corporate announcements (especially announcements about earnings) and stock returns. I will consider three kinds of motivations: those related to disclosure policies; those that extend some existing research on information content and those that are statistical/descriptive, i.e., "explaining the variance-covariance matrix of abnormal security returns."[15] The third of these appears as a suggested motivation, not one that has been widely implemented, but it is clearly consistent with the representation given in expression (1).

The specifics of information transfer motivations in research completed to date appear to emphasize documenting the existence of information transfers for common stock, often associated with earnings-related announcements. So far little attention has been given to explaining how such transfers operate. Seen in this light, the three motivations listed here give rise to three questions. First, why restrict the notion of information transfers to market settings, with such a heavy emphasis on earnings? Second, why focus on documenting existence? Third, within the context of market settings, why should accountants care about the covariance matrix of abnormal security returns? I will touch on these questions in the discussion of motivations which appears in the next three subsections.

Policy motivations for empirical information transfer research. Foster [1981] tests for a correlation between market-adjusted returns of firms making earnings announcements and non-announcing firms in the same SIC code. Part of the motivation involves establishing evidence of interdependencies among firms' share prices based on their earnings disclosures. He notes that documenting such interdependencies is just one step in considering whether disclosures create externalities that might attract the attention of policymakers. Baginski [1987] alludes to a similar idea (but with much less discussion) when he describes information transfers from firms that disclose earnings forecasts to non-forecasting firms as "cross-subsidies" under a voluntary disclosure system.

Pownall and Waymire [1989] come close to invoking a policy motivation when they interpret their results as tests of whether man-

---

[14] This characterization would fit much research on earnings response coefficients, on earnings management, on information content of accruals versus cash flows and on voluntary accounting changes. In contrast, a multilateral approach would require consideration of cross-sectional relations in (for example) earnings response coefficients (ERC's) in the sense of firm j's ERC revealing information about firm i's ERC. As another example, the information transfer perspective on share price effects of voluntary accounting changes would take explicit account of the "industry effects" that have been identified in previous research, under the view that one firm's decision to adopt LIFO conveys information about the propensity of other firms in the same industry to make the same adoption decision. Thus, once the first firm makes its LIFO adoption announcement, investors will capitalize in the prices of other comparable firms their revised expectations that those comparable firms will also adopt LIFO.

[15] The first two motivations appear in a number of papers, sometimes together. The third is given by Brown (1989, p. 214) in a discussion of past and future research on the earnings-stock price relation. In this context, one interpretation of this motivation involves exploring the economic forces that cause firms' abnormal returns (i.e., returns adjusted for general movements in a market index) to move together over time. This comovement is captured by the covariance matrix of returns.

agement earnings forecasts (voluntary disclosures) are substitutes for earnings information transfers (which arise from mandatory disclosures). They estimate earnings response coefficients along with earnings information transfer coefficients for forecasters and nonforecasters;[16] the basic hypothesis tested is that nonforecasting firms have larger earnings information transfer coefficients. (Note that the paper does not address the question of whether the management forecasts themselves generate information transfers, only whether earnings announcement do. The link to management forecasts occurs through sample selection).

Overall, the amount of explicit attention to a policy motivation for empirical earnings information transfer research appears to have diminished since Foster [1981]. As I noted earlier, the connection between information transfers and the usual policy questions of interest to accountants is indirect. Making this connection explicit would require, as Foster points out, establishing much more than the existence of interdependencies. It would require, for example, attention to the costs and benefits of such interdependencies. Dye [1990] and Foster [1990] provide non-empirical analyses and discussions of these issues.

Extending an existing set of results on information content. This motive appears in Foster [1981], as well as in a number of other papers. In Foster, the extension involves evaluating the information content of other-firm as well as own-firm earnings announcements. Baginski [1987] and Han, Wild and Ramesh [1989] investigate information transfers associated with management earnings forecasts as extensions to the literature which documents share price reactions when firms disclose such forecasts.[17] In addition to extending the literature on management forecasts, these two papers also propose methodological changes to testing for information transfers. Part of the motivation derives from these methodological issues, so they will be discussed here as well.[18]

Baginski is concerned with the share price reactions of nonforecasting firms when similar firms disclose management forecasts. His measure of the amount of information to be transferred is based on an accounting signal (the difference between the management forecast and an analyst's forecast) and not on the forecaster's return reaction. Such a direct, accounting-based estimate of the signal (the information available for transfer) may contain measurement error with unknown properties and effects on the estimation, but it is not likely to be susceptible to the same forces that could create the appearance of an earnings-based information transfer, when the only effect is in fact industry comovements in returns that occur in the absence of any such disclosures.[19]

Baginski's paper also illustrates the importance of sample selection in information transfer research. Specifically, if the goal is to document the existence of some phenomenon (as opposed to, say, explaining it or showing

---

[16] A forecaster is a firm that issued at least one management earnings forecast during the sample period, July 1969 to December 1973. Industries included in the sample had at least five management forecasts during the sample period.

[17] See Baginski [1987] and J. Han, J. Wild and K. Ramesh, "Managers' Earnings Forecasts and Intra-Industry Information Transfers," *Journal of Accounting and Economics* 11, 1989, pp. 3-33.

[18] It is not uncommon for extensions to substantive questions to include methodological critiques and illustrations of new (presumably better) approaches. The latter may in fact give rise to the former, in the sense that the methodological extension is developed to make it possible to evaluate the substantive extension. For example, Clinch and Sinclair [1987] develop a statistical approach for investigating the possibility, discussed in Foster [1981, p. 229], that evidence of information transfers based on tests using the market model in fact merely reflects the omission of explanatory variables which capture industry factors. (See G. Clinch and N. Sinclair, "Intra-Industry Information Transfers: A Recursive Systems Approach," *Journal of Accounting and Economics* 9, 1987, pp. 89-106.) Several questions of methods remain open in information transfer research; for a discussion and proposals see C. Frost, "Intra-industry Information Transfer: An Analysis of Research Methods, and Additional Evidence," working paper, Washington University, February 1990.

[19] The choice between accounting-based and return-based measures may be difficult. In general, the "surprise" in an earnings-related announcement explains an extremely modest portion of the cross-sectional variation in return reactions to the announcement; while the two measures are correlated, they do not necessarily carry the same information.

that it is widespread) it is advantageous to select a sample that is biassed in the sense of being especially likely to display the phenomenon. Baginski's approach is to select as potential recipients of information transfer firms that belong to a forecaster's four-digit SIC code and are similar in terms of market model parameters and leverage. (He includes as a comparison group firms in the same two-digit SIC code). The approach succeeds insofar as he finds statistical evidence supporting the existence of the posited information transfers, and provides support for the view that information transfers, while modest in magnitude over large random samples, are potentially larger in subsamples with special characteristics.

Han, Wild and Ramesh also evaluate information transfers associated with management earnings forecasts. A primary goal of the paper is to identify an announcement-induced information transfer as something separate from the general effects of industry comovement in returns.[20] The approach taken was to base tests for information transfer on returns adjusted for market index movements only and returns adjusted for both market and industry index movements. The results shift, based on which returns are evaluated; the evidence of information transfer is vitiated when returns are adjusted for industry effects.

This focus on identifying an information transfer as something distinct from a general covariability in returns appears in a number of papers, for example, Foster [1981] and Clinch and Sinclair [1987]. Note that such an approach is not necessarily required by either the casual definition given earlier or the framework given in expression (1); both are silent on the question of what should be held constant or abstracted from in measuring the effect of a firm's announcement on other firms. If, however, information transfers appear only in settings where general industry comovements in returns have not been controlled for, we may reach the conclusion that they are merely a specific instance of the general industry effects identified over two decades ago. such a conclusion would not, of course, settle the question of whether they are worth further investigation.

Accountants' interest in the covariance matrix of stock returns. The motive of explaining the covariance matrix of stock returns has at least two interpretations. (Recall that the covariance matrix is a numerical measure of the propensity of firms' returns to move together). Under the first interpretation, explaining the covariance matrix of returns could mean drawing a connection between accounting policy decisions and comovements in returns. Second, it could mean understanding how information transfers actually work by disentangling the causation which underlies covariances among returns. I will consider each of these two interpretations separately, since there is no necessary connection between them.

Another way to frame the policy question is to ask: Do the results concerning the existence of earnings information transfers (regardless of their strength or consistency) have implications for accounting policymakers? That is, do the results indicate anything about the quality of our disclosure system? The answer seems to depend on whether one believes information transfers are in some sense desirable and the accounting system should be configured to encourage them.

There is no strong indication in our current disclosure system that information transfers play much of a role when the rules are being formulated. The authoritative pronouncements of the Financial Accounting Standards Board do not state that a goal of accounting numbers disclosed by a firm is to provide information about other firms. Instead, the emphasis is squarely on own-firm informativeness. If earnings are not designed to be informative about other firms, it should come as no surprise that they very often aren't. But given the motivation of studying information transfers to understand the covariance

---

[20]Although he did not control for such industry effects, Baginski used the following approach to assess their likely importance. He estimated the comovement (i.e., the information transfer) in periods when there were no forecast announcements (but possibly other disclosures) and in periods when there were no information disclosures. He found evidence of comovement in the former but not in the latter.

matrix of returns, can an argument be made that earnings disclosed by a firm would be valuable to investors if they were informative about other firms?

Such an argument might be based on the principles of modern portfolio theory. This theory emphasizes the structuring of models and decisions about investments in terms of covariances. Optimal investment decisions take into account the effect of buying or selling a firm on the portfolio risk, and individual firms matter insofar as their characteristics combine to determine portfolio characteristics. If we literally adopted the portfolio approach to investing and used it as our guide to setting accounting rules, then the rules should lead to disclosures that will help investors estimate and evaluate portfolio covariances. Own-firm informativeness would not be the paramount consideration in setting accounting rules.

In thinking about the policy implications of information transfer research, it is important to distinguish between hypothetical accounting rules designed to help investors estimate and evaluate portfolio covariances and actual rules designed to foster comparability across firms. It may well be that one effect of movements toward standardization of procedures and disclosures designed to allow analysts to make inter-firm comparisons might be to enhance the likelihood of information transfers. But there is little or no basis for knowing that properties of the accounting rules which enhance comparability—such as requiring firms to report the same pension data using a standardized set of procedures—would (or would not) necessarily also enhance the usefulness of the data in evaluating portfolio covariances.

Finally, in considering the potential for policy implications, we should remind ourselves of the distinction between mandatory and voluntary disclosures. As previously mentioned, Dye [1990] compares these in the presence of two kinds of information transfers. Under the first, disclosures by one firm alter investors' perceptions about nondisclosers' cash flows; in this case, voluntary and mandatory disclosures often coincide. But under the second, where disclosures by one firm alter not perceptions of cash flows but rather the cash flows themselves, the situation is sufficiently complicated that no generalizations can be made.

Under the second interpretation of the proposed statistical motivation for studying information transfers—understanding the covariance matrix of returns means understanding how information transfers operate—research which addresses the question of what causes (or carries) information transfers is sparse. While a number of papers (see, for example, Baginski [1987]) conjecture that the potential for positive information transfers is greatest where firms have common determinants of earnings (similar size, capital structures, and production functions, for example), they do not necessarily distinguish between information signals that indicate changes in the size of market and information signals that indicate changes in market shares. Intuitively, it would seem that the former would lead to positive (similar sign) information transfers while the latter might well lead to negative information transfers, depending on the particulars of the setting.[21]

An example of research which structures the direction of hypothesized information transfers using the specifics of the setting is provided by Olsen and Dietrich [1985].[22] Their tests investigate the extent to which share prices of suppliers of large retailers respond to announcements of sales revenues by the retailers. In this study, the mechanism of information transfer is the implicit or explicit contractual relation between retailer and

---

[21]This issue is discussed, for example, in J. R. Dietrich, "Discussion of Voluntary Disclosure Choice and Earnings Information Transfer," *Journal of Accounting Research* 27 supplement, 1989, pp. 106-110. In addition, Scofield [1989] uses aggregate industry disclosures to structure situations when negative earnings information transfers would be expected; see B. Scofield, "Industry Disclosures and Information Transfer Associated with Quarterly Earnings Announcements," 1989, working paper, University of Florida.

[22]See C. Olsen and J. R. Dietrich, "Vertical Information Transfers: The Association Between Retailers' Sales Announcements and Suppliers' Security Returns," *Journal of Accounting Research* 23 supplement, 1985, pp. 144-166.

supplier which translates sales by the retailer into orders placed with the supplier (hence, sales for the supplier). The authors also investigate an alternative mechanism, which they do not label a contractually-induced information transfer: sales announcements by retailers affect share returns to suppliers because they reflect general economic conditions, not the specifics of the contract between a particular supplier-retailer pair.

Olsen and Dietrich's results provide some support for the view that suppliers, especially those with long-term contracts with specific retailers, receive information transfers from the retailers' sales announcements. There is no evidence that such transfers exist at non-announcement periods. In addition, the share returns of non-suppliers in the same industry as suppliers are affected when retailers make sales announcements. Taken together, these results suggest that sales announcements of large retailers carry two kinds of information relevant for pricing other firms. The first kind of information tells investors something about general conditions to be faced by suppliers—this would be a general industry-wide information transfer. The second kind of information is specific to a contractual relationship between a given retailer and its suppliers; the information transfer occurs because of the contract. Viewed this way, Olsen and Dietrich's results have provided a bit of evidence about what causes one kind of information transfer.

Olsen and Dietrich use a more-or-less conventional accounting setting (sales announcements and supplier contracts) to structure specific hypotheses about the causes of information transfer. In contrast, Dranove and Olsen [1990] structure tests of information transfer associated with announcements about dangerous drugs using the organizational and regulatory structure of the pharmaceutical industry. Specifically, they investigate whether anticipated regulation of all drug companies contributed to the substantial share price declines suffered by competitor firms when specific firms' products were subject to recalls, warning letters or lawsuits. Their hypothesis, which is supported by their results, is that competitors suffered losses as investors inferred impending regulation of all drug companies (i.e., industry-side sanctions) from announcements about specific drug companies. In this setting, the information transferred is released by a non-corporate entity and the mechanism of transfer is changing expectations of harsh regulation. The setting illustrates the potential for information transfer research—broadly construed—to help in gaining insights into a wide variety of questions.

BROADER CONSIDERATIONS OF THE INFORMATION TRANSFER CONCEPT

Broadening information transfer investigations beyond current research settings (which focus on the common shares of publicly traded firms) is consistent with the representation given in expression (1). To go a bit further, we can consider settings that do not involve exclusively assets with observable prices. This extension permits analysis of the role of information transfers in the design and operation of institutions and markets. If we accept that an information transfer has occurred when information on an economic entity "A" also provides relevant information on another economic entity "B," then it is easy to see that information transfers are or could be investigated in a number of market and non-market settings. Note that this very general approach to information transfers does not address questions of timing, of how the relevance of the information is assessed, of who supplies the information, or of the nature of the economic entities. I will use this general approach to discuss several non-capital-market settings in which information transfers (broadly construed) can be analyzed. Finally, I will discuss research which exploits the existence of information transfers which are presumed to exist in the data being analyzed.

Compensation research. In a relative performance evaluation (RPE) compensation scheme, it is assumed that comparing the performance of some individual agent to that of an appropriately chosen peer group filters out performance effects due to common uncertainties, leaving only the agent-specific performance component. In such a scheme, the performance of other agents provides information about a specific agent's performance. Clearly, empirical compensation research could investigate the existence and determinants of relative performance evaluation schemes as a form of information transfer.[23]

One feature of compensation research on RPE schemes, lacking in information transfer research in market settings, is its tie to a model of when information about other agents' performance will appear in a compensation contract. Roughly speaking, outcome measures for other agents are included when they are statistically associated with the outcome measure for the specific agent. One source of such statistical association is the common state-of-the-world assumed to be faced by all agents.[24] (In his paper on information transfers associated with management forecasts, Baginski attempts to maximize the statistical similarity of non-forecasters with the forecasting firms by clustering within industry on market model paramenters and leverage. The goal is presumably to structure the sample so that all sample firms face a common state-of-the-world. If the goal is achieved, the probability of observing information transfers is presumably increased).

Common stock analysis and pricing. Stock analysis and pricing are practical applications of the intuition behind information transfers as well as potential research settings. For example, investment bankers use the industry P/E multiple to capitalize the earnings of a private firm considering going public, or they use discount rates estimated from industry data to do a discounted cash flow valuation. In both cases, information from other (competitor) economic entities is informative about the specific entity of immediate interest. Furthermore, this application assumes the existence of an information transfer (as defined here).

As a second example, analysts who follow stocks (e.g., make buy and sell recommendations, forecast earnings) specialize by industry, and frequently refer to competitors when they write reports about a given firm. Thus, analysts' behavior appears to be predicated on the assumption of within-industry information transfers. There are several implications of this behavior. For example, an analyst following the automotive industry might revise the forecast of GM's earnings in light of *both* GM's and Ford's realized earnings. If so, one might ask how much of the industry commonality (i.e., the potential for information transfers) is extracted from earnings forecast errors computed using analyst forecasts. In an extreme case, researchers might find only very small (or no) information transfers associated with earnings releases not because there was little or no information about firm j in firm i's earnings, but rather because the analyst had already taken account of that information in making the forecast used by the researcher to compute the information measure.

Empirical research that assumes information transfers. The existence of information transfers (in the broad sense used in this section) is assumed and exploited in some event studies, in one of two senses. First, the structure of the setting sometimes creates an obvious connection among the returns to securities of several sample firms. An example is regulation research in which all sample firms belong to the same industry and are affected simultaneously by a regulatory event. Clearly, in this setting comovement among returns is expected, during both non-event periods (because of general industry effects) and event periods (because of industry effects and the shared impact of the regulatory events). The numerical measure of this comovement, the covariance matrix of returns for the sample firms, can be used to advantage in an event study to obtain more informative estimates of the wealth effects of the regulatory change. Such an approach assumes the existence of information transfers.

---

[23]See, for example, R. Antle and A. Smith, "An Empirical Investigation of the Relative Performance Evaluation of Corporate Executives," *Journal of Accounting Research* 24, 1986, pp. 1-39.

[24]The results which motivate RPE tests are found in B. Holmstrom, "Moral Hazard in Teams," *Bell Journal of Economics* 13, 1982, pp. 324-340.

Information transfers are in some sense assumed in event studies when the structure of the setting involves investigation of several securities of the same firm at a single event. These securities, for example, bonds, preferred stock and common stock, are linked by definition because they all represent claims on a common set of assets. Any information event with implications for one class of security has potential implications for the others as well. For example, research on whether going private transactions result in wealth transfers from creditors to stockholders assumes that an offer to buy the stock of a firm in a leveraged buyout is likely to have adverse wealth implications for the bonds of the same firm.[25]

The event study examples illustrate the same basic point as the valuation and compensation examples: information transfers (as defined here) are expected when two or more economic entities face a common state of the world. In the case of regulation research, the entities are firms which face the same regulatory environment. In the case of wealth transfer research, the entities are securities whose holders all face the same transaction. The commonalities in information events in these two cases are obvious.

The extent to which an empirical study can exploit information transfers depends in part on the extent to which the information event of interest carries state-of-the-world information, as opposed to firm-specific or idiosyncratic information. Announcements made by or about specific firms—such as earnings forecasts or earnings announcements—should by definition have a substantial firm-specific component. The greater this idiosyncratic component, the smaller the potential for information transfer (other things equal). This observation can in principle be used to structure tests that either rely on or assume information transfer by forcing a consideration of the nature of the information release to be studied: to what extent does the release carry general as opposed to idiosyncratic information? While regulation research seems a natural setting for assuming information transfers, it may be that the nature of earnings releases makes them a natural setting for testing for information transfers.

THE CURRENT STATE OF ACCOUNTING RESEARCH ON INFORMATION TRANSFERS

This commentary has used several examples of published and unpublished research to illustrate the current thinking about earnings information transfers and to explore the potential for linking information transfer research to accounting policy questions. I have focussed on how the question is framed, the motivation for the analysis, and some methodological issues, but I have commented only in passing on the strength of results. Briefly, they are not very strong and not very consistent, at least in the literature which considers earnings-related announcements.

The general weakness of results concerning the existence of information transfers is puzzling, especially in light of research which documents substantial commonalities among asset price movements. It may be that earnings information transfers exist, but are of sufficiently low magnitude that minor changes in design and estimation will greatly affect our ability to detect them. In that case, some may conclude that such small effects are not really worth pursuing for their own sake. That may well be an appropriate conclusion, but it certainly does not rule out the consideration of information transfers in service of pursuing some other research question which has a motivation independent of documenting the existence of information transfers. One such motivation might be based on incorporating information transfers into research on questions traditionally of interest to accountants. While there is no reason to discourage primarily methodological projects in this or any other area, it may be that the payoff from developing substantive questions in which information transfers play a role will be greater than the payoff from developing sharper ways of documenting and estimating the magnitude of information transfer effects.

---

[25]Empirical analysis of returns to securities other than common stock presents a number of practical and methodological difficulties. For an example of an event study approach to investigating the effects of management buyouts on all public securities of a firm, see L. Marais, K. Schipper, and A. Smith, "Wealth Effects of Going Private for Senior Securities," *Journal of Financial Economics* 23, 1989, pp. 155-191.

EVIDENCE THAT STOCK PRICES DO NOT FULLY REFLECT THE IMPLICATIONS OF CURRENT EARNINGS FOR FUTURE EARNINGS*

Victor L. BERNARD

Harvard Business School, Boston, MA 02163, USA
University of Michigan, Ann Arbor, MI 48109, USA

Jacob K. THOMAS

Columbia University, New York, NY 10027, USA

Received May 1990, final version received December 1990

Evidence presented here is consistent with a failure of stock prices to reflect fully the implications of current earnings for future earnings. Specifically, the three-day price reactions to announcements of earnings for quarters $t+1$ through $t+4$ are predictable, based on earnings of quarter t. Even more surprisingly, the signs and magnitudes of the three-day reactions are related to the autocorrelation structure of earnings, as if stock prices fail to reflect the extent to which each firm's earnings series differs from a seasonal random walk.

1. Introduction

Several studies have documented that estimated abnormal returns are predictable, based on previously-announced earnings [e.g., Ball and Brown (1968), Joy, Litzenberger, and McEnally (1977), Watts (1978), Rendleman, Jones, and Latane (1982), and Foster, Olsen, and Shevlin (1984)]. Repeated attempts to explain this 'post-earnings-announcement drift' as a product of research design flaws, including failure to adjust abnormal returns fully for

---

*We would like to acknowledge Thomas Lys, the referee, whose suggestions led to substantive improvements in the paper. We are grateful to Jim Wahlen for his research assistance and suggestions, and to Harry DeAngelo, Charles Jones, and members of Prudential Bache's Quantitative Research department, who helped plant the seeds that led to this research. We also appreciate comments received from Ray Ball, Robert Bowen, Michael Brennan, Larry Brown, Susan Chaplinsky, Gene Fama, Mark Grinblatt, Gautam Kaul, Han Kim, S.P. Kothari, Gene Imhoff, Maurice Joy, Robert Freeman, Robert Lipe, Jim McKeown, Pat O'Brien, Gordon Richardson, Jay Ritter, Michael Salinger, Nejat Seyhun, Doug Skinner, Ross Watts (the editor), and other participants in workshops at Baruch College, Columbia University, Florida State University, Harvard Business School, M.I.T., Notre Dame, Penn State University, and the Universities of Colorado, Illinois, Kansas, Michigan, Rochester, Southern California, and South Carolina. Victor Bernard is grateful for the support of the Price Waterhouse Foundation.

risk, have failed to resolve the anomaly.[1] Bernard and Thomas (1989) describe an implementable strategy, based upon the anomaly, that produces an estimated annualized abnormal return of 18 percent (before transactions costs) during the first quarter subsequent to the earnings announcement. Smaller abnormal returns appear to persist for at least two additional quarters.

It is difficult to understand why stock prices would appear not to respond completely and immediately to information as visible and freely available as publicly announced earnings. Although they do not purport to identify the reason for post-announcement drift, Bernard and Thomas (1989) and Freeman and Tse (1989) do provide one clue that could aid in the pursuit for an explanation. Specifically, they find that a disproportionately large fraction of the post-announcement drift is 'delayed' until the subsequent quarter's earnings announcement. In other words, given that a firm announces positive (negative) unexpected earnings for quarter t, the market tends to be positively (negatively) surprised in the days surrounding the announcement for quarter $t+1$. As Bernard and Thomas note, the evidence is consistent with a market that 'fails to adequately revise its expectations for quarter $t+1$ earnings upon receipt of the news for quarter t' (p. 27).

This paper investigates the possibility that stock prices fail to reflect fully the implications of current earnings for future earnings. Specifically, we entertain the hypothesis that prices fail to reflect the extent to which the time-series behavior of earnings deviates from a naive expectation: a seasonal random walk, where expected earnings are simply earnings for the corresponding quarter from the previous year.[2] It is well known that earnings

---

[1] A battery of tests in Bernard and Thomas (1989, p. 34) produces evidence that 'cannot plausibly be reconciled with arguments built on risk mismeasurement'. Specifically, Bernard and Thomas show that (1) contrary to the prediction of Ball, Kothari, and Watts (1988) shifts in beta are far too small to explain the drift; (2) five other measures of risk identified in the arbitrage pricing literature fail to explain the drift; (3) there is no evidence of any other (unidentified) risk surfacing in the form of a loss – that is, returns to a zero-investment trading strategy are consistently positive over time; and (4) in violation of plausible predictions of capital asset pricing theory as they would apply to a broad cross-section of stocks, the mean *raw* (total) post-announcement returns on 'bad news' stocks are significantly less than Treasury bill rates. Both Bernard and Thomas (1989) and Foster, Olsen, and Shevlin (1984) also cast doubt on the viability of other explanations based on potential research design flaws, such as various forms of hindsight bias, survivorship bias, and biases in return calculations.

[2] We are not the first to consider this possibility. That credit goes to Rendleman, Jones, and Latane (1987), who showed that when one controls for quarter $t+1$ earnings, much of the drift associated with quarter t earnings is eliminated. They conclude that post-announcement drift can be explained in part as a predictable response to the subsequent earnings announcement. However, since that study focuses on abnormal returns measured over long windows, it is difficult to rule out alternative explanations for the results (e.g., certain risk-based arguments). Freeman and Tse (1989) document (1) the predictability of the short-window response to quarter $t+1$ earnings that is also documented in Bernard and Thomas (1989) and (2) that when one controls for the effect of quarter $t+1$ earnings at least half of the drift associated with quarter t earnings is eliminated. On that basis, they conclude that 'the time-series behavior of earnings

forecast errors based on such a naive model are correlated through time [see, for example, Freeman and Tse (1989)]. In contrast, in a market that fully impounds all prior earnings information, forecast errors should not be autocorrelated (by definition). What we study here is the possibility that market prices can be modeled partially as reflections of naive expectations, and that as a result, the reactions of prices to future earnings are predictable, just as the forecast errors of a naive expectation model are predictable.

Our results are surprisingly consistent with this depiction of stock-price behavior. By assuming that stock prices are at least partially influenced by the above naive earnings expectation, we are able to predict with a significant degree of accuracy the three-day reaction to *future* earnings announcements (up to four quarters ahead), given only *current* earnings and information about the (historical) time-series behavior of earnings. Moreover, we can relate not only the *signs* but the relative *magnitudes* of the future reactions to the autocorrelation structure of forecast errors based on the naive seasonal random-walk earnings expectation.

One of the most surprising aspects of our evidence pertains to our predictions of market reactions four quarters ahead. In contrast to the well-documented *positive* relation between unexpected earnings for quarter t and post-announcement drift for quarter $t+1$, we find a *negative* relation between unexpected earnings of quarter t and the abnormal returns around the announcement of earnings for quarter $t+4$. This finding would not be predicted by any existing explanations for post-announcement drift based on concerns about potential research design flaws. However, this pattern in the data is precisely what would be expected if the prices failed to reflect fully that, while seasonally-differenced earnings are *positively* correlated for adjacent quarters, they are *negatively* correlated four quarters apart. That is, the data behave as if the market is consistently surprised that a portion of an earnings change tends to be reversed four quarters later.

A stock market in which prices are influenced by traders who anchor on a comparison of year-to-year changes in quarterly earnings, much like the financial press does in its coverage of earnings announcements (e.g., the Wall Street Journal's Digest of Earnings Reports), represents a disturbing departure from what would be predicted by existing models of efficient markets. For zero-investment portfolios constructed on the basis of the historical time-series behavior of earnings, the indicated abnormal returns from the day after the earnings announcement through the subsequent earnings announcement are approximately 8 to 9 percent, or 35 percent on an annualized basis, before transactions costs. Even higher abnormal returns per unit time (67

---

provides a partial explanation of the drift phenomenon'. However, that possibility was not the main focus of the Freeman and Tse paper, and thus they did not draw the links between post-announcement drift and the time-series properties of earnings that are documented here.

percent on an annualized basis) are available for portfolios constructed 15 days prior to the expected date for the upcoming announcement and held through the announcement.

The evidence in this paper offers two main contributions beyond the previous literature on post-announcement drift. First, the paper relates the signs and magnitudes of reactions to subsequent earnings announcements to the historical autocorrelation structure of earnings; this linkage may help identify the cause of post-announcement drift. Second, the evidence as a whole creates several added obstacles to contentions that the drift might ultimately be explained by errors in the methodology used to estimate expected returns. For example, an explanation based on failure to control for risk would now have to argue that 'good-news' firms experience 'delayed' increases in risk over three-day intervals that coincide with each of the next three earnings announcements, and then a decrease in risk over the three-day interval coinciding with the fourth subsequent announcement. The converse would have to hold for 'bad-news' firms. At a minimum, any rationale for such behavior must have a more complex structure than explanations suggested to date.

The nature of the evidence in this paper is also distinct in an important way from that in the growing body of other studies that question semi-strong or weak-form market efficiency [e.g., Ou and Penman (1989a, b), Poterba and Summers (1988)]. While such studies conclude that discrepancies appear to exist between stock prices and underlying fundamentals, they make only vague predictions about *when* the discrepancies will be eliminated and associated abnormal returns realized. In contrast, our assumption about earnings expectations allows us to successfully predict within days the timing of subsequent abnormal returns. By linking what appears to be the elimination of a discrepancy between prices and fundamentals to prespecified information events, the study presents perhaps the most direct evidence to date that a market-efficiency anomaly is rooted in a failure of information to flow completely into price. The evidence also emphasizes that even in a market where prices fail to reflect all available information, one can still observe unusual stock-price activity concentrated around news releases. The puzzling question is, if a portion of the 'news' became predictable months earlier, why did the associated price movements not occur then?

The rest of the paper is organized as follows. In section 2, we review the time-series behavior of earnings and develop hypotheses about how stock prices would behave if the earnings expectations embedded in such prices failed to reflect fully those time-series properties. Section 3 includes tests of those hypotheses. Questions raised by the evidence and potential alternative explanations for the results are discussed in section 4. We discuss the links between this and other research in section 5, and offer concluding remarks in section 6.

2. Hypothesis development

2.1. Time-series properties of quarterly earnings

Several studies have documented the time-series behavior of quarterly earnings [e.g., Watts (1975), Foster (1977), Griffin (1977), Brown and Rozeff (1979), Bathke and Lorek (1984), Brown, Hagerman, Griffin, and Zmijewski (1987)]. The cumulative evidence indicates that seasonal differences in quarterly earnings are correlated, and that the pattern of correlations can be viewed as including two components. First, there is a positive correlation between seasonal differences that is strongest for adjacent quarters, but that remains positive over the first three lags. Thus, a change in earnings of quarter t (relative to the comparable quarter of the prior year) tends to be followed by progressively smaller changes of the same sign in quarters $t + 1$, $t + 2$, and $t + 3$. Second, there is a negative correlation between seasonal differences that are four quarters apart. That is, a portion of the change for quarter t is 'reversed' in quarter $t + 4$.

To offer a more specific description of the time-series behavior of earnings, table 1 presents summary statistics for the sample to be studied here, which is based on the sample used in Bernard and Thomas (1989).[3] The earnings number used is net income before extraordinary items and discontinued items (item 8 from the quarterly Compustat tape). Panel A confirms that, consistent with prior research, the autocorrelations at the first three lags are positive but declining; the sample means of autocorrelations estimated separately for each firm are 0.34, 0.19, and 0.06 for lags 1, 2, and 3, respectively. Also consistent with prior research, there is a negative autocorrelation at the fourth lag (mean = -0.24). Beyond the fourth lag, the mean autocorrelations remain negative, but much smaller: -0.08, -0.07, -0.07, -0.06 for lags 5 through 8, respectively.

To obtain an intuitive sense for the implications of these autocorrelations, consider the following example. A firm reports quarterly earnings in year 0 of $10, $10, $10, and $20. Actual earnings for the first quarter of year 1 rise $1, to $11. Assuming no linear trend in earnings and that the autocorrelation structure of the firm's earnings is as depicted for the mean firm in table 1, the

---

[3]The sample is obtained from firms listed on the 1987 edition of the daily CRSP file and also listed on any edition of the Compustat quarterly files from 1982 to 1987. Based on earnings data beginning in 1970, we obtained estimates of unexpected earnings for 96,087 announcements over the period 1974–1986 for 2,649 firms. Abnormal returns data were available for up to 85,753 announcements, depending upon the return interval used. The number of observations reported in the tables varies across tests, depending upon factors such as the availability of measures of unexpected earnings at the specified lags and the interval over which abnormal returns are cumulated.

Table 1

Time-series behavior of quarterly earnings, 2,626 firms, 1974–1986.

Panel A: Autocorrelations in seasonally differenced quarterly earnings								
Lag	1	2	3	4	5	6	7	8

Distribution of firm-specific autocorrelations in seasonally-differenced earnings

Mean	0.34	0.19	0.06	−0.24	−0.08	−0.07	−0.07	−0.06
25th percentile	0.14	0.05	−0.10	−0.46	−0.26	−0.24	−0.24	−0.25
Median	0.36	0.18	0.06	−0.29	−0.09	−0.08	−0.06	−0.06
75th percentile	0.57	0.35	0.21	−0.07	0.08	0.08	0.09	0.11

Distribution of mean autocorrelations for 37 industries[a]

Number of positive mean autocorrelations (out of 37)	37	37	35	0	5	8	6	7
25th percentile (of 37 means)	0.29	0.14	0.00	−0.29	−0.13	−0.12	−0.12	−0.10
Median (of 37 means)	0.35	0.19	0.07	−0.24	−0.09	−0.08	−0.08	−0.08
75th percentile (of 37 means)	0.38	0.22	0.09	−0.18	−0.04	−0.01	−0.04	−0.03

Mean firm-specific autocorrelations within size categories[b]

Small (bottom 4 deciles)	0.28	0.14	0.03	−0.29	−0.09	−0.08	−0.08	−0.08
Medium	0.31	0.19	0.07	−0.23	−0.07	−0.08	−0.06	−0.04
Large (top 3 deciles)	0.36	0.20	0.06	−0.20	−0.09	−0.05	−0.06	−0.06

Panel B: Autocorrelations in seasonally-differenced earnings and standardized unexpected earnings (*SUE*)[c]								
Lag	1	2	3	4	5	6	7	8

Mean of firm-specific autocorrelations

Seasonally differenced earnings (as in panel A)	0.34	0.19	0.06	−0.24	−0.08	−0.07	−0.07	−0.06
*SUE*s	0.40	0.22	0.06	−0.21	−0.10	−0.09	−0.09	−0.08
SUE deciles	0.41	0.23	0.07	−0.18	−0.09	−0.09	−0.09	−0.08

[a] Mean of firm-specific autocorrelations is calculated for each industry to obtain distribution of 37 autocorrelations at each lag. Only the 37 two-digit SIC industries that contain at least 20 members are represented here.

[b] Small, medium, and large firms are in size deciles 1 to 4, 5 to 7, and 8 to 10, respectively, based on January 1 market values of equity for NYSE–AMEX firms.

[c] *SUE*s are forecast errors from a seasonal random walk with trend, scaled by their standard deviation within the trend estimation period (up to 36 observations). *SUE* deciles are based on rankings within calender quarters.

expected earnings for the next four quarters would be as indicated in italics below.

	Year 0	Year 1	Year 2
Quarter I	$10.00	$11.00	*$10.76*
Quarter II	10.00	*10.34*	
Quarter III	10.00	*10.19*	
Quarter IV	20.00	*20.06*	

For the next three quarters, one would expect additional increases over the prior year level, but the amounts of the expected increases decline over the three quarters. Looking four quarters ahead to the first quarter of year 2, we expect earnings will decline relative to this year; that is, a portion of the initial earnings change is not expected to persist.

Panel A also shows that this kind of autocorrelation pattern is quite consistent across firms. First, the pattern persists generally across the 37 two-digit SIC industries for which our sample includes 20 or more firms. For example, the signs of the within-industry means of the firm-specific autocorrelations calculated are in agreement for all 37 industries at lags 1, 2, and 4, and for 35 of 37 industries at lag 3. Second, the pattern of mean autocorrelations calculated within size categories is similar across small, medium, and large firms (those in the bottom four, middle three, and top three deciles of the NYSE/AMEX population). However, the autocorrelations over the first four lags tend to be somewhat more positive for large firms.

Panel B compares the autocorrelations in seasonally differenced earnings with those for *standardized unexpected earnings* (*SUE*), which will be a key variable in our empirical tests. The numerator of *SUE* is equal to actual earnings minus an expectation based on a seasonal random walk with trend (where the trend is estimated using up to 36 quarters of history, if available); that is, it is simply the detrended seasonal difference in earnings. The denominator is equal to the standard deviation of this measure of unexpected earnings over the trend estimation period. To reduce the influence of outliers, *SUE* values greater (less) than 5 (-5) are winsorized to 5 (-5). The autocorrelations in *SUE* are calculated for each firm in the sample, and a mean across firms is obtained for the autocorrelation at each lag.

The first two rows of panel B confirm that the pattern of autocorrelations in the *SUE*s is similar to the pattern already discussed for seasonally differenced earnings (although the magnitudes are slightly higher when *SUE* is the unit of analysis). The similarity indicates that the process of scaling the seasonal differences does not have a large influence on the degree of autocorrelation.

The last row of panel B presents autocorrelations in the *decile assignments* of *SUE*s (based on the distribution of all *SUE*s for a given calendar quarter), as opposed to *SUEs per se*. These statistics are of interest because much of our subsequent analysis is based on *SUE* deciles. As expected, the results indicate that *SUE* deciles have time-series properties very similar to those of the *SUE*s.

2.2. Hypothesis development

We now consider the behavior of stock prices in a market where earnings expectations fail to reflect the autocorrelation pattern described above. That is, we entertain the possibility that the earnings expectations reflected in stock prices follow a seasonal random walk with trend.[4] Even though market prices may reflect less naive expectations, our goal is to develop predictions for this extreme case and then test the extent to which such predictions are supported by the data. That is, we assume that the expectation of earnings for quarter t that is embedded in the market price, denoted by $E^M(Q_t)$, is as follows:

$$E^M[Q_t] = \delta + Q_{t-4}. \tag{1}$$

When earnings Q_t are announced, the market perceives the unexpected component of earnings to be $Q_t - E^M[Q_t]$. Given an 'earnings response coefficient' λ, the resulting abnormal return is

$$AR_t = \lambda(Q_t - E^M[Q_t]) = \lambda(Q_t - Q_{t-4} - \delta). \tag{2}$$

Note that the abnormal return reflects a component equal to the current detrended seasonal difference in earnings. Thus, the abnormal return should be correlated with past detrended seasonal differences in earnings, in the same way that the current detrended seasonal difference is correlated with past detrended seasonal differences. Specifically, we hypothesize the following:

Hypothesis 1. If prices reflect an earnings expectation described by a seasonal random walk with trend, there should be positive but declining associations between the abnormal return at the announcement of quarter t earnings and the detrended seasonal differences in earnings for quarters $t - 1$, $t - 2$, and $t - 3$. There should be a negative association between the abnormal return at the announcement of quarter t earnings and the detrended seasonal difference in earnings for quarter $t - 4$.

A useful feature of Hypothesis 1 is that it links the relation between abnormal returns and prior-period earnings data to the autocorrelation patterns presented in prior research and in table 1, and does so without the need to specify explicitly a particular model of the actual earnings process. However, the hypothesis represents a statement about the *simple* relation between abnormal returns and earnings changes of each prior period *taken individually*. If we are more precise about the actual time-series process of earnings, we can conveniently relate abnormal returns to earnings data from

---

[4] If we assume instead that the expectation is a seasonal random walk with *no* trend, then Hypothesis 1 below would be stated in terms of seasonal differences, *before* detrending. Empirical tests based on this alternative approach yield results similar to those reported here.

multiple prior periods simultaneously. This, in turn, will prove useful in assessing the economic importance of the predictable component of the abnormal returns.

Based on prior research, we assume that the most accurate univariate description of the time-series process of earnings is provided by the Brown and Rozeff (1979) model, modified to include a trend term:[5]

$$Q_t = \delta + Q_{t-4} + \phi(Q_{t-1} - Q_{t-5}) + \theta\varepsilon_{t-4} + \varepsilon_t, \qquad (3)$$

where ε_t is the white-noise earnings shock of period t, $\phi > 0$, and θ is sufficiently negative to ensure that the fourth-order autocorrelation in seasonally-differenced earnings is negative.

The Brown–Rozeff model includes a first-order autoregressive term $[\phi(Q_{t-1} - Q_{t-5})]$, which is designed to account for the positive but decaying autocorrelations in seasonally differenced earnings at lags 1 through 3. The model also includes a seasonal moving-average term ($\theta\varepsilon_{t-4}$) to account for the negative autocorrelation noted at the fourth lag. The earnings expectation implied by the Brown–Rozeff model is

$$E[Q_t] = \delta + Q_{t-4} + \phi(Q_{t-1} - Q_{t-5}) + \theta\varepsilon_{t-4}. \qquad (4)$$

Several studies [e.g., Brown and Rozeff (1979) and Bathke and Lorek (1984)] have documented that the Brown–Rozeff model fits earnings data well and generates more accurate out-of-sample earnings forecasts than other time-series models. However, the margin of superiority is not 'large'; Bathke and Lorek (1984) find a 9 percent reduction in mean absolute percentage forecast errors when moving from a seasonal random walk with trend to the Brown–Rozeff model. Thus, even if market expectations are characterized by a seasonal random walk with trend, the resulting predictable errors in those expectations might not be substantial. Any ability to predict stock-price reactions to future earnings announcements based on past earnings and the autocorrelation structure of earnings therefore becomes that much more surprising.

---

[5]Allowing for a trend in earnings was less of a concern for Brown and Rozeff, who dealt with per-share data. We assume that the trend term equals that embedded in stock prices [eq. (1)]. This assumption simplifies the development of Hypothesis 2, without altering the thrust of our conclusions. If a difference between the trend terms does exist and it varies across firms, then the observed association (in pooled cross-section) between abnormal returns and each past seasonal difference would be more positive; the negative association at the fourth lag would arise only if θ is sufficiently negative to overcome this effect. It turns out, however, that the observed association at the fourth lag is not only negative, but consistent in terms of magnitude with predictions based on the development of Hypothesis 2. Thus the benefits of a more complex treatment of the trend term appear minimal.

If the time-series process of earnings is best described by a Brown–Rozeff model, but earnings expectations embedded in prices are nevertheless based on a seasonal random walk with trend, then the abnormal return around earnings announcements presented in eq. (2) can be rewritten as shown below. We begin by decomposing the abnormal return in eq. (2) into an unpredictable component, $Q_t - \mathrm{E}[Q_t]$, and its complement, $\mathrm{E}[Q_t] - \mathrm{E}^M[Q_t]$, that is predictable based on knowledge about the time-series behavior of earnings:[6]

$$AR_t = \lambda(Q_t - \mathrm{E}^M[Q_t])$$
$$= \lambda(Q_t - \mathrm{E}[Q_t]) + \lambda(\mathrm{E}[Q_t] - \mathrm{E}^M[Q_t]). \tag{5}$$

Relying on the Brown–Rozeff model, we can replace $(Q_t - \mathrm{E}[Q_t])$ with the difference between eqs. (3) and (4), and replace $(\mathrm{E}[Q_t] - \mathrm{E}^M[Q_t])$ with the difference between eqs. (4) and (1):

$$AR_t = \lambda \varepsilon_t + \lambda \phi (Q_{t-1} - Q_{t-5}) + \lambda \theta \varepsilon_{t-4}. \tag{6}$$

Since $(Q_{t-1} - Q_{t-5})$ can be written in terms of prior period shocks, eq. (6) can also be written as

$$AR_t = \lambda \varepsilon_t + \lambda \phi \varepsilon_{t-1} + \lambda \phi^2 \varepsilon_{t-2} + \lambda \phi^3 \varepsilon_{t-3}$$
$$+ \lambda(\theta + \phi^4)\varepsilon_{t-4} + \lambda \nu, \tag{7}$$

where ν is a linear combination of earnings shocks from periods prior to $t - 4$, that are uncorrelated with the shocks of periods t through $t - 4$, and which have coefficients of order $\theta \phi$ or smaller.

Eqs. (6) and (7) provide the basis for our second hypothesis:

Hypothesis 2. If prices reflect an earnings expectation described by a seasonal random walk with trend, while the univariate times-series process of earnings is best described by the Brown–Rozeff (1979) model as written in eq. (3), then the abnormal return at the announcement of quarter t earnings should have a positive partial correlation with the seasonal difference in earnings for quarter t − 1, and a negative partial correlation with the earnings shock of period t − 4,

---

[6]The earnings response coefficient, λ, is assumed constant across the two components of the earnings change, because the market would have no way of distinguishing between the two components given that its expectations are based on a seasonal random walk with trend. The empirical tests, however, do not rely on this assumption as we estimate unrestricted coefficients for the regression models derived from eq. (5).

as specified in eq. (6). *Alternatively, the abnormal return at the announcement of quarter t earnings should have positive but declining partial correlations with the earnings shocks of quarters $t-1$, $t-2$, and $t-3$, and a negative partial correlation with the earnings shock of period $t-4$ as specified in eq. (7).*

Note that Hypothesis 1 and Hypothesis 2 lead to tests of the same fundamental notion that prices are based on an earnings expectation that fails to reflect fully the extent to which the earnings series departs from a seasonal random walk. Hypothesis 2 is distinct from Hypothesis 1 only in that it makes a more specific assumption about the actual time-series properties of earnings. This additional assumption can potentially increase the power of our tests, as well as facilitate the construction of portfolios based on multiple prior-period earnings signals.

3. Empirical tests

3.1. Portfolio tests of Hypothesis 1

Tests of Hypothesis 1 are conducted by forming ten portfolios for each calendar quarter, based on the *SUE* deciles of firms announcing earnings within that quarter. We then observe the relation between the *SUE* assignments and three-day market reactions to earnings announcements for subsequent quarters. (The three-day window includes the two days prior to and the disclosure date as reported on Compustat – from the Wall Street Journal or Dow Jones News Service.) If Hypothesis 1 is correct, then we should observe a positive relation for each of the next three announcements (but with the magnitude of the association declining over the three quarters) and a negative relation for the fourth subsequent announcement.

The measure of abnormal returns used is the same size-adjusted return described in Bernard and Thomas (1989). Daily abnormal returns for a given firm are obtained by subtracting from the total return the return on a portfolio of the NYSE/AMEX firms in the same size decile, based on January 1 market value of equity. Daily size-adjusted returns are summed across firms and cumulated over time to obtain portfolio cumulative abnormal returns.

Prior to reviewing the results, we offer one final comment on an econometric issue. Even though the primary tests focus on short (three-day) return intervals, there is some overlapping of event windows in calendar time. Thus, standard *t*-tests applied to mean abnormal returns would potentially be subject to bias due to cross-correlation in the data [see Bernard (1987)]. Therefore, for each of the major *t*-tests presented here, we also present an 'alternative *t*-test' designed by Jaffe (1974) and Fama and MacBeth (1973) to

Table 2

Predictions of market reactions to future earnings announcements based on current earnings information, 2,463 firms, 1974–1986 (72,076 to 85,482 observations).[a]

Panel A: Three-day percentage abnormal return in quarter $t+k$, for portfolios based on earnings information from quarter t (t-statistics in parentheses)

Portfolio held (based on SUE decile of quarter t)	Holding period (relative to announcement for quarter $t+k$)	$t+1$	$t+2$	$t+3$	$t+4$	$t+5$	$t+6$	$t+7$	$t+8$
10 (good news)	Three-day [−2, 0]	0.76 (13.21)	0.44 (8.05)	0.13 (2.21)	−0.22 (−4.11)	−0.05 (−0.85)	−0.04 (−0.76)	0.01 (0.21)	−0.04 (−0.66)
1 (bad news)	Three-day [−2, 0]	−0.56 (−8.04)	−0.26 (−4.16)	0.09 (0.13)	0.43 (6.82)	0.26 (4.10)	0.19 (2.99)	0.16 (2.43)	0.34 (5.22)
Long in 10/short in 1	Three-day [−2, 0]	1.32 (14.63)	0.70 (8.46)	0.04 (0.45)	−0.66 (−7.86)	−0.31 (−3.68)	−0.23 (−2.73)	−0.15 (−1.70)	−0.38 (−4.44)
Alternative t-test[b]		(7.40)	(5.56)	(1.63)	(−3.38)	(−2.53)	(−2.01)	(−0.89)	(−1.73)

Panel B: Comparison of three-day percentage abnormal returns with percentage abnormal returns since quarter t announcement

Portfolio held	Holding period	$t+1$	$t+2$	$t+3$	$t+4$	$t+5$	$t+6$	$t+7$	$t+8$
Long in 10/short in 1 (reversed after quarter $t+3$)	Sum of three-day abnormal returns for quarters $t+1,\ldots,t+k$	1.32	2.02	2.06	2.72	3.02	3.25	3.40	3.78
Long in 10/short in 1 (reversed after quarter $t+3$)	From day after announcement for quarter t through announcement for quarter $t+k$	5.69	7.48	8.10	8.61	8.72	8.39	8.03	8.63

| Ratio of three-day sum through $t+k$ to CAR since quarter t announcement, long in 10/short in 1 (reversed after quarter $t+3$) | 0.23 | 0.27 | 0.25 | 0.31 | 0.35 | 0.39 | 0.42 | 0.44 |

Panel C: Correlation between SUE for quarter t and three-day [−2, 0] percentage abnormal returns around subsequent earnings announcements[c]

Correlation between	Type	$t+1$	$t+2$	$t+3$	$t+4$	$t+5$	$t+6$	$t+7$	$t+8$
SUE deciles and abnormal return (for decile portfolio)	Spearman	1.00[d]	0.95[d]	0.36	−0.99[d]	−0.76[d]	−0.68[d]	−0.64[d]	−0.47
	Pearson	0.97[d]	0.94[d]	0.32	−0.96[d]	−0.79[d]	−0.77[d]	−0.65[d]	−0.45
SUE deciles and abnormal return (for firm-quarters)	Spearman	0.09[d]	0.05[d]	0.01[d]	−0.04[d]	−0.02[d]	−0.02[d]	−0.01[d]	−0.00
	Pearson	0.07[d]	0.03[d]	−0.00	−0.04[d]	−0.02[d]	−0.02[d]	−0.01[d]	−0.01[d]

[a] Standardized unexpected earnings (SUE) represent forecast errors from a seasonal random walk with drift, scaled by their estimation-period standard deviation. Earnings announcements are grouped into deciles, based on the distribution of SUE each calendar quarter, to generate the SUE deciles used to form portfolios. Abnormal returns are the difference between daily returns for individual firms in the portfolio and returns for NYSE-AMEX firms of the same size decile.

[b] Alternative t-test is conducted by calculating mean abnormal returns for each of 13 years, and dividing by the time-series standard error of that mean.

[c] In the top half of panel C, correlations are computed between the mean abnormal returns over the three-day holding periods for each SUE decile and the decile numbers (1 = lowest SUE, 10 = highest SUE). In the bottom half, the correlations are computed between the three-day abnormal returns and SUE deciles for individual announcements.

[d] Statistically significant at 0.05 level, two-tailed test.

eliminate bias from cross-sectional dependence. Specifically, we calculate the value of any given portfolio return (or in the regression tests of Hypothesis 2, any given coefficient) for each of the 13 years in the database. We then compare the mean of the resulting 13 values to its time-series standard error to construct the alternative t-test. In most cases, this alternative calculation generates a smaller t-statistic, probably reflecting both a loss of power and an elimination of some bias. (The loss of power arises because equal weight is placed on data from each year, which is generally suboptimal.)

The first test of Hypothesis 1 is presented in table 2, panel A. We form portfolios that are long in extreme 'good-news' ($SUE = 10$) firms and short in 'bad-news' ($SUE = 1$) firms based on quarter t earnings information, and then measure the mean abnormal returns for these portfolios around subsequent quarters' earnings announcements. We focus here on extreme deciles to enhance the power of our tests and provide results directly comparable to prior research. However, we later examine the behavior of all deciles.

The evidence shows that the three-day abnormal returns around earnings announcements are predictable, at least four quarters in advance. Moreover, the signs and magnitudes of the abnormal returns reflect the pattern of autocorrelations hypothesized in the previous section. The zero-investment portfolio created on the basis of quarter t earnings information generates a significant positive mean abnormal return (1.32 percent) upon the announcement of quarter $t + 1$ earnings, as if market prices fail to reflect fully that a given SUE in quarter t tends to be followed by an SUE of the same sign in quarter $t + 1$. As predicted, we also observe positive but smaller mean abnormal returns around the announcement of earnings for quarters $t + 2$ and $t + 3$. Finally, again consistent with our predictions, we observe significant negative mean abnormal returns around the announcement of earnings for quarter $t + 4$, as if prices fail to reflect fully that a given earnings change in quarter t is likely to be partially reversed in quarter $t + 4$.

We did not offer predictions about the behavior of market reactions around earnings announcements beyond quarter $t + 4$. However, based on the autocorrelations observed in table 1, we would expect small but negative market reactions to the announcements of quarters $t + 5$ through $t + 8$, for long (short) positions in quarter t's good-news (bad-news) firms. In fact, that is what we observe: the abnormal returns are -0.31 percent, -0.23 percent, -0.15 percent, and -0.38 percent for quarter $t + 5$ through $t + 8$, respectively. (The statistical significance of the last two amounts depends on the t-test used.) We hesitate to emphasize these particular results, however, because unlike the signs of the autocorrelations at the first four lags, the signs for lags 5 through 8 have not been robust across samples and time periods examined in prior studies [compare Foster (1977) with our evidence], and therefore might not have been predictable at the beginning of the test period.

Table 3

Correspondence between relative magnitude of *autocorrelations* in earnings data and relative magnitude of *abnormal returns* predicted on the basis of the past earnings.

Lag	1	2	3	4	5	6	7	8
Magnitudes of *autocorrelations* in *SUE* deciles at lag k, relative to autocorrelation at lag 1[a]	1.00	0.56	0.17	−0.44	−0.22	−0.22	−0.22	−0.20
Magnitudes of predictable *abnormal returns* at announcement for quarter $t + k$, relative to predictable abnormal return at announcement for quarter $t + 1$[b]	1.00	0.53	0.03	−0.50	−0.23	−0.17	−0.11	−0.28

[a]Autocorrelations are taken from table 1, panel B, which reports means of firm-specific autocorrelations in *SUE* deciles. Thus, the amount 0.56 shown above for lag 2 is the ratio of the mean autocorrelation in *SUE* deciles at lag 2 (0.23), divided by the mean autocorrelation in *SUE* deciles at lag 1 (0.41).

*SUE*s are forecast errors from a seasonal random walk with trend, scaled by their standard deviation within the trend-estimation period (up to 36 observations). *SUE* deciles are based on rankings within calendar quarters.

[b]Abnormal returns are taken from table 2, panel A, third section, which reports the return for the three-day window surrounding the announcement of earnings for quarter $t + k$, for a long position in firms with quarter t *SUE* in decile 10, combined with a short position in firms with quarter t *SUE* in decile 1. Thus, the amount 0.53 shown above for lag 2 is the ratio of the abnormal return around the announcement of earnings for quarter $t + 2$ (0.70 percent), divided by the corresponding amount for quarter $t + 1$ (1.32 percent).

Hypothesis 1 is borne out in the data not only in terms of the signs of future abnormal returns, but also in terms of magnitudes. That is, the relative magnitudes of the abnormal returns around subsequent earnings announcements are in general accordance with the relative magnitudes of the autocorrelations in *SUE*s documented earlier. The mean autocorrelations in *SUE* deciles at lag k (from the last row of table 1, panel B), relative to the autocorrelation at lag 1, are shown in the first row of table 3. They are compared with the mean abnormal returns around announcements for quarter $t + k$ (from the third section of table 2, panel A) relative to that for quarter $t + 1$. The strength of the correspondence between the two series is striking.

Returning to table 2, panel A, we note that the predictably positive abnormal returns around the first *three* subsequent announcements could simply reflect evidence already documented in prior research based on longer return intervals, if the three-day abnormal returns represented a proportionate allocation of the post-announcement drift already shown to exist over six to nine months [e.g., Watts (1978), Bernard and Thomas (1989)]. To check that possibility, table 2, panel B compares the three-day abnormal returns around subsequent earnings announcements to the abnormal return cumulated over periods from the day after the announcement for quarter t, through the announcements for subsequent quarters.[7] We assume a long (short) position in the good-news (bad-news) firms over the first three quarters after the earnings announcement, and then reverse that position at the beginning of the fourth subsequent quarter. The cumulative abnormal return is 5.7 percent through the announcement for quarter $t+1$ and 8.6 percent through the announcement for quarter $t+4$. The last row of panel B shows that the three-day abnormal returns (summed over announcements to date) account for 23 to 31 percent of the cumulative post-announcement drift through quarter $t+4$. Given that the three-day announcement periods account for only about 5 percent of the total trading days, the announcement period reactions clearly represent a disproportionate share of the drift. This constitutes an extension of similar evidence provided by Bernard and Thomas (1989) and Freeman and Tse (1989) for the first subsequent announcement.

The evidence in table 2, panel B suggests that some portion of the post-announcement adjustment to earnings is rapid even though it is delayed. The rapid adjustments went undetected in research prior to Bernard and Thomas (1989), because subsequent earnings-announcement dates were scattered in event time. By not realigning the data at each subsequent announcement date, researchers smoothed the sharp adjustments that occur at those dates.

Table 2, panel C shows that the phenomenon documented above is not driven by extreme deciles; it persists throughout the sample. Panel C presents the simple correlations between *SUE*s of quarter t and the three-day abnormal return surrounding each of the eight subsequent earnings announcements, at both the level of *SUE* decile portfolios and individual firm quarters. The Spearman and Pearson correlations indicate that the relation between *SUE* deciles for quarter t and the ten corresponding mean abnormal returns around the next four earnings announcements is not only close to monotonic, but is almost perfectly linear. The sole exception is the relation for quarter $t+3$, which was not expected to be strong. Movement from analysis at the portfolio level to the level of individual firm-quarters causes the correlations to decline considerably, as expected, but the predicted pattern remains.

---

[7]While the firm's *SUE* is known on the day prior to the commencement of this return interval, the firm's *SUE* decile assignment is not known until all firms have announced earnings for the quarter. Assuming the ability to calculate decile assignments prior to that time introduces a form of hindsight bias studied by Holthausen (1983). To overcome this potential bias, Foster, Olsen, and Shevlin (1984) and Bernard and Thomas (1989) assign *SUE*s to deciles by comparing them to the distribution of *SUE*s for the *prior* quarter. However, in this sample, the magnitude of post-announcement drift is insensitive to this adjustment.

Note that this form of hindsight bias is not an issue in the primary tests based on three-day return intervals, because by the time of the subsequent earnings announcement, the firm's *SUE* decile assignment would be known.

A final note on table 2 concerns an apparent asymmetry in the returns for 'good-news' and 'bad-news' firms in panel A. If one simply *adds* announcement-period abnormal returns across the two groups, rather than offsetting long and short positions, the result is a positive abnormal return of approximately 0.20 percent, regardless of the subsequent quarter examined. That announcement-period abnormal returns are on average positive has been documented previously by Chari et al. (1988) and Ball and Kothari (1990). Why this occurs is unclear. However, note that this effect would tend to 'work against' our prediction for bad-news firms for the first three lags and good-news firms for the fourth lag, and should cancel out in our combined long and short positions. Thus, while the effect is evident in our data, it cannot explain the results of our tests.

Table 4 presents evidence like that in table 2 for firms classified as small, medium, and large (those in size deciles 1 to 4, 5 to 7, and 8 to 10, respectively, based on January 1 market value of equity for all NYSE and AMEX firms). Fig. 1 summarizes the information from table 4 in the form of a *CAR* plot.[8] We are motivated to partition the data by firm size because it may be more plausible that published earnings information would fail to be impounded fully in the prices of small firms relative to large firms. For example, Foster, Olsen, and Shevlin (1984) suggest that the market for information might be less well developed for small firms, thus motivating their examination of post-announcement drift as a function of firm size.

The patterns noted above are present for each size group – in every case, positive but declining abnormal returns around the announcement of earnings for quarter $t + 1$, $t + 2$, and $t + 3$, and negative abnormal returns around the announcement of earnings for quarter $t + 4$. However, the effects are more pronounced for small firms. Note that this cannot be attributed to differences in the time-series behavior of earnings, since there is *less* autocorrelation in earnings changes for small firms (table 1) and *SUE*s actually vary *less* for small firms than large firms. Thus, the data are consistent with stock prices failing to reflect fully the implications of current earnings for future earnings for all firms, but the failure is more apparent for small stocks. Interestingly, however, the *fraction* of post-announcement drift that is delayed until subsequent earnings announcements is similar across the three size groups.

In addition to partitioning the data by firm size, we also checked the robustness of the results across fiscal quarters by partitioning on both the quarter of portfolio formation and the quarter to which the subsequent announcements pertain. The results (not reported here) are consistent across

---

[8] While Freeman and Tse (1989) present a similar plot for their overall sample (fig. 2), they offer no discussion of the reactions to announcements beyond quarter $t + 1$.

Table 4

Predictions of market reactions to future earnings announcements for portfolios based on current quarter's SUE; results by firm-size group.

	\multicolumn{4}{c}{Subsequent quarter for which earnings are announced}
	$t+1$	$t+2$	$t+3$	$t+4$

Small firms (28,877 to 30,904 observations)

Abnormal return three days $[-2, 0]$ around announcement, long (short) in quarter t SUE decile 10 (1)	1.92	0.82	0.10	−1.15
t-statistic	(8.26)	(4.09)	(0.48)	(−5.51)
Alternative t-test[b]	(4.76)	(2.80)	(0.97)	(−2.45)
Sum of above returns (position reversed in quarter $t+4$)	1.92	2.74	2.84	3.99
Ratio of sum of three-day abnormal returns through $t+k$ to CAR since quarter t announcement (with reversal of long and short positions in quarter $t+4$)	0.24	0.28	0.27	0.35

Medium firms (23,541 to 30,904 observations)

Abnormal return three days $[-2, 0]$ around announcement, long (short) in quarter t SUE decile 10 (1)	1.46	0.98	0.21	−0.44
t-statistic	(10.43)	(7.01)	(1.46)	(−3.05)
Alternative t-test	(4.86)	(4.26)	(1.83)	(−1.62)
Sum of above returns (position reversed in quarter $t+4$)	1.46	2.44	2.65	3.09
Ratio of sum of three-day abnormal returns through $t+k$ to CAR since quarter t announcement (with reversal of long and short positions in quarter $t+4$)	0.22	0.27	0.27	0.31

Large firms (27,342 to 29,088 observations)

Abnormal return three days $[-2, 0]$ around announcement, long (short) in quarter t SUE decile 10 (1)	0.84	0.48	0.04	−0.31
t-statistic	(8.84)	(5.10)	(0.40)	(−3.24)
Alternative t-test	(6.76)	(3.87)	(−0.30)	(−1.74)
Sum of above returns (position reversed in quarter $t+4$)	0.84	1.32	1.36	1.67
Ratio of sum of three-day abnormal returns through $t+k$ to CAR since quarter t announcement (with reversal of long and short positions in quarter $t+4$)	0.26	0.31	0.32	0.34

[a]Abnormal returns are the sum of daily returns for individual firms in the portfolio, less returns for NYSE–AMEX firms of the same size decile, based on January 1 market values of equity. Small, medium, and large firms are in size deciles 1 to 4, 5 to 7, and 8 to 10, respectively. CAR is the sum of abnormal returns over all days since the announcement for quarter t.

SUE represents the forecast error from a seasonal random-walk (with trend) earnings-expectation model, scaled by its estimation-period standard deviation. SUE decile portfolios are based on ranking of SUEs within the calendar quarter of the announcement of quarter t earnings.

[b]Alternative t-test is conducted by calculating mean abnormal return for each of 13 years, and dividing by the time-series standard error of that mean.

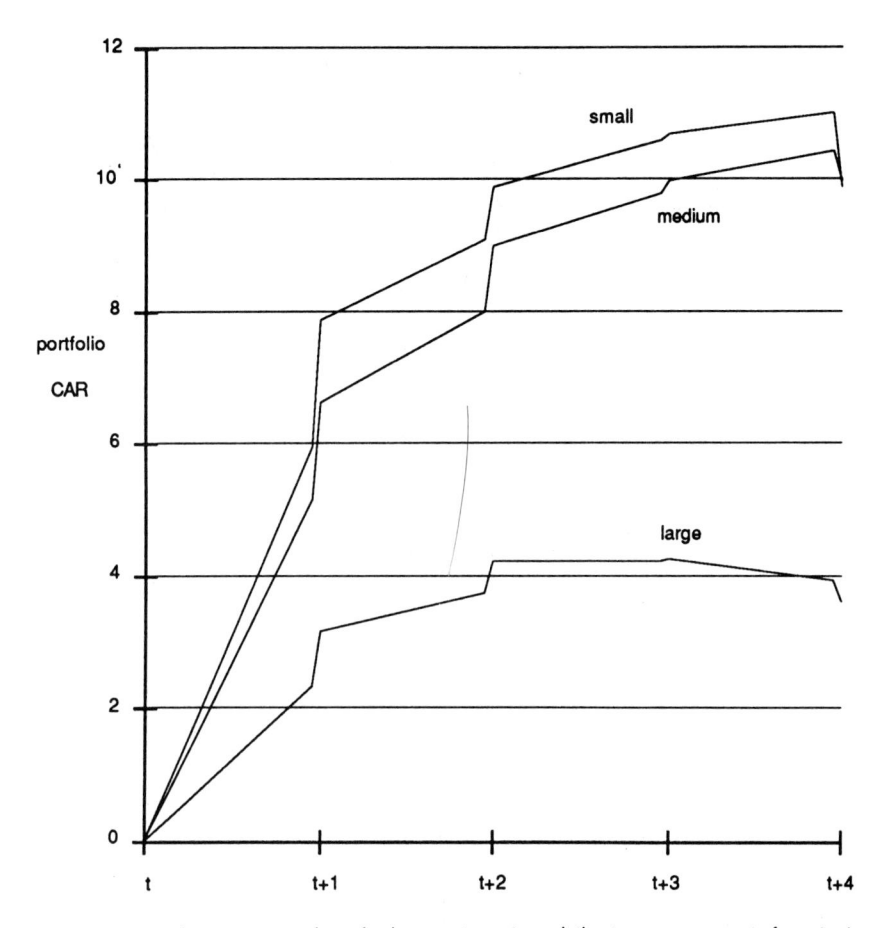

Fig. 1. Percentage cumulative abnormal returns for *SUE* portfolios: Returns aligned by subsequent earnings announcements.

Portfolio *CAR* is the percentage cumulative abnormal return over holding periods beginning after the earnings-announcement day for quarter t, for a portfolio invested long (short) in the highest (lowest) decile of standardized unexpected earnings (*SUE*) at quarter t. *SUE* represents forecast error from the seasonal random-walk (with trend) earnings-expectation model scaled by its estimation-period standard deviation. Abnormal returns are the differences between daily returns for individual firms in an *SUE* decile portfolio and returns for NYSE–AMEX firms of the same size decile, based on January 1 market values of equity. Small, medium, and large firms are in size deciles 1 to 4, 5 to 7, and 8 to 10, respectively. Holding periods are obtained by splitting the period between adjacent earnings-announcement dates into a three-day pre-announcement window (day -2 to day 0) and an inter-announcement window. While the actual inter-announcement windows vary in length, the mean value of 60 days is used to illustrate the differential price responses occurring in the two windows.

the quarters, with the following exception. When either the first or second subsequent announcements pertain to the first quarter of the fiscal year, the three-day abnormal returns are only about half as large as reported in table 2. Although this result may be partially due to the lower-than-average first-order autocorrelations between fourth-quarter and subsequent first-quarter SUEs, we are otherwise unable to explain this feature of the data.

3.2. Regression tests of Hypothesis 2

We now turn to tests of Hypothesis 2. These tests can be used to assess the economic importance of abnormal returns that are predicted using several prior earnings signals simultaneously. However, the tests require direct reliance on a specific model of earnings (the Brown–Rozeff model). Whether such reliance strengthens or weakens our tests depends on the validity of that model as a description of the actual univariate process of earnings.

Based on eqs. (6) and (7), we estimate regression models of the following form:

$$AR_{jt} = b_0 + b_1(Q_{j,t-1} - Q_{j,t-5}) + b_4 e_{j,t-4} + u_{jt}, \qquad (8)$$

$$AR_{jt} = b_0 + b_1 e_{j,t-1} + b_2 e_{j,t-2} + b_3 e_{j,t-3} + b_4 e_{j,t-4} + v_{jt}, \qquad (9)$$

where $e_{j,t-k}$ is an estimate of the earnings shock $\varepsilon_{j,t-k}$ from eqs. (6) and (7) as discussed below, u_{jt} and v_{jt} are residual errors, and other variables are as previously defined.

The earnings shocks called for on the right-hand side of eqs. (8) and (9) are the forecast errors from a Brown–Rozeff model. However, in time series as short as that used here, the iterative techniques necessary to estimate the Brown–Rozeff model are often unreliable. To deal with this problem, we produced two sets of estimates of (8) and (9). One is based on a subset (36 percent) of the sample for which 36 historical observations are available to estimate the Brown–Rozeff earnings forecasts; forecast errors for this sample are available only beginning in 1980. The second approach uses the full sample, extending from 1974 through 1986, but substitutes forecast errors from an alternative model developed by Foster (1977).[9] Such errors are highly correlated with Brown–Rozeff forecast errors, even though the Foster model differs by excluding the fourth-order moving-average term.[10] While

---

[9] The Foster model was estimated from the most recent 36 quarters of earnings data (after seasonal differencing), where available. Where fewer than 16 quarterly observations were available, we relied on a seasonal random walk to generate earnings expectations. This was necessary in about 6 percent of the cases.

[10] The correlation between the two forecast errors is 0.86, when each is converted to a winsorized SUE as was done previously with the seasonal differences; the correlation is 0.80, when each is converted to SUE deciles.

the substitution of Foster forecast errors weakens our tests by introducing some measurement error in the regressors, the impact should be small.[11] In fact, for the subsample where both Brown-Rozeff and Foster forecast errors are available, the results are essentially the same; those results are, in turn, similar to those based on the full sample and Foster model forecasts errors.

Given that the alternative approaches yield similar results, we choose to report only one in detail. The approach selected is that based on the full sample (using the Foster model), because the results of that approach are readily comparable to those in the previous tables. Moreover, by emphasizing that the predicted results hold when Foster model forecast errors are used, we can remove any doubt that the implied abnormal returns could only have been obtained through application of the computer-intensive statistical estimation required by the Brown-Rozeff model. The Foster model, in contrast, could easily have been estimated throughout our sample period, using a simple regression.

Another measurement issue concerns scaling of the regressors. Both the seasonal difference $Q_{t-1} - Q_{t-5}$ and the earnings shocks e_{t-1} through e_{t-4} are scaled by their historical standard deviations (using up to 36 observations, where available), just as the SUEs were in the previous section. [Thus, the regressors could themselves be viewed as SUEs based on forecasts from a seasonal random walk (for $Q_{t-1} - Q_{t-5}$) and a Foster model (for e_{t-1} through e_{t-4}).] The resulting scaled variables are then placed in deciles within quarters (to guard against the potential for difficulties with outliers) and the decile rankings (1 to 10) are reduced by one and then divided by nine so as to range between 0 and 1.

Given the way we have constructed the regressions, the coefficients can be interpreted as abnormal returns on portfolios with certain useful properties. [See Fama and MacBeth (1973) and Bernard (1984) for similar interpretations.] First, denoting the dependent variable as R and the matrix of regressors as X, note that the ordinary-least-squares (OLS) regression coefficients [written as $(X'X)^{-1}X'R$] represent abnormal returns on portfolios, where the portfolio weights are given by the rows of the matrix $(X'X)^{-1}X'$. Second, note that since the regression includes an intercept, the portfolio weights for the slope coefficients must sum to zero, and thus the slope coefficients can be viewed as abnormal returns to *zero-investment* portfolios. Third, to help interpret the economic meaning of the coefficient, note that a coefficient from a regression of abnormal returns can always be interpreted

---

[11]If the Brown-Rozeff and Foster model parameters could be estimated precisely, then movement from the former to the latter to estimate eq. (8) should introduce a bias toward zero in b_1 that is trivial and in b_4 that is on the order of 6 percent. (Details are available upon request.) For the subsample where both Brown-Rozeff and Foster forecast errors are available, the coefficient estimates based on the Foster model are indeed closer to zero, in the amount of 1 percent and 2 percent, respectively.

as the abnormal return on a portfolio with a value of 1 for the associated regressor, and a value of 0 for the remaining regressors. Thus, the amount $b_1 - b_4$ in eq. (8) represents the abnormal return on a zero-investment portfolio with a value of 1 for $Q_{t-1} - Q_{t-5}$ and -1 for e_{t-4}; the amount $b_1 + b_2 + b_3 - b_4$ in eq. (9) represents the abnormal return on a zero-investment portfolio with value of 1 for e_{t-1}, e_{t-2}, and e_{t-3} and -1 for e_{t-4}. (Of course, regressors for individual observations range from 0 to 1, spanning the ten deciles of the distribution, but the observations are weighted so that these statements hold for the *portfolio*.)

The above interpretations imply that, given how the regressors are scaled [with a value of 1 (0) representing the highest (lowest) decile of a regressor distribution], the portfolio underlying $b_1 - b_4$ in eq. (8) is comparable to a zero-investment portfolio with long (short) positions in firms within the highest (lowest) decile of $Q_{t-1} - Q_{t-5}$ and short (long) positions in firms within the highest (lowest) decile of e_{t-4}. Specifically, the two portfolios are comparable in the sense that both have values of 1 for $Q_{t-1} - Q_{t-5}$ and -1 for e_{t-4}.[12] Similarly, the portfolio underlying $b_1 + b_2 + b_3 - b_4$ in (9) is comparable to a zero-investment portfolio with long (short) positions in firms within the highest (lowest) deciles of e_{t-1}, e_{t-2}, and e_{t-3} and short (long) positions in firms within the highest (lowest) decile of e_{t-4}.

The essential point is that the linear combination of coefficients in regression (8) or (9) can be interpreted as abnormal returns on zero-investments portfolios that, unlike the portfolios in table 2 and prior research, are based on information about *multiple* earnings signals. Nevertheless, the portfolios implicit in the regression are scaled so as to permit comparisons with portfolios based on single earnings signals. In addition, the weights underlying them are determinable on the basis of information (the regressors) available prior to the beginning of the return interval.

Estimates of eqs. (8) and (9) are presented in table 5, panel A. The primary estimates based on three-day return intervals appear at the top of that panel. The abnormal returns implied by using the combination of prior period earnings signals [that is, $b_1 - b_4$ for eq. (8) and $b_1 + b_2 + b_3 - b_4$ for eq. (9)] appear in the rightmost column of panel A.

Coefficient estimates for both eqs. (8) and (9) at the top of panel A all have the predicted signs (b_1, b_2, and b_3 are all positive and b_4 is negative) and are always statistically significant. The relative magnitudes of the coefficients are also in accord with our expectations; that is, $b_1 > b_2 > b_3 > 0 > b_4$. The adjusted R^2 is low in regressions (8) and (9) – less than 1 percent – indicating that only a small fraction of the variance in stock returns is predictable

---

[12]The portfolio underlying $b_1 - b_4$ differs from the other portfolio in that, under the assumptions of OLS, the former is minimum variance. However, since the assumptions of OLS are unlikely to hold perfectly, the portfolio will not literally be minimum variance, thus weakening our tests.

Table 5
Regression tests of relation between market reactions to quarterly earnings announcements and earnings information.

Panel A: Predicting market reaction using lagged earnings information[a]

(8) $\quad AR_{jt} = b_0 + b_1(Q_{j,t-1} - Q_{j,t-5}) + b_4 e_{j,t-4} + u_{jt}$

(9) $\quad AR_{jt} = b_0 + b_1 e_{j,t-1} + b_2 e_{j,t-2} + b_3 e_{j,t-3} + b_4 e_{j,t-4} + v_{jt}$

Regression model	Holding period for abnormal returns	b_1	b_2	b_3	b_4	Adj. R^2	Implied portfolio abnormal return
		(t-statistic and alternative t-test)					
Equation 8 ($N=75{,}653$)	Three-day $[-2,0]$ announcement period for quarter t	1.30 (20.59) (12.22)			-0.84 (-13.29) (-6.06)	0.7%	2.14%
Equation 9 ($N=75{,}045$)	Three-day $[-2,0]$ announcement period for quarter t	0.98 (15.66) (9.14)	0.62 (9.89) (14.43)	0.28 (4.44) (2.83)	-0.71 (-11.41) (-9.04)	0.7%	2.59%
Equation 8 ($N=75{,}443$)	From day after prior announcement, to quarter t announcement (avg. 63 days)	6.24 (34.40) (9.41)			-2.44 (-13.41) (-9.64)	1.6%	8.68%
Equation 9 ($N=74{,}837$)	From day after prior announcement, to quarter t announcement (avg. 63 days)	5.38 (29.99) (6.56)	1.46 (8.10) (3.22)	0.53 (2.94) (0.18)	-1.56 (-8.68) (-5.32)	1.4%	8.93%

Panel B: Contemporaneous association: market reaction and earnings information[a]

(A) $\quad AR_{jt} = b_0 + b_1 e_{jt} + w_{jt}$

(B) $\quad AR_{jt} = b_0 + b_1(Q_{j,t} - Q_{j,t-4}) + z_{jt}$

Regression model	Holding period for abnormal returns	Regression coefficient, b_1 (t-statistic and alternative t-test)	Adj. R^2	Implied portfolio abnormal return
Equation A ($N=82{,}734$)	Three-day $[-2,0]$ announcement period for quarter t	4.18 (71.61) (26.34)	5.8%	4.18%
Equation B ($N=85{,}493$)	Three-day $[-2,0]$ announcement period for quarter t	4.43 (76.27) (19.27)	6.4%	4.43%

[a]Abnormal returns, AR_{jt}, represent the sum over the indicated holding periods of the differences between daily returns for firm j and returns for NYSE–AMEX firms of the same size decile, based on January 1 market values of equity. $Q_t - Q_{t-4}$ is seasonally differenced quarterly earnings and e_t is the forecast error from the Foster (1977) first-order autoregressive earnings-expectation model (in seasonal differences); both are scaled by their historical standard deviation. All regressors are assigned to deciles, based on the current quarter distribution, and then scaled so that they range from 0 (for the lowest decile) to 1 (for the highest decile). Implied portfolio abnormal returns are equal to $(b_1 - b_4)$ and $(b_1 + b_2 + b_3 - b_4)$ in panel A, and b_1 in panel B. Alternative t-test is conducted by estimating regressions for each of 13 years, and comparing each coefficient's mean to its time-series standard error.

based on previously announced earnings information. However, we will show later (table 7) that the remaining variance is largely diversifiable within annual cross-sections, yielding abnormal returns with the predicted signs consistently from year to year.

Turning to the implied portfolio abnormal return on the right-hand side of panel A, we see that a combination of prior period earnings signals improves our ability to predict future reactions to earnings announcements. Note that the implied abnormal returns are larger than any of the coefficients on individual regressors, and larger than any of the portfolio returns in table 2, each of which is based on a single earnings signal. Results based on eqs. (8) and (9) imply that, on average, historical earnings information could have been used to construct a portfolio with an abnormal return of 2.1 percent and 2.6 percent, respectively, over the three-day announcement-period interval.

Table 5 also provides two ways to assess the economic importance of the predictions. The first moves away from emphasis on three-day intervals surrounding subsequent earnings announcements, and focuses instead on portfolios formed immediately after the current announcement.[13] The portfolios are held until the next announcement (a period of approximately 63 trading days, on average). If an investor believes that post-announcement drift represents a delayed price response, there would be no good reason to wait until just prior to subsequent announcements to take a position. Moreover, the timing of the subsequent announcement cannot be predicted perfectly in advance. Thus, transacting just after the current announcement may represent a better depiction of the strategy an investor might pursue. However, the movement to longer windows increases the concerns about measurement error in abnormal returns.

Regressions using the longer return intervals are presented at the bottom of table 5, panel A. The implied abnormal return over one quarter for the portfolio constructed using information about two earnings signals – $(Q_{t-1} - Q_{t-5})$ and e_{t-4} – is 8.7 percent. When signals about each of the prior four earnings announcements are used – e_{t-1}, e_{t-2}, e_{t-3}, and e_{t-4} – the implied abnormal return is 8.9 percent. The magnitudes of these abnormal returns, corresponding to implied annualized abnormal returns on the order of 35 percent, are significant in economic as well as statistical terms.

There is a second approach to evaluating the economic importance of the effects documented here, that has more direct implications for methodology. We compare the implied three-day abnormal return from panel A, which is predicted solely on the basis of historical information, to the three-day abnormal return that could be generated if earnings were known with

---

[13]The values of two regressors, the decile assignments of $(Q_{t-1} - Q_{t-5})$ and e_{t-1}, depend on a firm's earnings *relative* to other firms, and thus cannot be calculated until all firms have announced earnings. However, as explained in footnote 7, the potential hindsight bias this introduces appears trivial in this sample.

certainty three days before the announcement. The latter abnormal return is presented in panel B, where we regress abnormal returns around the announcement of earnings for quarter t against measures of unexpected earnings (either $Q_t - Q_{t-4}$ or e_t) for that same quarter. (Consistent with our approach in panel A, the regressor ranges from 0 to 1, depending on the decile to which estimated unexpected earnings belongs.) The regression indicates that the zero-investment portfolio comparable to one with a long (short) position in stocks in the highest (lowest) decile of current unexpected earnings generates an abnormal return of 4.2 or 4.4 percent, depending on how unexpected earnings is defined. These amounts can then be compared to the three-day abnormal returns of 2.1 or 2.6 percent in panel A.

The above comparison indicates that, using only historical, publicly available earnings data, we are able to generate an abnormal return about half as large as that based on perfect foresight of earnings. *Thus, the abnormal return that can be predicted in advance is approximately half as large as the stock-price reaction to what is labeled 'unexpected earnings' in many accounting research studies.* This result calls into question the reliability of studies that rely heavily on the assumption that prices reflect all publicly available earnings information quickly. Of some consolation, however, is the observation that the fraction of variance in announcement-period abnormal returns explained by prior-period earnings information is small (0.7 percent), in both absolute terms and relative to the *R*-squared based on current earnings, which is 5.8 percent.

Eq. (8) is re-estimated within firm-size categories in table 6, panel A. Using the combination of indicators from prior earnings numbers, the mean three-day abnormal return on the implied zero-investment portfolio is 3.4 percent, 2.2 percent, and 1.2 percent for small, medium, and large firms, respectively. The regression results in panel B indicate that if one could forecast the *SUE* perfectly, the resulting mean three-day abnormal return would be 6.8 percent, 3.7 percent, and 2.3 percent, for small, medium, and large firms, respectively. In each case, the return based solely on historical information is about half as large as that based on perfect foresight.

A final note concerns the potential for further improvement in the ability to predict abnormal returns around future earnings announcements by considering cross-sectional differences in the parameters of individual firms' time-series processes. We examined this issue in two ways. First, in regressions not reported here, we used historical estimates of ϕ and θ in eq. (8), as called for by eq. (6). Predictive ability was not improved; the implied abnormal returns were similar to those reported in table 5. Second, we stratified the sample into four quartiles, first based on historical estimates of ϕ and then (separately) based on historical estimates of θ, and repeated the portfolio tests of table 2 within each group. As expected, the abnormal return at the announcement of quarter $t + 1$ earnings was most (least) positive for

Table 6

Regression tests of relation between market reactions to quarterly earnings announcements and earnings information; results by firm-size group.

Panel A: Predicting market reaction using lagged earnings information[a]

(8) $AR_{jt} = b_0 + b_1(Q_{j,t-1} - Q_{j,t-5}) + b_4 e_{j,t-4} + u_{jt}$

Firm-size category	b_1 (t-statistic and alternative t-test)	b_4	Adj. R^2	Implied portfolio abnormal return
Small firms ($N = 26{,}841$)	1.98 (13.37) (9.88)	−1.37 (−9.32) (−7.30)	0.8%	3.35%
Medium firms ($N = 22{,}204$)	1.49 (14.76) (5.40)	−0.71 (−7.00) (−4.66)	1.0%	2.20%
Large firms ($N = 26{,}438$)	0.80 (11.69) (1.88)	−0.43 (−6.52) (−1.30)	0.6%	1.23%

Panel B: Contemporaneous association: market reaction and earnings information[a]

$AR_{jt} = b_0 + b_1 e_{jt} + w_{jt}$

Firm-size category	Regression coefficient, b_1 (t-statistic and alternative t-test)	Adj. R^2	Implied portfolio abnormal return
Small firms ($N = 29{,}694$)	6.77 (50.58) (19.97)	7.9%	6.77%
Medium firms ($N = 24{,}163$)	3.74 (40.32) (24.57)	6.3%	3.74%
Large firms ($N = 28{,}482$)	2.28 (36.45) (15.92)	4.5%	2.28%

[a] Abnormal returns, AR_{jt}, represent the sum over the three-day $[-2, 0]$ holding period (relative to the announcement date for quarter t) of the differences between daily returns for firm j and returns for NYSE–AMEX firms of the same size decile, based on January 1 market values of equity. Small, medium, and large firms are in size deciles 1 to 4, 5 to 7, and 8 to 10, respectively. $Q_t - Q_{t-4}$ is seasonally differenced quarterly earnings and e_t is the forecast error from the Foster (1977) first-order autoregressive earnings-expectation model (in seasonal differences); both are scaled by their historical standard deviation. All regressors are assigned to deciles, based on the current-quarter distribution, and then scaled so that they range from 0 (for the lowest decile) to 1 (for the highest decile). Implied portfolio abnormal returns are equal to $(b_1 - b_4)$ in panel A and b_1 in panel B. Alternative t-test is conducted by estimating regressions for each of 13 years, and comparing each coefficient's mean to its time-series standard error.

the portfolio with the largest (smallest) historical value for ϕ (1.54 percent versus 1.21 percent), and the abnormal return at quarter $t+4$ was most (least) negative for the portfolio with the largest (smallest) historical value for θ (-1.09 percent versus -0.74 percent). However, the differences were not statistically significant. One possible explanation is that cross-sectional differences in time-series parameters are too small to provide much predictive power. (Recall the similarity in time-series behavior across industries in table 1.) Another possibility is that while cross-sectional differences exist, they are unstable or estimated with considerable error. Much of the time-series literature [e.g., Albrecht, Lookabill, and McKeown (1977), Foster (1977), Watts and Leftwich (1977)] is consistent with such cross-sectional differences not being predictable out of sample.

4. Alternative explanations and additional evidence

It is difficult to understand how stock prices could fail to reflect the implications of current earnings for future earnings in such a systematic way. The evidence naturally raises several questions, which we discuss below.

(1) *Can this evidence be explained in terms of rational investors' desire to await 'confirmation' that a previous earnings change is not transitory?*
An immediate problem with this explanation is that, at best, it fits only the patterns observed around the announcements of earnings for quarters $t+1$, $t+2$, and $t+3$; the reactions for quarter $t+4$ are consistent with investors treating previous earnings as if they were more permanent than they turned out to be.

There is a more fundamental problem with this explanation, however. No matter how much uncertainty surrounds the implications of earnings already announced for quarter t, prices in an efficient market would immediately reflect an unbiased expectation of future earnings, and future abnormal returns would be uncorrelated with past earnings changes. Even if increased uncertainty caused by extreme earnings changes is relevant for pricing, it could not explain the evidence. While it is true in that case that a post-announcement drift (actually, a risk premium) would be observed, *it would be positive for both extreme-bad-news and extreme-good-news firms*. [See Brown, Harlow, and Tinic (1988).] Both the existing literature on post-announcement drift and this study (see table 2) document a negative drift for bad-news firms.

(2) *Does the evidence reflect autocorrelations in earnings that were observable ex post, but not predictable ex ante?*
Two pieces of evidence contradict this explanation. First, the autocorrelation patterns we observed in our sample period were also observed by Foster for

Table 7

Consistency (over time) of relation between market reactions to future earnings announcements and current-quarter earnings information.

	Mean abnormal return during three-day $[-2,0]$ window around earnings announcement for quarter $t+k$, for portfolio including long (short) position in firms in highest (lowest) decile of SUE in quarter t[a] (predicted sign of abnormal return in parentheses)			
Year	$t+1$ (+)	$t+2$ (+)	$t+3$ (+)	$t+4$ (−)
1974	3.74[c]	3.05[c]	0.89	NA[b]
1975	2.28[c]	0.80[c]	−0.43	−1.32[c]
1976	1.30[c]	0.41	−0.15	−0.98[c]
1977	1.69[c]	0.87[c]	−0.01	−0.41
1978	1.06[c]	0.78[c]	0.69[c]	−0.15
1979	1.08[c]	0.76[c]	−0.10	−0.39
1980	1.48[c]	0.87[c]	0.21	−0.98[c]
1981	1.10[c]	0.78[c]	0.20	−0.57[c]
1982	1.08[c]	0.26	−0.19	−1.05[c]
1983	1.11[c]	0.73[c]	0.12	−0.75[c]
1984	0.70[c]	0.50[c]	0.27	−0.06
1985	1.12[c]	0.19	−0.70	−0.91[c]
1986	0.84[c]	0.81[c]	0.54	−0.19

[a] SUE represents forecast error from the seasonal random-walk (with trend) earnings-expectation model, scaled by its estimation-period standard deviation. Abnormal returns are the differences between daily returns for individual firms in the SUE decile portfolio and returns for NYSE–AMEX firms of the same size decile, based on January 1 market values of equity.
[b] Since SUEs are calculated beginning in the first quarter of 1974, four-quarter-ahead predictions are not possible for any quarter in that year.
[c] Statistically significant at 0.05 level, one-tailed test.

1946–1974. In fact, the positive autocorrelations in earnings changes at lags 1, 2, and 3 are *weaker* during our sample period than in Foster's earlier period, making it difficult to argue that the market was justified in being surprised at the degree of autocorrelation in earnings observed in our sample. [Our own expectations were based largely on the evidence in Foster (1977), and the evidence in tables 2 through 5 was generated *before* we produced the autocorrelations reported in table 1.]

The second piece of evidence is presented in table 7. Although the market might err in its expectations about the degree of autocorrelation in earnings, it is difficult to explain how it could justifiably err in the same direction year after year. Table 7 shows that the mean three-day abnormal returns around the announcement for quarter $t+1$ and $t+2$ (for portfolios formed based on earnings of quarter t, as they were for table 2) is positive for *13 consecutive years*. The mean abnormal return around the announcement of quarter $t+4$ earnings is negative for each of the 12 years for which we have data. (Results for quarter $t+3$ are weak, but that is not unexpected, given the weak third-order autocorrelation in seasonally differenced earnings.) Of course, the consistency in the results also makes it that much harder to understand how competitive market forces could fail to eliminate the anomaly.

Incidentally, there is a suggestion in table 7 that the predictable component of the reaction to earnings announcements is larger in the first two to four years of our sample period (that is, 1974, 1975, and perhaps 1976 and 1977) than in subsequent years. This may raise questions about whether the effect has for some reason dissipated over time. However, when we conduct similar tests for the years 1971–1973, the results are quite similar to those for years after 1977.[14]

(3) Is the evidence explainable in terms of transactions costs?

One immediate response to this question is that, when the entire period from one earnings announcement to the next is considered, the abnormal returns appear to be in excess of transactions costs, perhaps even for small investors. (Recall the implied abnormal returns between the announcements for quarters t and $t+1$ of about 9 percent for the combined long and short positions underlying the last two regressions in table 5, panel A; the more simple strategy of going long (short) in extreme-good-news (extreme-bad-news) firms yields an abnormal return over 180 days of 4.5 percent, 8.9 percent, and 9.9 percent for large, medium, and small firms [Bernard and Thomas (1989, table 1)]. Moreover, Freeman and Tse (1989, table 7) document that when *SUE*s are measured using analysts' forecasts, the indicated drift is even larger – by 50 percent – than when *SUE*s are based on the statistical forecasts used by Bernard and Thomas.

Even if the abnormal returns *are* within transactions costs for small investors, a transactions-cost argument can at best provide only a partial explanation. First, and most important, *even if transactions costs cause 'sluggishness' in prices, it is hard to understand why the resulting 'mispricing' would last for months, or why it would be related to the historical time-series behavior of earnings. It is particularly difficult to reconcile 'price sluggishness' with the 'return reversal' we detect upon the announcement of earnings for quarter $t+4$.* Second, any transactions-cost-based explanation raises questions about why information can't be impounded in prices by traders for whom transactions costs are low, or other traders for whom the transactions costs are irrelevant (because they have already committed to buy or sell for reasons unrelated to earnings information). Third, while transactions costs may prevent trades and therefore prevent the impounding of new information, they cannot explain why information is not completely impounded, *given that trades have occurred.*

---

[14]Since our earnings data begin only in 1970, we have insufficient data to calculate the denominator of the *SUE* for years prior to 1974. Thus, for this supplemental analysis, we scaled unexpected earnings by the beginning-of-quarter stock-market value of equity. For the years for which both scale factors were available (1974–1986), the choice of scale factor does not alter the general nature of the results.

(4) *Could a research design flaw, such as a failure to control for risk, explain the evidence?*

While these possibilities can never be completely dismissed, we believe the evidence is more difficult to explain as a research design flaw than any previous evidence on post-announcement drift. Consider, for example, what would be necessary to explain the results in terms of a failure to control for risk shifts. Firms announcing good (bad) news at quarter t would need to experience a temporary upward (downward) shift in risk that occurs three months later, six months later, and nine months later, and then a downward (upward) shift in risk twelve months later. In addition to requiring risk changes in *opposite* directions for the same portfolios, this explanation also requires that the changes occur over short periods that coincide with an earnings-announcement date. Moreover, one would have to explain why the risk shifts are large, relative to those that generate 'normal' risk premia. Note that the three-day abnormal return around the announcement for quarter $t+1$ in table 2, panel A represents an annualized amount on the order of 200 percent (with no compounding).

Even if an explanation based on risk shifts could accommodate each of the above-mentioned features of the data, one important feature would remain to be explained. If the positive mean abnormal returns to zero-investment portfolios represent only a compensation for risk-bearing, then that risk should surface from time to time in the form of a loss. However, the consistent behavior of the abnormal returns through time (see table 7) indicates that the zero-investment strategy suggested by the anomaly would have earned positive abnormal returns for 13 consecutive years.

Potential bias related to imbalances in bids and asks. Even though risk shifts seem unlikely to explain the evidence, other research design flaws remain to be considered. Marais (1989), in discussing the post-announcement drift documented by Bernard and Thomas, notes that one 'cannot rule out consideration' of measurement errors in CRSP returns caused by an imbalance of bids and asks at the end of earnings-announcement days. Note that since CRSP prices are not 'true' prices, but may equal either the closing bid or closing ask, CRSP returns may be biased for any portfolio where there are more end-of-day transactions recorded at the bid than the ask, or vice versa [Keim (1989)]. Although such a bias could possibly play a role in our results, there is no compelling reason to expect it *ex ante*. It is not obvious why earnings for quarter t would have any bearing on whether closing prices are recorded at the bid or the ask after announcements that occur three to twelve months later. Further, it is not obvious why the bias from the imbalance would be a function of quarter t *SUE*s, or why it would switch signs from quarter $t+3$ to quarter $t+4$. One possibility is that institutional arrangements might lead some investors to prefer to buy (sell) after a year-to-year earnings increase (decrease) in earnings, even though the increase (decrease) was predictable and already reflected in prices. If so, their actions could cause stocks with good (bad) earnings news for quarter t to tend to close at the ask (bid) after the earnings announcement for quarter $t+1$, $t+2$, and $t+3$, and at the bid (ask) for quarter $t+4$. The resulting measurement error in CRSP returns would then give the appearance of abnormal returns in the directions we hypothesize.

To investigate this explanation, we conducted a test for bias due to imbalances in bid–ask spreads. If there is an imbalance between bids and asks on a given earnings announcement day, the bias should be reversed in subsequent days as the proportion of bids and asks returns to normal. Therefore, the positive (negative) estimated abnormal returns in the announcement period would be offset by negative (positive) estimated abnormal returns over the subsequent days. However, we find no compelling evidence of such a reversal in the two-day returns subsequent to the earnings-announcement day. Recall from table 2 that the abnormal returns for the three days prior to and including announcements for quarters $t+1$, $t+2$, $t+3$, and $t+4$ are 1.32 percent, 0.70 percent, 0.04 percent, and −0.66 percent for portfolios based on extreme *SUE* deciles. The corresponding abnormal returns for the two days after the announcement are −0.04 percent, −0.07 percent, −0.03 percent, and 0.05 percent. The *signs* of these abnormal returns are all consistent with a reversal of a bid–ask bias, but the *magnitudes* are statistically insignificant and fall far short of the amounts necessary to offset the announcement period returns. (Upon detecting evidence at least weakly consistent with a partial reversal over the first *two* post-announcement days, we then examined the *ten*-day post-announcement period, but again there was little or no evidence of a reversal.)

Potential hindsight bias arising from restatements of Compustat data. Another possibility is that our results are biased by the use of earnings data that represent Compustat restatements, rather than the earnings information actually made available on the announcement day. Compustat restates prior quarter earnings when firms undergo major acquisitions, make accounting changes, or separately report income from discontinued operations. Evidence in at least two prior studies [Watts (1978) and Foster, Olsen, and Shevlin (1984)] suggests that these restatements are not responsible for inducing post-announcement drift.[15] Furthermore, we can conceive of no reason why such restatements would induce a bias related to the autocorrelation structure of earnings.

---

[15]In his study of post-announcement drift, Watts (1978) used earnings data as originally reported. Foster, Olsen, and Shevlin (1984) collected earnings data as it was originally reported for a subsample of firms and detected post-announcement drift for that sample. [Foster, Olsen, and Shevlin (1984, p. 580) report that they hand-collected earnings-announcement dates. However, conversation with Olsen revealed that the earnings information itself was also hand-collected for this subsample.]

Despite the indications that Compustat restatements are unlikely to explain our results, we conducted an additional test for this form of hindsight bias. Our approach was to identify the 275 sample firms for which Compustat's annual earnings amount (which is *not* restated) matched (within one thousand dollars) the sum of quarterly earnings per Compustat for each of the 13 years in the dataset. When Compustat restatements occur in the first three quarters of the year, prior-year quarterly numbers are affected, thus destroying the articulation between Compustat's quarterly and annual amounts. Thus, our subsample includes firms for which over a 13-year period there was either never a restatement or only restatements that occurred in the fourth quarter (affecting only the first three interim reports of the current year). Thus, this subsample includes firms for which restatements (1) were probably less frequent than for the sample as a whole and (2) should not have affected the reported fourth-quarter earnings. Therefore, if restatements of Compustat data explain our results, then within this subsample we would expect (1) a weakening of the results across all quarters and (2) no ability to predict reactions to future earnings announcements based on fourth-quarter earnings information. In contrast, however, whether we use earnings information from all quarters or the fourth quarter only, we obtain results that are similar to (and actually somewhat stronger than) those for the full sample.

(5) *Do the three-day abnormal returns documented here represent the return on an implementable trading strategy, particularly since earnings-announcement dates cannot be predicted perfectly in advance?*

The evidence based on three-day abnormal returns is not intended as a study of an implementable strategy; rather, it is intended to help us better understand a previously documented, more readily implementable trading strategy that involves holding stocks over much longer intervals beginning the day after an earnings announcement [see table 2, panel B, the bottom half of table 5, panel A, and Bernard and Thomas (1989, especially section 3.2.5)]. Nevertheless, since post-announcement drift is concentrated around subsequent earnings announcements and since the timing of those announcements is rather predictable [Chambers and Penman (1984)], an interesting question arises. How large an abnormal return per unit time could be generated by taking positions just prior to the *expected* dates of earnings announcements?

To examine the issue, we assume investors construct portfolios in the same way implicit in regression eq. (8), and that the positions are taken 15 trading days prior to the expected announcement date, where the expected date is the actual announcement date for the comparable quarter of the prior year. We hold the position until the day earnings are announced, or for 30 days, whichever occurs first. The actual holding period is, on average, 15 days. The implied abnormal return to this strategy is 4.2 percent. On an annualized basis (before compounding), this is equivalent to 67 percent.

5. Relation to other research

Aside from Bernard and Thomas (1989) and Freeman and Tse (1989), the evidence presented here is most closely related to that of Wiggins (1990) and Mendenhall (forthcoming). Wiggins documents abnormal returns around subsequent earnings announcements that are consistent with those reported in our table 2; the most important distinction between this paper and Wiggins is that we develop the detailed relations between the signs and magnitudes of the abnormal returns and the autocorrelation structure of earnings.[16]

Mendenhall tests the validity of the Bernard and Thomas (1989) conjecture that market prices 'fail to reflect the full implications of current earnings for future earnings.' Mendenhall first documents that Value Line earnings forecasts are not efficient with respect to information in the latest earnings announcement – which is consistent with at least one set of market participants failing to respond completely to recent earnings information. Mendenhall then documents that reactions to earnings announcements can be partially predicted in advance, based on the most recent Value Line earnings-forecast revision. Thus, in forming earnings expectations, stock prices appear to ignore not only the full implications of prior earnings information, as documented here, but also previously announced analyst forecasts.

The evidence summarized here is also related to several other streams of research that are not focused directly on the issue of post-announcement drift.

Alternative earnings forecasts as proxies for market expectations. Several studies have compared earnings-forecast errors from alternative sources (analysts, statistical models, etc.) in terms of their ability to explain contemporaneous stock returns. Surprisingly, Foster (1977) finds that forecast errors from a seasonal random-walk model yield marginally greater explanatory power than errors from more accurate statistical models. Bathke and Lorek (1984) and O'Brien (1988) provide evidence that is inconsistent with Foster's anomalous result, but O'Brien offers another anomaly that is at least as surprising. Specifically, she finds that forecast errors from the Foster model provide better explanations of contemporaneous stock returns than forecast errors of analysts who report to IBES, even though the analysts' forecasts are more accurate. [However, Brown, Griffin, Hagerman, and Zmijewski (1987) find that forecast errors based on Value Line are more highly associated with contemporaneous returns.]

The evidence presented here suggests that the 'anomalies' uncovered in prior research may in fact reflect predictable errors in the earnings expecta-

---

[16]Although the first draft of this paper predates the first draft of the Wiggins (1990) paper, the two papers were developed independently.

tions underlying stock prices, as opposed to a research design flaw or some other explanation. If prices fail to reflect the implications of all publicly available information for future earnings, then it is possible that contemporaneous movements in stock prices are better explained by forecast errors based on an inferior forecasting source.

'Rationality' of the contemporaneous stock-price response to earnings. Kormendi and Lipe (1987) and Easton and Zmijewski (1989) find evidence consistent with stock prices reflecting cross-sectional differences in the time-series behavior of earnings, in terms of differences in the response to current earnings. Freeman and Tse (1989) find evidence consistent with stock prices reflecting at least some of the implications of current earnings for future earnings. The evidence presented here suggests that, while stock prices may *partially* reflect such information, they evidently do not reflect *all* available information. In fact, given that post-announcement drift per unit time is not much smaller than pre-announcement drift [see Bernard and Thomas (1989), figs. 1 and 2)], the evidence suggests that the market's impounding of available information may be far from complete.

Other evidence on market efficiency. Several recent studies offer evidence interpreted as inconsistent with semi-strong market efficiency. At least two of these [Hand (1990) and Ou and Penman (1989)] could be viewed as indications that stock prices reflect a naive earnings expectation. In that sense, the studies are consistent with the evidence presented here. However, Hand focuses on an unusual sample (firms that reported gains from debt–equity swaps), and thus it is not clear that the phenomenon underlying his results is linked with that studied here. Ou and Penman (1989, p. 327) conclude that their ability to predict future abnormal returns based on fundamental analysis is distinct from the phenomenon of post-announcement drift. Perhaps no single theme could explain each of these anomalies.

6. Concluding remarks

The evidence summarized here is consistent with the hypothesis that stock prices partially reflect a naive earnings expectation: that future earnings will be equal to earnings for the comparable quarter of the prior year. We considered a variety of alternative explanations for the evidence, including problems with risk adjustment and the impact of transactions costs, but were unable to support the viability of any of them.

In some ways, evidence like that presented here raises more questions than it answers. Why markets as competitive as the NYSE or AMEX would behave as if they are influenced by naive earnings expectations is difficult to understand.

Another question concerns the economic importance of the effects documented here. In one sense, the degree of 'mispricing' that might be indicated by post-announcement drift is 'small' – less than 5 percent of price per position, even for cases of extreme earnings realizations [see Bernard and Thomas (1989) and the long-interval results in tables 2 and 4 of this paper]. However, in some other ways, the potential effect is large. First, previous studies [e.g., Bernard and Thomas (1989, table 1)] have found that what appears to be a delayed reaction to earnings is more than one-third as large as the anticipatory and contemporaneous reaction. Second, we find here that the three-day announcement-period returns on portfolios constructed with only *prior*-quarter earnings information are approximately half as large as the return to portfolios constructed using the *contemporaneous* earnings information. Such evidence may be cause for concern in interpreting the results of the many studies that assume that earnings information is fully impounded by the end of the earnings-announcement day. Moreover, if market prices fail to reflect fully the implications of information as freely available as earnings, how well do they reflect information that is not as well-publicized?

References

Albrecht, S., L. Lookabill, and J. McKeown, 1977, The time series properties of annual earnings, Journal of Accounting Research 15, 226–244.

Ball, R. and S.P. Kothari, 1990, Security returns around earnings announcements, Working paper (University of Rochester, Rochester, NY).

Ball, R., S.P. Kothari, and R. Watts, 1988, The economics of the relation between earnings changes and stock returns, Working paper (University of Rochester, Rochester, NY).

Bathke, A. and K. Lorek, 1984, The relationship between time-series models and the security market's expectation of quarterly earnings, The Accounting Review 59, 163–176.

Bernard, V., 1984, The use of market data and accounting data in hedging against consumer price inflation, Journal of Accounting Research 22, 445–466.

Bernard, V., 1987, Cross-sectional dependence and problems in inference in market-based accounting research, Journal of Accounting Research 25, 1–48.

Bernard, V. and J. Thomas, 1989, Post-earnings-announcement drift: Delayed price response or risk premium? Journal of Accounting Research, Suppl. 27, 1–36.

Brown, L., P. Griffin, R. Hagerman, and M. Zmijewski, 1987, An evaluation of alternative proxies for the market's assessment of unexpected earnings, Journal of Accounting and Economics 9, 159–194.

Brown, L.P. and M. Rozeff, 1979, Univariate time-series models of quarterly accounting earnings per share: A proposed model, Journal of Accounting Research 17, 179–189.

Brown, K., W. Harlow, and S. Tinic, 1988, Risk aversion, uncertain information, and market efficiency, Journal of Financial Economics 21, 355–386.

Chambers, A. and S. Penman, 1984, Timeliness of reporting and the stock price reaction to earnings announcements, Journal of Accounting Research 21, 21–47.

Chari, V., R. Jagannathan, and A. Ofer, 1988, Seasonalities in security returns: The case of earnings announcements, Journal of Financial Economics 21, 101–121.

Easton, P. and M. Zmijewski, 1989, Cross-sectional variation in the stock market response to the announcement of accounting earnings, Journal of Accounting and Economics 11, 117–142.

Fama, E. and J. MacBeth, 1973, Risk, return, and equilibrium: Empirical tests, Journal of Political Economy 38, 607–636.

Foster, G., 1977, Quarterly accounting data: Time series properties and predictive-ability results, The Accounting Review 52, 1–21.

Foster, G., C. Olsen, and T. Shevlin, 1984, Earnings releases, anomalies, and the behavior of security returns, The Accounting Review 59, 574–603.

Freeman, R. and S. Tse, 1989, The multi-period information content of earnings announcements: Rational delayed reactions to earnings news, Journal of Accounting Research, Suppl. 27, 49–79.

Hand, J.R., 1990, A test of the extended functional fixation hypothesis, The Accounting Review 65, 740–763.

Holthausen, R., 1983, Abnormal returns following quarterly earnings announcements, in: Proceedings of the CRSP seminar on the analysis of security prices (University of Chicago, Chicago, IL) 37–59.

Jaffe, J.F., 1974, Special information and insider trading, Journal of Business 47, 410–428.

Joy, O.M., R. Litzenberger, and R. McEnally, 1977, The adjustment of stock prices to announcements of unanticipated changes in quarterly earnings, Journal of Accounting Research 15, 207–225.

Keim, D.B., 1989, Trading patterns, bid–ask spreads and estimated security returns: The case of common stocks at calendar turning points, Journal of Financial Economics 25, 75–98.

Kormendi, R. and R. Lipe, 1987, Earnings innovations, earnings persistence, and stock returns, Journal of Business 60, 323–346.

Marais, M.L., 1989, Discussion of post-earnings-announcement drift: Delayed price response or risk premium?, Journal of Accounting Research, Suppl. 27, 37–48.

Mendenhall, R., forthcoming, Evidence of possible underweighting of earnings-related information, Journal of Accounting Research.

O'Brien, P., 1988, Analysts' forecasts as earnings expectations, Journal of Accounting and Economics 10, 53–83.

Ou, J. and S. Penman, 1989a, Financial statement analysis and the prediction of stock returns, Journal of Accounting and Economics 11, 295–330.

Ou, J. and S. Penman, 1989b, Accounting measurement, price–earnings ratios, and the information content of security prices, Journal of Accounting Research, Suppl. 27, 111–144.

Poterba, J.M. and L.H. Summers, 1988, Mean reversion in stock prices: Evidence and implications, Journal of Financial Economics 21, 27–59.

Rendleman, R.J., Jr., C.P. Jones, and H.A. Latane, 1982, Empirical anomalies based on unexpected earnings and the importance of risk adjustments, Journal of Financial Economics 10, 269–287.

Rendleman, R.J., Jr., C.P. Jones, and H.A. Latane, 1987. Further insight into the standardized unexpected earnings anomaly: Size and serial correlation effects, The Financial Review 22, 131–144.

Watts, R.L., 1975, The time series behavior of quarterly earnings, Working paper (University of Newcastle, Newcastle, NSW).

Watts, R.L., 1978, Systematic 'abnormal' returns after quarterly earnings announcements, Journal of Financial Economics 6, 127–150.

Wiggins, J.B., 1990, Do misperceptions about the earnings process contribute to post-announcement drift, Working paper (Cornell University, Ithaca, NY).

FINANCIAL STATEMENT ANALYSIS AND THE PREDICTION OF STOCK RETURNS*

Jane A. OU
Santa Clara University, Santa Clara, CA 95053, USA

Stephen H. PENMAN
University of California, Berkeley, CA 94720, USA

Received January 1988, final version received April 1989

This paper performs a financial statement analysis that combines a large set of financial statement items into one summary measure which indicates the direction of one-year-ahead earnings changes. Positions are taken in stocks on the basis of this measure during the period 1973–1983, which involve cancelling long and short positions with zero net investment. The two-year holding-period return to the long and short positions is in the order of 12.5%. After adjustment for 'size effects' the return is about 7.0%. These returns cannot be explained by nominated firm risk characteristics.

1. Introduction

Financial statement analysis identifies aspects of financial statements that are relevant to investment decisions. One goal of the analysis is to assess firm value from financial statements. Much empirical accounting research has attempted to discover value-relevant accounting attributes in order to enhance financial statement analysis. The approach taken in this work assumes that market price is sufficient for determining firms' values and thus serves as a benchmark against which to evaluate the information in accounting measures. Accounting attributes are inferred to be value-relevant because they are contemporaneously statistically associated with stock prices. For example, the seminal work of Ball and Brown (1968) and the many successive 'information content' papers indicate that accounting earnings and some of its components capture information that is contained in stock prices.

*We have benefited from many conversations with Jim Ohlson. The comments of participants in the Stanford University 1987 summer accounting conference and workshops at Berkeley, the University of Chicago, Michigan State University, and the University of Texas at Austin are also appreciated. In particular, Ray Ball, Dan Collins, George Foster, Prem Jain, Laurentius Marais, Maureen McNichols, Richard Sansing, Katherine Schipper, Peter Wilson, Ross Watts, Mark Wolfson, and Robert Holthausen (the referee) provided helpful comments.

Traditional 'fundamental analysis', however, embraces a different perspective. Firms' ('fundamental') values are indicated by information in financial statements. Stock prices deviate at times from these values and only slowly gravitate towards the fundamental values. Thus, analysis of published financial statements can discover values that are not reflected in stock prices. Rather than taking prices as value benchmarks, 'intrinsic values' discovered from financial statements serve as benchmarks with which prices are compared to identify overpriced and underpriced stocks. Because deviant prices ultimately gravitate to the fundamentals, investment strategies which produce 'abnormal returns' can be discovered by the comparison of prices to these fundamental values.

There have been many claims of market efficiency with respect to 'publicly available' accounting information, but (astonishingly, when one considers the many tests of technical analysis) little research into the competing claim of fundamental analysis.[1] This paper examines this claim. We outline a method of financial statement analysis that extracts a summary value measure from financial statements. This measure is an indicator of the direction of future earnings. Positions are taken in stocks on the basis of this measure and returns to the positions are observed. These procedures approximate the program of traditional fundamental analysis of discovering value-relevant attributes of firms from financial statements and taking market positions based on these. The results indicate that the summary measure robustly predicts future stock returns. Trading strategies based on predictions of future earnings from 'publicly available' financial statement information capture a significant portion of returns to the Ball and Brown (hypothetical) strategy based on perfect foreknowledge of those future earnings. Further, the returns to these strategies are not explained by aspects of firms that have been nominated as risk attributes.

In the next section we describe our financial statement analysis that extracts the summary value measure from financial statements. We also outline our preset program for utilizing this measure in investment strategies. Then, after summarizing the data in section 3, we describe the results of the execution of the program in section 4. Section 5 examines the extent to which returns predicted by the value measure are explained by firms' conjectured risk characteristics. Finally, a short summary of the results is given in section 6.

2. The approach

The tests in the paper involve observation of returns to investment strategies based on a measure that summarizes information in financial statements. In

---

[1] Many papers examine the ability of 'fundamentals' to predict returns, but test trading rules suggested by those with experience with the data on the same data from which that experience was gained. Exceptions are McKibben (1972) and Oppenheimer (1981).

this section we describe the financial statement analysis that produces this measure and outline features of the trading strategy that employs it.

2.1. The financial statement analysis

Fundamental analysis maintains that firms' values are indicated by information in financial statements. However, the methods by which these values are extracted from financial statements are unclear. Traditional financial statement analysis provides little guidance for this task. Textbooks describe the calculation of financial statement ratios but provide scant prescription as to how these should be used. Ratios are identified with such constructs as 'profitability', 'turnover', and 'liquidity', but the relationship of these operating characteristics to value is not apparent. Our financial statement analysis is an attempt to operationalize the notion of extracting values from financial statements. The large array of financial statement items are combined into a scalar that maps from the financial statements to the payoffs to securities.

A simple valuation model can be expressed as

$$V = \mathrm{E}(d)/r, \tag{1}$$

where V is a stock's value (equal to price in an efficient market), $\mathrm{E}(d)$ is expected future dividends, and r the rate at which future dividends are discounted. The discount rate reflects security risk. Both $\mathrm{E}(d)$ and r are assessed on the basis of financial statement and other information available. Thus, for determining firm values [and for taking market positions on the basis of information about either $\mathrm{E}(d)$ or r], the analyst desires to distinguish those accounting attributes that indicate positive-value expected payoffs in the numerator of (1) from those that indicate negative-value risk characteristics in the denominator.[2] We have in mind an accounting indicator of the numerator. Thus we identify those financial statement attributes that are correlated with future payoffs and combine these into one 'positive-value' measure. This approach is in contrast to but complements the financial statement analysis of Beaver, Kettler, and Scholes (1970) and Rosenberg and Marathe (1975), which seeks to discover financial statement measures that are related to risk [in the denominator of (1)] and which thus predict expected stock returns. As firm risk is not well-understood, one cannot guarantee that our measure will not reflect risk, but the procedure is likely to reduce the possibility.[3] As a check we

---

[2] There is some license taken with terminology here. In the theory of valuation under uncertainty [Rubinstein (1976)], risk adjustments appear in the numerator rather than the denominator. See also Ohlson (1988).

[3] An alternative way to proceed might be to discover those financial statement items that predict future stock returns directly [as in McKibbon (1972), for example]. This, however, poses an identification problem: if these items predict cross-sectional differences in stock returns, one cannot ascertain whether they distinguish differential expected returns due to risk differences or whether they predict 'abnormal' returns due to mispricing of fundamentals in the market. Our approach is an attempt to reduce this identification problem.

investigate whether returns predicted by the measure can be explained by firm characteristics that have been suggested as risk attributes in the literature.

The critical task in the endeavor is the identification of payoff indicators in the financial statements. Valuation theory [of which (1) is a crude representation] indicates that observables should be identified on the basis of their correlation with future dividends [see Rubinstein (1976) and Garman and Ohlson (1980)]. Unfortunately, the available history of dividend payouts is such that one cannot observe the full set of realizations of dividends that investors perceive as possible in their ex ante assessments. Indeed, Miller and Modigliani (1961) results suggest that payouts, exclusive of liquidation dividends (which typically are not observed), are arbitrary and unrelated to value, or driven by tax considerations. We are impressed, however, by one of the most robust results in empirical research in accounting, namely the Ball and Brown (1968) finding that accounting earnings are valued positively by investors. Higher (lower) earnings imply higher (lower) values. We are guided also by the intuition that future dividends are 'paid out of earnings'. Thus we identify future earnings as a value-relevant attribute of interest. Note that Grahamite principles stress the notion of 'future earnings power' as the most important valuation notion.[4]

Given future earnings are value-relevant, it is desirable to identify financial descriptors on the basis of their ability to predict earnings for many years in the future. We limit our investigation to one-year-ahead earnings. The disregard for information about earnings more than one year ahead produces a conservative bias to our tests, that is, towards the null hypothesis of market efficiency. The following year's earnings variable is specified as a binary outcome, an earnings increase or an earnings decrease. Thus financial statement descriptors published in a given annual report are selected on the basis of their ability to predict the direction of the annual earnings change in the following year. There is a loss of information in the binary specification, but we were concerned that, given outliers common to accounting data, estimation with dollar magnitudes might produce parameter estimates that perform poorly in out-of-sample prediction and result in investment strategies that give undue weight to estimation errors. The binary specification also permits a comparison of returns to the trading strategy with those of a Ball and Brown (1968) strategy which is based on perfect foreknowledge of the binary outcome.

Our estimation technique is LOGIT. Selected attributes are parsimoniously incorporated in a LOGIT model which, when estimated, delivers our summary

---

[4]'The most important single factor determining a stock's value is now held to be the *indicated average future earning power*, i.e., the estimated average earnings for a future span of years. Intrinsic value would then be found by first forecasting this earning power and then multiplying that prediction by an appropriate ' capitalization factor'. Graham, Dodd, and Cottle (1962, p. 28), emphasis in the original.

value measure. This is the estimated probability of an earnings increase in the subsequent year that is indicated jointly by descriptors in the financial statements and the LOGIT model. We denote the estimate of this for a given firm i in fiscal year t as $\hat{Pr}_{it}$. We will refer to this as $\hat{Pr}$, with the subscripts understood. This measure is an assessment of the relative ability of firms to generate earnings in the subsequent year. Thus it has the character of a 'future earning power' attribute referred to by traditional fundamental analysts.

In estimating $\hat{Pr}$, we choose, as the earnings variable in year $t+1$, the change in primary earnings-per-share before extraordinary items. Because earnings increases tend to outnumber earnings decreases, we define the variable as $\text{e.p.s.}_{it+1} - \text{e.p.s.}_{it} - \text{drift}_{it+1}$ to take out the firm-specific trend. The drift term was estimated as the mean earnings-per-share change over the four years prior to year $t+1$.

Because a limited number of observations of accounting variables are available for many individual firms, the LOGIT model is estimated based on data pooled over firms and time. This brings much more information to the estimates of parameters. However, if a general model is not a good representation for all firms (to the extent to which different characteristics generate future earnings in different firms in different ways), we again introduce a conservative bias to the tests.

2.2. The trading strategy

Stocks are assigned to investment positions on the basis of these $\hat{Pr}$ values. In designing an investment strategy, three principles are followed. First, information not available at the time the investment strategies could actually have been implemented is excluded in an attempt to minimize ex post bias. Second, we follow a fixed, preset program that does not reflect earlier experience with the data. We thus avoid statistical overfitting. Third, the analysis is carried out on a large sample of firms and replicated over a considerable period of time. Thus there is ability to evaluate robustness of results within the sample.

The trading strategy is developed as follows. Steps 1–3 involve the selection of accounting attributes and the consolidation of these into the summary measure. Step 4 involves the utilization of this summary measure in stock selection.

1. During an estimation period, the ability of a large number of financial statement attributes to predict future earnings is assessed by reference to observed correlations in the data. No conscious attempt is made to assess predictive ability on the basis of what we think should work or what we have observed to work from experience. Selected possible predictors are nominated after a survey of financial accounting and financial analysis texts

available at the beginning of the sample period. 'Let the data speak' is the motto here: the predictive ability of the financial statement attributes could have been observed by investors at the end of the estimation period.
2. Weights that combine financial statement attributes (that demonstrate predictive ability in step 1) into the $\hat{P}r$ summary measure are estimated from the data during the estimation period.
3. Using the selected accounting attributes and estimated weights, $\hat{P}r$ values are calculated for each stock in the sample from financial statements published for fiscal years after the estimation period.
4. Stocks are then assigned to long and short investment positions on the basis of this measure. The investment strategy is implemented according to a preset program describing execution dates (outside the estimation period and at a point in time when the financial statement attributes were publicly available), cut-off criteria for assignment to positions, weights given to securities in portfolios, and holding periods for the positions.

This approach is a conservative one. Our fixed program is only one of many possible and there is no guarantee that we have selected the best, or even a good one. Further, one might conjecture that had we 'thought a little' about the selection of accounting attributes, results could be 'improved'.

In assessing investment return performance, we do not compare observed returns to benchmarks described by a particular asset pricing model. Rather, we report returns to cancelling long and short positions (requiring zero net investment) which are indicated by the value measure. We then assess whether the returns to this position can be explained by attributes that are popular candidates for risk proxies – estimated market beta, return variance, firm size, earnings yield, market premium over book value, and leverage.

3. The sample

Annual financial statement information is obtained from the COMPUSTAT annual report files. These files contain an extensive list of 'above-the-line' accounting line items. The 1984 COMPUSTAT Annual Primary, Supplementary, and Tertiary File is merged with the 1984 COMPUSTAT Research File (which contains all firms dropped from COMPUSTAT files between 1971 and 1984) to obtain data on the complete set of firms covered by COMPUSTAT from 1970 to 1984. We thus reduce the ex post selection bias associated with the current COMPUSTAT file. COMPUSTAT claims that listed firms are comprehensive with respect to industrial firms whose common stock is traded on the NYSE or AMEX, and in addition includes a set of utilities and financial firms.

For these firms, the files provide a financial statement history from 1965 to 1984. Because accounting data from 1965 to 1972 are used to estimate the

Table 1

Selection of firms for analysis.

Year	Firms with at least one data item on COMPUSTAT Annual or Research file Annual	Research	Total	Firms rejected due to missing model descriptors Annual	Research	Total	Total firms available for predictions Annual	Research	Total	Firms not on CRSP files	Firms not listed on CRSP at month 1[a]	Firms in trading strategy	Firms with returns on CRSP files at April 1 of following year[b]
1973	1855	1042	2897	707	338	1045	1148	704	1852	50	170	1632	2687
1974	1946	993	2939	768	301	1069	1178	692	1870	49	172	1649	2641
1975	1961	934	2895	732	235	967	1229	699	1928	47	178	1703	2542
1976	1976	872	2848	715	206	921	1261	666	1927	41	171	1715	2562
1977	2005	777	2782	705	189	894	1300	588	1888	35	183	1670	2488
1978	2050	670	2720	715	171	886	1335	499	1834	31	178	1625	2423
1979	2101	561	2662	735	151	886	1366	410	1776	27	144	1605	2356
1980	2149	480	2629	777	147	924	1372	333	1705	25	98	1582	2340
1981	2190	372	2562	798	118	916	1392	254	1646	24	71	1551	2329
1982	2248	276	2524	831	96	927	1417	180	1597	24	51	1522	2276
1983	2317	183	2500	881	63	944	1436	120	1556	22	31	1503	2292
Total	22798	7160	29958	8364	2015	10379	14434	5145	19579	375	1447	17757	26936

[a] Month 1 is the first month in which firms are held in investment strategies. It is three months after the end of the fiscal year for which descriptors were reported.
[b] CRSP is the Center for Research in Security Prices at the University of Chicago.

earnings prediction model[5] and because portfolios are held for two years after financial statement dates (and 1985 CRSP returns files were used), investment strategies are implemented based on financial statement information for fiscal years 1973 to 1983. The number of observations with financial statement information in each of these years is indicated in the first 'Total' column in table 1. These numbers are greater than the number of observations with returns on CRSP files at (approximately) the financial statement date, indicated in the column to the extreme right of the table. The difference presumably represents firms included in the COMPUSTAT files but not traded on the NYSE or AMEX.

Our design calls for a comprehensive set of financial statement variables as descriptors in the earnings prediction model. Including all possible variables in such a model places too much of a demand on the data, however. If a model is estimated with a large set of descriptors from pooled data, firm observations will be lost in prediction out of sample if merely one accounting item is missing or not available for a firm.

For this reason, we reduce the number of descriptors in our estimation to a parsimonious set that captures the information in the complete set of descriptors, as described later. Despite the attempt to reduce the set of financial statement descriptors to a parsimonious set, firms are rejected in obtaining out-of-sample estimates of Pr if one or more of the descriptors in this set is missing or if a descriptor is one which is measuring an activity in which the firm is not involved. This reduces the set of firms for which the summary measure can be calculated to that indicated in the last 'Total' column in table 1. This amount, less firms without returns on CRSP files at the date that investment positions are taken, is the number of observations used in the trading strategies based on $\hat{Pr}$, as indicated in table 1.

The elimination of observations because of missing descriptors is the price of demanding a comprehensive financial statement analysis and using a general prediction model based on pooled data. It should be noted that this introduces ex post bias only if descriptors are available for eliminated firms but COMPUSTAT does not report them. It does, however, reduce the generality of the results to firms with operating characteristics summarized by the model. The industry composition of the final sample is similar to that on the COMPUSTAT files with the exception that there are very few electric and gas utilities (SIC code 49) and banks, financial, and real estate companies (SIC codes 60-69). These firms typically do not have the attributes identified by the prediction models.

---

[5]We extended this history back to 1961 by using data on firms listed on the 1980–1982 COMPUSTAT annual files. Because of the requirement to estimate an earnings drift parameter over four years, this significantly enlarged the number of observations. Note, however, that the earnings prediction model was estimated using data from 1965 on. The 1961–1964 data was used only to estimate drift parameters.

4. The execution

4.1. Calculation of the summary value measure, $\hat{P}r$

The predictive ability of financial statement attributes is assessed using annual report data over the period 1965–1972 and again over the period 1973–1977.[6] Table 2 lists the 68 descriptors investigated. In the first stage, each descriptor was included as the sole explanatory variable in a LOGIT earnings prediction model. To estimate the parameters of the models, observations are pooled across firms and across time. Thus every paired observation of each accounting descriptor and directional future earnings change (less estimated drift) that is available in the data is included, excluding any possible selection bias. Firms are not excluded because of 'missing model descriptors' at this stage.

The coefficient estimates for all 68 accounting descriptors are given in table 2 along with a χ_1^2 statistic (and p-value) relevant to the assessment of the estimated value relative to zero.[7] In both periods 34 (or 50%) of the coefficient estimates have p-values less than 0.10. The estimates within each estimation period are not from independent observations, however. The reader may wish to compare these estimates with his or her intuition about future earnings-generating attributes of firms. We choose to distance ourself from the data, so do not develop 'stories' that rationalize the signs of the coefficient estimates here. The consistency of the sign and significance levels of the estimated coefficients on the descriptors over the two mutually exclusive estimation periods requires emphasis, however. Of the 34 descriptors with p-values less than 0.10 in the first period, 32 have the same sign on the estimated coefficient in the second period and of these 32, only 6 did not have p-values less than 0.10. Similar consistency is observed (in the first period) for descriptors with p-values less than 0.10 in the second period. This indicates that we have captured attributes of firms that demonstrate some regularity in generating earnings and that predictive ability will hold up outside of the estimation periods.

To reduce these 68 descriptors to a parsimonious set, we follow the procedures. In a second stage we include in a multivariate model all descriptors for which coefficient estimates significant at the 0.10 level are observed in the univariate estimations. We then drop all variables for which coefficient estimates in this multivariate estimation are not significant at the 0.10 level, leaving 19 variables for the 1965–1972 period and 18 for the 1973–1977

---

[6]The first period is longer than the second because of the need to calculate an earnings drift term over four years preceding the relevant earnings prediction year and because the 1984 COMPUSTAT files used have data only from 1965 onwards. On this issue, see footnote 5.

[7]The Logist procedure in the Statistical Analysis System (SAS) was used in all LOGIT model estimations.

Table 2
Univariate LOGIT estimation results for all accounting descriptors selected.

Descriptor number	Accounting descriptor[a]	1965–1972 estimation				1973–1977 estimation			
		N^b	θ^c	χ_i^2	p-value	N^b	θ^c	χ_i^2	p-value
1	Current ratio	14683	0.0029	0.34	0.562	12679	−0.0009	0.98	0.323
2	%Δ in 1	14607	0.0037	0.01	0.921	12362	−0.0701	3.14	0.077
3	Quick ratio	14683	0.0019	0.14	0.710	12679	−0.0009	1.02	0.312
4	%Δ in 3	13376	0.0823	5.67	0.017	11828	0.1500	17.12	0.000
5	Days sales in accs. receivable	15632	0.0001	0.01	0.925	13712	−0.0001	0.60	0.438
6	%Δ in 5	13306	−0.0647	2.33	0.127	11732	−0.0090	0.31	0.581
7	Inventory turnover	12809	0.0024	0.08	0.775	11100	−0.0023	5.47	0.019
8	%Δ in 7	12708	0.1074	4.11	0.043	11032	0.4917	40.62	0.000
9	Inventory/total assets	15604	−0.0091	0.01	0.924	13724	−0.2181	4.93	0.026
10	%Δ in 9	12836	−0.0410	2.85	0.049	11116	−0.4151	48.08	0.000
11	%Δ in inventory	12843	−0.0691	9.73	0.002	11116	−0.4521	91.94	0.000
12	%Δ in sales	15594	−0.1134	11.81	0.001	13704	−0.2816	19.91	0.000
13	%Δ in depreciation	14598	−0.0999	10.02	0.002	12530	−0.2108	16.34	0.000
14	Δ in dividend per share	15840	−2.7033	176.91	0.000	13732	−1.5693	118.58	0.000
15	Depreciation/plant assets	15540	1.4788	38.55	0.000	13445	0.8490	13.44	0.000
16	%Δ in 15	14536	0.3553	34.31	0.000	12515	0.2636	16.36	0.000
17	Return on opening equity	15529	−2.9291	32.10	0.000	13607	−2.9960	389.99	0.000
18	Δ in 17	15477	−0.0362	0.91	0.341	13522	−0.3660	19.86	0.000
19	%Δ in (capital expenditure/ total assets)	13378	−0.0193	5.55	0.018	12466	−0.0531	10.71	0.001
20	19, one-year lag	12661	−0.0169	3.98	0.046	12396	−0.0631	16.17	0.000
21	Debt–equity ratio	15559	0.0145	13.86	0.000	13340	0.0296	28.28	0.000
22	%Δ in 21	15443	0.0514	6.79	0.009	13294	0.1029	6.27	0.012
23	LT debt to equity	15559	0.0400	9.72	0.002	13607	0.0004	0.03	0.861
24	%Δ in 23	13205	−0.0025	1.17	0.279	12407	0.0046	1.23	0.268
25	Equity to fixed assets	15559	−0.0013	0.95	0.329	13445	0.0003	0.50	0.481
26	%Δ in 25	15421	−0.0072	1.29	0.255	13342	−0.0269	1.83	0.176
27	Times interest earned	15023	−0.0001	0.86	0.350	12557	0.0003	1.85	0.174
28	%Δ in 27	11904	−0.0001	0.17	0.676	10891	0.0006	1.87	0.172
29	Sales/total assets	15604	−0.0241	2.15	0.142	13724	−0.0444	6.88	0.001
30	%Δ in 29	15527	0.1593	6.80	0.009	13704	0.1383	3.52	0.069
31	Return on total assets	15604	−6.4210	342.53	0.000	13724	−6.7617	361.45	0.000
32	Return on closing equity	15559	−4.0550	366.11	0.000	13607	−0.9786	60.87	0.000
33	Gross margin ratio	15833	−0.2577	20.77	0.000	13731	−0.0889	2.28	0.131
34	%Δ in 33	13388	0.0027	0.02	0.886	11936	0.0017	0.31	0.576

35	Op. profit (before dep.) to sales	15632	−0.9918	75.33	0.000	13712	−1.2560	108.82	0.000
36	%Δ in 35	15582	−0.0001	0.06	0.804	13688	−0.0000	0.40	0.343
37	Pretax income to sales	15632	−1.9240	162.73	0.000	13712	−1.6467	504.70	0.000
38	%Δ in 37	15578	−0.0001	0.02	0.860	13692	−0.0054	5.72	0.017
39	Net profit margin	15632	−2.3731	124.39	0.000	13712	−1.7202	475.99	0.000
40	%Δ in 39	15580	−0.0075	0.01	0.891	13692	0.0005	0.02	0.880
41	Sales to total cash	14296	0.0001	0.15	0.698	12886	−0.0002	4.42	0.035
42	Sales to accs. receivable	13402	−0.0011	2.54	0.108	11745	0.0003	1.21	0.271
43	Sales to inventory	12890	0.0008	2.21	0.137	11144	−0.0009	2.42	0.120
44	%Δ in 43	12799	0.1426	11.16	0.001	11091	0.4519	48.85	0.000
45	Sales to working capital	14687	−0.0001	0.01	0.925	12709	0.0003	0.21	0.648
46	%Δ in 45	14581	−0.0005	0.34	0.562	12357	−0.0016	1.26	0.261
47	Sales to fixed assets	15540	0.0001	0.00	0.980	13445	−0.0008	0.07	0.794
48	%Δ in production	12702	−0.1058	13.43	0.000	11022	−0.0380	3.07	0.080
49	%Δ in R&D	2338	−0.1762	5.11	0.024	5283	−0.0133	1.08	0.298
50	%Δ in (R&D/sales)	2337	−0.1017	1.82	0.177	5277	−0.0076	0.37	0.540
51	%Δ in advertising expense	657	0.0596	0.11	0.739	5699	0.0012	0.14	0.709
52	%Δ in (advertising/sales)	657	0.3493	2.56	0.109	5690	0.0038	0.42	0.517
53	%Δ in total assets	15552	−0.4691	69.77	0.000	13714	−1.1751	149.28	0.000
54	Cash flow to total debt	15592	−0.2258	32.75	0.000	13716	−0.0538	6.03	0.014
55	Working capital/total assets	15604	0.0850	1.16	0.282	13724	−0.1720	5.17	0.023
56	%Δ in 55	14464	0.0010	0.73	0.394	12707	−0.0006	0.01	0.932
57	Operating income/total assets	15604	−2.4455	182.86	0.000	13724	−2.8025	214.54	0.000
58	%Δ in 57	14198	0.0017	0.13	0.717	12272	−0.0023	0.07	0.795
59	%Δ in total uses of funds	2057	−0.0686	4.39	0.038	11817	−0.0077	0.79	0.374
60	%Δ in total sources of funds	2006	−0.0533	6.66	0.010	11621	−0.0028	1.02	0.313
61	Repayment of LT debt as % of total LT debt	13301	0.8894	70.47	0.000	12556	0.0405	2.90	0.089
62	Issuance of LT debt as % of total LT debt	12176	0.0391	5.06	0.025	9689	−0.0033	0.44	0.509
63	Purchase of treasury stock as % of stock	15840	−1.5440	39.15	0.000	13370	−0.0000	0.08	0.775
64	%Δ in funds	2052	−0.0035	2.26	0.133	11809	0.0003	0.54	0.464
65	%Δ in LT debt	13301	−0.0047	2.22	0.132	12556	−0.0039	0.59	0.444
66	Cash dividend as % of cash flows	15838	1.7335	158.05	0.000	13732	−0.0011	0.00	0.957
67	%Δ in working capital	14668	0.0002	0.09	0.769	12707	−0.0002	0.08	0.780
68	Net income over cash flows	15835	−0.0073	1.15	0.284	13732	−0.0019	0.04	0.847

[a] Δ indicates changes. In calculating %Δ, observations with zero denominators are excluded and absolute values are used in all denominators.
[b] N is the number of observations in the estimations.
[c] β̂ is the maximum likelihood estimate of the coefficient on the accounting descriptor.

period. In a third and final stage we investigate each of the remaining variables step-wise, deleting descriptors not significant at the 0.10 level with all other descriptors included. In this stage, 3 descriptors are dropped in the 1965–1972 period, but none in the 1973–1977 period. It is of course more desirable to proceed step-wise with the original 68 descriptors, but this calls for elimination of any firm without the full set of descriptors.

The final models (with 16 descriptors in the first estimation period and 18 in the second) are summarized in table 3. The various test statistics indicate significant ability of the descriptors to jointly describe subsequent earnings changes. At first glance there does not appear to be much consistency in the descriptors included in the models for the two periods. Of the 28 descriptors in either period, only 6 appear in both models. However, these are multivariate models and the inclusion of a particular variable and the sign on its estimated coefficient will depend on variables already in the model at the relevant step in the step-wise procedure. Notice that many of the descriptors capture similar operating characteristics. For example, inventories, sales, and deflated earnings appear in more than one descriptor. For the years 1973–1983 (the years for which investment positions are taken), we estimated $\hat{Pr}$ with both models and for each of these years estimated the correlation between the two values. The mean for the eleven years is 0.62. For a classification of $\hat{Pr}$ values above 0.5 and below 0.5, the two models classify firms consistently 78.7% of the time during these years. This indicates that the two models are capturing a similar phenomenon.

For each fiscal year 1973 to 1983, the summary value measure, $\hat{Pr}$, is calculated from financial statements for each firm with the set of model descriptors in table 3 available. For years 1973 to 1977, parameter estimates from the 1965–1972 estimations are used and for 1978 to 1983, estimates from 1973–1977 are used. The performance of the summary measure in predicting realized earnings changes is summarized in table 4. $\hat{Pr}$ values of 0.5 and 0.6 (chosen, somewhat arbitrarily, prior to the data analysis) are used alternatively as cutoffs for a predicted earnings increase with $(1 - \hat{Pr})$ being the cutoff for a predicted decrease. The x_1^2 values from a 2×2 contingency table are highly significant and the predictions appear to be correct about 60% of the time for a $\hat{Pr}$ cutoff of $(0.5, 0.5)$ and 66% of the time for a $(0.6, 0.4)$ cutoff. These results are similar over all years in the sample period.

4.2. Prediction of stock returns

Table 4 demonstrates that financial statement descriptors predict the sign of future earnings changes. Thus, if earnings are valued by investors, this financial statement analysis captures value-relevant information. However, the point is to assess whether it captures information that is not reflected in prices. If prices do not reflect the information in the descriptors about future earnings

Table 3

Summary of multivariate LOGIT earnings prediction models.

		1965–1972 estimation		1973–1977 estimation	
Accounting descriptor selected		No. of obs. 11322 Model χ^2_{16} 908.43 p-value 0.000 Likelihood ratio index[b] 0.28 % concordant pairs[c] 69.9% Rank correlation[c] 0.42		No. of obs. 11776 Model χ^2_{18} 855.97 p-value 0.000 Likelihood ratio index[b] 0.25 % concordant pairs[c] 65.4% Rank correlation[c] 0.33	
Descriptor number	Accounting descriptor	$\hat{\theta}$[d]	χ^2_1 (p-value)	$\hat{\theta}$[d]	χ^2_1 (p-value)
2	%Δ in current ratio			−1.2105	69.14 (0.00)
4[a]	%Δ in quick ratio			0.8185	53.13 (0.000)
8	%Δ in inventory turnover	0.1663	2.72 (0.100)		
9	Inventory/total assets			−1.0777	35.21 (0.000)
10	%Δ in 9	−0.1231	3.45 (0.063)	−0.7526	36.30 (0.000)
11	%Δ in inventory			0.2945	18.65 (0.000)
12	%Δ in sales			0.4846	21.77 (0.000)
13	%Δ in depreciation	−0.5107	40.61 (0.000)		
14	Δ in dividend per share	−3.0754	129.68 (0.000)	−1.5189	72.14 (0.000)
16	%Δ in (depreciation/ plant assets)	0.5613	23.39 (0.000)		
17[a]	Return on opening equity			−1.9197	44.84 (0.000)
18	Δ in 17			0.4124	10.13 (0.002)
19	%Δ in (capital expenditures/ total assets)	−0.0659	9.92 (0.002)		
20	19, one-year lag	−0.0758	16.10 (0.000)	−0.0288	4.32 (0.038)
21[a]	Debt–equity ratio			−0.0334	6.84 (0.009)
22	%Δ in 21	0.1514	7.25 (0.007)		
30	%Δ in (sales/total assets)	0.5754	13.15 (0.000)		
31	Return on total assets	−4.2089	8.62 (0.003)	−11.3727	90.95 (0.00)
32	Return on closing equity	−3.0088	28.97 (0.000)		
33	Gross margin ratio	0.8152	23.64 (0.00)		
38	% in (pretax income/sales)			0.0141	2.87 (0.090)
41	Sales to total cash			−0.003	3.81 (0.051)

Table 3 (continued)

		1965–1972 estimation		1973–1977 estimation	
Accounting descriptor selected		No. of obs. Model χ^2_{16} p-value Likelihood ratio index[b] % concordant pairs[c] Rank correlation[c]	11322 908.43 0.000 0.28 69.9% 0.42	No. of obs. Model χ^2_{18} p-value Likelihood ratio index[b] % concordant pairs[c] Rank correlation[c]	11776 855.97 0.000 0.25 65.4% 0.33
Descriptor number	Accounting descriptor	$\hat{\theta}$[d]	χ^2_1 (p-value)	$\hat{\theta}$[d]	χ^2_1 (p-value)
53	%Δ in total assets			−0.9628	37.19 (0.000) (0.051)
54	Cash flow to debt	0.3282	3.47 (0.062)		
55	Working capital/ total assets			0.9571	28.39 (0.000)
57	Operating income/ total assets	−0.2726	4.10 (0.43)	3.5859	43.76 (0.000)
61	Repayment of LT debt as % of total LT debt	0.5079	24.35 (0.000)	0.0576	3.87 (0.49)
66	Cash dividend/cash flows	2.4112	159.01 (0.000)		
Intercept		0.5162	95.57 (0.000)	0.7416	104.28 (0.000)

[a] This descriptor was dropped during the stepwise procedure in the 1965–1972 estimations.
[b] The likelihood ratio index is a measure of the goodness-of-fit of the model. It is defined as 1 − (log likelihood at convergence/log likelihood with all parameters equal to zero).
[c] For matched pairs of estimated probability of an earnings increase ($\hat{Pr}$) and directional realized earnings changes. Under the null hypothesis, % of concordant pairs is 50% and rank correlation is zero.
[d] $\hat{\theta}$ is the maximum-likelihood estimate of the coefficient on the accounting descriptor.

Table 4

Summary of prediction performance of earnings prediction models; earnings changes are predicted one year ahead on the basis of $\hat{Pr}$.[a]

	Predictions over 1973–1977		Predictions over 1978–1983	
	$\hat{Pr}$ cutoff		$\hat{Pr}$ cutoff	
	(0.5, 0.5)	(0.6, 0.4)	(0.5, 0.5)	(0.6, 0.4)
Number of observations[b]	9138	5791	9640	4779
% correct predictions	62%	67%	60%	67%
χ^2_1 from 2 × 2 table (and p-value)	299.94 (0.000)	271.63 (0.000)	387.46 (0.000)	444.54 (0.000)
% predicted e.p.s. increases correct	62%	67%	59%	66%
% predicted e.p.s. decreases correct	61%	66%	62%	67%

[a] $\hat{Pr}$ is the estimated probability of an earnings increase indicated by the prediction models summarized in table 3.
[b] The total number of observations over the two periods (18778) is less than 'Total firms available for predictions' in table 1 (19579) because some firms did not survive the year for which earnings were predicted.

and if prices gravitate later towards fundamentals (as the predicted earnings become known), then the descriptors should predict stock returns. Investment strategies designed to capture these predicted returns were implemented according to the following preset program:

(i) For each of the eleven years from 1973 to 1983, stocks are assigned to investment positions at the end of the third month after the end of the fiscal year for which the accounting descriptors (from which $\hat{P}r$ was calculated) were reported. It is assumed that annual report information was publicly available at this time.

(ii) Stocks are assigned to a 'long' position if $\hat{P}r$ is greater than 0.6 and to short position if $\hat{P}r$ is less than or equal to 0.4. We refer to this as the $\hat{P}r$ strategy. With concern for the power of the test, values of $\hat{P}r$ between these cutoff points are ignored because it is felt that values in the vicinity of 0.5 probably don't indicate the direction of earnings changes very well. Again, these cutoff points are chosen in the design stage prior to the analysis.

(iii) Stocks are held for a period of 24 months and mean return differences to the long and short positions at month 24 observed.

Cumulative returns to positions are reported at various points over the 24-month holding period. For each month, m, in the 24-month period a mean monthly return for all N_m stocks in the position in that month is calculated and added to the accumulation of such means at the end of the previous month. This yields a cumulative return, CR_m, from the first month ($\tau = 1$) to month m, as follows.

$$CR_m = \sum_{\tau=1}^{m} \sum_{i=1}^{N_m} \frac{1}{N_m} R_{im\tau}, \qquad (2)$$

where R_{im} is the rate-of-return for stock i in month m. This calculation results in the cumulative return of those stocks that stopped trading during the 24 months to be carried forward in the cumulative return for subsequent months. Thus the cumulative return at any point contains the total observed returns for all firms initially in the position.[8] However, the calculation involves monthly rebalancing of portfolios. Buy-and-hold returns are also calculated by compounding up returns for individual stocks each month and then averaging

---

[8]Cumulative returns were also calculated by multiplying one plus the cumulative mean return at the end of the previous month by one plus the mean return for the month (and subtracting one), with very similar results.

across firms in the portfolio, as follows:

$$BHR_m = \frac{1}{N_m} \sum_{i=1}^{N_m} \left[\prod_{\tau=1}^{m} (1 + R_{im\tau}) - 1 \right].$$ (3)

Buy-and-hold portfolios do not require monthly rebalancing and thus involve lower transactions costs. On these issues, see Blume and Stambaugh (1983) and Roll (1983). However, buy-and-hold returns at the end of the holding period (month 24) contain only the cumulative return experience of firms still trading at that time. One might calculate cumulative returns with the proceeds of the sale of stocks that stopped trading reinvested in the strategy. However, this assumes that these stocks can be liquidated, which may not be the case for some trading halts. Such reinvestment will, of course, involve the rebalancing of portfolios.

In the tables that follow, we report returns based on the calculation in (2) and report buy-and-hold returns in (3) in the text. Two sets of investment returns are reported. The first summarizes all observations in the sample and provides the basis for a comparison with the Ball and Brown strategy. Because firms have different fiscal year ends (and thus, for a given calendar year, the execution date differs over firms), the return for each firm/month in each position is defined as the firm's observed return for the month minus that for an equally weighted market return index for the month calculated from CRSP NYSE and AMEX monthly return indexes. Return to the position for the relevant month of the holding period (in event time) is calculated as the difference in mean returns for all such months for all stocks in the long and short sides of the position. The weights on securities are determined ex post here so it is not an implementable strategy.

The second set of returns reflects the result of an investment strategy that could have been executed at the time and so is appropriate for assessing market efficiency. Positions are taken on the basis of $\hat{Pr}$ values at each April 1 following each of the eleven years from 1973 to 1983 in December fiscal-year stocks only. For each month in the position, the return to the hedge position is again the difference between mean returns for the long and short sides of the position. Thus the same amount of money is invested in the long and short position for zero net investment, ignoring transaction costs. Reported returns for each month in the holding period are means of returns to the strategy over the eleven years (rather than means over stocks) and thus reflect the average profitability for the strategy implemented each year. Holding period months coincide in calendar time so the market return and other common factors drop out in the calculation of returns to the zero-investment hedge position if both sides of the position have the same sensitivity to these common factors.

Before presenting the results for positions based on values of $\hat{Pr}$, we present, in table 5, results from positions based on perfect foreknowledge of

Table 5

Mean cumulative market-adjusted monthly returns from hypothetical investment in stocks on the basis of the direction of one-year-ahead earnings changes;[a] 1973–1983.

Earnings change portfolio	N	\multicolumn{7}{c}{Month of holding period}
		3	6	9	12	18	24	36[e]
\multicolumn{9}{c}{Panel A: All firms[b]}
(Δ e.p.s. − drift) > 0	9207	0.0373	0.0655	0.0975	0.1159	0.1267	0.1371	0.1614
(Δ e.p.s. − drift) ≤ 0	7790	−0.0363	−0.0761	−0.1075	−0.1166	−0.1190	−0.1096	−0.0882
Hedge portfolio[c]	16997	0.0736	0.1416	0.2050	0.2325	0.2458	0.2467	0.2496
							(0.000)[d]	
\multicolumn{9}{c}{Panel B: Firms with $\hat{Pr} > 0.6$ or $\hat{Pr} \leq 0.4$}
(Δ e.p.s. − drift) > 0	5748	0.0311	0.0567	0.0858	0.1092	0.1196	0.1353	0.1790
(Δ e.p.s. − drift) ≤ 0	3774	−0.0390	−0.0841	−0.1180	−0.1282	−0.1362	−0.1292	−0.1051
Hedge portfolio[c]	9522	0.0702	0.1408	0.2038	0.2373	0.2558	0.2645	0.2841
							(0.000)[d]	

[a] Portfolio formation date is three months after end of the year prior to the earnings change year.
[b] All firms with returns over the holding period and one-year-ahead earnings.
[c] Long positions are taken in stocks with (Δ e.p.s. − drift) > 0 and short positions in stock with (Δ e.p.s. − drift) ≤ 0.
[d] Relative frequency of observing the 24-month return, or greater, in a random strategy repeated 2,000 times.
[e] Based on ten years, 1973–1982.

the realized values of subsequent years' earnings changes (minus the drift estimate) for all observations in the sample. Positions are taken at the same time as those for $\hat{Pr}$ (and prior to any earnings reports for the period predicted) and held for the same period of time. Long positions are taken in stocks with earnings increases and short positions in stocks with earnings decreases. This is the Ball and Brown (1968) hypothetical strategy. The results in panel A of table 5 (which are consistent over all years) demonstrate that earnings, one period ahead, are relevant for determining firms' relative values. Further, it is clear from the correspondence of signs on earnings changes and realized stock returns that (future) earnings are a positive-value attribute. Thus we feel comfortable in basing our summary value measure on the ability of financial statement descriptors to predict these earnings. Indeed, we propose to use the returns to this perfect-foresight (PF) strategy as a benchmark against which to compare the returns from the $\hat{Pr}$ strategy which reflects a (less than perfect) earnings prediction. The returns to the perfect foresight (PF) strategy for firms in the $\hat{Pr}$ strategy are given in panel B of table 5 for later reference.

Table 6 gives the results from the $\hat{Pr}$ strategy. The bottom of the table supplies mean cumulative market-adjusted returns from the hedge position at various months in the holding period, for all stocks and for the implementable positions in December 31 fiscal-year stocks. Although not part of our preset program, we also report mean cumulative market-adjusted returns on stocks with $\hat{Pr}$ values within the ten ranges indicated and mean cumulative market-adjusted returns on all portfolios 36 months after execution for a sensitivity analysis. However, our statistical inferences are restricted to the 24-month return on the hedge positions as determined by our preset program.[9] For these we give (in parentheses) the relative frequency of observing the reported return or greater in a strategy of assigning stocks to long and short sides of the position at random in 2,000 replications. In these replications, the number of randomly selected stocks assigned to each side of the position in each year is the same as the number of stocks in the corresponding side of the position in the $\hat{Pr}$ strategy for that year. The observed relative frequency is 0.000 in both cases. The 24-month return to the hedge position for all stocks (0.1453) is 55% of the 24-month return of 0.2645 to the perfect foresight (PF) strategy for firms with $\hat{Pr} > 0.6$ or $\hat{Pr} \leq 0.4$ which is given in panel B of table 5. The $\hat{Pr}$ partitioning variable does very well relative to not only a random strategy, but also to the Ball and Brown benchmark based on foreknowledge of the actual earnings realizations. The results for December 31 fiscal-year stocks indicate that a 24-month return of 0.1256 on average could have been earned during the sample period with zero net investment, and it is unlikely that this could have occurred by chance.[10] The mean cumulative 24-month return to the hedge position for December 31 fiscal-year firms using buy-and-hold calculations is 0.1684. As pointed out above, this return measures the return for stocks still trading at month 24.

The cumulative return to the $\hat{Pr}$ strategy is not diminished up to month 36. Further, it appears that the cumulative returns at this point vary almost monotonically in the predicted direction over levels of $\hat{Pr}$ in much the same way as percentage of earnings changes predicted correctly (in the fourth column) increase as $\hat{Pr}$ varies from 0.5. The ability of $\hat{Pr}$ to sort both subsequent stock returns and subsequent earnings changes appears to capture the realignment of prices to the fundamentals. It also could indicate persistent risk differences over $\hat{Pr}$ groups. Note that, whereas cumulative returns to the PF strategy in table 5 do not increase much after month 12 (when the actual earnings are public), those for the $\hat{Pr}$ strategy do so, indicating the prediction model (together with the $\hat{Pr}$ cutoff points of 0.6 and 0.4) may be capturing

---

[9]The zero net investment position applies only to the first month as price changes thereafter may result in investment on the long side not being equal to the amount in the short position. Note that the 'returns' to the hedge portfolio are not strictly returns as zero investment is involved. These figures should be interpreted as the sum of returns to each side of the position.

[10]As a 24-month investment position is taken every year, these results involve simultaneously running two portfolios, except in the first and last year. The mean return for positions taken in odd calendar years is 0.1139, while that taken in even calendar years is 0.1396. These involve returns that are not overlapping in calendar time.

Table 6

Mean cumulative market-adjusted monthly returns from investment in stocks on the basis of estimated probability of an earnings increase ($\hat{Pr}$);[a] 1973–1983.

| $\hat{Pr}$ portfolio | $\hat{Pr}$ values | N | % correct predictions ($\hat{pr} = 0.5$ cutoff) | \multicolumn{7}{c}{Month of holding period} |
				3	6	9	12	18	24	36[b]
1	$\hat{Pr} > 0.9$	658	85.2	−0.0029	0.0085	0.0118	0.0548	0.0443	0.0633	0.1864
2	$0.9 \geq \hat{Pr} > 0.8$	928	75.5	0.0015	0.0021	−0.0201	−0.0031	−0.0129	0.0058	0.0931
3	$0.8 \geq \hat{Pr} > 0.7$	2174	67.8	0.0184	0.0228	0.0346	0.0525	0.0576	0.0787	0.1008
4	$0.7 \geq \hat{Pr} > 0.6$	4359	59.2	0.0109	0.0124	0.0295	0.0384	0.0545	0.0719	0.1045
5	$0.6 \geq \hat{Pr} > 0.5$	4802	47.4	0.0086	0.0134	0.0188	0.0221	0.0330	0.0444	0.0560
6	$0.5 \geq \hat{Pr} > 0.4$	3007	60.4	0.0057	−0.0007	0.0034	0.0003	0.0000	−0.0013	−0.0083
7	$0.4 \geq \hat{Pr} > 0.3$	1174	68.5	−0.0124	−0.0242	−0.0293	−0.0379	−0.0557	−0.0629	−0.0804
8	$0.3 \geq \hat{Pr} > 0.2$	417	73.9	−0.0105	−0.0247	−0.0430	−0.0625	−0.1072	−0.1098	−0.1171
9	$0.2 \geq \hat{Pr} > 0.1$	154	72.7	−0.0000	0.0085	−0.0182	−0.0241	−0.0246	−0.0552	−0.1468
10	$\hat{Pr} \leq 0.1$	84	66.7	−0.0084	−0.0399	−0.0991	−0.1109	−0.1604	−0.2185	−0.1881
Hedge portfolio, all stocks[c]		9948	66.3	0.0214	0.0356	0.0577	0.0834	0.1152	0.1453 (0.000)[e]	0.2083
Hedge portfolio, 12/31 stocks[d]		5631	66.4	0.0093	0.0175	0.0302	0.0741	0.1001	0.1256 (0.000)[e]	0.1963

[a] Portfolios are formed three months after the fiscal year for which the accounting descriptors (on which $\hat{Pr}$ is based) were reported.
[b] Based on ten years, 1973–1982.
[c] Long positions are taken in all stocks with $\hat{Pr} > 0.6$ and short positions in all stocks with $\hat{Pr} < 0.4$, with zero net investment. Reported returns are mean differences for the holding month between mean cumulative returns of the two sides of the positions.
[d] Involves firms with December 31 fiscal-year ends only. Reported returns are means over years of returns to positions taken at April 1 of each year with long positions in stocks with $\hat{Pr} > 0.6$ and short positions in stocks with $\hat{Pr} \leq 0.4$, with zero net investment.
[e] Relative frequency of observing the 24-month return, or greater, in a random strategy repeated 2,000 times.

value attributes beyond one-year-ahead earnings. Indeed, we have found that $\hat{Pr}$ predicts the direction of earnings changes three years ahead on average [see Ou and Penman (1989)]. Note further that the perceived realignment of prices to fundamentals appears to be complete by month 36: the cumulative return to the $\hat{Pr}$ strategy from investing in stocks at the end of month 36 and holding them for 24 months (not reported in the table) is only 0.0191 (based on years 1973–1980 for which returns data are available).

The cumulative returns for the $\hat{Pr}$ groups in table 6 indicate that our choice of $\hat{Pr}$ values of 0.6 and 0.4 as cutoff points for assignment of stocks to long and short positions is conservative. The return could be improved by investing in more extreme $\hat{Pr}$ stocks. With fewer stocks in extreme $\hat{Pr}$ groups, it is likely that the variance of return to positions in these stocks would be higher, however.

Panel A of fig. 1 displays the mean cumulative market-adjusted returns to the hedge position in all stocks for each year from 1973 to 1983 and, to the extreme right, the mean over all years. These returns are positive in all years except 1983. A very similar picture emerges for December 31 fiscal-year stocks. This consistency assures us that the result in table 6 is not due to a fews years. Panel B of fig. 1 gives the cumulative market-adjusted returns to the long and short positions for each year (the difference of which is equal to the returns in the top panel). The returns are in the direction indicated by the position, except in 1982 and 1983. There are considerably more stocks in the long position than in the short position in all years. Over all years the short position contributes more to the total hedge portfolio return than the long side, with the mean return to the short position over years being -0.0799 and to the long position 0.0672. However, this is largely due to the (contrary) large negative return on the long side for 1983.

Three caveats must be given in interpreting the reported returns as returns to an implementable strategy. First, the returns are gross of transactions costs. The inability to use the proceeds from the short positions means that the strategy must be financed. Thus, in practice, it is not a zero net investment strategy. Second, any subsequent returns to stocks that stopped trading during the 24-month holding period are not included here (although returns up to the point of the trading halt are). This is the case with bankrupt firms that return a bankruptcy dividend. Of the December 31 fiscal-year firms in the position in the first month, 7.2% had dropped out by month 24, with 6.8% of firms in the long position dropping out and 8.5% on the short side. Unfortunately, CRSP does not give a code indicating whether firms went bankrupt, although they do indicate other reasons why stocks stopped trading.[11] On the long side of the position, 1.2% dropped out for reasons other than merger or exchange and

---

[11] CRSP gives six codes indicating the reason a stock stopped trading: merger, exchange, liquidation, delisting by exchange, trading halted by exchange, and suspended by SEC.

PANEL A: LONG AND SHORT POSITIONS TOGETHER

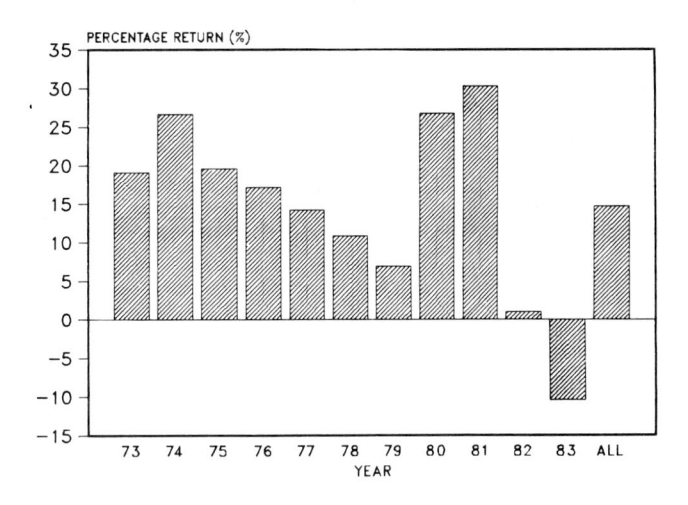

PANEL B: LONG AND SHORT POSITIONS SEPARATELY

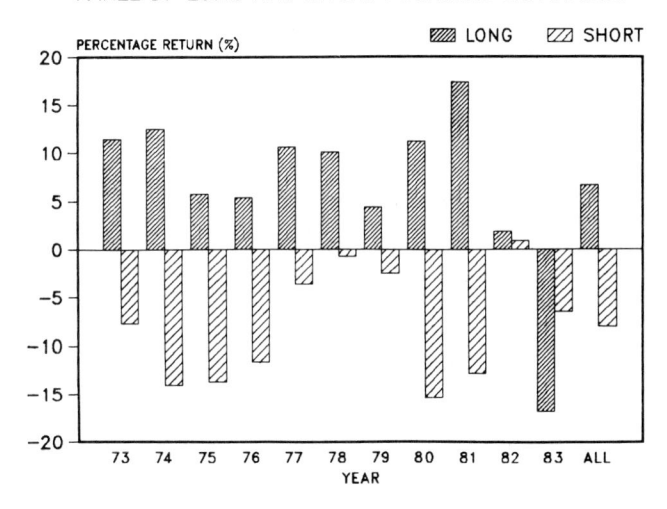

Fig. 1. Mean cumulative market-adjusted returns over 24 months to hedge positions based on the estimated probability of an earnings increase ($\hat{Pr}$), by year. Long positions are taken in stocks with $\hat{Pr} > 0.6$ and short positions are taken in stocks with $\hat{Pr} \leq 0.4$.

1.9% on the short side. These figures suggest that the omission of subsequent returns affects both sides of the position to a similar degree. In any case, this is not a problem if the last price before the trading halt is an unbiased predictor of the subsequent payoff. The third caveat concerns our assumption that the annual reports on which $\hat{Pr}$ is based are available at the date on which positions were taken, three months after fiscal-year end. An inspection of table 6 indicates that the returns to the strategy are not particularly sensitive to taking positions some months after this date.

5. The $\hat{Pr}$ summary measure and risk

These results demonstrate the ability of the value measure to predict stock returns in the sample period. It is possible that, despite our precautionary design, $\hat{Pr}$ is distinguishing firms on risk characteristics rather than delayed price adjustments to value fundamentals. If so, observed differences in realized returns across $\hat{Pr}$ portfolios may be differential rewards to differential risk. The approach has been to extract a value measure from financial statements that is correlated with positive-value attributes (namely, future earnings) and (hopefully) has low correlation with risk attributes. However, the latter is not guaranteed. This section investigates the risk explanation. We do so with the disclaimer that, as there is no generally universally accepted definition of risk, we can never be sure that we are comparing returns against the appropriate benchmark. We entertain as benchmarks the returns associated with a number of attributes that have been advocated as risk proxies.

5.1. A correlation profile

Table 7 summarizes, by $\hat{Pr}$ portfolio, values of certain characteristics that have been proposed as risk attributes, along with other attributes which may identify $\hat{Pr}$ as a positive-value descriptor rather than a risk descriptor. The values for the hedge position in this table are mean differences over years in the mean values over both sides of the position with all stocks included. t-values, based on the time series of mean differences over years, are given in parentheses.

The second column of table 7 demonstrates that $\hat{Pr}$ discriminates on the magnitude of subsequent percentage changes in earnings-per-share, the predicted attribute as well as the sign. Thus returns for different $\hat{Pr}$ levels in table 6 capture differential subsequent earnings performance. Note further that $\hat{Pr}$ is negatively related to percentage changes in earnings in the current year, the year for which the financial statement descriptors were reported. Thus these descriptors identify not only the direction of future earnings changes but also that of current earnings: high values of $\hat{Pr}$ indicate cases where current earnings are 'temporarily depressed' and low values of $\hat{Pr}$ identify cases where current earnings are 'abnormally high' (relative to the past and future). More

Table 7

Summary of selected attributes of $\hat{P}r$ portfolios; 1973–1983.

$\hat{P}r$ portfolio	Relative % e.p.s. changes in prediction year[a,h]	Relative % e.p.s. changes in current year[a,h]	Mean cumulative market-adjusted return over prior 24 months	Mean beta estimated over prior 60 months[b]	Mean beta estimated during holding period[b]	Mean std. dev. of returns over prior 60 months[b]	Mean std. dev. of returns over holding period[b]	Relative E/P ratios[a]	Relative equity market value (in $m)[a]	Relative market leverage[a,f]	Relative book leverage[a,g]	Relative market/book ratios[a]
1	81.3	−168.4	−0.4238	1.18	1.29	0.1300	0.1430	−0.330[d]	−56.10	0.188	0.116	−0.283
2	49.5	−74.3	−0.2925	1.10	1.21	0.1173	0.1197	−0.139[e]	−51.38	0.144	0.053	−0.309
3	31.8	−28.0	−0.1287	1.06	1.11	0.1109	0.1120	−0.048	−39.37	0.095	0.021	−0.243
4	3.1	−5.4	−0.0158	1.05	1.05	0.1155	0.0998	−0.005	−19.35	0.032	0.002	−0.144
5	−3.4	2.5	0.0700	1.02	1.01	0.1017	0.0928	0.017	14.76	−0.019	−0.009	0.034
6	−5.6	7.8	0.1445	1.01	1.00	0.1025	0.0912	0.023	66.50	−0.072	−0.021	0.264
7	−11.5	15.8	0.2709	1.03	1.01	0.1064	0.0904	0.020	118.67	−0.111	−0.016	0.541
8	−20.8	23.1	0.3502	1.09	1.03	0.1203	0.0956	0.038	97.18	−0.086	0.010	0.576
9	−17.8	45.8	0.5240	1.12	1.31	0.1290	0.1133	0.055	16.64	−0.019	0.058	0.695
10	−10.9	66.3	0.3668	1.17	1.12	0.1314	0.1098	0.042	55.18	−0.026	0.061	0.644
Hedge portfolio, all stocks[c]	26.1 (6.23)	−35.3 (−4.98)	−0.4243 (−7.99)	0.01 (0.39)	0.06 (1.83)	−0.0022 (−0.64)	0.0137 (4.63)	−0.064 (−6.74)	−132.07 (−3.35)	0.170 (5.88)	0.025 (1.99)	−0.763 (−5.86)

[a] Values are means (over eleven years) of differences (in each eleven years) in portfolio median values from median value for all firms in the year.
[b] Means calculated over portfolio means for eleven years.
[c] Figures given are mean differences in values for long and short sides of the $\hat{P}r$ hedge portfolio (described in note c to table 6). Figures in parentheses are t-statistics on mean differences over eleven years.
[d] Median E/P ratios are negative for all years except 1978.
[e] Median E/P ratios are negative in years 1978–1983.
[f] Market leverage defined as book value of debt/(market value of equity plus book value of debt). Market values are calculated from prices and shares outstanding at portfolio formation date, or, if these were unavailable, prices and shares outstanding at fiscal-year end.
[g] Book leverage defined as book value of debt/(book value of equity plus book value of debt).
[h] % e.p.s. changes are defined as change in e.p.s. divided by absolute value of prior year's e.p.s.

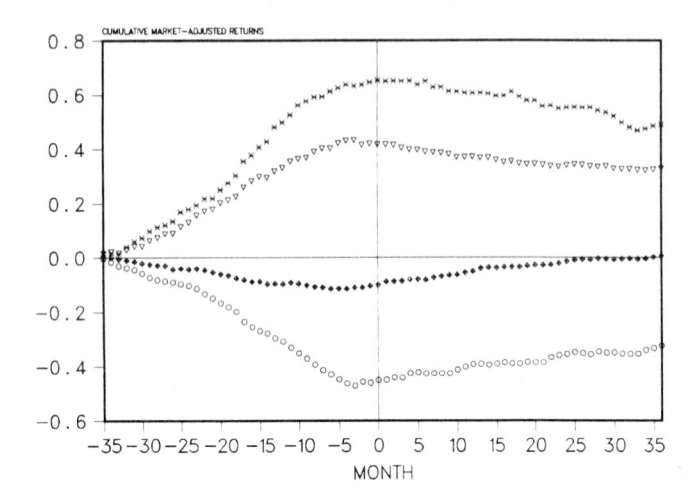

Fig. 2. Mean cummulative market-adjusted returns from 35 months prior to $\hat{P}r$ portfolio formation month, month 0, to 36 months after $\hat{P}r$ portfolio formation month, for selected $\hat{P}r$ portfolios, 1973–1982; ○ $\hat{P}r > 0.8$, ⊕ $0.6 < \hat{P}r \leq 0.8$, ▽ $0.2 < \hat{P}r \leq 0.4$, × $\hat{P}r \leq 0.2$.

significantly, the table indicates that $\hat{P}r$ is also negatively related to cumulative (market-adjusted) returns over the previous 24 months up to the portfolio formation date [while being positively related to cumulative (market-adjusted) returns over the subsequent 24 months, as described in table 6]. For extreme $\hat{P}r$ portfolios the prior returns are quite large. Thus $\hat{P}r$ identifies price reversals as well as earnings turning points: high values of $\hat{P}r$ are associated with prior price declines followed by price increases and low values of $\hat{P}r$ are associated with prior price increases followed by price declines. Fig. 2 graphically depicts these reversals for stocks with $\hat{P}r > 0.8$, stocks with $0.6 < \hat{P}r \leq 0.8$, stocks with $0.2 < \hat{P}r \leq 0.4$, and stocks with $\hat{P}r \leq 0.2$ in a window covering 72 months around $\hat{P}r$ portfolio formation dates, month 0. This phenomenon supports the interpretation that $\hat{P}r$ identifies cases where stock prices have previously 'moved away from fundamentals' as well as subsequent reversion to fundamentals.

These price reversals are inconsistent with $\hat{P}r$ capturing risk characteristics that are stationary over the periods before and after the observation of the $\hat{P}r$ values. However, the prior price changes could reflect risk *changes* that are associated with changing premiums in the future. Fama and French (1988) provide this explanation for similar price swings observed in their work. As returns both prior to and subsequent to month zero are market-adjusted, this explanation demands that $\hat{P}r$ measures substantially reorder firms' risks relative to the market portfolio (the average firm) at the relevant financial statement date. This seems a little implausible. Table 7 gives mean betas for $\hat{P}r$

groups estimated prior to and subsequent to the date when investment positions were taken. Higher estimated betas are associated with both extremes of the $\hat{Pr}$ distribution. Further, there is no indication of reversal in ordering of mean betas before and after the $\hat{Pr}$ observation dates that would explain the reversals in market-adjusted returns in fig. 2.

Mean betas for all stocks in table 7 cancel over the two sides of the hedge portfolio. For the hedge portfolio with December 31 fiscal-year firms, a hedge portfolio beta can be estimated. This is close to zero. As the holding period was 24 months after each portfolio-formation date, estimations were performed twice (on portfolio monthly returns using OLS techniques), first for portfolios formed in odd-numbered calendar years and second for portfolios formed in even-numbered years. For the first estimation, estimated hedge portfolio beta was 0.029 (with a t-statistic of 1.04) and for the second estimation, 0.074 (with a t-statistic of 2.02). These estimates are not independent.

Like estimated betas, higher standard deviations of returns are associated with both extremes of $\hat{Pr}$ in table 7. The figures reported in the standard deviation columns for the hedge portfolio in table 7 are the mean differences in the standard deviation of returns between the two sides of the hedge position for all stocks. These compare the variance characteristics of all stocks with $\hat{Pr} > 0.6$ and $\hat{Pr} \leq 0.4$. For the December 31 fiscal-year hedge portfolio, the standard deviations of portfolio monthly returns for each side of the hedge portfolio over the holding period are in the order of 0.06 (very close to that for the equally weighted market index). For this portfolio a standard deviation of returns for the portfolio can be calculated because returns are aligned in calendar time. This is only about 0.02. Further, the estimated correlation between returns on each side of the hedge position is about 0.93.[12] This high correlation indicates that both sides in the position have similar sensitivities to common (risk) factors affecting returns. These cancel in the hedge position resulting in the significant reduction in standard deviation of return for the position.

These investigations indicate that the predicted returns cannot be explained by return-based risk measures. Note further that there is no strong association of $\hat{Pr}$ values with industry groups (whose risks may differ) over the entire sample period. The rest of table 7 summarizes other attributes that have been conjectured as risk measures and which may indicate risk that is not captured by estimated beta or return standard deviation. These are all observed at the same time as $\hat{Pr}$. Referring to these measures as risk attributes is problematical, for with the exception of book leverage, they include market price. If

---

[12] For the set of returns from positions in odd-numbered years, the standard deviation of returns for the equally-weighted market index, the long side of the position, the short side of position, and the hedge portfolio were 0.0628, 0.0630, 0.0621, and 0.0203, respectively. For the second set of returns, the corresponding figures were 0.0559, 0.0598, 0.0574, and 0.0224.

market price reflects mispricing with respect to $\hat{P}r$, one cannot disentangle this mispricing from risk.[13]

E/P ratios are negatively related to $\hat{P}r$. If E/P ratios are risk proxies as has been suggested in Ball (1978), for example, the direction of the association is inconsistent with $\hat{P}r$ capturing this aspect of risk. $\hat{P}r$ is not capturing 'P/E effects'. Rather, the direction of the correlation can be explained by the fact that E/P ratios are negatively related to future earnings growth [Beaver and Morse (1978)]. Like $\hat{P}r$, E/P ratios are expressing an earnings prediction.[14] The remaining attributes in table 7 – market value of equity (size), market and book leverage, and market-to-book premiums – are all correlated with $\hat{P}r$ in a direction which indicates that if they are risk proxies, $\hat{P}r$ may be capturing risk differences across firms. Clearly more controls are necessary before inferences about fundamentals predicting risk-adjusted returns can be entertained.

5.2. Further controls

Table 7 indicates that $\hat{P}r$ is related to firm size, with the direction of the association suggesting that table 7 results capture a 'size effect'. Empirical work on security prices done in the last ten years indicates that size explains cross-sectional differences in mean returns, suggesting that it is a risk proxy. Table 8 provides results from the same investment positions as those in table 6, but with returns adjusted for size effects.[15] For each month in the position, the return for each firm was calculated as the observed return minus the mean return for that calendar month on a size control portfolio in which the firm was a member. Firms were assigned to one of ten size control portfolios (with the same number of securities) in each of the eleven years based on a ranking of firms in the sample at that time on market value of equity.

We carry out this size adjustment with some reservation. The rationale is that size proxies for risk. However, it could also indicate market inefficiency. In particular, if some small firms in our sample have low market values because of previous price declines which represent 'deviations from fundamentals' (with a similar argument for large firms), we may be taking out some of the mispricing of stocks as well as risk-related return. Indeed, table 7 indicated

---

[13] For example, book values (for given current earnings) predict future earnings [Freeman, Ohlson and Penman (1982)]. Thus the negative correlation between $\hat{P}r$ and market-to-book is consistent with the market's mispricing of predicted earnings as well as with market-to-book ratios capturing risk. With respect to market leverage, firms that have projects that they see as particularly profitable may finance them through debt rather than equity if they perceive equity to be undervalued. Thus market leverage can be construed as a signal of future profitability and of mispricing of equity.

[14] The similarity of $\hat{P}r$ and E/P as earnings predictors is explored in Ou and Penman (1989).

[15] The number of stocks in the position here is slightly less than in table 6 because price and shares outstanding data could not be discovered for a few firms.

Table 8

Mean cumulative size-adjusted monthly returns from investment in stocks on the basis of estimated probability of an earnings increase ($\hat{P}r$);[a] 1973–1983.

$\hat{P}r$ portfolio	$\hat{P}r$ values	N	\multicolumn{6}{c}{Month of holding period}
			3	6	9	12	18	24	36[b]
1	$\hat{P}r > 0.9$	658	−0.0162	−0.0149	−0.0216	0.0036	−0.0200	−0.0241	0.0286
2	$0.9 \geq \hat{P}r > 0.8$	928	−0.0094	−0.0165	−0.0453	−0.0419	−0.0681	−0.0656	−0.0330
3	$0.8 \geq \hat{P}r > 0.7$	2174	0.0071	0.0069	0.0097	0.0225	0.0168	0.0267	0.0219
4	$0.7 \geq \hat{P}r > 0.6$	4358	0.0017	−0.0013	0.0056	0.0149	0.0209	0.0295	0.0372
5	$0.6 \geq \hat{P}r > 0.5$	4800	0.0045	0.0054	0.0019	0.0068	0.0107	0.0150	0.0100
6	$0.5 \geq \hat{P}r > 0.4$	3005	0.0047	−0.0053	−0.0072	−0.0064	−0.0092	−0.0112	−0.0251
7	$0.4 \geq \hat{P}r > 0.3$	1159	−0.0099	−0.0248	−0.0369	−0.0362	−0.0519	−0.0565	−0.0713
8	$0.3 \geq \hat{P}r > 0.2$	417	−0.0010	−0.0282	−0.0554	−0.0630	−0.1116	−0.1045	−0.1083
9	$0.2 \geq \hat{P}r > 0.1$	154	−0.0013	0.0033	−0.0332	−0.0322	−0.0405	−0.0643	−0.1651
10	$\hat{P}r \leq 0.1$	84	−0.0110	−0.0451	−0.1079	−0.1291	−0.1797	−0.2474	−0.2165
Hedge portfolio, all stocks[c]		9932	0.0098	0.0220	0.0424	0.0554	0.0763	0.0908 (0.000)[e]	0.1185
Hedge portfolio, 12/31 stocks[d]		5631	−0.0009	0.0068	0.0244	0.0458	0.0654	0.0702 (0.000)[e]	0.1052

[a] See note a to table 6.
[b] Based on ten years, 1973–1982.
[c] See note c to table 6.
[d] See note d to table 6.
[e] Relative frequency of observing the 24-month return, or greater, in a random strategy repeated 2000 times.

that high $\hat{P}r$ values associated with small firms are also associated with prior price declines, while low $\hat{P}r$ values associated with large firms are also associated with prior price increases.

In spite of this, the hedge portfolios' size-adjusted returns at month 24 in table 8, though about 40% less than the market-adjusted returns in table 6, are significant, as indicated by the test statistic in parentheses under the returns.[16] The 24-month return to the hedge strategy for all firms is 35% of the 24-month size-adjusted return of 0.2582 to the PF strategy in stocks with $\hat{P}r > 0.6$ or $\hat{P}r \leq 0.4$. The relative frequency of observing this return, or greater, in 2,000 replications with randomly selected stocks was 0.000. This is so for positions in stocks with December 31 fiscal-year ends also.[17] Mean buy-and-hold size-adjusted returns for this position at month 24 are 0.0736.

Fig. 3 depicts the 24-month size-adjusted returns to the $\hat{P}r$ hedge strategy in all firms for each year from 1973 to 1983. Panel A gives the overall returns and panel B the returns to the long and short sides separately. It is evident that the strategy, net of returns to size, did not perform well in 1979, 1982, and 1983, with negative outcomes in 1979 and 1983. As the accuracy of $\hat{P}r$ in predicting directional earnings in these years was not inferior to that in other years for any of the $\hat{P}r$ groups, we decided to dig further to discover the reason for this inconsistency. The results for 1979, 1982, and 1983, as for other years, are not due to a few monthly return outliers. The holding periods for these years were not periods of prolonged bear markets so the exceptions cannot be attributed to the earnings prediction model capturing risk attributes related to market factors. For 1982 and 1983 (but not 1979) there is an aspect of the data that in part explains the results. The results for these years are largely attributable to negative return performance on the long side of the hedge position. 31.4% of the 1702 firms reporting current losses in the sample fell in these years (these were bad years for corporate profits) with 95.5% of these in portfolios 1–4. In fact, 35.2% of all stocks in these portfolios in 1982 and 1983 had current losses, compared to 17.7% over years 1973–1981. These loss firms performed well in earnings prediction tests. However, in partitioning returns on perfect-foresight realized earnings changes in the year predicted, the 210 loss firms in 1982 with positive subsequent earnings changes were associated with a mean 24-month size-adjusted return of -0.0296 and the 193 loss firms in 1983 with positive subsequent earnings changes were associated with a mean size-adjusted 24-month return of -0.2834. Hence the market valued positive earnings

---

[16] The observed return may still reflect some size effect if there is significant residual variation in size within the ten size portfolios and if $\hat{P}r$ is related to size within these portfolios. Investigation discovered that this residual size effect is very small.

[17] The estimated beta for size-adjusted returns to the hedge position taken in December 31 fiscal-year stocks in odd-numbered years was -0.001 (with a t-statistic of -0.05). For positions taken in December 31 fiscal-year stocks in even-numbered years it was -0.027 (with a t-statistic of -1.21).

PANEL A: LONG AND SHORT POSITIONS TOGETHER

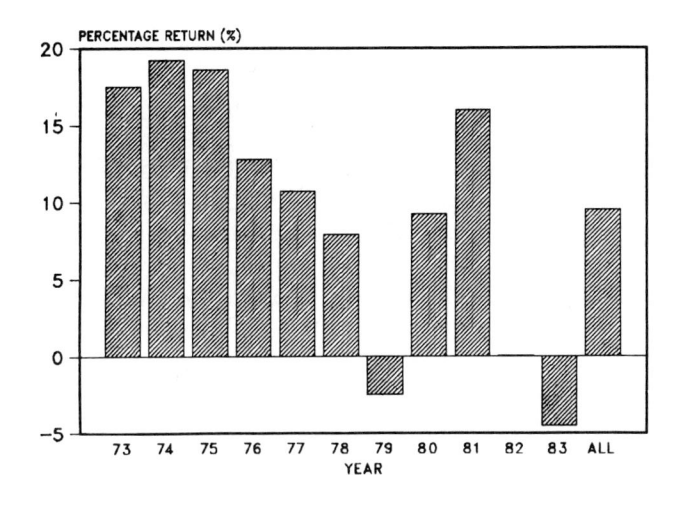

PANEL B: LONG AND SHORT POSITIONS SEPARATELY

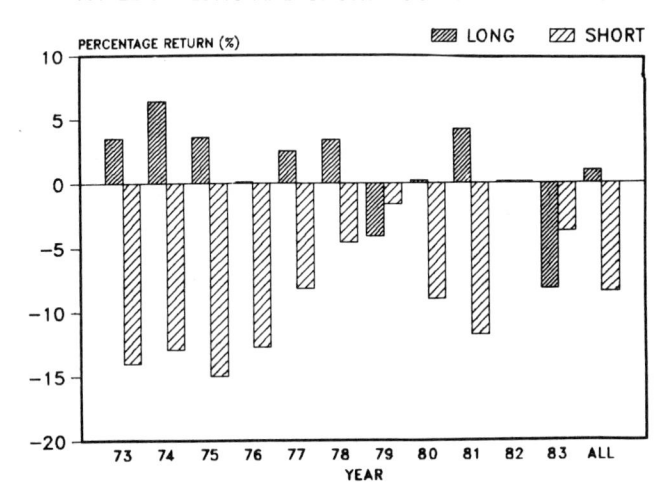

Fig. 3. Mean cumulative size-adjusted returns over 24 months to hedge positions based on the estimated probability of an earnings increase ($\hat{P}r$), by year. Long positions are taken in stocks with $\hat{P}r > 0.6$ and short positions are taken in stocks with $\hat{P}r \leq 0.4$.

changes for these firms negatively. This was not the case in other years[18] or for profitable firms in 1982 and 1983. The result appears to be attributable in part to the Ball and Brown strategy not working for loss firms in these years. The size-adjusted retuns to the $\hat{P}r$ hedge strategy in 1982 and 1983 excluding loss firms (on either side of the hedge position) were 0.0804 and 0.0855, respectively. (This calculation was not part of our preset program, of course.)

It is clear from panel B of fig. 3 that most of the size-adjusted return to the hedge position comes from the short side. The mean return to the long position over years, given at the extreme right of the figure, is 0.0105 while that for the short side is -0.0849. This, of course, is due to small-firm return premiums being subtracted from the returns to the long position. If these premiums are rewards to risk that is related to size, then our financial statement analysis is profitable primarily for sell positions. If small firms identified by high $\hat{P}r$ in the long position are small because they are undervalued, then the difference in returns over long and short sides of the positions is merely the result of an inappropriate size adjustment that takes out the price appreciation for these firms. The price reversals (from declining prices to increasing prices relative to the market) that are evident for these firms in table 7 and fig. 2 are consistent with both changing risk that reduces market values (size) and deviations of prices from the fundamentals captured in $\hat{P}r$ that also reduces market values.

Our fundamental analysis can be compared to the technical analysis of DeBondt and Thaler (1985, 1987). Their analysis documents price reversals associated primarily with 'loser' portfolios, that is, with stocks whose prices have previously declined. This phenomenon appears to be identified with small firms and price appreciations in January (see their 1987 paper) and, once size effects and January effects are controlled for, the phenomenon is not apparent [Zarowin (1988)]. The ability of our fundamental measure to predict returns survives after size adjustment of returns and, for size-adjusted returns, is associated primarily with 'winner' stocks (previous price increases relative to the market), not 'loser' stocks. It is not due to January effects. This is evident from the size adjustment (the January effect being a small-firm phenomenon) and by results (not reported) that are obtained when January returns are dropped in the accumulations.

A similar analysis was carried out for controls for market and book leverage and market-to-book premiums. The analysis was carried out on size-adjusted returns so the control for size was simultaneously maintained. The results indicated that the returns for the $\hat{P}r$ strategy could not be explained by returns

---

[18] An exception is 1979, a negative size-adjusted performance year. Here there were only 79 loss firms with actual earnings increases in the year predicted (out of 327) with a mean 24-month return of -0.0893 to a long position based on the actual increases. This cannot, by itself, explain the 1979 result: the 24-month hedge return excluding loss companies in 1979 was -0.0055.

predicted by these attributes. Details of these tests are available in an earlier version of the paper [Ou and Penman (1987)].

5.3. The $\hat{Pr}$ announcement effect

One further test indicates that $\hat{Pr}$ is not describing risk differences across firms. The accounting items on which $\hat{Pr}$ is based are published in annual accounting reports sometime between fiscal-year end and the time at which investment positions were taken, three months after fiscal-year end. If the $\hat{Pr}$ number conveys new information, a market price reaction to this information should be observed during this three-month period. If $\hat{Pr}$ is interpreted by investors as a (positive-value) indicator of future earnings, price changes should be positively related to the (unexpected) news in $\hat{Pr}$, similar to that observed for 'unexpected earnings', because $\hat{Pr}$ news is unexpected future earnings. If investors interpret $\hat{Pr}$ instead as a risk measure, price changes should be negatively related to values of $\hat{Pr}$.

Table 9 indicates the effect of the announcement of $\hat{Pr}$ on stock returns. It summarizes, for stocks in the $\hat{Pr}$ strategy, the cumulative size-adjusted returns over these three months from investing in stocks at fiscal-year end on the basis of foreknowledge of the forthcoming $\hat{Pr}$. Because we are unsure what aspect of $\hat{Pr}$ might convey news (that is, what is 'unexpected $\hat{Pr}$'), results are given for both levels of $\hat{Pr}$ (panel A) on the assumption that deviation of $\hat{Pr}$ from 0.5 is news and changes in $\hat{Pr}$ ($\Delta \hat{Pr}$) from one annual report to the next (panel B) on the assumption that revision in $\hat{Pr}$ levels is news. Further, as $\hat{Pr}$ is negatively correlated with earnings published at the same time (table 7), results are given for earnings increases and decreases separately to control for the earnings announcement concurrent with $\hat{Pr}$. It is clear from table 9 that returns over this announcement period are positively correlated with $\hat{Pr}$ and changes in $\hat{Pr}$. Market reactions to the publication of demonstrated earnings predictors are in the direction which indicates they are evaluated indeed as positive-attribute earnings predictors and not as risk changes. The result also indicates that the market recognizes some of the information in $\hat{Pr}$ when it is published. This is the result in Ou (1989). Our observations of returns following the publication of $\hat{Pr}$ indicate that the market is slow to appreciate that information fully.

The announcement effect in table 9 is likely to be understated because we have controlled only for the direction of current earnings changes, not the magnitude. As current earnings changes are negatively correlated with $\hat{Pr}$, remaining earnings announcement effects work against the observed result. It is likely that annual earnings changes measure 'unexpected earnings' reported in the three months poorly and some components of $\hat{Pr}$ may be available prior to the annual report. These considerations reinforce the null of no announce-

Table 9

Mean cumulative size-adjusted monthly returns over three months after fiscal-year end from hypothetical investment in stocks on the basis of foreknowledge of $\hat{P}r$; 1973–1983 (panel A), 1974–1983 (panel B).

Portfolios	Number of stocks[a]	Mean median % e.p.s. change in current year[b]	Month relative to fiscal-year end 1	2	3
		Panel A: Levels of $\hat{P}r$			
		$(\Delta e.p.s. - drift) > 0$			
$\hat{P}r > 0.6$	4001	50.0	0.0086	0.0203	0.0259
$\hat{P}r \leq 0.4$	1211	55.4	−0.0046	−0.0046	−0.0069
Hedge portfolio[c]	5212	−5.4	0.0132	0.0250	0.0328
		(−0.53)[d]			(3.79)[d]
		$(\Delta e.p.s. - drift) \leq 0$			
$\hat{P}r > 0.6$	4122	−50.3	0.0023	−0.0049	−0.0081
$\hat{P}r \leq 0.4$	608	−0.1	−0.0126	−0.0148	−0.0196
Hedge portfolio[c]	4730	−50.3	0.0149	0.0100	0.0115
		(−6.56)[d]			(0.22)[d]
		Panel B: Changes in $\hat{P}r$ ($\Delta\hat{P}r$)			
		$(\Delta e.p.s. - drift) > 0$			
$\Delta\hat{P}r > 0$	1400	35.0	0.0133	0.0262	0.0350
$\Delta\hat{P}r \leq 0$	2841	64.3	0.0047	0.0128	0.0149
Hedge portfolio[c]	4241	−29.2	0.0086	0.0134	0.0201
		(−3.85)[d]			(2.97)[d]
		$(\Delta e.p.s. - drift) \leq 0$			
$\Delta\hat{P}r > 0$	3467	−59.7	0.0014	−0.0054	−0.0081
$\Delta\hat{P}r \leq 0$	781	−20.9	−0.0084	−0.0146	−0.0171
Hedge portfolio[c]	4248	−38.7	0.0098	0.0093	0.0090
		(−7.82)[d]			(0.65)[d]

[a] For panel B only stocks for which consecutive values of $\hat{P}r$ were observed (from 1974–1983) are involved.
[b] Mean of median %e.p.s. changes observed over the sample period.
[c] Long positions are taken in stocks satisfying the first condition and short positions in stocks satisfying the second condition.
[d] t-statistic calculated from the time series of observations to the position over the sample period.

ment effect, however, not the observed result. In any case, the result is similar when returns are observed over the twelve months during which the four quarterly and annual earnings reports that contain both the annual earnings change and $\hat{P}r$ are published [see Ou (1989)].

Table 7 indicated that high $\hat{P}r$ values are associated with large negative current earnings changes and low $\hat{P}r$ values with large positive current earnings changes. One might conjecture, then, that the returns to the $\hat{P}r$

strategy might be predicted by current earnings changes without the other financial statement information involved in the calculation of $\hat{P}r$. A number of papers have documented that 'post-earnings-drifts' in returns are predicted by extreme earnings changes [for example, Foster, Olsen, and Shevlin (1984) and Bernard and Thomas (1989)] and extreme earnings relative to price [Basu (1983)]. In Ou and Penman (1989) we show that return drifts predicted by E/P ratios (which are positively correlated with earnings changes) are in fact negatively correlated with returns to positions based on $\hat{P}r$. This is indeed suggested by the negative correlation between $\hat{P}r$ and current earnings changes and E/P ratios that is evident in table 7. Thus, $\hat{P}r$ is not predicting 'post-earnings-drifts' in returns. Note, however, that Ball, Kothari, and Watts (1988), in their investigation of 'post-earnings-drifts' in stock returns, find that extreme positive earnings changes (the top 10% in cross-section) are followed by negative returns after their unique beta-risk adjustment. This is in the opposite direction to 'post-earnings-drifts' documented in other studies. These extreme positive earnings changes are likely to be associated with $\hat{P}r$ values less than 0.4 (table 7) and so are in the same direction as those indicated by $\hat{P}r$. For both sides of the $\hat{P}r$ position, we partitioned firms into those with contemporaneous earnings increases and contemporaneous earnings decreases and calculated the mean 24-month cumulative market-adjusted returns from three months after fiscal-year end for each group. For firms with $\hat{P}r \leq 0.4$, the mean 24-month return following the 1220 cases with earnings increases was -0.0820 and for the 609 cases with earnings decreases it was -0.0764, little different. Likewise, for firms with $\hat{P}r > 0.6$, the mean 24-month return following the 4012 cases with earnings increases was 0.0784, and for the 4107 cases with earnings decreases it was 0.0525. Thus the returns to $\hat{P}r$ positions cannot be replicated by positions based on contemporaneous earnings changes.[19]

6. Conclusion

On the basis of an extensive financial statement analysis we have derived a summary measure from financial statements that predicts future stock returns. Although we cannot be absolutely sure that this measure is not solely a risk attribute, the analysis indicates that this is not so. It appears that this fundamental measure captures equity values that are not reflected in stock prices.

We feel reasonably confident in our conclusion because of the conservative approach to the data. We followed a fixed, preset program of investing in stocks which may not be optimal. We derived the value measure based on observed correlations with one-year-ahead earnings and ignored earnings for years further in the future. The model estimated to predict these earnings did

---

[19]Similar inferences are drawn from size-adjusted returns.

not exploit all aspects of the data. It was based on a dichotomous specification of future earnings rather than on actual dollar amounts and was not re-estimated every year in the sample period. Further, it was based on a pooling of all firms and one suspects that industry-specific or firm-specific models would produce improvements, provided enough data were available to estimate coefficients with precision.

The evidence here suggests that financial statements capture fundamentals that are not reflected in prices. Thus, it points to limitations in the traditional approach in empirical analysis in accounting of making inferences about accounting numbers on the basis of contemporaneous associations with prices. Much of that research stems from the work of Ball and Brown (1968). The findings here indicate that the predictive associations between earnings predictors and future stock returns capture a good deal of the contemporaneous association between earnings and stock returns documented in the Ball and Brown paper.

In closing, it should be noted that there is one aspect of fundamental analysis that has not been incorporated in our program. Fundamental analysis extracts value measures from financial statements and compares them to prices to identify mispriced stocks. Our trading strategies involve cross-sectional comparisons of the value measure, $\hat{P}r$, rather than comparisons with prices. It is quite possible that, given market inefficiency, some high (low) values of $\hat{P}r$ are associated with overpricing (underpricing). In taking investment positions one would want to distinguish such cases from those where the mispricing was in the direction implied by the long and short positions taken here. Unfortunately, direct comparison of $\hat{P}r$ to prices is difficult because it is not in dollar-per-share form. However, Ou and Penman (1989) indicate that the return to the $\hat{P}r$ strategy is improved if one restricts investment in the long position to stocks with $\hat{P}r > 0.6$ and price low relative to earnings in cross-section and the short position to stocks with $\hat{P}r \leq 0.4$ and price high relative to earnings in cross-section.

References

Ball, R., 1978, Anomalies in relationships between securities' yields and yield-surrogates, Journal of Financial Economics, June-Sept., 103–106.

Ball, R. and P. Brown, 1968, An empirical evaluation of accounting income numbers, Journal of Accounting Research, Autumn, 159–178.

Ball, R., S.P. Kothari, and R.L. Watts, 1988, The economics of the relation between earnings changes and stock returns, Manuscript (William E. Simon Graduate School of Business Administration, University of Rochester, Rochester, NY).

Basu, S., 1983, The relationship between earnings yield, market value and the return for NYSE stocks: Further evidence, Journal of Financial Economics, June, 129–156.

Beaver, W., P. Kettler, and M. Scholes, 1970, The association between market determined and accounting determined risk measures, Accounting Review, Oct., 654–682.

Beaver, W.H. and D. Morse, 1978, What determines price–earnings ratios?, Financial Analysts' Journal, July-Aug., 65–76.

Bernard, V.L. and J.K. Thomas, 1989, Post-earnings announcement drift: Delayed price response or risk premium?, Journal of Accounting Research, forthcoming.

Blume, M.E. and R.F. Stambaugh, 1983, Biases in computed returns: An application to the size effect, Journal of Financial Economics, Oct., 387–404.

DeBondt, W.F.M. and R.H. Thaler, 1985, Does the stock market overreact?, Journal of Finance, July, 793–805.

DeBondt, W.F.M. and R.H. Thaler, 1987, Further evidence of investor overreaction and stock market seasonality, Journal of Finance, July, 557–581.

Fama, E.F. and K.R. French, 1988, Permanent and temporary components of stock prices, Journal of Political Economy, April, 246–273.

Foster, G., C. Olsen, and T. Shevlin, 1984, Earnings releases, anomalies, and the behavior of security returns, Accounting Review, Oct., 574–603.

Freeman, R.N., J.A. Ohlson, and S.H. Penman, 1982, Book rate-of-return and prediction of earnings changes: An empirical investigation, Journal of Accounting Research, Autumn, 639–653.

Garman, M.B. and J.A. Ohlson, 1980, Information and the sequential valuation of assets in arbitrage-free economics, Journal of Accounting Research, Autumn, 420–440.

Graham, B., D.L. Dodd, and S. Cottle, 1962, Security analysis: Principles and techniques, 4th ed. (McGraw-Hill, New York, NY).

McKibben, W., 1972, Econometric forecasting of common stock investment returns: A new methodology using fundamental operating data, Journal of Finance, May, 371–380.

Miller, M. and F. Modigliani, 1961, Dividend policy, growth and the valuation of shares, Journal of Business, Oct., 411–433.

Ohlson, J.A., 1988, A synthesis of security valuation theory and the role of dividends, cash flows, and earnings, Manuscript (Graduate School of Business, Columbia University, New York, NY).

Oppenheimer, H.R., 1981, Common stock selection: An analysis of Benjamin Graham's 'intelligent investor' approach (YMI Research Press, Ann Arbor, MI).

Ou, J.A., 1989, The incremental information content of non-earnings accounting numbers as earnings predictors, Manuscript (Leavey School of Business Administration, Santa Clara University, Santa Clara, CA).

Ou, J.A. and S.H. Penman, 1987, Financial statement analysis and the prediction of stock returns, Manuscript (University of California, Berkeley, CA).

Ou, J.A. and S.H. Penman, 1989, Accounting measurement, P/E ratios and the information content of security prices, Journal of Accounting Research, forthcoming.

Roll, R., 1983, On computing mean returns and the small firm premium, Journal of Financial Economics, Oct., 371–386.

Rosenberg, B. and V. Marathe, 1975, The prediction of investment risk: Systematic and residual risk, in: Proceedings of the seminar on the analysis of security prices, Nov. (Center for Research in Security Prices, University of Chicago, Chicago, IL) 185–226.

Rubinstein, M., 1976, The valuation of uncertain income streams and the pricing of options, Bell Journal of Economics, Autumn, 407–425.

Zarowin, P., 1988, Size, seasonality and stock market overreaction, Manuscript (New York University, New York, NY).

The earnings–price anomaly

Ray Ball*

University of Rochester, Rochester, NY 14627, USA

Received March 1992, final version received April 1992

This review explores systematic explanations for the anomalous evidence in the relation between accounting earnings and stock prices. The anomaly is that estimated future abnormal returns are predicted by public information about future earnings, contained in (1) current earnings and (2) current financial statement ratios. The current-earnings anomaly appears due to either market inefficiency or substantial costs of investors acquiring and processing information, the choice depending on one's priors concerning these costs and one's definition of market 'efficiency'. The financial-statement-information anomaly appears due to accounting ratios proxying for stocks' expected returns. Anomaly seems likely to be a permanent state.

1. Introduction

The apparent predictability of abnormal returns after earnings announcements has become one of the most significant anomalies in financial markets research, for several reasons. First, the magnitude is daunting: for example, the estimated abnormal return from trading on 'old' earnings information exceeds the normal return on the market.[1] Second, the anomaly is ubiquitous: earnings announcements occur every quarter for every stock. Third, the anomaly is scientifically indisputable: it appeared in Ball and Brown (1968) and has been replicated, consistently and with increasing precision, in one of the most carefully and thoroughly researched areas of the empirical financial economics literature.[2] Fourth, taken at face value the anomaly implies that share markets, which are central to the economy and which one would think are paradigm examples of the competitive model, grossly fail the test of competitive economic theory. Fifth, the anomaly challenges the theory underlying most of the widely-used models in modern financial economics. It therefore is not surprising that, while it

---

*I am grateful to Andrew Christie, S.P. Kothari, G. William Schwert, Ross Watts, Jerold Zimmerman, and workshop participants at UCLA for helpful comments. Financial support was received from the Bradley Policy Research Center at the Simon School, University of Rochester and from the John M. Olin Foundation.

[1] The magnitude of the estimated abnormal returns is reviewed in sections 4 and 5 below.

[2] Surveys of the evidence are in Ball (1978), Joy and Jones (1979), and Bernard (1989, 1992).

is only one property of the relation between accounting earnings and stock prices, the earnings–price anomaly has attracted considerable attention.

For some time, the contentious issue has not been the existence of the earnings–price anomaly, but its explanation. This paper addresses that issue. The following section describes the properties of an anomaly in the context of the theory of efficient markets and canvasses the principal feasible explanations. One possibility is that errors in estimating abnormal returns are correlated with earnings information, so the third section discusses controlling for variables (notably, size) that could proxy for expected returns in an efficient market. Section 4 reviews the evidence on the two principal versions of the anomaly: (1) the 'drift' in abnormal returns after quarterly earnings announcements documented by a sequence of studies, culminating in the novel evidence of Rendleman, Jones, and Latané (1987), confirmed by Freeman and Tse (1989) and Bernard and Thomas (1989, 1990) among others, that current earnings predicts abnormal returns at future earnings announcement dates; and (2) the evidence of Ou and Penman (1989a, b), extending the prior work of McKibben (1972) and others, that current financial statement information predicts abnormal returns via its capacity to predict future earnings. In both versions of the anomaly, the market seems unaware of the full implications of current accounting information for predicting future earnings. As a prelude to the analysis of the evidence in section 6, the fifth section briefly describes the economic magnitude of the unexploited profit opportunities allegedly involved. The sixth section then draws the previous sections together, exploring the consistency of the principal anomaly explanations outlined in sections 2 and 3 with the evidence summarized in sections 4 and 5.

The anomaly takes the form of current earnings (or current financial statement information about future earnings) predicting future abnormal returns. This could reflect a true association between earnings information and abnormal returns, which implies market inefficiency. Alternatively, it could reflect an association between earnings information and errors in estimating abnormal returns, which does not imply market inefficiency. Evaluating the evidence therefore involves evaluating the sensitivity of the research designs to errors in estimating abnormal returns.

I conclude that the Ou and Penman (1989a, b) evidence most likely results from an association between current accounting information and errors in estimating abnormal returns, whereas the evidence in Rendleman, Jones, and Latané (1987), Freeman and Tse (1989), and Bernard and Thomas (1989, 1990), among others, reflects either market inefficiency or substantial costs of investors acquiring and processing information. In one, the failure appears to lie with the research design, by not implementing an unbiased control for expected returns; in the other, the failure appears to lie either with the market or with how scholars have modelled an efficient stock market. Nevertheless, choice among hypotheses is hampered by the low power of the tests.

2. Interpreting earnings–price anomalies in the context of efficient market theory

In the context of the theory of efficient stock markets, an anomaly is a predictable abnormal return. The reasoning is as follows. Market efficiency is a simple application of the theory of competition, in which there are competitive returns, at the margin, to economic activity. If it is assumed to be costless for investors to use (i.e., acquire and process) an item of information, then in a competitive market they can expect no return from using it. Investment positions based on costless information therefore can expect to earn only the normal competitive return for those positions, with no additional compensation for using the information.[3] If investors can costlessly acquire and process information that allows them to earn predictable abnormal returns, then they can earn pure economic profits. In the context of the theory of efficient markets, this is anomalous (i.e., inconsistent).[4]

There are two classes of explanation for earnings–price anomalies:

1. The market truly is inefficient: that is, systematic mispricing allows true abnormal returns to be obtained, at zero cost, from using earnings information; or

2. The market is efficient and measured abnormal returns are biased estimates of pure economic profits, because:

    2.1. Costs of acquiring and processing earnings information are large enough to cause detectable returns to this economic activity; and/or

    2.2. Investors' rates of return are misestimated, for reasons that include failing to allow for taxes and using price estimates based on price quotations, with the estimation error being correlated with the earnings variables studied by researchers; and/or

    2.3. Abnormal rates of return (i.e., returns adjusted for expected or normal returns on investment) are misestimated, due to limitations in our knowledge of the determinants of expected returns (i.e., asset pricing models) or misestimation of relevant parameters such as risk, with the

---

[3]The theory of efficient markets is surveyed from different perspectives in Fama (1970, 1991), LeRoy (1989), and Ball (1991). This review is based on the perspective taken in the latter survey, in which items of information are distinguished economically, according to their costs of acquisition and processing. Consequently, there are different predictions concerning returns from publicly-available information about past prices and announced earnings, for example, versus returns from privately-held information such as managers' inside knowledge or security analysts' researched recommendations. That is, the so-called 'strong' form is distinguished in terms of information costs from the 'weak' and 'semi-strong' forms of Fama (1970).

[4]The term 'anomaly' was taken from Kuhn (1970, esp. sect. VI), whose definition can be paraphrased as: 'systematic evidence that appears scientifically precise but is inconsistent with the tenets of basic theory'.

estimation error being correlated with the earnings variables studied by researchers.

The first explanation is failure of the capital market, whereas the second is failure of researchers to construct either adequate theory or adequate empirical measures of price behavior in an efficient market. The remainder of this section explores the second explanation, in the spirit of Kuhn's (1970, p. 80) admonition: 'It is a poor carpenter who blames his tools.' Discussion of the consistency of the explanations with the evidence, including the pattern and magnitude of estimated abnormal returns, is deferred to section 6.

2.1. Information costs

In Fama, Fisher, Jensen, and Roll (1969) and Ball and Brown (1968), the issue of information acquisition and processing costs was finessed by studying items of simple, publicly-available information. Firms' quarterly and annual earnings reports are widely disseminated in the financial press, on the wire services, to analysts, and to interested parties. The reasoning then is that the cost to investors of *acquiring* (i.e., reproducing) an earnings number, in contrast to the firm's initial cost of producing that earnings number, becomes trivial as a consequence of its public-domain property. Further, provided the information variable studied by the researcher requires little *processing* cost to investors, such as in calculating the change in earnings per share (*EPS*), the combined cost of acquisition and processing remains trivial. This reasoning seems particularly persuasive when, for comparison with rates of return, information acquisition and processing costs are expressed as a percentage of market value, either of the firm or of a typical shareholding in the firm. If there are competitive returns relative to costs, then trivial information costs can be assumed to have only a trivial (and probably undetectable) effect on expected returns

Subsequent tests of the efficient market theory have come to rely on the researcher identifying information that, to an acceptable approximation, is costless to acquire and process. In contexts where information costs are substantial, they could have a detectable effect on security returns. This could be associated with an upward bias in abnormal returns that investors are estimated as earning. It thus is a potential explanation of the observed anomalies. This is a troublesome issue, because there is little the researcher can rely on, in the form of either theory or data, to gauge the magnitude of information processing and acquisition costs in practice.

The assumption of costless acquisition and processing is unlikely to be equally valid in all research contexts. It seems more valid in the earlier earnings–price research designs, which study simple variables such as increases and decreases in annual *EPS* [Ball and Brown (1968)]. Later designs involve the hypothetical investor in more (and more complex) information acquisition and processing, such as obtaining the dates of the following four quarters' earnings announcements and computing cross-sectionally standardized prediction errors from a model that exploits the information in the autocorrelation function in seasonally-differenced quarterly earnings [Rendleman, Jones, and Latané (1987), Bernard and Thomas (1990)]. The assumption of zero cost of using information thus has been increasingly tested over time.

The notion of information processing costs is not new to economists. Pioneering contributions include Coase (1937) and Stigler (1961) on the costs of observing prices, Hayek (1945) on the role of information in markets, and Simon (1955, 1957) on the concept of bounded rationality. Information costs are not inconsistent with competitive markets, though they do require a different characterization of price behaviour in competitive markets. This arguably is the central issue in the theory of efficient capital markets, because 'efficiency' is a property of the response of prices to information in competitive markets.[5] Nevertheless, it largely is an unresolved issue. In addition, little is known about the magnitude of information acquisition and processing costs in relation to accounting information, so their role in explaining the earnings–price anomaly remains unclear.

A related issue is *investor heterogeneity*. Investors differ in prior beliefs and face different costs of acquiring and processing new information. Yet homogeneity is assumed by most relevant theory, including versions of the capital asset pricing model (CAPM) used in testing efficiency and even the models of efficiency that characterize the market as responding essentially mechanistically to objective information.[6] Questions that remain unanswered include: Whose information costs determine expected returns in an efficient market? The highest-cost investor who is attracted to trade? Are infra-marginal investors (with lower information costs and thus higher net returns) consistent with efficiency?

A more challenging issue is raised by Hayek's (1945) characterization of markets. In his celebrated defence of the price mechanism, Hayek argues that the total information set reflected in prices is unknown, or even unknowable, to individuals. The immediate implication for share markets is that each investor trades without knowing the full information set that other investors have used in trading and thus without knowing the full information set that has influenced prices. An investor who possesses an item of information must process that information, to form a view of its effect on price, but also must decide whether other investors have used that information in setting the transacted price. The Hayekian characterization of markets transforms the role of information processing costs for an investor trading on the basis of information, as distinct

---

[5]The relation between competitive and efficient markets, including its historical development, is discussed in Ball (1991).

[6]Models incorporating heterogeneity are proposed in Merton (1987), Admati and Pfleiderer (1988), and Shleifer and Vishny (1990), among others.

from a liquidity trader. It is facile to conclude that the role of information processing costs, in tests of simulated information-based trading rules, is not well understood.

2.2. Errors in estimating rates of return

The dependent variable in market efficiency tests is the return earned from trading on information, adjusted for normal or expected returns. Rates of return derived from widely-accessible data files, notably those supplied by the Center for Research in Security Prices (CRSP), provide estimates of the returns from trading on information, but are not true returns. They incorporate errors from at least two sources.

First, the price estimates recorded on the data files are not necessarily prices at which one could trade on the basis of earnings information. Either they are last-trade prices (which might be executed at the bid or the ask price) or, particularly for thinly-traded stocks, they are bid-ask averages. Keim (1989, table 6) reports the average bid-ask spread for NYSE/AMEX stocks as 2.8%, suggesting that their rates of return cannot be estimated within this magnitude of accuracy.[7] Keim also reports systematic changes, correlated with time (e.g., at the turn of the year), in the frequency with which trades occur at ask prices. Systematic movements from bid to ask, or vice versa, appear to bias estimated returns at particular times. Because the level of precision involved is independent of the return interval, short-interval returns are most likely to be affected (i.e., when either studying short periods or requiring repeated trading over longer periods). Abnormal returns over long holding-period intervals are unlikely to be explained by trading-mechanism effects, except for very-low-price stocks.

Second, the return estimates ignore the possible effects on security returns of differential taxation of dividend income and capital gains.[8] These effects could be correlated with earnings due to: (1) the correlation between dividends and earnings and (2) nonlinearity in the capital gains tax function, due to gains and losses being taxed at different rates, which makes the value of capital gains taxes an increasing function of stock price volatility and thus of the magnitude of information in announced earnings.[9]

Errors induced by quotation-mechanism effects and by imperfect allowance for taxes illustrate the general point that researchers use estimates of rates of

---

[7] Jones, Kaul, and Lipson (1991, table 1) report an equivalent figure of 4.7% for NASDAQ-NMS stocks.

[8] See Brennan (1973) and Litzenberger and Ramaswamy (1979) for analyses.

[9] The relation between earnings information and volatility was first observed by Beaver (1968). The effect of price volatility on the value of capital gains taxes is analyzed in Ball and Bowers (1983).

return, not true returns.[10] In the context of earnings–price studies, the primary issue is not the effect of errors on efficiency in estimation, due to the large sample sizes available [Bernard and Thomas (1989, 1990) study over 100,000 earnings announcements]. The concern is the potential for bias arising from correlation between errors in measuring returns and the earnings variables studied. This issue is largely unexplored.[11]

2.3. Errors in measuring normal (expected) returns

Abnormal return estimates involve an adjustment for 'normal' or 'expected' returns. This typically is performed by controlling for risk, as suggested by the simple Sharpe–Lintner form of the CAPM. Yet the CAPM is an abstraction that has clear limitations, some of which are discussed below.

1. The CAPM is a pure-exchange model, ignoring properties of the supply of securities.

2. The CAPM is a partial-equilibrium model, defining 'normal' returns relative to returns on the population of assets, as measured by returns on the market index. It thus can only address efficiency with respect to microeconomic information, that is information whose effect on security prices is not reflected in the index.

Due to these limitations, the simple CAPM allows no statements about how an efficient market would behave in several dimensions. One dimension is its response to the component of firms' earnings variation that is due to economy-wide factors.[12] The following conjecture illustrates this point. Suppose increases in market-wide earnings are associated with opposing effects on share prices: (1) increases, due to the good earnings news, and (2) decreases, due to an increase in the demand for capital by firms, which react to the good news by revising upward their assessment of the profitability of new investment opportunities (thus requiring expected returns to increase, to attract more capital from investors). The net effect on market-wide expected returns would evolve over time, as a function of the time path of new capital creation. In the absence of

---

[10]The related issue of transactions costs, and their effect on estimated returns from simulated trading strategies, is discussed in section 6.2 below.

[11]Skinner (1991), discussed below, finds no evidence of significant trading-mechanism biases to estimated abnormal returns at earnings announcements. Bernard and Thomas (1989) report that their estimated abnormal returns are not associated with dividend yields (a test of tax effects).

[12]See Brown and Ball (1967) for evidence on the economy-wide 'market' factor in earnings and Sloan (1993) for evidence on the relation between it and the equivalent factor in returns. Note that Ball and Brown (1968) and Ball, Kothari, and Watts (1992) remove the market factor in earnings before studying the earnings–price relation.

a macroeconomic theory that provides precise, time-dated predictions of market-wide expected returns, the researcher can neither model nor test the behaviour of an efficient market in response to the market factor in earnings.[13]

Balvers, Cosimano, and McDonald (1990) show that aggregate output predicts the future return on the market and argue this is consistent with market efficiency. Fama (1990) and Chen (1991) report related results. Fama (1990, p. 1090) views the implications for efficiency as unclear: is the response of expected returns to current aggregate variables too large, too small, or 'correct'? These results link to accounting variables because, as Brown and Ball (1967) for example show, indexes of current earnings are correlated with aggregate output. In general, when portfolios are formed on the basis of accounting variables such as changes in earnings, inventories, liquidity, or leverage [Ou and Penman (1989a, b)], a proportion of the individual-firm variability is eliminated by diversification, and the contribution of aggregate economic factors to their remaining time-series variability is increased. Yet this is the component of the accounting variables for which the simple CAPM makes no predictions concerning market reaction. In principle, this problem can be eliminated in research designs that remove the market component of earnings, either by earnings 'market model' regression or by simulating hedge portfolios that have zero beta and no net investment in the market portfolio, but in practice that is not always accomplished.

A second dimension in which the simple CAPM is silent is predictions about securities' risks. Yet risk (and change in risk) likely is endogenous in many research contexts. For example, Ball and Kothari (1991) show that betas estimated from daily returns change in the days surrounding earnings announcements. Ball, Kothari, and Watts (1992) show that betas estimated from annual returns change as a decreasing function of firms' annual earnings. This is due in part to the association of earnings with stock prices and thus with debt/equity ratios. Adjusting for the observed risk changes removes a portion of the 'drift' after announcements of annual earnings. Again, is the observed response of betas to earnings (and thus the adjustment of the estimated 'drift') too large, too small, or 'correct'?

3. Being a partial-equilibrium model, the CAPM is susceptible to deficiencies in sampling from the population of assets, for example when using a sharemarket 'index' portfolio as a proxy.

---

[13]An advantage of the CAPM is the precision, in both magnitude and time, of its predicted post-announcement return behavior in an efficient market. It predicts a zero expected disturbance, immediately after public information announcements. A disadvantage is that the model addresses only 'micro' information, with zero-sum valuation implications in cross-section.

Share indexes exclude most small corporations, unincorporated businesses, human capital, real estate, and consumer durables, among other assets.[14] Market indexes are dominated by large corporate equities, particularly when they are weighted by sharemarket capitalization. This suggests that sharemarket indexes provide a more effective control for the expected return on large corporate equities than on other assets. Conversely, market indexes seem a less effective control for expected returns on the smallest listed stocks, which are the likely closest substitutes for the assets omitted from the index.

4. The CAPM assumes security returns are continuous and mean-variance.

Fama (1976, ch. 1) concludes that stock returns generally are leptokurtic. There appears to be a higher frequency of 'large' market-wide falls than rises. McNichols (1988) shows that returns are more positively skewed around earnings announcements than during nonannouncement periods. The implications of such results for short-interval expected returns, in general and around earnings announcement dates, are largely unknown.

These and other limitations in our knowledge of security pricing in an efficient market do not in themselves imply that research is fruitless. They do suggest at least three things. First, the power of tests of efficiency or inefficiency hypotheses is an important issue. Second, research designs that are more sensitive to suspected limitations in our knowledge of security pricing can be interpreted more as providing clues concerning those limitations, and less as providing substantive evidence on market efficiency. Third, research can be made less sensitive to these limitations by careful selection of proxies for expected returns in an efficient market.

3. Size as a proxy for expected returns

A promising proxy for expected returns is market value of equity (size). Reasons include the following:

(1) Over extended periods, size consistently is a better predictor of expected returns than estimated betas.[15] While not fully understood, this 'size effect' does not challenge the efficient market theory. There is no serious alternative hypothesis that the information in firm size, which is public information and easy to process, is so comprehensively ignored by investors in their pursuit of abnormal returns that it predicts abnormal returns over extended

---

[14]This point is due to Roll (1977). Stambaugh (1982) incorporates other assets into CAPM tests.
[15]See, for example, Banz (1981), Jaffe, Keim, and Westerfield (1989), and Fama and French (1991).

periods.[16] The only serious hypothesis is that size is proxying for expected returns.

(2) Information acquisition and processing costs are likely to be a deceasing percentage of market capitalization. If there are competitive returns to incurring information costs, then expected returns also are a decreasing function of size.

(3) The effect of personal taxes on returns is likely to depend on size. Size is correlated with dividend yield and thus with taxes on the divided component of returns. Size also is correlated and with stock return variance, which affects the value of capital gains taxes.[17] For legal and other reasons, small stocks are less likely to be held by tax-exempt institutions. These factors suggest that pre-tax returns could be a function of size.

(4) Sharemarket indexes incorporate a nonrepresentative sample of assets by size (see section 2 above). It is feasible that betas estimated from sharemarket data provide biased estimates of expected returns, as a function of size.[18]

(5) Proportional bid–ask spreads, and thus the quality of stock return data used to estimate CAPM betas, are a decreasing function of size.

(6) Amihud and Mendelson (1986) hypothesize that expected returns are an increasing function of spreads, which constitute a round-trip transactions cost. Spreads arise because the flow of buy and sell orders to the market is discrete, both in time and quantity, and thus they decrease with size.

(7) Handa, Kothari, and Wasley (1989) show that when betas are estimated from longer-interval returns, they have greater cross-sectional dispersion, the cross-sectional risk/return relation is more consistent with the Sharpe–Lintner CAPM, and the relation between size and expected returns becomes statistically insignificant. This suggests that the 'size effect' in part is due to errors in measuring betas from short-interval returns.

(8) Size (market value of equity) by definition is a function of past equity returns. Ball and Kothari (1989) show that betas are a function of past equity returns. Size at a point in time thus can proxy for beta changes up to that instant.

The arguments collectively suggest that size be used in addition to estimated beta as a control for expected returns, in the absence of a better alternative.[19]

---

[16]Models that classify investors as informed and uninformed or sophisticated and unsophisticated would predict a size effect in the opposite direction, if the likelihood of being informed or sophisticated is an increasing function of size.

[17]Size also is correlated and with stock return variance at earnings announcements.

[18]Evidence consistent with this possibility is provided by Stambaugh (1982), in which the performance of the Sharpe–Lintner CAPM is sensitive to the set of assets employed in the tests.

[19]The evidence of Fama and French (1991) further suggests that size and the market/book ratio be used *instead of* estimated beta. This could reflect the phenomenon observed in Ball and Kothari (1989), since market/book is highly positively correlated with past equity returns and thus positively correlated with leverage and expected return on equity.

They also suggest there is little to learn about market efficiency from studies that demonstrate predictable CAPM-estimated abnormal returns, if the abnormal returns disappear after controlling for size. Such results are not likely to be either: (1) novel, being a manifestation of the well-documented size effect, or (2) relevant to market efficiency, if size simply is proxying for expected returns. The more interesting research question in these studies is *why* size proxies for expected returns.

4. The anomalous earnings–price evidence

This section reviews the two principal categories of earnings–price anomaly: the 'drift' in the apparent market response to earnings and the unexploited implications of financial statement information for future earnings and abnormal returns. These are chosen because they are the largest and most comprehensive earnings-related anomalies and because of the contrasting interpretations placed on them in section 6 below.

4.1. Quarterly earnings information

The 'drift' in the apparent market response was first observed by Ball and Brown (1968), using annual earnings. It subsequently was shown to be even more pronounced for quarterly earnings, by a string of researchers: Jones and Litzenberger (1970), Brown and Kennelly (1972), Joy, Litzenberger, and McEnally (1977), Watts (1978), Foster, Olsen, and Shevlin (1984), Rendleman, Jones, and Latané (1987), Bernard and Thomas (1989, 1990), Freeman and Tse (1989), Wiggins (1991), and Bartov (1992), among others.

Bernard and Thomas (1989, 1990) report an exhaustive investigation of approximately 100,000 quarterly earnings announcements over 1974–86. Their salient results are:

1. A portfolio that every calendar quarter takes equal-weighted long positions in the top decile of earnings performers, and short positions in the bottom decile, earns + 4.19% average estimated abnormal return over the 60 trading days (approximately one quarter) following the earnings announcement.[20] The estimated post-announcement abnormal return is positive for 46 of the 50 calendar quarters studied.

---

[20]Following Foster, Olsen, and Shevlin (1984), Bernard and Thomas convert the 4.19% return earned from the average quarter's earnings announcement to an annualized rate of approximately 18%. This is misleading if the anomaly is due in part to once-off effects such as information costs or Keim's (1989) bid/ask effect. For example, a 0.25% abnormal return over 5 days might seem comparable to reasonable information acquisition and processing costs, or to bid–ask spreads, but when expressed as a 12.5% annual rate it might not seem comparable at all. Note that Bernard and Thomas standardize the earnings variable and are careful to avoid any hindsight biases in the design.

2. Estimated post-announcement abnormal returns from this trading rule are a decreasing function of size.
3. Over the first five trading days (approximately one week), the portfolio earns + 0.70%, i.e., one sixth of the estimated 60-day abnormal returns.
4. Trading days 61–80 exhibit additional estimated abonormal returns of approximately the same magnitude as those in days 1–60. By day 180 (approximately three quarters) the estimated abnormal return from the trading strategy climbs to + 7.74%.
5. Little or no further 'drift' occurs beyound day 180.

These results are consistent with over two decades of prior research. The most intriguing result in Bernard and Thomas (1989, 1990) builds on the hypothesis and evidence of Rendleman, Jones, and Latané (1987), who link a component of the post-announcement 'drift' to the market not fully appreciating the time series behaviour of quarterly earnings. Bernard and Thomas report that:

6. A significant component of the predictable post-announcement abnormal return occurs at the announcement of following quarters' earnings. The sign of *this* quarter's deseasonalized change in *EPS* is associated with estimated abnormal returns of + 1.32%, + 0.70%, + 0.04%, and − 0.66% at the time of the *following* four quarters' announcements (*t*-statistics are + 14.63, + 8.46, + 0.45, and − 7.86). What makes this result remarkable is that the pattern of the estimated abnormal returns mimics the (+ , + , 0, −) pattern of autocorrelation in changes in the average firm's seasonally-adjusted quarterly *EPS*.

Similar results are obtained by Freeman and Tse (1989), Wiggins (1991), and Bartov (1992). The market seems to assume a seasonal random walk in quarterly earnings, unaware of the complete implications of current *EPS* for the next four quarters' *EPS*. Bernard and Thomas (1990, p. 338) conclude: 'The evidence is consistent with the hypothesis that stock prices partially reflect a naive earnings expectation: that future earnings will be equal to earnings for the comparable quarter of the prior year.'

4.2. Annual report information

Ou and Penman (1989a,b) propose a more general version of this hypothesis. In the spirit of Graham, Dodd, and Cottle (1962) and McKibben (1972), they hypothesize there is underutilized information about future earnings contained in a variety of financial statement variables, not just in current earnings. This information can be used to predict future earnings, even though it is not so used by the market, and thus it can generate abnormal returns. They state (1989a, p. 296, parentheses in original):

> Firms' ('fundamental') values are indicated by information in financial statements. Stock prices deviate at time from these values and only slowly gravitate towards the fundamental values. Thus, analysis of published financial statements can discover values that are not reflected in stock prices.

They develop a LOGIT model for predicting changes in annual *EPS* one year ahead, using publicly-available financial statement information. Lacking a specific theory of what financial statement information is underutilized by the market, Ou and Penman select 28 financial-statement variables (16 in one subperiod and 18 in the other, with only six in common) from a wide set of 68 variables, purely on the basis of their ability to predict earnings. Those selected include return on assets, return on equity, change in return on equity, debt/equity ratio, percent change in dividend per share, and percent change in inventories. The model parameters then are fitted to subsequent (i.e., out-of-sample) values of firms' financial statement variables, to generate predictions of future earnings. Predictions are based on the estimated LOGIT probability of a future earnings increase, denoted *Pr*. This variable is ranked in pooled cross-section and time-series and extreme observations are selected by a programmed trading rule.

Ou and Penman program a strategy of long positions in the 45.3% of stocks with the highest predicted probability of an earnings increase and short positions in the lowest 10.8%, weighted to produce zero net investment. They report estimated out-of-sample abnormal returns from this strategy over 1973–83. These average +8.3% in the first year after the *EPS* predictions are made (i.e., in the year leading up to and including the announcement of the actual *EPS* outcome), +6.2% in the second year, and +6.3% in the third (i.e., two years after the actual *EPS* is announced). Ou and Penman (1989a, p. 328) conclude: 'The evidence here suggests that financial statements capture fundamentals that are not reflected in prices.'

Ou and Penman use a similar research design, and obtain qualitatively similar results, to McKibben (1972). The approach is similar to Value Line's long-standing method of stock selection.[21] Their results are replicated, albeit with some qualifications and with more a skeptical interpretation, in three studies published in this issue: Greig (1992), Holthausen and Larcker (1992), and Stober (1992). Lev and Thiagarajan (1991) adopt a different approach in

---

[21] The ability of financial variables to predict estimated abnormal returns has been known for some time. In the 'modern' literature, P/E ratios and market/book ratios have been studied by Basu (1983), Jaffe, Keim, and Westerfield (1989), and Fama and French (1991), among others.

selecting financial statement variables, but obtain qualitatively similar results.

5. Economic significance of the anomalies

As a prelude to discussing the interpretation of these anomalies in the following section, it is useful to reflect on their magnitude, particularly in dollar (rather than rate of return) terms. Bernard and Thomas (1989) estimate that *every quarter* the total feasible pure profit from trading on the 20% extreme-earnings-announcing stocks is 7.74% times 10% of the aggregate market value of all NYSE–AMEX firms. After only thirteen quarters of running their strategy, the total feasible pure profit would be approximately 10% of the total market value of all NYSE–AMEX firms, without reinvestment. Calculated conservatively, it accumulates to the value of the entire NYSE–AMEX market after approximately 34 years.[22]

The Ou and Penman result, taken at face value, implies pure profits of far greater scale. Once every year, their strategy earns a +20.8% abnormal return over the following three years, on 55% of the firms in the market. It takes only eight years to earn pure profits in the order of the entire market's capitalization, without compounding.[23] Some free lunch.

6. A survey of feasible interpretations

Several feasible interpretations are surveyed in this section. None appears sufficient to explain all the anomalous evidence, though they are not mutually-exclusive.

6.1. CAPM 'beta' risk

One possibility is beta estimation error that is correlated with earnings. For example, the 'market factor' in quarterly earnings could proxy for errors arising from omitting assets in the market index or from using an incorrectly-specified estimation system.

Beta estimation error also could be due to risk varying with quarterly earnings. Consistent with this explanation, Ball, Kothari, and Watts (1992) and Ball and Kothari (1989, 1990) show that risk is a function of stocks' earnings

---

[22]These calculations are intended to give only a first-order approximation to the scale of the anomaly. They are not intended to be precise or implementable. They assume equal weighting, as in Bernard and Thomas (1989), and take positions equal to the entire amount of outstanding stock in all firms. They assume no reinvestment and ignore possible pure profits from the 80% of firms that are not in the extreme earnings-performance portfolios.

[23]If account was taken for Stober's (1991) finding, that the estimated abnormal returns continue beyond three years (discussed below), then this period would be shortened further.

outcomes, past returns, and quarterly earnings announcements, respectively. Bernard and Thomas (1989) replicate these endogenous beta changes in their sample. While endogenous beta changes predict the sign of the estimated abnormal returns, they cannot explain its magnitude. Ibbotson and Sinquefield (1989, exhibit A-8) report an average risk premium of 3.6% per year over the period studied by Bernard and Thomas. For beta bias to fully explain their estimated abnormal returns over days 1–180, betas thus would need to be underestimated (overestimated) by approximately 1.3 (3.0) for the long (short) position stocks, which is implausible. The corresponding numbers for days 61–180 are 0.3 (2.6). In addition, beta bias cannot explain: (1) the seasonal pattern of the earnings anomaly over the ensuing four quarters of the earnings event cycle, (2) the consistency of the anomaly in chronological time,[24] or (3) the high abnormal returns over the short intervals immediately after earnings announcements and at subsequent earnings announcement periods. Risk estimation bias thus is a potential explanation for only a minor part of the quarterly-earnings anomaly. Similar reasoning applies to the Ou and Penman anomaly.

6.2. Transactions costs

Nor is transactions costs a sufficient explanation, for a variety of reasons. First, the numbers generally are too large to be explained by transactions costs alone. This is not the case over short periods: Bernard and Thomas estimate trading-rule abnormal returns of only 0.70%, 1.32%, 0.70%, 0.04%, and 0.66% over the five days immediately after earnings announcements, and the three days surrounding each of the four following quarters' announcements, respectively. However, their +7.74% estimate over the first 180 post-announcement days is comfortably in excess of reasonable transactions cost estimates, as is the Ou and Penman (1989a, b) anomaly.

Second, the role of transactions costs in any definition of market efficiency is unclear. Jensen (1978) proposes that predictable abnormal returns are consistent with market efficiency, provided they are less than transactions costs. This has an undesirable implication, that the likelihood a given sequence of prices will be judged consistent with efficiency is an *increasing* function of transactions costs. For example, a predictable abnormal return of 2.5% would be treated as

---

[24]In dismissing beta-estimation error as an explanation of the earnings anomaly, Bernard and Thomas (1989, p. 15) take comfort in the fact that the estimated abnormal returns are uncorrelated with the return on the market portfolio. But this result would have been guaranteed if they had used the market model to control for beta risk, and is a characteristic of all CAPM-based tests, because CAPM abnormal returns by construction are uncorrelated with the index. The result cannot shed light upon whether the correct market index (and thus the correct set of betas) is being used, or upon whether the CAPM is a well-specified model of expected returns in this context.

evidence of inefficiency at 2% cost of transacting, but not if the cost is increased to 3%.

Third, it is not even obvious that transactions costs logically can be used to predict abnormal returns. Transactions costs might predict a delayed price response to information in cases where costs inhibit trading upon its announcement. For example, good (bad) earnings news that implies price increases (decreases) of less than 2% might not generate transactions when the cost of trading is 2%. When no trading occurs, the price bias then is bounded by the magnitude of transactions costs. But there is no predicted price bias when a transaction has occurred, for whatever reason, and thus when any transactions cost inertia has been overcome. As demonstrated by Beaver (1968) and others, trading volume increases around earnings announcements, so essentially all of the estimated rates of return in the studies under review are computed from actual transactions prices. The market thus has overcome any inertia of transactions cost in setting most prices studied. Transactions costs of x% then might explain unremoved price *errors* of $\pm x$%, independent of the sign of the earnings news, but they cannot explain a systematic *bias* of that magnitude.

The role of transactions costs is clouded by other issues. For example, whose transactions costs are relevant? The lowest-cost trader's? If so, are these zero at the margin, because transactions occur in the absence of information announcements? All factors considered, there is a strong case that transactions costs are an illogical and implausible explanation of the anomalies.

6.3. Liquidity and trading-mechanism effects

Amihud and Mendelson (1986) propose an asset-pricing model in which expected returns increase in illiquidity, measured by the bid–ask spread. In this model, the spread influences expected returns because it is a round-trip transactions cost paid by the investor. This raises the possibility that abnormal returns from simulated trading strategies are estimated with error when no allowance is made for spreads. For this effect to explain the earnings–price anomaly, it is necessary that spreads be a function of earnings news.

A related issue, raised by Keim (1989), is the effect of the trading mechanism on prices recorded on the CRSP files, and whether these are biased estimates of prices at which trades could be executed. Any effect would be bounded by the bid–ask spread, which Keim reports averages 2.8% for NYSE/AMEX stocks. It thus would most likely occur in short-interval returns, such as those observed around current and subsequent quarters' announcements. For this effect to explain the earnings–price anomaly, it is necessary that the likelihood of trading at the bid or the ask be a function of earnings news.

The evidence suggests these effects do not explain the anomaly. Skinner (1991, table 6) reports an increase in post-announcement spreads for firms with above-median magnitudes of earnings news, but the increase is at most 0.11%

of price. Skinner (1991, table 9) also reports no change in the frequency of trading at the bid or the ask as a function of earnings news. Liquidity and trading-mechanism effects thus do not appear sufficient to explain the estimated abnormal returns.

A related issue is the variety of seasonals observed in recorded returns. Cross (1973), French (1980), Rogalski (1984), and Harris (1986, 1989), among others, report that returns estimated from transactions prices vary systematically with day-of-the-week, weekends, time-of-day, and overnight versus during trading. Keim (1989) and Lakonishok and Maberly (1990) link these empirical regularities to trading-mechanism effects. Lee (1992) reports a rapid increase in large trades initiated by buyers (sellers) during good (bad) earnings announcements, but a puzzling increase in small buy orders regardless of the sign of earnings news. Patell and Wolfson (1984) report that 35% of their sample announced earnings while the market was closed. These results suggest caution in interpreting estimated average abnormal returns over small intervals, notably the days surrounding current and future quarters' earnings, lest they be trading-mechanism effects.

An intriguing possibility is that: (1) the time and date of earnings announcements is a function of the earnings news, (2) estimated abnormal returns are a function of time and date, and thus (3) a relation is induced between earnings news and estimated abnormal returns. Further, serial correlation in earnings news could induce serial correlation in announcement timing and thus predictable estimated abnormal returns at earnings announcement, as reported in Bernard and Thomas (1990). Such seasonals in announcement effects could explain only a small portion of the total 'drift', but a potentially higher portion of the estimated abnormal returns at subsequent quarters' announcement dates. Further research on trading-mechanism effects appears warranted.

6.4. Overstated t-statistics

It is possible that researchers have systematically understated the standard errors of various statistics, due (say) to some undetected form of cross-sectional correlation or to an over-fitting bias.[25] This seems unlikely. It is not consistent with the replication of the basic results over different time periods.[26] Nor is it

---

[25]Typically, portfolios are formed (i.e., securities are grouped) on the rank of the independent variable. Lo and MacKinlay (1989) demonstrate that even weak correlation at the individual-security level, between the independent variable and errors in estimating expected returns, then becomes significant at the portfolio level. Because portfolios are formed in part on the basis of information about errors in estimating expected returns, the distribution of the test statistic (under the null hypothesis that the earnings variable is uninformative concerning errors in estimating expected returns) typically is misrepresented in favor of rejecting the null.

[26]The exception is Holthausen and Larcker (1992), who cannot replicate Ou and Penman (1989, 1990) beyond 1983, the last year Ou and Penman study, or on OTC stocks.

consistent with the Bernard and Thomas (1990) result that the abnormal returns from their trading rule are positive in each of the thirteen years studied.

6.5. Earnings variables proxy for expected returns

An alternative interpretation is that either the CAPM or the empirical market portfolio used in its implementation is misspecified, and the independent variables proxy for errors in estimating expected returns.[27] The proxy effect is compounded by: (1) differencing the independent variables which then can contain information about errors in observing nonstationarities in expected returns, (2) ignoring the intermediate range of the independent variables and thus focussing on the extreme nonstationarities, and (3) because earnings changes are leptokurtic [Ball, Kothari, and Watts (1992)] extreme-decile earnings changes tend to be unusually large, thus magnifying potential nonstationarities and proxy effects.

There are several factors suggesting that the Ou and Penman (1989a, b) result is due to their *Pr* variable proxying for expected returns.

(1) Ou and Penman use several independent variables (*ROA*, *ROE*, debt/equity ratio, dividend payout, gross margin ratio) that individually seem likely to proxy for expected returns. They also use several differenced variables (change in inventories, change in debt/equity ratio, change in *ROE*, growth in total assets) that individually seem likely to proxy for change in expected returns, thus increasing the difficulty of controlling for post-announcement differences in expected returns on the long- and short-position stocks.[28] When a combination of 16 or 18 such variables is selected from a set of 68, their combined potential to proxy for expected returns and changes in expected returns is magnified.

(2) Ou and Penman offer no hypotheses as to which variables predict abnormal returns. Variables are chosen purely on the basis of their empirical association with one-year-ahead earnings in the pre-test period. No theory is involved in the choice. This research design increases the likelihood of discovering an association with estimated future abnormal returns that is due to factors other than those hypothesized.[29] Note that there is little

---

[27]This hypothesis was raised in Ball (1978).

[28]See Ball and Kothari (1989).

[29]Lev and Thiagarajan (1991) attempt to overcome this limitation by pre-specifying the variables. However, their selection process leaves open the possibility of *ex post* selection biases. For example, they appear to choose labor force changes as a predictor of abnormal returns in part because of the favorable reaction of analysts to workforce reductions during the late 1970s and 1980s. They then test the variable as a predictor of abnormal returns over the period 1975–88. It seems unlikely that the favorable analyst reaction to this variable was completely established before 1975.

overlap between the two subperiods in the variables selected and in their weightings.

(3) Ou and Penman's fundamental hypothesis, that the market underutilizes the earnings implications of publicly-available information contained in firms' financial statements (such as debt/equity ratios, dividend changes, gross margins on sales, working capital ratios, and inventory changes), seems implausible in this context. None of this information can reasonably be viewed as obscure: it is routine accounting information. It seems unlikely to be the type of information that would *routinely* (i.e., for at least the duration of Ou and Penman's sample period) escape the attention of the market *for years into the future*. Nor does it seem consistent with pure profits of such a large magnitude.

(4) Stober (1992) replicates their analysis and shows that the estimated abnormal returns continue at an almost constant rate for at least six years beyond the earnings prediction date. This suggests the financial statement variables used by Ou and Penman are proxying for expected returns.[30]

(5) Stober's result, that the abnormal returns extend for at least six years after the earnings prediction is made, is qualitatively inconsistent with Ou and Penman's own hypotheses and model. Their research design predicts only *one-year-ahead* earnings. It specifically identifies and trades on information about *next* year's earnings that is contained in this year's financial statements [see Ou and Penman (1989a, p. 298), for example]. It does not address six-years-ahead earnings. But not one of the studies on post-announcement drift, surveyed in section 4.1 above, has price responses to earnings lagging by more than three quarters.[31] The continuation of the estimated abnormal returns for at least four and one quarter years beyond the horizon predicted by the Ou and Penman hypothesis is grossly inconsistent with that hypothesis. It implies that the hypothesis has failed to describe the empirical phenomenon that is observed.

(6) Holthausen and Larcker (1992) show that the Ou and Penman hypothesis essentially adds noise to our understanding of the behavior of abnormal returns, in the following sense. The hypothesis is that there is an unexploited link from financial statement data to abnormal returns, via the unexploited implications of that data for future earnings. Holthausen and Larcker test the unexploited-implications hypothesis by correlating the financial-statement data directly with abnormal returns, without any hypothesis about earnings. The resulting strategy dominates the Ou and Penman strategy,

---

[30]In addition, Holthausen and Larcker (1991) report that the abnormal returns *increase* each year, for the four event-time years after the earnings predictions are made.

[31]Ignoring reversals at quarter +4, which go in the other direction.

thus implying that the unexploited-implications hypothesis is not what is driving the results.

(7) Greig (1992) shows that size outperforms Ou and Penman's *Pr* measure in predicting abnormal returns. While size *per se* hardly is a satisfactory explanation, there are reasons to expect that size generally proxies for expected returns (see section 3 above).[32]

(8) Greig (1992) shows that Ou and Penman's research design allows the frequency of long and short positions in stocks to change over time. Their simulated portfolio has positive risk. There is evidence that *Pr* predicts the market index. After controlling for beta and implementing a more precise control for size than Ou and Penman (1989a), *Pr* loses its apparent ability to predict abnormal returns.

For these reasons, the evidence of Ou and Penman (1989a, b) seems consistent with the hypothesis that their *Pr* variable, which is a composite of various financial statement variables, proxies for differences in securities' expected returns.

6.6. Substantial information production costs or market inefficiency?

One explanation for the earnings–price anomaly is that substantial costs of information acquisition and/or processing would be encountered in implementing the trading rules simulated by researchers. The principal remaining alternative is that the market consistently has used accounting information inefficiently, leaving unexploited pure economic profit opportunities.[33] These explanations are difficult to distinguish in theory, because the role of information costs in an efficient market is largely unexplored. They also are difficult to

---

[32]Size also is associated with past returns (by definition) and past earnings performance (due to the association between earnings and returns, particularly over long intervals). In the Ou and Penman study, size thus could be related to *Pr* because high (low) *Pr* firms have experienced large past earnings decreases (increases) [Ou and Penman (1989a, table 7) and Brooks and Buckmaster (1976) for evidence]. Thus, the Ou and Penman anomaly overlaps that reported by DeBondt and Thaler (1985, 1987). The ongoing debate on how to measure expected returns in this context thus is relevant [see Ball and Kothari (1989) and Chopra, Lakonishok, and Ritter (1991)].

[33]Bernard and Thomas (1989, 1990) provide a variety of evidence aimed at eliminating other explanations. They report that their estimated abnormal returns are not due to the five APT factors identified by Chen, Roll, and Ross (1986) as being priced (a test of CAPM misspecification), are not associated with dividend yields (a test of tax effects), and are positive in 90% of the quarters studied. They argue reasonably that the almost consistently-positive sign of the estimated return to the trading strategy is evidence that it is not a compensation for risk. However, that is not evidence against mismeasurement of expected returns, because risk is not the only feasible determinant of rates of return (though the CAPM induces us to think that way). They also note that Watts' (1978) results are not obtained from Compustat earnings data, thus suggesting that the general 'drift' over the following two or three quarters is not due to Compustat reporting revised earnings data. The clustering of estimated abnormal returns at subsequent quarters' earnings announcements is another matter.

distinguish in practice, because they offer identical predictions about the signs of abnormal returns and because (as discussed in section 2.1 above) little is known about the magnitudes of information costs.

The issue in theory is whether information acquisition and processing costs are consistent with one's definition of market efficiency. Competitive returns on information acquisition and processing costs certainly are consistent with competitive securities markets. If it is too costly for investors to determine the full implications of current financial statement information for future earnings, then they will not do so. They will wait for future earnings (and/or any other information that is less costly to process) to be announced before adjusting prices.[34] There will remain a cost-efficient amount of unexploited information in current earnings and other accounting numbers. The term 'efficient' therefore could be used to describe a market in which there is a cost-efficient amount of predictability in security prices, and there are competitive returns from acquiring and processing information, without violating either fundamental economic principles or the spirit in which of the efficient markets hypothesis was developed.[35] To date, however, the term has been used to describe price behavior in the absence of information acquisition and processing costs, possibly due to difficulties in developing both the theory and information-cost measures for empirical research.

Here also, the question is whether the explanation is consistent with the magnitude of the estimated abnormal returns. Because little is known about the magnitude of information processing costs and their effect on security returns, one's priors on the cost of processing accounting information in the simulated trading strategies are relevant when interpreting the evidence. In the case of the Ou and Penman (1989a, b) results, several factors assist in forming priors. First, it is difficult to imagine that a competitive market would allow returns of the magnitude they report, viewed either in rate of return or total dollar terms, for processing the financial-statement information incorporated in their *Pr* variable. Second, an information-cost explanation seems inconsistent with the duration of the abnormal returns, which are estimated by Stober (1992) to continue for at least six years. One would imagine that considerable information, less costly than *Pr* information to process, would arrive in the meantime, including but not limited to the actual one-year-ahead earnings announcement that *Pr* information is alleged to be predicting. Third, Stober reports a substantial overlap between the information in *Pr* and in analysts' forecasts. For example, they agree 78% of the time on the sign of their predicted one-year-ahead earnings changes. This suggests the information in *Pr* has been

---

[34]Bartov (1992) expands the event window at following-quarters' announcements to encompass the entire quarter, compared with the three-day window in Bernard and Thomas (1989, 1990). One rationale is to capture the market response to all information that is relatively low-cost to process.

[35]See Ball (1991, sect. 1) for a review of the hypothesis development.

largely acquired and processed by analysts before the estimated abnormal returns emerge. Proxy effects appear to offer the most likely explanation for these results.

Similar doubts apply in the case of the general quarterly-earnings anomaly, where the estimated abnormal returns over the six or nine months following earnings announcements appear well in excess of reasonable costs of discovering the 'drift'. The component of the 'drift' uncovered by Rendleman, Jones, and Latané (1987) is another matter. Here, the market seems unaware of the autocorrelation function for quarterly earnings, and thus its pattern is mimicked in abnormal returns. Compared with what we know about the time-series behaviour of quarterly earnings from the academic literature, this is a relatively unsophisticated use of earnings information.[36] It is feasible that the costs of acquiring, processing, and implementing the relevant academic research, on both the time-series behavior of quarterly earnings and its implication for security returns, exceed the additional expected returns generated from trading on it. Factors supporting this view include the complexity of the academic literature and the Hayekian argument (developed in section 2.1 above) that information-processing costs include the cost of determining whether the information one possesses has already been used by other investors, and whether it is reflected in price. An investor might have some knowledge of the pattern of serial correlation in quarterly earnings, but not of whether other investors know it and of whether and how prices incorporate it. Processing costs thus offer a plausible explanation for the anomaly, due to the apparent complexity of the simulated trading strategies in the studies under review, and it correctly predicts both the sign of the post-announcement price behavior and its apparent clustering around subsequent earnings announcements.

A counter-argument is that the information used in Bernard and Thomas' (1990) trading rule is not as costly to process as it first appears. In statistical terms, the market is hypothesized as not fully processing exploitable information in the autocorrelation function of changes in quarterly earnings and as acting as if earnings are a seasonal random walk. Put in simpler language, this says only that investors do not realize that if first-quarter earnings is up on last year's first quarter, then second-quarter earnings tends to be up on last year's second quarter too. One does not have to be much of a statistician to observe that tendency. My reading of the financial press is that reporters and analysts routinely assume that one quarter's earnings result alters expectations for at

---

[36]The hypothesis requires investors to be sophisticated enough to realize that earnings are seasonal and to compare earnings with the equivalent past quarter, but not enough to realize that earnings changes are sustained across quarters.

least the following quarter's. The case for substantial information processing costs as an explanation of the anomaly is not clear-cut.[37]

In sum, it seems difficult to distinguish between information costs and market inefficiency as explanations for the pattern of predictable abnormal returns around future earnings announcement dates. One's choice depends on: (1) whether the concept of 'efficiency' is defined to allow information acquisition and processing costs and (2) priors about information costs. Both of these issues are largely unexplored, in part because the need has not arisen previously.

6.7. The inefficient-markets hypothesis

The market-inefficiency explanation requires market prices to systematically provide unexploited pure-profit opportunities from using accounting information. It is important to view market inefficiency as a theory to be tested against the evidence, not as the residual claimant on the evidence. Evidence that is anomalous for the efficient markets hypothesis does not logically prove inefficiency: it simply is anomalous (i.e., inconsistent). Rather, the conclusion that markets are inefficient emerges from failing to reject a specific inefficiency hypothesis, not by a process of eliminating all other known explanations for the evidence. However, direct testing of inefficiency hypotheses is made difficult by the paucity of plausible, testable theory on when and why systematic pricing errors occur in an inefficient market.[38]

The scarcity of testable inefficiency theories has risked making efficiency an almost irrefutable hypothesis. Thus, it has been the accumulation of anomalous evidence, rather than the creation of clearly preferable alternative theories, that has reduced the appeal of efficient market theory. Correspondingly, treating market inefficiency as the residual claimant on the evidence risks making it an almost irrefutable hypothesis also, because its acceptance then requires only a similar paucity of competing explanations of the anomalies. This overlooks the possibility, argued in section 2 above to be substantial, that the anomalous evidence is inconsistent with theories of *both* efficiency and inefficiency. Even after a generation of research on earnings and prices, substantially incomplete knowledge of the determinants of security prices suggests that one must live with tests of both efficiency and inefficiency theories that are low in power. The literature seems destined to live with anomaly.

---

[37]For comparison with rates of return, information costs must be scaled by the market value of the firm or of individual investments in the firm. Thus, their *relative* magnitude is questionable in this context.

[38]Notable exceptions include De Bondt and Thaler (1985, 1987). If information-acquisition and processing costs are treated as inconsistent with market efficiency, then so is the earnings seasonal hypothesis of Rendleman, Jones, and Latané (1987).

7. Concluding observations

The anomalies reviewed in this paper take the form of current earnings (or current information about future earnings) predicting future abnormal returns. This could reflect a true association between earnings information and abnormal returns, which implies market inefficiency. Alternatively, it could reflect research design biases such as an association between earnings information and errors in estimating abnormal returns, which does not imply market inefficiency. The objective of the review has been to sift the evidence for clues as to which explanation seems most likely.

To conclude that estimated abnormal returns of a given sign, magnitude, or level of significance are inviolate evidence of either efficiency or inefficiency would be to assume a one-for-one correspondence between a construct (efficiency) and its proxy (predictable estimated abnormal returns). This would place absolute reliance on both a theory of asset pricing, to define expected returns, and on its implementation in the research design that produced the estimates. The survey in section 2 above suggests that there are limits to how much one can reasonably rely upon such knowledge. One must examine the evidence and the research designs for clues that are not always transparent.

The pattern of the evidence suggests different explanations for the two principal versions of the earnings–price anomaly. The anomaly documented by Ou and Penman (1989a, b), building on the prior work of McKibben (1972) and others, seems most likely to result from an association between accounting variables and errors in estimating abnormal returns. The anomaly due to Rendleman, Jones, and Latané (1987), Freeman and Tse (1989), and Bernard and Thomas (1989, 1990), among others, is another matter. It seems most likely due to either substantial information-processing costs or market inefficiency. One's choice between these explanations depends on one's priors about information costs and one's preferences for defining 'efficiency'. The anomaly is unlikely due to accounting variables proxying for expected returns, endogenous risk shifts, transaction costs, liquidity, or trading-mechanism effects. It possibly is due to some combination of these.

Nevertheless, the implications of the evidence are not totally clear, as might be expected. Hopefully, future research will provide greater clarity, though our substantially incomplete knowledge of security pricing in a competitive market suggests anomalies are likely to continue. It perhaps is worth recalling that anomalies are not the only property of the relation between accounting earnings and stock prices, that stock prices are not the only measure of the use of accounting earnings by stockholders, and that stockholders are not the only users of accounting information.

References

Admati, A.R. and P. Pfleiderer, 1988, A theory of intraday trading patterns: Volume and price variability, Review of Financial Studies 1, 3–40.
Amihud, Y. and H. Mendelson, 1986, Asset pricing and the bid–ask spread, Journal of Financial Economics 15, 223–249.
Ball, R., 1978, Anomalies in relationships between securities' yields and yield-surrogates, Journal of Financial Economics 6, 103–126.
Ball, R., 1991, What do we know about market efficiency?, Unpublished manuscript (University of Rochester, Rochester, NY).
Ball, R. and J. Bowers, 1983, Distortions created by taxes which are options on value creation: The Australian resources rent tax proposal, Australian Journal of Management 8, 1–14.
Ball, R. and P. Brown, 1968, An empirical evaluation of accounting numbers, Journal of Accounting Research 6, 159–178.
Ball, R. and S.P. Kothari, 1989, Nonstationary expected returns: Implications for serial correlation in returns, apparent price reversals, and tests of market efficiency, Journal of Financial Economics 25, 51–74.
Ball, R. and S.P. Kothari, 1991, Security returns around earnings announcements, The Accounting Review 66, 718–738.
Ball, R., S.P. Kothari, and R.L. Watts, 1992, Economic determinants of the relation between earnings changes and stock returns, Unpublished manuscript (University of Rochester, Rochester, NY).
Balvers, R.J., T.F. Cosimano, and B. McDonald, 1990, Predicting stock returns in an efficient market, Journal of Finance 45, 1109–1128.
Banz, R.W., 1981, The relationship between return and market value of common stocks, Journal of Financial Economics 9, 3–18.
Bartov, E., 1992, Patterns in unexpected earnings as an explanation for post-announcement drift, The Accounting Review, forthcoming.
Basu, S., 1983, The relationship between earnings yield, market value and return for NYSE common stocks: Further evidence, Journal of Financial Economics 12, 129–156.
Beaver, W.H., 1968, The information content of annual earnings announcements, Journal of Accounting Research 6, Suppl., 67–92.
Bernard, V.L., 1989, Capital markets research in accounting during the 1980s: A critical review, in: T.J. Frecka, ed., Ph.D. jubilee (University of Illinois, Department of Accountancy, Urbana, IL).
Bernard, V.L., 1992, Stock price reactions to earnings announcements: A summary of recent anomalous evidence and possible explanations, in: R. Thaler, ed., Advances in behavioral finance (Russell Sage Foundation, New York, NY).
Bernard, V.L. and J. Thomas, 1989, Post-earnings-announcement drift: Delayed price response or risk premium, Journal of Accounting Research 27, Suppl., 1–36.
Bernard, V.L. and J. Thomas, 1990, Evidence that stock prices do not fully reflect the implications of current earnings for future earnings, Journal of Accounting and Economics 13, 305–340.
Brennan, M.J., 1973, Taxes, market valuation and corporate financial policy, National Tax Journal 23, 417–427.
Brooks, L. and D. Buckmaster, 1976, Further evidence on the time series property of accounting income, Journal of Finance 31, 1359–1373.
Brown, P.R. and R. Ball, 1967, Some preliminary findings on the association between the earnings of a firm, its industry, and the economy, Journal of Accounting Research 5, Suppl., 55–77.
Brown, P. and J.W. Kennelly, 1972, The information content of quarterly earnings: An extension and some further evidence, Journal of Business 45, 403–415.
Chari, V., R. Jagannathan, and O. Ofer, 1988, Seasonalities in security returns: The case of earnings announcements, Journal of Financial Economics 21, 101–121.
Chen, N., 1991, Financial investment opportunities and the microeconomy, Journal of Finance 46, 529–554.
Chen, N., R. Roll, and S. Ross, 1986, Economic forces and the stock market, Journal of Business 59, 383–404.

Chopra, N., J. Lakonishok, and J. Ritter, 1991, Performance measurement methodology and the question of whether stocks overreact, Unpublished manuscript (University of Illinois, Urbana, IL).
Coase, R.H., 1937, The nature of the firm, Economica N.S. 4, 386–405.
Cross, F., 1973, The behavior of stock prices on Fridays and Mondays, Financial Analysts Journal 29, 67–69.
De Bondt, W.F.M. and R.H. Thaler, 1985, Does the stock market overreact?, Journal of Finance 40, 793–805.
De Bondt, W.F.M. and R.H. Thaler, 1987, Further evidence on investor overreaction and stock market seasonality, Journal of Finance 42, 557–581.
Fama, E.F., 1970, Efficient capital markets: A review of theory and empirical work, Journal of Finance 25, 383–417.
Fama, E.F., 1976, Foundations of finance (Basic Books, New York, NY).
Fama, E.F., 1990, Stock returns, expected returns and real activity, Journal of Finance 45, 1089–1108.
Fama, E.F., 1991, Efficient capital markets: II, Journal of Finance 46, 1575–1617.
Fama, E.F. and K.R. French, 1988, Permanent and temporary components of stock prices, Journal of Political Economy 96, 246–273.
Fama, E.F. and K.R. French, 1991, The cross-section of expected stock returns, Unpublished manuscript (University of Chicago, Chicago, IL).
Fama, E.F., L. Fisher, M.C. Jensen, and R. Roll, 1969, The adjustment of stock prices to new information, International Economic Review 10, 1–21.
Foster, G., C. Olsen and T. Shevlin, 1984, Earnings releases, anomalies, and the behavior of securities returns, The Accounting Review 59, 574–603.
Freeman, R. and S. Tse, 1989, The multi-period information content of accounting earnings: Confirmations and contradictions of previous earnings reports, Journal of Accounting Research 27, Suppl., 49–79.
French, K., 1980, Stock returns and the weekend effect, Journal of Financial Economics 8, 55–69.
Graham, B., D. Dodd, and S. Cottle, 1962, Security analysis: Principles and techniques, 4th ed. (McGraw-Hill, New York, NY).
Greig, A.C., 1992, Fundamental analysis and subsequent stock returns, Journal of Accounting and Economics, this issue.
Handa, P., S.P. Kothari, and C. Wasley, 1989, The relation between the return interval and betas: Implications for the size-effect, Journal of Financial Economics 23, 79–100.
Harris, L., 1986, A transaction data study of weekly and intradaily patterns in stock returns, Journal of Financial Economics 16, 99–118.
Harris, L., 1989, A day-end transaction price anomaly, Journal of Finance and Quantitative Analysis 24, 29–46.
Hayek, F., 1945, The use of knowledge in society, American Economic Review 35, 519–530.
Holthausen, R.W. and D.F. Larcker, 1992, The prediction of stock returns using financial statement information, Journal of Accounting and Economics, this issue.
Ibbotson, R.G. and R.A. Sinquefield, 1989, Stocks, bonds, bills and inflation: Historical returns (1926–1987) (Institute of Chartered Financial Analysts, Charlottesville, VA).
Jaffe, J., D.B. Keim, and R. Westerfield, 1989, Earnings yields, market values, and stock returns, Journal of Finance 44, 135–148.
Jensen, M.C., 1978, Some anomalous evidence regarding market efficiency, Journal of Financial Economics 6, 95–101.
Jones, C.M., G. Kaul, and M.L. Lipson, 1991, Information, trading and volatility, Unpublished manuscript (University of Michigan, Ann Arbor, MI).
Jones, C.P. and R. Litzenberger, 1970, Quarterly earnings reports and intermediate stock price trends, Journal of Finance 25, 143–148.
Joy, O.M. and C.P. Jones, 1979, Earnings reports and market efficiencies: An analysis of the contrary evidence, Journal of Financial Research, Spring, 51–63.
Joy, O.M., R. Litzenberger, and R. McEnally, 1977, The adjustment of stock prices to announcements of unanticipated changes in quarterly earnings, Journal of Accounting Research 15, 207–225.

Keim, D.B., 1989, Trading patterns, bid–ask spreads and estimated security returns: The case of common stocks at calendar turning points, Journal of Financial Economics 25, 75–98.
Kuhn, T.S., 1970, The structure of scientific revolutions (University of Chicago Press, Chicago, IL).
Lakonishok, J. and E. Maberly, 1990, The weekend effect: Trading patterns of individual and institutional investors, Journal of Finance 45, 231–243.
Lee, C.M.C., 1992, Earnings news and small traders: An intraday analysis, Journal of Accounting and Economics, this issue.
LeRoy, S.F., 1989, Efficient capital markets and martingales, Journal of Economic Literature 27, 1583–1621.
Lev, B. and S.R. Thiagarajan, 1991, Fundamental information analysis, Unpublished manuscript (University of California, Berkeley, CA).
Litzenberger, R.H. and K. Ramaswamy, 1979, The effect of personal taxes and dividends on capital asset prices, Journal of Financial Economics 7, 163–195.
Lo, A.W. and A.C. MacKinlay, 1990, Data-snooping biases in tests of financial asset pricing models, Review of Financial Studies 3, 431–467.
Mendenhall, R.R., 1991, Evidence on the possible underweighting of earnings-related information, Journal of Accounting Research 29, 170–179.
McKibben, W., 1972, Econometric forecasting of common stock investment returns: A new methodology using fundamental operating data, Journal of Finance 27, 371–380.
McNichols, M., 1988, A comparison of the skewness of stock return distributions at earnings and non-earnings announcement dates, Journal of Accounting and Economics 10, 239–273.
Ou, J.A. and S.H. Penman, 1989a, Financial statement analysis and the prediction of stock returns, Journal of Accounting and Economics 11, 295–330.
Ou, J.A. and S.H. Penman, 1989b, Accounting measurement, price–earnings ratios, and the information content of security prices, Journal of Accounting Research 27, 111–144.
Patell, J.M. and M.A. Wolfson, 1984, The intraday speed of adjustment of stock prices to earnings and dividend announcements, Journal of Financial Economics 13, 223–252.
Rendleman, R.J., C.P. Jones, and H.A. Latané, 1987, Further insight into the standardized unexpected earnings anomaly: Size and serial correlation effects, Financial Review 22, 131–144.
Rogalski, R., 1984, New findings regarding day of the week returns over trading and non-trading periods, Unpublished manuscript.
Roll, R., 1977, A critique of the asset pricing theory's tests, Part 1: On past and potential testability of the theory, Journal of Financial Economics 4, 129–176.
Shleifer, A. and R.W. Vishny, 1990, Equilibrium short run horizons of investors and firms, American Economic Review, Papers and Proceedings 80, 148–153.
Simon, H., 1955, A behavioral model of rational choice, Quarterly Journal of Economics 69, 99–118.
Simon, H., 1957, Models of man (Wiley, New York, NY).
Skinner, D.J., 1991, Stock returns, trading volume, and bid-ask spreads around earnings announcements: Evidence from the NASDAQ national market system, Unpublished manuscript (University of Michigan, Ann Arbor, MI).
Sloan, Richard G., 1993, Accounting earnings and top executive compensation, Journal of Accounting and Economics 16, forthcoming.
Stambaugh, R.F., 1982, On the exclusion of assets from tests of the two-parameter model: A sensitivity analysis, Journal of Financial Economics 10, 237–268.
Stigler, G.J., The economics of information, Journal of Political Economy 69, 213–225.
Stober, T.L., 1992, Summary financial statement measures and analysts' forecasts of earnings, Journal of Accounting and Economics, this issue.
Watts, R., 1978, Systematic 'abnormal' returns after quarterly earnings announcements, Journal of Financial Economics 6, 817–837.
Wiggins, J.B., 1991, Do misperceptions about the earnings process contribute to post-announcement drift?, Manuscript (Cornell University, Ithaca, NY).

II

ACCRUALS, CASH FLOWS, AND ALTERNATIVE ACCOUNTING METHODS

1 Livnat, Joshua, and Paul Zarowin, 1990, "The Incremental Information Content of Cash-Flow Components," *Journal of Accounting and Economics*, 13 (1990), pp. 25–46.

2 Stephens, Ray G., and Vijay Govindarajan, "On Assessing a Firm's Cash Generating Ability," *The Accounting Review*, 65 (1990), pp. 242–257.

3 Dopuch, Nicholas, and Morton Pincus, "Evidence on the Choice of Inventory Accounting Methods: LIFO versus FIFO," *Journal of Accounting Research*, 26 (1988), pp. 28–59.

4 Dawson, James P., Peter M. Neupert, and Clyde P. Stickney, "Restating Financial Statements for Alternative GAAPs: Is it Worth the Effort?," *Financial Analysts Journal*, November–December (1980), pp. 38–46.

5 Beaver, William H., and Stephen G. Ryan, "How Well Do Statement No. 33 Earnings Explain Stock Returns," *Financial Analysts Journal*, September–October (1985), pp. 66–71.

6 Barth, Mary E., William H. Beaver, and Wayne Landsman, "The Market Valuation Implications of Net Periodic Pension Cost Components," *Journal of Accounting and Economics*, 15 (1992), pp. 27–62.

Current and potential claimholders of a firm seek information about the firm's expected future cash flows. The information should be helpful to them in stock valuation and in assessing the probability of interest and principal payments to bondholders on a timely basis, and payments to creditors and employees, among others. One source of the desired information to market participants is the firm's financial statements. Financial statements provide information about the various sources and uses of cash by the firm over the past year. While it only reveals the net cash flow realized by the firm over the current period, the cash flow information in the financial statements is expected to be helpful in revising market participants' beliefs about future cash flows. Naturally, considerable research in accounting has focused on evaluating the information content of cash flows.

Since the early work by Ball and Brown (1968), several studies assess the degree of contemporaneous association between changes in cash flows over an accounting period and stock returns. More recently, the focus is on whether the information in the various components of cash flows is richer than that in a summary cash flow number. **Livnat and**

Zarowin (1990) decompose annual cash flow to a firm into cash flows from operating, financing, and investing activities, and into various subactivities within each. They motivate their analysis by arguing that various theories in economics, finance, and accounting suggest that cash flows from operating, financing, and investing activities do not signal homogeneous information about future cash flows. For example, unanticipated increases in investments signal management's expectation of increased demand for the firm's goods and services and therefore increased operating cash flows in the future. Yet, the current period's operating cash flow might reveal little about the management's expectations, and the current period's investing activities would indicate a negative cash flow. Financial analysts likely engage in a similar thought process in analyzing financial statement information and then making forecasts of future earnings and cash flows. Of course, analysts and other market participants gather information beyond that in financial statements in forming their expectations. Therefore, prices reflect a richer information set than that in the current and past time series of cash flows.

Results of analyzing financial data on about 400 firms from 1974 to 1986 in **Livnat and Zarowin (1990)** indicate that disaggregating a firm's cash flows into operating, financing, and investing cash flows and further into subcomponents (e.g., cash flows from receivable collections, tax payments, dividend payments, investments in property, plant, and equipment, and investment in unconsolidated subsidiaries) considerably enhances their association with annual stock returns. In particular, cash flows by themselves explain about 8 percent of the cross-sectional variation in annual stock returns, whereas disaggregated cash flows account for roughly a quarter of the stock return variation, a twofold increase.

Financial analysts are faced with the practical task of processing the information in financial statements and making forecasts of a firm's future cash flows. While analysts supplement the information in financial statements with other information, including management plans and forecasts and industry and macroeconomic data, financial statements often are the starting point in their formulation of forecasts. **Stephens and Govindarajan (1990)** offer insightful guidance on using operating funds flow information from financial statements to assess a firm's cash-generating ability. They separate operating activities from financing activities, and within the operating activities they make a distinction between "capital maintenance" investments and growth or expansion investments. The basic idea is that knowledge of what a dollar of cash flow is being used for is informative because the magnitudes of future cash flows are intimately related to the quality of investments made by a firm.

In addition to cash flow information, financial statements provide, as the main element of the historical cost accounting earnings measurement process, information on accounting accruals. Operating accruals transform the operating cash flow number into accounting earnings, the bottom line figure from an income statement. The role of accruals is to make the earnings number a better measure of firm performance than cash flows. Through accruals, accountants calculate earnings that exhibit a greater degree of matching of revenues with expenses than earnings on a cash basis. For example, in accrual accounting earnings determination, credit sales are recognized as revenue, net of expected bad debt expense. Cash received during the current period against credit sales in prior periods is not recorded as revenue for the current period. Expenses deducted from revenues to calculate earnings accordingly are only toward the cost of goods sold, regardless of when the goods were produced or the amount of current period cash outflow toward producing goods. Dechow (1993) provides evidence that the accrual process indeed results in earnings being a better measure of firm performance (i.e., greater contemporaneous correlation with stock returns) than cash flows. Dechow (1993) also shows that the negative serial correlation in cash flow changes arising because cash flows lack "matching" is reduced by accruals. Consequently, the well-known result dating back to Ball and Watts (1972) on the time series property of earnings is obtained. Unlike cash flow changes, earnings changes exhibit only a mild negative serial correlation (see Part III).

Accrual adjustments by firm managers, however, potentially have some adverse effects on earnings as an indicator of firm performance or future cash flows. Since there is no unique and objective method of arriving at accruals, over time and across firms, the accrual adjustment of cash flows to obtain earnings varies. Managers have discretion within GAAP in terms of choosing among alternative accounting methods to account for inventories, fixed assets, research and development expenditures, investment tax credit etc. Also, many accrual adjustments are based on the management's estimates, forecasts, and intent. Examples include determination of pension liabilities, useful life of fixed assets, and restructuring leases to attract operating versus capital lease accounting. Managers can use the discretion in accrual adjustments and accounting method choice for more efficient contracts between the firm and various claimholders, for tax-related reasons, to signal their private information, or to use it to opportunistically influence reported earnings. Therefore, financial analysts' assessment of a firm's future cash flows should be based, in part, on an analysis of the firm's accruals and various components of accruals. The last five papers in this section provide useful guidance to financial statement analysts in dealing with the diversity in firms' use of alternative accounting methods in income statement and balance sheet preparation.

Dopuch and Pincus (1988) examine firms' choice between LIFO and FIFO inventory practice. They test whether tax or nontax reasons explain firms' inventory method choice. During inflationary periods and assuming a firm not shrinking, the use of LIFO inventory method results in lower (present value of) tax payments compared to FIFO, but reported LIFO income also is lower. The tax explanation thus predicts a widespread use of LIFO inventory method for financial and tax reporting. Nontax explanations include management compensation contracts and debt contracts, stock market's mechanical fixation on reported earnings (LIFO earnings are generally lower), and "best" fit with the operating, financing, and investment characteristics, assuming criteria for judging a "best" fit can be specified. Their results indicate that neither tax nor nontax explanation alone explains firms' inventory method choice. Perhaps more interestingly, **Dopuch and Pincus (1988, p. 273)** find that "significant differences in the ratios which use either reported inventory or reported cost-of-sales numbers in their calculations were mainly induced by the different accounting methods" by LIFO and FIFO inventory method firms. Thus, analysts should consider making adjustments for LIFO/FIFO inventory methods in drawing inferences about a firm's financial health. The next study, however, indicates that the benefits from such adjustments may be limited.

Dawson, Neupert, and Stickney (1980) assess the benefits of restating financial statements prepared using alternative accounting methods. They restate financial statements of ninety-six large firms so that all firms' data are converted to FIFO, depreciation expense and net asset values to tax reporting, unconsolidated to consolidated wholly owned subsidiaries, unrecognized to recognized pension liabilities, and deferred tax accounting to flow through accounting. Their results are striking. Adjustments for inventories, depreciation, and deferred taxes have virtually no effect on the correlations between reported and restated net income and financial ratios. Adjustments due to consolidation and pension obligations affect the correlations considerably. Interestingly, the Financial Accounting Standards Board has since changed GAAP to require consolidation of wholly owned subsidiaries and recognition of unfunded pension obligations as liabilities on the balance sheet.

One perceived shortcoming of historical cost financial statements is that they cannot reflect the impact of changing prices (inflation) on the economic well-being of a firm. It is well known that inflation adversely affects firm values [e.g., Fama (1981)]. With a view to making the information in financial statements more timely and relevant to users, the Financial Accounting Standards Board issued Statement of Financial Accounting Standards No. 33 requiring firms to disclose the effects of changing prices on certain assets, such as inventory, property, plant, and equipment, in supplementary financial statements. **Beaver and Ryan (1985)** test whether inflation-adjusted accounting data provide information that historical cost earnings do not. Information content, as usual, is inferred from the correlation of accounting data with firms' stock returns. Using samples of 260 to 368 firms from 1979 to 1982, **Beaver and Ryan (1985, p. 313)** conclude that "Statement No. 33 variables provide no incremental information beyond that already provided by historical cost earnings. . . ." Their results reinforce findings of previous research by Beaver, Griffin, and Landsman (1983) using "Replacement Cost Income" data and Beaver and Landsman (1983) using Statement No. 33 data for only two years. Overall, the results suggest that either the inflation-adjusted financial numbers are too noisy to be informative or the impact of unanticipated inflation on the revision in expectation of net future cash flows is more complicated than that captured by rules prescribed in Statement No. 33. Thus, financial analysts must rely on their individual expertise in factoring in the effects of inflation on expected future cash flows.

The focus of the **Barth, Beaver, and Landsman (1992)** study is on the market's valuation of pension cost components that Statement of Financial Accounting Standards No. 87, *Employers' Accounting for Pensions*, requires to be disclosed in financial statements. The required disclosure began for early-adopting firms in 1986, and was required in 1987 for the remaining firms. Since some of the pension cost components represent a one-shot gain or loss, whereas other components reflect more permanent changes in pension costs, **Barth, Beaver, and Landsman** expect the market's valuation to differ across pension-cost components. Their evidence supports the hypothesis. Indeed, the findings of their research appear to have influenced the thinking at the Financial Accounting Standards Board, which has recently issued Statement of Financial Accounting Standard No. 106, *Employers' Accounting for Postretirement Benefits Other than Pensions*. This Standard recognizes that market participants rationally decompose pension and other costs based on their permanence and value those components accordingly. The disclosure requirements in Statement of Financial Accounting Standard No. 106 accordingly dictate decomposition of firms' postretirement benefit obligations and recognition of some gains and losses immediately in net income, instead of amortizing those over long time periods.

THE INCREMENTAL INFORMATION CONTENT OF CASH-FLOW COMPONENTS

Joshua LIVNAT and Paul ZAROWIN*

New York University, New York, NY 10006, USA

Received September 1988, final version received January 1990

This study examines whether components of operating, financing, and investing cash flows are differentially associated with annual security returns, as predicted by theoretical models in finance and economics. The results of the study indicate that disaggregation of net income into cash from operations and accruals does not contribute significantly to the association with security returns beyond the contribution of net income alone. However, further disaggregation of financing and operating cash flows into their components significantly improves the degree of association, as predicted by theory. In contrast, we find no evidence of differential associations across components of investing cash flows.

1. Introduction

This study examines the information content of *components* of cash flows that are required by Financial Accounting Standard (FAS) No. 95 [FASB (1987)]. Theoretical models in finance, economics, and accounting imply that various components of cash flows should be associated with annual security returns in a manner that differs predictably in terms of both sign and magnitude of the association. This study investigates whether the components of cash flows required by FAS No. 95 indeed exhibit differential associations with stock returns, and whether these associations are consistent with theory.

Recent studies examine the incremental information content of cash flows given earnings [Wilson (1986, 1987) and Bowen et al. (1987)] and given accruals [Rayburn (1986)] and generally document the existence of incremental information content of cash-flow data. More recently, Bernard and Stober (1989) show that disaggregating net income into cash from operations and

---

*The authors are grateful to Ray Ball (editor), Victor Bernard (referee), Ashiq Ali, Ross Jennings, April Klein, Baruch Lev, Robert Lipe, Victor Pastena, Grace Pownall, Judy Rayburn, Joshua Ronen, George Sorter, and participants of the Accounting Seminars at Baruch College, Columbia University, and New York University for their helpful comments. All errors remain our responsibility. We are thankful for obtaining Summer Research Grants from the Stern Graduate School of Business, New York University. The second author acknowledges financial support provided by the KPMG Peat Marwick Foundation.

0165-4101/90/$3.50 © 1990, Elsevier Science Publishers B.V. (North-Holland)

accruals does not provide additional information content beyond net income. However, these studies focus on a single aspect of cash flows, namely, cash from operations (or working capital from operations), and generally ignore information about components of cash flows. In contrast, our study examines the components of cash flows from financing, investing, and operating activities, as required by FAS No. 95.

The results indicate that individual components of financing and operating cash flows are differentially associated with security returns, with signs predicted by theory. These results imply that the accounting signals required by FAS No. 95 reflect the various economic events that relate to financing and operating events. Furthermore, this study shows that there is incremental information content in disaggregating net income into accruals and *components* of cash flows from financing, investing, and operating activities, as compared to the information content of earnings alone. Thus, consistent with Lipe (1986) and Ou and Penman (1989), the results of this study indicate that financial statements contain more information than the 'bottom-line' earnings figure.[1] These results are robust to various specifications of the variables and research designs.

The next section discusses the estimation of cash-flow components. Section 3 develops the hypotheses. Section 4 describes the data, variables, and research design. Section 5 provides the empirical results, as well as results of robustness tests. The last section summarizes and concludes the study.

2. Identification of cash-flow components

This study uses available data in the Compustat Annual Industrial File to estimate the following components of cash flows, which are described more fully in the appendix:

1. Cash from operating activities
    (a) Cash collections from customers,
    (b) Cash payments to suppliers, employees, etc.,

---

[1]Bernard (1989, p. 32) summarizes the literature on the information content of accounting data other than 'bottom line' historical cost earnings by stating:
'The recurring lesson from this research is that bottom-line historical cost earnings is not only 'hard to beat', but that it is difficult to demonstrate convincingly that other data convey any information beyond that reflected in earnings. That is, once one knows the bottom-line historical cost earnings, it is not clear one can achieve much improvement in the ability to explain stock returns by using inflation-adjusted earnings, cash flow data, or disclosures of the present value of oil and gas reserves.'

(c) Cash payments to tax authorities,
   (d) Net interest paid,
   (e) Other operating cash flows.

2. Cash from financing activities
   (a) Cash received in net debt issuance,
   (b) Cash received in net-preferred-stock issuance,
   (c) Cash received in net common-stock issuance,
   (d) Cash dividends paid.

3. Cash used for investing activities
   (a) Cash used for new investments in Property, Plant, and Equipment (PPE),
   (b) Cash used for acquisitions of new businesses,
   (c) Cash used to acquire additional interest from minority shareholders,
   (d) Cash invested in new unconsolidated subsidiaries,
   (e) Cash obtained through the retirement of PPE.

This breakdown of cash-flow components is motivated by FAS No. 95, which provides detailed definitions of operating, investing, and financing activities.

2.1. Estimation of cash-flow components

Although the components of operating cash flows were not reported in the format described by FAS No. 95 prior to 1988, they can be estimated reasonably from data reported in the balance sheet, the income statement, and the statement of changes in financial position. For example, we estimate cash collections by subtracting from sales the change in accounts receivable during the period. However, this estimate does not include the change in uncollectible accounts (because sample size would have been severely reduced had we required it) or changes in accounts receivable that are not related to operating activities (e.g., notes received in sale of PPE). We estimate the components of cash flows for investing and financing activities using similar procedures. For example, we use information about the additions to PPE available in the statement of changes in financial position as an approximation to cash spent for new investments in PPE.

Our estimates of cash-flow components from financial statements seem reasonable as an approximation to the components of cash flows that would have been required by the FASB. Indeed, Livnat and Sondhi (1989) show that estimation errors of our procedures are immaterial for a sample of firms that use the 'direct' method to report operating cash flows.

3. Testable hypotheses about associations between components of cash flows and returns

3.1. Hypotheses

This section discusses economic hypotheses concerning financing, investing, and operating events. These hypotheses are stated in terms of associations between cash flows and annual security returns. To test these hypotheses, we use the following regression model:

$$\begin{aligned} CAR = {} & a_0 + a_1 \text{ Collections} + a_2 \text{ Payments} + a_3 \text{ Taxes} \\ & + a_4 \text{ Interest} + a_5 \text{ Other} \\ & + b_1 \text{ Debt} + b_2 \text{ Common} \\ & + b_3 \text{ Preferred} + b_4 \text{ Dividend} \\ & + c_1 \text{ PPE} + c_2 \text{ Acquisition} \\ & + c_3 \text{ Minority} + c_4 \text{ Subsidiary} \\ & + c_5 \text{ RetPPE} + d_1 \text{ Accrual} + \tilde{e}, \end{aligned} \qquad (1)$$

where *CAR* is a measure of annual abnormal return and the independent variables are estimates of unexpected components of cash flows in the order that the components appear in the previous section (expectation models are discussed below).[2] Accrual equals net income minus total operating cash flows. We use the term cash-flow response coefficients to refer to the coefficients of the cash-flow components in eq. (1).

3.2. Economic hypotheses about financing cash flows

1. Irrelevance of financing cash flows

In one of the most fundamental theories in finance, Miller and Modigliani (1961) postulate the irrelevancy of capital structure or dividend policy for security valuation. Under their assumptions, a firm's value is unaffected by its decision to finance its cash needs through issuance of debt, common or preferred stock. Similarly, security values are unaffected by a firm's dividend policy. Thus, components of financing cash flows should not contribute to the association of unexpected cash flows with annual market returns. We test the irrelevance of financing cash flows by examining the individual coefficients of the financing cash flows in eq. (1). The null hypotheses for these coefficients

---

[2] For ease of exposition, eq. (1) omits the subscripts j and t, which denote a particular firm j in year t, respectively. Eq. (1) is estimated cross-sectionally for each year. Results are then aggregated across years.

are:

$$b_1 = 0, \quad b_2 = 0, \quad b_3 = 0, \quad b_4 = 0.$$

2. Signalling effects of financing cash flows

(i) *Debt issuance.* Assumptions about asymmetric information between owners and investors lead Ross (1977) and Leland and Pyle (1977) to suggest that debt issuance may be perceived as a good signal about future cash flows, because owners retain a larger proportion of equity than when stock is issued. Thus, based on these theories, one expects a positive market reaction to the announcement of debt issuance, i.e., $b_1 > 0$. On the other hand, Miller and Rock (1985) suggest negative market reactions to announcements of any external financing, because such announcements imply that future operating cash flows will be lower than previously expected, i.e., $b_1 < 0$. The empirical evidence of Mikkelson and Partch (1986) and Eckbo (1986) documents small (statistically insignificant) negative reactions to announcements of debt financing.

(ii) *Common-stock issuance.* Smith (1986) discusses finance theories that postulate the effects of common-stock issuances and repurchases on security returns. Managers, who are assumed to have private information about their firms, engage in stock issuances (repurchases) when they believe that security prices are too high (low) relative to fundamental (intrinsic) value. Anticipating this behavior, investors react negatively (positively) to announcements of stock issuances (repurchases), i.e., $b_2 < 0$. Mikkelson and Partch (1986), Masulis and Korwar (1986), and Asquith and Mullins (1986) provide evidence of negative reactions to announcements of stock issuances. Dann (1981) and Vermaelen (1981) provide evidence of positive market reactions to announcements of stock repurchases.

(iii) *Preferred-stock issuance.* Smith (1986) discusses the implications of theories based on asymmetric information to issuance of preferred stock. When a security is less sensitive to the underlying value of the firm, because it has senior claims (e.g., debt or preferred stock) or because it cannot be converted into common stock, then announcements of its issuance are expected to be accompanied by smaller market reactions than announcements about issuance of common stock, i.e., $b_3 < b_2 < 0$. Empirical evidence in Smith (1986, table 1) confirms weaker negative market reactions to the issuance of more senior and nonconvertible securities than to the issuance of common stock.

(iv) *Dividends.* The theoretical model of Miller and Rock (1985) predicts that dividend changes are associated with security returns. Increased dividends signal greater future cash flows which are expected to be associated with positive market reactions, i.e., $b_4 > 0$. The empirical evidence of Asquith and Mullins (1983), Charest (1978), Aharony and Swary (1980), and Brickley (1983) is consistent with these expectations.

The above discussion suggests that the associations between security returns and the four components of cash flows from financing activities could be different; $b_1 \gtrless 0$, $b_2 < b_3 < 0$, $-b_4 > 0$. Thus, the disaggregation of total cash flows from financing activities into their components could yield incremental association with annual returns. The following hypothesis, therefore, is tested:[3]

$$H_1: \quad b_1 = b_2 = b_3 = -b_4.$$

H_1 tests whether the four financing cash flows have the same association with security returns. The hypothesis (as well as later hypotheses) postulates certain relations among the coefficients in eq. (1), holding all other independent variables constant. For example, like Miller and Modigliani (1961), we test for the effects of different financing techniques (or dividends), *given* the investment decisions of a firm. To the extent that the four components of financing cash flows reflect different economic events (as suggested by finance theories), hypothesis H_1 should be rejected by the data. If H_1 is not rejected by the data, the components of cash flows might not reflect well the economic events they are purported to represent. The above discussion also implies specific hypotheses regarding the following pairwise relations:

$$H_2: \quad b_1 = b_2, \qquad H_3: \quad b_1 = b_3, \qquad H_4: \quad b_2 = b_3.$$

3.3. Economic hypotheses concerning investing cash flows

3. Irrelevance of investing cash flows

The Miller and Rock (1985) model also can aid in predicting the effects of investments on security returns. Generally, increases in investments are associated with higher future cash flows, and, therefore, positive associations with security returns are expected for announcements of new investments, i.e., $c_1 > 0$. Evidence that is consistent with these expectations is reported in McConnell and Muscarella (1986). However, to the extent that investors anticipate capital investments, there might not be any association between security returns and capital investments. Hence, as for financing cash flows, we test whether each of the individual coefficients corresponding to investing

---

[3] Throughout the study, the hypotheses are postulated in null form. The alternative hypotheses can be easily understood from the discussion. It should be noted that the coefficients of cash outflows are hypothesized to have negative signs.

cash flows in eq. (1) is equal to zero. The null hypotheses are:

$$c_1 = 0, \quad c_2 = 0, \quad c_3 = 0, \quad c_4 = 0, \quad c_5 = 0.$$

4. Differential effects of investing cash flows

The form of corporate investment might have different implications for equity shareholders. Amihud and Lev (1981) suggest that managers hold an undiversified personal portfolio because of their large nontradable human investments in their firms. Hence, managers might engage in negative net present-value acquisitions to diversify their firms, and, indirectly, their own personal portfolios. This theory predicts negative market reactions to announcements of investments in other firms, i.e., $c_2 < 0$. Jensen and Ruback (1983) summarize evidence that documents small and negative market reactions to bidders' announcements of takeover attempts.

Following Leland and Pyle (1977) and Ross (1977), it is expected that increases in the proportion of ownership through purchases of minority interests will be positively associated with security returns, due to the increase of owners' share of the firm, i.e., $c_3 > 0$. Similarly, according to Miller and Rock (1985) new investments in unconsolidated subsidiaries should have positive implications about future cash flows, and, hence, for returns, i.e., $c_4 > 0$. Indeed, the empirical evidence cited in Smith (1986, table 4) generally suggests that increasing ownership control is associated with positive security returns. Thus, we expect different market reactions to the various investing cash flows and test:

$$H_5: \quad c_1 = c_2 = c_3 = c_4 = -c_5.$$

3.4. Economic hypotheses of operating cash flows

5. Irrelevance of operating cash flows

Most valuation models suggest that unexpected cash inflows or outflows from operations in the current period should affect security prices through their effects on current and future cash flows. Thus, we expect the components of operating cash flows to be significantly associated with security returns. Therefore, as a check on our research design, we test whether the individual coefficients corresponding to operating cash flows in eq. (1) are equal to zero. The null hypotheses are:

$$a_1 = 0, \quad a_2 = 0, \quad a_3 = 0, \quad a_4 = 0, \quad a_5 = 0.$$

6. Recurring and nonrecurring events

Gonedes (1979) documents different market reactions to the disclosure of ordinary and extraordinary income. Barnea, Ronen, and Sadan (1976) provide evidence that the market reacts more to the permanent component of earnings than to the transitory component of earnings. Lipe (1986) shows that whether a component of earnings is expected to recur in the future is important for security valuation. The 'other' operating cash flows might be less likely to recur than collections from customers, because they represent items like settlements of law suits, receipt of payments for insured damages, etc. Consequently, the association of security returns with unexpected cash inflows from sales to customers is postulated to be greater than that with 'other' operating cash inflows, i.e., $a_1 > a_5$. Formally, we test

$$H_6: \quad a_1 = a_5.$$

7. Cash from operations and accruals

The current accounting literature seems to provide contradictory findings about the decomposition of earnings into cash from operations and accruals. Wilson (1986, 1987) shows that cash from operations has information content beyond earnings, while Bernard and Stober (1989) show that Wilson's results are not obtained beyond his sample period. Bowen et al. (1987) show that cash from operations has incremental association with security returns beyond earnings, but their results seem to be driven by data from two years (see their table 7), and are not robust to treatment of statistical outliers (see their pp. 744–746). Rayburn's (1986) results indicate that the associations of security returns with cash from operations and total accruals are of about the same magnitude (see her tables 5 and 6). Because prior studies provide inconclusive results, we examine whether disaggregation of net income into cash from operations and accruals in our sample improves the association with security returns. We first estimate the following regression model:

$$CAR = f_0 + f_1\ CFO + g_1\ Accrual + u, \qquad (2)$$

where CAR, CFO, and $Accrual$ represent the abnormal return, unexpected total cash from operations, and unexpected total accruals, respectively. Then, we test the hypothesis:

$$H_7: \quad f_1 = g_1.$$

8. Components of operating cash flows

The FASB requires firms to disclose information about components of investing and financing cash flows, and encourages firms to disclose information about components of operating cash flows [the direct approach in FASB (1987)]. If all components of operating cash flows have equal associations with annual security returns, then disaggregation of total cash from operations into its components would not provide incremental association beyond that of total cash from operations. However, in its discussion of FAS No. 95, the FASB (1987) notes that 'amounts of major classes of operating cash receipts and payments presumably would be more useful than information only about their arithmetic sum – net cash flow from operating activities – in assessing an enterprise's ability to generate sufficient cash from operating activities to pay its debt, to reinvest in its operations, and to make distributions to its owners' (para. 107). Thus, we test the following hypothesis:

$$H_8: \quad a_1 = -a_2 = -a_3 = -a_4 = a_5.$$

4. Methodology

4.1. Data

The sample firms are selected from the Compustat Annual Industrial File and from the CRSP Monthly Returns File according to the following criteria:

1. December fiscal year-end,
2. Availability of financial data to estimate the cash-flow components and market value of equity,
3. Availability of monthly returns on the CRSP File to estimate cumulative abnormal returns.

The first selection criterion is included to ensure comparable return accumulation periods for all firms. The other selection criteria ensure availability of data. Over 1,000 firms satisfy the first two selection criteria for at least one year during the period 1973–1986. These years are selected because information regarding sources and uses of funds is available on the Compustat Annual Industrial File after 1971, when the Accounting Principles Board (APB) issued its Opinion No. 19 [AICPA (1971)]. 434 firms have available returns data *and* financial data to estimate the components of cash flows for two consecutive years.[4] However, not every firm is represented in the sample in every year; 281 firms have available data in all years during 1974–1986. The study uses all firms with available data for a particular year (at least 345 firms each year).

4.2. Variables

The cash-flow components are estimated as described in the appendix. Our research design calls for assessments of the associations between estimates of unexpected components of cash flows and security returns. As a first approximation of the unexpected components of cash flows, we use the change in the

---

[4]Two consecutive years were necessary for estimation of unexpected cash flows.

component from the previous year, assuming a random-walk-generating process for these components.[5] We describe below additional tests that estimate the unexpected cash-flow components differently. The results are insensitive to these alternative specifications of the expectations model.

Since our tests are based on cross-sectional comparisons of firms, it is important to scale the unexpected cash-flow components by some measure of size to minimize heteroskedasticity in the data. As Christie (1987) recommends, this study uses the market value of equity at the beginning of the year as a deflator.[6]

Previous research has used abnormal returns cumulated over the contemporaneous year with the earnings report, or over the twelve months since the disclosure of the previous year's data, i.e., April of the previous year to March of the current year [e.g., Bowen et al. (1987) and Rayburn (1986)]. We use both in our study, with very little difference between the two sets of results, and thus, unless otherwise indicated, the results are presented for the second definition alone. The abnormal returns are estimated by the market model, using all available observations (with a minimum of 30 observations) over a 60-month period that ends in December of the preceding year.

Table 1 provides some summary statistics about the components of cash flows. For each component the unexpected portion is estimated as the realized value of the component in year t minus its realized value in year $t-1$, scaled by market value of equity at the end of year $t-1$. As can be seen in the table, most components have a mean that is very close to zero, consistent with a random walk. Some components (e.g., investment in subsidiaries and net debt issuance) have high standard deviations due to the presence of extreme observations. This can be ascertained by the information on the 10th and 90th percentiles of the distributions reported in the table, which show that observations in these percentiles are not extreme. Extreme observations occur due to scaling by market value of equity, which is extremely small for some firm-years. We test the sensitivity of our results to outliers in the data.

The table also reports average annual Pearson correlations between cumulative abnormal returns and components of cash flows. Generally, operating cash flows exhibit the most significant associations with security returns. Financing cash flows exhibit some significant associations with security returns, with signs that are generally consistent with those expected by finance theories. The least significant correlations are obtained for investing cash flows.

---

[5]The random-walk model was also used by Bowen et al. (1987) and Rayburn (1986) to estimate unexpected cash from operations and accruals.

[6]We have also used the total assets at the beginning of the year as a deflator with very similar results.

Table 1

Summary statistics – Components of cash flows, accruals, and net income.

Variable	Mean difference[a]	Standard deviation[a]	Percentile[a] 10%	Percentile[a] 90%	Correlation with CAR[b]
Operating cash flows					
Collections from customers	0.241	1.255	−0.386	1.147	0.09
Payments to suppliers, etc.	0.190	1.656	−0.456	1.134	0.05
Tax payments	0.006	0.124	−0.082	0.100	0.08
Interest payments	−0.001	0.087	−0.025	0.046	−0.05
Other operating cash flows	−0.001	0.541	−0.139	0.161	0.04
Financing cash flows					
Net debt issuance	0.005	1.019	−0.408	0.410	−0.02
Net stock issuance	0.011	0.199	−0.085	0.113	0.00
Net preferred stock issuance	−0.001	0.103	−0.001	0.001	0.01
Dividends paid	0.003	0.022	−0.003	0.014	0.06
Investing cash flows					
Investment in PPE	0.008	0.169	−0.108	0.137	0.05
Acquisitions	0.009	0.219	−0.021	0.038	0.04
Investment in subsidiaries	0.017	1.254	−0.077	0.091	0.01
Purchases of minority interest	0.001	0.070	−0.001	0.001	0.01
Retirement of PPE	0.002	0.091	−0.022	0.026	0.01
Aggregates of cash flows					
Operating cash flows	0.037	1.457	−0.331	0.437	0.05
Financing cash flows	0.013	1.058	−0.425	0.452	−0.02
Investing cash flows	0.033	1.332	−0.236	0.292	0.03
Net income	0.036	0.865	−0.126	0.149	0.18
Accruals	−0.005	2.194	−0.413	0.365	0.02

[a] The means, standard deviations, and 10th and 90th percentiles are estimated for first differences of the variables, deflated by market value of equity at the beginning of the year $[(CF_t - CF_{t-1})/MV_{t-1}]$. These estimates are based on all firm-years, totalling 4805 observations for the years 1974–1986, with a minimum of 345 firms in 1974 and a maximum of 382 in 1986.

[b] Correlations with annual Cumulative Abnormal Returns (*CAR*) represent average annual Pearson correlations during 1974–1986.

An examination of the average annual correlations among the independent variables in eq. (1) (not reported in the table) reveals that only three pairs of variables (out of 105 pairs – 14 components of cash flows plus accruals) have an average correlation coefficient greater than 0.50 (in absolute value), indicating that the degree of multicollinearity in the data is not severe. A correlation of 0.56 is found between collections from customers and payments to suppliers and employees, probably due to random shocks in demand that also affect production costs. High correlations are also found between accruals and payments to suppliers (0.63) and between accruals and investment in subsidiaries (−0.52).

5. Results

5.1. Tests of hypotheses about individual regression coefficients

To examine the associations between returns and individual components of cash flows, we estimate separate annual cross-sectional regressions and use the average coefficient and its standard error over the 13 years 1974–1986, as in Fama and MacBeth (1973).[7] We follow this approach to nullify the effect of possible cross-correlation in the data [Bernard (1987)]. The Fama and MacBeth approach uses only point estimates of the coefficients, which are unbiased even in the presence of cross-correlation, but not their annual standard errors. The average coefficients for regression eq. (1) and their t-statistics are reported in table 2. As can be seen from the table, the components of operating cash flows are highly associated with security returns, and all of these coefficients have the expected signs. Tax payments do not have a significant coefficient, either because this information is irrelevant for investors, or because it was anticipated, or because it can be derived from other cash flows, i.e., some multicollinearity exists.

Turning to financing cash flows, we observe that, consistent with signalling theory, debt issuance has a positive coefficient and preferred-stock issuance a negative coefficient, although the latter is statistically insignificant. Common-stock issuance has a positive but insignificant coefficient, although a negative coefficient is predicted by signalling theory. The coefficient for dividends is positive and statistically significant, as predicted by theory.

The coefficients for investing cash flows are generally small and statistically insignificant, except for the investments in unconsolidated subsidiaries, which has a sign that is contrary to expectations. The insignificant coefficients on investing cash flows are consistent with McConnell and Muscarella (1985, fn. 18) who report that cross-sectional regressions of abnormal returns on capital expenditures yield coefficients that are statistically indistinguishable from zero. These results suggest that capital investments might be anticipated by investors.[8]

In summary, the examination of the individual coefficients of cash-flow components indicates that operating cash flows are strongly associated with

---

[7] For comparative purposes, we also combined all firm-years into a pooled cross-sectional time-series regression for the subset of firms that had available data in all years. The results of pooling were similar to those reported here.

[8] Note that the results reported in table 2 are based on a different methodology than those usually reported in the finance literature. The results in the table are based on linear regression, where the magnitude of the independent variable is considered. The results usually reported in the finance literature are based on an announcement-event methodology, where one does not necessarily consider the magnitude of the economic event. For example, McConnell and Muscarella (1985) report significant effects for announcements of capital expenditures, but fail to find a significant association with abnormal returns, when the magnitude of these investments is incorporated into a regression equation (their footnote 18).

Table 2

Regression results and tests of coefficients.[a,b]

Eq. (1) $CAR = a_0 + a_1\ Collections + a_2\ Payments + a_3\ Taxes + a_4\ Interest + a_5\ Other$
$+ b_1\ Debt + b_2\ Common + b_3\ Preferred + b_4\ Dividend$
$+ c_1\ PPE + c_2\ Acquisition + c_3\ Minority + c_4\ Subsidiary + c_5\ RetPPE$
$+ d_1\ Accrual + e$

Eq. (2) $CAR = f_0 + f_1\ CFO + g_1\ Accrual + u$

Eq. (3) $CAR = h_0 + h_1\ AggOp + h_2\ AggFin + h_3\ AggInv + h_4\ Accrual + q$

Eq. (4) $CAR = p_0 + p_1\ NetInc + v$

Independent variable	Eq. (1)[c] Coefficient Mean	Eq. (1)[c] t-stat	Eq. (3)[c] Coefficient Mean (t-stat)	Eq. (2)[c] Coefficient Mean (t-stat)	Eq. (4)[c] Coefficient Mean (t-stat)
Aggregate operating cash flows			0.217 (5.86)	0.169 (4.23)	
Collections from customers	0.273	6.04			
Payments to suppliers and employees	−0.268	−5.43			
Tax payments	−0.059	−0.70			
Interest payments	−0.645	−3.67			
Other operating cash flows	0.217	4.47			
Aggregate financing cash flows			0.041 (1.64)		
Debt issuance	0.063	2.51			
Common-stock issuance	0.051	0.48			
Preferred-stock issuance	−0.019	−0.14			
Dividend payment	1.379	2.68			
Aggregate investing cash flows			−0.048 (−2.40)		
Investment in PPE	0.005	0.08			
Acquisitions	0.062	0.67			
Retirement of PPE	0.092	1.39			
Investment in unconsolidated subsidiaries	−0.088	−4.40			
Purchase of minority interest	0.020	0.14			
Accruals	0.179	(3.84)	0.159 (3.79)	0.159 (3.70)	
Net income					0.163 (3.93)
Mean (unadjusted) R^2	0.248		0.116	0.085	0.081

[a] The table is based on data from all available firm-years. Similar results are obtained for 281 firms that had available data in every year during 1974–1986.

[b] The dependent variable is annual cumulative abnormal return (*CAR*).

[c] The mean is the average coefficient over the 13 annual cross-sectional regression eqs. (1)–(4) for the years 1974–1986. The *t*-statistics are computed as the mean annual coefficient divided by the standard error of the mean coefficient over the 13 annual cross-sectional regressions.

security returns and have the expected signs. Individual components of cash flows from financing activities are generally consistent with prior studies and expectations, albeit they tend to be less stable over the years and do not exhibit the same significance levels as the coefficents of cash flows from operations. The coefficients of investing cash flows are generally insignificant.

Table 2 also provides the coefficient means, t-statistics, and mean R^2's of eq. (2) and of the following regression equations:

$$CAR = h_0 + h_1 \, AggOp + h_2 \, AggFin + h_3 \, AggInv$$
$$+ h_4 \, Accruals + q, \qquad (3)$$

$$CAR = p_0 + p_1 \, NetInc + v, \qquad (4)$$

where the dependent variable is the cumulative abnormal return and the independent variables are aggregate cash flows from operating, financing, investing activities, accruals, and net income, respectively. The results of eqs. (2)–(4) are included to facilitate comparisons with prior studies and to provide insights into the results with disaggregated data. Consistent with prior studies that examine regression (4) for annual returns, the mean (unadjusted) R^2 over the 13 years is 0.081 [Lev (1989)]. This is very close to the mean (unadjusted) R^2 of regression eq. (2), which decomposes net income into aggregate operating cash flows and accruals (0.085). Likewise, the coefficients of operating cash flows and accruals in eq. (2) are similar. These results indicate that disaggregating net income into cash from operations and accruals might not contribute to the association with returns. The table also reveals an increase in (unadjusted) R^2 when aggregate cash flows from financing and investing are added (0.116) and a marked increase in (unadjusted) R^2 when all cash flows are disaggregated (0.248). Formal tests of these observations are provided below.

5.2. Tests of hypotheses about groups of regression coefficients

To test the hypotheses about groups of coefficients (i.e., H_1–H_8), we estimate regression eqs. (1)–(2) for each year and use the estimated annual coefficients in a procedure similar to Fama and MacBeth (1973). For example, to test whether the coefficients of the four components of financing cash flows are all equal (H_1), we use the 13 annual sets of coefficients for financing events from the cross-sectional regressions. We then test for the equality of these four coefficients of financing cash flows using analysis of variance, with 13 observations on each coefficient.[9] Table 3 reports the hypotheses, the

---

[9]We have also performed direct tests of the equality of these coefficients for each year (an F-test) and aggregated the results over all years using a χ^2-statistic as in Healy et al. (1987). The results are similar to those reported here.

Table 3

Results of hypotheses tests.

Eq. (1) $\quad CAR = a_0 + a_1\ Collections + a_2\ Payments + a_3\ Taxes + a_4\ Interest + a_5\ Other$
$\quad\quad\quad + b_1\ Debt + b_2\ Common + b_3\ Preferred + b_4\ Dividend$
$\quad\quad\quad + c_1\ PPE + c_2\ Acquisition + c_3\ Minority + c_4\ Subsidiary + c_5\ RetPPE$
$\quad\quad\quad + d_1\ Accrual + e$

Eq. (2) $\quad CAR = f_0 + f_1\ CFO + g_1\ Accrual + u$

Hypothesis	Description of null hypothesis	Test	F[a]	Significance[b]
Financing				
H_1	Components of financing cash flows have identical associations with returns.	$b_1 = b_2 = b_3 = -b_4$	6.81	0.001
H_2	Debt and common stock have identical associations.	$b_1 = b_2$	0.01	0.914
H_3	Debt and preferred stock have identical associations.	$b_1 = b_3$	0.37	0.546
H_4	Common and preferred stock have identical associations.	$b_2 = b_3$	0.17	0.682
Investing				
H_5	Components of investing cash flows have identical associations with returns.	$c_1 = c_2 = c_3 = c_4 = -c_5$	0.63	0.640
Operating				
H_6	Collections and other operating cash flows have identical associations.	$a_1 = a_5$	0.70	0.410
H_7	Cash from operations and accruals have identical associations with returns.	$f_1 = g_1$	0.01	0.925
H_8	Components of operating cash flows have identical associations with returns.	$a_1 = -a_2 = -a_3 = -a_4 = a_5$	5.16	0.001

[a] The F-statistic is estimated by using ANOVA for 13 annual observations of cash-flow response coefficients estimated by eqs. (1)–(2) for each year 1974–1986.
[b] The significance level measures the probability of observing the F-statistic under the null hypothesis.

restrictions on coefficients they imply, F-statistics that are obtained to test these hypotheses, and their associated significance levels.

Consistent with signalling theories of finance (which postulate that the form of financing has an effect on security returns), the test of hypothesis H_1 indicates that the components of financing cash flows do, indeed, have different associations with security returns. However, the data cannot distinguish between various pairs of financing cash inflows (H_2 through H_4).

Turning to the hypothesis of investing cash flows (H_5), we find that the coefficients of investing cash flows are statistically indistinguishable from each other. These results are consistent with market anticipation of future investments by firms.

Contrary to intuition about the recurring nature of cash collected from customers as compared to that from 'other' sources, the hypothesis that the two differ in associations with returns (H_6) is not rejected by the data. Consistent with Bernard and Stober (1989) and inconsistent with Bowen et al. (1987) and Wilson (1986, 1987), the disaggregation of net income into cash from operations and accruals (H_7) does not increase the association with security returns. The results in table 3 also indicate that the null hypothesis that associations with security returns do not differ across components of operating cash flows (H_8) is easily rejected by the data. Thus, individual components of operating cash flows have information content beyond total operating cash flows.

5.3. Sensitivity analyses

The above results are dependent on correct specifications of the models and could be sensitive to the underlying assumptions. To test for the robustness of the results, we perform the following additional tests:

1. *Return accumulation period*: We accumulate abnormal returns over a period that coincides with year t, instead of April of year t through March of year $t + 1$. We also use raw returns instead of risk-adjusted returns. The results are unaffected by these changes.
2. *Size*: For each year, we split the sample into above- and below-median in terms of market value of equity at the beginning of the year. The results are similar for the two groups.
3. *Outliers*: We eliminate every observation which contains at least one component that is more than four standard deviations away from its cross-sectional mean. On average, 9.5% of the sample firms are deleted in any particular year due to component outliers. Wilson (1986), using the same definition of outliers, reports that more than 7% of the firm-years in his sample are deleted due to outliers, although he uses fewer components than we do. The results of this study are insensitive to the deletion of outliers.
4. *Predictions based on prior returns*: Following Beaver et al. (1980) and Collins et al. (1987), we use prior cumulative abnormal returns to predict the expected components of cash flows. Like Collins et al. (1987), we first classify firms in each year into five size groups according to market value of equity at the beginning of the year. Within each size group, we then estimate the following regression equation for each of the components of

cash flows, for the total cash flows from financing, investing, and operating activities, for accruals, and for net income:

$$SCF_{jtk} = a_0 + a_1 CAR_{jt-1} + w, \tag{5}$$

where SCF_{jtk} is the scaled difference in the kth component of cash flow for year t and firm j, expressed as $(CF_{jtk} - CF_{jt-1k})/MV_{jt-1}$, where CF_{jtk} is the level of the cash-flow component k for firm j in year t and MV_{jt-1} is market value of firm j's equity at the beginning of year t. CAR_{jt-1} is the abnormal return for firm j in year $t-1$ cumulated over April through March. The estimated coefficients, a_0 and a_1 (for each of the five size groups), are used together with CAR_{jt} to predict SCF_{jt+1k}, from which we derive a prediction of CF_{jt+1k}. This prediction is subtracted from the actual CF_{jt+1k}, and scaled by the market value of firm j's equity at the beginning of year $t+1$. This process is repeated for all the components of cash flows, the total cash flows, accruals, and net income. Thus, we have a different specification of 'surprises' in the components of cash flows, which are tested for their associations with security returns. The results are insensitive to this specification of unexpected cash flows.

5. *Predictions based on all other components*: Following Lipe (1986), each component change of cash flows in year t is predicted by using all changes in the components of cash flows in year $t-1$. Thus, we first estimate the equation:

$$SCF_{jtk} = a_0 + \sum_k a_k SCF_{jt-1k} + z, \qquad t = 1975, \ldots, 1986, \tag{6}$$

where SCF_{jtk} is defined as before. This equation is estimated by using pooled data from all years and all firms. We then use the residuals from (6) as independent variables in our returns regressions.[10] The results are insensitive to this specification of the unexpected components of cash flows.

Based on these additional tests, we believe that the results reported in the study are robust, and are not caused by specification errors or by the particular construction of unexpected components of cash flows.

---

[10] Our procedure is different from Lipe's (1986), who estimates his models separately for each firm. Since we have only 13 time-series observations for each firm (as compared to 34 observations for Lipe) and 15 components of cash flows and accruals, estimating separate models for each firm is infeasible.

6. Summary and conclusions

This study investigates whether the disaggregation of total cash flows into their components as required by FAS No. 95 yields greater associations with annual security returns than aggregate cash flows or accruals. The study formulates and tests several hypotheses about the relations between cash flows and returns.

Consistent with theory and prior studies, we find that individual components of cash flows are differentially associated with security returns. Individual components that designate cash inflows from operations are positively associated with stock returns, whereas those that designate cash outflows from operating activities are negatively associated with stock returns. We also find that individual components of operating cash flows (excluding tax payments) have strong associations with security returns. Individual coefficients of cash-flow components from financing activities are generally consistent with theories about information asymmetries; issuance of debt is positively associated with security returns, issuance of common stock is positively (but weakly) associated with returns, and issuance of preferred stock is negatively associated with returns, albeit less than common stock. Dividends are positively associated with stock returns. Most of the individual components of investing cash flows do not exhibit significant associations with security returns.

Consistent with Bernard and Stober (1989), the disaggregation of net income into operating cash flows and accruals is insufficient to improve the association with annual returns. However, the disaggregation of total cash from operations and total financing cash flows into their components does improve the association with annual returns. These results are consistent with theories about different effects of financing and operating events. However, our evidence indicates that the level of aggregation for investing activities is not important in improving the association with security returns.

The empirical results are robust to various specifications of the variables. In particular, the results are insensitive to the specific accumulation period of abnormal returns, size of firms, and whether the scaling of the prediction error is performed by market value of equity or by total assets. The results also are insensitive to whether predictions of cash-flow components are generated by the random-walk model, or by a model that uses the prior year's cumulative abnormal returns to predict the current year's components of cash flows, or by a model that uses data about all components of cash flows in the preceding year.

Finally, this study indicates that financial statements contain more information than just the 'bottom-line' earnings figure; i.e., financing and operating cash flows capture additional information about valuation-relevant economic events, beyond that which is captured by earnings alone.

Appendix: Estimation of cash-flow components

Following Sondhi et al. (1987), estimation of cash-flow components is based on information taken from the income statement, changes in balance-sheet accounts from the beginning of the accounting period till its end, and from the statement of changes in financial position. The components of cash flows correspond to those required by FAS No. 95. Specifically, we estimate the following components:

Cash from operating activities

1. Collections from customers = Sales − Change in accounts receivable.
2. Payments to suppliers, employees etc. = Cost of goods sold (excluding depreciation) + Change in inventory − Change in accounts payable + Change in other assets − Change in other current liabilities − Change in other liabilities.
3. Taxes paid = Tax expense − Change in deferred taxes − Change in taxes payable.
4. Interest paid, net = Interest expense − Interest income.
5. Other operating cash flows = Special items + Nonoperating income (excluding interest income) − Extraordinary expenses.

Total cash from operations = (1) + (5) − (2) − (3) − (4).

Cash flows from financing activities

6. Net issuance of debt = Change in long-term debt + Change in current maturities of long-term debt.
7. Net issuance of common stock = Change in total stockholders equity − Net income + Common dividends + Dividends on preferred stock.
8. Net issuance of preferred stock = Change in the carrying value of preferred stock.
9. Dividends paid = Dividends on common stock + Dividends on preferred stock.

Total cash flows from financing = (6) + (7) + (8) − (9).

Cash flows from investing activities

10. Capital expenditures = Capital expenditures from the statement of changes in financial position.
11. Acquisitions = Acquisitions from the statement of changes in financial position.

12. Investments and advances to unconsolidated subsidiaries, net = Change in investments and advances to unconsolidated subsidiaries (equity method or other).
13. Net purchases of minority interests = Minority interest in income − Change in minority interest.
14. Proceeds from the retirement of PPE = Capital expenditures from (9) + Acquisitions from (10) − Change in gross PPE − Change in intangibles − Depreciation and amortization + Change in accumulated depreciation.

Total cash from investing activities = (10) + (11) + (12) + (13) − (14).

Total increase in cash = Total cash from operations + Total cash from financing activities + Total cash from investing activities.

As a check of the estimation procedure, for each firm and for each year we compare the change in the cash account to the total increase in cash obtained as above. Absent rounding-off errors, the change in the cash account should be identical to the cumulative effect of the cash-flow components. Firms for which we find differences that cannot be considered rounding-off errors are omitted from the analysis. Such differences can occur due to missing data, erroneous data recorded by Compustat, etc. However, for most firms the cumulative effect of cash-flow components is identical to the change in the cash account for the year. Only 50 out of 10,911 observations (firm-years) are deleted due to a difference of over one million dollars between the change in cash and the cumulative effect of the cash-flow components.

References

Aharony, Joseph and Itzhak Swary, 1980, Quarterly dividend and earnings announcements and stockholder's returns: An empirical analysis, Journal of Finance 35, 1–12.

AICPA, 1971, Reporting changes in financial position, APB opinion no. 19 (AICPA, New York, NY).

Amihud, Yakov and Baruch Lev, 1981, Risk reduction as a managerial motive for conglomerate mergers, Bell Journal of Economics 12, 605–617.

Asquith, Paul and David Mullins, 1983, The impact of initiating dividend payments on shareholder wealth, Journal of Business 56, 77–96.

Asquith, Paul and David Mullins, 1986, Equity issues and offering dilution, Journal of Financial Economics 15, 61–89.

Barnea, Amir, Joshua Ronen, and Simcha Sadan, 1976, Classificatory smoothing of income with extraordinary items, The Accounting Review 51, 110–122.

Beaver, William, Richard Lambert, and Dale Morse, 1980, The information content of security prices, Journal of Accounting and Economics 2, 3–28.

Bernard, Victor L., 1987, Cross-sectional dependence and problems in inference in market-based accounting research, Journal of Accounting Research 25, 1–48.

Bernard, Victor L., 1989, Capital market research in accounting during the 1980s: A critical review, Paper prepared in honor of the University of Illinois Accountancy Ph.D. program golden jubilee symposium (University of Michigan, Ann Arbor, MI).

Bernard, Victor L. and Thomas L. Stober, 1989, The nature and amount of information reflected in cash flows and accruals, The Accounting Review 64, 624–652.

Bowen, Robert M., David Burgstahler, and Lane A. Daley, 1987, The incremental information content of accrual versus cash flows, The Accounting Review 62, 723–747.

Brickley, James, 1983, Shareholder wealth, information signaling and the specially designated dividend: An empirical study, Journal of Financial Economics 12, 187–209.

Charest, Guy, 1978, Dividend information, stock returns, and market efficiency – II, Journal of Financial Economics 6, 297–330.

Christie, Andrew A., 1987, On cross-sectional analysis in accounting research, Journal of Accounting and Economics 9, 231–258.

Collins, Daniel W., S.P. Kothari, and Judy D. Rayburn, 1987, Firm size and the information content of prices with respect to earnings, Journal of Accounting and Economics 9, 111–138.

Dann, Larry, 1981, Common stock repurchases: An analysis of returns to bondholders and stockholders, Journal of Financial Economics 9, 113–138.

Eckbo, B. Espen, 1986, Valuation effects of corporate debt offerings, Journal of Financial Economics 15, 119–151.

Fama, Eugene F. and James D. MacBeth, 1973, Risk, return and equilibrium: Empirical tests, Journal of Political Economy 71, 607–636.

FASB, 1987, Statement of Financial Accounting Standards No. 95.

Gonedes, Nicholas J., 1979, Corporate signaling, external accounting and capital market equilibrium: Evidence on dividends, income and extraordinary items, Journal of Accounting Research 17, 26–79.

Healy, Paul M., Sok-Hyon Kang, and Krishna G. Palepu, 1987, The effect of accounting procedure changes on CEO's cash salary and bonus compensation, Journal of Accounting and Economics 9, 7–34.

Jensen, Michael C. and Richard S. Ruback, 1983, The market for corporate control: The scientific evidence, Journal of Financial Economics 11, 5–50.

Kormendi, Roger and Robert Lipe, 1987, Earnings innovations, earnings persistence and stock returns, Journal of Business 60, 323–345.

Leland, Hayne and David Pyle, 1977, Information asymmetries, financial structure, and financial intermediation, Journal of Finance 32, 371–387.

Lev, Baruch, 1989, On the usefulness of earnings: Lessons and directions from two decades of empirical research, Journal of Accounting Research, forthcoming.

Lipe, Robert, 1986, The information contained in the components of earnings, Journal of Accounting Research 24, 37–64.

Livnat, Joshua and Ashwinpaul Sondhi, 1989, Estimating the components of operating cash flows, Working paper (New York University, New York, NY).

Masulis, Ronald W. and Ashok Korwar, 1986, Seasoned equity offerings: An empirical investigation, Journal of Financial Economics 15, 91–118.

McConnell, John and Chris J. Muscarella, 1985, Corporate capital expenditure decisions and the market value of the firm, Journal of Financial Economics 14, 399–422.

Mikkelson, Wayne H. and M. Megan Partch, 1986, Valuation effect of security offerings and the issuance process, Journal of Financial Economics 15, 31–60.

Miller, Merton and Franco Modigliani, 1961, Dividend policy, growth, and the valuation of shares, Journal of Business 34, 411–433.

Miller, Merton and Kevin Rock, 1985, Dividend policy under asymmetric information, Journal of Finance 40, 1031–1052.

Ou, Jane A. and Stephen H. Penman, 1989, Financial statement analysis and the prediction of stock returns, Journal of Accounting and Economics 11, 295–329.

Rayburn, Judy, 1986, The association of operating cash flow and accruals with security returns, Journal of Accounting Research 24, 112–138.

Roll, Richard, 1986, The hubris hypothesis of corporate takeovers, Journal of Business 59, 197–216.

Ross, Stephen, 1977, The determination of capital structure: The incentive-signalling approach, Bell Journal of Economics 8, 23–40.

Smith, Clifford W. Jr., 1986, Investment banking and the capital acquisition process, Journal of Financial Economics 15, 3–29.

Sondhi, Ashwinpaul C., George H. Sorter, and Gerald White, 1987, Transactional analysis, Financial Analysts Journal 43, 57–64.

Vermaelen, Theo, 1981, Common stock repurchases and market signalling, Journal of Financial Economics 9, 139–183.

Wilson, G. Peter, 1986, The relative information content of accruals and cash flows: Combined evidence at the earnings announcement and annual report date, Journal of Accounting Research 24, 165–200.

Wilson, G. Peter, 1987, The incremental information content of the accrual and funds components of earnings after controlling for earnings, The Accounting Review 62, 293–321.

On Assessing a Firm's Cash Generating Ability

Ray G. Stephens
The Ohio State University
Vijay Govindarajan
Dartmouth College

ABSTRACT: Focusing on funds flow from operations, a way for analysts to use financial statement information to obtain additional insights when assessing a firm's cash generating ability is proposed. The method provides a clearer focus on a firm's cash generating ability from operations. Results from applying the proposed method are compared with information from traditional funds flow statements (APBO No. 19 and SFAS No. 95) for 20 firms, highlighting the incremental insights available.

THIS paper proposes a way for analysts to use currently disclosed accounting information to obtain additional insights in assessing a firm's cash generating ability.[1] The method involves identifying and classifying cash flows such that the various effects and implications of a firm's operating and financing activities can be measured and understood. The differences between the information available from applying this method and that from applying APBO No. 19 and SFAS No. 95 are illustrated using data from the fiscal 1982 financial statements of The Limited, Inc.[2] Results of applying the method are then compared with information available from traditional funds flow statements for 20 firms over the period 1980–1984.[3]

We wish to express our debt to Pearson Hunt whose unpublished manuscript (1979) provided the impetus for this paper, to W. W. Cooper and J. K. Shank for many valuable lessons, and to Andrew Bailey, Douglas Schroeder, Felix Kollaritsch, Thomas Selling, Clyde Stickney, M. Edgar Barrett, and two anonymous referees for helpful comments on earlier versions of this paper.

Manuscript received November 1986.
Revisions received October 1987, December 1988, and April 1989.
Accepted June 1989.

There is a significant and growing body of literature concerning both the disclosure and the use of funds flow information. One group of authors has noted inconsistency in how firms classify certain events as operating or nonoperating (such as interest revenue and expenses, sales of long-term assets, and early debt extinguishments) between the income statement and the funds flow statement (Ketz and Largay 1987; Nurnberg 1972).

Other authors have focused on the best indicator of a firm's financial state. Rappaport (1979) proposed the concept of "distributable funds," the periodic amount said to be available for distribution to stockholders. Hunt (1975, 1979) proposed the concept of "funds position," which focused on the difference between the amount of internally generated operating funds in a period and the amount of funds devoted to capital investment in that same period. According to Hunt, a series of negative "funds positions" indicates fundamental problems in a firm's operations and investment policies. A similar approach is Hawkins' (1986, 127–129) "total cash flow analysis."

We expand Hunt's concept by distinguishing between "capital maintenance" investments and "capital expansion" investments. Different assessments of a firm's cash generating ability are thus made available. For example, growing firms and firms not replacing capital would receive different assessments under Hunt's concept and this proposal. Additional information about cash generating ability is also obtainable from the application of this proposal via the inclusion of the concepts of dispensable, distributable, and discretionary funds as well as from several additional refinements. While the underlying concept of "distributable funds" has the same definition as Rappaport, the determination of the amount differs.

A Focus on Funds Flows From Operating Activities

The principal focus of financial analysis is on the amount of funds generated from operating activities.[4] The focus assumes that the assessment of a firm's cash generating ability from operations should not be influenced by financing activities. This flows from the fact that financial leverage allocates funds flow, changes resulting from it do not reflect changes in cash generating ability. Fur-

---

[1] Until recently, much of the information was provided by the Statement of Changes in Financial Position prepared under the requirements of Accounting Principles Board Opinion (APBO) No. 19, *Reporting Changes in Financial Position* (AICPA 1971). Currently, much of that information is provided by the Statement of Cash Flows prepared under the requirements of SFAS No. 95, *Statement of Cash Flows* (FASB 1987b).

[2] The insights available from applying this method are both similar to and distinct from those that may be obtained using the data now available in a Statement of Cash Flows prepared in accordance with SFAS No. 95.

[3] These statements have had a variety of titles over the years (see fn. 1 above). For purposes of clarity and simplicity the term "funds flow statement" will be used here.

[4] Dorfman (1987, 37) reports in *The Wall Street Journal*, "Follow the money. That's a guiding principle for the increasing number of stock analysts and investors who study corporate cash flows. While none of them advocates using cash flow analysis by itself, they say it can be an important tool in piercing the camouflage that sometimes makes reported earnings misleading." Bankers also desire and like the funds flow statement (see Stephens 1980; Abdel-khalik et al. 1983).

ther, the cash generating process for operations—which requires one type of managerial decisions and reflects operating risk—is different from the cash generating process for financing activities, which requires another type of managerial decisions and reflects financial risk. An analysis of operating funds flows should also provide insight into the ability of the firm and its management to generate these flows in the future.[5]

The important questions, therefore, are: (1) how should funds flows from operating activities be distinguished from funds flows from other activities? and, (2) how should funds flow from operating activities be determined. Each of these questions will be discussed separately below.

Separation of Operating Activities from Financing Activities

Financial leverage should not influence an assessment of operating funds flow since the presence of such leverage affects only the allocation of funds flow between creditors and investors. Its presence does not indicate a change in cash generating ability. An analysis of firms' cash generating ability prior to considering any allocation of the funds flow—even though there may be different requirements for making specific payments—is important even if financial leverage changes as it might under a leveraged buyout.

Only two types of a firm's activities, operating and financing, need be separated for purposes of funds flow analysis. Investment activities need not be shown as a separate activity.[6] Such an elimination is rooted in the premise that investments are undertaken either: (1) to earn a return from providing goods and services (the purchasing, producing, and selling operations), or (2) to earn a return from nonoperating (financial) assets. The first category of investing activities is undertaken to generate operating funds flows. The second category is undertaken to generate financing funds flows.

Separating activities into operating and financial categories leads to another difference from current practice. Currently available funds flow statements do not fully separate operating activities from financing activities since financial revenues (such as interest revenue and investment income) and financial expenses (such as interest expense) are included in the current calculation of funds from operations under SFAS No. 95. The effects of operating activities need to be completely separated from financing activities.[7,8]

---

[5] The focus on the future is consistent with the user orientation in accounting which states that the purpose of accounting is to provide information for estimating future cash flows (AICPA 1973a; FASB 1980, 1981, 1986a; Elliott 1986).

[6] The stated objective of APBO No. 19 was to summarize the financing and investing activities of firms, including the extent to which a firm has generated funds from operations during a period, and to provide complete disclosure of changes in financial position. SFAS No. 95 clearly provides for this in its formatted disclosures.

[7] Accounts receivable and accounts payable are financial instruments arising from operations. We classify these items as affecting the operating cash flows to conform to current practice. Analysts will have to decide whether major changes in these items reflect changes in operations or changes in methods of financing business operations.

[8] The ability to analyze a firm's cash generating ability prior to considering the effect of the firm's financing activities has become even more important with the required consolidation of finance subsidiaries (SFAS No. 94, FASB 1987a).

Capital Maintenance Considerations and Operating Activities

There is an inseparable relation between a firm's future ability to generate funds from operating activities and its current need to make investments to maintain itself as a going concern. The latter need is sometimes referred to as "capital maintenance" (that is, a level of current investment is required in order to enable a firm to maintain operating capacity). In other words, not all investments in operating assets are equivalent. A level of operating investment is required to maintain the operating capacity and this amount should be separated from other funds flow uses. Any remainder of the operating investment is made either to increase the operating capacity of existing business or to invest in new types of businesses.

This distinction is important to an understanding of a firm's funds flows. Expansion of the current business or entry into new types of businesses can be undertaken using new debt or equity financing. Unlike capital maintenance investments, such investments need not be able to be funded from current operating funds flow in order for the firm to avoid a real terms reduction of the per share value of owners equity.

The Basic Data Implementation

Reorganizing the items reported on the funds flow statement is all that is necessary for implementing the parts of the proposal discussed so far. The following revisions to traditional funds flow statements provide for a separation of operating from financing activities and allow the user to focus on assessing the ability of a firm to generate operating funds flows in the future:

1. Add (subtract) interest expense (income) to income from continuing operations and treating it as a subtraction (addition) under financing activities. This is done in order to separate the cost of (return from) financing from the cost of (return from) operations.
2. Adjust revenues and expenses for collections from customers and payments to suppliers, in order to reflect cash receipts and expenditures.
3. Classify as operating funds flow the funds used to maintain the real level of operating assets (such as inventory and property, plant, and equipment).
4. Separate those investments in operating assets which are not required for "capital maintenance."
5. Separate financing activities into debt and equity components.

The first revision may be used to generate what is termed "Gross Funds from Operations." The second adjusts accrual basis income to reflect cash receipts from customers and cash payments to suppliers.[9] The third change allows for the generation of "Net Funds from Operations before Expansion," while the fourth change provides a subtotal that might be called "Net Funds from Operations"—that is, it reflects the separation of "steady state" from "growth" investments. The final alteration can be used to show burdens of financing, and extensions

---

[9] This adjustment is unnecessary for statements of cash flows prepared under the direct method of SFAS No. 95. The information is available on the face of the financial statements.

and receipts from financing by type of financing. This separation is especially important when net funds from operations are negative because of the differing "requirements" for paying the burden of debt and the burden of equity.[10]

The effect of income taxes on the segregated disclosures also needs to be considered. Following Nurnberg (1983) and intraperiod tax allocation in APBO No. 30, we use the concept that taxes follow the transaction; that is, income taxes will be allocated to individual transactions as operating and financing activities are separated on the funds flow statement. Thus, adjustments of income will use after tax amounts at the marginal tax rate for the individual transaction.[11]

Dispensable, Distributable, and Discretionary Funds Flows

The revisions just outlined may provide three additional items of information. These new items are: (1) dispensable funds generated; (2) distributable funds generated; and (3) discretionary funds generated. The amount shown as *dispensable funds generated* provides information about the "self financing" ability of the firm. A positive number indicates that enough funds have been generated by operations to cover the investments required to maintain "steady state" operations. The amount shown represents either the amount of funds generated from operations which a firm can use for financing activities or the amount that it must make up from financing activities. When there are no debt requirements, it represents the amount available for dividends without any element of liquidation. If the firm has debt and the dispensable funds number is negative, the firm must still pay interest, and by implication, the firm had to borrow to pay interest.

The amount of *distributable funds generated* provides an indication of the ability of a firm to maintain itself given its current financial leverage. It provides information about the joint effects of operating and leveraging characteristics. A positive number indicates that enough funds have been generated by operations to cover the required interest on current debt in addition to meeting investments to maintain "steady state" operations. A negative number accompanied by cash dividends implies that the firm had to borrow to pay dividends, thus, resulting in a partial liquidation of the firm.

The *discretionary funds generated* indicates the funds available after both maintaining "steady state" operations and covering interest and dividends. A positive number indicates that the firm has available funds for growth or other activities such as stock repurchase or debt reduction.

Refinements

There are other items that affect an analyst's ability to estimate both a firm's future funds flow and their uncertainty. Among the more prominent are: "one

---

[10] The funds flow burden of debt financing consists of the after tax cost of interest. A firm must pay this amount to avoid financial complications, including bankruptcy. Our concern is whether this amount is being generated by operations after coverage of "steady state" investment. The funds flow burden of equity financing consists of cash dividends. While no legal requirements may exist for paying dividends, an economic requirement may exist (Dielman and Oppenheimer 1984; Watts 1973).

[11] The marginal rates used are the maximum rates for income tax purposes unless the adjustment carries specific income tax effects.

shot" effects; peripheral and incidental operating activities; and information about financing activities.

Sustainable Funds Generation

There is a need to differentiate between sustainable funds generating activities—activities which are expected to continue to generate funds in future periods—and "one shot" funds generations from operations. APBO No. 30 requires firms to separate extraordinary items, discontinued operations and the cumulative effect of accounting changes from income from continuing operations on the income statement and that these items should also be shown separately on the funds flow statement.[12] There are two different issues: (1) the separation of these items into operating and financing activities, and (2) the handling of "one shot" operating funds flow.

Extraordinary items may be either one-time effects on operating activities (e.g., an extraordinary gain resulting from the receipt of insurance from a fire loss) or on financing activities (e.g., an extraordinary gain resulting from the redemption of debt). Funds generated by operations should be adjusted for each of these items. Those items classified as financing activities also should be removed from the operations section and placed under the appropriate financing activity (debt or equity). By definition, discontinued operations would always be an operating activity. The funds flow effects of gains and losses from discontinued operations should be shown after net funds from continuing operations. Since the cumulative effect of accounting changes is normally an income item not requiring the use of funds, this item has already been removed from funds generated from operations under present disclosure rules. Thus, no further adjustment is necessary.

Operating related "one shot" effects can be handled by using income from continuing operations as the starting point and moving the after tax effect of all "one shot" operating earnings items to yield a new category, "net funds from *continuing* operations before expansion." Effecting this change also allows one to properly show dispensable, distributable, and discretionary funds by deleting any "one shot" funds flow items from their calculation. As the primary rationale behind analyzing the funds flow statement is to assess future cash generating ability, "one shot" funds flows need to be shown separately since they provide little guidance in respect to the prediction of future cash flows. Thus, dispensable funds is defined as net funds from continuing operations (before expansion), and distributable funds and discretionary funds would be this amount less the appropriate burdens.

Separation of Peripheral and Incidental Operating Activities

Beyond the "one shot" effects, so called peripheral and incidental operating activities may have different risks (different distributions of future funds flow)

---

[12] The purpose of APBO No. 30 (AICPA 1973b) was to further implement the "all inclusive income statement concept" by prohibiting charges to retained earnings. The separation of "one shot earnings" from an amount termed herein as income from continuing operations, was felt to be needed in order to allow an analyst to project future amounts of sustainable net income.

than will the central operating activities. In other words, the funds flow from central operating activities may be more or less likely to be different in the future than will funds from incidental and/or peripheral operating activities. The separation of central operating activities from peripheral and incidental activities involves the activities by which firms generated funds and the disclosure of these activities. For instance, gains and losses on the sale of marketable securities should be seen as incidental to a firm's main activities, unless it is a financial institution (Ketz and Largay 1987, 13).

The separation of peripheral and incidental operating activities from a firm's central operating activities may be especially difficult for diversified firms. The analyst will have to determine in these situations if some segments are core activities and other segments are separable. Peripheral and incidental operating activities will have no meaning for conglomerates. For other firms, some segments may be related around such things as a common technology, a common customer base, or common distribution channels.

Separate disclosures are also desirable when different levels of perceived riskiness exist between different funds flow streams. From a financial analysis standpoint, this would result in two parts of the funds from operations: (1) funds generated by central operating activities, and (2) funds generated by peripheral and incidental activities.

An Example: The Limited, Inc.

Funds Flow Under APBO No. 19

The funds flow statement of The Limited, Inc., as reported in their 1982 fiscal year Report to Stockholders and prepared under APBO No. 19, is shown in Exhibit 1. This statement used the "Cash and Equivalents" definition of funds.[13] That is, the statement showed the items that caused an increase or decrease in the amount of cash and equivalents available to The Limited. Exhibit 1 shows The Limited reported a decrease of $5,837,000 in cash and short-term investments during the fiscal year ended January 29, 1983.

Formats for the funds flow statement, acceptable under APBO No. 19, showed funds from operations obtained as an adjustment to net income for expenses not requiring the expenditures of funds. In Exhibit 1, these are the adjustments shown to "net income" for "depreciation and amortization" and for "deferred income taxes and other" in order to reach an amount for "working capital from operations." This illustrates three points: (1) there was no usual classificatory separation of operating, investing, and financing activities within specific financial reports prepared under APBO No 19; (2) the distinction between operations, investing, and financing activities was not always handled in a similar fashion across firms (note that The Limited, by placing the adjustment for working capital prior to summing to an amount for funds provided by operations, was

---

[13] The definition of funds for a funds flow statement was irrelevant to the preparation of a statement under APBO No. 19. The definition affected only what items would be included on the statement. A funds flow statement could have been prepared for any balance sheet items (Clemente 1982). SFAS No. 95 adopted either cash or cash equivalents as the definition of funds.

Exhibit 1
The Limited, Inc. & Subsidiaries
Consolidated Statement of Changes in Financial Position*
Year Ended January 29, 1983
(thousands)

Cash was provided from:	
Operations	
Net income	$ 33,592
Add expenses not requiring working capital	
Depreciation and amortization	22,509
Deferred income taxes and other	10,322
Working capital from operations	$ 66,423
Cash flow additions (requirements) resulting from (includes acquired subsidiaries since acquisition dates in 1982)	
Inventories	$ 7,005
Payables	(22,607)
Income taxes	8,775
Other current assets and liabilities	(7,416)
Cash provided from operations	$ 52,180
Sale of receivables to Limited Credit Corp., net of equity investment	47,947
Long-term debt incurred to acquire subsidiaries	110,439
Cash balances of acquired subsidiaries at dates of acquisition	14,304
Total cash provided	$224,870
Cash was used for:	
Purchase of net assets of acquired subsidiaries	$111,452
Investment in property and equipment	35,506
Reduction of long-term debt, net of $7,104,000 conversion of debentures in 1982	80,130
Cash dividends and other, net	3,619
Total cash used	$230,707
Increase (decrease) in Cash and Equivalents	(5,837)
Cash and Equivalents, beginning of year	11,326
Cash and Equivalents, end of year	$ 5,489

* Source: 1982 Annual Report

terming changes in current assets and current liability items except cash and equivalents as operational items); and (3) since no specific format was required by GAAP, The Limited could present the funds flow statement as it desired.

The APBO No. 19 funds flow statement format provided an amount termed funds generated from operations ($52,180,000 for The Limited). After this amount, the funds flow statement showed: (1) financing and investing activities that affected funds flow, and (2) other significant financing and investing activities (that is, activities that did not directly result in funds flow, such as the purchase of investments by stock issuance).

Exhibit 2
The Limited, Inc.
Estimated Statement of Cash Flows[1]
(Prepared under SFAS No. 95)
Year Ended January 29, 1983

Operating Activities	
Net Income	$ 33,592
Add expenses not requiring cash:	
Depreciation and amortization	22,509
Deferred income taxes and other	10,322
Changes in accounts:	
Receivables	47,947
Inventory	7,005
Payables	(22,607)
Income taxes	8,775
Other current accounts	(7,416)
Total from operating activities	$100,127
Investing Activities	
Purchase of plant and equipment	$ (35,506)
Purchase of new subsidiaries, net of cash received	13,291
Total from investing activities	$ (22,215)
Financing Activities	
Financing from long-term debt	$ (80,130)
Cash dividends	(3,619)
Total from financing activities	$ (83,749)
Decrease in cash and equivalents	$ (5,837)

Schedule of Noncash Investing and Financing Activities

Purchase of subsidiaries through issuance of long-term debt	$110,439

[1] Presumes, based upon information in the report to stockholders, that all items affected cash. Note that some long-term debt and investments in property and equipment may have been capital leases and, thus, may not be shown within the appropriate section of this particular statement of cash flows.

Funds Flow Under SFAS No. 95

A funds flow statement using the guidelines of SFAS No. 95 for The Limited, Inc. prepared by the authors based upon the information in the fiscal 1982 Report to Stockholders is shown in Exhibit 2. SFAS No. 95 established specific criteria for separating operating, investing, and financing activities on the statement of cash flows. It overcame two format shortcomings of APBO No. 19 through separating by type of activities and presenting noncash investing and financing activities in a separate statement. Exhibit 2 shows that The Limited reported a decrease of $5,837,000 in cash and short-term investments during the fiscal year, the same as under APBO No. 19. The Exhibit 2 Statement of Cash

Flows also provides an amount termed cash (funds) generated from operations ($100,127,000), that is significantly different from the amount shown for cash provided from operations in Exhibit 1.

A Revised Funds Flow Statement

The fiscal 1982 funds flow statement of The Limited, Inc., as revised to illustrate the method proposed in this paper, is shown in Exhibit 3. Among other things, the amount of investments in productive assets for "capital maintenance" has to be estimated by the analyst. This estimate of capital maintenance can be made using additional information contained in the firm's financial statements—such as the expenditure to acquire additional stores shown in Exhibit 3. The estimate can also be made using information accompanying the financial statements such as the liquidity and capital expenditures information in the Management Discussion and Analysis section.[14] Finally, the estimate can be made using generalized techniques for estimating the effects of cost changes such as general price level or specific price level adjustments. The use of replacement cost disclosures, previously required by SFAS No. 33 (FASB 1979), is illustrated later in making the comparative analysis for 20 firms.

Exhibit 3 shows the fiscal 1982 funds flow statement of The Limited, Inc. adjusted for the changes discussed above to: (1) separate operating activities from financing activities, and (2) to separate "steady state" investments from growth. This Exhibit shows *Gross Funds from Operations* of $98,111,000 after separating operating activities from financing activities, *Net Funds from Operations Before Expansion* of $69,610,000, and *Net Funds From Operations* of ($27,538,000) after separating steady state operating investments from growth operating investments.[15]

Comparative Analyses

If the proposed funds flow statement analysis has incremental benefit, it should be able to identify firms with fundamental funds flow problems when such problems could not be easily detected from traditional funds flow statements. Funds flow data for 20 firms were collected and analyzed to compare the

---

[14] A substantial amount of information is required for publicly reporting firms under Regulation S-K that can prove useful for making such estimates, especially the requirements for discussing future investment needs under Item 303, Management Discussion and Analysis (17 Code Federal Regulations 229, 303).

[15] The Limited made major expansion during 1982. Note that if capital expansion was not considered and the first approximation—that all investments in inventory and fixed assets constituted capital maintenance—was used, the "net funds generated before expansion" (dispensable funds generated) would be a negative ($27,538,000), indicating a severe cash flow problem for The Limited. However, when the "steady state" investments are separated from the "growth" investments, the dispensable funds generated are a positive $69,610,000, indicating a very healthy firm from an operating cash flow standpoint. We have further assumed for The Limited that all investments in plant and equipment are for capital maintenance and all investments in acquisitions of other companies are for capital expansion. A more sophisticated analysis would involve examination of investments in plant and equipment ($35,506,000) to further separate maintenance and growth investments included in this amount. Otherwise, potential for bias exists where firms that spend money on internal growth might look worse than firms that expand through acquisitions.

Exhibit 3
The Limited, Inc.
Illustrative Reformatted Funds Flow Statement
Year Ended January 29, 1983
(thousands)

Net Income	$ 33,592
Add expenses not requiring funds:	
Depreciation and amortization	22,509
Deferred income taxes and other	10,322
Add: Revenues of prior period collected	47,947
Subtract: Payments of prior period expenses	(22,607)
Add: Interest burden (net of taxes)	6,348[1]
GROSS FUNDS FROM OPERATIONS	**$ 98,111**
Investments:	
Inventories	7,005
Property and Equipment	(35,506)
NET FUNDS FROM OPERATIONS BEFORE EXPANSION	**$ 69,610[2]**
Purchase of new subsidiaries	(97,148)
NET FUNDS FROM OPERATIONS	**$(27,538)**
Financing—Debt:	
Long-term debt	30,309
Income taxes	8,775
Other current accounts	(7,416)
Interest Burden	(6,348)
FUNDS PROVIDED (USED) BY DEBT FINANCING	$ 25,320
Financing—Equity:	
Dividends	$ (3,619)
FUNDS PROVIDED (USED) BY EQUITY FINANCING	$ (3,619)
NET FUNDS PROVIDED BY FINANCING	**$ 21,701**
INCREASE (DECREASE) IN CASH	**$ (5,837)**

Additional Information

DISPENSABLE FUNDS GENERATED[3]	$ 69,610
Less Burden of Debt (interest)	(6,348)
DISTRIBUTABLE FUNDS GENERATED[4]	$ 63,262
Less Burden of Equity (dividends)	(3,619)
DISCRETIONARY FUNDS GENERATED[5]	$ 59,643

[1] After tax interest cost from 1982 annual report.
[2] May be understated as it presumes all investments in (1) inventory, and (2) property, plant, and equipment are "steady state" except for purchase of new subsidiaries.
[3] This amount is equal to Net Funds From Operations Before Expansion.
[4] This is the amount available for stockholders.
[5] This is the amount available for real growth.

funds flow amounts under APBO No. 19 and SFAS No. 95 with funds flow amounts under the proposals discussed in this paper. The 20 firms were chosen because each was operating in an industry (such as auto, steel, tires, or paper) generally believed to be having financial difficulties. Thus, the analysis should reveal whether these specific firms were having fundamental funds flow problems and, if so, provide some indication of the magnitude of these problems. The results of the analysis are shown in Table 1.

Five years of data were used for the comparative analysis in order to provide a reasonably long time frame. For the period 1980 to 1984, only two of the 20 firms (American Can and International Harvester) showed negative funds from continuing operations in the funds flow statements included in their annual reports. As can be seen from the first column in Table 1, the majority of the firms reported huge positive funds from operations, seeming to indicate very healthy funds flow positions. The results were not much different when the operating funds flow were recast to a SFAS No. 95 cash-type basis (col. 3). For the period 1980 to 1984 only International Harvester showed negative funds flow from continuing operations under this basis.

A dramatically different conclusion emerges when the funds flow statements were recast based upon the proposals in this paper. Using "steady state" approximations for necessary investment in inventories and fixed assets obtained from SFAS No. 33 replacement cost disclosures in the annual reports, dispensable, distributable, and discretionary funds flow for the five-year period 1980 to 1984 were calculated. The approximations involved: (1) the difference between replacement cost of goods sold and historical cost of goods sold as the necessary "steady state" operating investment in inventory, and (2) replacement depreciation as the necessary "steady state" operating investment in property, plant, and equipment.

Seventeen of the 20 firms showed negative dispensable funds flow for the five-year period (col. 4 of Table 1). These 17 firms were not generating sufficient funds from operations to cover "steady state" investments required to maintain the operating capacity of existing businesses. Nineteen of the firms showed negative distributable funds flow for the five-year period (col. 5). These 19 firms were not generating sufficient funds from operations to cover "steady state" investments and pay interest; for 17, it indicates that if steady state investments were covered, then they had to borrow to pay interest. All 20 firms showed substantial negative discretionary funds flows for the five-year period (col. 6). Since each of these firms paid dividends, by implication, they had to borrow to pay dividends! Further, the adjusted funds flow statements of no firm indicated the ability to provide funds from current businesses for growth. These conclusions confirm that individual firms in industries such as autos, tires, steel, and paper faced significant funds flows difficulties in modernizing their plant facilities during this period.

Conclusion

Proper classification, definition, and presentation of funds flow is important if investors and creditors are to gain the maximum analytical insight from funds flow statements. To aid analysts, several proposals to provide insights in addition

Table 1
Comparative Analysis of Funds From Operations
Fiscal Years 1980–1984
(all amounts in millions)

Company	Funds from Operations per Annual Report[1]	Basis[2]	Funds from Operations Adjusted to Cash-Type Basis Before Investments[3]	Dispensable Funds Flow[4]	Distributable Funds Flow[5]	Discretionary Funds Flow[6]
American Can	(34.1)	C&MS	730.4	(405.9)	(543.6)	(890.1)
Bethlehem Steel	1,031.6	C&MS	1,293.7	(5,711.6)	(5,942.5)	(6,193.5)
B. F. Goodrich	786.0	C&MS	753.9	(1,100.2)	(1,327.2)	(1,504.3)
Crown Zellerbach	985.2	C&ST	897.1	(135.3)	(255.9)	(545.8)
Eastern Gas & Fuel	552.4	C&CE	570.4	27.3	(85.3)	(216.8)
Ford Motors	16,445.1	C&MS	16,457.1	(629.8)	(2,067.3)	(2,984.4)
General Motors	31,784.7	C&MS	29,681.6	(4,024.3)	(6,884.3)	(11,655.0)
Georgia-Pacific[7]	2,313.0	C	2,448.0	228.7	(165.0)	(708.0)
Goodyear	3,010.8	C&ST	3,144.1	(1,190.6)	(1,693.4)	(2,120.5)
Interlake	289.6	C	264.7	(488.4)	(517.0)	(590.2)
International Harvester	(514.9)	C&MS	(1,204.9)	(2,469.5)	(3,253.7)	(3,367.7)
International Paper[8]	2,864.1	C&TI	2,867.2	530.8	349.5	(365.2)
Kaiser Aluminum	608.6	WC	371.9	(2,174.7)	(2,461.6)	(2,667.8)
Lukens	108.9	C&ST	114.0	(226.4)	(247.0)	(261.7)
National Can	455.0	WC	415.9	(51.0)	(132.2)	(186.2)
National Steel	411.0	C&ST	483.7	(2,454.0)	(2,614.8)	(2,760.8)
Owens Illinois	1,685.5	NLF	1,752.9	(896.0)	(1,082.5)	(1,319.2)
Reynolds Metals	750.4	C	830.6	(3,750.6)	(3,983.4)	(4,156.7)
U.S. Steel	5,109.0	C&MS	4,750.0	(10,921.2)	(12,725.0)	(13,643.0)
Weyerhauser	3,307.0	C&ST	3,336.7	(194.6)	(522.2)	(1,481.2)

[1] The funds flow from continuing operations shown on the corporation's annual reports for the period 1980–1984 ("one-shot" earnings (losses) eliminated) adjusted to the basis used for reporting in 1984.
[2] The basis in preparing the funds flow statement by the company in 1984. The codings are: C&MS = Cash and Marketable Securities; C&ST = Cash and Short-Term Investments; C&CE = Cash and Cash Equivalents; C = Cash; C&TI = Cash and Temporary Investments; WC = Working Capital; and NLF = Net Liquid Funds.

Table 1—*Continued*

[3] This column shows the "Funds from Operations per Annual Report" adjusted as necessary (1) to provide a cash-type basis (the 1984 annual report basis except for Working Capital and Net Liquid Fund bases which are adjusted to cash), and (2) to provide an amount prior to any operating investments in inventory and property, plant, and equipment. Within the limits of the data in the Statement of Changes in Financial Position, this approximates the amount that would be reported as cash from operating activities in the Statement of Cash Flows prepared under SFAS No. 95.

[4] Amounts in "Funds from operations adjusted to cash-type basis before investments" adjusted (1) for leverage by adding the after tax interest expense for the period 1980–1984, and (2) for required investments in inventories and fixed assets by subtracting the replacement cost approximations for the period 1980–1984.

[5] Amounts in "Dispensable Funds Flow" less the burden of debt (the after tax interest expense) for the period 1980–1984.

[6] Amounts in "Dispensable Funds Flow" less the burden of debt (the after tax interest expense) and burden of equity (dividends) for the period 1980–1984.

[7] Georgia-Pacific had negative dispensable funds in four of the five years. The positive dispensable funds from one year (1980) was so large that the cumulative five-year period showed positive dispensable funds.

[8] International Paper had positive dispensable funds in four of the five years. Like Georgia-Pacific and most other fully integrated paper companies, 1980 was the significant positive year.

to those available from a SFAS No. 95 Statement of Cash Flows have been provided.

The first proposal was to separate operating activities from financing activities. The second proposal was to separate "steady state" operating investments from "growth" operating investments. This separation refined the concept of "steady state" investments and distinguished those amounts that need to be covered by internal funds flow from those that could be externally financed. This approach allows for the provision of information about the firm's ability to: self-finance its operations (summarized in the dispensable funds generated concept), to cover its burden of debt financing (summarized in the distributable funds generated concept), and to cover its burden of equity financing (summarized in the discretionary funds generated concept).

The financial analyst still must estimate both the amount of capital maintenance investments in productive assets and the capital expansion investments that change the operating capacity of existing business or that represent investments in new types of businesses. Operating funds flow presentations that assume that all investments in operating assets are capital maintenance expenditures cannot accurately reflect the state of affairs at all businesses. One disclosure which previously could have been used to approximate this information is no longer required—vis., SFAS No. 89 (FASB 1986b) makes voluntary the replacement cost information required by SFAS No. 33. The FASB rejected specifically requiring firms to provide such information in SFAS No. 95 (FASB 1987b, 97-99) due to subjectivity (lack of reliability) of such amounts. This means that analysts usually must supply their own estimates of steady state investments. Two other sources of information useful in making these estimates were noted earlier.

Three other specific suggestions for refining future estimates were made. Continuing earnings need to be separated from "one shot" earnings. Such a separation would refine the dispensable funds, distributable funds, and discretionary funds generated concept for the appropriate role of financial analysis—estimates of future amounts. The effects of incidental/peripheral activities should be separately disclosed to provide information about the riskiness of future estimates. This is important as incidental and/or peripheral activities may have different risk characteristics than central operating activities. The separate classification into debt and equity financing, the final proposal, also yields information about the financing activities of a firm. Information about financing activities is especially important when a firm has funds flow deficits in dispensable, distributable, and discretionary funds—as it can be used to show the source of funds with which a firm covered the deficit.

These changes yield insights useful in assessing a firm's cash generating ability. Revising the funds flow statements of several firms in troubled industries showed large negative numbers for dispensable, distributable, and discretionary funds. Such an insight is not readily available from traditional funds flow statements.

References

Abdel-khalik, R., W. A. Collins, P. D. Shields, D. A. Snowball, R. G. Stephens, and J. H. Wragge. 1983. *Financial reporting by private companies: Analysis and diagnosis.* Financial Accounting Standards Board.

American Institute of Certified Public Accountants. Accounting Principles Board. 1971. *Reporting changes in financial position.* Opinion no. 19. AICPA.

——. Study Group on the Objectives of Financial Statements. 1973a. *Objectives of financial statements.* AICPA.

——. Accounting Principles Board. 1973b. *Reporting the results of operations—reporting the effects of disposal of a segment of a business, and extraordinary, unusual, and infrequently occurring events and transactions.* AICPA.

Clemente, H. A. 1982. The funds flow statement: Striving for greater accuracy. *Financial Executive.* (December): 27-32.

Dielman, T. E., and H. R. Oppenheimer. 1984. An examination of investor behavior during periods of large dividend changes. *Journal of Financial and Quantitative Analysis.* (June): 197-216.

Dorfman, J. R. 1987. Stock analysts increase focus on cash flow. *The Wall Street Journal.* (17 February): 37.

Elliott, R. K. 1986. Financial accountants must move beyond the mandated accounting model. *World.* (May): 32-35.

Financial Accounting Standards Board. 1979. *Financial reporting and changing prices.* Statement of financial accounting standards no. 33. (September). FASB.

——. 1980. *Reporting funds flow, liquidity, and financial flexibility.* Discussion memorandum. (15 December). FASB.

——. 1981. *Reporting income, cash flows, and financial position of business enterprises.* Exposure draft. (November). FASB.

——. 1986a. *Statement of cash flows.* Exposure draft. (31 July). FASB.

——. 1986b. *Financial reporting and changing prices.* Statement of financial accounting standards no. 89. (December). FASB.

——. 1987a. *Consolidation of all majority owned subsidiaries.* Statement of financial accounting standards no. 94. (October). FASB.

——. 1987b. *Statement of cash flows.* Statement of financial accounting standards no. 95. (November). FASB.

Hawkins, D. F. 1986. *Corporate financial reporting: Text and cases.* 2d ed. Irwin.

Hunt, P. 1975. Funds position: Keystone in financial planning. *Harvard Business Review.* (May-June): 106-115.

——. 1979. A cure for the dysfunction of the funds statement. Manuscript.

Ketz, J. E., and J. A. Largay, III. 1987. Reporting income and cash flows from operations. *Accounting Horizons.* (June): 9-17.

Nurnberg, H. 1972. APB opinion no. 19—pro and con. *Financial Executive.* (December): 58-70.

——. 1983. Issues in funds statement presentation. *The Accounting Review.* (October): 799-812.

Rappaport, A. 1979. Measuring company growth capacity during inflation. *Harvard Business Review.* (January-February): 91-100.

Stephens, R. G. 1980. *Uses of financial information in bank lending decisions.* UMI Research Press.

Watts, R. 1973. The information content of dividends. *Journal of Business.* (April): 191-211.

Evidence on the Choice of Inventory Accounting Methods: LIFO Versus FIFO

NICHOLAS DOPUCH AND MORTON PINCUS*

1. Introduction

1.1 OVERVIEW

In this paper, we describe various systematic properties of *LIFO* and *FIFO* firms' accounting numbers. Included are assessments of these properties for firms' reported annual numbers and for their "as-if" counterparts, obtained by estimating what *LIFO* (*FIFO*) firms would have reported had they used the *FIFO* (*LIFO*) inventory method instead. Our purpose in conducting these assessments is to provide additional evidence on tax and nontax explanations of firms' choices of inventory accounting methods. In the next subsection, we elaborate on these two classes and suggest that the nontax explanations may have attracted adherents partly because existing empirical evidence is not entirely consistent with the tax explanation of *LIFO/FIFO* choices of inventory accounting methods. Although data limitations prevent us from performing direct tests of these alternative explanations, our empirical results

---

* Washington University (St. Louis). We wish to acknowledge the useful comments received on earlier drafts of this paper from the anonymous referees, from accounting workshop participants at Michigan, Minnesota, Oklahoma State, Pennsylvania State, Queensland, Rice, Stanford, Toronto, Washington (Seattle), Wharton, and the 1987 annual meetings of the American Accounting Association, especially Gary Biddle, Bala Dharan, John Dickhaut, George Foster, Don Gribbin, Bob Lipe, Maureen McNichols, Dale Morse, Eric Noreen, Jim Patell, Earl Spiller, Tom Stober, Pete Wilson, and Mark Wolfson, and from Laurentius Marais, Walter Teets, and Greg Waymire. The computing assistance of David Nasser is gratefully acknowledged. [Accepted for publication December 1987.]

lead us to conclude that the tax explanation remains a viable one underlying managers' choices of inventory accounting methods.

1.2 EXPLANATIONS OF INVENTORY ACCOUNTING CHOICES

Perhaps the most popular explanation of firms' inventory accounting method choices is simply that firms choose that method which results in the lowest expected present value of future tax payments. The U.S. tax code does not allow firms to use *LIFO* for tax purposes unless they also use that method for financial reporting purposes. It is generally assumed, then, that firms choose *LIFO* for their accounting reports primarily because they wish to use that method for tax reporting, and analogously, that firms choose *FIFO* for their accounting reports because they intend to use that method for their tax reports as well. Assuming both classes of firms choose methods which minimize the present value of their expected future tax payments, net of any implementation costs, we can assume that *LIFO* is the optimal tax-reporting choice for some firms, whereas *FIFO* is the optimal tax-reporting choice for others.

Disagreement with this last statement has encouraged the development of nontax explanations of inventory choices. The disagreement arises from an apparent belief that the potential tax savings from the adoption of *LIFO* are so large, dominating any implementation costs, that most (if not all) U.S. firms would have switched to *LIFO* by this decade if this motive were the driving force. In fact, however, the majority of U.S. firms have continued to keep the bulk of their inventories on *FIFO* or other non-*LIFO* bases. This would indicate either that the tax savings foregone by *FIFO* firms are not as large as some would believe or that other considerations outweigh these potential benefits.

One of these considerations might be that firms remain on *FIFO* because they fear their security prices will be adversely affected when they report lower earnings under *LIFO*, even though the switch should reduce their future tax payments. Another possible explanation is that *FIFO* firms wish to continue to report higher earnings and asset values because of contracting considerations, but in the process again foregoing the (large) potential tax savings noted above.

The first test of stock market effects on firms that chose *LIFO* was conducted by Sunder [1973], who observed that firms which switched from *FIFO* to *LIFO* experienced positive cumulative abnormal returns in the switch year. This finding has been interpreted as evidence that the market rewarded these firms for switching to *LIFO*. Subsequent studies extended and replicated these results by incorporating adjustments for unexpected earnings (e.g., Abdel-khalik and McKeown [1978], R. Brown [1980], and Ricks [1982]). Their results led them to conclude that, on average, negative abnormal returns accompanied the switch to *LIFO*. These results conflict with Sunder's in that they imply the market reacted negatively to the *LIFO*-induced lower reported earnings. Such evidence might motivate firms to retain *FIFO*, sacrificing whatever tax savings they might otherwise have realized. Subsequently, Biddle and Lindahl [1982] partially resolved these conflicting results in a cross-sectional study which showed a positive association between abnormal returns and tax savings. However, their experimental design has been criticized by Ricks [1986]. Recently, Biddle and Ricks [1987] have noted that Ricks' [1982] results on 1974 switch-firms may be attributed to a systematic bias contained in his measures of expected earnings, so the controversy has still not been totally resolved.[1] The failure to demonstrate a systematic positive market reaction at the time of *LIFO* adoptions is disconcerting to some since it allows for the possibility that managers will be rewarded by sacrificing tax savings (real cash flows) in favor of reporting higher accounting earnings. The contract theory of accounting method choices provides what some believe to be a more appealing alternative explanation.

Under this explanation firms remain on *FIFO* because a switch to *LIFO* would increase contracting costs of one type or another. This is part of a more general view that firms' accounting choices can be predicted on the basis of the relationships between accounting numbers and contracts involving firms' managers and outsiders. Applied to inventory accounting specifically, the prediction would be that firms which face constraints imposed by debt covenants or whose managers would suffer from lower reported accounting earnings because of their compensation contracts will choose *FIFO*; otherwise they are predicted to choose *LIFO* in order to minimize future tax payments. Here again it must be assumed that *FIFO* firms are willing to forego tax savings in order to report higher accounting income, presumably because income-related contracting costs would exceed these tax savings. Unfortunately, direct tests of a contracting theory explanation of inventory accounting method choices are often not feasible because data on the actual costs of contracting or recontracting under one method of accounting versus another are difficult (if not impossible) to obtain.

Recently, less direct tests of contracting hypotheses of firms' inventory accounting choices were conducted by Abdel-khalik [1985], Hunt [1985], and Lee and Hsieh [1985]. These authors conclude that managerial compensation plans do not explain the inventory choices of their samples of firms, but that debt constraints may. Other studies (e.g., Dhaliwal,

---

[1] In discussion comments, Kaplan [1974] speculated about whether market studies of accounting changes could be improved by first analyzing the differential impact of the changes across firms' earnings and, if so, for how many years. Biddle and Lindahl [1982] encountered a similar question trying to estimate the total tax savings which would be realized by firms which switched to *LIFO* inventory accounting. They finally used the tax savings in the year of switch on the assumption that this provided a lower bound on the total benefits of *LIFO*. Our as-if vs. as-reported accounting number comparisons provide an indirect method of testing that assumption. Also, regarding a recent paper by Stevenson [1987], see n. 14.

Salamon, and Smith [1982]) also provide some limited support of contracting hypotheses as they might apply to inventory accounting choices.

Finally, still another explanation of inventory accounting method choices can be derived from the assumption that firms choose accounting methods which "best" fit the characteristics of their operating, financing, and investment decisions, assuming the existence of appropriate criteria for doing so.[2] Among the several ways in which this explanation could manifest itself in accounting method choices is the possibility that firms' managers and owners wish to select accounting methods that lead to more accurate assessments of their firms' future operating cash flows. For example, some years ago it was fashionable to argue that the use of current value (replacement) accounting methods improved users' ability to forecast future operating cash flows by separately disclosing operating profit and holding gains and losses (e.g., see Edwards and Bell [1961, pp. 222–27]). A similar argument can be made for the use of the *LIFO* since it effectively removes holding gains due to inflation from calculations of accounting income.

As we would surmise, tax and nontax explanations of inventory accounting method choices are not completely independent. That is, the selection of inventory accounting methods may require a simultaneous consideration of the interactions between operating results (costs of sales), asset management (levels of inventory), and financing methods (taxes payable). However, we are unaware of any model that successfully incorporates all of these factors as endogenous to the inventory accounting method choice, although Biddle and Martin [1985] provide one which includes the trade-offs between inventory management policies and tax savings.

1.3 SUMMARY OF RESULTS

In order to obtain additional evidence on the extent to which these alternative explanations are consistent with firms' actual choices of inventory accounting methods, we compared the interactions between method choices and firms' characteristics. We first compared the cross-

---

[2] This explanation can be traced back to debates over whether firms should be required to adopt uniform accounting methods or be allowed flexibility in the selection of methods (see, e.g., Keller and Zeff [1969] and the references therein). Chapter 4, "Inventory Pricing," of the 1953 restatement and revision of the AICPA Committee on Accounting Procedure's [1961] *Accounting Research Bulletin No. 43*, contains the following discussion of Statement 4, in which generally accepted inventory cost flow assumptions are codified: "Although selection of the method should be made on the basis of individual circumstances, it is obvious that financial statements will be more useful if uniform methods of inventory pricing are adopted by all companies within a given industry."

Interest in the uniformity vs. flexibility (or diversity) debate was heightened in the late 1950s and 1960s because of the newly formed Accounting Principles Board whose major objective was to reduce the accounting alternatives available to firms (see, e.g., Hendriksen [1982, pp. 36–39] and Merino and Coe [1978]).

sectional differences in operating, financing, and investment characteristics of firms which have remained on *FIFO* or on *LIFO* for at least 20 years, as these are reflected in various accounting numbers and ratios using data reported by the two classes of firms. Our initial results support the notion that several operating and investment characteristics of *FIFO* and *LIFO* firms vary systematically. But after we repeated the calculations using our estimate of firms' as-if numbers, we observed that the significant differences in the ratios which use either reported inventory or reported costs-of-sales numbers in their calculations were mainly induced by the use of different accounting methods by the two classes of firms. Effectively, only various size measures, including estimates of yearly holding gains for the two sets of firms, were significantly different over the 20-year span of our analyses. We extended these results by examining the same kinds of characteristics for a sample of firms which switched to *LIFO* mainly during the mid 1970s, vis-à-vis the long-term users of *FIFO* and *LIFO*. In doing so we found that the size measures and even some of the inventory variables for this class of firms were more like those of the *LIFO* group in the years preceding and subsequent to the year of switch, using both reported and as-if numbers in the calculations.

These results at least partially support both tax and nontax explanation of inventory accounting method choices. Unfortunately, we were not able to obtain additional data, such as the direct costs and benefits underlying nontax explanations and the actual tax rates experienced by our firms, that would allow us to distinguish further between these alternative explanations.

Nevertheless, we wish to highlight some of the results which seem especially supportive of a tax explanation of inventory accounting method choices. First, only a few marginally significant differences were observed for our operating and investment variables, and none for our contracting variable, the debt/equity ratio. Second, the long-term *FIFO* firms in our sample have not been foregoing significant tax savings, in which case remaining on that method is certainly consistent with *FIFO* being an optimal tax choice for that set of firms, given other considerations. In contrast, long-term *LIFO* firms would have foregone significant tax savings (i.e., tax deferrals) during the same time period had they been computing their taxes on the basis of the *FIFO* method (instead of on *LIFO*). Finally, using the long-term *FIFO* sample's average holding gains as a base, our change-firms' average holding gains became significantly larger than the *FIFO* average as they approached the year in which they switched, and this difference continued to grow subsequently. Still, the difference in holding gains between the change-firms and the long-term *FIFO* users was much smaller than that observed for the long-term *LIFO* users, which suggests that the change-firms would not have obtained anything like the large amounts of tax savings achieved by our *LIFO* firms, except perhaps during the year of the switch.

This pattern of significantly increasing holding gains for the change-firms, vis-à-vis the long-term *FIFO* users, also has implications for market studies of the switch to *LIFO*. That is, external market agents making similar conversion estimates would have been able to increase their priors that these firms were more likely to switch to *LIFO* in advance of the period during which they made their switch. This would suggest that market studies which use an event date near the end of the year in which firms first provide an announcement of their switch could miss a large part of the potential market responses to such an event.

In the next section, we provide details on our assessments of the cross-sectional properties of long-term *FIFO* and long-term *LIFO* users' accounting numbers. Section 3 provides results from our cross-sectional tests applied to our third subsample, those firms that switched from *FIFO* to *LIFO* during the past two decades. Conclusions appear in section 4.

2. Cross-Sectional Analyses of Long-Term FIFO and Long-Term LIFO Users

2.1 SAMPLES OF FIRMS

Our first sample consists of 102 firms which used *FIFO* as their primary (as defined by *Compustat*) inventory method for the years 1962–81 and our second one consists of 29 firms which used *LIFO* for the same time period. We refer to these as our long-term *FIFO* and long-term *LIFO* firms. All of these firms were taken from *Compustat* (Annual Industrials or OTC), provided they were U.S. firms (see V. Brown [1980]), had a complete series for annual income before extraordinary and discontinued items, a complete history of their inventory methods for these same years, did not change fiscal year-end, and for which industry-specific Bureau of Labor Statistics producer price index data were available. Our decision to include only firms which had not changed their primary inventory method for at least 20 years increased the probability of detecting significant differences between the two sets of firms, but at the cost of sharply reducing our sample sizes, especially of the *LIFO* firms. In addition, this requirement may prevent our results from generalizing to firms which use *LIFO* for a substantial portion of their inventories but still retain *FIFO* as their primary inventory method. However, the comparisons we make among long-term users of *FIFO* and *LIFO* and our change-firms may be viewed as constituting an analysis of short-term *LIFO* users.

Based on two-digit SIC codes, the industry composition of these samples is as follows. For the long-term *LIFO* firms, 17 industries are represented, with concentrations only in the primary metals group (8 firms). Thirty-one industries are included in the long-term *FIFO* sample, with the following concentrations: food and kindred products (9 firms);

chemicals (13 firms); fabrication metals (6 firms); nonelectrical machinery (10 firms); electrical machinery and appliances (16 firms); measuring instruments and the like (7 firms); and wholesale trade-durable goods (7 firms).

Our third sample consists of 70 firms which switched from *FIFO* to *LIFO* during the period 1965–78, with 49 (70%) switching in 1974 and another 13 (19%) switching in the 1976–78 period. These firms are analyzed in section 3 and were chosen using the same criteria indicated above, plus the requirement of only one inventory method switch.[3] Multiple switches would have made cross-sectional analyses impractical. Some 20 two-digit SIC code industries were represented in this subsample, with concentrations in the following six industries: chemicals (7 firms); rubber and miscellaneous plastics (6 firms); fabrication metals (8 firms); nonelectrical machinery (7 firms); electrical machinery and appliances (8 firms); and transportation equipment and parts (8 firms).

The industry concentrations of our subsamples are consistent with other studies (e.g., Morse and Richardson [1983]) which suggest an association between industry and inventory method choices. The implication of this industry influence for our statistical tests is noted below.

2.2 COMPUTING AS-IF INVENTORY VARIABLES

Our analyses require computations either of inventory or costs-of-sales numbers which would have been reported had *FIFO* (*LIFO*) firms used *LIFO* (*FIFO*) inventory accounting instead of their actual method. The algorithm used to obtain these as-if numbers is taken from Biddle [1980], with some minor modifications.[4] Appendix A provides a more detailed description of our conversion procedures. Based on these procedures we estimate holding-gain differences (sometimes called costs-of-sales differences) which are then used to convert variables which incorporate reported costs of sales. These same procedures are also used to estimate firms' ending inventories as-if they had used the alternative inventory method. The resulting holding-gain differences were further adjusted to include estimates of the tax savings (or tax savings foregone) for firms using *LIFO* instead of *FIFO* (or using *FIFO* instead of *LIFO*).

These estimated holding-gain calculations, along with the tax effects, are based on several simplifying assumptions, some of which are highlighted here. First, we focused exclusively on inventory tax effects, with all other tax items assumed constant (see Scholes and Wolfson [1987] regarding interactions among different tax items). For example, it is conceivable that a *FIFO* firm has a larger supply of other tax shields than a *LIFO* firm, thereby reducing the need to use *LIFO* for tax savings. The effect of assuming constant other tax shields is potentially to

---

[3] Seven firms meeting all selection criteria noted above switched from *LIFO* to *FIFO*. However, this sample was too small for meaningful analysis.

[4] We wish to thank Gary Biddle for the computer programs he provided.

overstate the maximum tax savings a *FIFO* firm could obtain by shifting to *LIFO*. Second, we ignored two partially offsetting factors in our conversion procedures. Technically, the tax effects accruing from the use of *LIFO* should be reduced by the present value of any future tax liability resulting from a *LIFO* reserve liquidation, and increased by the value of the tax timing option that *LIFO* firms possess regarding the timing of inventory liquidations. Third, we assumed that all of our sample firms paid marginal tax rates equal to the U.S. statutory rates in effect during the years under study. The reason is a practical one since it is quite difficult to estimate the actual marginal tax rates faced by firms based on information contained in published annual reports. Later, we comment on the sensitivity of our results to alternative marginal rate assumptions and on our attempt to examine financial and investment characteristics of firms which have the potential to affect (and reflect) their marginal tax rates. Finally, we assumed that if a firm were on *FIFO*, it could convert all of its inventories to *LIFO*. However, *LIFO* is rarely used for the entire inventory holdings of firms; in fact, the typical percentage in our sample was less than 75%. As an ad hoc adjustment, we converted only 75% of each *LIFO* firm's inventories to an as-if *FIFO* basis, even though we allowed a *FIFO* firm to convert 100% to *LIFO*. If anything, our resulting calculations will overstate amounts of holding gains a *FIFO* firm could have obtained had it switched.[5]

As a diagnostic test of our algorithm, we compared our estimated costs-of-sales differences to those reported by a sample of 41 firms that switched from *FIFO* to *LIFO* in 1974.[6] Disclosures of these differences have been required for all SEC firms switching from *FIFO* to *LIFO* since the early 1970s. On a firm/year basis, the median of the Spearman rank-correlations between computed and disclosed costs-of-sales differences over at least six years was .53.[7]

2.3 DESCRIPTIVE STATISTICS

Descriptive statistics on various measures of firm size for the long-term *FIFO* and long-term *LIFO* firms appear in table 1. The most consistent observation from that table is the relatively larger size of *LIFO* firms using all measures of size,[8] even though the average *FIFO* firm has grown more rapidly. Like most accounting series, however, the

---

[5] Clearly, the use of the 75% adjustment yields a lower estimated holding gain (and hence tax saving) for *LIFO* firms than if it were not used.

[6] This is a subset of our sample of change-firms for which we could obtain microfiche copies of annual reports for at least six years from *Disclosure, Inc.*

[7] A *t*-test of differences in the mean costs-of-sales differences could not reject the null of no difference at the 10% level in 85% of the cases. However, these *t*-tests are probably not very powerful since they are based on sample sizes of six to eight observations.

[8] This was also true for the costs-of-sales and inventory balances. The link between firm size and inventory accounting choice is examined more closely in the following subsection. Not surprisingly, the firm size variables were highly correlated with each other and with the estimated holding gains.

TABLE 1
Firm-Size-Related Descriptive Statistics of Long-Term FIFO and Long-Term LIFO Firms Selected Years 1963–81
(millions of $)

FIFO Firms (n = 102)		1963	1972	1981
Total Assets	(mean)	59.0	221.2	608.8
	(median)	19.4	67.4	151.5
	(range)	0.8—769.1	2.6—1,993.1	5.5—6,062.9
Total Sales	(mean)	86.5	280.2	774.9
	(median)	27.2	94.1	250.6
	(range)	0.8—790.2	1.3—2,217.5	8.8—6,508.0
Total Market Value of Equity	(mean)	124.5	452.4	429.4
	(median)	20.0	413.7	75.6
	(range)	0.5—3,387.7	1.2—9,665.9	0.5—6,390.2
Net Income	(mean)	4.4	15.3	38.6
	(median)	1.1	3.4	8.9
	(range)	−5.6—90.6	−13.4—244.4	−9.4—673.0
LIFO Firms (n = 29)		1963	1972	1981
Total Assets	(mean)	811.8	1,640.1	4,416.7
	(median)	370.0	866.1	2,193.3
	(range)	6.3—5,139.3	16.7—7,401.8	38.6—20,942.0
Total Sales	(mean)	798.5	1,618.2	5,543.9
	(median)	467.7	814.4	2,186.0
	(range)	16.7—4,918.7	40.8—10,239.5	73.2—27,797.4
Total Market Value of Equity	(mean)	964.3	1,389.9	2,025.9
	(median)	438.7	493.3	433.2
	(range)	2.5—7,848.9	6.4—13,256.7	4.4—13,050.7
Net Income	(mean)	48.9	79.8	320.3
	(median)	27.7	43.1	80.4
	(range)	0.3—270.6	0.9—530.0	−11.0—1,671.3

distributions of size measures are positively skewed. Because of this, we often use medians in our tests, although adjusting for skewness would not change our conclusion that the typical *LIFO* firm is larger than the typical *FIFO* firm (for each of the 20 years under study).

Table 2 provides summary statistics of our (ex post) estimates of the tax savings for these samples of firms. Similar statistics for (pretax) holding-gain estimates appear in Appendix A (table 12). The data indicate significantly larger holding gains for *LIFO* firms, with median amounts for *LIFO* and *FIFO* firms of $1.88 million and $329,000 per firm/year, respectively. Hence, the median estimated tax savings foregone by the *FIFO* firms not switching to *LIFO* were small, both in absolute amounts ($161,000 per firm/year) and relative to the taxes saved

TABLE 2

Panal A: Descriptive Statistics of Estimated Tax Savings (i.e., Deferrals) by *LIFO* Firms Not Having Used *FIFO* (1963–81)
(millions of $)

29 *LIFO* Firms		Selected Percentiles	
Mean	14.563	0th	−107.311
Median	0.942	1st	−15.274
Standard Deviation	46.531	5th	−1.652
IQR*	8.282	95th	96.868
Number of Annual Firm/Year Observations	551	99th	215.668
		100th	566.574

Panel B: Descriptive Statistics of Estimated Tax Savings Foregone by *FIFO* Firms Not Having Used *LIFO* (1963–81)
(millions of $)

102 *FIFO* Firms		Selected Percentiles	
Mean	1.493	0th	−10.135
Median	0.161	1st	−1.083
Standard Deviation	4.690	5th	−0.064
IQR*	0.856	95th	8.345
Number of Annual Firm/Year Observations	1,938	99th	22.578
		100th	79.263

* *IQR* = interquartile range.

(i.e., deferred) by the *LIFO* firms ($942,000 per firm/year). On the face of it, the data are consistent with the assumption that both sets of firms followed tax minimization strategies over the entire time-span, assuming *FIFO* firms would have incurred nontrivial implementation costs in using *LIFO*.

As indicated above, these median figures assume the same marginal tax rate for all firms. Although we have no data on the range of possible marginal rates faced by firms, our long-term *LIFO* firms would have had to face a marginal tax rate of less than 10% in order for the median tax savings of the *LIFO* and *FIFO* groups to be equal over the entire time period. This would be less than one-fourth the rate assumed for the *FIFO* firms. It seems unlikely that our *FIFO* firms would have been facing a marginal tax rate that much higher than our *LIFO* firms during the period of our analyses.

2.4 UNIVARIATE CROSS-SECTIONAL TESTS

We selected accounting ratios (and other numbers) to reflect differences in the operating, financing, and investment characteristics of *FIFO* and *LIFO* firms based on the results of previous studies—in particular, Biddle [1980], Lee and Hsieh [1985], Morse and Richardson [1983]—and on our intuition. Linking some of the selections to those used in previous studies allows us to replicate their results using our samples of firms. Of course, like others we would have preferred to select our variables based on some formal theory linking choices of inventory accounting methods to firms' characteristics; however, we are unaware of the existence of such theories.

To begin, Biddle [1980] and Morse and Richardson [1983] found that firms switched to *LIFO* after their estimated tax savings reached a rather high plateau. This would be consistent with the existence of a fixed level of costs of switching. Such costs would be more easily absorbed by large firms, which would also have a higher probability of reaching a critical plateau in any given year (or in a couple of adjacent years). Large firms are also more likely to acquire specialized managerial skills and diversified product lines which could be reflected in lower overall inventory variability. A lower inventory variability should reduce the probability of dipping into *LIFO* layers. Similarly, large firms are generally more capital intensive, and the attendant fixed costs of capital are more easily absorbed if operations, and inventories, are kept at a relatively stable level.

Based on the above, size, capital intensity, and variability of inventory should be associated with the selection of inventory accounting methods. We chose sales and levels of holding gains as measures of size, and, like Lee and Hsieh [1985], fixed assets/total assets as a measure of capital intensity and the coefficient of variation of inventory as the main measure of variability. We also included their coefficient of variation of income as a related measure of variability, first, because less income variability should lead to more stable inventory levels (demands) and, second, because it increases a firm's ability to take advantage of *LIFO*'s tax benefits year after year.

Lee and Hsieh hypothesized that *LIFO* firms would have lower inventory/sales and inventory/total assets ratios due to more efficient inventory management. They termed the former a type of inventory turnover ratio (more accurately a reciprocal of one). However, since *LIFO* firms are typically larger than *FIFO* firms, they might show lower inventory/sales ratios simply because inventory levels may not increase linearly with sales. Moreover, ratios which use inventory (or its complement costs of sales) might vary between *LIFO* and *FIFO* firms simply because the former firms will carry older (lower) nominal prices in inventory but more current (higher) ones in costs of sales. The overall net effect of the above factors on ratios using costs-of-sales and/or inventory numbers for our classes of firms (as opposed to an individual firm) is not easy to model. However, the effect of using nominal prices on inventory ratios will be assessed later when we use our as-if numbers in place of reported numbers for such ratios. As benchmarks for comparisons, we selected the two Lee and Hsieh inventory ratios, as well as the conventional turnover ratio, costs of sales/average inventory, and its reciprocal.

We limited our selection of a contracting variable to the debt/equity ratio, since this ratio seems to achieve significance in other accounting method studies (e.g., Hunt [1985] and Lee and Hsieh [1985]). The typical assumption is that *LIFO* firms would have lower average debt/equity ratios, because their lower reported *LIFO* earnings and *LIFO* assets could lead to a higher probability of violations of debt covenants.[9] However, taxes may enter as a confounding variable, given that interest payments on debt are deductible for tax purposes. For example, if firms choose *LIFO* because they face higher marginal tax rates, then they might issue more debt than *FIFO* firms to obtain additional tax deductions. Alternatively, *FIFO* firms might issue more debt because they choose to use the interest deductibility feature of the tax laws in lieu of adopting *LIFO* for tax purposes. Since either possibility seems equally likely, we do not adopt an unambiguous prediction regarding the association between inventory method choices and debt/equity ratios.

As stated earlier, in their studies of choices of inventory accounting methods Abdel-khalik [1985] and Hunt [1985] tested whether these choices could be linked to compensation variables, which is another hypothesis derived from contract theory. Abdel-khalik used a continuous variable for compensation, whereas Hunt merely used a dummy variable to indicate the existence or nonexistence of a bonus plan based on accounting earnings. A continuous variable is more appealing, but it is also more costly to implement. Since neither study found evidence of such a link between compensation and inventory accounting method choices, we decided not to make the additional investment to obtain the data needed to test the compensation hypothesis directly.

Finally, since it is generally assumed that *LIFO* results in the maximum tax benefits for those firms which experience a steady pattern of increasing prices of their inventory items and higher marginal tax rates, we included measures of the average price changes for *FIFO* and *LIFO* firms, the coefficient of variation of these price changes, and an estimate of the effective tax rates faced by each set of firms (a proxy for their marginal rates).

As a form of caveat, several of the inventory variables selected for this study may reflect responses to what might be termed exogenous factors, rather than more (or less) efficient inventory tax-management policies. For example, firms that hold inventory items which are less susceptible to obsolescence (fungible items) may be able to hold higher levels of inventories even in the face of expected declines in sales since their storage costs incurred would be less than the extra taxes they would have to pay if they reduced their year-end inventory levels below their beginning levels. In contrast, firms that carry items which can become obsolete if held too long in inventories might have to sell (dump) the items in

---

[9] As a consequence of the existence of accounting-number-based restrictions in debt covenants, contracting theory argues for a positive relation between debt covenant restrictions and income-increasing accounting techniques (Holthausen and Leftwich [1983]). Since *FIFO* generally results in higher assets and income, contracting theory predicts higher debt/equity ratios for *FIFO* firms. Problems in computing debt/equity ratios are discussed below in the text and in n. 12. Like others, we did not examine debt contracts to determine the specific provisions involving accounting-number-based stipulations. Hence our tests of contracting hypotheses are limited for this reason as well.

response to predictions of declining sales and, if on *LIFO*, run the risk of liquidating inventories with low historical costs. High-obsolescence items could also benefit from the lower-of-cost-or-market accounting rule, which is not applicable under *LIFO* tax accounting. These factors suggest that firms which choose *FIFO* are firms which face higher storage costs relative to stock-out costs. Note also that by liquidating much of its inventory items each period a *FIFO* firm could significantly reduce the taxes paid on holding gains. In effect, the types of inventory items held by *FIFO* and *LIFO* firms may actually permit (encourage) them to follow different inventory policies (see Biddle [1980]). While there is evidence that certain industries are more likely to have *LIFO* firms than *FIFO* ones, perhaps because of this phenomenon, our *LIFO* sample is too small to perform formal tests of within-industry differences in inventory characteristics between the two classes of firms.

2.5 RESULTS

The results for univariate directional tests of our hypothesized inventory-method choice variables are presented in table 3. Included in the table is a column indicating agreement or disagreement with the results obtained by Lee and Hsieh [1985]. The test results are based on two-sample, Mann-Whitney tests of differences in location, with significance assessed at conventional levels.[10]

In addition to having significantly larger holding-gain differences and higher sales levels relative to firms using *FIFO*, *LIFO* firms on average are more capital intensive, have a lower variability of inventories, lower inventory/total assets, a lower average inventory/costs-of-sales ratio, and a higher conventional turnover ratio. Generally, these results are consistent with those obtained by Lee and Hsieh (for those variables common to both studies). One exception is their inventory/sales ratio. They find a significantly lower ratio for *LIFO* firms; in contrast, our results merely indicate a marginally significant difference. Also, consistent with Lee

---

[10] The Mann-Whitney test used throughout the paper assumes independent *LIFO* and *FIFO* samples. This assumption may be violated because of autocorrelation in some of the accounting series and the presence of some industry concentrations within the samples. Hence the 551 and 1,938 figures in table 2 overstate the degrees of freedom associated with the 29 *LIFO* and 102 *FIFO* firms. However, following Pratt [1964], the Mann-Whitney test employed includes an adjustment for differing sample sizes (see note d to table 3) which involves computing $\lambda = n_L/(n_L + n_F)$ where n_L and n_F are the *LIFO* and *FIFO* sample sizes, respectively. Hence, $\lambda = 551/(551 + 1,938) = .22$. If we assume, for example, the absence of independent observations over time for each firm, that is, if we assume there were only 29 *LIFO* and 102 *FIFO* observations, we would still have the same ratio: $\lambda = 29/(29 + 102) = .22$. Further, even in this case the sample sizes would be large enough to assess significance using a normal approximation (see Siegel [1956, pp. 120–21]). It therefore is unlikely that the statistically significant Mann-Whitney results which we report would lose significance at conventional levels even if the actual degrees of freedom of the tests fell substantially below that implied by the 551 and 1,938 observations.

TABLE 3
Univariate Analysis of Inventory Method Choice Variables: 1963–81

Variable[a]	(1) Median for LIFO Firms	(2) Median for FIFO Firms	(3) Hypothesis[c]	(4) Test Statistics[d]	(5) Agree with Lee & Hsieh?[e]
V_1 Net Sales	$1,044[b]	$109[b]	$L > F$	4.92***	Yes
V_3 C.V. of Inventory	0.42	0.63	$L < F$	−4.26***	Yes
V_4 C.V. of Before-Tax Income[f]	0.74	0.79	$L < F$	−0.52	Yes
V_5 Long-Term Debt/S.E.	0.33	0.32	$L < F$	−0.32	Yes
V_6 Inventory/Net Sales	0.16	0.20	$L < F$	−1.54	(Yes)
W_1 Avg. Inventory/C.G.S.[g]	0.21	0.27	$L < F$	−2.50**	—
W_2 C.G.S./Avg. Inventory[g]	4.97	3.88	$L > F$	2.55**	—
V_7 Inventory/Total Assets	0.21	0.29	$L < F$	−2.00*	Yes
V_{10} Gross F.A./Net Sales	0.66	0.30	$L > F$	4.65***	Yes
V_{11} Relative Frequency of Price Increases[h]	0.92	0.94	$L > F$	−1.32	No
V_{14} C.V. of Price Changes[h]	1.18	1.02	$L < F$	1.98*	(Yes)
W_3 Mean Price Change[h]	0.11	0.09	$L > F$	1.96*	—
V_{15} Effective Tax Rate	0.41	0.44	$L \neq F$	−0.70	Yes
W_4 Holding-Gain Differences	$1.88[b]	$0.33[b]	$L > F$	9.01***	—

Abbreviations:
- C.V. = coefficient of variation = standard deviation/mean
- S.E. = stockholders' equity
- C.G.S. = costs-of-goods sold
- F.A. = fixed assets.

One-tailed significance levels:
  * = .05 level; ** = .005 level; *** = .0005 level.

[a] Lee and Hsieh [1985] include several variables with very high pair-matched correlations. Since our results are not sensitive to the choice of correlated variables, we report parsimoniously. Variables denoted V_i (W_i) were (were not) used by Lee and Hsieh.

[b] Dollar amounts in columns (1) and (2) are in millions.

[c] See the text for an explanation of the directional hypotheses listed in column (3). Also see Lee and Hsieh's table 3 and their accompanying text. To be consistent with Lee and Hsieh a directional hypothesis is shown for V_5 even though a directionless alternative is argued for in section 2.4.

[d] A Mann-Whitney U-statistic adjusted for differences in sample sizes and variances (Pratt [1964]) is computed, and a normal approximation is used. (Also see n. 10.) Lee and Hsieh use a difference-in-means t-test. With one exception our results are robust across both tests, although the t-test for the following variables is only approximate because of significantly different variances: Net Sales, C.V. of Before-Tax Income, Long-Term Debt/S.E., Gross F.A./Net Sales, C.V. and Mean Price Change, and Holding-Gain Differences. The exception, Long-Term Debt/S.E., had a significant t-statistic in the hypothesized direction.

[e] (Yes) indicates results are consistent with Lee and Hsieh's results but were or were not statistically significant, depending on the specific case.

[f] One LIFO and 16 FIFO firms with negative denominators were not included. Their inclusion yields a MW statistic significant at the .08 level in the predicted direction, and an approximate t-statistic significant at the .005 level.

[g] For Mann-Whitney purposes, variables W_1 and W_2 are essentially equivalent. However, we report W_1 to facilitate direct comparison with V_6 and V_7, and we report W_2 since it is the conventional measure of inventory turnover.

[h] For variables V_{11}, V_{14}, and W_3, industry-specific annual price changes were determined using (i) an average of monthly producer price index changes for a year, and (ii) year-end to year-end price changes. The results were not sensitive to the method of calculation; results based on (i) are reported here. Also, a specific industry is included in a sample only once. Hence, sample sizes are as follows: 31 for FIFO and 17 for LIFO.

and Hsieh, we do not find a statistically significant difference in the debt/equity ratio or in the average effective tax-rate variable. Although there is some disagreement regarding how to treat deferred tax balances and changes in these balances in computing the debt/equity and effective tax-rate variables (for a discussion of the latter, see Zimmerman [1983]), our results remain fairly robust using alternative measures of these variables (not reported).

A major difference between our results and those obtained by Lee and Hsieh is the lack of a statistically significant finding at conventional levels for the price-change variable (V_{11}). This variable summarizes the relative frequency of price increases in the industries in which the two sets of firms operate. An alternative is to measure the difference in the average price changes for the two sets of firms, which is captured in our variable W_3. There we obtain a statistically significant difference (at the .05 level) in the hypothesized direction. However, like Lee and Hsieh, we obtain significantly greater variability of inventory prices for the *LIFO* firms, which is contrary to expectations. We might note here that both price-change variables could have significant measurement error since each uses producer output (i.e., product) price indexes rather than inventory input costs, and the selection of the appropriate index for each firm is limited to that index which best matches each firm's primary SIC code. In other words, a single product index is used for each firm's inventories.

One of the problems in comparing our results with those obtained by Lee and Hsieh is that they were able to obtain a larger sample of *LIFO* firms because they required each firm in their sample to use its primary inventory method for only 7 consecutive years. Our firms remained on the same method for at least 20 years. As a result, our firms adopted *LIFO* much earlier, when inflation rates were relatively lower. This might also account for the fact that on average our firms are larger.

An implicit assumption in cross-sectional assessments of accounting variables is that the distributions of these variables are stationary over time. To test this assumption, we repeated the significance tests using data from three distinct subperiods: 1963–69; 1970–75; and 1976–81. Most of the results were consistent across these different time periods, so we do not report them here. Nevertheless, there were some inconsistencies. For example, statistical significance was not obtained in the 1963–69 subperiod for the turnover variables, V_6, W_1, W_2, and V_7, and the two price-change variables, V_{14} and W_3. Moreover, the latter two were also not significantly different during the last subperiod. Finally, the income variability variable, V_4, exhibited very irregular behavior. *LIFO* firms had significantly lower income variability (as hypothesized) in the first subperiod, significantly higher income variability in the middle period, but were not different from *FIFO* firms in the last period. The net effect was an insignificant difference overall. As stated in the notes to table 3, negative denominators hampered the calculation of this variable; in fact, 13% of the observations had to be dropped for this reason.

2.6 AS-IF RESULTS

Significant differences in the ratios of *LIFO* firms versus *FIFO* firms could be due either to substantive differences in the economic characteristics of the two classes of firms or to the use of two different inventory accounting methods. To gain some insight into this potentially confounding issue, we recomputed those variables directly affected by the choice of inventory accounting methods using our as-if data.[11] The ratios affected were those which used inventory balances or costs of goods sold in the numerator or denominator.[12] The results are summarized in four ways. First, all ratios are recomputed as-if the *LIFO* firms were on the *FIFO* method (table 4), and these were assessed relative to the reported ratios of the *FIFO* firms. Next, all ratios of the *FIFO* firms were recomputed as-if they were on the *LIFO* basis, and these were then assessed relative to the *LIFO* firms' reported ratios (table 5). The third and fourth comparisons, termed within-firms comparisons, consist of assessments of the *FIFO* firms' reported ratios against their recomputed (as-if *LIFO*) ratios (table 6) and assessments of the *LIFO* firms' reported ratios against their recomputed (as-if *FIFO*) ratios (table 7).

Recall that in table 3, we observed statistically significant differences at conventional levels for three of the four inventory ratios, and almost so for the fourth. However, none of these differences is statistically significant in tables 4 and 5. Hence, the differences observed previously between firms' inventory ratios are entirely artifacts of the use of alternative inventory accounting methods. Moreover, the highly significant difference (.0005 level) in inventory variability (*C.V.* of Inventory) using reported data is considerably less so when all firms are stated on a *LIFO* basis (.05 level), and is not significant at conventional levels when all firms are placed on the *FIFO* basis. These accounting-method effects are supported in the within-firms comparisons shown in tables 6 and 7. The statistically significant differences in ratios which use either inventory balances or costs of sales shown in those tables are completely induced by the different accounting methods since the comparisons are for the same firms under two different methods.

Our findings indicate, then, that in our cross-sectional tests of the relation between certain explanatory variables and inventory accounting choices the significant results obtained were due more to the confounding

---

[11] Derstine and Huefner [1974] followed a similar approach in computing several risk-oriented accounting ratios for a sample of change-firms. See also Chasteen [1971] for a similar approach.

[12] We did not attempt to trace completely through the effects of different inventory methods on the computation of the debt/equity and effective tax-rate variables. Although the cumulative after-tax costs-of-sales difference could be added to stockholders' equity, it is not clear how additional amounts (from *LIFO* to *FIFO*) or lower amounts of taxes (from *FIFO* to *LIFO*) would affect the total liabilities of firms, should they move to an alternative inventory method. A complete treatment would require modeling cash, debt, dividends, etc. Similarly for the effective tax-rate variable, the denominator, before-tax earnings, can be adjusted for the *LIFO/FIFO* costs-of-sales difference. However, should the numerator, tax expense, be adjusted for the additional tax (or tax savings) amounts?

TABLE 4
Univariate Analysis of Inventory Choice Variables—FIFO Based: 1963-81

Variable	(1) Median for LIFO Firms As-If FIFO[a]	(2) Median for FIFO Firms[b]	(3) Hypothesis	(4) Test Statistic	(5) Agree with Table 3?
V_3 C.V. of Inventory	0.67	0.63	$L < F$	0.94	No
V_4 C.V. of Before-Tax Income	0.77	0.79	$L < F$	0.10	Yes
V_6 Inventory/Net Sales	0.22	0.20	$L < F$	1.11	No
W_1 Avg. Inventory/C.G.S.	0.26	0.27	$L < F$	−0.49	No
W_2 C.G.S./Avg. Inventory	4.03	3.88	$L > F$	0.44	No
V_7 Inventory/Total Assets	0.24	0.29	$L < F$	−0.43	No

[a] The amounts in column (1) are median values of the specified variables (ratios) for long-term LIFO firms computed under the assumption that the FIFO method had been used instead.
[b] Same as in table 3 except for W_1 and W_2 which are computed over 1964-81 (no as-if data for 1962).

TABLE 5
Univariate Analysis of Inventory Choice Variables—LIFO Based: 1963-81

Variable	(1) Median for LIFO Firms[a]	(2) Median for FIFO Firms As-If LIFO[b]	(3) Hypothesis	(4) Test Statistic	(5) Agree with Table 3?
V_3 C.V. of Inventory	0.42	0.52	$L < F$	−2.29*	Yes
V_4 C.V. of Before-Tax Income	0.74	0.81	$L < F$	−0.77	Yes
V_6 Inventory/Net Sales	0.16	0.17	$L < F$	0.30	No
W_1 Avg. Inventory/C.G.S.	0.21	0.23	$L < F$	−0.95	No
W_2 C.G.S./Avg. Inventory	4.97	4.72	$L > F$	0.67	No
V_7 Inventory/Total Assets	0.21	0.25	$L < F$	−0.87	No

[a] Same as in table 3 except for W_1 and W_2 which are computed over 1964-81 (no as-if data for 1962).
[b] The amounts in column (2) are median values of the specified variables (ratios) for long-term FIFO firms computed under the assumption that the LIFO method had been used instead.
* Significant at the .05 level (one-tailed).

TABLE 6
Univariate Analysis of Inventory Choice Variables—FIFO Firms: 1963-81

Variable	(1) Median for FIFO Firms As-If LIFO[a]	(2) Median for FIFO Firms[b]	(3) Hypothesis	(4) Test Statistic
V_3 C.V. of Inventory	0.52	0.63	$L \neq F$	−3.47***
V_4 C.V. of Before-Tax Income	0.81	0.79	$L \neq F$	0.25
V_6 Inventory/Net Sales	0.17	0.20	$L \neq F$	−3.05**
W_1 Avg. Inventory/C.G.S.	0.23	0.27	$L \neq F$	−2.51*
W_2 C.G.S./Avg. Inventory	4.72	3.88	$L \neq F$	3.04**
V_7 Inventory/Total Assets	0.25	0.29	$L \neq F$	−2.38*

[a] Same as table 5.
[b] Same as table 3.
* Significant at the .05 level (two-tailed).
** Significant at the .005 level (two-tailed).
*** Significant at the .0005 level (two-tailed).

TABLE 7
Univariate Analysis of Inventory Choice Variables—LIFO Firms: 1963-81

Variable	(1) Median for LIFO Firms[a]	(2) Median for LIFO Firms As-If FIFO[b]	(3) Hypothesis	(4) Test Statistic
V_3 C.V. of Inventory	0.42	0.67	$L \neq F$	−4.34***
V_4 C.V. of Before-Tax Income	0.74	0.77	$L \neq F$	−0.76
V_6 Inventory/Net Sales	0.16	0.22	$L \neq F$	−2.08*
W_1 Avg. Inventory/C.G.S.	0.21	0.26	$L \neq F$	−1.85
W_2 C.G.S./Avg. Inventory	4.97	4.03	$L \neq F$	1.88
V_7 Inventory/Total Assets	0.21	0.24	$L \neq F$	−1.57

[a] Same as table 3.
[b] Same as table 4.
* Significant at the .05 level (two-tailed).
*** Significant at the .0005 level (two-tailed).

effects of the accounting methods than to substantive (real decision) differences between *FIFO* and *LIFO* firms. Of course, the findings might also suggest that comparisons of medians of traditional kinds of accounting ratios may not provide a very good basis for testing whether there are substantive differences between firms which use different inventory accounting methods. To illustrate, suppose firms' inventory balances are related to sales in some square-root manner. In the absence of tax considerations, the percentage relation between inventory balances and sales for growing firms should be decreasing, and we might expect the same decreasing relation between inventory and total assets. The fact that the average ratios computed on a uniform basis for our two classes of firms are very similar, even though the *LIFO* firms are several times larger than the *FIFO* firms, may merely indicate that substantive differences cannot be detected when using a simple model which posits that average ratios between these two classes of firms should be larger (or smaller), particularly if firms are growing at different rates.

In summary, the only variables which consistently show significant differences between the *FIFO* and *LIFO* samples are firm size, holding gains, capital intensity, and mean price changes, with the *LIFO* firms having larger median values for each. Significant differences in other ratios seem to have been induced by the use of different inventory accounting methods by the two samples of firms. In the next section, we repeat these kinds of comparisons for our sample of firms which switched from *FIFO* to *LIFO*.

3. Cross-Sectional Tests of Change-Firms

In this section we provide results from our cross-sectional tests applied to firms which switched from *FIFO* to *LIFO* during the period 1965-78. Selection criteria and industry composition of our sample of change-firms are described above in section 2.1.

3.1 HOLDING-GAIN DEVIATIONS

For each change-firm, we computed the costs-of-sales difference (i.e., holding gain) between the inventory method the firm actually used and its alternative. This meant that in the years prior to the switch, we estimated the costs-of-sales differences as-if each of these firms had been on *LIFO*; and during the year of the switch and subsequent years, we estimated the costs-of-sales difference as-if each firm had remained on *FIFO*. We then subtracted the corresponding year's median costs-of-sales difference of our long-term *FIFO* sample (i.e., our sample of *FIFO* firms that did not switch) from each firm/year costs-of-sales difference of the switching firms, thereby obtaining a holding-gain deviation for each change-firm for each calendar year. Change-firms were then aligned in event time, with year 0 being the year of change. To facilitate discussion, we present the median deviations for the change-firms for each event year in table 8.

With the exception of year −10, the median costs-of-sales difference of the change-firms is always greater than the median of the long-term *FIFO* firms. Prior to year −4, the median deviation never exceeds $139,000 per firm/year. However, it ranges between $184,000 and $249,000 per firm/year in event years −4 through −1, and in year 0, the year of change, it jumps to $1,641,000. Subsequently, the median deviation is never less than $614,000, and rises to over $1.5 million per firm/year in years +5 through +7, the last year examined. For each event year, a Wilcoxon signed rank test for location was computed which compares the entire change-firm sample with the entire long-term *FIFO* sample.[13] The test rejects the null hypothesis of a zero deviation in favor of the upper-tail alternative at the .01 level or beyond in every event year except years −11 and −10.

As another benchmark, we also show in table 8 the median deviation of the costs-of-sales difference of the long-term *LIFO* firms from that of the long-term *FIFO* firms, aligned in time with the median deviation of the change-firms. That is, we use the median costs-of-sales differences of the long-term *LIFO* and long-term *FIFO* firms from the same calendar year as the median change-firm. The correlation between the median deviations of the change-firms and the long-term *LIFO* firms is .77 over the 19-year period (.80 over the prechange period). Nevertheless, the overall median deviation of the long-term *LIFO* sample is almost 18 times larger than the median deviation of the change-firm sample.

To provide additional insight into the pattern of holding-gain deviations, we report separate results in table 9 for the 1974 and non-1974 subsamples of the change-firm. Several differences can be noted. First,

---

[13] The Wilcoxon signed rank test is used because the focus is on deviations between paired observations (e.g., change-firm costs-of-sales differences and long-term *FIFO* firm costs-of-sales differences), and these deviations can be ranked in order of absolute magnitude.

TABLE 8
Wilcoxon Signed Rank Test Results and Median Deviations in Event Time: Change-Firm Less Long-Term FIFO Firm Cost-of-Sales Differences and Long-Term LIFO Firm Less Long-Term FIFO Firm Cost-of-Sales Differences
(millions of $)

Event Year	n	Median Deviation of Change-Firms	z-Statistic (Entire Sample)	Corresponding Median Deviation of Long-Term LIFO Firms
−11	62	0.004	0.04	0.253
−10	67	−0.003	−0.01	−0.077
−9	67	0.019	2.23*	0.253
−8	67	0.045	2.56*	0.274
−7	68	0.116	3.61**	0.299
−6	68	0.139	3.85***	1.055
−5	69	0.067	3.06**	1.055
−4	69	0.210	3.58**	3.031
−3	69	0.231	3.43**	4.964
−2	70	0.184	3.18**	0.009
−1	70	0.249	3.49**	5.192
0	70	1.641	3.61**	41.273
1	70	1.293	4.36***	4.221
2	70	0.614	3.04**	4.083
3	70	0.682	3.39**	4.221
4	66	0.734	3.38**	8.227
5	63	1.548	3.71**	43.261
6	57	2.335	4.00***	44.095
7	55	1.963	4.11***	23.341
Mean (of median deviations)		0.583		9.949
Median		0.231		4.083
Standard Deviation		0.705		15.576

z-statistic for Wilcoxon signed rank test for location (see Gibbons [1976, pp. 123–35]) with continuity correction for normal approximation. All firms' observations in a given event year are used. The null hypothesis is a zero median deviation; the alternative is a median greater than zero.

$$z = \frac{T_+ - .5 - [n(n+1)/4]}{\sqrt{[n(n+1)(2n+1)]/24}}$$

where T_+ = the sum of positive deviation ranks.
Significance levels (one-tailed): * = .01; ** = .001; *** = .0001.
Also, see note to table 9.

in the years immediately preceding the change in methods, the non-1974 change-group reflects positive and typically larger median costs-of-sales deviations (from the long-term *FIFO* sample) than does the 1974 change-group. Second, the 1974 change-group's year 0 median deviation ($1.8 million) is much larger than the non-1974 group's year-of-change deviation but still much smaller than the corresponding median deviation of the long-term *LIFO* firms. Finally, the 1974 group's postchange deviations are larger than those of the non-1974 group, both in absolute terms and relative to the median deviations of the long-term *LIFO* firms, for years +1 through +4; however, they then fall below those of the non-1974 group for years +5 through +7. Over the entire time period examined, both change-subsamples reflect a similar pattern, with a correlation between the median deviations of the change-firms and the long-term

TABLE 9
Median Deviations in Event Time: 1974 Change-Firms and Non-1974 Change-Firms
(millions of $)

Event Year	1974 Change-Firms (n = 49) Median Deviation of Change-Firms	Corresponding Median Deviation of Long-Term LIFO Firms	Non-1974 Change-Firms Median Deviation of Change-Firms	Corresponding Median Deviation of Long-Term LIFO Firms	n
−11	0.003	−0.404	0.004	0.253	15
−10	−0.003	−0.077	0.006	0.274	18
−9	0.019	0.253	0.020	1.055	19
−8	0.044	0.274	0.121	0.253	19
−7	0.157	0.299	−0.058	2.652	19
−6	0.254	1.055	−0.063	0.299	19
−5	0.179	2.652	0.020	4.964	20
−4	0.210	3.031	0.253	0.009	20
−3	0.223	4.964	0.534	3.031	20
−2	−0.029	0.009	0.224	4.964	21
−1	0.249	5.192	0.240	4.221	21
0	1.810	41.273	0.059	4.083	21
1	1.943	31.682	0.124	4.221	21
2	0.614	4.083	0.504	8.287	21
3	1.004	4.221	−0.022	4.964	21
4	0.947	8.287	0.338	4.221	17
5	1.548	43.261	3.356	3.031	14
6	2.016	44.095	5.598	43.261	8
7	1.963	23.341	2.257	31.682	6

Median deviations are for descriptive purposes only. They are computed as the difference between the holding gain of each change-firm in a given calendar year and the median holding gain of the long-term *FIFO* sample in the same calendar year. Change-firms are then aligned in event time and the median deviation of the change-firms is reported. Basically, the same procedure is employed for the median deviation of the long-term *LIFO* firms, where the median holding gain of the long-term *LIFO* sample is from the same calendar year as the change-firm whose deviation is reported as the median.

LIFO firms in excess of .81 for each subgroup. One interpretation of these data is that the high rates of inflation, which typically produce large immediate *LIFO* tax savings, were major factors inducing the 1974 change-firms to switch in that year. Nevertheless, even for this group the cumulative holding-gain deviation from years −6 to −1 of $1.1 million is quite close to the cumulative holding-gain deviation of approximately $1.2 million over the same event time-span for the non-1974 group. In both cases, the cumulative deviations represent a consistent pattern relative to our sample of long-term *FIFO* firms.

In summary, median holding gains of the change-firms significantly exceeded those of long-term *FIFO* firms over the time-span prior to the year of switch. However, the median dollar amount of the excess for any one year was substantially less than that in the actual year of change for the overall change-firm sample. From that point on, the deviations generally became larger over time. Although these deviations were highly correlated with those of the long-term *LIFO* firms, they were dwarfed by the magnitude of the deviations of the latter. Consistent with Biddle

[1980] and Morse and Richardson [1983], the 1974 change-firms apparently waited to switch until the year in which there were substantially larger tax savings. Nevertheless, the deviations from the long-term *FIFO* firms' costs-of-sales differences for this and the other group of change-firms reflected a consistently growing difference prior to the switch. Hence, there is some evidence of a foreshadowing of the switch to *LIFO*. This suggests that the typical capital market study of the switch to *LIFO* might not be able to pick up the total abnormal return behavior associated with firms' decisions to switch to *LIFO* if the analysis were restricted to a narrow time period surrounding the "announcement" of the switch.[14]

3.3 CROSS-SECTIONAL ANALYSES

The variables and methods described in section 2 are again employed in order to assess whether we can detect systematic differences between the operating, financing, and investment decisions of change-firms vis-à-vis the long-term user firms, as captured by particular accounting numbers and ratios. In table 10 (columns labeled (2), (3), and (4)), we show the median values of these variables for the change-firm sample computed under three different bases over the 1963–81 period: as reported, as-if *LIFO* for the entire period, and as-if *FIFO* for the entire period. Also reproduced there are the corresponding median values for the long-term *LIFO* (column (1)) and the long-term *FIFO* (column (5)) samples. The median values of several of the variables for the change-firms lie between those of the long-term *LIFO* and the long-term *FIFO* median values. Pair-matched statistical tests of differences in location were employed to assess the significance of these differences and the results appear in table 11.

Using conventional levels of significance, these tests indicate that change-firms are significantly larger than long-term *FIFO* firms, but smaller than long-term *LIFO* firms (V_1); have significantly lower variability of inventory levels than the *FIFO* firms, but not as low as the *LIFO* firms (V_3); have inventory turnover generally similar to *LIFO* firms, but significantly different from *FIFO* firms (W_1 and W_2); and have inventory/total asset ratios similar to *FIFO* firms, but significantly different from *LIFO* firms (V_7). As noted above, change-firms' holding gains lie between the amounts for the two long-term user samples (W_4). Finally, change-firms have a higher effective tax rate than both long-term user samples.

---

[14] In a recent study, Stevenson [1987] found specific announcements of the switch to *LIFO* that were made prior to the announcement of annual earnings for approximately two-thirds of his sample of change-firms. Another form of advance announcement can come from the tendency of *LIFO* adoptions to cluster in time and industry. For example, our change-firm sample reflects this since it is dominated by 1974 switch firms and includes concentrations in six two-digit SIC industries. It seems reasonable to assume that when the first firm in an industry announces a switch to *LIFO*, the likelihood of other firms in the same industry switching in the same year should rise, inducing a market reaction at the time of the first switching firm's announcement.

TABLE 10
Change-Firms: Univariate Analyses of Inventory Choice Variables, 1963–81

Variable	(1) Long-Term LIFO Firms ($n = 29$)	(2) Change-Firms ($n = 70$) Reported Numbers	(3) LIFO Basis	(4) FIFO Basis	(5) Long-Term FIFO Firms ($n = 102$)
V_1 Net Sales	$1,044	$164			$109
V_3 C.V. of Inventory	0.42	0.53	0.55	0.66	0.63
V_4 C.V. of Before-Tax Income	0.74	0.67	0.66	0.76	0.79
V_5 Long-Term Debt/S.E.	0.33	0.26			0.32
V_6 Inventory/Net Sales	0.16	0.13	0.17	0.20	0.20
W_1 Avg. Inventory/C.G.S.	0.21	0.22	0.22	0.21	0.27
W_2 C.G.S./Avg. Inventory	4.97	4.68	4.82	5.25	3.88
V_7 Inventory/Total Assets	0.21	0.30	0.29	0.32	0.29
V_{10} Gross F.A./Net Sales	0.66	0.35			0.30
V_{11} Relative Frequency of Price Increases	0.92	0.94			0.94
V_{14} C.V. of Price	1.18	1.01			1.02
W_3 Mean Price Changes	0.11	0.10			0.09
V_{15} Effective Tax Rate	0.41	0.43			0.44
W_4 Holding-Gain Differences	$1.88	$0.69			$0.33

Median values shown. Dollar amounts, variables V_1 and W_4, are in millions. Amounts left blank in columns (3) and (4) are unaffected by the switch in accounting methods. (Regarding variables V_5 and V_{15}, see n. 12.)

With the exception of inventory variability, these differences do not appear to be induced by different accounting methods (see the within-firms assessments of the change-firms in table 11). While not reported here, these relationships generally held up in both the pre- and post-change periods.

Overall, then, the average differences between the values of several variables of the change-firms are different from, and fall between, those of long-term users of *FIFO* and *LIFO*. Further, these rankings hold up both before and after the switch to *LIFO*. These results provide further evidence that market participants might be able to identify which set of *FIFO* firms are most likely to switch to *LIFO* prior to any actual announcement of their decision to do so.

4. Summary and Conclusions

In this paper, we provide results from various cross-sectional analyses of differences in accounting numbers and accounting ratios of long-term users of *FIFO* versus long-term users of *LIFO* versus change-firms, assuming these numbers and ratios capture differences in these firms' operating, financing, and investment decisions. Our analyses were performed on firms' reported accounting numbers and estimates of those numbers which they would have reported had they used an alternative inventory method instead, called as-if series. By using both reported and as-if accounting series we attempted to address the extent to which firms'

TABLE 11
Mann-Whitney Test Statistics on Table 10 Data: 1963–81

Variable	Long-Term *LIFO* Firms vs. Δ(R)	Long-Term *LIFO* Firms vs. Δ(L)	Long-Term *LIFO* Firms vs. Δ(F)	Long-Term *FIFO* Firms vs. Δ(R)	Long-Term *FIFO* Firms vs. Δ(L)	Long-Term *FIFO* Firms vs. Δ(F)	Within-Firms Δ(R) vs. Δ(L)	Within-Firms Δ(R) vs. Δ(F)	Within-Firms Δ(L) vs. Δ(F)
V_1 Net Sales	3.76[c]			1.96[a]					
V_3 C.V. of Inventory	−2.43[a]	−2.89[b]	−4.79[c]	−3.00[b]	−2.17[a]	0.93	−0.80	−3.65[c]	−2.89[b]
V_4 C.V. of Before-Tax Income	0.67	0.98	−0.11	−1.22	−1.62	−0.73	0.51	−0.76	−1.14
V_5 Long-Term Debt/S.E.	0.85			−1.24					
V_6 Inventory/Net Sales	−0.67	−0.23	−1.63	−1.40	−2.11[a]	0.01	0.77	−1.41	−2.04[a]
W_1 Avg. Inventory/C.G.S.	−1.20	−0.81	0.34	−2.60[a]	−3.19[b]	−3.70[c]	0.74	1.46	0.78
W_2 C.G.S./Avg. Inventory	1.31	0.88	−0.08	2.42[a]	3.00[b]	4.02[c]	−0.73	−1.99[a]	−1.37
V_7 Inventory/Total Assets	−2.91[b]	−2.59[a]	−3.41[b]	1.10	−0.57	2.14[a]	0.64	−1.14	−1.65
V_{10} Gross F.A./Net Sales	3.83[c]			1.58					
V_{11} Relative Frequency of Price Increases	−1.67			0.40					
V_{14} C.V. of Price Changes	2.04[a]			−0.15					
W_3 Mean Price Change	0.87			1.54					
V_{15} Effective Tax Rate	−2.97[b]			3.24[b]					
W_4 Holding-Gain Differences	5.27[c]			6.47[c]					

Change-Firms:
Δ(R) = reported numbers
Δ(L) = *LIFO* basis
Δ(F) = *FIFO* basis.
[a] = significant at the .05 level (two-tailed).
[b] = significant at the .005 level (two-tailed).
[c] = significant at the .0005 level (two-tailed).

choices of inventory accounting methods were consistent with tax and nontax explanations of such accounting decisions.

Overall we find considerable evidence that inventory choice and tax savings are related. We cannot conclude, however, that the results are more consistent with the tax explanation because of an identification problem which is exacerbated by our inability to estimate reliably the costs and benefits associated with nontax explanations of inventory method choices, and the extent to which firms face different marginal tax rates. That is, we also find evidence that the characteristics of firms' operating, investment, and financing decisions differ in a manner consistent with certain nontax explanations of accounting choices. However, most of these differences between long-term *FIFO* and *LIFO* firms are induced by the inventory accounting methods themselves. Further, we find that long-term *LIFO* firms enjoyed the largest magnitude of tax savings (i.e., deferrals) based on their *LIFO* choice, with change-firms next and the long-term *FIFO* firms falling at the lower end of the spectrum. Our estimates of the potential tax savings the long-term *FIFO* firms could have obtained had they used the *LIFO* method over the time period, 1963–81, were quite small relative to what the *LIFO* firms attained over the same period, and relative to what the change-firms attained after they switched (mostly in 1974). Given that our estimates of foregone tax savings may be biased upward, since we assumed all of the long-term *FIFO* firms' inventories would have been switched to *LIFO*, we conclude that long-term *FIFO* users have not been foregoing significant tax savings by remaining on *FIFO*, certainly not of the magnitude that others have suggested in the past. There seems to be some threshold level of potential tax savings which has to be met before firms choose to switch to *LIFO*, and the long-term users of *FIFO* apparently have not reached that level (see Morse and Richardson [1983] and Lee and Petruzzi [1987]).

A more direct test of alternative explanations of inventory accounting method choices would entail comparing costs of implementing different accounting methods with the tax benefits from using *LIFO* versus *FIFO*. The comparisons would also have to include assessing other tax-saving options available to firms and whether these are less costly to implement than choosing *LIFO*. In an attempt to gain some insights in this regard, we examined various financial statement accounts and disclosures having the potential to suggest differences in expected levels of taxable income or marginal tax rates—e.g., net operating loss carryforwards, pension funding, holdings of municipal bonds, etc.—across a subsample of each of our three classes of firms. No systematic differences were detected, which suggests that the inventory method choice represents a significant tax option in itself. Direct tests of alternative explanations of inventory method choices would also require more information on the expected marginal tax rates faced by the various classes of firms. We assumed all of our firms faced the same marginal tax rate. Nevertheless, the use of actual marginal tax rates in our calculations of median tax savings for each class of firms would not change our conclusions that tax savings are significantly linked to the inventory method choice unless such rates were considerably lower for long-term *LIFO* firms, relative to the other two classes.

APPENDIX A

Converting FIFO (LIFO) Earnings, Costs of Sales, and Ending Inventory Series to As-If LIFO (FIFO) Series

A. Overview and Conversion of FIFO Ending Inventory to Constant Dollar Amounts

We convert the nominal dollar *FIFO* and *LIFO* ending inventory time-series to constant dollar values. For *FIFO*, this is accomplished by dividing the series by the appropriate industry-specific producer price index. The procedure is similar to general price-level adjustments. The conversion procedure for the as-reported *LIFO* series is described in the next section. Then, as explained in section C below, we infer from the constant dollar series the realized holding gains experienced under both *FIFO* and *LIFO* (see Biddle [1980]). A direct application of the identity:

$$HG_F - HG_L \equiv CGS_L - CGS_F$$

where:

$HG_F \equiv$ Realized holding gain with *FIFO*,
$HG_L \equiv$ Realized holding gain with *LIFO*,
$CGS_F \equiv$ Costs of sales under *FIFO*,
$CGS_L \equiv$ Costs of sales under *LIFO*,

yields the difference in costs of sales under the two inventory methods. Sufficient information is then available to estimate as-if ending inventories. Additionally, we apply the appropriate marginal tax rate (see section D below) to the costs-of-sales holding-gain difference to estimate, first, the tax savings (i.e., deferrals) reaped or foregone by using one inventory method vs. the other and, second, the after-tax difference between reported and as-if earnings.

The following assumptions hold throughout: acquisition and sales transactions occur uniformly throughout the year; a single industry classification covers all units of inventory (based on a firm's primary SIC code), to which a single producer price index is applied (see Sunder and Waymire [1983]); for *FIFO* firms, 100% of the inventory is costed using *FIFO*; 75% of inventory is covered by *LIFO* for *LIFO* firms (see section C below); a firm either began operations using *LIFO* or switched to *LIFO* in 1962, the first year under study.

B. Converting Nominal LIFO Ending Inventory to Constant Dollar Amounts

It is necessary to identify *LIFO* layers for each year of the time-series. Let:

$$EIDIF_t = EI_t - EI_{t-1},$$

i.e., $EIDIF_t$ is the first difference in the nominal dollar inventory series. Let:

$$LIFLAY_t = \text{the } LIFO \text{ layer added in year } t,$$

where: $LIFLAY_1 = EI_1$ in year 1.

We assign $LIFLAY_t = EIDIF_t$ for $EIDIF_t \geq 0$ and search back through previous layers to liquidate $EIDIF_t < 0$. Hence, for a liquidation, we have:

$$LIFLAY_t = 0 \quad \text{and,}$$

$$LIFLAY_{t-1} = \begin{cases} 0 & \text{if } |EIDIF_t| \geq LIFLAY_{t-1} \\ (LIFLAY_{t-1} + EIDIF_t) & \text{if } \\ |EIDIF_t| < LIFLAY_{t-1} \end{cases}$$

since $EIDIF_t < 0$.

If resultant $LIFLAY_{t-1} = 0$, then:

$$LIFLAY_{t-2} = \begin{cases} 0 & \text{if } |LIFLAY_{t-1} + EIDIF_t| \geq LIFLAY_{t-2} \\ (LIFLAY_{t-2} + LIFLAY_{t-1} + EIDIF_t) & \text{if } \\ |LIFLAY_{t-1} + EIDIF_t| < LIFLAY_{t-2}. \end{cases}$$

If necessary, this continues back to year 1. Hence, at the end of year t, the constant dollar ending inventory quantity (denoted with *) under *LIFO* is estimated as follows:

$$EI_t^* = \sum_{i=1}^{t} [LIFLAY_i / \overline{WPI}_{i,(1,12)}]$$

where $\overline{WPI}_{i,(1,12)}$ is the 12-month average of the producer price index in a particular year i.

C. Estimation of Realized Holding Gains

1. FIFO REALIZED HOLDING GAINS

Let:

$$TURN_t = CGS_t / EI_{t-1}$$

where: $TURN_t$ is a metric for inventory turnover in period t;
CGS_t is costs of sales in period t;
EI_{t-1} is ending inventory in period $t-1$ (beginning inventory in period t).

We infer from $TURN_t \geq 1$ that beginning inventory for period t, EI_{t-1}, was sold (on average) in the first $(12/TURN_t)$ months of period t. We infer from $TURN_{t-1} \geq 1$ that beginning inventory for period t was purchased (on average) in the last $(12/TURN_{t-1})$ months of period $t-1$. This gives rise to a FIFO holding gain (realized on beginning inventory) which is assigned as follows:

$$HG_{F,t} = EI^*_{t-1}\{\overline{WPI}_{t,(1,[12/TURN_t])} - \overline{WPI}_{t-1,([13-(12/TURN_{t-1})],12)}\}$$

where: $\overline{WPI}_{t,(j,k)}$ is the average of the producer price index over months j through k of year t;

* denotes constant dollar quantities.

When $TURN_{t-1} < 1$ (which rarely happened), the computation is similar but a portion of beginning inventory in year t must be identified with the producer price index of year $t-2$.[15]

2. LIFO REALIZED HOLDING GAINS

Let:

$$EIDIF_t^* = EI_t^* - EI_{t-1}^*,$$

i.e., $EIDIF_t^*$ = is the first difference in the constant dollar inventory series. Let $LIFLAY_t^*$ = the constant dollar LIFO layer added in year t, where $LIFLAY_1^* = EI_1^*$ in year 1; and let $\overline{LIQ}_t^*$ be a $(t-1) \times 1$ vector of constant dollar inventory quantities liquidated in year t.

We assign $LIFLAY_t^* = EIDIF_t^*$ for $EIDIF_t^* \geq 0$ and search back through previous layers to liquidate any $EIDIF_t^* < 0$. Hence, for $EIDIF_t^* = 0$, we have:

$$LIFLAY_t^* = 0, \text{ and}$$

$$LIFLAY_{t-1}^* = \begin{cases} 0 & \text{if } |EIDIF_t^*| \geq LIFLAY_{t-1}^* \\ (LIFLAY_{t-1}^* + EIDIF_t^*) & \text{if} \\ |EIDIF_t^*| < LIFLAY_{t-1}^* \end{cases}$$

If resultant $LIFLAY_{t-1}^* = 0$, then:

$$LIFLAY_{t-2}^* = \begin{cases} 0 & \text{if } |LIFLAY_{t-1}^* + EIDIF_t^*| \geq LIFLAY_{t-2}^* \\ (LIFLAY_{t-2}^* + LIFLAY_{t-1}^* + EIDIF_t^*) & \text{if} \\ |LIFLAY_{t-1}^* + EIDIF_t^*| < LIFLAY_{t-2} \end{cases}$$

etc., back to year 1 as necessary.

$\overline{LIQ}_t^*$ will be the zero vector for any year in which constant dollar

---

[15] In section 2.6 we document that differences in LIFO and FIFO firms' inventory turnover ratios are due primarily to the use of alternative inventory accounting methods. Here we use reported numbers to compute TURN. Although these are price adjusted, their use may induce differences that show up as systematic differences in holding gains of FIFO firms, vis-à-vis LIFO firms as-if FIFO had been used. Since the LIFO method typically yields a higher turnover rate, beginning inventory would be treated as being held a shorter time (acquired later in the prior year and sold earlier in the current year) than had (as-if) FIFO numbers been used. However, assuming uniform price increases throughout a year, this implies a smaller price increase and therefore a lower estimated holding gain for the LIFO firms as-if FIFO had been used.

inventories have not decreased (i.e., $EIDIF_t^* \geq 0$). Where $EIDIF_t^* < 0$, we have:

$$LIQ_{t-1}^* = \begin{cases} LIFLAY_{t-1}^* & \text{if } |EIDIF_t^*| \geq LIFLAY_{t-1}^* \\ (LIFLAY_{t-1}^* + EIDIF_t^*) & \text{if } |EIDIF_t^*| < LIFLAY_{t-1}^* \end{cases}$$

$$LIQ_{t-2}^* = \begin{cases} 0 & \text{if the second condition for } LIQ_{t-1}^* \text{ above holds} \\ LIFLAY_{t-2}^* & \text{if } |LIFLAY_{t-1}^* + EIDIF_t^*| \geq LIFLAY_{t-2}^* \\ (LIFLAY_{t-2}^* + LIFLAY_{t-1}^* + EIDIF_t^*) \\ \quad \text{if } |LIFLAY_{t-1}^* + EIDIF_t^*| < LIFLAY_{t-2}^* \end{cases}$$

where LIQ_i^* is the indicated element of $\overline{LIQ_t}^*$.

LIQ_{t-3}^* through LIQ_1^* are assigned in a like manner.

Liquidated quantities (in constant dollar amounts) are associated with the average producer price index of the year in which each of the *LIFO* layers was established to compute the *LIFO* realized holding gain:

$$HG_{L,t} = \begin{cases} 0 \text{ if } EIDIF_t^* \geq 0 \\ \sum_{i=1}^{t-1} LIQ_i^* [\overline{WPI}_{t,(1,12)} - \overline{WPI}_{i,(1,12)}] \\ \quad \text{if } EIDIF_t^* < 0. \end{cases}$$

D. Final Conversion from Reported to As-If Earnings

Because:

$$HG_F - HG_L = CGS_L - CGS_F$$

we have (using reported *FIFO* to as-if *LIFO* as an example, and suppressing temporal subscripts):

$$NI_L^0 = NI_F + MTR(HG_L - HF_F)$$

where:

NI_L^0 is as-if *LIFO* earnings for a *FIFO* firm;
NI_F is *FIFO* reported earnings;
MTR is the marginal tax rate, defined as the maximum statutory federal corporate tax rate in a given year;
HG_F and HG_L are the estimated holding gains realized with *FIFO* and *LIFO*, respectively.

Recall that exclusive use of one inventory method is assumed for *FIFO* firms. We examined the annual reports for a sample of our firms included in *Disclosure, Inc.* For *FIFO* firms, in the vast majority of cases, substantially all of the inventory was accounted for under *FIFO*. On the other hand, an average of 25% of *LIFO* firms' inventories were carried on a basis other than *LIFO*. Accordingly, the holding-gain difference computed for *LIFO* firms was reduced by 25% to eliminate an otherwise built-in bias in our conversion procedure.

Statutory tax rates ranged from .46 to .53 over the 1963–81 period. Operating loss carryforwards were ignored. For firms having carryforwards that would otherwise be used in the future, the relevant tax rate is the future statutory rate discounted back to the present at the appropriate cost of capital. The marginal rate would be zero in the extreme case where carryforwards would otherwise expire unused. (An examination of subsets of all three samples did not reveal significant differences across the samples in the prevalence of net operating loss carryforwards and other factors potentially giving rise to or reflecting differing expected marginal tax rates.) Our use of the statutory rate coupled with our assumption of 100% conversion from *FIFO* to *LIFO* means that our estimate of tax savings foregone for *FIFO* firms is biased upward. For *LIFO* firms, use of the statutory rate also biases upward the implied tax savings, but our assumption of conversion of only 75% of *LIFO* inventory serves to at least partially offset that bias.

Table 12 presents descriptive statistics of firm/year holding gains for the long-term *LIFO* and *FIFO* subsamples. These data are briefly discussed in the text in conjunction with the estimated tax savings shown in table 2. Two additional points may be noted here. First, for the long-term *LIFO* firms, liquidations are not uncommon, occurring in approximately 20% of the firm/years in our sample. We determined, however, that liquidations were always immediately preceded by at least one year (typically more years) where the *LIFO* tax savings exceeded the tax costs implied by the *LIFO* liquidation. Second, for the long-term *FIFO* firms, firm/years in which substantial tax savings were foregone were noted. In

TABLE 12

Panel A: Descriptive Statistics of Estimated Pretax Differences Between *LIFO* Firms' Costs of Sales As-Reported and As-If *FIFO* (1963–81)
(millions of $)

29 *LIFO* Firms		Selected Percentiles	
Mean	31.067	0th	−233.284
Median	1.883	1st	−32.514
Standard Deviation	100.533	5th	−3.386
IQR*	17.264	95th	207.840
Number of Annual Firm/Year Observations	551	99th	468.842
		100th	1,231.680

Panel B: Descriptive Statistics of Estimated Pretax Differences Between *FIFO* Firms' Costs of Sales As-Reported and As-If *LIFO* (1963–81)
(millions of $)

102 *FIFO* Firms		Selected Percentiles	
Mean	3.163	0th	−21.114
Median	0.329	1st	−2.311
Standard Deviation	10.042	5th	−0.127
IQR*	1.797	95th	17.814
Number of Annual Firm/Year Observations	1,938	99th	468.842
		100th	172.310

* *IQR* = interquartile range.

following these up we discovered in every case that these were for firms having significant non-U.S. operations (typically in excess of 40% of total sales). While we purged non-U.S. firms from our sample because *LIFO* is rarely a tax option for them, we did include U.S. firms having non-U.S. activities. To the extent that *LIFO* is not an option for a substantial portion of the inventories of these long-term *FIFO* firms as well, we have overestimated their tax savings foregone.

REFERENCES

ABDEL-KHALIK, R. "The Effect of LIFO-Switching and Firm Ownership on Executives' Pay." *Journal of Accounting Research* (Autumn 1985): 427–47.

———, AND J. MCKEOWN. "Understanding Accounting Changes in an Efficient Market: Evidence of Differential Reaction." *The Accounting Review* (October 1978): 851–68.

BIDDLE, G. "Accounting Methods and Management Decisions: The Case of Inventory Costing and Inventory Policy." *Journal of Accounting Research* (Supplement 1980): 235–80.

———, AND F. LINDAHL. "Stock Price Reactions to LIFO Adoptions: The Association Between Excess Returns and LIFO Tax Savings." *Journal of Accounting Research* (Autumn 1982, pt. II): 551–88.

———, AND K. MARTIN. "Inflation, Taxes, and Optimal Inventory Policies." *Journal of Accounting Research* (Spring 1985): 57–83.

———, AND W. RICKS. "Analyst Forecast Errors and Stock Price Behavior Near the Earnings Announcement Dates of LIFO Adopters." Working paper, 1987.

BROWN, R. "Short-Range Market Reactions to Changes to LIFO Accounting Using Preliminary Earnings Announcement Dates." *Journal of Accounting Research* (Spring 1980): 38–63.

BROWN, V. "Discussion of Accounting Methods and Management Decisions: The Case of Inventory Costing and Inventory Policy." *Journal of Accounting Research* (Supplement 1980): 281–85.

CHASTEEN, L. "An Empirical Study of Differences in Economic Circumstances as a Justification for Alternative Inventory Pricing Methods." *The Accounting Review* (July 1971): 504–8.

COMMITTEE ON ACCOUNTING PROCEDURE. *Accounting Research and Terminology Bulletins.* Final ed. New York: AICPA, 1961.

DERSTINE, R., AND R. HUEFNER. "LIFO-FIFO, Accounting Ratios, and Market Risk." *Journal of Accounting Research* (Autumn 1974): 216–34.

DHALIWAL, D., G. SALAMON, AND E. SMITH. "The Effect of Owner Versus Management Control on the Choice of Accounting Methods." *Journal of Accounting and Economics* (July 1982): 41–53.

EDWARDS, E., AND P. BELL. *The Theory and Measurement of Business Income.* Berkeley: University of California Press, 1961.

GIBBONS, J. *Nonparametric Methods for Quantitative Analysis.* New York: Holt, Rinehart & Winston, 1976.

HENDRIKSEN, E. *Accounting Theory.* 4th ed. Homewood, Ill.: Richard D. Irwin, 1982.

HOLTHAUSEN, R., AND R. LEFTWICH. "The Economic Consequences of Accounting Choice: Implications of Costly Contracting and Monitoring." *Journal of Accounting and Economics* (August 1983): 77–117.

HUNT, H., III. "Potential Determinants of Corporate Inventory Accounting Decisions." *Journal of Accounting Research* (Autumn 1985): 448–67.

KAPLAN, R. "Discussion of Capital Market Equilibrium, Information Production, and Selecting Accounting Techniques: Theoretical Framework and Review of Empirical Work." *Journal of Accounting Research* (Supplement 1974): 130–37.

KELLER, T., AND S. ZEFF, eds. "Problem of Comparability of Financial Statements." Part

III of *Financial Accounting Theory II: Issues and Controversies.* New York: McGraw-Hill, 1969.

LEE, C. J., AND D. HSIEH. "Choice of Inventory Accounting Methods: Comparative Analyses of Alternative Hypotheses." *Journal of Accounting Research* (Autumn 1985): 468–85.

LEE, C. J., AND C. PETRUZZI. "Inventory Accounting Choice and Uncertainty." Working paper, 1987.

MERINO, B., AND T. COE. "Uniformity in Accounting: A Historical Perspective." *Journal of Accountancy* (August 1978): 48–54.

MORSE, D., AND G. RICHARDSON. "The LIFO/FIFO Decision." *Journal of Accounting Research* (Spring 1983): 106–27.

PRATT, J. "Robustness of Some Procedures for the Two-Sample Location Problem." *Journal of the American Statistical Association* (September 1964): 665–80.

RICKS, W. "The Market's Response to the 1974 LIFO Adoptions." *Journal of Accounting Research* (Autumn 1982, pt. I): 367–87.

———. "Firm Size Effects and the Association Between Excess Returns and LIFO Tax Savings." *Journal of Accounting Research* (Spring 1986): 206–16.

SCHOLES, M., AND M. WOLFSON. "Issues in the Theory of Optimal Capital Structure." In *Frontiers in Modern Finance*, edited by S. Bhattachara and G. Constantinidas. New York, 1987.

SIEGEL, S. *Nonparametric Statistics.* New York: McGraw-Hill, 1956.

STEVENSON, F. "New Evidence on LIFO Adoptions: The Effects of More Precise Event Dates." Working paper, 1987.

SUNDER, S. "Relationship Between Accounting Changes and Stock Prices: Problems of Measurement and Some Empirical Evidence." *Journal of Accounting Research* (Supplement 1973): 1–45.

———, AND G. WAYMIRE. "Marginal Gains in Accuracy of Valuation from Increasingly Specific Price Indexes: Empirical Evidence for the U.S. Economy." *Journal of Accounting Research* (Autumn 1983): 565–80.

ZIMMERMAN, J. "Taxes and Firm Size." *Journal of Accounting and Economics* (August 1983): 119–49.

by James P. Dawson, Peter M. Neupert and Clyde P. Stickney

Restating Financial Statements for Alternative GAAPs: Is It Worth the Effort?

Evidence suggests that share prices react rationally to changes in accounting method, "seing through" changes that have no real economic effect. Research has been less conclusive on whether share prices accurately reflect differences in accounting methods across firms. Are such differences large enough to justify analysts' time and effort in adjusting financial statement data?

Using a sample of 96 firms randomly selected from the largest 250 industrial firms in the 1978 *Fortune* 500, the authors converted all firms to FIFO, converted depreciation expense and net asset values to amounts consistent with those reported for income tax purposes, consolidated wholly owned unconsolidated subsidiaries, recognized pension obligations as liabilities, and eliminated the effects of deferred tax accounting. In order to obtain a measure of the impact of restatement, they correlated net incomes and common financial ratios based on the restated figures with net incomes and ratios based on the figures as reported.

With relatively minor exceptions, the correlations between reported net incomes and financial ratios and their values restated for FIFO exceeded 99 per cent. In the case of the depreciation adjustment, correlation between reported and restated figures exceeded 98 per cent, even though 80 of the 96 firms required adjustment. Correlations between reported incomes and ratios and those restated for elimination of deferred tax amounts exceeded 97 per cent.

Consolidation of wholly owned subsidiaries had by far the largest impact on financial ratios: Despite the fact that only 23 of the 96 companies had unconsolidated subsidiaries, correlations for the quick ratio and receivables turnover were only 81 and 43 per cent, respectively. The adjustment for the prior service pension obligation also produced a low correlation—only 83 per cent for the comprehensive debt-equity ratio. Obviously, pension obligations can have a substantial effect on measures of capital structure risk.

RESEARCH on capital market efficiency suggests that market prices fully reflect publicly available information and react quickly and unbiasedly to new information.[1] One type of information available to the market is the set of accounting principles, or methods, used by a firm in preparing its financial statements. Previous research has shown that market prices react "correctly" to *changes* in accounting methods. That is, changes that have real economic effects (e.g., a switch from FIFO to LIFO for tax and

---

James Dawson is Manager of Teradyne, Inc., Boston. Peter Neupert is Controller of Consolidated Supply Company, Portland, Oregon. Clyde Stickney is Professor of Accounting at The Amos Tuck School of Business Administration, Dartmouth College.

1. Footnotes appear at the end of article

book) affect share prices, whereas changes without real economic effects (e.g., a switch from deferral to flow through for the investment credit) do not.[2]

Research has been less conclusive on whether market prices accurately reflect the effects of *differences* across firms in the methods of accounting used.[3] That is, do market participants restate reported financial statement amounts, either explicitly or implicitly, so that all firms are placed on a comparable reporting basis? One question of particular concern to analysts is whether different accounting methods create significant enough differences in financial statement data to justify the time and effort required to make such adjustments.[4] Another is identifying the conditions under which a particular choice of accounting method (e.g., FIFO versus LIFO) can materially affect financial statement data.

This article examines the relative effect on net income and conventional financial statement ratios of restating reported data to make accounting methods comparable across firms. Specifically, we made the following adjustments to the financial statement data of sample firms:

1. We converted all firms to a FIFO cost-flow assumption.
2. We based depreciation expense and the amounts for property, plant and equipment on the amounts reported for income tax purposes. In all cases, this entailed using an accelerated depreciation method (declining balance or sum of the years' digits).
3. We consolidated wholly-owned unconsolidated subsidiaries (generally captive finance and insurance companies).
4. We recognized pension obligations as liabilities, performing separate analyses recognizing both the unfunded prior service obligation and the excess of vested benefits over pension fund assets.
5. We eliminated the effects of deferred tax accounting.

We make no attempt to judge which accounting method is "best" in each case. For example, opinions differ as to whether FIFO or LIFO more accurately reflects operating performance and financial position during a period of inflation; we are concerned only with the effects of changing from the latter to the former. Discussions of alternative accounting principles will be more fruitful if interested parties can differentiate between those instances when the choice leads to material differences and those instances when it does not.

The Study

From the largest 250 industrial firms in the 1978 *Fortune* 500 we randomly selected 96. Appendix A lists the firms, along with their industry designations and the adjustments made for accounting methods. (The analysis was replicated using data for 1977 as well, with no significant differences in results).

We classified the 1978 financial statement data for each firm into a standardized set of accounts (e.g., construction contracts in process were placed in a separate account from merchandise inventory), and computed from these data net income and various financial statement ratios (e.g., rate of return on assets, current ratio, etc.; see Appendix B). We also restated the reported data for differences in accounting methods (Appendix C) and computed net income and financial statement ratios from the restated data.

We then calculated the correlation between the reported and the restated amounts for net income and each financial statement ratio. If little or no change occurred as a result of the restatement, we would expect the data to plot along a line at a 45-degree angle to the axis and the correlation coefficient (R) to be near 1.0. If significant changes occurred, the plot of data points would vary from the 45-degree line, and the correlation coefficient would fall below 1.0. Table I presents the correlation coefficients.

FIFO Adjustment

With the exception of the inventory turnover and current ratios, the correlations between net income and each of the financial ratios as reported and as restated using FIFO exceed 99 per cent. Given that 73 of the 96 firms required adjustments to convert to a FIFO basis, these high correlations are somewhat surprising. Two factors explain these results.

First, the effect of the FIFO restatement on income numbers (e.g., cost of goods sold, income tax expense, net income) is based on the *change* in the excess of FIFO over LIFO between the beginning and end of the year, rather than on the absolute size of the excess. The change in the excess (which depends primarily on the rate of price change during the current year and the proportion of inventories accounted for on LIFO) will be significantly smaller than the absolute size of the excess (which depends on how long the firm has been on LIFO and the cumulative amount of price change over that period). Thus the effect of the restatement on profit margin, cost of goods sold to sales and net income is

Table I Correlation Between Reported and Restated Ratios and Net Incomes

	FIFO	Accelerated Depreciation	Consoli- dation of Subsidiary	Prior Service Obligation	Vested Pension Benefits	Deferred Taxes	Combined
Return on Assets	0.995	0.993	0.929	*	*	0.976	0.909
Profit Margin	0.994	0.989	0.986	*	*	0.982	0.975
Asset Turnover	0.998	0.997	0.891	*	*	0.999	0.877
Cost of Goods Sold/Sales	0.999	*	*	*	*	*	0.999
Income Tax Expenses/Sales	0.993	0.987	0.974	*	*	0.970	0.881
Sell. & Admin./Sales	*	*	0.989	*	*	*	0.987
Receivables Turnover	*	*	0.431	*	*	*	0.431
Inventory Turnover	0.944	*	*	*	*	*	0.944
Fixed Asset Turnover	*	0.993	0.993	*	*	*	0.990
Return on Common Share- holders' Equity	0.994	0.987	*	0.955	0.986	0.916	0.896[a] 0.914[b]
Current Ratio	0.944	*	0.911	*	*	0.944	0.815
Quick Ratio	*	*	0.815	*	*	0.953	0.815
Total Liabilities/Total Equities	0.993	0.997	0.848	0.832	0.925	0.981	0.743[a] 0.800[b]
Long-Term Liabilities/ Total Equities	0.998	0.999	0.897	0.871	0.944	0.980	0.808[a] 0.859[b]
Interest Coverage	0.999	0.999	0.995	*	*	0.999	0.994
Net Income	0.996	0.994	*	*	*	0.987	0.995

* Ratio not affected by this adjustment.
[a] Combined including unfunded prior service obligation.
[b] Combined including unfunded vested benefits.

relatively small.

Second, the effect of restatement on rate of return measures is relatively small because both the numerator and denominator are affected similarly. Converting to FIFO increases the income measure in the numerator of return on assets and return on shareholders' equity, but it also increases the denominator in each case. While increases in the numerator and denominator are not of the same magnitude, their proportional effects are not so different as to change the ratios dramatically.

The inventory turnover and current ratios—two measures used for assessing short-term liquidity—exhibit lower correlations than the other ratios. The conversion to FIFO reduces the numerator while increasing the denominator of the inventory turnover, hence the numerator and denominator effects do not neutralize each other. Forty-seven firms had a change greater than 10 per cent in their inventory turnover ratios as a result of the adjustment, and 37 firms had a change greater than 20 per cent. Petroleum and steel firms showed the largest changes in inventory turnover ratio (greater than 50 per cent).

The conversion to FIFO increases the numerator of the current ratio by the excess of FIFO over LIFO inventory value (net of taxes) at the end of the year, but has no effect on the denominator. Since the year-end excess reflects cumulative inflation since each LIFO layer was established, the longer a firm has been on LIFO, the larger the change in the current ratio as a result of conversion. During 1978, 36 firms had a change greater than 10 per cent in the current ratio as a result of the restatement, and 12 firms had a change greater than 20 per cent. The steel companies, which have been on LIFO for decades, exhibited the largest change. In future years, the effect of LIFO versus FIFO on the current ratio will likely become even more significant as the cumulative time since adoption of LIFO lengthens.

Accelerated Depreciation Adjustment

Table I shows very high correlations between the reported net incomes and financial ratios and the restated values based on accelerated depreciation. Eighty of the 96 firms required such adjustment; the remaining firms already used accelerated depreciation for financial reporting. Three factors explain these high correlations.

First, except for heavily capital intensive firms, depreciation represents a relatively small percentage of total expense. Even when accelerated depreciation is 1.5 to 2.0 times larger than straight line depreciation, the impact on net income tends to be relatively small. The steel and petroleum companies—highly capital intensive—exhibited the largest changes in net income and financial ratios as a result of conversion.

Second, as was the case with the FIFO adjustment, the adjustments for accelerated depreciation decrease both the numerator and denominator of the rate of return measures. Again, while the decreases were not always of the same magnitude, their proportional effects were not different enough to change the ratios dramatically.

Third, because of the lack of publicly available data, we based our computation of the balance sheet effect of accelerated depreciation (see Appendix C) on the deferred tax provision relating to depreciation for the preceding four years only. This probably understates the actual difference between accelerated and straight line amounts. A deferred tax provision over the average life of depreciable assets is usually preferred when making the adjustment for accelerated depreciation, but disclosure of the relevant data has been required only since 1973. If more years of data were available, the ratios would change by a greater amount, and the correlations would probably decrease. However, judging by the very high correlations when four years of data are used, they probably wouldn't decrease significantly.

Consolidation of Unconsolidated Subsidiaries

Of all the accounting methods studied, the consolidation of wholly-owned finance, insurance and similar subsidiaries had by far the largest impact on the sample's financial ratios (see the lower correlation coefficients in Table I). Despite the fact that only 23 of the 96 companies had unconsolidated subsidiaries requiring consolidation, the impact of consolidation on these firms' reported data was so material that the correlation coefficients for the total sample were driven down. Those firms having a substantial portion of their sales funneled through these subsidiaries (primarily automobile and heavy equipment manufacturers) exhibited the most significant differences between the unadjusted and adjusted ratios.

In consolidating a subsidiary, the Investment in Subsidiary account on the parent's books is replaced with the individual assets and liabilities of the subsidiary. The primary assets of finance subsidiaries comprise accounts and notes receivable from customers. The consolidation of such receivables, generally large in amount relative to receivables on the parent's books, accounts for the low correlation coefficients for accounts receivable turnover, current ratio and quick ratio.

The primary effect of consolidation on the equity side is the recognition of a subsidiary's long-term debt. Captive finance subsidiaries generally rely heavily on long-term debt financing. Consolidation drives up the debt to equity ratios relative to their unadjusted values, decreasing the observed correlations.

Note that consolidation of a finance subsidiary affects the rate of return on assets, but not the rate of return on shareholders' equity. Consolidation of a finance subsidiary accounted for using the equity method increases the numerator of return on assets by the amount of the subsidiary's after-tax interest expense. The denominator is increased by the excess of the subsidiary's total assets over the balance in the parent's investment account. There is no incremental effect on either the numerator or denominator of return on shareholders' equity.

Recognition of Pension Obligations

Considerable controversy centers on whether unfunded pension obligations represent liabilities of a firm. Those who agree that liabilities exist disagree about whether the appropriate measure of that liability is the unfunded prior service obligation or the excess of vested benefits over pension fund assets. And those who can agree on the appropriate measure of the pension obligation point out that differences in the actuarial methods used inhibit the comparability of amounts across firms.[5]

Seventy-six of the sample firms disclosed an unfunded prior service obligation. Sixty firms reported an excess of vested benefits over pension fund assets. We restated financial statement ratios to reflect each of these measures of the pension obligation. Such recognition primarily affects debt to equity ratios (observe the correlations in Table I). The automotive, rubber and steel companies, each of which is heavily unionized, experienced the largest changes in ratios.

While recent pronouncements from the Financial Accounting Standards Board aimed at making the measurement of pension obligations more uniform across firms, it is clear from the results in Table I that, even with less uniform data, the effect of pension obligations on measures of capital structure risk can be substantial.

Elimination of Deferred Income Taxes

Controversy likewise exists as to whether deferred income taxes represent a legitimate expense and liability. Generally accepted accounting principles require that deferred taxes be recognized for timing differences between pretax book income and taxable income. Opponents argue that, for a growing firm, pretax book income will continually exceed taxable income, hence the deferred taxes will never become payable. According to this view, deferred income tax expense should be eliminated from the income statement and deferred tax liabilities (and prepaid income taxes) should be eliminated from the balance sheet.[6]

To examine the effect of eliminating deferred tax accounting, we recomputed net income and the financial statement ratios assuming deferred taxes had never been recognized. While elimination of all deferred tax amounts is probably inappropriate (i.e., some portion will likely become payable), complete elimination provides some indication of what the *maximum* effect would be.

Table I shows that, with the exception of the rate of return on shareholders' equity, the correlations between the reported and restated amounts exceed 97 per cent. The lower correlation for return on shareholders' equity can be traced to the reclassification of deferred tax liabilities as part of shareholders' equity.

Combined Effect of Adjustments

The last column of Table I shows the correlations between (1) net income and the financial statement ratios based on reported data and (2) net income and the ratios recomputed to reflect all the adjustments discussed above. In general, measures of profitability (net income, rates of return, profit margin, expense to sales ratios) show reasonably high correlations. Lower correlations emerge for short-term liquidity ratios (receivables turnover, current and quick ratios), primarily because of the effect of FIFO and the consolidation of finance subsidiaries. The consolidation of finance subsidiaries and the recognition of pension obligations result in lower correlations for measures of capital structure risk (debt to equity ratios).

Implications for Financial Statement Analysis

Wholly-owned unconsolidated finance subsidiaries should be consolidated with the parent before any financial statement analysis is performed. The potential bias in the data from not consolidating can be substantial, particularly when a significant portion of the parent's sales are funneled through the subsidiary—as occurs frequently in the automobile, farm equipment and industrial equipment manufacturing industries.

Furthermore, unfunded pension obligations should be considered in assessing risk, especially in the case of heavily unionized firms. The assumptions underlying the calculation of pension obligations should become more uniform over the next several years, however, improving the comparability of data across firms.

On the other hand, LIFO/FIFO inventory differences and accelerated/straight line depreciation differences do not affect net income and financial ratios significantly. Except in the case of some capital-intensive firms in the steel and petroleum industries, the benefits of adjusting net incomes and financial statement ratios for differences in accounting method hardly seem worth the effort.

Finally, controversies surrounding the recognition of deferred taxes appear to be of more theoretical than practical significance. The correlations between the unadjusted ratios and the ratios adjusted for deferred tax accounting exceeded 90 per cent. ■

Footnotes

1. Nicholas J. Gonedes and Nicholas Dopuch, "Capital Market Equilibrium, Information Production, and Selected Accounting Techniques: Theoretical Framework and Review of Empirical Work," *Studies on Financial Statement Objectives: 1974*, Supplement to Vol. 12 of the *Journal of Accounting Research*, pp. 48-129.
2. Shyam Sunder, "Relationships Between Accounting Changes and Stock Prices: Problems of Measurement and Some Empirical Evidence," *Empirical Research in Accounting: Selected Studies, 1973*, Supplement to Vol. 11 of the *Journal of Accounting Research*, pp. 1-45.
3. For a review of this research, see Gonedes and Dopuch, "Capital Market Equilibrium," or Robert S. Kaplan, "Information Content of Financial Accounting Numbers: A Survey of Empirical Evidence," in *Symposium on Impact of Accounting Research in Financial Accounting and Disclosure in Accounting Practice*, ed. by T. Keller and R. Abdel-khalik (Durham, NC: Duke University, 1978).
4. The potential significance of this question was raised by Lasman and Weil in an earlier article in this journal. See Daniel A. Lasman and Roman L. Weil, "Adjusting the Debt-Equity Ratio," *Financial Analysts Journal*, September/October 1978, pp. 49-58.
5. Ann M. Morrison, "Those Pension Plans Are Even Weaker Than You Think," *Fortune*, November 1977, pp. 104-114; Paul A. Gewirtz and Robert C. Phillips, "Unfunded Pension Liabilities...The New Myth," *Financial Executive*, August 1978, pp. 18-24.
6. For an interchange of various positions on deferred tax accounting, see the April 1977 issue of the *Journal of Accountancy*, pp. 53-59.

Appendix A Sample of Firms Studied and Adjustments Made for Accounting Methods

Industry and Company	FIFO	Accelerated Depreciation	Unconsolidated Subsidiary	Unfunded Prior Service Obligation	Unfunded Vested Benefits	Deferred Taxes
Food Products						
General Foods	x	x		x		x
General Mills	x	x		x	x	x
Quaker Oats	x	x		x		x
Pillsbury		x		x		x
Dairy Products						
Beatrice		x	x	x		x
Borden		x		x	x	x
Carnation	x					x
Kraft	x	x		x	x	x
Canned Foods						
Campbell	x	x				x
Heinz		x		x	x	x
Corn Milling						
CPC International	x	x		x	x	x
A.E. Staley	x	x		x	x	x
Soft Drinks						
Coca Cola	x	x				x
Pepsi		x	x	x		x
Textiles						
Burlington	x	x			x	x
J.P. Stevens		x		x		x
Lumber						
Champion	x	x		x	x	x
Weyerhaeuser	x	x	x	x	x	x
Paper Products						
International Paper	x	x	x	x	x	x
Scott Paper	x	x			x	x
Union Camp	x	x	x	x	x	x
Westvaco	x	x			x	x
Publishing						
Time	x	x		x	x	x
Times Mirror	x	x		x	x	x
Chemicals						
American Cyanamid	x	x			x	x
Dow Chemical	x	x	x		x	x
E.I. du Pont	x	x		x	x	x
W.R. Grace	x	x				x
Hercules	x	x		x	x	x
Union Carbide	x	x		x	x	x
Drugs						
Lilly		x		x	x	x
Merck				x		x
Squibb	x	x		x	x	x
Sterling Drug	x	x		x	x	x
Soaps						
Colgate	x	x		x		x
Procter & Gamble	x	x				x
Perfumes & Cosmetics						
Bristol-Myers	x	x		x	x	x
Agricultural Chemicals						
International Minerals & Chemicals		x		x	x	x
Williams Companies		x				x
Petroleum						
Amerada Hess		x		x		x
American Petrofina	x	x		x		x
Ashland	x	x		x		x
Arco	x	x		x	x	x
Cities Service	x	x		x		x
Gulf	x	x		x	x	x

Appendix A Continued

Industry and Company	FIFO	Accelerated Depreciation	Unconsolidated Subsidiary	Unfunded Prior Service Obligation	Unfunded Vested Benefits	Deferred Taxes
Kerr McGee	x	x		x		x
Pennzoil	x	x				x
Phillips	x	x		x		x
Standard Oil (Calif.)	x	x		x		x
Sun	x	x		x	x	x
Tesoro	x	x		x		x
Texaco	x	x				x
Union	x	x				x
Rubber						
Firestone	x	x		x	x	x
Goodyear	x	x	x	x	x	x
Footwear						
Genesco			x	x	x.	x
Interco	x	x		x	x'	x
Flat Glass						
Corning	x	x		x	x	x
Libbey-Owens-Ford	x	x		x	x	x
Containers						
American Can	x	x		x	x	x
Continental Group	x	x	x	x	x	x
Steel						
Armco Steel	x	x	x	x	x	x
Bethlehem Steel	x	x		x	x	x
Inland Steel	x	x		x	x	x
U.S. Steel	x	x		x	x	x
Metals						
Phelps Dodge	x	x		x	x	x
Reynolds Metals	x	x		x	x	x
Metal Products						
Gillette	x	x		x	x	x
Farm Machinery						
Allis Chalmers		x	x	x	x	x
Deere	x	x	x	x	x	x
Office Machines						
Control Data	x	x	x	x		x
Digital Equipment						x
Hewlett Packard				x		x
IBM	x			x	x	x
3M	x	x		x		x
Xerox	x	x				x
Electrical Machinery						
General Electric	x	x	x	x	x	x
Westinghouse	x	x	x	x	x	x
Household Appliances						
Sunbeam		x		x		x
Whirlpool	x	x	x	x	x	x
Radio, Television Transmission						
Motorola		x				x
Raytheon				x	x	x
Motor Vehicles						
American Motors			x	x	x	x
Chrysler			x	x	x	x
Ford	x	x	x	x	x	x
General Motors	x		x	x	x	x
Missiles & Space						
Grumman	x	x			x	x
Martin Marietta	x	x		x	x	x

307

Appendix A Concluded

Industry and Company	FIFO	Accelerated Depreciation	Unconsolidated Subsidiary	Unfunded Prior Service Obligation	Unfunded Vested Benefits	Deferred Taxes
Sports Goods						
AMF	x	x		x		x
Brunswick	x			x		x
Radio, Television Broadcasting						
ABC		x		x	x	x
CBS						x
Conglomerates						
Gulf & Western	x		x	x	x	x
Litton					x	x
Teledyne	x		x	x	x	x
Textron	x		x	x		x
TOTAL	73	80	23	76	60	96

Appendix B Summary of Financial Statement Ratios

Ratio	Numerator	Denominator
Rate of Return on Assets	Net Income + Interest Expense (net of tax effects)	Average Total Assets During the Period
Profit Margin Ratio (before interest effects)	Net Income + Interest Expense (net of tax effects)	Sales
Total Assets Turnover Ratio	Sales	Average Total Assets During the Period
Various Expense Ratios	Various Expenses	Sales
Accounts Receivable Turnover Ratio	Net Sales	Average Accounts Receivable During the Period
Inventory Turnover Ratio	Cost of Goods Sold	Average Inventory During the Period
Fixed Asset Turnover Ratio	Sales	Average Plant Assets During the Period
Rate of Return on Common Stock Equity	Net Income—Preferred Stock Dividends	Average Common Shareholders' Equity During the Period
Current Ratio	Current Assets	Current Liabilities
Quick or Acid-Test Ratio	Cash, Marketable Securities and Receivables	Current Liabilities
Long-Term Debt Ratio	Total Noncurrent Liabilities	Total Equities (liabilities plus shareholders' equity)
Debt-Equity Ratio	Total Liabilities	Total Equities (liabilities plus shareholders' equity)
Times Interest Charges Earned	Net Income Before Interest and Income Taxes	Interest Expense

Appendix C Journal Entries to Adjust Financial Statements for Differences in Accounting Methods

I. FIFO Cost Flow Assumption

1. Inventory (Excess of FIFO Over LIFO at Beginning of Period) x
   Assets (0.48 of Excess of FIFO Over LIFO at Beginning of Period) x
   Retained Earnings (0.52 of Excess of FIFO Over LIFO at Beginning of Period) x
   To restate beginning inventory to a FIFO basis.
2. Inventory (Increase in Excess of FIFO Over LIFO During Period) x
   Cost of Goods Sold x
   To restate cost of goods sold to a FIFO basis.
   Income Tax Expense (0.48 of Change in Cost of Goods Sold) x
   Assets x
   To recognize the change in income tax expense from using FIFO.

II. Accelerated Depreciation

1. Deferred Income Taxes (0.48 of Cumulative Difference in Depreciation) x
   Retained Earnings (0.52 of Cumulative Difference in Depreciation) x
   Property, Plant and Equipment (Cumulative Difference in Depreciation) x
   To restate property, plant and equipment to accelerated depreciation at the beginning of the period.

   The cumulative difference in depreciation is equal to the deferred tax provision relating to depreciation for the preceding four years divided by 0.48

2. Depreciation Expense (Deferred Tax Provision for Current Year Relating to Depreciation Divided by 0.48) x
   Property, Plant and Equipment x
   To restate depreciation expense to an accelerated basis.
3. Deferred Income Taxes (Deferred Tax Provision for Current Year Relating to Depreciation) x
   Income Tax Expense x
   To eliminate deferred taxes for current year relating to depreciation.

III. Consolidated Subsidiary

1. Cash x
   Accounts Receivable x
   Inventory x
   Other Current Assets x
   Property, Plant and Equipment x
   Notes Payable x
   Accounts Payable x
   Other Current Liabilities x
   Long-Term Debt x
   Deferred Income Taxes x
   Other Long-Term Debt x
   Investment in Unconsolidated Subsidiary x
   To eliminate investment account and recognize individual assets and liabilities of subsidiary.
2. Interest Expense x
   Selling & Administrative Expenses x
   Income Tax Expense x
   Other Expenses x
   Equity in Earnings of Subsidiary x
   Interest Revenue x
   To eliminate equity in earnings of subsidiary and recognize individual revenues and expenses.

IV. Unfunded Prior Service Obligation

1. Deferred Income Taxes (0.48 of Unfunded Prior Service Obligation) x
   Retained Earnings (0.52 of Unfunded Prior Service Obligation) x
   Pension Liability x
   To recognize unfunded prior service obligation.

V. Unfunded Vested Benefits

1. Deferred Income Taxes (0.48 of Unfunded Vested Benefits) x
   Retained Earnings (0.52 of Unfunded Vested Benefits) x
   Pension Liability x
   To recognize unfunded vested benefits.

VI. Deferred Income Taxes

1. Deferred Income Taxes (Both Current and Noncurrent Liabilities) x
   Deferred Income Taxes (Both Current and Noncurrent Assets) x
   Retained Earnings x
   To eliminate deferred taxes at the beginning of the period.
2. Deferred Income Taxes x
   Income Tax Expense x
   To eliminate deferred tax provision for the current period. Debit and credit accounts may be reversed in some cases.

by William H. Beaver and Stephen G. Ryan

How Well Do Statement No. 33 Earnings Explain Stock Returns?

Inflation-adjusted accounting data mandated by the Financial Accounting Standards Board's Statement No. 33 have the potential to provide valuable information on inflation's impact on income and stock returns. In particular, these data can reflect the effects of inflation on certain assets, such as inventory, property, plant and equipment, that are not treated explicitly by historical cost measures.

Do Statement No. 33 data provide information that historical cost earnings do not? The authors calculated cross-sectional correlations between actual stock returns and seven earnings variables—historical cost earnings plus six Statement No. 33 income measures. The results indicate that historical cost earnings dominate the other earnings measures.

In particular, knowledge of Statement No. 33 data does not significantly increase the ability of historical cost earnings to explain stock returns. In contrast, historical cost earnings do add to the explanatory power provided by the FASB's data.

PREVIOUS RESEARCH has indicated that replacement cost earnings derived from disclosures mandated by the Securities and Exchange Commission's Accounting Series Release No. 190 (ASR 190) do not have explanatory power for stock market returns beyond that provided by historical cost earnings.[1] Since 1979, the Financial Acounting Standards Board's Statement No. 33 has required disclosure of the effects of changing prices in annual reports. But there is little evidence that analysts use such data.[2] This study concentrates on the ability of various earnings measures derived from FASB Statement No. 33 data to explain stock returns for the years 1979 through 1982.[3]

The Theory
According to the FASB, the purpose of financial reporting in general, and income measurement in particular, is to provide investors with information on the magnitude, timing and uncertainty of prospective cash flows.[4] Thus earnings information can affect analysts' and investors' judgments, which in turn can affect stock prices. At any point in time, stock prices reflect the collective, or consensus, judgment of analysts and others as to the future earning power of a stock. Changes in stock price (i.e., returns) reflect changes in investors' expectations regarding future earning power.

Two conditions must be met if earnings are to convey information. First, reported earnings must differ from expected earnings. Second, the unexpected portion of earnings must be capable of changing expectations about future earning power. Prior research has demonstrated that unexpected changes in historical cost earnings explain a significant portion of changes in stock prices. This finding, one of the most robust empirical results observed in security price research, is consistent with the perception that earnings provide information about prospective cash flows and future earning power.

It has been asserted that various forms of earnings adjusted for inflation (and for changes in prices of specific assets) provide information on operating performance beyond that provided by historical cost earnings.[5] In particular, historical cost earnings do not reflect the effects

---

1. Footnotes appear at end of article.

William Beaver is Joan E. Horngren Professor of Accounting at the Graduate School of Business, Stanford University, and a member of the Editorial Board of this journal. Stephen Ryan is a doctoral student at the Graduate School of Business, Stanford University.

of inflation upon certain assets such as inventory, property, plant and equipment.

The merits of Statement No. 33 data rest upon two major considerations. The potential value of such data lies in their ability to provide information about the effects of inflation upon the prospective cash flows, hence the value of firms' securities. But measurement errors can creep into the data and impair their potential informational content. Which effect dominates? The answer depends upon the magnitude of unanticipated inflation relative to the magnitude of the measurement errors. We conducted an empirical analysis to provide evidence on this issue.

The Data

From the 1,137 nonfinancial firms recorded on the FASB's Statement No. 33 research tape, we chose those firms with December 31 fiscal year-ends and with the components necessary to compute all seven of the earnings variables (to be described below) in a given year.[6]

For each firm, stock return was calculated as the annual cash dividend plus capital gains or losses divided by price at the end of the previous year. Seven variables were used to explain stock returns—historical cost earnings (HC) plus six earnings measures based on Statement No. 33 (PRE, PREP, CD, CDP, POST, POSTP).[7]

PRE represents percentage change in per share *income from continuing operations under current cost*; adjustments are made here for the current cost of depreciation and cost of goods sold. CD is the percentage change in per share *income from continuing operations under constant dollar*, with adjustments made to depreciation and the cost of goods sold to reflect changes in the general price level since the date of acquisition of the assets.

PREP and CDP represent *adjustments for purchasing power gain (or loss)*. Purchasing power gain or loss is added to income from continuing operations under both current cost (PREP) and constant dollar (CDP), and the new earnings number expressed in terms of percentage change in a per share figure.

POST is a current cost *adjustment for holding gains*. Income from continuing operations under current cost does not include the holding gain or loss due to the change in current costs of assets during the year. A more comprehensive measure of income would include such gains. The *gross* holding gain (before reflecting the effects of changes in the general price index) is added to income from continuing operations under current cost, and the resulting number is divided by net assets (essentially stockholders' equity) under current cost to obtain the variable POST.

Income from continuing operations *after* the purchasing power gain and loss adjustment is also further adjusted by adding the *net* holding gain (after reflecting the effects of the change in the general price index). The resulting number is then divided by net assets under current cost to obtain the variable POSTP.

Historical cost earnings available for common shareholders before extraordinary items are expressed in percentage change in the per share figure, for the variable HC.

As noted, the merits of Statement No. 33 data rest on a tradeoff between the magnitude of unanticipated inflation and measurement errors in the data. Each earnings measure represents an imperfect alternative. The issue is not which earnings measure possesses the greatest information content. Rather, the issue is whether Statement No. 33 earnings variables provide information that historical cost earnings do not.

The Results

We initially conducted cross-sectional correlations between stock returns and each of the income measures. Table I reports the correlation coefficients, which indicate the extent to which differences in stock return across firms in a given year can be explained by each of the earnings variables. HC has a higher correlation than any of the six Statement No. 33 variables across all four years. The only exception is the behavior of PRE in 1981, which has the same correlation with stock returns as HC does. PRE is unable to sustain this performance in the other years.[8] The explanatory power of historical cost is remarkable in that it had to compete against six challengers and might be expected to lose occasionally simply by chance.

These simple correlations suggest that historical cost income has greater explanatory power with respect to stock returns than any of its rivals. However, this perspective treats the other earnings variables as competitors and does not address the question of gains from using more than one earnings measure. Once we have knowledge of HC, do we gain further explanatory power by also knowing the Statement No. 33 variables?

To answer this question, we compared the proportions of variance explained (R-squared)

Table I Correlation Between Annual Security Returns and Various Earnings Measures, 1979–1982[a]

	1979	1980	1981	1982
Percentage Change In Historical Cost Earnings (HC)	0.48	0.47	0.30	0.46
Percentage Change In IFCO: Current Cost (PRE)[b]	NA[c]	0.32	0.30	0.35
Percentage Change In IFCO: Current Cost Plus Purchasing Power Gains (PREP)	NA	0.33	0.24	0.39
Percentage Change In IFCO: Constant Dollar (CD)	NA	0.33	0.20	0.39
Percentage Change In IFCO: Constant Dollar Plus Purchasing Power Gains (CDP)	NA	0.35	0.19	0.36
IFCO: Current Cost Plus *Gross* Holding Gains Divided by Net Assets: Current Cost (POST)	−0.04	0.29	0.02	0.12
IFCO: Current Cost Plus *Net* Holding Gains Plus Purchasing Power Gains Divided by Net Assets: Current Cost (POSTP)	0.46	0.35	0.03	0.18
Number of Observations	368	301	298	260

[a] The correlation coefficients are Pearson (product moment) correlations. The correlation coefficient is significant at the 5 per cent level if it is larger than 0.11 in absolute value.
[b] IFCO denotes income from continuing operations.
[c] NA = not available, because percentage change variables require previous year's data. Statement No. 33 data start in 1979.

under two regressions. The first regression used only HC earnings to explain cross-sectional differences in returns. The second regression included both HC earnings and one additional Statement No. 33 earnings variable. We tested to determine if the increase in R-squared was significant.[9]

Table II compares the R-squared attained by using HC only with the R-squared attained by adding each of the Statement No. 33 variables.

Table II Contribution To Proportion of Variance Explained (R^2) Attained by Adding Statement No. 33 Variable, 1979–1982

Variable in Addition to HC	Proportion of Variance Explained After Adding Variable			
	1979	1980	1981	1982
PRE	NA	0.22	0.10	0.21
PREP	NA	0.22	0.09	0.21
CD	NA	0.22	0.09	0.21
CDP	NA	0.22	0.09	0.21
POST	0.24	0.24*	0.09	0.22
POSTP	0.31*	0.25*	0.09	0.22
HC only[†]	0.23	0.22	0.09	0.21

* Increase in R^2 relative to the R^2 of the HC-only regression is significant at the 5 per cent level.
[†] The R^2 refers to the proportion of variance explained by a regression which includes only HC.

For the years 1979 through 1982, HC has R-squares of 23, 22, 9 and 21 per cent. Adding POSTP increases these by 8, 3, zero and 1 per cent, respectively.

No one Statement No. 33 variable is able to add significant explanatory power on a consistent basis.[10] PRE, PREP, CD and CDP do not provide significant additional explanatory power in any of the four years. POST provides a significant addition in only one year. POSTP is significant in the first two years, but insignificant in the two most recent years. Although not reported here, the signs of the regression coefficients on the Statement No. 33 variables also fluctuate over time.[11]

We also performed a multiple regression analysis, where all the variables were included in a single equation. The results were similar to those reported in Table II. There was essentially no increase in the proportion of variance explained beyond the results reported in Table II, largely because the Statement No. 33 variables are correlated with one another and little is added by including all six instead of just one.

We also addressed the question of the incremental explanatory power of HC over and above that provided by the Statement No. 33 variables. The results reported in Table II may arise because the HC and the Statement No. 33

Table III Contribution To Proportion of Variance Explained (R^2) Attained by Adding the Historical Cost Variable, 1979–1982*

	1979 No. 33 Variable	1979 Both Variables	1980 No. 33 Variable	1980 Both Variables	1981 No. 33 Variable	1981 Both Variables	1982 No. 33 Variable	1982 Both Variables
PRE	NA	NA	0.10	0.22	0.09	0.10	0.12	0.21
PREP	NA	NA	0.11	0.22	0.06	0.09	0.15	0.21
CD	NA	NA	0.11	0.22	0.04	0.09	0.15	0.21
CDP	NA	NA	0.12	0.22	0.04	0.09	0.13	0.21
POST	0.0016	0.24	0.08	0.24	0.0004	0.09	0.01	0.22
POSTP	0.21	0.31	0.12	0.25	0.0004	0.09	0.03	0.22

* The increase in R^2 relative to using the Statement No. 33 variable only is significant at the 5 per cent level in all cases, except for PRE in 1981. Here, the level of significance is 0.053.

variables are so highly correlated with each other that nothing is gained by adding a second variable.

From one perspective, knowing the incremental explanatory power of HC may seem of little importance, since HC is already provided in the primary financial statements and Statement No. 33 data are merely intended to be supplemental. From a purely statistical point of view, however, if HC provides no additional explanatory power beyond that provided by the other variables we might be indifferent as to which were used. More importantly, examining the incremental explanatory power of HC earnings may provide insights about the extent to which the results reported in Table II are merely due to high correlation between HC and each of the Statement No. 33 earnings variables. If the results *are* due to high correlation, then HC earnings would not be expected to provide incremental explanatory power beyond that already provided by the Statement No. 33 variables.

We compared the R-squared of one Statement No. 33 variable with the R-squared obtained when that variable was used in conjunction with HC. Table III reports the results. For 1979 through 1982, POSTP has R-squares of 21, 12, 0.04 and 3 per cent; adding HC increases these R-squares by 10, 13, 9 and 19 per cent, respectively.

Whatever the Statement No. 33 variable used, adding HC earnings significantly increased the R-squared in all four years, with only one exception. In 1981 the increase in R-squared with respect to PRE was significant at the 5.3 per cent level (i.e., it "just misses" the conventional 5 per cent). HC earnings data do provide significant incremental explanatory power beyond that provided by Statement No. 33 earnings.

Moreover, the regression coefficients on HC (not reported here) are positive without exception.

These results and those reported in Table II indicate that it is not a matter of indifference which set of data is used to explain stock returns. HC data "dominate" Statement No. 33 data in this context. The explanatory power of historical cost earnings is significant, whether or not Statement No. 33 variables are included in the regression. By contrast, none of the Statement No. 33 variables is able to explain stock returns beyond historical cost earnings.

The combined results suggest that high correlation between Statement No. 33 variables and HC is not the sole reason for the poor performance of the FASB variables. To be sure, there is correlation. Despite it, however, HC demonstrated significant incremental explanatory power; the FASB data did not. Furthermore, in contrast to the Statement No. 33 variables, the HC data demonstrated stability in the sign of the regression coefficient over time. Differences in the quality of the data may be another explanation for the differences in incremental explanatory power.

Implications

Statement No. 33 variables provide no incremental information beyond that already provided by historical cost earnings, when explanatory power is defined in terms of the ability to explain cross-sectional stock returns.

Negative results are usually difficult to interpret. Is there really no incremental explanatory power or have we failed to detect it because of some flaw in our research design? Previous research using a variety of other analyses has found no effect.[12] Moreover, our finding is consistent with earlier research on ASR 190 data and analyst nonusage of Statement No. 33 data.

It is important to state what these results do *not* imply, however. They do not imply that it is unimportant to make adjustments for inflation in an analysis of security prices. They do *not* imply that analysts are not making adjustments for inflation in their analysis. They do imply that, if the adjustments are being made, either Statement No. 33 data are not capturing that adjustment process very well or the magnitude of the adjustment is small.

While it was possible that the results could have differed for 1982 relative to earlier years, they do not. Either the magnitude of unanticipated inflation is still too small to be material, even in 1982, or the magnitude of the measurement errors in the Statement 33 data is large enough to overwhelm the potential informational value.

What does the future hold for the Statement No. 33 disclosures? The FASB has voted to extend changing prices disclosures beyond 1984. Will the data perform better in the future? The answer depends upon the magnitude of future unexpected inflation and upon improvements in the quality of the data. ∎

Footnotes

1. See, for example, William H. Beaver, Paul A. Griffin and Wayne R. Landsman, "How Well Does Replacement Cost Income Explain Stock Return?" *Financial Analysts Journal*, March/April 1983, pp. 26-39.
2. See Robert W. Berliner, "Do Analysts Use Inflation-Adjusted Information? Results of a Survey," *Financial Analysts Journal*, March/April 1983, pp. 65-72, and William C. Norby, "Applications of Inflation-Adjusted Accounting Data," *Financial Analysts Journal*, March/April 1983, pp. 33-39.
3. Our study differs from earlier work reported in this journal in three respects. First, it focuses on Statement No. 33 data rather than ASR 190 data. Statement No. 33's reliance on current costs rather than replacement costs could result in improvements in the quality of the disclosures relative to ASR 190 data. This is because current cost differs from replacement cost in that it reflects adjustments for the value of operating advantages of replacement assets (e.g., anticipated cost savings from newer technology). (See, for example, Financial Accounting Standards Board, "Invitation to Comment: Supplementary Disclosures about the Effects of Changing Pricing," December 27, 1983, pp. 11-12.) Second, it examines more recent years than those covered by the ASR 190 data. Third, it includes additional earnings variables derived from the more comprehensive Statement No. 33 disclosures.

   The study extends an earlier investigation of Statement No. 33 data based on the years 1979 through 1981 (see William H. Beaver and Wayne R. Landsman, "Incremental Information Content of Statement 33 Disclosures: Research Report" (Stamford, Conn.: Financial Accounting Standards Board, November 1983)). The inclusion of 1982 is of particular importance for two reasons. First, our experience with Statement No. 33 data is brief, and an additional year's data can be informative. Second, 1982 differed markedly from earlier years. Stock prices rose dramatically in late 1982, both short and long-term interest rates declined substantially, and the magnitude of unanticipated inflation (negative, in this case) was larger than it was in the 1979-81 period.
4. For further discussion see *Concepts Statement No. 1: Objectives of Financial Reporting by Business Enterprises* (Stamford, Conn.: Financial Accounting Standards Board, November 1983).
5. Statement No. 33 provides for disclosures related to inflation and to changes in prices of specific assets. For brevity, the article will merely refer to inflation, but it is intended to apply to changes in prices of specific assets as well.
6. Observations were also deleted if earnings in that year were negative or if the percentage change in earnings was extremely large (i.e., greater than 300 per cent in absolute value).
7. The reason for the variable names, further rationale for each of the variables, and a precise definition of the variables are discussed in William H. Beaver and Wayne R. Landsman, "Incremental Information Content of Statement 33 Disclosures: Research Report," *op. cit.*, pp. 48-52.
8. Further analysis indicated that PRE failed to perform as well as HC in 1981 on a larger set of data (common to both PRE and HC only) and on a smaller set of nonutility firms. For further discussion, see William H. Beaver and Wayne R. Landsman, "Incremental Information Content of Statement 33 Disclosures: Research Report," *op. cit.*, p. 59.
9. The test is an F test on the reduction in sum of the squared residuals as a result of using two instead of one earnings variable. This approach is not the econometrically unique way to test for incremental explanatory power. For further discussion see William H. Beaver and Wayne R. Landsman, "Incremental Information Content of Statement 33 Disclosures: Research Report," *op. cit.*, p. 57; William H. Beaver, Paul A. Griffin and Wayne R. Landsman, "Testing for Incremental Information Content in the Presence of Collinearity: A Comment," *Journal of Accounting and Economics*, December 1984, pp. 219-223; and A. Christie, M. Kennelly, J. King and T. Schaeffer, "Testing for

Incremental Information Content in the Presence of Collinearity," *Journal of Accounting and Economics*, December 1984, pp. 205–217.

10. The F test assumes normality and independence of the regression residuals. Empirical evidence indicates that positive correlation in the residuals may be present (e.g., due to industry effects). If so, the tests of significance are biased against accepting the null hypothesis of no incremental explanatory power. For convenience, levels of significance rather than F ratios are reported, and the conventional 5 per cent significance level has been used here. The results reported for 1979 through 1981 are essentially the same as those reported in William H. Beaver and Wayne R. Landsman, "Incremental Information Content of Statement 33 Disclosures: Research Report." The only exception is for POSTP in 1979 and 1980. Qualitatively, the conclusions regarding the performance of POSTP are the same, but we cannot literally replicate the results for 1979 and 1980 using the latest version of the Statement No. 33 research tape. After further investigation, we are convinced that the results reported here for POSTP are the correct ones. We are indebted to Professor James McKeown of the University of Illinois for alerting us to this difference.

11. The statement regarding the stability of the signs has to be tempered somewhat because each of the Statement No. 33 variables is correlated with the HC variable. However, as we shall see, the sign of the HC variable is consistent over time, even in the presence of the correlation.

12. The variations include examining a larger set of observations, which requires that the data be available only for the one Statement No. 33 variable currently being examined, instead of requiring that they be available for all of the variables. Another extension was to repeat the regression analysis on a smaller set of firms, which excluded the utility firms. Under both analyses, the results are essentially the same as those reported here. Further discussion appears in William H. Beaver and Wayne R. Landsman, "Incremental Information Content of Statement 33 Disclosures: Research Report," *op. cit.*

The market valuation implications of net periodic pension cost components*

Mary E. Barth
Harvard University, Boston, MA 02163, USA

William H. Beaver
Stanford University, Stanford, CA 94305-5015, USA

Wayne R. Landsman
University of North Carolina, Chapel Hill, NC 27599-3490, USA

Received August 1990, final version received November 1991

This paper examines whether market participants implicitly assign different coefficients to pension cost components when determining security prices. The major findings are: (1) The pension cost components' coefficients generally differ from one another. As predicted, the transition asset amortization coefficient is lower than other pension coefficients, and is insignificantly different from zero. (2) Consistent with the market viewing pension-related income streams as less risky, the pension coefficients are generally larger than the nonpension coefficients. Additional specification tests permitting nonpension coefficients to vary with risk, taxpayer status, and industry membership, generally support the basic findings, although the significance levels are generally higher.

1. Introduction

Statement of Financial Accounting Standards No. 87 (SFAS 87), *Employers' Accounting for Pensions*, requires separate disclosure of the major components of pension cost because of their diverse nature. These disclosure

---

*We acknowledge the assistance of the Business Information Analysts at Harvard Business School, especially Philip Hamilton, and thank Mike Constas for assistance in data collection. Our paper also benefited from comments provided by accounting workshop participants at Harvard Business School, the University of Michigan, New York University, the University of North Carolina, Stanford University, and Southern Methodist University, and by Jerry Zimmerman (the editor) and Doug Skinner (the referee). The first author also acknowledges funding from the Division of Research, Harvard Business School.

0165-4101/92/$05.00 © 1992—Elsevier Science Publishers B.V. All rights reserved

requirements imply that the FASB believes that such disclosure is incrementally informative to financial statement users. Our research investigates whether this contention is supported empirically. The primary purpose of our study is to determine whether market participants implicitly assign different multiples to the components of pension cost when assessing the market value of common equity. We expect this to be the case because of potential differences in the information each component contains regarding the firm's permanent earnings potential. A primitive assumption in the determination of net income is that each revenue and expense component is given equal weight. Prior security-price research has largely accepted this convention when examining the price–earnings relation.

To examine whether different multiples are applied to different components of pension cost in the determination of security prices, the market value of common equity is expressed as a linear function of various nonpension- and pension-related components of net income. To estimate this relation empirically, market value of common equity is regressed on the various components of net income. The regressions are estimated cross-sectionally on a year-by-year basis. Statistical tests are conducted to determine: (1) whether the regression coefficients for the pension coefficients are significantly different from one another, and (2) whether the pension component coefficients are significantly different from the nonpension-related coefficients. Arguments are offered below with respect to each of these hypotheses.

We find: (1) The coefficients on the pension cost components generally differ from each other, as predicted based on the information each contains regarding the firms' permanent earnings potential. In particular, the coefficient on the one component with no permanent earnings implications, the amortization of the transition asset, is not significantly different from zero. The evidence is consistent with market participants using other available data to decompose pension cost components even further than explicitly disclosed in the financial statements. (2) Consistent with predictions based on the relative riskiness of earnings streams generated by the respective underlying assets, the pension-related components generally have larger coefficients than nonpension components of income. However, firms which adopted SFAS 87 before they were required to do so generally have insignificant pension cost component coefficients. Our findings are generally robust to specifications which consider risk, taxpayer status, and industry membership. The motivation for considering these alternative specifications is explained below.

This study extends prior research which examines whether different multiples are applied to different components of income. Lipe (1986) estimates coefficients for broad revenue and expense categories. More recently, Barth, Beaver, and Wolfson (1990) determine that in valuing banks' common equity, market participants implicitly assign different multiples to the earnings before security gains and losses component and the securities gains and losses component of bank income. A major feature common to this research and our primary estimating equation is the assumption that the coefficient on a given component is a cross-sectional constant. Prior research suggests that the coefficient on aggregate earnings varies cross-sectionally as a function of risk, growth, and persistence [Collins and Kothari (1989) and Easton and Zmijewski (1989), among others]. A major theme of this study is that persistence varies across pension cost components, predictably leading to different coefficients for each component. By permitting each component to have its own coefficient, we effectively allow the earnings coefficient to vary cross-sectionally as a function of the pension and nonpension asset mix. We also examine specifications which permit the earnings coefficient to vary with proxies for risk and growth.

Prior pension research has also been concerned with the effect of factors that influence firms' use of pensions (versus wages) and pension funding levels. Our primary concern is the extent to which these factors (to be described below) affect the inferences we draw with respect to the pension cost component coefficients. Ippolito (1985) offers evidence that firms' owners choose deferred compensation and pension funding levels to 'bond' employees to the long-run interests of the firm. Although the Ippolito study is based on pre-ERISA (Employee Retirement Income Security Acts of 1974) data, and Ippolito contends that the bonding effect offered by pensions was dissipated by the provisions of ERISA, the general issue of incentive-based reasons for pension-related behavior remains. Scholes and Wolfson (1991) offer a general treatment of the tradeoff between incentive-based and tax-based motivations affecting corporate financial decisions, such as pension funding. Although their primary concern is with tax motivations, they provide some illustrations where the incentive-based motivations reinforce the tax-based ones, and others where they conflict. This makes identification of the primary motivation difficult. Viewed as an identification problem, the pension variables are endogenous from the perspective of the firm's portfolio of financial decisions.

Thomas (1988) controls for incentive-based factors in studying corporate taxes as an explanation for differences in pension funding levels over time and across firms. Thomas discusses the difficulty associated with distinguishing tax-based incentives from those associated with maximizing the value of the pension put with the Pension Benefit Guarantee Corporation. As Thomas notes, tax loss and financial difficulty (a condition under which maximizing the value of the pension put is likely to lead to pension underfunding) are likely to be highly correlated. Moreover, prior research has been unsuccessful in disentangling these two effects, and as a result, his study is unable to provide a separate control for the put option effect. This is important in Thomas' study because he is primarily interested in assessing the incremental importance of tax factors. In this study, both tax and nontax factors may impact the inferences drawn from our reported results. However, having one variable that is a good proxy for either or both effects is adequate for our purposes because estimating their separate effects is not of interest here.

The tax and nontax factors influencing funding levels impact our study to the extent they are proxies for factors that affect the coefficient applied to earnings or one of its components. As Thomas notes, tax status could be a proxy for both future profitability (growth) and financial difficulty (risk). Industry membership could be a proxy for both factors. Following Thomas, this study uses a dichotomous variable to denote taxpayer status and includes industry membership as a separate variable to control for nontax effects. A direct measure of risk, systematic risk, is also separately examined. Ultimately, of course, we can never be sure that we have included all of the potential omitted variables or that the reported results are not attributable to some unidentified correlated omitted variable. However, given the factors identified in prior research, risk, taxpayer status, and industry membership are the most likely factors to impact our results. The task of identifying and empirically examining other potential candidates is left for future research.

The remainder of the paper is organized as follows. Section 2 discusses the research design issues. The empirical results for both the primary estimation equations and alternative specifications are reported in section 3. Section 4 consists of the summary and concluding remarks.

2. Research design issues

There are two primary categories of research design issues: (1) the theoretical relation between market value of equity and income, including the pension cost components, and (2) the institutional setting in which such data are disclosed. Each is discussed below.

2.1. Theoretical relation

One model of the relation between the market value of a firm's common equity and net income is given by

$$MVE = \beta NI, \tag{0}$$

where MVE is market value of equity, $\beta = 1/r$, r is a discount rate, and NI is net income.[1] In a setting such as perfect and complete markets [see, e.g., Beaver and Demski (1979)], net income is well-defined as the firm's perma-

---

[1]Ohlson (1989) has developed an alternative valuation model in terms of a 'clean surplus' theory. The primary focus in Ohlson is on linking the income statement and balance sheet via a 'retained earnings' account. His modelling assumptions are more restrictive than those used here.

nent earnings and r is the cost of capital [Miller and Modigliani (1958)].[2] Typically, earnings valuation formulations do not decompose earnings into its components and thus implicitly assume the same coefficient is applied to all earnings components. Indeed, absent measurement and estimation issues, there is little motivation to decompose earnings.

Even in this simple setting, there are reasons to expect that different multiples apply to different earnings components. For example, the mix of assets with respect to risk likely varies across firms. Hence, the multiple applied to earnings varies cross-sectionally. Bodie et al. (1985) and Landsman, Miller, and Yeh (1990) find that a significant portion of pension fund assets are invested in fixed-income instruments, which exhibit lower systematic risk than other securities. Thus, pension assets are likely to be systematically less risky than nonpension assets. By permitting each component to have its own coefficient, we allow earnings multiples to vary cross-sectionally as a function of the pension and nonpension asset mix. In addition, if the relative proportion of transitory elements differ among *accounting* net income components, then the empirical coefficients will also differ among the components.

Although earnings could be partitioned in a variety of ways, our primary interest is pension cost and its components, which leads to the following decomposition:[3]

$$MVE = \beta_0 + \beta_1 NI + \varepsilon, \tag{1}$$

$$MVE = \beta_0 + \beta_1 REVENUES + \beta_2 NPENX + \beta_3 PENX + \varepsilon, \tag{2}$$

$$MVE = \beta_0 + \beta_1 REVENUES + \beta_2 NPENX + \sum_{k=3}^{7} \beta_k PEN_k + \varepsilon, \tag{3}$$

where *REVENUES* is nonpension revenues, *NPENX* is nonpension expenses, and *PENX* is pension expense.[4] The PEN_ks are the five components

---

[2] In richer settings, such as those in which the perfect and complete markets assumptions are relaxed, the relation would reflect other factors such as growth, investors' marginal rate of time preference, and a risk premium.

[3] For ease of exposition, the notation for coefficients and disturbance terms is the same across specifications. In actuality, they probably differ.

[4] The SFAS 87 disclosures report the components of pension cost, yet the modelling contains the amount of pension expense. Analogous to depreciation cost versus depreciation expense, the two will differ by the net amount of pension cost that is not expensed, but instead is reflected as, e.g., a cost layer in inventories of manufactured goods. The difference is likely to be related to changes in inventory levels. Under steady state conditions (i.e., zero growth and a constant pension cost) – which are likely to be violated particularly in the year of adoption of SFAS 87 – pension cost will equal pension expense. Because the difference is not disclosed and because the difference is likely to be 'small' barring massive changes in inventory levels, we assume that pension cost equals pension expense. To the extent this assumption is incorrect, measurement error is introduced.

of pension expense described in section 2.2. The eq. (0) and (1) models imply that β_1 through β_7 in eq. (3) are the same. A primary focus of our study is to determine if β_k differs by component. Also of interest are differences between β_1 and β_2 and the β_ks. The motivation for introducing β_0 and ε will be discussed later. Estimation of coefficients based on the eq. (0) through (3) models ignores the potential impact of endogenous determinants of pension funding levels (e.g., cross-sectional differences in risk, taxpayer status, and industry membership). Alternative specifications which include these factors are considered in section 3.3.

2.2. The institutional setting

SFAS 87 comprises generally accepted accounting principles with respect to employers' reporting of pension obligations. The effects of a firm's pension obligation and its pension assets are primarily reflected in the income statement via net periodic pension cost. SFAS 87 requires only four components of pension cost to be reported separately: service cost (SVC), interest cost (INT), actual return on plan assets ($RPLNA$), and a component that reflects the net deferral and amortization of the effects of a variety of transactions that have occurred in the past ($TAMOR$). We decompose $TAMOR$ into its two principal components, the deferred return on plan assets ($DEFRET$) and the amortization of the transition asset ($ATRANS$), to yield a total of five components.[5] The FASB defines service cost as the addition to the pension obligation attributable to services rendered by employees during the period. Interest cost represents the increase in the pension obligation related to the passage of time. Actual return on plan assets, $RPLNA$, is the difference between the fair value of plan assets at the end and the beginning of the period, adjusted for contributions and payments of benefits during the period. The sum of $RPLNA$ and $DEFRET$ is the expected return on plan assets, $EXPRET$. This critical relation is exploited in the research design.

Although reporting the components of $TAMOR$ is not required, in the years immediately after adoption of SFAS 87 $TAMOR$ consisted almost exclusively of two components, $DEFRET$ and $ATRANS$. $DEFRET$, the unexpected portion of the actual return on plan assets, is deferred for later recognition. $ATRANS$ is the amortization of the unrecognized net obligation or asset existing at the date of initial application of SFAS 87 (i.e., amortization of the 'transition' asset/obligation). Using an excerpt from FMC Corporation's pension footnote, appendix B shows how the pension variables used in this study relate to one another. Appendix C describes how we estimate

[5]A glossary of all variables used in this study is provided in appendix A.

$\overline{DEFRET}$ and $\overline{ATRANS}$ ($\overline{DEFRET}$ and $\overline{ATRANS}$) from other SFAS 87 disclosures.[6]

In the context of the permanent earnings model introduced earlier and expressed by eq. (3), we expect those earnings components that are largely permanent, such as service cost and interest cost, to have coefficients of approximately $1/r$. Other earnings components which are partly transitory should have coefficients less than $1/r$. We expect this to be the case, for example, for the actual return on plan assets. Its coefficient is a weighted average of the coefficients assigned to the expected and unexpected returns on plan assets. The expected return component ($EXPRET$) should have a coefficient of $1/r$. The unexpected portion of the actual return on plan assets is transitory, for reasons similar to those offered by Barth, Beaver, and Wolfson (1990) for securities gains and losses. That is, if the expected return on plan assets were properly measured, the unexpected gain or loss would be zero and an ex post gain or loss in a given year would not be expected to recur. Thus, the expected coefficient would be one because the ex post gain or loss would affect market value of equity dollar-for-dollar.

A distinctive feature of SFAS 87 disclosures is that a measure of the unexpected component of the actual return on plan assets (i.e., the deferred return, $DEFRET$) is reflected in total net deferrals and amortizations ($TAMOR$), implicitly permitting the actual return ($RPLNA$) to be decomposed into the expected and unexpected elements. When jointly estimating the coefficients on $RPLNA$ and $DEFRET$ in eq. (3), a coefficient of $1/r$ would be expected for $RPLNA$ and a coefficient of $1/r - 1$ would be expected for $DEFRET$.[7]

---

[6] Fewer than 25% of our sample firms report either component. Evidence contained in appendix C supports our contention that, for our sample, $DEFRET$ and $ATRANS$ comprise almost all of $TAMOR$, and several internal validity checks indicate our estimates are reliable.

[7] Derivation of the coefficients expressed in terms of eq. (3) is

$$MVE = \beta_0 + \beta_1 REVENUES + \beta_2 NPENX + \sum_{k=3}^{7} \beta_k PEN_k + \varepsilon,$$

$$MVE = \beta_0 + \beta_1 REVENUES + \beta_2 NPENX + \beta_3 SVC + \beta_4 INT + \beta_5 EXPRET + \alpha DEFRET + \beta_7 ATRANS + \varepsilon,$$

where $EXPRET \equiv RPLNA + DEFRET$, and

$$MVE = \beta_0 + \beta_1 REVENUES + \beta_2 NPENX + \beta_3 SVC + \beta_4 INT + \beta_5 [RPLNA + DEFRET] + \alpha DEFRET + \beta_7 ATRANS + \varepsilon,$$

$$MVE = \beta_0 + \beta_1 REVENUES + \beta_2 NPENX + \beta_3 SVC + \beta_4 INT + \beta_5 RPLNA + \beta_6 DEFRET + \beta_7 ATRANS + \varepsilon,$$

where pension expense equals $SVC + INT - (RPLNA + DEFRET) - ATRANS$. In the simple permanent earnings model underlying eq. (3), $\beta_5 = 1/r$, $\alpha = -1$, and $\beta_6 = \beta_5 + \alpha = (1/r - 1)$. Note that if $RPLNA$ is greater than expected, $DEFRET$ (the unexpected gain deferred) is a negative number. This convention leads to a negative sign for α. Also by convention, $ATRANS$ and $DEFRET$ are positive numbers if they represent a credit to pension cost.

The other major component of *TAMOR*, *ATRANS*, is the amortization of past gains and losses cumulated prior to the date of adoption of SFAS 87. In a permanent earnings model this component provides no incremental information content about future earnings, not reflected in the other components of earnings, because it is 'stale', assuming that management does not signal its private information through a discretionary change in the amortization rate. For example, *ATRANS* may reflect a cumulative gain because of large unexpected increases in plan assets created by unexpected returns in prior years. However, the earnings implications of this are, in principle, reflected in the expected return on plan assets. From this perspective, the coefficient on this variable would be expected to be zero, unless it is a proxy for some other valuation-relevant information.

A formal statement of our major predictions in terms of eq. (4) is

$$MVE = \beta_0 + \beta_1 REVENUES + \beta_2 NPENX + \beta_3 SVC + \beta_4 INT$$
$$+ \beta_5 RPLNA + \beta_6 DEFRET + \beta_7 ATRANS + \varepsilon, \quad (4)$$

where $-\beta_3, -\beta_4, \beta_5 > 0$ (in the permanent earnings model, $-\beta_3 = -\beta_4 = \beta_5 = 1/r$), $\beta_5 > \beta_6 > \beta_7$ (in the permanent earnings models, $\beta_5 = 1/r$, $\beta_6 = 1/r - 1$, $\beta_7 = 0$). In a setting where there are differences in risk among earnings components (e.g., between pension and nonpension assets or between the pension asset and the pension obligation), β_1 through β_6 could differ from one another. The substantial fixed-income security components of pension plan assets is one basis for positing such a difference.

The above discussion has largely taken place without considering potential measurement errors in the accounting data. In the valuation model, earnings and its components represent market participants' consensus expectations concerning future revenues and expenses, and the market price reflects a consensus among market participants. By measurement error, we mean the difference between a measured variable (i.e., accounting earnings) and the unobserved construct implicit in security prices (i.e., permanent earnings). Potential measurement error in the nonpension earnings components is discussed elsewhere and is not elaborated upon here.[8] Each pension component is also potentially measured with error, which is not explicitly modelled here.[9] However, these characteristics of the pension and nonpension compo-

---

[8] Here, we refer to the cross-sectional valuation literature since Miller and Modigliani (1966). See Foster (1986, ch. 12) for a more complete discussion. Also, Barth (1991) considers measurement errors in both pension and nonpension assets and liabilities.

[9] Economic factors such as expected future salaries, interest rates, mortality rates, and turnover rates may be implicitly reflected in share prices differently from in the accounting measures. Additionally, accounting conventions such as those relating to the expected return on plan assets may introduce measurement error. A further potential source of measurement error is that the components of pension expense are subject to choice variables over which management has some discretion. Management may make these choices for incentive-based or debt-covenant-based reasons. A general argument appears in Watts and Zimmerman (1986). Specific empirical examples are offered in Healy (1985) and Barth, Beaver, and Wolfson (1990).

nents can lead to different estimated coefficients for each component, which also may differ from their theoretical values. Moreover, measurement error is one reason for the intercept (β_0) and the residual (ε) to be nonzero, although either could also reflect the effects of omitted variables (i.e., unrecorded intangible assets or unrecorded liabilities).

3. Empirical results

3.1. Data and sample firms

Three hundred sample firms were selected randomly from the largest half (based on 1987 sales) of the population of Compustat firms which (1) were publicly traded, (2) had fiscal years ending December 31, and (3) disclosed SFAS 87 data in 1987. By sampling with replacement, we ensured that, in the sample, the proportion of firms which adopted SFAS 87 before it was mandatory (the 'early adopters') was the same as the proportion in the Compustat population.[10] Representative sampling of early/nonearly adopters (hereafter EARLY and NEARLY firms) is potentially important because of the possible self-selection bias of early adopter firms. SFAS 87 was issued in December 1985, with a requirement to adopt by December 1987. Results are presented here for three sample years: 1986, 1987, and 1988. The 1986 sample includes only early adopter firms. Pension cost component data were obtained directly from annual reports (or Forms 10K); all other data were obtained from the Compustat database.

December 31 market value of equity is the dependent variable for eqs. (1) and (2). Using December 31 market values is appropriate as the independent variables are also measured at the same date. However, an implicit assumption in using December 31 market values is that earnings and earnings component information is reflected in share price as of that date. Previous research [e.g., Beaver, Lambert, and Morse (1980) and Collins and Kothari (1989), among others] regarding earnings suggests that this assumption is reasonable. However, because the pension cost component information is detailed enough that it may be obtainable only from the annual financial statements, the assumption that pension cost component information is reflected in December 31 share prices is open to question. As a result, we estimate eq. (3) using both December 31 market value of common equity and March 31 market value of equity in the subsequent year to select a date after the publication of the annual financial statements. Relating March 31 market values and December 31 earnings components may introduce specification error because March 31 market values reflect the impact of events which occurred during the three-month interval but which were not reflected in previous year's earnings. The unresolved empirical issue is when information

---

[10] The names of the sample firms are available upon request.

Table 1

Descriptive statistics for 1986–1988, variables in per-share form (sample of calendar-year-end Compustat firms).[a]

	1988 EARLY		1988 NEARLY		1987 EARLY		1987 NEARLY		1986 EARLY	
Variable	Mean	Std. dev.	Mean	Std. dev.	Mean	Std. dev.	Mean	Std. dev.	Mean	Std. dev.
MVE	34.63	18.53	35.54	34.78	30.96	16.50	31.23	31.97	31.00	14.57
NI	3.25	2.28	3.29	3.66	2.56	1.81	2.72	3.23	2.18	1.33
REVENUES	66.81	58.25	58.58	58.93	59.90	54.84	51.88	48.08	60.64	69.71
PENX	0.08	0.35	0.13	0.61	0.08	0.36	0.10	0.57	0.05	0.28
NPENX	63.47	57.33	55.16	56.55	57.26	53.88	49.05	46.45	58.40	69.31
SVC	0.30	0.43	0.27	0.43	0.32	0.45	0.26	0.44	0.26	0.30
INT	0.76	0.97	0.75	1.18	0.70	0.85	0.65	1.06	0.64	0.74
RPLNA	1.07	1.36	1.10	2.34	0.57	1.37	0.44	0.93	1.37	1.79
TAMOR	−0.09	0.75	−0.21	0.93	0.37	1.14	0.37	1.58	−0.52	1.02
TR_ASSET	1.41	1.95	1.26	6.07	1.46	2.09	1.34	6.07	1.30	1.70
N	115		116		115		116		114	

[a] MVE   December 31 market value of common equity.
NI   Income to common shareholders before extraordinary items.
REVENUES Nonpension revenues.
PENX   Pension expense (= SVC + INT − RPLNA − TAMOR).
NPENX   Nonpension expenses.
SVC   Service cost.
INT   Interest cost.
RPLNA   Actual return on plan assets.
TAMOR   Net deferral and amortization pension cost component.
TR_ASSET Transition asset at the date of adoption of SFAS 87.
EARLY   Early adopters of SFAS 87.
NEARLY   Nonearly adopters of SFAS 87.

about the pension cost components is in the public domain. The timing may differ for the year of adoption of SFAS 87 and subsequent years. Because our sample period includes data for the year of adoption and at least one post-adoption year for all sample firms, we can provide insight into this issue.

Descriptive statistics for the sample firms appear in table 1, with all variables deflated by the number of shares outstanding.[11] Although the statistics for the deflated variables in table 1 reveal no notable differences between the samples, NEARLY firms are smaller than EARLY firms as measured by the market value of equity and revenues before per share deflation. The undeflated mean values for the market value of equity (revenues) are (in $ million) 3,040, 2,852, and 3,206 (3,663, 3,895, and 4,552) for the NEARLY firms in 1986, 1987, and 1988. The corresponding numbers for the EARLY firms are 4,916, 4,433, and 4,899 (6,147, 6,653, and 7,381). However, these differences are not statistically significant. In addition, no other differences, as measured by the other undeflated variables, are observed.

3.2. Empirical results for market value equations

F-tests for our primary hypotheses and regression summary statistics for eqs. (1) through (4) for 1986–1988 appear in panels A through D of table 2.[12]

---

[11]All valuation models are estimated after deflating all variables by the number of shares outstanding at year-end, adjusted for stock splits and dividends, because of the presence of heteroscedastic disturbances in undeflated form. The inferences we draw with respect to our primary hypotheses are the same in deflated and undeflated forms, with the exception of the EARLY sample in 1986. The final sample sizes for each year reflect missing data and the elimination of firms with net income less than or equal to zero. The number of firms eliminated from the regressions relating to our primary hypotheses (table 2, panel C) are 20, 34, and 34 in 1986, 1987, and 1988. In this study, net income is income before extraordinary items available to common shareholders. The restriction on net income for the sample firms was imposed as the relation in eq. (1) is not expected to hold for firms with negative net income. The criterion is also adopted by Barth, Beaver, and Stinson (1991) and Barth, Beaver, and Wolfson (1990).

[12]F-tests relating to other subsidiary hypotheses are reported in the text. All empirical relations are estimated in levels using cross-sectional data in per share form. The White (1980) test for model specification was performed for eq. (4). The null of correct model specification could not be rejected at the 0.05 level for any version of eq. (4) in any year except for the March 31 regression for the EARLY sample in 1986. We do not use the alternative first-differences formulation for the following reasons. First, using first-differences would severely limit the sample size. Only one year of observations would be available for the NEARLY sample. Second, a first-differences formulation presumes an expectations model. It is not clear what would be reasonable expectations models for the various components, nor do we have sufficient time-series data to use a statistical model. Modelling such expectations could introduce more noise than benefits received. Third, Landsman and Magliolo (1988) note that first-differences formulations implicitly assume constancy of the coefficients over time. Given the lack of experience with SFAS 87 data, it is not clear that this is a reasonable assumption. Moreover, research by Beaver and Landsman (1983), Barth, Beaver, and Wolfson (1990), and Ryan (1989) indicates that the coefficients on earnings are substantially closer to $1/r$ in levels than in first-differences, where the coefficients are uniformly closer to zero, which is consistent with introducing greater error in first-differences form.

Table 2

Estimation of market value equations for 1986–1988, variables in per-share form (sample of calendar-year-end Compustat firms).[a]

Panel A: $MVE = \beta_0 + \beta_1 NI + \beta_{1E} ENI + \varepsilon$

		1988		1987		1986	
Coeff.	(Variable)	Est.	(t)	Est.	(t)	Est.	(t)
β_0	(Intercept)	14.32	(11.20)	13.29	(11.04)	13.69	(7.52)
β_1	(NI)	7.14	(23.55)	7.28	(21.99)	7.90	(11.03)
β_{1E}	(ENI)	−1.69	(−4.19)	−1.29	(−2.69)	—	—
Adj. R^2			0.6101		0.5119		
N			476		116		

Panel B: $MVE = \beta_0 + \beta_1 REVENUES + \beta_{1E} EREVENUES + \beta_2 NPENX + \beta_{2E} ENPENX + \beta_3 PENX + \beta_{3E} EPENX + \varepsilon$

		1988		1987		1986	
Coeff.	(Variable)	Est.	(t)	Est.	(t)	Est.	(t)
β_0	(Intercept)	15.02	(10.44)	13.87	(9.51)	15.38	(8.03)
β_1	(REVENUES)	6.97	(16.30)	7.22	(17.01)	7.80	(10.41)
β_{1E}	(EREVENUES)	−2.26	(−3.83)	−1.54	(−2.20)	—	—
β_2	(NPENX)	−6.96	(−15.59)	−7.22	(−16.40)	−7.83	(−10.42)
β_{2E}	(ENPENX)	2.30	(3.73)	1.56	(2.15)	—	—
β_3	(PENX)	−16.16	(−8.40)	−13.78	(−6.66)	−1.94	(−0.55)
β_{3E}	(EPENX)	12.45	(2.82)	6.10	(1.41)	—	—
Adj. R^2			0.6390		0.5273		
N			462		115		

H_0: Nonpension and pension expense coefficients are equal ($\beta_2 = \beta_3$ and $\beta_2 + \beta_{2E} = \beta_3 + \beta_{3E}$)

| F-statistic | 11.76 | 5.36 | 3.28 |
| (p-value) | (0.0001) | (0.0050) | (0.0728) |

Panel C: $MVE = \beta_0 + \beta_1 NONPEN + \beta_{1E} ENONPEN + \beta_3 SVC + \beta_{3E} ESVC + \beta_4 INT + \beta_{4E} EINT + \beta_5 RPLNA + \beta_{5E} ERPLNA + \beta_6 \overline{DEFRET} + \beta_{6E} \overline{EDEFRET} + \beta_7 \overline{ATRANS} + \beta_{7E} \overline{EATRANS} + \varepsilon$

(using MVE at December 31)

Coeff.	(Variable)	1988 Est.	(t)	1987 Est.	(t)	1986 Est.	(t)
β_0	(Intercept)	16.06	(11.29)	14.51	(10.11)	13.19	(6.93)
β_1	(NONPEN)	5.67	(11.64)	5.77	(9.22)	7.34	(9.17)
β_{1E}	(ENONPEN)	−1.16	(−1.86)	−0.64	(−0.78)	—	—
β_3	(SVC)	17.91	(1.83)	3.77	(0.36)	7.01	(1.08)
β_{3E}	(ESVC)	−13.71	(−1.20)	−7.44	(−0.64)	—	—
β_4	(INT)	−18.02	(−4.36)	−14.61	(−3.36)	−5.76	(−1.13)
β_{4E}	(EINT)	17.68	(2.58)	14.81	(1.68)	—	—
β_5	(RPLNA)	15.38	(3.83)	15.98	(3.17)	3.39	(1.01)
β_{5E}	(ERPLNA)	−15.61	(−2.27)	−15.12	(−1.73)	—	—
β_6	($\overline{DEFRET}$)	18.38	(4.72)	12.68	(2.53)	4.75	(1.40)
β_{6E}	($\overline{EDEFRET}$)	−19.60	(−3.00)	−10.77	(−1.22)	—	—
β_7	($\overline{ATRANS}$)	−2.43	(−0.22)	2.35	(0.22)	19.27	(1.69)
β_{7E}	($\overline{EATRANS}$)	12.13	(0.64)	13.49	(0.76)	—	—
Adj. R^2		0.6377				0.5511	
N		432				114	

H_0: Pension expense coefficients are equal ($\beta_3 = \cdots = \beta_7$ and $\beta_3 + \beta_{3E} = \cdots = \beta_7 + \beta_{7E}$)

F-statistic	3.13	2.22	1.60
(p-value)	(0.0019)	(0.0249)	(0.1802)

H_0: Amortization of transition asset coefficients equal zero ($\beta_7 = 0$ and $\beta_7 + \beta_{7E} = 0$)

F-statistic	0.25	0.70	2.84
(p-value)	(0.7798)	(0.4963)	(0.0949)

Table 2 (continued)

Panel D: $MVE = \beta_0 + \beta_1 NONPEN + \beta_{1E} ENONPEN + \beta_3 SVC + \beta_{3E} ESVC + \beta_4 INT + \beta_{4E} EINT + \beta_5 RPLNA + \beta_{5E} ERPLNA + \beta_6 \overline{DEFRET} + \beta_{6E} \overline{EDEFRET} + \beta_7 \overline{ATRANS} + \beta_{7E} \overline{EATRANS} + \varepsilon$

(using MVE at March 31 of following year)

Coeff. (Variable)	1988 Est.	(t)	1987 Est.	(t)	1986 Est.	(t)
β_0 (Intercept)	17.38	(11.72)	15.67	(11.09)	16.17	(6.24)
β_1 (NONPEN)	5.79	(11.67)	6.10	(9.82)	9.71	(8.88)
β_{1E} (ENONPEN)	−0.76	(−1.18)	−0.38	(−0.47)	—	—
β_3 (SVC)	19.92	(1.87)	9.15	(0.85)	4.22	(0.49)
β_{3E} (ESVC)	−16.51	(−1.35)	−12.80	(−1.08)	—	—
β_4 (INT)	−22.45	(−5.39)	−15.28	(−3.70)	−6.66	(−0.99)
β_{4E} (EINT)	23.63	(3.43)	23.97	(2.85)	—	—
β_5 (RPLNA)	19.20	(4.70)	15.85	(3.29)	2.97	(0.67)
β_{5E} (ERPLNA)	−21.53	(−3.08)	−22.49	(−2.70)	—	—
β_6 ($\overline{DEFRET}$)	20.37	(5.13)	12.19	(2.54)	5.23	(1.17)
β_{6E} ($\overline{EDEFRET}$)	−23.77	(−3.59)	−17.61	(−2.09)	—	—
β_7 ($\overline{ATRANS}$)	−8.97	(−0.77)	−0.72	(−0.07)	36.78	(2.42)
β_{7E} ($\overline{EATRANS}$)	17.29	(0.89)	13.18	(0.77)	—	—
Adj. R^2	0.6728				0.5078	
N	410				105	

H_0: Pension expense coefficients are equal ($\beta_3 = \cdots = \beta_7$ and $\beta_3 + \beta_{3E} = \cdots = \beta_7 + \beta_{7E}$)

F-statistic	2.84	2.82	2.02
(p-value)	(0.0045)	(0.0048)	(0.0971)

H_0: Amortization of transition asset coefficients equal zero ($\beta_7 = 0$ and $\beta_7 + \beta_{7E} = 0$)

F-statistic	0.48	0.46	5.86
(p-value)	(0.6342)	(0.4963)	(0.0173)

[a]*MVE*   Market value of common equity at calendar year-end for panels A–C and March 31 of the following year for panel D.
NI   Income to common shareholders before extraordinary items.
REVENUES   Nonpension revenues.
NPENX   Nonpension expenses.
PENX   Pension expense per SFAS 87 (= $SVC + INT - (RPLNA + DEFRET) - ATRANS$).
NONPEN $REVENUES - NPENX$.
SVC   Service cost.
INT   Interest cost.
RPLNA   Actual return on plan assets.
DEFRET   Estimate of deferred return on plan assets (*DEFRET*).
ATRANS   Estimate of amortization of transition asset (*ATRANS*).
EARLY   Early adopters of SFAS 87. In 1986, all firms are early adopters.
NEARLY   Nonearly adopters of SFAS 87.
E before variable denotes $E \times$ variable, where $E = 1$ for EARLY firms and $E = 0$ for NEARLY firms.
t-statistics are in parentheses. R^2 is system R^2 for 1987 and 1988.
F-statistics are based on SUR estimation for 1987 and 1988 and test a joint null for the EARLY and NEARLY samples, permitting the coefficients to differ between the groups and in each year.

In 1987 and 1988, the coefficients for the NEARLY and EARLY firms are estimated in a single pooled regression for each year, permitting separate slope coefficients for each group of firms in each year. We test the joint null that coefficients for the EARLY sample are equal to one another and that coefficients for the NEARLY sample are equal to one another. We use Seemingly Unrelated Regressions (SUR) to jointly estimate the regression equations for the two years because we expect the disturbance terms from each regression equation to be correlated across years. 1986 observations are not included in the SUR estimation because the statistical procedure we use requires a common set of observations across equations. Including 1986 observations would eliminate approximately one-half of our sample firms (all NEARLY firms). Because the null hypotheses of interest are not that each coefficient is equal to zero, the t-statistics reported in table 2 (and subsequent tables) should be viewed as descriptive statistics.[13]

In panel A, the coefficient on *NI* for the NEARLY sample is 7.28 and 7.14 for 1987 and 1988, and is significant at conventional levels. These coefficients imply a discount rate of approximately 14%. For the EARLY firms, the coefficients on *NI* are smaller than for the NEARLY firms, as indicated by the negative incremental slope coefficient on net income for these firms (*ENI*). As will be seen below, the difference in *NI* coefficients for the NEARLY and EARLY samples is attributable to differential pricing of the pension components.

In panel B, the coefficients on *REVENUES* and nonpension expense, *NPENX*, are not significantly different, nor have we offered any reason to expect them to differ. Because they are not statistically different, *REVENUES* and *NPENX* are netted to form *NONPEN* in panels C and D. However, for the NEARLY sample, the absolute value of the coefficient on pension expense, *PENX*, is significantly larger than those on *REVENUES* and *NPENX* in 1987 and 1988. This is consistent with a lower discount rate being applied to pension expense. As discussed earlier, this is expected given a lower risk level associated with pension assets and liabilities. Equality of coefficient values for *NPENX* and *PENX* is rejected at the 0.0050 level in 1987 and at the 0.0001 level in 1988. In 1986, the null is rejected at only the 0.0728 level.[14]

In panel C, each pension component is permitted to have its own coefficient. Consistent with panel B, most of the coefficients for the NEARLY

---

[13] Without relying on asymptotic theory, taking t- or F-statistics at face value in finite samples assumes the residuals are normally and independently distributed. No such assumption is made here and no formal checks for normality were conducted. Hansen (1982) discusses weaker conditions necessary for asymptotic normality of ordinary least squares regressions. For purposes of discussion, we will consider as significant coefficients with t-statistics greater than 1.96 for two-sided tests and 1.65 for one-sided tests.

[14] To determine which group of firms is responsible for rejection of the null in 1987 and 1988, the F-test was repeated on each group of firms separately. Our unreported findings reveal that rejection is attributable to the NEARLY firms in both years.

sample are larger than that on net nonpension revenues and expenses (*NONPEN*). The principal exceptions are service cost (*SVC*) and the amortization of the transition asset ($\overline{ATRANS}$), both of which will be discussed shortly. With respect to our primary hypothesis, the coefficients on the pension components are significantly different from one another at the 0.0249 and 0.0019 levels for 1987 and 1988. Rejection of the null of equality of coefficients is attributable to the NEARLY sample. The null cannot be rejected for the EARLY sample in 1986. As predicted, $\overline{ATRANS}$'s coefficient is never significantly different from zero, which is consistent with the transition asset amortization being viewed as 'stale' data which does not provide any incremental valuation-relevant information beyond that reflected in the other components.[15] However, the explanatory power of the model is not greatly enhanced by including the pension cost components, partly because of the inclusion of a variable with little or no explanatory power, $\overline{ATRANS}$.

Although the deferred return on plan assets (*DEFRET*) and the amortization of the transition asset (*ATRANS*) are reported as a combined figure in *TAMOR*, for the NEARLY sample, their coefficients are 12.68 and 2.35 in 1987 and 18.38 and −2.43 for 1988. $\overline{DEFRET}$'s coefficient is significantly different from zero at the 0.0306 level ($F = 3.52$) and at the 0.0001 level ($F = 12.19$) in 1987 and 1988. The difference in findings for $\overline{DEFRET}$ and $\overline{ATRANS}$ is consistent with market participants decomposing pension cost components even further than explicitly disclosed in the financial statements. The lower coefficients on $\overline{ATRANS}$ are also consistent with estimating $\overline{ATRANS}$ with greater error.[16,17]

The coefficients on the net nonpension revenues and expenses (*NONPEN*) are not statistically different for the EARLY and NEARLY firms in panel C. The apparent difference of net income coefficients for the two samples noted in panel A was created by imposing a constraint that the pension and nonpension coefficients be the same [in terms of eq. (4), $\beta_1 = \beta_2 = \cdots = \beta_7$],

---

[15] To determine the effect of including $\overline{ATRANS}$ in the test for equality of coefficients, the test was repeated, leaving out $\overline{ATRANS}$'s coefficient. The differences are significant at the 0.0210 and 0.0019 in 1987 and 1988, and insignificant in 1986. Note that because $\overline{ATRANS}$ and $\overline{DEFRET}$ are estimates of *ATRANS* and *DEFRET*, the two principal components of total net deferrals and amortizations (*TAMOR*), the model in panel C is not a strict decomposition of the model in panel B, i.e., the models are nonnested. Therefore, it is inappropriate to compare the adjusted R^2s in the two panels. The appropriate test for the significance of the decomposition is the reported *F*-test.

[16] The $\overline{DEFRET}$ and $\overline{ATRANS}$ coefficients are not significantly different from each other. Taken at face value, this could also be interpreted as evidence of greater estimation error for $\overline{ATRANS}$.

[17] The regression associated with panel C was also estimated with *TAMOR* in place of $\overline{DEFRET}$ and $\overline{ATRANS}$. Although point estimates of the remaining coefficients differ from those reported, the test for equality of coefficients yields similar conclusions.

when in fact the market was assigning lower (essentially zero) multiples to the pension components for the EARLY firms than for the NEARLY firms. Panel B presents an intermediate case which permits the pension and nonpension components to have different coefficients, but still constrains the pension coefficients to be the same [i.e., in terms of eq. (4), $\beta_3 = \beta_4 = \cdots = \beta_7$].

The reason for the insignificant coefficients for the EARLY firms is not immediately obvious. This result may be attributable to the nature of the decision of when to adopt an accounting standard.[18] However, this is only a conjecture, and a full treatment of this question is beyond the scope of this study.

The positive, albeit insignificant, coefficients on *SVC* in panel C are inconsistent with our predictions. One explanation is that *SVC* fails to measure the pension liability. To the extent this is true, the appropriateness of *SVC* as a component of pension cost is called into question. To explore this possibility, we estimated a regression relating the projected benefit obligation measure of the pension liability to its two related cost components, *SVC* and *INT*. Barth (1991) provides evidence that the projected benefit obligation is significantly related to the market value of equity. Even though a complete specification of the pension liability would include consideration of payments, contributions, and plan amendments and terminations, in addition to *SVC* and *INT*, unreported findings indicate that *SVC* and *INT* are each significantly positively related to the projected benefit obligation. Moreover, these two variables explain more than 95 percent of the cross-sectional variation in the projected benefit obligation. This evidence suggests that *SVC* does not fail to measure the pension liability, leaving unresolved the anomalous finding for its coefficient.

Another result in table 2, panel C that is inconsistent with our predictions is that the estimated coefficient on the deferred return on plan assets ($\widehat{DEFRET}$) is not always less than its actual return on plan assets counterpart (*RPLNA*). It is significantly less at the 0.0274 level ($F = 3.63$) in 1987, but the two coefficients are statistically indistinguishable at more than the 0.05 level in 1988. Note, however, that we are predicting a relatively small difference, $1/r$ versus $1/r - 1$. To investigate this inconsistency, we estimated the relation between pension assets and *RPLNA* and *DEFRET*, its two related cost components. The unreported findings indicate that the magnitude of $\widehat{DEFRET}$'s coefficient is significantly less than *RPLNA*'s coefficient in all years for both the NEARLY and EARLY firms. This result is consistent with the expected permanent versus transitory nature of these two components.

---

[18]Reasons for, and implications of, the decision to adopt accounting standards is not addressed in this study. See Stone and Ingram (1988) and Scott (1989) for evidence regarding early adopters of SFAS 87.

Table 2, panel D presents analogous statistics to those in panel C except that market value of equity at March 31 in the subsequent year is used in place of December 31 market value of equity. The findings are very similar to those presented in panel C. With respect to our primary hypotheses, the inferences are unaffected, except that the coefficient on $\overline{ATRANS}$ is significantly different from zero in 1986.

3.3. Risk, taxpayer status, and industry membership specification tests

With some exceptions relating to the EARLY firms and the SVC variable, the evidence thus far supports our primary contentions that: (1) the pension coefficients are significantly different from one another, with the coefficient on the amortization of the transition asset ($\overline{ATRANS}$) not being significantly different from zero, and (2) the pension coefficients are significantly higher than the nonpension coefficients. This section explores specification tests to examine the robustness of our findings with respect to consideration of risk, taxpayer status, and industry membership. These analyses indicate that the coefficients on nonpension components of income are sensitive to cross-sectional differences in these factors. In addition, the significance levels for the test of equality of the pension cost component coefficients are somewhat weaker than those from our primary specification, even though the relative magnitude of their coefficients are similar.

Our research design allows the earnings coefficient to vary cross-sectionally as a function of the pension versus nonpension mix of assets and liabilities. In these specification tests, we also allow the coefficients on net nonpension revenues and expenses (NONPEN) to differ cross-sectionally as a function of risk, taxpayer status, or industry membership. Our motivation is to determine whether the coefficients for the pension components differ from those of NONPEN – and from one another – in compensating for the misspecification of constraining the NONPEN coefficient to be a cross-sectional constant.

We use beta to measure systematic risk. For each year, beta for each sample firm was obtained from Compustat, and it measures the sensitivity of a firm's stock return to the overall fluctuation in the Standard and Poor's 500 Index. Compustat uses the most recent sixty months of data in its calculation. As in Thomas (1988), a tax status indicator variable denotes whether the firm is a taxpayer. A firm is considered a taxpayer in a given year if the current portion of its Federal tax expense is greater than zero, and it has no net operating loss carryforward. Also consistent with Thomas (1988), we examine possible industry differences for two broad industry categories: defense and automobile manufacturing (SIC 37) and utilities (SIC 49). In the spirit of Ippolito (1985), we also examine possible industry differences for metals (SIC 33 and 34), which are associated with high a degree of unionization. Except for utilities, industry membership is indicated by indicator variables, which take on a value of one if a firm is a member of a given industry group and zero otherwise. Since there were only four utilities in the sample, they were deleted for purposes of this analysis.

In each case (risk, taxpayer status, and industry membership), the indicator variables were multiplied by *NONPEN* to produce additional variables.[19] A coefficient on these additional variables that is statistically significantly different from zero indicates that the coefficient for *NONPEN* for that subgroup differs significantly from that of the rest of the sample. The *NONPEN* coefficient for that subgroup is the sum of the sample-wide coefficient plus the coefficient assigned to the respective additional variable.

The regression summary statistics are reported in table 3, which extends table 2, panels C and D, to include these additional variables. Panel A considers risk, panel B taxpayer status, and panel C industry membership. Part 1 of each panel presents regression summary statistics using December 31 market value of equity, and part 2 using March 31 market value of equity.

As expected, in panel A the *NONPEN* coefficients are significantly lower for the high beta group. A higher beta implies a higher discount rate and a lower multiple applied to (nonpension) earnings components. In panel B, the *NONPEN* coefficients are significantly lower for the nontaxpayer firms. Although we have no prediction for the sign of these coefficients, a lower coefficient is consistent with lower future expected earnings growth for the nontaxpayer group. In any event, the purpose of examining taxpayer status is not because we can predict the sign, but rather to examine the effects of this additional specification on the pension coefficients. The results for the industry analysis in panel C indicate that only the incremental *NONPEN* coefficients for defense and automobiles (β_{2aE}) for the EARLY sample are significant. Given the number of variables for which industry membership is a proxy, it would be impossible to predict the sign of, or even interpret, the observed coefficients. Again, that is not our concern.

The coefficient point estimates in table 3 are comparable to, but smaller than, those in table 2, panels C and D. With respect to our primary hypotheses, using December 31 market value of equity, equality of the pension cost components' coefficients is rejected at the following levels in 1987 and 1988: (1) for risk, 0.0903 and 0.0558 ($F = 1.73$ and $F = 1.92$), (2) for taxpayer status, 0.0707 and 0.0050 ($F = 1.83$ and $F = 2.80$), and (3) for industry membership, 0.0070 and 0.0029 ($F = 2.69$ and $F = 3.02$). Using March 31 market value of equity, equality of the pension cost components' coefficients is rejected at the following levels in 1987 and 1988: (1) for risk, 0.0334 and 0.0848 ($F = 2.12$ and $F = 1.75$), (2) for taxpayer status, 0.0417 and

---

[19] For risk, an indicator variable is assigned a value of one for firms with high betas (where beta is above the median) and zero for firms with low betas (where beta is below the median). Median values are 1.0, 1.1, and 1.1 in 1986, 1987, and 1988.

Table 3

Specifications with risk, taxpayer status, and industry membership indicator variables, estimated in per share form 1986–1988 (sample of calendar-year-end Compustat firms).[a]

Panel A.1: Risk (using MVE at calendar-year-end)

$$MVE = \beta_0 + \beta_1 NONPEN + \beta_{1E} ENONPEN + \beta_2 BNONPEN + \beta_{2E} EBNONPEN + \beta_3 SVC + \beta_{3E} ESVC + \beta_4 INT + \beta_{4E} EINT$$
$$+ \beta_5 RPLNA + \beta_{5E} ERPLNA + \beta_6 \overline{DEFRET} + \beta_{6E} \overline{EDEFRET} + \beta_7 \overline{ATRANS} + \beta_{7E} \overline{EATRANS} + \varepsilon$$

Coeff.	(Variable)	1988 Est.	(t)	1987 Est.	(t)	1986 Est.	(t)
β_0	(Intercept)	15.00	(11.74)	13.93	(9.95)	13.06	(6.76)
β_1	(NONPEN)	7.74	(14.79)	6.81	(10.20)	7.21	(8.50)
β_{1E}	(ENONPEN)	−1.68	(−2.43)	−0.38	(−0.42)	—	—
β_2	(BNONPEN)	−3.57	(−6.17)	−2.38	(−3.37)	0.37	(0.48)
β_{2E}	(EBNONPEN)	1.26	(1.59)	0.54	(0.54)	—	—
β_3	(SVC)	10.65	(1.21)	0.86	(0.08)	7.46	(1.13)
β_{3E}	(ESVC)	−4.88	(−0.48)	−4.26	(−0.38)	—	—
β_4	(INT)	−10.08	(−2.52)	−10.68	(−2.38)	−6.65	(−1.22)
β_{4E}	(EINT)	10.59	(1.66)	9.02	(1.02)	—	—
β_5	(RPLNA)	8.01	(2.06)	12.98	(2.52)	3.98	(1.11)
β_{5E}	(ERPLNA)	−10.15	(−1.59)	−11.55	(−1.32)	—	—
β_6	($\overline{DEFRET}$)	9.85	(2.57)	9.81	(1.94)	5.19	(1.47)
β_{6E}	($\overline{EDEFRET}$)	−13.85	(−2.25)	−7.09	(−0.81)	—	—
β_7	($\overline{ATRANS}$)	−1.82	(−0.18)	1.49	(0.14)	18.92	(1.65)
β_{7E}	($\overline{EATRANS}$)	16.20	(0.96)	19.25	(1.11)	—	—
Adj. R^2		0.7017				0.5224	
N		432				114	

H_0: Pension expense coefficients are equal ($\beta_3 = \cdots = \beta_7$ and $\beta_3 + \beta_{3E} = \cdots = \beta_7 + \beta_{7E}$)

	1988	1987	1986
F-statistic	1.92	1.73	1.63
(p-value)	(0.0558)	(0.0903)	(0.1725)

H_0: Amortization of transition asset coefficients equal zero ($\beta_7 = 0$ and $\beta_7 + \beta_{7E} = 0$)

	1988	1987	1986
F-statistic	0.63	1.22	2.71
(p-value)	(0.5318)	(0.2970)	(0.1030)

Table 3 (continued)

Panel A.2: Risk (using MVE at March 31)

$$MVE = \beta_0 + \beta_1 NONPEN + \beta_{1E} ENONPEN + \beta_2 BNONPEN + \beta_{2E} EBNONPEN + \beta_3 SVC + \beta_{3E} ESVC + \beta_4 INT + \beta_{4E} EINT$$
$$+ \beta_5 RPLNA + \beta_{5E} ERPLNA + \beta_6 \overline{DEFRET} + \beta_{6E} \overline{EDEFRET} + \beta_7 \overline{ATRANS} + \beta_{7E} \overline{EATRANS} + \varepsilon$$

Coeff.	(Variable)	1988 Est.	(t)	1987 Est.	(t)	1986 Est.	(t)
β_0	(Intercept)	16.49	(12.25)	15.10	(11.11)	16.29	(6.16)
β_1	(NONPEN)	7.84	(14.62)	7.31	(11.20)	9.81	(8.40)
β_{1E}	(ENONPEN)	−1.55	(−2.18)	−0.30	(−0.34)	—	—
β_2	(BNONPEN)	−3.71	(−6.19)	−2.76	(−4.10)	−0.28	(−0.27)
β_{2E}	(EBNONPEN)	1.88	(2.28)	0.94	(0.99)	—	—
β_3	(SVC)	14.47	(1.49)	6.45	(0.62)	3.82	(0.44)
β_{3E}	(ESVC)	−9.78	(−0.88)	−10.14	(−0.89)	—	—
β_4	(INT)	−14.12	(−3.45)	−10.67	(−2.52)	−5.96	(−0.82)
β_{4E}	(EINT)	15.42	(2.36)	17.19	(2.06)	—	—
β_5	(RPLNA)	11.33	(2.80)	12.02	(2.46)	2.50	(0.52)
β_{5E}	(ERPLNA)	−14.72	(−2.23)	−17.78	(−2.15)	—	—
β_6	($\overline{DEFRET}$)	11.49	(2.87)	8.75	(1.81)	4.88	(1.04)
β_{6E}	($\overline{EDEFRET}$)	−16.64	(−2.63)	−13.05	(−1.57)	—	—
β_7	($\overline{ATRANS}$)	−9.12	(−0.86)	−2.14	(−0.21)	37.10	(2.42)
β_{7E}	($\overline{EATRANS}$)	21.02	(1.19)	19.68	(1.19)	—	—
Adj. R^2		0.7259				0.5030	
N		410				105	

H_0: Pension expense coefficients are equal ($\beta_3 = \cdots = \beta_7$ and $\beta_3 + \beta_{3E} = \cdots = \beta_7 + \beta_{7E}$)

F-statistic	1.75	2.12	2.00
(p-value)	(0.0848)	(0.0334)	(0.1012)

H_0: Amortization of transition asset coefficients equal zero ($\beta_7 = 0$ and $\beta_7 + \beta_{7E} = 0$)

F-statistic	0.78	0.98	5.87
(p-value)	(0.4574)	(0.3755)	(0.0172)

Panel B.1: Taxpayer status (using MVE at calendar-year-end)

$$MVE = \beta_0 + \beta_1 NONPEN + \beta_{1E} ENONPEN + \beta_2 TNONPEN + \beta_{2E} ETNONPEN + \beta_3 SVC + \beta_{3E} ESVC + \beta_4 INT + \beta_{4E} EINT$$
$$+ \beta_5 RPLNA + \beta_{5E} ERPLNA + \beta_6 \overline{DEFRET} + \beta_{6E} \overline{EDEFRET} + \beta_7 \overline{ATRANS} + \beta_{7E} \overline{EATRANS} + \varepsilon$$

Coeff.	(Variable)	1988 Est.	(t)	1987 Est.	(t)	1986 Est.	(t)
β_0	(Intercept)	15.96	(11.67)	14.01	(10.03)	13.16	(6.86)
β_1	(NONPEN)	6.57	(12.57)	6.53	(10.08)	7.39	(8.95)
β_{1E}	(ENONPEN)	−1.64	(−2.52)	−0.54	(−0.66)	—	—
β_2	(TNONPEN)	−2.41	(−3.71)	−1.60	(−2.64)	−0.21	(−0.25)
β_{2E}	(ETNONPEN)	0.10	(0.11)	−1.19	(−1.30)	—	—
β_3	(SVC)	14.60	(1.55)	2.28	(0.22)	7.63	(1.09)
β_{3E}	(ESVC)	−8.40	(−0.77)	−1.28	(−0.11)	—	—
β_4	(INT)	−11.38	(−2.56)	−10.83	(−2.45)	−6.07	(−1.15)
β_{4E}	(EINT)	12.46	(1.80)	7.03	(0.80)	—	—
β_5	(RPLNA)	9.22	(2.14)	11.96	(2.36)	3.55	(1.03)
β_{5E}	(ERPLNA)	−10.54	(−1.52)	−7.70	(−0.89)	—	—
β_6	($\overline{DEFRET}$)	12.31	(2.95)	8.85	(1.76)	4.75	(1.39)
β_{6E}	($\overline{EDEFRET}$)	−15.26	(−2.31)	−4.05	(−0.46)	—	—
β_7	($\overline{ATRANS}$)	3.09	(0.28)	5.97	(0.58)	18.57	(1.57)
β_{7E}	($\overline{EATRANS}$)	9.61	(0.52)	3.12	(0.18)	—	—
Adj. R^2		0.6503		0.6503		0.5217	
N		432		432		114	

H_0: Pension expense coefficients are equal ($\beta_3 = \cdots = \beta_7$ and $\beta_3 + \beta_{3E} = \cdots = \beta_7 + \beta_{7E}$)

	1988	1987	1986
F-statistic	2.80	1.83	1.60
(p-value)	(0.0050)	(0.0707)	(0.1802)

H_0: Amortization of transition asset coefficients equal zero ($\beta_7 = 0$ and $\beta_7 + \beta_{7E} = 0$)

	1988	1987	1986
F-statistic	0.46	0.41	2.46
(p-value)	(0.6308)	(0.6620)	(0.1196)

Table 3 (continued)

Panel B.2: Taxpayer status (using MVE at March 31)

$$MVE = \beta_0 + \beta_1 NONPEN + \beta_{1E} ENONPEN + \beta_2 TNONPEN + \beta_{2E} ETNONPEN + \beta_3 SVC + \beta_{3E} ESVC + \beta_4 INT + \beta_{4E} EINT$$
$$+ \beta_5 RPLNA + \beta_{5E} \overline{ERPLNA} + \beta_6 \overline{DEFRET} + \beta_{6E} \overline{EDEFRET} + \beta_7 \overline{ATRANS} + \beta_{7E} \overline{EATRANS} + \varepsilon$$

Coeff.	(Variable)	1988 Est.	(t)	1987 Est.	(t)	1986 Est.	(t)
β_0	(Intercept)	17.04	(11.91)	15.05	(10.95)	16.04	(6.14)
β_1	(NONPEN)	6.64	(12.42)	6.82	(10.71)	9.84	(8.71)
β_{1E}	(ENONPEN)	−1.08	(−1.60)	−0.22	(−0.27)	—	—
β_2	(TNONPEN)	−2.25	(−3.34)	−1.43	(−2.42)	−0.59	(−0.50)
β_{2E}	(ETNONPEN)	−0.19	(−0.20)	−0.90	(−1.02)	—	—
β_3	(SVC)	18.10	(1.75)	7.41	(0.71)	5.97	(0.64)
β_{3E}	(ESVC)	−12.63	(−1.07)	−7.42	(−0.64)	—	—
β_4	(INT)	−16.15	(−3.52)	−12.09	(−2.87)	−7.56	(−1.08)
β_{4E}	(EINT)	18.93	(2.67)	17.36	(2.06)	—	—
β_5	(RPLNA)	13.22	(2.93)	12.50	(2.57)	3.43	(0.76)
β_{5E}	($\overline{ERPLNA}$)	−16.88	(−2.36)	−16.32	(−1.96)	—	—
β_6	($\overline{DEFRET}$)	14.56	(3.34)	9.05	(1.88)	5.24	(1.16)
β_{6E}	($\overline{EDEFRET}$)	−20.03	(−2.94)	−12.10	(−1.44)	—	—
β_7	($\overline{ATRANS}$)	−4.37	(−0.38)	2.25	(0.22)	34.78	(2.21)
β_{7E}	($\overline{EATRANS}$)	16.02	(0.85)	4.44	(0.26)	—	—
Adj. R^2		0.6967				0.5040	
N		410				105	

H_0: Pension expense coefficients are equal ($\beta_3 = \cdots = \beta_7$ and $\beta_3 + \beta_{3E} = \cdots = \beta_7 + \beta_{7E}$)

F-statistic	2.53	2.03	1.97
(p-value)	(0.0109)	(0.0417)	(0.1048)

H_0: Amortization of transition asset coefficients equal zero ($\beta_7 = 0$ and $\beta_7 + \beta_{7E} = 0$)

F-statistic	0.41	0.16	4.86
(p-value)	(0.6656)	(0.8492)	(0.0298)

Panel C.1: Industry membership (using MVE at calendar-year-end)

$$MVE = \beta_0 + \beta_1 NONPEN + \beta_{1E} ENONPEN + \beta_{2a} DNONPEN + \beta_{2aE} EDNONPEN + \beta_{2b} MNONPEN + \beta_{2bE} EMNONPEN$$
$$+ \beta_3 SVC + \beta_{3E} ESVC + \beta_4 INT + \beta_{4E} EINT + \beta_5 RPLNA + \beta_{5E} ERPLNA$$
$$+ \beta_6 \overline{DEFRET} + \beta_{6E} \overline{EDEFRET} + \beta_7 \overline{ATRANS} + \beta_{7E} \overline{EATRANS} + \varepsilon$$

Coeff.	(Variable)	1988 Est.	(t)	1987 Est.	(t)	1986 Est.	(t)
β_0	(Intercept)	13.56	(9.00)	12.47	(7.61)	12.94	(6.72)
β_1	(NONPEN)	6.25	(11.61)	6.31	(7.98)	7.49	(9.40)
β_{1E}	(ENONPEN)	−0.50	(−0.76)	−0.19	(−0.21)	—	—
β_{2a}	(DNONPEN)	−0.17	(−0.25)	−0.12	(−0.16)	−3.40	(−2.47)
β_{2aE}	(EDNONPEN)	−3.63	(−2.87)	−4.34	(−3.16)	—	—
β_{2b}	(MNONPEN)	−2.48	(−1.60)	0.71	(0.32)	−0.30	(−0.09)
β_{2bE}	(EMNONPEN)	−0.94	(−0.53)	−2.31	(−0.74)	—	—
β_3	(SVC)	13.70	(1.41)	3.74	(0.36)	6.80	(1.05)
β_{3E}	(ESVC)	−12.99	(−1.15)	−5.90	(−0.50)	—	—
β_4	(INT)	−17.26	(−4.13)	−15.17	(−3.25)	−6.52	(−1.29)
β_{4E}	(EINT)	14.63	(2.15)	6.60	(0.68)	—	—
β_5	(RPLNA)	16.35	(4.05)	16.16	(3.07)	5.30	(1.54)
β_{5E}	(ERPLNA)	−10.58	(−1.52)	−4.49	(−0.46)	—	—
β_6	($\overline{DEFRET}$)	19.73	(4.79)	12.43	(2.37)	4.92	(1.46)
β_{6E}	($\overline{EDEFRET}$)	−15.70	(−2.31)	0.08	(0.01)	—	—
β_7	($\overline{ATRANS}$)	−4.17	(−0.38)	3.18	(0.29)	5.23	(0.41)
β_{7E}	($\overline{EATRANS}$)	2.86	(0.16)	−5.41	(−0.29)	—	—
Adj. R^2		0.6914				0.5409	
N		424				112	

H_0: Pension expense coefficients are equal ($\beta_3 = \cdots = \beta_7$ and $\beta_3 + \beta_{3E} = \cdots = \beta_7 + \beta_{7E}$)

F-statistic	3.02	2.69	1.16
(p-value)	(0.0029)	(0.0070)	(0.3342)

H_0: Amortization of transition asset coefficients equal zero ($\beta_7 = 0$ and $\beta_7 + \beta_{7E} = 0$)

F-statistic	0.08	0.06	0.17
(p-value)	(0.9202)	(0.9427)	(0.6838)

Table 3 (continued)

Panel C.2: Industry membership (using MVE at March 31)

$$MVE = \beta_0 + \beta_1 NONPEN + \beta_{1E} ENONPEN + \beta_{2a} DNONPEN + \beta_{2aE} EDNONPEN + \beta_{2b} MNONPEN + \beta_{2bE} EMNONPEN$$
$$+ \beta_3 SVC + \beta_{3E} ESVC + \beta_4 INT + \beta_{4E} EINT + \beta_5 RPLNA + \beta_{5E} ERPLNA$$
$$+ \beta_6 \overline{DEFRET} + \beta_{6E} E\overline{DEFRET} + \beta_7 \overline{ATRANS} + \beta_{7E} E\overline{ATRANS} + \varepsilon$$

Coeff.	(Variable)	1988 Est.	(t)	1987 Est.	(t)	1986 Est.	(t)
β_0	(Intercept)	15.16	(9.41)	13.93	(8.45)	16.12	(6.07)
β_1	(NONPEN)	6.36	(11.33)	6.61	(8.30)	9.79	(8.90)
β_{1E}	(ENONPEN)	−0.19	(−0.28)	0.02	(0.02)	—	—
β_{2a}	(DNONPEN)	−0.17	(−0.25)	−0.04	(−0.06)	−3.87	(−2.10)
β_{2aE}	(EDNONPEN)	−3.11	(−2.36)	−3.80	(−2.84)	—	—
β_{2b}	(MNONPEN)	−2.18	(−1.36)	0.41	(0.19)	−0.65	(−0.15)
β_{2bE}	(EMNONPEN)	−0.94	(−0.51)	−3.46	(−1.14)	—	—
β_3	(SVC)	15.03	(1.39)	7.60	(0.69)	4.32	(0.50)
β_{3E}	(ESVC)	−14.84	(−1.19)	−10.78	(−0.89)	—	—
β_4	(INT)	−21.41	(−4.96)	−15.55	(−3.45)	−7.62	(−1.13)
β_{4E}	(EINT)	20.19	(2.87)	16.59	(1.76)	—	—
β_5	(RPLNA)	19.90	(4.73)	16.06	(3.14)	5.31	(1.16)
β_{5E}	(ERPLNA)	−16.71	(−2.31)	−13.07	(−1.38)	—	—
β_6	($\overline{DEFRET}$)	21.75	(5.09)	11.98	(2.34)	5.55	(1.24)
β_{6E}	($E\overline{DEFRET}$)	−20.22	(−2.87)	−7.93	(−0.84)	—	—
β_7	($\overline{ATRANS}$)	−8.63	(−0.75)	0.76	(0.07)	19.58	(1.13)
β_{7E}	($E\overline{ATRANS}$)	8.11	(0.43)	−2.92	(−0.16)	—	—
Adj. R^2		0.7141		0.5131			
N		402				103	

H_0: Pension expense coefficients are equal ($\beta_3 = \cdots = \beta_7$ and $\beta_3 + \beta_{3E} = \cdots = \beta_7 + \beta_{7E}$)			
F-statistic	2.38	2.80	0.85
(p-value)	(0.0164)	(0.0051)	(0.4943)
H_0: Amortization of transition asset coefficients equal zero ($\beta_7 = 0$ and $\beta_7 + \beta_{7E} = 0$)			
F-statistic	0.31	0.01	1.28
(p-value)	(0.7351)	(0.9852)	(0.2610)

[a] MVE Market value of common equity.
NONPEN Nonpension revenues minus nonpension expenses.
SVC Service cost.
INT Interest cost.
RPLNA Actual return on plan assets.
DEFRET Estimate of deferred return on plan assets (DEFRET).
ATRANS Estimate of amortization of transition asset (ATRANS).
EARLY Early adopters of SFAS 87. In 1986, all firms are early adopters.
NEARLY Nonearly adopters of SFAS 87.
Pension expense equals $SVC + INT - (RPLNA + DEFRET) - ATRANS$.
E before variable denotes $E \times$ variable, where $E = 1$ for EARLY firms and $E = 0$ for NEARLY firms.
B before variable denotes $B \times$ variable, where $B = 1$ for beta > median, $B = 0$ otherwise.
T before variable denotes $T \times$ variable, where $T = 1$ for taxpayer firm, $T = 0$ otherwise.
D before variable denotes $D \times$ variable, where $D = 1$ for defense and autos, $D = 0$ otherwise.
M before variable denotes $M \times$ variable, where $M = 1$ for metals, $M = 0$ otherwise.
t-statistics are in parentheses. R^2 is system R^2 for 1987 and 1988.
F-statistics are based on SUR estimation for 1987 and 1988 and test a joint null for the EARLY and NEARLY samples, permitting the coefficients to differ between the groups and in each year.

0.0109 ($F = 2.03$ and $F = 2.53$), and (3) for industry membership, 0.0051 and 0.0164 ($F = 2.80$ and $F = 2.38$).[20] In both the December 31 and March 31 regressions, $\overline{ATRANS}$'s coefficient is never significantly different from zero in 1987 and 1988.

Although the relative magnitude of the coefficients in table 3 are similar to those of the primary specification (table 2, panel C), the significance levels for the test of equality of pension cost component coefficients are somewhat weaker under these additional specifications. This is most evident with respect to the risk specification (panel A), where we fail to reject the null hypothesis of equal coefficients at the conventional 5 percent level for 1987 and 1988 using December 31 market values and for 1987 using March 31 market values. The inferences from the industry specification (panel C) are essentially the same as those from the primary specification. The inferences from the taxpayer status specification (panel B) are less (more) consistent with the primary specification than those from the industry (risk) specification. Note, however, the null hypothesis of equal coefficients is rejected at the 10 percent level for both 1987 and 1988 for all three specifications. The implications of the lower significance levels are not immediately obvious. A potential problem in incorporating the effects of omitted variables by using such generic proxies as risk, taxpayer status, and industry membership is that these proxies may also partially remove the effects of interest [see, e.g., Beaver (1987)]. Including all three proxies at once might further reduce significance levels. However, resolving the issue of the relative costs and benefits of including these proxies is beyond the scope of the current study.

4. Summary and concluding remarks

The paper examines whether market participants implicitly assign different multiples to the components of pension cost in determining security prices. Our major finding is that the coefficients on the pension cost components significantly differ from one another. Moreover, the coefficient on the amortization of the transition asset is lower than the other pension coefficients and, as predicted, is not significantly different from zero. The findings are robust to the choice of date of measurement of the market value of equity.

In SFAS 106, *Employers' Accounting for Postretirement Benefits Other Than Pensions*, the FASB has adopted policies consistent with this study's findings regarding the valuation implications of the amortization of the transition amount. First, our study provides evidence that market participants decompose disclosed pension cost components to estimate the amortization of the transition amount. In SFAS 106, firms are required to disclose

---

[20] In addition, for both the December 31 and March 31 regressions, the significance levels are similar when testing equality of the pension cost coefficients without $\overline{ATRANS}$.

separately the analogous postretirement cost component. Second, our findings are consistent with market participants assigning a zero multiple to the amortization of the transition amount. SFAS 106 permits firms to recognize immediately in net income the transition amount.

We also examine whether the multiples assigned to nonpension-related components of net income differ from those assigned to pension-related components. Our findings are that pension cost has a significantly higher coefficient than nonpension components of income. This finding is consistent with differences in the asset mix between nonpension and pension assets, which consist of large portions of fixed-income securities.

Findings from specifications which consider risk, taxpayer status, and industry membership indicate that the nonpension coefficients often vary as a function of these factors. However, the significance levels for the test of equality of the pension cost component coefficients are somewhat weaker than those from our primary specification, even though the relative magnitude of their coefficients are similar.

Although the results generally support our predictions, there are some unresolved questions. First, the service cost components' coefficients are not significantly different from zero, and they often have signs opposite to our prediction. Second, we can offer no obvious explanation for the general insignificance of the pension variables for the early adopters. Third, although the coefficient on the transition asset amortization is lower than those of the other pension components, evidence indicates that it might be estimated with greater error than the deferred portion of the return on plan assets. Better estimates or direct disclosure of the amount would permit more powerful tests.

Finally, the predictions are based on a valuation relation developed in a simple setting. Our findings are robust to specifications of the valuation equation which include proxies for several factors found in prior research to affect pension funding levels. However, because the precise way in which these factors impact share prices is unknown, we may not have appropriately identified their effects in our specifications. A more complete valuation model which treats the pension-related components endogenously is a promising but ambitious avenue for future research.

Appendix A: Variable definitions

$ATRANS$	Amortization of the transition asset at the date of adoption of SFAS 87
$\overline{ATRANS}$	Estimate of $ATRANS$
$DEFRET$	Deferred return on plan assets
$\overline{DEFRET}$	Estimate of $DEFRET$

EXPRET	Expected return on plan assets
INT	Interest cost
MVE	Market value of equity
NI	Income before extraordinary items available to common shareholders
NONPEN	REVENUES − NPENX
NPENX	Nonpension expenses
PENX	Pension expense per SFAS 87
REVENUES	Nonpension revenues
RPLNA	Actual return on plan assets
SVC	Service cost
TAMOR	Net deferral and amortization pension cost component
TR_ASSET	Unrecognized net obligation or asset existing at the date of initial application of SFAS 87 ('transition' asset)

Appendix B: Sample pension footnote

Below is an excerpt from Note 13 (Retirement Plans) of the 1987 FMC Corporation Annual Report. To illustrate the variables used in the study, the amounts reported in the footnote are labelled [1] through [10]. All amounts are expressed in thousands of dollars and are for the year ended December 31, 1987.

The four components of pension cost that are required to be reported are: [1] service cost (SVC), [2] interest cost (INT), [3] actual return on plan assets ($RPLNA$), and [4] a component that reflects the net deferral and amortization of the effects of a variety of transactions that have occurred in the past ($TAMOR$).

The four components of $TAMOR$ are: [5] amortization of the unrecognized net obligation or asset existing at the date of initial application (i.e., amortization of the 'transition' obligation or asset) ($ATRANS$), [6] the amortization of unrecognized prior service cost, [7] the amortization of the gain or loss from earlier periods, and [8] the net gain or loss during the period deferred for later recognition (in effect, the unexpected portion of the actual return on plan assets) ($DEFRET$). Under SFAS 87 only the total is reported for most firms. FMC was chosen as an illustration because it reported each of the components. Although $TAMOR$ is the sum of [5] through [8], $TAMOR$ will consist almost exclusively of the components $ATRANS$ and $DEFRET$ ([5] and [8]) because [6] and [7] are likely to be zero or small in the years immediately following adoption of SFAS 87. [6] pertains only to plan amendments since the date of adoption. [7] comprises only the amortization of the unrealized gains and losses accumulated since adoption of SFAS 87 in excess of 10 percent of the greater of the projected benefits obligation or the market-related value of assets. For FMC $TAMOR$ amounts to − $17,430. The net amount of [6] and [7] is $87 and represents less than one-half of 1 percent (0.005) of *TAMOR*. Even the gross amounts are less than 2 percent of the total. Total pension cost (benefit), [9] (*PENX*), is the net of [1] through [4], where [4] is the sum of [5] through [8].

Three measures of the pension obligation are reported under SFAS 87, the accumulated benefit obligation, the vested portion of the accumulated benefit obligation, and the projected benefit obligation. The disclosure also includes pension assets and the unrecognized net obligation or asset existing at the date of initial application of SFAS 87 [10] (*TR_ASSET*).

Excerpt from the 1987 pension footnote of FMC Corporation

Note 13 Retirement plans

Effective January 1, 1986, the company adopted the provisions of FASB Statement No. 87, 'Employers' Accounting for Pensions', for all domestic retirement plans. Provisions of this standard were adopted prospectively, and income prior to 1986 has not been restated. The following... components were used to develop the net pension benefit:

(in thousands)	Year ended December 31, 1987
Components:	
[1] Service cost-benefits earned during the period	$19,324
[2] Interest cost on projected benefit obligation	43,230
[3] Actual return on plan assets	(74,656)
[4] Net amortization and deferral:	
[5] Net transition asset amortization	(27,529)
[6] Prior service cost amortization	344
[7] Net (gain) loss amortization	(257)
[8] Net asset gain (loss) deferred	10,012
[9] Net pension benefit	$(29,532)

The funded status of the plans and amounts recognized in the company's consolidated financial statements as of December 31 were as follows:

(in thousands)	1987
Actuarial present value of benefits for service rendered to date:	
Accumulated benefit obligation based on salaries to date, including vested benefits of $288,344	$(301,161)
Additional benefits based on estimated future salary levels	(30,836)
Projected benefit obligation	(331,997)
Plan assets at fair value	426,110
[10] Unrecognized net transition asset	(307,926)

Appendix C: Estimation of *DEFRET* and *ATRANS*

As noted in section 2.2, reporting the components of *TAMOR* is not required. The two primary components of *TAMOR* are *DEFRET* and *ATRANS*. Because we expect different coefficients for these two components, and they are often not separately disclosed, it is necessary to estimate them. This appendix describes the estimation of these components from available data. Estimation is possible because *DEFRET* and *ATRANS* are structurally related to other disclosed data.

DEFRET is the difference between expected return on plan assets (*EXPRET*) and the actual return on plan assets (*RPLNA*). Under SFAS 87, *EXPRET* is the product of an assumed long-term projected rate of return ('rate') and a measure of plan assets. For the purpose of calculating expected return, firms may use either the beginning-of-year plan assets or a 'market-related' value of plan assets.[21] In estimating *EXPRET*, we use beginning-of-year plan assets (*PALAG*). The use of beginning-of-year plan assets may be associated with less measurement error than the use of a market-related value of plan assets in terms of the market's valuation of the firm. The transition asset at the time of adoption, *TR_ASSET*, is amortized on a straight-line basis over the remaining service life (l) of the employees covered by the pension plan. These relations are depicted below.

$$DEFRET = EXPRET - RPLNA,$$

$$EXPRET = \text{rate} \times PALAG$$

$$ATRANS = 1/l \times TR\_ASSET,$$

$$TAMOR = DEFRET + ATRANS + e,$$

$$TAMOR + RPLNA = (\text{rate} \times PALAG) + (1/l \times TR\_ASSET) + e.$$

Although *DEFRET* and *ATRANS* are the two primary components of *TAMOR*, there are other components which are assumed to be on average equal to zero, and are represented as e.[22]

---

[21] Market-related values are moving averages (but not to exceed five years) of estimates of fair value of plan assets.

[22] As noted in appendix B, in the years immediately after adoption of SFAS 87, *TAMOR* consists primarily of *DEFRET* and *ATRANS*.

Based on the relations above, the following cross-sectional regression equation is used to estimate *DEFRET* and *ATRANS*:

$$TAMOR + RPLNA = \alpha_0 + \alpha_1 PALAG + \alpha_2 ED\_PALAG$$

$$+ \alpha_3 D\_PALAG6 + \alpha_4 D\_PALAG7$$

$$+ \alpha_5 TR\_ASSET + \alpha_6 ED\_TR + \varepsilon, \quad (C.1)$$

ED_PALAG and *ED_TR* are defined as $ED \times PALAG$ and $ED \times TR\_ASSET$, where *ED* is an indicator variable which equals one if a firm is an early adopter and zero otherwise, permitting different slope coefficients (and, thus, different estimates of 'rate' and *l*) for early adopter firms. *D_PALAG6* and *D_PALAG7* are defined as $D \times PALAG$, where *D* is an indicator variable which equals one if a firm observation is from 1986 (in the case of *D_PALAG6*) or 1987 (in the case of *D_PALAG7*), and zero otherwise. This permits 'rate' to differ across the three sample years, as SFAS 87 requires firms to update their rate of return estimates each year. The amortization period for the transition asset is assumed not to change across years. All coefficients are assumed to be cross-sectional constants.[23,24]

Table 4, panel A, contains the regression summary statistics for eq. (C.1). The estimate of 'rate' is 7.8% for 1988, 8.1% for 1987, and 8.8% for 1986. For early adopters, the respective rates are 0.6% higher. The estimate of *l* is 28 years $(1 + 1/0.037)$ for nonearly adopters and 17 years $(1 + 1/0.062)$ for early adopters. These estimates are reasonable as SFAS 87 requires amortization over the average remaining service life of employees or fifteen years, whichever is longer.

The empirical estimates for *DEFRET* ($\widetilde{DEFRET}$) and *ATRANS* ($\widetilde{ATRANS}$) are constructed as follows. If *DEFRET* is available ($N = 51$, 59, and 39 in 1988, 1987, and 1986), then $\widetilde{DEFRET}$ is set equal to *DEFRET*. Otherwise, estimates are based on eq. (C.1) ($N = 191$, 190, and 75) as follows:

$$\widetilde{DEFRET} \equiv \hat{\alpha}_1 PALAG + \hat{\alpha}_2 ED\_PALAG + \hat{\alpha}_3 D\_PALAG6$$

$$+ \hat{\alpha}_4 D\_PALAG7 - RPLNA.$$

---

[23]Reported rates are not used for estimating $\widetilde{DEFRET}$ as they are applied to the market-related value of plan assets which is not available to us.

[24]Two items related to eq. (C.1) need clarification. First, *TR_ASSET* is not generally available. In eq. (C.1) we use the unamortized amount of *TR_ASSET* at the end of the year of adoption of SFAS 87 (*UNAM_TR*) in place of *TR_ASSET*. As a result, *l* in eq. (C.1) is actually *l* − 1. Second, the assumption that *e* is on average equal to zero does not hold empirically for firms which separately disclose *ATRANS*. These firms were not included in the estimation of eq. (C.1). However, inclusion of these firms, with the exception of one outlier based on Cook's *D* statistic [Cook (1977)], yields qualitatively similar results.

Table 4

Estimation of $\widehat{DEFRET}$ and $\widehat{ATRANS}$ from other disclosures (sample of calendar-year-end Compustat firms).[a]

Panel A: $TAMOR + RPLNA = \alpha_0 + \alpha_1 PALAG + \alpha_2 ED\_PALAG + \alpha_3 D\_PALAG6 + \alpha_4 D\_PALAG7 + \alpha_5 TR\_ASSET + \alpha_6$

	α_0	α_1	α_2	α_3	α_4	α_5	α_6
Coefficient estimate	2.97	0.08	0.01	0.01	0.00	0.04	0.03
t-statistic	(2.10)	(65.93)	(4.69)	(6.21)	(4.40)	(5.58)	(2.63)
N	568						
Adj. R^2	0.9898						

Panel B: Descriptive statistics 1986–1988, variables in per-share form

	1988		1987		1986	
Variable	Mean	Std. dev.	Mean	Std. dev.	Mean	Std. dev.
$\widehat{DEFRET}$	−0.26	0.96	0.25	1.28	−0.64	1.14
$\widehat{ATRANS}$	0.07	0.23	0.08	0.24	0.09	0.12
N	241		248		113	

[a] $\widehat{DEFRET}$ Estimate of deferred return on plan assets (DEFRET).
$\widehat{ATRANS}$ Estimate of amortization of transition asset (ATRANS).
TAMOR   Net deferral and amortization pension cost component.
RPLNA   Actual return on plan assets.
PALAG   Beginning-of-year plan assets.
ED_PALAG $ED \times PALAG$, where $ED = 1$ for early adopters of SFAS 87, $ED = 0$ otherwise.
D_PALAG $D \times PALAG$, where $D = 1$ for the year indicated, $D = 0$ otherwise.
ED_TR $ED \times TR\_ASSET$, where $ED = 1$ for early adopters of SFAS 87, $ED = 0$ otherwise.
TR_ASSET   Transition asset at the date of adoption of SFAS 87.
$TAMOR = ATRANS + DEFRET + error^*$.
$TAMOR = \widehat{ATRANS} + \widehat{DEFRET} + error$.
$error = error^* + (ATRANS - \widehat{ATRANS}) + (DEFRET - \widehat{DEFRET})$.
Variables in panel A are not deflated by number of shares.

If $\widehat{ATRANS}$ is available ($N = 38$, 43, and 33), then $\widehat{ATRANS}$ is set equal to ATRANS. Otherwise, estimates are based on eq. (C.1) ($N = 204, 206$, and 81) as follows:

$$\widehat{ATRANS} \equiv \hat{\alpha}_5 TR\_ASSET + \hat{\alpha}_6 ED\_TR.$$

Table 4, panel B, also contains sample summary statistics for $\widehat{DEFRET}$ and $\widehat{ATRANS}$. Note that negative values for $\widehat{DEFRET}$ imply that actual return on plan assets exceeded expected return. Negative mean values for $\widehat{DEFRET}$ are observed in 1986 and 1988, but not in 1987, which may reflect the rise in the stock market in 1986, the crash in 1987, and rebound in 1988. Although the mean value of $\overline{ATRANS}$ is highest in 1988, the mean values are of similar magnitude across the three years. This is consistent with straight-line amortization of the transition asset.

As an internal validity check, $\overline{DEFRET}$ and $\overline{ATRANS}$ were computed as if $DEFRET$ and $ATRANS$ were not available, and then correlations were computed between $\overline{DEFRET}$ and $DEFRET$ and $\overline{ATRANS}$ and $ATRANS$, using observations for which $DEFRET$ and $ATRANS$ are available. For $\overline{DEFRET}$ and $DEFRET$, correlations are 0.988 ($N = 59$), 0.984 ($N = 63$), and 0.988 ($N = 44$) in 1988, 1987, and 1986. For $\overline{ATRANS}$ and $ATRANS$, correlations are 0.964 ($N = 38$), 0.971 ($N = 43$), and 0.977 ($N = 33$).

As a further validity check, $TAMOR$ was regressed on $\overline{DEFRET}$ and $\overline{ATRANS}$. Under the assumption of no estimation error, the coefficients are expected to be equal to one. Under the assumption that $\overline{ATRANS}$ and $ATRANS$ are the primary components of $TAMOR$, the R^2 is expected to be very high. The coefficients (t-statistics) on $\overline{DEFRET}$ are 0.92, 0.99, and 0.93 (36.1, 99.5, and 56.7), the coefficients (t-values) on $\overline{ATRANS}$ are 0.77, 0.95, and 0.76 (3.2, 18.3, and 11.5), with R^2 of 0.95, 0.98, and 0.94 for 1986, 1987, and 1988, respectively. The somewhat lower coefficient for $\overline{ATRANS}$ may be reflecting somewhat greater estimation error relative to $\overline{DEFRET}$.

References

Barth, M.E., 1991, Relative measurement errors among alternative pension asset and liability measures, The Accounting Review 66, 433–463.
Barth, M.E., W.H. Beaver, and C.H. Stinson, 1991, Supplemental data and the structure of thrift share prices, The Accounting Review 66, 56–66.
Barth, M.E., W.H. Beaver, and M.A. Wolfson, 1990, Components of bank earnings and the structure of bank share prices, Financial Analysts Journal 46, May/June, 53–60.
Beaver, W.H., 1987, Properties of sequential regressions with multiple explanatory variables, The Accounting Review 62, 137–144.
Beaver, W.H. and J. Demski, 1979, The nature of income measurement, The Accounting Review 54, 38–46.
Beaver, W.H. and W. Landsman, 1983, Incremental information content of statement 33 disclosures (FASB, Stamford, CT).
Beaver, W.H., R. Lambert, and D. Morse, 1980, The information content of security prices, Journal of Accounting and Economics 2, 3–28.
Belsley, D.A., E. Kuh, and R.E. Welsch, 1980, Regression diagnostics (Wiley, New York, NY).
Bodie, Z., J. Light, R. Morck, and R. Taggert, 1985, Corporate pension policy: An empirical investigation, Financial Analysts Journal 41, Sept./Oct., 10–16.
Collins, D. and S.P. Kothari, 1989, An analysis of intertemporal and cross-sectional determinants of earnings response coefficients, Journal of Accounting and Economics 11, 143–181.
Cook, R.D., 1977, Detection of influential observation in linear regression, Technometrics 19, 15–18.
Easton, P. and M. Zmijewski, 1989, Cross-sectional variation in the stock market response to accounting earnings announcements, Journal of Accounting and Economics 11, 117–141.
Financial Accounting Standards Board, 1984, Statement of financial accounting standards no. 87, Employers' accounting for pensions (FASB, Stamford, CT).

Financial Accounting Standards Board, 1990, Statement of financial accounting standards no. 106, Employers' accounting for postretirement benefits other than pensions (FASB, Norwalk, CT).

Foster, G., 1986, Financial statement analysis (Prentice-Hall, Englewood Cliffs, NJ).

Hansen, L.P., 1982, Large sample properties of generalized method of moments estimators, Econometrica 50, 1029–1054.

Healy, P., 1985, The impact of bonus schemes on the selection of accounting principles, Journal of Accounting and Economics 7, 85–107.

Ippolito, R.A., 1985, The economic function of underfunded pension plans, Journal of Law and Economics 28, 611–651.

Landsman, W., 1986, An empirical investigation of pension fund property rights, The Accounting Review 61, 662–691.

Landsman, W.R. and J. Magliolo, 1988, Cross-sectional capital market research and model specification, The Accounting Review 63, 586–604.

Landsman, W.R., B.L. Miller, and S. Yeh, 1991, An empirical examination of the pension fund asset allocation decision, Working paper (University of California, Los Angeles, CA).

Lipe, R., 1986, The information contained in the components of earnings, Journal of Accounting Research (Suppl.) 24, 37–68.

Miller, M. and F. Modigliani, 1966, Some estimates of the cost of capital to the electric utility industry, American Economic Review 56, 333–391.

Modigliani, F. and M. Miller, 1958, The cost of capital, corporation finance and the theory of investment, American Economic Review 48, 261–297.

Ohlson, J.A., 1989, Accounting earnings, book value, and dividends: The theory of the clean surplus equation (Part I), Working paper (Columbia University, New York, NY).

Ryan, S., 1989, A note on measurement error in earnings and bias in valuation models, Working paper (Yale School of Organization and Management, New Haven, CT).

Scholes, M.S. and M.A. Wolfson, 1991, Taxes and business strategy: A global planning approach (Prentice-Hall, Englewood Cliffs, NJ).

Scott, T.W., 1989, Pension disclosures under SFAS 87: Theory and evidence, Working paper (University of Alberta, Edmonton).

Stone, M. and R.W. Ingram, 1988, The effect of statement no. 87 on the financial reports of early adopters, Accounting Horizons 2, 48–61.

Thomas, J.K., 1988, Corporate taxes and defined benefit pension plans, Journal of Accounting and Economics 10, 199–237.

Watts, R.L. and J.L. Zimmerman, 1986, Positive accounting theory (Prentice-Hall, Englewood Cliffs, NJ).

White, H., 1980, A heteroskedasticity-consistent covariance matrix estimator and a direct test for heteroskedasticity, Econometrica 48, 817–838.

III

FORECASTING EARNINGS AND INVESTMENT PERFORMANCE USING FINANCIAL STATEMENT INFORMATION

1 Ball, Ray, and Ross L. Watts, "Some Time Series Properties of Accounting Income," *Journal of Finance*, 27 (1972), pp. 663–681.
2 Brooks, Leroy D., and Dale A. Buckmaster, "Further Evidence of the Time Series Properties of Accounting Income," *Journal of Finance,* 31 (1976), pp. 1359–1373.
3 Ou, Jane, "The Information Content of Nonearnings Numbers as Earnings Predictors," *Journal of Accounting Research,* 28 (1990), pp. 144–163.
4 Brown, Larry D., Paul A. Griffin, Robert L. Hagerman, and Mark E. Zmijewski, "An Evaluation of Alternative Proxies for the Market's Assessment of Unexpected Earnings," *Journal of Accounting & Economics,* 9 (1987), pp. 159–193.
5 Ali, Ashiq, April Klein, and James Rosenfeld, "Analysts' Use of Information about Permanent and Transitory Earnings Components in Forecasting Annual EPS," *The Accounting Review*, 67 (1992), pp. 183–198.
6 Stickel, Scott E., "The Effect of Value Line Investment Survey Rank Changes on Common Stock Prices," *Journal of Financial Economics*, 14 (1985), pp. 121–143.

This part deals with forecasting, using financial statement information. Because of the primary role of earnings in the stock market (discussed in the previous part), most of the literature is concerned with forecasting future earnings. Earnings forecasts fall into three categories: (1) statistical time series forecasts, which utilize only the past sequence of earnings; (2) statistical forecasting models, which utilize financial statement information other than earnings; and (3) security analysts' and managers' forecasts, which utilize whatever information the forecaster chooses. The final article in the part studies forecasts of future stock price performance made by analysts at The Value Line Investment Survey. Value Line's forecasts make extensive use of financial statement information, and are not limited to forecasting earnings.

Random Walks in Earnings

In a fetchingly titled publication, "Higgledy Piggledy Growth," I. M. D. Little (1962) presents the first systematic evidence that the growth rates in firms' earnings are independent across time. Little studied a very small sample of British firms. A follow-up study by Rayner and Little (1966) confirms this result in a wider sample, again of British firms. **Ball and Watts (1972)** study a broad sample of large NYSE firms and employ a wider range of statistical tests. They report that to a first approximation, changes in EPS are uncorrelated across time.

In statistical parlance this means that earnings behave like a "random walk" in time, though with a predominantly upward trend.[1] The term "random" is not meant to imply anything about the meaningfulness or the information content of earnings; it simply means that future earnings changes cannot be forecast from past changes. The random walk result in annual earnings also is confirmed by Albrecht, Lookabill, and McKeown (1977), by Watts and Leftwich (1977), and by researchers in several countries.

The result that changes in earnings are approximately uncorrelated across time has important implications for financial statement analysis. First, it explains the emphasis that analysts attach to the most recent period's earnings (as distinct from, say, an average of the most recent three years). In a random walk process, the best statistical forecast of the next observation is its most recent value (that is, it is optimum to forecast no change apart from the trend). Second, the random walk model for earnings can be used as a simple statistical benchmark for evaluating the accuracy of analysts' earnings forecasts: it is a model that analysts should beat. It implies that the best time series model for forecasting future earnings simply adjusts last year's actual earnings for the upward trend in earnings. Third, the random walk result has important implications for how large the price response to earnings should be. Ball and Watts observe that in a strict random walk process, any change in earnings causes a corresponding revision in the expected value of all future earnings. This in turn implies that stock prices should be very sensitive to earnings: the price response to an earnings change should normally be in the order of a normal P/E ratio times that change. **Kothari and Sloan (1992)** make use of a version of this result (see Part I). They estimate an average "earnings response coefficient" of 5.45 over four years. This implies that a $1 change in EPS on average is associated with a $5.45 change in share price. They calculate that a strict random walk process in earnings is consistent with a coefficient of approximately 7 to 8.[2] The conclusion thus is that prices are very sensitive to earnings when one adjusts for prices anticipating earnings.

The Temporary Component of Earnings

It is implausible that all firms' annual earnings follow a strict random walk process. All earnings changes then would be "permanent," in the sense that they would be incorporated into the expectation of all future years' earnings.[3] But some type of temporary component of earnings changes seems likely as well.

One need only consider the fact that firms occasionally report negative earnings. If earnings followed a strict random walk process, then for these firms the expectation of all

---

[1] The upward trend presumably is due at least in part to companies reinvesting earnings.

[2] An alternative calculation, based on average P/E ratios, would suggest a factor of approximately 11.

[3] Random walks have the property that the level at time t is the sum of all the changes up to that time. Each change thus permanently affects the future level.

future earnings would be negative. Start-up companies, which tend to report negative earnings in the early years before their revenues begin flowing, then would possess value only as "real options." More generally, earnings seem likely to be affected by one-off "temporary" events such as uninsured fires, strikes, lawsuits, and accidents, which tend to induce effects of opposite sign on successive earnings differences. In addition, accounting accruals seem likely to induce some negative dependence in successive earnings changes; for example, undervaluing closing inventories or accounts receivable will increase this year's earnings but will also decrease next year's.

The random walk model is only a parsimonious description of the earnings process. It is not surprising that researchers can detect a temporary component in annual earnings, in addition to the permanent random walk component. This causes some negative correlation in first differences in annual earnings. However, the improvements in the accuracy of annual earnings forecasts obtained from utilizing this dependence are not great, except for extreme earnings cases, because temporary effects do not appear to be a large component of annual earnings.

Ball and Watts (1972, Table 3) report that first differences in the average firm's EPS exhibit first-order serial correlation (i.e., at lag one) of approximately -0.2. This is consistent with a small temporary component in annual earnings. They note that it explains only 4 percent of the variability in changes in EPS. In a follow-up study of a sample of fifty firms over the much longer period 1916–1965, Ball and Watts (1979) replicate this result surprisingly closely. They also report (1979, Table 5) that first differences in firms' revenues are essentially independent over time, and conclude that this "indicates that expenses, rather than revenues, are the source of the negative serial correlation. Depreciation and inventory valuation methods would be prime suspects in this regard" [Ball and Watts (1979, p. 205)].

Brooks and Buckmaster (1976) demonstrate the temporary (or mean-reverting) component of earnings by focussing on extreme earnings changes. They show a tendency for extreme changes to be followed by changes of the opposite sign. This means that there are temporary effects on the level of earnings, which violates the strict random walk model. Reversal of extreme changes thus is one source of the negative correlation in EPS changes at the first lag.

Quarterly Earnings
Foster (1977) investigates the time series properties of quarterly earnings. These properties are unlikely to be identical to those of annual earnings, if only due to the within-year production and sales seasonals that occur in many businesses. Foster concludes that the best one-quarter-ahead earnings forecasting model has the following properties: (1) it allows for seasonals in quarterly earnings; (2) the earnings variable it works with is the difference between earnings in the corresponding quarters of adjacent years;[4] and (3) it allows for positive correlation between adjacent quarters in the seasonally adjusted first differences. The latter property means that seasonally adjusted quarterly earnings do not follow a strict random walk process, in which changes would be uncorrelated across time.
Bernard and Thomas (1990) believe that this property of quarterly earnings is not completely recognized by the stock market (see Part I). In effect, they believe that the market

---
[4] The earnings variable thus is, for example, first quarter 1993 EPS minus first quarter 1992 EPS.

understands the first two, but not the third, of Foster's conclusions about the optimal quarterly earnings forecasting model.

Forecasts Using Other Information

The research surveyed above deals only with statistical time series forecasts of earnings, in which future earnings are forecast using only the information in the past time series of earnings. An additional category of earnings forecasts utilizes statistical models that incorporate financial statement information other than earnings. **Ou and Penman (1989)** report that several variables are useful in predicting one-year-ahead earnings, including return on assets, return on equity, change in return on equity, debt/equity ratio, percent change in dividend per share, and percent change in inventories (see Part I). **Ou (1990)** reports related results.

Analysts' Earnings Forecasts

Forecasts made either by security analysts or by corporate managers should be superior to those of statistical models. Since both of these parties have access to considerable information in addition to past earnings and past financial statement information (including information released after the end of the last accounting period), their forecasts seem likely to be more accurate than time series forecasts.[5]

Brown and Rozeff (1978) study forecasts of fifty firms' earnings made by analysts at The Value Line Investment Survey. They find them to be more accurate than sophisticated statistical time series forecasting methods, which in turn are more accurate than simple random walk forecasts. Brown, Hagerman, Griffin, and Zmijewski (1987) extend this to a sample involving over two hundred firms' forecasts from the same source. They show that the higher accuracy of analysts' forecasts is due to analysts' possessing more information than past earnings at the time earnings were announced, and also to their acquiring additional subsequent information. In a related paper, **Brown, Griffin, Hagerman and Zmijewski (1987)** change the criterion for evaluating alternative forecasts from accuracy (i.e., predicting future earnings) to one of how closely the earnings forecast error corresponds with the revision of share prices at the time earnings are announced. Assuming that the immediate post-announcement price incorporates the complete market reaction to earnings (i.e., ignoring the evidence of "drift" in Part I), the revision in price over the announcement period reflects the difference between actual earnings and the market's pre-announcement forecast. The announcement periods studied begin from one up to forty days before the announcement. The criterion for alternative forecasts thus amounts to one of how closely they correspond to those of the market, and is based on the theory of market efficiency. Using this criterion, the authors report several interesting results, including the effects of firm size and forecast age.

Ali, Klein, and Rosenfeld (1992) report that a sample of analysts' earnings forecasts is biased and inefficient. The sample is more than 5,000 median analyst forecasts recorded on the IBES data file over 1976–1990. There is evidence that the analysts do not make statistically optimal forecasts. First, they are overoptimistic on average, so they are statistically biased. Second, they do not use all available information, so they are statistically

---

[5] This statement assumes that the single role of analysts' earnings forecasts is to be informative about future earnings. Ball (1994) offers the hypothesis that earnings forecasts also provide valuable information about the subjective beliefs underlying other investors' actions.

inefficient. They do not even exploit all the information in past forecasts (i.e., there is positive serial correlation on average in forecast errors). The latter result could be due in part to taking medians of forecasts made at different times.[6] These results raise several fundamental questions, including whether the sole objective of analysts is to forecast earnings accurately [Ball (1994)] and whether forecasting is a costly production activity with only a cost-efficient degree of bias or accuracy.

Value Line Rankings

Stickel (1985) examines the decision of The Value Line Investment Survey to change its published rating of a company's stock. The rating, on a scale of one through five, is meant as an indicator of the attractiveness of the stock as an investment. The criteria used by Value Line are based on changes in earnings and stock prices, over the immediate past as well as periods up to ten years. This rating system assumes that the market is slow in digesting earnings information, so that prices diverge from and only slowly return to fundamentals, and thus it overlaps the stock selection schemes of **Ou and Penman (1989)** and **Bernard and Thomas (1990).** Perhaps as a consequence, Stickel's Figure 1 looks somewhat familiar. It resembles the graph reproduced from Ball and Brown (1968) in the introduction to Part I, and the equivalent Figure 1 in **Foster, Olsen, and Shevlin (1984)**, the third article in that part. It shows: (1) most of the information in the rating change is incorporated in prices before the change; (2) price reaction occurs at the time to some of the rating changes; and (3) there is a slow response or "drift" in prices over the following period for some of the rating changes, suggesting an opportunity to earn abnormal returns from the Value Line system. As is true in most studies, the above effects are stronger for smaller firms' stocks.

---

[6] There are problems with the bias result as well. The distribution of the forecast errors, scaled by price, is skewed (the minimum eight-month-ahead error is -631 percent). The mean eight month-ahead error appears to be -3.02 percent of price (assuming the reported numbers are percentages), which is implausibly large as a percentage of earnings. The median bias is much closer to zero.

SOME TIME SERIES PROPERTIES OF ACCOUNTING INCOME

Ray Ball and Ross Watts*

I. Introduction

The time series behavior of corporate incomes has generated considerable interest. The early work of Little [28] suggests that successive changes in corporate incomes in the U.K. are independent. Subsequent empirical work suggests that the same conclusion applies to corporate incomes in the U.S. This article applies different methods from those of previous researchers, but the conclusion is unchanged. We conclude that, in general, measured annual accounting incomes for U.S. corporations follow either a submartingale or some very similar process.[1] Because of small sample problems this conclusion is based on mean and median results; no attempt has been made to determine whether specific firms are systematic outliers.

The conclusion that corporate incomes are submartingales has important implications for forecasters and researchers in accounting and finance. For example, it implies that attempts to smooth corporate incomes in the manner suggested in the accounting and finance literatures are not successful. It also affects the interpretation of the growth and decline of firms.

II. The Smoothing of Income

The accounting and finance literatures are replete with the suggestion that accountants smooth the incomes of firms. That is, it is commonly hypothesized that accountants manipulate their income-measuring techniques in order to soften the effect of hard times upon income and, conversely, in order to diminish the extent to which good times are contemporaneously reflected in income.

The hypothesis that accountants do smooth income and the belief that they should smooth income have existed for decades. Hepworth [25], Gordon [21, 22], Gordon et al. [23], Schiff [36], Dopuch and Drake [14], Copeland [10], Copeland and Licastro [11], and Gagnon [20] all investigate income

---

* Graduate School of Business, University of Chicago and Graduate School of Management, University of Rochester, respectively. The authors are indebted to Philip Brown, Eugene Fama, Nicholas Gonedes, Merton Miller, Robert Officer and a referee for their assistance. An earlier version of this paper was delivered at the Workshop in Accounting Research and the Workshop in Finance at the University of Chicago on April 23, 1968.

1. Let $Y_1, Y_2 \ldots$ be random variables with expectations. Then the sequence $\{Y_t\}$ is a submartingale if

$$E(Y_{t+1} | Y_0, \ldots, Y_t) \geq Y_t \quad \text{for all } t,$$

where E is an expectation operator.

The martingale is a specific case of a submartingale.
The sequence $\{Y_t\}$ is a martingale if

$$E(Y_{t+1} | Y_0, \ldots, Y_t) = Y_t \quad \text{for all t.}$$

smoothing. To our knowledge, no study has addressed the possible futility of alleged smoothing practices.

As it is presented in the literature, smoothing is an attempt to reduce the variance of income around its expectation. Income is assumed to be generated by a process whose expectation is constant or is a deterministic function of time.[2] For example, Schiff writes [36, p. 66]:

> Some years ago, Boulding referred to the "homeostasis of the balance sheet—that there is some desired quantity of all the various items in the balance sheet, and that any disturbance of this structure immediately sets in motion forces which restore the status quo." It can be suggested that we now have a "homeostasis of earnings per share" and that the application of generally accepted accounting principles facilitates the reporting of earnings per share in a constant or rising pattern . . . .

Gordon writes [22, p. 223]:

> If the variation of the observations around the curve are smaller [when accountants adopt a specific accounting practice], income smoothing has been the consequence . . . .

Copeland says essentially the same thing [10, p. 102]:

> Income smoothing involves the repetitive selection of accounting measurement or reporting rules in a particular pattern, the effect of which is to report a stream of income with a smaller variation from trend than would otherwise have appeared.

These and other sources imply that the expectation of income is a function of time or is constant. Smoothing implies a return to good times, on average, after bad times, during which income decreases are artificially reduced by smoothing practices. It implies that many increases in income are also temporary, and can therefore be smoothed in order to avoid the impression of permanence.

Apart from ignoring the substantial evidence that the market can decide for itself whether in fact income changes are permanent or temporary,[3] the smoothing of income by the accounting profession would seem to ignore the possibility that good times are not followed, on average, by bad times. A submartingale implies that a firm is stuck with good and bad times (deviations of realized incomes from expectations) when they occur since a submartingale, by definition, is a process in which any one observation becomes the basis for the expectation of the next. Given the uncertainty of the world, there is always a probability distribution around the expectation. But the behavior of the expectation of a submartingale over time would be such as to make nonsense of the notion of income smoothing.[4]

---

2. If $Y_1, Y_2 \ldots$ are random variables with expectations, the assumption is

$$E(Y_{t+1} | Y_0, \ldots, Y_t) = \psi \quad \text{for all } t,$$

where ψ is a constant or

$$E(Y_{t+1} | Y_0, \ldots, Y_t) = f(t+1)$$

where $f(t+1)$ is some function of $t+1$, and which incorporates trends in expectations in an analogous fashion to a submartingale.

3. See the theory and evidence summarized by Fama [16]. Some specific studies of market ingenuity in reacting to information, such as income, are [2] and [18].

4. Attempting to smooth an underlying submartingale mechanism would *increase* the variance of future income changes, simply by making the probability distribution of changes asymmetric.

One could initially be tempted to argue that this is not true, because the evidence of independence of income changes applies only to measured income numbers—which are observed *after* accountants have decided upon which measurement rules to use. This argument does not go far enough, for smoothing of a series generated by a process with an expectation that is constant or a deterministic function of time produces another series of the same form.[5] Since the observed series is not of this form, smoothing of this type does not appear to occur. If accountants try to smooth in the manner which we outline, then they attempt a futile exercise.[6]

III. Growth and Decline

The interpretation of growth and decline (and their extreme counterparts, survival and failure) depends heavily upon the income-generating process. Growth in a martingale mechanism occurs as frequently as decline; and either, once experienced, is permanent, on average. Growth in a process whose expectation is constant over time is nonexistent.[7]

The implications of income variability for the survival of a firm depend upon the process which generates income. A constant-expectation finite-variance process implies the relative insignificance of variability in income. Deviations of income from the expectation are then *once-and-for-all* increments or decrements in the value of the firm. Value changes are relatively small—the value of the firm changes in the order of the size of the deviation in income, given the (known) expectation of the process. If the expectation of income is known and stationary (and it surely would become known), then investors face very little risk. It is difficult to see why individual firms would ever fail; even the possibility of gambler's ruin and its consequential reorganization costs seem to be avoidable by borrowing when the expectation of income is constant. While borrowing is not without cost, it is then difficult to see the *ex ante* importance of variability to the valuation of the firm, conditional upon a (known) long-run expectation.

In contrast, a process whose expectation is not constant or a deterministic function of time implies the importance of variability. For a martingale (that is, ignoring trend), there is a finite probability, which is a function of the variability of the process, that the expectation of income at some future time will be negative or zero, and that the firm will on average fail. The expectation of *all* future incomes is changed with each observation. Hence, investors face greater risk than under the other type of income process. The value of the

---

5. The variance of income changes and higher moments are reduced, but the covariance of successive changes is reduced in the same order. Hence, the correlation coefficient for successive changes is roughly the same for the observed and unsmoothed series. We observe essentially zero serial correlation.

6. Of course, other types of smoothing can be investigated. In a paper which provides valuable insights in other ways, Beaver [4] adopts a different definition of "smoothing." He hypothesizes a non-manipulative type of smoothing, different from that which exists in the literature, and demonstrates its consistency with our results.

7. Either process, when superimposed with a trend, produces growth. A submartingale therefore can exhibit either or both of two kinds of growth: on average, due to the expectation of trend; and by chance, in spite of the zero expectation of non-trend change.

firm should change in the order of a normal proportionality factor times the change in income, reflecting the changed expected profitability.

The interpretation of decline and growth processes and of income variability are therefore significantly different when income is generated by a submartingale mechanism.

Given that the nature of the income process has importance both for the successful smoothing of income and for the interpretation of growth in the incomes of firms, what is the prior evidence and what does it imply about the income generating process?

IV. Prior Evidence

The original work of Little [28] and the later and larger study of Little and Rayner [29] indicate that successive growth rates in the incomes of British companies are random. Both studies use percentage changes in incomes to measure growth rates and are concerned with the period-to-period stability of those growth rates. As the authors recognize, the use of such period-to-period percentage changes biases the results towards randomness.

Lintner and Glauber [27] also investigate the relationship between growth rates in successive periods. However, the periods are longer, namely 5 and 10 years, and the sample consists of the 309 U.S. corporations on the Compustat industrial tapes with positive dividends in each of the years 1946 to 1965 inclusive. Using log arithmetic data, growth is measured as the slope coefficient in the regressions of various income variables on time over the 5 and 10 year periods.[8] Although they find very small cross-sectional correlation between the growth rates of successive periods, Lintner and Glauber are not prepared to accept the hypothesis that the successive growth rates are independent:

"any conclusion to the effect that nothing but a table of random numbers is relevant to growth in the real world itself would be premature and unwise." [27, p. 8].

Brealey [6 and 7] follows Lintner and Glauber in studying the incomes of U.S. corporations. However, he investigates changes in incomes instead of growth rates in incomes. From cross-sectional correlations of changes in incomes for various lags, runs tests and financial analysts' predictions based on past accounting data only, Brealey effectively concludes that incomes follow a martingale [6, p. 13]. In his later book Brealey [7] reviews his own study and that of Lintner and Glauber and does not change his conclusions.

Other evidence comes from less direct analyses. Fama and Babiak [17] note in their dividend study that signs of earnings changes are nearly independent over time. Ball and Brown [2] find that changes in earnings capture the new information which the stock market sees in an income number. Ball and Brown [3] find that the assumption $E(Y_t) = Y_{t-1}$, where Y_t is the income number in year t, leads to less error in measurement of the expectation of Y than using an average of past Y's.[9]

---

8. The income variables used by Lintner and Glauber are sales, operating income, earnings before interest and taxes, aggregate dollar earnings, earnings per share and dividends per share.

9. Specifically, a covariance between Y and another series is measured with less error in first differences (which assumes $E(Y_t) = Y_{t-1}$) than in levels (which averages Y over the whole time series).

This evidence suggests that incomes conform to the specific kinds of non-randomness which are implicitly assumed by using specific tests. In our examination of the incomes of U.S. corporations, we do not impose such restrictive assumptions since it is difficult to hypothesize a specific form of time series behavior for incomes. While the theory of efficient markets may yield specific hypotheses for the time series behavior of market prices of securities, there is no such theory for firms' incomes. The theory of the firm is comparative static rather than stochastic, and the properties of accounting measurement rules are not well understood. Consequently, our investigation is essentially a descriptive exercise and it uses a number of different tests.

Since we are concerned with the income generating process per se, we do not use the cross-sectional approach of Brealey, Little, and Little and Rayner.

Our analysis is deliberately confined to the expectations of the probability distributions of change, ignoring other distributional features.[10]

V. Data

Data are from Standard and Poor's *Compustat* file for the twenty years 1947-1966.[11] Firms with less than twenty years of data are excluded from the sample because the estimating procedures are sensitive to both few and missing observations. As a consequence, the incomes of fewer than the approximately 900 firms on the S & P file are investigated, the number differing according to the specific definition of net income which is used.

The effect of our sample selection procedure probably is to over-estimate the importance of trends which are imposed upon expectations. Because the S & P file contains only survived firms, because it contains only large firms which are presumably older survivors than average, and because we do not accept firms without early data and are presumably left with even older survivors than the S & P average, we probably have fewer average decreases in income in our sample than have occurred over the time period under study. Failed firms represent an obvious bias; age represents another. A proportion of unexpected positive deviations from expectation will appear to constitute an *expectation* of upward trend, since a proportion of offsetting chance negative deviation will have been removed by the selection of only surviving and older firms.[12]

The importance of this upward bias in income relative to genuine expectations of trend (due, say, to reinvestment) cannot be determined within the selected sample of firms. In an extension of this study we consider the effects of these biases by investigating different samples of firms over different time periods. Preliminary results indicate that the effects are minimal.

Four definitions of "income" in year t, Y_t, are studied. They are:

---

10. For example we do not test directly whether incomes arise from a single constant process. The more general form $g(Y_{t+1} \mid Y_0, \ldots, Y_t)$, where g is the distribution function for Y_{t+1}, is not considered.

11. Tape used is dated July 7, 1967.

12. Any competitive situation with selection of succeeding entities faces this same *ex post* sample selection bias, unless records are available of failures after they drop out. The construction of an unbiased sample of firms is thus a delicate procedure. We do not use log transformations in this paper because we do not wish to eliminate zero and negative incomes.

(1) Net income, after income taxes, as defined by Standard and Poor's.[13]
(2) Adjusted earnings per share, adjusted for stock splits and dividends.
(3) Net income, deflated by total assets, which might reduce reinvestment effects.
(4) Net sales, which is chosen because of its possible dominance of the income series, and because it could be less affected by income "smoothing" practices of accountants.

VI. Tests and Results

As we suggested above, this study is a descriptive exercise since we do not have theories of the firm or of the measurement of income. Further, due to our limited number of observations for each firm, the results we obtain may be sensitive to violations of the assumptions of each test. Analytical results for most tests are for "large" samples.[14] We attempt to avoid both issues by subjecting the income data to a number of different tests. Some of their characteristics are noted below; conclusions are based upon their broad tenor.[15]

Average changes—One indication of trend in a series is the number of increases relative to decreases [29, p. 390]. However, the test assumes symmetrically-distributed changes. An alternative test for trend is to investigate changes for the *average* firm; that is, to aggregate incomes over firms and then to look at signs of changes in the aggregate series. The test is sensitive to asymmetry, but the asymmetry possibly has been removed by the averaging process.

Table 1 shows the time series of average net income and E.P.S. for 1947-65. The averages are those used in [8]. Average net income is calculated as a single average over 451 *Compustat* firms. Average E.P.S. is a weighted average over the same firms, the weights being the adjusted number of common shares outstanding at the end of each year for each firm.

An *ex post* upward trend in both series is apparent. Unfortunately, the sample cannot reveal the importance of an *ex post* sample selection bias against decreases in income, relative to an *ex ante* expectation of increase.

Runs tests—A "weak" test of independence is afforded by comparing the actual and expected numbers of runs in a series. The test is "weak" because it tests for independence conditional upon known probabilities of increases and decreases in income, which must be estimated from the sample itself. Thus it tends to fit the data too closely to the distribution which is assumed to generate the observations.[16] Furthermore, it tests a specific form of independence: the randomness of the sequential arrangement in signs of deviations within a finite series.

---

13. S & P exclude "extraordinary items" which are shown in company reports net of tax. Where gross figures are available, extraordinary items are included. Using *Moody's Industrial Manual* as a reference, it would appear that S & P thereby include most extraordinary items.

14. Kendall and Stuart [26].

15. Bennett and Franklin [5, p. 688] also suggest this procedure.

16. Roberts [35], Chapter 5, p. 24. Partly for this reason, the distribution of runs by length of run is not considered. Another reason for the omission is the sensitivity of this test to discontinuities in a series.

TABLE 1
TIME SERIES OF INCOME AVERAGED OVER 451 Compustat FIRMS

Year	Net Income Levels ($m)	Net Income Changes ($m)	E.P.S. Levels ($P.S.)	E.P.S. Changes ($P.S.)
1947	11.17		1.207	
1948	14.43	+3.26	1.550	+0.343
1949	13.12	−1.31	1.399	−0.151
1950	17.27	+4.15	1.829	+0.430
1951	15.96	−1.31	1.646	−0.183
1952	15.32	−0.64	1.551	−0.095
1953	16.93	+1.61	1.696	+0.145
1954	18.18	+1.25	1.775	+0.079
1955	23.72	+5.54	2.250	+0.475
1956	24.57	+0.85	2.259	+0.009
1957	24.63	+0.06	2.221	−0.038
1958	21.27	−3.36	1.867	−0.354
1959	25.26	+3.99	2.188	+0.321
1960	25.16	−0.10	2.143	−0.045
1961	25.59	+0.43	2.143	0.000
1962	28.66	+3.07	2.393	+0.250
1963	32.17	+3.51	2.659	+0.266
1964	37.08	+4.91	3.020	+0.361
1965	42.47	+5.39	3.420	+0.400
Increases		13		11
Decreases		5		6

Source: Brown and Ball [8, p. 61]. The 451 firms were those which met the more stringent data requirements of those authors.

Wald and Wolfowitz [38] calculate the exact distribution of the number of runs, R, under the assumption of independence, and show that:

$$\mu_R = \frac{2N_1 N_2}{N} + 1,$$

and

$$\sigma_R^2 = \frac{2N_1 N_2 (2N_1 N_2 - N)}{N^2 (N+1)},$$

where μ_R and σ_R^2 are the expectation and variance of R respectively, N_1 is the number of cases when $Y_t > Y_a$ (for any Y_a), N_2 is the number of cases when $Y_t < Y_a$, and $N = N_1 + N_2$. Further assuming that both N_1 and N_2 are "large," the statistic

$$Z = \frac{R - \mu_R}{\sigma_R}$$

is normally distributed, with limiting distribution normal (0, 1). The normal approximation holds "closely" for $N_1, N_2 > 10$ ([13], p. 289; [31], pp. 414-16), which requires at least five more observations than our sample possesses.[17]

---

17. An adjustment for the normal approximation to the binomial distribution [37, p. 280] is omitted because we are describing the data, not testing a specific hypothesis.

Results for $Y_a = Y_{t-1}$ (that is, for runs in signs of changes) are reported in Table 2. The Table gives the deciles of the cross-sectional distribution of

TABLE 2
RUNS IN SIGNS OF INCOME CHANGES

	Mean	Decile								
		.1	.2	.3	.4	.5	.6	.7	.8	.9
Net Income z value	−0.03	−1.37	−0.94	−0.49	−0.22	−0.12	0.34	0.50	0.74	1.20
E.P.S. z value	−0.04	−1.22	−0.04	−0.61	−0.22	−0.13	0.25	0.39	0.72	1.01

	Net Income		E.P.S.	
	Number	per cent	Number	per cent
Firms with more runs than expected under independence	348	48.7	326	48.0
Firms with fewer runs than expected under independence	366	51.3	353	52.0
	714	100.0	679	100.0
Total runs in sample	6522	100.0	6338	99.8
Total expected runs, assuming independence	6524	100.0	6350	100.0

Z scores for the 714 firms with net income data and the 679 firms with E.P.S. data. It also gives two comparisons of the observed number of runs in the series with the expected number of runs under the assumption of independence.

The runs tests reveal that, on average, changes in both net income and E.P.S. are essentially independently distributed. The mean Z for both series is extremely close to zero.[18] The actual number of runs is very close to the expected number under the assumption of independence.

Serial correlation—The analytical serial covariance of *changes* in equally-lagged drawings from an independently-distributed process is zero. The expectation of the computed serial correlation coefficient of "large" samples from an independent process also is zero. With "large" samples, the computed coefficient is insensitive to non-normality [26]. With "small" samples, and assuming normality,

$$\mu_S = -\frac{1}{N-1},$$

and

$$\sigma_S^2 = \frac{T-2}{(T-1)^2},$$

where μ_S and σ_S^2 are the expectation and variance of the computed coefficient S, N is the number of changes in the series, and T is N less the size

---

18. The median Z is sensitive to the fact that R is an integer. However, it should also be noted that there will be cross-sectional correlation in firms' incomes.

of the lag (N − 1 for successive differences). The distribution of S is approximately normal[19] and hence the statistic

$$Z = \frac{S - \mu_S}{\sigma_S}$$

is approximately normal (0, 1).

Estimated coefficients are presented in Table 3 for net income and E.P.S. with lag of one (that is, for successive first differences), and in Table 4 for lags of two to five. The tables once again give cross-sectional data. Table 3 also gives the cross-sectional distribution of the standard normal deviate Z, calculated on the assumption of independence.

The serial correlation coefficients are in agreement with the tenor of the runs tests, indicating that net income changes are essentially independent and that there is only a very low probability of a compensating mechanism for E.P.S. Most mean and median coefficients are very close to the expectation for an independent normal process. For example, with lag one, N = 19 and assuming independence and normality, the expectation of the computed coefficient is −0.056 and its standard deviation is 0.228. The mean coefficient for net income is −0.075, and for E.P.S. it is −0.198. Table 4 reveals that the coefficients for lags two and five are even closer to their expectations than those for lag one. The most extreme mean or median coefficient in either table is −0.200. This is not only an extreme observation; it also implies a mere 4 per cent explanatory power for an autoregressive prediction model.[20]

Mean squared successive difference—Runs tests give some indication of the source of any nonrandomness in a series. An excess of actual over expected runs suggests a compensating mechanism, while a deficit is evidence of either persistence, or of a mixture of processes with alternating parameter values.[21] The serial correlation coefficient has the added advantage of being sensitive to the size of successive differences and not merely their sign. The ratio of the mean squared successive difference to an estimate of the variance possesses some of the characteristics of both of these tests.

Define

$$\delta^2 = \sum_{t=1}^{N-1} (Y'_{t-1} - Y'_t)^2 / 2(N - 1),$$

where Y'_t are successive *differences*. Then δ^2 is an unbiased estimate of the variance of Y', if Y' is identically and independently distributed with finite variance.

Define

$$s^2 = \sum_{t=1}^{N} (Y'_t - \overline{Y'})^2 / N,$$

---

19. Anderson [1, p. 7] and Malinvaud [30, pp. 292-94].

20. The analytical serial correlation coefficient for first differences in a stable stationary process is −0.5. The computed coefficients clearly are of a lesser magnitude.

21. See Roberts [35, pp. 5-13].

TABLE 3
DISTRIBUTION OF SERIAL CORRELATION COEFFICIENTS, NET INCOME CHANGES
Lag 1

	Mean	.1	.2	.3	.4	.5	.6	.7	.8	.9
Net Income										
Coefficient	−0.030	−0.386	−0.286	−0.233	−0.150	−0.075	0.009	0.085	0.213	0.388
z value	+0.01	−1.45	−1.01	−0.78	−0.41	−0.08	0.29	0.62	1.18	1.94
E.P.S.										
Coefficient	−0.200	−0.453	−0.371	−0.307	−0.247	−0.198	−0.151	−0.090	−0.036	0.057
z value	−0.42	−1.74	−1.38	−1.10	−0.84	−0.62	−0.42	−0.15	0.09	0.49

TABLE 4
DISTRIBUTION OF SERIAL CORRELATION COEFFICIENTS, NET INCOME CHANGES
Lags 2-5

	Mean	.1	.2	.3	.4	Decile .5	.6	.7	.8	.9
Net Income										
Lag 2	−.040	−.368	−.275	−.197	−.129	−.067	−.002	+.087	+.209	+.315
3	+.006	−.306	−.202	−.131	−.068	+.001	+.053	+.120	+.205	+.321
4	−.007	−.320	−.221	−.128	−.070	−.013	+.050	+.111	+.184	+.313
5	+.055	−.277	−.165	−.085	−.008	+.047	+.118	+.193	+.262	+.403
E.P.S.										
Lag 2	−.076	−.375	−.255	−.182	−.131	−.081	−.030	+.020	+.098	+.208
3	−.061	−.331	−.231	−.163	−.115	−.073	−.027	+.035	+.132	+.259
4	+.023	−.300	−.163	−.150	−.088	−.052	−.009	+.069	+.159	+.319
5	+.010	−.346	−.150	−.140	−.079	−.024	+.031	+.096	+.200	+.318

TABLE 5
RATIO OF MSSD TO ESTIMATED VARIANCE (STANDARDIZED)[a]

	Mean	.1	.2	.3	.4	Decile .5	.6	.7	.8	.9
Net Income	+0.366	−1.37	−0.86	−0.48	−0.13	0.22	0.63	1.04	1.67	2.36
E.P.S.	−0.584	−1.91	−1.44	−1.15	−0.92	−0.73	−0.45	−0.18	0.26	0.84

[a] Expressed as standard normal deviates.

where $\overline{Y}'$ is the average difference. Then s^2 is the usual estimate of the variance under the same assumptions. If the assumptions are violated, then the ratio δ^2/s^2 measures the strength and sources of the violation. If, for example, a persistent trend exists, then the ratio will be small, or if the series fluctuates highly, then the ratio will be large. Hart and von Neumann show that under the assumption of an identically and independently distributed process with defined variance, and for "large" N, $\varepsilon = \delta^2/s^2$ has

$$\mu_\varepsilon = 1$$

$$\sigma_\varepsilon^2 = \frac{N-2}{N^2-1},$$

and is distributed approximately normally.[22] Hence the statistic

$$Z = \frac{1-\varepsilon}{\sigma_\varepsilon}$$

is normal (0, 1).

Values for the standardized ε value are reported in Table 5. Zero would indicate an independent process, while positive and negative values would indicate persistence and fluctuations, respectively. The results are, on the whole, consistent with previous tests. The median estimated ε for net income is +0.22 standard deviations from its expected value, assuming independence, and is −0.73 standard deviations from its conditional expectation for E.P.S. Once again, independence of changes in income is suggested.

It is helpful to bear in mind that the computed serial correlation coefficients do not constrain the average change to be zero, and therefore linearly detrend the income series. Further, the MSSD tests are conducted on changes in income, and the runs tests do not constrain the probabilities of increases and decreases to be equal. Hence, each of these three tests is a different test of the independence of deviations from a constant trend mechanism. Taken together with the observed trends in the aggregate time series of Table 1, the tests consistently imply that net income and E.P.S. behave, on average, as a submartingale.[23]

Partial Adjustment Models—We initially distinguished two extreme types of processes: processes with means which are a deterministic function of time and submartingales. The first type implies the independence of the expectation of income from the *observed* past incomes; in contrast, a submartingale implies total dependence in the sense that the expected value becomes the most immediate past observed income.

Partial adjustment models provide a natural method of determining the extent of dependence of the expectation of income upon past income. Let

---

22. Hart and von Neumann [24, p. 211]. Note the close similarity with the familiar tests for autocorrelation in regression analysis, where Y' is constrained to equal zero.

23. Some of the tests assume normal distributions, in which case the implication would be a random walk with an upward trend, i.e. a submartingale with a normal distribution. The term submartingale includes random walks and martingales (see footnote 1).

$\hat{Y}_t$ represent a forecast of income in period t. Then let $\hat{Y}_t$ be a function of the prior period's forecast $\hat{Y}_{t-1}$, and the observed income Y_{t-1}:

$$\hat{Y}_t = \alpha Y_{t-1} + (1-\alpha)\hat{Y}_{t-1}, \quad 0 \leq \alpha \leq 1.$$

Our objective is to estimate α from the income data. The α which produces, *ex post* and on average, the "best" forecast of income is deemed to characterize the *ex ante* degree of dependence of the expectation of income upon past observed values. That is, we define:

$$\hat{Y}_t^0 = E(Y_t \mid Y_0, \ldots, Y_{t-1})$$

where $\hat{Y}_t^0$ is the optimal forecast of Y_t on average.[24] An α of unity implies a martingale. An α of zero implies a process with a constant expectation. Intermediate values of α provide a linear measurement of the extent to which the time series can be described by a process with a constant expectation.

Two complications immediately arise. First, there is the problem of specifying what a "best" average forecaster of income would be. We choose mean absolute error as a measure of forecasting accuracy,

$$\sum_t |e_t| = \sum_t |Y_t - \hat{Y}_t|,$$

in order to avoid assumptions concerning the distribution of the errors. However, mean absolute error gives almost identical results to those of mean squared error. (unreported)

Second, there is the problem of growth in incomes over time. The partial-adjustment models described above do not perform well under the upward trend of the past twenty years. For example, a process with an expectation which is a strong positive function of time would be best fitted by the model which gives the most weight to the most recent observation: by a martingale. In order to accommodate trends, and therefore to avoid biasing the estimate of α upward, the range of smoothing models is generalized beyond the simple partial-adjustment models which assume that variables are unrelated to time. As well as these "constant" models we investigate models which allow for linear and quadratic dependence on time.[25] Detailed proofs and some explanation of the models are given by Muth [32] and Brown [9].

Values of α ranging between zero and one and with increments of 0.05 are used in making forecasts of Y_t. These 21 values of α, combined with the three levels employed, give 63 forecasting models which are tested. Thus, 63 forecasts of income are generated for each firm and each year. For α equal to zero or unity, the three broad models degenerate into a process with a constant mean and a martingale, respectively, for both of which time is not an argu-

---

24. The identity is also conditional upon the class of forecasting models used to calculate the various $\hat{Y}_t$.

25. There are reasons for confining the analysis to the three broad classes of constant, linear, and quadratic models: we doubt whether, given the available data, one could differentiate between a large number of models; and the estimation procedures make it desirable to limit the study from a computational point of view.

ment. Thus, we are left with 59 sub-models overall, although there are 21 sub-models within each broad class.

Results from Partial Adjustment Models—Actual Data

Forecasts in a given year are based upon actual observations in the series up to the previous year. The 1948 forecast is the actual value for 1947, since that is the only prior observation available.[26] Forecasts for subsequent years employ progressively more observations.

For each firm and each variable, the sub-models are then ranked on their total absolute errors over the 19 forecasts. Two sets of rankings are computed for each firm: an overall ranking of the 50 sub-models and individual rankings of the 21 sub-models within each of the three broad classes of models. The ranks of each sub-model are then summed over all firms, giving two sets of sums of ranks for each of the four income variables. The final precedure is to rank these sums, giving ranks of 1 through 59 overall and 1 through 21 for each class of models.

TABLE 6
SUB-MODELS RANKED FIRST FOR EACH VARIABLE ON THE BASIS OF MINIMUM SUM OF OVERALL RANKS OVER N FIRMS
RANKS FOR EACH FIRM ARE BASED ON MEAN ABSOLUTE ERROR

Variable	Model	α	Firms
Net Income	Constant	1.00	714
Earnings Per Share	Constant	0.95	679
Deflated Net Income	Constant	0.90	669
Sales	Linear	0.55	690

The sub-model which ranks first on the basis of overall rankings is shown in Table 6. Except for sales, the generating process which best fits the data is close to a martingale. A martingale is indicated for net income, and a slight degree of serial dependence in changes in E.P.S. and deflated net income is indicated. The most recent observation in the time series appears, if we take the results at face value and concentrate on expected values, to contain 100 per cent, 95 per cent, and 90 per cent of all the predictive information in the series, for net income, E.P.S. and deflated net income respectively.[27] The fact that models which incorporate growth are not selected, except for sales, probably reflects a misspecification of the growth process. Evidence is presented below that this interpretation is reasonable. These results are consistent with those for the average series (Table 1).

The rankings of the models change slightly when computed within each group. Ranking models 1 through 59 attaches a greater penalty to large fore-

---

26. As discussed below, this "starting problem" biases our estimate of α. This is met in two ways. First, the simulations reported below assess this bias to be minimal. Second, in an unreported analysis, the forecasting models rank in essentially the same order over only the last 15 observations, giving the low α models time to "settle down."

27. Since the best sales forecast model under this criterion falls with the linear class, there is no similarly natural interpretation for the sales variable. Note, however, that the absolute weight given by the linear model to the most recent observation is *twice* times the value of α for that model.

TABLE 7
Sub-Models Ranked First in Each Class for Each Variable on the Basis of Minimum Sum of Ranks Within Each Class
Ranks for Each Firm are Based on Mean Absolute Error

Variable	Constant	α's Linear	Quadratic	Firms
Net Income	0.95	1.00	1.00	714
Earnings Per Share	0.95	1.00	1.00	679
Deflated Net Income	0.85	1.00	1.00	669
Sales	1.00	0.60	0.35	690

cast errors than does within-class ranking of 1 through 21. Table 7 presents the rankings on a within-group basis. Again, the extreme relative importance of the most recent observation is indicated, except for sales. The best "linear" and "quadratic" models for each of the income variables all have α's of unity, and therefore collapse into the martingale model. The best constant model for sales is a martingale, but middle-sized α's outperform the martingale in both the linear and quadratic models, as well as overall. Since a linear model with $\alpha = .6$ gives a weight of 1.2 to Y_{t-1}, sales might be similar to a submartingale (with a trend). We present more evidence on this point later.

The partial-adjustment models confirm that net income is, on average, a martingale or a similar process. However, since the analytical properties of partial adjustment models are not well known, we cannot place full reliance upon them. Further, the availability of relatively few observations for the forecasts of early years biases the findings against low α's. The importance of such a bias is difficult to treat analytically. We therefore adopt further tests in the following section.

Results from Partial Adjustment Models—Simulated Data

Data are simulated for twenty observations and four different generating processes:

(a) a constant process, with stationary expectation and error term distributed normally;

(b) a linear process, with linearly increasing expectation and error term distributed normally;

(c) a specific type of martingale, namely a random walk process with error distributed normally; and

(d) a specific type of submartingale, namely a random walk with normally-distributed error, and with a linear trend through time.[28]

---

28. The generating equations are:

(a) $y_t = z_t$

(b) $y_t = 8(t-1) + 4z_t$

(c) $y_t = y_{t-1} + 4z_t$

(d) $y_t = y_{t-1} + 4z_t + 1$

where z_t is drawn from the standardized normal distribution, and $t = 1, \ldots, 20$. The expectations,

TABLE 8

Sub-Models Ranked First for Each Simulated Process on the Basis
of Minimum Sum of Overall Ranks for N Simulated Firms
Ranks for Each Firm are Based on Mean Absolute Error

Simulated Process	Model	α	N
Constant with Noise	Constant	.20	200
Linear with Noise	Linear	.20	200
Martingale	Constant	.90	714
Submartingale with Trend	Constant	.95	200

TABLE 9

Sub-Models Ranked First in Each Class for Each Simulated Process
on the Basis of Minimum Sum of Ranks Within Each Class
Ranks for Each Firm are Based on Mean Absolute Error

Simulated Process	Constant	α's Linear	Quadratic	N
Constant with Noise	.20	.10	.05	200
Linear with Noise	.55	.20	.15	200
Martingale	.90	1.00	1.00	714
Submartingale with Trend	.95	1.00	1.00	200

Tables 8 and 9 contain the rankings of the models, with simulated firms ranked overall and within groups respectively. The partial adjustment models discriminate submartingales from other processes even with only twenty observations available. There is some bias against low α's, as expected, since α is estimated at 0.20 for a simulated stable and constant process (that is, with α = 0). Whether this constitutes an effective bias in favor of the α's close to unity is another question. The high α of .55 which the constant model gives to the process whose expectation is a deterministic function of time shows that more recent observations capture trend information. This is removed by the linear and quadratic models.

While these results establish the discriminating power of the techniques, they give no appealing measure of that power, and they do not assist in solving the equation of unconsidered forms of generating functions.[29] Thus, we compare the rankings given the various models under the four actual income series and the four simulated series. Table 10 quantifies the comparisons by reporting the computed matrix of rank order correlation coefficients between the rankings of the models when fitted to first the actual and then the simulated series. Rankings are computed overall (1 through 59).

We draw the following conclusions from the table:
(1) Deflated net income and E.P.S. behave very similarly to the simulated martingale series, and the correspondence between the rankings for

---

variance, and trends are roughly estimated from a random sample of fifty of the actual firms. Specification of the distribution of z_t implies (c) and (d) are random walks. Experimenting with several variances for the error terms reveals that the results are not sensitive to the size of the variances.

29. See footnote 24.

TABLE 10
RANK ORDER CORRELATION COEFFICIENTS BETWEEN THE RANKINGS OF THE FOUR VARIABLES AND THE RANKINGS OF FOUR SIMULATED PROCESSES BASED OF MINIMUM SUM OF OVERALL RANKS

	Actual Variables				Simulated Processes			
Variable or Process	N.I.	E.P.S.	D.I.	S	C	L	M	S.T.
Net Income	1.0000							
Earnings Per Share	.9210	1.0000						
Deflated Net Income	.9015	.9952	1.0000					
Sales	.7528	.4798	.4327	1.0000				
Constant with Noise	−.0270	.2405	.2974	−.5342	1.0000			
Linear with Noise	.5467	.7181	.7406	.0751	.6135	1.0000		
Martingale	.9742	|.9788|	|.9671|	.6232	.0932	.6325	1.0000	
Submartingale with Trend	|.9950|	.9272	.9063	|.7436|	−.0586	.5389	.9802	1.0000

The boxed numbers represent the highest correlation between the ranks of the particular variable and the simulated processes.

The hypothesis that there is no relationship between the rankings of two variables cannot be rejected if $|r| \geq .22$ at the 95 per cent level, and if $|r| \geq .302$ at the 99 per cent level.

net income and the simulated submartingale with a linear trend is amazingly close. The deflated and undeflated income variables do not look like processes with means which are deterministic functions of time.

(2) Sales corresponds most closely to a submartingale with a trend, as we earlier speculated. However, the association is not as strong as that for the other variables. One interpretation of the "low" rank order correlation of 0.74 between the rankings given to the sales series and the simulated submartingale with a trend is that partial-adjustment models do not perform well for such series. Table 8 presents some evidence in this regard: the trend in a simulated submartingale with a trend is not identified by the partial-adjustment models.

(3) The actual net income data give similar rankings to both a martingale and a submartingale with a trend. This is most likely due to the higher growth rate in net income and the consequential selection of high α models which we referred to earlier.

(4) The partial-adjustment class of forecasting models differentiates processes with expectations which are constant or deterministic functions of time from submartingale processes. Hence the simulation results add credence to our earlier conclusions. Their discriminatory power is greatest in non-trend situations, as evidenced by the rank order correlations of 0.09 and −0.06 between the rankings given to simulated submartingale processes and the simulated stationary constant mean process.

In general, the simulations support the previous section. In that section it was concluded that net income is best described by a martingale. However, that section did not fit submartingales with trends to the net income time series and the simulation data suggests that those processes may also be good descriptions of net income. Consequently, our conclusion from both sections is that income can be characterized on average as a submartingale or some similar process. The term submartingale includes the martingale process.

VII. Summary of Results

The evidence of independence in detrended income changes is compelling. Results from a variety of testing procedures lead us to the conclusion that measured accounting income is a submartingale or some very similar process. We do not investigate income which is calculated in ways which differ from conventional accounting practice. Further, our conclusions are necessarily based upon mean and median results (because of small-sample problems) and do not investigate whether specific firms are systematic outliers. Subsequent research addresses the latter issue.[30]

The conclusion that measured income is a submartingale is consistent with the earlier research reported at the beginning of this paper. This conclusion has important implications, some of which are spelled out above.

REFERENCES

1. R. L. Anderson. "Distribution of the Serial Correlation Coefficient," *Annals of Mathematical Statistics* XIII (1942), 207-14.
2. Ray Ball and Philip Brown. "An Empirical Evaluation of Accounting Income Numbers," *Journal of Accounting Research* VI, No. 2 (Autumn, 1968), 159-78.
3. ——————— and ———————. "Portfolio Theory and Accounting," *Journal of Accounting Research* VII, No. 2 (Autumn, 1969), 300-23.
4. William H. Beaver. "Time Series Behavior of Earnings." Paper presented at the Conference on Empirical Research in Accounting, Graduate School of Business, University of Chicago, May 21, 1970.
5. Carl A. Bennett and Normal L. Franklin. *Statistical Analysis in Chemistry and the Chemical Industry*. New York: John Wiley & Sons, Inc., 1954.
6. Richard A. Brealey. "Statistical Properties of Successive Changes in Earnings," unpublished paper, March, 1967. Keystone Custodian Funds, p. 13.
7. ———————. *An Introduction to Risk and Return from Common Stocks*. Boston: M.I.T. Press, 1969.
8. Philip Brown and Ray Ball. "Some Preliminary Findings on the Association Between the Earnings of a Firm, Its Industry, and the Economy," *Empirical Research in Accounting: Selected Studies, 1967.* Supplement to Vol. V, *Journal of Accounting Research*, 55-77.
9. Robert G. Brown. *Smoothing, Forecasting and Prediction of Discrete Time Series*. Englewood Cliffs, N.J.: Prentice-Hall, 1962.
10. Ronald M. Copeland. "Income Smoothing." *Empirical Research in Accounting: Selected Studies, 1968.* Supplement to Vol. VI, *Journal of Accounting Research*, 101-16.
11. ——————— and Ralph D. Licastro. "A Note on Income Smoothing," *Accounting Review* XLIII, No. 3 (July, 1968), 540-45.
12. John Y. Cragg and Burton Y. Malkiel. "The Consensus and Accuracy of Some Predictions of the Growth of Corporate Earnings," *Journal of Finance* XXIII, No. 1 (March, 1968), 67-84.
13. Wilfrid J. Dixon and Frank J. Massey, Jr. *Introduction to Statistical Analysis*. New York: McGraw-Hill, 1957, second edition.
14. Nicholas Dopuch and David Drake. "The Effect of Alternative Accounting Rules for Non-

---

30. In a subsequent paper Watts [39] investigates the incomes of 32 firms over the 38 year period 1927-1964. He uses an identification and estimation technique which allows a much broader range of processes than the partial adjustment models we use. For 6 of the 32 firms Watts is able to reject at the .01 probability level the hypothesis that the incomes of those firms are random walks with or without trend.

subsidiary Investments." *Empirical Research in Accounting: Selected Studies, 1966.* Supplement to Vol. IV, *Journal of Accounting Research*, 192-219.
15. Eugene F. Fama. "The Behavior of Stock Market Prices," *Journal of Business* XXXVIII (January, 1965), 34-105.
16. ———. "Efficient Capital Markets: A Review of Theory and Empirical Work," *Journal of Finance* XXV, No. 2 (May, 1970), 383-417.
17. ——— and Harvey Babiak. "Dividend Policy: An Empirical Analysis," *Journal of the American Statistical Association* LXIII (December, 1968), 1132-61.
18. ———, Lawrence Fisher, Michael C. Jensen, and Richard Roll. "The Adjustment of Stock Prices to New Information," *International Economic Review* X (February, 1969), 1-21.
19. Lawrence Fisher. "Some New Stock Market Indices," *Journal of Business* XXXIX (Supplement, 1966), 191-225.
20. Jean-Marie Gagnon. "Purchase Versus Pooling of Interests: The Search for a Predictor," *Empirical Research in Accounting: Selected Studies, 1967.* Supplement to Vol. IV, *Journal of Accounting Research*, 187-204.
21. Myron J. Gordon. "Postulates, Principles and Research in Accounting," *Accounting Review* XXXIX, No. 2 (April, 1964), 251-263.
22. ———. Discussion of Dopuch and Drake [14]. *Empirical Research in Accounting: Selected Studies, 1966.* Supplement to Vol. IV, *Journal of Accounting Research*, 220-223.
23. ———, Bertrand N. Horwitz and Philip T. Meyers. "Accounting Measurements and Normal Growth of the Firm," in *Research Accounting Measurement*, Robert K. Jaedicke, Yuji Ijiri and Oswald Nielsen (eds.). Evanston, Ill.: American Accounting Association, 1966.
24. B. I. Hart and John von Neumann. "Tabulation of the Probabilities of the Ratio of the Mean Square Successive Difference to the Variance," *Annals of Mathematical Statistics* XIII (1942), 207-214.
25. Samuel R. Hepworth. "Smoothing Periodic Income," *Accounting Review*, XXVIII, No. 1 (January, 1953), 32-39.
26. Maurice G. Kendall and Alan Stuart. *The Advanced Theory of Statistics.* Vol. III. London: Charles Griffin & Co., 1966.
27. John Lintner and Robert Glauber. "Higgledy Piggledy Growth in America?" Paper presented to the Seminar on the Analysis of Security Prices, Graduate School of Business, University of Chicago, May 11-12, 1967.
28. I. M. D. Little. "Higgledy Piggledy Growth," *Institute of Statistics, Oxford* XXIV, No. 4 (Nov., 1962).
29. ——— and A. C. Rayner. *Higgledy Piggledy Growth Again.* Oxford, U. K.: Basil Blackwell, 1966.
30. E. Malinvaud. *Statistical Methods of Econometrics.* Chicago, Illinois: Rand McNally, 1966.
31. Alexander M. Mood and Franklin A. Graybill. *Introduction to the Theory of Statistics.* New York: McGraw-Hill, 1963.
32. J. F. Muth. "Optimal Properties of Exponentially Weighted Forecasts," *Journal of American Statistical Association* LV, No. 290 (June, 1960), pp. 299-306.
33. P. D. Praetz. "Australian Share Prices and the Random Walk Hypothesis." *Australian Journal of Statistics* XI, No. 3 (November, 1969), 123-139.
34. S. James Press. "Security Prices and the Compound Poisson Process." Report No. 6707, Center for Mathematical Studies in Business and Economics, Graduate School of Business, University of Chicago, 1967.
35. Harry V. Roberts. "Statistical Inference and Decision." Chicago, Illinois: The University of Chicago, 1966. (Mimeographed.)
36. Michael Schiff. "Accounting Tactics and the Theory of the Firm," *Journal of Accounting Research* IV, No. 1 (Spring, 1966), 62-67.
37. Robert Schlaiffer. *Probability and Statistics for Business Decisions.* New York: McGraw-Hill, 1959.
38. A. Wald and J. Wolfowitz. "On a Test of Whether Two Samples are from the Same Population," *Annals of Mathematical Statistics* XI, 147-162.
39. Ross Watts. Appendix A to "The Informational Content of Dividends," unpublished paper, Graduate School of Business, University of Chicago, October, 1970.

FURTHER EVIDENCE OF THE TIME SERIES PROPERTIES OF ACCOUNTING INCOME

LeRoy D. Brooks and Dale A. Buckmaster*

I. Introduction

THE BEHAVIOR OF ACCOUNTING INCOME TIME-SERIES is of considerable interest to researchers in accounting, finance, and related disciplines. For example, the properties of accounting income time-series are directly related to accounting questions of management manipulation of accounting income and interim reporting. However, increased knowledge of income time-series behavior will be of most benefit to the extent that it contributes to the improvement of models in finance and improvement of the quality of accounting income numbers that are variables in predictive models [4], [5], [6]. Beaver compiled an impressive list of studies that required assumptions concerning the time-series behavior of accounting income or used accounting income as a predictive variable. The studies included in the Beaver list related to: valuation models of the firm, valuation of firm securities, dividend policies, earnings growth rate forecasts, evaluation of the informational content of accounting numbers, forecasting the failure of firms, and industrial concentration and accounting rates of return [6, p. 64].

Most previous research provided convincing evidence that income changes are independent [1], [2], [8], [18], [19]. Without exception, these studies have examined the total sample of time series selected for study. However, earlier work by Brooks and Buckmaster [9], [12] and Beaver [6] suggests that some subsets of series that are homogeneous with respect to configuration behave in a different manner than other income time-series. Specifically, the results of these studies suggested that series containing what appear to be non-systematic disturbances or shocks have special characteristics. These characteristics are obscured by the averaging process when the sample is not stratified.

Strong evidence has been provided by Ball and Watts [2] that income time-series follow a submartingale or some similar process. This present study identifies systematic conditions where income time-series do not follow a submartingale process. This has substantial impact on conclusions stated in previous studies concerning firm survival, effectiveness of income manipulation, and efficient market pricing.

The tests and results presented in this study are exploratory and descriptive. Thus, they are intended only as an incremental step towards the development of a general theory of income time-series behavior.

The approach used in this study was to stratify the sample according to distance of a given observation from an operationally defined normal income for each company. Iterative procedures were then used to determine the best exponential smoothing model and smoothing constant (α) for each stratum. This procedure was performed for each of three separate stratification rules. The outcome of our tests

---

* Associate Professors of Business Administration, University of South Carolina and University of Delaware.

suggests that the series included in the outer strata (from the norm) do not follow a martingale process. Also, the results indicate that the observations subsequent to the outer strata classificatory observations tend to revert to the income levels that preceded the classificatory observation.

II. Prior Evidence

The authors are aware of four studies that have been primarily concerned with examining the properties of accounting income time-series. One of these, Brown and Ball [10], was unrelated to the problem being investigated in this paper. The object of the Ball and Brown research was to identify the portions of firm income that can be associated with the economy and the industry to which the firm belongs.

Beaver [6] conducted an exploratory study on accounting rates of return series. His primary conclusion of relevance to this research was that these measures tended to be mean reverting. He was careful, however, to point out that undeflated income series do not necessarily behave in the same manner as rates of return series.

Ball and Watts [2] concentrated on examining the dependence in undeflated income time-series. Earlier research that had used income time-series as predictor model inputs seemingly established that there was little or no dependence in the series.[1] Much of the evidence obtained from these studies was derived from examination of changes in income. Ball and Watts, since their interest in the behavior of income series was primary, added exponential smoothing models as their primary analytical tool. Their study indicated that, in general, accounting income follows a submartingale process. That is, the best predictor of period "t" income is the income of period $t-1$.

Buckmaster and Brooks [12] also were primarily concerned with the time-series behavior of accounting income and utilized exponential models as the primary analytical tool. This study was, however, very limited in both scope and objective. The objective was to determine if the income of companies taking what appeared to be a "financial bath" returned to previous income levels. The sample consisted of compustat firms that had: (1) observations of both operating income and extraordinary item series that were extremely low relative to the *ex-post* linear structure, and (2) the extremely low observations occurred in the same accounting period. The investigators found that: (1) in the year subsequent to the extremely low observations, both operating income and extraordinary items tended to move back up towards the levels preceding the period containing the extremely low observations, and (2) the best predictions of operating income in the period following the low observations were provided by the first order smoothing model with a smoothing constant (α) of .333.

III. Some Implications of Martingale or Similar Processes

Ball and Watts identify two implications of their study which arise from the evidence that time-series follow a martingale or similar process: (1) Conceptually,

---
1. For a review of these studies, see [2], pp. 666–667.

every firm can be expected to fail; and (2) "Income Smoothing" efforts by management cannot be successful. They describe why firms can be expected to fail by stating:

> For a martingale (that is, ignoring trend), there is a finite probability, which is a function of the variability of the process, that the expectation of income at some future time will be negative or zero, and that the firm will on average fail. The expectation of *all* future incomes is changed with each observation. Hence, investors face greater risk than under the other type of income process [a series that is not a submartingale]. The value of the firm should change in the order of a normal proportionality factor times the change in income, reflecting the changed expected profitability. [2, pp. 665–666]

Despite the significance of the above inference, Ball and Watts may have been even more concerned with the implications related to income smoothing. In very general terms, the income smoothing hypothesis is that management will attempt to minimize the volatility of the income series. The hypothesis has, however, been stated with widely varying degrees of rigor. Ball and Watts chose to discuss smoothing in its most general form. They state:

> Smoothing implies a return to good times, on average, after bad times, during which income decreases are artificially reduced by smoothing practices. It implies that many increases in income are also temporary, and can therefore be smoothed in order to avoid the impression of permanence...the smoothing of income by the accounting profession would seem to ignore the possibility that good times are not followed, on average, by bad times. A submartingale implies that a firm is stuck with good and bad times (deviations of realized incomes from expectations) when they occur since a submartingale, by definition, is a process in which any one observation becomes the basis for the expectation of the next...the behavior of the expectation of a submartingale over time would be such as to make nonsense of the notion of income smoothing. [1, p. 664]

If (1) income time-series of companies with major shifts in income levels do not follow a submartingale process, and (2) income in the year subsequent to an extremely large gain or loss tends to regress to previous levels, then the Ball and Watts statements do not hold. The validity of their conclusions relies on the nature of the independence in accounting income-series that they found.

If income does tend to improve after an extremely bad period, then it cannot necessarily be concluded that every firm can be expected, on average, to fail. If income time-series contain this characteristic, failure, and thus risk, is less than what might be expected. Conversely, we can expect that an extremely high income period is only temporary and that income is likely to shift downward toward income levels of periods preceding the high income year.

Even if series with observations in the outer strata of the population are dependent and tend to be mean regressive, these properties do not indicate that income smoothing as identified in some of the more rigorous statements of the smoothing hypothesis ([3], [7], [13], [16]) can be achieved. The existence of these properties would, however, negate the conclusion that income smoothing cannot be maintained.

The income smoothing question is quite complicated and there may be many factors that have prevented the accumulation of strong evidence of smoothing behavior. For example, Beaver pointed out that many accounting rules dictate that the "unexpected" component of firm income be averaged over several periods and subsequently found evidence that "a moving average procedure would produce a measure where these properties [serial correlation] would be obscured, even though the underlying process was mean reverting" [6, p. 81]. Furthermore, management may engage in income manipulation behavior other than smoothing. Brooks and Buckmaster [9] found that the "financial bath" may be widely practiced by those firms having an unusually large operating loss and that many firms may, at times, attempt short-run income maximization.[2] The results of this paper support the possibility that both types of behavior are practiced. These types of behavior may also tend to obscure the effects of income smoothing efforts. Certainly, if the martingale process fails to hold systematically for identifiable series, then more evidence is required to prove that income smoothing efforts are ineffectual.

IV. Methodology

The research is composed of three separate sets of tests, each set being based upon a different decision rule which is used to stratify the sample. In very general terms, the stratification rules are:

(1) A linear regression rule that stratifies by likelihood of an income observation falling a specific distance from time trended earnings estimates;

(2) A modified percentage change rule that stratifies by the percent change of a given year's income from the previous year's income; and

(3) A normalized first difference rule that stratifies according to the first difference in income divided by the standard deviation of the first differences for that firm.

Obviously, all three of the stratification rules are rather primitive. However, emphasis is directed toward determining the characteristics of different subsets of income time-series, not toward finding a superior stratification rule. One can expect that the partitioning rules will not be successful in separating observations into strata having different best predictor models if they do not systematically include some characteristic that affects prediction and, thereby, the choice of the best predictor model. The rules employed were selected because they provide crude, but operational, measures of change from previous performance levels and trends. The research discussed in Part II of this paper [9], [12] suggested that identification of companies with shifts in relative performance levels might provide productive stratification rules for examining the properties of income time-series. Our results indicate that the primitive partitioning rules, even with their serious limitations, were successful in classifying observations into subsets having different "best predictor" models.

The methodology applied to each of the three stratification rules may be separated into three phases. The sample of income time-series observations for the specific decision rule is drawn in phase one. In phase two, the stratification rule is applied to the sample in order to determine the members of each stratum. In the final phase, each stratum of observations is subjected to tests to determine the best smoothing model and the best smoothing constant for that particular stratum.

---

2. Also, see Copeland and Moore [14] for evidence of the financial bath and Copeland and Wodjak [15], and White [20] for evidence of income maximization or loss minimization.

A. *The Linear Regression Rule*

1. *Sample selection.* The income observations used in the study are from a July, 1974 edition of the COMPUSTAT annual industrial tape containing financial data for 2630 companies.[3] Net income after both taxes and all extraordinary items is used.

All firms having net income data reported for a sequential period of nine or more years over the period 1954 through 1973 are included in the sample. A minimum of nine years of sequential income data is required to satisfy the requirements of the linear regression stratification rule. Thus, with sufficient data, as many as twelve sets of nine-year income sequences may be obtained for any one company on the tapes. A total of 15,661 observations of nine-year income series are obtained with this procedure.

2. *Stratifying the sample.* The fifth through seventh years of each nine-year income series are used in deriving a time-trended linear regression equation.[4] Thus the postulated linear relation is

$$y_t = \alpha + \beta X_t + \mu_t,$$

where: for $t = 5, 6, 7$, we have $X_t = 1, 2, 3$ and the observations of actual income numbers, y_t. Applying simple least squares, an estimate of income for the eighth year, $t = 8$, is derived

$$\hat{Y}_8 = \hat{\alpha} + \hat{\beta} X_8,$$

where: $\hat{\alpha}$ and $\hat{\beta}$ are the estimated model parameters based on the sample of three observations, $X_8 = 4$, and $\hat{Y}_8$ is the derived estimate of the eighth year income. A t-test statistic is obtained from the eighth year's actual income variation from the estimated income, $(Y_8 - \hat{Y}_8)$.[5] The eleven strata for this rule are defined in terms of t-test statistics and are illustrated in column 1 of Table 1. The statistic determined for the variation from the regression line in the eighth year determines in which of the strata an income series is classified.

3. *Tests for best predictor model.* Estimates of the ninth year income of each of the nine-year series provide the basis for selecting the best predictor model for each of the strata. First, second, and third order exponential smoothing models are applied to years one through eight of each nine-year time-series of each stratum to

---

3. The number of companies on the compustat tapes has increased greatly in the past few years, thus reducing much of the bias from size that concerned researchers in the late sixties and early seventies. Clearly, a survival bias also exists. However, our results on the extreme upper stratum indicate mean reversion and at least part of the mean reversion on the extreme lower strata are probably not due to the survival bias. The predominance of observations from the later years in the study also decreases the survival bias; i.e., some of the companies may fail.

4. The three year series was used in preference to longer time series since it explained a larger portion of the variation of the income observations about the least-square-line. Three through seventeen year trend lines were tested.

5. This partitioning method was chosen for its simplicity and computational efficiency, not for its statistical superiority. The existence of autocorrelation decreases the predictive ability of the linear regression model employed in this study. First, since it does not account for recent disturbances, it is biased. Second, the simple least-squares estimators are less efficient than estimators derived from a model considering the auto-correlated disturbance. It follows that biases in the t-statistic also exist. See [17, pp. 196–197].

derive a ninth period estimate of income.[6] Sixteen different smoothing constants are used with each of the smoothing models.[7]

The smoothing models provide a means by which the nature of the historical time dependence in the income series can be judged.[8] The degree of dependence on previous periods is indicated by the smoothing constant that generated the best predictor model. Thus, for example, with the first order smoothing model,

$$\hat{Y}_n = \alpha Y_{n-1} + (1-\alpha)\hat{Y}_{n-1},$$

if a smoothing constant equal to one, $\alpha = 1$, generated the best estimate of income, $\hat{Y}_n$; then the best predicator model will be a martingale (i.e., the most recent outcome in a time-series is the best predictor of the next outcome).[9] Greater dependence of the estimate on periods preceding the most recent outcome occurs as α decreases from one and approaches zero. When α equals zero, a process with a constant expectation is implied.

Iterative procedures were used to determine the best smoothing model and smoothing constant for each stratum. The first error measure used to select the best smoothing model and constant was the mean absolute error of the ninth year income for the I time-series of each strata

$$m = \frac{1}{I} \cdot \sum_{i=1}^{I} |Y_{i9} - \hat{Y}_{i9}|.$$

As in the Ball and Watts study [2, p. 675], the mean absolute error is chosen as the dominant error measure to avoid assumptions concerning the distribution of errors. The standard error of the estimate (SEE)

$$s = \left[\frac{\sum_{i=1}^{I} (Y_{i9} - \hat{Y}_{i9})^2}{I-2} \right]^{1/2}$$

is calculated as a secondary error estimate on each strata. As the results will indicate, the two error measures are quite similar, though the SEE seems much more unstable in providing consistent results. Slight changes in strata boundaries (not reported) occasionally cause substantial shifts in the optimal smoothing

---

6. See Appendix A for a description of the three smoothing models.

7. Iterations were made for each of the smoothing models using the following α-levels: .05, .10, .20, .30, .333, .40, .45, .50, .55, .60, .65, .70, .80, .90, .95 and .999 where .999 will be considered approximately equal to 1.0.

8. Ball and Watts tested the validity of exponential smoothing models as they are used in this study. They concluded, "The partial adjustment class of forecasting models [exponential smoothing models] differentiates processes with expectations which are constant or deterministic functions of time from sub-martingale processes." [2, p. 697].

9. A sequence is a martingale if we have the expectation,

$$e(Y_{n+1} | Y_0 \cdots Y_n) = Y_n \quad \text{for all } n$$

constant and smoothing model with the SEE measure. This condition does not occur with the absolute mean error measure.

The smoothing models are used because of their ability to provide information on the historical time dependence of income series, not because they are superior to other available time-series data fitting models. They provide a computationally feasible, and quite efficient, means to test the large samples we employed to determine if the submartingale is the optimal model over the various defined strata. The intent is directed toward determining if the submartingale does not hold over some definable subset of observations. It is beyond the scope of this paper, although quite likely the task of some future empiricist, to attempt to specify the optimal models, of the broader class of data fitting models for time-series analysis, that apply when the submartingale is non-optimal. This paper purposely restricts this initial investigation to the first, second, and third order smoothing models.

B. A Modified Percentage Change Rule

1. *Sample selection.* The same COMPUSTAT data used for the first partitioning model is employed. All firms having net income data reported for a sequential period of seven or more years over the 1954 through 1973 time period are included in the sample. A minimum of seven years of sequential income data is used to provide the smoothing models with a minimum of six observations. Thus, with sufficient data, as many as fourteen seven-year income sequences may be obtained for any one company. A total of 19,935 observations were obtained with the procedure.

2. *Stratifying the sample.* The fifth and sixth year of each seven-year income series are used to calculate the modified percentage change, p, in income,

$$p = \frac{Y_6 - Y_5}{|Y_5|}$$

An absolute value is used in the denominator to enable the specification of a measure of change for firms having negative income in the fifth year of an income time-series. This also will show that decreases in income always result in a negative-change number and that increases in income always result in a positive-change number. The cut-off p values used to form the strata are given in column 1 of Table 2.

A major weakness of the percent-change based model can occur since very large change numbers can exist if the fifth year income observation is near zero. The effect would be to introduce more randomness in defining extreme outer strata since these strata would contain many observations where large changes in performance, as perceived by analysts or measured by other stratification measures, had not occured. The reliability of the selected optimal model and optimal smoothing constant for the extreme strata is weakened by the distortion caused by incomes near zero. To partially control against this problem, an arbitrary cut-off point of 1600 percent, plus or minus, is used to exclude extreme changes from the sample. The footnotes in Table 2 indicate the effects of including these extreme 135 observations. Examination of the observations with this large change indicates that the base year income, year 5, is near zero for most of the observations.

3. *Tests for best predictor model.* Estimates of the seventh year income of each of the seven-year series provide the basis for selecting the best predictor model for each stratum. The same smoothing models and smoothing constants utilized with the first stratification rule are then applied to years one through six of each seven-year time series of each stratum to derive the seventh period estimate of income. The actual and estimated seventh year income are used in calculating both a mean absolute error and standard error of the estimate for each model and constant within each stratum. The error measures are in turn used to define the best smoothing model and constant for each stratum.

C. *The Normalized First Difference Stratification Rule*

1. *Sample selection.* The data source is the same one used for the two rules just discussed. A minimum of seven years of sequential income data is used so that the smoothing models will have a minimum of six observations. Thus, with sufficient data there can be fourteen possible income sequences for each company.

2. *Stratifying the sample.* This stratification rule, unlike the previous two, is based upon a varying number of observations. Each company series is stratified by a normalized first difference measure.

$$d_n = \frac{Y_n - Y_{n-1}}{\sigma_{d_{n-1}}}$$

where Y_n is the income reported in year n and $\sigma_{d_{n-1}}$ is the standard deviation of the first differences of yearly income. The standard deviation, $\sigma_{d_{n-1}}$, is calculated with the first differences of years one through n-1. At a minimum, the standard deviation would be based on the first differences of income for years one through five. Thus, for each subsequent observation in the time-series, the additional year's data is incorporated into the computation of the standard deviation of first differences. For example, a company having income data for all years in the twenty-year period would have a normalized first difference calculated for year nineteen,

$$d_{19} = \frac{Y_{19} - Y_{18}}{\sigma_{d_{18}}}$$

where $\delta_{d_{18}}$ is calculated using the first differences of years one through eighteen. The "roll forward" addition of observations in calculating the standard deviation of first differences is used in an attempt to both avoid the controversy of selecting, or searching for, an "optimal" historical time frame for calculating a variance measure. Additionally, the same size was much smaller, 10,619 observations, than with either of the previous stratification rules since data was required from the first year available on the tapes. Thus, a greater likelihood of survival bias exists with this stratification rule. The first column of Table 3 indicates the cut-off d values used to stratify the sample.

3. The testing using the normalized first difference rule is identical to that used with the modified percentage change rule.

V. RESULTS

A. The Linear Regression Stratification Rule

The results of our tests for best predictor models and smoothing constants when the linear regression stratification rule is used are presented in Table 1. Column 1 describes the strata. The strata are ordered from the extremely high income observations to the extremely low observations. Column 2 describes the stratum as a percentage of the total sample and Column 3 indicates the number of observations in the stratum. Using the mean absolute error (MAE) as a measure, Column 4 indicates which of the smoothing models provides the best predictions when the best smoothing model is used with the best α-level. Column 5 indicates the best α-level for the best smoothing model in terms of lowest MAE. Columns 6 and 7 indicate the same results as column 5 and 6 except that the standard error of the estimate (SEE) is used as the error measure.

Strata on the extremes (over 35% of the sample for the MAE and 15.2% for the SEE) follow a process other than a submartingale. This outcome is contrary to the Ball and Watts outcome for their entire sample. Obviously, however, if this sample had not been stratified, the best predictor model would have been the first order model with an α-level of one. This outcome is what would be expected from earlier research.

TABLE 1

LINEAR REGRESSION STRATIFICATION RULE
PARAMETERS OF THE BEST PREDICTION MODEL FOR EACH STRATUM

1	2	3	4	5	6	7
Likelihood of t-test Statistic	% of Sample	Sample Size	Order of Best Smoothing Model (MAE)	Best Smoothing Constant for the Best Model (MAE)	Order of Best Smoothing Model (SEE)	Best Smoothing Constant for the Best Model (SEE)
$.99 \leqslant X$	1.4	227	1	.8	1	.5
$.95 \leqslant X < .99$	5.7	889	1	1.0	1	1.0
$.9 \leqslant X < .95$	6.6	1038	1	1.0	1	1.0
$.8 \leqslant X < .9$	11.7	1828	1	1.0	1	1.0
$.7 \leqslant X < .8$	10.5	1647	1	1.0	1	1.0
$.3 < X < .7$	30.4	4765	1	1.0	1	1.0
$.2 < X \leqslant .3$	9.1	1431	1	.95	1	1.0
$.1 < X \leqslant .2$	10.8	1696	1	.9	1	1.0
$.05 < X \leqslant .1$	6.1	949	1	.45	3	.3
$.01 < X \leqslant .05$	6.2	962	2*	.3*	2	.3
$X \leqslant .01$	1.5	229	1	.5	1	.8
	100.0	15661				

* On this stratum and with this error measure the third order model with an $\alpha = .95$ gave nearly identical results. Additional interations with α near .3 and .95 were run with the minimum mean absolute error at $\alpha = .291$.

"Best" smoothing constants of less than one for extreme strata, using the MAE as a measure, show that the income in the period following a high income $(.99 \leq X)$ or a low income $[(.05 < X \leq .3)$ and $(X \leq .01)]$ period are best described by a process with a constant expectation.[10] Likewise, smoothing constants of less than one for the second order model for the stratum $(.01 < X \leq .05)$ indicate a linear expectation with both error measures. For the stratum $(.05 < X \leq .1)$ and the SEE measure, the best predictor is a third order model, and an exponential expectation exists. The mean error terms (not presented) of the first order model that had a smoothing constant of one were examined.[11] We found that in all the strata where the best model has an $\alpha < 1$ that there was a return toward income levels preceding the disturbance period. Thus, for example, the mean error for the stratum $(.05 < X \leq .1)$ for the first order model with an $\alpha = 1$ is 2.155 million. Since the first order model with $\alpha = 1.0$ for this low income stratum had an average error of 2.155, we can conclude that the actual income exceeds the submartingale estimated income and partially reverts to earlier reported income levels.

B. *The Percentage Change Stratification Rule*

Table 2 presents the outcome of our results from applying the percentage change rule. The format of Table 2 is identical with that of Table 1. The outcome using the percentage change rule is, in most ways, almost identical to the outcome of the application of the linear regression stratification rule. Again, strata on the extremes follow a process other than a submartingale process and, if the sample is not stratified, the best predictor model for the entire sample is the first order model with an α-level of one (a submartingale).

There are, of course, some differences from the linear regression rule. First, there is a slight decrease in the percentage of the sample having a best α-level of less than one for the MAE measure. The proportion of the sample having this property was 30.4%, still quite substantial. The SEE measure defines a larger percentage, 29.7%, of the sample as being nonsubmartingale than the SEE measure with the regression stratification rule, 15.2%. This change in the percentage of the sample having a best smoothing constant of less than one between the regression and percentage stratification rule is mainly accounted for on the income decrease side; there was somewhat of a weakening in the income increase strata (a decrease in population proportion of .7% for MAE and .2% for SEE). It should also be noted that the best smoothing model for both the highest stratum and the lowest stratum is the second order model rather than the first order model as it was for the linear

---

10. This contention is supported by tests in a related situation [12]. The movement of operating income subsequent to an extreme deviation from trend on the low side was examined. It was found that the series tended to move back toward previous trends and that the "best" smoothing constant with the first order smoothing model was 1.0 for the average observation and was .333 in the period subsequent to the extreme deviation.

11. Where the mean error, m', for the sample of I income observations, Y_i, for each stratum and σ-level is

$$m' = \frac{1}{I} \cdot \sum_{i=1}^{I} (Y_i - \hat{Y}_i)$$

where $\hat{Y}_i$ is the predicted income.

TABLE 2

PERCENTAGE CHANGE STRATIFICATION RULE
PARAMETER OF THE BEST PREDICTION MODEL FOR EACH STRATUM

			Mean Absolute Error		Standard Error of the Estimate	
1	2	3	4	5	6	7
Percentage Change	% of Sample	Sample Size	Order of Best Smoothing Model	Best Smoothing Constant for the Best Model	Order of Best Smoothing Model	Best Smoothing Constant for the Best Model
900 < Change ≤ 1600*	.3	66	2	.1	2	.1
600 < Change ≤ 900	.4	77	1	.8	1	.8
400 < Change ≤ 600	.5	108	1	1.0	1	.05
200 < Change ≤ 400	2.1	424	1	1.0	1	1.0
100 < Change ≤ 200	5.2	1031	1	1.0	1	1.0
0 ≤ Change ≤ 100	61.8	12310	1	1.0	1	1.0
−100 ≤ Change < 0	25.7	5119	1	.55	3	.5
−200 ≤ Change < −100	1.7	333	1	.3	1	.2
−400 ≤ Change < −200	1.2	241	1	.1	3	1.0
−600 ≤ Change < −400	.5	99	1	.1	1	.1
−900 ≤ Change < −600	.3	69	2	.2	2	.2
−1600 ≤ Change < −900**	.3	58	2	.3	2	.4
	100.0	19935				

* When the 77 additional observations having a percentage change in excess of 1600 are included in this stratum the submartingale (model 1, α = 1.0) is the optimal model.

** When the 58 additional observations having a percentage change less than −1600 are included in this stratum the third order, α = .2, provided the lowest mean absolute error and the second order, α = .2, provided the lowest standard error of the estimate.

regression rule. Examination of the mean error terms also indicated mean reversion with this, and the next, stratification rule.

C. *The Normalized First Difference Stratification Rule*

The outcome of our tests utilizing the normalized first difference rule is presented in Table 3. The format of this table is identical to that of Table 2.

The outcome using this stratification rule supports the findings of the other two rules in that the best α-level for the strata on the extremes is less than one (not a submartingale process) and, for the sample as a whole, the best α-level would have been one. The mean absolute error measure produced results that were quite similar to those produced by the percentage change rule. Using mean absolute error, .8% of the sample on the income increase side had an α-level less than one and 27.7% on the decrease side had a best α-level less than one.

With the SEE measure, 52.9% of the sample had a best α-level less than one. The pattern of σ-levels is not as nearly consistent as with the MAE measure even though a larger proportion of the sample is not submartingale. Despite the increased instability of results that occured when using the standard error of the

TABLE 3

NORMALIZED FIRST DIFFERENCE STRATIFICATION RULE
PARAMETERS OF THE BEST PREDICTION MODEL FOR EACH STRATUM

1	2	3	4	5	6	7
				Mean Absolute Error	Standard Error of the Estimate	
Normalized First Difference	% of Sample	Sample Size	Order of Best Smoothing Model	Best Smoothing Constant for the Best Model	Order of Best Smoothing Model	Best Smoothing Constant for the Best Model
9 < Difference	.8	89	1	.9	1	.65
6 < Difference ≤ 9	1.9	205	1	1.0	1	1.0
4 < Difference ≤ 6	4.4	466	1	1.0	2	.1
2 < Difference ≤ 4	16.7	1781	1	1.0	1	1.0
1 < Difference ≤ 2	20.0	2136	1	1.0	3	.1
0 ≤ Difference ≤ 1	28.4	2977	1	1.0	1	1.0
−1 ≤ Difference < 0	14.3	1531	1	.65	3	.45
−2 ≤ Difference < −1	6.4	686	1	.45	1	.333
−4 ≤ Difference < −2	4.4	478	1	.333	3	.333
−6 ≤ Difference < −4	1.3	137	1	.1	1	.05
−9 ≤ Difference < −6	.8	81	1	.3	1	.45
Difference < −9	.5	52	2	.2	2	.2
	100.0	10619				

estimate, the outcome of these tests further supports the results produced by the other stratification rules and the mean absolute error measure.

VI. SUMMARY AND CONCLUSION

The research reported in this paper represents the initial stage of research using a different approach to the examination of time-series properties of income. Previous studies have tested the entire sample without attempting an examination of subsets of series having homogeneous characteristics.

Three stratification rules were used to see if some consistent variations from the submartingale process occured in different strata. The best smoothing constant for first, second, and third order exponential smoothing models was then determined for each stratum to test for the existence of the submartingale.

Despite the limited scope of the research results being reported, three interesting properties of income time-series are suggested:

1. For the entire set of tests, a smoothing constant of one provided the best predictions. This supports other research that indicates that income time-series normally follow a submartingale or similar process.

2. However, series that fall in the outer strata have a best smoothing constant of less than one for predicting income in the period subsequent to the stratification period for all of the stratification rules and error measures used in the study. Thus, a substantial and identifiable portion of income time-series do not appear to follow a submartingale process.

3. The tendency of the best smoothing constant to change from one to some number less than one in those series included in the outer strata, together with an analysis of mean errors, indicates that income tends to revert to previous levels in the period subsequent to a substantial deviation from an operationally defined norm.

There are two important implications of the outcome of our study that are related to the Ball and Watts study discussed in Part II of this paper. First, the apparent temporal dependence of the series in the outer strata and the tendency of income to revert to previous levels make the conclusion that "all firms will, on the average, fail" [2, p. 665] questionable at best. Also, given Ball and Watts' definition of income smoothing, the evidence seems to provide a contradiction to their inference that management cannot be successful in efforts to smooth income.

We do not maintain that management does smooth income. The greater smoothness of series containing a material deviation from previous income levels may be management induced or inherent in the income determination process.

Perhaps the most interesting aspect of the results presented in this paper relates to the questions that are suggested but not investigated. A much broader and detailed examination of income time-series is called for in order to investigate further the phenomena suggested by this preliminary study. For example, the study can be expanded to include other stratification rules, prediction models, and both undeflated and deflated (rate of return measures) series. Other extensions include detailed examination of a random sample of series from each stratum to provide possible further evidence on the income smoothing controversy. Additionally, the inclusion of several periods subsequent to the stratification period in the tests might provide evidence on time-series behavior subsequent to a substantial disturbance.

REFERENCES

1. Ray Ball and Philip Brown. "Portfolio Theory and Accounting," *Journal of Accounting Research*, VII, No. 2 (Autumn, 1969), 300–323.
2. ———— and Ross Watts. "Some Time Series Properties of Accounting Income," *Journal of Finance*, XXVII, No. 3 (June, 1972), 663–681.
3. Russell M. Barefield and Eugene E. Comisky. "The Smoothing Hypothesis: An Alternative Test," *The Accounting Review*, XLVII, No. 2 (April, 1972) 291–298.
4. William H. Beaver. "The Behavior of Security Prices and Its Implications for Accounting Research (Methods)," *Committee Reports, 1972*, Supplement to Volume XLVII, *The Accounting Review*, 407–437.
5. ————, John W. Kennelly and William M. Voss. "Predictive Ability as a Criterion for the Evaluation of Accounting Data," *The Accounting Review*, XLIII, No. 4 (October, 1968), 678–683.
6. ————. "The Time Series Behavior of Earnings," *Empirical Research in Accounting: Selected Studies, 1970*, Supplement to Vol. 8, *Journal of Accounting Research*, 62–89.
7. Carl R. Beidleman. "Income Smoothing: The Role of Management," *The Accounting Review*, XLVIII, No. 4 (October, 1973) 653–667.
8. Richard A. Brealey. *An Introduction to Risk and Return from Common Stocks*. Boston: M.I.T. Press, 1969.
9. LeRoy D. Brooks and Dale Buckmaster. "Income Manipulation," Paper presented at the Annual Meeting of the American Accounting Association, New Orleans, August 19–21, 1974.
10. Philip Brown and Ray Ball. "Some Preliminary Findings on the Association Between the Earnings of a Firm, Its Industry, and the Economy," *Empirical Research in Accounting: Selected Studies, 1967*. Supplement to Vol. 5, *Journal of Accounting Research*, 55–77.

11. Robert G. Brown. *Smoothing, Forecasting and Prediction of Discrete Time Series*. Englewood Cliffs, N. J.: Prentice-Hall, 1962.
12. Dale Buckmaster and LeRoy D. Brooks. "Accounting Income Time Series and Unusually Large Pre-Opinion 30 Extraordinary Losses." *AIDS Proceedings*. Atlanta: American Institute of Decision Sciences, 1974, 226–228.
13. Ronald M. Copeland. "Income Smoothing," *Empirical Research in Accounting: Selected Studies, 1968*, Supplement to Vol. 6, *Journal of Accounting Research*, 101–106.
14. ——— and Michael L. Moore. "The Financial Bath: Is It Common?" *MSU Business Topics*, XX (Autumn, 1972) pp. 63–69.
15. Ronald M. Copeland and Joseph F. Wodjak. "Income Manipulation and the Purchase—Pooling Choice," *Journal of Accounting Research*, VII, No. 2 (Autumn, 1969) 188–195.
16. Barry E. Cushing. "An Empirical Study of Changes in Accounting Policy," *Journal of Accounting Research*, VII, No. 2 (Autumn, 1969), 196–203.
17. J. Johnston. *Econometric Methods*. New York: McGraw-Hill Book Co., 1963.
18. I. M. D. Little. "Higgledy Piggledy Growth," *Institute of Statistics, Oxford XXIV*, No. 4 (Nov., 1962).
19. ——— and A. C. Raynor. *Higgledy Piggledy Growth Again*. Oxford, U. K.: Basil Blackwell, 1966.
20. Gary E. White. "Effects of Discretionary Accounting Policy and Declining Performance Trends," *Journal of Accounting Research*, X, No. 2 (Autumn, 1972) 351–358.

Appendix A

Exponential Smoothing Models

(1) *First-order smoothing*:

$$I_{t+1} = (I_t)\alpha + (1-\alpha)(_1F_t), \quad \text{where:}$$

I_t = actual income for period t;

$_nF_t$ = forecasted income for period t. The prescript n indicates the order of the smoothing model.

α = smoothing constant

(2) *Second-order smoothing*:

$$_2F_{t+1} = a_t + b_t, \quad \text{where}$$

$$a_t = 2S_t(x) - {_2S_t(X)};$$

$$b_t = \left[\frac{\alpha}{1-\alpha}\right]\left[{_1S_t(x)} - {_2S_t(x)}\right];$$

$$_1S_t(x) = \alpha I_t + (1-\alpha){_1S_{t-1}(x)}; \quad \text{and}$$

$$_2S_t(x) = \alpha S_t(x) + (1-\alpha){_2S_{t-1}(x)},$$

where, $_nS_t$ = the smoothing function introduced in the nth order model.

(3) *Third-order smoothing*:

$$_3F_{t+1} = a_t + b_t + \frac{1}{2}c_t^2, \quad \text{where}$$

$$a_t = 3S_t(x) - 3\,_2S_t(x) + \,_3S_t(x);$$

$$b_t = \left[\frac{\alpha}{2(1-\alpha)}\right]\left[(6-5\alpha)S_t(x) - 2(5-4\alpha)\,_2S_t(x) + (4-3\alpha)\,_3S_t(x)\right];$$

$$c_t = \left[\frac{\alpha^2}{(1-\alpha)^2}\right]\left[S_t(x) - 2\,_2S_t(x) + \,_3S_t(x)\right]; \quad \text{and}$$

$$_3S_t(x) = \alpha\,_2S_t(x) + (1-\alpha)\,_3S_{t-1}(x).$$

The Information Content of Nonearnings Accounting Numbers as Earnings Predictors

JANE A. OU*

1. Introduction

This paper provides empirical evidence on the predictive ability and information content of nonearnings annual report numbers beyond that contained in earnings.[1] I take an "earnings prediction" approach to address the incremental information content issue.[2] Under this approach, nonearnings accounting numbers, jointly, play the role of predictors of future earnings changes. Specifically, I investigate whether nonearnings accounting numbers convey information about future earnings that is not reflected in current earnings; and if they do, whether this incremental predictive content is reflected in stock prices.

---

* Santa Clara University. This paper is based on my dissertation at the University of California, Berkeley. I gratefully acknowledge the helpful comments and suggestions of William Beaver, George Foster, James Ohlson, Stephen Penman, James Sepe, Neal Ushman, Peter Wilson, and the workshop participants at U.C. Berkeley and Stanford. I also wish to thank an anonymous referee for providing many insightful suggestions. I am especially indebted to Stephen Penman, my dissertation chairman, for his guidance and assistance throughout the development and revisions of this paper.

[1] In this paper, "nonearnings accounting numbers" refer to all data items reported in annual financial statements other than earnings, including earnings components.

[2] Much prior research had identified nonearnings items that are marginally useful in explaining contemporaneous stock returns. Examples include Lipe [1986] on components of earnings, Kaplan and Patell [1977], Rayburn [1986], and Wilson [1986; 1987] on cash flow and/or accrual components of earnings, Griffin [1976] on dividends, Gonedes [1975; 1978] and Eskew and Wright [1976] on extraordinary items, and Gonedes [1974] on several financial ratios. Many of these studies found incremental information content in various accounting items. For a review of earlier studies, see Lev and Ohlson [1982].

Copyright ©, Institute of Professional Accounting 1990

The information perspective of accounting implies that the contemporaneous association between nonearnings accounting numbers and stock returns can be viewed as resulting from a predictive information link between these accounting numbers and some unobservable, value-relevant attributes of the firm.[3] Although future dividends and future cash flows have commonly been cited as proxies for these primitive attributes, evidence suggests that future earnings are also value-relevant.[4] Thus, the incremental information content of nonearnings accounting numbers previously found in tests based on their associations with stock returns may have arisen partly from these numbers' ability to predict future earnings.[5] This paper complements the existing literature by offering this predictive perspective on, and interpretation of, the incremental information content of nonearnings accounting numbers. The main results of this study provide evidence for both a "predictive information link" between some nonearnings annual report numbers and future earnings changes and a "valuation link" between predicted future earnings changes and stock returns during the annual report dissemination period.

The predictive information link is established by fitting binary one-year-ahead earnings prediction models to selected annual report data and comparing these models' predictions with those of a random walk model.[6] Predictive ability of the annual-report-based models over and above that of a random walk model must be attributed to the nonearnings predictors. My results indicate that some nonearnings accounting numbers contain information about future earnings changes not reflected in current and prior earnings.

---

[3] In this framework, the observed contemporaneous association between accounting data and stock prices is the result of an "information link" between accounting data and future streams of benefits from equity investments and a "valuation link" between future benefits and stock prices. Information disclosure triggers revisions of investors' expectation of the future benefits. These revisions are then reflected in current stock prices. This framework is formally presented in Ohlson [1979] and Garman and Ohlson [1980], and empirically tested by Easton [1985].

[4] For example, the findings of Ball and Brown [1968], Beaver and Morse [1978], and Beaver, Lambert, and Morse [1980] all are consistent with the notion that stock prices reflect information regarding future earnings. Moreover, the efforts expended by security analysts, corporate management, and the general investing public in forecasting earnings seem to indicate that future earnings must be value-relevant.

[5] Nonearnings accounting numbers may convey predictive information about future earnings for at least the following reasons. First, some nonearnings numbers may help to identify the "transitory component" of current earnings which does not persist in the long run. Second, nonearnings data may reflect managerial decisions that have implications for future earnings. The current earnings figure, prepared under *GAAP*, is commonly believed to reflect some value-relevant information with a lag.

[6] Most studies examining the time series properties of accounting earnings have concluded that annual earnings in general follow a martingale type of process (for example, Ball and Watts [1972]). Thus, changes in future earnings (net of drift) cannot be predicted based on current and prior earnings. This has been referred to as annual earnings following a "random walk" or "random walk with a drift."

Given this predictive information link, annual reports can be viewed as providing both current earnings and a prediction of next year's change in earnings. Ball and Brown [1968] have shown differential returns to portfolios based on current earnings. Using their portfolio approach to analyze the "valuation link" between stock returns and the second signal, I find that during the annual report dissemination period, stock returns reflect both current earnings changes and the annual-report-based predictions of future earnings changes. In other words, stock prices behave as if investors do (at least to some extent) use nonearnings annual report numbers to revise their future earnings expectations and thereby bid up (down) the prices of stocks with favorable (unfavorable) predictions.

My results also provide an additional explanation for a result in Ball and Brown [1968]. They report that the information in reported earnings is anticipated by the market as early as 12 months prior to the preliminary earnings announcement. They speculate that other news events, such as dividend and interim earnings announcements, might explain why "unexpected earnings" are anticipated. The predictive information link documented in this study suggests that the release of the previous year's complete annual report, an event included in Ball and Brown's abnormal return accumulation period, also provides useful information for forming expectations about the current year's earnings.

Section 2 introduces the logit earnings prediction models. Section 3 describes the test samples and the study periods. Section 4 presents the empirical results. Section 5 contains the conclusion.

2. A Probabilistic Model of Earnings Changes

This study investigates the ability of nonearnings annual accounting numbers to predict the *sign* of the change in one-year-ahead earnings. A correctly specified prediction model with a continuous dependent variable capturing both the sign and the magnitude of the change would be more efficient. However, given that outliers are very common in accounting data series and that available data series are typically short, it is not clear whether such a model would perform better in a new prediction space. A binary model mitigates this problem since an extreme change in earnings has no greater influence on the model parameter estimates than any other observation.

Let $\mathbf{A}_{it}$ denote a vector of firm i's accounting descriptors based on its annual reports of year t and prior years, and Θ be a vector of estimated parameters. Now denote the probability of observing an earnings increase in year $t + 1$, the subsequent year, for a given $\mathbf{A}_{it}$ and Θ by $Pr(\mathbf{A}_{it}, \Theta)$. For simplicity in computation and interpretation, the following logistic distribution function is assumed for $Pr(\mathbf{A}_{it}, \Theta)$: $Pr(\mathbf{A}_{it}, \Theta) = (1 + exp(-\mathbf{A}_{it}'\Theta))^{-1}$. Given any $\mathbf{A}_{it}$, the output of the logit model is an estimated probability of an earnings increase in year $t + 1$ for firm i. This probability measure, denoted Pr_{it}, or Pr for short, summarizes the information contained in $\mathbf{A}_{it}$ about firm i's earnings of year $t + 1$.

Because of the limited number of time-series observations for individual firms, the maximum likelihood estimate of the parameter vector Θ is derived from pooling data across all sample firms over the model estimation period. Therefore, a general prediction model is applied to all firms. To the extent that firm-specific characteristics (such as industry membership) imply differing earnings processes, using a general model rather than industry-specific or even firm-specific models may weaken the model's predictive ability.

To translate each probablistic prediction, Pr, into a binary prediction of an earnings increase or decrease, I use two preset probability cutoff schemes: (.5, .5) and (.6, .4). Under the (.5, .5) scheme, the prediction is an earnings increase for $Pr > 0.5$ and a decrease otherwise. Alternatively, under the (.6, .4) scheme, the prediction is an earnings increase when $Pr \geq 0.6$ and a decrease when $Pr \leq 0.4$; observations with Pr between 0.6 and 0.4 are dropped.

The change in firm i's earnings in year $t + 1$, denoted ΔX_{it+1}, is specified as: $\Delta X_{it+1} = EPS_{it+1} - EPS_{it} - drift_{it}$, where EPS_{it+1} and EPS_{it} are firm i's "as reported" earnings per share before extraordinary items for years $t + 1$ and t, respectively. The drift term for year t is estimated as firm i's mean earnings-per-share change over the four years prior to year $t + 1$. This specification of earnings changes approximates "unexpected earnings" under a submartingale process.[7]

Although it may be desirable to include a large set of accounting predictors in the model in order to explore fully the information content of nonearnings accounting numbers, such a model would inevitably place too heavy demands on the data. Firm observations will have to be dropped if just one accounting item is not available. For this reason, and partly for simplicity, I construct simple logit models based on a parsimonious set of predictors.

To identify these predictors, I screened 61 predictor candidates (mostly financial ratios) over the period 1965–77.[8] The screening took two steps. First, a univariate logit model was fitted for each candidate and only those 13 descriptors with an estimated coefficient significant at the 10% level were retained. Second, multivariate logit models were fitted for these 13 descriptors on two independent data sets. Eight descriptors with a coefficient significant at the 10% level in at least one of these two data sets were kept as predictors to fit the final logit models:

(1) *GWINVN*: percentage growth in the "inventory to total assets" ratio;

---

[7] Since earnings increases significantly outnumber earnings decreases in the test period, this specification of earnings changes also removes firm-specific trends and balances the number of observations on the two sides of earnings changes. The main results of this study are unchanged when earnings changes are not adjusted for the drift term, and when earnings are deflated by owners' equity rather than by the number of outstanding shares. These results are reported in Ou [1984].

[8] These 61 accounting descriptors are reported in Ou [1984, appendix A].

(2) *GWSALE*: percentage growth in the "net sales to total assets" ratio;
(3) *CHGDPS*: change in "dividends per share," relative to that of the previous year;
(4) *GWDEP*: percentage growth in "depreciation expense";
(5) *GWCPX1*: percentage growth in the "capital expenditure to total assets" ratio;
(6) *GWCPX2*: *GWCPX1*, with a one-year lag;
(7) *ROR*: the accounting rate of return, i.e., "income before extraordinary items" divided by "total owners' equity as of the beginning of the year";
(8) ΔROR: change in *ROR*, relative to the previous year's *ROR*.

Most of these eight descriptors have been directly or indirectly tested in prior incremental information content studies under different approaches.[9]

3. Data and Study Periods

The logit prediction models were estimated based on a pooled data set of 391 firms over the period 1965–77. The sample firms met the following data requirements in each year: (1) all data items needed for computing the eight earnings predictors and the subsequent year's earnings change (net of drift) were available on the 1982 *Compustat Industrial Annual File*, and (2) fiscal year ended in December.

The predictive ability of the logit models was then assessed over the period 1978–83. Use of a test period independent of the model estimation period avoids potential bias from statistical overfitting. The test sample for predictive performance includes 637 firms with a December fiscal year-end and complete data on the 1986 *Compustat* file for calculating the eight accounting predictors and earnings change in each year of the test period. Of the 637 firms, 303 are among the 391 model estimation firms.[10]

About 1,700 *Compustat* firms were eliminated from the test sample. Taken together, the fiscal year-end requirement and the requirement

---

[9] For example, Wilson [1986] and Rayburn [1986] report that the current accruals component of earnings has incremental information content beyond cash (and/or working capital) from operations. A significant portion of current accruals can be attributed to changes in inventory levels. In examining the incremental information content of earnings components over the aggregate earnings, Lipe [1986] includes depreciation expense and gross profit as earnings components; sales is a major element of gross profit. Other tests include Wilson [1986] on capital expenditures, Freeman, Ohlson, and Penman [1982] on accounting rate of return (*ROR*), and Griffin [1976] and Gonedes [1978] on dividends.

[10] The predictive performance of the logit models was very similar for these two groups of firms examined separately. Therefore, this paper reports only the results based on the aggregate sample.

that data be continuously available for the years 1978–83 eliminated about 48% of all *Compustat* firms. Of the eight accounting predictors, inventory and capital expenditure are the top two contributors to missing data. Of all firms with at least one data item available on *Compustat* in each of the six years, approximately 29% have missing data on inventory and 18% have missing data on capital expenditure.

The relation between stock returns and the earnings predictions was examined over the same six-year period: 1978–83. For each year, a test sample for security return analysis was selected from the original 637 firms. To be included in the test sample for a particular year, a firm must have daily returns data available on the Daily Returns Tape of the Center for Research in Security Prices (*CRSP*) during a period starting 72 months prior to, and ending 3 months after, the end of the fiscal year covered by the annual report. A sample of 3,692 firm-year observations was obtained: 598, 605, 612, 622, 626, 629 firms for the six years 1978–83, respectively.

4. Results

4.1 THE MODELS

The Logist procedure of Statistical Analysis System (*SAS*) was used to fit multivariate logit models to the pooled data. Three estimated models are reported in table 1. Model 1, based on all eight accounting descriptors, is the primary prediction model of this study. To demonstrate that the predictive power of model 1 does not depend on *ROR* or Δ*ROR* (which include the current earnings figure in the conditioning information set), model 2 (which eliminates *ROR* and Δ*ROR*) is also presented. In model 3, *ROR* is the only predictor, so it includes only one nonearnings accounting number, common equity, in the conditioning information set. Test results based on model 3 will be compared with those based on model 1 to examine the effects of expanding the conditioning information set to include more nonearnings numbers (see table 1).

The signs of the estimated coefficients in these models show that growth in inventory (*GWINVN*), change in dividends per share (*CHGDPS*), growth in depreciation (*GWDEP*), growth in capital expenditures and its lagged term (*GWCPX1* and *GWCPX2*), and accounting rate of return (*ROR*) are negatively correlated with the chance of observing an earnings increase in the following year.[11] On the other hand, growth in sales (*GWSALE*) and change in accounting rate of return (Δ*ROR*) correlate positively with the chance of observing an earnings

---

[11] To investigate the negative correlation between current dividend changes and future earnings changes, changes in dividends per share were standardized (by standard deviation) for each firm, and observations with zero dividend change were dropped from the sample. The sign of the dividend coefficient remained negative after these modifications.

TABLE 1
Multivariate Logit Earnings Prediction Models (1965–77)

$$Pr(\Delta X_{it+1}>0|\mathbf{A}_{it},\Theta) = (1+exp(-\mathbf{A}_{it}'\Theta))^{-1a}$$

	Model 1		Model 2		Model 3	
Number of Observations	5,083		5,083		5,083	
$\Delta X_{t+1} > 0$	2,852		2,852		2,852	
$\Delta X_{t+1} \leq 0$	2,231		2,231		2,231	
Model χ^2 (d.f.)[b]	323.20 (8)[b]		175.42 (6)[b]		226.80 (1)[b]	
D-statistic[c]	.221		.168		.186	
% of Concordant Pairs[d]	.664		.648		.628	
Rank Correlation[d]	.329		.298		.257	
Accounting Descriptor	Θ	χ^{2e}	Θ	χ^{2e}	Θ	χ^{2e}
Intercept	+1.07	265.78	+0.44	162.13	+1.03	279.36
GWINVN	−0.58	15.58	−0.65	19.54		
GWSALE	+0.33	1.68*	+0.70	8.78		
GHGDPS	−1.77	47.16	−2.67	105.37		
GWDEP	−0.10	0.75*	−0.39	12.01		
GWCPX1	−0.11	9.81	−0.11	10.22		
GWCPX2	−0.12	11.40	−0.12	12.43		
ROR	−5.09	134.32			−5.72	211.22
ΔROR	+1.69	9.66				

[a] $Pr(\Delta X_{it+1}>0|\mathbf{A}_{it},\Theta)$ is the estimated probability that firm i will have an increase in earnings per share (net of the estimated drift) in year $t+1$, given $\mathbf{A}_{it}$ and Θ. $\mathbf{A}_{it}$ is a vector of accounting descriptors obtained from firm i's annual reports of year t and prior years. Θ is a vector of maximum likelihood estimates of the coefficients of the accounting descriptors. This vector is estimated based on pooled cross-sectional and time-series data.

[b] This statistic tests the null hypothesis that all coefficients in the model are equal to zero. These χ^2 values are significant at the .0001 level.

[c] This value is a measure of the goodness-of-fit of the model. It is the value such that $D(n-p)(1-D)$ = model χ^2, where p is the number of variables in the model including the intercept, and n is the number of observations.

[d] For matched pairs of estimated probability of an earnings increase (Pr) and directional realized earnings changes. Under the null hypothesis, % concordant pairs is 50% and rank correlation is zero.

[e] The p-values of these χ^2 values are all significant at the .01 level or better except those with *.

increase.[12] The negative sign of the ROR coefficient is consistent with results in Freeman, Ohlson, and Penman [1982].

Descriptive statitics for the estimated logit models are also reported in table 1. For each model, the "model χ^2," which tests the null hypothesis that all coefficients in the model are zero, is significant at the .0001 level. For model 1, the D-statistic, which measures the goodness-of-fit of the logit model, is .221.[13] The rank correlation between the predicted proba-

---

[12] To examine the consistency of coefficient signs across time and across samples, I reestimated model 1 for two subperiods and for two random (and exhaustive) subsets of the 391 firms. No sign of any coefficient changed.

[13] The D-statistic is an analogue of the R^2 value in the ordinary least squares (OLS) setting. It is the value such that $D(n-p)(1-D)$ = model χ^2, where p is the number of variables in the model including the intercept, and n is the number of observations. The adjusted R^2 from the OLS regression on the same data with the magnitude of earnings changes as dependent variable was 13.2%.

bility of an earnings increase and the realized directional earnings change is 0.329. The percentage of concordant pairs between these two measures is 66.4%. Under the null hypothesis of no association, the rank correlation is zero and the percentage of concordant pairs is 50%. The tests statistics for model 2 and model 3 show similar but slightly weaker results.

4.2 PREDICTIVE PERFORMANCE

Table 2 presents each model's predictive performance during the period 1978–83 under the two probability cutoff schemes: (.5, .5) and (.6, .4). The accuracy of the earnings predictions under each model is assessed relative to random walk predictions in a 2 × 2 contingency table setting. Given that I define an earnings change as the difference between two consecutive years' earnings per share *net of the estimated drift*, the "random walk with drift" model implies predictive performance equivalent to the outcome of a random-guess strategy in this setting.

Panel A of the table 2 reports model 1's performance. Under the (.5, .5) scheme, the resulting χ^2 value under a "fixed row" χ^2 test is 174.10, significant at the 1% level. Since this χ^2 value does not distinguish between a better-than-random-guess prediction and a worse-than-random-guess prediction, the percentage of correct predictions (61%) is also reported; both the "increase" predictions and the "decrease" predictions have the same predictive accuracy. Moreover, when one moves into the (.6, .4) scheme where relatively vague predictions have been deleted, both the χ^2 statistic and the percentage values show substantial improvement. Now 69% of all "increase" predictions and 67% of all "decrease" predictions are correct. Compared with the expected outcome under the random-guess strategy, these results are consistent with the notion that annual earnings do not follow a "random walk" if nonearnings accounting numbers are also included in the conditioning information set.[14]

The predictive performance of model 2 (with *ROR* and ΔROR omitted) is presented in panel B of table 2. The χ^2 value is still significant at the 1% level, and 58% of all predictions are correct under the (.5, .5) scheme. Under the (.6, .4) scheme, 64% of the predictions are correct. Furthermore, both the "increase" and the "decrease" predictions still have a better than 50% chance of being correct. These results indicate that nonearnings accounting numbers *alone* do convey information about future earnings.

Panel C reports the predictive ability of model 3, where *ROR* is the only predictor. The predictive performance of this most parsimonious

---

[14] The predictive performance of model 1 was also compared to that of a "trend model," where the subsequent earnings change is in the same direction as the current earnings change, and a "reversal model," where the subsequent earnings change is in the opposite direction to the current earnings change. In a binomial test, model 1 outperforms both earnings-based models at the 1% significance level.

TABLE 2
Predictive Performance of Earnings Prediction Models (1978–83)
Earnings Changes Are Predicted One Year Ahead on the Basis of Pr[a]

Panel A: Model 1, Based on All Eight Accounting Descriptors

Probability Cutoff Scheme[b]	(.5, .5)		(.6, .4)	
Number of Observations	3,822		1,968	
χ^2 of 2×2 Table[c]	174.10		230.15	
% of Predictions Correctly Made	61%		68%	
Further Breakdown According to Model's Prediction	Predicted As Increase	Predicted As Decrease	Predicted As Increase	Predicted As Decrease
Number of Observations	2,348	1,474	1,314	654
Correct	1,422	905	904	440
Incorrect	926	569	410	214
% Correct	61%	61%	69%	67%

Panel B: Model 2, Based on Six Accounting Descriptors

Probability Cutoff Scheme[b]	(.5, .5)		(.6, .4)	
Number of Observations	3,822		1,365	
χ^2 of 2×2 Table[c]	109.94		75.63	
% of Predictions Correctly Made	58%		64%	
Further Breakdown According to Model's Prediction	Predicted As Increase	Predicted As Decrease	Predicted As Increase	Predicted As Decrease
Number of Observations	2,954	868	1,113	252
Correct	1,675	552	703	169
Incorrect	1,279	316	410	83
% Correct	57%	64%	63%	67%

Panel C: Model 3, Based Only on *ROR* (Accounting Rate of Return)

Probability Cutoff Scheme[b]	(.5, .5)		(.6, .4)	
Number of Observations	3,822		1,751	
χ^2 of 2×2 Table[c]	88.28		120.40	
% of Predictions Correctly Made	58%		66%	
Further Breakdown According to Model's Prediction	Predicted As Increase	Predicted As Decrease	Predicted As Increase	Predicted As Decrease
Number of Observations	2,426	1,396	1,250	501
Correct	1,404	809	840	308
Incorrect	1,022	587	410	193
% Correct	58%	58%	67%	61%

[a] Pr is the estimated probability of an earnings increase indicated by the prediction models summarized in table 1.

[b] Under the (.5, .5) scheme, the prediction is an earnings increase for $Pr > 0.5$, and a decrease otherwise. Under the (.6, .4) scheme, the prediction is an earnings increase when $Pr \geq 0.6$, and a decrease when $Pr \leq 0.4$; observations with Pr between 0.6 and 0.4 are dropped.

[c] Based on a "fixed row" χ^2 test. A χ^2 value of 6.63 is significant at the .01 level.

model is similar to that of model 2. Since the current earnings figure is used in calculating *ROR*, it is desirable to examine whether the predictive power of models 3 and 1 is indeed "incremental" to that of current earnings. For this purpose, I estimated a logit model with "earnings before extraordinary items" (the numerator of *ROR*) as the sole predictor and applied this model to the same test sample. The resulting χ^2 is not significant at the 10% level. The model predicts 99% of all observations as "increase" and has a correct prediction rate of 52%. It thus seems fair to infer that nonearnings accounting numbers do contain information about future earnings that is not available in current earnings.

As an exception to the "random walk" properties of earnings, Brooks and Buckmaster [1976; 1980] have found that an extreme earnings change tends to be followed by one in the opposite direction. To ensure that the results presented in table 2 did not arise from observations with extreme current earnings changes, the predictive performance test was replicated on a sample in which observations with absolute current earnings change exceeding one standard deviation were deleted. For this sample, model 1's percentage of correct predictions dropped from 61% to 58% under the (.5, .5) scheme, and from 68% to 64% under the (.6, .4) scheme; but the χ^2 values of the 2 × 2 tables were still significant at the 1% level. When I further narrowed down the allowed absolute magnitude of current earnings changes to below one standard deviation (and thus trimmed away more observations), model 1's predictive accuracy did not deteriorate any further. It seems that at least a significant portion of model 1's predictive ability is independent of Brooks and Buckmaster's finding and thus truly represents *incremental* predictive content over current earnings.

The models' predictive performance on a yearly basis is reported in table 3. The results indicate that the superiority of the three logit models over the random-guess strategy is consistent across individual years, except for 1981 (in the prediction of 1982 earnings). Under model 1, the χ^2 value in each of the six years is significant at the 1% level. The percentages of correct predictions range from 57% to 70% under the (.5, .5) scheme, except for 1981; and each model's prediction accuracy consistently improves when the (.6, .4) scheme is used.

Comparing the predictive performance of model 1, based on all eight accounting descriptors, with that of model 3, based only on one nonearnings number, isolates the effects of expanding the conditioning information set to include more nonearnings numbers. Results in tables 2 and 3 indicate that model 1 outperforms model 3 in the 2 × 2 setting, although the significance of the difference is not clear. An additional test (not presented in the tables) shows that model 1 and model 3 predict differently in 534 of 3,822 cases under the (.5, .5) cutoff scheme. In these 534 cases, 61% of the time model 1 produced the correct prediction. A binomial test yields a z-value of 4.93, significant at the 1% level.[15] Thus, the additional predictors used in model 1 seem to have conveyed information about future earnings that is not available in *ROR*.

---

[15] Under the (.6, .4) cutoff, these two models produce different predictions in 85 cases. Model 1 has the correct prediction in 59 of these cases (61%) (binomial test z-value of 2.061).

TABLE 3
Yearly Performance of Earnings Prediction Models
Earnings Changes Are Predicted One-Year Ahead on the Basis of Pr[a]

Probability Cutoff Scheme[b]		(.5, .5)			(.6, .4)	
Year	Number of Observations	χ^2 of 2 × 2 Table[c]	Correct Predictions (%)	Number of Observations	χ^2 of 2 × 2 Table[c]	Correct Predictions (%)
Panel A: Model 1, Based on All Eight Accounting Descriptors						
1978	637	15.88	59%	274	21.25	65%
1979	637	7.14	57%	283	16.59	64%
1980	637	32.68	61%	310	42.32	69%
1981	637	15.31	50%	326	22.45	56%
1982	637	51.63	69%	370	35.91	76%
1983	637	21.08	70%	405	30.42	76%
Panel B: Model 2, Based on Six Accounting Descriptors						
1978	637	13.79	65%	164	2.80	66%
1979	637	5.85	51%	158	5.81	58%
1980	637	31.53	59%	207	22.45	66%
1981	637	18.86	42%	228	5.30	42%
1982	637	19.45	65%	280	6.87	71%
1983	637	2.45	68%	328	0.0	73%
Panel C: Model 3, Based Only on ROR (Accounting Rate of Return)						
1978	637	1.92	55%	229	12.36	64%
1979	637	1.25	53%	242	6.35	59%
1980	637	12.65	57%	270	23.64	66%
1981	637	7.46	48%	286	8.94	50%
1982	637	28.96	66%	358	15.44	76%
1983	637	20.71	68%	366	25.45	73%

[a] See n. a to table 2.
[b] See n. b to table 2.
[c] See n. c to table 2.

So far, the logit models have been evaluated based on the frequency of correct predictions without regard to magnitudes. Since the magnitude of unexpected earnings is known to be positively correlated with residual stock returns (Beaver, Clarke, and Wright [1979]), an ability to predict large earnings changes is more desirable than an ability to predict small changes. Table 4 shows that, on average, model 1 predicts large earnings changes more successfully than small earnings changes. For firms whose earnings increase (panel A) and decrease (panel B) in year $t + 1$, table 4 reports the magnitudes of these earnings changes. The average magnitude of the earnings increase or decrease is substantially higher for firms whose earnings changes have been correctly predicted than for those incorrectly predicted. This relation is consistent across years in the test period with two exceptions (in panel B, 1978 and 1983, under the (.6, .4) scheme) where the differences seem to be immaterial. Thus, the results in table 4 suggest that the overall predictive accuracy rate of 61% reported

TABLE 4
Magnitude of Realized Subsequent Earnings Changes for the Correct and the Incorrect Predictions[a]

Panel A: Cases Where the Subsequent Earnings Changes Are an Increase (i.e., $\Delta X_{it+1} > 0$)

Probability Cutoff Scheme[b]	(.5, .5)		(.6, .4)	
Prediction of Earnings Change	As Increase (Correct)	As Decrease (Incorrect)	As Increase (Correct)	As Decrease (Incorrect)
Number of Observations	1,422	569	904	214
Mean Standardized Subsequent Earnings Change:[c]				
1978	1.05	0.74	2.32	0.72
1979	0.91	0.65	1.69	0.55
1980	1.03	0.65	1.88	0.65
1981	1.09	0.90	1.54	0.92
1982	1.56	1.16	2.14	1.12
1983	1.82	1.29	2.53	1.60
Mean Difference Across Six Years[d]	+0.34		+1.09	

Panel B: Cases Where the Subsequent Earnings Changes Are a Decrease (i.e., $\Delta X_{it+1} \leq 0$)

Probability Cutoff Scheme[b]	(.5, .5)		(.6, .4)	
Prediction of Earnings Change	As Decrease (Correct)	As Increase (Incorrect)	As Decrease (Correct)	As Increase (Incorrect)
Number of Observations	905	926	440	410
Mean Standardized Subsequent Earnings Change:[c]				
1978	−0.83	−0.79	−0.88	−0.90
1979	−1.23	−1.02	−1.27	−0.93
1980	−1.31	−0.98	−1.51	−0.95
1981	−2.01	−1.67	−1.96	−1.50
1982	−1.74	−1.28	−2.06	−1.20
1983	−2.38	−2.37	−1.64	−1.77
Mean Difference Across Six Years[d]	−0.31		−0.34	

[a] Predictions of these earnings changes are based on prior years' annual reports and model 1 in table 1.
[b] See n. b to table 2.
[c] Standardized by each firm's standard deviation of yearly earnings changes.
[d] Yearly difference between the mean standardized subsequent earnings change of the correctly predicted firms and that of the incorrectly predicted firms, averaged across six years.

in table 2 might have captured most of the large, and presumably more important, earnings changes.

4.3 ASSOCIATION WITH STOCK RETURNS

In this study, a firm's annual report of year t is viewed as containing two binary signals. First, signal E (Earnings) indicates the direction of the change in current (year t) earnings. This signal is usually released in a preliminary earnings announcement[16] prior to the publication of the

---

[16] Using quarterly *Compustat* data, I examined reporting lags between the end of December and preliminary earnings announcements for my sample firms during the test period 1978–83. In each year, about 80% of the sample firms made preliminary earnings announcements by the end of February. The yearly median reporting lags range from 40 to 43 days. This is similar to Chambers and Penman's [1984] finding of a mean and median reporting lag of 44 days during 1970–76.

complete annual report. Second, signal F (Forecast) is an ex ante forecast of the direction of the firm's earnings change in the following year (year $t + 1$). This forecast is based on the accounting numbers contained in the year t annual report. This subsection examines stock returns' incremental association with signal F over signal E during the year t annual report dissemination period.[17]

Ball and Brown [1968] partitioned sample firms into portfolios according to the direction of current earnings changes (signal E) and demonstrated differential returns between good news firms ($E+$, those with an increase in current earnings) and bad news firms ($E-$, those with a decrease in current earnings) during the 12 months prior to preliminary earnings announcements. I use annual report data and a logit prediction model to produce forecasts of the direction of next year's earnings changes (signal F) and further partition each of the $E+$ and $E-$ portfolios into two subsets: (1) $F+$, those with an "increase" forecast, and (2) $F-$, those with a "decrease" forecast. This procedure yields four portfolios in each year: $E+F+$, $E+F-$, $E-F+$, and $E-F-$. This study assesses the incremental stock return response to signal F over signal E by examining the differential return behavior between portfolios $E+F+$ and $E+F-$, and that between portfolios $E-F+$ and $E-F-$ over the period 1978–83. Similar results were obtained for all three prediction models; reported results are based on model 1, unless specified otherwise.

I assume that sample firms' complete annual reports are available within three months after the end of December (month 0);[18] some of the predictors are usually known earlier. Therefore, the three-month period following the year-end, January through March (months +1, +2, and +3), is designated the dissemination period of the predictors.

Each portfolio's performance was measured by its cumulative abnormal return (CAR). The CAR of a portfolio held from month m to month n (both relative to month 0) was computed as follows:

$$CAR(m, n) = \frac{1}{N} \sum_s \sum_i \left(\prod_{t=m}^{n} (1 + e_{ist}) - 1 \right)$$

where e_{ist} is the market model residual of month t for firm i in year s,[19] and N is the total number of firm-year observations in the portfolio.[20]

---

[17] A correlation between signal E and signal F is expected since my logit prediction models incorporate current earnings changes and some components of current earnings in the calculation of the predictors. This makes controlling for the effects of signal E necessary.

[18] This assumption is based on the SEC requirement that companies file annual 10-K reports within 90 days of the fiscal year-end.

[19] Monthly stock returns of individual firms were calculated from the CRSP daily returns tape. For calculating e_{ist}, α_i and β_i were estimated from an OLS regression of firm i's monthly returns on the equally weighted monthly market returns of all NYSE firms over a 60-month period prior to month t. Note that α_i and β_i were reestimated each month.

[20] Using monthly returns and an assumed announcement period runs the risk of including various confounding events. Tests based on exact information dates, such as those in Wilson [1987], will probably produce stronger results.

Panel A of table 5 reports the CARs of the four portfolios $E+F+$, $E+F-$, $E-F+$, and $E-F-$ over the 12-month period $[-8, +3]$, assuming that the portfolios were formed at the beginning of month -8 (April) based on knowledge of year t's annual reports. The CARs of the $E+$ portfolio and the $E-$ portfolio, based only on the change in current

TABLE 5

Cumulative Abnormal Returns of Portfolios Based on Current Earnings Changes (Signal E) and Predictions[a] of Next Year's Earnings Changes (Signal F) (1978–83)

Month Relative to the End of Year t	(1) All Firms	$E+$	$E-$	(3) $E+F+$	$E+F-$	(4) $E-F+$	$E-F-$
Panel A: CARs of Portfolios Formed at the Beginning of Month −8, Based on the (.5, .5) Scheme							
−8 (Apr)	−.0002	.0191	−.0209	.0153	.0241	−.0234	−.0155
−7 (May)	.0023	.0311	−.0286	.0344	.0270	−.0285	−.0288
−6 (Jun)	−.0043	.0365	−.0479	.0378	.0348	−.0475	−.0488
−5 (Jul)	−.0055	.0480	−.0626	.0505	.0448	−.0626	−.0624
−4 (Aug)	−.0082	.0507	−.0710	.0513	.0499	−.0695	−.0742
−3 (Sep)	−.0130	.0537	−.0843	.0543	.0530	−.0849	−.0829
−2 (Oct)	−.0213	.0597	−.1078	.0564	.0641	−.1086	−.1059
−1 (Nov)	−.0235	.0688	−.1221	.0619	.0777	−.1253	−.1154
0 (Dec)	−.0218	.0729	−.1229	.0661	.0816	−.1214	−.1261
+1 (Jan)	−.0153	.0829	−.1202	.0917	.0715	−.1104	−.1406
+2 (Feb)	−.0130	.0880	−.1209	.0997	.0729	−.1067	−.1506
+3 (Mar)	−.0157	.0809	−.1189	.1035	.0519	−.1023	−.1539
Number of Observations	3,692	1,907	1,785	1,073	834	1,210	575
Panel B: CARs of Portfolios Formed at the Beginning of Month +1, Based on the (.5, .5) Scheme							
+1 (Jan)	.0083	.0104	.0060	.0265	−.0102	.0167	−.0165
+2 (Feb)	.0098	.0158	.0034	.0366	−.0109	.0191	−.0295
+3 (Mar)	.0076	.0109	.0041	.0405	−.0272	.0227	−.0350
Median CAR over $[+1, +3]$	−.0038	.0003	−.0080	.0221	−.0289	.0050	−.0358

Panel C: Portfolio CARs over the Three-Month Period [+1, +3], Based on the (.6, .4) Scheme[c]

	$E+F+$	$E+F-$	$E-F+$	$E-F-$
CAR over $[+1, +3]$	.0751	−.0509	.0381	−.0489
Number of Observations	580	388	717	233

[a] All predictions are based on model 1 of table 1.
[b] These portfolios are formed based on the sample firms' current earnings changes (ΔX_{it}) and model 1's predicted probabilities (Prs) of an earnings increase in the subsequent year (year $t+1$):
$E+$ consists of firms with $\Delta X_{it} > 0$;
$E-$ consists of firms with $\Delta X_{it} \leq 0$;
$E+F+$ consists of firms with $\Delta X_{it} > 0$ and $Pr > 0.5$;
$E+F-$ consists of firms with $\Delta X_{it} > 0$ and $Pr \leq 0.5$;
$E-F+$ consists of firms with $\Delta X_{it} \leq 0$ and $Pr > 0.5$;
$E-F-$ consists of firms with $\Delta X_{it} \leq 0$ and $Pr \leq 0.5$.
[c] Under the (.6, .4) scheme, portfolios are formed as follows:
$E+F+$ consists of firms with $\Delta X_{it} > 0$ and $Pr \geq 0.6$;
$E+F-$ consists of firms with $\Delta X_{it} > 0$ and $Pr \leq 0.4$;
$E-F+$ consists of firms with $\Delta X_{it} \leq 0$ and $Pr \geq 0.6$;
$E-F-$ consists of firms with $\Delta X_{it} \leq 0$ and $Pr \geq 0.4$.

earnings, are also reported. These reproduce Ball and Brown's results: portfolio $E+$ shows positive and continuously increasing CAR; while portfolio $E-$ has negative and continuously decreasing CAR during this period. However, these trends stop before month $+3$, possibly because preliminary earnings are usually announced prior to month $+3$.

Columns (3) and (4) of table 5 report the CAR behavior of the four portfolios conditional on the signals E and F (based on a (.5, .5) cutoff scheme). Differential CAR behavior between portfolios $E+F+$ and $E+F-$ first appears in month $+1$ (January), when the CAR of $E+F-$ begins to drop, while the CAR of $E+F+$ continues to rise. Similarly, the differential behavior between portfolios $E-F+$ and $E-F-$ begins in month 0 (December), when the CAR of $E-F+$ begins to rise, while the CAR of $E-F-$ continues to drop. This incremental response of stock returns to signal F over signal E is illustrated in figure 1.

Since the stock returns' response to signal F did not begin until toward

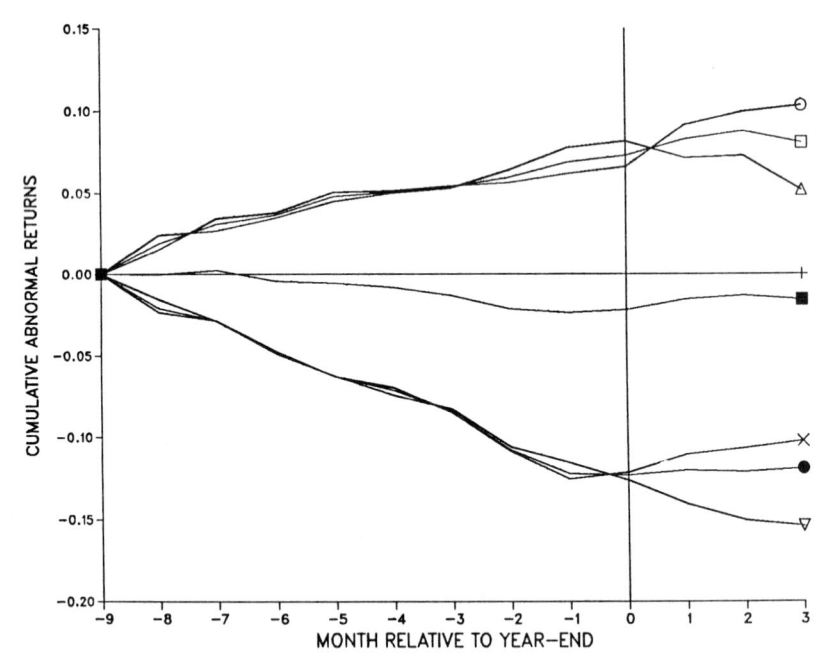

FIG. 1.—Cumulative abnormal returns of portfolios based on current earnings changes (signal E) and predictions of next year's earnings changes (signal F), 1978–83. In this figure, ■ denotes all firms; □ denotes the $E+$ portfolio (firms with an increase in current earnings); ● denotes the $E-$ portfolio (firms with a decrease in current earnings); ○ denotes the $E+F+$ portfolio (firms with an increase in current earnings and a predicted increase in next year's earnings); △ denotes the $E+F-$ portfolio (firms with an increase in current earnings and a predicted decrease in next year's earnings); × denotes the $E-F+$ portfolio (firms with a decrease in current earnings and a predicted increase in next year's earnings); ▽ denotes the $E-F-$ portfolio (firms with a decrease in current earnings and a predicted decrease in next year's earnings). All earnings predictions are based on the (.5, .5) probability cutoff scheme.

the end of December (month 0), the CAR behavior was reexamined in the three-month period January through March. This period contains preliminary earnings announcements and annual reports release dates.[21] Panel B of table 5 shows that although the CARs of both the E+ and the E− portfolios are relatively low in magnitude during this period, stock returns react substantially to signal F. The CARs of the F+ portfolios (i.e., E+F+ and E−F+, firms with good news regarding future earnings) are positive and continuously increasing throughout this period. The CARs of the F− portfolios (i.e., E+F− and E−F−, firms with bad news regarding future earnings) are negative and continuously decreasing. The mean three-month CARs are +4.05% and −2.72% for E+F+ and E+F−, and +2.27% and −3.50% for E−F+ and E−F−, respectively. A simulation test which randomly assigned the sample firms to these portfolios showed that the probablity of obtaining CARs with magnitudes similar to those reported in table 5 was less than one out of 10,000.

Qualitatively similar results were obtained when signal F was calculated based on model 2 or model 3. For the four portfolios E+F+, E+F−, E−F+, and E−F−, the mean three-month CARs during [+1, +3] are +2.10%, −2.34%, +1.54%, and −3.47% under model 2, and +4.07%, −2.14%, +1.60%, and −3.55% under model 3, respectively. This is consistent with the conjecture that ROR and other nonearnings predictors contain similar information about future earnings.

Panel C of table 5 shows that under the (.6, .4) scheme, the differences in CARs between the portfolios with a favorable forecast and those with an unfavorable forecast widen substantially. The CARs of the four portfolios E+F+, E+F−, E−F+, and E−F− are now +7.51%, −5.09%, +3.81%, and −4.89%, respectively.

The CAR behavior in each year over the three-month period [+1, +3] is reported in table 6. For each of the six years, portfolio E+F+ consistently outperforms E+F−, and portfolio E−F+ outperforms E−F−. A Mann-Whitney rank-sum U-statistic was calculated for each of the portfolio pairs [E+F+ versus E+F−] and [E−F+ versus E−F−] for each year. In most cases, the resulting asymptotic z-values of the U-statistics are significant at the 1% level. When portfolios are pooled across the six years, the resulting z-values are significant at the 0.1% level.

Results presented so far suggest that the logit predictions of future earnings changes have incremental explanatory power for cross-sectional differences in return distributions over that of the *direction* of current earnings changes. One might question whether the observed incremental return response to signal F is a proxy for the stock market's response to the *magnitude* of signal E. To examine this possibility, I calculated each portfolio's mean change in current (year t) earnings per share (scaled by

---

[21] This period does not include the announcement of the following year's first-quarter earnings, thus the test results are not affected by the market's response to this announcement.

TABLE 6
Portfolio[a] Cumulative Abnormal Returns over the Three-Month Period [+1, +3]:[b]
Yearly Results

	(1) All Firms	(2) E+	(2) E−	(3) E+F+	(3) E+F−	(4) E−F+	(4) E−F−
1978	.0011	.0071	.0209	.0539	−.0444	.0418	−.0079
1979	.0250	.0376	−.0021	.0541	.0282	.0040	−.0100
1980	−.0004	−.0133	.0075	.0608	−.0693	.0301	−.0227
1981	−.0153	−.0075	−.0221	.0234	−.0551	−.0076	−.0475
1982	.0114	.0248	.0071	.0391	−.0101	.0302	−.0820
1983	.0142	.0098	.0218	.0286	−.0650	.0329	−.0361
Pooled Across Years	.0076	.0109	.0041	.0405	−.0272	.0227	−.0350

Mann-Whitney Rank-Sum U-Test:

	E+F+ vs. E+F− z-Value	E−F+ vs. E−F− z-Value
1978	6.12*	1.18
1979	1.01	0.15
1980	4.77*	2.81*
1981	3.69*	2.36*
1982	1.64	6.63*
1983	5.43*	2.68*
Pooled Across Years	8.50*	6.85*

[a] All predictions are based on model 1 and the (.5, .5) probability cutoff scheme. See n. b to table 5 for the assignment of sample firms to portfolios.

[b] This period covers January through March, the three months immediately following the sample firms' fiscal year-end.

[c] Significant at the .01 level.

standard deviation). These mean changes are +.810 and +1.058 for $E+F+$ and $E+F-$, and −.989 and −.318 for $E-F+$ and $E-F-$. In addition, the Spearman rank correlation between the magnitude of the scaled current earnings change and the predicted probability (Pr) of an earnings increase in the following year is negative: −.0401, significant at the 5% level. Thus, on average, firms with a favorable future earnings prediction ($F+$) are experiencing a relatively unfavorable current earnings change (signal E), while firms with an unfavorable future earnings prediction ($F-$) are experiencing a relatively favorable current earnings change. This result is inconsistent with the notion that the incremental stock return response to signal F simply proxies for the return response to the magnitude of current earnings changes.

Results in section 4.2 indicate that model 1, based on more nonearnings accounting descriptors, outperforms model 3 in predicting future earnings changes. To see whether this superior predictive power is also reflected in stock returns, I examined whether a portfolio strategy based only on model 3 is outperformed by one based on both model 1 and model 3. Table 7 reports the results. Under the first strategy, two portfolios, $F3+$ and $F3-$, were formed according to each firm's signal F (earnings forecast) based on model 3 and a (.5, .5) probability cutoff scheme. Under the second stategy, $F3+$ was further partitioned into two subportfolios,

TABLE 7

Comparison of CARs of Portfolios Based on Model 3 Alone with CARs of Portfolios Based on Model 1 and Model 3 Together (1978–83)

	Portfolios[a] Based Only on Model 3's Prediction		Portfolios[a] Based on Both Model 1's and Model 3's Predictions			
	(1)		(2)		(3)	
	$F3+$	$F3-$	$F3+F1+$	$F3+F1-$	$F3-F1+$	$F3-F1-$
Three-Month CAR over $[+1, +3]$[b]	.0264	−.0258	.0335	−.0223	.0084	−.0326
Number of Observations	2,365	1,327	2,064	301	219	1,108
Mann-Whitney Rank-Sum U-Test:						
		$F3+F1+$ vs. $F3+F1-$		$F3-F1+$ vs. $F3-F1-$		
z-Value		4.79*			3.08*	

[a] All predictions are based on the (.5, .5) cutoff scheme.
$F3+$ consists of firms with $Pr > 0.5$ based on model 3;
$F3-$ consists of firms with $Pr \leq 0.5$ based on model 3;
$F3+F1+$ consists of firms with $Pr > 0.5$ based on both model 3 and model 1;
$F3+F1-$ consists of firms with $Pr > 0.5$ based on model 3, but $Pr \leq 0.5$ based on model 1;
$F3-F1+$ consists of firms with $Pr \leq 0.5$ based on model 3, but $Pr > 0.5$ based on model 1;
$F3-F1-$ consists of firms with $Pr \leq 0.5$ based on both model 3 and model 1.

[b] This period covers January through March, the three months immediately following the sample firms' fiscal year-end.

* Significant at the .01 level.

$F3+F1+$ and $F3+F1-$, according to each firm's signal F based on model 1 and a (.5, .5) cutoff. Similarly, $F3-$ was partitioned into $F3-F1+$ and $F3-F1-$. The three-month CARs presented in table 7 indicate that model 1 significantly screens the predictions based on model 3, and the stock returns reflect this incremental predictive power.

In sum, results presented in this subsection indicate that stock returns not only reflect changes in current earnings, but also respond to the logit models' predictions of future earnings changes during a period surrounding the release of annual report data. In other words, stock prices behave as if investors revise their expectations of future earnings based on nonearnings annual report numbers.

5. Conclusion

This paper takes an earnings prediction approach to investigate the incremental information content of nonearnings annual report numbers over earnings. It provides empirical evidence for a predictive information link between these nonearnings numbers and future earnings changes. The findings suggest that a firm's nonearnings annual report numbers contain information concerning the direction of its next year's earnings change that is not reflected in its current earnings. A valuation link between stock returns and this annual-report-based prediction is also documented. During the annual report dissemination period, the stock return response to the prediction of future earnings changes is over and beyond its response to current earnings. This result is consistent with the view that the disclosure of nonearnings annual report numbers triggers revisions of investors' future earnings expectations.

REFERENCES

BALL, R., AND P. BROWN. "An Empirical Evaluation of Accounting Income Numbers." *Journal of Accounting Research* (Autumn 1968): 159–78.

BALL, R., AND R. WATTS. "Some Time-Series Properties of Accounting Income." *Journal of Finance* (June 1972): 663–82.

BEAVER, W. H., AND D. MORSE. "What Determines Price-Earnings Ratios?" *Financial Analysts' Journal* (July/August 1978): 65–76.

BEAVER, W. H., R. CLARKE, AND W. WRIGHT. "The Association Between Unsystematic Security Returns and the Magnitude of the Earnings Forecasting Error." *Journal of Accounting Research* (Autumn 1979): 316–40.

BEAVER, W. H., R. LAMBERT, AND D. MORSE. "The Information Content of Security Prices." *Journal of Accounting and Economics* (March 1980): 3–28.

BROOKS, L., AND D. BUCKMASTER. "Further Evidence of the Time Series Properties of Accounting Income." *Journal of Finance* (December 1976): 1359–73.

———. "First Differences Signals and Accounting Income Time Series Properties." *Journal of Business Finance and Accounting* 7, no. 3 (1980): 437–55.

CHAMBERS, A., AND S. PENMAN. "Timeliness of Reporting and the Stock Price Reaction to Earnings Announcements." *Journal of Accounting Research* (Spring 1984): 21–47.

EASTON, P. "Accounting Earnings and Security Valuation: Empirical Evidence of the Fundamental Links." *Journal of Accounting Research* (Supplement 1985): 54–77.

ESKEW, R., AND W. WRIGHT. "An Empirical Analysis of Differential Capital Market Reactions to Extraordinary Accounting Items." *Journal of Finance* (May 1976): 651–74.

FREEMAN, R., J. OHLSON, AND S. PENMAN. "Book Rate of Return and Prediction of Earnings Changes: An Empirical Investigation." *Journal of Accounting Research* (Autumn 1982, pt. II): 639–53.

GARMAN, M., AND J. OHLSON. "Information and Sequential Valuation of Assets in Arbitrage-Free Economies." *Journal of Accounting Research* (Autumn 1980): 420–40.

GONEDES, N. "Capital Market Equilibrium and Annual Accounting Numbers: Empirical Evidence." *Journal of Accounting Research* (Spring 1974): 26–62.

———. "Risk, Information, and the Effects of Special Accounting Items on Capital Market Equilibrium." *Journal of Accounting Research* (Autumn 1975): 220–56.

———. "Corporate Signaling, External Accounting, and Capital Market Equilibrium: Evidence on Dividends, Income, and Extraordinary Items." *Journal of Accounting Research* (Spring 1978): 26–79.

GRIFFIN, P. A. "Competitive Information in the Stock Market: An Empirical Study of Earnings, Dividends and Analysts' Forecasts." *Journal of Finance* (May 1976): 631–50.

KAPLAN, R., AND J. PATELL. "The Information Content of Cash Flow Data Relative to Annual Earnings." Working paper, Stanford University, 1977.

LEV, B., AND J. A. OHLSON. "Market-Based Empirical Research in Accounting: Review, Interpretation, and Extension." *Journal of Accounting Research* (Supplement 1982): 249–322.

LIPE, R. "The Information Contained in the Components of Earnings." *Journal of Accounting Research* (Supplement 1986): 37–64.

OHLSON, J. "Risk, Return, Security Valuation, and the Stochastic Behavior of Accounting Numbers." *Journal of Financial and Quantitative Analysis* (June 1979): 317–36.

OU, J. "The Information Content of Nonearnings Accounting Numbers as Earnings Predictors." Ph.D. dissertation, University of California, Berkeley, 1984.

RAYBURN, J. "The Association of Operating Cash Flow and Accruals with Security Returns." *Journal of Accounting Research* (Supplement 1986): 112–33.

WILSON, G. P. "The Relative Information Content of Accruals and Cash Flows: Combined Evidence at the Earnings Announcement and Annual Report Release Date." *Journal of Accounting Research* (Supplement 1986): 165–200.

———. "The Incremental Information Content of the Accrual and Funds Components of Earnings After Controlling for Earnings." *The Accounting Review* (April 1987): 293–322.

AN EVALUATION OF ALTERNATIVE PROXIES FOR THE MARKET'S ASSESSMENT OF UNEXPECTED EARNINGS*

Lawrence D. BROWN and Robert L. HAGERMAN

State University of New York, Buffalo, NY 14260, USA

Paul A. GRIFFIN

University of California, Davis, CA 95616, USA

Mark E. ZMIJEWSKI

University of Chicago, Chicago, IL 60637, USA

Received October 1985, final version received April 1987

This study examines the association between abnormal returns and five alternative proxies for the market's assessment of unexpected quarterly earnings. We examine the role that measurement error potentially has in multiple regression tests of abnormal returns (occurring around the time of earnings announcements) on an unexpected earnings proxy and other non-earnings variables. The results indicate a potential measurement error interpretation of such multiple regression tests. We examine three procedures which reduce, to an unknown degree, the measurement error problem. Our procedures appear to be more (less) effective at reducing measurement error for small (large) firms and recent (non-recent) forecasts.

1. Introduction

Numerous studies have shown that stock market prices respond to the sign and magnitude of earnings that are unexpected by the market.[1] These studies use a proxy for the market's assessment of unexpected earnings ('market unexpected earnings') that is conditioned on a particular earnings forecast. If the unexpected earnings proxy measures the market's assessment with error,

---

*The authors acknowledge comments on earlier versions from workshop participants at the University of California at Berkeley, University of Chicago, Columbia University, Duke University, University of Iowa, University of Michigan, New York University, University of North Carolina at Chapel Hill, Northwestern University, Purdue University, University of Rochester, State University of New York at Buffalo, and the University of Southern California. We extend special thanks to R. Castanias II, A. Christie, R. Holthausen, W. Landsman, R. Leftwich, T. Lys, P. O'Brien, R. Watts, and an anonymous reviewer for advice on various topics.

[1]See Foster (1986, ch. 11), Watts and Zimmerman (1986, ch. 3), or Brown (1987, ch. 2) for a review of this literature.

the results can, in certain experimental designs, lead to incorrect inferences. This issue is potentially important when the researcher attempts to hold constant the effects of unexpected earnings while testing hypotheses for other financial variables (e.g., accounting changes, non-earnings information). In tests of this type, any correlation between the measurement error in the unexpected earnings proxy and the other financial variables results in biased statistics.[2]

This study examines the association between abnormal (stock) returns and alternative proxies for market unexpected earnings and the significance of the measurement error in those unexpected earnings proxies. Three procedures are used to detect and reduce the measurement error effects. Daily security returns, assumed to impound the market's knowledge of earnings, are used to investigate unexpected earnings from five one-quarter-ahead expectation models. Four of the expectation models are based on the time series of quarterly earnings numbers; the fifth consists of quarterly earnings forecasts made by security analysts.[3]

The empirical analysis proceeds in five stages. First, we examine five alternative measures of unexpected earnings individually (i.e., five alternative unexpected earnings proxies). This allows us to link our findings with those of prior studies using a single proxy. Second, we assess the incremental explanatory power of a single unexpected earnings proxy vis-a-vis a combination of proxies that includes the single proxy; the emphasis is on combining alternative unexpected earnings proxies to detect and reduce measurement error. Third, we examine factors that might explain differences in measurement error across firms. Fourth, we examine the effects of using the stock return prior to the abnormal return holding period to control for measurement error. Finally, we examine the effects of using instrumental variable procedures to reduce measurement error.

The results indicate that no single proxy consistently dominates in the simple association (e.g., regression) tests across the various abnormal return holding periods we examine. However, unexpected earnings that are based on financial analysts' earnings forecasts, in general, explain abnormal returns better than other proxies. Further, the results indicate a significant amount of measurement error in all earnings proxies and that our procedures may be useful for reducing (to an unknown degree) measurement error, especially for small firms and recent forecasts. Nevertheless, while our procedures do appear to mitigate the measurement error problem, we are unable to determine whether they produce reliable parameter estimates in a multiple regression

---

[2] The effects of measurement error are of less concern in studies of the relation between stock price changes and unexpected earnings when the null hypothesis of no relation is rejected, see Beaver et al. (1987) and Collins et al. (1987).

[3] The proxy variables are conditioned on a seasonal random walk model, three Box and Jenkins (1976) models, and forecasts from *The Value Line Investment Survey*.

research design (i.e., regressing abnormal returns on unexpected earnings and one or more additional non-earnings explanatory variables).

Overall, our results indicate that measurement error is a significant problem for the researcher using this multiple regression research design. Researchers must interpret the coefficients for the additional explanatory variables conditional on an assumed correlation between the additional variables and the measurement error in the unexpected earnings proxy variable. A non-zero correlation potentially results in a measurement error interpretation of the coefficients for the additional explanatory variables.

The paper is organized as follows. Section 2 describes the underlying empirical model and discusses the research design incorporating the potential effects of measurement error. The data, the forecasting models, and the variables for stock price adjustment and unexpected earnings are described and defined in section 3. Section 4 presents and discusses the results. Section 5 contains a summary and conclusions.

2. The underlying model, measurement error, and empirical tests

2.1. The model

The model below is used to show the effects of measurement error in a specific context. Although the model that underlies the empirical tests is consistent with models underlying many tests of association between stock price changes and unexpected earnings (as well as multiple regression models incorporating other financial variables), it is not the only specification. For alternative specifications, see Christie (1985), Miller and Rock (1985), and Watts and Zimmerman (1986). The model states

$$R_{it} = \alpha + \beta S_{it} + \mu_{it}, \qquad (1)$$

where

R_{it} = stock return resulting from the earnings announcement of firm i at time t,

S_{it} = the market unexpected earnings associated with the earnings announcement of firm i at time t,

μ_{it} = a random error term for firm i at time t with properties $\mu_{it} \sim N(0, \sigma^2(\mu_{it}))$ and $\sigma(\mu_{it}, \mu_{j,t+k}) = 0$ for all k and $i \neq j$.

The parameters α and β are assumed to be identical across firms and stationary over time.[4] This assumption would be valid, for example, if S_{it} equals the change in the expectations of the appropriately discounted future

---

[4] For evidence on the cross-sectional variation in β, see Easton and Zmijewski (1987).

cash flows available to equity holders when the conditioning signal for the change in expectations is the earnings announcement. In this case, $\alpha = 0$ and $\beta = 1$. However, due to alternative specifications of eq. (1), including alternatives regarding the stochastic processes underlying S_{it}, we are unable to form definitive expectations on the magnitude of β, except that it is expected to be positive.

2.2. Measurement error

Since S_{it} is unobservable, a proxy variable, $P_{it\lambda}$, must be used in the empirical tests. Let

$$P_{it\lambda} = S_{it} + \epsilon_{it\lambda} \quad \text{for} \quad \lambda = 1, \ldots, P \text{ models (proxies)}, \tag{2}$$

where $\epsilon_{it\lambda}$ is a random error term for firm i at time t with properties

$$\epsilon_{it\lambda} \sim N(0, \sigma^2(\epsilon_{it\lambda})),$$

$$\sigma(\epsilon_{it\lambda}, \epsilon_{jt\lambda}) = 0 \quad \text{for all} \quad i \neq j,$$

$$\sigma(\epsilon_{it\lambda}, R_{j,t+k}) = 0 \quad \text{for all} \quad i, j, k,$$

$$\sigma(\epsilon_{it\lambda}, S_{j,t+k}) = 0 \quad \text{for all} \quad i, j, k,$$

$$\sigma(\epsilon_{it\lambda}, \mu_{j,t+k}) = 0 \quad \text{for all} \quad i, j, k.$$

Substituting $P_{it\lambda}$ for S_{it} in eq. (1) yields

$$R_{it} = \alpha' + \beta' P_{it\lambda} + \mu'_{it}. \tag{3}$$

It is well known that α' and β' are biased and inefficient estimates of α and β [Madalla (1977)]. In particular, the slope coefficient, β, is biased towards zero and the error variance is biased upwards. The direction of the bias in α depends on the signs of β and the mean of S_{it}. If β and the mean of S_{it} have identical signs, then the bias in α is positive; if they have opposite signs, the bias is negative; and if either is equal to zero, there is no bias in α. Researchers often assume that the measurement error in the proxy is small and can be ignored, especially in simple association tests, since the tests are biased against rejecting the null hypothesis of no association. Additionally, if it can be assumed that the dependent variable R_{it} is measured without error, a reverse regression can be conducted [see Beaver et al. (1987) for an example of this technique], resulting in unbiased estimates of α and β.

The impact of measurement error in the earnings proxy is less clear and more troublesome when using a multiple regression research design, i.e., using explanatory variables in addition to market unexpected earnings to explain R_{it}. To demonstrate this point, we add another independent variable to eq. (1), Z_{it}. We assume initially that this variable is uncorrelated with R_{it}, S_{it}, and μ_{it}. Let

$$R_{it} = \alpha + \beta S_{it} + \delta Z_{it} + \mu_{it}, \tag{4}$$

where, in addition to the above assumptions,

$$\sigma(Z_{it}, R_{j,t+k}) = 0 \quad \text{for all} \quad i, j, k,$$

$$\sigma(Z_{it}, S_{j,t+k}) = 0 \quad \text{for all} \quad i, j, k,$$

$$\sigma(Z_{it}, \mu_{j,t+k}) = 0 \quad \text{for all} \quad i, j, k.$$

In this special case of eq. (4), that is, in the case where Z_{it} is uncorrelated with R_{it}, S_{it}, and μ_{it}, $\delta = 0$, and the estimates of α and β are unbiased and efficient [Madalla (1977)].

Now, suppose eq. (4) can be estimated only by using proxies for S_{it}, namely, $P_{it\lambda}$, and assume that Z_{it} is perfectly correlated with the measurement error in $P_{it\lambda}$. In this extreme situation we have

$$R_{it} = \alpha'' + \beta'' P_{it\lambda} + \delta'' Z_{it} + \mu''_{it}, \tag{5}$$

where

$$\sigma(Z_{it})\sigma(\epsilon_{it\lambda}) = |\sigma(Z_{it}, \epsilon_{it\lambda})|.$$

In this case, the estimates of α'' and δ'' are biased estimates of α and δ, respectively, and estimates of β'' and $\sigma(\mu''_{it})$ are unbiased estimates of β and $\sigma(\mu_{it})$. The sign of the bias in δ'' (and the sign of δ'', since $\delta = 0$) depends on the sign of β and the sign of the correlation between Z_{it} and $\epsilon_{it\lambda}$, $\rho(Z_{it}, \epsilon_{it\lambda})$; $\delta'' > 0$ if β and $\rho(Z_{it}, \epsilon_{it\lambda})$ have opposite signs; and $\delta'' < 0$ if β and $\rho(Z_{it}, \epsilon_{it\lambda})$ have identical signs. However, Z_{it} does not have to be perfectly correlated with the measurement error in $P_{it\lambda}$ to result in biased estimates of δ. Bias in δ, i.e., $\delta \neq 0$, results whenever Z_{it} has a non-zero correlation with the measurement error in $P_{it\lambda}$.

Additionally, the estimates of β'' and $\sigma(\mu''_{it})$ are unbiased estimates of β and $\sigma(\mu_{it})$ in this special case because Z_{it} is perfectly correlated with the measurement error in $P_{it\lambda}$. Since Z_{it} is not, most likely, perfectly correlated with the measurement error in $P_{it\lambda}$ [i.e., $0 < \rho(Z_{it}, \epsilon_{it\lambda}) < 1$], estimates of β'' and $\sigma(\mu''_{it})$ are biased estimates of β and $\sigma(\mu_{it})$. However, this bias decreases with increases in $|\rho(Z_{it}, \epsilon_{it\lambda})|$.

If significant measurement error exists in the unexpected earnings proxies, studies using a multiple regression approach similar to eq. (5) may report estimates for the coefficients for the additional explanatory variables (e.g., δ'') that are significantly different from zero, not because there exists a relation between the additional explanatory variable (Z_{it}) and the dependent variable (R_{it}), conditional on market unexpected earnings (S_{it}), but because these coefficients may be 'picking up' the measurement error in the unexpected earnings proxy variable.[5] The measurement error in an unexpected earnings proxy may be mitigated if another explanatory variable is added to eq. (3) that is highly correlated with the measurement error in $P_{it\lambda}$, yet uncorrelated with R_{it}, S_{it}, and μ_{it}. We use the above result in an attempt to reduce the measurement error in estimating eq. (3).[6]

2.3. Approaches to assessing measurement error

(i) *Using two or more proxy variables:* Based on the preceding model, our first approach to document the existence of significant measurement error in alternative earnings proxies is to use jointly two or more proxies to estimate eq. (1). Consider a two proxy model of the form

$$R_{it} = \gamma_0 + \gamma_1 P_{it1} + \gamma_2 P_{it2} + \eta_{it}, \qquad (6)$$

where P_{it1} and P_{it2} are alternative unexpected earnings proxies as defined in eq. (2).

The sum of the coefficients of the unexpected earnings proxy variables (i.e., $\gamma_1 + \gamma_2$) is an estimate of the coefficient for unexpected earnings. If the sum of the proxy variable coefficients increases as the number of proxy variables in the regression increases, this suggests the existence of measurement error in the unexpected earnings proxy variables and a reduction in the bias of the estimates of β and $\sigma(\mu_{it})$ in eq. (1). That is, for P_{it1} and P_{it2} less than perfectly correlated,

$$\beta - (\gamma_1 + \gamma_2) < \beta - \beta',$$

and

$$\sigma(\eta_{it}) - \sigma(\mu_{it}) < \sigma(\mu'_{it}) - \sigma(\mu_{it}).$$

For the above specification of eq. (6), significant coefficients for both γ_1 and γ_2 indicate significant measurement error in both proxy variables P_{it1} and

---

[5]An alternative explanation for observing that $\delta'' \neq 0$ is that the additional independent variable(s) 'pick up' misspecification of the basic model (e.g., cross-sectional variation in β). We assume throughout the paper that eq. (1) is the true model (i.e., we do not have an omitted variables problem) and that R_{it} is measured without error.

[6]See also Lys and Sivaramakrishnan (1986).

P_{it2}.[7] In order to examine the extent to which the use of multiple proxy variables may reduce measurement error, we examine the incremental explanatory power (i.e., the partial F-statistic) of adding an additional proxy variable to the (ex post) 'best' proxy variable among the alternative single proxy variable regressions, of adding an additional proxy variable to the 'best' set of two proxy variables among the alternative two proxy variable regressions, of adding an additional proxy variable to the 'best' set of three proxy variables among the alternative three proxy variable regressions, and of adding an additional proxy variable to the 'best' set of four proxy variables among the alternative four proxy variable regressions.[8]

(ii) *Using variables that are ex ante correlated with measurement error:* As a second approach for assessing measurement error, we incorporate potentially relevant stock return data as an additional explanatory variable in an attempt to control for the measurement error in the unexpected earnings proxies. We add the stock return from 100 trading days before the earnings announcement through the trading day before the dependent variable (abnormal return) is measured as an additional explanatory variable to eq. (3). Since the forecasts that are used to condition unexpected earnings are typically made prior to the period over which the abnormal return is calculated (in other words we use dated forecasts to condition unexpected earnings), we assume that the measurement error in the proxy for market unexpected earnings is positively correlated with this stock return.

We assume that $\beta > 0$, and hence, estimates of β are biased downward. Thus, an indication of the degree to which measurement error is reduced is given by the increase in the coefficient for unexpected earnings from estimating eq. (5) rather than eq. (3). Additionally, since we assume $\beta > 0$ and a positive correlation between the additional explanatory variable and the measurement error in the unexpected earnings proxy variable, the coefficient for the additional explanatory variable should be negative [see the discussion of eq. (5)].

(iii) *Using instrumental variables procedures:* Finally, as a third approach for assessing measurement error, we apply an instrumental variables technique. We follow the standard procedure [see Judge et al. (1984)]; namely, we (1) regress the earnings proxy, $P_{it\lambda}$, on K instruments, I_{ikt}, $k = 1, \ldots, K$, calculating a 'predicted' value of the proxy, and (2) regress the original dependent

---

[7]Non-zero coefficients may also indicate misspecification of the underlying model of the form of the measurement error in the proxies. See section 2.1 for the required assumptions of the underlying model.

[8]'Best' is determined on the basis of adjusted R-squares. The model with the highest adjusted R-square is deemed the 'best' of a particular set of proxy variable alternatives. It is most likely (but not necessary) that the 'best' $N + 1$ variable model includes all the variables in the 'best' N variable model.

variable, R_{it}, on the predicted proxy from the first regression. This two-stage procedure assumes that the instrument, I_{ikt}, is correlated with the true independent variable, S_{it}, and uncorrelated with (a) residuals from the stage 1 regression, (b) the eq. (1) residuals, μ_{it}, and (c) the measurement error in the proxy, $\epsilon_{it\lambda}$. Unfortunately, we have no guidance as to the choice of instrumental variables and it is unlikely that the required assumptions hold literally for any set of instrumental variables we could choose.

For this reason, we examine four alternative sets of instrumental variables in an attempt to gain some insights on the usefulness of this approach. For a given proxy, the four sets of instrumental variables are (a) the four unexpected earnings proxy variables that are not the dependent variable in the stage 1 regression, (b) the signs of the five unexpected earnings proxy variables, (c) a stock return variable and the instrumental variables in (a), and (d) a stock return variable and the instrumental variables in (b). The stock return instrumental variable is the stock return from 100 days before the earnings announcement (day -100) through the day before R_{jt} is measured (day $d-1$).[9] However, the stock return variable most likely violates the assumption (c) above.

3. Sample and variable definitions

3.1. Sample

Two samples are obtained for this study. The first sample includes forecasts for the five-year period 1975–1979. The second sample is a subset of firms included in the first sample, with appropriate forecasts for the year 1980. All firms included in the first (second) sample satisfy three criteria:

(1) 1960–1979 (1960–1980) quarterly earnings per share available in *Moody's Handbook of Common Stocks*,
(2) the same fiscal year end between 1960 and 1979 (1960 and 1980),
(3) covered by *The Value Line Investment Survey* between 1975 through 1979 (1975 through 1980).

The number of firms satisfying these criteria is 233 for the first (1975–1979) sample and 212 for the second (1980) sample. We require additional data for the empirical tests and thus impose two more sample selection criteria:

(4) Sufficient data on the CRSP Daily Master file to deflate unexpected earnings by price and on the CRSP Daily Return file to calculate abnormal returns,
(5) *Wall Street Journal Index* availability of the quarterly earnings announcement date.

---

[9]Given the instrumental variables we examine, this approach is similar to estimating a cross-sectional ex post composite forecast from alternative forecasting models.

The first criterion provides a source of quarterly earnings data that is used to generate time series forecasts based on the Box and Jenkins (1976) procedure. The second ensures that a firm's quarterly earnings reflects the same degree of seasonality each year. The third criterion is imposed because a source of analysts' forecasts of quarterly earnings is needed.[10] Criteria (4) and (5) are required for calculating the earnings proxy and stock return variables. Overall, there are at most 5,508 firm/year/quarter observations, but due to data requirements, the samples for various analyses range in size from 1,611 observations (for the longest abnormal return holding period) to 4,177 observations (for the shortest abnormal return holding period).[11] These criteria bias the sample toward larger firms.[12] Thus, the extent to which our results are generalizable to all firms is unknown. Nevertheless, our criteria are similar to the assumptions that have been made in previous research, so our results should be comparable to those of other studies.

3.2. Variable definitions

We specify the proxy for market unexpected earnings for firm i in quarter t, conditional on forecasting model λ, as

$$UE_{it\lambda} = (E_{it} - F_{it\lambda})/D_{it}, \qquad (7)$$

where

E_{it} = earnings for firm i in quarter t,
$F_{it\lambda}$ = earnings forecast for firm i in quarter t by forecasting model λ,
D_{it} = stock price of firm i the day before the abnormal return holding period begins (i.e., the deflator for quarter t).[13]

We use five alternative forecasting models to generate $F_{it\lambda}$. The first is the seasonal random walk (SRW) model, defined as the most recently reported earnings number for the *quarter* whose earnings are being forecast. For

---

[10] *The Value Line Investment Survey* is the only publicly available source of quarterly analysts' forecasts for the period under study.

[11] The maximum number of firm/year/quarter observations of 5,508 is calculated as (233 firms × 5 years × 4 quarters) + (212 firms × 4 quarters).

[12] An examination of the percentage of sample firms contained in each size decile of all American and New York Stock Exchange firms (based on market value of common equity) revealed that over half the firms are in the largest size decile, and over 85 percent of the firms are in the largest four size deciles in every year under study.

[13] While a common stock price deflator for earnings forecast errors has not been widely used in the literature, Christie (1985), Easton and Zmijewski (1987), and others have argued that such a deflator is appropriate. We use the stock price the day before the period over which the abnormal return is measured (day $d+1$). An earlier version of this paper reported results using three alternative deflators: actual earnings, forecasted earnings, and the mean and standard deviation of earnings. Those results are similar to the results presented here, except that the use of actual earnings as a deflator appears to increase measurement error.

example, the earnings forecast for the first quarter of 1979 conditional upon knowledge of the first, second, third, or fourth quarter of 1978 equals the earnings number reported for the first quarter of 1978. The second to fourth models, TS1, TS2, and TS3, respectively, are the forecasting models introduced by Brown and Rozeff (1979), Foster (1977), and Watts (1975) – Griffin (1977), respectively. The fifth model (VL) is the forecast reported in *The Value Line Investment Survey* after the quarter $t-1$ earnings announcement, but before the quarter t earnings announcement. These models have commonly been used in the forecasting literature and performed well relative to other naive benchmarks over short horizons [Hopwood et al. (1982)]. The SRW and TS models use information up to and including the latest earnings number, and hence, assume approximately a ninety-day forecast horizon. Brown et al. (1987a) report that *Value Line* forecasts are made approximately thirty-nine calendar days before the earnings announcement.

We use four alternative holding periods to generate abnormal returns (CR): a short, two-day holding period, representing the day before and the day of the earnings announcement $(-1,0)$; a long, forty-one-day holding period, representing a return cumulated from forty days before the earnings announcement through the day of the earnings announcement $(-40,0)$; and two intermediate holding periods, $(-10,0)$ and $(-20,0)$. While the holding periods are admittedly ad hoc, they include those commonly used by researchers and they enable us to examine the sensitivity of the validity of our techniques to alternative holding periods.

Eq. (8) defines firm i's excess stock return for the holding period, trading day d through day 0, as

$$CR_{it}(d,0) = \sum_{t=d}^{0} (r_{it} - \hat{a}_0 - \hat{a}_1 r_{mt}), \qquad (8)$$

where

$CR_{it}(d,0)$ = abnormal return for firm i, cumulated from day d ($d = -1, -10, -20, -40$) prior to the earnings announcement (i.e., day 0) through day 0,

r_{it} = continuously compounded return on firms i's common stock on trading day t,

r_{mt} = continuously compounded return on the CRSP value weighted market index on trading day t,

$\hat{a}_0, \hat{a}_1$ = ordinary least squares regression parameters.[14]

---

[14] For all holding periods (the period from day d through day 0), the regression parameters are estimated using returns from day -361 to day -61, where day 0 is the earnings announcement date. We require a minimum of 100 daily returns over the estimation period and all returns over the holding period for an observation to be included in a particular test.

Table 1

Comparison of individual proxy variables for unexpected earnings based on weighted portfolio excess stock returns and correlations with excess stock returns.

Cumulative residuals[a]	Number of obs.[b]	Unexpected earnings $(UE_{it\lambda})$[c]				
		SRW	TS1	TS2	TS3	VL
Panel A. Weighted portfolio percentage abnormal returns[d]						
$CR(-1,0)$	4,177	1.174	1.470	1.422	1.478	1.666
$CR(-10,0)$	3,431	1.392	1.947	1.964	2.058	2.202
$CR(-20,0)$	2,931	1.334	1.669	2.027	2.122	2.006
$CR(-40,0)$	1,611	1.137	1.542	1.726	2.137	2.346
Panel B. Pearson correlations between $CR_{it}(d,0)$ and $UE_{it\lambda}$						
$CR(-1,0)$	4,177	0.210	0.252	0.234	0.243	0.272
$CR(-10,0)$	3,431	0.136	0.180	0.177	0.182	0.198
$CR(-20,0)$	2,931	0.101	0.123	0.139	0.144	0.136
$CR(-40,0)$	1,611	0.076	0.093	0.093	0.110	0.117
Panel C. Rank correlations between $CR_{it}(d,0)$ and $UE_{it\lambda}$						
$CR(-1,0)$	4,177	0.210	0.286	0.302	0.281	0.317
$CR(-10,0)$	3,431	0.144	0.202	0.234	0.207	0.227
$CR(-20,0)$	2,931	0.177	0.154	0.176	0.180	0.175
$CR(-40,0)$	1,611	0.097	0.124	0.155	0.149	0.137

[a] Cumulative residual, $CR(d,0)$, is the cumulated market model residual, cumulated from d days before the earnings announcement date through the earnings announcement date (day 0).

[b] Number of observations available for the test. The number of observations decreases as the cumulation period increases because an observation is constrained so that each observation's *Value Line* report date occurs before the first day of the cumulation period, d.

[c] Unexpected earnings for firm i, in quarter t, conditional on forecasting model λ is denoted as $UE_{it\lambda}$. There are five unexpected earnings proxy variables. SRW denotes the seasonal random walk forecasting model, TS1 the Brown and Rozeff (1979) model, TS2 the Foster (1977) model, TS3 the Watts (1975) – Griffin (1977) model, and VL the forecast in *The Value Line Investment Survey*.

[d] Weighted portfolio abnormal returns in percentages, conditional on forecasting model λ, are calculated as

$$\sum_{i=1}^{N} CR_{it}(d,0) \left[UE_{it\lambda} \bigg/ \sum_{j=1}^{N} |UE_{jt\lambda}| \right],$$

where $CR_{it}(d,0)$ is the cumulative residual for firm i in quarter t, N the number of observations, and $|\cdot|$ the absolute value operator.

4. Results

4.1. Comparison of individual proxies

Table 1 presents individual analyses of the five unexpected earnings proxies, SRW, TS1, TS2, TS3, and VL. For each $CR(d,0)$ calculation, the sample is constrained so that each company's *Value Line* report date occurs before the first day of the cumulation (day d) period. Thus, the longer the cumulation period, the fewer the number of observations in the sample. This constraint achieves a consistency between the holding period and the market's presumed knowledge of the *Value Line* forecast, and it enables researchers requiring measures of earnings expectations to ensure that the proxy variables they utilize are available to the market as of the start of the presumed holding period.

Panel A reports the weighted average excess (portfolio) returns (stated in percentages) from an investment strategy of (1) buying long (selling short) on the first day of the holding period (day d) common stock with positive (negative) unexpected earnings, $UE_{it\lambda}$, and (2) holding the portfolio of firms through the end of the earnings announcement date (day 0). The weighted abnormal returns (for a sample of N observations) are calculated as follows:

$$\sum_{i=1}^{N} CR_{it}(d,0) \left[UE_{it\lambda} \bigg/ \sum_{j=1}^{N} |UE_{jt\lambda}| \right],$$

where $|\cdot|$ is the absolute value operator.

The results in panel A indicate that SRW has the lowest abnormal return in every holding period. VL has the highest abnormal return for the $(-1,0)$, $(-10,0)$, and $(-40,0)$ holding periods. However, TS2 and TS3 have slightly higher abnormal returns than VL for the $(-20,0)$ holding period. Panels B and C, respectively, present pairwise Pearson and rank correlation coefficients between CR_{it} and $UE_{it\lambda}$. Consistent with panel A, VL has the highest correlation for the $(-1,0)$ holding period.

In sum, proxies for unexpected earnings based on analysts' forecasts (VL) have the highest association with abnormal returns for one of the four holding periods. One of the time series models (SRW) is the 'worst' proxy in that it consistently exhibits the poorest measure of association. Although not reported, weighted return measures which are based on the rank of the unexpected earnings measures are qualitatively identical. Also, tests based on unweighted abnormal returns display a similar pattern.[15]

4.2. Multiple earnings proxies

Table 2 summarizes the results of using multiple unexpected earnings proxies in explaining abnormal returns for various holding periods. More

---

[15]Additional results indicate: (1) The five $UE_{it\lambda}$ proxy variables have identical signs in approximately 48 percent of the cases, (2) four of the five $UE_{it\lambda}$ variables have identical signs for approximately 78 percent of the cases, and (3) when the proxies disagree in the sign of $UE_{it\lambda}$, the magnitudes of the $UE_{it\lambda}$'s are closer to zero than they are when the proxies agree in sign. The latter finding suggests that grouping on the basis of consistency of sign of $UE_{it\lambda}$ is positively correlated with grouping on the basis of magnitude of $UE_{it\lambda}$.

specifically, it reports an adjusted R-square and the sum of cross-sectional regression coefficients (sum of γ_λ) for the regression of abnormal returns on P ($P = 1, \ldots, 5$) unexpected earnings proxy variable(s):

$$CR_{it}(d,0) = \gamma_0 + \sum_{\lambda=1}^{P} \gamma_\lambda UE_{it\lambda} + \text{error}. \tag{9}$$

Because we estimate regression eq. (9) for all combinations of proxies, the results are presented in five panels. Panel A reports the regressions with one proxy variable in eq. (9) (five regressions for each of the four holding periods), panel B with two proxy variables (ten regressions for each of four holding periods), panel C with three proxy variables (ten regressions for each of the four holding periods), panel D with four proxy variables (five regressions for each of four holding periods), and panel E with five proxy variables (one regression for each of four holding periods). The principal findings from these analyses follow.

First, the γ_λ coefficient values for the single proxy variable forms of eq. (9), that is, the twenty regressions in panel A, are all highly significant with t-statistics significant at less than the 0.001 probability level. These results essentially confirm the results in table 1 and in the extant literature.

Second, the sum of coefficients tends to increase and the adjusted R-squares always decrease as the holding period for the regressions increases. These results are consistent with the measurement error discussion in section 2. The earnings forecasts we use are dated in that the forecast is made before the first day of the holding period and, as such, are not conditioned on the earnings related information that is released between the forecast date and the day before the holding period begins ($d+1$). Increasing the holding period reduces the datedness of the earnings forecast which should result in an increase in the estimate of β. Decreases in the adjusted R-squares over longer holding periods are consistent with the hypothesis that abnormal returns with longer holding periods contain more variation due to factors unrelated to the firm's earnings.[16]

Third, table 2 shows that the sum of γ_λ coefficients generally increases when additional proxies are added to regression eq. (9). While the increase in the sum of coefficients with respect to holding period is seldom monotonic, an examination of the table reveals that the sum of coefficients for the three longer holding periods ($-10,0$), ($-20,0$), and ($-40,0$) is always greater than it is for the shortest holding period ($-1,0$).

---

[16]The actual timing of the analyst's forecast is also critical here. We would expect, for instance, that if all analysts' forecasts are made just before earnings announcements, the coefficient for the ($-1,0$) holding period would be higher. Unfortunately, we cannot examine this issue with our analyst data, as the average forecast in our sample is made approximately 39 days prior to the earnings announcement date (our day 0).

Table 2

Summary of cross-sectional regressions between cumulative residuals and one or more unexpected earnings proxy variable(s).

Regression: $CR_{it}(d,0) = \gamma_0 + \sum_{\lambda=1}^{P} \gamma_\lambda UE_{it\lambda} + \text{error}.$[a]

Regression No.	Independent variable(s)[c]	$CR_{it}(-1,0)$ 4,177 observations[b]		$CR_{it}(-10,0)$ 3,431 observations		$CR_{it}(-20,0)$ 2,931 observations		$CR_{it}(-40,0)$ 1,611 observations	
		Adjusted R-square	Sum of coeff.[d]	Adjusted R-square	Sum of coeff.	Adjusted R-square	Sum of coeff.	Adjusted R-square	Sum of coeff.
Panel A. Regressions with one earnings proxy ($P=1$)									
1.	SRW	0.0437	0.3170	0.0182	0.3822	0.0099	0.3911	0.0044	0.3507
2.	TS1	0.0631	0.4740	0.0321	0.6299	0.0149	0.6140	0.0081	0.6230
3.	TS2	0.0547	0.3859	0.0311	0.5577	0.0189	0.6027	0.0080	0.5473
4.	TS3	0.0590	0.4220	0.0329	0.5866	0.0205	0.6523	0.0115	0.6613
5.	VL	0.0738	0.6985	0.0388	0.9335	0.0183	0.8927	0.0131	1.0096
Panel B. Regressions with two earnings proxies ($P=2$)									
6.	TS1, TS2	0.0660	0.4871	0.0346	0.6565	0.0189	0.6505	0.0083	0.6444
7.	TS1, TS3	0.0649	0.4809	0.0340	0.6372	0.0203	0.6279	0.0109	0.6433
8.	TS1, SRW	0.0674	0.5029	0.0328	0.6555	0.0157	0.6531	0.0082	0.6715
9.	TS1, VL	0.0886	0.7680	0.0445	0.9990	0.0208	0.9671	0.0133	1.0670
10.	TS2, TS3	0.0644	0.4588	0.0360	0.6473	0.0223	0.7178	0.0112	0.7010
11.	TS2, SRW	0.0675	0.4826	0.0341	0.6408	0.0203	0.6891	0.0089	0.6630
12.	TS2, VL	0.0905	0.7769	0.0472	1.0239	0.0252	1.0185	0.0147	1.1259
13.	TS3, SRW	0.0648	0.4662	0.0336	0.6200	0.0206	0.6828	0.0112	0.7067
14.	TS3, VL	0.0891	0.7639	0.0463	0.9989	0.0251	0.9955	0.0156	1.1015
15.	VL, SRW	0.0826	0.7335	0.0409	0.9666	0.0199	0.9383	0.0128	1.0294

Panel C. Regressions with three earnings proxies (P = 3)

16.	TS1, TS2, TS3	0.0669	0.4906	0.0359	0.6599	0.0233	0.6585	0.0109	0.6615
17.	TS1, TS2, SRW	0.0709	0.5193	0.0354	0.6845	0.0199	0.6928	0.0085	0.7000
18.	TS1, TS2, VL	0.0918	0.7837	0.0470	1.0260	0.0251	1.0119	0.0142	1.1251
19.	TS1, TS3, SRW	0.0684	0.5058	0.0343	0.6568	0.0205	0.6535	0.0107	0.6809
20.	TS1, TS3, VL	0.0899	0.7715	0.0460	1.0005	0.0259	0.9722	0.0158	1.0718
21.	TS1, VL, SRW	0.0898	0.7718	0.0444	1.0032	0.0210	0.9770	0.0128	1.0713
22.	TS2, TS3, SRW	0.0702	0.5038	0.0366	0.6776	0.0223	0.7441	0.0109	0.7442
23.	TS2, TS3, VL	0.0924	0.7834	0.0480	1.0272	0.0262	1.0294	0.0152	1.1271
24.	TS2, VL, SRW	0.0933	0.7868	0.0472	1.0309	0.0252	1.0289	0.0142	1.1305
25.	TS3, VL, SRW	0.0903	0.7687	0.0461	1.0018	0.0248	0.9988	0.0150	1.1018

Panel D. Regressions with four earnings proxies (P = 4)

26.	TS1, TS2, TS3, SRW	0.0711	0.5198	0.0363	0.6827	0.0236	0.6884	0.0109	0.7055
27.	TS1, TS2, TS3, VL	0.0923	0.7845	0.0480	1.0246	0.0291	1.0111	0.0164	1.1243
28.	TS1, TS2, VL, SRW	0.0934	0.7888	0.0470	1.0311	0.0253	1.0232	0.0138	1.1316
29.	TS1, SRW, TS3, VL	0.0908	0.7743	0.0458	1.0027	0.0257	0.9772	0.0152	1.0737
30.	TS2, SRW, TS3, VL	0.0938	0.7889	0.0478	1.0299	0.0259	1.0321	0.0146	1.1274

Panel E. Regressions with five earnings proxies (TS1, TS2, TS3, SRW, VL) (P = 5)

31.	All models	0.0936	0.7890	0.0478	1.0281	0.0290	1.0178	0.0158	1.1280

[a] $CR_{it}(d,0)$ is the cumulative residual for firm i in quarter t. It is calculated as the cumulated market model residual, cumulated from d days before the earnings announcement date through the earnings announcement date (day 0). $UE_{it\lambda}$ is the unexpected earnings proxy for firm i, in quarter t, conditional on forecasting model λ (see note c). γ_0 is the estimated regression intercept coefficient. P is the number of proxy variables for unexpected earnings in the regression, $P = 1, \ldots, 5$. γ_λ is the estimated regression coefficient for $UE_{it\lambda}$.

[b] Number of observations available for the test. The number of observations decreases as the cumulation period increases because an observation is constrained so that each observation's *Value Line* report date occurs before the first day of the cumulation period, d.

[c] The independent variable(s) in the regressions are proxy variables for unexpected earnings. There are five unexpected earnings proxy variables. SRW indicates that the unexpected earnings proxy is calculated conditional on the seasonal random walk forecasting model, TS1 the Brown and Rozeff (1979) model, TS2 the Foster (1977) model, TS3 the Watts (1975) – Griffin (1977) model, and VL the forecast in *The Value Line Investment Survey*.

[d] Sum of coeff. is the sum of the coefficients for the proxy variables in the regression, i.e., the sum of γ_λ. Since all independent variables are proxy variables for unexpected earnings, the sum of the coefficients represents the estimated coefficient for unexpected earnings. For the single proxy variable regressions (regressions 1 through 5), the sum of coefficients is the coefficient for the single proxy variable.

The following results pertain to the $(-1,0)$ holding period. The highest sums of coefficients in panels A through E are 0.6985 (panel A, #5, VL), 0.7769 (panel B, #12, TS2, VL), 0.7868 (panel C, #24, TS2, VL, SRW), 0.7889 (panel D, #30, TS2, SRW, TS3, VL), and 0.7890 (panel E, #31, all five models), respectively; the lowest sum of coefficients in panels A through E are 0.3170 (panel A, #1, SRW), 0.4588 (panel B, #10, TS2, TS3), 0.4906 (panel C, #16, TS1, TS2, TS3), 0.5198 (panel D, #26, TS1, TS2, TS3, SRW), and 0.7890 (panel E, #31, all five models), respectively.

As discussed in section 2.3, a finding that the sum of γ_λ coefficients increases when additional proxies are included in regression eq. (9) suggests that the proxy variables contain measurement error and the regressions with two or more proxy variables reduce (to an unknown degree) the measurement error. To examine the extent to which the use of multiple proxy variables reduces (ex post) measurement error, we examine the incremental explanatory power (i.e., the partial F-statistic) of adding an additional proxy variable to the (ex post) 'best' proxy variable among the alternative single proxy variable regressions, of adding an additional proxy variable to the 'best' set of two proxy variable regressions, and so on. Assuming that eq. (1) is the 'true' model for R_{it}, a significant partial F-statistic suggests the existence of measurement error and that our procedure of combining earnings proxies reduces (to an unknown degree) measurement error.

Fig. 1 presents a bar graph of the maximum adjusted R-squares from table 2 for a given number of proxy variables for each of the four holding periods. For example, for the $(-1,0)$ holding period, the proxy variables represented by the bar graph are regressions #5 (VL), #12 (TS2, VL), #24 (TS2, VL, SRW), #30 (TS2, SRW, TS3, VL), and #31 (all five models) for the regressions with one through five proxy variables, respectively. We first examine the t-statistic of TS2 in regression #12 to ascertain whether addition of a second proxy variable significantly reduces measurement error. Finding a significant t-statistic, we conclude that a two proxy variable equation reduces measurement error in this case. Similarly, we examine the t-statistic of SRW in regression #24, of TS3 in regression #30, and of TS1 in regression #31, respectively, to ascertain whether addition of a third, fourth, and fifth explanatory variable to a set of two, three, and four explanatory variables significantly reduces measurement error. The incremental t-statistics of SRW and TS3 in regressions #24 and #30 were significant, but the t-statistic of TS1 in equation #31 was not significant.

The bar graph in fig. 1 representing the four proxy variable equation for the $(-1,0)$ holding period is designated by an asterisk to indicate that the four variable set appears to be (ex post) 'best' for this holding period. Similar analyses are conducted for the longest holding period $(-40,0)$ and the two intermediate holding periods $(-10,0)$ and $(-20,0)$. The 'best' set of proxy

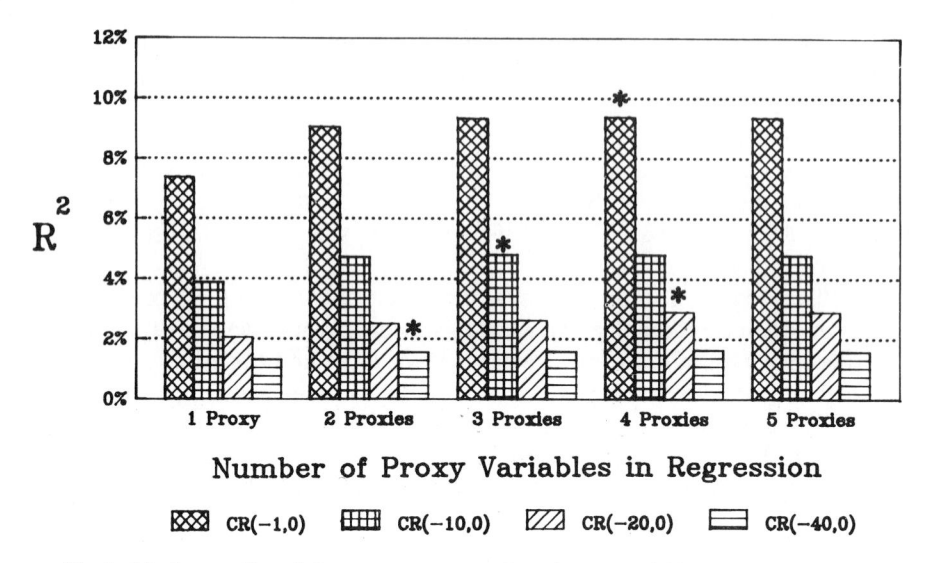

Fig. 1. Maximum adjusted R-squares across number of proxy variables – table 2 regressions.

variable equations for these holding periods is also represented by an asterisk in fig. 1. Comparing the longest holding period $(-40,0)$ with the shortest holding period $(-1,0)$, it is evident that our procedure is more successful for reducing measurement error for the shortest holding period. More specifically, the 'best' set of proxy variable equations for the shortest holding period is represented by four proxy variables, while it is represented by two proxy variables for the longest holding period.

In summary, the results presented in table 2 and fig. 1 suggest that our procedures are more effective for reducing measurement error for shorter abnormal return holding periods than they are for reducing measurement error for the longest $(-40,0)$ holding period. We cannot distinguish between the explanations that our procedure is not sufficiently powerful for detecting measurement error over the longest $(-40,0)$ holding period and that measurement error is not a significant problem in our sample for the longest holding period. However, for shorter holding periods, our results indicate that measurement error is a significant problem for the researcher using a multiple regression research design.

While we have demonstrated an increase in the explanatory power of the relation between CR_{it} and $UE_{it\lambda}$ by using multiple proxies for unexpected earnings – which we attribute in part to the reduction of the error in measuring the market's expectation of unexpected earnings – we realize that we do not purge all the error, and thus, the coefficient values that are estimated do

Table 3

Summary of cross-sectional regressions between cumulative residuals and one or more unexpected earnings proxy variable(s), comparison of large and small firms.

Regression: $CR_{it}(d,0) = \gamma_0 + \sum_{\lambda=1}^{P} \gamma_\lambda UE_{it\lambda} + \text{error}.$ [a]

Dependent variable: Cumulative residual ($CR_{it}(d,0)$)

		$CR_{it}(-1,0)$				$CR_{it}(-40,0)$			
		1,044 small firms[b]		1,044 large firms		403 small firms		403 large firms	
Regression No.	Independent variable(s)[c]	Adjusted R-square	Sum of coeff.[d]	Adjusted R-square	Sum of coeff.	Adjusted R-square	Sum of coeff.	Adjusted R-square	Sum of coeff.

Panel A. Regressions with one earnings proxy ($P=1$)

1.	SRW	0.0560	0.3220	0.0035	0.1393	0.0108	0.4464	-0.0025	-0.0449
2.	TS1	0.0810	0.4659	0.0146	0.3192	0.0108	0.6015	0.0054	1.1356
3.	TS2	0.0632	0.3583	0.0116	0.2527	0.0071	0.4325	0.0176	1.6575
4.	TS3	0.0880	0.4451	0.0146	0.3142	0.0218	0.7682	0.0049	1.0106
5.	VL	0.0945	0.6416	0.0383	0.7824	0.0252	1.0711	-0.0010	0.5796

Panel B. Regressions with two earnings proxies ($P=2$)

6.	TS1, TS2	0.0828	0.4789	0.0138	0.3205	0.0084	0.6052	0.0164	1.4482
7.	TS1, TS3	0.0904	0.4834	0.0144	0.3302	0.0215	0.6832	0.0031	1.1428
8.	TS1, SRW	0.0873	0.5055	0.0150	0.3079	0.0138	0.7411	0.0121	1.1704
9.	TS1, VL	0.1158	0.7391	0.0383	0.8036	0.0234	1.1166	0.0030	1.0511
10.	TS2, TS3	0.0894	0.4674	0.0139	0.3177	0.0194	0.7532	0.0156	1.5445
11.	TS2, SRW	0.0843	0.4840	0.0107	0.2568	0.0137	0.7127	0.0207	1.3563
12.	TS2, VL	0.1162	0.7468	0.0384	0.8043	0.0246	1.1711	0.0153	0.5051
13.	TS3, SRW	0.0938	0.4939	0.0151	0.3017	0.0230	0.8971	0.0093	0.9098
14.	TS3, VL	0.1239	0.7445	0.0389	0.8147	0.0290	1.2070	0.0024	0.9517
15.	VL, SRW	0.1071	0.6996	0.0376	0.7749	0.0258	1.1532	-0.0028	0.5279

Panel C. Regressions with three earnings proxies ($P = 3$)

16.	TS1, TS2, TS3	0.0903	0.4897	0.0134	0.3303	0.0195	0.6936	0.0140	1.4522
17.	TS1, TS2, SRW	0.0901	0.5239	0.0141	0.3087	0.0119	0.7594	0.0186	1.4242
18.	TS1, TS2, VL	0.1187	0.7589	0.0376	0.8060	0.0224	1.1703	0.0140	1.4651
19.	TS1, TS3, SRW	0.0944	0.5148	0.0153	0.3208	0.0238	0.8114	0.0101	1.1835
20.	TS1, TS3, VL	0.1232	0.7475	0.0381	0.8157	0.0317	1.1512	0.0007	1.0446
21.	TS1, VL, SRW	0.1175	0.7495	0.0396	0.7986	0.0235	1.1698	0.0097	1.2494
22.	TS2, TS3, SRW	0.0955	0.5186	0.0142	0.3042	0.0206	0.8853	0.0188	1.4271
23.	TS2, TS3, VL	0.1248	0.7612	0.0380	0.8147	0.0266	1.1952	0.0132	1.4961
24.	TS2, VL, SRW	0.1210	0.7698	0.0387	0.7957	0.0247	1.2341	0.0185	1.5271
25.	TS3, VL, SRW	0.1246	0.7543	0.0411	0.8159	0.0280	1.2504	0.0070	1.0313

Panel D. Regressions with four earnings proxies ($P = 4$)

26.	TS1, TS2, TS3, SRW	0.0950	0.5260	0.0144	0.3203	0.0226	0.8406	0.0163	1.4311
27.	TS1, TS2, TS3, VL	0.1240	0.7602	0.0372	0.8161	0.0316	1.2195	0.0115	1.4597
28.	TS1, TS2, VL, SRW	0.1210	0.7725	0.0387	0.7996	0.0232	1.2428	0.0162	1.5486
29.	TS1, SRW, TS3, VL	0.1238	0.7550	0.0402	0.8159	0.0316	1.2011	0.0077	1.2426
30.	TS2, SRW, TS3, VL	0.1256	0.7722	0.0402	0.8158	0.0256	1.2408	0.0165	1.5405

Panel E. Regressions with five earnings proxies (TS1, TS2, TS3, SRW, VL) ($P = 5$)

31.	All models	0.1251	0.7707	0.0393	0.8154	0.0322	1.2898	0.0140	1.5407

[a] $CR_{it}(d,0)$ is the cumulative residual for firm i in quarter t. It is calculated as the cumulated market model residual, cumulated from d days before the earnings announcement date through the earnings announcement date (day 0). $UE_{it\lambda}$ is the unexpected earnings proxy for firm i, in quarter t, conditional on forecasting model λ (see note c). γ_0 is the estimated regression intercept coefficient. P is the number of proxy variables for unexpected earnings in the regression, $P = 1, \ldots, 5$. γ_λ is the estimated regression coefficient for $UE_{it\lambda}$.

[b] Number of observations available for the test. The number of observations decreases as the cumulation period increases because an observation is constrained so that each observation's *Value Line* report date occurs before the first day of the cumulation period, d. The total number of observations for a particular cumulation period is partitioned into quartiles on the basis of size, then the upper quartile (large firms) is compared to the lower quartile (small firms) in the columns of the table. For $CR_{it}(-1,0)$, small firms have equity with a market value of less than $274 million and large firms have equity with a market value of more than $1,269 million; for $CR_{it}(-40,0)$ small firms have equity with a market value of less than $328 million and large firms have equity with a market value of more than $1,356 million.

[c] The independent variable(s) in the regressions are proxy variables for unexpected earnings. There are five unexpected earnings proxy variables. SRW indicates that the unexpected earnings proxy is calculated conditional on the seasonal random walk forecasting model, TS1 the Brown and Rozeff (1979) model, TS2 the Foster (1977) model, TS3 the Watts (1975) – Griffin (1977) model, and VL the forecast in *The Value Line Investment Survey*.

[d] Sum of coeff. is the sum of the coefficients for the proxy variables in the regression, i.e., the sum of γ_λ. Since all independent variables are proxy variables for unexpected earnings, the sum of the coefficients represents the estimated coefficient for unexpected earnings. For the single proxy variable regressions (regressions 1 through 5), the sum of coefficients is the coefficient for the single proxy variable.

not reveal the magnitude of the 'true' β implicit in eq. (1). Also, recall that the coefficients are based on a cross-sectional estimation procedure, a technique that makes the simplifying assumption that the β coefficient is cross-sectionally invariant.

4.3. Effects of firm size

Measurement error in unexpected earnings may differ on the basis of firm characteristics. Larger firms are subject to closer scrutiny by equity analysts [e.g., Advisory Committee on Corporate Disclosure (1977)] and earnings information of large firms generally is available earlier to the market. For large firms, the market obtains information from primary and secondary sources on a relatively continuous basis. On the other hand, for small firms, new information tends to be released less frequently, for example, at the time of earnings announcements.

In order to examine whether or not the results differ on the basis of firm size (i.e., the market value of equity measured two days before the earnings announcement), we segment our sample into four quartiles conditional on firm size, and present, in table 3, the results for the smallest and the largest quartiles for the shortest $(-1,0)$ and longest $(-40,0)$ holding periods. For the short holding period, $(-1,0)$, small firms have equity with a market value of less than $274 million and large firms have equity with a market value of more than $1,269 million; for the long holding period, $(-40,0)$, small firms have equity with a market value of less than $328 million and large firms have equity with a market value of more than $1,356 million. Consistent with the format of table 2, panel A of table 3 summarizes regressions with one proxy, panel B with two proxies, etc. In a manner similar to fig. 1, fig. 2 presents a bar graph of the maximum adjusted R-squares from table 3 for a given number of proxy variables (one to five) for the $(-1,0)$ and $(-40,0)$ holding period for the small and large firms. The principal results follow.

First, the γ_1 coefficient values for the single variable forms of eq. (9) are highly significant for the small firms for both the shortest and longest holding periods. However, they are not always significant for the large firms. The adjusted R-squares are actually negative in two instances for the large firms for the longest holding period. Second, the sum of the γ_λ coefficients always increases and the adjusted R-squares always decrease as the holding period increases for the small firms. Such is not the case, however, for the large firms. Third, the partitioning of the sample on firm size appears to have opposite effects for *Value Line* and the Box–Jenkins time series conditioned proxies. For the shortest (longest) holding period, the Box–Jenkins time series models' γ_1 (see regressions #2 through #4) are larger (smaller) for small firms than

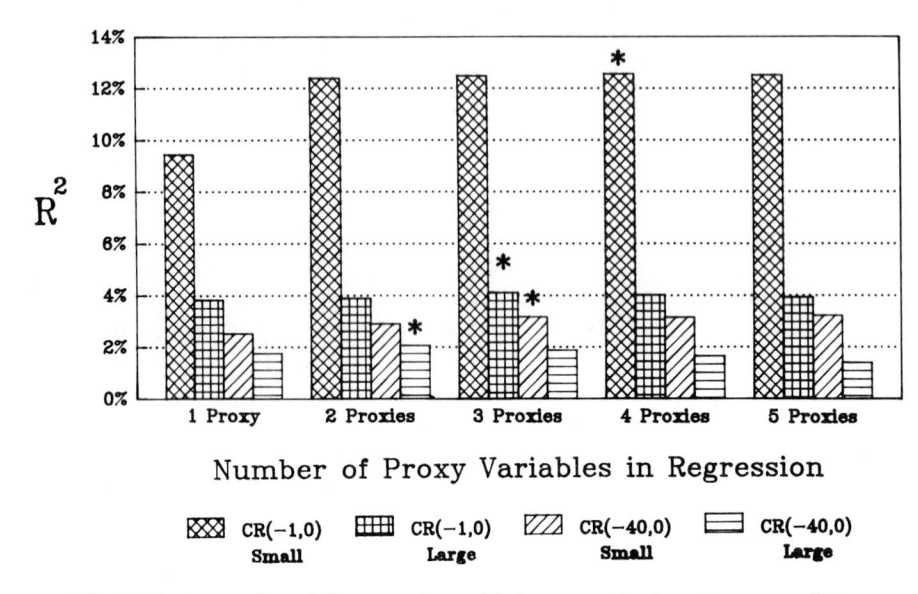

Fig. 2. Maximum adjusted R-squares from table 3 – comparing large firms to small firms.

for large firms, while the opposite is observed for VL (see regression #5). Fourth, the sum of the γ_λ coefficients generally increases when additional proxy variables are added to eq. (9), regardless of firm size or length of holding period.

Similar to fig. 1, the asterisks for fig. 2 designate the N proxy variable set that is (ex post) 'best' for the particular firm size/holding period. Fig. 2 reveals that our procedures appear to be more effective at reducing measurement error for small than for large firms and for short than for long holding periods. More specifically, for the (−1,0) holding period, a four variable set appears to be 'best' for small firms, while a three variable set appears to be 'best' for large firms. For the (−40,0) holding period, a three variable set appears to be 'best' for small firms, while a two variable set appears to be ex post 'best' for large firms.

In sum, the results presented in table 3 and fig. 2 again suggest the existence of measurement error in unexpected earnings proxies, that our procedures are more effective at reducing measurement error for the short holding period than they are for the long holding period, and that these results hold for both small and large firms. However, the results also suggest that the relation between abnormal returns and unexpected earnings is better specified for small than for large firms, and that our procedures are more effective at ameliorating measurement error for the small firms.

Table 4

Summary of cross-sectional regressions between cumulative residuals and one or more unexpected earnings proxy variable(s), comparison of recent and non-recent forecasts.

Regression: $CR_{it}(d,0) = \gamma_0 + \sum_{\lambda=1}^{P} \gamma_\lambda UE_{it\lambda} + \text{error}.$ [a]

No.	Regression Independent variable(s)[c]	$CR_{it}(-1,0)$ 1,056 recent[b] Adjusted R-square	Sum of coeff.[d]	1,095 non-recent Adjusted R-square	Sum of coeff.	$CR_{it}(d,0)$ 429 recent Adjusted R-square	Sum of coeff.	$CR_{it}(-40,0)$ 409 non-recent Adjusted R-square	Sum of coeff.
		Panel A. Regressions with one earnings proxy ($P=1$)							
1.	SRW	0.0640	0.3536	0.0173	0.1852	0.0005	0.2795	0.0057	0.4041
2.	TS1	0.0746	0.4458	0.0359	0.3684	0.0169	0.8631	0.0013	0.4197
3.	TS2	0.0672	0.3762	0.0226	0.2561	0.0358	1.0467	−0.0001	0.3139
4.	TS3	0.0676	0.4032	0.0387	0.3711	0.0197	0.7269	0.0036	0.5185
5.	VL	0.0860	0.7544	0.0526	0.5572	0.0118	1.1926	0.0037	0.6183
		Panel B. Regressions with two earnings proxies ($P=2$)							
6.	TS1, TS2	0.0784	0.4619	0.0350	0.3681	0.0356	0.9039	−0.0010	0.4091
7.	TS1, TS3	0.0756	0.4562	0.0386	0.3871	0.0180	0.8230	0.0024	0.4596
8.	TS1, SRW	0.0820	0.4795	0.0370	0.3892	0.0147	0.8324	0.0038	0.5277
9.	TS1, VL	0.1096	0.8318	0.0565	0.6005	0.0169	1.2389	0.0014	0.6317
10.	TS2, TS3	0.0746	0.4360	0.0383	0.3825	0.0337	1.0325	0.0021	0.4704
11.	TS2, SRW	0.0889	0.4972	0.0289	0.3257	0.0338	0.9845	0.0035	0.4834
12.	TS2, VL	0.1134	0.8513	0.0560	0.6073	0.0344	1.2993	0.0013	0.6241
13.	TS3, SRW	0.0788	0.4581	0.0394	0.3914	0.0176	0.6775	0.0050	0.6199
14.	TS3, VL	0.1088	0.8358	0.0588	0.6096	0.0204	1.1990	0.0024	0.6846
15.	VL, SRW	0.1037	0.7890	0.0524	0.5628	0.0096	1.2044	0.0047	0.6492

Panel C. Regressions with three earnings proxies (P = 3)

16.	TS1, TS2, TS3	0.0781	0.4662	0.0378	0.3887	0.0334	0.8950	0.0001	0.4500
17.	TS1, TS2, SRW	0.0887	0.5069	0.0361	0.3898	0.0333	0.8940	0.0014	0.5195
18.	TS1, TS2, VL	0.1144	0.8547	0.0560	0.6093	0.0358	1.2984	−0.0010	0.6259
19.	TS1, TS3, SRW	0.0819	0.4851	0.0391	0.4030	0.0161	0.7701	0.0043	0.5573
20.	TS1, TS3, VL	0.1103	0.8399	0.0579	0.6087	0.0181	1.2035	0.0022	0.6639
21.	TS1, VL, SRW	0.1115	0.8288	0.0557	0.6007	0.0150	1.2113	0.0022	0.6498
22.	TS2, TS3, SRW	0.0882	0.5009	0.0390	0.4019	0.0317	0.9851	0.0035	0.5716
23.	TS2, TS3, VL	0.1142	0.8572	0.0582	0.6181	0.0326	1.3132	0.0011	0.6446
24.	TS2, VL, SRW	0.1189	0.8548	0.0553	0.6080	0.0328	1.2630	0.0022	0.6406
25.	TS3, VL, SRW	0.1113	0.8321	0.0579	0.6095	0.0188	1.1571	0.0028	0.6949

Panel D. Regressions with four earnings proxies (P = 4)

26.	TS1, TS2, TS3, SRW	0.0878	0.5069	0.0383	0.4054	0.0312	0.8797	0.0019	0.5500
27.	TS1, TS2, TS3, VL	0.1138	0.8569	0.0577	0.6204	0.0337	1.2897	−0.0002	0.6542
28.	TS1, TS2, VL, SRW	0.1180	0.8548	0.0552	0.6095	0.0337	1.2810	−0.0002	0.6412
29.	TS1, SRW, TS3, VL	0.1116	0.8358	0.0571	0.6087	0.0165	1.1625	0.0026	0.6741
30.	TS2, SRW, TS3, VL	0.1181	0.8551	0.0574	0.6181	0.0308	1.2784	0.0014	0.6564

Panel E. Regressions with five earnings proxies (TS1, TS2, TS3, SRW, VL) (P = 5)

31.	All models	0.1172	0.8552	0.0568	0.6204	0.0316	1.2677	0.0002	0.6666

[a] $CR_{it}(d,0)$ is the cumulative residual for firm i in quarter t. It is calculated as the cumulated market model residual, cumulated from d days before the earnings announcement date through the earnings announcement date (day 0). $UE_{it\lambda}$ is the unexpected earnings proxy for firm i, in quarter t, conditional on forecasting model λ (see note c). γ_0 is the estimated regression intercept coefficient. P is the number of proxy variables for unexpected earnings in the regression, $P = 1, \ldots, 5$. γ_λ is the estimated regression coefficient for $UE_{it\lambda}$.

[b] Number of observations available for the test. The number of observations decreases as the cumulation period increases because an observation is constrained so that each observation's *Value Line* report date occurs before the first day of the age of the forecast, the recent forecasts (non-recent forecasts) is for the particular cumulation period is partitioned into quartiles on the basis of the age of the forecast. For $CR_{it}(-1,0)$, the recent forecasts are less than 21 days old and the compared to the lower quartile (recent forecasts) in the columns of the table. For $CR_{it}(-40,0)$ the recent forecasts are less than 62 days old and the non-recent forecasts are more than 67 days old; for $CR_{it}(-40,0)$ the recent forecasts are less than 62 days old and the non-recent forecasts are more than 75 days old.

[c] The independent variable(s) in the regressions are proxy variables for unexpected earnings. There are five unexpected earnings proxy variables. SRW indicates that the unexpected earnings proxy is calculated conditional on the seasonal random walk forecasting model, TS1 the Brown and Rozeff (1979) model, TS2 the Foster (1977) model, TS3 the Watts (1975) – Griffin (1977) model, and VL the forecast in *The Value Line Investment Survey*.

[d] Sum of coeff. is the sum of the coefficients for the proxy variables in the regression, i.e. the sum of γ_λ. Since all independent variables are proxy variables for unexpected earnings, the sum of the coefficients represents the estimated coefficient for unexpected earnings. For the single proxy variable regressions (regressions 1 through 5), the sum of coefficients is the coefficient for the single proxy variable.

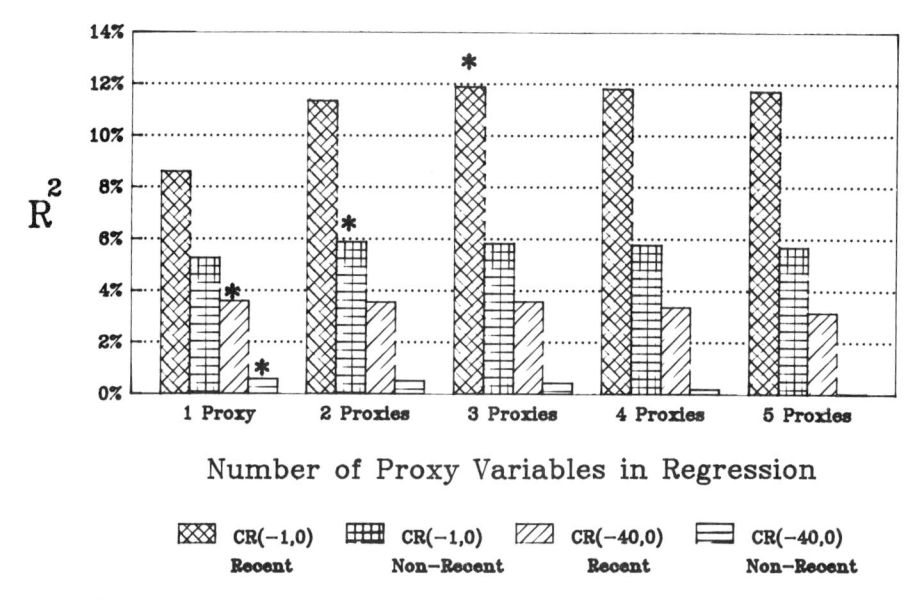

Fig. 3. Maximum adjusted *R*-squares from table 4 – comparing recent to non-recent forecasts.

4.4. Effects of forecast timing

Another characteristic of our data is that all forecasts are not equally timely; some forecasts are more recent than others relative to the earnings announcement date. Time series model forecasts have approximately a 90 day forecast horizon. However, security analysts make their forecasts with varying horizons [median forecast horizon (age) of 39 days]. It is possible that the older the forecast, the greater the measurement error, and hence the lower the estimated β coefficient. Table 4 examines this issue by presenting the adjusted *R*-squares and sum of γ_λ coefficients for recent and non-recent forecasts in a format similar to tables 2 and 3.

Firms with recent (non-recent) forecasts are partitioned into the lowest (highest) quartile of days between the *Value Line* report date and the earnings announcement date for the entire sample. As a result, recent and non-recent forecasts for the $(-1,0)$ holding period are less than 21 days old and more than 67 days old, respectively, where 'days old' is defined as the number of days the VL forecast precedes the earnings announcement day (day 0). Recent and non-recent forecasts for the $(-40,0)$ holding period are less than 62 days old and more than 75 days old, respectively. Fig. 3 presents a bar graph of the maximum adjusted *R*-squares from table 4 for a given number of proxy variables for each of the two holding periods for both recent and non-recent forecasts similar to figs. 1 and 2. The principal results follow.

First, the γ_1 coefficient values for the single firm variable forms of eq. (9) are highly significant for the recent forecasts for both the shortest and longest holding periods. However, they are not always significant for the non-recent forecasts. The adjusted R-square for TS2 in panel A is actually negative for the non-recent forecasts for the longest holding period. Second, with one exception (i.e., SRW in panel A), the sum of the γ_λ coefficients always increases and the adjusted R-squares always decrease as the holding period increases for the recent forecasts. Similarly, the sum of the γ_λ coefficients always increases and the adjusted R-squares always decrease for the non-recent forecasts. Third, for the short holding period, the sum of the γ_λ coefficients and the adjusted R-squares are always higher for the recent than for the non-recent forecasts. Similarly, for the long holding period, with the sole exception of SRW in panel A, the sum of the γ_λ coefficients and the adjusted R-squares for the recent forecasts are larger than those of firms with non-recent forecasts. These results are consistent with the conjecture that unexpected earnings proxies that are conditioned on non-recent forecasts contain more measurement error than proxies that are conditioned on more recent forecasts. Fourth, the sum of the γ_λ coefficients generally increases when additional proxy variables are added to eq. (9), regardless of recency of forecast or length of holding period.

Similar to figs. 1 and 2, the asterisks in fig. 3 designate the N proxy variable set that is (ex post) 'best' for the particular recency of forecast/holding period. Fig. 3 reveals that our procedures appear to be more effective at reducing measurement error for recent than non-recent forecasts, and for short rather than long holding periods. More specifically, for the $(-1,0)$ holding period, a three variable set appears to be 'best' for the recent forecasts, while a two proxy variable set appears to be 'best' for non-recent forecasts. For the $(-40,0)$ holding period, the multiple proxy variable procedure is ineffectual in the sense that the goodness of fit of the 'best' two proxy variable equation is not significantly better than the goodness of fit of the 'best' single variable equation, regardless of the recency of the forecast.

In sum, the results in table 4 and fig. 3 again suggest the existence of measurement error in unexpected earnings proxies and that our procedures are more effective at reducing measurement error for the short abnormal return holding period than they are for the long holding period. However, the results suggest that the relation between abnormal returns and unexpected earnings is better specified for recent forecasts than for non-recent forecasts, and that our procedures are more effective at reducing measurement error for the recent forecasts.

Table 5

Summary of cross-sectional regressions between cumulative residuals and one or more unexpected earnings proxy variable(s) using stock return to control for measurement error in unexpected earnings.

$$CR_{it}(d,0) = \gamma_0 + \sum_{\lambda=1}^{P} \gamma_\lambda UE_{it\lambda} + \omega R'_{jt} + \text{error.}[a]$$

No.	Regression Independent variable(s)[c]	$CR_{it}(-1,0)$ 4,177 observations[b] Sum of coeff.[d]	Table 2 change	$CR_{it}(-10,0)$ 3,431 observations Sum of coeff.	Table 2 change	$CR_{it}(-20,0)$ 2,931 observations Sum of coeff.	Table 2 change	$CR_{it}(-40,0)$ 1,611 observations Sum of coeff.	Table 2 change
		Panel A.	Regressions	with one earnings	proxy ($P=1$)				
1.	SRW	0.3182	0.36%	0.3829	0.20%	0.3882	−0.73%	0.3630	3.50%
2.	TS1	0.4788	1.01%	0.6434	2.15%	0.6198	0.95%	0.6550	5.15%
3.	TS2	0.3910	1.33%	0.5790	3.83%	0.6180	1.35%	0.5814	6.23%
4.	TS3	0.4273	1.26%	0.6048	3.10%	0.6587	0.99%	0.6887	4.15%
5.	VL	0.7163	2.54%	0.9728	4.21%	0.9198	3.03%	1.1341	12.33%
		Panel B.	Regressions	with two earnings	proxies ($P=2$)				
6.	TS1, TS2	0.4927	1.14%	0.6736	2.61%	0.6575	1.07%	0.6790	5.38%
7.	TS1, TS3	0.4861	1.10%	0.6520	2.32%	0.6340	0.98%	0.6757	5.04%
8.	TS1, SRW	0.5073	0.88%	0.6667	1.71%	0.6566	0.54%	0.7038	4.80%
9.	TS1, VL	0.7860	2.35%	1.0375	3.85%	0.9917	2.54%	1.1827	10.84%
10.	TS2, TS3	0.4652	1.39%	0.6700	3.51%	0.7260	1.16%	0.7364	5.05%
11.	TS2, SRW	0.4875	1.01%	0.6567	2.48%	0.6928	0.54%	0.6984	5.34%
12.	TS2, VL	0.7975	2.65%	1.0688	4.38%	1.0461	2.71%	1.2507	11.08%
13.	TS3, SRW	0.4708	1.00%	0.6338	2.22%	0.6859	0.46%	0.7350	4.00%
14.	TS3, VL	0.7834	2.55%	1.0405	4.17%	1.0212	2.58%	1.2194	10.70%
15.	VL, SRW	0.7498	2.22%	1.0023	3.69%	0.9607	2.38%	1.1487	11.58%

Panel C. Regressions with three earnings proxies ($P = 3$)

16.	TS1, TS2, TS3	0.4965	1.20%	2.72%	0.6779	0.6657	1.09%	0.6964	5.27%
17.	TS1, TS2, SRW	0.5246	1.01%	2.16%	0.6993	0.6973	0.65%	0.7354	5.06%
18.	TS1, TS2, VL	0.8035	2.53%	4.26%	1.0697	1.0398	2.67%	1.2502	11.13%
19.	TS1, TS3, SRW	0.5105	0.94%	1.80%	0.6686	0.6572	0.56%	0.7134	4.77%
20.	TS1, TS3, VL	0.7903	2.43%	3.98%	1.0403	0.9975	2.60%	1.1876	10.80%
21.	TS1, VL, SRW	0.7892	2.25%	3.68%	1.0402	0.9998	2.32%	1.1853	10.64%
22.	TS2, TS3, SRW	0.5095	1.12%	2.66%	0.6956	0.7491	0.67%	0.7802	4.84%
23.	TS2, TS3, VL	0.8040	2.63%	4.35%	1.0719	1.0562	2.60%	1.2509	10.98%
24.	TS2, VL, SRW	0.8062	2.46%	4.10%	1.0732	1.0538	2.43%	1.2526	10.80%
25.	TS3, VL, SRW	0.7873	2.41%	3.94%	1.0413	1.0226	2.38%	1.2177	10.51%

Panel D. Regressions with four earnings proxies ($P = 4$)

26.	TS1, TS2, TS3, SRW	0.5252	1.04%	2.20%	0.6977	0.6929	0.67%	0.7410	5.03%
27.	TS1, TS2, TS3, VL	0.8047	2.57%	4.34%	1.0690	1.0386	2.71%	1.2494	11.13%
28.	TS1, TS2, VL, SRW	0.8079	2.42%	4.08%	1.0732	1.0481	2.44%	1.2549	10.90%
29.	TS1, SRW, TS3, VL	0.7924	2.34%	3.81%	1.0410	1.0008	2.42%	1.1879	10.64%
30.	TS2, SRW, TS3, VL	0.8085	2.48%	4.12%	1.0724	1.0572	2.43%	1.2491	10.80%

Panel E. Regressions with five earnings proxies (TS1, TS2, TS3, SRW, VL) ($P = 5$)

| 31. | All models | 0.8084 | 2.46% | 4.15% | 1.0707 | 1.0433 | 2.51% | 1.2513 | 10.94% |

[a] $CR_{it}(d,0)$ is the cumulative residual for firm i in quarter t. It is calculated as the cumulative market model residual, cumulated from d days before the earnings announcement date through the earnings announcement day (day 0). UE_{itA} is the unexpected earnings proxy for firm i, in quarter t, conditional on the forecasting model λ (see note c). γ_0 is the estimated regression intercept coefficient. P is the number of proxy variables for unexpected earnings in the regression, $P = 1, \ldots, 5$. γ_λ is the estimated regression coefficient for UE_{itA}. ω is the coefficient for R'_{jt} which is firm i's stock return from day -100 through the day before the cumulation period begins (day $d - 1$).

[b] Number of observations available for the test. The number of observations decreases as the cumulation period increases because an observation is constrained so that each observation's Value Line report date occurs before the first day of the cumulation period, d.

[c] There are five unexpected earnings proxy variables. SRW indicates that the unexpected earnings proxy is calculated conditional on the seasonal random walk forecasting model, TS1 the Brown and Rozeff (1979) model, TS2 the Foster (1977) model, TS3 the Watts (1975) – Griffin (1977) model, and VL the forecast in The Value Line Investment Survey.

[d] Sum of coeff. is the sum of the coefficients for the proxy variables in the regression, i.e., the sum of γ_λ, estimated via eq. (10). Table 2 change is the percentage change in the sum of the coefficients from table 2 [estimated via eq. (9)] to table 5 [estimated via eq. (10)]. Since all independent variables are proxy variables for unexpected earnings, the sum of the coefficients represents the estimated coefficient for the unexpected earnings. For the single proxy variable regressions (regressions 1 through 5), the sum of coefficients is the coefficient for the single proxy variable. To the extent R'_{jt} is correlated with the measurement error in the proxy variable, the sum of the coefficients should increase.

4.5. Using stock returns to control for measurement error

Given the model and underlying assumptions in section 2, we show that including another independent variable in eq. (3) reduces the bias in estimating β in eq. (1) when the additional independent variable, Z_{it}, is correlated with the measurement error in the proxy, $\epsilon_{it\lambda}$, and uncorrelated with the dependent variable, R_{it}, the independent variable, S_{it}, and the eq. (1) residuals, μ_{it}. For present purposes, we use as Z_{it} the firm's stock return from 100 days before the earnings announcement (day -100) through the day before the cumulation period begins (day $d-1$) and re-estimate eq. (9) with this additional variable. More formally, the model we estimate is

$$CR_{it}(d,0) = \gamma_0 + \sum_{\lambda=1}^{P} \gamma_\lambda UE_{it\lambda} + \omega R'_{jt} + \text{error}, \qquad (10)$$

where R'_{jt} is our proxy for Z_{it}.

If earnings revisions and stock returns are positively correlated, then this additional stock return variable would be positively correlated with the measurement error in the (dated) unexpected earnings proxy variables. We assume that the stock return variable is positively correlated with the measurement error in the unexpected earnings proxy variables and uncorrelated with the dependent variable, the independent variable, and the residuals from the eq. (1) regression model. Since the additional return variable is assumed to be positively correlated with the measurement error in the unexpected earnings proxy variable, and β is assumed to be positive, we expect R'_{jt} to have a negative coefficient (i.e., $\omega < 0$).

Each of the regressions in table 2 [see eq. (9)] is re-estimated with inclusion of this additional stock return variable [see eq. (10)]. The percentage increase in the sum of the γ_λ coefficients resulting from the addition of this additional variable is reported in table 5 for each of the 124 regressions in table 2. The coefficients for ω (not reported in the table) are, as expected, negative and have t-statistics which reject the null hypothesis that ω is greater than or equal to 0 at less than the 0.01 probability level for every proxy variable combination and for every holding period (i.e., for all 124 regressions).

Further, with the sole exception of regression #1 (SRW) for the $(-20,0)$ holding period, the percentage change in the sum of the γ_λ coefficients is positive; that is, the sum of the γ_λ coefficients increases with the addition of the return variable for 123 of the 124 regressions. However, the percentage increases are small, the 124 regressions are not independent tests, and we do not conduct statistical tests for the significance of the increases. For the $(-1,0)$ holding period, the percentage increases range from 0.36 percent to 2.65 percent. The amount of the increase does not generally appear to be affected by the number of proxy variables in the regression. The increase in the percentage change increases as the holding period increases from $(-1,0)$ to $(-10,0)$ and from $(-10,0)$ to $(-40,0)$. The percentage increase is greatest for the $(-40,0)$ holding period, ranging from 3.50 to 12.33 percent.

In sum, the results from the addition of the stock return variable to the multiple proxy variable regression [eq. (9)] are consistent with the discussion of the measurement error problem above. These results indicate the existence of measurement error for long as well as short abnormal return holding periods. Further, the use of a multiple proxy variable research design does not appear to be a substitute for the addition of the stock return variable in that the addition of the stock return variable to a multiple proxy regression research design appears to reduce additional measurement error.

4.6. Instrumental variables

As discussed in section 2.2, an instrumental variables procedure regresses a proxy variable on a set of instrumental variables; the predictions from this regression are then used in a second regression of $CR(d,0)$ on the predicted variable. More specifically, the following two regressions are estimated:

$$UE_{it\lambda} = \delta_0 + \sum_{k=1}^{K} \delta_k I_{ikt} + \text{error}_1, \tag{11}$$

$$CR_{it}(d,0) = \beta_0 + \beta_1 \left[\hat{\delta}_0 + \sum_{k=1}^{K} \hat{\delta}_k I_{ikt} \right] + \text{error}_2, \tag{12}$$

where

δ_0, β_0 = regression intercept coefficients for eqs. (11) and (12), respectively,
I_{ikt} = instrumental variable k for firm i, in quarter t; k is the number of instrumental variables that are used in eq. (a) in table 6, $k = 4$, 5, or 6,
δ_k = regression coefficient for I_{ikt},
β_1 = slope coefficient in eq. (12).

Since it is unlikely that any variable exists that precisely meets the instrumental variable requirements discussed in section 2.2, we examine four alternative sets of instrumental variables which are based on earnings and stock returns. The four sets of instrumental variables are: (i) the four unexpected earnings proxy variables that are not the dependent variable in eq. (11), (ii) the signs of the five unexpected earnings proxy variables, (iii) a stock return variable and the instrumental variables in (i), and (iv) a stock return variable and the instrumental variables in (ii). The stock return instrumental variable is the stock return from 100 trading days before the earnings announcement through the day before the abnormal return holding period.

Table 6

Summary of cross-sectional regressions between cumulative residuals and instrumental variables for unexpected earnings.

Regressions: (a) $UE_{it\lambda} = \delta_0 + \sum_{k=1}^{K} \delta_k I_{ikt} + \text{error}_1$, (b) $CR_{it}(d,0) = \beta_0 + \beta_1 \left[\hat{\delta}_0 + \sum_{k=1}^{K} \hat{\delta}_k I_{ikt} \right] + \text{error}_2$.[a]

Dependent variable: Cumulative residual ($CR_{it}(d,0)$)

Eq. (b) regression		$CR_{it}(-1,0)$ 4,177 observations[b]		$CR_{it}(-10,0)$ 3,431 observations		$CR_{it}(-20,0)$ 2,931 observations		$CR_{it}(-40,0)$ 1,611 observations	
No.	Initial proxy[c]	Adjusted R-square	β_1 coeff.	Adjusted R-square	β_1 coeff.	Adjusted R-square	β_1 coeff.	Adjusted R-square	β_1 coeff.

Panel A. *Instrumental variables are the four unexpected earnings proxies not used as the initial unexpected earnings proxy variable (K = 4)*

1.	TS1	0.0753	0.5663	0.0402	0.7600	0.0246	0.8500	0.0135	0.8618
2.	TS2	0.0618	0.5049	0.0331	0.7005	0.0160	0.6833	0.0072	0.6317
3.	TS3	0.0686	0.5096	0.0342	0.6612	0.0165	0.6552	0.0088	0.6652
4.	SRW	0.0750	0.6307	0.0393	0.8686	0.0207	0.9035	0.0131	1.0450
5.	VL	0.0675	1.1734	0.0333	1.4175	0.0157	1.3759	0.0082	1.2856

Panel B. *Instrumental variables are the signs of the five unexpected earnings proxy variables (K = 5)*

6.	TS1	0.0838	0.8590	0.0396	1.1239	0.0346	1.4667	0.0307	1.9088
7.	TS2	0.0844	0.9504	0.0329	1.1243	0.0255	1.3849	0.0235	1.8538
8.	TS3	0.0818	0.9982	0.0343	1.2280	0.0329	1.6828	0.0286	2.1560
9.	SRW	0.0818	0.9982	0.0343	1.2280	0.0329	1.6828	0.0286	2.1560
10.	VL	0.0743	1.7908	0.0290	2.0073	0.0247	2.5671	0.0230	3.4194

Panel C. *Instrumental variables are the four unexpected earnings proxies not used as the initial unexpected earnings proxy variable and the stock return variable ($K = 5$)*

11.	TS1	0.0757	0.5679	0.0411	0.7681	0.0247	0.8531	0.0140	0.8752
12.	TS2	0.0611	0.5017	0.0317	0.6848	0.0157	0.6772	0.0066	0.6064
13.	TS3	0.0681	0.5077	0.0334	0.6529	0.0164	0.6525	0.0088	0.6648
14.	SRW	0.0762	0.6349	0.0414	0.8904	0.0217	0.9229	0.0141	1.0834
15.	VL	0.0627	1.1149	0.0296	1.3280	0.0141	1.2993	0.0051	1.0301

Panel D. *Instrumental variables are the signs of the five unexpected earnings proxy variables and the stock return variable ($K = 6$)*

16.	TS1	0.0871	0.9990	0.0395	1.2701	0.0368	1.7160	0.0342	2.2544
17.	TS2	0.0751	0.9374	0.0267	1.0559	0.0258	1.4571	0.0215	1.8788
18.	TS3	0.0817	0.9324	0.0305	1.0801	0.0253	1.3782	0.0234	1.8509
19.	SRW	0.0822	1.0009	0.0365	1.2632	0.0348	1.7190	0.0305	2.2240
20.	VL	0.0644	1.6118	0.0234	1.7749	0.0216	2.3701	0.0143	2.6530

[a] UE_{itk} is the unexpected earnings proxy for firm i, in quarter t, conditional on forecasting model λ (see note c). δ_0 and β_0 are the regression intercept coefficients for eqs. (a) and (b), respectively. I_{ikt} is instrumental variable k for firm i, in quarter t. K is the number of instrumental variables that are used in eq. (a), $k = 4, 5, 5, 6$. The instrumental variables are (i) the four unexpected earnings proxy variables that are not the dependent variable in eq. (a), see note c, (ii) the signs of the five unexpected earnings proxy variables, (iii) a stock return variable and the instrumental variables in (i), and (iv) a stock return variable and the instrumental variables in (ii). The stock return instrumental variable is the stock return from day -100 through the day before the cumulation period (day $d + 1$). δ_k is the regression coefficient for I_{ikt}. $CR_{it}(d, 0)$ is the cumulative residual for firm i in quarter t. It is calculated as the cumulated market model residual, cumulated from d days before the earnings announcement date through the earnings announcement date (day 0). β_1 is the slope coefficient in eq. (b) and it is denoted as β_1 coeff. in the table.

[b] Number of observations available for the test. The number of observations decreases as the cumulation period increases because an observation is constrained so that each observation's *Value Line* report date occurs before the first day of the cumulation period, d.

[c] The initial proxy variable in the regressions are proxy variables for unexpected earnings. There are five unexpected earnings proxy variables. SRW indicates that the unexpected earnings proxy is calculated conditional on the seasonal random walk forecasting model, TS1 the Brown and Rozeff (1979) model, TS2 the Foster (1977) model, TS3 the Watts (1975) – Griffin (1977) model, and VL the forecast in *The Value Line Investment Survey*.

Panels A through D of table 6 summarize the tests examining four alternative sets of instrumental variables for each of the five proxy variables. The table 6 results suggest that the instrumental variables technique has the desired effect of reducing measurement error. The β coefficient estimates are higher than in any of the regression estimates (based on the sum of the γ_λ coefficients) reported earlier in table 2. For example, the highest coefficient estimates in table 2 are 0.7890, 1.0311, 1.0321, and 1.1316 for the $(-1,0)$, $(-10,0)$, $(-20,0)$, and $(-40,0)$ holding periods, respectively. These estimates are dominated by the highest coefficient estimates based on the instrumental variables approach in table 6 for these same holding periods: 1.7908, 2.0073, 2.5671, and 3.4194, respectively.

These results reveal the importance of using analysts' forecasts in conjunction with non-VL proxies as measures of unexpected earnings. The magnitudes of the β coefficients are generally highest in regressions #5, #10, #15, and #20; that is, where the instrumental variable technique uses non-VL proxies to purge error from the VL proxy. Moreover, relative to using the VL proxy without attempting to purge error, the magnitude of the coefficient increases considerably (more than 100 percent in some cases, e.g., compare regression #5, table 2, with regressions #5, #10, #15, and #20, table 6, for the various holding periods).[17]

In sum, relative to the multiple regression approach with and without the inclusion of prior stock return data, and despite possible violations of the underlying assumptions, the instrumental variables approach apparently improves the estimation of the β coefficient. The effects of the instrumental variable procedure are most evident when the technique is used to purge error from an unexpected earnings proxy derived from *Value Line* analysts' forecasts.

5. Summary and conclusions

This study compares and evaluates five alternative proxy variables for the market's assessment of unexpected earnings for four alternative abnormal return holding periods. Since such proxy variables measure the market's assessment of unexpected earnings with error, we examine procedures to

---

[17] We do not claim that the reported coefficient estimates are 'close' to what they would be if all variables are measured without error. Such predictions depend on a particular model of the earnings change versus price change relation. These models make numerous simplifying assumptions about earnings behavior, the relation of earnings to cash flow, and the mapping of earnings or cash flows into prices. The models, however, generally predict that the β coefficient should be positive. Recent examples of models linking earnings to prices include Miller and Rock (1985) and Watts and Zimmerman (1986).

detect and potentially reduce the measurement error in these proxy variables. The procedures we examine are (i) the use of multiple unexpected earnings proxy variables in a regression of abnormal returns on unexpected earnings (multiple proxy procedure), (ii) the addition of an explanatory variable that is, ex ante, uncorrelated with the abnormal return (dependent) variable and correlated with the measurement error in the unexpected earnings proxies (additional explanatory variable procedure), and (iii) the use of an instrumental variables procedure (instrumental variable procedure). Additionally, we examine the relation of abnormal returns and unexpected earnings conditional on the size of the firm and on the age of the financial analyst's forecast. The major results follow.

For short holding periods, the results consistently indicate significant measurement error in all five unexpected earnings proxy variables and the reduction (to an unknown degree) in measurement error using any of the three procedures we examine. For the longest holding period, the results are mixed. The multiple proxy procedure is less effective for reducing measurement error for the longest holding period than for the shorter holding periods. However, the additional explanatory variable procedure and the instrumental variables procedure detect and appear to reduce measurement error for all holding periods.

The multiple proxy procedure is used to examine the sensitivity of our results to firm size and forecast age. This procedure appears to be more effective at detecting and/or reducing measurement error for the shortest holding period than for the longest holding period, regardless of firm size or forecast age. The relation between abnormal returns and unexpected earnings appears to be better specified for small firms and firms with more recent forecasts than for large firms and firms with non-recent forecasts. Moreover, our procedures appear to be more effective at reducing measurement error for small firms and firms with more recent forecasts than for large firms and firms with non-recent forecasts.

The more critical caveat to this study concerns the unknown effects of misspecifying the underlying relation between abnormal returns and unexpected earnings. For instance, our evidence suggests that earnings variables explain only a small portion of the market's response at the time of an earnings announcement (e.g., our largest adjusted R-square equals 0.1256). Future research may consider additional variables in conjunction with earnings surprise (e.g., extent of analyst coverage, stochastic nature of the process generating cash flows or earnings, confounding events) for the purpose of detecting measurement error and controlling for omitted variables. Also, we may have misspecified the properties of the error in measuring unexpected earnings. The sensitivity of our results to the unbiasedness property of earnings measurement error may be evaluated. In addition, we examine only two factors that potentially explain measurement error – firm size and age of forecast. Future research could consider other potential explanatory factors.[18]

Overall, our results indicate that measurement error is a significant problem for the researcher using a multiple regression research design; that is, regressing abnormal returns (capturing the information content of accounting earnings) on an unexpected earnings proxy variable and additional non-earnings explanatory variable(s). For expositional purposes, assume a researcher is regressing abnormal returns on an unexpected earnings proxy variable and one additional non-earnings explanatory variable. Our results indicate that the researcher must interpret the coefficient for the additional non-earnings explanatory variable conditional on an assumed correlation between the additional variable and the measurement error in the unexpected earnings proxy variable. A non-zero correlation potentially results in a measurement error interpretation of the coefficient for the additional non-earnings explanatory variable.

The procedures we examine to reduce measurement error, while reducing the measurement error problem to some extent, do not eliminate the problem. Our results indicate that it may be useful to use multiple unexpected earnings proxy variables and a stock return variable (observed before the abnormal return holding period) in a multiple regression research design. If inclusion of multiple unexpected earnings proxy variables or the stock return variable alters the estimates of the coefficient of the additional non-earnings explanatory variable, then a measurement error interpretation of this variable is likely. Unfortunately, if inclusion of the additional unexpected earnings proxy variables and the stock return variable does not alter the estimate of the coefficient of the additional non-earnings explanatory variable, our results do not imply that a measurement error interpretation of the additional non-earnings explanatory variable is invalid.

References

Advisory Committee on Corporate Disclosure, 1977, Report of the advisory committee on corporate disclosures to the securities and exchange commission (U.S. Government Printing Office, Washington, DC).
Beaver, W.H., R.A. Lambert and S. Ryan, 1987, The information content of security prices: A second look, Journal of Accounting and Economics 9, this issue.
Box, G.E. and G.M. Jenkins, 1976, Time series models: Forecasting and control (Holden Day, San Francisco, CA).

---

[18] One possibility would be to consider the firm's information environment. Brown et al. (1987b) show that analyst superiority in predicting firms' earnings relative to time series model forecasts is positively related to firm size and the extent of analyst agreement regarding their ex ante earnings predictions. Our finding that it is easier to reduce measurement error for small firms than for large firms is consistent with Brown et al. (1987b). Future research may examine whether it is easier to reduce measurement error in earnings proxies for firms for which analyst have heterogeneous rather than homogeneous ex ante earnings expectations.

Brown, L.D., 1987, The modern theory of financial reporting (Business Publications, Inc., Plano, TX).

Brown, L.D., P.A. Griffin, R.L. Hagerman and M.E. Zmijewski, 1987a, Security analyst superiority relative to univariate time-series models in forecasting quarterly earnings, Journal of Accounting and Economics 9, 61–87.

Brown, L.D., G.D. Richardson and S.A. Schwager, 1987b, An information interpretation of financial analyst superiority in forecasting earnings, Journal of Accounting Research 25, 49–67.

Brown, L.D. and M.S. Rozeff, 1979, Univariate time-series models of quarterly accounting earnings per share: A proposed model, Journal of Accounting Research 17, 179–189.

Christie, A.A., 1985, On cross-sectional analysis in accounting research, Unpublished working paper (University of Southern California, Los Angeles, CA).

Collins, D.W., S.P. Kothari and J.D. Rayburn, 1987, Firm size and the information content of prices with respect to earnings, Journal of Accounting and Economics 9, this issue.

Easton, P.E. and M.E. Zmijewski, 1987, Cross-sectional variation in the stock market's response to corporate earnings, Unpublished paper (University of Chicago, Chicago, IL).

Foster, G., 1977, Quarterly accounting data: Time-series properties and predictive-ability results, The Accounting Review 52, 1–21.

Foster, G., 1986, Financial statement analysis (Prentice-Hall, Englewood Cliffs, NJ).

Griffin, P.A., 1977, The time-series behavior of quarterly earnings: Preliminary evidence, Journal of Accounting Research 15, 71–83.

Hopwood, W.S., J.C. McKeown and P.A. Newbold, 1982, The additional information content of quarterly earnings reports: Intertemporal disaggregation, Journal of Accounting Research 20, 343–349.

Judge, G., R. Hill, W. Griffiths, H. Lutkepohl and T. Lee, 1984, Introduction to the theory and practice of econometrics (Wiley, New York).

Kross, W. and D. Shroeder, 1985, Firm prominence and the differential information content of quarterly earnings announcements, Unpublished working paper (Purdue University, West Lafayette, IN).

Lys, T. and S. Sivaramakrishnan, 1986, Earnings expectations and capital restructuring: The case of equity-for-debt swaps, Unpublished paper (Northwestern University, Evanston, IL).

Madalla, G.S., 1977, Econometrics (McGraw Hill, New York).

Miller, M.H. and K. Rock, 1985, Dividend policy under asymmetric information, Journal of Finance 40, 1031–1051.

Watts, R.L., 1975, The time series behavior of quarterly earnings, Unpublished paper (University of Newcastle, Newcastle, New South Wales).

Watts, R.L. and J.L. Zimmerman, 1986, Positive accounting theory (Prentice-Hall, Englewood Cliffs, NJ).

Analysts' Use of Information about Permanent and Transitory Earnings Components in Forecasting Annual EPS

Ashiq Ali
Columbia University and New York University
April Klein
New York University
James Rosenfeld
Emory University

SYNOPSIS AND INTRODUCTION: An intriguing anomaly in recent market-based accounting research is that both the market and analysts appear not to recognize properly the time-series properties of quarterly earnings shocks. Bernard and Thomas (1990) and Freeman and Tse (1989) present evidence that the market underestimates the implications of previous period earnings for future earnings. Mendenhall (1991) and Abarbanell and Bernard (1991) find that analysts do not seem to utilize time-series information about earnings correctly when setting their forecasts. Specifically, these last two studies document a positive serial correlation in analysts' quarterly forecast errors and interpret this finding as analysts systematically underestimating the persistence of past earnings forecast errors in forecasting future earnings.

The purpose of this article is to examine whether analysts properly recognize the time-series properties of *annual* earnings when setting their estimates of future earnings. Givoly (1985) investigates this issue and finds that analysts' forecasts of annual earnings per share (EPS) are unbiased and that prediction errors are not serially correlated. He concludes that

---

We gratefully acknowledge the valuable comments and suggestions from George Benston, Larry Brown, Richard Mendenhall, Shehzad Mian, Jacob Thomas, Nicholas Valerio, Larry Wall, Greg Waymire, two anonymous referees, and the participants of the NYU Accounting and Emory Finance Workshops. We also would like to thank IBES for supplying us with the analysts' forecast data.

Submitted January 1990.
Accepted July 1991.

forecasts are formed in an efficient manner. In contrast, this study finds that, on average, analysts set overly optimistic estimates of the next period's annual EPS and that forecast errors display significantly positive serial correlation. These results hold for short-term as well as for longer-term IBES consensus forecasts.

Bias and positive serial correlation in forecast errors suggest that analysts do not properly recognize the time-series properties of earnings when setting expectations of future earnings. Studies show that, for any given year, earnings shocks have both permanent and transitory (i.e., mean-reverting) components (see, e.g., Brooks and Buckmaster 1976; Ou 1990; Ou and Penman 1989b) and that the level of earnings persistence varies across firm-years. We examine whether analysts are aware of the differences between permanent and temporary components in the previous year's earnings when predicting future earnings.

The findings show that analysts are able to differentiate partially between permanent and temporary components in previous period earnings. We also find that the overestimation bias in forecasts is most pronounced for firms that recently experienced negative earnings. In contrast, the positive serial correlation is most evident for firms that had predominantly permanent earnings. These results suggest that the overestimation bias and serial correlation are not uniform across firms.

To address the economic significance of our findings, estimates of bias and serial correlation in forecast errors are used to adjust existing forecasts. The accuracy of the adjusted forecasts are then compared to the unadjusted forecasts. A significant improvement in forecasting ability is found for the adjusted longer-term forecasts, as evidenced by a 12 percent improvement in the mean squared error. Further, the bias and serial correlation in the adjusted forecasts are significantly less than in the actual forecasts for both longer and short terms. These results further support the view that analysts do not utilize available information efficiently when setting forecasts.

Key Words: *Analysts' forecast errors, Overprediction bias, Serial correlation in forecast errors, Permanent and temporary components of earnings.*

Data Availability: *Analysts' forecast data are available from Lynch, Jones and Ryan's Institutional Brokers Estimate System (IBES) 1990 database. Stock market prices and returns are available on the Center for Research in Security Prices (CRSP) monthly and CRSP NASDAQ databases.*

THE article is organized as follows. Section I describes the data and the test variables. Section II documents the overprediction bias and serial correlation in longer-term forecast errors for the entire sample. Section III examines whether analysts utilize the time-series properties of earnings when setting forecasts. Section IV explores the economic implications of our findings. Section V repeats the analyses with one-month forecasts, and section VI presents our conclusions.

I. Data and Variable Definitions

Analysts' forecasts errors for firm i for year t, $FEPR_{it}$, is defined as:

$$FEPR_{it} = (EPS_{it} - F_{it})/P_{it}, \qquad (1)$$

where EPS_{it} is reported annual earnings per share for firm i for year t, F_{it} is the median analysts' forecast for annual EPS of year t, and P_{it} is the market price of the stock at the beginning of the month in which analysts' forecasts are released by IBES.[1] The initial sample of analysts' forecasts consists of firms included in the IBES 1990 database, which contains forecasts of annual earnings from 1976 to 1990. We use the median forecast as our measure of the analysts' consensus forecast. To help insure that the median is a meaningful statistic, we require each firm to have at least three earnings estimates. Short-term forecasts for year t are taken one month prior to the end of fiscal-year t. Longer-term forecasts are taken eight months prior to the end of the fiscal year. Selection of an eight-month forecast horizon is based on our requirement that the previous year's EPS be known by analysts when making their current year's forecast.[2] We further require that EPS for year $t-1$ be known at the time the EPS forecast for year t is made.

Stock prices are taken from the *Center for Research in Security Prices* (CRSP) monthly database (which contains all firms listed on the NYSE) and the CRSP NASDAQ database (which contains over-the-counter firms through 1988). If prices are unavailable from either source, the IBES database is used. (The IBES database does not contain price information before 1983.)[3]

To be included in the final sample, each firm must have at least three consecutive years of data (from year $t-2$ to year t) for reported and forecasted EPS, as well as price data at the beginning of the forecast month. We do not limit our sample on the basis of listing status and/or fiscal year-end month.[4] Retaining OTC firms allows for the inclusion of smaller firms; including firms with non-December fiscal year-ends produces a sample with a broader number of industries (Smith and Pourciau 1988).

These restrictions yield a sample of 5,365 firm-years over the 12-year period 1978-1989. Table 1 presents a breakdown of the firm-years according to firms' listing status as well as the month of their fiscal year-ends.

For the sample, the mean and median eight-month forecast errors (deflated by price) are -3.02 and -0.24, significant at the 0.01 level, which suggest that analysts' forecasts are, on average, upwardly biased over the period 1978-1989.[5] The Pearson and Spearman correlation coefficients between $FEPR_{it}$ and $FEPR_{it-1}$ are 0.36 and 0.33,

---

[1] To evaluate the sensitivity of our analyses to the selection of the deflator, we re-estimated our equations with the standard deviation of analysts' forecasts at the time of the forecast (available from IBES) as an alternate deflator and also on raw, undeflated data. The results with these two measures are qualitatively the same as those reported in this article and can be obtained from the authors.

[2] Penman (1987) reports that 92 percent of all annual reports are filed with the SEC within 12 weeks after the end of the fiscal year. We allow an extra month in view of O'Brien's (1988) finding that an average lag of 34 trading days exists between the analysts' forecast date and the date of the forecast's publication in the IBES database.

[3] All of the data are adjusted for stock splits and stock dividends.

[4] Givoly (1985) restricts his sample to 27 firms listed on the NYSE with December 31 fiscal year-ends.

[5] The eight-month forecast error has a maximum value of 102.25 and a minimum value of -631.13. The first and third quartiles of the distribution are -2.08 and 0.33, respectively.

Table 1
Distribution of Sample Observations According to Firms' Listing Status and Month of Fiscal Year-End (1978–1989)

Firm Characteristics	Firm-Years	Percentage Firm-Years
Listing Status		
New York Stock Exchange	4,195	78.2
American Stock Exchange	188	3.5
Over-the-Counter	982	18.3
Total	5,365	100.0
Fiscal Year-End		
January	134	2.5
February	59	1.1
March	129	2.4
April	91	1.7
May	80	1.5
June	381	7.1
July	97	1.8
August	96	1.8
September	322	6.0
October	150	2.8
November	86	1.6
December	3,740	69.7
Total	5,365	100.0

significant at the 0.01 level, and are preliminary evidence that longer-term annual forecast errors may be serially correlated.[6]

The mean and median one-month forecast errors are -1.38 and -0.03, each significant at the 0.01 level.[7] The Pearson and Spearman correlation coefficients between yearly forecast errors are 0.27 and 0.18, also significant at the 0.01 level. Thus, both long-term and short-term forecast errors display evidence of bias and first-order serial correlation.

II. Serial Correlation and Bias in Analysts' Forecast Errors: Eight-Month Forecasts

We test for the bias and serial correlation in analysts' forecast errors by estimating:

$$FEPR_{it} = a_o + a_1 FEPR_{it-1} + a_2 Ret_{it-1} + e_{it}, \qquad (2)$$

---

[6] In this section, we do not control for possible cross-sectional dependencies. Thus, these significance levels must be viewed with caution.

[7] The maximum value is 120.5 and the minimum value is -815.0. The first and third quartiles are -0.51 and 0.23, respectively.

Table 2
Bias and Serial Correlation in Analysts' Eight-Month Forecast Errors
(N=5,365 Firm-Years; Dependent Variable = $FEPR_{it}$)

Independent Variable	OLS Coefficient	White Method Standard Error	t-statistic	Bootstrap Method Coefficient	Standard Error	t-statistic
Intercept	−1.99*	0.38	5.16*	−1.58	0.38	4.13*
$FEPR_{it-1}$	0.40*	0.17	2.30**	0.64	0.18	3.61*
	Adjusted R^2=0.13; Chi-square Coefficient = 4.08					
Intercept	−2.71*	0.43	6.31*	−2.53	0.42	6.10*
$FEPR_{it-1}$	0.39*	0.17	2.26**	0.36	0.17	2.10**
Ret_{it-1}	10.05*	1.27	7.94*	9.57	1.32	7.25*
	Adjusted R^2=0.15; Chi-square Coefficient = 15.28*					

Note: The standard errors and the t-statistics for the OLS coefficients are determined before and after adjusting for heteroscedasticity via the White (1980) method. The chi-square coefficient tests for the degree of heteroscedasticity.

$FEPR_{it}$ ($FEPR_{it-1}$) = eight-month forecast error for firm i for fiscal year t ($t-1$) divided by the stock market price at the time of the forecast; and

Ret_{it-1} = one-year stock return ending at the beginning of the month of the forecast.

* Significant at the 0.01 level (two-tailed test).
** Significant at the 0.05 level (two-tailed test).

where $FEPR_{it}$($FEPR_{it-1}$) is the analysts' eight-month forecast error for firm i for year t ($t-1$) and Ret_{it-1} is the one-year stock return ending on the month of the current forecast.

Rejecting the null that a_0 equals zero indicates that, on average, analysts' forecasts display a levels bias. Rejecting the null that a_1 equals zero shows that analysts' forecasts do not fully incorporate the information contained in past forecast errors. Rejecting the null that a_2 equals zero indicates that analysts do not fully use the past stock returns when forming expectations of future earnings. Beaver et al. (1980, 1987) and Collins et al. (1987) show that past stock returns reveal information about future earnings. If analysts' forecasts are efficient, this information should be reflected in their estimates.

Table 2 contains the pooled cross-sectional time-series regression results for equation (2), estimated with and without Ret_{it-1}. The statistical significance of the OLS coefficients are presented before and after the White (1980) adjustment for heteroscedasticity. To adjust for possible cross-sectional correlation, a bootstrapping procedure is used (Noreen 1989) to estimate the coefficients and their standard errors.[8]

The coefficient on $FEPR_{it-1}$ is significantly positive at the 0.05 level (using White's method) or 0.01 level (using OLS and bootstrap methods), indicating that forecast errors

---

[8] This procedure controls for possible cross-sectional dependence for each year's residuals. We also used yearly dummy variables to control for possible cross-sectional correlations in forecast errors, as has been done by O'Brien (1988), and Collins and Kothari (1989), who use the change in earnings as their dependent variable. The results are qualitatively the same as those reported in table 2. We do not control for time-series dependence because tests on the residuals show a lack of significant serial correlation.

of annual earnings are correlated in adjacent years. In contrast, Givoly (1985) finds no evidence of serial correlation in annual forecast errors. One interpretation compatible with our results is that analysts systematically underestimate the permanence of past forecast errors when forecasting future earnings (see, e.g., Mendenhall 1991, 170). That is, they do not appear to properly incorporate information about the time-series properties of earnings into their forecasts.

The significantly negative intercept terms suggest that analysts, on average, overestimate earnings. This result supports the findings of Stober (1991) who finds that although the number of realized increases in annual EPS is 68 percent greater than the number of decreases, the frequency of forecasted increases outnumbers forecasted decreases by a margin of three to one. It is also consistent with the findings of Barefield and Comiskey (1975) and Fried and Givoly (1982).

O'Brien (1988) notes that pooled cross-sectional, time-series regressions may, *ex post*, falsely reject the hypothesis that analysts' forecasts are unbiased. For example, an adverse macroeconomic shock could lead to a significantly negative forecast error when, in fact, analysts may have efficiently set their forecasts.

We examine this possibility by re-estimating equation (2) on a year-by-year basis to see if the bias and serial correlations reported in table 2 are driven by a few years. We find that the intercept term is significantly negative at the 0.01 level for nine of the 12 sample years. Similarly, the coefficient on the previous year's forecast error is significantly different from zero at the 0.01 level for every year except 1989, when it is significant at the 0.05 level. The mean (median) values for the intercept and for the coefficient on the previous year's forecast error are -1.20 (-1.05) and 0.38 (0.36), each significantly different from zero.[9] Thus, the observed bias and serial correlation from the pooled regression are not specific to any one year (or a subset of years).

The bottom section of table 2 shows that the coefficient on Ret_{it-1} is significantly positive at the 0.01 level for all three statistical methods.[10] This suggests that analysts are not using past stock returns efficiently when setting their current annual forecasts, a result consistent with Abarbanell (1990), who documents a similar finding for quarterly earnings forecasts. Further, since Ret_{it-1} represents the information available to market participants, our finding is consistent with Abdel-khalik (1990), who finds that analysts' forecasts are not good proxies for market earnings expectations. It also supports Brown et al. (1987b) who find that analysts' forecasts and past stock returns together provide a better proxy of the market's expectations of future earnings than analysts' forecasts alone.

III. Analysts' Forecasts and the Time-Series Properties of Earnings

Cross-sectional Variation in Bias and Serial Correlation of Forecast Errors

In this section, we explicitly examine whether the bias and positive serial correlation shown in table 2 are observed across the full sample, or are more likely to occur

---

[9] The *t*-statistic is the mean value divided by the standard deviation of the 12 yearly coefficients. A sign rank test confirms that the number of positive coefficients is different from a random selection of 12 positive/negative draws.

[10] To check if past returns are indeed related to future earnings, we regress EPS (normalized by price) for time *t* on Ret_{it-1}. The coefficient on Ret_{it-1} is 3.71, significant at the 0.01 level (with both OLS and White standard errors).

when the previous period's earnings are predominantly permanent or transitory. To examine this question, we estimate:

$$FEPR_{it} = b_0 + b_1 PERM_{it-1} + b_2 FEPR_{it-1} + b_3(FEPR_{it-1} * PERM_{it-1}) + b_4 Ret_{it-1} + u_{it}, \quad (3)$$

where $PERM_{it-1}$ is a dummy variable equal to one if last year's change in earnings for firm i is deemed to be relatively permanent and zero if it is relatively transitory.[11]

To differentiate between permanent and transitory earnings components, we rely on the results presented in Beaver and Morse (1978), Ou and Penman (1989b), and in Jaffe et al. (1989), showing that earnings/price (E/P) ratios proxy for the extent to which the previous year's earnings are transitory. In particular, they show that firms with relatively high, low, or negative E/P ratios experience mean reversion in the following year's earnings, whereas firms in the middle range experience fairly stationary earnings.

Accordingly, firms are ranked each year by their current E/P ratios, which are calculated by using the previous year's earnings per share and stock price at the beginning of the month of the eight-month forecast. Ten portfolios are formed. Portfolio 1 consists of negative E/P ratios (Ou and Penman 1989b; Jaffe et al. 1989); portfolios 2–10 are formed by ranking positive E/P firms from low to high and then dividing the ranked sample into nine portfolios of equal size. Re-ranking firms each year by their current E/P ratios is equivalent to assuming that the permanence of earnings for a firm is not stationary over time (e.g., see Freeman and Tse 1989; Ou and Penman 1989b).

We define the permanent group ($PERM_{it-1} = 1$) as those firm-years in portfolios 4–8 and the transitory group ($PERM_{it-1} = 0$) as those in portfolios 1–3 and in 9–10.[12] We further divide the temporary group into two subgroups: firm years with negative E/P ratios (portfolio 1) and firm-years with positive, but relatively small or large E/P ratios (portfolios 2, 3, 9, and 10). Segregating negative E/P ratios is based on Jaffe et al. (1989), who show that these firms display different firm and stock return characteristics from positive E/P firms, and Ou and Penman (1989b), who present evidence that firm-years with negative E/P ratios display dramatic mean reversion.[13]

We also estimate:

$$FEPR_{it} = c_0 + c_1 PERM_{it-1} + c_2 NEG_{it-1} + c_3 FEPR_{it-1} + c_4(FEPR_{it-1} * PERM_{it-1}) \\ + c_5(FEPR_{it-1} * NEG_{it-1}) + c_6 Ret_{it-1} + u_{it}, \quad (3a)$$

---

[11] Although prior studies present evidence that annual earnings, in general, follow a random walk (e.g., Albrecht et al. 1977; Ball and Watts 1972; Watts and Leftwich 1977), other studies show that, on a year-to-year basis, earnings have both permanent and transitory (i.e., mean-reverting) components (e.g., Brooks and Buckmaster 1976; Ou 1990; Ou and Penman 1989a, 1989b).

[12] To examine whether these classifications are reasonable, we examine the time-series properties of each class of firms. Specifically, we estimate: $CEPSPR_{it} = a_0 + a_1 CEPSPR_{it-1} + e_{it}$ for each group, where $CEPSPR_{it}$ ($CEPSPR_{it-1}$) is the change in annual EPS for firm i deflated by price for year $t(t-1)$. For the permanent group, we expect a_1 to be indistinguishable from zero. For the temporary group, we expect mean-reversion in earnings, i.e., a_1 to be significantly negative.

For the permanent group, a_1 equals 0.047, insignificantly different from zero (two-tailed test) at the 0.10 level. For the temporary group, a_1 equals -0.354, significantly different from zero at the 0.01 level. The Pearson and Spearman correlations between $CEPSPR_{it}$ and $CEPSPR_{it-1}$ for the permanent group are 0.03 and 0.07; for the temporary group, they are -0.32 and -0.16. Thus, E/P appears to be a reasonable instrument for differentiating between permanent and temporary earnings.

[13] Regressing current changes in earnings on last year's change in earnings for the subsample of negative E/P firms yields a slope coefficient of -0.407, significant at the 0.01 level. This confirms that, on average, firm-years with negative earnings experience a larger degree of mean-reversion than firm-years with positive temporary earnings (see footnote 12).

Table 3
Cross-Sectional Variation in Bias and Serial Correlation in Analysts' Eight-Month Forecast Errors
($N=5,305$ Firm-Years; Dependent Variable $= FEPR_{it}$)

Independent Variable	Equation (3) (Permanent vs. Temporary Earnings Groups)		Equation (3a) (Permanent vs. Positive Temporary and Negative Earnings Groups)	
Intercept	−1.94 (14.35)*	−2.46 (18.32)*	−1.82 (13.06)*	−2.36 (17.09)*
$PERM_{it-1}$	1.21 (6.54)*	1.32 (7.37)*	1.09 (5.78)*	1.23 (6.77)*
NEG_{it-1}			−2.88 (4.87)*	−2.16 (3.76)*
$FEPR_{it-1}$	0.23 (15.80)*	0.21 (14.84)*	0.34 (11.40)*	0.32 (10.88)*
$FEPR_{it-1}*PERM_{it-1}$	0.42 (8.30)*	0.37 (7.61)*	0.31 (5.41)*	0.27 (4.85)*
$FEPR_{it-1}*NEG_{it-1}$			−0.24 (6.03)*	−0.21 (5.40)*
Ret_{it-1}		5.44 (18.73)*		5.36 (18.49)*
Adjusted R^2	0.09	0.14	0.09	0.15

Note: The numbers in parentheses are t-statistics.

$FEPR_{it}$ ($FEPR_{it-1}$) = eight-month forecast error for firm i for fiscal year t ($t-1$) divided by the stock market price at the time of the forecast;

$PERM_{it-1}$ = dummy variable equal to 1 if the firm's previous period's earnings is predominantly permanent, and 0 otherwise;

NEG_{it-1} = dummy variable equal to 1 if the firm's previous period's earnings is negative, and 0 otherwise; and

Ret_{it-1} = one-year stock return ending at the beginning of the month of the forecast.

* Significant at the 0.01 level (two-tailed test).

where NEG_{it-1} is a dummy variable equal to one if the E/P ratio portfolio is one (the negative E/P group) and zero otherwise.

The regression results for equations (3) and (3a) are contained in table 3, which shows that the overestimation bias (intercept and dummy intercept terms) in analysts' forecasts and the serial correlation between successive years (slope and dummy slope coefficients) are not homogeneous among groups.[14]

First, the significantly negative intercept terms and the significantly positive coefficients on $PERM_{it-1}$ in both equations indicate that the level of overestimation bias is less

---

[14] For these and the remaining tests reported, we eliminated outliers in which the absolute value of the forecast errors or change in earnings for year t or $t-1$ (scaled by price) is greater than 100 percent. This reduced the sample from 5,365 to 5,305 observations. To determine the sensitivity of our results to the presence of outliers, we used the SAS subcommand INFLUENCE to remove extreme observations systematically from the data and then re-estimated the equations with the purged data. The results with the purged data are qualitatively the same as those reported and are available from the authors.

when the previous period's earnings are predominantly permanent.[15] The significantly negative coefficient on NEG_{it-1} in equation (3a) implies that the degree of overestimation is most evident for firms with negative earnings. This latter result is consistent with Klein (1990), who finds that analysts tend to overpredict EPS most for the group of firms that recently experienced the most negative stock returns (many of which also had negative earnings).

Next, the coefficients on both $FEPR_{it-1}$ and $FEPR_{it-1}*PERM_{it-1}$, are significantly positive in equation (3), which suggests that analysts systematically omit information contained in last year's forecast error for all firms. Moreover, the tendency to omit this information is greater when previous period earnings are predominantly permanent, and less so when such earnings are predominantly transitory. The significantly negative coefficient on $FEPR_{it-1}*NEG_{it-1}$ in equation (3a), coupled with the evidence that firms with negative earnings display the most transitory earnings (see footnote 13), lends further support to this conclusion.[16] Thus, the degree of bias and serial correlation of analysts' forecast errors does not appear to be homogeneous across firm-years. Finally, the significantly positive coefficient on Ret_{it-1} implies that analysts do not completely utilize the information about future earnings contained in past stock returns.

Adaptive Expectations Model

Previous empirical studies using adaptive expectations models for analysts' forecasts support the view that analysts use this last period's forecast error to formulate the present period's forecast (see, e.g., Abdel-khalik and Espejo 1978; Brown and Rozeff 1979; Givoly 1985). However, these studies do not explicitly examine whether analysts incorporate the degree of permanence of earnings in last year's forecast errors in making their forecasts.[17]

The adaptive expectations model for analysts' forecasts of annual EPS is:

$$(FPR_{it} - FPR_{it-1}) = d_0 + d_1 FEPR_{it-1} + v_{it}, \qquad (4)$$

where FPR_{it} (FPR_{it-1}) is the eight-month forecast for year t ($t-1$), and $FEPR_{it-1}$ is the forecast error for year $t-1$. All variables are deflated by stock price at the beginning of the month of the eight-month forecast for year $t-1$. According to the adaptive expectations hypothesis, the more permanent the last year's earnings, the closer d_1 will be to one. Conversely, the more transient the last year's earnings, the closer d_1 will be to zero.

To examine if analysts recognize the time-series properties of earnings when setting their forecasts, we estimate:

$$(FPR_{it} - FPR_{it-1}) = f_0 + f_1 PERM_{it-1} + f_2 FEPR_{it-1} + f_3 (FEPR_{it-1}*PERM_{it-1}) + v_{it} \qquad (5)$$

---

[15] To determine if the permanent group exhibits significant negative bias, we test separately the null hypotheses that the sum of the intercept term and the coefficient on $PERM_{it-1}$ in the first and third columns of table 3 equals zero. We reject each null at the 0.01 level, and conclude that analysts tend to overestimate earnings for the permanent group.

[16] For example, adding the coefficients in the third column of table 3 on $FEPR_{it-1}$ and $FEPR_{it-1}*NEG_{it-1}$ produces a serial correlation coefficient of 0.10 (significant at the 0.05 level) for the negative group. In contrast, the serial correlation for the permanent group (the sum of $FEPR_{it-1}$ and $FEPR_{it-1}*PERM_{it-1}$) is 0.65. The latter value is significantly greater than the values for the positive temporary and negative groups.

[17] For example, Givoly (1985, 383) finds that the adaptation coefficient for more than 60 percent of his companies was below one and concludes that this "... may imply that the earnings process of most companies is perceived by analysts as being different from a random walk." However, he does not test for this.

Table 4
Adaptive Expectation Model of Setting Eight-Month Forecasts
($N=5,305$ Firm-Years; Dependent Variable $= FPR_{it} - FPR_{it-1}$)

Independent Variable	Equation (5) (Permanent vs. Temporary Earnings Groups)	Equation (5a) (Permanent vs. Positive Temporary and Negative Earnings Groups)
Intercept	0.35 (4.71)*	0.32 (4.43)*
$PERM_{it-1}$	0.44 (4.34)*	0.47 (4.80)*
NEG_{it-1}		−1.30 (4.25)*
$FEPR_{it-1}$	0.27 (33.30)*	0.60 (38.49)*
$FEPR_{it-1}*PERM_{it-1}$	0.38 (13.73)*	0.04 (1.44)
$FEPR_{it-1}*NEG_{it-1}$		−0.48 (22.92)*
Adjusted R^2	0.25	0.33

Note: The numbers in parentheses are t-statistics.

FPR_{it} (FPR_{it-1}) = eight-month forecast of year-end EPS for firm i for year t ($t-1$) divided by the stock market price at the time of the previous period's forecast;
$FEPR_{it}$ ($FEPR_{it-1}$) = eight-month forecast error for firm i for fiscal year t ($t-1$) divided by the stock market price at the time of the forecast;
$PERM_{it-1}$ = dummy variable equal to 1 if the firm's previous period's earnings is predominantly permanent, and 0 otherwise; and
NEG_{it-1} = dummy variable equal to 1 if the firm's previous period's earnings is negative, and 0 otherwise.

* Significant at the 0.01 level (two-tailed test).

and

$$(FPR_{it} - FPR_{it-1}) = g_0 + g_1 PERM_{it-1} + g_2 NEG_{it-1} + g_3 FEPR_{it-1} + g_4(FEPR_{it-1}*PERM_{it-1}) + g_5(FEPR_{it-1}*NEG_{it-1}) + v_{it}, \quad (5a)$$

where the variables are defined as before. If analysts utilize the time-series properties of earnings, then f_3 and g_4, the slope-dummy coefficients for the permanent group, should be significantly positive. Further, g_5, the coefficient on the slope-dummy for the negative group should be significantly negative.

The regression results for equations (5) and (5a) are presented in table 4. In equation (5), the coefficient on $FEPR_{it-1}*PERM_{it-1}$ is significantly positive, indicating that d_1, the adaptation coefficient in equation (4), is significantly greater when previous period earnings are predominantly permanent. This supports the view that analysts at least partially recognize the difference between permanent and transitory earnings components. In equation (5a), the coefficient on $FEPR_{it-1}*NEG_{it-1}$ is significantly negative, signifying that analysts correctly perceive that the earnings of negative E/P firms are the least permanent. However, the coefficient on $FEPR_{it-1}*PERM_{it-1}$ in equation (5a), is not significant at the 0.05 level, suggesting that analysts may not materially differentiate the degree of permanence of earnings among firms in the permanent and the positive temporary groups. One explanation for this finding is that analysts underestimate the permanence of earnings for firms in the permanent group much more than they do for firms in the positive temporary group. This explanation is consistent with the results shown in table 3; the serial correlation of forecast errors is greater for the permanent group than for the positive temporary group.

Taken together, tables 3 and 4 suggest that analysts recognize some of the time-series properties of earnings when making forecasts. However they do not fully recognize the temporary versus permanent components of previous period earnings when forecasting future earnings.

IV. Adjusting Analysts' Forecasts of Earnings

To address the economic significance of our findings, estimates of bias and serial correlation in forecast errors are used to adjust existing forecasts, and improvements in the adjusted forecasts are examined. Specifically, we use the following mechanical procedure to adjust analysts' forecasts of earnings. First, the model given by equation (3a), without Ret_{it-1}, is estimated separately for each year. Second, simple averages of the regression coefficient estimates for five consecutive years are computed. The five-year mean coefficient is used because of the non-stationarity of coefficients found for our yearly regressions.[18] These mean estimates are then used to adjust the following year's forecast. For example, the data from 1978 to 1982 is used to estimate the coefficients. We then use the mean coefficients to adjust the actual forecasts of 1983 earnings made by analysts. This procedure is repeated with data from 1979 to 1983 to obtain the coefficients to adjust the forecasts of 1984, and so on.[19]

Table 5 reports the results for the adjustments in analysts' forecasts. Panel A presents a comparison of the forecast bias and serial correlation in forecast errors associated with the unadjusted and adjusted analysts' forecasts. Since we require five years of leading data, the number of firm-years is reduced to 3,892, spanning from 1983 through 1989. For these sample years, the bias (−1.66, $t=13.9$) and the serial correlation (0.26, $t=15.9$) are significant for the unadjusted forecasts. The adjusted analysts' forecasts exhibit very little bias (0.17, $t=1.5$) and serial correlation (0.03, $t=2.2$). Thus, the mechanical procedure yields a significant reduction in both bias and serial correlation.

In panel B, we compare the accuracy, as measured by the mean squared error, of the unadjusted and adjusted forecasts. The mean squared error for the adjusted forecasts is 12.2 percent less than for the actual forecasts. Further, the improvement in accuracy is similar across firm type; the mean squared error is reduced by 15.3, 9.9, and 12.9 percent for firms in the permanent, the positive temporary, and the negative groups, respectively.[20] We, therefore, conclude that our findings of bias and serial cor-

---

[18] We also use one-year coefficients and, as expected, find similar but weaker results.

[19] Conroy and Harris (1987) and Stickel (1990) use alternative methods to update analysts' forecasts. The first study uses a simple average of analysts' and time-series forecasts. The second updates individual analyst forecasts by using the information in consensus forecasts.

[20] An interesting result in table 5 is that the mean squared errors for the unadjusted analysts' forecasts differ across groups. They are lowest for the permanent group (26.39), followed by the positive temporary group (63.74), and highest for the negative group (238.74). A similar pattern of mean squared errors is observed for the

Table 5
Effect of a Mechanical Adjustment to Analysts' Forecasts of Earnings—Eight-Month Forecasts
($N = 3,892$ Firm-Years)

Panel A. Change in Bias and Serial Correlation:

Analysts' Forecast (Dependent Variable = $FEPR_{it}$)		Adjusted Analysts' Forecast (Dependent Variable = $AFEPR_{it}$)	
Intercept	−1.66 (13.90)*	Intercept	0.17 (1.50)
$FEPR_{it-1}$	0.26 (15.90)*	$AFEPR_{it-1}$	0.03 (2.20)**
Adjusted R^2	0.061	Adjusted R^2	0.001

Panel B. Change in Accuracy (Mean Squared Error):

	Analysts' Forecast	Adjusted Analysts' Forecast	Percentage Change
All firms	59.15	51.96	−12.2
Permanent group	26.39	22.35	−15.3
Positive temporary group	63.74	57.46	−9.9
Negative group	238.74	207.96	−12.9

Note: The numbers in parentheses are t-statistics.

$FEPR_{it}$ ($FEPR_{it-1}$) = eight-month forecast error for firm i for year t ($t-1$) divided by the stock market price at the time of the forecast; and

$AFEPR_{it}$ ($AFEPR_{it-1}$) = adjusted forecast error for year t ($t-1$) divided by the stock market price at the time of the forecast.

* Significant at the 0.01 level (two-tailed test).
** Significant at the 0.05 level (two-tailed test).

---

relation are economically significant (rather than being period-specific statistical oddities) in that they allow us to improve significantly the accuracy of analysts' eight-month forecasts significantly by using past time-series properties of earnings.

V. One-Month Forecast Errors

Empirical evidence suggests that analysts' ability to predict year-end EPS improves as the forecast horizon shrinks (see, e.g., Brown et al. 1987a; Elton et al. 1984; Klein 1990; O'Brien 1988). To examine the effect of a decrease in the forecast horizon on the informational efficiency of analysts' forecasts, we repeat all of the above analyses for one-month forecasts.

Table 6 contains the bias and serial correlation for one-month forecast errors and the coefficients for the adaptive expectations model. A total of 4,530 firm-years are available on IBES. The results provide evidence that bias, serial correlation, and

---

adjusted analysts' forecasts. One possible explanation for this result is that smaller firms are classified more often in the positive temporary and negative groups and that earnings for smaller firms can be predicted with less accuracy. We leave further investigation of this issue for future research.

Table 6
Analysis of One-Month Forecast Errors
(N=4,530 Firm-Years)

Independent Variable	Bias and Serial Correlation in Forecast Errors (Dependent Var. = $FEPR_{it}$)		Adaptive Expectation Model of Setting Forecasts (Dependent Var. = $FPR_{it} - FPR_{it-1}$)	
Intercept	−0.76 (7.32)*	−0.64 (5.83)*	−0.07 (0.45)	−0.69 (4.49)*
$PERM_{it-1}$	0.24 (1.81)***	0.14 (0.98)	0.33 (1.64)	1.08 (5.22)*
NEG_{it-1}		−1.03 (3.32)*		5.89 (13.44)*
$FEPR_{it-1}$	0.09 (5.96)*	0.11 (3.95)*	0.18 (8.35)*	0.29 (13.33)*
$FEPR_{it-1}*PERM_{it-1}$	0.12 (2.40)**	0.10 (1.70)***	0.33 (4.31)*	0.29 (6.87)*
$FEPR_{it}*NEG_{it-1}$		−0.07 (1.92)***		−0.45 (12.06)*
Ret_{it-1}	0.56 (2.30)**	0.51 (2.10)**		
Adjusted R^2	0.01	0.02	0.03	0.09

Note: The numbers in parentheses are t-statistics.

FPR_{it} (FPR_{it-1}) = one-month forecast of year-end EPS for firm i for year t ($t-1$) divided by the stock market price at the time of the previous period's forecast;

$FEPR_{it}$ ($FEPR_{it-1}$) = one-month forecast error for firm i for fiscal year t ($t-1$) divided by the stock market price at the time of the forecast;

$PERM_{it-1}$ = dummy variable equal to 1 if the firm's previous period's earnings is predominantly permanent, and 0 otherwise;

NEG_{it-1} = dummy variable equal to 1 if the firm's previous period's earnings is negative, and 0 otherwise; and

Ret_{it-1} = one-year stock return ending at the beginning of the month of the forecast.

* Significant at the 0.01 level (two-tailed test).
** Significant at the 0.05 level (two-tailed test).
*** Significant at the 0.10 level (two-tailed test).

adjusted R^2 levels are dramatically less than those found for the sample of eight-month forecast errors (table 3). Nevertheless, even at this late juncture, analysts' forecasts exhibit overprediction bias and serial correlation, as evidenced by the significantly negative intercept terms and the significantly positive coefficients on $FEPR_{it-1}$. Further, the pattern of underestimation for the one-month forecasts is similar to the sample of eight-month forecasts in that the coefficient on $FEPR_{it-1}*RM_{it-1}$ is significantly positive, whereas the coefficient on $FEPR_{it-1}*NEG_{it-1}$ is significantly negative.[21] Results similar to those in table 3 are also reported for the intercept dummy variables $PERM_{it-1}$ and NEG_{it-1}.

The regression results for the adaptive expectations model for one-month forecasts in table 6 show that analysts partially recognize the time-series properties of earnings

---

[21] The same criterion as in section IV is used to categorize firm-years into permanent, temporary positive, and negative groups.

Table 7
Effect of a Mechanical Adjustment to Analysts' Forecasts of Earnings—One-Month Forecasts
(N = 3,184 Firm-Years)

Panel A. Change in Bias and Serial Correlation:

Analysts' Forecast (Dependent Variable = $FEPR_{it}$)		Adjusted Analysts' Forecast (Dependent Variable = $AFEPR_{it}$)	
Intercept	−0.73 (8.30)*	Intercept	0.23 (2.50)**
$FEPR_{it-1}$	0.09 (5.30)*	$AFEPR_{it-1}$	0.03 (1.60)
Adjusted R^2	0.009	Adjusted R^2	0.001

Panel B. Change in Accuracy (Mean Squared Error):

	Analysts' Forecast	Adjusted Analysts' Forecast	Percent Change
All firms	24.29	25.09	3.3
Permanent group	12.55	12.47	−0.6
Positive temporary group	22.52	23.20	3.0
Negative group	105.47	112.15	6.3

Note: The numbers in parentheses are t-statistics.

$FEPR_{it}$ ($FEPR_{it-1}$) = one-month forecast error for firm i for year t ($t-1$) divided by the stock market price at the time of the forecast; and

$AFEPR_{it}$ ($AFEPR_{it-1}$) = adjusted forecast error for year t ($t-1$) divided by the stock market price at the time of the forecast.

* Significant at the 0.01 level (two-tailed test).
** Significant at the 0.05 level (two-tailed test).

when setting short-term forecasts. This is demonstrated by the significantly positive coefficients on $FEPR_{it-1}*PERM_{it-1}$ and the significantly negative coefficient on $FEPR_{it-1}*NEG_{it-1}$. Thus, similar conclusions about analysts recognizing the degree of permanence for these respective groups can be made for both one-month and eight-month forecasting horizons.

Table 7 examines whether the observed serial correlations and biases documented in table 6 can be used to improve the accuracy of short-term forecasts. The same procedure employed for adjusting the longer-term forecasts is used. Panel A shows that the adjusted forecasts display less bias and serial correlation in forecast errors than the unadjusted forecasts.

Panel B reports the change in the mean squared error for the one-month forecasts. As the horizon shrinks from eight months to one, analysts show considerable improvement in their forecasting ability, evident in the reduction of the mean squared error for unadjusted forecasts from 59.15 (table 5) to 24.29. However, the adjustment procedure does not improve the accuracy of analysts' one-month forecasts any further. For the full sample, the mean squared error actually increases by 3.3 percent, and no significant increase in accuracy is found for any of the individual groups. We attribute this latter result to the low explanatory power (R-squared values) of the regressions of one-month forecast errors on prior forecast errors. Thus, even though the adjustment procedure leads to reductions in bias and serial correlation, it does not improve the accuracy of the short-term forecasts.

VI. Summary and Conclusions

In this study, we examine whether analysts correctly use the time-series properties of annual earnings when setting their forecasts of annual EPS. We document significantly positive serial correlation in eight-month and one-month forecast errors, a result consistent with the hypothesis that analysts, on average, underestimate the permanence of the last year's forecast error when setting forecasts. We also find a significant overprediction bias for both forecast horizons.

Further examination of our results reveals that the observed bias and serial correlation of the prediction errors are not uniform across firm-years. Specifically, the over-prediction bias is most pronounced for firms that previously reported negative annual earnings. Also, the positive serial correlation in the prediction errors is greatest for firms with previous period earnings that are predominantly permanent.

To evaluate the economic significance of our findings, we use our estimates of bias and serial correlation to adjust existing forecasts. The adjusted eight-month forecasts are found to be more accurate predictors of future earnings than the actual forecasts made by analysts. In addition, the adjustment procedure leads to a significant reduction in the bias and serial correlation for both the one-month and eight-month forecast errors.

References

Abarbanell, J. 1990. Analysts' earnings forecasts as market expectations around stock price changes. Working paper, University of Michigan, Ann Arbor.
———, and V. L. Bernard. 1991. Do analysts underreact or overreact to earnings? Working paper, Harvard University, Cambridge, MA.
Abdel-khalik, A. R. 1990. Specification problems with information content of earnings: Revisions and rationality of expectations and self-selection bias. *Contemporary Accounting Research* 7 (Fall): 142–72.
———, and J. Espejo. 1978. Expectations data and the predictive value of interim reporting. *Journal of Accounting Research* 16 (Spring): 1–13.
Albrecht, W. S., L. L. Lookabill, and J. C. McKeown. 1977. The time series properties of annual earnings. *Journal of Accounting Research* 15 (Autumn): 226–44.
Ball, R., and R. Watts. 1972. Some time-series properties of accounting income. *Journal of Finance* 27 (June): 663–82.
Barefield, R. M., and E. E. Comiskey. 1975. The accuracy of analysts' forecasts of earnings per share. *Journal of Business Research* 3 (July): 241–51.
Beaver, W. H., and D. Morse. 1978. What determines price-earnings ratios? *Financial Analysts Journal* 34 (July/August): 65–76.
———, R. A. Lambert, and D. Morse. 1980. The information content of security prices. *Journal of Accounting & Economics* 2 (March): 3–28.
———, ———, and S. G. Ryan. 1987. The information content of security prices: A second look. *Journal of Accounting & Economics* 9 (July): 139–57.
Bernard, V. L., and J. Thomas. 1990. Evidence that stock prices do not fully reflect the implications of current earnings for future earnings. *Journal of Accounting & Economics* 13 (December): 305–40.

Line provides valuable new information to the marketplace, market prices should adjust to reflect the information in a rank change.[2]

In addition to examining an equally weighted portfolio reaction to a Value Line rank change, this study investigates the cross-sectional relationship between individual firm size and individual firm unexpected returns. Recent work by Ohlson (1979) and Holthausen and Verrecchia (1982) provides a basis for predicting cross-sectional differences in firm reaction to reports such as earnings announcements, management forecasts, and security analyst recommendations. Ohlson models the variance of price change resulting from information disclosure as a function of the frequency of disclosure, predicting greater price variance on disclosure when information is disclosed less frequently. Holthausen and Verrecchia model the price change resulting from a sequence of information releases as a function of the precision of information, predicting greater price variance as the precision of new information increases, the precision of prior information decreases, or the correlation between information releases decreases. As an empirical matter, the predictions of the Ohlson model would be similar to the predictions of the Holthausen and Verrecchia model. If reports on firm value arrive less frequently, the precision of prior information decreases and any single report would, ceteris paribus, have greater marginal information content.[3]

This study also provides evidence on the differential impact of the various types of rank change. One issue is whether or not the reaction of upgraded securities is of the same magnitude as the reaction of downgraded securities (e.g. do reclassifications from rank 2 to rank 1 and from rank 1 to rank 2 have equal, but opposite effects on prices). Provided firms do not systematically differ across ranking by frequency of report arrival or precision of prior information, there is no apparent reason to predict any difference. Another

---

[2] Ison (1980), examining the behavior of firms added or dropped from Value Line rank 1, concluded the majority of the abnormal returns found by Black occur immediately after the rank change. Copeland and Mayers (1982) found a 'combined' portfolio, which buys securities moving up in Value Line rank and sells short securities moving down in rank, had significant performance during the first two weeks after recommendation. However, grouping all rank changes into a 'combined' portfolio may dilute the Value Line recommendation effect if subscribers perceive a difference in the information content of the various types of rank changes.

[3] Recent empirical work supports the Ohlson (1979) and Holthausen and Verrecchia (1982) models. Stickel (1980), examining security price reaction of firms recommended for purchase by Growth Stock Outlook (an investment advisory service), found smaller firms have a greater reaction than larger firms. Grant (1980) found OTC firms react more strongly to an annual earnings announcement than NYSE firms. Assuming small and OTC firms have less precise prior information or less frequent report arrival, the results of Stickel and Grant support the models. McNichols and Manegold (1983), examining the variability of security returns around annual report release dates before and after the initiation of interim reports, found a significant decrease in the variance of returns after firms initiate interim reporting (increase the precision of prior information and the frequency of report arrival). Pincus (1983), examining the association of earnings predictability and market reaction to earnings announcements, found firms with less predictable earnings (less precise prior information or less frequent report arrival) had greater market reaction to an earnings announcement.

issue is whether different types of upgraded (or downgraded) rank changes have similar effects (e.g. does a reclassification from rank 2 to rank 1 have the same impact as a reclassification from rank 5 to rank 4?). While a change from rank 2 to rank 1 is undoubtedly 'good news', the information in a change from rank 5 to rank 4 is not as clear. Although a security reclassified from rank 5 to rank 4 has been upgraded, it remains in a rank that is predicted to underperform the general market.

Finally, evidence on the speed of adjustment of individual security prices to new information is presented. Value Line provides an interesting speed of price adjustment test because rank change information is disseminated by mail, which results in a sequential dissemination of information to subscribers rather than an immediate release to all market participants. Copeland (1976) models price adjustment to sequentially released information and provides an hypothesis for empirical predictions. Copeland assumes aggregate price adjustment depends on the summation of individual price changes caused by shifts in individual investor demand curves, which suggests the period of aggregate price adjustment is the length of time over which individual investors become aware of new information. If Value Line rank changes are disseminated over a multiple-day period, the Copeland model assumes a multiple-day price adjustment period for individual securities. A competing hypothesis is that price adjustment to new information is completed by the first individual to receive new information, as opposed to the summation of individual actions. If price adjustment to a Value Line rank change is completed by the first subscriber to receive rank change information, price adjustment is immediate.

Summarizing the results, Value Line rank changes have information content, but the effect varies by the type of rank change. Changes from rank 2 to rank 1 have the most dramatic effect on prices. A cross-sectional analysis finds smaller firms have a greater reaction to a rank change than larger firms, which supports the models of Ohlson and Holthausen and Verrecchia. Finally, a speed of adjustment test suggests individual securities with significant abnormal performance on event day 0 or +1 adjust to the information in a rank change over a multiple-day period.

The remainder of the paper is outlined as follows. The Value Line ranking process and the sample subjected to empirical testing are described in section 2. Section 3 describes the methodology used to calculate and test the significance of abnormal performance. Section 4 reports empirical results. Section 5 concludes.

2. Data description

2.1. The Value Line ranking process

Summarizing Bernhard (1977), the criteria used by Value Line in establishing timeliness ranks are (1) current year relative earnings (relative to other firms) and relative prices in comparison to the past 10 years' relative earnings

Brooks, L., and D. Buckmaster. 1976. Further evidence of the time series properties of accounting income. *Journal of Finance* 31 (December): 1359–73.

Brown, L. D., R. L. Hagerman, P. A. Griffin, and M. E. Zmijewski. 1987a. Security analyst superiority relative to univariate time-series models in forecasting quarterly earnings. *Journal of Accounting & Economics* 9 (April): 61–87.

———, ———, ———, and ———. 1987b. An evaluation of alternative proxies for the market's assessment of unexpected earnings. *Journal of Accounting & Economics* 9 (July): 159–93.

———, and M. Rozeff. 1979. Adaptive expectations, time-series models and analyst forecast revision. *Journal of Accounting Research* 17 (Autumn): 341–51.

Collins, D. W., and S. P. Kothari. 1989. An analysis of intertemporal and cross-sectional determinants of earnings response coefficients. *Journal of Accounting & Economics* 11 (July): 143–81.

———, ———, and J. D. Rayburn. 1987. Firm size and the information content of prices with respect to earnings. *Journal of Accounting & Economics* 9 (July): 111–38.

Conroy, R., and R. Harris. 1987. Consensus forecasts of corporate earnings: Analysts' forecasts and time-series methods. *Management Science* 33 (June): 725–38.

Elton, E., M. Gruber, and M. Gultekin. 1984. Professional expectations: Accuracy and diagnosis of errors. *Journal of Financial and Quantitative Analysis* 19 (December): 351–63.

Freeman, R., and S. Tse. 1989. The multi-period information content of earnings announcements: Rational delayed reactions to earnings. *Journal of Accounting Research* 27 (Supplement): 49–79.

Fried D., and D. Givoly. 1982. Financial analysts' forecasts of earnings—A better surrogate for market expectations. *Journal of Accounting & Economics* 4 (October): 85–107.

Givoly, D. 1985. The formation of earnings expectations. *The Accounting Review* 60 (July): 372–86.

Jaffe, J. J., D. B. Keim, and R. Westerfield. 1989. Earnings yields, market values and stock returns. *Journal of Finance* 44 (March): 135–48.

Klein, A. 1990. A direct test of the cognitive bias theory of share price reversals. *Journal of Accounting & Economics* 13 (July): 155–66.

Mendenhall, R. 1991. Evidence of possible underweighting earnings-related information. *Journal of Accounting Research* 29 (Spring): 170–79.

Noreen, E. 1989. *Computer-Intensive Methods for Testing Hypotheses: An Introduction.* New York: John Wiley & Sons.

O'Brien, P. 1988. Analysts' forecasts as earnings expectations. *Journal of Accounting & Economics* 10 (January): 53–83.

Ou, J. A. 1990. The information content of non-earnings accounting numbers as earnings predictors. *Journal of Accounting Research* 28 (Spring): 144–63.

———, and S. H. Penman. 1989a. Financial statement analysis and the prediction of stock returns. *Journal of Accounting & Economics* 11 (November): 295–329.

———, and ———. 1989b. Accounting measurement, price-earnings ratio, and the information content of security prices. *Journal of Accounting Research* 27 (Supplement): 111–44.

Penman, S. H. 1987. The distribution of earnings news over time and seasonalities in aggregate stock returns. *Journal of Financial Economics* 18 (June): 199–228.

Smith, D. B., and S. Pourciau. 1988. A comparison of the financial characteristics of December and non-December year-end companies. *Journal of Accounting & Economics* 10 (December): 335–44.

Stickel, S. E. 1990. Predicting individual analyst earnings forecasts. *Journal of Accounting Research* 28 (Autumn): 409–17.

Stober, T. L. 1991. Summary financial statement measures and analysts' forecasts of earnings. Working paper, Indiana University, Bloomington, IN.

Watts, R. L., and R. W. Leftwich. 1977. The time series properties of annual accounting earnings. *Journal of Accounting Research* 15 (Autumn): 253–71.

White, W. H. 1980. A heteroskedasticity-consistent covariance matrix estimation and a direct test for heteroskedasticity. *Econometrica* 48 (May): 817–38.

THE EFFECT OF VALUE LINE INVESTMENT SURVEY RANK CHANGES ON COMMON STOCK PRICES*

Scott E. STICKEL

University of Chicago, Chicago, IL 60637, USA

Received May 1984, final version received September 1984

The information content of *Value Line Investment Survey* rank changes is investigated. The results suggest rank changes affect common stock prices, but the effect varies by the type of rank change. Changes from rank 2 to rank 1 have the most dramatic impact on prices. A cross-sectional analysis finds small firms have a greater reaction to a rank change than larger firms, which supports theories on the frequency of report arrival and precision of information. A speed of adjustment test concludes the prices of individual securities adjust to the information in a rank change over a multiple-day period.

1. Introduction

The *Value Line Investment Survey* is published every Friday by Arnold Bernhard and Co., one of the largest investment advisory services. Value Line provides a wide range of financial information on common stocks, including a weekly ranking of 1700 common stocks into 5 groups based on projected relative price performance over the next 12 months. Rank 1 securities are expected to have the best relative price performance over the next 12 months, rank 5 securities are expected to perform the worst. This paper investigates the information content of Value Line rank changes, which may be interpreted as recommendations to purchase or sell the securities.

Value Line has attracted attention because of its reported ability to predict future common stock price movements better than empirical versions of theoretical models of asset pricing. Performance evaluation studies by Black (1973), Holloway (1981), and Copeland and Mayers (1982) conclude Value Line has predictive ability.[1] This evidence provides motivation for examining the immediate impact of rank change on a common stock price. If Value

---

*The helpful comments of Eugene Fama, Robert Holthausen, Richard Leftwich, Clifford Smith, and Thomas Copeland (the referee) are gratefully acknowledged.

[1] Black (1973), constructing portfolios of firms grouped by rank and revising the portfolios monthly, found rank 1 firms outperform rank 5 firms by 20% per year on a risk-adjusted basis over the 1965–1970 period. Holloway (1981) found significant performance for rank 1 firms over the 1974–1977 period. Copeland and Mayers (1982) found rank 1 firms outperform rank 5 firms by 6.8% per year on a risk-adjusted basis over the 1965–1978 period for portfolios updated semi-annually.

and relative prices, (2) price momentum, (3) quarterly earnings momentum, and (4) unexpected quarterly earnings.[4] Although a general description of how the criteria are used to obtain rankings is provided by Value Line, the precise manner is (understandably) not revealed.

The Value Line ranking process begins with statistical regressions every Wednesday using Wednesday closing prices. The preliminary rankings as of Wednesday may be changed by unusual events on Thursday or Friday. On Friday the ranks are sent to a printer. Mailings are staggered in an attempt to ensure all subscribers receive the issue on the following Friday, and thus the information in a Value Line issue is approximately a week old at the time of subscriber receipt. However, variability in the U.S. Postal Service results in subscribers receiving any particular issue on different days. Although Value Line does not formally test their system of staggered mailings, management believes a small percentage of subscribers receive issues on Thursday. As such, the Thursday prior to the Friday publication date is defined as event day 0 in the subsequent empirical tests.

2.2. Data

Weekly ranks of all securities followed by Value Line within the period July 16, 1976 to March 7, 1980 (191 weeks) were obtained from Value Line. The ranks supplied by Value Line were the preliminary ranks as of Wednesday using Wednesday closing prices, not the final ranks as of Friday.[5] Value Line management estimates that approximately four ranks per week are changed between Wednesday and Friday due to unusual events. If there is an announcement effect and preliminary ranks are used, the empirical tests probably understate the effect of a rank change on security prices and bias the results against finding a rank change effect.

For inclusion in the subsequent empirical tests, a firm must have been included in the Center for Research in Security Prices (CRSP) Daily Stock Files at the date of recommendation. Of the 1792 companies followed by Value Line within the sample period, 365 were not included in the CRSP files, leaving

---

[4] The literature investigating abnormal returns following earnings announcements is voluminous. Most researchers find significant abnormal returns after quarterly earnings announcements [for example, see Rendleman, Jones, and Latane (1982) and Watts (1978)]. Thus, the significant abnormal performance of Value Line found by Black (1973), Holloway (1981), and Copeland and Mayers (1982) may be partly due to the use of the earnings surprise criterion.

[5] Value Line has maintained a machine-readable listing of their preliminary weekly rankings since July 1976. March 1980 is approximately the month the rankings were requested. In addition, the three weeks of rankings from September 8, 1978 to September 22, 1978 were missing from the data supplied by Value Line. Any rank change between September 1, 1978 and September 29, 1978 was disregarded because of the inability to determine the exact week of rank change without reference to the original publication.

1427 companies for the initial rank change tests in section 4.1. For the subsequent cross-sectional tests of the relationship between firm characteristics and abnormal returns a firm must have been included on a 1982 version of the Value Line Data Base-II. This requirement eliminated 255 companies, leaving 1172 companies for the cross-sectional tests.

3. Methodology

Event study methodology models expected returns, then computes the deviation of actual returns from expectations and the significance of the deviation. In the empirical results presented below the benchmark expected return is estimated from the market model [see Fama (1976) and Brown and Warner (1980)]

$$\tilde{R}_{it} = \alpha_i + \beta_i \tilde{R}_{mt} + \tilde{\varepsilon}_{it},$$

where

R_t = return to security i on day t,
R_{mt} = return to an equally weighted market portfolio on day t,
α_i, β_i = regression parameters,
ε_{it} = error term for security i on day t, assumed to be i.i.d. normal through time with mean zero and constant variance.

Returns from event days $+51$ to $+290$ are used to obtain OLS parameter estimates. Following Copeland and Mayers (1982), the period preceding the event is rejected as the benchmark period because the Value Line ranking system tends to increase the ranking of firms recently experiencing positive abnormal returns and decrease the ranking of firms recently experiencing negative abnormal returns. Using the period prior to a rank change as the benchmark period would imply this 'unusual' performance is expected to continue in the event period. Event day $+51$ was chosen as the beginning of the benchmark period because Copeland and Mayers (1982) found no abnormal performance after approximately 13 weeks. Use of a combined benchmark period of event days -170 to -51 and $+51$ to $+170$ produced results very similar to those reported in section 4 for event days 0, $+1$, and $+2$, but biased the results for the cumulative periods from event days -50 to -7 and $+7$ to $+50$.

The deviation of actual return from expectations, abnormal return, is defined for security i in period t as

$$AR_{it} = R_{it} - (\hat{\alpha}_i + \hat{\beta}_i R_{mt}).$$

Average abnormal return (AAR) for portfolio j in period t is calculated as

$$AAR_{jt} = \sum_{i=1}^{N} AR_{it}/N,$$

where N is the number of securities having a computed abnormal return in period t. Finally, defining $t=0$ as the recommendation date, portfolio abnormal returns are cumulated over time as

$$CAAR_{jT} = \sum_{t=0}^{T} AAR_{jt},$$

where $CAAR_{jT}$ is the cumulative average abnormal return of portfolio j over T periods.

The results are robust to alternative specifications of expected returns. Tests replicated with Scholes and Williams (1977) estimates of market model parameters and the mean-adjusted returns model had similar results that are not reported. In the mean-adjusted returns model abnormal returns are defined as the difference between actual returns and an average return computed from the benchmark period and assumed to be equal to the expected return during the event period [see Fama (1976) and Brown and Warner (1980)].

The statistical significance of the deviation of (cumulative) average abnormal returns from zero is tested by Z-statistics [see Patell (1976)], which are assumed to be distributed approximately unit normal in the absence of an 'event'. Z-statistics are calculated by first standardizing abnormal returns for each security i by the square root of their estimated forecast variance

$$SAR_{it} = AR_{it} \bigg/ \left(S_i^2 \left(1 + 1/L_i + \left((R_{mt} - \bar{R}_m)^2 \bigg/ \sum_{v=1}^{L_i} (R_{mv} - \bar{R}_m)^2 \right) \right) \right)^{\frac{1}{2}},$$

where S_i^2 is the estimated residual variance from the market model regression and $\bar{R}_m$ is the average market return for the L_i days used in the regression. Assuming the AR_{it} are normally distributed with mean zero and constant variance, SAR_{it} is distributed Student-t with $L_i - 2$ degrees of freedom, approximately unit normal because L_i is not less than 200. Standardized abnormal returns are used to compute Z-statistics by the formula

$$Z_{jT} = \sum_{i=1}^{N} \left(\sum_{t=1}^{T} SAR_{it}/T^{\frac{1}{2}} \right) \bigg/ N^{\frac{1}{2}},$$

where T is the number of days over which SAR_{it} is cumulated and N is the number of securities in portfolio j. Assuming the standardized abnormal returns are independent across securities and over time, Z is distributed approximately unit normal.

In addition, the significance of daily AAR was tested by a parametric t-statistic and a non-parametric binomial statistic, which are also assumed to be distributed approximately unit normal. T-statistics are calculated from the formula

$$T_{jt} = AAR_{jt} \bigg/ \left(\sum_{t=+11}^{t=+50} \left(AAR_{jt} - \overline{AAR_j} \right)^2 / 39 \right)^{\frac{1}{2}},$$

where $\overline{AAR_j}$ is the average daily abnormal return for portfolio j over event days $+11$ to $+50$. Binomial statistics are calculated from the formula

$$B_{jt} = \left(\%POS_{jt} - E(\%POS) \right) \bigg/ \left(E(\%POS)^2 / N_{jt} \right)^{\frac{1}{2}},$$

where $\%POS_{jt}$ is the percentage of positive abnormal returns for portfolio j on day t, $E(\%POS)$ is the expected percentage of postive abnormal returns, and N is the number of individual security non-zero abnormal returns in portfolio j at time t [e.g. Lehmann (1975)]. Following Stickel (1984), $E(\%POS)$ is estimated from the empirical distribution of abnormal returns in the absence of abnormal performance using randomly selected securities and hypothetical event dates and is assumed constant over time and across portfolios. Although the binomial statistic is probably less powerful because it uses only the sign and not the magnitude of abnormal returns, it avoids any potential bias in the benchmark period of event days $+51$ to $+290$ and is not affected by event period variance changes [see Brown and Warner (1984)]. Because T-statistics and B-statistics did not alter the conclusions of the paper, only Z-statistics are reported.

4. Empirical findings

4.1. Abnormal return behavior surrounding a Value Line rank change

Rank changes were sorted into one of twenty possible groups. Table 1 reports the number of observations for the most frequently observed rank change groups, which contain approximately 98% of all rank changes in the sample period.[6] Tests of securities moving two ranks (e.g. 3 to 1) were

---

[6] Seven of the rank changes noted on table 1 (approximately 0.06% of the total number of observations before the cross-sectional tests) were excluded from the subsequent empirical analyses because the security stopped trading between event days 0 and $+50$ and the benchmark period begins with event day $+51$. The resulting bias, if any, is inconsequential because of the large number of remaining observations. All seven rank changes involved securities moving to or from ranks 3, 4, and 5.

Table 1

Number of observations for the most frequently observed types of Value Line rank changes between July 1976 and March 1980. The number of observations in the cross-sectional tests is lower because 255 of the 1427 CRSP listed firms did not have sufficient data on the Value Line Data Base-II.

From rank	2	1	3	2	4	3	5	4
To rank	1	2	2	3	3	4	4	5
Number of observations before cross-sectional tests	786	774	2131	2153	2239	2277	1065	1072
Number of observations in cross-sectional tests	682	670	1807	1816	1927	1957	913	915
Representation on fig. 1	1	2	3	4	5	6	7	8

consistent with the tests of securities moving one rank and are not reported. The effect of Value Line rank changes on stock prices is first analyzed by rank change group to see if there is a difference in the information content of different types of rank changes.

Segregating rank changes by type of rank change, fig. 1 plots percentage cumulative average abnormal returns for 50 trading days prior and subsequent to event day 0. Reclassifications from rank 2 to rank 1 are plotted by the number '1', reclassifications from rank 1 to rank 2 are plotted by the number '2', and so on up to reclassifications from rank 4 to rank 5 by the number '8'. Supporting fig. 1 is table 2, which presents percentage daily average abnormal returns (AAR), Z-statistics, and percentage cumulative average abnormal returns ($CAAR$) for the rank change group portfolios.

The behavior of abnormal returns prior to event day 0, displayed on fig. 1 and summarized on table 2, is the result of the Value Line ranking system, which upgrades firms recently experiencing positive abnormal returns and downgrades firms recently experiencing negative abnormal returns. Fig. 1 also reveals some unusual movement of $CAAR$ after event day 0 (defined as the Thursday prior to the Friday publication date of a rank change) for some rank change groups. The tests of significance on table 2 reject the null hypothesis of no information content for most types of Value Line rank change, but the results vary by type of rank change and by event day. The evidence suggests portfolio price adjustment to the information in a Value Line rank change requires approximately three days. The most significant rank change effect occurs for firms reclassified from rank 2 to rank 1. The AAR for events days 0, +1, and +2 are 0.86%, 0.86%, and 0.72% (Z-statistics of 10.91, 11.27, and 9.93, T-statistics of 11.49, 11.55, and 9.66, B-statistics of 7.64, 9.14, and 7.83),

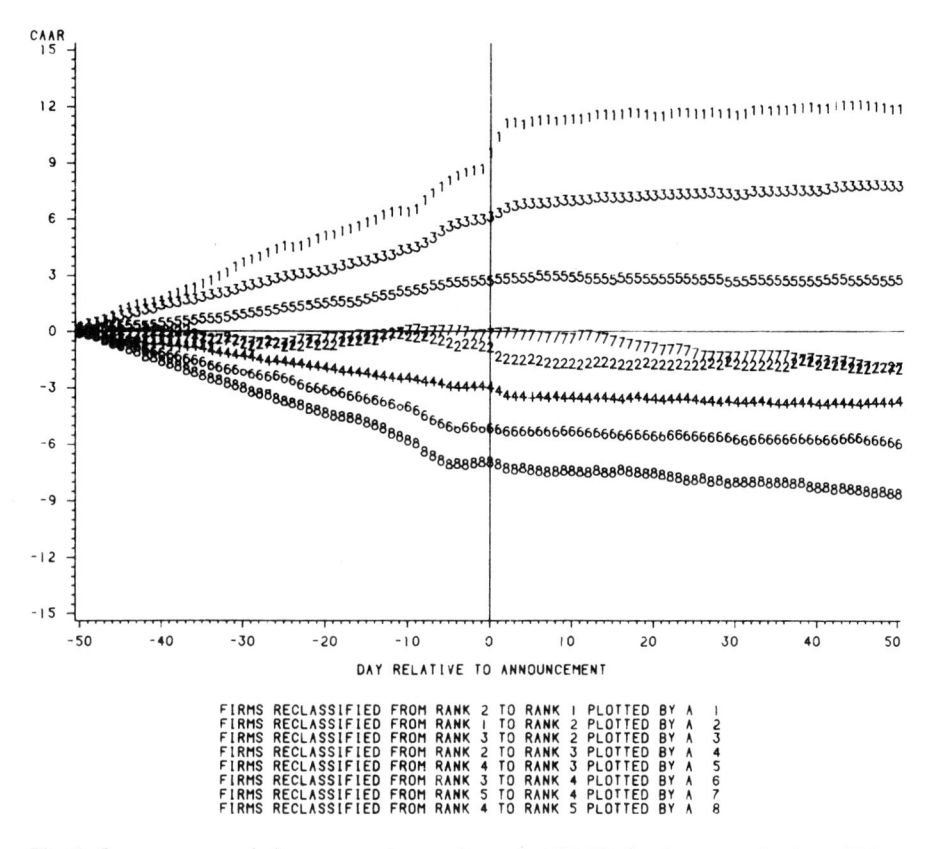

Fig. 1. Percentage cumulative average abnormal returns (*CAAR*) for firms experiencing a Value Line rank change between July 1976 and March 1980. Firms segregated by type of rank change.

all significant at greater than the 0.01 level.[7] This is strong evidence of the effect of Value Line rank changes on prices. For rank changes from 1 to 2, 3 to 2, and 2 to 3, the Z-statistics for event days 0, +1, and +2 are in excess of 1.96 a combined total of 7 (out of 9) times. However, the magnitudes of the *AAR* are roughly 25% of that found for changes from 2 to 1. The *AAR* and

---

[7] Because of the Friday publication date, the rank change effect is related to the 'day of the week' effect [see French (1980) and Gibbons and Hess (1981)]. However, Gibbons and Hess found the 'day of the week' effect in market model residuals to be much smaller than that found in raw returns. To some extent, market model residuals are adjusted for the 'day of the week' effect found in the CRSP equally weighted common stock index. From Gibbons and Hess (1981, fig. 3), the daily average market model residual for each day of the week appears to be less than $\pm 0.05\%$ over the 1962–1978 period. In addition, the 'day of the week' effect in market model residuals appears to be smaller over the 1974–1978 period (which overlaps the period of this study) than the entire 1962–1978 period [Gibbons and Hess (1981, table 8)]. Thus, the 'day of the week' effect in the market model residuals on tables 2 and 4 is very small relative to the magnitudes reported.

Table 2

Percentage daily average abnormal returns (AAR) and percentage cumulative average abnormal returns ($CAAR$) for firms experiencing a Value Line rank change between July 1976 and March 1980. Firms segregated by type of rank change. Event day 0 is the Thursday prior to the Friday publication date of a Value Line rank change.[a]

Event day(s)	Rank 2 to 1 ($N = 786$) AAR	Z	CAAR	Rank 1 to 2 ($N = 774$) AAR	Z	CAAR
(−50, −7)	0.17	15.12	7.38	−0.01	−1.59	−0.40
−6	0.33	4.63	7.70	−0.08	−1.08	−0.49
−5	0.34	4.73	8.04	−0.14	−2.54	−0.63
−4	0.27	3.57	8.31	−0.16	−2.63	−0.80
−3	0.17	2.94	8.48	0.12	2.05	−0.68
−2	0.09	1.97	8.57	0.00	−0.12	−0.67
−1	0.10	1.59	8.67	−0.12	−1.85	−0.80
0	0.86	10.92	9.53	−0.05	−0.60	−0.85
1	0.86	11.27	10.39	−0.48	−6.38	−1.34
2	0.72	9.93	11.12	−0.13	−1.73	−1.46
3	0.03	0.28	11.14	−0.04	−1.20	−1.51
4	−0.11	−1.64	11.03	−0.02	−0.52	−1.52
5	0.15	2.30	11.18	0.05	0.39	−1.47
6	0.06	0.98	11.25	−0.08	−1.27	−1.55
(7, 50)	0.01	0.74	11.82	−0.01	−1.21	−2.02

Event day(s)	Rank 3 to 2 ($N = 2131$) AAR	Z	CAAR	Rank 2 to 3 ($N = 2153$) AAR	Z	CAAR
(−50, −7)	0.11	17.56	4.97	−0.06	−9.64	−2.66
−6	0.35	8.58	5.33	−0.10	−2.26	−2.75
−5	0.25	6.24	5.58	−0.15	−4.17	−2.91
−4	0.15	3.21	5.73	−0.02	−0.51	−2.93
−3	0.10	2.90	5.83	0.01	0.48	−2.92
−2	0.09	1.89	5.92	0.03	1.45	−2.89
−1	0.03	0.34	5.95	0.01	0.63	−2.88
0	0.14	2.55	6.09	−0.06	−2.23	−2.94
1	0.21	4.49	6.29	−0.20	−4.51	−3.15
2	0.27	6.62	6.57	−0.24	−5.48	−3.39
3	0.11	2.98	6.68	−0.05	−0.68	−3.43
4	0.10	2.17	6.78	−0.00	0.14	−3.43
5	0.03	0.12	6.80	−0.01	−0.72	−3.45
6	−0.01	−0.35	6.80	0.01	0.31	−3.44
(7, 50)	0.02	3.71	7.69	−0.01	0.20	−3.71

Table 2 (continued)

Event day(s)	Rank 4 to 3 ($N = 2239$) AAR	Z	CAAR	Rank 3 to 4 ($N = 2277$) AAR	Z	CAAR
(−50, −7)	0.05	9.81	2.42	−0.11	−15.63	−4.73
−6	0.00	0.90	2.42	−0.19	−4.35	−4.92
−5	0.14	4.00	2.56	−0.16	−4.46	−5.08
−4	0.02	0.96	2.58	−0.08	−1.63	−5.16
−3	0.03	0.72	2.61	0.06	1.75	−5.10
−2	0.03	1.20	2.63	−0.00	0.49	−5.10
−1	0.05	1.03	2.68	−0.04	−1.43	−5.15
0	−0.03	−0.28	2.65	−0.01	−0.37	−5.16
1	0.10	1.64	2.75	−0.06	−1.46	−5.22
2	0.01	1.51	2.76	−0.10	−2.33	−5.32
3	0.03	0.97	2.79	0.00	0.52	−5.32
4	0.01	0.53	2.80	0.00	−0.24	−5.31
5	0.01	−0.03	2.82	−0.00	−0.23	−5.31
6	0.11	2.41	2.92	0.00	−0.28	−5.31
(7, 50)	−0.01	0.01	2.65	−0.02	−1.28	−5.99

Event day(s)	Rank 5 to 4 ($N = 1065$) AAR	Z	CAAR	Rank 4 to 5 ($N = 1072$) AAR	Z	CAAR
(−50, −7)	−0.00	0.56	−0.11	−0.15	−14.26	−6.64
−6	0.03	−0.20	−0.08	−0.24	−3.79	−6.89
−5	0.01	0.25	−0.07	−0.22	−3.21	−7.11
−4	−0.01	−0.95	−0.08	0.04	0.83	−7.06
−3	−0.07	−0.46	−0.15	−0.05	−1.12	−7.12
−2	−0.19	−1.26	−0.33	0.09	1.87	−7.03
−1	0.03	0.38	−0.30	0.04	0.62	−6.99
0	0.06	1.16	−0.24	0.02	−0.58	−6.97
1	0.01	1.23	−0.23	−0.13	−2.22	−7.10
2	0.03	0.99	−0.20	−0.22	−2.22	−7.31
3	−0.04	−0.64	−0.25	−0.04	−0.43	−7.36
4	−0.07	−0.88	−0.32	0.07	0.63	−7.29
5	−0.01	−0.34	−0.33	−0.09	−1.24	−7.38
6	−0.06	−1.06	−0.39	−0.06	0.09	−7.44
(7, 50)	−0.04	−3.12	−2.06	−0.03	−2.25	−8.66

[a] AAR for a multiple-day observation period is the average daily AAR within the observation period.

A Z-statistic (Z) of 2.58 (1.96) indicates the AAR is significantly different from zero at the 0.01 (0.05) level.

Z-statistics diminish further for firms reclassified to or from ranks 4 and 5. For rank changes from 4 to 3, 3 to 4, 5 to 4, and 4 to 5, the *AAR* for event days 0, +1, and +2 are relatively small and Z-statistics are in excess of 1.96 a combined total of 3 (out of 12) times. The behavior of *AAR* between days +3 and +50 reveals little or no drift for all rank change groups and is consistent with unbiased estimated returns.

4.2. The association between firm market value and abnormal returns

Testing the Ohlson model of frequency of disclosure or the Holthausen and Verrecchia model of information precision as a determinant of the magnitude of price changes requires the selection of appropriate observable proxies. This study considered various measures of firm size and the uncertainty of earnings forecasts as possible proxies. Ceteris paribus, smaller firms and firms with greater earnings uncertainty were assumed to have less frequent report arrival and less precise prior information. Using the sample of securities experiencing a change from rank 2 to rank 1 and their standardized abnormal returns on event days 0, +1, and +2, cross-sectional regressions of standardized abnormal returns on various firm characteristics found firm market value (market value of common stock plus book value of liabilities) to be a good explanatory variable of the magnitude of standardized abnormal returns.[8]

To investigate cross-sectional differences in the information content of the various types of Value Line rank changes, the association between firm size (market value of common stock plus book value of liabilities) and *standardized* abnormal returns was estimated by Spearman rank correlations for all rank change groups.[9] For upgraded (downgraded) securities the predicted association is negative (positive), smaller firms are predicted to have larger positive

---

[8]An earlier version of this paper, which is available from the author on request, detailed the procedure for selecting a proxy for the frequency of report arrival and precision of prior information. The five proxies considered were (1) the rank ordered 'Relative Position' earnings reliability data item from the Value Line Data Base-II, which is intended to be a measure of the uncertainty in earnings forecasts, (2) the market value of common stock (price per share times the number of shares outstanding), (3) the market value of common stock plus the book value of total liabilities (from the Value Line Data Base-II), (4) the number of employees of the company (from the Value Line Data Base-II), and (5) common stock price per share. Because of their high correlation (0.98), results using market value of common stock and market value of common stock plus book value of liabilities were virtually identical.

[9]Cross-sectional differences in information content could be predicted from cross-sectional differences in abnormal return variances. Following Jain (1982), if smaller firms have larger abnormal return variances than larger firms, smaller firms could be predicted to have a larger reaction to new information. Stickel (1980) found smaller firms have larger abnormal return variances. However, the relationship between *standardized* abnormal returns and firm size abstracts from differences in individual security abnormal return variances provided the returns are cross-sectionally independent [see Jain's (1982, p. 218) Solution 2]. Since rank changes in this study occurred on 186 different days, a relationship between *standardized* abnormal returns and firm-specific variables is not predictable from the empirical relationship between abnormal return variances and firm-specific variables.

(negative) standardized abnormal returns.

The hypotheses are

If upgraded, $H_0: r \geq 0$, $H_a: r < 0$,

If downgraded, $H_0: r \leq 0$, $H_a: r > 0$.

The significance of rank correlations is tested by the statistic

$$t = r\left((N-2)/(1-r^2)\right)^{\frac{1}{2}},$$

where r is the sample rank correlation and N is the number of observations.

Table 3

Spearman rank correlations (r) between firm size (market value of common stock plus book value of liabilities) and *standardized* abnormal returns for event days -5 to $+5$. Firms segregated by type of rank change. Event day 0 is the Thursday prior to the Friday publication date of a Value Line rank change.

Event day	Rank 2 to 1 ($N = 682$) r	Rank 1 to 2 ($N = 670$) r	Rank 3 to 2 ($N = 1807$) r	Rank 2 to 3 ($N = 1816$) r
−5	−0.032	−0.038	−0.016	0.007
−4	−0.047	0.040	0.011	0.002
−3	0.099	0.068	0.056	−0.001
−2	0.016	0.011	0.023	0.059[b]
−1	0.003	0.079[b]	−0.022	0.036
0	−0.164[a]	0.111[a]	−0.017	−0.008
1	−0.254[a]	0.102[a]	−0.072[a]	0.019
2	−0.080[b]	0.053	−0.019	0.058[b]
3	−0.003	0.063	−0.006	0.081[a]
4	0.023	−0.010	0.037	0.055[b]
5	−0.005	−0.059	0.004	0.012

Event day	Rank 4 to 3 ($N = 1927$) r	Rank 3 to 4 ($N = 1957$) r	Rank 5 to 4 ($N = 913$) r	Rank 4 to 5 ($N = 915$) r
−5	−0.002	0.005	−0.018	−0.007
−4	−0.000	0.011	0.003	−0.009
−3	0.018	0.031	0.083	0.069[b]
−2	0.015	0.048[b]	0.083	0.044
−1	0.051	−0.008	0.053	0.030
0	0.065	−0.010	0.005	0.013
1	−0.046[b]	−0.023	0.007	−0.001
2	0.045	0.053[b]	0.090	0.069[b]
3	−0.005	0.054[b]	0.004	0.024
4	0.034	0.022	−0.018	−0.045
5	−0.020	0.017	−0.027	0.000

[a] Null hypothesis rejected at greater than the 0.005 level using a one-tail test.
[b] Null hypothesis rejected at greater than the 0.025 level using a one-tail test.

The statistic is approximately t-distributed with $N - 2$ degrees of freedom.[10] Table 3 presents rank correlations between standardized abnormal returns and firm size for event days -5 to $+5$ for each rank change group.

For changes from rank 2 to rank 1, the null hypothesis of positive correlation is rejected by a one-tail test on event days 0 and $+1$ (p-values of 0.0001) and day $+2$ (p-value of 0.0176). Although the correlations are weaker for other rank change groups, as long as the change involves a firm moving to or from rank 1 or 2 there are significant correlations of the predicted sign. Evidence of a firm size effect for firms moving to or from rank 4 or 5 is weak. Unexpectedly, there are many large correlations of the sign opposite of predictions for firms moving to or from rank 4 or 5.

Although table 3 documents a significant association between firm size and *standardized* abnormal returns, the magnitude of the *abnormal* returns for small firms is important for economic interpretations. Fig. 2 segregates observations reclassified from rank 2 to rank 1 into size quintiles and plots percentage cumulative average abnormal returns for a period of 5 trading days prior and subsequent to event day 0 (defined as the Thursday prior to the Friday publication date of a Value Line rank change). Quintile 1, the smallest firms, is plotted by the number '1', quintile 2 by the number '2', and so on up to quintile 5, the largest firms, by the number '5'. Supporting fig. 2 is table 4 which presents percentage daily average abnormal returns (AAR), Z-statistics, and percentage cumulative average abnormal returns ($CAAR$) by size quintile. Although the cumulation of AAR begins with day -5 to be consistent with the plots, the daily average AAR and Z-statistics for days -50 to -6 and $+6$ to $+50$ are reported.

Fig. 2 and table 4 plot and summarize the inverse relationship between firm size and the magnitude of abnormal returns for firms reclassified from rank 2 to rank 1. Smaller firms have a larger reaction to the rank change. Quintile 1, the smallest firms, has AAR of 2.08%, 2.00%, and 1.10% on event days 0, $+1$, and $+2$, whereas quintile 5, the largest firms, has AAR of 0.30%, -0.05%, and 0.45% for the same three-day period.[11] Despite the differences in the magnitude

---

[10] Testing the relationship between firm size and standardized abnormal returns may contaminate the announcement effect with the January size effect. Keim (1983) documents abnormally high returns for small firms during the first few trading days in January. The results of this paper could be biased to the extent Value Line upgrades the ranks of small firms during the first few trading days in January. To check for contamination all tests for an announcement effect were also performed excluding rank changes that occurred during the first eight calendar days of January. Results of these tests were virtually identical to the results for all observations.

[11] Blume and Stambaugh (1983) and Roll (1983) show portfolio average returns are biased upwards if daily returns are cross-sectionally averaged before cumulating. More importantly, the bias is greater for smaller firms than larger firms. Blume and Stambaugh estimate the amount of the bias by calculating the difference between the average daily returns to a portfolio that is rebalanced daily and a buy-and-hold portfolio that is rebalanced yearly. Using firms in the two smallest size deciles (which roughly corresponds to the smallest quintile in this study) the bias is approximately 0.07% ((0.093% + 0.045%)/2) per day during the 1975–1980 period [Blume and Stambaugh (1983, table 1)]. For firms in the two largest size deciles, the bias is less than 0.01%

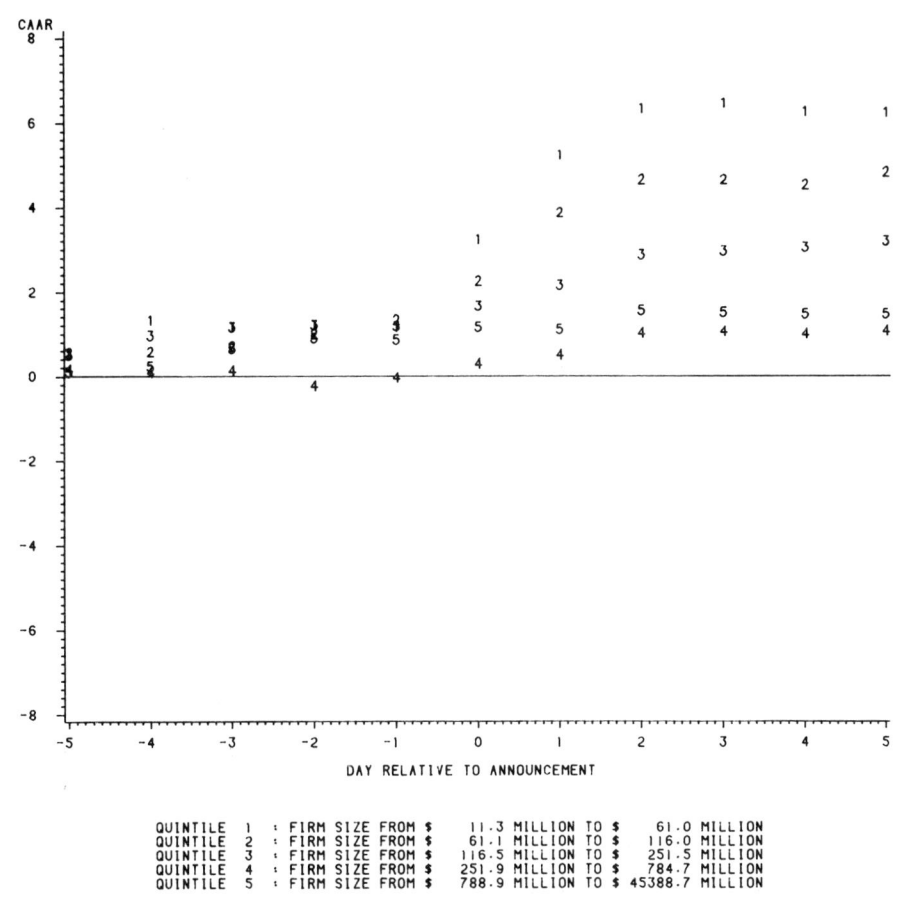

Fig. 2. Percentage cumulative average abnormal returns (*CAAR*) for 682 firms changed from Value Line rank 2 to rank 1 between July 1976 and March 1980. Firms segregated into quintiles based on firm size.

of abnormal returns, the abnormal returns of all size quintiles are significantly different from zero at the 0.05 level or greater on event days 0, +1, and +2, except for quintiles 4 and 5 on event day +1. By event day +3 the rank change effect has mostly dissipated.

The relationship between firm size and abnormal returns for the other rank change groups was also examined. For firms reclassified from rank 1 to 2, 3 to 2, and 2 to 3, the rank change effect is generally larger and more significant for the smaller firms. For changes from rank 4 to 3, 3 to 4, 5 to 4, and 4 to 5

---

during the 1975–1980 period. In both cases, this potential bias is very small relative to the magnitudes of the abnormal returns on table 4.

Table 4

Percentage daily average abnormal returns (AAR) and percentage cumulative average abnormal returns ($CAAR$) for 682 firms changed from Value Line rank 2 to rank 1 between July 1976 and March 1980. Firms segregated into quintiles based on firm size. Event day 0 is the Thursday prior to the Friday publication date of a Value Line rank change.[a]

Event day(s)	Quintile 1 (small firms) AAR	Z	CAAR	Quintile 2 AAR	Z	CAAR
(−50, −6)	0.21	6.80	0.0	0.19	7.18	0.0
−5	0.50	2.43	0.50	0.55	3.19	0.55
−4	0.82	4.02	1.32	0.02	−0.06	0.57
−3	−0.15	−0.54	1.17	0.13	0.56	0.70
−2	0.05	0.40	1.22	0.29	2.00	0.99
−1	−0.06	−0.03	1.16	0.34	2.20	1.32
0	2.08	9.43	3.24	0.93	5.19	2.25
1	2.00	9.75	5.24	1.61	9.49	3.86
2	1.10	5.71	6.34	0.78	4.84	4.65
3	0.12	0.75	6.46	−0.01	0.11	4.64
4	−0.20	−0.65	6.26	−0.11	−0.37	4.52
5	−0.02	0.07	6.23	0.29	1.96	4.82
(6, 50)	0.03	0.55	7.47	0.01	0.79	5.38

Event day(s)	Quintile 3 AAR	Z	CAAR	Quintile 4 AAR	Z	CAAR	Quintile 5 (large firms) AAR	Z	CAAR
(−50, −6)	0.16	6.06	0.0	0.18	7.38	0.0	0.12	5.54	0.0
−5	0.49	2.95	0.49	0.15	0.81	0.15	0.09	1.02	0.09
−4	0.46	2.83	0.95	−0.06	−0.31	0.09	0.13	1.20	0.22
−3	0.20	1.55	1.15	0.03	0.35	0.12	0.42	3.33	0.64
−2	0.05	1.02	1.20	−0.36	−1.67	−0.23	0.25	1.92	0.90
−1	−0.03	0.20	1.17	0.19	0.91	−0.04	−0.04	−0.51	0.86
0	0.48	2.94	1.65	0.32	2.13	0.28	0.30	2.11	1.15
1	0.50	3.31	2.15	0.21	1.42	0.50	−0.05	−0.59	1.10
2	0.72	4.31	2.87	0.52	3.13	1.02	0.45	3.19	1.55
3	0.09	0.40	2.96	0.03	0.14	1.05	−0.05	−0.45	1.50
4	0.08	−0.09	3.04	−0.06	−0.43	0.99	−0.04	−0.46	1.46
5	0.15	0.75	3.19	0.07	0.51	1.06	0.00	0.28	1.46
(6, 50)	0.01	0.14	3.49	0.02	0.75	2.10	0.03	0.58	2.61

[a] AAR for a multiple-day observation period is the average daily AAR within the observation period.

A Z-statistic (Z) of 2.58 (1.96) indicates the AAR is significantly different from zero at the 0.01 (0.05) level.

evidence of a rank change effect is generally weak for all size quintiles. Detailed results of these tests are available from the author on request.

Abnormal return behavior surrounding a change from rank 2 to rank 1 confirms the description of the Value Line ranking process in section 2.1. The Value Line ranking process uses Wednesday closing prices to determine preliminary rankings (which are used in this study), sends the final rankings to the printer on Friday for publication the following Friday. Using quintile 1 firms on fig. 2 as an example, $CAAR$ drift upward on days -5 and -4, then level off until the following Thursday (day 0), where the initial subscribers receive their issue and the rank change effect occurs. In the absence of holidays, event day -5 corresponds to the Thursday of the week prior to the Friday publication date of rankings. If two weekdays between the Wednesday of the week prior to the Friday publication date and the following Thursday (day 0) are holidays, the Wednesday of the week before publication corresponds to event day -4. Since Value Line uses daily data up to the Wednesday of the week prior to the Friday publication date in the ranking process, holidays could explain the significant abnormal performance on event days -5 and -4 for some quintiles. In the absence of a three-day holiday significant abnormal returns on event days -3, -2, and -1 are not expected, but are observed for some quintiles. Significant abnormal returns on these days may be the result of rank change information leakage prior to subscriber receipt. Event days 0, $+1$, and $+2$ correspond to Thursday, Friday, and the following Monday in calendar time, unless there are holidays.

The evidence suggests prices adjust to some types of Value Line rank change for approximately three trading days at the portfolio level. Using event days 0, $+1$, and $+2$, table 5 summarizes the differential effect of a Value Line rank change across firm size, across type of rank change, and by the direction (upgraded or downgraded) of the rank change. Firms reclassified from rank 2 to 1 have an average $CAAR$ of 2.39%, which is approximately 3 times greater than the absolute magnitude of the $CAAR$ for any other rank change group

Table 5

Percentage cumulative average abnormal returns ($CAAR$) for event days 0, $+1$, and $+2$. Firms segregated into quintiles based on firm size ($Q1$ = smallest firms,..., $Q5$ = largest firms) and cross-classified by type of Value Line rank change. Event day 0 is the Thursday prior to the Friday publication date of a Value Line rank change.

Size quintile Rank change group	Percentage $CAAR$ for event days 0, $+1$, and $+2$					
	$Q1$ (small firms)	$Q2$	$Q3$	$Q4$	$Q5$ (large firms)	Average
Rank 2 to rank 1 (fig. 2)	5.18	3.32	1.70	1.05	0.70	2.39
Rank 1 to rank 2	−1.66	−0.88	−0.71	−0.58	0.20	−0.73
Rank 3 to rank 2	1.53	0.55	0.59	0.34	0.15	0.63
Rank 2 to rank 3	−0.54	−0.82	−0.47	−0.46	−0.31	−0.52
Rank 4 to rank 3	−0.13	0.35	0.15	−0.03	0.14	0.10
Rank 3 to rank 4	−0.17	−0.27	−0.17	−0.11	−0.11	−0.17
Rank 5 to rank 4	0.16	−0.01	−0.16	0.45	0.32	0.14
Rank 4 to rank 5	−0.72	−0.19	−0.14	−0.33	−0.13	−0.30
Average for upgraded	1.69	1.05	0.57	0.45	0.32	0.81
Average for downgraded	−0.77	−0.54	−0.37	−0.37	−0.09	−0.43

over the same three-day period. Small firms (quintile 1) that were upgraded (downgraded) have an average *CAAR* of 1.69% (−0.77%), which is greater in absolute magnitude than any other size quintile. Upgraded firms have an average *CAAR* of 0.81%, which is larger in absolute magnitude than the average *CAAR* of −0.43% for downgraded firms. Quintile 1 firms experiencing a change from rank 2 to 1, which range in market value of common stock from $8.8 million to $58.2 million, have a 5.18% *CAAR* for event days 0, +1, and +2. Using $33.5 million as an approximate average of equity value, a 5.18% *CAAR* for event days 0, +1, and +2 implies an average change of $1.74 million in the total equity value of the smallest firms because of the Value Line rank change. Schultz (1983), studying NYSE and ASE securities, and Stoll and Whaley (1983), studying NYSE securities, found round-trip transactions costs for small firms of 11.4% and 6.77%, respectively. In either case a trading strategy of buying quintile 1 firms experiencing a 2 to 1 rank change on Thursday and selling those firms on the following Monday would not be profitable after such transactions costs.

4.3. Speed of adjustment of individual securities to a rank change

The evidence presented has found the period of adjustment of portfolio returns to new information to be approximately three days. However, the three-day adjustment period for portfolios could be driven by different firms on different days with individual firms adjusting within one day, as well as individual firms adjusting over a multiple-day period. To test the speed of adjustment of individual securities we examine the marginal distribution of average abnormal returns for event day $t + s$, $t = 0, 1$ and $s \geq 1$, conditional on a security having significant abnormal performance on event day t. Given significant abnormal performance on event day t and the assumptions of the methodology from section 3, the distribution of average abnormal returns on day $t + s$, $s \geq 1$ is assumed normal with mean zero. Firms experiencing a change from rank 2 to rank 1 were chosen for speed of adjustment analysis because of their relatively large rank change reaction. Defining significant abnormal performance on event day t as a standardized abnormal return (*SAR*) greater than 1.65 (significantly different from zero at the 0.10 level), 78 and 93 of the 682 firms experiencing a change from rank 2 to rank 1 had significant abnormal performance on event days 0 and +1, respectively. To test for a multiple-day adjustment period for individual securities, average abnormal returns and Z-statistics were calculated for event days subsequent to the day of significance. The hypotheses tested are stated as: For securities with significant abnormal performance on

event day 0, $\quad$ H_0: $E(AAR_{j,0+s}|SAR_{i,0} \geq 1.65) = 0.0,$
H_a: $E(AAR_{j,0+s}|SAR_{i,0} \geq 1.65) \neq 0.0,$

Table 6

Percentage average abnormal returns (AAR) for securities experiencing a Value Line rank change from rank 2 to rank 1 between July 1976 and March 1980 and a significant abnormal return on event day 0 or +1. Event day 0 is the Thursday prior to the Friday publication date of a Value Line rank change.[a]

For 78 securities with significant abnormal performance on event day 0

	AAR	Z
Event day +1	1.40	5.74
Event day +2	1.21	4.41
Event day +3	−0.62	−3.04
Event day +4	−0.39	−1.68
Event day +5	0.11	0.08

For 93 securities with significant abnormal performance on event day +1

	AAR	Z
Event day +2	1.33	6.71
Event day +3	−0.19	−0.85
Event day +4	−0.33	−1.83
Event day +5	−0.14	−1.03
Event day +6	−0.12	−0.23

[a] A significant abnormal return is defined as a standardized abnormal return (SAR) greater than 1.65, which is significantly different from zero at the 0.10 level.
A Z-statistic of 2.58 (1.96) indicates the AAR is significantly different from zero at the 0.01 (0.05) level.

event day 1, $\quad$ H_0: $E(AAR_{j,1+s}|SAR_{i,1} \geq 1.65) = 0.0$,
$\qquad\qquad\quad$ H_a: $E(AAR_{j,1+s}|SAR_{i,1} \geq 1.65) \neq 0.0$,

for $s \geq 1$. Results of these tests are presented on table 6.

The hypothesis of a single-day price adjustment period is rejected for securities experiencing significant abnormal performance on event day 0 or event day +1. For the 78 (out of 682) securities with significant abnormal performance on event day 0, the AAR on event days +1 and +2 are 1.40% and 1.21%, respectively (Z-statistics of 5.74 and 4.41), both significantly different from zero at greater than the 0.01 level.[12] Even more surprising is the significantly negative AAR of −0.62% (Z-statistic of −3.04) on event day +3. The AAR for event days +4 and +5 are not significant. For the 93 (out of 682) securities with significant abnormal performance on event day +1, the AAR on event day +2 is 1.33% (Z-statistic of 6.71), which is significantly

---

[12] Finding a multiple-day adjustment period for some securities does not preclude the possibility that variation in the day of arrival of Value Line reports is contributing to the abnormal performance for event days +1 and +2 on tables 2 and 4.

different from zero at greater than the 0.01 level. The AAR for event days $+3$ through $+5$ are not significant.[13]

5. Conclusions

The Value Line ranking process is almost entirely based on publicly available information. Value Line management believes the only part of the ranking process that does not rely on publicly available information is the 'earnings surprise' criterion which uses a quarterly earnings estimate to compare against actual quarterly earnings. Because Value Line uses some non-public information in the ranking process, one cannot view the evidence that rank changes affect security prices as inconsistent with the semi-strong definition of market efficiency, that prices reflect all publicly available information. Even if Value Line rank changes were entirely based on publicly available information they may affect prices if individual investors believe the expected costs of gathering and processing information to be greater than the expected benefits. Value Line may be an efficient processor of costly, publicly available information. Finding information content in Value Line rank changes adds to the literature on the value of investment advisory services and is consistent with the performance evaluation studies by Black (1973), Holloway (1981), and Copeland and Mayers (1982).[14]

Cross-sectional differences in firm reaction to Value Line rank change were found. The empirical results support the theoretical work of Ohlson (1979) and Holthausen and Verrecchia (1982), which propose the frequency of report arrival and the precision of information as determinants of price change. Using firm market value as a proxy for the frequency of report arrival and the precision of prior information, smaller firms were found to have a larger

---

[13] If the returns of the securities used to compute the AAR on table 6 are generally slow to adjust to new information, a multiple-day adjustment to a Value Line rank change would not be surprising. Using the set of securities from the analysis on table 6, 'normal' conditional AAR were calculated conditional on an SAR greater than 1.65 for any day between event days $+7$ and $+45$. For 378 observations of SAR greater than 1.65, the AAR for the following five days were $+0.28\%$, -0.24%, -0.10%, -0.07%, and $+0.05\%$. Using the assumptions of section 3 and a parametric test of difference in means, the significance of the difference between the conditional AAR on table 6 and the 'normal' conditional AAR was calculated. Although there is marginal evidence the prices of these firms are generally slow to adjust, the difference between the conditional AAR on table 6 and the 'normal' conditional AAR is significant at greater than the 0.01 level for event days $+1$, $+2$, and $+3$ for the 78 securities with significant abnormal performance on event day 0 and for event day $+2$ for the 93 securities with significant abnormal performance on event day $+1$.

[14] Throughout this paper we have implicitly assumed Value Line causes security price changes. A valid alternative hypothesis is Value Line does not cause price adjustment, but predicts it. The lack of immediate price adjustment may be attributed to the market not believing the predictive ability of Value Line. Although it seems unlikely that Value Line could consistently predict, not cause, a three-day abnormal return of 5.18% for small firms, we have not distinguished between predictive ability and causality.

reaction to a rank change. As with any empirical work, alternative interpretations are possible. A price pressure hypothesis would suggest there is a smaller supply of small firm securities available to meet the demand caused by a change in rank. However, evidence on price pressure [e.g. Kraus and Stoll (1972)] suggests the effect, if any, is very temporary. Because the effect of a rank change appears permanent, at least through event day +50, the results support an information effect, not a price pressure effect. An alternative, information-related hypothesis is Value Line more accurately predicts the future of smaller firms than larger firms. However, there is nothing in the Value Line ranking process to suggest they concentrate their evaluation efforts on small firms. Finding price reaction to a report on firm value is a function of firm size has important implications for 'event studies' testing for information content. To avoid a Type II error, incorrectly accepting the null hypothesis of no information content, researchers should include cross-sectional tests for predictable cross-sectional differences in information content.

The effect of Value Line rank changes on prices varies by the type of rank change. For example, reclassifications from rank 2 to rank 1 and rank 5 to rank 4 both upgrade projected relative price performance, but investors assess the reclassifications differently. Reclassification from rank 2 to rank 1 is 'very good news', but reclassification from rank 5 to rank 4 is 'no news'. A plausible explanation is that although a reclassification from rank 5 to 4 increases projected relative price performance, the security remains in a rank that is predicted to underperform the general market. Another finding was that the reaction of upgraded securities is greater in magnitude than the reaction of downgraded securities. The immediate impact of a reclassification from rank 2 to rank 1 is approximately three times as large as the immediate impact of a reclassification from rank 1 to rank 2. Although no complete explanation is offered, restrictions on short selling may be contributing to limiting the immediate effect of a downgraded ranking.

Speed of adjustment tests suggest individual securities with significant abnormal returns on event day 0 or +1 adjust to the information in a rank change over a multiple-day period. This is in sharp contrast to other studies that have found much faster price adjustment to new information.[15] However, the dissemination of rank change information is dependent on the U.S. Postal Service, thus the information is released sequentially to subscribers rather than immediately to all market participants. The results are consistent with the hypothesis that price adjustment to new information is dependent on the

[15] Dann, Mayers, and Raab (1977), examining intra-day price reaction to large block trades, found the period of price adjustment to be approximately fifteen minutes. Hillmer and Yu (1979), examining price changes, the variance of price changes, and trading intensity for five companies experiencing an 'unexpected' information release, found the period of adjustment for price changes to be at least within one hour of the announcement. Interestingly, Hillmer and Yu found the period of adjustment for the variance of price changes and for trading intensity to be the longest (in excess of one day) for the smallest firm.

summation of individual actions, and the period of aggregate price adjustment is the length of time over which individual investors become aware of new information.[16] Nonetheless, it is surprising to find new information that is not immediately reflected in security prices. Apparently, the subscribers who receive Value Line on Thursday do not complete the price adjustment process. Although roundtrip transactions costs probably preclude arbitrage profits from active trading, a buy-and-hold policy would benefit by receiving Value Line issues on Thursdays.

[16] These results are similar to Lloyd Davies and Canes (1978), which found price reaction to analysts' recommendations reported in the Wall Street Journal's 'Heard on the Street' column after the recommendations had been given to the analysts' clients.

References

Bernhard, Arnold, 1977, Value Line methods of evaluating common stocks (Arnold Bernhard, New York).

Black, Fisher, 1973, Yes, Virginia, there is hope: Tests of the Value Line ranking system, Financial Analysts Journal 29, 10–14.

Blume, Marshall E. and Robert F. Stambaugh, 1983, Biases in computed returns: An application to the size effect, Journal of Financial Economics 12, 387–404.

Brown, Stephen J. and Jerold B. Warner, 1980, Measuring security price performance, Journal of Financial Economics 8, 205–258.

Brown, Stephen J. and Jerold B. Warner, 1984, Using daily stock returns: The case of event studies, Journal of Financial Economics, this issue.

Copeland, Thomas E., 1976, A model of asset trading under the assumption of sequential information arrival, Journal of Finance 31, 1149–1163.

Copeland, Thomas E. and David Mayers, 1982, The Value Line enigma (1965–1978): A case study of performance evaluation issues, Journal of Financial Economics 10, 289–321.

Dann, Larry Y., David Mayers and Robert J. Raab, Jr., 1977, Trading rules, large blocks and the speed of price adjustment, Journal of Financial Economics 4, 3–22.

Fama, Eugene F., 1976, Foundations of finance (Basic Books, New York).

French, Kenneth R., 1980, Stock returns and the weekend effect, Journal of Financial Economics 8, 55–69.

Gibbons, Michael R. and Patrick Hess, 1981, Day of the week effects and asset returns, Journal of Business 54, 579–596.

Grant, Edward B., 1980, Market implications of differential amounts of interim information, Journal of Accounting Research 18, 255–268.

Hillmer, S.C. and P. Yu, 1979, The market speed of adjustment to new information, Journal of Financial Economics 7, 321–346.

Holloway, Clark, 1981, A note on testing an aggressive investment strategy using Value Line ranks, Journal of Finance 36, 711–719.

Holthausen, Robert W. and Robert E. Verrecchia, 1982, The change in price resulting from a sequence of information releases, Working paper (Graduate School of Business, University of Chicago, Chicago, IL).

Ison, Bryan N., 1980, More tests of the Value Line ranking system, Manuscript (Graduate School of Business, University of Chicago, Chicago, IL).

Jain, Prem C., 1982, Cross-sectional association between abnormal returns and firm specific variables, Journal of Accounting and Economics 4, 205–228.

Keim, Donald, 1983, Size-related anomalies and stock return seasonality: Further empirical evidence, Journal of Financial Economics 12, 13–32.

Kraus, Alan, and Hans R. Stoll, 1972, Price impacts of block trading on the New York Stock Exchange, Journal of Finance 27, 569–588.

Lehmann, E.L., 1975, Nonparametrics: Statistical methods based on ranks (Holden-Day, San Francisco, CA).
Lloyd Davies, Peter and Michael Canes, 1978, Stock prices at the publication of second hand information, Journal of Business 51, 43–56.
McNichols, Maureen and James G. Manegold, 1983, The effect of the information environment on the relationship between financial disclosure and security price variability, Journal of Accounting and Economics 5, 49–74.
Ohlson, James A., 1979, On financial disclosure and the behavior of security prices, Journal of Accounting and Economics 1, 211–232.
Patell, James, 1976, Corporate forecasts of earnings per share and stock price behavior: Empirical tests, Journal of Accounting Research 14, 246–274.
Pincus, Morton, 1983, Information characteristics of earnings announcements and stock market behavior, Journal of Accounting Research 21, 155–183.
Rendelman, Richard J. Jr., Charles P. Jones and Henry A. Latane, 1982, Empirical anomalies based on unexpected earnings and the importance of risk adjustments, Journal of Financial Economics 10, 269–287.
Roll, Richard, 1983, On computing mean returns and the small firm premium, Journal of Financial Economics 12, 371–386.
Scholes, Myron and Joseph Williams, 1977, Estimating betas from nonsynchronous data, Journal of Financial Economics 5, 309–327.
Schultz, Paul, 1983, Transactions costs and the small firm effect: A comment, Journal of Financial Economics 12, 81–88.
Stickel, Scott E., 1980, The effect of costly information on capital asset prices, Manuscript (Graduate School of Business, University of Chicago, Chicago, IL).
Stickel, Scott E., 1984, Detecting information effects using daily preferred stock returns, Working paper (Graduate School of Business, University of Chicago, Chicago, IL).
Stoll, Hans R. and Robert E. Whaley, 1983, Transactions costs and the small firm effect, Journal of Financial Economics 12, 57–79.
Watts, Ross L., 1978, Systematic 'abnormal' returns after quarterly earnings announcements, Journal of Financial Economics 6, 127–150.

IV

FINANCIAL STATEMENT INFORMATION IN DEBT AND EQUITY RISK ASSESSMENT

1 Hand, John R. M., Robert W. Holthausen, and Richard W. Leftwich, "The Effect of Bond Rating Agency Announcements on Bond and Stock Prices," *Journal of Finance*, 47 (1986), pp. 733–752.

2 Ohlson, James A., "Financial Ratios and the Probabilistic Prediction of Bankruptcy," *Journal of Accounting Research*, 18 (1980), pp. 109–131.

3 Altman, Edward I., and Joseph Spivack, "Predicting Bankruptcy: The Value Line Relative Financial Strength System vs. the ZETA Bankruptcy Classification Approach," *Financial Analysts Journal*, November–December (1983), pp. 60–67.

4 Rosenberg, Barr, and James Guy, "Prediction of Beta from Investment Fundamentals: Part I," *Financial Analysts Journal*, May–June (1976), pp. 60–72.

5 Rosenberg, Barr, and James Guy, "Prediction of Beta from Investment Fundamentals: Part II," *Financial Analysts Journal*, July–August (1976), pp. 62–70.

6 Beaver, William H., and Dale Morse, "What Determines Price-Earnings Ratios?," *Financial Analysts Journal*, July–August (1978), pp. 65–76.

7 Lev, Baruch, "On the Association between Operating Leverage and Risk," *Journal of Financial and Quantitative Analysis*, 9 (1974), pp. 627–641.

8 Ball, Ray, S.P. Kothari, and Ross L. Watts, "Economic Determinants of the Relation between Earnings Changes and Stock Returns," *The Accounting Review*, 68 (1993), pp. 622–638.

9 Fama, Eugene F., and Kenneth R. French, "The Cross-Section of Expected Returns," *Journal of Finance*, 47 (1992), pp. 427–465.

Debtholders and equityholders, as claimants to a firm's future cash flows, are interested in assessing their riskiness. Debtholders are primarily interested in assessing whether the firm's cash flows will be sufficient to make interest and principal payments on a timely basis. The lower the probability that the firm will have a shortfall in cash to make promised interest and principal payments, the safer the debt. Debtholders therefore gather information about the firm's liquidity, debt capacity, and liquidation value of assets. Debt capacity of assets is a function of the level and uncertainty (variance) of cash flows expected to be generated through their use.

Unlike debtholders, equityholders are residual claimants of the firm's cash flows. Shareholders in effect hold an option on the value of the firm's assets, with the exercise price equal to the face value of debt [e.g., Black and Scholes (1973) and Galai and Masulis (1976)]. It is well known that the option component of equity value increases with the variance of expected future cash flows [Black and Scholes (1973)] and with the firm's debt to its equity ratio.[1] Therefore, when equity has a large component of option-like characteristics, financial statement analysis focusses on assessing both the expected level and the variance of future cash flows when valuing equity. At less extreme debt levels, the equity is a deep-in-the-money option and its valuation does not require the use of the option pricing model. More traditional valuation models will suffice. For example, equity valuation can be based on discounting the firm's expected cash flows at a rate that, according to the Sharpe-Lintner-Black Capital Asset Pricing Model (CAPM), linearly increases in the relative risk, β, of the firm's cash flows. The risk measure that affects the discount rate thus is the covariance of the firm's equity cash flows with the (cash flows of the) economy (or the market), rather than total variance of the firm's cash flows. Financial analysts and investors are interested in assessing a firm's beta risk so that they can perform valuation of traded stocks, seasoned equity issues, and initial public offerings.

The papers included in this part focus on various issues with respect to debt and equity risk assessment. The first three papers deal with riskiness of debt, whereas the last six are about equity risk assessment. The topics encompassed in these papers include the information in bond ratings, bankruptcy prediction models, prediction of systematic risk from fundamentals, determinants of systematic risk of equity, information in earnings yield about risk and growth, and empirical measures of risk in addition to the CAPM beta.

Bond Ratings

Financial statement information is useful in assessing corporate and municipal bond risks. Wakeman (1981) argues that the explanations offered by the rating agencies, the timing of rating changes, and ability of financial ratios to explain cross-sectional variation in the ratings of bonds collectively suggest that rating agencies like Standard and Poor's and Moody's use financial statement information in issuing rating changes of publicly traded corporate and municipal debt. **Hand, Holthausen, and Leftwich (1992)** extend previous research by Weinstein (1977) and Wakeman (1978) on the information content of changes in ratings of corporate bonds announced by Standard and Poor's and Moody's. They find that unanticipated (possible and actual) ratings changes are associated with significant bond and stock price effects, particularly when bonds are being downgraded.

---

[1] The variance of a firm's cash flows obviously is a function of the nature of its investments. When equity assumes the characteristics of an option because the firm is highly leveraged, equityholders have an incentive to undertake high-variance investment projects and increase the value of equity. Assuming no change in the expected level of cash flows to the firm, all the increase in equity value comes at the expense of debtholders, because higher variance of cash flows diminishes the value of debt. This develops an agency conflict between debtholders and bondholders. This conflict is discussed in detail in Smith and Warner (1979).

Bankruptcy Prediction

Creditors and equity investors alike are interested in knowing the likelihood of a firm's experiencing bankruptcy or financial distress in the near future. A high probability of distress would indicate both debt and equity are highly risky. An investor would factor this information in making portfolio investment decisions, and potential lenders would use the bankruptcy probability in their lending decisions (e.g., whether to lend, how much to lend, and what interest rate to charge). Thus, bankruptcy prediction is a useful exercise even in an efficient capital market. Early work on the usefulness of financial statement information for bankruptcy prediction is by Beaver (1966) and Altman (1968). These studies reveal that economically intuitive financial ratios like leverage, earnings before interest and taxes over assets, and working capital over assets are useful predictors of financial distress or bankruptcy. Altman's bankruptcy prediction models have been enormously popular in the financial community because they are easily applicable and are capable of correctly identifying potential bankrupt firms with considerable accuracy.

Ohlson (1980) makes an important contribution to the bankruptcy-prediction literature by pointing out that Altman (1968) and others overstate the predictive accuracy of their models. Predictive ability is overstated because the accuracy of bankruptcy-prediction models is often tested using a sample consisting of roughly equal numbers of bankrupt and nonbankrupt firms. In reality, however, the proportion of firms that go bankrupt in a year in the economy is far below 50 percent, probably no more than 5 percent. Therefore, when tested using a randomly selected sample of firms, most bankruptcy-prediction models erroneously identify a large number of firms as potential bankruptcies. Unless the cost of erroneously identifying a firm as potentially bankrupt is relatively low compared to the cost of failing to identify a bankrupt firm, the benefit of bankruptcy-prediction models is diminished. This weakness notwithstanding, bankruptcy and other prediction models continue to be popular. One reason is that they serve as a cost-effective preliminary screen to segregate a large number of firms, loan applicants, credit-card applicants, etc,. into high-, medium-, and low-risk categories.

Altman and Spivack (1983) compare the predictive ability of Altman's ZETA bankruptcy classification approach with that of the Value Line relative financial strength approach. Their results suggest that the models rank firms similarly in terms of their likelihood of going bankrupt. In addition, their rankings are highly correlated with bond ratings. Thus, bankruptcy prediction models are useful in assessing the riskiness of both stocks and bonds.

Equity Risk

Perhaps the most common measure of equity risk is the CAPM beta. One way of estimating the expected rate of return on equity is to add the risk-free interest rate to an allowance for bearing risk, equal to the estimated beta times the historical average risk premium of about 8 to 10 percent per annum.[2] For publicly traded stocks, beta can be estimated using stock-return data, and for nontraded stocks accounting betas can be used as proxies for market-return betas [see Beaver, Kettler, and Scholes (1970)]. As an alternative to accounting betas of nontraded stocks, market-return betas of traded stocks that are matched on the basis of industry membership and/or other characteristics can be used.

---

[2] The recent recommendation by **Fama and French (1992)** to augment the CAPM by adding size and book-to-market factors in estimating expected rates of returns on equities is discussed below.

One limitation of market-return betas or accounting betas is that they are obtained using historical data and they therefore are less useful if there is reason to believe the true beta has changed. An understanding of determinants of beta is helpful in dealing with situations when there are economic reasons to expect a beta change. **Rosenberg and Guy (1976, Parts I and II)** give examples of macroeconomic events like energy shocks and inflation and firm-specific events like acquisitions (investment) and financial leverage changes, and describe these events' impacts on the betas of equities. Depending on the sensitivity of a firm to a particular macroeconomic shock, its beta will change, and depending upon the nature of an investment-financing decision the equity beta will change (e.g., investment in a low-risk project or a leverage-reducing financing transaction will lower equity beta). The **Lev (1974)** and **Ball, Kothari, and Watts (1993)** papers provide evidence on the determinants of risk changes. **Lev (1974)** shows that changes in a firm's operating leverage (i.e., the ratio of fixed to variable operating costs) should be positively associated with beta risk changes. Thus, if a firm expands by investing in a capital-intensive project or acquires another firm that is fixed-cost–intensive, then the equity risk is expected to rise.

Ball, Kothari, and Watts (1993) provide evidence that earnings changes are positively associated with beta changes. The normal rate of return (or cost of capital) commensurate with the riskiness of the investments (assets) of a firm is a component of a firm's revenues. In calculating accounting earnings, accountants deduct the cost of debt capital, but not equity capital. So accounting earnings include the cost of equity capital. Thus, when the cost of capital changes due to changes in the riskiness of the underlying assets, it is expected to be reflected in earnings changes. Therefore, **Ball, Kothari, and Watts (1993)** hypothesize and document, a portion of the observed earnings changes is positively related to beta changes.

Beaver and Morse (1978) analyze the usefulness of earnings yield as a measure of risk and earnings growth. Following the analysis in Miller and Modigliani (1961) and Litzenberger and Rao (1971), **Beaver and Morse (1978)** argue that earnings yield would be decreasing in the beta risk of a stock. This makes intuitive sense: *ceteris paribus*, the market would assign a higher multiple on a relatively low risk stream of earnings and therefore the earnings yield would be low. **Beaver and Morse (1978)** also show that, perhaps better than as a risk measure, earnings yield forecasts earnings growth. In periods when the market anticipates high earnings growth for a firm, its stock price today rises to reflect these expectations, driving the current earnings yield lower.

For over two decades, academics and practitioners have used the CAPM beta as the sole determinant of the expected rate of return on equity. In recent years, several studies provide evidence contradicting the CAPM. These studies show that firm size, earnings yield, dividend yield, leverage, and book-to-market ratio explain cross-sectional variation in average return that beta cannot. The anomalous evidence in these studies is important to the investment community because investment decisions and performance evaluation are almost invariably guided by a benchmark model of expected rate of return. The anomalous evidence also brings into question the efficient markets hypothesis. An important contribution to this literature is by **Fama and French (1992)**. They evaluate various variables (e.g., size, earnings yield, and book-to-market) that previous research indicates explain cross-sectional variation in average returns. Their major conclusions are that (1) beta is not particularly helpful in explaining variation in average returns; and (2) two easily measured variables, size and book-to-market, are successful in explaining variation in average returns. Thus, once the set of determinants of risk and expected rates of return is expanded to include firm size and book-to-market ratio, variation in average returns is better explained and doubts about capital market efficiency are mitigated. Fama and French (1993) provide additional guidance to those interested in using an empirical model employing the market return, firm size, and book-to-market ratio as determinants of expected rates of return. Recent research by Kothari, Shanken, and Sloan (1993) and Chan and Lakonishok (1992) casts doubts on the Fama and French (1992) claim that beta is unhelpful in explaining cross-sectional variation in average returns over the past fifty years.

The Effect of Bond Rating Agency Announcements on Bond and Stock Prices

JOHN R. M. HAND, ROBERT W. HOLTHAUSEN, and RICHARD W. LEFTWICH*

ABSTRACT

This paper examines daily excess bond returns associated with announcements of additions to Standard and Poor's Credit Watch List, and to rating changes by Moody's and Standard and Poor's. Reliably nonzero average excess bond returns are observed for additions to Standard and Poor's Credit Watch List when an expectations model is used to classify additions as either expected or unexpected. Bond price effects are also observed for actual downgrade and upgrade announcements by rating agencies. Excluding announcements with concurrent disclosures weakens the results for downgrades, but not upgrades. The stock price effects of rating agency announcements are also examined and contrasted with the bond price effects.

THIS PAPER EXAMINES DAILY excess bond and stock returns associated with two types of bond rating agency announcements; warnings of possible rating changes via additions to Standard and Poor's Credit Watch List between 1981 and 1983, and actual rating changes announced by Moody's and Standard and Poor's between 1977 and 1982. Prior work that has used bond price data to examine the effect of rating changes has been mixed. Weinstein (1977) (monthly bond returns), and Wakeman (1978) (monthly stock and weekly bond returns) do not find a price reaction at the time of rating changes. Other studies, such as Katz (1974) (monthly changes in bond yields), Grier and Katz (1976) (average monthly bond prices) and Ingram, Brooks and Copeland (1983) (monthly changes in municipal bond yields), find significant bond price reactions. One potential advantage of our study is the

---

* Hand and Leftwich are from the Graduate School of Business at the University of Chicago. Holthausen is from the Wharton School at the University of Pennsylvania. We wish to thank John Elliott, Paul Healy, Gene Imhoff, Wayne Mikkelson, Dale Morse, Pat O'Brien, Scott Stickel, Tom Stober, an anonymous referee and David Mayers (editor) for their comments on a previous version of this paper, as well as workshop participants at Cornell University, Massachusetts Institute of Technology, the University of Michigan, Ohio State University, the University of Pennsylvania, and the University of Rochester. We wish to thank the Interactive Data Corporation for a research grant allowing access to the daily bond prices used in this study. Holthausen and Leftwich gratefully acknowledge the financial support of the Institute of Professional Accounting of the University of Chicago and the Center for Research in Security Prices.

use of daily data to isolate the announcement effect on bond prices, although nontrading of bonds does not always allow the use of short windows for estimating the price response. Another potential advantage is the separate examination of warnings of possible rating changes via additions to the Standard and Poor's Credit Watch List, and of actual rating changes that are not preceded by such warnings. Standard and Poor's began the Credit Watch List in November 1981, and companies are added to the list when Standard and Poor's believes a rating change is likely, with additions designated as "indicated upgrades" or "indicated downgrades", or "developing" if a rating change of unknown direction is likely. As a result, a rating change announcement may occur after a firm's debt is placed on the Credit Watch List, or it may occur without being preceded by a Credit Watch designation. We also develop an expectations model of rating changes to distinguish between those rating changes that are expected and those that are unexpected.

Overall results on the announcement effects of additions to the Credit Watch List do not indicate significant average excess bond returns. However, when we study those additions classified as unexpected additions by our expectations model, a significant negative average excess bond return of -1.39% is associated with indicated downgrades and a significant positive average excess bond return of 2.25% is associated with indicated upgrades. Significant average excess stock returns are observed at the time of indicated downgrades but not at the time of indicated upgrades.

The average excess bond return on the announcement of actual rating downgrades by Moody's and Standard and Poor's is -1.27% and the median excess return is -0.45%. Investment grade bonds experience a mean excess return of -0.55%, with a similar median excess return. Below investment grade bonds on average lose 3.82%, but the median bond loses only 0.62%. Downgrade announcements also affect the equity price of the rerated firm, and the negative average effects on the debt and equity are similar, though the effects on equity are somewhat more negative than the effect on the debt. The evidence on upgrades is weaker; the mean and median announcement effects are both approximately 0.35%, and little difference is observed between above and below investment grade bonds. Finally, there is little evidence of positive excess returns for the equity of upgraded firms.

To determine whether our results are the product of the rating announcement or of simultaneously announced news from other known sources, we classify observations as either "contaminated" or "noncontaminated" by other news. In general, the excess bond returns associated with Credit Watch announcements are even more supportive of price effects when the noncontaminated observations are examined. However, the significant negative average excess bond returns associated with actual rating downgrades disappear when we examine noncontaminated observations, though evidence of negative average excess stock returns is still apparent. For upgrades, elimination of contaminated events causes the measured average excess bond returns to become more positive, but stocks still evidence little impact associated with the rating change.

Results in previous studies on the effect of rating agency announcements on daily common and preferred stock prices are generally consistent with the results in this paper. Holthausen and Leftwich (1986) examine the common stock price response to Credit Watch announcements and bond rating changes, and find evidence consistent with a stock price response to all of those announcements except actual rating upgrades. Stickel (1986) examines the effect of preferred stock rating changes on preferred stock returns and finds evidence consistent with price effects for both upgrades and downgrades.

Section I of the paper describes the sample of additions to the Credit Watch List, and of actual rating changes by Moody's and Standard and Poor's. Section II describes the bond and stock price tests, and Section III reports results. A cross-sectional analysis of the excess bond returns associated with rating changes is given in Section IV. Concluding remarks are in Section V.

I. Data: Moody's and Standard and Poor's Rating Changes

We analyze two types of bond rating agency announcements. First, we examine a sample of approximately 250 additions to the Standard and Poor's Credit Watch List. Second, we examine a sample of approximately 1,100 bond rating change announcements by Moody's and Standard and Poor's.

Standard and Poor's began the Credit Watch List in November 1981. Companies are added to the list when Standard and Poor's believes a rating change is likely, with additions designated as "indicated upgrades", "indicated downgrades", or "developing" if a rating change of unknown direction is likely (for example, due to a potential merger). Additions to the Credit Watch List are published every Friday.[1] We sampled observations from the inception of the Credit Watch List to December 31, 1983. Observations are included if they relate to taxable straight-debt other than commercial paper and if the firm's common stock was publicly traded on the New York or American Stock Exchanges at the time of the announcement.

The sample of actual rating change announcements consists of bond rating changes announced by Moody's and Standard and Poor's during the period 1977–1982. Moody's rating changes are obtained from the section "Taxable Corporate Securities—Ratings Reviewed and Revised" of *Moody's Bond Survey*. Standard and Poor's rating changes are obtained from a listing entitled "Standard and Poor's Corp. Corporate Finance Rating Changes" supplied by officials of the Standard and Poor's Corporation. Only rating changes for fully taxable corporate straight-debt bonds are included in the study (i.e., tax-free industrial revenue bonds, convertible debt, and floating

---

[1] The announcements usually take place during trading. If Friday is a holiday, the announcement is made on Thursday. The *Wall Street Journal* story about Credit Watch additions typically appears on Monday. We define Friday as Day 0 unless the *Wall Street Journal* story precedes Monday, in which case Day 0 is the day before the *Wall Street Journal* story.

[2] All Moody's rating changes on April 20, 1982 are eliminated. On that day, Moody's announced a large number of rating changes to reflect a new rating system incorporating three rating grades within each class between AA and B.

rate notes are excluded).[2] The announcement date, Day 0, for each observation is the press release date indicated by Moody's and Standard and Poor's.[3]

If several bonds of the same firm are affected simultaneously, we select a maximum of five bonds with the longest time to maturity for both the samples of Credit Watch additions and actual rating changes. Long maturities are sampled to increase the likelihood of detecting excess bond returns. If bonds of the same firm in two different rating classes are affected, we sample from both classes. No firm in the sample has bonds in more than two rating categories.

Daily bond prices and volume, coupon amounts, payment dates and maturity dates were collected from the Interactive Data Corporation (IDC) Corporate Bond Data Base from 11 days before to 60 days after the announcement of an addition to the Credit Watch List or a rating change. Only transactions prices are used in this study. Many corporate bonds trade infrequently, and often only bid prices are reported. We performed extensive filtering on the price data, visually inspected every series, and decided to exclude all bid data. Large reversals are common in the price series if both bid and transaction prices are included. Even if transaction prices adjust to news announcements or interest rate shocks, many bid prices adjust only with a lag. Consequently, for some series the bid prices are consistently either above or below transaction prices (by more than half any plausible bid-ask spread) for one or two months.

Table I provides information on the trading frequency for the 1,548 bonds in the sample of bonds experiencing rating changes. At the extremes, no trades occur in the sample period (11 days before to 60 days after the rating change announcement) for 6.9% of the sample, and 9.7% of the sample trades on at least 61 of the 72 days in the sample period. Table I reveals that the trading frequency is considerably higher for bonds below investment grade (below BAA) than for investment grade bonds (BAA and above). For example, 25.2% of the 238 bonds below investment grade trade on at least 61 of the 72 sample days, while only 6.9% of the investment grade bonds trade that frequently. Further inspection reveals that 50% of the bonds below investment grade trade on at least half of the sample days while only 22.8% of the investment grade bonds trade that regularly.

Table II summarizes the distribution of differences between the original and the revised rating categories for the 1,133 bonds with at least one transaction price in the 11 days before the rating change and at least one transaction price in the 60 days after the rating change. Relative to Table I, the sample size declines from 1,548 to 1,133 because a bond is only included in Table II if it has a transaction price both before and after the rating change announcement. There are 841 downgrades and 292 upgrades. The imbalance in the number of downgrades and upgrades is probably due to the time period chosen. For the vast majority of observations, the difference

---

[3] We are grateful for the officials of Moody's and Standard and Poor's for providing this information.

Table I
Distribution of Frequencies of Days with Trades for Sample of 1548 Bonds having Rating Changes by Moody's or Standard and Poor's during 1977–1982: Trading Period of 72 Tradings Days from 11 Days before to 60 Days after the Rating Change

Number of Days with Trades	Investment Grade Number of Bonds	Investment Grade Percent of Bonds	Investment Grade Cumulative Percent of Bonds	Below Investment Grade Number of Bonds	Below Investment Grade Percent of Bonds	Below Investment Grade Cumulative Percent of Bonds	All Grades Number of Bonds	All Grades Percent of Bonds	All Grades Cumulative Percent of Bonds
61–72	90	6.9	6.9	60	25.2	25.2	150	9.7	9.7
49–60	87	6.6	13.5	24	10.1	35.3	111	7.2	16.9
37–48	122	9.3	22.8	35	14.7	50.0	157	10.1	27.0
25–36	171	13.1	35.9	41	17.2	67.2	212	13.7	40.7
13–24	257	19.6	55.5	38	16.0	83.2	295	19.1	59.8
1–12	481	36.7	92.2	35	14.7	97.9	516	33.3	93.1
0	102	7.8	100.0	5	2.1	100.0	107	6.9	100.0
Total	1310			238			1548		

Table II
Distribution of Differences between Original and Revised Rating Categories for a Sample of 841 Downgrades and 292 Upgrades of Corporate Taxable Debt Ratings Revised by Moody's and Standard and Poor's during 1977-1982[a]

The grading of the rating categories is based on the rating scheme introduced April 20, 1982. Grades are a cardinal variable measured on a scale of 28 (for rating AAA) to 1 (for rating D). Since some of the 10 classes (AAA to D) have three grades, each class is assigned three numbers. Classes without grades (D, C, CC, CCC, AAA, and all Moody's classes before April 20, 1982) are assigned the midpoint of the three numbers.

Number of Ratings Categories Changed	Downgrades	Upgrades	Total
1	345	116	461
2	258	84	342
3	216	84	300
4	13	1	14
5	4	4	8
6	0	1	1
7	1	0	1
8	2	1	3
9	0	1	1
10	0	0	0
11	2	0	2
Total	841	292	1133

[a] The sample includes only bonds that have prices both before and after the rating change.

between the original and the revised rating category is only either one category (461 observations) or two categories (342 observations). Nevertheless, 330 observations change three or more categories. Though not shown in Table II, 50 bonds change from above investment grade (rating categories BBB− and above) to below investment grade (rating categories BB+ and below) and 17 are upgraded to an investment grade category from a below-investment grade category.

Some of the subsequent excess returns tests depend on whether the rating agency announcement is accompanied by one or more concurrent disclosures. To identify concurrent disclosures for each announcement, we searched the *Wall Street Journal* index for potential new stories in the window spanning the first trading day with an available bond price prior to the rating change announcement through the first trading day with an available bond price after the rating change announcement. For each news item found, we read the story to determine if it discussed the rating agency announcement and if it contained information from any source other than the rating agency. If a story containing information other than the rating agency announcement appeared in the *Wall Street Journal* during the period used to measure the price effect (defined later), the observation is classified as contaminated. All remaining observations are classified as noncontaminated. Of course, investors may obtain information from sources other than the *Wall Street Journal*, and our tests will not detect that "contaminating" news. However, conditional on employing only one source for news releases, our test is particularly stringent because we exclude observations even if the contaminating disclosure is triggered by the bond rating agency's announcement. For example, we classify an observation as contaminated if a rating change causes a firm to announce postponement of a new debt issue or reduction in a capital expenditure program.

II. Measurement of Excess Bond and Stock Returns

A. *Estimation of Excess Bond Returns*

'Window-spanning' excess returns are employed because bonds trade infrequently, and bond prices are often not available on Days 0 and +1, the preferred window. The window-spanning raw return for each bond is measured from the last transaction price in the period −11 to −1 to the first transaction price on or after Day +1. For example, if a bond trades on Days −10, −3, +2, and +5, the window spanning return is calculated from transactions prices on Day −3 and Day +2. Accrued interest is added to the price change to calculate the bond's return over the period. If there are more than 20 days between the two prices the observation is eliminated.[4] For most of the following tests, the median number of days in the window-spanning return is five or six days. Excess returns for each bond for a given firm are equally weighted and the average is treated as a single observation.[5]

We measure excess bond returns as raw bond returns minus the return on a risk free bond (a long-term U.S. Treasury bond) for the window-spanning period. The benchmark controls for shifts in interest rates due to changes in real rates or expectations of inflation, but it does not control for variations in term or default premiums since we use one relatively long-term riskless bond as the benchmark for all bonds, regardless of maturity. Since default premia are positive, this measure overstates (understates) the impact for upgrades (downgrades). For short estimation periods, this bias is negligible.[6]

Estimation of the return variances and covariances between individual bonds is hampered by the overall paucity of trades. Consequently, we use relatively simple test statistics to determine whether the average excess bond

---

[4] The results reported are not sensitive to reducing the maximum number of days allowed in a window spanning return. For example, we obtain similar results with smaller sample sizes if we restrict the sample to firms that have window spans of no greater than five days.

[5] The results are similar if tests are conducted on individual bonds, or on a weighted-least squares estimate of mean abnormal performance. The weighted-least squares estimate assumes that each observation is independent with the same mean and a variance proportional to the length of the window. Each observation is weighted inversely according to the window length.

[6] We obtain similar results with the mean-adjusted excess return model used by Handjinicolaou and Kalay (1984). In that model, abnormal performance is defined as the bond's return less the return on a long-term U.S. Treasury bond, less the bond's default premium estimated using data after Day 0.

return differs from zero. We calculate a t-statistic based on the cross-sectional standard deviation of window-spanning excess returns, assuming that excess window-spanning returns of the firms are cross-sectionally independent and identically distributed. This t-statistic has one degree of freedom fewer than the number of firms in the sample.

The estimated excess returns for bonds are slightly skewed so we also report both median excess bond returns and the proportion of positive window-spanning excess bond returns. A binomial test (a Z-statistic) indicates whether the observed proportion of positive window-spanning excess bond returns is reliably different from 50%.[7]

B. Estimation of Excess Stock Returns

Excess stock returns are defined as stock prediction errors calculated from a market model, summed over event Days 0 and +1. Market model parameters are estimated using the 300 day post-rating change period from Day +62 to +361, because there is evidence in previous studies that downgrades (upgrades) are preceded by negative (positive) average excess returns. The index is the CRSP equally weighted New York and American Stock Exchange Index. Median excess stock returns and the proportion of positive excess stock returns are also reported. The t-test on the mean excess stock return is based on the cross-sectional standard deviation.[8]

C. Expectations Model for Bond Rating Agency Announcements

We develop an expectations model of bond rating changes based on yields-to-maturity, and use that model to increase the likelihood of detecting announcement effects associated with Credit Watch additions and bond rating changes. We measure the expectation of a bond rating change by comparing the yield-to-maturity on a bond of interest (Credit Watch or actual rating change), estimated from the price available just prior to the rating agency announcement, with the yield-to-maturity of a benchmark, namely the median yield to maturity of other bonds with the same bond rating.[9]

---

[7] Since our measure of the excess bond return does not control for variation in term or default premia, and default premia are positive, the expected proportion of positive window-spanning excess bond returns is actually slightly higher than 50%.

[8] We also estimated, but do not report, t-statistics based on the time-series standard deviation of the common stock prediction errors of the portfolio. The t-statistics based on the time-series standard deviation always exceed (in absolute value) the t-statistics based on the cross-sectional standard deviation.

[9] The yield-to-maturity of a rating class at a point in time is estimated from the yields-to-maturity of our sample of rerated bonds in the sixty trading days after they are rerated. A bond is used to estimate the yield-to-maturity of a rating class if its post-rating change rating class matches the pre-rating change rating class of the bond of interest, and if it trades within 10 trading days of the date on which the yield-to-maturity of the bond of interest is estimated. This procedure does not allow us to form an expectation for every announcement, hence the sample size is reduced for results based on the expectations model.

If the yield-to-maturity of a bond of interest is greater than the benchmark, we argue that investors believe that bond has greater default risk than comparable bonds. Thus, if the bond is downgraded, we classify it as an expected downgrade. If the bond is upgraded, we would classify it as an unexpected upgrade. If the bond's yield-to-maturity is lower than the benchmark, a subsequent downgrade would be classified as unexpected, while an upgrade would be considered expected. Some tests which follow use the relative size of the expectation error, defined as the yield-to-maturity of the bond of interest less the yield-to-maturity of the benchmark, divided by the yield-to-maturity of the benchmark.

We selected a price-based expectations model to capture the expectation of a rating change just prior to its announcement, because the prior literature on rating changes indicates that downgrades (upgrades) are preceded by negative (positive) excess returns for both bonds and stocks. We tested other price-based expectations models, including yield-to-maturity benchmarks based on matching rating class and duration, and matching rating class and maturity, but did not discover superior models.

III. Results

A. Standard and Poor's Credit Watch Announcements

The results for the entire sample of Credit Watch additions in Table III provide little evidence of excess bond and stock returns associated with either indicated downgrades or indicated upgrades. However, use of the expectations model increases the observed price effects considerably. For the entire sample of Credit Watch downgrades, mean and median excess bond returns are -0.35% (t-statistic of -1.37) and -0.37%, and 40.4% of the excess bond returns are positive (Z-statistic of -1.96). The mean excess stock return is -0.79% (t-statistic of -1.81). The 75 bonds of 50 firms classified as unexpected downgrades have a mean excess bond return of -1.39% (t-statistic of -3.15), with only 28% positive (Z-statistic of -3.11). The mean excess stock return for these observations is -1.78% (t-statistic of -2.63). Average excess stock and bond returns for the sample of indicated downgrades classified as expected are not reliably different from zero. Moreover, comparisons of the expected and unexpected samples suggest reliable differences between the two portfolios. For example, for all Credit Watch indicated downgrades, the difference in mean bond returns of the expected and unexpected portfolios is 1.59% with a t-statistic of 2.20. Moreover, regressions of excess bond returns on the magnitude of the expectation error indicate that the coefficient is positive (4.1) as expected and significantly different from zero with a p-value of 0.037.

Results for the noncontaminated subsample of indicated downgrades are even more supportive of price effects for unexpected announcements. Mean excess bond and stock returns are each -0.83% (t-statistics of -2.08 and -1.07) for all noncontaminated observations. Splitting the sample into ex-

Table III
Mean and Median Excess Bond and Stock Announcement Returns for Sample of Firms Placed on Standard and Poor's Credit Watch List during 1981–1983

Excess bond returns are defined as bond returns minus the risk free rate, calculated over the window spanning the announcement. The window runs from the last day on which the bond is traded before the announcement through the first day the bond is traded after the announcement. Excess stock returns are defined as market model prediction errors for the day of and the day after the announcement. t- and Z-statistics are given in parentheses directly below the mean % excess return, and the percent of excess returns > 0 respectively.

Sample	Number of Bonds	Number of Firms	Bonds Mean % Excess Return	Bonds Median % Excess Return	Bonds Percent of Excess Returns > 0	Stocks Mean % Excess Return	Stocks Median % Excess Return	Stocks Percent of Excess Returns > 0
Panel A: Indicated Downgrades								
All	215	104	−0.35 (−1.37)[a]	−0.37	40.4 (−1.96)[b]	−0.79 (−1.81)	−0.43	45.5 (−0.90)
Expected	92	54	0.20 (0.57)	−0.02	50.0 (0.00)	−0.36 (−0.76)	−0.48	45.1 (−0.70)
Unexpected	75	50	−1.39 (−3.15)	−0.87	28.0 (−3.11)	−1.78 (−2.63)	−0.91	40.0 (−1.41)
Noncontaminated	91	47	−0.83 (−2.08)	−0.82	36.2 (−1.90)	−0.83 (−1.07)	−0.23	46.8 (−0.44)
Expected	41	24	−0.02 (−0.04)	−0.13	45.8 (−0.41)	−0.05 (−0.08)	−0.23	50.0 (0.00)
Unexpected	40	26	−1.79 (−2.31)	−1.09	30.8 (−1.96)	−2.14 (−1.84)	−1.11	42.3 (−0.78)

Table III—Continued

Panel B: Indicated Upgrades

All	38	23	−0.69	0.04	52.2	−0.33	−0.03
			(−0.79)		0.21	(−0.62)	
Expected	24	16	−2.12	−0.85	31.3	−0.13	0.01
			(−2.22)		(−1.50)	(−0.21)	
Unexpected	10	8	2.25	1.13	87.5	−0.88	−0.79
			(1.53)		(2.12)	(−1.04)	
Noncontaminated	22	13	−0.15	0.08	53.8	0.44	0.01
			(−0.11)		(0.28)	(0.99)	
Expected	15	8	−2.26	−1.19	25.0	0.53	0.01
			(−1.44)		(−1.41)	(0.82)	
Unexpected	5	4	4.15	1.08	100.0	−0.22	−0.79
			(1.76)		(2.00)	(−0.43)	

50.0	(0.00)
53.3	(0.26)
25.0	(−1.41)
66.7	(1.15)
75.0	(1.41)
25.0	(−1.00)

[a] The t-statistic on the mean return is based on the cross-sectional standard deviation of the excess returns.
[b] The Z-statistic on the proportion positive is based on a binomial test of whether that proportion is > 50%.

pected and unexpected downgrades has the predicted effect for both bond and stock returns. For the unexpected sample, the average excess bond (stock) return is -1.79% (-2.14%), with a t-statistic of -2.31 (-1.84). The medians for excess bond and stock returns suggest similar conclusions.

For the indicated upgrades, comprised of 38 bonds representing 23 different firm-observations, average excess bond and stock returns are not reliably different from zero. Splitting the sample into expected and unexpected subsamples reveals some evidence of positive average excess returns for bonds in the unexpected sample, but not for the stocks. A regression of excess bond returns on the magnitude of the expectation error again produces a coefficient that is significantly greater than zero with a p-value of 0.019. Results for the noncontaminated Credit Watch upgrades are marginally significant for the bonds but these results are based on a small number of observations.

B. Moody's and Standard and Poor's Bond Rating Changes

When the sample of actual rating changes by Moody's and Standard and Poor's is analyzed, the results are difficult to interpret because of several apparent inconsistencies; for example, we observe significantly negative average excess bond and stock returns for downgrades, but weaker positive average excess bond and stock returns for upgrades. Moreover, because the expectations model does not sharpen the results as it did in the case of Credit Watch announcements, we do not present subsamples of rating changes based on expected and unexpected classifications. The results obtained from analyzing the rating changes are summarized in Table IV.

Detailed results for downgrades are reported in Table V. Announcements of rating downgrades are associated with statistically significant negative average excess bond and stock returns. For the entire sample of 785 downgrades representing 356 firm-observations, the average excess bond return is -1.27% (t-statistic of -4.33) for the window spanning return which has a median length of 4 days. These results are inconsistent with Weinstein (1977), Pinches and Singleton (1978), and Wakeman (1978), who do not find significant bond price effects associated with rating changes. Even though the average excess bond return includes some large negative individual

Table IV
Summary of Excess Return Results for Moody's and Standard and Poor's Rating Change Announcements

Sample of 841 downgrades and 292 upgrades of corporate taxable debt ratings revised by Moody's and Standard and Poor's during 1977–1982.

	Downgrades		Upgrades	
	Bonds	Stocks	Bonds	Stocks
Entire sample	Negative	Negative	Positive	Zero
Noncontaminated	Zero	Negative	Positive	Zero

Table V
Mean and Median Excess Bond and Stock Announcement Returns for Sample of Firms with Rating Downgrade Announcements by Moody's and Standard and Poor's during 1977–1982

Excess bond returns are defined as bond returns minus the risk free rate, calculated over the window spanning the rating change announcement. The window runs from the last day on which the bond is traded before the rating change announcement through the first day the bond is traded after the rating change announcement. Excess stock returns are defined as market model prediction errors for the day of and the day after the rating change announcement. t- and Z-statistics are given in parentheses below the mean % excess return and the percent of excess returns > 0.

			Bonds			Stocks		
Sample	Number of Bonds	Number of Firms	Mean % Excess Return	Median % Excess Return	Percent of Excess Returns > 0	Mean % Excess Return	Median % Excess Return	Percent of Excess Returns > 0

Panel A: Downgrades

All	785	356	−1.27 (−4.33)[a]	−0.45	41.1 (−3.37)[b]	−1.52 (−4.11)	−0.75	39.1 (−3.99)
Investment grade	638	273	−0.55 (−3.45)	−0.45	41.5 (−2.82)	−0.83 (−3.72)	−0.65	38.4 (−3.76)
Below investment grade	147	87	−3.82 (−3.22)	−0.62	40.2 (−1.82)	−4.22 (−2.95)	−2.22	40.8 (−1.61)

Panel B: Noncontaminated Downgrades

All	205	90	−0.37 (−1.16)	−0.23	45.6 (−0.84)	−1.12 (−1.82)	−1.10	30.7 (−3.62)
Investment grade	176	79	−0.09 (−0.39)	−0.09	46.8 (−0.56)	−1.06 (−2.17)	−1.06	28.6 (−3.76)
Below investment grade	29	13	−1.91 (−1.13)	−1.00	30.8 (−1.39)	−1.89 (−0.60)	−1.28	46.2 (−0.28)

[a] The t-statistic for the mean return is based on the cross-sectional standard deviation of the excess returns.
[b] The Z-statistic for the proportion positive is based on a binomial test of whether that proportion is greater than 50%.

returns,[10] the median excess bond return is still −0.45%, and the percentage of firms with positive returns is 41.1% (Z-statistic of −3.37). Over the period Day 0 to +1, the mean excess stock return for these firms is −1.52% (t-statistic of −4.11), and the median return is −0.75%, with only 39.1% of the excess stock returns positive (Z-statistic of −3.99).

The remainder of Table V provides information about certain strata of downgrades. The (pre-rating change) investment grade bonds represent 273 firm-observations and have mean and median excess bond returns of −0.55% and −0.45%. The stock of these firms loses 0.83% on average. The test statistics indicate that the negative mean excess returns are reliably different from zero for both bonds and stocks. The 87 firms below investment grade experience mean and median excess bond returns of −3.82% and −0.62%, reflecting large losses experienced by 12 of the 87 observations. Only 40.2% of the observations have positive excess bond returns. The mean and median excess stock returns for these firms are −4.22% and −2.22%. Test statistics indicate the bond and stock returns are significantly different from zero. The average excess bond and stock returns for below investment grade bonds are reliably more negative than for investment grade bonds driven in part by the number of firms with bonds losing more than 10%.

While the entire sample of downgrades provides strong evidence of bond and stock price effects, the results based on noncontaminated observations provide little evidence that those bonds experience negative average excess returns (mean of −0.37% with a t-statistic of −1.16). Paradoxically, for the same observations, the stocks experience an average excess return of −1.12% (t-statistic of −1.82). Table V also presents separate evidence for noncontaminated bond rating changes on bonds above or below investment grade. Of the 205 noncontaminated observations, 176 are bonds which were above investment grade prior to the rating change. The mean and median excess bond returns are generally close to zero for investment grade bonds. Nevertheless, firms with downgraded investment grade bonds classified as noncontaminated experience mean and median excess stock returns of −1.06% (t- and Z-statistics of −2.17 and −3.76). The below-investment grade downgrades are associated with excess stock and bond returns of approximately −1.90%, but those results are not reliably different from zero due to the large standard deviation of returns (in excess of 6%) and because of the small sample size. The difference in mean returns between noncontaminated investment grade and below-investment grade bonds of −1.82% is insignificantly different from zero.

There is some evidence of a significant positive mean excess bond return for upgrades, but there is no evidence of a significant positive mean excess stock return. Table VI contains results for upgrades of 263 bonds of 141 different firms. The mean excess bond return is 0.35% (t-statistic of 1.93). The median return is 0.36%, and 62% are positive (Z-statistic of 2.85). The

---

[10] Thirteen firms have bonds with window spanning returns below −10%, including one of −63.3%, and five in the range −30% to −45%.

Table VI
Mean and Median Excess Bond and Stock Announcement Returns for Sample of Firms with Rating Upgrade Announcements by Moody's and Standard and Poor's during 1977–1982

Excess bond returns are defined as bond returns minus the risk free rate, calculated over the window spanning the rating change announcement. The window runs from the last day on which the bond is traded before the rating change announcement through the first day the bond is traded after the rating change announcement. Excess stock returns are defined as market model prediction errors for the day of and the day after the rating change announcement. t- and Z-statistics are given in parentheses below the mean % excess return and the percent of excess returns > 0.

			Bonds			Stocks		
Sample	Number of Bonds	Number of Firms	Mean % Excess Return	Median % Excess Return	Percent of Excess Returns > 0	Mean % Excess Return	Median % Excess Return	Percent of Excess Returns > 0

Panel A: Upgrades

All	263	141	0.35 (1.93)[a]	0.36	62.0 (2.85)[b]	0.24 (1.13)	0.16	55.5 (1.28)
Investment grade	200	98	0.33 (1.49)	0.15	56.6 (1.31)	0.23 (0.97)	0.15	55.7 (1.12)
Below investment grade	63	43	0.40 (1.23)	0.59	74.4 (3.20)	0.28 (0.59)	0.17	55.0 (0.63)

Panel B: Noncontaminated Upgrades

All	66	29	0.60 (2.77)	0.71	72.4 (2.41)	−0.07 (−0.16)	0.02	55.2 (0.56)
Investment grade	54	22	0.55 (2.16)	0.70	72.7 (2.13)	0.09 (0.25)	0.02	59.1 (0.85)
Below investment grade	12	7	0.75 (1.69)	0.71	71.4 (1.13)	−0.59 (−0.38)	−0.91	42.9 (−0.38)

[a] The t-statistic for the mean return is based on the cross-sectional standard deviation of the excess returns.
[b] The Z-statistic for the proportion positive is based on a binomial test of whether that proportion is greater than 50%.

mean excess stock return is 0.24% (*t*-statistic of 1.13). The differences between investment and below-investment grade bond returns are small.

Of the 263 upgrades, 66 are classified as noncontaminated. The mean and median excess return estimates for the noncontaminated upgrades are 0.60% (*t*-statistic is 2.77) and 0.71%, with 72.4% excess returns being positive (*Z*-statistic is 2.41). Thus, unlike downgrades, the noncontaminated upgrade sample is more supportive of a positive mean bond price reaction to the rating change announcement. There is no evidence of positive mean excess stock returns for upgraded bonds classified as noncontaminated.

IV. Cross-Sectional Analysis of Excess Bond Returns

We estimate multivariate regressions to try to explain cross-sectional variation in the window-spanning excess bond returns. Separate regressions are estimated for downgrades and upgrades, and for contaminated and noncontaminated observations. The regressions are based on individual bonds (not firm-observations) because the independent variables are primarily bond characteristics, not firm characteristics. Consequently, there is probably some cross-sectional dependence in the residuals of the regression. The following variables are included in the regression:

a) a cardinal variable representing the number of grades changed (new rating less old rating, measured on a scale of 28 for rating AAA to 1 for rating D);
b) the magnitude of the yield-to-maturity expectation error (defined previously);
c) a dummy variable set equal to one if the rating change is a resolution of a Standard and Poor's Credit Watch Listing;
d) a dummy variable set equal to one if the rating change moves the bond into or out of investment grade;
e) a dummy variable set equal to one if the rating change occurs after December 31, 1980; and
f) the time lapse since a similar rating change by the other agency.

The excess bond return should depend positively on the number of grades changed by the rerating, and should be closer to zero for resolutions of a Credit Watch Listing. The yield-to-maturity expectation error is designed to capture the degree of the market's expectation of the rating change—stronger (meaning larger in absolute value) excess bond returns should be observed for reratings that are more unexpected. If there are separate clienteles for investment and below-investment grade bonds, rating changes that cross the investment/below-investment grade boundary should result in stronger excess returns. The dummy variable for pre- and post-1980 splits the sample period approximately in half because the financial press conjectures that competition forced rating agencies to begin monitoring companies more closely in the early 1980's.[11] Post-1980 rating change announcements are expected to result in stronger price effects. The time lapse variable tests whether a change by one rating agency has the same impact if it follows a similar rating change by the other agency. Bond ratings which immediately follow a similar rating by the other agency are not expected to produce strong excess bond returns.

The results in Table VII indicate little consistency other than the finding that the number of grades is significantly related to the excess bond return in the downgrade and upgrade sample for the contaminated observations. In the regression using contaminated downgrade observations, the t-statistic on the number of grades changed is 16.17 and the coefficient of 1.87 implies that holding all else constant, the marginal effect of an additional one grade decline (e.g., from AA + to AA) on average results in a 1.87% decline in the value of the bonds. The variable PREV is also significant and has the predicted sign, indicating less of a price impact when there was a recent prior rating change on the same company by the other agency. The adjusted-R^2 of the regression is 37.7%. While the number of grades changed is significant in the regression using contaminated upgrades, the explanatory power is much lower (t-statistic of 2.32) and no other variable is significant. While the results on the contaminated observations do not reveal whether the excess returns around the time of bond rating change announcements result from the rating change or the contaminating announcement, at a minimum the evidence on #GRADES suggests that rating agencies respond relatively quickly to some events. In the regressions using noncontaminated observations, not a single variable is both significant and has the predicted sign.

V. Summary and Conclusion

Excess bond returns for additions to the Credit Watch List are generally insignificant until the expected rating changes are excluded. Examination of noncontaminated observations which are classified as unexpected, generally increases the measured bond and stock price effects of the Credit Watch announcements. In addition, statistically significant average excess bond and stock returns to announcements of downgrades of straight debt are observed, with less reliable effects for upgrades. Moreover for downgrades, the average excess bond returns are stronger for below investment grade bonds than for investment grade bonds. When observations with concurrent disclosures are eliminated, the negative average excess returns associated with downgrades disappear, but those for stocks remain. For upgrades, significant bond price

---

[11] See, for example, "Moody's Dominance in Municipals Market is Slowly Being Eroded", *Wall Street Journal*, November 2, 1981, pp. 1 and 20. In addition, it is likely that the start of Standard and Poor's Credit Watch List was a response to the long standing charge that rating agencies reacted slowly to changes in default risk.

Table VII
Regression Tests on Excess Bond Announcement Returns for Bonds with Rating Changes by Moody's or Standard and Poor's during 1977–1982

$$BER_j = \beta 0 + \beta 1\, (\#GRADES_j) + \beta 2\, (YTMERR_j) + \beta 3\, (CR\ WATCH_j) + \beta 4\, (INV\ GRADE_j) + \beta 5\, (PRE/POST_j) + \beta 6\, (PREV_j) + e_j$$

BER_j is the window-spanning excess return on bond j, defined as the raw return on bond j less the risk free rate, calculated over the window spanning the rating change announcement. $\#GRADES_j$ is the number of grades changed (new rating less old rating)—a cardinal variable measured on a scale of 28 (for rating AAA) to 1 (for rating D). Since some of the 10 classes (AAA to D) have three grades, each class is assigned three numbers. Classes without grades (D, C, CC, CCC, AAA, and all Moody's classes before April 20, 1982) are assigned the midpoint of the three numbers. $YTMERR_j$ is a yield-to-maturity expectation error designed to capture the market's expectation of the rating change. $CRWATCH_j$ is a dummy variable set equal to one if the rating change is a resolution of Standard and Poor's Credit Watch, zero otherwise. $INV\ GRADE_j$ is a dummy variable set equal to one if the rating change moves a bond into investment grade (BBB, or above) from below, or out of investment grade from above, zero otherwise. $PRE/POST_j$ is a dummy variable set equal to one if the rating change occurs after December 31, 1980, zero otherwise. $PREV_j$ is the natural log of the reciprocal of the maximum number of days since the previous rating change in the same direction by the other agency. The number of days is set equal to 60 if both reratings are within four days (the average return window length), if the previous rating change by the other agency was not in the same direction, or if the previous rating change occurred more than 60 days previously.

Panel A: Downgrades

Predicted Sign	INTERCEPT	#GRADES (+)	YTMERR (+)	CRWATCH (+)	INV GRADE (−)	PRE/POST (−)	PREV (+)	Adj-R^2	Number of Obs.	F-Stat
Noncontaminated observations										
Estimated coefficient	0.72	0.03	−1.34	0.32	0.65	−0.33	0.14	−2.90	177	0.17
t-statistic	(0.27)	(0.10)	(−0.51)	(0.37)	(0.63)	(−0.64)	(0.22)			
Mean of variable	1.00	−1.70	0.01	0.08	0.05	0.72	−4.01			
Standard deviation of variable	0.00	0.79	0.09	0.27	0.22	0.45	0.38			
Contaminated observations										
Estimated coefficient	5.95	1.87	−2.68	0.78	1.16	0.42	0.97	37.70	472	48.50
t-statistic	(3.91)	(16.17)	(−1.56)	(1.12)	(1.36)	(0.92)	(2.68)			
Mean of variable	1.00	−2.19	0.02	0.10	0.07	0.69	−3.88			
Standard deviation of variable	0.00	1.83	0.12	0.30	0.25	0.46	0.57			

Table VII—*Continued*

Panel B: Upgrades

Predicted Sign	INTERCEPT	#GRADES	YTMERR	CRWATCH	INV GRADE	PRE/POST	PREV	Adj-R^2	Number of Obs.	F-Stat
		(+)	(+)	(−)	(+)	(+)	(−)			
Noncontaminated observations										
Estimated coefficient	0.35	0.14	−8.90	0.46	NA	0.31	NA	8.20	46	2.00
t-statistic	(0.58)	(0.49)	(−2.42)	(0.66)	NA	(0.62)	NA			
Mean of variable	1.00	1.74	−0.01	0.15	NA	0.52	−4.09			
Standard deviation of variable	0.00	0.80	0.06	0.36	NA	0.51	0.00			
Contaminated observations										
Estimated coefficient	2.54	0.40	0.29	1.94	1.32	−0.34	0.78	5.70	153	2.50
t-statistic	(0.95)	(2.32)	(0.20)	(1.50)	(1.28)	(−0.79)	(1.20)			
Mean of variable	1.00	2.16	−0.05	0.04	0.05	0.47	−4.01			
Standard deviation of variable	0.00	1.27	0.14	0.19	0.21	0.50	0.38			

effects are observed for the noncontaminated sample, but no stock price effect is detected.

There are some inconsistencies in the results; in particular, we find asymmetric results with respect to rating change downgrades and upgrades. For example, we observe significantly negative average excess bond and stock returns for downgrades, but weaker positive average excess bond and stock returns for upgrades. When we examine the noncontaminated samples the asymmetries disappear in the bond results (or if anything, they reverse, that is, there is a greater absolute effect for the upgrades than downgrades). The asymmetry persists for stocks in the noncontaminated subsample. However, we do find symmetric results for the excess bond returns of indicated downgrades and upgrades for additions to the Credit Watch List, especially when we control for prior expectations. Despite the inconsistencies, our overall conclusion is that there are both bond and stock price effects associated with announcements of additions to the Credit Watch list, and with announcements of actual rating changes by Moody's and Standard and Poor's.

REFERENCES

Grier, P. and S. Katz, 1976, The differential effects of bond rating changes on industrial and public utility bonds by maturity, *Journal of Business* 49, 226–239.

Handjinicolaou, G. and A. Kalay, 1984, Wealth redistributions or changes in firm value: An analysis of returns to bondholders and stockholders around dividend announcements, *Journal of Financial Economics* 14, 35–63.

Holthausen, R. and R. Leftwich, 1986, The effect of bond rating changes on common stock prices, *Journal of Financial Economics* 17, 57–89.

Ingram, R., L. Brooks and R. Copeland, 1983, The information content of municipal bond rating changes: A note, *Journal of Finance* 38, 997–1003.

Katz, S., 1974, The price adjustment process of bonds to rating reclassifications: A test of bond market efficiency, *Journal of Finance* 29, 551–559.

Pinches, G. and J. Singleton, 1978, The adjustment of stock prices to bond rating changes, *Journal of Finance* 33, 29–44.

Stickel, S., 1986, The effect of preferred stock rating changes on preferred and common stock prices, *Journal of Accounting and Economics* 8, 197–216.

Wakeman, L., 1978, Bond rating agencies and the capital markets, Working paper, University of Rochester, Rochester NY.

Weinstein, M., 1977, The effect of a rating change announcement on bond price, *Journal of Financial Economics* 5, 329–350.

Financial Ratios and the Probabilistic Prediction of Bankruptcy

JAMES A. OHLSON*

1. Introduction

This paper presents some empirical results of a study predicting corporate failure as evidenced by the event of bankruptcy. There have been a fair number of previous studies in this field of research; the more notable published contributions are Beaver [1966; 1968a; 1968b], Altman [1968; 1973], Altman and Lorris [1976], Altman and McGough [1974], Altman, Haldeman, and Narayanan [1977], Deakin [1972], Libby [1975], Blum [1974], Edmister [1972], Wilcox [1973], Moyer [1977], and Lev [1971]. Two unpublished papers by White and Turnbull [1975a; 1975b] and a paper by Santomero and Vinso [1977] are of particular interest as they appear to be the first studies which logically and systematically develop probabilistic estimates of failure. The present study is similar to the latter studies, in that the methodology is one of maximum likelihood estimation of the so-called conditional logit model.

The data set used in this study is from the seventies (1970–76). I know of only three corporate failure research studies which have examined data from this period. One is a limited study by Altman and McGough [1974] in which only failed firms were drawn from the period 1970–73 and only one type of classification error (misclassification of failed firms) was analyzed. Moyer [1977] considered the period 1965–75, but the sample of bankrupt firms was unusually small (twenty-seven firms). The

---

* Associate Professor, University of California, Berkeley. I gratefully acknowledge the financial support from the Wells Fargo Bank. My thanks are also due to R. Wagner and R. Benin, who provided able and valuable assistance in the course of the project. G. Feltham, R. Hamilton, V. Anderson, W. Beaver, and R. Holland supplied valuable comments on earlier versions of this paper. [Accepted for publication March 1979.]

third study, by Altman, Haldeman, and Narayanan [1977], which "updates" the original Altman [1968] study, basically considers data from the period 1969 to 1975. Their sample was based on fifty-three failed firms and about the same number of nonfailed firms. In contrast, my study relies on observations from 105 bankrupt firms and 2,058 nonbankrupt firms. Although the other three studies differ from the present one so far as methodology and objectives are concerned, it is, nevertheless, interesting and useful to compare their results with those presented in this paper.

Another distinguishing feature of the present study which I should stress is that, contrary to almost all previous studies, the data for failed firms were not derived from *Moody's Manual*.[1] The data were obtained instead from 10-K financial statements as reported at the time. This procedure has one important advantage: the reports indicate at what point in time they were released to the public, and one can therefore check whether the company entered bankruptcy prior to or after the date of release. Previous studies have not explicitly considered this timing issue. Some studies, but by no means all, seem implicitly to presume that a report is available at the fiscal year-end date. The latter may or may not be appropriate, depending on the purpose of the study. However, if the purpose is one of investigating pure forecasting relationships, as is the case in this study, then the latter procedure is inadequate. This follows because it is possible that a company files for bankruptcy at some point in time after the fiscal year date, but prior to releasing the financial statements. This is not a trivial problem and neglecting this possibility may lead to "back-casting" for many of the failed firms.

The major findings of the study can be summarized briefly. First, it was possible to identify four basic factors as being statistically significant in affecting the probability of failure (within one year). These are: (i) the size of the company; (ii) a measure(s) of the financial structure; (iii) a measure(s) of performance; (iv) a measure(s) of current liquidity (the evidence regarding this factor is not as clear as compared to cases (i)–(iii)). Second, previous studies appear to have overstated the predictive (in the sense of forecasting) power of models developed and tested. The point of concern is the one alluded to above, that is, if one employs predictors derived from statements which were released after the date of bankruptcy, then the evidence indicates that it will be easier to "predict" bankruptcy. However, even if one allows for this factor, for the sample of firms used in this study, the prediction error-rate is larger in comparison to the rate reported in the original Altman [1968] study as well as most other studies using data drawn from periods prior to 1970. More important, the prediction error-rate is also larger than the one reported in Altman et al. [1977]. On the other hand, the Altman and McGough [1974]

---

[1] The only exception appears to be the Altman and McGough [1974] study. Altman et al. [1977] do not describe how they derived their data.

and Moyer [1977] studies report significantly larger error-rates, which are comparable to those found in this study. I have not been able completely to account for this most significant difference in the error-rates reported here, in Altman and McGough [1974], and in Moyer [1977], as compared to Altman et al. [1977]. (Any period dependence should after all be relatively minor.)

The model(s) are relatively simple to apply and may be of use in practical applications. The data requirements are such that all of the predictors are easily retrieved from the *Compustat* file. A potential disadvantage is that the model does not utilize any market transactions (price) data of the firms. One may, of course, expect that the predictive power of the model could be enhanced by incorporating such data.[2]

However, one might ask a basic and possibly embarrassing question: why forecast bankruptcy? This is a difficult question, and no answer or justification is given here. It could, perhaps, be argued that we are dealing with a problem of "obvious" practical interest. This is questionable since real-world problems concern themselves with choices which have a richer set of possible outcomes. No decision problem I can think of has a payoff space which is partitioned naturally into the binary status bankruptcy versus nonbankruptcy. (Even in the case of a "simple" loan decision, the payoff configuration is much more complex.) Existing empirical studies reflect this problem in that there is no consensus on what constitutes "failure," with definitions varying significantly and arbitrarily across studies. In other words, the dichotomy bankruptcy versus no bankruptcy is, at the most, a very crude approximation of the payoff space of some hypothetical decision problem. It follows that it is essentially a futile exercise to try to establish the relative decision usefulness of alternative predictive systems. Accordingly, I have not concerned myself with how bankruptcy (and/or failure) "ought" to be defined; I also have refrained from making inferences regarding the relative usefulness of alternative models, ratios, and predictive systems (e.g., univariate versus multivariate). Most of the analysis should simply be viewed as descriptive statistics—which may, to some extent, include estimated prediction error-rates—and no "theories" of bankruptcy or usefulness of financial ratios are tested. Even so, there are a large number of difficult statistical and methodological problems which need to be discussed. Many important problems pertaining to the development of data for bankrupt firms have gone mostly unnoticed in the literature.

2. Some Comments Regarding Methodology and Data Collection

The econometric methodology of conditional logit analysis was chosen to avoid some fairly well known problems associated with Multivariate

---

[2] I am currently undertaking work in this direction. I should note further that the use of price data implicitly is another way of using more information. Hence, it can also be viewed as another way of indirect use of accounting data.

Discriminant Analysis (*MDA*, for short). The *MDA* approach has been the most popular technique for bankruptcy studies using vectors of predictors. Among some of the problems with these studies are:[3] (*i*) There are certain statistical requirements imposed on the distributional properties of the predictors. For example, the variance–covariance matrices of the predictors should be the same for both groups (failed and nonfailed firms); moreover, a requirement of normally distributed predictors certainly mitigates against the use of dummy independent variables. A violation of these conditions, it could perhaps be argued, is unimportant (or simply irrelevant) if the only purpose of the model is to develop a discriminating device. Although this may be a valid point, it is nevertheless clear that this perspective limits the scope of the investigation. Under many circumstances, it is of interest to go through more traditional econometric analysis and test variables for statistical significance, etc. (*ii*) The output of the application of an *MDA* model is a score which has little intuitive interpretation, since it is basically an ordinal ranking (discriminatory) device. For decision problems such that a misclassification structure is an inadequate description of the payoff partition, the score is not directly relevant.[4] If, however, prior probabilistics of the two groups are specified, then it is possible to derive posterior probabilities of failure. But, this Bayesian revision process will be invalid or lead to poor approximations unless the assumptions of normality, etc. are satisfied. (*iii*) There are also certain problems related to the "matching" procedures which have typically been used in *MDA*. Failed and nonfailed firms are matched according to criteria such as size and industry, and these tend to be somewhat arbitrary. It is by no means obvious what is really gained or lost by different matching procedures, including no matching at all. At the very least, it would seem to be more fruitful actually to include variables as predictors rather than to use them for matching purposes.

The use of conditional logit analysis, on the other hand, essentially avoids all of the problems discussed with respect to *MDA*. The fundamental estimation problem can be reduced simply to the following statement: given that a firm belongs to some prespecified population, what is the probability that the firm fails within some prespecified time period? No assumptions have to be made regarding prior probabilities of bankruptcy and/or the distribution of predictors. These are the major advantages. The statistical significance of the different predictors are obtained from asymptotic (large sample) theory. To be sure, as is the case in any parametric analysis, a model must be specified, so there is always room for misspecification of the basic probability model. (Al-

---

[3] See also Eisenbeis [1977] and Joy and Tollefson [1975] for extensive discussions.

[4] The payoff partition will be inadequate if it is not feasible to define a utility function over the two types of classification errors. Any economic decision problem would typically require a richer state partition.

though it is possible to test for misspecification, it is beyond the confines of this paper to discuss and report on the results of such tests.)

Regardless of the virtues of probabilistic prediction over *MDA*, there are important problems with respect to data collection of bankrupt firms which deserve preliminary discussion. This matter was alluded to in the introduction. Realistic evaluation of a model's predictive relationships requires that the predictors are (would have been) available for use prior to the event of failure. Now, it is of course true that annual reports are not publicly available at the end of the fiscal year, since the financial statements must be audited. Previous studies have not mentioned this problem, at least not explicitly. This is not surprising since most previous studies have used *Moody's Manual* to derive the pertinent financial ratios, and the *Manual* does not indicate at what point in time the data were made available. Another reason is that not all studies have been concerned with strict forecasting relationships. That is, whether accounting statements were publicly available or not had no direct bearing upon the subject at hand. One such case is Beaver [1968a; 1968b], who studied whether financial ratios will reflect impending failure. The timing issue can be expected to be serious for firms which have a large probability of failure in the first place. Such firms are in poor shape and the auditing process could be particularly problematic and time-consuming. Thus, it is somewhat risky to assume that financial reports were available, say, three months after the end of the fiscal year. There are other disadvantages associated with *Moody's Manual*. The data are often highly condensed, and it is generally complicated, if not impossible, to reconstruct actual balance sheets and income statements.[5] Again, firms which are in poor shape are particularly difficult, since one can never be sure whether some of the many possible special items have been given special treatment in *Moody's* tabulation.[6] Moreover, it should be noted that the comparative schedules over the different years are ex-post reconstructions, and items from previous years may have been restated and may differ from the amounts originally reported. At a nontrivial cost, this problem can be circumvented if one uses several annual editions of *Moody's* for the same firm.

Clearly, much can be gained by improving the data base. The evaluation of the predictive classification power of a model should be more realistic, and, more important here, the same should apply for standard tests of statistical significance. This is not to suggest that it is important to have "super accurate" data for purposes of developing (as opposed to evaluating) a discriminatory device. It might well be that the predictive quality of any model is reasonably robust across a variety of data-gathering and estimating procedures.

---

[5] The conclusion is based on a few "case studies."

[6] The summaries of taxes (loss carry-forward, in particular) and measures of operating performance appear to be the most difficult items to deal with.

3. Collection of Financial Statement Data

The collection of data for bankrupt firms requires a definition of failure and specification of the population from which firms are drawn. In this study, the definition is purely legalistic. The failed firms must have filed for bankruptcy in the sense of Chapter X, Chapter XI, or some other notification indicating bankruptcy proceedings.[7] The population boundaries are restricted by: (*i*) the period from 1970 to 1976; (*ii*) the equity of the company had to have been traded on some stock exchange or over-the-counter (*OTC*) market; (*iii*) the company must be classified as an industrial. The first criterion was chosen simply because it is the most recent period, and the cutoff point of 1970 was selected as a matter of practicality. The second criterion excludes small or privately held corporations. This is crucial, since otherwise the use of *Compustat* firms as a source of nonbankrupt firms would be precluded. The third criterion excludes utilities, transportation companies, and financial services companies (banks, insurance, brokerage, REITs, etc.). Companies in these industries are structurally different, have a different bankruptcy environment, and appropriate data are, in some cases, difficult to obtain.

The following procedures were used to generate a list of failed firms satisfying the inclusion criteria. (1) A primary listing of failed firms was tabulated from the *Wall Street Journal Index* (*W.S.J.I.*). Type and date of bankruptcy were recorded. If the name of the company indicated that the firm in question was a nonindustrial, then it was excluded. (2) A secondary listing of firms was tabulated by excluding all firms on the primary listing which had not been traded on one of the stock exchanges (or *OTC*) during the three-year period prior to the date of bankruptcy. If a company could be traced to one of the exchanges, then the exchange was recorded. This kind of information was derived from various stock guides issued by *Moody's* and *Standard and Poor's*. Of course, as a practical matter, it was assumed that a stock had not been traded if no evidence could be found to that effect. (3) Attempts were made to augment the secondary listing by examining other miscellaneous sources of data. This led to some relatively minor additions to the listing of bankrupt firms. However, in tracing bankrupt firms it seemed to me that very few firms were omitted from the *W.S.J.I.*, so long as the firms satisfied the inclusion criteria.

The next phase was one of actually collecting financial data for the bankrupt firms. The objective was to obtain three years of data prior to the date of bankruptcy. Each report had to include the balance sheet, income statement, funds statement, and the accountants' report. In case the last available accountants' report explicitly stated that the company had filed for bankruptcy, then a fourth report was collected. All reports were retrieved from the Stanford University Business School Library,

---

[7] See Altman [1971] for a discussion of the difference between different types of bankruptcy proceedings.

TABLE 1
Bankrupt Firms: Year, Type of Bankruptcy, and Exchange Listing

Type	1970	1971	1972	1973	1974	1975	1976	Totals
Chapter X	0	2	2	1	1	0	0	6
Chapter XI	1	4	14	20	18	14	14	85
Other or unknown	0	0	5	6	0	1	2	14
Totals	1	6	21	27	19	15	16	105

New York Stock Exchange	8
American Stock Exchange	43
Other*	54

* Over-the-counter market or regional exchange.

which has an extensive microfilm file of 10–K reports. The relevant parts of the 10–K reports were photocopied and subsequently coded. Some firms had to be deleted from the sample because no report whatsoever was available, but these were few. Other firms, again very few, were deleted because they were corporate shells and had no sales. On the other hand, no firm was deleted because of its young (exchange) age, and some firms had only one set of reports.

In the process of coding items from the annual reports, I noted that all but one firm which went bankrupt in 1970, and some of the 1971 firms, had no funds statement in their annual report. This was not true for firms which filed for bankruptcy in subsequent years. Similar observations are applicable for firms on the *Compustat* file, although omissions were much less frequent. The SEC did not require a funds statement until the early seventies.[8] I decided that firms without a funds statement should be deleted, since it would have been impossible otherwise to use ratios derived from the funds statement.

The final sample was made up of 105 bankrupt firms. Basic information regarding year, exchange, and type of bankruptcy is given in table 1. As one would suspect, relatively few firms were listed on the NYSE, compared to the other two categorizations. Furthermore, Chapter XI bankruptcy was apparently much more frequent than Chapter X.

I noted that while eighteen of the 105 firms (17 percent) had accountants' reports which disclosed that the company had entered bankruptcy, the fiscal year-end was prior to the date of bankruptcy. These reports were deleted and reports from the previous fiscal year were substituted. As a consequence, the average lead time between the date of the fiscal year of the last relevant report and bankruptcy is quite long, approximately thirteen months. Table 2 shows the entire frequency distribution. This lead time is quite a bit longer, compared to what has been reported in previous studies. A cursory review of the data indicated that the time lag between the fiscal year-end and the date of the accountants' report

---

[8] Funds statements have been required since September 30, 1971; see *APB opinion No. 19*.

TABLE 2
Lead Times of Last Set of Annual Reports (Not Indicating Bankruptcy) Prior to Bankruptcy*

Months	3	3.5	4.5	5.5	6	6.5	7	7.5	8	8.5	9	9.5	10	10.5	11	11.5	12	12.5	13	13.5	14	14.5	15	15.5
Number of Reports	2	1	1	1	3	4	5	2	2	4	2	4	3	4	4	7	3	2	2	2	3	8	15	4
Months	16	16.5	17	17.5	18	18.5	19.5	20	20.5	21.5	23	23.5	25	26	27.5	28	33.5							
Number of Reports	4	4	3	1	1	1	1	1	2	1	1	1	1	2	1	1	1							

* Mean: 13 months; mode: 14.5 months; median: 12.5 months.

can be quite long. In fact, for the group of eighteen firms, the lag was always longer in the year which was closer to bankruptcy. The following example is reasonably representative. Hers Apparel Ind. filed for bankruptcy May 31, 1974; the accountants' report for the fiscal year-end February 28, 1974 is dated July 19, 1974. In the previous year, the report was dated April 24, 1973. Note that the lead time between fiscal year date of last "relevant" report and date of bankruptcy is approximately thirteen months in this case (i.e., April 24, 1973 to May 31, 1974). In 1974, it took approximately four and one-half months to complete the audit. (I found many cases which exceeded four and one-half months.) There were also a number of firms for which additional relevant reports could have existed. Under such circumstances, search procedures were attempted, but with little success. For most of these cases, it appears as if the firms simply never filed any additional reports with the S.E.C. This is by no means implausible, since firms can apply for extension of their deadline, and after bankruptcy has actually occurred there may simply be no point in going through an audit and preparing a standard annual report. Of course, it is also possible that additional reports did exist, but never got to the Stanford University Library. In order to play it "safe," I decided that no firm was to be deleted because reports were potentially missing. As a consequence, any evaluation of a model based on this data set probably understates the predictive classification performance.

A sample of nonbankrupt firms was obtained from the *Compustat* tape. Ideally, all reports for all firms satisfying the population constraints should have been included as a control sample. However, this was deemed to be too costly and impractical (due to core memory constraints). I decided instead that every firm on the *Compustat* tape (excluding utilities, etc.) should contribute with only one vector of data points; the year of any given firm's report was obtained by random procedure. This led to 2,058 vectors of data points for nonbankrupt firms. The breakdown into exchange listings was as follows: New York Stock Exchange = 42%, American Stock Exchange = 32%, Other = 26%.

4. A Probabilistic Model of Bankruptcy

Let $\mathbf{X}_i$ denote a vector of predictors for the ith observation; let β be a vector of unknown parameters, and let $P(\mathbf{X}_i, \beta)$ denote the probability of bankruptcy for any given $\mathbf{X}_i$ and β. P is some probability function, $0 \le P \le 1$. The logarithm of the likelihood of any specific outcomes, as reflected by the binary sample space of bankruptcy versus nonbankruptcy, is then given by:

$$l(\beta) \equiv \sum_{i \in S_1} \log P(\mathbf{X}_i, \beta) + \sum_{i \in S_2} \log(1 - P(\mathbf{X}_i, \beta)),$$

where S_1 is the (index) set of bankrupt firms and S_2 is the set of nonbankrupt firms. For any specified function P, the maximum likelihood estimates of $\beta_1, \beta_2 \cdots$, are obtained by solving:

$$\max_{\beta} l(\beta).$$

In the absence of a positive theory of bankruptcy, there is no easy solution to the problem of selecting an appropriate class of functions P. As a practical matter, all one can do is to choose on the basis of computational and interpretative simplicity. One such function is the logistic function:

$$P = (1 + \exp\{-y_i\}^{-1}), \quad \text{where } y_i \equiv \sum_j \beta_j X_{ij} = \boldsymbol{\beta}'\mathbf{X}_i.$$

There are two implications which should be mentioned. First, P is increasing in y; second, y is equal to $\log[P/(1-P)]$. The model is thus relatively easy to interpret, and this is its main (and perhaps only) virtue.[9]

5. Ratios and Basic Results

For purposes of the present report, no attempt was made to develop any "new or exotic" ratios. The criterion for choosing among different predictors was simplicity. The first three models estimated, Models 1–3, were composed of an intercept and the following nine independent variables:[10]

1. $SIZE = \log(\text{total assets/GNP price-level index})$. The index assumes a base value of 100 for 1968. Total assets are as reported in dollars. The index year is as of the year prior to the year of the balance sheet date. The procedure assures a real-time implementation of the model. The log transform has an important implication. Suppose two firms, A and B, have a balance sheet date in the same year, then the sign of $P_A - P_B$ is independent of the price-level index. (This will not follow unless the log transform is applied.) The latter is, of course, a desirable property.
2. $TLTA$ = Total liabilities divided by total assets.
3. $WCTA$ = Working capital divided by total assets.
4. $CLCA$ = Current liabilities divided by current assets.
5. $OENEG$ = One if total liabilities exceeds total assets, zero otherwise.
6. $NITA$ = Net income divided by total assets.
7. $FUTL$ = Funds provided by operations divided by total liabilities.

---

[9] See McFadden [1973] for a comprehensive analysis of the logit model.

[10] No attempt was made to select predictors on the basis of rigorous theory. To put it mildly, the state of the art seems to preclude such an approach. (The first six predictors were partially selected simply because they appear to be the ones most frequently mentioned in the literature.)

8. *INTWO* = One if net income was negative for the last two years, zero otherwise.
9. $CHIN = (NI_t - NI_{t-1})/(|NI_t| + |NI_{t-1}|)$, where NI_t is net income for the most recent period. The denominator acts as a level indicator. The variable is thus intended to measure change in net income. (The measure appears to be due to McKibben [1972]).

Previous studies, "common sense," and perhaps even theory, would suggest that the sign of the coefficients of the different ratios should be as follows:

Positive	Negative	Indeterminate
TLTA	SIZE	OENEG
CLCA	WCTA	
INTWO	NITA	
	FUTL	
	CHIN	

OENEG serves as a discontinuity correction for *TLTA*. A corporation which has a negative book value is a special case. Survival would tend to depend upon many complicated factors, and the effect of the extreme leverage position needs to be corrected. A positive sign would suggest almost certain bankruptcy, while a negative sign suggests that the situation is very bad indeed (due to *TLTA*), but not *that* bad. (Granted, this is a very heuristic procedure to capture something very complicated.)

A "profile" analysis of the data supports the hypotheses regarding the signs. Table 3 shows the means and standard deviations of the predictors for three sets of data: one year prior to bankruptcy, nonbankruptcy firms, and two years prior to bankruptcy. The results are hardly surprising. The ratios deteriorate as one moves from nonbankrupt firms to two years prior to bankruptcy to one year prior to bankruptcy. Although the data

TABLE 3
Profile Analysis

Variable	One Year Prior to Bankruptcy mean	stdv	Nonbankrupt Firms mean	stdv	Two Years Prior to Bankruptcy mean	stdv
SIZE	12.134	1.38	13.26	1.570	12.234	1.414
TLTA	0.905	0.637	0.488	0.181	0.718	0.311
WCTA	0.041	0.608	0.310	0.182	0.157	0.320
CLCA	1.32	2.52	0.525	0.740	0.814	0.671
NITA	−0.208	0.411	0.0526	0.0756	−0.052	0.155
FUTL	−0.117	0.421	0.2806	0.360	−0.0096	0.332
INTWO	0.390	0.488	0.0432	0.2034	0.180	0.384
OENEG	0.18	0.385	0.0044	0.0660	0.060	0.237
CHIN	−0.322	0.644	0.0379	0.458	0.00308	0.8673
N	105		2,058		100	

and ratios are not quite comparable with those of Beaver [1966], the results here are quite similar to the profiles he presented [1966, p. 82]. It should also be noted that the standard deviations of the predictors (except for size) are larger for year-1 firms, compared to nonbankrupt firms. These differences are significant at a 5-percent level or better. Hence, as discussed in Section 2, standard assumptions of *MDA* are unlikely to be valid.

Three sets of estimates were computed for the logit model using the predictors previously described. Model 1 predicts bankruptcy within one year; Model 2 predicts bankruptcy within two years, given that the company did not fail within the subsequent year; Model 3 predicts bankruptcy within one or two years. A summary of the results are shown in table 4. This table indicates that all of the signs were as predicted for Model 1. Only three of the coefficients (*WCTA*, *CLCA*, and *INTWO*) have t-statistics less than two, so the others are all statistically significant at a respectable level. This includes *SIZE*, which has a relatively large t-statistic. An overall measure of goodness-of-fit is given by the likelihood ratio index. The index is similar to a R^2 in the sense that it equals one in case of a perfect fit, and zero if the estimated coefficients are zero.[11] For Model 1, the ratio is 84 percent, and this is significant at an extremely low α-level. The statistic "Percent Correctly Predicted" equals 96.12 percent; it is tabulated on the basis of a cutoff point of .5. That is, classify the company if and only if $P(\mathbf{X}_i, \hat{\beta}) > 0.5$. Whether this is a "good" or "bad" result is not easy to answer at this stage, so further discussion regarding the model's predictive power is postponed until the next section. At this point, we can note that if all firms were classified as nonbankrupt, then 91.15 percent would be correctly classified (2,058/(105 + 2,058)). Thus the marginal (unconditional, prior) probability of bankruptcy is an important quantity in the above type of statistic. Further, there is no apparent reason why .5 is an appropriate cutoff point, since it presumes implicitly that the loss function is symmetric across the two types of classification errors.

Table 5 shows the correlation coefficients of the estimation errors in Model 1. The coefficients of the financial state variables (variables 1–4 in the table) are uncorrelated with those of the performance variables (variables 5–9). Hence, both sets of variables contribute significantly and independently of each other to the likelihood function. This strongly supports the contention that both sets of variables are important in establishing the predictive relationship.

Models 2 and 3 have somewhat weaker goodness-of-fit statistics, which

---

[11] The likelihood ratio index is defined to be:

1 − log likelihood at convergence/log likelihood at zero.

The index will take on the value of one in case of a perfect fit, since log likelihood at convergence then equals zero. If there is no fit, then obviously the index equals zero. See McFadden [1973] for further details.

TABLE 4
Prediction Results

	Variable								
	SIZE	TLTA	WCTA	CLCA	NITA	FUTL	INTWO	OENEG	CHIN	CONST
Model 1
Estimates	−.407	6.03	−1.43	.0757	−2.37	−1.83	0.285	−1.72	−.521	−1.32
t-statistics	−3.78	6.61	−1.89	.761	−1.85	−2.36	.812	−2.450	−2.21	−.970
Model 2
Estimates	−.519	4.76	−1.71	−.297	−2.74	−2.18	−.780	−1.98	.4218	1.84
t-statistics	−5.34	5.46	−1.78	−.733	−1.80	−2.73	−1.92	−2.42	2.10	1.38
Model 3
Estimates	−.478	5.29	−.990	.062	−4.62	−2.25	−.521	−1.91	.212	1.13
t-statistics	−6.23	7.72	−1.74	.738	−3.60	−3.42	−1.73	−3.11	1.30	1.15

	Likelihood Ratio Index	Percent Correctly Predicted
Model 1	0.8388	96.12
Model 2	0.7970	95.55
Model 3	0.719	92.84

TABLE 5
Correlation Matrix of (Estimated) Estimation Errors in Model 1

	SIZE	TLTA	WCTA	CLCA	OENEG	NITA	FUTL	INTWO	CHIN
SIZE	1	−.28	*	*	*	*	*	*	*
TLTA		1	.32	*	−.49	*	*	*	*
WCTA			1	.46	*	*	*	*	*
CLCA				1	*	*	*	*	*
OENEG					1	*	*	*	*
NITA						1	−.41	.40	−.44
FUTL							1	*	*
INTWO								1	−.32
CHIN									1

* = Absolute value of coefficient less than .20.

is exactly what one would expect in view of the profile analysis. Note also that the signs of *INTWO* and *CHIN* differ from those of Model 1. The positive and significant coefficient for *CHIN* in Model 2 can perhaps be explained by a scenario proposed by Deakin [1972]. Firms with a positive change in earnings may be particularly tempted to raise external capital through borrowing, and this will then imply that they become higher-risk firms at a subsequent point. Of course, this is only one possible explanation and the evidence is far too weak even vaguely to suggest that it is in fact the case.

In all three models, size appears as an important predictor. This finding is consistent with Horrigan's [1968] study of bond ratings, wherein he too found that size was an important determinant. One could perhaps argue that the conclusion is invalid because the bankrupt and nonbankrupt firms are drawn from different populations. Specifically, one cannot be sure that all the nonbankrupt firms would have been on the *Compustat* tape if they had not failed.[12] No direct test of the problem is therefore feasible. The *Compustat* tape is heavily biased toward the relatively large firms listed on the two major exchanges. If size is a spurious variable, then it is likely that dummy variables reflecting exchange listings are more important than size. This test was implemented, and the results are shown in table 6. The *t*-statistic for *SIZE* is larger than two, whereas the two exchange dummies NYSE and AMSE are essentially insignificant. These results again support the contention that size is an important predictor of bankruptcy. Even so, the test and conclusion must be viewed with great caution, since *Compustat* firms are different from non-*Compustat* firms on a number of complex dimensions. Therefore, we cannot be sure that size is a surrogate which is superior to exchange listing. If size, in fact, is a superior surrogate, then the statistical significance of size may simply reflect a general *Compustat* bias.[13]

---

[12] The *Compustat* file does not include all firms which have (or have had) their equity traded.

[13] It would have been preferable to obtain data for nonbankrupt firms by sampling 10-K reports from the Stanford Library. However, this would have been a very costly procedure.

TABLE 6
Model 4

Variable	Estimates	t-Statistics
SIZE	−.267	−2.02
TLTA	5.63	6.04
WCTA	−1.43	−1.91
CLCA	.0585	.595
NITA	−2.35	−1.82
FUTL	−1.99	−2.53
INTWO	.307	.877
OENEG	−1.56	−2.20
CHIN	−.5092	−2.15
NYSE	−.854	−1.71
AMSW	−.0513	−.186
CONST	−2.63	−1.70
Percent Correctly Predicted		96.30%
Likelihood Ratio Index		.8399

Subject to the qualification above, the results indicate that the four factors derived from financial statements which are statistically significant for purposes of assessing the probability of bankruptcy are: (*i*) size (*SIZE*); (*ii*) the financial structure as reflected by a measure of leverage (*TLTA*); (*iii*) some performance measure or combination of performance measures (*NITA* and/or *FUTL*); (*iv*) some measure(s) of current liquidity (*WCTA* or *WCTA* and *CLCA* jointly).[14] In an attempt to determine whether other factors can be obtained from financial statements which could increase the predictability of failure, I estimated an additional model. This model was Model 1 supplemented by a measure of profit margin, computed as funds from operations divided by sales, and a ratio of assets with little or no cash value (intangibles plus deferred assets) divided by total assets. The estimation results showed not only that both of these variables were completely insignificant, but also that the estimated coefficients had "incorrect" signs. (The *t*-statistics were .14 and −.42, respectively.) Whether other accounting predictors could have done a better job in improving upon the likelihood function is not clear, but, in my view, it is not overly likely.[15] On the other hand, nonaccounting data, such as information based on equity prices and changes in prices might prove to be most useful. I intend to test these kinds of models once adequate data have been gathered.

---

[14] If *CLCA* is deleted in the equation estimated, then the *t*-statistic of *WCTA* is slightly greater than two. For all practical purposes, this will be the only difference.

[15] One possible exception would be measures of "trends" of ratios and/or volatility of ratios (and performance measures). Due to the considerable costs of gathering and organizing data, such a refinement was judged to be cost-benefit inefficient.

6. Evaluation of Predictive Performance

There is no way one can completely order the predictive power of a set of models used for predictive (decision) purposes. As a minimum, this requires a complete specification of the decision problem, including a preference structure defined over the appropriate state-space. Previous work in the area of bankruptcy prediction has generally been based on two highly specific and restrictive assumptions when predictive performance is evaluated. First, a (mis)classification matrix is assumed to be an adequate partition of the payoff structure. Second, the two types of classification errors have an additive property, and the "best" model is one which minimizes the sums of percentage errors. Both of these assumptions are arbitrary, although it must be admitted that the first assumption is of some value if one is to describe at least one implication of using a model. Much of this discussion will therefore focus on such a (mis)classification description. Nevertheless, the second assumption will also be used at some points, since it would otherwise be impossible to compare the results here with those of previous studies. The comparison cannot be across models because the time periods, predictors, and data sets are different. Rather, the question of interest is one of finding to what extent the results conform with each other.

Without loss of generality, one may regard the estimated probability of failure, $P(\mathbf{X}_i, \hat{\beta})$, as a signal which classifies firm i into one of the two groups. Hence, it is of interest to describe the conditional distributions of these signals. Figure 1 shows the empirical frequency of $P(\mathbf{X}_i, \hat{\beta})$ for the 105 firms which failed within a year; $\hat{\beta}$ is the vector of estimated coefficients obtained from Model 1. Figure 2 shows the frequency for the 2,058 nonfailed firms where $\hat{\beta}$ is again taken from Model 1. Figure 3 shows the probabilities for 100 firms two periods prior to bankruptcy; the β's

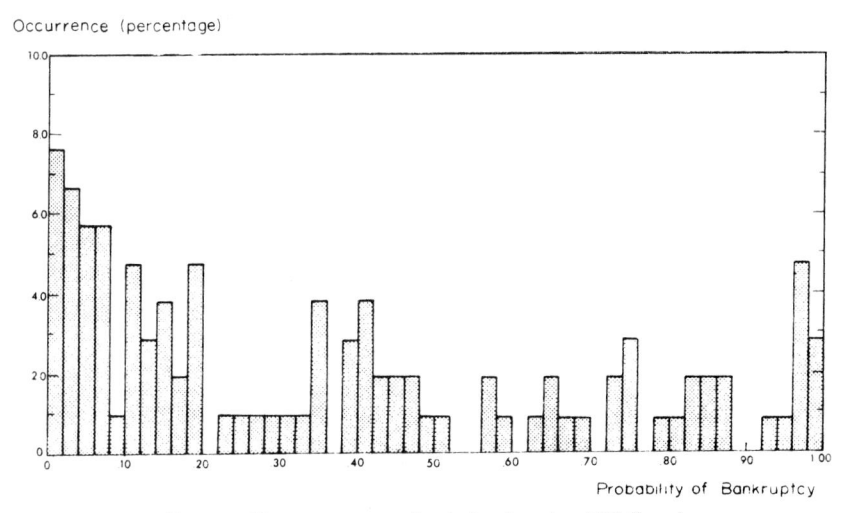

FIG. 1.—Firms one year prior to bankruptcy (105 firms)

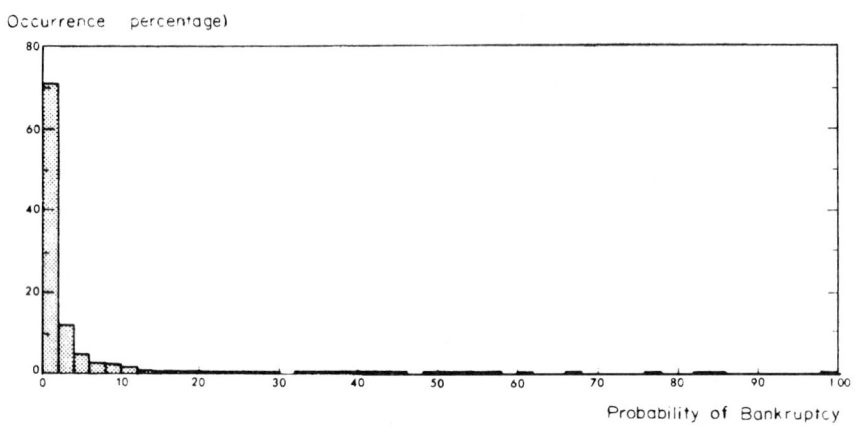

Fig. 2.—Nonbankrupt firms (2,058 firms)

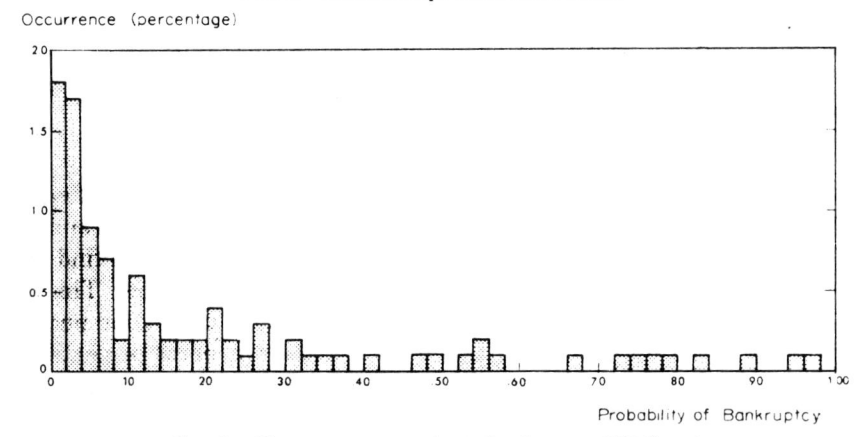

Fig. 3.—Firms two years prior to bankruptcy (100 firms)

were taken from Model 2. The mean probabilities are .39, .03, and .20, respectively. This is, of course, in accordance with what one would expect on the basis of prior reasoning.

Using the data which underlie figures 1–3, one can readily perform analysis of classification errors for different cutoff points. The focus will be on a prediction of bankruptcy within one year. A Type-I error will be said to occur if $P(\mathbf{X}_i, \hat{\boldsymbol{\beta}})$ is greater than the cutoff point and the firm is nonbankrupt; in a similar fashion, one defines a Type-II error for bankrupt firms if the probability is less than the cutoff point. It would have been preferable to perform the error analysis on a "fresh" data set and thereby (in)validate the models estimated.[16] Due to the lack of data beyond 1976, this was not possible at the time of the study. This should not be a serious problem, however, for the following reasons. First, I have

---

[16] It would, of course, have been possible to cut the sample in half and then go through the usual kind of procedures. However, the primary purpose of this paper is not one of getting a precise evaluation of a predictive model. Hence, it was decided that the full sample would be used in order to produce the smallest possible errors of the estimated coefficients.

Type I (percentage)

FREQUENCY OF ERROR

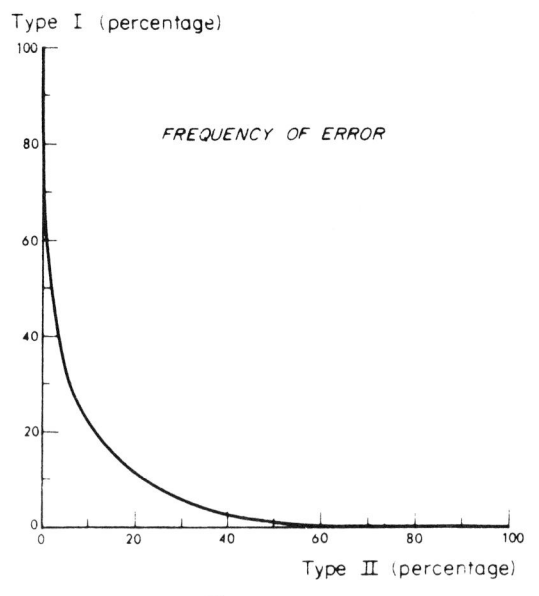

Type II (percentage)

Fig. 4.

not indulged in any "data dredging" and no attempt was made to find a "best" model or even a model which is "superior" to Model 1. Second, a logit analysis is not an econometric method which is designed to find an "optimal" frontier, trading off one type of error against another. This is in contrast to *MDA* models which satisfy optimality conditions under appropriate assumptions. Third, as it turns out, the sum of the percentage of errors is relatively robust across a wide range of cutoff points. Finally, the sample size is relatively large, so the estimates should not be too sensitive to the particular sample used.[17]

Figure 4 depicts the frontier trading of one error against another, when the errors are expressed as percentages. Figure 5 shows the mapping from cutoff points to the two different types of errors. The cutoff point which minimizes the sum of errors is .038. At that point, 17.4 percent of the nonbankrupt firms and 12.4 percent of the 105 bankrupt firms are misclassified. Given an (infinite) population, in which half of the firms are failed and the other half nonfailed, the expected error rate would then be 14.9 percent, provided that the cutoff point is .038, and provided that the distribution of the predictors is representative of the population. I might also note that if one selects a cutoff point equal to .0095, then no Type-II error occurs and Type-I errors equal .47.

It is not easy to compare the results above with those reported by others. First, the lead time from last fiscal year-end to the date of

---

[17] The points just made will be invalid in a real-world application of the model if the β-parameters are significantly different in future periods. This is a fairly obvious observation which has been made by others (see, e.g., Moyer [1977]).

Cut Off Point (Pc) (percentage)

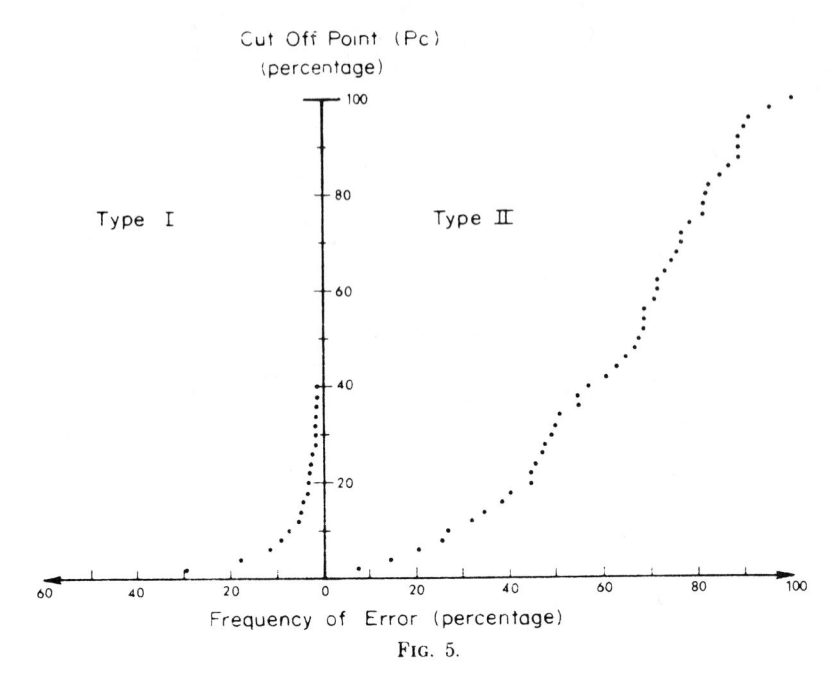

Type I   Type II

Frequency of Error (percentage)

FIG. 5.

bankruptcy is much longer in the present study. Second, most studies, except for the ones by Altman and McGough [1974], Moyer [1977], and Altman et al. [1977], have not considered data from the seventies. Third, studies have differed in their selection of predictors. However, it is hard to believe that the latter is of great significance once a fair number of "basic" ratios and predictors are incorporated. One potentially important exception to the latter is the use of nonaccounting-based data such as market-price data. Such data have not been used here. Fourth, it is possible that the predictive results could be sensitive to choice of estimation procedures (e.g., the logit model versus *MDA*).

A review of previous studies indicates that most of these reported error rates which are less than those given here, with several studies reporting rates in the vicinity of 5 percent. Some of the potential sources that may account for this differential are considered below.

The first point mentioned (the lead time) can be investigated to some extent. If it is true that this is an important consideration, then the average lead time should be larger for misclassified bankrupt firms, compared to correctly classified bankrupt firms. The difference is approximately 1.75 months, so the factor may be of some importance. The difference is significant at the 20-percent level (approximately). Indeed, three of the misclassified firms would have been "correctly" classified if I had used data from the subsequent annual report (i.e., these firms belong to the group of eighteen firms discussed in a previous section). Under these circumstances the minimum of the average error is somewhat less than 13 percent, the cutoff point is somewhat larger, and both types of errors are reduced. Hence, the lead time accounts for some of the differences. But it is hard to believe that this is the entire explanation.

As previously indicated, evidence exists regarding the second issue. Altman and McGough [1974] applied the model which Altman [1968] developed in 1968 to twenty-eight firms that failed during the period 1970–73. The predictors were computed from data one year prior to bankruptcy; the definition of "one year prior to bankruptcy" appears to be completely equivalent to that of the present study. In the 1968 study Altman reported a misclassification rate of approximately 5 percent for failed firms. The same model applied to the second group of firms yielded a misclassification rate of 18 percent (5/28). This is a substantial and significant increase, since the probability of getting five or more misclassifications out of twenty-eight observations is approximately one in one thousand if the true parameter is 5 percent. The study lacks a systematic analysis of the other type of error, so the evidence is not conclusive. More important, Altman et al. [1977] reworked much of what Altman did in 1968 using data from 1969–75 (94 percent of the total sample was from this period). The model development included a number of refinements in the utilization of discriminant analysis, as well as in the computation of financial ratios. The authors report: "... bankruptcy classification accuracy ranges from over 96 (93% holdout) one period prior to bankruptcy" (Altman et al. [1977, p. 50]). Needless to say, such results are not in accordance with those of the present study or, for that matter, the two other studies which used data from the seventies. I am unable to account for this difference. Unfortunately, Altman et al. [1977] do not report on the average lead time, so it is impossible to evaluate the importance of this factor. Also, they did not apply (or report) the predictive performance of their recent *ZETA* model on the 1974 sample. However, the authors do seem to suggest some sample dependence (see Altman et al. [1977, n. 16]). There are also differences in the definition of bankruptcy.

In sum, differences in results are most difficult to reconcile. Moyer [1977] recently reexamined the Altman model using data from the 1965–75 period. (The Altman [1968] sample was from the 1946–65 period.) The error rate reported by Moyer for the Altman model was no less than 25 percent! Reestimation of the parameters of the Altman model (using 1965–75 data and using the estimated model to classify firms) yielded an error rate of 10 percent. The latter result must be qualified (downward bias) due to the small sample size (twenty-seven bankrupt and twenty-seven nonbankrupt firms). The data were derived from *Moody's Manual* leading to additional downward bias.

Would the use of other predictors have affected the predictive power? The question cannot really be answered unless one tries out a large number of models and thereafter, necessarily, cross-validates the "best" model. The results from the model which added two predictors to Model 1 are not very encouraging, so at this point I must be quite skeptical. As previously suggested, a significant improvement in goodness-of-fit is more likely to occur by augmenting the accounting-based data with market-price data.

At this point, I want to emphasize that the reports of the misclassified bankrupt firms seem to lack any "warning signals" of impeding bankruptcy. All but two of the thirteen companies reported a profit. The two losses were relatively minor (*NITA* was −0.022 and −0.044, respectively), and these two companies had strong financial positions (*TLTA* was .23 and .37, respectively). The median *TLTA* ratio is .55, and the range is .23–.70. The median *NITA* is 3.4 percent with a range of −0.44 to 0.156. (The firm which had *TLTA* = .70 had *NITA* = .156.) Other ratios analyzed showed the same "healthy" patterns. It is not surprising that these firms were misclassified, especially if one considers the profile of the nonbankrupt firms shown in table 3.

Moreover, the accountants' reports would have been of little, if any, use. None of the misclassified bankrupt firms had a "going-concern qualification" or disclaimer of opinion. A review of the opinions revealed that eleven of these companies had completely clean opinions, and the two that did not had relatively minor uncertainty exceptions. Curiously, some of the firms even paid dividends in the year prior to bankruptcy. Hence, if any warning signals were present, it is not clear what these actually were.[18]

There is always the possibility that an alternative estimating technique, other than the logit model used, could yield a more powerful discriminatory device. Unfortunately, a priori reasoning appears to be of no use in finding such an "optimal" estimating technique. All one can do is to try some alternatives. One approach I tried, *MDA*, produced results which were somewhat "worse" than those previously reported, in that the minimum average error rate was 16 percent. More generally, I would hypothesize that many "reasonable" procedures will lead to results which will not differ too much. This robustness property can be illustrated as follows. If we use the estimates from Model 2 for the purpose of predicting bankruptcy within one year, the β-estimates from Model 2 will be evaluated in terms of their predictive power with respect to firms one year prior to bankruptcy and the 2,058 *Compustat* firms. Again, different cutoff points yield a trade-off between the two types of errors. Table 7 displays the two types of errors at selected cutoff points for Models 1 and 2. Interestingly enough, if a cutoff point of .08 is selected for Model 2, then the average error is 14.4 percent, and this is slightly better than the minimum attained by Model 1. Model 2 performs better at some other

---

[18] Ratios other than those used in the estimating equations were also examined. For all of the misclassified firms, I was unable to detect any ratio which was clearly out of line. However, it is quite possible that a time-series analysis of an extended period would indicate that some of the firms had "significant" above-average operating risks. By the use of market data, this problem will be investigated in the future.

TABLE 7
*Type I-Type II Analysis for Selected Cutoff Points**

Estimates from: Cutoff Point	Model 1 Type I**	Model 1 Type II	Model 2 Type I	Model 2 Type II
0.0	100%	0%	100%	0%
0.02	28.7	7.6	54.3	0%
0.04	16.7	14.3	37.7	0.95
0.06	11.8	20.0	26.8	4.76
0.08	9.3	25.7	20.2	8.6
0.10	7.2	26.7	17.0	12.4
0.20	3.3	44.8	7.2	31.4
0.30	1.75	48.6	3.6	43.8
0.40	1.07	57.1	2.0	50.5
0.42	0.92	61.0	1.75	51.4
0.50	0.63	67.6	1.07	57.1
0.54	0.44	68.6	0.82	61.0
0.60	0.29	71.4	0.68	62.9
0.70	0.19	76.2	0.49	70.5
0.80	0.15	81.9	0.24	74.3
0.90	0.049	88.6	0.19	82.9
1.00	0	1.00	0	1.00

* Data sets: nonbankrupt firms and one year prior to bankruptcy.
** Type I: predict bankruptcy; actual nonbankrupt.

points too; that is, for a fixed level of one type of error for both models, the complementary error is lower for Model 2. A close examination of table 7 will verify this. To be sure, for some error rates Model 1 is better than Model 2. It seems reasonable to suggest that the models are essentially equivalent as predictive tools.

7. Conclusions

There are two conclusions which should be restated. First, the predictive power of any model depends upon when the information (financial report) is assumed to be available. Some previous studies have not been careful in this regard. Second, the predictive powers of linear transforms of a vector of ratios seem to be robust across (large sample) estimation procedures. Hence, more than anything else, significant improvement probably requires additional predictors.

REFERENCES

ALTMAN, E. "Financial Ratios, Discriminant Analysis and the Prediction of Corporate Bankruptcy." *Journal of Finance* (September 1968).
———. *Corporate Bankruptcy in America*. Lexington, Mass.: Heath Lexington, 1971.
———. "Predicting Railroad Bankruptcies in America." *Bell Journal of Economics and Management Science* (Spring 1973).
———, R. HALDEMAN, AND P. NARAYANAN. "ZETA Analysis: A New Model to Identify Bankruptcy Risk of Corporations." *Journal of Banking and Finance* (June 1977).
———, AND B. LORRIS. "A Financial Early Warning System for Over-the-Counter Broker Dealers." *Journal of Finance* (September 1976).

———, AND T. MCGOUGH. "Evaluation of a Company as a Going Concern." *Journal of Accountancy* (December 1974).

BEAVER, W. "Financial Ratios as Predictors of Failure." *Empirical Research in Accounting: Selected Studies, 1966.* Supplement to *Journal of Accounting Research* 4.

———. "Alternative Financial Ratios as Predictions of Failure." *The Accounting Review* (January 1968a).

———. "Market Prices, Financial Ratios and the Prediction of Failure." *Journal of Accounting Research* (Autumn 1968b).

BLUM, M. "Failing Company Discriminant Analysis." *Journal of Accounting Research* (Spring 1974).

DEAKIN, E. B. "A Discriminant Analysis of Predictors of Business Failure." *Journal of Accounting Research* (Spring 1972).

EDMISTER, R. O. "An Empirical Test of Financial Ratio Analysis for Small Business Failure Prediction." *Journal of Financial and Quantitative Analysis* (March 1972).

EISENBEIS, R. A. "Pitfalls in the Application of Discriminant Analysis in Business, Finance, and Economics." *Journal of Finance* (June 1977).

HORRIGAN, J. "The Determination of Long-Term Credit Standing with Financial Ratios." *Empirical Research in Accounting: Selected Studies, 1968.* Supplement to *Journal of Accounting Research* 6.

JOY, M. O., AND J. O. TOLLEFSON. "On the Financial Applications of Discriminant Analysis." *Journal of Financial and Quantitative Analysis* (December 1975).

LEV, B. "Financial Failure and Informational Decomposition Measures." In *Accounting in Perspective Contributions to Accounting Thoughts by Other Disciplines,* edited by R. R. Sterling and W. F. Bentz, pp. 102–11. Cincinnati: Southwestern Publishing Co., 1971.

LIBBY, R. "Accounting Ratios and the Prediction of Failure: Some Behavioral Evidence." *Journal of Accounting Research* (Spring 1975).

MCFADDEN, D. "Conditional Logit Analysis of Qualitative Choice Behavior." In *Frontiers in Econometrics,* edited by P. Zarembka. New York: Academic Press, 1973.

MCKIBBEN, W. "Econometric Forecasting of Common Stock Investment Returns: A New Methodology Using Fundamental Operating Data." *Journal of Finance* (May 1972).

MOYER, R. "Forecasting Financial Failure: A Re-Examination." *Financial Management* (Spring 1977).

SANTOMERO, A., AND J. D. VINSO. "Estimating the Probability of Failure for Commercial Banks and the Banking System." *Journal of Banking and Finance* (September 1977).

WHITE, R. W., AND M. TURNBULL. "The Probability of Bankruptcy: American Railroads." Working paper, Institute of Finance and Accounting, London University Graduate School of Business, February 1975a.

———. "The Probability of Bankruptcy for American Industrial Firms." Working paper, July 1975b.

WILCOX, J. "A Prediction of Business Failure Using Accounting Data." *Empirical Research in Accounting: Selected Studies, 1973.* Supplement to *Journal of Accounting Research* 11.

by Edward I. Altman and Joseph Spivack

Predicting Bankruptcy: The Value Line Relative Financial Strength System vs. The Zeta® Bankruptcy Classification Approach

Both the Zeta® model of bankruptcy classification and the Value Line Relative Financial Strength System classify public corporations according to characteristics of financial health. Zeta® uses financial variables to discriminate between bankrupt and nonbankrupt firms, whereas Value Line relates similar types of variables to the observed yields of outstanding debt securities. Zeta® is essentially an objective system; Value Line's ratings are a function of both mathematical relations and human judgment. Both models employ measures of profitability, leverage, size, variability and market value. Zeta®, however, measures earnings variability, whereas Value Line evaluates stock price stability. Value Line's size measure involves earnings; Zeta® uses total assets.

Despite these differences, a comparison of the two systems reveals that Value Line's scores exhibit a high correlation with Zeta® scores, which have been shown to discriminate well between bankrupt and nonbankrupt firms. Both systems' scores also correlate well with published bond ratings.

IN THE TWO YEARS 1980–81, over one dozen major industrial corporations, each with liabilities exceeding $150 million, succumbed to the economic reality of legal insolvency and petitioned the courts for protection and reorganization under Chapter 11 of the Bankruptcy Code (see Table I). Stockholders in these corporations saw the prices of their shares plummet, on average, 50 per cent around the bankruptcy declaration day.[1] Bondholders, whose potential returns are a function not only of the probability of failure, but also of the prospects for successful reorganization, may have an equal or even greater stake in the financial viability of corporations.

This article describes and compares two of the more prominent measures of corporate financial viability available to the investment community—the Zeta® model of bankruptcy classification and the Value Line *Relative Financial Strength System*. Although these systems differ in a number of respects, both classify public corporations according to characteristics of financial health. Furthermore, both employ similar multivariate statistical techniques in constructing their models and both utilize weighted measures to summarize the financial strength or viability of the firm in a single score or rating. Based on a comparative sample of 87 manufacturing companies, we find that there is a 0.85 correlation between the two systems. In addition, tests on a smaller sample indicate that the results of both systems correlate well with bond ratings.

---

1. Footnotes appear at end of article.

Edward Altman is Professor of Finance and Chairman of the MBA Program at New York University. Joseph Spivack, a recent MBA graduate of New York University, is Senior Analyst at The Value Line Investment Survey.

This article is adapted from a speech presented at the Institute for Quantitative Research in Finance meeting in Orlando in the spring of 1983.

Table I Major U.S. Bankruptcies in 1981 and 1982
(*millions of dollars*)

Company	Bankruptcy Date	Total Liabilities
Wickes & Co.	April 1982	$2,000
Itel Corp.	January 1981	1,700
Manville Corp.	August 1982	1,116
Braniff Int'l Airlines	May 1982	1,100
Seatrain Lines	February 1981	785
AM International	April 1982	510
Saxon Industries	April 1982	461
Sambo's Restaurants	June 1981	370
McLouth Steel	December 1981	323
Revere Copper & Brass	October 1982	237
KDT Industries	August 1982	185
HRT Industries	November 1982	182
Lionel Corp.	February 1982	165

Source: E. Altman, *Corporate Financial Distress: A Complete Guide to Predicting, Understanding and Dealing with Bankruptcy* (New York: John Wiley & Sons, 1983).

Table II Zeta® Model Variables

Variable	Description
1	Overall profitability (Return on Assets)
2	Size (Based on Tangible Assets)
3	Debt Service (Interest Coverage)
4	Liquidity (Current Ratio)
5	Cumulative Profitability (Retained Earnings/Total Assets)
6	Capitalization (Based on a Five-Year Average Market Value of Common Stock)
7	Stability of Earnings over a 10-Year Period

The Zeta® System

The Zeta® credit worthiness and financial viability system, available through Zeta Services, Inc., Mountainside, New Jersey, was developed in 1976 and first published in 1977.[2] It is basically an expansion and update of the original Z-Score model developed and published by Altman in 1968, combining readily available financial statement data and adjusting the information to reflect current accounting standards.[3]

Working with an original sample of bankrupt firms and a control sample of healthy entities, Altman *et al.* utilized a combination of traditional financial ratio analysis and a sophisticated statistical technique known as discriminant analysis to construct and test a financial model for assessing the likelihood that a firm would go bankrupt.[4] The model combined seven financial measures (given in Table II), utilizing both reported accounting figures and stock market variables to arrive at an objective overall measure of corporate health. The model has proved to be durable and is accepted as an important indicator for analysts and decision-makers in many spheres of work.

Of course, the real test is whether the model has been able to predict the fate of observed companies; the "proof is in the eating." Table III shows how well the model did on the basis of 73 bankruptcies that occurred after the model's development. Zeta® correctly anticipated 68 of the 73 (93 per cent) using data from one statement prior to failure and 62 of 71 (87 per cent) using data from two statements prior to failure. The model provides a reliable gauge of potential failure.

Any firm with a Zeta® score less than zero (i.e., a negative score) has a greater than 50 per cent chance of being classified as a bankrupt, with its probabilities increasing as its score deteriorates. The absolute Zeta® score, however, is not the only indicator of financial distress. The trend in Zeta® is perhaps even more important. A major decline—say, two or three points—into the negative zone suggests a serious deterioration in financial strength.

The Value Line Relative Financial Strength System

The *Value Line Investment Survey*, published in New York by Arnold Bernhard & Co., is one of the largest and best known investment advisory publications in the United States. The survey follows and reports on about 1,700 companies, both listed and over-the-counter. A full-page report, comprising historical data, financial analysis and written comments, is published quarterly for each company under review.

In the lower right-hand corner of each review is a rating of the financial strength of the company in question. There are nine possible Relative Financial Strength System (RFSS) ratings, ranging from A++ (highest) down to C (lowest). Value Line introduced them in 1977, at approximately the same time that Zeta® became available. The ratings, which are based on publicly available financial data, resemble the bond ratings published by agencies such as Moody's and Standard & Poor's, but apply to all companies in the survey, not just those with publicly traded bonds outstanding.

A computerized model generates the ratings, which are subject to analytical and editorial review. The basic concept of the model is straightforward: The year-end closing yields of several hundred publicly traded bonds are regressed on a number of financial variables calculated from the Value Line data base. A formula producing a weighted score is derived, then applied to most of the 1,700 companies in the survey. Letter-grade ratings are based on this weighted score.

To arrive at the ratings, values for each of 21 financial variables (described in Table IV) are calculated for all nonfinancial companies in the survey. (The ratios for financial companies such as banks and insurance companies are not easily comparable to those of industrial firms, hence are excluded.) The values of each variable for all included companies are placed in ascending order, then divided into eight equal groups. Each variable for each company is then assigned a rank from one to eight, according to which group it falls into. All subsequent calculations employ these *rank numbers*, rather than the actual values; this has the effect of standardizing the ranges for all the variables, both between variables and between years.

Suppose, for example, that there are 1,500 com-

Table III Companies that have Failed since Zeta® was Developed

Company Name	Bankruptcy Date	Final Statement Date	Zeta® F.S.D. −1	F.S.D. −2	F.S.D. −3	F.S.D. −4	No. of Mos with Neg. Score Prior to Failure
AM International	4/14/82	7/81	−4.60	−0.18	0.35	1.01	0.32	20
Acme Hamilon Mfg	2/28/78	10/76	−5.54	−4.40	−4.25	−4.00	−4.12	124
Advent	3/17/81	3/80	−6.10	−4.22	−1.41			36
Alan Wood Steel	6/10/77	12/76	−4.92	−3.18	−0.31	−0.84	−1.33	89
Allied Artists	4/5/79	3/78	−7.07	−8.18	−7.14	−2.29	−1.40	120
Allied Supermkts	11/6/78	6/78	−6.11	−5.28	−4.59	−2.92	−2.41	88
Apeco Corp	10/19/77	11/76	−8.29	−1.53	−2.16	0.94	4.67	35
Arctic Enterprses	2/17/81	3/80	−4.12	−2.06	−0.78	0.26	0.54	35
Auto Train Corp	9/80	12/79	−9.30	−8.42	−5.76			33
Barclay Inds Inc	6/81(?)	7/80	−10.47	−4.80	−3.78	−2.83	−0.17	59
Berven Carpets	8/10/82	12/81	−7.10	−2.02	−0.92	1.35	−0.01	31
Bobbie Brooks	1/17/82	4/81	−1.98	−1.69	−0.29	−0.97	−3.03	103
Braniff Airlines	5/13/82	12/80	−3.40	−2.18	1.21	1.02	0.63	28
B Brody Seating	2/4/80	8/79	−4.87	−3.02	−1.15	−0.41	−1.32	53
Capehart Corp	2/16/79	3/78	−11.34	−6.54				24
Combustion Equp As	10/20/80	3/80	−4.22	−1.60	4.23	3.38	2.65	19
Commonwealth Oil	3/3/78	12/76	−2.57	−1.72	0.26	0.63	1.12	26
Cooper Jarrett	12/28/81	12/80	−8.56	−6.93	−5.18	−4.04	−3.98	120
Eagle Clothes	11/1/77	12/75	−2.89	−2.38	−2.30	−1.83	−1.18	70
Ernst, E C	12/4/78	3/78	−4.49	0.78	2.00	1.81	2.04	8
FDI Inc	12/1/78	4/77	−5.75	−5.93	−5.06	−0.58	−0.45	79
Filigree Foods	4/2/76	7/74	−3.99	−3.97	−3.80	−4.87	−5.62	68
First Hartford	2/23/81	4/79	−10.00	−7.30	−7.67	−5.45	−5.42	123
Food Fair Inc	10/3/78	7/77	−0.61	−0.68	−1.01	0.52	0.62	38
Frigitemps	3/24/78	12/76	−1.65	−1.08				27
GRT Corp	7/14/79	3/78	−3.46	−1.62	−2.92			39
Garcia Corp	8/8/78	7/77	−4.69	−2.49	0.61			24
Garland Corp	4/29/80	10/79	−1.85	−0.61	−0.04	2.54	0.70	30
Gen'l Recreation	12/21/78	12/77	−14.41	−6.79	−4.39	−0.67		48
Goldblatt Bros	6/16/81	1/80	−2.35	−1.71	−0.59	0.36	0.46	41
Good, L S & Co	5/27/80	1/79	−2.75	−2.17	−1.63	−1.37	−1.31	64
HRT Inds Inc.	11/23/82	1/82	−2.29	−2.38	−2.21	−2.64	−3.36	118
Inforex	10/79	12/78	−3.69	−4.22	−3.66	−4.43		46
Itel	1/19/81	12/79	−6.62	−1.79	−1.88	−1.15	−1.68	85
KDT Inds Inc	8/5/82	1/82	−3.37	0.08	4.11	3.70	3.68	6
Keydata Corp	11/31/80	7/80	−15.79	−9.55	−8.44	−7.25	−7.17	64
Lionel	2/82	12/80	−1.61	−1.91	−2.19	−1.23	−1.70	121
Lynnwear Corp	2/81	11/79	−5.46	−2.05	−2.10	−1.80	−0.94	98
Mansfield Tire	10/79	12/78	−8.20	−1.09	1.31	0.90	0.84	22
Manville Corp	8/25/82?	12/81	3.12	4.10	3.52	3.29	6.21	0*
Mays, J W Inc	1/26/82	7/81	−2.03	−1.04	−0.44	−0.40	−0.74	78
McLouth Steel	12/8/81	12/80	−2.17	0.32	0.34	−0.45	2.29	11
Mego Int'l	6/15/82	2/81	−7.46	−0.36	0.12	0.22	1.61	27
Metropltn Greetings	1/18/79	12/77	−5.94	−3.89	−3.63	−2.45		49

Table III Continued →

Table III Continued

Company Name	Bankruptcy Date	Final Statement Date	Zeta® Final Statement Date	F.S.D. −1	F.S.D. −2	F.S.D. −3	F.S.D. −4	No. of Mos with Neg. Score Prior to Failure
Morton Shoe Cos	1/1/82(?)	6/81	−5.05	−2.72	−1.32	−2.05	−2.26	137
National Shoes	12/12/80	1/79	−2.56	−1.05	−0.41			46
Neisner Bros Inc	12/77	1/77	−2.84	−3.02	−1.81	−0.98	−1.07	58
Nelly Don Inc	11/29/78	11/77	−16.73	−7.11	−4.28	−3.40	−1.70	72
Novo Corp	9/78	12/76	−5.03	−4.66	−3.36	−3.07	−3.23	128
Nucorp Energy Inc	7/28/82	12/80	−2.13	−3.16				31
Pacific Far East	1/2/78	12/76	−3.52	−3.95	−4.28	−4.74	−2.41	72
Pathcom	11/30/81	12/80	−29.56					11
Penn Dixie Inds	4/7/80	12/78	−2.88	−3.54	−1.71	−1.28	0.15	51
Piedmont Inds	2/22/79	5/78	−1.90	−1.38				21
Red Ball Express (Telecom Score)	4/26/82	12/80	−2.75	−0.58	−0.62	−0.78	−2.46	94
Revere Copper & Br	10/27/82	12/81	1.49	1.36	0.40	−0.37	−0.98	0*
Richton Int'l	3/13/80	4/79	0.15	1.08	0.49	0.25	−0.59	0*
Sambo's Rstrnts	11/81	12/80	−3.51	−4.28	−0.54	1.10	1.32	35
Saxon Inds	4/15/82	12/80	0.27	−0.06	0.14	−0.34	−0.50	0*
Seatrain Lines	2/11/81	6/80	−2.41	−2.69	−2.58	−2.77	−3.27	115
Shulman Trans Ent	8/21/78	12/77	−7.31	−4.23	−2.58			32
Sitkin Smlt & Ref	3/13/78	6/77	−4.07	−3.12	−1.24	−1.52	−0.17	68
Solomon, Sam Inc	8/29/80	1/79	−2.03	−2.09				31
Stelber Industries	3/10/76	6/73	−5.97	−2.40	−2.21	−2.93	−3.94	80
Stevcoknit Inc	11/81	1/81	−2.47	−2.45	−0.07	0.01	0.70	34
Tenna Corp	6/25/81	1/79	−0.70	−1.52	1.87	2.21	3.36	41
United Merch & Mfg	7/12/77	6/76	−0.38	0.24	1.72	3.23	3.04	12
Universal Cont'r	3/22/78	11/76	−5.03	−5.32	−4.02	−2.96	−2.26	111
UNR Industries	7/30/82	12/81	−0.24	−0.59	0.42	0.79	1.23	19
West Chem Prods	2/29/78	11/78	−0.31	0.35	5.70	5.98	5.44	3*
White Motor Corp	9/4/80	12/79	−1.41	−1.95	−1.80	−1.85	−2.39	116
Wickes Cos	4/25/82	1/81	−0.92	0.39	0.48	0.77	0.91	15
Wilson Freight Co	7/80	12/79	−3.87					7
Average Score			−4.72	−2.62	−1.44	−0.79	−0.53	
No. of Cos. Correctly Classified			68	62	47	37	34	
No. of Cos. Incorrectly Classified			5	9	19	23	23	
Total Number of Companies			73	71	66	60	57	
% Correct			93	87	71	62	60	
% Incorrect			7	13	29	38	40	
Average Number of Months' Lead Time							53	

*Error if less than four months of lead time.

Table IV Variables Tested for Inclusion in the Value Line RFSS

Variable	Description	Variable	Description
1	Stock Price Stability	12	(Profit − Total Dividends) / Common Equity
2	Stock Price / Long-Term Debt per Share	13	Debt Due in Next Five Years
3	Net Income Trend Point	14	Tangible Book Value per Share Trend Point
4	Return on Equity Trend Point	15	Percentage Change in Stock Price over last 13 Weeks
5	Quick Ratio	16	Percentage Change in Stock Price over last 26 Weeks
6	Long-Term Debt / Total Capital	17	Bond Yield / AAA Bond Yield
7	Accounting Code	18	Operating Income / Total Interest
8	(Total Capital + Deferred Charges) / Debt Due in Next Five Years	19	Last Five Years' Average Net Income
9	Net Worth / (Deferred Charges + Intangibles)	20	Five-Year Compound Growth Rate of Tangible Book Value per Share
10	Cash Tax Rate	21	Net Worth / Unfunded Vested Pension Liability
11	Operating Income / (Total Interest + Depreciation)		

panies, hence 1,500 values for each variable. The values are first sorted by increasing order, then divided into eight groups of 187 values per group (1500/8) with the remaining four firms assigned to the last group. The lowest group of 187 values is ranked number one, the next group two, and so on up to eight. This process is repeated for each of the 21 variables.

Those companies with nonconvertible, noncallable, unsecured debt with about 10 years to maturity are further scrutinized. The yields on a sample of some 300 bonds are regressed against the rank-number values of the 21 financial variables, a regression coefficient and t-statistic being calculated for each variable. Only those variables shown to be significant are retained; a recent analysis indicated that Variables 1, 2, 3, 5, 6, 7, 9, 10, 13, 14 and 21 from Table IV were significant. A new regression is performed using the smaller number of variables, and new coefficients are obtained; this becomes the final equation.

This equation is then applied to all nonfinancial companies in the survey. A weighted score is calculated for each by applying the regression coefficients to the rank-number values for each variable, adding the products, then dividing the sum by the sum of the absolute values of the regression coefficients. This last adjustment normalizes the weighted score, assuring that even if the regression coefficients differ from run to run, the weighted scores produced will be comparable. This feature is a prerequisite for the operation of the "buffer" routine, which will be described below.

All companies are sorted in ascending order according to the weighted scores assigned them. They are then divided into nine equal groups, corresponding to the nine financial strength ratings. The regression equation is structured so that the lowest weighted scores corespond to the highest rating, and vice versa.

Next, each stock's position in the weighted score universe and its computer-assigned financial strength rating are compared between the current run and the previous year's run. This is where the normalization feature comes into play. If a relatively small change in a stock's position in the weighted score universe (e.g., less than 25 positions) has moved it into another rating category, the change is overridden and the previous year's rating is preserved. This means that small changes in weighted score that happen to cross a boundary between ratings will not produce an actual change in rating. The process is intended to reduce rank volatility from year to year. The result of this process is called the "buffered" rating.

Once buffered ratings have been produced, nine "switches" are applied. These have three main purposes—(1) to limit the number of stocks rated A++; (2) to limit the number of stocks rated A+; and (3) to raise all utility stocks by one rating. While one can understand why Value Line has added these various subjective modifications to the system, it is also true that they will "sanitize" the data and may result in loss of information.

Once a complete listing of all buffered and switched ratings has been produced, each rating is carefully evaluated by the analyst who follows the company and by the editor who supervises the analyst. This is the most crucial step of the process, because it assures that the published rating is not contrary to the judgment of the analyst or editor. It also allows the most recent quarterly financial data, known to the analyst but not to the computer, to be factored into the rating. The final rating is a joint product, therefore, of the computerized model and the judgment of professional analysts. In fact, the editorial review process resulted in revisions of the ratings of 33 of the 87 firms studied in our analysis.

Comparing Zeta® with the Value Line System

The two systems differ in three principal ways. The first difference is a conceptual one. Zeta® utilizes financial variables to discriminate between bankrupt and nonbankrupt firms, whereas the Value Line model relates similar types of variables to the observed bond yields of outstanding debt securities. Conceptually, Value Line builds upon the earlier work of Fisher, who postulated that bond yield risk premiums are a function of credit worthiness and marketability, and West, who utilized the Fisher model to explain observed bond ratings.[5] Zeta® may also be considered a type of credit worthiness model, with the event of legal bankruptcy serving as the basis for comparison. In this sense, the first "difference" is in some respects actually a similarity.

Second, the systems differ in the degree of subjectivity of their ratings or scores. Zeta® is essentially an objective system with little or no room for human judgment to affect the scores. The Value Line system has built into it a series of adjustments and comparisons resulting in ratings that are a function of both mathematical associations and human assessment. In general, it is the human element that causes reality to diverge from models. If a model can replicate human evaluation with a high degree of reliability, however, then costs as well as human errors may be significantly reduced.

The third difference involves the choice of variables included in the two models. Although both models have profitability, leverage, size, variability and market value elements, the specific reference data are not uniform. For example, Zeta® measures earnings variability, whereas the Value Line model evaluates stock price stability. Zeta® uses market prices in its definition of equity. Value Line's size measure involves earnings; Zeta® uses total assets. It is interesting to note that the final Value Line equation does not contain the interest coverage measure found in the Zeta® model, although it was originally considered (see Table IV). Value Line's accounting code measure contains a quality of earnings variable encompassing such factors as investment tax credits, depreciation and inventory methods and capitalized leases; Zeta® includes most of these factors by adjusting the data directly.

What specific effects, if any, these differences have on the two systems' results is difficult to determine. An examination of the Zeta® scores and the Value Line ratings, however, should indicate whether the two systems yield significantly different results.

Statistical Comparisons and Tests

We performed several statistical tests on a sample of 87 manufacturing companies divided about equally between the financial strength ratings published in the *Value Line Investment Survey* for the fourth quarter of 1981. We tried to ensure roughly equal representation from about 20 industry groups, and to include both well-known and little-known firms and both large and small firms. Table V gives the characteristics of some of the sample companies.

We used the computer-determined Value Line score (not the final published rating) and the Zeta® score for our sample of industrials. We then arrayed the scores from highest to lowest and performed a rank correlation test between the scores for each firm. A perfect −1.0 would result if each Value Line score corresponded exactly with each of the 87 Zeta® scores (e.g., lowest Value Line equals highest Zeta®). The result was a highly significant (at the 0.001 level of confidence) −0.857 correlation. By any standards, this indicates a very high level of similarity. The product moment correlations on the scores yielded almost identical results (−0.854).

We also compared the Zeta® scores and the Value Line scores and ratings with the Standard & Poor's October 1981 bond ratings for a smaller sample of 20 bonds. The S&P ratings correlated as follows:

with published Value Line ratings 0.867,
with Zeta® scores .... −0.854,
with Value Line weighted scores 0.824,
with Value Line computer-assigned
  ratings .... 0.767.

Despite the smallness of the sample, this test indicates that the Value Line published ratings replicate bond ratings fairly well. Furthermore, the application of the analysts' and editors' judgment to the computer-generated ratings improves the correlation with the S&P ratings. The manually adjusted Value Line ratings and the objective Zeta® scores show essentially the same association with the S&P bond ratings; the application of the human element apparently helps to reconcile the two models. Finally, the correlations observed with both the Value Line scores and the Zeta® scores tend to support the correlation observed earlier between the two sets of scores themselves.

A further investigation was conducted to determine if the Value Line editors could have used Zeta® scores in their evaluation of the ratings supplied to them by the computer model. Two basic approaches were used. First, we examined the score rank differentials (see Table V). The *direction* of the differential (i.e., whether a given company was ranked higher by its Value Line score or by its Zeta® score) was compared with the direction of rating changes made by the editors.

Second, we constructed a scale of Zeta® bond rank equivalents, using the average Zeta® score for each S&P rating category (in 1981). Table VI reproduces the scale. Each company in the sample was assigned a Zeta® "bond rank." The direction of the difference between this Zeta® bond rank and the Value Line computer rating (i.e., whether a higher rank was assigned by the Value Line model or by the Zeta® bond rank method) was again compared with the direction of editorial changes.

The Value Line editors accepted the computer rating in 54 of 87 cases (62 per cent), rejecting the

Table V Scores and Ratings of Selected Firms as of October 1981

Company and Computer Rating	Value Line Computed Score	Zeta® Score	Score Rank Differential*	Zeta® "Bond Rank"
A. Published Rating = A++				
CBI—A+	1.2322	7.97	−7	AA
Coors Brewing—A+	1.0322	12.80	+8	AAA
Grainger—A++	1.1879	10.15	+2	AAA
Harsco—A++	1.1664	9.14	−2	AAA
Lubrizol—A++	0.8725	11.86	+2	AAA
Maytag—A+	0.8584	11.75	−2	AAA
Minnesota Mining & Manufacturing—A++	0.1879	12.62	−3	AAA
Moore—A++	0.6195	11.85	−3	AAA
Thomas and Betts—A++	0.7564	11.10	−5	AAA
Timken—A++	0.6765	13.81	+3	AAA
B. Published Rating = B+				
Allis Chalmers—B++	2.0148	2.08	−18	BB
Bell and Howell—B+	2.0570	3.74	−4	BBB
Bethlehem Steel—B+	1.9564	4.10	−2	BBB
Chicago Pneumatic—B+	2.0027	4.00	−2	BBB
Ennis Business Forms—B	2.2255	6.34	+26	A
Ford Motor—A	1.6416	2.42	−34	BB
Fleetwood Enterprises—B	2.1134	4.74	+9	A
Lukens Steel—B+	2.0738	5.19	+11	A
Murray Ohio—B+	2.2027	3.31	−1	BBB
C. Published Rating = C				
AM International—C+	3.3685	−0.18	+14	B
Chrysler—C+	3.0470	−3.55	−4	CCC
Facet Enterprises—C+	2.9792	−2.78	−4	CCC
Martin Processing—C+	3.5188	2.15	+26	BB
McLouth Steel—C++	2.6040	−2.17	−13	CCC
Mesta Machine—C++	2.5134	−1.35	−13	B
Phoenix Steel—C+	3.3618	−8.53	−2	C
Ronson Corp.—C+	3.3262	−5.44	−2	CC
Wurlitzer—C+	2.7248	−2.45	−10	CCC

*Calculated by placing Value Line weighted scores and Zeta® scores in rank order, then subtracting the Value Line weighted score rank from the Zeta® score rank.

remaining 33 cases (38 per cent). For the rejected cases, the direction of the rank differential between Zeta® scores and Value Line scores agreed with the direction of editorial revisions in 30 out of 33 cases (91 per cent). The direction of the difference between Zeta® bond ranks and Value Line computer ratings agreed with the direction of editorial revisions in 16 of the 33 cases (48 per cent).

Thus if Value Line editors had used the direction of rank differentials between Zeta® scores and Value Line scores as a guide to revising computer ratings they had already independently rejected, they might have duplicated actual results for the entire sample in 84 (= 54 + 30) out of 87 cases (97 per cent). (This assumes the editors have access to both Zeta scores and score rank differentials.) If they had used the direction of the difference between Zeta® bond ranks and Value Line computer ratings in a similar fashion (access to Zeta® again assumed) they would have duplicated actual results in 70 (= 54 + 16) out of 87 cases (80 per cent). The "direction of score rank differentials" method appears to dominate.

It must be stressed that this is a two-step procedure. The editors would first determine independently whether to accept a given Value Line computer rating. They would then use data from the Zeta® model to confirm the proper direction for revision. If a discrepancy existed between a directional change indicated by Zeta® and the editorial determination, further analysis would be indicated.

Conclusions

Despite conceptual, statistical and behavioral

Table VI Average Zeta® Scores by Rating Agency, by Rating Category and by Type of Debt Rated

Moody's Ratings	Senior Debt	Subordinated Debt	Convertible Subordinated Debt	Subordinated & Convertible Subordinated Debt	Secured Debt	U.S. Government Guaranteed Debt	Telephone Companies
AAA	10.10		8.15	8.15		3.39	4.77
AA	7.60	7.10		7.10			2.86
A	5.59	4.70	6.61	6.13	5.10		4.67
BAA	3.57	7.14	6.83	6.86	1.40		3.46
BA	0.91	2.36	3.97	3.59			
B	0.05	−0.07	−0.27	−0.19			0.21
CAA	−3.89	−4.08	−3.58	−3.78			
CA			−4.00	−4.00			
C			−4.62	−4.62			
NR	1.17	1.35	0.44	0.68	2.05	4.09	
S & P Ratings							
AAA	10.32		8.15	8.15		4.09	5.37
AA	7.54		6.30	6.30	6.28		3.21
A	5.65	4.49	4.50	4.49	4.35		4.67
BBB	3.56	4.30	6.07	5.80	1.74		4.34
BB	1.23	2.22	4.20	3.81			2.58
B	−0.64	−0.09	−0.02	−0.05	−2.86		0.21
CCC	−2.68	−3.55	−3.51	−3.52			
NR	0.92	2.03	0.45	0.94		3.39	

Source: Zeta® Services, Inc., Mountainside, New Jersey.

differences between the Zeta® and Value Line approaches, the areas of agreement appear to be substantial and significant. The fact that Value Line's weighted scores correlate well with Zeta® scores, which have been shown to discriminate well between bankrupt and nonbankrupt firms, indicates that the Value Line scores contain significant information about companies' financial strengths. Our tests do not, however, address the timing factor—that is, whether the information is made available to subscribers early enough for meaningful use. The early warning nature of the Zeta® system is fairly well established.

Furthermore, both the Value Line weighted scores and the Zeta® scores correlate well with bond ratings; the Value Line computer-assigned ratings correlate somewhat less well. The computer-assigned ratings obviously deviate in some way from the weighted scores on which they are based, and further investigation of this discrepancy is probably warranted. The subsequent application of analysts' and editors' judgment tends to "correct" this deviation and to bring the final ratings more into line with agency bond ratings. As the Value Line editors are aware of the bond ratings when they make their revisions, this result is perhaps not surprising. ∎

Footnotes

1. T. Clark and M. Weinstein, "The Behavior of the Common Stocks of Bankrupt Firms," *Journal of Finance*, May 1983; the so-called bankruptcy effect was also observed by E. Altman, "Bankrupt Firms' Equity Securities As An Investment Alternative," *Financial Analysts Journal*, July/August 1969, pp. 129-133.

2. See E. Altman, R. Haldeman and P. Narayanan, "Zeta® Analysis: A New Model for Bankruptcy Classification," *Journal of Banking and Finance*, June 1977, pp. 29-54, for an in-depth description and tests of accuracy.

3. E. Altman, "Financial Ratios, Discriminant Analysis and the Prediction of Corporate Bankruptcy," *Journal of Finance*, September 1968, pp. 589-609.

4. Altman, Haldeman and Narayanan, "Zeta® Analysis," *op cit*. Discriminant analysis is a multivariate technique that analyzes the characteristics (e.g., financial ratios) of entities (e.g., corporations) belonging to two or more populations or groups (e.g., bankrupt vs. nonbankrupt firms, Aaa vs. Aa-rated bonds) in order to identify the relative importance of these characteristics to the entity's classification into its identified group. The trick is to maximize the classification accuracy of the original test observations and to test the model on many relevant samples in order to verify the model's statistical reliability.

5. L. Fisher, "Determinants of Risk Premiums on Corporate Bonds," *Journal of Political Economy*, 1959, pp. 217-237 and R. West, "An Alternative Approach to Predicting Corporate Bond Ratings," *Journal of Accounting Research*, 8, pp. 112-125.

Prediction of Beta from Investment Fundamentals

by Barr Rosenberg and James Guy

To understand why true beta changes, consider two imaginary future events with uncertain outcomes and two common stocks, A and B. One event has strong energy implications, the other stong inflation implications. Assuming that, relative to the market, stock A responds two-thirds as much to energy and two times as much to inflation, whereas stock B responds four-thirds as much to energy and nil to inflation, stock B will show the higher volatility if the energy situation changes and stock A the higher volatility if the inflation situation changes. Depending whether energy or inflation is currently the greater source of uncertainty, stock A or stock B will have the higher beta.

Reprinted from Financial Analysts Journal, May/June 1976—all rights reserved
Copyright © The Financial Analysts Federation, 1976

by Barr Rosenberg and James Guy

Prediction of Beta from Investment Fundamentals

Part One
Prediction Criteria

Systematic risk, as measured by beta, captures that aspect of investment risk that cannot be eliminated by diversification. Consequently, it plays the crucial role in evaluating *ex post* the degree of risk undertaken in a diversified investment program, hence in judging the ability of that investment program to achieve a desirable risk-return posture. Again, the prediction of beta essentially predicts the future risk of a diversified portfolio, hence its influence on portfolio beta is one of the key considerations in any investment decision. Therefore, among many possible risk measures beta deserves particular attention and will be the central topic of this article. In the first section, beta will be defined, and then, in our discussions of the applications of beta, criteria for optimal prediction and estimation of beta will emerge. In the second section (to be published in the July/August issue), we develop alternative methods of estimating and predicting beta from a fundamental perspective, in which beta is seen as the consequence of economic variables.

Beta

If the investment return on the market portfolio in any time period assumes any certain value, what return can be expected, on the average, for a security

Barr Rosenberg is an associate professor at the University of California, Berkeley, schools of Business Administration, and is principal of Barr Rosenberg & Associates, a consulting firm in finance. James Guy is an assistant professor at the schools of Business Administration, Berkeley.

in the same time period? For example, if the market return in that period will be 10 per cent, can the security return be expected, on the average, to be 20 per cent, or five per cent?

Notice that this question refers to the value of the security return to be expected "on the average," although it applies to a single security in a single period. The expectation is to be taken in the following sense. Suppose that, in view of everything we now know about the economy and the specific firm n, we imagine repeating many times the uncertain events that may occur in the time period with each repetition having the nature of an experiment. Each experiment yields some market return r_M and some security return r_n.

Each pair of returns (r_M, r_n) may be graphed, with the security return r_n on the vertical axis and the market return r_M on the horizontal axis. The slope of a regression line fitted through these points, which measures the degree to which higher market return leads to an expectation of greater security return, is the beta of the security (see Figure 1). When the stock market index rises or falls, the security price will tend to rise or fall also, and the rise will tend to be more or less than one. Typically, the slope (i.e., beta) will be greater than zero but less than three. Many securities have betas around one, and they tend to rise and fall in price roughly by the same percentage that the market index rises or falls. A security with a negative beta would tend to move against the market, but such securities are rare.

When each repetition is viewed in hindsight, a unique pair of returns (r_M, r_n) will have occurred, but we are concerned with the expectation that held looking forward in time, before the actual returns have occurred. The values actually realized will not ordinarily correspond to expectations: *Ex post* (i.e., hindsight) observation that $r_M = 10$ per cent and $r_n = 20$ per cent does not imply that the security's beta was two. The true beta could have been one with the additional 10 per cent in security return being caused by random factors unique to that security. Beta gives an expected value just as a probabilistic prediction for the profit in a gamble does: *Ex post*, the gamble will have either succeeded or failed, but the result need not be equal to the expected value.

Beta is often explained by plotting a time series of pairs of returns. This corresponds to repeating the above experiment at a sequence of dates. In this way, we are able to observe more than one outcome and, therefore, to illustrate the relationship. Repetition is somewhat misleading, however, since it suggests that beta is unchanging over the sequence. Actually, as we will discuss below, there are reasons to expect that beta changes. The sequence is actually that of repeating similar but changing experiments. The es-

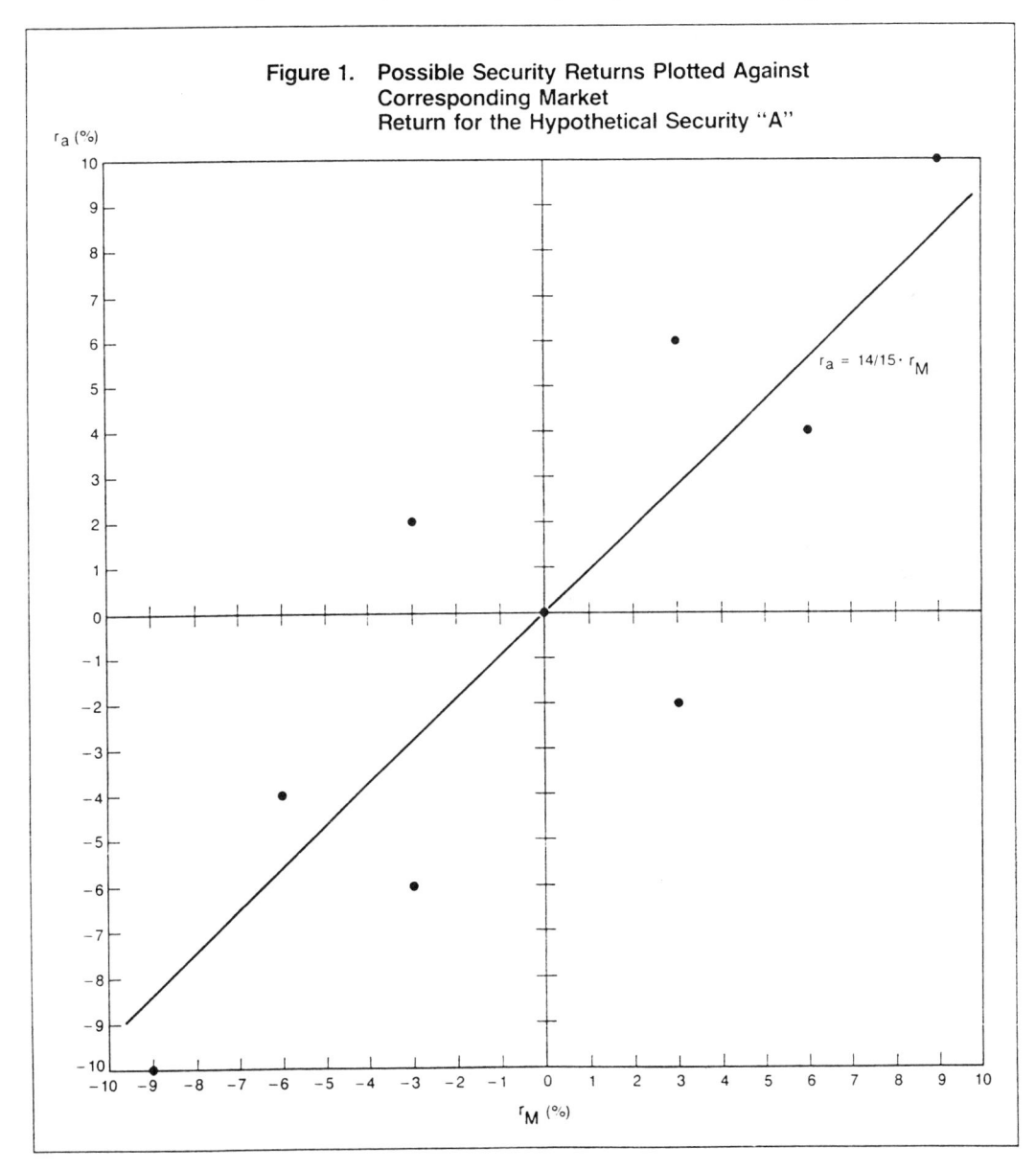

Figure 1. Possible Security Returns Plotted Against Corresponding Market Return for the Hypothetical Security "A"

$r_a = 14/15 \cdot r_M$

sential meaning of beta applies distinctly at each point in time.

Note that, from an economic viewpoint, the market return does not cause the security return. Instead, both are caused by economic events. This point has created some confusion among analysts who interpret beta, which is a regression coefficient, as necessarily stating the causal relationship of market returns upon the security returns: That is, if beta is two, a market return of 10 per cent *causes* a security return of 20 per cent. The correct wording of this statement is that, as a consequence of the dependence of both market return and security return upon economic events, if a market return of 10 per cent is observed, then the most likely value for the associated security return is 20 per cent. The words "most likely" include the following pattern of inference: If the market return is 10 per cent, then the associated economic events must be of certain types; if for each set of events that could induce a market return of 10 per cent we compute the security return that would result, then on average the return, weighted by the probability of the events, is 20 per cent.

Beta as the Consequence of Underlying Economic Events

It is instructive to reach a judgment about beta by carrying out an imaginary experiment as follows. One can imagine all the various events in the economy that may occur, and attempt to answer in each case the two questions: (1) What would be the security return as a result of that event? and (2) What would be the market return as a result of that event? Looking forward in time we can see that the market will be significantly affected by changes in the expected rate of inflation, interest rates, institutional regulations of alternative investment media, growth rate of real GNP, and many other factors. Further, there are a number of less broad events that also deserve attention: movements in international oil and other raw material prices, developments in alternative domestic energy supplies, changes in public attitudes toward pollution and consumer durables, and possible changes in tax law, among others. Each of these events is important in contributing to the uncertainty of future market returns. And for each we can anticipate the effect upon any particular security. Consider, for example, a domestic oil stock. "Energy crisis"-related events will have a proportionally greater effect upon such a stock, inflation-related events probably a relatively smaller effect, than for the market as a whole. As a result, if we foresee that the major source of uncertainty in future returns is from developments in the energy picture, we will anticipate an unusually high beta, but if we foresee that the major source of uncertainty lies in inflation-related events, we will anticipate an unusually low beta.

One could easily devote as much time to predicting beta as is usually devoted to predicting security returns in conventional security analysis. This parallel is, in fact, a valuable one to draw on in thinking about beta. In security analysis, it is customary to distinguish between the component of return resulting from events specific to the firm in question, and the component of return stemming from events affecting the economy or the market as a whole. When the sum of these two is expected to be positive, then the security is considered to be a good buy. Now, in enumerating the events specific to the firm in question, the analyst will formulate a prediction of the expected impact on return and also a forecast of the uncertainty of realizing that expectation. The former determines the expected specific return and the latter the magnitude of specific risk. Thus the tasks of predicting expected return and risk of return are clearly related in this case.

Similarly, in predicting the component of security return arising from economywide events rather than from events specific to that particular firm, the analyst estimates the probabilities of the various possible outcomes of the event, and the magnitude of the response of the security return to that event. The product of these two is the expected effect of the event upon the security return. These effects are then summed over all economywide events that may impact the stock to obtain the expected security return due to economywide factors. Here again, all that is needed is a judgment as to the uncertainty attaching to the economywide events, and we find a prediction of the uncertainty of the security return due to economic events. The return on the market portfolio is the weighted average of the individual security returns, so this same approach yields a prediction of the uncertainty of the market return due to economywide events. Since the events specific to individual firms will tend to average out and contribute little to the market return, the economywide events will account for the great bulk of market risk.

Thus the risk of market return is largely accounted for by economic events that impact many stocks. For each stock, we find that these events also have an effect that can be predicted by security analysis. As an illustration, consider Table 1, where we give two imaginary future events with equal probability of good, bad, and no-change outcomes, and describe the resulting percentage returns on the market, stock A and stock B. Relative to the market, stock A responds two-thirds as much to the energy event and two times as much to the inflation event. Relative to the market, stock B responds four-thirds as much to energy and responds nil to inflation. (These are later referred to as relative response coefficients.)

Table 1

Event	Outcome	% Contribution to Return		
		Market	Stock A	Stock B
Energy	good	+6	+4	+8
	no change	0	0	0
	bad	−6	−4	−8
Inflation	good	+3	+6	0
	no change	0	0	0
	bad	−3	−6	0

Because the effects of the two events are independent, the information given in this table can be represented by the tree diagram given in Figure 2. Using this diagram, it is easy to derive the expected value and variance of returns on the market, r_M, as a result of the two events.

$$E(r_M) = 0$$
$$VAR(r_M) = 1/9\,(9^2 + 6^2 + 3^2 + 3^2 + 3^2 + 3^2 + 6^2 + 9^2) = 30.$$

This variance of future market returns can be decomposed into the variances induced by the two independent events. The variance in market returns caused by energy uncertainty alone is equal to $1/3[6^2 + 0^2 + (-6)^2] = 24$, while that caused by inflation uncertainty alone is equal to $1/3[3^2 + 0^2 + (-3)^2] = 6$. Because these two events are independent, the sum of these two subvariances should equal the total variance of market returns, and indeed we have:

$$24 + 6 = 30.$$

The variance of the future market return stems from uncertainty in energy and inflation. Energy is the greater source of future variance (actually four-fifths of the total in this example). Stock B is more responsive to the energy factor than the market, and it will show a high volatility if the energy situation changes. Stock A will show the higher volatility if the inflation situation changes, since its response coefficient to inflation is higher. Since energy is the greater source of uncertainty, it turns out that stock B has the higher beta.

The betas of companies A and B can be easily calculated using this tree diagram. Consider, for example, the beta of company A, which is defined as:[1]

$$\beta_a \equiv \frac{COV(r_a, r_M)}{VAR(r_M)} = \frac{E[(r_a - E[r_a])(r_M - E[r_M])]}{E[(r_M - E[r_M])^2]}.$$

We know that $VAR(r_M) = 30$, so that all that remains is to calculate $COV(r_a, r_M)$. Remembering that $E(r_a) = 0$, we have

$$\begin{aligned}COV(r_a, r_M) &= 1/9[9.10 + 6.4 + 3(-2) + 3.6\\&\quad + 0.0 + (-3)(-6) + (-3).2\\&\quad + (-6)(-4) + (-9)(-10)]\\&= 28, \text{ substituting this result in the}\end{aligned}$$

formula for β_a, we have,

$$\beta_a = 28/30 = 14/15.$$

This beta for company A can be decomposed into the component betas due to the two events. Let us define r_M^e, r_a^e, and r_b^e as the returns on the market, stock A and stock B due to the energy event alone, and r_M^i, r_a^i, and r_b^i as the corresponding returns due to the inflation event alone. Then:[2]

$$\begin{aligned}COV(r_a, r_M) &= COV(r_a^e, r_M^e) + COV(r_a^i, r_M^i)\\&= 1/3[4.6 + 0.0 + (-4)(-6)] +\\&\quad 1/3[6.3 + 0.0 + (-6)(-3)]\\&= 2/3\{1/3[6.6 + 0.0 + (-6)(-6)]\}\\&\quad + 2\{1/3[3.3 + 0.0 + (-3)(-3)]\}\\&= 2/3\,VAR(r_M^e) + 2\,VAR(r_M^i)\end{aligned}$$

$$\beta_a = 2/3\,\frac{VAR(r_M^e)}{VAR(r_M)} + 2\,\frac{VAR(r_M^i)}{VAR(r_M)}.$$

Substituting in the values for $VAR(r_M^e)$, $VAR(r_M^i)$, and $VAR(r_M)$, we obtain:

$$\begin{aligned}\beta_a &= 2/3 \cdot 24/30 + 2 \cdot 6/30 = 2/3 \cdot 4/5\\&\quad + 2 \cdot 1/5 = 14/15.\end{aligned}$$

The first component of β_a reflects the behavior of the security relative to energy, and the second considers the effect of inflation. As indicated in the derivation, 4/5 and 1/5 are the proportional contributions of the energy and inflation events to market variance, and 2/3 and two measure the relative response coefficients of stock A to these events.

Similarly, it is possible to show that, for security B

---

1. Footnotes appear at end of article.

we have,

$$\beta_b = 4/5 \cdot 4/3 + 1/5 \cdot 0 = 16/15.$$

The foregoing discussion illustrates the proposition that the level of beta is determined by two kinds of parameters: (1) the degree of uncertainty attached to various categories of economic events (the proportional contributions of the events to market variance), and (2) the response of the security returns to these events (relative response coefficients).

In general, if we assume, for expository purposes, that economic events are independent of each other, then the beta of the security n will be:

$$\beta_n = \frac{\sum_{j=1}^{J} \gamma_{jn} V_j}{\sum_{j=1}^{J} V_j}$$

where V_j is the contribution of economywide event j to market variance in any period, and where γ_{jn} is the ratio of the responses of the nth security and the market to the jth event or the "relative response coefficient."[3] This expression can be rewritten as:

$$\beta_n = \sum_{j=1}^{J} \left(\frac{V_j}{\sum_{j=1}^{J} V_j} \right) \gamma_{jn} ,$$

which clearly shows that the beta for any one security is the weighted average of its relative response coefficients, each weighted by the proportion of total variance in market return due to the event.

This insight into the fundamental determinants of beta will be exploited at many points in this article. For the moment it provides a grasp on the behavior of a security's beta over time. Is beta likely to be constant over time, to drift randomly, or to change in some predictable or understandable way? The answer is that beta will change when either the rela-

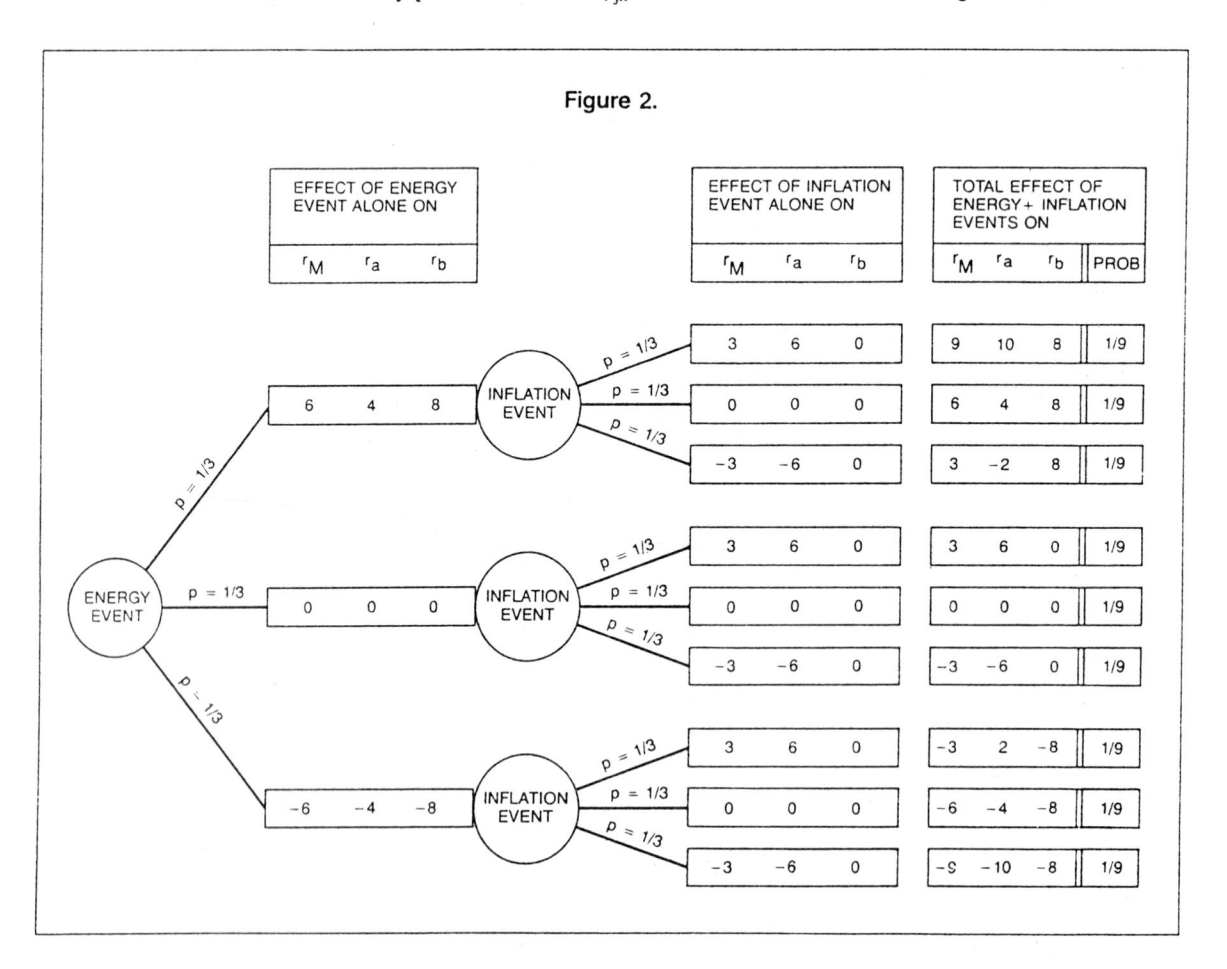

Figure 2.

ENERGY EVENT		EFFECT OF ENERGY EVENT ALONE ON				EFFECT OF INFLATION EVENT ALONE ON			TOTAL EFFECT OF ENERGY + INFLATION EVENTS ON			PROB
		r_M	r_a	r_b		r_M	r_a	r_b	r_M	r_a	r_b	
p = 1/3		6	4	8	INFLATION EVENT p=1/3	3	6	0	9	10	8	1/9
					p=1/3	0	0	0	6	4	8	1/9
					p=1/3	-3	-6	0	3	-2	8	1/9
p = 1/3		0	0	0	INFLATION EVENT p=1/3	3	6	0	3	6	0	1/9
					p=1/3	0	0	0	0	0	0	1/9
					p=1/3	-3	-6	0	-3	-6	0	1/9
p = 1/3		-6	-4	-8	INFLATION EVENT p=1/3	3	6	0	-3	2	-8	1/9
					p=1/3	0	0	0	-6	-4	-8	1/9
					p=1/3	-3	-6	0	-9	-10	-8	1/9

548

tive response coefficients or the relative variances of economic events change. To the degree that these changes can be predicted or explained, changes in beta can be predicted or explained. For example, the monthly dates on which the Bureau of Labor Statistics announces inflation rates will be dates upon which the inflation-oriented events will explain a larger proportion of market variance, and will therefore be dates when firms with high relative response to inflation will have higher than usual betas. For another example, if a firm changes its capital structure, thereby increasing its leverage, its relative response coefficient to virtually all economic events will increase, and so as a result will its beta.

Because beta need not be constant over time, it follows that estimating the average value of beta for a security in some past period is not the same problem as predicting the value of beta in some future period. This is the first distinction between historical estimation and future prediction. A second equally important distinction arises from the use of beta.

Uses of Beta

It is important to examine the uses of beta, not only as an aid in understanding it, but also because the criteria for prediction and estimation probably arise from the requirements of usage. In other words, in each application, that estimator or predictor should be used that will function best in that application. If different applications impose different requirements, then different estimators should be used. Recall that we never observe the "true" beta but rather outcomes that are randomly distributed about an expected value that is equal to beta. As a consequence, we must estimate from the observed outcomes the underlying value of beta that generated them. Similarly, we must predict from this same data the value of beta to be expected in the future, as distinct from the true value of beta in the past.

Performance Evaluation

The most widely recognized use of beta, at this writing, is in the evaluation of past investment performance. For reasons repeatedly discussed in the literature, this use of beta is strongly suggested by the theory of capital markets; the wisdom of this course has been confirmed by the extraordinary increase in the clarity with which investment performance is now being assessed and perceived.

For this purpose, the portfolio as a whole is the appropriate entity: One is interested in the degree of portfolio risk (the beta of the portfolio). There is only a derivative interest in the risks of the individual securities, to the degree that knowledge of these can be helpful in assessing risk for the overall portfolio.

Investment Strategy

We now turn to the use of beta in the selection of an investment policy, that is, to decision making as opposed to *ex post* evaluation.

Because the value of beta measures the expected response to market returns and because the vast majority of returns in diversified portfolios can be explained by their response to the market, an accurate prediction of beta is the most important single element in predicting the future behavior of a portfolio. To the degree that one believes that one can forecast the future direction of market movement, a forecast of beta, by predicting the degree of response to that movement, provides a prediction of the resultant portfolio return. To the degree that one is uncertain about the future movement of the market, the forecast of beta, by determining one's exposure to that uncertainty, provides a prediction of portfolio risk. For a less well diversified portfolio, the residual returns associated with the component investments assume greater proportional importance, but the influence of the overall market factor remains important even in a portfolio containing only one security.

Thus there is little doubt that, if one could make an accurate prediction of future beta for the portfolio, it would be an important ingredient in his investment decision making. And equally, if he could make accurate predictions of the betas for individual securities, these would be important ingredients of his portfolio revision decisions. For instance, if the manager decides to increase the portfolio beta, then he will seek to exchange current holdings with low beta for new purchases with high beta, and the success of this exchange will depend on his ability to forecast the difference in beta.[4]

In this same context it must also be noted that the decision to revise the portfolio cannot be separated from an implicit time horizon. If the asset is to be held for a four-year period, perhaps the average duration in large portfolios, then the appropriate horizon for the forecast of beta will be four years. However, if the asset is purchased with a view to exploiting an anticipated market movement in the short term, say the next half year, then the beta forecast should be made with a horizon of six months.

Thus far, two kinds of uses of beta in the decision-making aspects of portfolio management have been delineated: (a) By forecasting the response to market movement, it allows a forecast of security return when a forecast of market movement is made. (b) To the degree that the market movement is uncertain, beta, in determining the response, determines the expected uncertainty of security or portfolio return. To develop criteria for predictors of beta, it is convenient to refer to a typical investment decision strategy (in the spirit of Treynor and Black) that relies, in part, on beta. This will be referred to as a "typical control strategy."[5] We assume that the strategy includes a target for the portfolio beta, which changes over time in response to (a) changing forecasts of the direction of market movement, or (b) changing assessments of the permissible level of systematic risk to be assumed. Transactions are motivated in part by considerations of security analysis, in the sense that securities regarded as overvalued are sold and securities regarded as undervalued are purchased. Transactions are also influenced by a desire to maintain an appropriate level of diversification. Also, each time that the beta target is changed, a set of transactions is undertaken with the intention of reaching the new target. To reach the new target with a minimum of transactions (hence a minimum of transaction costs), there is a preference for the purchase of securities with values of beta that differ from the existing portfolio in the direction of the new target, and for the sale of securities that differ in the opposite direction. Thus transactions are undertaken with the multiple goals of (1) reaching an appropriate portfolio beta with a minimal number of transactions; (2) increasing expected return; and (3) retaining an appropriate degree of portfolio diversification.

During periods when the target beta for the portfolio is not changing, there will be transactions motivated by the desire to increase expected return and to control diversification. Beta will remain an important consideration in these transactions, because the need to keep the portfolio beta near the target will serve as an indirect constraint on purchases and sales. Transactions involving stocks with betas differing from the target will require offsetting adjustments in other transactions. And, recalling that the beta of the portfolio, just as the beta of a security, may change over time, transactions may sometimes be required simply to adjust for an undesirable drift in the portfolio beta.

Thus a typical control strategy will involve a constraint on the portfolio beta that induces a preference for the purchase (or sale) of stocks with particular kinds of individual betas; in other words, the beta of each individual stock assumes importance as a means to achieve a portfolio target value. The portfolio beta being the average value of the individual betas, weighted by investment proportions, the importance of the individual betas will be determined by the investment proportions. Since the typical portfolio will by definition involve investments in securities that are proportional to their market capitalizations, it follows that the typical weight of an individual beta, as an ingredient in the control strategy, will be in proportion to the capitalization of the firm.

Valuation

Finally, a third class of uses applies to the valuation of convertible assets. Consider any asset, such as convertible bonds, convertible preferred stock, warrants and options, that provides the opportunity to exercise a conversion into the underlying security. An important determinant of the value of any such asset is the total risk of the underlying security, for the simple reason that such assets provide one-sided claims on the underlying security. The higher the underlying risk, the more likely that the security price will change significantly. Since one profits (loses) if the security price goes in one direction and is unaffected if the security goes in the other, the greater the expected risk, the greater the expected profit (loss). Knowledge of the value of beta permits prediction of one important element of risk. Notice that this use of beta arises because its usefulness as a measure of risk of the underlying common implies an estimate of the value of the convertible asset.

Criteria for Prediction

For each use of beta described above, one should ask what properties an appropriate measure of beta should have. It is beyond the scope of this article to discuss criteria for the estimator of beta to be used in historical performance evaluation. We may note in passing that the appropriate measure relates to an average level of risk assumed in the portfolio during the evaluation period, so that it is an estimator of a past risk level. The problem of choosing among alternative estimators of the average value in the past provides a good vehicle for introducing the concepts of bias, variance, and mean square error as employed in the context of estimation problems.

How are we to choose among several alternative estimates of the average value of the portfolio beta over the historical period? (Recall that beta is no more than an underlying tendency and that the actual results observed *ex post* do not tell us what the exact underlying tendency was.) The distributions of estimated values for four imaginary estimators are plotted in Figure 3.

Suppose that the true average for a portfolio or security beta was β_n, and that $\hat{\beta}_n$ is an estimator of this and has an expected value $\bar{\hat{\beta}}_n$. The quality of this estimator can be judged by three criteria: bias, variance, and mean square error.[6] If the estimator is unbiased, its expected value equals the true underlying average, and the bias, $\bar{\hat{\beta}}_n - \beta_n$, is zero. Estimators (a) and (b) are unbiased in Figure 3. Freedom from bias is obviously desirable.

Of a group of unbiased estimators, the most desirable is the one that is the most accurate. Accuracy may be defined by the smallness of the variance of estimation error. Thus the best unbiased estimator is the unbiased estimator with the smallest variance, i.e., minimum $E[\hat{\beta}_n - \bar{\hat{\beta}}_n]^2$. In Figure 3, a is the most desirable unbiased estimator. A criterion for comparing biased and unbiased estimators when it is not important whether the error in $\hat{\beta}_n$ is derived from the bias or estimation error is the mean square error, MSE. Whereas the variance of the estimator is the expected squared deviation of the estimated beta from its mean, the mean square error is the mean of the squared deviation of the estimated beta from the true value, i.e., $E[\hat{\beta}_n - \beta_n]^2$. Of course, when the estimator is unbiased these two measures are equivalent. For any estimator $\hat{\beta}_n$, the formal relationship between bias, $BIAS(\hat{\beta}_n)$, variance, $VAR(\hat{\beta}_n)$, and mean square error, $MSE(\hat{\beta}_n)$, is given by[7]

$$MSE(\hat{\beta}_n) = VAR(\hat{\beta}_n) + [BIAS(\hat{\beta}_n)]^2.$$

As can be seen, by minimizing the MSE of the estimate, we are in fact minimizing the sum of the variance and the squared bias of that estimator. As such, minimizing the MSE imposes an arbitrary judgment as to the relative importance of the bias and variance. If it is thought critical to have an unbiased estimator, then minimizing the MSE would not automatically provide one. It is quite possible that a biased estimator with low variance would be chosen in preference to an unbiased estimator with high variance. This point is amplified graphically in

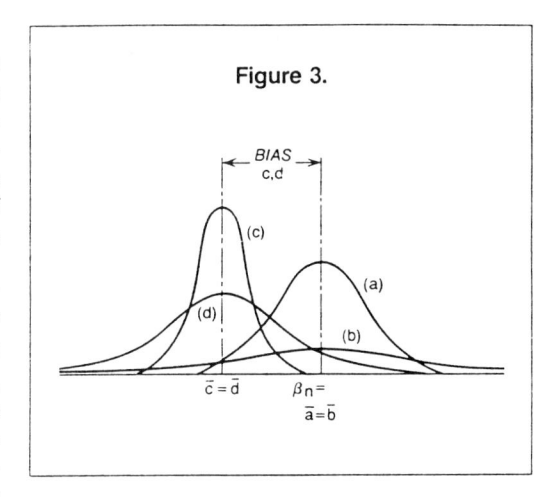

Figure 3.

Figure 3. Estimates (c) and (d) are both biased to the same extent, but (c) is superior to (d) because it has a lower variance. Can (c) be superior to either (a) or (b), even though (c) is biased and (a) and (b) are not? Using the MSE criterion, it is quite possible that (c) is superior to (b) so long as,

$$VAR(c) + [BIAS(c)]^2 < VAR(b).$$

Let us now turn to the main topic of this article, namely, the prediction of beta and the criteria for good prediction. Consider the case where the criteria are concerned with the management of a portfolio of stocks and other nonconvertible assets, as distinct from convertible assets. Clearly, the first requirement is a prediction of the beta of the existing portfolio. This will provide an indication of the portfolio's response to anticipated market movements as well as a prediction of the portfolio's exposure to market risk. Naturally, the prediction should relate to the planning horizon. That is, we are concerned with an estimate of beta for the future period for which plans are being made.

The portfolio beta in the future is the weighted average of the individual security betas, each weighted by the proportionate investment in that security[8],

$$\beta_P = \sum_n W_{Pn} \beta_n,$$

where W_{Pn} is the proportion of the total investment now in stock n, with $\sum_n W_{Pn} = 1$. The predicted portfolio beta is[9]

$$\hat{\beta}_P = \sum_n W_{Pn} \hat{\beta}_n.$$

The prediction error will therefore be $\sum_n W_{Pn}(\hat{\beta}_n - $

β_n). Thus the prediction error for the portfolio beta is the weighted average of the prediction errors for the individual securities, each weighted in proportion to the value of the investment in that security. In order for the prediction error to be small, it is necessary that the prediction errors for the individual stocks be small and average out to zero. If the estimation errors are independent and are expected to equal zero (which will be the case if the estimators are unbiased) then the estimation error will tend to average out to zero.

The quality of the forecast beta for any one stock can be judged using the same criteria as was suggested in the evaluation of estimates of the historical average beta. If the true future beta is β_n, and the forecast beta is $\hat{\beta}_n$ and has an expected value of $\bar{\hat{\beta}}_n$, then the forecast is unbiased if $\bar{\hat{\beta}}_n - \beta_n = 0$. From a group of such unbiased forecasts, the optimal estimate is that with the minimum forecast variance. If, on the other hand, we are considering biased and unbiased forecasts of beta we should choose that one with the minimum mean square forecast error, MSE. Notice that it is the true future value of β_n, not the present value, that is to be predicted.

If we were concerned with estimating the beta for a single stock n, β_n, the preceding considerations would suffice. But since we are estimating beta for a number of securities, n=1, ..., N, we must consider criteria for a collection of estimates $\hat{\beta}_n$, ... n=1, ... N such that the collection will perform optimally in use. Suppose that a prediction rule is defined that produces, for each n, a prediction $\hat{\beta}_n$. Then a criterion for this prediction rule might take the form of a condition applying to a weighted average of the properties of the estimator for the individual securities.

Consider, for example, the question of *unbiasedness*. The strongest requirement of unbiasedness would be that the expected value of the estimator for each and every individual security should equal the value of beta for that security. A weaker requirement would be that the average estimated beta for each industry should equal the true average beta for that industry. Comparing the requirement with the previous one, the difference here is that some estimators within the industry could be upward biased and others downward biased as long as the average bias were zero. A still weaker statement would be that the average predicted beta for all stocks should equal the true average value. This last statement is equivalent to asserting that the expected value for a predicted beta of a stock selected at random from the stock exchange should equal the expected true value for a security selected at random. This condition requires only that the average bias, averaged over all securities, is zero.

Each of these prediction criteria involve an average over many securities. Over what group of securities should this average be taken? How should the securities be weighted? These two questions can be collapsed into a single question of weighting within the universe of securities, because those securities not included in the group over which the average is taken would automatically have a weight of zero.

The answer to the weighting problem follows directly from the criterion that the errors in the predicted betas should average out when weighted by the future proportionate investments in the portfolio. What is desired is unbiasedness, when weighted by the future investment proportions.[10] Thus, ideally, a slightly different set of weights must be used to evaluate unbiasedness for each future investment portfolio. In practice, it is simpler and probably sufficient to achieve unbiasedness relative to the average investment weights to be expected for the user of the prediction rule. Since the sum of the investment weights, summed across all potential institutional users of the prediction rule, approximates the aggregate market values, a natural criterion is to define unbiasedness relative to a capitalization-weighted average.

Having settled the question of weighting, the next issue is that of the strictness of the unbiasedness condition: Must the prediction be unbiased for every security, for groups of securities such as industries, or only for the entire sample? The answer is again that the average expected prediction error for the group of securities in any portfolio should be zero. If all portfolios were identical to the market portfolio, then the absence of bias for the capitalization-weighted market would suffice. But in fact individual portfolios differ. Some emphasize one industry group, some emphasize another. Some concentrate on stocks with a particular fundamental characteristic, some on stocks with a particular technical characteristic. It follows that, if the average expected prediction error is to be zero for all portfolios, it is desirable that the predictor be unbiased for each industry group and for each fundamental or technical characteristic that may serve as a basis for portfolio selection.

The question of the appropriate criterion for *ac-*

curacy of the estimators may be approached in a similar fashion. From the point of view of predicting portfolio risk, it is the size of the error in predicting the portfolio beta that is important, as distinct from the betas of individual stocks in the portfolio. Moreover, it is the error itself that matters, not the source from which it derives. Thus it is immaterial whether an error results from bias or from variance in the estimator. It follows that the appropriate criterion for accuracy in the prediction of portfolio risk is a Minimum Mean Square Error Predictor. We are not only concerned with predictions of beta for the prediction of portfolio risk, but also for making decisions with regard to possible portfolio revisions. The respective criteria for prediction of individual security betas and of the present risk of the portfolio must be such as to yield a good control of risk for the eventual portfolio constructed using these predictions. Thus the form of these criteria must be derived from the decision procedure. If, for example, the manager follows a typical control strategy with a desired portfolio beta of 1.3, then a good beta predictor is one such that by relying on the predictor he will indeed tend to achieve a portfolio beta of 1.3. Because the portfolio revision decision entails the sale of specific securities within the portfolio and the purchase of others, it becomes necessary to predict the betas of individual securities—highlighting another essential distinction between future prediction and historical evaluation: In prediction, the risk levels of individual securities assume primary importance. Again, any error in the prediction of risk for the existing portfolio, regardless of its source or nature, will be equally serious as long as we accept the predicted value as the basis for subsequent portfolio revision.

However, in modifying the portfolio, we will consider alternative combinations of sales and purchases, following the "typical control strategy" outlined previously. Our decision will depend in some form on the predictions of the betas for the individual securities. Presumably, we will select a group of sales and purchases that move in the direction of the desired beta, while also achieving an increase in expected return. It is likely that certain "characteristics" of the stocks will influence the choice. Thus we consider currently "popular" stocks for purchase, and currently "unpopular" stocks for sale. Or we consider currently high P/E stocks for purchase, and currently low P/E stocks for sale. Any one of an infinite number of decision rules may be used in which the major ingredient is a forecast of excess return on the individual security. But if this forecast of excess return shows any dependence at all across different stocks, it is probable that the dependence will take the form of a belief on the part of the manager that stocks with more of some characteristics or groups of characteristics are desirable. Another form of this approach would be based on the belief that stocks in some sectors will outperform others.

Obviously, we want the prediction of beta to be as accurate as possible for each stock, so that its contribution to the expected change in beta is as accurately measured as possible. But it is also important that the law of averages will operate to reduce toward zero over a number of decisions the average value of the errors in the individual stocks selected. In other words, we want the prediction rule to be unbiased relative to the decision rule being used.

The importance of this point can be indicated by an illustration that we shall develop in some detail. Consider a portfolio manager who constructs his portfolio using stocks currently experiencing trading volume above their historical average. Then, when revising his portfolio, that portfolio manager might sell from the existing portfolio those stocks with below average volume, and might buy stocks with currently high trading volume. Now, suppose that at the same time the portfolio manager attempts to control the portfolio risk and limit beta to, for example, 1.2. If the predicted beta value on his current portfolio is 1.3, he might reasonably select for sale those stocks from the portfolio that were high in predicted beta, and replace these with stocks from among the actively traded list that were low in beta, while also meeting his other criteria for higher expected return.

Having set up this illustration, consider now the effects of a prediction rule that is negatively biased relative to changes in share trading volume in comparison to historical averages. In other words, if the stock is currently popular, the predicted beta wil be too low, and, if the stock is currently unpopular, the predicted beta will be too high. It should be apparent that the portfolio manager would not achieve his goal of controlling risk by using such a rule. The average predicted beta for the stocks that he sold would be too high so that the sale would reduce the beta of his portfolio less than he expected, and the average predicted beta for the stocks he bought would be too low, resulting in a greater increase in beta from the purchase than he expected. These two effects combine to result in the transactions reducing beta less than expected. In fact, if the bias is large enough, the transactions might actually increase beta despite the fact that a reduction is predicted.

This example was developed at some length because the conventional methods now being used to predict beta *do show this kind of bias* and, as a result, this kind of error is being made on an everyday basis. It is quite conceivable for a portfolio manager, with the best intentions, to continue to produce a beta of 1.3 on a regular basis, although continually revising his portfolio to achieve an apparent beta of 1.2, simply because the prediction rule, by being biased relative to one of the characteristics employed for stock selection, asserts that beta will be reduced, when in fact it will not.

Thus we see that in selecting stocks it is desirable that the prediction rule for individual security betas again be unbiased relative to the characteristics employed in the decision rule.[11] Subject to this requirement, the prediction rule should be as accurate as possible—i.e., should exhibit minimum mean square error.

Finally, let us turn to the third use of predicted beta, namely, the valuation of convertible assets. Consider an investor in convertible assets who will repeatedly use the prediction rule to value a convertible asset prior to making a buy or sell decision. For this purpose the important point is that he make profitable decisions on average. So in this case our criterion for the choice of a prediction rule for beta is derived from the requirement that "good" valuations of convertible assets result, where "goodness" is measured by the profitability of an investment strategy based upon the valuations. Any error in the predicted beta feeds through to a consequent error in the valuation of the convertible asset, and the relationship between the former and the latter is a complicated one. It follows that a simple criterion applied to the valuation rule for convertible assets will result in a complicated criterion for the underlying prediction of risk. In particular the desire for a minimum-variance unbiased predictor of convertible asset value (not a bad criterion for a valuation rule), yields a highly complex criterion for the nature of the predictor of risk on the underlying common, that, among other things, does not require that the underlying predictor be unbiased.[12] Thus the criteria for beta predictions to be used for asset valuation are crucially dependent on the exact context. ■

Footnotes

1. For an explanation of subscript notation, see Jerome L. Valentine and Edmund A. Mennis, *Quantitative Techniques for Financial Analysis* (Homewood, Ill.: Richard D. Irwin, Inc., 1971).

2. Note that $r_M = r_M^i + r_M^e$ and $r_a = r_a^i + r_a^e$. Because the events are independent, $E(r_M^i, r_M^e) = 0 = E(r_a^i, r_a^e)$. Further, because there is no reason to expect any dependence between r_a^e and r_M^i or r_a^i and r_M^e, $E(r_M^i, r_a^e) = 0 = E(r_M^e, r_a^i)$. Consequently,

$$COV(r_a, r_M) = E[r_a^i + r_a^e][r_M^i + r_M^e]$$
$$= E[r_a^i, r_M^i] + E[r_a^i, r_M^e] + E[r_a^e, r_M^i]$$
$$\quad + E[r_a^e, r_M^e]$$
$$= E[r_a^i, r_M^i] + E[r_a^e, r_M^e]$$
$$= COV(r_a^i, r_M^i) + COV(r_a^e, r_M^e).$$

3. A formal proof of this equation is given as follows: Let the market return generated by the jth factor be denoted by f_j, with $r_M = \sum_j f_j$, and the market variance resulting from the jth factor $= VAR(f_j) = V_j$. For expository convenience, let us assume that the factors are independent, so $COV(f_i, f_j) = 0$ for $i \neq j$. Without loss of generality, the factors are standardized so that the market response coefficient is 1.

Then $r_n = \sum_j \gamma_{jn} f_j + u_n$, where γ_{jn} is the security return caused by the jth factor divided by the market return caused by the same factor, and u_n is the specific component of return for security n, independent of the factors. Therefore

$$\beta_n = COV(r_n, r_M) / VAR(r_M)$$

$$= \frac{COV\left(\sum_j \gamma_{jn} f_j + u_n, \sum_j f_j\right)}{VAR(\sum_j f_j)}$$

$$= \frac{\sum_j \gamma_{jn} V_j + \sum_i \sum_{j \neq i} 0}{\sum_j V_j + \sum_i \sum_{j \neq i} 0}.$$

This equation can be viewed in another light. γ_{jn} can be considered to be that component of beta arising from a specific economic event. Consequently, to derive the overall beta, we should weight each one of these components by the importance of that specific event to overall market variance.

4. The discussion in the text indicates that an investor will make use of his predictions about the future and his attitude toward risk to derive a portfolio with a particular beta value. In this process, the investor is choosing between many portfolios with different beta values. When confronted with such a decision pro-

cess, some market participants simplify the portfolio problem by advocating that an investor has to choose between just two extreme portfolios. If he expects the stock market to rise, he should be fully invested in common stocks with as high a beta value as is possible. If he expects the stock market to decline, however, he should hold no common stocks and should be fully invested in some fixed-interest assets whose value does not depend on movements in the stock market. Such an approach is based on the naive belief that we know with certainty whether the market will rise or fall. We can never be so certain. To reduce the exposure to this uncertainty, it is prudent to select an intermediate portfolio that balances the risks of an exposed position against the benefits from the expected movement. Consequently, at any point in time, the optimal portfolio will be some mixture of fixed-interest and equity securities, and, depending on the uncertainty of our predictions and our risk attitude, the portfolio could have one of many different beta levels.

5. Jack L. Treynor and Fischer Black, "How to Use Security Analysis to Improve Portfolio Selection," *Journal of Business* (January 1973), pp. 66-86.

6. In principle, none of these criteria is really appropriate. One should first consider the investment strategy and evaluate the cost of making an error. Once this is decided, the error is measured in such a way as to maximize the present value of the contemplated investment strategy.

7. The derivation of this formula is simple:

$$MSE[\hat{\beta}_n] = E[\hat{\beta}_n - \beta_n]^2$$
$$= E[\hat{\beta}_n - E(\hat{\beta}_n) + E(\hat{\beta}_n) - \beta_n]^2$$
$$= E[\hat{\beta}_n - \bar{\beta}_n + \bar{\beta}_n - \beta_n]^2$$
$$= E[\hat{\beta}_n - \bar{\beta}_n]^2 + E[\bar{\beta}_n - \beta_n]^2$$
$$+ 2E[\hat{\beta}_n - \bar{\beta}_n][\bar{\beta}_n - \beta_n].$$

Now, $E(\hat{\beta}_n - \bar{\beta}_n)^2 = VAR(\hat{\beta}_n)$, by definition

$E(\bar{\beta}_n - \beta_n)^2 = [BIAS(\hat{\beta}_n)]^2$, since $\bar{\beta}_n$ and β_n are both parameters, whose difference is equal to $BIAS(\hat{\beta}_n)$, the expectation of the $BIAS(\hat{\beta}_n)^2$ is equal to $BIAS(\hat{\beta}_n)^2$.

and $E[\hat{\beta}_n - \bar{\beta}_n][\bar{\beta}_n - \beta_n] = [\bar{\beta}_n - \beta_n]E[\hat{\beta}_n - \bar{\beta}_n]$
$$= [\bar{\beta}_n - \beta_n][\bar{\beta}_n - \bar{\beta}_n]$$
$$= 0.$$

8. The variance of returns on an individual security, n, is related to its beta, and the variance of returns on the market by the following expression:

$$VAR(r_n) = \beta_n^2 VAR(r_M) + VAR(u_n),$$

where $VAR(u_n)$ is the unsystematic risk of the security n. If we combine N securities in a portfolio with each security weighted by W_n, the expected return and variance of returns for the portfolio are:

$$E(r_P) = \sum_{n=1}^{N} E[W_{Pn}(\alpha_n + \beta_n r_M + u_n)]$$

and

$$VAR(r_P) = \sum_{n=1}^{N} W_{Pn}^2 \beta_n^2 VAR(r_M)$$
$$+ \sum_{n=1}^{N} W_{Pn}^2 VAR(u_n).$$

In a diversified portfolio, the last term is close to zero and

$$VAR(r_P) = VAR(r_M) \sum_{n=1}^{N} W_n^2 \beta_n^2 \approx \beta_P^2 VAR(r_M).$$

Also,

$$\beta_P = \frac{COV(r_P, r_M)}{VAR(r_M)} = \frac{COV\left(\sum_{n=1}^{N} W_n r_n, r_M\right)}{VAR(r_M)}$$

$$= \frac{\sum_{n=1}^{N} W_n COV(r_n, r_M)}{VAR(r_M)} = \sum_{n=1}^{N} W_n \beta_n.$$

9. In future periods, the investment proportions will change as a consequence of stock price changes, and the portfolio beta will therefore also change. Nevertheless, the expected weights in the future will be close to the existing investment proportions, so that the predicted portfolio beta using current investment proportions is appropriate even when the uncertain future changes in investment proportions are taken into account.

10. There exists a problem of circularity here. The estimates of beta are used to determine the investment properties in any future portfolio, but yet these future investment proportions are needed in order to choose between the various estimates of $\hat{\beta}$. The choice of "typical investment proportions" suggested in the text sidesteps this problem.

11. As in the prediction of portfolio beta, there is the question of appropriate weights for the definition of unbiasedness. Paralleling the previous discussion, a natural criterion is to define the unbiasedness relative to a capitalization weighted average. For purposes of portfolio revision, however, this weighting is less clearly indicated. The problem is that the entire set of beta predictors for securities being considered for purchase and sale influences the transaction decision, although only a fraction of the securities under consideration may actually be traded. For instance, among eight securities regarded as candidates for above-average appreciation, the one with the highest predicted beta may be chosen for purchase. Whether

this is also the stock with the highest true beta depends on the errors in estimating all eight statistics, regardless of the capitalization of those securities. Nevertheless, it is a reasonable approximation to assert that the expected influence of an error in estimating $\hat{\beta}_n$ is proportional to the capitalization of that asset.

12. To see this, note that the typical valuation rule for the estimated value $\hat{V}$ of a convertible asset, as a function of the estimated mean $\hat{\bar{r}}$ and variance $\hat{s}$ of the return to the underlying common stock, has the properties of the integral

$$V \propto \int_{X_0}^{\infty} X \exp\{-1/2(X-\hat{\bar{r}})^2/\hat{s}\}dX.$$

The integral is a nonlinear function of $\hat{\bar{r}}$ and $\hat{s}$, so that a linear or quadratic criterion on $\hat{V}$ (e.g., $E[\hat{V}] = E[V]$, or MINIMIZE VAR$[\hat{V}]$) implies a non-quadratic criterion on $\hat{s}$. Indeed, the criterion can only be written in the form of an integral equation.

References

Beaver, William; Kettler, Paul; and Scholes, Myron. "The Association Between Market Determined and Accounting Determined Risk Measures." *The Accounting Review* 45 (October 1970), 654-682.

Lintner, John. "The Valuation of Risk Assets and the Selection of Risky Investments in Stock Portfolios and Capital Budgets." *Review of Economics and Statistics* 47 (February 1965), 13-37.

Rosenberg, Barr and Guy, James. "The Prediction of Systematic Risk." Research Program in Finance, Working Paper No. 33. Berkeley: Institute of Business and Economic Research, University of California, 1975.

Rosenberg, Barr and Marathe, Vinay. "Tests of Capital Asset Pricing Hypotheses." Research Program in Finance, Working Paper No. 32. Berkeley: Institute of Business and Economic Research, University of California, 1975.

Rosenberg, Barr and McKibben, Walt. "The Prediction of Systematic and Specific Risk in Common Stocks." *Journal of Financial and Quantitative Analysis* 8 (March 1973), 317-333.

Rosenberg, Barr; Houglet, Michael; Marathe, Vinay; and McKibben, Walt. "Components of Covariance in Security Returns." Research Program in Finance, Working Paper No. 13. Berkeley: Institute of Business and Economic Research, University of California, 1973. [Revised 1975.]

Sharpe, William F. *Portfolio Theory and Capital Markets*. New York: McGraw-Hill Book Company, 1970.

Treynor, Jack and Black, Fischer. "How to Use Security Analysis to Improve Portfolio Selection." *Journal of Business* 46 (January 1973), 66-86.

Prediction of Beta from Investment Fundamentals

by Barr Rosenberg and James Guy

Whether one can legitimately use the same estimator of beta for predicting portfolio behavior as for evaluating historical performance depends on whether one expects the value of beta to change. Examples of cases in which the expected change is not zero are (1) a firm that has recently acquired another, less risky firm and (2) a firm that uses the proceeds of a new equity offering to retire debt, reducing its leverage. In order to avoid error in cases like these, it is necessary to incorporate into predictions of future beta knowledge about fundamentals. The authors demonstrate that betas predicted from fundamental considerations are considerably superior to betas based purely on historical experience.

Reprinted from Financial Analysts Journal, July/August 1976—all rights reserved
Copyright © The Financial Analysts Federation, 1976

by Barr Rosenberg and James Guy

Prediction of Beta from Investment Fundamentals

◂ Is it legitimate to use the same estimator of beta both to predict portfolio behavior and to evaluate historical performance? The answer depends on whether one can reasonably expect the value of beta not to change. Examples of cases in which this expectation is unwarranted are (1) a firm that has recently acquired another, less risky firm and (2) a firm that uses the proceeds of a new equity offering to retire debt, reducing its leverage.

If the firm's beta has been consistently rising or falling over the period for which its historical beta is computed, its average value will lag behind the current true value, and still further behind a projection for the future that allows for continuation of this trend. Or, if a firm is exposed to a macroeconomic event whose uncertainty is known to be increasing, its historical beta will underestimate its future beta.

When there is a discrepancy between past and future beta, it is necessary to incorporate into predictions of future beta knowledge about fundamentals of the firm. Thus, for example, if there is a demonstrated tendency for a company's beta to revert toward the norm for the industry, then any estimate of future beta should allow for this tendency toward reversion.

The more information brought to bear in predicting beta, the smaller will be the average prediction error. If the information is properly used, it will always pay to incorporate fundamental as well as purely technical, or price historical, information into prediction of beta. ▸

Barr Rosenberg is an associate professor at the University of California, Berkeley, Schools of Business Administration, and is principal of Barr Rosenberg & Associates, a consulting firm in finance. James Guy is an assistant professor at the Schools of Business Administration, Berkeley. Part One of this article appeared in the May/June 1976 issue of this journal.

Part Two
Alternative Prediction Methods

Of necessity, forecasting entails an extrapolation of some past relationships into the future. It also entails the use of currently available information to which the relationship is applied to predict a future value. Of course, one wishes to use as much information as possible and to extrapolate those relationships most likely to remain stable.

The Historical or Technical Beta: Its Limitations

At this writing, the most popular method of predicting beta is to take an estimate of the historical value of beta, β_n, and to use this in an unadjusted fashion as a predictor. The estimate of the past average beta can be obtained by regressing historical security returns on market returns.[13] This "historical beta" is an unbiased estimator of the true historical beta averaged over past periods; it is the minimum variance unbiased estimator of the true historical value if certain common assumptions hold—namely, the regression model is correctly specified, and the specific returns have zero mean, constant variance, and no correlation with each other.

One of the forces behind this approach has been to use the same estimator of beta for prediction purposes as for evaluation of historical performance, since the historical beta is also somewhat suitable for performance measurement. We may ask, however, whether this estimator meets our criteria of minimum variance subject to unbiasedness relative to characteristics for individual securities. Does it meet

---

1. Footnotes appear at end of article.

the criterion of minimum mean square error for portfolios?

Whether the historical beta is an unbiased predictor of the future value of beta depends entirely on whether the change from the past average to the future value is expected to be zero. If the expected change is zero, then the average prediction error will be the sum of the average estimation error in the historical period (or zero) plus the expected change from the historical to the future value (or zero). However, if any information currently available to implement a decision rule contains implications about the difference between the future beta and the historical average, then the expected value of the change in beta, conditional on that information, will be non-zero, and the prediction rule will be biased.

Figure 4 illustrates several circumstances in which the expected change from the historical average to the future value is non-zero. In Figure 4a, the beta of an imaginary security is plotted over a fairly long period, perhaps 15 years. Two pronounced drops in beta occurred in the past, one perhaps arising from the acquisition of a less risky firm, another from a recent offering of equity that reduced leverage. One of these occurred in the recent past, so that the average value of beta in the historical period indicated by the dashed line is substantially higher than the current value. The best forecast of beta is indicated by the heavy line extending out to the right, and the probable range of future values of beta, taking into account the possible future changes in the fundamentals of the firm, is shown by dotted lines that spread wider as time elapses and the likelihood of cumulative change grows.

The historical average is a biased predictor of future beta because the fundamentals of the firm have changed within the historical interval, illustrating the first defect of the historical beta: Because it ignores possible changes in the fundamentals of the firm, it is potentially out of date and inaccurate. Moreover, it is biased with respect to any change in the fundamentals that took place within the historical period. *It is necessary to incorporate the current fundamental position of the firm into risk prediction in order to remove this defect.*

Figure 4b graphs the beta of another stock that tends to drift about an industry norm, assumed equal to 1.2. Sometimes the firm's beta is substantially above the norm, sometimes it is below, but the economic conditions of the industry, together with the standards of management in that industry, cause the tendency to revert toward the norm. The reversion may be the result of management's overt decision to achieve a more normal risk posture, or it may result from the disappearance of transitory abnormalities in the position of the firm within the industry. In either case, the best prediction for future beta includes a tendency for reversion to the industry norm, shown by the declining heavy line of best forecast. Again the historical average provides a biased forecast, this time because of the intrinsic tendency for the beta to return toward the norm from any abnormal historical average. *The only way to remove this defect in the historical beta is to employ a weighted average including the industry norm and the historical beta.*

Figure 4c graphs the beta of a company whose intrinsic exposure to economic events is changing over time as the result of unknown causes—for example, a consulting firm in pollution control, whose specialties are changing over time so that its fortunes are linked to different industries. Recently, the beta of the firm has been much higher than the historical average. The best forecast for the future, in the absence of information about future changes in the situation of the firm, is that beta will persist at its present value. Thus the historical average is out of date and provides a biased estimator with respect to any decision rule that responds to recent changes in beta. *The only way to remove this defect is to obtain a more timely estimator of beta, either by changing the estimation procedure for historical beta itself or by obtaining other indicators of the current beta of the security.*

Figure 4d graphs the beta of a security that has had a relatively constant level of risk in the past and for which the exposure to economic events is unchanging. However, this security is heavily exposed to one kind of economic event—the energy crisis—and the variance of that event is known to be increasing in the future. The exposure of the firm to that event will consequently contribute to a progressively higher beta in the future, so that the best forecast of beta is shown by the rising heavy line. The historical average is a biased predictor because the variance of economic events is changing. *The only way to remove this defect is to predict the relative response coefficient of the security to economic events and use the forecast of increasing variance for energy-related events to deduce a higher future beta.*

There is one further defect of the historical beta as

Figure 4.

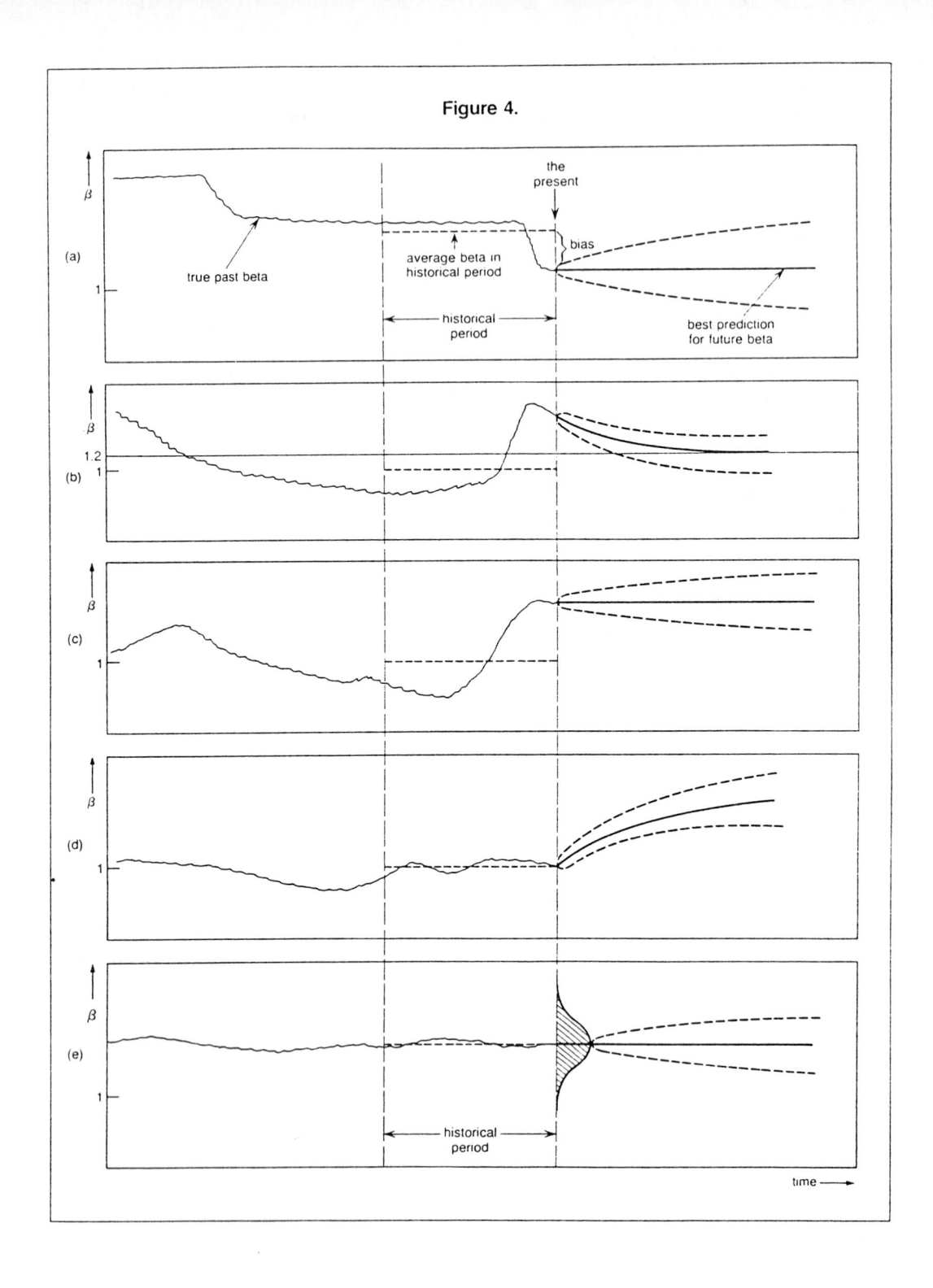

a predictor—it inevitably involves estimation error. Specific events occurring to the firm in the past that really had nothing to do with the economic events affecting the general market level will have matched the direction of market movement purely by chance, thereby causing the estimated value to differ from the underlying tendency. Figure 4e graphs a firm for which there have been no changes in the fundamentals, hence in the underlying beta. Nevertheless, the estimated historical beta will not be exactly equal to the underlying tendency, exhibiting instead a random error as shown in the superimposed distribution. When an estimator exhibits error and when other information on the underlying quantity is available, the use of an appropriate weighted average of the two sources of information always reduces the mean square error of the predictor. Thus, even if beta is unchanging, we will want to include both fundamental and technical information in the predictor in order to improve accuracy.

There are a number of possible improvements that lie strictly in the realm of greater efficiency in deducing from historical stock behavior the most likely current value of the beta. All can be viewed as improvements in the historical beta *per se,* and all amount to different forms of regression. All maintain the advantage of being unbiased estimators of some historical average of past beta for the stock. Some increase the timeliness of the estimate by weighting more recent observations more heavily than past observations, thus moving the weighting forward toward the present. Others attempt to deduce the underlying true value of beta more accurately by differential weights for observations at different time intervals when more or less noise (specific risk) was present to obscure the underlying beta. Still others use different time intervals for observations. But the crucial point is that none escape the limitations discussed above.

An implied predictor for the portfolio beta is found by summing the predictors for the individual stocks in the portfolio, with each weighted by the investment proportion in that stock. It turns out that the properties of this predictor as a predictor of future beta are similar to those for individual securities, so that an amelioration of the problems considered above would improve portfolio risk prediction as well.

The Use of Fundamental Information in Prediction

It is intriguing to consider using other information to predict beta. At this point, an analogy may be helpful. Suppose that it is desired to estimate the volume of fluid in a human being, in order to determine the correct dosage of a drug that will be detected in proportion to this volume when administered to him. Direct measurement of his fluid volume is impossible, because it would entail invading the patient. A good indirect measure, based on the "fundamentals" of physiology, is provided by the patient's weight, but this is imperfect, since other characteristics of the patient obscure the relationship between weight and volume. Other good "fundamental" measures can be based on his height, age, the amount of fat in his body as measured by skinfold thickness, and on knowledge of the manner in which the amount of fluid in the body is being self-regulated. To be even more precise, measurements of his body may be taken to estimate volume constructively. Now, each one of these measurements can add some information as to the prevailing volume. Alternatively, the volume concept can be measured directly by observing how much dilution actually occurs when the drug is administered—i.e., by observing the concentration in the blood after administering some dosage. This latter approach is akin to a "technical" measure, for it measures the system's response to the drug. This measure may be unbiased, but it will have the associated problems of error (if concentration is perturbed by random factors) and of untimeliness (if the volume has changed since the time of the last measurement).

There is no theory that will tell us which of these two procedures to use. Each has a natural appeal. The former gets down to reliance on an intuitively appealing fundamental view of the patient, one that can be related to our understanding of physiology. The latter is a direct measurement of the construct that we are trying to estimate.

Precisely the same distinction arises in contrasting fundamental and technical approaches for predicting beta. In fundamental prediction, the fundamental characteristics of the stock and the market are analyzed in order to predict the responsiveness of the stock to the market. The fundamental approach allows us to rely on our understanding of the firm in its economic setting and on our understanding of the market's view of the firm. The technical approach is a direct measurement of the market's treatment of the firm that can be neither improved nor polluted by "knowledge" about the economy and the market.

In order to highlight the advantages of fundamental prediction relative to technical prediction, it is instructive to distinguish between "conditional" and "unconditional" prediction of beta. In the unconditional prediction of beta, the response coefficients to economic events are predicted, but the variances of the underlying events are considered unchanged. Consequently, beta is determined solely by the predicted response coefficients. This approach deals with the problem illustrated in Figure 4a. Consider, as another illustration, a small undiversified automobile parts supplier, under the assumption that the future variance of economic events will be the same as in the past. Then if the company's response to economic events is the same in the future as in the past, the unconditional forecast of beta will be the same as the best estimate of its value in the past. If this company decides to increase its long-term debt liability, however, its response coefficient will change, and there will be a different unconditional forecast of beta.

In the conditional forecast of beta, the variance of economic events and the response coefficients are both predicted, and the future beta is predicted conditional on the macroeconomic forecast. Although the energy crisis affects the stock market adversely, it has a more severe effect on the automobile industry. If the severity of the energy crisis increases, the prices of automobile stocks will fall more than the market. Consequently, if we believe the future variance of the macroeconomic event called "energy crisis" will increase, then the predictions of future beta for automobile companies, including the parts supplier introduced above, will be higher. Thus the conditional approach deals with the problem illustrated in Figure 4d.

Fundamental predictions specifically attempt to measure the effects on beta of changes in the response coefficients and the variances of the underlying events. Nonfundamental predictions can never predict a change in beta due to a change in the firm's response coefficient arising, say, from a change in its leverage. But unconditional fundamental forecasting can. Furthermore, nonfundamental predictions can never predict a change in beta due to a change in the variance of underlying macroeconomic events. But conditional fundamental forecasting can.

Estimation of an Unconditional Fundamental Prediction Rule

To estimate an unconditional prediction rule, it is only necessary to observe the pattern of systematic risk realized in the past, because the unconditional forecast presumes that the future economic variance is similar to the observed historical variance and extrapolates that pattern directly into the future. For example, if utilities have shown lower systematic risk in the recent past than airlines, then an unconditional forecast asserts that they will do so in the future.

TABLE 2
Industry Differentials in Beta[a]

Industry	Average Industry Values of Beta	Industry Risk Differences Not Explained by Other Fundamental Firm Characteristics[b] Adjustment to Beta
Nonferrous metals	.99	−.142***
Energy raw materials	1.22	−.030
Construction	1.27	.062
Agriculture, food	.99	.140***
Liquor	.89	−.165***
Tobacco	.80	−.279***
Apparel	1.27	.019
Forest products, paper	1.16	−.016
Containers	1.01	−.140**
Media	1.39	.124*
Chemicals	1.22	.011
Drugs, medicine	1.14	−.099***
Soaps, cosmetics	1.09	−.067*
Domestic oil	1.12	−.103*
International oil	.85	−.143*
Tires, rubber goods	1.21	.050
Steel	1.02	−.086*
Producer goods	1.30	.043
Business machines	1.43	.065
Consumer durables	1.44	.132*
Motor vehicles	1.27	.045
Aerospace	1.30	.020
Electronics	1.60	.155**
Photographic, optical	1.24	.026
Nondurables, entertainment	1.47	.042
Trucking, freight	1.31	.098
Railroads, shipping	1.19	.030
Air transport	1.80	.348***
Telephone	.75	−.288***
Energy, utilities	.60	−.237***
Retail, general	1.43	.073
Banks	.81	−.242***
Miscellaneous finance	1.60	.210**
Insurance	1.34	.103
Real property	1.70	.339***
Business services	1.28	.029
Travel, outdoor recreation	1.66	.186**
Gold	.36	−.827***
Miscellaneous, conglomerate	1.14	.089*

a. These results are taken from "The Prediction of Investment Risk: Systematic and Residual Risk," Barr Rosenberg and Vinay Marathe. In Proceedings: Seminar on the Analysis of Security Prices, November 1975. Center for Research in Security Prices, Graduate School of Business, The University of Chicago.

b. One asterisk indicates significance at the 95% level of confidence; two asterisks, significance at the 99% level; and three asterisks, significance at the 99.9% level.

This point is illustrated by some empirical results presented in a study by Rosenberg and Marathe.[14] Column 1 of Table 2 lists the average betas for a number of industry groups. These average betas were generated using 101 months of data from April 1966 to August 1974. Although it is beyond the scope of this article to discuss these results in detail, the standard errors were small and highly significant differences in average beta conform, in the main, to the analysts' intuitions concerning industry risk. Because industry betas maintained these differences over the period studied, it is appealing to incorporate in an unconditional prediction of beta the assertion that the future beta for stocks in each industry will tend to be close to the historical average for that industry. Thus the predicted beta for a stock will give some weight to the average historical beta for the industry.

If the future industry average beta for the utilities, for example, will not change relative to this historical average, this prediction rule will be unbiased across utilities, in the sense of yielding a predicted beta that is equal, on the average, to the true beta across all utilities. This rule will be biased upward, however, for any one utility that, for unknown reasons, differs from the usual utility and has an inordinately low value of beta. This error arises because the utility is assumed to be similar to the other utilities, when in fact it is not.

Besides the industry effect, it is necessary to capture those other characteristics of a firm—for example, financial structure, aggressiveness of management or diversification—that influence its risk. Using these characteristics, it is possible to deduce the variables that are likely to affect risk and the direction of the influence. Increases in the firm's financial leverage or variability of earnings are likely to increase the firm's risk. But increases in the payout ratio or dividend yield are likely to lower risk as the management reduces its attempts to provide returns to the investors from uncertain capital gains on new projects.

The problem is to quantify these and similar concepts in a usable prediction rule. As one solution, the relation between future risk and the fundamental characteristics of the firm may be estimated by regression methods. For this to be possible, a firm's characteristics must be quantified. *Descriptors* of the current condition of the firm are then used to predict future risk, and the best prediction rule is obtained by linear regression. The better the descriptors, the more successful the prediction of risk will be.

This approach was used in Rosenberg and Marathe.[15] It is not the purpose of this article to review those results in detail but, as an illustration of this approach, we give a few selected results in Table 3. The table gives the adjustments to predicted beta for a few descriptors. These adjustments are additive: In other words, the value of each descriptor for the firm is computed, and the adjustment for that descriptor is added to the adjustments for all other descriptors.

The final prediction is a weighted sum of many descriptors. A good prediction can be obtained by using only the variability of earnings; by adding the debt/asset ratio, one obtains a better prediction and the importance of earnings variability diminishes because it was, in part, serving to measure the effects of financial leverage. Similarly, as dividend yield is added, the importance of both earnings variability and leverage diminishes, because they were both serving, in part, as measures of management conservatism, which is also measured by yield. If one characteristic of the firm cannot be measured accurately, the measurement, once obtained, may be useless, because the accurate measurements of other charac-

TABLE 3
Optimal Adjustments to Short-Term Beta Forecasts, $\hat{\beta}$, for Selected Fundamental Characteristics[a]

Descriptor	Adjustment in $\hat{\beta}$ for a Difference of One Standard Deviation from the Mean of All Firms[b]
Variance of cash flow	0.022***
Variance of earnings	0.023*
Growth in earnings per share	−0.004***
Market capitalization	−0.043***
Current dividend yield	−0.044***
Total debt to assets	0.041***

a. These results taken from Rosenberg and Marathe (1975b), table 4.

b. These figures are standardized so as to be comparable with one another. For example, the coefficient of 0.022 for the variance of cash flow, VFLO, indicates that if the VFLO for a firm lies one standard deviation from the mean VFLO of all firms, the predicted beta for that firm is increased by 0.022. Roughly 17 per cent of all firms will lie more than one standard deviation above the mean, and these will experience upward adjustments of 0.022 or more. Similarly, roughly three per cent of all firms will lie two standard deviations or more above the mean and will experience upward adjustments of 0.044 or more as a result of this descriptor. And, of course, equally as many firms will lie below the mean and receive negative adjustments of the same amount.

The significance of estimated coefficients is indicated as follows: "*" indicates significance at the 95% level of confidence; "**" at the 99% level of confidence; and "***" at the 99.9% level of confidence.

teristics serve as better predictors of this one characteristic than does the doubtful measurement itself. This explains the quite low weight given to the variability of past earnings in the final prediction rule: The measure used in this study, the variability of annual historical earnings, apparently has less content than other fundamental variables, not all of which are included in this table, that serve as predictors of the intrinsic earnings variability.

Taken as a group, the fundamental variables provided excellent predictors of risk. In fact, they were substantially better predictors than the historical beta in the sense that they achieved a smaller measurement error. The prediction rule combining the fundamental variables and the industry differences in an optimal way performed still better. In this combined prediction rule, industry differences need account for only those aspects of the firms in the industry not otherwise measured by fundamental characteristics. The differences remaining after the contribution of the fundamental characteristics are given in the second column of Table 2. The differences are now much smaller but remain highly significant statistically. These remaining differences may be interpreted as true "industry characteristics" as distinct from fundamental characteristics typical of firms in the industry.

Will this prediction rule, as fitted by regression, be unbiased? It may be shown that, if any characteristic is included within this regression, the resulting prediction rule will necessarily be unbiased relative to that characteristic. However, if unbiasedness is taken with the items weighted by market capitalization, the data in a regression must be weighted in the same way.

This approach provides a very powerful method of constructing a prediction rule for beta using fundamental information. To clarify this point, suppose that we have initially a fundamental prediction rule that does not employ the distinction between utilities and other firms as one of its sources of information. Suppose, further, that this characteristic has a profound effect upon beta over and above all other observable fundamental characteristics that might have already been employed in the prediction rule. Because this item is correlated with the difference between the previous fundamental prediction and the actual beta, the previous fundamental prediction rule will be biased relative to this characteristic. In fact, it will be biased upward relative to this characteristic, because utilities have lower betas than could otherwise be accounted for by balance-sheet and income-statement characteristics.

The foregoing prediction rule would have been fitted by a regression in which the information about utilities was not included. The bias and inefficiency of that prediction rule can be overcome if an additional descriptor capturing the "utility" characteristic is added to the right-hand side of the equation. Since this variable carries significant new information about beta, the modified regression fits significantly better. On the average, the predictions of beta for utilities will drop by the desired amount, so that the resulting predictions will no longer be biased and will show an average error of zero across the group. Thus, by adding this additional item, the efficiency of the overall predictive performance has improved, and the bias of the predictor relative to the utility industry has been removed.

There is a clear-cut moral here. Whenever an item of information will be helpful in predicting beta, it should be employed in the prediction rule because it always improves efficiency in prediction and, whenever that characteristic may be used as the basis for a selection rule, removes bias with respect to that selection rule.

Combining Fundamental and Technical Approaches

In making an estimate, it is natural to combine information from several sources. In developing the fitted fundamental prediction rule, we combined a variety of descriptors of fundamental characteristics and industry groups into a prediction rule by least squares regression. It is not widely realized that these same sources of information may be further combined with technical predictors for beta by simply including the latter as additional descriptors in the regression. In the augmented regression, descriptors may be any measures of risk-relevant aspects of the firm based upon published information—fundamental, technical, or otherwise. The dependent variable is the future beta, and the fitted prediction rule provides an optimal predictor of future beta from currently published descriptors of all sorts, in the sense of providing a minimum mean square error prediction rule that is also unbiased with respect to any descriptors included in the fitted rule, relative to the weights on firms used in the regression.

Intuitively, the regression places weight on a descriptor whenever it helps provide accurate information about future risk. If individual security risk is not changing over time, and if past risk can be accurately estimated by an historical technical measure, then that technical measure will be given heavy weight and fundamental information will be given relatively little weight. If, on the other hand, the individual security betas are changing over time, or the historical risk cannot be accurately estimated by a technical measure, then the technical measure will be downweighted and heavy weight will be placed on fundamental information.

The fundamental information turns out to carry the lion's share of the weight in the fitted prediction rule. The historical beta added only four per cent to the total predictable variance, and the weight given to historical beta was only 0.2. That is, if the estimated historical beta were 2.5—1.5 above the average value of 1.0—then the predicted beta would be increased by 0.2 × 1.5 = 0.3.

Compared to technical betas, fundamental betas have certain advantages and disadvantages. The technical beta uses the historical data of the stock to derive a direct measurement of the characteristic of interest, beta. Its weakness lies in measurement error and in inadequate response to changes in the company's characteristics and in the variances of the underlying economic events. In contrast, the weakness of the fundamental prediction rule, or of the most naïve rule that all betas are akin to the norm, is that it applies a general pattern to an individual stock. Its strength lies in the ability to respond to changes in characteristics and in less measurement error, since the pattern is observed over many cases. The combined rule attains some of the strengths of both approaches.

Combining Predictions for Individual Security Betas into a Prediction for a Portfolio Beta

So far, the question of combining predictors of individual security betas into a predictor for the portfolio beta has been sidestepped. At first sight, the answer appears obvious: Since the portfolio beta is the sum of the individual security betas, each weighted by the appropriate investment proportion, the predictor of the portfolio beta should be just the weighted average of the predictors for the individual betas. The problem, however, is that the individual predictors were constructed so as to be optimal predictors for individual securities, and it is not necessarily true that they are also optimal as ingredients in a weighted sum used to predict a portfolio beta.

We need to begin with the criterion of minimum mean square error for portfolio beta prediction and to deduce from it new criteria that can be applied to individual stocks. When we do this, we find that, if the individual predictors are optimal relative to some criterion, then their weighted sum will be optimal for the portfolio relative to that criterion, if and only if 1) the prediction rule exhibits errors that are uncorrelated with the weights in the portfolio (i.e., the prediction rule is unbiased relative to the method of constructing the portfolio) and 2) the prediction rule is optimal with respect to the weights used in the portfolio.

These two conditions must be satisfied. The second condition can be approximately satisfied by a single overall prediction rule, provided that it is unbiased with respect to capitalization weights. These weights will tend to reflect the weights used in institutional portfolios, and an optimized prediction rule, unbiased with respect to these weights, will, in practice, be very similar to one optimized with respect to the weights in the individual portfolio.

The first condition turns out to be equivalent to the requirement that the predictor be unbiased relative to the characteristics employed in the selection rule. As a consequence, introducing these characteristics as ingredients in a fundamental prediction rule for individual securities has the additional advantage of allowing us to use the individual forecasts unhesitatingly as ingredients for the portfolio forecast.

The estimated fundamental prediction rule suggested that shares that have recently exhibited high (low) share turnover rates will exhibit higher (lower) betas in the near future than would otherwise be expected. This implies that a prediction rule that did not employ this characteristic would be downward biased for currently popular stocks. To confirm this expectation, an experiment was carried out using data subsequent to that employed in the previously mentioned study. Among the 700 largest capitalized industrial firms, the 25 with the highest share turnover ratios (STO) in the year 1972 were grouped into a portfolio, as were the 25 firms with the lowest STO. It was expected that the historical beta for the high STO portfolio would underpredict the actual future beta for that portfolio, while that for the low STO portfolio would overpredict. Historical betas were taken from the Merrill Lynch beta file, as of December 1972. Returns for the portfolios were observed for the first six months of 1973, a period in which the average stock in the sample of 700 stocks fell by 23 per cent. The high STO portfolio had a high estimated historical beta of 1.27. Reliance on the technical prediction rule, using information available on December 31, 1972, would therefore have forecast a six-month decline of 28.8 per cent for the portfolio, conditional on the market return. The portfolio actually declined by 39.1 per cent, exhibiting a much higher beta than the historical beta. This was expected on the basis of the high STO rate in 1972. The low STO portfolio had a low estimated historical beta of 0.725. Relying on this technical forecast, the portfolio would have been expected to decline by 15.1 per cent. It actually exhibited a still lower beta, declining by only six per cent! This experiment shows the magnitude of the biases inherent in a technical rule that ignores recent fundamental changes in the nature of the firm.

SUMMARY

The systematic risk (or beta) of a security arises from the dependence of the security return, on the one hand, and the market return, on the other, on economic events. A measure of this joint dependence, beta is determined by the relative responses of security return and market return to economic events and by the variance of those events. As such, beta will change if the fundamental characteristics of the firm change, thereby altering responsiveness relative to economic events, or if the variance in the economy is redistributed.

The estimates of beta now commonly available rely on historical security price behavior. Such estimates are appropriate as estimators of the level of risk assumed in the past for purposes of measuring past performance, but they are not necessarily appropriate for portfolio management, where a prediction of risk in a future period is required.

If a portfolio management process is to achieve effective control of beta, its prediction rule must satisfy two criteria. First, the prediction rule should be unbiased relative to any characteristics of securities used to select portfolios—i.e., the average expected error for any group of securities likely to show up in a portfolio should be zero, with the average being weighted by capitalization. Second, the mean square predictor error for each stock, and on the average across all stocks, should be minimized. These criteria are not drawn arbitrarily from a statistics textbook but are deduced from exigencies of portfolio management.

The historical estimate of beta is suboptimal on both these counts. The strength of the technical approach is that it directly estimates the past value of beta. The strength of fundamental prediction is that it responds to the current condition of the company and exhibits less measurement error. The two techniques are easily coalesced into a single prediction rule, which weights fundamental and technical data optimally according to their predictive potential.[16] ∎

Footnotes:

13. The form of the regression equation that is commonly used is as follows:

$$R_{nt} = \hat{\alpha} + \hat{\beta}_n R_{Mt} + u_t \text{ where } E(u_t) = 0$$
$$E(u_t u_s) = \sigma_u^2 \quad t = s$$
$$= 0 \quad t \neq s.$$

If one believes in the market model of Sharpe, Lintner, and Mossin, then one would also believe that the above equation was misspecified. In this case, the following regression would be run:

$$[R_{nt} - R_{Ft}] = \hat{\alpha}_n + \hat{\beta}_n [R_{Mt} - R_{Ft}] + u_t \text{ where}$$
$$E(u_t) = 0$$
$$E(u_t u_s) = \sigma_u^2 \quad t = s$$
$$= 0 \quad t \neq s.$$

The minimum variance unbiased estimates of the historical average beta would be slightly but not significantly different. In the first method, beta would equal $COV(R_{Mt}, R_{nt})/VAR(R_{Mt})$, while in the second method, it would equal $COV(R_{Mt} - R_{Ft}, R_{nt} - R_{Ft})/VAR(R_{Mt} - R_{Ft})$.

14. Barr Rosenberg and Vinay Marathe, "Tests of Capital Asset Pricing Hypotheses," Research Program in Finance, Working Paper No. 32 (Berkeley: Institute of Business and Economic Research, University of California, 1975).

15. Rosenberg and Marathe, "The Prediction of Investment Risk: Systematic and Residual Risk," Proceedings: Seminar on the Analysis of Security Prices, Graduate School of Business, University of Chicago, 1975.

16. Rosenberg and James Guy, "The Prediction of Systematic Risk," Research Program in Finance, Working Paper No. 33 (Berkeley: Institute of Business and Economic Research, University of California, 1975).

by William Beaver and Dale Morse

What Determines Price-Earnings Ratios?

▶ Recent studies on the behavior of earnings growth over time raise doubt about the ability of past growth to explain differences in price-earnings ratios. Either future growth is difficult to predict, or investors are basing their predictions on information other than past growth.

Grouping common stocks into portfolios on the basis of price-earnings ratios, the authors find that the initial P/E differences among the portfolios persist up to 14 years. Growth appears to explain little of the persisting P/E differences, however. Price-earnings ratios correlate negatively with earnings growth in the year of the portfolio's formation, but positively with earnings growth in the subsequent year, suggesting that investors are forecasting only short-lived earnings distortions.

Nor does risk supply the explanation for these differences. Although price-earnings ratios can vary either positively or negatively with market risk, depending on the market conditions in a given year, market risk is of little assistance in explaining the observed persistence in price-earnings ratios over periods longer than two or three years.

The authors conclude that the most likely explanation of the evident persistence in price-earnings ratios is not growth or risk, but differences in accounting method. ▶

THE PRICE-EARNINGS ratio (hereafter P/E ratio) is of considerable interest, yet little is known about how it behaves over time or about the relative importance of the factors believed to influence its behavior. Differences in expected growth are commonly offered as a major explanation for differences in P/E ratios. Yet recent research raises doubt about this interpretation; past growth and analysts' forecasts appear to have little ability to explain subsequent growth.[1] Using a portfolio approach, we examine the behavior of P/E ratios and explore the ability of earnings growth (hereafter growth) and risk to explain P/E ratio differences across stocks. We find that, although differences in P/E ratios persist for up to 14 years, growth and risk appear to explain little of this persistency. In particular, growth appears to have virtually no effect beyond two years.[2]

Valuation Theory

Under perfect markets and certainty, the price of a security is equal to the present value of the future cash flows. Over an infinite horizon, the current price will reflect the stream of dividends. Under the further assumptions of (1) a constant dividend payout ratio (K), (2) constant growth in earnings per share (g) and (3) a constant riskless rate (r), P/E is given by the Gordon-Shapiro valuation equation:

$$P/E = \frac{K}{r - g} \qquad (1)$$

In a certainty world, earnings per share (E) can be defined as that constant cash flow whose present value is equivalent to the present value of the cash flows generated from current equity investment. Where the investment involves assets with finite lives, this definition implicitly reflects the fact that the value of the assets will depreciate over their lives.[3] We adopt this definition, which is often referred to as permanent earnings. Absent further investment, or if the earnings rate on future investment

---

1. Footnotes appear at end of article.

William Beaver is Thomas D. Dee, II Professor of Accounting at the Graduate School of Business, Stanford University. Dale Morse is a Ph.D. candidate at the Graduate School of Business, Stanford. Financial support for their research was provided by the Stanford Program in Professional Accounting, the major sponsors of which are Arthur Andersen & Co., Arthur Young & Co., Coopers & Lybrand, Ernst & Ernst, Peat, Marwick, Mitchell & Co. and Price Waterhouse.

Copyright © The Financial Analysts Federation, 1978
Reprinted from Financial Analysts Journal, *July/August 1978 — all rights reserved*

is r, the P/E ratio is simply the reciprocal of the riskless rate (1/r). The P/E ratio will reflect a growth "premium" (or discount) only when the rate of return on future investment exceeds (or falls below) the riskless rate, r.[4]

When the world is no longer certain, it is no longer clear what the "earnings term" in Equation 1 is intended to represent. The earnings concept underlying market prices is future-oriented, hence is defined in terms of the expectations of market participants. As such, it is not directly observable, but presumably represents some form of *expected* permanent earnings per share attributable to the current equity investment.

A second consequence of uncertainty is that, along with E, the actual values of the variables r, g and K are also unknown. Each symbol in Equation 1 is often interpreted as the expected value of the corresponding variable. When Equation 1 is used to analyze the behavior of current prices, these variables are commonly interpreted as a "consensus" expectation across investors.[5] While there are problems in using Equation 1 in this manner, it may still be a reasonable approximation of a more complex valuation process.

A third consequence of uncertainty is that the expected return is no longer the riskless rate, but rather a risky rate. Since stocks will differ with respect to risk, the expected risky rate for stock i will be denoted r_i. In the one-period capital asset pricing model (CAPM), differences in the expected risky rate of return are due solely to differences in beta—the sensitivity of the stock to return on the general market r_m. In particular:

$$r_i = r_f + b_i(r_m - r_f), \quad (2)$$

where r_i is the *expected* rate of return on security i, r_f the riskless rate, r_m the *expected* rate of return on the market portfolio and b_i security i's sensitivity to market risk, or beta.

Moreover, actual earnings per share (EPS) will vary from year to year because of transitory (i.e., temporary) factors peculiar to a particular year. Therefore, actual earnings may differ from the expected earnings upon which market prices are based. This leads to the distinction between the transitory versus the permanent component of EPS. This distinction will become crucial in interpreting our results.[6]

Research Design

A portfolio approach potentially diversifies out some of the "noise" at the individual stock level.[7] We selected stocks that satisfied the following criteria: (1) five consecutive years of data on the Compustat and CRSP tapes (the latter implies New York Stock Exchange membership) and (2) a fiscal year ending on December 31.

For each year from 1956 through 1974 we computed the P/E for each stock with data available in

TABLE 1: Median Values of Variables

Year	No. of Stocks	Median P/E	Median Percentage Growth in EPS	Median Beta*
1956	270	11.55	—	0.981
1957	279	10.08	−3.63	0.952
1958	284	17.61	−8.94	0.959
1959	295	15.75	20.73	0.954
1960	354	15.29	−4.83	0.964
1961	373	19.68	1.56	0.959
1962	398	14.98	8.39	1.007
1963	409	15.46	9.00	0.981
1964	435	14.45	19.42	0.960
1965	464	15.18	18.19	0.952
1966	493	11.60	13.01	0.975
1967	514	16.91	−0.69	0.967
1968	548	19.43	7.52	0.991
1969	581	14.04	5.31	0.998
1970	600	15.58	−10.16	0.939
1971	600	17.06	9.92	—
1972	600	14.07	20.46	—
1973	600	7.45	23.10	—
1974	600	5.01	12.37	—
1975	600	8.04	−1.21	—

*A stock's beta for 1956 is computed over the 60-month period following December 1956 (January 1957 through December 1961), according to the method described in Footnote 8.

568

that year. We defined P/E as price per share on December 31 divided by earnings per share for the year, computed on a pre-extraordinary item basis. Using data from the Compustat tape, we defined earnings growth as the percentage change in the year's earnings per share relative to the previous year and measured risk as the stock's beta, computed from monthly stock price return data available on the CRSP tape.[8]

We then ranked each year's stocks according to P/E and formed 25 portfolios, with Portfolio One comprising those four per cent with the highest P/E's and Portfolio 25 comprising the stocks with the lowest P/E's. We then compared the median P/E for each portfolio in its base year (year of formation) with the median P/E, median realized growth and median risk for the portfolio in subsequent years.[9] Note that, in all cases, once formed the portfolio's composition was fixed (i.e., a buy and hold strategy was used).[10]

Table 1 reports some summary statistics.[11] Once a stock appears on the tape in a given year, its data are available from that year onward. The similarity of stocks appearing later relative to those appearing earlier is supported by the median beta, which shows no trend over time and is close to one. When we correlated the median P/E for each year with the aggregate P/E ratio for Standard & Poor's Composite stocks for the years 1956 through 1975, we obtained a positive rank correlation of 0.85, which is reasonable, given the differences in the stocks and the methods used to compute the average P/E for a given year. Furthermore, the rank correlation between the median annual growth rates reported in Table 1 and the growth in aggregate EPS for S&P Industrials yielded a positive correlation of 0.89.[12]

How Do P/E Ratios Behave Over Time?

Table 2 reports the rank correlation between P/E ratios in the year of formation and P/E ratios in subsequent years.[13] The first row of Table 2 displays the correlations between the P/E ratios of portfolios formed in 1956 and the P/E ratios of the same portfolios in subsequent years. The second row displays results for portfolios formed in 1957 and the final row the correlation between the P/E ratios of the portfolios formed in 1974 and the P/E ratios of those same portfolios in 1975. For example, for the portfolios formed at the end of 1956, the correlation between portfolio P/E ratios in 1956 (the year of formation) and 1957 (one year later) is 0.96. The rank correlation between the P/E ratios in 1956 and 1966 (10 years later) is 0.74.

The median correlation of each column is reported at the bottom of the table. The median correlations are not strictly comparable for several reasons. First, the group of calendar years over which the median is computed gradually changes as one moves across the columns: One year after formation includes calendar years 1957 through 1975, while 14 years after formation includes only calendar years 1970 through 1975. Then, too, the median P/E ratio varies considerably by calendar years, as Table 1 indicates, dropping sharply in 1973, 1974 and 1975. Table 1 also shows that the average number of stocks per portfolio differs; in 1956 the number of

TABLE 2: Rank Correlations of Portfolios Formed By P/E Ratios With P/E Ratios in Subsequent Years

Base Year	1	2	3	4	5	6	7	8	9	10	11	12	13	14
1956	0.96	0.87	0.88	0.65	0.78	0.70	0.82	0.85	0.69	0.74	0.62	0.36	0.41	0.59
1957	0.85	0.91	0.83	0.84	0.89	0.89	0.90	0.81	0.86	0.72	0.51	0.67	0.78	0.44
1958	0.95	0.73	0.64	0.52	0.43	0.55	0.49	0.30	0.60	0.22	0.24	0.49	0.41	0.18
1959	0.96	0.91	0.91	0.73	0.57	0.88	0.74	0.69	0.33	0.46	0.69	0.56	0.40	0.56
1960	0.94	0.94	0.93	0.89	0.88	0.79	0.70	0.63	0.80	0.73	0.61	0.61	0.50	0.24
1961	0.98	0.96	0.86	0.89	0.85	0.76	0.74	0.87	0.83	0.87	0.76	0.72	0.55	0.64
1962	0.92	0.89	0.93	0.94	0.87	0.69	0.86	0.73	0.78	0.76	0.87	0.78	0.77	
1963	0.99	0.98	0.95	0.89	0.71	0.77	0.75	0.61	0.79	0.93	0.77	0.76		
1964	0.95	0.96	0.94	0.72	0.88	0.89	0.72	0.88	0.90	0.81	0.82			
1965	0.99	0.93	0.83	0.83	0.77	0.86	0.93	0.91	0.80	0.71				
1966	0.96	0.89	0.95	0.96	0.84	0.95	0.89	0.80	0.79					
1967	0.98	0.98	0.94	0.89	0.85	0.58	0.57	0.69						
1968	0.98	0.95	0.88	0.84	0.63	0.53	0.35							
1969	0.89	0.92	0.95	0.74	0.80	0.82								
1970	0.95	0.79	0.63	0.72	0.73									
1971	0.96	0.80	0.70	0.67										
1972	0.96	0.96	0.96											
1973	0.99	0.97												
1974	0.97													
Median Correlation	0.96	0.92	0.91	0.83	0.80	0.78	0.74	0.76	0.79	0.73	0.69	0.64	0.50	0.44

stocks is 10, while the base years 1970 through 1974 average 24 per portfolio. On purely statistical grounds, the correlation coefficient should rise as the number of stocks per portfolio increases. However, Table 2 does not display any obvious tendency for the correlations to increase systematically in the later base years.[14]

With these caveats in mind, we interpret the correlations in Table 2 as supporting a long-term persistency in the portfolios' P/E ratios. With only two minor disruptions, the median correlation declines steadily with the number of years since portfolio formation. Five years after formation the median correlation is 0.80, while 10 years after formation the median correlation is 0.73. Fourteen years after formation, the median is 0.44. We tentatively conclude that, although much of the effect of the factors that determine P/E ratios dissipates over the 14 years, a portion still clearly remains after five, 10 or perhaps even 14 years.

This conclusion is supported by Table 3, which displays a composite picture of six of the 25 portfolios.[15] We averaged the P/E ratios across the base years, weighting each year by the number of stocks in that year.[16] The striking feature of Table 3 is the shrinkage over time in the P/E differences among the portfolios. Not surprisingly, this tendency is most evident in the extreme portfolios (i.e., Portfolios One and 25). The P/E of Portfolio One is less than half its value one year after formation, and less than one-third its value two years after formation. Portfolio 25 shows a similar reversion toward a central value, as do other portfolios, for which the pattern is, however, less pronounced.

As a convenient summary, Table 3 reports the ratio of the P/E values for Portfolio One relative to those for Portfolio 25. In the year of formation, Portfolio One's P/E is over eight times that of Portfolio 25's, while in the next year it has shrunk to slightly over three times and by three years after formation it is less than twice Portfolio 25's P/E. Apart from this dramatic convergence of the P/E ratios, their most striking feature is the stability of the relative difference from the third year through the eleventh year after formation. After the eleventh year, further convergence occurs until, in the fourteenth year, Portfolio 25 has a P/E greater than that of Portfolio One's.

We take this to mean that the effect of the factors determining P/E ratios in the year of formation dissipates dramatically by the third year after formation. On the other hand, the fact that the convergence of P/E ratios is by no means complete implies that certain factors are still causing differences in P/E ratios through at least the eleventh year after formation.

The pattern of reversion toward a central value is a common phenomenon among economic variables. Research on the behavior of beta indicates a similar pattern. Two factors explain such behavior: (1) The variable being ranked normally contains a transitory component; in our context, this means that earnings in a given year result in part from factors peculiar to that year whose effects will either not persist beyond that year or will dissipate in subsequent years. (2) The underlying, permanent value is reverting toward the average. Such a reversion in the ratio of price to expected earnings per share could be caused by a change in expected earnings growth or by a change in risk.

Examining the time series behavior of the P/E ratio provides some insight into the nature of the factors that influence it. Apparently, some of these factors dissipate substantially within the first three years after formation. On the other hand, some continue effective through at least the eleventh year after formation. We will consider three potential factors—growth, risk and accounting method.

Does Growth Explain Differences in P/E Ratios?

Table 4 displays correlations between median P/E ratios in the year of formation and median earnings growth in the year of and in the years subsequent to formation.[17] Column zero indicates the correlation between the P/E ratio and growth in the year of formation. The correlation of earnings growth in 1957 with the P/E ratio computed at the end of 1957 is

TABLE 3: Price-Earnings Ratios

Portfolio	\multicolumn{15}{c}{Years After Formation}
	0	1	2	3	4	5	6	7	8	9	10	11	12	13	14
1	50.0	22.7	16.4	13.8	12.3	13.2	13.5	13.2	17.2	14.9	13.0	13.2	10.5	9.3	8.3
5	20.8	17.5	16.9	15.9	15.9	13.7	13.0	12.8	12.5	11.8	11.9	10.9	10.1	10.2	8.4
10	14.3	11.9	11.5	11.1	10.3	10.1	9.4	9.0	10.0	10.0	9.9	11.0	10.6	9.5	8.3
15	11.1	10.8	10.4	10.8	10.0	10.0	9.4	9.7	9.3	9.5	8.6	9.2	8.3	8.6	7.1
20	8.9	9.1	9.6	9.3	9.4	9.3	9.3	9.0	8.8	8.8	9.0	8.2	7.6	7.0	7.7
25	5.8	6.9	8.0	7.8	7.9	7.9	8.2	8.8	8.3	8.5	7.8	7.5	7.5	7.5	8.9
Port. 1 / Port. 25	8.6	3.3	2.1	1.8	1.6	1.7	1.6	1.5	2.1	1.8	1.7	1.8	1.4	1.2	0.9

negative 0.28. The median correlation over the 19 years from 1957 through 1975 is also negative 0.28, and 16 of the 19 correlations are negative.

The negative correlation implies that stocks with relatively low earnings growth during the year tend to have relatively high P/E ratios. This is consistent with the contention that market participants perceive that earnings contain transitory components and price stocks accordingly.[18] Since we formed portfolios on the basis of the ratio of price to *realized* earnings, we expect that the ranking will systematically group together stocks with transitory earnings of the same sign. In other words, the portfolio with the highest P/E ratio will tend to include firms with negative transitory components (i.e., realized earnings below expected earnings) and conversely for the portfolio with the lowest P/E ratio.

Table 4 displays a strong correlation between P/E and earnings growth in the year subsequent to portfolio formation. The median correlation for base years 1957 through 1975 is 0.53, and all 19 correlations are positive. Market participants' perceptions of the transitory nature of earnings were confirmed by actual earnings behavior. While, in the year of formation, current earnings were abnormally low relative to expected permanent earnings, in the subsequent year earnings tended to "catch up" to investors' expectations about permanent earnings.[19]

In the second year after formation, the median correlation is 0.25 and, from there on, growth is essentially uncorrelated with P/E in the year of formation. The rapid dissipation in subsequent growth rates is similar to the pattern for P/E ratios observed in Table 2. In general, the pattern behaves as if market participants, in determining prices, cannot forecast differential growth beyond two years.[20]

One may ask what this tells us about the ability of market participants to isolate and detect transitory elements in current earnings versus their ability to forecast unusual earnings situations with respect to additional investment. Although the distinction may seem arbitrary, the implications can differ substantially. The first process concerns unusual factors due to events of this year that will not persist (e.g., an abnormally high rate of inflation or abnormally high interest rates), while the second asks questions related to future unusual earnings opportunities.[21]

As far as we can tell, the data provide no basis for assessing how much of the observed growth differential is due to each factor (although the introduction of other evidence may permit such a basis).[22] As a result, we cannot preclude the possibility that the results may be entirely due to the detection of transitory components that take more than one year to disappear from reported earnings. It is not our intention to be unduly pessimistic, but rather to caution against interpreting the figures as solely the result of market participants' ability to forecast unusual earnings opportunities on future investments.

Magnitude of Differential Growth

Table 4's correlation matrix does not provide information on the magnitude of differential earnings growth. Table 5 displays this information for the

TABLE 4: Rank Correlations of Portfolios Formed By P/E Ratios With Earnings Growth in Subsequent Years

Base Year	0	1	2	3	4	5	6	7	8	9	10	11	12	13	14	15
1956		0.12	0.13	−0.30	0.48	0.00	−0.12	−0.62	−0.17	−0.19	−0.32	−0.08	−0.31	0.07	0.05	−0.48
1957	−0.28	0.53	−0.23	0.51	−0.07	0.02	−0.73	−0.26	0.26	−0.23	−0.01	−0.14	0.22	0.21	−0.33	−0.03
1958	−0.28	0.52	0.32	0.03	0.18	−0.15	0.19	0.29	0.11	−0.54	0.16	0.32	−0.20	−0.40	0.39	0.23
1959	−0.37	0.62	0.40	−0.12	−0.16	0.27	0.15	0.30	0.04	−0.22	0.32	0.04	−0.48	0.17	0.21	0.36
1960	−0.10	0.49	−0.15	−0.04	−0.04	0.04	−0.01	0.26	0.29	0.26	0.06	−0.13	0.09	−0.05	−0.45	0.10
1961	−0.45	0.53	0.13	0.07	−0.05	−0.03	0.27	−0.11	0.22	0.40	0.08	0.36	−0.16	−0.51	0.27	
1962	−0.35	0.17	0.12	0.05	−0.26	−0.40	0.20	−0.39	0.49	−0.17	−0.19	−0.44	−0.46	0.31		
1963	−0.42	0.26	0.24	0.13	0.35	0.08	0.13	0.56	−0.03	−0.27	−0.12	−0.47	0.28			
1964	−0.43	0.11	−0.14	0.68	0.08	0.44	0.71	0.06	−0.21	−0.30	−0.31	0.04				
1965	0.12	0.47	0.55	0.04	0.22	0.61	−0.16	−0.14	−0.15	−0.26	0.26					
1966	−0.02	0.77	0.02	0.30	0.66	−0.35	−0.14	−0.38	−0.16	0.35						
1967	0.18	0.74	0.41	0.12	0.05	0.39	0.01	−0.31	−0.07							
1968	−0.02	0.77	0.74	0.54	0.42	−0.14	0.15	0.32								
1969	0.15	0.75	0.48	0.05	−0.17	−0.42	0.58									
1970	−0.19	0.90	0.58	−0.09	−0.63	0.34										
1971	−0.22	0.71	0.27	−0.02	0.32											
1972	−0.18	0.45	−0.09	0.39												
1973	−0.31	0.52	0.51													
1974	−0.66	0.89														
1975	−0.66															
Median Correlation	−0.28	0.53	0.25	0.05	0.06	0.02	0.14	−0.11	0.01	−0.22	0.02	−0.08	−0.18	0.07	0.24	0.10

same six composite portfolios reported in Table 3, using the same composite process. The results support the contentions made earlier. Portfolio One (the highest P/E portfolio) experienced a median *drop* in earnings of 4.1 per cent, while Portfolio 25 experienced a median earnings *increase* of 26.4 per cent. In simplest terms, the prices of the stocks in Portfolio One did not change proportionately with their earnings; as a result, their P/E ratios were relatively high. Similarly, the stocks in Portfolio 25 experienced a price change that, on average, was less than 26 per cent, and their P/E ratios were relatively low. Again, this implies a price formation process whereby participants view changes in earnings as containing a transitory element.

In Table 5, Portfolio One shows a median earnings growth of 95.3 per cent in the first year after formation, while Portfolio 25 shows a drop in earnings of 3.3 per cent. This is consistent with the results reported in Table 4: The perceptions of market participants regarding the transitory element in earnings were confirmed by subsequent earnings behavior.

The results in Table 5 differ from those in Table 4 in one major respect—the highest P/E portfolio maintains its distinctive earnings growth behavior for seven years after formation. This is neither contradictory nor surprising. Whereas correlations in Table 4 reflect the strength of the relationship for all 25 portfolios, where growth and P/E are essentially unrelated after two years, the comparison described above involves only one of those portfolios. For that one "extreme" portfolio we would expect non-normal growth to be larger and to last longer.

The results in Table 5 can be deceptive in at least two respects. First, they reflect the average effect across a number of base years and do not reveal variation from one base year to another. A more detailed examination, not reported here, revealed considerable variation across base years. Second, while it is intuitively appealing to focus solely on the high P/E portfolio, it constitutes only four per cent of the observations. It is important to remember that, with the remaining portfolios included, there is little or no apparent relation beyond the second year.

Comparing the P/E analysis with the growth analysis, we conclude that some of the initial dissipation of the P/E ratio in the first three years after formation can be explained by differential growth in earnings. Beyond that, however, there clearly exists a P/E differential that cannot be explained by differential earnings growth.

Before leaving growth analysis, we'd like to comment on one aspect of the data. In contrast to P/E ratios, which exhibit a high degree of correlation over time, previous evidence indicates that earnings growth rates possess near-zero correlation over time. To ensure that the same behavior held for the stocks in our sample, we constructed a portfolio strategy based on earnings growth in the year of formation and then observed subsequent growth. Our results confirmed previous findings of near-zero correlation of earnings growth rates. While a mechanical process relying on past growth rates is largely unsuccessful in predicting future differential growth, the P/E ratio is successful because price reflects a process whereby market participants rely on more information than past earnings in distinguishing the transitory and permanent components of earnings.

Risk Analysis

The expected sign of the correlation between P/E and beta may be either positive or negative. The argument is developed in greater detail in the appendix, but it essentially proceeds as follows: Stocks' earnings move together because of economy-wide factors. In years of transitorily low earnings, the market-wide P/E will tend to be high, but stocks with high betas will tend to have even higher P/E ratios because their earnings are most sensitive to economy-wide events. Conversely, in years of transitorily high earnings, high beta stocks will have even lower P/E ratios than most. Therefore we expect a positive correlation in "high" P/E years and a negative correlation in "low" years.

Table 6 reports the rank correlations between P/E and beta. We compared beta for a given base year over the 60 months subsequent to formation; thus the beta for 1956 was computed over the years 1957

TABLE 5: Earnings Growth

Portfolio	Years After Formation														
	0	1	2	3	4	5	6	7	8	9	10	11	12	13	14
1	−4.1	95.3	37.2	28.2	16.4	18.9	18.1	19.7	13.1	14.8	15.3	10.8	10.9	10.2	11.8
5	10.7	14.9	12.1	13.1	14.2	10.9	10.4	11.8	10.5	11.6	8.0	11.9	8.3	13.3	18.1
10	9.6	12.9	11.5	12.3	12.6	9.2	10.1	10.8	12.8	8.3	12.9	22.2	16.6	20.6	29.6
15	10.0	8.8	8.5	8.1	8.2	14.3	11.6	5.4	13.3	10.3	11.0	10.8	11.9	12.8	33.4
20	10.8	5.2	9.3	12.6	12.4	6.0	8.4	13.0	10.2	11.3	11.1	25.0	12.9	17.7	18.0
25	26.4	−3.3	7.5	10.8	8.3	12.9	17.1	13.6	18.0	12.8	16.7	14.2	10.9	12.4	10.1
Port. 1 / Port. 25	−0.155	*	5.0	2.61	1.98	1.47	1.06	1.45	0.73	1.16	0.92	0.76	1.00	0.82	1.17

*Not meaningful because of negative growth in denominator.

TABLE 6: Rank Correlations of Portfolio Median P/E Ratios and Median Beta

Year	Rank Correlation	Rank of Median P/E[a]	Predicted Sign of Correlation
1956	−0.34	14	−
1957	−0.23	15	−
1958	0.22	3	+
1959	0.41	5	+
1960	0.50	8	+
1961	0.55	1	+
1962	−0.48	10	−
1963	−0.42	7	+[b]
1964	−0.63	11	−
1965	−0.26	9	−
1966	−0.44	13	−
1967	0.50	4	+
1968	0.53	2	+
1969	0.58	12	−[b]
1970	0.28	6	+
Median Adjusted for Predicted Sign	0.41		

[a] Computed from Table 1.
[b] 1963 and 1969 are the two years incorrectly predicted.

through 1961.

To predict the sign of the correlation in a given base year, we ranked the market-wide P/E ratios (as reported in Table 1) from high to low.[23] We hypothesized that the years with the eight highest values of market-wide P/E ratios would have a positive correlation between P/E and beta, while the years with the seven lowest values of market-wide P/E would have a negative correlation. Over the 15 base years 1956 through 1970, the actual correlations are positive eight times and negative seven times. We correctly predicted the sign of the correlation for 13 of the 15 years. This is impressive, given the crudeness of the test. (The test's limitations are discussed in the appendix.)

Table 7 reports the magnitude of the betas for the six portfolios presented in Tables 3 and 5. Because the relation between P/E and beta can be either positive or negative, we averaged results over two sets of years—those in which the correlation was positive

Table 7: Relation of P/E and Beta

Portfolio	Average Beta in All Years	Average Beta in Years of Positive Correlation	Average Beta in Years of Negative Correlation
1	1.22	1.28	1.13
5	1.01	1.03	0.98
10	1.05	1.09	1.00
15	0.96	0.94	1.00
20	1.03	0.96	1.11
25	1.04	0.95	1.14

and those in which the correlation was negative. The third column reports the beta differences for the years of positive correlation. The differences are small for Portfolios Five through 25, where beta ranges from 1.09 to 0.94. The largest difference occurs in the highest P/E portfolio, with its beta of 1.28. In the fourth column, negative correlation is evident for Portfolios Five through 25, with a pronounced aberrant behavior for Portfolio One. For this set of stocks, a "U-shaped" relationship is present. Given the consistently high betas of the highest P/E portfolio, it is imperative that some form of risk-adjusted performance standard be introduced to avoid spuriously inferring superior stock price performance.

While beta clearly holds some explanatory power, the crucial issue is, to what extent does it explain the P/E ratio behavior reported in Tables 2 and 3? We think it explains little: If beta were an important explanatory variable, then the predicted behavior of P/E over time would be much different from what Tables 2 and 3 report. Stocks in Portfolio One during years of high market-wide P/E would tend to move to Portfolio 25 (or its neighbors) in years of low market-wide P/E. Looking across a row of Table 2, we would expect to see a pattern of positive and negative correlations similar to that reported in the last column of Table 6. Instead, we observe a strong positive serial correlation throughout.[24] Furthermore, the relative differences in betas are not of the same magnitude as the relative differences in P/E ratios. Before considering another source of P/E differences, however, we report the results of a regression analysis that combines both growth and risk analysis.

Regression Analysis

Table 8 displays the results of a simple linear regression that included beta and earnings growth as independent variables. We used the E/P, rather than P/E, ratio because the Litzenberger and Rao model posits linearity in E/P (not in P/E).[25] The expected sign of the E/P and beta relationship is thus the reverse of that shown in the final column of Table 6. The actual regression coefficients have the predicted sign in 13 of the 15 years; again, 1963 and 1969 are exceptions.

The predicted signs of the growth coefficients are also negative, since we're using E/P as the dependent variable. For growth in the year subsequent to portfolio formation (g_1), all 15 coefficients have the predicted sign. Growth two years subsequent to formation (g_2) has the predicted sign in 12 years. By the third year (g_3), however, the signs of the coefficients are evenly divided. Table 4 suggests there is little merit to introducing additional growth variables.

TABLE 8: E/P Regression Results

Base Year	Constant	Beta	g_1	g_2	g_3	Adjusted R^2	F Statistic
1956	0.070	0.030 (0.71)	−0.046 (−1.38)	−0.035 (−0.73)	0.053 (0.93)	0.185	2.36
1957	0.348	0.086* (1.74)	−0.142* (−4.13)	−0.066 (−1.57)	−0.123* (−2.29)	0.581	9.30*
1958	0.136	0.000 (0)	−0.019* (−2.57)	−0.070 (−1.69)	0.013 (0.26)	0.270	3.96
1959	0.076	−0.053* (−1.76)	−0.157* (−4.45)	0.098 (1.29)	0.086 (1.62)	0.505	7.13*
1960	0.155	−0.075* (−2.83)	−0.161* (−3.55)	0.046 (0.71)	0.092 (1.17)	0.502	7.06*
1961	0.077	−0.054* (−1.89)	−0.063 (−1.25)	0.064 (0.93)	0.023 (0.57)	0.289	3.44*
1962	0.119	0.116* (4.68)	−0.055* (−2.10)	−0.026 (−0.50)	−0.064 (−1.02)	0.524	7.61*
1963	0.239	0.097* (3.10)	−0.106* (−1.93)	−0.089* (−1.84)	−0.034 (−0.62)	0.370	4.52*
1964	0.260	0.076* (2.36)	−0.085 (−1.26)	−0.045 (−0.67)	−0.114* (−2.24)	0.572	9.03*
1965	0.300	0.071* (2.00)	−0.167* (−2.54)	−0.091* (−1.73)	−0.022 (−0.32)	0.475	6.44*
1966	0.501	0.112* (3.53)	−0.304* (−7.06)	−0.068 (−0.96)	−0.138* (−1.80)	0.783	22.63*
1967	0.447	−0.065* (−2.15)	−0.164* (−2.87)	−0.106 (−1.67)	−0.034 (−0.94)	0.575	9.10*
1968	0.285	−0.031 (−1.71)	−0.033 (−1.71)	−0.108* (−5.23)	−0.060 (−1.62)	0.738	17.91*
1969	0.380	−0.054 (−1.40)	−0.159* (−4.64)	−0.134* (−2.09)	0.030 (0.57)	0.658	12.56*
1970	0.185	−0.029 (−0.71)	−0.003 (−0.28)	−0.167* (−2.58)	0.089 (1.42)	0.391	4.86*

* Significant at five per cent level (one-tail test on regression coefficients).

The R^2 (proportion of variance explained) adjusted for degrees of freedom ranges from 18.5 per cent to 78.3 per cent, with a median of 50.5 per cent. The F-statistic, which tests the null hypothesis that all of the coefficients are zero, is significant at the five per cent level in 13 of the 15 years.[26]

While risk and growth on the average explain approximately 50 per cent of the variance of the E/P ratio, they obviously leave an equal proportion unexplained. Thus the regression results presented in Table 8 provide only the crude beginnings of an attempt to explain cross-sectional P/E differences. We suggest further research in a number of areas: (1) Even if the realized values of beta and growth are unbiased estimates of expectations, they may still measure those expectations with error; better specification could lead to higher R^2, which is understated when measurement error is present. (2) Better specification of the denominator of the P/E ratio might yield better results.[27] (3) Accounting rules could be creating P/E differences; our final comments are devoted to this area.

Accounting Method

The finding that P/E ratio differences persist well beyond three years after portfolio formation suggests the influence of some factor other than risk or growth. Accounting effects are obvious candidates. Accounting method effects are of two types— use of different rules (e.g., depreciation methods) by different firms for essentially the same or similar circumstances and errors introduced by applying a uniform accounting rule (e.g., historical cost) to differing economic circumstances (e.g., current value of assets).

The P/E ratio will be influenced by the effect on earnings of differing accounting methods. Assuming prices are not dependent on the accounting method used in annual reports, firms that use conservative accounting methods (e.g., accelerated depreciation or LIFO inventory valuation) would tend to have higher P/E ratios than firms that use less conservative methods, holding constant the effects of risk and growth.[28] For example, Beaver and Dukes found the P/E ratios of a portfolio of firms using accelerated depreciation were greater than the P/E ratios of a portfolio of firms using straight-line depreciation.[29] The two portfolios were essentially the same with respect to risk (beta) and growth. Moreover, when the earnings of the straight-line portfolio were converted according to the accelerated method, the P/E ratios were essentially the same for both portfolios. In other words, the P/E differences in the two portfolios disappeared when earnings were computed on a uniform depreciation method. We suggest an extension of this type of analysis to other accounting methods as an obvious candidate for future research.[30] ∎

APPENDIX

If the EPS used to compute P/E ratios contained no transitory elements, we would expect a positive relation between E/P and beta and a negative relation between P/E and beta. However, the evidence suggests that transitory elements in EPS are present. How does this affect the analysis of risk?

Previous empirical research indicates that a stock's E/P ratio can be characterized by the following (linear) process:

$$E/P_t = \hat{a} + \hat{b} M_t + u_t , \qquad (a)$$

where E/P_t = earnings-price ratio for a stock in year t,

M_t = a market-wide E/P ratio for year t,

u_t = a non-market residual for a stock in year t and

$\left.\begin{array}{r}\hat{a} \\ \hat{b}\end{array}\right\}$ = the intercept and slope of the linear relationship.

Moreover, this research has shown that, at the portfolio level, $\hat{b}$ (the earnings-price "beta") is highly correlated with beta.

In a given year where the actual, realized earnings may differ from the expected earnings, what relation can we expect between E/P and beta? Rearranging (a) we have:

$$(E/P_t - \overline{E/P}) = \hat{b}(M_t - \overline{M}) + u_t , \qquad (b)$$

where $\overline{E/P}$ = expected value of E/P_t and
$\overline{M}$ = expected value of M_t

Ignoring u_t and taking $\hat{b}$ equal to b, we have:

$$(E/P_t - \overline{E/P}) = b(M_t - \overline{M}) \qquad (c)$$

When the realized M_t is above its expected value, stocks with higher betas will have higher E/P's (expressed as a deviation from the expected value). However, when the realized M_t is below its expected value, stocks with higher betas will have lower E/P's (expressed in terms of a deviation from its mean).

Limitations of the Empirical Test

One obvious limitation is the failure to express P/E (or E/P) as a deviation from its expected value, as indicated by Equation (c). This test implicitly assumes that inter-stock P/E differences are zero. This is obviously not the case, as Tables 2 and 3 indicate. However, we did not take this latter step since our concern throughout has been with the risk differences of a simple, P/E-oriented portfolio strategy, not a strategy that expresses P/E as a deviation from its expected value. A second limitation is the assumption that 15 years taken as a whole contain approximately an equal number of realizations above and below the expected value, which in turn is assumed to be a constant over 15 years.

In the absence of any other evidence, this assumption seems as reasonable as any other. However, the assumption of a constant expected value cannot be strictly true. Factors such as changing interest rates would lead us to expect that market-wide P/E ratios change over time. Third, the test ignores the influence of u_t (the unsystematic component) as expressed in Equation (b).

Further Analysis of Table 7

Evidence in our article supports the contention that transitory elements in earnings exist. We would expect high P/E stocks to have greater earnings variability to the extent that transitory elements account for P/E differences. Research by Beaver and Manegold, among others, confirms that stocks with greater earnings variability have higher betas. However, the argument is not complete: If earnings volatility were exclusively systematic, we would have observed no U-shaped behavior in the years with negative correlation. If unsystematic earnings volatility (the variance of u_t from Equation (a)) is positively correlated with beta, and if high P/E stocks have greater unsystematic volatility, the result would be a consistently higher beta for the highest P/E portfolio. However, a similar argument could be offered for the lowest P/E portfolio. Yet consistently higher betas are not observed here. We offer no explanation for this result.

Footnotes

1. See I. Little, "Higgledy Piggledy Growth" (Institute of Statistics, Oxford, November 1962), the seminal work. See also R. Ball and R. Watts, "Some Time Series Properties of Accounting Earnings Numbers," *Journal of Finance* (June 1972), pp. 663-682; J. Cragg and B. Malkiel, "The Consensus and Accuracy of Some Predictions of the Growth of Corporate Earnings," *Journal of Finance* (March 1968), pp. 67-84; I. Little and Raynor, *Higgledy Piggledy Growth Again* (Oxford: Basil Blackwell, 1966); and J. Murphy, "Relative Growth in Earnings Per Share—Past and Future," *Financial Analysts Journal* (November/December 1966), pp. 73-76. Excellent summaries appear in R. Brealey, *An Introduction to Risk and Return from Common Stocks* (Cambridge: MIT Press, 1969) and in J. Lorie and M. Hamilton, *The Stock Market: Theories and Evidence* (Homewood, Illinois: Irwin, 1973).
2. Previous studies have attempted to use the P/E ratio itself as a growth predictor—with little success. Two examples are Cragg and Malkiel, "Consensus and Accuracy" and J. Murphy and H. Stevenson, "Price/Earnings Ratios and Future Growth of Earnings and Dividends," *Financial Analysts Journal* (November/December 1967), pp. 111-114. The portfolio strategy adopted in our study provides an opportunity to uncover relations that may have been undetected by previous research.
3. Let CF_t equal the cash flow generated t periods from now from current equity investment. Assuming r is constant:

$$\frac{E}{r} \equiv \sum_{t=1}^{\infty} CF_t(1+r)^{-t} = \text{Present Value of Current Equity Investment,}$$

$$E \equiv r\left[\sum_{t=1}^{\infty} CF_t(1+r)^{-t}\right] = \text{Permanent Earnings}$$

4. It appears to us that a basic inconsistency may exist when perfect markets are invoked to motivate present value formulas and yet abnormal returns in productive opportunities are posited to explain growth premiums or discounts in P/E ratios. However, this is a puzzle we are not prepared to resolve. Stocks may still be priced "as if" a discounted cash flow model were applied even in the presence of abnormal returns in the productive sector (i.e., the product and factor markets).
5. Consensus expectations in general depend on the wealth, risk preferences and beliefs of market participants. ("Market participants" is a generic term intended to include individuals whose expectations directly or indirectly influence market prices—i.e., analysts as well as investors.) In a one-period setting, expressing price as a function of expected values is an arbitrary, although innoucuous, way to view valuation. In a multi-period setting, however, such a valuation scheme will not necessarily hold.
6. Previous attempts by researchers to remove transitory elements from earnings vary from subjective adjustments of the components of earnings to statistical data fitting via Box-Jenkins techniques. For an example of the latter, see P. Griffin, "The Time Series Behavior of Quarterly Earnings," *Journal of Accounting Research* (Spring 1977), 71-83.

    We would like to be able to say a portfolio approach will permit us to diversify out the transitory earnings components. Clearly we cannot make such a statement. To the contrary, since the portfolios will be formed on the basis of the ratio of price to *realized* earnings, we expect the ranking will systematically group together stocks with transitory earnings of the same sign. In other words, the portfolio with the highest P/E ratios will tend to include firms where the transitory component is negative (i.e., realized earnings are below expected earnings) and conversely for the portfolio with the lowest P/E ratios. Our evidence will support these contentions, and it is a major point to keep in mind in interpreting the results.
7. For a more detailed discussion of the effects of aggregation into portfolios see W. Beaver and J. Manegold, "The Association Between Market-Determined and Accounting-Determined Risk Measures," *Journal of Financial and Quantitative Analysis* (June 1975), pp. 231-284. In this context, "noise" refers to the fact that our growth and risk measures may differ from the growth and risk expected at the time of portfolio formation.
8. Beta was estimated as the slope of a linear regression of the form:

    $$R_{it} = a_i + b_i R_{mt} + e_{it} \quad , \quad t = 1,60$$

    where R_{it} equals monthly percentage change in price (adjusted for dividends) for security i in month t and R_{mt} equals monthly percentage change in a market index of price changes (adjusted for dividends) of all NYSE firms (provided as part of CRSP tape).
9. The median was used because it was a nonparametric measure that would place less demands on the data. Various weighting schemes (e.g., weighting by market value) were also applied with essentially the same results as reported here. Since it is unclear how to define growth off of negative earnings, the portfolios were formed only over those stocks with positive earnings in the base year. However, the sign of earnings was unrestricted in the years subsequent to formation. Hence earnings could be negative in later years.
10. The Compustat tape contains those firms that have survived mergers and bankruptcy. We would expect that this could induce a potential bias in the levels of the variables to be studied. However, the study focuses on differences in these variables across portfolios of stocks. It is not obvious to what extent survivorship imparts a bias for this purpose. This would require knowledge of how non-surviving firms sys-

tematically differ from surviving ones. In any event, because of the survivorship criteria, the portfolio strategies described here could not have been literally followed by an investor.
11. The number of stocks increases over time because of availability on the Compustat tape. In virtually all instances, the firms with incomplete histories on Compustat existed throughout the 1956-75 period but were picked up at some later date by Compustat. In other words, the firms being added do not tend to be new firms.
12. These aggregate statistics were obtained from S&P's *Trade and Securities Statistics, 1976*.
13. It is important to realize that a correlation matrix like that of Table 2 invariably leaves out certain information. For example, does a correlation coefficient of one mean the P/E difference between portfolios remains approximately the same as it was in the year of formation? Not necessarily. We can draw no inference about the magnitude of portfolio differences; the rank correlation coefficient merely indicates a similarity in the rankings of the portfolios. A coefficient of one indicates that the rankings of two portfolios remain the same, but it does not tell us anything about the spread between the portfolios. The spread between the portfolios may have shrunk or grown. However, we do know that, even if the spread has changed, at least the relative positions remained unaltered.
14. Since the P/E ratios are highly correlated, we cannot view elements in one cell as unrelated to the other cells; the results in two adjacent rows should be highly related. In other words, the results for the base year 1957 are, not surprisingly, similar to the results for the base year 1956. Because the results are not perfectly correlated, however, some additional information is conveyed by repeating the portfolio strategy for different base years.
15. Table 3 is subject to the same caveats as Table 2. For example, the years 1971 through 1975 play a relatively more important role in the later years after formation, so the P/E ratios exhibit a downward drift. The real focal point of the table is the difference in P/E ratios across portfolios, rather than the common movement by all portfolios. Moreover, the results of a more extensive examination of the data, which held constant the calendar year composition of each year, did not differ from the findings shown in Table 3. We chose Table 3's composite because it was the most comprehensive and the simplest method of presentation.
16. For example, for Year 0 (the year of formation), the average P/E ratio for Portfolio One was computed by taking a weighted average of each of the median P/E ratios for Portfolio One for the years 1956-74 inclusive. The weights were determined by the number of securities in that portfolio in that year. 1956, with 10 securities per portfolio, carried a weight of 0.029, while 1970-74 carried weights of 0.070 each with the sum of the weights over the 1956-74 period equalling one.
17. Since earnings could be negative in any subsequent year, a problem rose as to how to define growth when the denominator is negative. When earnings changed from negative to positive, the growth was defined to be greater than the median (i.e., "very large"). When earnings remained negative in both years, the observation was deleted. Typically, this caused a deletion of less than two per cent of the observations, with the exception of Portfolio One, where deletions ranged from two to three per cent of the observations.
18. We regard the transitory earnings argument as one, but by no means the only, interpretation to place on the results.
19. Suppose expected earnings per share are $1.00. For convenience, assume that realized earnings per share were $1.00 and $0.75 in 19x1 and 19x2. The actual growth rate of 19x2 is -25 per cent, while the expected growth in 19x3 is 33 per cent. Assuming price remains essentially unchanged (because permanent earnings are unchanged) at $10.00, the P/E ratio would be 10 and 13.3 for 19x1 and 19x2, while the expected P/E in 19x3 would be 10. Note that in 19x2 there was an abnormal low earnings growth associated with a high P/E (negative correlation) and that a high P/E in 19x2 was followed by abnormal high growth in 19x3 (positive correlation). This is discussed in more detail in W. Beaver, "The Information Content of the Magnitude of Unexpected Earnings" (Stanford Research Seminar, 1974).
20. This conclusion is contingent upon the way we chose to measure the variables and to rank the portfolios. For example, a longer term measure of growth (i.e., five or 10 years) might produce different results.
21. By unusual earnings opportunities we essentially mean opportunities to earn a return on future investments greater than the cost of capital. Valuation theory tells us that this form of future earnings growth will induce a growth premium in the P/E. Note that it is crucial to distinguish between unusual earnings opportunities on *future*, rather than current, investment. To the extent there are abnormal returns earned on the current investment, this will not affect the P/E ratio, although the ratio of market price to book value per share would be affected.
22. For example, if one believes that product and factor markets are reasonably competitive, then there exist little or no unusual earnings opportunities and the observed growth differences are almost entirely due to transitory factors.
23. Operationally, the market-wide P/E was defined to be the median P/E as reported in Table 1.
24. Although not reported here, the analysis of the serial correlation in P/E behavior was augmented by an analysis of a transition matrix. This analysis also confirmed the lack of any material tendency to move from one extreme portfolio to extreme portfolios at the other end of the P/E spectrum.
25. Since our study is concerned with differences across P/E ratios at a given point in time, beta (b_i) will be the sole determinant of differences in P/E resulting from differences in r_i. Assuming a finite growth horizon, Litzenberger and Rao ("Estimates of the Marginal Rate of Time Preference and Average Risk Aversion

of Investors in Electric Utility Shares: 1960-66," *The Bell Journal of Economics and Management Science* (Spring 1971), pp. 265-277) have shown the E/P ratio (the reciprocal of P/E) is a simple linear function of beta and a growth variable, with the following form:

$$\frac{E_i}{P_i} = \gamma_0 + \gamma_1 b_1 = \gamma_2 f(g)$$

The sign of γ_1 is expected to vary, f(g) is some function of growth and γ_2 is expected to be negative.

26. An analysis of the residuals indicated that they are well approximated by normality. This is not surprising in the sense that each observation is an "average" for a portfolio of stocks. By the Central Limit Theorem, we would expect the sampling distributions of averages to approach normality. Note, however, that the results from any one year's regression are not independent of those of other years.

27. Two approaches immediately come to mind—the application of Box-Jenkins techniques to the past earnings series or the use of analysts' forecasts of earnings. Either method might produce better assessments of expected earnings per share.

28. This ordinal statement holds for both depreciation and inventory, even though inventory also implies a "real" difference due to taxes. Obviously, the specific adjustments to be made would have to distinguish between accounting differences that imply tax differences versus those that do not.

29. W. Beaver and R. Dukes, "Delta-Depreciation Methods: Some Empirical Results," *Accounting Review* (April 1972), pp. 320-332. In this study, all sample firms were using an accelerated method for tax purposes. Therefore the difference was solely due to the depreciation method used for annual report purposes.

30. Another approach would be to introduce variables related to the accounting effect. Recent works by Watts and Zimmerman ("Toward a Positive Theory of the Determination of Accounting Standards," *Accounting Review* (April 1978)) suggest that conservativeness of accounting method varies positively with firm size. Van Breda ("The Prediction of Corporate Earnings" (Stanford University, 1976)) indicates that average age of assets is one of the variables that explains cross-sectional differences in return on equity (i.e., earnings available to common dividend by the book value of common equity).

ON THE ASSOCIATION BETWEEN OPERATING LEVERAGE AND RISK

Baruch Lev[*]

A major part of financial research is concerned with the effect of managerial decisions on the market value of the firm. Thus, the effect of changes in capital structure, dividend policy, and investment strategy on stock prices and risk has been extensively investigated on both the conceptual and empirical levels. This research is concerned with the effect of the firm's operating leverage on the riskiness and, hence, market value of its shares. The firm's operating leverage is defined as the ratio of the fixed to variable operating costs; a high operating leverage refers to a high share of fixed costs relative to variable costs. Given the substitutability among production factors, the degree of operating leverage can be substantially changed by managerial decisions. Thus, for example, an increase in the capital intensiveness of the production process (e.g., a switch from steam generating to nuclear production of electricity) will result in an increase in the relative share of fixed costs (e.g., depreciation, maintenance, etc.) to variable costs (e.g., coal, wages, etc.).

The main objective of investigating the relationship between operating leverage and risk is to advance the understanding of the risk-generating process operating in capital markets, a process about which little is yet known. Knowledge of the real determinants (i.e., those resulting from the firm's input and output decisions) of a stock's risk is obviously crucial for decisions on both the firm and investor levels. On the firm level, the relationship between operating decisions and risk (and hence, stock prices) is important since it is generally assumed that management attempts to maximize stockholders' wealth. On the investor level, knowledge of this relationship will improve the prediction of *ex ante* risk (and hence portfolio selection), given information on expected operational changes.

---

[*] *Tel-Aviv University, Israel, and the University of Chicago. The helpful comments of Robert S. Hamada, Eugene F. Fama, and a referee are gratefully acknowledged.*

JOURNAL OF FINANCIAL AND QUANTITATIVE ANALYSIS

September 1974

The relationship between operating leverage and risk is examined analytically in the next section. It is shown that a positive relationship between the two variables is expected. As operating leverage increases (decreases), both the overall and systematic volatility of the stock's return increases (decreases). These *a priori* expectations are found to be consistent with results of an empirical test conducted on the electric utility, steel, and oil industries.

I. Operating Leverage and Risk

A firm's before-tax net earnings during period t, x_{jt}, may be defined as:

$$(1) \quad x_{jt} = R_{jt} - V_{jt} - F_{jt},$$

where

R_{jt} = total revenues (sales) during t;

V_{jt} = total variable costs, which are a function of the number of units sold during t; and

F_{jt} = total fixed costs (including interest and preferred dividend) unaffected by volume changes during t.

The after-tax earnings, where τ is the average (and marginal) corporate tax rate, are:

$$(2) \quad x_{jt}(1 - \tau) = (R_{jt} - V_{jt} - F_{jt})(1 - \tau).$$

The relationship between the firm's earnings and the return on its common stock during period t, r_{jt}, is:

$$(3) \quad r_{jt} = d_{jt} + cg_{jt} = \frac{x_{jt}(1 - \tau) + \Delta g_{jt}}{S_{j,t-1}},$$

where

d_{jt} = dividends per share during t;

cg_{jt} = capital gains per share during t;

Δg_{jt} = change in capitalized growth during t; and

$S_{j,t-1}$ = total market value of common stock at the beginning of t.

The periodic rate of return on a stock is thus equal to the after-tax earnings accruing to common stockholders, $x_{jt}(1 - \tau)$, plus the change in the capitalized growth, Δg_{jt}, divided by the total market value of the common stocks, $S_{j,t-1}$.

580

The change in the capitalized growth is added to earnings in order to equate them to market returns:

> To this [net earnings] must be added any change in capitalized growth since we are trying to explain the common stockholder's market holding period dollar return. ΔG_t must be added for growth firms to the current period's profits from existing assets since capitalized growth opportunities of the firm--future earnings from new assets over and above the firm's cost of capital which are already reflected in the stock price at $(t-1)$--should change over the period and would accrue to the common stockholder.[1]

In an uncertain environment, future demand, Q_{jt} (in physical units), is of course a random variable. Hence, sales, variable costs, and earnings are also random variables.[2] The effect of demand fluctuations on earnings can be examined by rewriting (1) as:

$$(4) \qquad x_{jt} = (pQ)_{jt} - (vQ)_{jt} - F_{jt},$$

where

p = average price per unit of the product, and

v = average variable costs per unit of the product.

Differentiating (4) with respect to Q_{jt} yields:

$$(5) \qquad x'_{jt} = p_{jt} - v_{jt}.$$

The term involving the fixed costs, F_{jt}, vanishes since, by definition, these costs are not affected by demand fluctuations within a specified range. The derivative of earnings with respect to demand, x'_{jt}, thus equals the difference between the product's average price and the average variable costs (known by accountants as the "contribution margin"). Recall that differences in operating leverage among firms belonging to a homogeneous industry will be reflected in different average variable unit costs, v_{jt}, and hence in different earnings

---

[1] R. S. Hamada, "The Effect of the Firm's Capital Structure on the Systematic Risk of Common Stocks," *Journal of Finance,* vol. 27 (May 1972), pp. 437-438. More on the relationship between earnings and returns for growth companies in E. F. Fama and M. H. Miller, *The Theory of Finance* (New York: Holt, Rinehart and Winston, 1972), pp. 96-97.

[2] The fixed costs element F_{jt} is, of course, also a random variable, but it is independent of demand, Q_{jt}.

derivatives, x'_{jt}.[3/] Consider, for example, two firms, 1 and 2, where the former has a higher operating leverage than the latter. Accordingly, $v_{1t} < v_{2t}$, and $x'_{1t} > x'_{2t}$; i.e., earnings volatility of firm 1 induced by demand fluctuations will be larger than that of firm 2. In general, the higher the operating leverage, the higher the earnings volatility with respect to demand fluctuations.

Since earnings are related by (3) to stock returns, it can be expected that, other things being equal, the higher the operating leverage the larger the volatility of returns. Thus, when $v_{1t} < v_{2t}$, the derivative of the first firm's stock returns with respect to demand, $\partial r_{1t}/\partial Q_{1t}$ will be larger than that of the second firm's returns, $\partial r_{2t}/\partial Q_{2t}$. The volatility of returns is usually known as the overall riskiness of the firm's stock, and will be measured below by the standard deviation of monthly returns.

Note the analogy between the preceding argument and the better-known "financial leverage effect" which states that within a given risk class (a homogeneous industry in our case) the higher the financial leverage, i.e., the relative share of fixed interest charges (fixed costs in our case), the larger the volatility of the earnings residual accruing to common stockholders, and hence, the higher the financial risk associated with the common stocks.

In the portfolio theory, "capital asset pricing model," the relevant risk variable for portfolio selection is that associated with the *systematic*, or undiversifiable risk component, measured by the β value of Sharpe's market model:

$$(6) \qquad \beta_j = \frac{\text{cov}(r_{jt}, r_{Mt})}{\sigma^2(r_{Mt})},$$

where

r_{Mt} = return on the "market portfolio" during period t.

Substituting expressions (2) and (3) for r_{jt} in (6) yields:

---

[3] This assumes, of course, that in equilibrium the averate product price is identical for all firms in the industry, an assumption which seems tenable for a homogeneous and competitive industry.

(7) $$\beta_j = \frac{\text{cov}\left[\frac{(R_{jt} - V_{jt} - F_{jt})(1-\tau) + \Delta g_{jt}}{S_{j,t-1}}, r_{Mt}\right]}{\sigma^2(r_{Mt})},$$

(7a) $$S_{j,t-1}\beta_j = \frac{\text{cov}[R_{jt} - V_{jt} - F_{jt})(1-\tau) + \Delta g_{jt}, r_{Mt}]}{\sigma^2(r_{Mt})}$$

$$= \frac{\text{cov}[R_{jt}(1-\tau), r_{Mt}]}{\sigma^2(r_{Mt})} - \frac{\text{cov}[V_{jt}(1-\tau), r_{Mt}]}{\sigma^2(r_{Mt})} + \frac{\text{cov}[\Delta g_{jt}, r_{Mt}]}{\sigma^2(r_{Mt})}.[4]$$

Consider two firms, 1 and 2, in a homogeneous industry with a different degree of operating leverage (input mix) but an identical pattern of sales (output) across the states of nature:

(8) $$R_{1t}(\theta) = R_{2t}(\theta)$$

where

$R_{jt}(\theta)$ = sales of firm j during period t if state θ occurs.

In this case, the first covariance term, on the right-hand side of (7a) between sales and the market return, will be equal for the two firms. The last covariance term, between Δg_{jt} and r_{Mt}, can also be assumed to be equal for the two firms, since there seems to be no reason why the future growth of the firm, depending mainly on the output pattern, would be affected by differences in the mix of fixed and variable costs. However, the middle covariance term, between variable costs and the market return, will clearly differ for the two firms. The firm with the higher operating leverage, firm 1, will have a lower level (expected value) of variable costs than firm 2, and hence, a lower covariance with the market return. Thus, since

---

[4] The covariance of the fixed costs, F_{jt}, with the market portfolio return, r_{Mt}, is, of course, equal to zero.

(9) $$\frac{\text{cov}[V_{1t}(1-\tau), r_{Mt}]}{\sigma^2(r_{Mt})} < \frac{\text{cov}[V_{2t}(1-\tau), r_{Mt}]}{\sigma^2(r_{Mt})},$$

then from (7a):

(10) $$S_{1,t-1}\beta_1 > S_{2,t-1}\beta_2.$$

The product of the total stock value of the higher operating leverage firm and its systematic risk (left-hand side of (10)) is larger than the similar product for the lower operating leverage firm. Assuming equality of the total stock values of the firms, i.e., $S_{1,t-1} = S_{2,t-1}$, the systematic risk of the higher operating leverage firm will be larger than that of the lower operating leverage firm: $\beta_1 > \beta_2$.

The assumption regarding the equality of the total stock values of the two firms seems tenable given the identity of the sales pattern across the states of nature (8). It has been shown[5] that in equilibrium the market value of stocks plus the present value of future factor payments will be identical for all firms having the same output stream, $R_{jt}(\theta)$, *despite different efficiencies or input mixes*.[6] Accordingly, if different levels of operating leverage do not systematically affect the present value of total factor payments, then the market value of stocks of firms having identical output streams will be equal, and the preceding conclusion (10) regarding the positive association between operating leverage and systematic risk (β_j), holds.

Summarizing, the preceding analysis suggests that both the overall risk (volatility) and the systematic risk of common stocks will be positively associated with the degree of operating leverage, or negatively associated with the firm's level of variable costs. The validity of this hypothesis, resting on several *ceteris paribus* assumptions, will be empirically examined in the following section.

---

[5] P. A. Diamond, "The Role of a Stock Market in a General Equilibrium Model with Technological Uncertainty," *American Economic Review*, vol. 57 (September 1967), pp. 759-776, especially p. 767.

[6] This equivalence is also shown to be analogous to the Modigliani-Miller propositions that the total value of the firm is independent of the debt-equity mix.

II. Test Design and Results

Three homogeneous industries (mainly from the product point of view) were chosen for the test: the electrical utility industry, and steel and oil production.[7] Industry homogeneity was required to approximate as far as possible the *ceteris paribus* conditions set in the preceding section, in particular, the cross-sectional equality of sales patterns across states of nature.[8] Industry homogeneity also assures a relatively small diversity of accounting techniques and hence greater cross-sectional comparability of financial statement data.

Data were derived from both Standard and Poor's Compustat tape and the CRSP tape of monthly stock returns.[9] The first stage of analysis involved the determination of average variable costs for each firm, which were shown in (5) and (9-10) to be inversely associated with risk. These data cannot be obtained directly from the firms' financial statements since most reported cost items (e.g., cost of sales, maintenance, etc.) include both variable and fixed components. To break down total operating costs into the variable and fixed elements, a time-series regression of the following general form was run for each firm:

$$(11) \quad TC_{jt} = a_j + v_j Q_{jt} + u_{jt}, \qquad t = \begin{matrix} 1, \ldots, 20 \\ 1, \ldots, 12 \end{matrix}.[10]$$

where

TC_{jt} = total operating costs of firm j during year t, and

Q_{jt} = physical output (e.g., kilowatt-hours) of firm j during year t. Physical output for the steel and oil firms was unavailable, hence volume of sales was used as a surrogate for Q_{jt}.

---

[7] See Appendix for complete sample listing.

[8] This again is analogous to the industry homogeneity requirement in cost-of-capital studies (e.g., M. H. Miller and F. Modigliani, "Some Estimates of the Cost of Capital to the Electric Utility Industry," *American Economic Review*, vol. 56 (June 1966), pp. 334-391), set to meet the equivalent risk-class assumption.

[9] A few firms with incomplete data series were omitted.

[10] For electric utilities also producing gas, a second independent variable, $Q(G)_{jt}$, measuring gas output, was incorporated into (11).

The estimated coefficient $\hat{v}_j$ is thus a surrogate for the firm's average variable costs per unit of output. It indicates the change in total operating costs induced by a unit of volume change which is, by definition, equal to average variable costs per unit.[11] Such an estimation procedure implicitly assumes that no substantial changes in the production process (i.e., the fixed-variable cost mix) have taken place during the period over which the regression was run. To examine the restrictiveness of this stationary process assumption, we experimented with two different periods: 20 years (1949-1968) and 12 years (1957-1968). As shown in Table 1, the differences in the unit variable costs were relatively small. Accordingly, subsequent tests were based on variable costs calculated over a 12-year period. Note also in Table 1 the extremely high coefficients of multiple determination, R^2, and the large t-values which indicate the goodness of fit of the linear equation (11).

It should be noted that since firms usually use the full (absorption) costing method, in which fixed cost items are allocated to production, these costs might appear in the financial reports as if they were variable. This will bias upward the regression coefficient, v_j, in (11). However, a serious bias will exist only if periodic inventory changes are substantial. Since as is well known, when periodic sales equal production (i.e., no inventory changes), costs under the absorption method will equal those under the direct cost method in which no fixed cost allocation is made. Accordingly, no bias can be expected with respect to the electric utilities in the sample due to the lack of inventories. Regarding the oil and steel firms, the average annual change in inventory during the examined period was 10.3 and 12.1 percent, respectively, indicating the possibility of some bias in the estimation of the variable cost component, v_j. Obviously, a complete separation of fixed from variable costs cannot be done without access to internal (unpublished) data.

Risk measures for each firm were obtained from the CRSP tape. Overall volatility was measured as the standard deviation of monthly returns over the 10-year period, 1958-1967. Systematic risk estimates, β_j's, were obtained from the following diagonal or market model:[12]

---

[11] In empirical studies dealing with cost behavior and production function determination, firms' costs are usually deflated by price indexes in order to concentrate on real values. This procedure was felt to be inappropriate here since the volatility of return measures, with which the variable costs are to be associated, are based on nominal values (i.e., nominal dividends and capital gains).

[12] This estimation procedure assumes, of course, that the *ex post* determined β values are unbiased estimates of the "true" systematic risk.

TABLE 1

SELECTED DATA FOR EQUATION (11)

	No. of Firms	20-Year Interval $\bar{R}^2$ [a]	20-Year Interval $\bar{\bar{v}}$ [b]	20-Year Interval $\sigma(v)$ [c]	12-Year Interval $\bar{R}^2$	12-Year Interval $\bar{\bar{v}}$	12-Year Interval $\sigma(v)$
Electric Utilities	75	.98	.00815 (26.85)	.00444	.96	.00762 (18.67)	.00455
Steel Manufacturers	21	.96	.82922 (31.98)	.07930	.93	.81503 (20.97)	.08034
Oil Producers	26	.98	.74806 (68.12)	.15885	.95	.71677 (43.27)	.17459

[a] Sample average of the coefficient of multiple determination.

[b] Sample average of unit variable costs; average t-value in parentheses.

[c] Sample standard deviation of unit variable costs.

(12) $\quad r_{jt} = \alpha_j + \beta_j r_{Mt} + u_{jt}, \quad t = 1, \ldots, 120 \ (1958-1967)$,

where

r_{jt} = monthly return on stock j, and

r_{Mt} = New York Stock Exchange arithmetic average index of monthly returns.

The residual, u_{jt}, conditions are those assumed by OLS model.

The two risk measures were then cross-sectionally regressed for each industry on the unit variable cost estimate, $\hat{v}_j$, obtained from equation (11):

(13) $\quad \sigma(r_j) = a_1 + b_1 \hat{v}_j + \varepsilon_{1j}$, and

(14) $\quad \beta_j = a_2 + b_2 \hat{v}_j + \varepsilon_{2j}$.

Estimated coefficients for regressions (13) and (14) are reported in Tables 2 and 3.

The empirical results are indeed consistent with the hypothesized relationships: the average variable cost component is negatively associated with both the overall and systematic risk measures (see coefficients $\hat{b}_1$ and $\hat{b}_2$), for all three industries examined. In all cases, except for oil producers in Table 3, this association is statistically significant at the .05 level or higher.[13] The explanatory power of the variable cost component, in terms of the coefficient of multiple determination, R^2, is modest. Generally, the unit variable cost component explains a larger portion of the cross-sectional variability of the overall risk measure than that of the systematic risk measure. In both cases, it is evident that operating leverage is not the only (and may not even be the major) variable contributing to cross-sectional risk differentials. The poor performance of the variable cost measure with respect to the systematic risk of oil producers may be explained by the relative heterogeneity

---

[13] The above regressions were also run with the *size* of the firm (measured by total sales) as an additional independent variable. This was done since size might be related to operation leverage and also to risk. However, the addition of the size variable did not significantly change the estimates reported in Tables 2 and 3.

TABLE 2

REGRESSION ESTIMATES FOR EQUATION 13, OVERALL RISK

(t-values are shown in parentheses.)

Industry	No. of Firms	R^2	F-value	$\hat{a}_1$	$\hat{b}_1$	$\hat{c}_1$ [a]
Electric utilities	75	.12	3.122	.0560 (21.650)	-.4953 (-1.989)	-.0017 (-.725)
Steel manufacturers	21	.38	11.434	.1620 (6.306)	-.1061 (-3.381)	
Oil producers	26	.31	10.639	.0823 (10.274)	-.0358 (-3.262)	

[a] $\hat{c}_1$ is the coefficient of a dummy variable, taking the value of 1 for electrical utilities also producing gas, and zero for utilities producing electricity only.

TABLE 3

REGRESSION ESTIMATES FOR EQUATION 14, SYSTEMATIC RISK

(t-values are shown in parentheses.)

Industry	No. of Firms	R^2	F-value	$\hat{a}_2$	$\hat{b}_2$	$\hat{c}_2$
Electric utilities	75	.08	1.958	.5149 (14.790)	-6.912 (-2.060)	.0422 (1.378)
Steel manufacturers	21	.23	5.807	2.2833 (5.014)	-1.3401 (-2.4097)	
Oil producers	26	.05	1.338	.8101 (4.673)	-.2748 (-1.157)	

of this industry (which includes integrated domestic, integrated international, and crude oil producers). This heterogeneity is evident in the sample coefficients of variation reported in Table 4. The coefficient of variation for the systematic risk measures of oil producers, .357, is substantially larger than the other coefficients.

TABLE 4

SAMPLE COEFFICIENTS OF VARIATION (STANDARD DEVIATIONS DIVIDED BY THE MEANS) OF RISK MEASURES

	Overall Risk, $\sigma(r_j)$			Systematic Risk, β_j		
	$\bar{\sigma}$	$\bar{\mu}$	$\bar{\sigma}/\bar{\mu}$	$\bar{\sigma}$	$\bar{\mu}$	$\bar{\sigma}/\bar{\mu}$
Electric Utilities	.0097	.0489	.199	.1280	.5000	.256
Steel Manufacturers	.0139	.0755	.184	.2225	1.1910	.187
Oil Producers	.0122	.0587	.207	.2299	.6442	.357

III. Summary

A link between the firm's operating decisions and the riskiness of its stocks was established. Differences in the production process affecting the relative shares of fixed and variable costs (i.e., the operating leverage) were found, both analytically and empirically, to be associated with risk differentials. Specifically, other things equal, the higher the operating leverage (i.e., the lower the unit variable costs) the larger the overall and systematic risk of the stocks.

Various practical implications are suggested by these findings. On the firm level, it can be expected that large capital expenditures associated with an operating leverage increase will increase stock riskiness. In these cases, the cut-off rate used for the capital budgeting decision (i.e., the cost of capital) should allow for the increased risk. The use of the current cost of capital as the cut-off rate would probably result in a decrease in stock prices, adversely affecting stockholders' wealth. On the investor level, these findings might assist in the estimation of common stocks' risk given expected changes in the firm's operating leverage. Specifically, they suggest that, if a firm will experience a significant operating leverage change, the estimation of risk measures based exclusively on historical returns would be inappropriate.

APPENDIX

Sample Listing

Electric Utilities (Industry No. 4911 on Compustat)

1. Allegheny Power System Inc.
2. American Electric Power Co.
3. Arizona Public Services
4. Atlantic City Electric Co.
5. Boston Edison Co.
6. Carolina Power and Light Co.
7. Central Hudson Gas and Electric
8. Central Illinois Light
9. Central Illinois Public Service Co.
10. Central Main Power Co.
11. Central and Southwest Corp.
12. Cincinnati Gas and Electric Co.
13. Cleveland Electric Illuminating Co.
14. Columbus and Southern Ohio Electric
15. Commonwealth Edison Co.
16. Consolidated Edison Co.
17. Consumers Power Co.
18. Dayton Power and Light Co.
19. Delmarva Power and Light Co.
20. Detroit Edison Co.
21. Duke Power Co.
22. Duquesne Light Co.
23. Florida Power Corp.
24. Florida Power and Light Co.
25. General Public Utilities Corp.
26. Gulf States Utilities Co.
27. Hawaiian Electric Co.
28. Hudson Lighting and Power Co.
29. Idaho Power Co.
30. Indianapolis Power and Light
31. Interstate Power Co.
32. Iowa Power and Light
33. Iowa Public Service Co.
34. Kansas City Power and Light Co.
35. Kansas Gas and Electric
36. Kentucky Utilities Co.
37. Long Island Lighting Co.
38. Louisville Gas and Electric Co.
39. Middle South Utilities Inc.
40. Minnesota Power and Light
41. Montana Dakota Utilities
42. Montana Power Co.
43. Nevada Power Co.
44. New England Electric System
45. New York State Electric and Gas Co.
46. Niagara Mohawk Power Corp.
47. Northern Indiana Public Service Co.
48. Northern States Power Co.
49. Ohio Edison Co.
50. Oklahoma Gas and Electric Co.
51. Orange and Rockland Utilities
52. Pacific Gas and Electric Co.
53. Pacific Power and Light

54. Pennsylvania Power and Light
55. Philadelphia Electric Co.
56. Potomac Electric Power
57. Public Service Co. of Colorado
58. Public Service Co. of Indiana
59. Public Service Electric and Gas Co.
60. Puget Sound Power and Light
61. Rochester Gas and Electric
62. San Diego Gas and Electric Co.
63. South Carolina Electric and Gas Co.
64. Southern California Edison Co.
65. Southern Co.
66. Southwestern Public Service Co.
67. Tampa Electric Co.
68. Texas Utilities Co.
69. Toledo Edison Co.
70. Union Electric Co.
71. Utah Power and Light
72. Virginia Electric and Power Co.
73. Washington Water Power
74. Wisconsin Electric Power Co.
75. Wisconsin Public Service

Steel Manufacturers (Industry No. 3310 on Compustat)

1. Allegheny Ludlum Steel Corp.
2. Armco Steel Corp.
3. Bethlehem Steel Corp.
4. Bliss and Laughlin Industries
5. C. F. and I. Steel
6. Carpenter Steel Co.
7. Continental Steel Corp.
8. Copperweld Steel
9. Detroit Steel Corp.
10. Florida Steel Corp.
11. Granite City Steel Co.
12. Inland Steel Co.
13. Interlake Steel Co.
14. Jones and Laughlin Steel Corp.
15. Lukens Steel Co.
16. Mclouth Steel Corp.
17. National Steel Corp.
18. Pittsburgh Steel Co.
19. Republic Steel Corp.
20. U.S. Steel Corp.
21. Youngstown Sheet and Tube Co.

Oil Producers (Industries No. 1311, 2912, and 2913 on Compustat)

1. Amerada Petroleum
2. General American Oil Texas
3. Midwest Oil Corp.
4. Superior Oil Co.
5. Ashland Oil and Refining Co.
6. Atlantic Richfield Co.
7. Cities Service Co.
8. Continental Oil Co.
9. Standard Oil Co. (New Jersey)
10. Kerr McGee Corp.
11. Marathon Oil Co.
12. Phillips Petroleum Co.
13. Quaker State Oil Refining
14. Shell Oil Co.
15. Sinclair Oil Corp.
16. Skelly Oil Co.
17. Standard Oil Co. (Indiana)
18. Standard Oil Co. (Ohio)
19. Sun Oil
20. Sunray DX Oil Co.
21. Union Oil Co. of California
22. Gulf Oil Corp.
23. Mobil Oil Corp.
24. Royal Dutch Petroleum
25. Standard Oil Co. (California)
26. Texaco Inc.

Economic Determinants of the Relation Between Earnings Changes and Stock Returns

Ray Ball
S. P. Kothari
Ross L. Watts
University of Rochester

SYNOPSIS AND INTRODUCTION: In competitive product markets, product prices and thus firms' revenues incorporate the cost of equity capital. In a competitive capital market, the cost of equity capital (the expected return on equity) increases with the risk of firms' investments. Because accounting earnings are calculated without deducting the cost of equity capital, they are expected to be an increasing function of firms' investment risks. This simple competitive equilibrium analysis predicts a positive relation between changes in investment risk and expected earnings. The presence of corporate debt complicates the analysis because leverage effects seem likely to affect the relation between changes in investment risk and expected earnings.

Using annual earnings and return data from 1950 to 1988, we document a statistically significant positive association between changes in equities' relative risks and in earnings. However, on average, only a small proportion of changes in earnings can be attributed to changes in risk. A much larger proportion is attributable to changes in economic rents (windfall gains and losses). The observed positive association between changes in earnings and changes in equities' risks suggests that leverage effects do not fully offset the effect of changes in investment risks. This

---

We are grateful for the comments of participants in workshops at the University of California at Berkeley, University of Chicago, Columbia University, Baruch College CUNY, Duke University, Michigan State University, New York University, University of Southern California, SUNY at Buffalo, University of Washington at Seattle, and the 1988 European Finance Association meetings at Istanbul. We also benefitted from the comments of Mike Barclay, Vic Bernard, John Bildersee, Jim Brickley, Dan Collins, George Foster, Robert Holthausen, Wayne Landsman, Richard Leftwich, Wayne Marr, Jim Ohlson, Katherine Schipper, Terry Shevlin, Dee Shores, John Wild, and Jerry Zimmerman. We acknowledge excellent research assistance by David Atlas, Tony Greig, and Richard Sloan. We acknowledge financial support from the Managerial Economics Research Center at the Simon School, University of Rochester, and from the John M. Olin Foundation.

Submitted January 1991.
Accepted September 1992.

association is robust with respect to subperiod analysis, alternative specifications of the earnings change variable, alternative data-availability requirements, and the number of portfolios formed.

Key Words: *Earnings, Stock prices, Risk, Leverage, Windfall gains and losses.*

Data Availability: *All data used are publicly available from sources identified in the text.*

IN section I, we discuss the economic determinants of changes in accounting earnings and propose that they are associated with changes in equity risk. In section II, our research design, data, and sample selection process are described. The empirical results are given in section III, and the results of a range of diagnostic tests are given in section IV. Conclusions are presented in section V.

I. Economic Determinants of Earnings Changes and Their Implications

Standard valuation models (see, e.g., Fama and Miller 1972, chap. 2) suggest that earnings changes can be attributable to changes in expected returns on equity (the cost of equity capital) as well as to changes in economic rents (windfall gains and losses). However, research on the relation between changes in earnings and stock returns has implicitly interpreted changes in earnings as information about economic rents, commonly describing them as earnings "news," "surprises," or "innovations."[1] We propose that changes in expected earnings and stock returns are jointly determined by changes in firms' investment risks and in their leverage. Thus, part of the observed association between changes in earnings and stock returns is predicted to be attributable to changes in equities' risks and, hence, expected returns. We discuss the relation between risk and changes in earnings initially in the context of an all-equity capital structure, then add the complication of debt financing.

Investment Risk Changes as Determinants of Changes in Earnings

A firm's investment risk is the market-value-weighted sum of the risks of its individual investments. The weights vary with the amounts invested in new projects, with the success (and hence value) of individual projects or lines of business, and with mergers, acquisitions, divestitures, restructurings, and plant closings. In addition, investment risk is affected by changes in operating leverage (see, e.g., Christie 1989; Lev 1974), which varies with product prices and factor costs. Finally, investment risk varies over time as individual products or lines of business mature or are repositioned in their markets. In summary, for a variety of reasons we expect that firms' investment risks, and thus the expected returns on their equity, change continuously.

---

[1] See Foster (1977), Beaver et al. (1979, 1980). The random-walk earnings model in Ball and Watts (1972) encourages an economic rents interpretation of earnings changes, as does the earnings increase/decrease research design of Ball and Brown (1968). However, in discussing the form of the earnings-returns relation, Ball and Brown (1968, fn. 40) conjecture that "income numbers convey information about the convariablity of the income process." More recently, the literature on earnings response coefficients recognizes that riskiness of the earnings stream affects the price-earnings relation (see, e.g., Collins and Kothari 1989; Easton and Zmijewski 1989; Kormendi and Lipe 1987).

We also expect variations in expected returns to be reflected in accounting earnings changes because accounting earnings are calculated without deducting the cost of equity capital. In competitive product markets, product prices, and thus firms' sales revenues, reflect the cost of capital for the level of risk involved. Without any deduction of cost of capital, earnings will also reflect the cost of capital and thus risk. If a firm increases its proportion of sales and investment in a higher-risk line of business, it not only increases its relative risk, but also its expected accounting return.[2]

Since changes in expected return are reflected in both equity returns and accounting earnings, we hypothesize that changes in investment risk induce a relation between returns and changes in accounting earnings.

Effect of Leverage

In a Miller-Modigliani world without taxes, leverage does not affect the *firm's* expected return, but it does affect the *stock's* risk and expected return, which raises the potential for another form of relation between changes in earnings and stock returns. Specifying the effect of leverage on the relation between changes in earnings and returns is complex and requires general equilibrium modelling. We consider only the direct effect of leverage on the relation between returns and changes in earnings. In this simple setting, leverage affects the interest expense deducted from earnings as well as the risks of firms' equities. A negative relation between changes in earnings and in equity risk is implied. This negative effect of leverage is hypothesized to offset, at least in part, our earlier expectation of a positive relation between change in earnings and in equity risk.

II. Research Design

We require a research design that is sensitive to annual changes in risk, so we use an annual-returns version of the Ibbotson (1975) risk-estimation technique (see Ball and Kothari 1989, for further details).[3] We investigate the association between annual changes in earnings (scaled by price) and stocks' risks and returns in the year before, the year of, and the year following the changes in earnings.

Risk and Abnormal Return Estimates

All firms on COMPUSTAT with December 31 fiscal year-ends are ranked on their unexpected earnings (defined below) in each of the 37 years during the 1951–1987 period, and are assigned to decile portfolios in equal numbers. The first (tenth) portfolio therefore is rebalanced annually to contain each year's 10 percent worst (best) earnings performers. The earnings-performance year is designated as year 0 in event time and is

---

[2] The simple economic model of the firm implied in the above reasoning abstracts from several factors. First, it ignores the effects of imperfect accounting methods and mandatory or voluntary changes in accounting method. Second, it ignores that part of investment risk variation that is inframarginal and absorbed by the firm, rather than passed on to consumers.

[3] Annual returns are used because annual-return beta estimates appear more consistent with the CAPM and are effective in identifying risk changes in a similar context. Handa et al. (1989) show that, when returns are measured annually, there is more dispersion in estimated betas, the cross-section risk/return intercept is more consistent with CAPM predictions, and the "size effect" is insignificant. Ball and Kothari (1989) show that, for portfolios formed on the basis of ranked *ex post* security returns, annual-return betas estimated from the same procedure used here successfully identify associated annual risk (and expected return) changes. Ex *post* security return portfolios overlap *ex post* earnings change portfolios, so the latter results are particularly relevant.

the year whose earnings are used to sort firms into portfolios. For event year 0, the annual buy-and-hold excess return (net of the riskless rate) on each of the ten earnings-performance portfolios is calculated for each of the 37 calendar years. From this time series, we estimate the beta and average annual abnormal return for each portfolio. These statistics are, therefore, functions only of each earnings-performance portfolio's returns *in the year in which its earnings performance occurs*; returns in no other event-year are used in obtaining the estimated event-year risks and abnormal returns.

The above procedure is repeated for event years -1 and $+1$. A time series of 37 annual excess returns is constructed for each portfolio, and market model parameters are estimated, over 1950–1986 for the event year -1, and over 1952–1988 for event year $+1$. The three resulting 37-year time series (for event years -1, 0, and $+1$) have two important properties. First, for each earnings-performance portfolio, the three time series are independent in that they utilize non-overlapping security returns. Second, individual return observations within each time series are non-overlapping, so the procedure does not induce autocorrelation in the market model regression residuals.

We estimate the market model in risk-premium form to measure relative risk, thus controlling for the effects of interest rates and the market risk premium on returns. The market model for portfolio p ($p=1,\ldots,10$) in event-year τ ($\tau=-1,0,+1$) is:

$$(R_{pt}-R_{ft})=\alpha_{p,\tau}+\beta_{p,\tau}(R_{mt}-R_{ft})+\epsilon_{pt}, \tag{1}$$

where R_{pt} = equal-weighted return on portfolio p in year t; R_{mt} = equal-weighted return on the market portfolio in year t; R_{ft} = riskless rate of return in year t; $\alpha_{p,\tau}$ and $\beta_{p,\tau}$ are the intercept and slope coefficients in event year τ; and ϵ_{pt} is the error term. The intercept $\alpha_{p,0}$ is the estimated abnormal return of portfolio p in the earnings-performance year ($\tau=0$), under the maintained hypothesis of the capital asset pricing model (CAPM). The slope $\beta_{p,0}$ is portfolio p's relative risk during the earnings-performance year. Neither $\alpha_{p,0}$ nor $\beta_{p,0}$ is influenced by returns in any other event-time year. To assess the risk variation from the year before to the year after the earnings-performance year, we also estimate equation (1) in event years $\tau=-1$ and $+1$.

Although we use data over a 37-year period, we neither assume parameter stationarity for *individual* stocks nor require that each stock be available throughout the 37-year period. Instead, parameter stationarity is assumed at the portfolio level. For example, the beta of the worst-performance portfolio is assumed constant over chronological time, even though its composition of stocks varies every calendar year.[4] Stationarity is assumed only at the relation between earnings and market return parameters, the process being studied.

Sample Selection, Data, and Variable Definitions

The sample is all firms with a December 31 fiscal year-end, earnings data for at least six years during 1950–1988, and monthly return data on the Center for Research in Security Prices (CRSP) monthly tape. Earnings data are obtained from the COM-

---

[4] Even then, beta stationarity of earnings-performance portfolios is not a critical assumption. If the portfolio betas are not stationary and the riskiness of stocks assigned to portfolios is independent of the market return, then the portfolio betas estimated from the 37-year series are statistically less precise, but still unbiased and consistent. Nevertheless, in section IV we report subperiod results, betas estimated separately in good and bad market-performance years, and results of estimating betas separately in each year by using daily returns. These results are consistent with a positive association between risk changes and earnings changes.

PUSTAT annual industrial, research, and history tapes. The resulting sample consists of 28,294 firm-years, an average of 764 firms per year.

We use annual primary earnings per share excluding extraordinary items and discontinued operations, adjusted for stock splits and stock dividends. We ignore the effect of accounting method changes because they are relatively infrequent.[5] However, because of income smoothing or other reasons, the incidence of accounting method changes among the extreme good and bad earnings-performance stocks could be greater than among other stocks. The power of the test would be reduced to the extent that stocks are misclassified into the ten earnings-performance portfolios because of accounting method changes.

The scaled earnings change variable for firm i is defined as:

$$\Delta X_{it} = (X_{it} - X_{it-1})/P_{it-1}, \qquad (2)$$

where X_{it} is earnings per share in year t, and P_{it-1} is share price at the close of year $t-1$.[6] The scaled earnings change then is orthogonalized with respect to the market return by estimating the following firm-specific time-series regression with all available data (minimum of five observations):

$$\Delta X_{it} = \gamma_{0i} + \gamma_{1i}(R_{mt} - R_{ft}) + \eta_{it}, \qquad (3)$$

where R_{mt} is the CRSP equal-weighted annual return obtained by summing monthly returns or the sample mean annual return on the available securities, and R_{ft} is the annual T-bill interest rate. This avoids any correlation between the market return and the assignment of stocks to portfolios that could induce a spurious association between changes in risk and changes in earnings. Earnings performance is defined as:

$$UX_{it} = \gamma_{0i} + \eta_{it}. \qquad (4)$$

The ten earnings-performance portfolios are formed on the basis of annually ranked UX_{it}.

III. Empirical Results

Unexpected Earnings and Total Returns: Descriptive Statistics

We report the average earnings performance and total returns on each of the ten portfolios during $\tau = -1, 0,$ and $+1$ in table 1. The CRSP equal-weighted return and the sample average return also are reported. By construction, UX increases monotonically with the portfolio rank. The distribution of the earnings-performance variable is leptokurtic. The worst portfolio's earnings change is -27.44 percent of its market value; that of the best is 26.44 percent. An implication of leptokurtosis is that the extreme earnings-performance portfolios are likely to exhibit relatively large risk changes.

---

[5] A virtually exhaustive sample of accounting method changes from 1969 to 1988 in Pincus and Wasley (1991, table 4) indicates that the probability that a firm's earnings are affected by either voluntary or mandatory accounting method changes is 0.084 (our calculation).

[6] Analysts' forecast errors are an alternative to the earnings variable used in this study. Since analysts' forecasts are unavailable in machine-readable form prior to the seventies and the early coverage is generally limited to large market-capitalization stocks, we begin with earnings change as a proxy for the market-unexpected earnings. The advantage of analysts' forecast errors would be that they are less likely to be serially correlated, particularly compared to the behavior of extreme earnings changes through time. As discussed below, the effect of ignoring the negative serial correlation in extreme earnings changes biases against the risk-change hypothesis.

Table 1
Earnings-Performance Portfolio Average Annual Returns in the Three Years Around the Earnings-Performance Year: 1951–1987

Earnings-Performance Rank (p)[a]	$UX_{p,0}$	$R_{p,-1}$[b] (S.D.)	$R_{p,0}$ (S.D.)	$R_{p,+1}$ (S.D.)	$R_{p,+1JM}$[c] (S.D.)	$R_{p,+AD}$ (S.D.)
1	−27.44%	14.5% (31.6)	−2.1% (27.5)	15.1% (29.1)	11.0% (16.9)	4.0% (23.6)
2	−3.76	16.7 (28.3)	3.6 (22.1)	13.2 (24.0)	7.6 (12.5)	4.9 (18.1)
3	−1.48	16.5 (21.4)	5.94 (20.0)	13.8 (21.2)	6.7 (11.4)	6.5 (16.1)
4	−0.39	18.0 (20.8)	8.4 (19.1)	13.7 (18.9)	5.7 (10.4)	7.6 (14.8)
5	0.32	19.8 (21.2)	12.3 (19.4)	14.2 (17.6)	5.8 (9.1)	7.9 (14.4)
6	1.01	20.2 (21.2)	17.6 (20.1)	16.9 (19.4)	6.6 (9.2)	9.5 (16.4)
7	1.75	22.5 (22.2)	23.6 (24.0)	18.0 (22.5)	7.3 (10.5)	9.9 (18.4)
8	2.93	21.8 (23.3)	25.8 (24.0)	18.5 (22.4)	9.2 (11.6)	8.4 (27.8)
9	5.43	21.7 (27.2)	32.0 (28.6)	22.2 (28.4)	10.8 (12.4)	9.6 (21.2)
10	26.44	10.6 (30.4)	43.3 (38.1)	25.3 (37.4)	15.9 (16.6)	7.5 (27.0)
Equal-Weighted CRSP Average Return	—	17.8 (26.4)	16.7 (26.5)	16.8 (26.5)	9.5 (13.2)	6.6 (20.6)
Equal-Weighted Sample Average Return	—	18.2 (23.5)	17.0 (23.5)	17.1 (23.0)	8.6 (11.7)	7.5 (18.0)

[a] Portfolio 1 (10) consists of the 10 percent worst (best) earnings performers in every calendar year. The sample is all 28,294 firm-years with December 31 fiscal year-end and earnings and return data available on the COMPUSTAT annual industrial or research files and the CRSP monthly returns tape for at least six years. Earnings-performance years, designated as event year 0, cover 1951–1987. Each calendar year, firms are ranked on their earnings performance and assigned to ten earnings-performance portfolios. Earnings performance, $UX_{p,0}$, is earnings change, scaled by year-beginning price and orthogonalized with respect to the annual market return; see equations (2) to (4).

[b] Averages of the 37 annual portfolio returns over 1951–1987, for event years −1, 0, and +1 relative to the earnings-performance year. Buy-and-hold security returns inclusive of dividends are used.

[c] $R_{p,+1JM}$ ($R_{p,+1AD}$) is average return over 1951–1987 in January–March (April–December) of year +1.

As expected, portfolio returns in year $\tau=0$ increase monotonically with UX. The average return of the worst portfolio in year 0 is −2.1 percent and that of the best is 43.3 percent. The sample mean is 17 percent. Returns in year −1 exhibit an inverted-U-shaped relation with earnings rank in year 0, which suggests the presence of factors other than earnings anticipation. These could include (1) correlated variables omitted from the CAPM and (2) negative correlation between earnings changes in years −1 and 0 (Brooks and Buckmaster 1976).

Returns in year +1 include those of the earnings announcement period as well as those of the post-announcement period. We therefore expect portfolio 10's (1's) return to be highest (lowest) in year +1. As shown in table 1, returns are highest for portfolio 10, but are not lowest for portfolio 1. Table 1 also includes returns for the January to March and the April to December components of year +1, which roughly correspond to the earnings announcement and post-announcement periods. The January to March returns reveal a return seasonality for the portfolios (see, e.g., Keim 1983; Rozeff and Kinney 1976). Much of the high return in year +1 for portfolio 10 is concentrated in the January to March quarter, reflecting both the announcement and January seasonal effects. The April to December return for portfolio 1 is 4 percent, compared to 7.5 percent for portfolio 10, which might reflect either risk differences or post-announcement drift.

Risk Changes

The estimated betas and standard errors of the ten earnings-performance portfolios for years −1, 0, and +1 are reported in table 2. The evidence is consistent with the hypothesis that risk shifts occur as a function of changes in earnings.

Estimated changes in beta from year −1 to year 0 are a statistically significant function of changes in year 0 earnings. The rank correlation between $\Delta\beta_{p,0}$ and contemporaneous earnings performance is 0.98 (p-value<0.01), thus the null hypothesis that beta shifts are not associated with changes in earnings is rejected. Consistent with this pattern, the estimated betas of the first six portfolios (essentially the "bad news" portfolios) decrease, while the estimated betas of the remaining four portfolios increase. Changes in individual portfolio betas are not significant, except in the portfolios formed at the extremes of ranked changes in earnings. The estimated beta of the worst earnings-performance portfolio declines from 1.17 to 1.01; since the standard errors of β_{-1} and β_0 are 0.056 and 0.054, and the estimates are independent, the t-statistic for the −0.16 estimated change in beta is −2.05 (p-value<0.05). Similarly, the estimated beta of the best earnings-performance portfolio increases by +0.27, from 1.07 to 1.34, and the t-statistic for the difference is 2.30 (p-value<0.05). As is the case with earnings, changes in portfolio betas appear leptokurtic. Overall, these results are consistent with our hypothesis that changes in earnings and changes in risk are related.[7]

The estimated changes in year +1 beta are not significantly related to prior earnings performance. The rank correlation between $\Delta\beta_{p,+1}$ and year 0 earnings is −0.48 (p-value=0.16), and no individual change is significant. The negative correlation raises the possibility of a partial reversal of the beta shifts observed in the earnings-performance year. The last column of table 2 reports the overall estimated change in beta from year −1 to +1. The rank correlation between portfolio earnings and $\Delta\beta_{p,-1,+1}$ is 0.82 (p-value<0.01), which is consistent with the hypothesis that changes in earnings are positively associated with changes in risk. Portfolio 1's estimated beta decreases by

---

[7] The changes in risk ($\Delta\beta_{p,0}s$) cannot be explained by mean reversion in betas alone (see Blume 1975, Vasicek 1973, among others). Mean reversion predicts positive changes for portfolios whose year −1 beta is less than 1, and negative changes for the others. The changes in risk reported in table 2 are consistent with mean reversion in five out of ten portfolios. For two of the five instances where the sign is as predicted by mean reversion, the beta estimates in year 0 go beyond or below unity, which is inconsistent with mean reversion (mean reversion predicts that betas approach 1 from below or above).

Table 2
Relation Between Earnings Performance and Relative Risk in the Three Years Around the Earnings-Performance Year: 1951–1987

Earnings-Performance Rank (p)[a]	$UX_{p,0}$ %	$\beta_{p,-1}$[b] (Std Err)	$\beta_{p,0}$ (Std Err)	$\beta_{p,+1}$ (Std Err)	$\Delta\beta_{p,0}$[c]	$\Delta\beta_{p,+1}$	$\Delta\beta_{p,-1,+1}$
1	−27.44	1.17 (0.056)	1.01 (0.054)	1.05 (0.059)	−0.16*	+0.04	−0.12
2	−3.76	1.04 (0.050)	0.82 (0.041)	0.89 (0.033)	−0.22*	+0.07	−0.15*
3	−1.48	0.80 (0.030)	0.74 (0.043)	0.76 (0.046)	−0.06	+0.02	−0.04
4	−0.39	0.73 (0.055)	0.69 (0.046)	0.68 (0.044)	−0.03	−0.02	−0.05
5	0.32	0.74 (0.056)	0.71 (0.043)	0.62 (0.046)	−0.03	−0.10	−0.12
6	1.01	0.75 (0.051)	0.73 (0.042)	0.68 (0.049)	−0.02	−0.05	−0.07
7	1.75	0.81 (0.037)	0.88 (0.039)	0.83 (0.037)	+0.07	−0.06	0.01
8	2.93	0.84 (0.047)	0.88 (0.034)	0.82 (0.040)	+0.04	−0.07	−0.03
9	5.43	0.98 (0.056)	1.05 (0.043)	1.04 (0.048)	+0.07	−0.01	0.06
10	26.44	1.07 (0.080)	1.34 (0.085)	1.34 (0.074)	+0.27*	0.00	0.28*
Average		0.89	0.89	0.87	−0.01	−0.02	−0.02
Rank Correlations with Earnings Performance[d]					0.98	−0.48	0.82
p-Value					<0.01	0.16	<0.01

[a] See notes to table 1.

[b] $\beta_{p,-1}$ from regressing annual excess returns for portfolio p in the 37 event years −1 on the annual CRSP equal-weighted market portfolio excess return ($\beta_{p,0}$ and $\beta_{p,+1}$ are estimated similarly):

$$(R_{pt} - R_{ft}) = \alpha_{p,-1} + \beta_{p,-1}(R_{mt} - R_{ft}) + \epsilon_{pt} \quad \text{for } p = 1, \ldots, N.$$

[c] $\Delta\beta_{p,0} = \beta_{p,0} - \beta_{p,-1}$, $\Delta\beta_{p,+1} = \beta_{p,+1} - \beta_{p,0}$, and $\Delta\beta_{p,-1,+1} = \beta_{p,+1} - \beta_{p,-1}$.

[d] Spearman rank correlation between earnings performance and $\Delta\beta_{p,0}$, $\Delta\beta_{p,+1}$, and $\Delta\beta_{p,+1,-1}$; p-values that the correlations are zero assume ten degrees of freedom.

* Significant at p-value of 0.05.

−0.12 and portfolio 10's increases by 0.28. Again, only the changes in the extreme portfolios (2 and 10) are individually significant.

The beta estimates of the earnings-performance portfolios in years −2 and +2 reveal that the risk changes associated with changes in earnings are not permanent beyond year +1. This result is addressed further in section IV.

Leverage Effects

In table 3, we report average debt/equity ratios for firms in each earnings-performance portfolio, at the end of years −1, 0, and +1. Market values are used for equity,

Table 3
Earnings-Performance Portfolios' Debt-to-Equity Ratios in the Three Years Around the Earnings-Performance Year: 1951–1987

Earnings-Performance Rank (p)[a]	$UX_{p,0}$ %	$D/E_{p,-1}$[b]	$D/E_{p,0}$	$D/E_{p,+1}$	$\Delta D/E_{p,0}$[c]	$\Delta D/E_{p,+1}$
1	−27.44	1.07 (0.12)	1.30 (0.14)	1.30 (0.13)	0.23	0.00
2	−3.76	0.70 (0.07)	0.81 (0.09)	0.85 (0.09)	0.11	0.04
3	−1.48	0.65 (0.07)	0.72 (0.07)	0.74 (0.07)	0.07	0.02
4	−0.39	0.57 (0.06)	0.61 (0.06)	0.64 (0.06)	0.04	0.03
5	0.32	0.54 (0.05)	0.56 (0.05)	0.58 (0.05)	0.02	0.02
6	1.01	0.54 (0.05)	0.55 (0.05)	0.57 (0.05)	0.01	0.02
7	1.75	0.59 (0.06)	0.58 (0.05)	0.60 (0.06)	−0.01	0.02
8	2.93	0.68 (0.07)	0.66 (0.06)	0.67 (0.06)	−0.02	0.01
9	5.43	0.80 (0.07)	0.74 (0.07)	0.75 (0.07)	−0.06	−0.01
10	26.44	1.26 (0.13)	1.06 (0.10)	1.05 (0.10)	−0.20	−0.01
Rank Correlations with Earnings Performance[d]					−1.00	−0.44
p-value					<0.01	0.20

[a] See notes to table 1. The sample is reduced to 27,680 firm-year observations by requiring long-term debt and preferred stock data.

[b] $D/E_{p,-1}(D/E_{p,0}, D/E_{p,+1})$ is ratio of book value of long-term debt plus preferred stock to market value of common equity, both at the end of event year −1 (0, +1). Reported values are averages of 37 annual portfolio debt-to-equity ratios and their standard errors. Ratios exceeding 5 are set equal to 5.

[c] $\Delta D/E_{p,0} = D/E_{p,0} - D/E_{p,-1}$ and $D/E_{p,+1} = D/E_{p,+1} - D/E_{p,0}$.

[d] Spearman rank correlations between earnings performance and $\Delta D/E_{p,0}$ and $\Delta D/E_{p,+1}$; p-values that the correlations are zero assume ten degrees of freedom.

but book values are used for long-term debt and preferred stock.[8] Although none of the individual portfolio changes in leverage is significant, they exhibit a perfect negative rank correlation with earnings performance. The leverages of the first six earnings-performance portfolios increase in the earnings-performance year, while they decrease for

---

[8] Data are for 27,680 firm-years, a reduction of 2.2 percent from the 28,294 observations used earlier, because book values of some debt and preferred stock are not available. Debt/equity ratios exceeding 5 are set equal to 5. The tenor of the results is unchanged when alternative truncation rules are used or when outliers are included.

the other four portfolios.[9] This evidence suggests that when earnings-induced changes in equity values alter firms' debt/equity ratios, the firms do not fully adjust their capital structures to previous levels. This is consistent with the results of Ball et al. (1976). Nevertheless, the significant positive correlation between changes in earnings and in equity risks (reported above) suggests that changes in leverage do not fully offset the hypothesized relation between changes in earnings and in investment risks.

We also examine the portfolios' leverage ratios in year +1 to determine whether firms make delayed capital structure adjustments. We do not expect a complete capital structure adjustment because there is a negative relation between investment risk and leverage (see, e.g., Smith and Watts 1992). There is no evidence in table 3 of a lagged capital structure adjustment. The absolute magnitudes of the changes in leverage are small compared to those in year 0 (none exceeds 0.05), and the rank correlation between earnings performance and change in leverage in year +1 is insignificant (-0.44, p-value=0.20).

Abnormal Returns

We report abnormal returns for the three years around the earnings-performance year in table 4. Not surprisingly, portfolio abnormal returns in event year 0 (denoted as $\alpha_{p,0}$) exhibit a perfect positive rank correlation with earnings. The relation is not linear. In the extreme performance portfolios, abnormal returns are similar in magnitude to scaled unexpected earnings; in the interior portfolios, they exceed scaled unexpected earnings. This is consistent with prior studies, including Beaver et al. (1979).

The pattern of the abnormal returns in the year prior to the earnings-performance year (denoted as $\alpha_{p,-1}$) is partially consistent with early anticipation by the security market, as reported by prior studies (see, e.g., Beaver et al. 1980; Collins et al. 1987; Freeman 1987). However, the abnormal returns exhibit an inverted-U-shaped function of changes in earnings possibly reflecting other phenomena occurring in year -1 or misspecification of the CAPM.[10] The rank correlation between portfolio abnormal returns in year -1 and change in year 0 earnings is only 0.32 (p-value=0.37).

Portfolio average abnormal returns in year +1 (denoted as $\alpha_{p,+1}$) are generally small but are consistent with post-announcement drift. Their rank correlation with change in earnings is 0.96 ($p<0.01$). These abnormal returns include pre-announcement and earnings-announcement effects in the early months of year +1, and thus are biased in

---

[9] Leverage changes are exaggerated by using book values for debt. For bad-news portfolios, market values of debt decrease because of increased bankruptcy risk, and the leverage ratios therefore are overestimated. The converse is true for good-news portfolios. The precise effect of earnings outcomes on market-valued leverage ratios is unknown. However, given the magnitude of change in the ratios of book value of debt to market value of equity for the extreme portfolios, it seems unlikely that the use of market values of debt would substantially alter the results. It is possible, though, that market-valued leverage changes are less dramatic and that correlations between leverage changes and earnings performance are weaker than those reported in table 3. A second possibility is that, since the extreme earnings-performance stocks are relatively more leveraged, they are more sensitive to macroeconomic variables, including interest rates, which potentially induce a greater correlation between their earnings performance and aggregate economic activity. A detailed examination of this issue is potentially interesting but is beyond the scope of this study.

[10] The declining abnormal returns for the good-news portfolios and the -8.07 percent abnormal return on the best-news portfolio could be explained by some firms' achieving 10th-portfolio earnings performance in year 0 by making write-offs in year -1. Write-offs usually accompany poor earnings performance at the time, which could explain the negative abnormal return in year -1, but they reduce deductions from future earnings. See Healy (1985) and DeAngelo (1988) for evidence on such write-offs. The phenomenon is commonly known as the "big bath."

Table 4
Earnings Performance and Abnormal Returns in the Three Years Around the Earnings-Performance Year: 1951–1987

Earnings-Performance Rank (p)[a]	$UX_{p,0}$	$\alpha_{p,-1}$[b] (Std Err)	$\alpha_{p,0}$ (Std Err)	$\alpha_{p,+1}$ (Std Err)	$\alpha_{p,+1JM}$[c] (Std Err)	$\alpha_{p,+1AD}$ (Std Err)
1	−27.44	−5.48** (1.65)	−18.85** (1.56)	−2.24 (1.70)	−0.61 (0.66)	−2.87 (1.18)
2	−3.76	−1.65 (1.47)	−10.91** (1.18)	−2.41 (0.96)	−1.29* (0.52)	−1.29 (0.75)
3	−1.48	1.22 (1.07)	−7.74** (1.24)	−0.22 (1.35)	−1.49 (0.55)	0.59 (1.00)
4	−0.39	3.58 (1.62)	−4.71** (1.34)	0.61 (1.28)	−1.88** (0.54)	1.83 (0.82)
5	0.32	5.32** (1.65)	−1.02 (1.24)	1.89 (1.32)	−1.00 (0.49)	2.23 (0.93)
6	1.01	5.57* (1.51)	4.04** (1.22)	3.75 (1.41)	−0.25 (0.47)	3.63** (1.05)
7	1.75	7.11** (1.09)	8.28** (1.12)	3.24 (1.08)	−0.30 (0.55)	3.71** (0.81)
8	2.93	6.05** (1.39)	10.54** (0.98)	3.79* (1.15)	0.88 (0.55)	2.33 (0.86)
9	5.43	4.14 (1.66)	14.76* (1.24)	4.98** (1.38)	2.01** (0.63)	2.99* (0.80)
10	26.44	−8.07** (2.36)	22.70** (2.47)	4.54 (2.14)	4.67** (0.95)	0.21 (1.32)
Average		1.78	1.71	1.79	0.07	1.34
Rank Correlations with Earnings Performance[d]		0.32	1.00	0.96	0.82	0.56
p-Value		0.37	<0.01	<0.01	<0.01	0.09

[a] See notes to table 1.

[b] $\alpha_{p,-1}$ is estimated by regressing annual excess returns for portfolio p in the 37 event years −1 on the annual CRSP equal-weighted market portfolio excess return ($\alpha_{p,0}$ and $\alpha_{p,+1}$ are estimated similarly):

$$(R_{pt}-R_{ft}) = \alpha_{p,-1} + \beta_{p,-1}(R_{mt}-R_{ft}) + \epsilon_{pt} \quad \text{for } p=1,\ldots,N.$$

[c] $\alpha_{p,+1JM}$ ($\alpha_{p,+1AD}$) is average abnormal return over 1951–1987 in January–March (April–December) of year +1, estimated as in footnote c above, but using only January–March (April–December) returns.

[d] Spearman rank correlations between earnings performance and $\alpha_{p,-1}$, $\alpha_{p,0}$, $\alpha_{p,+1}$, $\alpha_{p,+1JM}$, and $\alpha_{p,+1AD}$; p-values that the correlations are zero assume ten degrees of freedom.

* Significantly different from the cross-sectional average at p-value=0.05.
** Significantly different from the cross-sectional average at p-value=0.01.

favor of finding a post-announcement drift. Virtually all firms announce their annual earnings by April 1, so we reestimate abnormal returns over the nine-month period from April to December of year +1 (denoted as $\alpha_{p,+AD}$) by regressing portfolio excess returns during April to December of year +1 on excess returns over the same period for the market index. The results suggest that post-announcement drift persists after controlling for risk changes, but it is weaker than reported previously. The rank correlation between abnormal returns and portfolio earnings is 0.56, with a p-value of 0.09. The weaker drift results are attributable in part to (1) a better control for risk changes, (2) assuming April earnings announcements, and (3) ignoring interim earnings announcements.

To gain some insight into the ability of risk changes to explain a portion of the post-announcement drift observed in constant-beta research designs, consider the effect in our study of assuming risk to be constant (i.e., projecting the year −1 beta estimates into years 0 and +1) As shown in table 2, a portfolio that is long (short) in stocks with the 10 percent largest (smallest) changes in earnings experiences a change in risk of 0.40 over the two years [+0.28−(−0.12)]. Because the annual realized risk premium on the CRSP equal-weighted portfolio averaged 9.5 percent over 1951–1987, ignoring changes in risk would underestimate the annual CAPM expected return of the portfolio by 3.8 percent [0.40 • 9.5 percent].

There is clear evidence in table 4 against the joint hypotheses that the market is efficient and that the CAPM describes expected returns. But the pattern of the estimated abnormal returns in year +1 does not appear consistent with *any* credible alternative hypothesis of which we are aware. We note three intriguing features of the year +1 abnormal returns.[11] First, $\alpha_{p,+1AD}$ is an inverted-U-shaped function of earnings performance. This general pattern is inconsistent with the hypothesis that the market systematically underutilizes earnings. In particular, the low abnormal returns earned by the extreme *good-news* portfolio in April to December of year +1 is inconsistent with prior research that suggests "drifts" in prices. The pattern begs an explanation.[12] Second, the correlation between the abnormal returns in years −1 and +1 is 0.72 (p-value<0.02) when using April to December abnormal returns in year +1 (which are unlikely to be affected by earnings announcements).[13] Third, there is a symmetric seasonal pattern in the abnormal returns of the extreme-earnings portfolios. The worst news portfolio earns only a −0.61 percent abnormal return in January to March of year +1, which is surprising because it includes pre-announcement and announcement effects. It earns a larger negative return of −2.87 percent in April to December. The pattern is reversed for the best news portfolio, which earns a large positive abnormal return during January to March and little during April to December. This suggests a stock return seasonality, such as the January seasonal (Rozeff and Kinney [1976], among others) or CAPM misspecification. Taken together, these three features are anomalous; that is, they escape systematic explanation.

IV. Diagnostic Tests

This section summarizes a series of diagnostic tests that examine whether the results reported in the previous section are robust.

---

[11] Year +1 abnormal returns are *ex post* estimates for portfolios of large numbers of stocks. Lo and MacKinlay (1990) show that misleading inferences occur when variables correlated with abnormal returns (here, *ex post* earnings performance) are used to construct the portfolios.

[12] Ou and Penman (1989, table 8) also use annual earnings data and report negative abnormal returns, for both extreme good- and bad-news portfolios, over a nine-month post-announcement period.

[13] Abnormal returns in years +2 and −2 (reported below) are not highly correlated with each other or with abnormal returns over April to December of year +1. The correlation between years −1 and +1 therefore seems unlikely to indicate a simple CAPM misspecification.

Sample Selection Issues

We obtain similar results in a sample of 360 firms with a December 31 fiscal year-end and continuous listing during 1965–1985. This increases the number of time-series observations in the regression that orthogonalizes changes in earnings with respect to the market return. We also obtain similar (but not independent) results over subperiods of 18 and 19 years, addressing the concern that the research design assumes stationarity over the 37-year period in the relation between returns and changes in earnings. We again obtain similar (but not independent) results using 20 portfolios to investigate changes in earnings that are more extreme. As expected, risk shifts are larger in the extreme portfolios. The results are virtually indistinguishable when the average return for the sample proxies for the market portfolio, thus constraining the sample average beta and abnormal return to unity and zero, repectively. Finally, we obtain similar results without orthogonalizing scaled changes in earnings with respect to annual market returns.

Analysis of Years −2 and +2

We study event years −2 and +2 to assess whether (1) abnormal returns on the earnings-performance portfolios are correlated through time and (2) risk shifts are transitory or continue beyond year +1. The estimation technique is as described in section II, with 35 instead of 37 years now available.

The portfolio abnormal returns in years +2 and −2 are not highly correlated with each other or with abnormal returns over April to December of year +1. If the abnormal returns were correlated, then CAPM misspecification would be a more likely explanation of their "drift."

The earnings-performance portfolios' systematic risk estimates in years −2, 0, and +2 are reported in table 5. Changes in risk associated with changes in earnings do not appear to be permanent beyond year +1. The worst earnings-performance portfolio's systematic risk increases from 1.11 in year −2 to 1.18 in year +2, whereas the best news portfolio's systematic risk remains unchanged at 1.12 from year −2 to +2. In conformance with our hypothesis, risk changes from year −2 to 0, $\Delta\beta_{p,-2,0}$, are positively correlated with earnings performance (rank correlation, 0.73; p-value, 0.02). These risk changes are reversed over the following two years because $\Delta\beta_{p,0,+2}$ is negatively correlated with earnings performance. Risk changes from year −2 to +2, $\Delta\beta_{p,-2,+2}$, thus exhibit no relation with earnings performance (rank correlation, 0.03, p-value, 0.93). These results suggest that firms, particularly those with extreme earnings performance, adjust their investment policies as a function of risk changes.[14] An alternative possibility is that risk changes are a short-term function of earnings performance.

Beta Estimation Issues

The tenor of the results is unchanged when we estimate portfolio betas from daily returns in each year 1965–1985.[15] The beta change magnitudes generally are lower,

---

[14] We also examine leverage in years −2 and +2. There is little evidence of a systematic adjustment of leverage beyond year +1. Leverage ratios in year −2 are very similar to those in year −1, and the leverage ratios in year +2 are similar to those in year +1. Leverage changes from year −2 to +2 are highly correlated with earnings performance (rank correlation, −0.98; p-value, 0.01), which is similar to the behavior of leverage changes from year −1 to 0 reported in table 3.

[15] CRSP daily returns are not available for the pre-1963 period.

Table 5
Relation Between Earnings Performance and Relative Systematic Risk in the Earnings-Performance Year and in Years −2 and +2 Relative to the Earnings-Performance Year: 1951–1987

Earnings-Performance Rank (p)[a]	$\beta_{p,-2}$[b] (Std Err)	$\beta_{p,0}$ (Std Err)	$\beta_{p,+2}$ (Std Err)	$\Delta\beta_{p,-2,0}$[c]	$\Delta\beta_{p,0,+2}$	$\Delta\beta_{p,-2,+2}$
1	1.11 (0.060)	1.02 (0.058)	1.18 (0.074)	−0.09	+0.16*	0.07
2	0.92 (0.046)	0.79 (0.043)	0.84 (0.046)	−0.13*	+0.05	−0.08
3	0.83 (0.058)	0.74 (0.043)	0.60 (0.055)	−0.10	−0.14*	−0.23*
4	0.76 (0.035)	0.67 (0.049)	0.65 (0.062)	+0.09	−0.01	−0.11
5	0.67 (0.041)	0.69 (0.046)	0.68 (0.055)	+0.02	−0.01	−0.01
6	0.72 (0.048)	0.69 (0.046)	0.70 (0.040)	−0.02	+0.01	−0.01
7	0.73 (0.050)	0.87 (0.033)	0.80 (0.043)	+0.14*	−0.07	+0.07
8	0.96 (0.045)	0.87 (0.052)	0.89 (0.043)	−0.08	+0.01	−0.07
9	1.04 (0.048)	1.00 (0.046)	0.94 (0.039)	−0.04	−0.06	−0.10
10	1.12 (0.068)	1.39 (0.093)	1.12 (0.056)	+0.26*	−0.27*	−0.01
Average	0.89	0.87	0.84	−0.01	−0.03	−0.05
Rank Correlation with Earnings Performance[d]				0.73	−0.55	0.03
p-Value				0.02	0.10	0.93

[a] See notes to table 1.

[b] $\beta_{p,-2}$ is estimated by regressing annual excess returns for portfolio p in the 37 event years −1 on the annual CRSP equal-weighted market portfolio excess return ($\beta_{p,0}$ and $\beta_{p,+2}$ are estimated similarly):

$$(R_{pt}-R_{ft}) = \alpha_{p,-2} + \beta_{p,-2}(R_{mt}-R_{ft}) + \epsilon_{pt} \quad \text{for } p=1,\ldots,N.$$

[c] $\Delta\beta_{p,-2,0} = \beta_{p,0} - \beta_{p,-2}$, $\Delta\beta_{p,0,+2} = \beta_{p,+2} - \beta_{p,0}$, and $\Delta\beta_{p,-2,+2} = \beta_{p,+2} - \beta_{p,-2}$.

[d] Spearman rank correlations between earnings performance and $\Delta\beta_{p,-2,0}$, $\Delta\beta_{p,0,+2}$, and $\Delta\beta_{p,+2,-2}$; p-values that the correlations are zero assume ten degrees of freedom.

* Significant at $\alpha=5$ percent.

which is expected because betas estimated from daily returns are biased toward unity by the larger relative effect of market microstructure on measured returns (see, e.g., Ball 1977; Foster et al. 1984).

Our earnings-performance variable, defined in equation (4), is orthogonalized with respect to the market return, in part to mitigate concern that our portfolio formation procedure induces a spurious association between changes in risk and changes in earnings. A dependence between changes in risk and earnings might arise if the stocks assigned to good-news portfolios are relatively high-risk in years when the market performs well and low-risk when it performs poorly, and conversely for bad-news portfolios. With bivariate normality, portfolio beta estimates are unbiased even if there is a dependence between the market return and the beta of stocks assigned to a portfolio. However, higher-order dependence between the market performance and portfolios' risks could yield biased beta estimates.[16] We therefore perform several diagnostic tests.

First, to verify the orthogonalization procedure at the portfolio level, we estimate correlations between each portfolio's earnings performance and the market return, using the time series of 37 years. None of the ten portfolios' earnings performance is reliably correlated with the market through time. The estimated correlation for the extreme good-news portfolio is only 0.11 (p-value, 0.50), and it is negative for the extreme bad-news portfolio. Thus, a priori, there is little concern that the estimated betas are biased.

Second, we reestimate the event-year 0 betas of each portfolio, allowing them to differ with the sign of the realized market risk premium. If the worst (best) earnings-performance portfolio consists of more (less) risky stocks in years with low market returns, then its beta will be higher (lower) in such years. However, both the worst and the best earnings-performance portfolios' estimated betas are lower in years with low market returns, which is inconsistent with the bias argument. The rank correlation between earnings performance and the deviation of the portfolios' betas from their 37-year average is only −0.21 (p-value, 0.56) in the years with negative risk premiums.[17] Further, the rank correlation between earnings performance and the change from year −1 to 0 in the deviations from their average is 0.12 (p-value, 0.75). The corresponding correlation coefficient when using the change from year 0 to +1 is 0.35 (p-value, 0.33); from year −1 to +1, it is 0.47 (p-value, 0.17).

Third, we estimate the time-series correlation between the annual market return and the calendar-year beta of each earnings-performance portfolio, which is estimated with daily or monthly returns within each calendar year. The time series is 25 years for daily betas and 37 years for monthly betas. For both daily and monthly returns, the point estimates of the correlation between betas and market returns are positive for both the worst- and best-performance portfolios. This is similar to the finding reported previously that annual beta estimates of both portfolio 1 and 10 are lower in years of poor market returns. The correlation between the market return and betas estimated from daily returns is insignificant for both portfolio 1 and 10. The beta of the worst-performance portfolio, when estimated from daily returns, correlates reliably and *positively* with the annual market return. None of the remaining nine betas exhibit a reliable correlation with the market return.

Overall, a variety of diagnostic tests yields no reliable evidence that the research design is biased in favor of finding risk changes consistent with our hypothesis.

V. Conclusions

Changes in earnings have systematic economic determinants that are likely to be associated with variation in securities' expected returns, particularly since earnings is the accounting return on equity. Identifying the economic determinants of earnings variation should improve our understanding of the earnings-price relation.

---

[16] We thank an anonymous referee for raising this issue.

[17] By construction, the corresponding correlation in the positive risk-premium years is identical in magnitude, but of opposite sign.

Ignoring endogenous variation in expected returns implies the assumption that earnings variation is attributable entirely to variation in firms' economic rents. By and large, this assumption is implicit in the "event-study" literature to date and can contribute to anomalous results. Research designs investigating cross-sectional or cross-temporal variation in earnings, or similar variables, are likely to induce variation in securities' expected returns.

This study implements a research design that allows the economic determinants of earnings to vary with the same periodicity as earnings. Specifically, we estimate and control for annual, event-time betas. We rely on the single-period CAPM, even though it is implemented over a 37-year period. The continued use of the single-period CAPM in the literature presumably reflects the absence of an empirically tractable multiperiod model.[18] A second limitation is the loss of information from data aggregation into portfolios. However, using portfolios enables more powerul tests, by allowing us to estimate annual event time betas with annual returns. A third limitation arises from errors in measuring the news in earnings. Brooks and Buckmaster (1976) show that extreme changes in earnings exhibit negative serial correlation. By ignoring this, we could assign some stocks to extreme portfolios, whereas their changes in earnings are expected to be largely reversed. We also could be failing to capture risk changes that occur earlier in event time. These measurement problems seem likely to bias the results against the risk-change hypothesis.

The results suggest a predictable positive association between changes in earnings and changes in equity risk. The results also suggest that leverage-change effects do not fully offset the hypothesized relation between changes in earnings and investment risk changes. The conclusions are robust with respect to a variety of changes in the research design.

---

[18] An anonymous referee and the editor pointed out this as a limitation of our research design. A recent study of changing-composition portfolios over long time periods is Fama and French (1992).

References

Ball, R. 1977. A note on errors in variables and estimates of systematic risk. *Australian Journal of Management* 2: 79–84.

———, and P. Brown. 1968. An empirical evaluation of accounting income numbers. *Journal of Accounting Research* 6 (Autumn): 159–78.

———, and S. P. Kothari. 1989. Nonstationary expected returns: Implications for tests of market efficiency and serial correlation in returns. *Journal of Financial Economics* 25 (November): 51–74.

———, B. Lev, and R. Watts. 1976. Income variation and balance sheet compositions. *Journal of Accounting Research* 14 (Spring): 1–9.

———, and R. Watts. 1972. Some time-series properties of accounting income. *Journal of Finance* 27 (July): 663–82.

Beaver, W., R. Clarke, and W. Wright. 1979. The association between unsystematic security returns and the magnitude of earnings forecast errors. *Journal of Accounting Research* 17 (Autumn): 316–40.

———, R. Lambert, and D. Morse. 1980. The information content of security prices. *Journal of Accounting & Economics* 2 (March): 3–28.

Blume, M. 1975. Betas and their regression tendencies. *Journal of Finance* 3 (July): 785–95.

Brooks, L., and D. Buckmaster. 1976. Further evidence on the time-series properties of accounting income. *Journal of Finance* 31 (December): 1359–73.

Christie, A. 1989. Equity risk, the opportunity set, production costs and debt. Working paper, University of Rochester, NY.
Collins, D., and S. P. Kothari. 1989. An analysis of intertemporal and cross-sectional determinants of earnings response coefficients. *Journal of Accounting & Economics* 11 (July): 143–81.
———, ———, and J. Rayburn. 1987. Firm size and the information content of prices with respect to earnings. *Journal of Accounting & Economics* 9 (July): 111–38.
DeAngelo, L. 1988. Managerial competition, information costs, and corporate governance: The use of accounting performance measures in proxy contests. *Journal of Accounting & Economics* 10 (January): 3–36.
Easton, P., and M. Zmijewski. 1989. Cross-sectional variation in the stock market response to the announcement of accounting earnings. *Journal of Accounting & Economics* 11 (July): 117–41.
Fama, E., and K. French. 1992. Common risk factors in the returns on bonds and stocks. *Journal of Financial Economics* (forthcoming).
———, and M. Miller. 1972. *The Theory of Finance.* Hinsdale, IL: Dryden.
Foster, G. 1977. Quarterly accounting data: Time-series properties and predictive ability results. *The Accounting Review* 52 (January): 1–21.
———, C. Olsen, and T. Shevlin. 1984. Earnings releases, anomalies and the behavior of security returns. *The Accounting Review* 59 (October): 574–603.
Freeman, R. 1987. The association between accounting earnings and security returns for large and small firms. *Journal of Accounting & Economics* 9 (July): 195–228.
Handa, P., S. P. Kothari, and C. Wasley. 1989. The relation between the return interval and betas: Implications for the size effect. *Journal of Financial Economics* 23 (June): 79–100.
Healy, R. 1985. The effect of bonus schemes on accounting decisions. *Journal of Accounting & Economics* 7 (April): 85–107.
Ibbotson, R. 1975. Price performance of common stock new issues. *Journal of Financial Economics* 2 (September): 235–72.
Keim, D. 1983. Size-related anomalies and stock return seasonality: Further empirical evidence. *Journal of Financial Economics* 12 (June): 13–32.
Kormendi, R., and R. Lipe. 1987. Earnings innovations, earnings persistence and stock returns. *Journal of Business* 60 (July): 323–45.
Lev, B. 1974. On the association between operating leverage and risk. *Journal of Financial and Quantitative Analysis* 9 (December): 627–41.
Lo, A., and C. MacKinlay. 1990. Data-snooping biases in tests of financial asset pricing models. *Review of Financial Studies* (3): 431–67.
Ou, J., and S. Penman. 1989. Accounting measurement, P/E ratios and the information content of security prices. *Journal of Accounting Research* 27 (Supplement): 111–44.
Pincus, M., and C. Wasley. 1991. Time-series and cross-sectional characteristics of accounting changes. Working paper, Washington University, St. Louis.
Rozeff, M., and W. Kinney. 1976. Capital market seasonality: The case of stock returns. *Journal of Financial Economics* 3 (October): 379–402.
Smith, C., and R. Watts. 1992. The investment opportunity set and corporate financing, dividend, and compensation policies. *Journal of Financial Economics* 32 (December): 263–92.
Vasicek, O. 1973. A note on using cross-sectional information in Bayesian estimation of security betas. *Journal of Finance* 28 (December): 1233–39.

The Cross-Section of Expected Stock Returns

EUGENE F. FAMA and KENNETH R. FRENCH*

ABSTRACT

Two easily measured variables, size and book-to-market equity, combine to capture the cross-sectional variation in average stock returns associated with market β, size, leverage, book-to-market equity, and earnings-price ratios. Moreover, when the tests allow for variation in β that is unrelated to size, the relation between market β and average return is flat, even when β is the only explanatory variable.

THE ASSET-PRICING MODEL OF Sharpe (1964), Lintner (1965), and Black (1972) has long shaped the way academics and practitioners think about average returns and risk. The central prediction of the model is that the market portfolio of invested wealth is mean-variance efficient in the sense of Markowitz (1959). The efficiency of the market portfolio implies that (a) expected returns on securities are a positive linear function of their market βs (the slope in the regression of a security's return on the market's return), and (b) market βs suffice to describe the cross-section of expected returns.

There are several empirical contradictions of the Sharpe-Lintner-Black (SLB) model. The most prominent is the size effect of Banz (1981). He finds that market equity, ME (a stock's price times shares outstanding), adds to the explanation of the cross-section of average returns provided by market βs. Average returns on small (low ME) stocks are too high given their β estimates, and average returns on large stocks are too low.

Another contradiction of the SLB model is the positive relation between leverage and average return documented by Bhandari (1988). It is plausible that leverage is associated with risk and expected return, but in the SLB model, leverage risk should be captured by market β. Bhandari finds, however, that leverage helps explain the cross-section of average stock returns in tests that include size (ME) as well as β.

Stattman (1980) and Rosenberg, Reid, and Lanstein (1985) find that average returns on U.S. stocks are positively related to the ratio of a firm's book value of common equity, BE, to its market value, ME. Chan, Hamao, and Lakonishok (1991) find that book-to-market equity, BE/ME, also has a strong role in explaining the cross-section of average returns on Japanese stocks.

---

*Graduate School of Business, University of Chicago, 1101 East 58th Street, Chicago, IL 60637. We acknowledge the helpful comments of David Booth, Nai-fu Chen, George Constantinides, Wayne Ferson, Edward George, Campbell Harvey, Josef Lakonishok, Rex Sinquefield, René Stulz, Mark Zmijeweski, and an anonymous referee. This research is supported by the National Science Foundation (Fama) and the Center for Research in Security Prices (French).

Finally, Basu (1983) shows that earnings-price ratios (E/P) help explain the cross-section of average returns on U.S. stocks in tests that also include size and market β. Ball (1978) argues that E/P is a catch-all proxy for unnamed factors in expected returns; E/P is likely to be higher (prices are lower relative to earnings) for stocks with higher risks and expected returns, whatever the unnamed sources of risk.

Ball's proxy argument for E/P might also apply to size (ME), leverage, and book-to-market equity. All these variables can be regarded as different ways to scale stock prices, to extract the information in prices about risk and expected returns (Keim (1988)). Moreover, since E/P, ME, leverage, and BE/ME are all scaled versions of price, it is reasonable to expect that some of them are redundant for describing average returns. Our goal is to evaluate the joint roles of market β, size, E/P, leverage, and book-to-market equity in the cross-section of average returns on NYSE, AMEX, and NASDAQ stocks.

Black, Jensen, and Scholes (1972) and Fama and MacBeth (1973) find that, as predicted by the SLB model, there is a positive simple relation between average stock returns and β during the pre-1969 period. Like Reinganum (1981) and Lakonishok and Shapiro (1986), we find that the relation between β and average return disappears during the more recent 1963–1990 period, even when β is used alone to explain average returns. The appendix shows that the simple relation between β and average return is also weak in the 50-year 1941–1990 period. In short, our tests do not support the most basic prediction of the SLB model, that average stock returns are positively related to market βs.

Unlike the simple relation between β and average return, the univariate relations between average return and size, leverage, E/P, and book-to-market equity are strong. In multivariate tests, the negative relation between size and average return is robust to the inclusion of other variables. The positive relation between book-to-market equity and average return also persists in competition with other variables. Moreover, although the size effect has attracted more attention, book-to-market equity has a consistently stronger role in average returns. Our bottom-line results are: (a) β does not seem to help explain the cross-section of average stock returns, and (b) the combination of size and book-to-market equity seems to absorb the roles of leverage and E/P in average stock returns, at least during our 1963–1990 sample period.

If assets are priced rationally, our results suggest that stock risks are multidimensional. One dimension of risk is proxied by size, ME. Another dimension of risk is proxied by BE/ME, the ratio of the book value of common equity to its market value.

It is possible that the risk captured by BE/ME is the relative distress factor of Chan and Chen (1991). They postulate that the earning prospects of firms are associated with a risk factor in returns. Firms that the market judges to have poor prospects, signaled here by low stock prices and high ratios of book-to-market equity, have higher expected stock returns (they are penalized with higher costs of capital) than firms with strong prospects. It is also possible, however, that BE/ME just captures the unraveling (regression toward the mean) of irrational market whims about the prospects of firms.

Whatever the underlying economic causes, our main result is straightforward. Two easily measured variables, size (ME) and book-to-market equity (BE/ME), provide a simple and powerful characterization of the cross-section of average stock returns for the 1963–1990 period.

In the next section we discuss the data and our approach to estimating β. Section II examines the relations between average return and β and between average return and size. Section III examines the roles of E/P, leverage, and book-to-market equity in average returns. In sections IV and V, we summarize, interpret, and discuss applications of the results.

I. Preliminaries

A. Data

We use all nonfinancial firms in the intersection of (a) the NYSE, AMEX, and NASDAQ return files from the Center for Research in Security Prices (CRSP) and (b) the merged COMPUSTAT annual industrial files of income-statement and balance-sheet data, also maintained by CRSP. We exclude financial firms because the high leverage that is normal for these firms probably does not have the same meaning as for nonfinancial firms, where high leverage more likely indicates distress. The CRSP returns cover NYSE and AMEX stocks until 1973 when NASDAQ returns also come on line. The COMPUSTAT data are for 1962–1989. The 1962 start date reflects the fact that book value of common equity (COMPUSTAT item 60), is not generally available prior to 1962. More important, COMPUSTAT data for earlier years have a serious selection bias; the pre-1962 data are tilted toward big historically successful firms.

To ensure that the accounting variables are known before the returns they are used to explain, we match the accounting data for all fiscal yearends in calendar year $t - 1$ (1962–1989) with the returns for July of year t to June of $t + 1$. The 6-month (minimum) gap between fiscal yearend and the return tests is conservative. Earlier work (e.g., Basu (1983)) often assumes that accounting data are available within three months of fiscal yearends. Firms are indeed required to file their 10-K reports with the SEC within 90 days of their fiscal yearends, but on average 19.8% do not comply. In addition, more than 40% of the December fiscal yearend firms that do comply with the 90-day rule file on March 31, and their reports are not made public until April. (See Alford, Jones, and Zmijewski (1992).)

We use a firm's market equity at the end of December of year $t - 1$ to compute its book-to-market, leverage, and earnings-price ratios for $t - 1$, and we use its market equity for June of year t to measure its size. Thus, to be included in the return tests for July of year t, a firm must have a CRSP stock price for December of year $t - 1$ and June of year t. It must also have monthly returns for at least 24 of the 60 months preceding July of year t (for "pre-ranking" β estimates, discussed below). And the firm must have COMPUSTAT data on total book assets (A), book equity (BE), and earnings (E), for its fiscal year ending in (any month of) calendar year $t - 1$.

Our use of December market equity in the E/P, BE/ME, and leverage ratios is objectionable for firms that do not have December fiscal yearends because the accounting variable in the numerator of a ratio is not aligned with the market value in the denominator. Using ME at fiscal yearends is also problematic; then part of the cross-sectional variation of a ratio for a given year is due to market-wide variation in the ratio during the year. For example, if there is a general fall in stock prices during the year, ratios measured early in the year will tend to be lower than ratios measured later. We can report, however, that the use of fiscal-yearend MEs, rather than December MEs, in the accounting ratios has little impact on our return tests.

Finally, the tests mix firms with different fiscal yearends. Since we match accounting data for all fiscal yearends in calendar year $t - 1$ with returns for July of t to June of $t + 1$, the gap between the accounting data and the matching returns varies across firms. We have done the tests using the smaller sample of firms with December fiscal yearends with similar results.

B. Estimating Market βs

Our asset-pricing tests use the cross-sectional regression approach of Fama and MacBeth (1973). Each month the cross-section of returns on stocks is regressed on variables hypothesized to explain expected returns. The time-series means of the monthly regression slopes then provide standard tests of whether different explanatory variables are on average priced.

Since size, E/P, leverage, and BE/ME are measured precisely for individual stocks, there is no reason to smear the information in these variables by using portfolios in the Fama-MacBeth (FM) regressions. Most previous tests use portfolios because estimates of market βs are more precise for portfolios. Our approach is to estimate βs for portfolios and then assign a portfolio's β to each stock in the portfolio. This allows us to use individual stocks in the FM asset-pricing tests.

B.1. β Estimation: Details

In June of each year, all NYSE stocks on CRSP are sorted by size (ME) to determine the NYSE decile breakpoints for ME. NYSE, AMEX, and NASDAQ stocks that have the required CRSP-COMPUSTAT data are then allocated to 10 size portfolios based on the NYSE breakpoints. (If we used stocks from all three exchanges to determine the ME breakpoints, most portfolios would include only small stocks after 1973, when NASDAQ stocks are added to the sample.)

We form portfolios on size because of the evidence of Chan and Chen (1988) and others that size produces a wide spread of average returns and βs. Chan and Chen use only size portfolios. The problem this creates is that size and the βs of size portfolios are highly correlated (-0.988 in their data), so asset-pricing tests lack power to separate size from β effects in average returns.

To allow for variation in β that is unrelated to size, we subdivide each size decile into 10 portfolios on the basis of pre-ranking βs for individual stocks. The pre-ranking βs are estimated on 24 to 60 monthly returns (as available) in the 5 years before July of year t. We set the β breakpoints for each size decile using only NYSE stocks that satisfy our COMPUSTAT-CRSP data requirements for year $t-1$. Using NYSE stocks ensures that the β breakpoints are not dominated after 1973 by the many small stocks on NASDAQ. Setting β breakpoints with stocks that satisfy our COMPUSTAT-CRSP data requirements guarantees that there are firms in each of the 100 size-β portfolios.

After assigning firms to the size-β portfolios in June, we calculate the equal-weighted monthly returns on the portfolios for the next 12 months, from July to June. In the end, we have post-ranking monthly returns for July 1963 to December 1990 on 100 portfolios formed on size and pre-ranking βs. We then estimate βs using the full sample (330 months) of post-ranking returns on each of the 100 portfolios, with the CRSP value-weighted portfolio of NYSE, AMEX, and (after 1972) NASDAQ stocks used as the proxy for the market. We have also estimated βs using the value-weighted or the equal-weighted portfolio of NYSE stocks as the proxy for the market. These βs produce inferences on the role of β in average returns like those reported below.

We estimate β as the sum of the slopes in the regression of the return on a portfolio on the current and prior month's market return. (An additional lead and lag of the market have little effect on these sum βs.) The sum βs are meant to adjust for nonsynchronous trading (Dimson (1979)). Fowler and Rorke (1983) show that sum βs are biased when the market return is autocorrelated. The 1st- and 2nd-order autocorrelations of the monthly market returns for July 1963 to December 1990 are 0.06 and -0.05, both about 1 standard error from 0. If the Fowler-Rorke corrections are used, they lead to trivial changes in the βs. We stick with the simpler sum βs. Appendix Table AI shows that using sum βs produces large increases in the βs of the smallest ME portfolios and small declines in the βs of the largest ME portfolios.

Chan and Chen (1988) show that full-period β estimates for portfolios can work well in tests of the SLB model, even if the true βs of the portfolios vary through time, if the variation in the βs is proportional,

$$\beta_{jt} - \beta_j = k_t(\beta_j - \beta), \qquad (1)$$

where β_{jt} is the true β for portfolio j at time t, β_j is the mean of β_{jt} across t, and β is the mean of the β_j. The Appendix argues that (1) is a good approximation for the variation through time in the true βs of portfolios (j) formed on size and β. For diehard β fans, sure to be skeptical of our results on the weak role of β in average stock returns, we can also report that the results stand up to robustness checks that use 5-year pre-ranking βs, or 5-year post-ranking βs, instead of the full-period post-ranking βs.

We allocate the full-period post-ranking β of a size-β portfolio to each stock in the portfolio. These are the βs that will be used in the Fama-MacBeth cross-sectional regressions for individual stocks. We judge that the precision of the full-period post-ranking portfolio βs, relative to the imprecise β estimates that would be obtained for individual stocks, more than makes up for the fact that true βs are not the same for all stocks in a portfolio. And note that assigning full-period portfolio βs to stocks does not mean that a stock's β is constant. A stock can move across portfolios with year-to-year changes in the stock's size (ME) and in the estimates of its β for the preceding 5 years.

B.2. β Estimates

Table I shows that forming portfolios on size and pre-ranking βs, rather than on size alone, magnifies the range of full-period post-ranking βs. Sorted on size alone, the post-ranking βs range from 1.44 for the smallest ME portfolio to 0.92 for the largest. This spread of βs across the 10 size deciles is smaller than the spread of post-ranking βs produced by the β sort of *any* size decile. For example, the post-ranking βs for the 10 portfolios in the smallest size decile range from 1.05 to 1.79. Across all 100 size-β portfolios, the post-ranking βs range from 0.53 to 1.79, a spread 2.4 times the spread, 0.52, obtained with size portfolios alone.

Two other facts about the βs are important. First, in each size decile the post-ranking βs closely reproduce the ordering of the pre-ranking βs. We take this to be evidence that the pre-ranking β sort captures the ordering of true post-ranking βs. (The appendix gives more evidence on this important issue.) Second, the β sort is not a refined size sort. In any size decile, the average values of ln(ME) are similar across the β-sorted portfolios. Thus the pre-ranking β sort achieves its goal. It produces strong variation in post-ranking βs that is unrelated to size. This is important in allowing our tests to distinguish between β and size effects in average returns.

II. β and Size

The Sharpe-Lintner-Black (SLB) model plays an important role in the way academics and practitioners think about risk and the relation between risk and expected return. We show next that when common stock portfolios are formed on size alone, there seems to be evidence for the model's central prediction: average return is positively related to β. The βs of size portfolios are, however, almost perfectly correlated with size, so tests on size portfolios are unable to disentangle β and size effects in average returns. Allowing for variation in β that is unrelated to size breaks the logjam, but at the expense of β. Thus, when we subdivide size portfolios on the basis of pre-ranking βs, we find a strong relation between average return and size, but no relation between average return and β.

A. Informal Tests

Table II shows post-ranking average returns for July 1963 to December 1990 for portfolios formed from one-dimensional sorts of stocks on size or β. The portfolios are formed at the end of June each year and their equal-weighted returns are calculated for the next 12 months. We use returns for July to June to match the returns in later tests that use the accounting data. When we sort on just size or 5-year pre-ranking βs, we form 12 portfolios. The middle 8 cover deciles of size or β. The 4 extreme portfolios (1A, 1B, 10A, and 10B) split the bottom and top deciles in half.

Table II shows that when portfolios are formed on size alone, we observe the familiar strong negative relation between size and average return (Banz (1981)), and a strong positive relation between average return and β. Average returns fall from 1.64% per month for the smallest ME portfolio to 0.90% for the largest. Post-ranking βs also decline across the 12 size portfolios, from 1.44 for portfolio 1A to 0.90 for portfolio 10B. Thus, a simple size sort seems to support the SLB prediction of a positive relation between β and average return. But the evidence is muddied by the tight relation between size and the βs of size portfolios.

The portfolios formed on the basis of the ranked market βs of stocks in Table II produce a wider range of βs (from 0.81 for portfolio 1A to 1.73 for 10B) than the portfolios formed on size. Unlike the size portfolios, the β-sorted portfolios do not support the SLB model. There is little spread in average returns across the β portfolios, and there is no obvious relation between β and average returns. For example, although the two extreme portfolios, 1A and 10B, have much different βs, they have nearly identical average returns (1.20% and 1.18% per month). These results for 1963–1990 confirm Reinganum's (1981) evidence that for β-sorted portfolios, there is no relation between average return and β during the 1964–1979 period.

The 100 portfolios formed on size and then pre-ranking β in Table I clarify the contradictory evidence on the relation between β and average return produced by portfolios formed on size or β alone. Specifically, the two-pass sort gives a clearer picture of the separate roles of size and β in average returns. Contrary to the central prediction of the SLB model, the second-pass β sort produces little variation in average returns. Although the post-ranking βs in Table I increase strongly in each size decile, average returns are flat or show a slight tendency to decline. In contrast, within the columns of the average return and β matrices of Table I, average returns and βs decrease with increasing size.

The two-pass sort on size and β in Table I says that variation in β that is tied to size is positively related to average return, but variation in β unrelated to size is not compensated in the average returns of 1963–1990. The proper inference seems to be that there is a relation between size and average return, but controlling for size, there is no relation between β and average return. The regressions that follow confirm this conclusion, and they produce another that is stronger. The regressions show that when one allows

Table I
Average Returns, Post-Ranking βs and Average Size For Portfolios Formed on Size and then β: Stocks Sorted on ME (Down) then Pre-Ranking β (Across): July 1963 to December 1990

Portfolios are formed yearly. The breakpoints for the size (ME, price times shares outstanding) deciles are determined in June of year t ($t = 1963-1990$) using all NYSE stocks on CRSP. All NYSE, AMEX, and NASDAQ stocks that meet the CRSP-COMPUSTAT data requirements are allocated to the 10 size portfolios using the NYSE breakpoints. Each size decile is subdivided into 10 β portfolios using pre-ranking βs of individual stocks, estimated with 2 to 5 years of monthly returns (as available) ending in June of year t. We use only NYSE stocks that meet the CRSP-COMPUSTAT data requirements to establish the β breakpoints. The equal-weighted monthly returns on the resulting 100 portfolios are then calculated for July of year t to June of year $t + 1$.

The post-ranking βs use the full (July 1963 to December 1990) sample of post-ranking returns for each portfolio. The pre- and post-ranking βs (here and in all other tables) are the sum of the slopes from a regression of monthly returns on the current and prior month's returns on the value-weighted portfolio of NYSE, AMEX, and (after 1972) NASDAQ stocks. The average return is the time-series average of the monthly equal-weighted portfolio returns, in percent. The average size of a portfolio is the time-series average of monthly averages of ln(ME) for stocks in the portfolio at the end of June of each year, with ME denominated in millions of dollars.

The average number of stocks per month for the size-β portfolios in the smallest size decile varies from 70 to 177. The average number of stocks for the size-β portfolios in size deciles 2 and 3 is between 15 and 41, and the average number for the largest 7 size deciles is between 11 and 22.

The All column shows statistics for equal-weighted size-decile (ME) portfolios. The All row shows statistics for equal-weighted portfolios of the stocks in each β group.

	All	Low-β	β-2	β-3	β-4	β-5	β-6	β-7	β-8	β-9	High-β
				Panel A: Average Monthly Returns (in Percent)							
All	1.25	1.34	1.29	1.36	1.31	1.33	1.28	1.24	1.21	1.25	1.14
Small-ME	1.52	1.71	1.57	1.79	1.61	1.50	1.50	1.37	1.63	1.50	1.42
ME-2	1.29	1.25	1.42	1.36	1.39	1.65	1.61	1.37	1.31	1.34	1.11
ME-3	1.24	1.12	1.31	1.17	1.70	1.29	1.10	1.31	1.36	1.26	0.76
ME-4	1.25	1.27	1.13	1.54	1.06	1.34	1.06	1.41	1.17	1.35	0.98
ME-5	1.29	1.34	1.42	1.39	1.48	1.42	1.18	1.13	1.27	1.18	1.08
ME-6	1.17	1.08	1.53	1.27	1.15	1.20	1.21	1.18	1.04	1.07	1.02
ME-7	1.07	0.95	1.21	1.26	1.09	1.18	1.11	1.24	0.62	1.32	0.76
ME-8	1.10	1.09	1.05	1.37	1.20	1.27	0.98	1.18	1.02	1.01	0.94
ME-9	0.95	0.98	0.88	1.02	1.14	1.07	1.23	0.94	0.82	0.88	0.59
Large-ME	0.89	1.01	0.93	1.10	0.94	0.93	0.89	1.03	0.71	0.74	0.56

Table I—Continued

	All	Low-β	β-2	β-3	β-4	β-5	β-6	β-7	β-8	β-9	High-β
Panel B: Post-Ranking βs
All		0.87	0.99	1.09	1.16	1.26	1.29	1.35	1.45	1.52	1.72
Small-ME	1.44	1.05	1.18	1.28	1.32	1.40	1.40	1.49	1.61	1.64	1.79
ME-2	1.39	0.91	1.15	1.17	1.24	1.36	1.41	1.43	1.50	1.66	1.76
ME-3	1.35	0.97	1.13	1.13	1.21	1.26	1.28	1.39	1.50	1.51	1.75
ME-4	1.34	0.78	1.03	1.17	1.16	1.29	1.37	1.46	1.51	1.64	1.71
ME-5	1.25	0.66	0.85	1.12	1.15	1.16	1.26	1.30	1.43	1.59	1.68
ME-6	1.23	0.61	0.78	1.05	1.16	1.22	1.28	1.36	1.46	1.49	1.70
ME-7	1.17	0.57	0.92	1.01	1.11	1.14	1.26	1.24	1.39	1.34	1.60
ME-8	1.09	0.53	0.74	0.94	1.02	1.13	1.12	1.18	1.26	1.35	1.52
ME-9	1.03	0.58	0.74	0.80	0.95	1.06	1.15	1.14	1.21	1.22	1.42
Large-ME	0.92	0.57	0.71	0.78	0.89	0.95	0.92	1.02	1.01	1.11	1.32
Panel C: Average Size (ln(ME))
All	4.11	3.86	4.26	4.33	4.41	4.27	4.32	4.26	4.19	4.03	3.77
Small-ME	2.24	2.12	2.27	2.30	2.30	2.28	2.29	2.30	2.32	2.25	2.15
ME-2	3.63	3.65	3.68	3.70	3.72	3.69	3.70	3.69	3.69	3.70	3.68
ME-3	4.10	4.14	4.18	4.12	4.15	4.16	4.16	4.18	4.14	4.15	4.15
ME-4	4.50	4.53	4.53	4.57	4.54	4.56	4.55	4.52	4.58	4.52	4.56
ME-5	4.89	4.91	4.91	4.93	4.95	4.93	4.92	4.93	4.92	4.92	4.95
ME-6	5.30	5.30	5.33	5.34	5.34	5.33	5.33	5.33	5.33	5.34	5.36
ME-7	5.73	5.73	5.75	5.77	5.76	5.73	5.77	5.77	5.76	5.72	5.76
ME-8	6.24	6.26	6.27	6.26	6.24	6.24	6.27	6.24	6.24	6.24	6.26
ME-9	6.82	6.82	6.84	6.82	6.82	6.81	6.81	6.81	6.81	6.80	6.83
Large-ME	7.93	7.94	8.04	8.10	8.04	8.02	8.02	7.94	7.80	7.75	7.62

Table II
Properties of Portfolios Formed on Size or Pre-Ranking β: July 1963 to December 1990

At the end of June of each year t, 12 portfolios are formed on the basis of ranked values of size (ME) or pre-ranking β. The pre-ranking βs use 2 to 5 years (as available) of monthly returns ending in June of t. Portfolios 2–9 cover deciles of the ranking variables. The bottom and top 2 portfolios (1A, 1B, 10A, and 10B) split the bottom and top deciles in half. The breakpoints for the ME portfolios are based on ranked values of ME for all NYSE stocks on CRSP. NYSE breakpoints for pre-ranking βs are also used to form the β portfolios. NYSE, AMEX, and NASDAQ stocks are then allocated to the size or β portfolios using the NYSE breakpoints. We calculate each portfolio's monthly equal-weighted return for July of year t to June of year $t+1$, and then reform the portfolios in June of $t+1$.

BE is the book value of common equity plus balance-sheet deferred taxes, A is total book assets, and E is earnings (income before extraordinary items, plus income-statement deferred taxes, minus preferred dividends). BE, A, and E are for each firm's latest fiscal year ending in calendar year $t-1$. The accounting ratios are measured using market equity ME in December of year $t-1$. Firm size ln(ME) is measured in June of year t, with ME denominated in millions of dollars.

The average return is the time-series average of the monthly equal-weighted portfolio returns, in percent. ln(ME), ln(BE/ME), ln(A/ME), ln(A/BE), E/P, and E/P dummy are the time-series averages of the monthly average values of these variables in each portfolio. Since the E/P dummy is 0 when earnings are positive, and 1 when earnings are negative, E/P dummy gives the average proportion of stocks with negative earnings in each portfolio.

β is the time-series average of the monthly portfolio βs. Stocks are assigned the post-ranking β of the size-β portfolio they are in at the end of June of year t (Table I). These individual-firm βs are averaged to compute the monthly βs for each portfolio for July of year t to June of year $t+1$.

Firms is the average number of stocks in the portfolio each month.

	1A	1B	2	3	4	5	6	7	8	9	10A	10B
Panel A: Portfolios Formed on Size
Return	1.64	1.16	1.29	1.24	1.25	1.29	1.17	1.07	1.10	0.95	0.88	0.90
β	1.44	1.44	1.39	1.34	1.33	1.24	1.22	1.16	1.08	1.02	0.95	0.90
ln(ME)	1.98	3.18	3.63	4.10	4.50	4.89	5.30	5.73	6.24	6.82	7.39	8.44
ln(BE/ME)	−0.01	−0.21	−0.23	−0.26	−0.32	−0.36	−0.36	−0.44	−0.40	−0.42	−0.51	−0.65
ln(A/ME)	0.73	0.50	0.46	0.43	0.37	0.32	0.32	0.24	0.29	0.27	0.17	−0.03
ln(A/BE)	0.75	0.71	0.69	0.69	0.68	0.67	0.68	0.67	0.69	0.70	0.68	0.62
E/P dummy	0.26	0.14	0.11	0.09	0.06	0.04	0.04	0.03	0.03	0.02	0.02	0.01
E(+)/P	0.09	0.10	0.10	0.10	0.10	0.10	0.10	0.10	0.10	0.10	0.09	0.09
Firms	772	189	236	170	144	140	128	125	119	114	60	64

Table II—Continued

Panel B: Portfolios Formed on Pre-Ranking β

	1A	1B	2	3	4	5	6	7	8	9	10A	10B
Return	1.20	1.20	1.32	1.26	1.31	1.30	1.30	1.23	1.23	1.33	1.34	1.18
β	0.81	0.79	0.92	1.04	1.13	1.19	1.26	1.32	1.41	1.52	1.63	1.73
ln(ME)	4.21	4.86	4.75	4.68	4.59	4.48	4.36	4.25	3.97	3.78	3.52	3.15
ln(BE/ME)	−0.18	−0.13	−0.22	−0.21	−0.23	−0.22	−0.22	−0.25	−0.23	−0.27	−0.31	−0.50
ln(A/ME)	0.60	0.66	0.49	0.45	0.42	0.42	0.45	0.42	0.47	0.46	0.46	0.31
ln(A/BE)	0.78	0.79	0.71	0.66	0.64	0.65	0.67	0.67	0.70	0.73	0.77	0.81
E/P dummy	0.12	0.06	0.09	0.09	0.08	0.09	0.10	0.12	0.12	0.14	0.17	0.23
E(+)/P	0.11	0.12	0.10	0.10	0.10	0.10	0.10	0.09	0.10	0.09	0.09	0.08
Firms	116	80	185	181	179	182	185	205	227	267	165	291

for variation in β that is unrelated to size, the relation between β and average return is flat, even when β is the only explanatory variable.

B. Fama-MacBeth Regressions

Table III shows time-series averages of the slopes from the month-by-month Fama-MacBeth (FM) regressions of the cross-section of stock returns on size, β, and the other variables (leverage, E/P, and book-to-market equity) used to explain average returns. The average slopes provide standard FM tests for determining which explanatory variables on average have non-zero expected premiums during the July 1963 to December 1990 period.

Like the average returns in Tables I and II, the regressions in Table III say that size, ln(ME), helps explain the cross-section of average stock returns. The average slope from the monthly regressions of returns on size alone is -0.15%, with a t-statistic of -2.58. This reliable negative relation persists no matter which other explanatory variables are in the regressions; the average slopes on ln(ME) are always close to or more than 2 standard errors from 0. The size effect (smaller stocks have higher average returns) is thus robust in the 1963–1990 returns on NYSE, AMEX, and NASDAQ stocks.

In contrast to the consistent explanatory power of size, the FM regressions show that market β does not help explain average stock returns for 1963–1990. In a shot straight at the heart of the SLB model, the average slope from the regressions of returns on β alone in Table III is 0.15% per month and only 0.46 standard errors from 0. In the regressions of returns on size and β, size has explanatory power (an average slope -3.41 standard errors from 0), but the average slope for β is negative and only 1.21 standard errors from 0. Lakonishok and Shapiro (1986) get similar results for NYSE stocks for 1962–1981. We can also report that β shows no power to explain average returns (the average slopes are typically less than 1 standard error from 0) in FM regressions that use various combinations of β with size, book-to-market equity, leverage, and E/P.

C. Can β Be Saved?

What explains the poor results for β? One possibility is that other explanatory variables are correlated with true βs, and this obscures the relation between average returns and measured βs. But this line of attack cannot explain why β has no power when used alone to explain average returns. Moreover, leverage, book-to-market equity, and E/P do not seem to be good proxies for β. The averages of the monthly cross-sectional correlations between β and the values of these variables for individual stocks are all within 0.15 of 0.

Another hypothesis is that, as predicted by the SLB model, there is a positive relation between β and average return, but the relation is obscured by noise in the β estimates. However, our full-period post-ranking βs do not seem to be imprecise. Most of the standard errors of the βs (not shown) are

Table III

Average Slopes (*t*-Statistics) from Month-by-Month Regressions of Stock Returns on β, Size, Book-to-Market Equity, Leverage, and E/P: July 1963 to December 1990

Stocks are assigned the post-ranking β of the size-β portfolio they are in at the end of June of year t (Table I). BE is the book value of common equity plus balance-sheet deferred taxes, A is total book assets, and E is earnings (income before extraordinary items, plus income-statement deferred taxes, minus preferred dividends). BE, A, and E are for each firm's latest fiscal year ending in calendar year $t - 1$. The accounting ratios are measured using market equity ME in December of year $t - 1$. Firm size ln(ME) is measured in June of year t. In the regressions, these values of the explanatory variables for individual stocks are matched with CRSP returns for the months from July of year t to June of year $t + 1$. The gap between the accounting data and the returns ensures that the accounting data are available prior to the returns. If earnings are positive, E(+)/P is the ratio of total earnings to market equity and E/P dummy is 0. If earnings are negative, E(+)/P is 0 and E/P dummy is 1.

The average slope is the time-series average of the monthly regression slopes for July 1963 to December 1990, and the *t*-statistic is the average slope divided by its time-series standard error.

On average, there are 2267 stocks in the monthly regressions. To avoid giving extreme observations heavy weight in the regressions, the smallest and largest 0.5% of the observations on E(+)/P, BE/ME, A/ME, and A/BE are set equal to the next largest or smallest values of the ratios (the 0.005 and 0.995 fractiles). This has no effect on inferences.

β	ln(ME)	ln(BE/ME)	ln(A/ME)	ln(A/BE)	E/P Dummy	E(+)/P
0.15 (0.46)						
	−0.15 (−2.58)					
−0.37 (−1.21)	−0.17 (−3.41)					
		0.50 (5.71)				
			0.50 (5.69)	−0.57 (−5.34)		
					0.57 (2.28)	4.72 (4.57)
	−0.11 (−1.99)	0.35 (4.44)				
	−0.11 (−2.06)		0.35 (4.32)	−0.50 (−4.56)		
	−0.16 (−3.06)				0.06 (0.38)	2.99 (3.04)
	−0.13 (−2.47)	0.33 (4.46)			−0.14 (−0.90)	0.87 (1.23)
	−0.13 (−2.47)		0.32 (4.28)	−0.46 (−4.45)	−0.08 (−0.56)	1.15 (1.57)

0.05 or less, only 1 is greater than 0.1, and the standard errors are small relative to the range of the βs (0.53 to 1.79).

The β-sorted portfolios in Tables I and II also provide strong evidence against the β-measurement-error story. When portfolios are formed on pre-ranking βs alone (Table II), the post-ranking βs for the portfolios almost perfectly reproduce the ordering of the pre-ranking βs. Only the β for portfolio 1B is out of line, and only by 0.02. Similarly, when portfolios are formed on size and then pre-ranking βs (Table I), the post-ranking βs in each size decile closely reproduce the ordering of the pre-ranking βs.

The correspondence between the ordering of the pre-ranking and post-ranking βs for the β-sorted portfolios in Tables I and II is evidence that the post-ranking βs are informative about the ordering of the true βs. The problem for the SLB model is that there is no similar ordering in the average returns on the β-sorted portfolios. Whether one looks at portfolios sorted on β alone (Table II) or on size and then β (Table I), average returns are flat (Table II) or decline slightly (Table I) as the post-ranking βs increase.

Our evidence on the robustness of the size effect and the absence of a relation between β and average return is so contrary to the SLB model that it behooves us to examine whether the results are special to 1963–1990. The appendix shows that NYSE returns for 1941–1990 behave like the NYSE, AMEX, and NASDAQ returns for 1963–1990; there is a reliable size effect over the full 50-year period, but little relation between β and average return. Interestingly, there is a reliable simple relation between β and average return during the 1941–1965 period. These 25 years are a major part of the samples in the early studies of the SLB model of Black, Jensen, and Scholes (1972) and Fama and MacBeth (1973). Even for the 1941–1965 period, however, the relation between β and average return disappears when we control for size.

III. Book-to-Market Equity, E/P, and Leverage

Tables I to III say that there is a strong relation between the average returns on stocks and size, but there is no reliable relation between average returns and β. In this section we show that there is also a strong cross-sectional relation between average returns and book-to-market equity. If anything, this book-to-market effect is more powerful than the size effect. We also find that the combination of size and book-to-market equity absorbs the apparent roles of leverage and E/P in average stock returns.

A. Average Returns

Table IV shows average returns for July 1963 to December 1990 for portfolios formed on ranked values of book-to-market equity (BE/ME) or earnings-price ratio (E/P). The BE/ME and E/P portfolios in Table IV are formed in the same general way (one-dimensional yearly sorts) as the size and β portfolios in Table II. (See the tables for details.)

The relation between average return and E/P has a familiar U-shape (e.g., Jaffe, Keim, and Westerfield (1989) for U.S. data, and Chan, Hamao, and Lakonishok (1991) for Japan). Average returns decline from 1.46% per month for the negative E/P portfolio to 0.93% for the firms in portfolio 1B that have low but positive E/P. Average returns then increase monotonically, reaching 1.72% per month for the highest E/P portfolio.

The more striking evidence in Table IV is the strong positive relation between average return and book-to-market equity. Average returns rise from 0.30% for the lowest BE/ME portfolio to 1.83% for the highest, a difference of 1.53% per month. This spread is twice as large as the difference of 0.74% between the average monthly returns on the smallest and largest size portfolios in Table II. Note also that the strong relation between book-to-market equity and average return is unlikely to be a β effect in disguise; Table IV shows that post-ranking market βs vary little across portfolios formed on ranked values of BE/ME.

On average, only about 50 (out of 2317) firms per year have negative book equity, BE. The negative BE firms are mostly concentrated in the last 14 years of the sample, 1976–1989, and we do not include them in the tests. We can report, however, that average returns for negative BE firms are high, like the average returns of high BE/ME firms. Negative BE (which results from persistently negative earnings) and high BE/ME (which typically means that stock prices have fallen) are both signals of poor earning prospects. The similar average returns of negative and high BE/ME firms are thus consistent with the hypothesis that book-to-market equity captures cross-sectional variation in average returns that is related to relative distress.

B. Fama-MacBeth Regressions

B.1. BE/ME

The FM regressions in Table III confirm the importance of book-to-market equity in explaining the cross-section of average stock returns. The average slope from the monthly regressions of returns on ln(BE/ME) alone is 0.50%, with a t-statistic of 5.71. This book-to-market relation is stronger than the size effect, which produces a t-statistic of -2.58 in the regressions of returns on ln(ME) alone. But book-to-market equity does not replace size in explaining average returns. When both ln(ME) and ln(BE/ME) are included in the regressions, the average size slope is still -1.99 standard errors from 0; the book-to-market slope is an impressive 4.44 standard errors from 0.

B.2. Leverage

The FM regressions that explain returns with leverage variables provide interesting insight into the relation between book-to-market equity and average return. We use two leverage variables, the ratio of book assets to market equity, A/ME, and the ratio of book assets to book equity, A/BE. We interpret A/ME as a measure of market leverage, while A/BE is a measure

Table IV
Properties of Portfolios Formed on Book-to-Market Equity (BE/ME) and Earnings-Price Ratio (E/P): July 1963 to December 1990

At the end of each year $t-1$, 12 portfolios are formed on the basis of ranked values of BE/ME or E/P. Portfolios 2–9 cover deciles of the ranking variables. The bottom and top 2 portfolios (1A, 1B, 10A, and 10B) split the bottom and top deciles in half. For E/P, there are 13 portfolios; portfolio 0 is stocks with negative E/P. Since BE/ME and E/P are not strongly related to exchange listing, their portfolio breakpoints are determined on the basis of the ranked values of the variables for all stocks that satisfy the CRSP-COMPUSTAT data requirements. BE is the book value of common equity plus balance-sheet deferred taxes, A is total book assets, and E is earnings (income before extraordinary items, plus income-statement deferred taxes, minus preferred dividends). BE, A, and E are for each firm's latest fiscal year ending in calendar year $t-1$. The accounting ratios are measured using market equity ME in December of year $t-1$. Firm size $\ln(\text{ME})$ is measured in June of year t, with ME denominated in millions of dollars. We calculate each portfolio's monthly equal-weighted return for July of year t to June of year $t+1$, and then reform the portfolios at the end of year t.

Return is the time-series average of the monthly equal-weighted portfolio returns (in percent). $\ln(\text{ME})$, $\ln(\text{BE/ME})$, $\ln(A/\text{ME})$, $\ln(A/\text{BE})$, $E(+)/P$, and E/P dummy are the time-series averages of the monthly average values of these variables in each portfolio. Since the E/P dummy is 0 when earnings are positive, and 1 when earnings are negative, E/P dummy gives the average proportion of stocks with negative earnings in each portfolio.

β is the time-series average of the monthly portfolio βs. Stocks are assigned the post-ranking β of the size-β portfolio they are in at the end of June of year t (Table I). These individual-firm βs are averaged to compute the monthly βs for each portfolio for July of year t to June of year $t+1$. Firms is the average number of stocks in the portfolio each month.

Panel A: Stocks Sorted on Book-to-Market Equity (BE/ME)

Portfolio	0	1A	1B	2	3	4	5	6	7	8	9	10A	10B
Return		0.30	0.67	0.87	0.97	1.04	1.17	1.30	1.44	1.50	1.59	1.92	1.83
β		1.36	1.34	1.32	1.30	1.28	1.27	1.27	1.27	1.27	1.29	1.33	1.35
$\ln(\text{ME})$		4.53	4.67	4.69	4.56	4.47	4.38	4.23	4.06	3.85	3.51	3.06	2.65
$\ln(\text{BE/ME})$		−2.22	−1.51	−1.09	−0.75	−0.51	−0.32	−0.14	0.03	0.21	0.42	0.66	1.02
$\ln(A/\text{ME})$		−1.24	−0.79	−0.40	−0.05	0.20	0.40	0.56	0.71	0.91	1.12	1.35	1.75
$\ln(A/\text{BE})$		0.94	0.71	0.68	0.70	0.71	0.71	0.70	0.68	0.70	0.70	0.70	0.73
E/P dummy		0.29	0.15	0.10	0.08	0.08	0.08	0.09	0.09	0.11	0.15	0.22	0.36
$E(+)/P$		0.03	0.04	0.06	0.08	0.09	0.10	0.11	0.11	0.12	0.12	0.11	0.10
Firms		89	98	209	222	226	230	235	237	239	239	120	117

Table IV—Continued

Panel B: Stocks Sorted on Earnings-Price Ratio (E/P)

Portfolio	0	1A	1B	2	3	4	5	6	7	8	9	10A	10B
Return	1.46	1.04	0.93	0.94	1.03	1.18	1.22	1.33	1.42	1.46	1.57	1.74	1.72
β	1.47	1.40	1.35	1.31	1.28	1.26	1.25	1.26	1.24	1.23	1.24	1.28	1.31
ln(ME)	2.48	3.64	4.33	4.61	4.64	4.63	4.58	4.49	4.37	4.28	4.07	3.82	3.52
ln(BE/ME)	-0.10	-0.76	-0.91	-0.79	-0.61	-0.47	-0.33	-0.21	-0.08	0.02	0.15	0.26	0.40
ln(A/ME)	0.90	-0.05	-0.27	-0.16	0.03	0.18	0.31	0.44	0.58	0.70	0.85	1.01	1.25
ln(A/BE)	0.99	0.70	0.63	0.63	0.64	0.65	0.64	0.65	0.66	0.68	0.71	0.75	0.86
E/P dummy	1.00	0.00	0.00	0.00	0.00	0.00	0.00	0.00	0.00	0.00	0.00	0.00	0.00
E(+)/P	0.00	0.01	0.03	0.05	0.06	0.08	0.09	0.11	0.12	0.14	0.16	0.20	0.28
Firms	355	88	90	182	190	193	196	194	197	195	195	95	91

of book leverage. The regressions use the natural logs of the leverage ratios, ln(A/ME) and ln(A/BE), because preliminary tests indicated that logs are a good functional form for capturing leverage effects in average returns. Using logs also leads to a simple interpretation of the relation between the roles of leverage and book-to-market equity in average returns.

The FM regressions of returns on the leverage variables (Table III) pose a bit of a puzzle. The two leverage variables are related to average returns, but with opposite signs. As in Bhandari (1988), higher market leverage is associated with higher average returns; the average slopes for ln(A/ME) are always positive and more than 4 standard errors from 0. But higher book leverage is associated with lower average returns; the average slopes for ln(A/BE) are always negative and more than 4 standard errors from 0.

The puzzle of the opposite slopes on ln(A/ME) and ln(A/BE) has a simple solution. The average slopes for the two leverage variables are opposite in sign but close in absolute value, e.g., 0.50 and -0.57. Thus it is the difference between market and book leverage that helps explain average returns. But the difference between market and book leverage is book-to-market equity, $\ln(BE/ME) = \ln(A/ME) - \ln(A/BE)$. Table III shows that the average book-to-market slopes in the FM regressions are indeed close in absolute value to the slopes for the two leverage variables.

The close links between the leverage and book-to-market results suggest that there are two equivalent ways to interpret the book-to-market effect in average returns. A high ratio of book equity to market equity (a low stock price relative to book value) says that the market judges the prospects of a firm to be poor relative to firms with low BE/ME. Thus BE/ME may capture the relative-distress effect postulated by Chan and Chen (1991). A high book-to-market ratio also says that a firm's market leverage is high relative to its book leverage; the firm has a large amount of market-imposed leverage because the market judges that its prospects are poor and discounts its stock price relative to book value. In short, our tests suggest that the relative-distress effect, captured by BE/ME, can also be interpreted as an involuntary leverage effect, which is captured by the difference between A/ME and A/BE.

B.3. E/P

Ball (1978) posits that the earnings-price ratio is a catch-all for omitted risk factors in expected returns. If current earnings proxy for expected future earnings, high-risk stocks with high expected returns will have low prices relative to their earnings. Thus, E/P should be related to expected returns, whatever the omitted sources of risk. This argument only makes sense, however, for firms with positive earnings. When current earnings are negative, they are not a proxy for the earnings forecasts embedded in the stock price, and E/P is not a proxy for expected returns. Thus, the slope for E/P in the FM regressions is based on positive values; we use a dummy variable for E/P when earnings are negative.

The U-shaped relation between average return and E/P observed in Table IV is also apparent when the E/P variables are used alone in the FM regressions in Table III. The average slope on the E/P dummy variable (0.57% per month, 2.28 standard errors from 0) confirms that firms with negative earnings have higher average returns. The average slope for stocks with positive E/P (4.72% per month, 4.57 standard errors from 0) shows that average returns increase with E/P when it is positive.

Adding size to the regressions kills the explanatory power of the E/P dummy. Thus the high average returns of negative E/P stocks are better captured by their size, which Table IV says is on average small. Adding both size and book-to-market equity to the E/P regressions kills the E/P dummy and lowers the average slope on E/P from 4.72 to 0.87 ($t = 1.23$). In contrast, the average slopes for ln(ME) and ln(BE/ME) in the regressions that include E/P are similar to those in the regressions that explain average returns with only size and book-to-market equity. The results suggest that most of the relation between (positive) E/P and average return is due to the positive correlation between E/P and ln(BE/ME), illustrated in Table IV; firms with high E/P tend to have high book-to-market equity ratios.

IV. A Parsimonious Model for Average Returns

The results to here are easily summarized:

(1) When we allow for variation in β that is unrelated to size, there is no reliable relation between β and average return.
(2) The opposite roles of market leverage and book leverage in average returns are captured well by book-to-market equity.
(3) The relation between E/P and average return seems to be absorbed by the combination of size and book-to-market equity.

In a nutshell, market β seems to have no role in explaining the average returns on NYSE, AMEX, and NASDAQ stocks for 1963–1990, while size and book-to-market equity capture the cross-sectional variation in average stock returns that is related to leverage and E/P.

A. Average Returns, Size and Book-to-Market Equity

The average return matrix in Table V gives a simple picture of the two-dimensional variation in average returns that results when the 10 size deciles are each subdivided into 10 portfolios based on ranked values of BE/ME for individual stocks. Within a size decile (across a row of the average return matrix), returns typically increase strongly with BE/ME: on average, the returns on the lowest and highest BE/ME portfolios in a size decile differ by 0.99% (1.63% − 0.64%) per month. Similarly, looking down the columns of the average return matrix shows that there is a negative relation between average return and size: on average, the spread of returns across the size portfolios in a BE/ME group is 0.58% per month. The average return matrix gives life to the conclusion from the regressions that,

Table V
Average Monthly Returns on Portfolios Formed on Size and Book-to-Market Equity; Stocks Sorted by ME (Down) and then BE/ME (Across): July 1963 to December 1990

In June of each year t, the NYSE, AMEX, and NASDAQ stocks that meet the CRSP-COMPUSTAT data requirements are allocated to 10 size portfolios using the NYSE size (ME) breakpoints. The NYSE, AMEX, and NASDAQ stocks in each size decile are then sorted into 10 BE/ME portfolios using the book-to-market ratios for year $t - 1$. BE/ME is the book value of common equity plus balance-sheet deferred taxes for fiscal year $t - 1$, over market equity for December of year $t - 1$. The equal-weighted monthly portfolio returns are then calculated for July of year t to June of year $t + 1$.

Average monthly return is the time-series average of the monthly equal-weighted portfolio returns (in percent).

The All column shows average returns for equal-weighted size decile portfolios. The All row shows average returns for equal-weighted portfolios of the stocks in each BE/ME group.

	All	Low	2	3	4	5	6	7	8	9	High
All	1.23	0.64	0.98	1.06	1.17	1.24	1.26	1.39	1.40	1.50	1.63
Small-ME	1.47	0.70	1.14	1.20	1.43	1.56	1.51	1.70	1.71	1.82	1.92
ME-2	1.22	0.43	1.05	0.96	1.19	1.33	1.19	1.58	1.28	1.43	1.79
ME-3	1.22	0.56	0.88	1.23	0.95	1.36	1.30	1.30	1.40	1.54	1.60
ME-4	1.19	0.39	0.72	1.06	1.36	1.13	1.21	1.34	1.59	1.51	1.47
ME-5	1.24	0.88	0.65	1.08	1.47	1.13	1.43	1.44	1.26	1.52	1.49
ME-6	1.15	0.70	0.98	1.14	1.23	0.94	1.27	1.19	1.19	1.24	1.50
ME-7	1.07	0.95	1.00	0.99	0.83	0.99	1.13	0.99	1.16	1.10	1.47
ME-8	1.08	0.66	1.13	0.91	0.95	0.99	1.01	1.15	1.05	1.29	1.55
ME-9	0.95	0.44	0.89	0.92	1.00	1.05	0.93	0.82	1.11	1.04	1.22
Large-ME	0.89	0.93	0.88	0.84	0.71	0.79	0.83	0.81	0.96	0.97	1.18

controlling for size, book-to-market equity captures strong variation in average returns, and controlling for book-to-market equity leaves a size effect in average returns.

B. The Interaction between Size and Book-to-Market Equity

The average of the monthly correlations between the cross-sections of ln(ME) and ln(BE/ME) for individual stocks is −0.26. The negative correlation is also apparent in the average values of ln(ME) and ln(BE/ME) for the portfolios sorted on ME or BE/ME in Tables II and IV. Thus, firms with low market equity are more likely to have poor prospects, resulting in low stock prices and high book-to-market equity. Conversely, large stocks are more likely to be firms with stronger prospects, higher stock prices, lower book-to-market equity, and lower average stock returns.

The correlation between size and book-to-market equity affects the regressions in Table III. Including ln(BE/ME) moves the average slope on ln(ME) from −0.15 ($t = -2.58$) in the univariate regressions to −0.11 ($t = -1.99$) in the bivariate regressions. Similarly, including ln(ME) in the regressions lowers the average slope on ln(BE/ME) from 0.50 to 0.35 (still a healthy 4.44 standard errors from 0). Thus, part of the size effect in the simple regressions is due to the fact that small ME stocks are more likely to have high book-to-market ratios, and part of the simple book-to-market effect is due to the fact that high BE/ME stocks tend to be small (they have low ME).

We should not, however, exaggerate the links between size and book-to-market equity. The correlation (−0.26) between ln(ME) and ln(BE/ME) is not extreme, and the average slopes in the bivariate regressions in Table III show that ln(ME) and ln(BE/ME) are both needed to explain the cross-section of average returns. Finally, the 10 × 10 average return matrix in Table V provides concrete evidence that, (a) controlling for size, book-to-market equity captures substantial variation in the cross-section of average returns, and (b) within BE/ME groups average returns are related to size.

C. Subperiod Averages of the FM Slopes

The message from the average FM slopes for 1963–1990 (Table III) is that size on average has a negative premium in the cross-section of stock returns, book-to-market equity has a positive premium, and the average premium for market β is essentially 0. Table VI shows the average FM slopes for two roughly equal subperiods (July 1963–December 1976 and January 1977–December 1990) from two regressions: (a) the cross-section of stock returns on size, ln(ME), and book-to-market equity, ln(BE/ME), and (b) returns on β, ln(ME), and ln(BE/ME). For perspective, average returns on the value-weighted and equal-weighted (VW and EW) portfolios of NYSE stocks are also shown.

In FM regressions, the intercept is the return on a standard portfolio (the weights on stocks sum to 1) in which the weighted averages of the explanatory variables are 0 (Fama (1976), chapter 9). In our tests, the intercept is weighted toward small stocks (ME is in millions of dollars so ln(ME) = 0 implies ME = $1 million) and toward stocks with relatively high book-to-market ratios (Table IV says that ln(BE/ME) is negative for the typical firm, so ln(BE/ME) = 0 is toward the high end of the sample ratios). Thus it is not surprising that the average intercepts are always large relative to their standard errors and relative to the returns on the NYSE VW and EW portfolios.

Like the overall period, the subperiods do not offer much hope that the average premium for β is economically important. The average FM slope for β is only slightly positive for 1963–1976 (0.10% per month, $t = 0.25$), and it is negative for 1977–1990 (−0.44% per month, $t = -1.17$). There is a hint that the size effect is weaker in the 1977–1990 period, but inferences about the average size slopes for the subperiods lack power.

Unlike the size effect, the relation between book-to-market equity and average return is so strong that it shows up reliably in both the 1963–1976 and the 1977–1990 subperiods. The average slopes for ln(BE/ME) are all more than 2.95 standard errors from 0, and the average slopes for the

Table VI
Subperiod Average Monthly Returns on the NYSE Equal-Weighted and Value-Weighted Portfolios and Subperiod Means of the Intercepts and Slopes from the Monthly FM Cross-Sectional Regressions of Returns on (a) Size (ln(ME)) and Book-to-Market Equity (ln(BE/ME)), and (b) β, ln(ME), and ln(BE/ME)

Mean is the time-series mean of a monthly return, Std is its time-series standard deviation, and $t(Mn)$ is Mean divided by its time-series standard error.

	7/63–12/90 (330 Mos.)			7/63–12/76 (162 Mos.)			1/77–12/90 (168 Mos.)		
Variable	Mean	Std	$t(Mn)$	Mean	Std	$t(Mn)$	Mean	Std	$t(Mn)$
NYSE Value-Weighted (VW) and Equal-Weighted (EW) Portfolio Returns									
VW	0.81	4.47	3.27	0.56	4.26	1.67	1.04	4.66	2.89
EW	0.97	5.49	3.19	0.77	5.70	1.72	1.15	5.28	2.82
$R_{it} = a + b_{2t}\ln(ME_{it}) + b_{3t}\ln(BE/ME_{it}) + e_{it}$									
a	1.77	8.51	3.77	1.86	10.10	2.33	1.69	6.67	3.27
b_2	−0.11	1.02	−1.99	−0.16	1.25	−1.62	−0.07	0.73	−1.16
b_3	0.35	1.45	4.43	0.36	1.53	2.96	0.35	1.37	3.30
$R_{it} = a + b_{1t}\beta_{it} + b_{2t}\ln(ME_{it}) + b_{3t}\ln(BE/ME_{it}) + e_{it}$									
a	2.07	5.75	6.55	1.73	6.22	3.54	2.40	5.25	5.92
b_1	−0.17	5.12	−0.62	0.10	5.33	0.25	−0.44	4.91	−1.17
b_2	−0.12	0.89	−2.52	−0.15	1.03	−1.91	−0.09	0.74	−1.64
b_3	0.33	1.24	4.80	0.34	1.36	3.17	0.31	1.10	3.67

subperiods (0.36 and 0.35) are close to the average slope (0.35) for the overall period. The subperiod results thus support the conclusion that, among the variables considered here, book-to-market equity is consistently the most powerful for explaining the cross-section of average stock returns.

Finally, Roll (1983) and Keim (1983) show that the size effect is stronger in January. We have examined the monthly slopes from the FM regressions in Table VI for evidence of a January seasonal in the relation between book-to-market equity and average return. The average January slopes for ln(BE/ME) are about twice those for February to December. Unlike the size effect, however, the strong relation between book-to-market equity and average return is not special to January. The average monthly February-to-December slopes for ln(BE/ME) are about 4 standard errors from 0, and they are close to (within 0.05 of) the average slopes for the whole year. Thus, there is a January seasonal in the book-to-market equity effect, but the positive relation between BE/ME and average return is strong throughout the year.

D. β and the Market Factor: Caveats

Some caveats about the negative evidence on the role of β in average returns are in order. The average premiums for β, size, and book-to-market equity depend on the definitions of the variables used in the regressions. For example, suppose we replace book-to-market equity (ln(BE/ME)) with book equity (ln(BE)). As long as size (ln(ME)) is also in the regression, this change will not affect the intercept, the fitted values or the R^2. But the change, in variables increases the average slope (and the t-statistic) on ln(ME). In other words, it increases the risk premium associated with size. Other redefinitions of the β, size, and book-to-market variables will produce different regression slopes and perhaps different inferences about average premiums, including possible resuscitation of a role for β. And, of course, at the moment, we have no theoretical basis for choosing among different versions of the variables.

Moreover, the tests here are restricted to stocks. It is possible that including other assets will change the inferences about the average premiums for β, size, and book-to-market equity. For example, the large average intercepts for the FM regressions in Table VI suggest that the regressions will not do a good job on Treasury bills, which have low average returns and are likely to have small loadings on the underlying market, size, and book-to-market factors in returns. Extending the tests to bills and other bonds may well change our inferences about average risk premiums, including the revival of a role for market β.

We emphasize, however, that different approaches to the tests are not likely to revive the Sharpe-Lintner-Black model. Resuscitation of the SLB model requires that a better proxy for the market portfolio (a) overturns our evidence that the simple relation between β and average stock returns is flat and (b) leaves β as the only variable relevant for explaining average returns. Such results seem unlikely, given Stambaugh's (1982) evidence that tests of the SLB model do not seem to be sensitive to the choice of a market proxy. Thus, if there is a role for β in average returns, it is likely to be found in a multi-factor model that transforms the flat simple relation between average return and β into a positively sloped conditional relation.

V. Conclusions and Implications

The Sharpe-Lintner-Black model has long shaped the way academics and practitioners think about average return and risk. Black, Jensen, and Scholes (1972) and Fama and MacBeth (1973) find that, as predicted by the model, there is a positive simple relation between average return and market β during the early years (1926–1968) of the CRSP NYSE returns file. Like Reinganum (1981) and Lakonishok and Shapiro (1986), we find that this simple relation between β and average return disappears during the more recent 1963–1990 period. The appendix that follows shows that the relation between β and average return is also weak in the last half century (1941–1990) of returns on NYSE stocks. In short, our tests do not support the central prediction of the SLB model, that average stock returns are positively related to market β.

Banz (1981) documents a strong negative relation between average return and firm size. Bhandari (1988) finds that average return is positively related to leverage, and Basu (1983) finds a positive relation between average return and E/P. Stattman (1980) and Rosenberg, Reid, and Lanstein (1985) document a positive relation between average return and book-to-market equity for U.S. stocks, and Chan, Hamao, and Lakonishok (1992) find that BE/ME is also a powerful variable for explaining average returns on Japanese stocks.

Variables like size, E/P, leverage, and book-to-market equity are all scaled versions of a firm's stock price. They can be regarded as different ways of extracting information from stock prices about the cross-section of expected stock returns (Ball (1978), Keim (1988)). Since all these variables are scaled versions of price, it is reasonable to expect that some of them are redundant for explaining average returns. Our main result is that for the 1963–1990 period, size and book-to-market equity capture the cross-sectional variation in average stock returns associated with size, E/P, book-to-market equity, and leverage.

A. Rational Asset-Pricing Stories

Are our results consistent with asset-pricing theory? Since the FM intercept is constrained to be the same for all stocks, FM regressions always impose a linear factor structure on returns and expected returns that is consistent with the multifactor asset-pricing models of Merton (1973) and Ross (1976). Thus our tests impose a rational asset-pricing framework on the relation between average return and size and book-to-market equity.

Even if our results are consistent with asset-pricing theory, they are not economically satisfying. What is the economic explanation for the roles of size and book-to-market equity in average returns? We suggest several paths of inquiry.

(a) The intercepts and slopes in the monthly FM regressions of returns on ln(ME) and ln(BE/ME) are returns on portfolios that mimic the underlying common risk factors in returns proxied by size and book-to-market equity (Fama (1976), chapter 9). Examining the relations between the returns on these portfolios and economic variables that measure variation in business conditions might help expose the nature of the economic risks captured by size and book-to-market equity.

(b) Chan, Chen, and Hsieh (1985) argue that the relation between size and average return proxies for a more fundamental relation between expected returns and economic risk factors. Their most powerful factor in explaining the size effect is the difference between the monthly returns on low- and high-grade corporate bonds, which in principle captures a kind of default risk in returns that is priced. It would be interesting to test whether loadings on this or other economic factors, such as those of Chen, Roll, and Ross (1986), can explain the roles of size and book-to-market equity in our tests.

(c) In a similar vein, Chan and Chen (1991) argue that the relation between size and average return is a relative-prospects effect. The earning prospects of distressed firms are more sensitive to economic conditions. This results in a distress factor in returns that is priced in expected returns. Chan and Chen construct two mimicking portfolios for the distress factor, based on dividend changes and leverage. It would be interesting to check whether loadings on their distress factors absorb the size and book-to-market equity effects in average returns that are documented here.

(d) In fact, if stock prices are rational, BE/ME, the ratio of the book value of a stock to the market's assessment of its value, should be a direct indicator of the relative prospects of firms. For example, we expect that high BE/ME firms have low earnings on assets relative to low BE/ME firms. Our work (in progress) suggests that there is indeed a clean separation between high and low BE/ME firms on various measures of economic fundamentals. Low BE/ME firms are persistently strong performers, while the economic performance of high BE/ME firms is persistently weak.

B. Irrational Asset-Pricing Stories

The discussion above assumes that the asset-pricing effects captured by size and book-to-market equity are rational. For BE/ME, our most powerful expected-return variable, there is an obvious alternative. The cross-section of book-to-market ratios might result from market overreaction to the relative prospects of firms. If overreaction tends to be corrected, BE/ME will predict the cross-section of stock returns.

Simple tests do not confirm that the size and book-to-market effects in average returns are due to market overreaction, at least of the type posited by DeBondt and Thaler (1985). One overreaction measure used by DeBondt and Thaler is a stock's most recent 3-year return. Their overreaction story predicts that 3-year losers have strong post-ranking returns relative to 3-year winners. In FM regressions (not shown) for individual stocks, the 3-year lagged return shows no power even when used alone to explain average returns. The univariate average slope for the lagged return is negative, -6 basis points per month, but less than 0.5 standard errors from 0.

C. Applications

Our main result is that two easily measured variables, size and book-to-market equity, seem to describe the cross-section of average stock returns. Prescriptions for using this evidence depend on (a) whether it will persist, and (b) whether it results from rational or irrational asset-pricing.

It is possible that, by chance, size and book-to-market equity happen to describe the cross-section of average returns in our sample, but they were and are unrelated to expected returns. We put little weight on this possibility, especially for book-to-market equity. First, although BE/ME has long been touted as a measure of the return prospects of stocks, there is no evidence that its explanatory power deteriorates through time. The 1963–1990 relation between BE/ME and average return is strong, and remarkably similar for the 1963-1976 and 1977-1990 subperiods. Second, our preliminary work on economic fundamentals suggests that high-BE/ME firms tend to be persistently poor earners relative to low-BE/ME firms. Similarly, small firms have a long period of poor earnings during the 1980s not shared with big firms. The systematic patterns in fundamentals give us some hope that size and book-to-market equity proxy for risk factors in returns, related to relative earning prospects, that are rationally priced in expected returns.

If our results are more than chance, they have practical implications for portfolio formation and performance evaluation by investors whose primary concern is long-term average returns. If asset-pricing is rational, size and BE/ME must proxy for risk. Our results then imply that the performance of managed portfolios (e.g., pension funds and mutual funds) can be evaluated by comparing their average returns with the average returns of benchmark portfolios with similar size and BE/ME characteristics. Likewise, the expected returns for different portfolio strategies can be estimated from the historical average returns of portfolios with matching size and BE/ME properties.

If asset-pricing is irrational and size and BE/ME do not proxy for risk, our results might still be used to evaluate portfolio performance and measure the expected returns from alternative investment strategies. If stock prices are irrational, however, the likely persistence of the results is more suspect.

Appendix
Size Versus β: 1941-1990

Our results on the absence of a relation between β and average stock returns for 1963-1990 are so contrary to the tests of the Sharpe-Lintner-Black model by Black, Jensen, and Scholes (1972), Fama and MacBeth (1973), and (more recently) Chan and Chen (1988), that further tests are appropriate. We examine the roles of size and β in the average returns on NYSE stocks for the half-century 1941-1990, the longest available period that avoids the high volatility of returns in the Great Depression. We do not include the accounting variables in the tests because of the strong selection bias (toward successful firms) in the COMPUSTAT data prior to 1962.

We first replicate the results of Chan and Chen (1988). Like them, we find that when portfolios are formed on size alone, there are strong relations between average return and either size or β; average return increases with β and decreases with size. For size portfolios, however, size (ln(ME)) and β are almost perfectly correlated (-0.98), so it is difficult to distinguish between the roles of size and β in average returns.

One way to generate strong variation in β that is unrelated to size is to form portfolios on size and then on β. As in Tables I to III, we find that the resulting independent variation in β just about washes out the positive simple relation between average return and β observed when portfolios are formed on size alone. The results for NYSE stocks for 1941-1990 are thus much like those for NYSE, AMEX, and NASDAQ stocks for 1963-1990.

This appendix also has methodological goals. For example, the FM regressions in Table III use returns on individual stocks as the dependent variable. Since we allocate portfolio βs to individual stocks but use firm-specific values of other variables like size, β may be at a disadvantage in the regressions for individual stocks. This appendix shows, however, that regressions for portfolios, which put β and size on equal footing, produce results comparable to those for individual stocks.

A. Size Portfolios

Table AI shows average monthly returns and market βs for 12 portfolios of NYSE stocks formed on the basis of size (ME) at the end of each year from 1940 to 1989. For these size portfolios, there is a strong positive relation between average return and β. Average returns fall from 1.96% per month for the smallest ME portfolio (1A) to 0.93% for the largest (10B) and β falls from 1.60 to 0.95. (Note also that, as claimed earlier, estimating β as the sum of the slopes in the regression of a portfolio's return on the current and prior month's NYSE value-weighted return produces much larger βs for the smallest ME portfolios and slightly smaller βs for the largest ME portfolios.)

The FM regressions in Table AI confirm the positive simple relation between average return and β for size portfolios. In the regressions of the size-portfolio returns on β alone, the average premium for a unit of β is 1.45% per month. In the regressions of individual stock returns on β (where stocks are assigned the β of their size portfolio), the premium for a unit of β is 1.39%. Both estimates are about 3 standard errors from 0. Moreover, the βs of size portfolios do not leave a residual size effect; the average residuals from the simple regressions of returns on β in Table AI show no relation to size. These positive SLB results for 1941–1990 are like those obtained by Chan and Chen (1988) in tests on size portfolios for 1954–1983.

There is, however, evidence in Table AI that all is not well with the βs of the size portfolios. They do a fine job on the relation between size and average return, but they do a lousy job on their main task, the relation between β and average return. When the residuals from the regressions of returns on β are grouped using the pre-ranking βs of individual stocks, the average residuals are strongly positive for low-β stocks (0.51% per month for group 1A) and negative for high-β stocks (−1.05% for 10B). Thus the market lines estimated with size-portfolio βs exaggerate the tradeoff of average return for β; they underestimate average returns on low-β stocks and overestimate average returns on high-β stocks. This pattern in the β-sorted average residuals for individual stocks suggests that (a) there is variation in β across stocks that is lost in the size portfolios, and (b) this variation in β is not rewarded as well as the variation in β that is related to size.

B. Two-Pass Size-β Portfolios

Like Table I, Table AII shows that subdividing size deciles using the (pre-ranking) βs of individual stocks results in strong variation in β that is

Table AI
Average Returns, Post-Ranking βs and Fama-MacBeth Regression Slopes for Size Portfolios of NYSE Stocks: 1941–1990

At the end of each year $t - 1$, stocks are assigned to 12 portfolios using ranked values of ME. Included are all NYSE stocks that have a CRSP price and shares for December of year $t - 1$ and returns for at least 24 of the 60 months ending in December of year $t - 1$ (for pre-ranking β estimates). The middle 8 portfolios cover size deciles 2 to 9. The 4 extreme portfolios (1A, 1B, 10A, and 10B) split the smallest and largest deciles in half. We compute equal-weighted returns on the portfolios for the 12 months of year t using all surviving stocks. Average Return is the time-series average of the monthly portfolio returns for 1941–1990, in percent. Average firms is the average number of stocks in the portfolios each month. The simple βs are estimated by regressing the 1941–1990 sample of post-ranking monthly returns for a size portfolio on the current month's value-weighted NYSE portfolio return. The sum βs are the sum of the slopes from a regression of the post-ranking monthly returns on the current and prior month's VW NYSE returns.

The independent variables in the Fama-MacBeth regressions are defined for each firm at the end of December of each year $t - 1$. Stocks are assigned the post-ranking (sum) β of the size portfolio they are in at the end of year $t - 1$. ME is price times shares outstanding at the end of year $t - 1$. In the individual-stock regressions, these values of the explanatory variables are matched with CRSP returns for each of the 12 months of year t. The portfolio regressions match the equal-weighted portfolio returns with the equal-weighted averages of β and ln(ME) for the surviving stocks in each month of year t. Slope is the average of the (600) monthly FM regression slopes and SE is the standard error of the average slope. The residuals from the monthly regressions for year t are grouped into 12 portfolios on the basis of size (ME) or pre-ranking β (estimated with 24 to 60 months of data, as available) at the end of year $t - 1$. The average residuals are the time-series averages of the monthly equal-weighted portfolio residuals, in percent. The average residuals for regressions (1) and (2) (not shown) are quite similar to those for regressions (4) and (5) (shown).

Portfolios Formed on Size

	1A	1B	2	3	4	5	6	7	8	9	10A	10B
Ave. return	1.96	1.59	1.44	1.36	1.28	1.24	1.23	1.17	1.15	1.13	0.97	0.93
Ave. firms	57	56	110	107	107	108	111	113	115	118	59	59
Simple β	1.29	1.24	1.21	1.19	1.16	1.13	1.13	1.12	1.09	1.05	1.00	0.98
Standard error	0.07	0.05	0.04	0.03	0.02	0.02	0.02	0.02	0.01	0.01	0.01	0.01
Sum β	1.60	1.44	1.37	1.32	1.26	1.23	1.19	1.17	1.12	1.06	0.99	0.95
Standard error	0.10	0.06	0.05	0.04	0.03	0.03	0.03	0.02	0.02	0.01	0.01	0.01

Table AI—Continued

Portfolio Regressions

	(1) β	(2) ln(ME)	(3) β and ln(ME)
Slope	1.45	−0.137	3.05 0.149
SE	0.47	0.044	1.51 0.115

Individual Stock Regressions

	(4) β	(5) ln(ME)	(6) β and ln(ME)
Slope	1.39	−0.133	0.71 −0.060
SE	0.46	0.043	0.81 0.062

Average Residuals for Stocks Grouped on Size

	1A	1B	2	3	4	5	6	7	8	9	10A	10B
Regression (4)	0.17	0.00	−0.04	−0.06	−0.05	−0.04	0.00	−0.03	0.03	0.08	0.01	0.04
Standard error	0.11	0.06	0.04	0.04	0.04	0.04	0.03	0.03	0.03	0.03	0.05	0.06
Regression (5)	0.30	0.02	−0.05	−0.06	−0.08	−0.07	−0.03	−0.04	0.02	0.08	0.01	0.13
Standard error	0.14	0.07	0.04	0.04	0.04	0.04	0.04	0.03	0.03	0.03	0.04	0.07
Regression (6)	0.20	0.02	−0.05	−0.07	−0.08	−0.06	−0.01	−0.02	0.04	0.09	0.00	0.06
Standard error	0.10	0.06	0.04	0.04	0.04	0.04	0.03	0.03	0.03	0.03	0.05	0.05

Average Residuals for Stocks Grouped on Pre-Ranking β

	1A	1B	2	3	4	5	6	7	8	9	10A	10B
Regression (4)	0.51	0.61	0.38	0.32	0.16	0.12	0.03	−0.10	−0.27	−0.31	−0.66	−1.05
Standard error	0.21	0.19	0.13	0.08	0.04	0.03	0.04	0.05	0.09	0.11	0.18	0.23
Regression (5)	−0.10	0.00	0.02	0.09	0.05	0.07	0.05	0.00	−0.03	−0.01	−0.11	−0.33
Standard error	0.11	0.10	0.07	0.05	0.04	0.03	0.03	0.04	0.05	0.07	0.10	0.13
Regression (6)	0.09	0.25	0.13	0.19	0.11	0.14	0.09	0.01	−0.11	−0.12	−0.38	−0.70
Standard error	0.41	0.37	0.24	0.14	0.07	0.04	0.04	0.09	0.16	0.21	0.34	0.43

Table AII
Properties of Portfolios Formed on Size and Pre-Ranking β: NYSE Stocks Sorted by ME (Down) then Pre-Ranking β (Across): 1941–1990

At the end of year $t - 1$, the NYSE stocks on CRSP are assigned to 10 size (ME) portfolios. Each size decile is subdivided into 10 β portfolios using pre-ranking βs of individual stocks, estimated with 24 to 60 monthly returns (as available) ending in December of year $t - 1$. The equal-weighted monthly returns on the resulting 100 portfolios are then calculated for year t. The average returns are the time-series averages of the monthly returns, in percent. The post-ranking βs use the full 1941–1990 sample of post-ranking returns for each portfolio. The pre- and post-ranking βs are the sum of the slopes from a regression of monthly returns on the current and prior month's NYSE value-weighted market return. The average size for a portfolio is the time-series average of each month's average value of ln(ME) for stocks in the portfolio. ME is denominated in millions of dollars. There are, on average, about 10 stocks in each size-β portfolio each month. The All column shows parameter values for equal-weighted size-decile (ME) portfolios. The All rows show parameter values for equal-weighted portfolios of the stocks in each β group.

	All	Low-β	β-2	β-3	β-4	β-5	β-6	β-7	β-8	β-9	High-β
Panel A: Average Monthly Return (in Percent)
All	1.78	1.22	1.30	1.32	1.35	1.36	1.34	1.29	1.34	1.14	1.10
Small-ME	1.78	1.74	1.76	2.08	1.91	1.92	1.72	1.77	1.91	1.56	1.46
ME-2	1.44	1.41	1.35	1.33	1.61	1.72	1.59	1.40	1.62	1.24	1.11
ME-3	1.36	1.21	1.40	1.22	1.47	1.34	1.51	1.33	1.57	1.33	1.21
ME-4	1.28	1.26	1.29	1.19	1.27	1.51	1.30	1.19	1.56	1.18	1.00
ME-5	1.24	1.22	1.30	1.28	1.33	1.21	1.37	1.41	1.31	0.92	1.06
ME-6	1.23	1.21	1.32	1.37	1.09	1.34	1.10	1.40	1.21	1.22	1.08
ME-7	1.17	1.08	1.23	1.37	1.27	1.19	1.34	1.10	1.11	0.87	1.17
ME-8	1.15	1.06	1.18	1.26	1.25	1.26	1.17	1.16	1.05	1.08	1.04
ME-9	1.13	0.99	1.13	1.00	1.24	1.28	1.31	1.15	1.11	1.09	1.05
Large-ME	0.95	0.99	1.01	1.12	1.01	0.89	0.95	0.95	1.00	0.90	0.68

Table AII—Continued

	All	Low-β	β-2	β-3	β-4	β-5	β-6	β-7	β-8	β-9	High-β
Panel B: Post-Ranking β										
All		0.76	0.95	1.05	1.14	1.22	1.26	1.34	1.38	1.49	1.69
Small-ME	1.52	1.17	1.40	1.31	1.50	1.46	1.50	1.69	1.60	1.75	1.92
ME-2	1.37	0.86	1.09	1.12	1.24	1.39	1.42	1.48	1.60	1.69	1.91
ME-3	1.32	0.88	0.96	1.18	1.19	1.33	1.40	1.43	1.56	1.64	1.74
ME-4	1.26	0.69	0.95	1.06	1.15	1.24	1.29	1.46	1.43	1.64	1.83
ME-5	1.23	0.70	0.95	1.04	1.10	1.22	1.32	1.34	1.41	1.56	1.72
ME-6	1.19	0.68	0.86	1.04	1.13	1.20	1.20	1.35	1.36	1.48	1.70
ME-7	1.17	0.67	0.88	0.95	1.14	1.18	1.26	1.27	1.32	1.44	1.68
ME-8	1.12	0.64	0.83	0.99	1.06	1.14	1.14	1.21	1.26	1.39	1.58
ME-9	1.06	0.68	0.81	0.94	0.96	1.06	1.11	1.18	1.22	1.25	1.46
Large-ME	0.97	0.65	0.73	0.90	0.91	0.97	1.01	1.01	1.07	1.12	1.38
Panel C: Average Size (ln(ME))										
All		4.39	4.39	4.40	4.40	4.39	4.40	4.38	4.37	4.37	4.34
Small-ME	1.93	2.04	1.99	2.00	1.96	1.92	1.92	1.91	1.90	1.87	1.80
ME-2	2.80	2.81	2.79	2.81	2.83	2.80	2.79	2.80	2.80	2.79	2.79
ME-3	3.27	3.28	3.27	3.28	3.27	3.27	3.28	3.29	3.27	3.27	3.26
ME-4	3.67	3.67	3.67	3.67	3.68	3.68	3.67	3.68	3.66	3.67	3.67
ME-5	4.06	4.07	4.06	4.05	4.06	4.07	4.06	4.05	4.05	4.06	4.06
ME-6	4.45	4.45	4.44	4.46	4.45	4.45	4.45	4.45	4.44	4.45	4.45
ME-7	4.87	4.86	4.87	4.86	4.87	4.87	4.88	4.87	4.87	4.85	4.87
ME-8	5.36	5.38	5.38	5.38	5.35	5.36	5.37	5.37	5.36	5.35	5.34
ME-9	5.98	5.96	5.98	5.99	6.00	5.98	5.98	5.97	5.95	5.96	5.96
Large-ME	7.12	7.10	7.12	7.16	7.17	7.20	7.29	7.14	7.09	7.04	6.83

independent of size. The β sort of a size decile always produces portfolios with similar average ln(ME) but much different (post-ranking) βs. Table AII also shows, however, that investors are not compensated for the variation in β that is independent of size. Despite the wide range of βs in each size decile, average returns show no tendency to increase with β. AII

The FM regressions in Table AIII formalize the roles of size and β in NYSE average returns for 1941–1990. The regressions of returns on β alone show that using the βs of the portfolios formed on size and β, rather than size alone, causes the average slope on β to fall from about 1.4% per month (Table AI) to about 0.23% (about 1 standard error from 0). Thus, allowing for variation in β that is unrelated to size flattens the relation between average return and β, to the point where it is indistinguishable from no relation at all.

The flatter market lines in Table AIII succeed, however, in erasing the negative relation between β and average residuals observed in the regressions of returns on β alone in Table AI. Thus, forming portfolios on size and β (Table AIII) produces a better description of the simple relation between average return and β than forming portfolios on size alone (Table AI). This improved description of the relation between average return and β is evidence that the β estimates for the two-pass size-β portfolios capture variation in true βs that is missed when portfolios are formed on size alone.

Unfortunately, the flatter market lines in Table AIII have a cost, the emergence of a residual size effect. Grouped on the basis of ME for individual stocks, the average residuals from the univariate regressions of returns on the βs of the 100 size-β portfolios are strongly positive for small stocks and negative for large stocks (0.60% per month for the smallest ME group, 1A, and -0.27% for the largest, 10B). Thus, when we allow for variation in β that is independent of size, the resulting βs leave a large size effect in average returns. This residual size effect is much like that observed by Banz (1981) with the βs of portfolios formed on size and β.

The correlation between size and β is -0.98 for portfolios formed on size alone. The independent variation in β obtained with the second-pass sort on β lowers the correlation to -0.50. The lower correlation means that bivariate regressions of returns on β and ln(ME) are more likely to distinguish true size effects from true β effects in average returns.

The bivariate regressions (Table AIII) that use the βs of the size-β portfolios are more bad news for β. The average slopes for ln(ME) are close to the values in the univariate size regressions, and almost 4 standard errors from 0, but the average slopes for β are negative and less than 1 standard error from 0. The message from the bivariate regressions is that there is a strong relation between size and average return. But like the regressions in Table AIII that explain average returns with β alone, the bivariate regressions say that there is no reliable relation between β and average returns when the tests use βs that are not close substitutes for size. These uncomfortable SLB results for NYSE stocks for 1941–1990 are much like those for NYSE, AMEX, and NASDAQ stocks for 1963–1990 in Table III.

C. Subperiod Diagnostics

Our results for 1941-1990 seem to contradict the evidence in Black, Jensen, and Scholes (BJS) (1972) and Fama and MacBeth (FM) (1973) that there is a reliable positive relation between average return and β. The βs in BJS and FM are from portfolios formed on β alone, and the market proxy is the NYSE equal-weighted portfolio. We use the βs of portfolios formed on size and β, and our market is the value-weighted NYSE portfolio. We can report, however, that our inference that there isn't much relation between β and average return is unchanged when (a) the market proxy is the NYSE EW portfolio, (b) portfolios are formed on just (pre-ranking) βs, or (c) the order of forming the size-β portfolios is changed from size then β to β then size.

A more important difference between our results and the earlier studies is the sample periods. The tests in BJS and FM end in the 1960s. Table AIV shows that when we split the 50-year 1941-1990 period in half, the univariate FM regressions of returns on β produce an average slope for 1941-1965 (0.50% per month, $t = 1.82$) more like that of the earlier studies. In contrast, the average slope on β for 1966-1990 is close to 0 (-0.02, $t = 0.06$).

But Table AIV also shows that drawing a distinction between the results for 1941-1965 and 1966-1990 is misleading. The stronger tradeoff of average return for β in the simple regressions for 1941-1965 is due to the first 10 years, 1941-1950. This is the only period in Table AIV that produces an average premium for β (1.26% per month) that is both positive and more than 2 standard errors from 0. Conversely, the weak relation between β and average return for 1966-1990 is largely due to 1981-1990. The strong negative average slope in the univariate regressions of returns on β for 1981-1990 (-1.01, $t = -2.10$) offsets a positive slope for 1971-1980 (0.82, $t = 1.27$).

The subperiod variation in the average slopes from the FM regressions of returns on β alone seems moot, however, given the evidence in Table AIV that adding size always kills any positive tradeoff of average return for β in the subperiods. Adding size to the regressions for 1941-1965 causes the average slope for β to drop from 0.50 ($t = 1.82$) to 0.07 ($t = 0.28$). In contrast, the average slope on size in the bivariate regressions (-0.16, $t = -2.97$) is close to its value (-0.17, $t = -2.88$) in the regressions of returns on ln(ME) alone. Similar comments hold for 1941-1950. In short, any evidence of a positive average premium for β in the subperiods seems to be a size effect in disguise.

D. Can the SLB Model Be Saved?

Before concluding that β has no explanatory power, it is appropriate to consider other explanations for our results. One possibility is that the variation in β produced by the β sorts of size deciles in just sampling error. If so, it is not surprising that the variation in β within a size decile is unrelated to average return, or that size dominates β in bivariate tests. The standard errors of the βs suggest, however, that this explanation cannot save the SLB

Table AIII
Average Slopes, Their Standard Errors (SE), and Average Residuals from Monthly FM Regressions for Individual NYSE Stocks and for Portfolios Formed on Size and Pre-Ranking β: 1941–1990

Stocks are assigned the post-ranking β of the size-β portfolio they are in at the end of year $t-1$ (Table AII). ln(ME) is the natural log of price times shares outstanding at the end of year $t-1$. In the individual-stock regressions, these values of the explanatory variables are matched with CRSP returns for each of the 12 months in year t. The portfolio regressions match the equal-weighted portfolio returns for the size-β portfolios (Table AII) with the equal-weighted averages of β and ln(ME) for the surviving stocks in each month of year t. Slope is the time-series average of the monthly regression slopes from 1941–1990 (600 months); SE is the time-series standard error of the average slope.

The residuals from the monthly regressions in year t are grouped into 12 portfolios on the basis of size or pre-ranking β (estimated with 24 to 60 months of returns, as available) as of the end of year $t-1$. The average residuals are the time-series averages of the monthly equal-weighted averages of the residuals in percent. The average residuals (not shown) from the FM regressions (1) to (3) that use the returns on the 100 size-β portfolios as the dependent variable are always within 0.01 of those from the regressions for individual stock returns. This is not surprising given that the correlation between the time-series of 1941–1990 monthly FM slopes on β or ln(ME) for the comparable portfolio and individual stock regressions is always greater than 0.99.

	Portfolio Regressions				Individual Stock Regressions			
	(1) β	(2) ln(ME)	(3) β and ln(ME)		(4) β	(5) ln(ME)	(6) β and ln(ME)	
Slope	0.22	−0.128	−0.13	−0.143	0.24	−0.133	−0.14	−0.147
SE	0.24	0.043	0.21	0.039	0.23	0.043	0.21	0.039

Average Residuals for Stocks Grouped on Size

	1A	1B	2	3	4	5	6	7	8	9	10A	10B
Regression (4)	0.60	0.26	0.13	0.06	−0.01	−0.03	−0.03	−0.09	−0.10	−0.11	−0.25	−0.27
Standard error	0.21	0.10	0.06	0.04	0.04	0.04	0.04	0.04	0.04	0.05	0.06	0.08
Regression (5)	0.30	0.02	−0.05	−0.06	−0.08	−0.07	−0.03	−0.04	0.02	0.08	0.01	0.13
Standard error	0.14	0.07	0.04	0.04	0.04	0.04	0.04	0.03	0.03	0.03	0.04	0.07
Regression (6)	0.31	0.02	−0.05	−0.06	−0.09	−0.07	−0.03	−0.04	0.02	0.08	0.01	0.13
Standard error	0.14	0.07	0.04	0.04	0.04	0.04	0.04	0.03	0.03	0.03	0.04	0.07

Table AIII—Continued

Average Residuals for Stocks Grouped on Pre-Ranking β

	Portfolio Regressions			Individual Stock Regressions		
	(1) β	(2) ln(ME)	(3) β and ln(ME)	(4) β	(5) ln(ME)	(6) β and ln(ME)

	1A	1B	2	3	4	5	6	7	8	9	10A	10B
Regression (4)	−0.08	0.03	−0.01	0.08	0.04	0.08	0.04	0.02	−0.03	0.02	−0.11	−0.32
Standard error	0.07	0.05	0.03	0.03	0.03	0.03	0.04	0.04	0.04	0.04	0.06	0.07
Regression (5)	−0.10	0.00	0.02	0.09	0.05	0.07	0.05	0.00	−0.03	−0.01	−0.11	−0.33
Standard error	0.11	0.10	0.07	0.05	0.04	0.03	0.03	0.04	0.05	0.07	0.10	0.13
Regression (6)	−0.17	−0.07	−0.02	0.07	0.04	0.06	0.05	0.03	0.00	0.04	−0.04	−0.23
Standard error	0.05	0.04	0.03	0.03	0.03	0.03	0.03	0.03	0.04	0.04	0.06	0.07

Table AIV
Subperiod Average Returns on the NYSE Value-Weighted and Equal-Weighted Portfolios and Average Values of the Intercepts and Slopes for the FM Cross-Sectional Regressions of Individual Stock Returns on β and Size (ln(ME))

Mean is the average VW or EW return or an average slope from the monthly cross-sectional regressions of individual stock returns on β and/or ln(ME). Std is the standard deviation of the time-series of returns or slopes, and t(Mn) is Mean over its time-series standard error. The average slopes (not shown) from the FM regressions that use the returns on the 100 size-β portfolios of Table AII as the dependent variable are quite close to those for individual stock returns. (The correlation between the 1941–1990 month-by-month slopes on β or ln(ME) for the comparable portfolio and individual stock regressions is always greater than 0.99.)

Panel A

	1941–1990 (600 Mos.)			1941–1965 (300 Mos.)			1966–1990 (300 Mos.)		
Variable	Mean	Std	t(Mn)	Mean	Std	t(Mn)	Mean	Std	t(Mn)

NYSE Value-Weighted (VW) and Equal-Weighted (EW) Portfolio Returns

VW	0.93	4.15	5.49	1.10	3.58	5.30	0.76	4.64	2.85
EW	1.12	5.10	5.37	1.33	4.42	5.18	0.91	5.70	2.77

$$R_{it} = a + b_{1t}\beta_{it} + e_{it}$$

a	0.98	3.93	6.11	0.84	3.18	4.56	1.13	4.57	4.26
b_1	0.24	5.52	1.07	0.50	4.75	1.82	−0.02	6.19	−0.06

$$R_{it} = a + b_{2t}\ln(ME_{it}) + e_{it}$$

a	1.70	8.24	5.04	1.88	6.43	5.06	1.51	9.72	2.69
b_2	−0.13	1.06	−3.07	−0.17	1.01	−2.88	−0.10	1.11	−1.54

$$R_{it} = a + b_{1t}\beta_{it} + b_{2t}\ln(ME_{it}) + e_{it}$$

a	1.97	6.16	7.84	1.80	4.77	6.52	2.14	7.29	5.09
b_1	−0.14	5.05	−0.66	0.07	4.15	0.28	−0.34	5.80	−1.01
b_2	−0.15	0.96	−3.75	−0.16	0.94	−2.97	−0.13	0.99	−2.34

Table AIV—Continued

Panel B:

NYSE Value-Weighted (VW) and Equal-Weighted (EW) Portfolio Returns

Return	1941–1950 Mean	t(Mn)	1951–1960 Mean	t(Mn)	1961–1970 Mean	t(Mn)	1971–1980 Mean	t(Mn)	1981–1990 Mean	t(Mn)
VW	1.05	2.88	1.18	3.95	0.66	1.84	0.72	1.67	1.04	2.40
EW	1.59	3.16	1.13	3.76	0.88	1.96	1.04	1.82	0.95	2.01

$$R_{it} = a + b_{1t}\beta_{it} + e_{it}$$

a	0.24	0.66	1.41	6.36	0.64	1.94	0.27	0.62	2.35	5.99
b_1	1.26	2.20	−0.19	−0.63	0.32	0.72	0.82	1.27	−1.01	−2.10

$$R_{it} = a + b_{2t}\ln(ME_{it}) + e_{it}$$

a	2.63	3.47	1.08	2.73	1.78	2.50	2.18	2.03	0.82	1.20
b_2	−0.37	−2.90	0.03	0.53	−0.17	−2.19	−0.20	−1.57	0.04	0.57

$$R_{it} = a + b_{1t}\beta_{it} + b_{2t}\ln(ME_{it}) + e_{it}$$

a	2.14	3.93	1.38	4.03	2.01	4.16	1.50	2.12	2.84	4.25
b_1	0.34	0.75	−0.17	−0.53	−0.11	−0.27	0.41	0.75	−1.14	−2.16
b_2	−0.34	−2.92	0.01	0.20	−0.18	−2.89	−0.16	−1.50	−0.07	−0.84

model. The standard errors for portfolios formed on size and β are only slightly larger (0.02 to 0.11) than those for portfolios formed on size alone (0.01 to 0.10, Table AI). And the range of the post-ranking βs within a size decile is always large relative to the standard errors of the βs.

Another possibility is that the proportionality condition (1) for the variation through time in true βs, that justifies the use of full-period post-ranking βs in the FM tests, does not work well for portfolios formed on size and β. If this is a problem, post-ranking βs for the size-β portfolios should not be highly correlated across subperiods. The correlation between the half-period (1941–1965 and 1966–1990) βs of the size-β portfolios is 0.91, which we take to be good evidence that the full-period β estimates for these portfolios are informative about true βs. We can also report that using 5-year βs (pre- or post-ranking) in the FM regressions does not change our negative conclusions about the role of β in average returns, as long as portfolios are formed on β as well as size, or on β alone.

Any attempt to salvage the simple positive relation between β and average return predicted by the SLB model runs into three damaging facts, clear in Table AII. (a) Forming portfolios on size and pre-ranking βs produces a wide range of post-ranking βs in every size decile. (b) The post-ranking βs closely reproduce (in deciles 2 to 10 they exactly reproduce) the ordering of the pre-ranking βs used to form the β-sorted portfolios. It seems safe to conclude that the increasing pattern of the post-ranking βs in every size decile captures the ordering of the true βs. (c) Contrary to the SLB model, the β sorts do not produce a similar ordering of average returns. Within the rows (size deciles) of the average return matrix in Table AII, the high-β portfolios have average returns that are close to or less than the low-β portfolios.

But the most damaging evidence against the SLB model comes from the univariate regressions of returns on β in Table AIII. They say that when the tests allow for variation in β that is unrelated to size, the relation between β and average return for 1941–1990 is weak, perhaps nonexistent, even when β is the only explanatory variable. We are forced to conclude that the SLB model does not describe the last 50 years of average stock returns.

REFERENCES

Alford, Andrew, Jennifer J. Jones, and Mark E. Zmijewski, 1992, Extensions and violations of the statutory SEC Form 10-K filing date, Unpublished manuscript, University of Chicago, Chicago, IL.

Ball, Ray, 1978, Anomalies in relationships between securities' yields and yield-surrogates, *Journal of Financial Economics* 6, 103–126.

Banz, Rolf W., 1981, The relationship between return and market value of common stocks, *Journal of Financial Economics* 9, 3–18.

Basu, Sanjoy, 1983, The relationship between earnings yield, market value, and return for NYSE common stocks: Further evidence, *Journal of Financial Economics* 12, 129–156.

Bhandari, Laxmi Chand, 1988, Debt/Equity ratio and expected common stock returns: Empirical evidence, *Journal of Finance* 43, 507–528.

Black, Fischer, 1972, Capital market equilibrium with restricted borrowing, *Journal of Business* 45, 444–455.

———, Michael C. Jensen, and Myron Scholes, 1972, The capital asset pricing model: some empirical tests, in M. Jensen, ed.: *Studies in the Theory of Capital Markets* (Praeger).

Chan, Louis K., Yasushi Hamao, and Josef Lakonishok, 1991, Fundamentals and stock returns in Japan, *Journal of Finance* 46, 1739–1789.

Chan, K. C. and Nai-fu Chen, 1988, An unconditional asset-pricing test and the role of firm size as an instrumental variable for risk, *Journal of Finance* 43, 309–325.

———, and Nai-fu Chen, 1991, Structural and return characteristics of small and large firms, *Journal of Finance* 46, 1467–1484.

———, Nai-fu Chen, and David A. Hsieh, 1985, An exploratory investigation of the firm size effect, *Journal of Financial Economics* 14, 451–471.

Chen, Nai-fu, Richard Roll, and Stephen A. Ross, 1986, Economic forces and the stock market, *Journal of Business* 56, 383–403.

DeBondt, Werner F. M., and Richard H. Thaler, 1985, Does the stock market overreact, *Journal of Finance* 40, 557–581.

Dimson, Elroy, 1979, Risk measurement when shares are subject to infrequent trading, *Journal of Financial Economics* 7, 197–226.

Fama, Eugene F., 1976, *Foundations of Finance* (Basic Books, New York).

———, and James MacBeth, 1973, Risk, return and equilibrium: Empirical tests, *Journal of Political Economy* 81, 607–636.

Fowler, David J. and C. Harvey Rorke, 1983, Risk measurement when shares are subject to infrequent trading: Comment, *Journal of Financial Economics* 12, 279–283.

Jaffe, Jeffrey, Donald B. Keim, and Randolph Westerfield, 1989, Earnings yields, market values, and stock returns, *Journal of Finance* 44, 135–148.

Keim, Donald B., 1983, Size-related anomalies and stock return seasonality, *Journal of Financial Economics* 12, 13–32.

———, 1988, Stock market regularities: A synthesis of the evidence and explanations, in Elroy Dimson, ed.: *Stock Market Anomalies* (Cambridge University Press, Cambridge).

Lakonishok, Josef, and Alan C. Shapiro, 1986, Systematic risk, total risk and size as determinants of stock market returns, *Journal of Banking and Finance* 10, 115–132.

Lintner, John, 1965, The valuation of risk assets and the selection of risky investments in stock portfolios and capital budgets, *Review of Economics and Statistics* 47, 13–37.

Markowitz, Harry, 1959, *Portfolio Selection: Efficient Diversification of Investments* (Wiley, New York).

Merton, Robert C., 1973, An intertemporal capital asset pricing model, *Econometrica* 41, 867–887.

Reinganum, Marc R., 1981, A new empirical perspective on the CAPM, *Journal of Financial and Quantitative Analysis* 16, 439–462.

Roll, Richard, 1983, Vas ist Das? The turn-of-the-year effect and the return premia of small firms, *Journal of Portfolio Management* 9, 18–28.

Rosenberg, Barr, Kenneth Reid, and Ronald Lanstein, 1985, Persuasive evidence of market inefficiency, *Journal of Portfolio Management* 11, 9–17.

Ross, Stephen A., 1976, The arbitrage theory of capital asset pricing, *Journal of Economic Theory* 13, 341–360.

Sharpe, William F., 1964, Capital asset prices: a theory of market equilibrium under conditions of risk, *Journal of Finance* 19, 425–442.

Stambaugh, Robert F., 1982, On the exclusion of assets from tests of the two-parameter model: A sensitivity analysis, *Journal of Financial Economics* 10, 237–268.

Stattman, Dennis, 1980, Book values and stock returns, *The Chicago MBA: A Journal of Selected Papers* 4, 25–45.

V

FINANCIAL STATEMENT INFORMATION AND CORPORATE CONTROL

1 Myers, Stewart, "The Evaluation of an Acquisition Target," *Midland Corporate Finance Journal,* 4, Winter (1983), pp. 39–46.
2 Palepu, Krishna, "Predicting Takeover Targets: A Methodological and Empirical Analysis," *Journal of Accounting & Economics*, 8 (1986), pp. 3–35.
3 Kaplan, Steven N., "The Effects of Management Buyouts on Operations and Value," *Journal of Financial Economics,* 24 (1989), pp. 217–254.
4 Kaplan, Steven N., "Campeau's Acquisition of Federated: Value Destroyed or Added?," *Journal of Financial Economics*, 25 (1989), pp. 191–212.
5 Palepu, Krishna, "Consequences of Leveraged Buyouts," *Journal of Financial Economics*, 27 (1990), pp. 247–262.

The eighties heralded an unprecedented level of corporate control transactions. Billions of dollars' worth of control transactions including mergers, takeovers, acquisitions, and leveraged buyouts and corporate restructurings involving spinoffs, divestitures, and equity carveouts take place every year in America. These transactions are not limited only to small market-capitalization firms. In fact, the purchase price in many transactions individually exceeds one billion dollars. The multibillion-dollar leveraged buyout of RJR Nabisco suggests that virtually no firm in the economy is immune to the threat of a corporate control transaction. Financial analysts therefore cannot ignore the possibility of corporate control transactions, and their financial implications, in performing a valuation analysis of any firm.

To reduce the threat of takeovers, many corporations have built an elaborate takeover defense by adopting by-law and charter amendments. Since these amendments make corporate control transactions more costly to potential acquirers, and therefore corporate control changes less likely, they effectively make incumbent management's jobs more secure, potentially at the expense of the current shareholders. An entrenched management that is insulated from the corporate control disciplining mechanism is more likely to be inefficient than a firm exposed to the competitive corporate control market. The implication for shareholders of a firm with an entrenched management is that they are more likely to experience lower cash flows in the future due to management efficiencies. Perhaps more relevant to analysts' valuation, a firm with an antitakeover defense has forgone some of the value of the option of being taken over in the future. The current valuation of such a firm will be lower than that of an otherwise identical firm without an antitakeover defense. To correctly value the option of being taken over in the future requires forecasting the probability that individual firms will be takeover candidates. The forecast would be a function of the characteristics that make a firm an attractive takeover candidate [e.g., poor industry-adjusted performance, low leverage, and high free cash flow].

In the event of an actual corporate control transaction, the transacting parties make their own assessment of the market value of the corporate entity or its division. Valuation analysis in the context of a corporate transaction is a bit trickier than under normal circumstances. Valuation must not be based just on the current fundamentals of a company; more importantly, an analyst must factor in the financial implications of the corporate control transaction taking place. For example, effects of changes in investment and operating decisions, effects of changes in leverage on tax payments, potential financial distress costs arising from increased leverage, synergistic benefits of mergers and acquisitions, etc., must be incorporated in projecting cash flows for the future, thereby affecting valuation. Indeed, Jensen and Ruback (1983) report that target shareholders have on average earned a 30 to 40 percent takeover premium. Assuming acquirers, on average, do not over- or underpay for the targets, the takeover premium reflects the present value of the forecasted change in the target's fundamentals as a result of the takeover. The rise in a target's stock price (i.e., the takeover premium) in anticipation of better than previously expected fundamentals indicates that the information set in prices is richer than that in a firm's current fundamentals. Consistent with this idea, the evidence summarized in the readings included in Part I suggests that prices anticipate firms' future earnings performance as many as three years in advance.

Myers (1983) provides some very useful suggestions to those interested in valuing an acquisition target. He discusses the importance of identifying the stream of net benefits (cash flows) from a merger, valuing these benefits, the relevant discount rate applicable in valuing the benefits, and valuing real options. **Myers (1983)** suggests that considerable effort must be exerted in identifying the net synergistic benefits of a merger and valuing these benefits, rather than attempting to value the target firm as a whole. The present value of these net benefits would then be the upper bound on the takeover premium the acquirer would be willing to pay to the target shareholders. Caution should, however, be exercised to avoid overpaying for the target because the target's current price may very well reflect a portion of the present value of these benefits. If a takeover is much anticipated in the marketplace, then much of the synergistic benefits and efficiency improvements may have been anticipated by the market. If the present value of net benefits is added on to the current price as the takeover premium, then the acquirer would be overpaying for the target. Nevertheless, **Myers (1983)** offers the sensible recommendation to not acquire another firm unless there are easily identifiable benefits from acquiring a target that cannot be realized without a merger. Financial valuation of a target without any clear benefits from acquisition will often incorrectly indicate that the target is underpriced. Besides, one can easily invest in an underpriced stock and derive the benefits, rather than expend resources to acquire the firm to capture the same benefits.

Firms that are takeover targets generally have certain characteristics that distinguish those firms from the nontarget firms. Since target shareholders receive a substantial takeover premium, there naturally is considerable interest in accurately identifying potential targets prior to their takeover announcements. **Palepu (1986)** reexamines the claim in previous literature that acquisition targets can be predicted accurately using publicly available data six to twelve months prior to the takeover announcements. As with the bankruptcy prediction models examined in Part IV of this book, **Palepu (1986)** concludes that the predictive ability of takeover target prediction models is no better than that of the stock market. In particular, he reports that a strategy of investing in firms identified to be potential targets fails to beat the market. Target prediction models are nevertheless useful in identifying a broad set of potential takeover candidates that analysts and takeover specialists can analyze in detail to decide on the subset of firms to acquire.

The next three papers in this part focus on leveraged corporate control transactions, i.e., debt-financed acquisitions, management buyouts, and leveraged buyouts. Leveraged corporate control transactions became common in the eighties, with acquirers, on average, paying a premium in excess of 40 percent of the target's pre-acquisition equity market value. Despite their popularity in recent years, leveraged corporate control transactions have sparked a controversy among academics, practitioners, and politicians about their economic consequences. In particular, critics of the leveraged transactions argue that the takeover premium largely reflects redistribution of wealth from taxpayers and employees to target shareholders [e.g., Shliefer and Summers (1988)]. In contrast, Jensen (1986, 1989), one of the ardent proponents of leveraged transactions, suggests these transactions result in superior operating and investment decisions because post-buyout managers have strong incentives to undertake wealth-enhancing actions and reduce wasteful negative net present value investments.

In a careful study of the post-buyout performance of a large sample of management buyouts, **Kaplan (1989a)** describes the sources of wealth gains to target shareholders. He reports substantial increases in operating income and net cash flows from the pre- to the post-buyout periods. These increases are adjusted for industry performance. Management buyouts are also associated with cutbacks in capital expenditures, but the change in employment is positive, though only 0.9 percent. Thus, evidence in **Kaplan (1989a)** strongly supports the Jensen (1989) view that leveraged transactions improve operating and investment performance, and thereby create wealth. Evidence consistent with the wealth-transfer hypothesis is limited because employment does not decline and changes in tax liabilities do not fully explain the wealth gains from leveraged transactions. In particular, even though an increased interest-expense tax shield is a source of value in leveraged transactions, it constitutes only a small fraction of the total wealth change, and once increases in many other tax payments are accounted for, the net effect on tax revenues may be positive, not negative.

Kaplan (1989b) is a case study of a leveraged acquisition of Federated Department Stores by Campeau Corporation that apparently went awry even though evidence suggests that the acquisition resulted in a substantial value increase. **Kaplan (1989b)** argues that Campeau overestimated the future cash flows and thus overpaid for the acquisition of Federated, but since the deal was almost entirely debt-financed, *ex post* Campeau defaulted on payments to debtholders and ended in bankruptcy courts. Post-buyout value nevertheless was more than a billion dollars in excess of the pre-buyout value, which means the leveraged transaction was value-increasing. The wealth transfer was largely from debtholders to the Federated shareholders since Campeau overpaid for the acquisition using debt financing.

Palepu (1990) provides an excellent summary of the various issues surrounding leveraged buyout transactions. In particular, he discusses arguments of the critics and proponents of leveraged corporate control transactions and summarizes the empirical evidence from various studies of leveraged transactions.

The Berkeley Conference

The Evaluation of an Acquisition Target

Stewart Myers,
Massachusetts Institute of Technology

Over the past two days, we have been talking about mergers in two different senses. At times, we have put our scientific hat on, and tried to develop some theory which would explain what's really going on. At other times we've concentrated on the institutional or practical side. Most of my talk will be concerned with this practical side. But, just for a moment, let's keep our scientific hat on and remember that the list of things we actually know about mergers is pretty short. We know that sellers win; we know that buyers—at least buying stockholders—win sometimes and lose sometimes, but probably not very much in either direction on average. We know that merger activity is volatile. I could go on for a little while, but it still would be a relatively short list. On the other hand, the list of the things we don't know about mergers is probably sufficient to fill up a two-and-a-half-day conference. But, fortunately, not this one.

Occasionally, though, there is a little flash of insight that comes through. I want to tell you about a flash that came to me last Fall when I spent a day as a token academic at a roundtable populated mostly by high-priced merger lawyers, anti-trust people from Washington, and investment bankers who were big in the merger business. This was right after the Bendix-Martin Marietta-Allied brouhaha; and that takeover battle, along with similar kinds of fun and games, was the main topic of conversation all day. I kept trying to put up my hand and say, "Yeah, those are interesting cases but, remember, Mike Bradley and Rick Ruback have shown that mergers, *on average*, benefit buying as well as selling companies stockholders." But they just weren't interested in the averages. And it finally came to me that, in mergers, the ratio of "noise" to "signal" is very high, and that the noise is a helluva lot more fun. All of the things that make Bendix interesting are noise and not signal. They're idiosyncratic things that happen in a particular case, once people get into it, and once people start trying to win.

As we move back to the subject of this talk and take the manager's point of view, I think that the lesson about noise and signal is really very important. If we pose the problem as one of valuing a merger candidate, what you want to do is find the signal and avoid the noise. The great danger is that you start out trying to be rational and end up as a noisemaker. What you'd like to do is get a net reduction in noise, but I'm afraid that some analyses lead to a net increase. People start out trying to be rational but they end up making mistakes in the analysis: they end up getting carried away in the heat of the battle, and they lose the kind of rationality, the kind of power, that financial analysis can bring to this kind of a problem. As Pogo used to say, "We've met the enemy and he is us."

Now if I were faced with the problem of evaluating a merger candidate, armed with that warning, armed with the idea that I wanted to do everything possible to make sure that I don't end up creating more noise than I eliminate, I would want to arm myself with some pretty clear rules. I would want to impose some discipline on myself. I would want to set up a structure that ensures that I ask the right questions. And I think that's the secret of it all: ask the right questions, don't make mistakes, and get the answer approximately right.

I'm going to start out by talking about how to define benefits and costs. That may seem to be a pedestrian thing to do, but I personally think it's critical. Because if you define the benefits and costs correctly, you end up asking the right questions. Next, I will talk about how to *value* the benefits that may come out of a merger. The main point I'm making here is that the benefits, the incremental cash flows, that come out of merger are of different types. The stream is not just one pure flow, but a mixture of different flows; and the best way to value those flows is to look at the different types and try to value them separately. The phrase that my colleague Don Lessard has been using lately is "valuation by components." That is, you break up the total stream into similar pieces, and then evaluate each of the pieces

If you assume that the valuation of a merger target is simply another discounted cash flow calculation, you're effectively ignoring some very valuable information.

separately. When you do break them up, you will see that the evaluation techniques you use for each of these three categories is different.

The Benefits and Costs of Merger

The first thing, then, is to define benefits and costs. Let's begin with a simple illustration, and suppose that a Firm A, which has a value V_A, wants to acquire a Firm B, with a value V_B. I want to define the benefits of the merger as the *gain in value from putting these two firms together.* In other words, I'm going to compare the value of the combined firm, V_{AB}, with the sum of what the two firms are worth separately. That difference is what we normally think of as the present value of expected synergy—the value of whatever it is that makes the two firms worth more together than apart.

If we define the benefit purely in terms of the expected synergy, then we have to define the cost as the *value given up by A's shareholders to B's shareholders*. I would measure this economic cost as the price paid for B minus V_B, where V_B is what the target is worth as a separate organization. For example, if it is a merger for cash, you would simply take the amount of cash and subtract what you think B is worth standing alone.

It is possible, of course, that A could pay less than the value of B (if B were significantly undervalued) to acquire its assets. In such a case, even if the expected gains from synergy were zero, we could still have a rationale for a merger. That is, even if the firms are not worth more together than apart, A's stockholders can still come out ahead if you're able to strike a deal at B's expense, get B for less than it's worth. In this case, the "cost" of the merger would be negative.

Let me pause here to say that my definitions and classifications of benefits and costs probably seem to complicate things needlessly. So let me explain why I like to do it this way. First of all, on the benefits side, the exercise of calculating the benefits from merger is important because it forces management to ask the right question. It forces them to ask whether the two firms really are worth more together than apart. It forces you to look at the synergy "incrementally," so to speak; it forces you to identify the addition to economic value.

For example, let's suppose that the rationale for the merger is that the firm wants to enter a new business and believes it may be cheaper to do so by buying a going concern rather than starting from scratch. If we define and segregate the expected benefits this way, it more or less forces the manager to ask, "How much would it cost us to enter that new line of business from scratch? If we went ahead with the merger and bought a going concern, how much more would we have to put into that going concern to get where we want to be? How much will we end up saving by buying the going concern?"

The second reason for recommending this approach is that it takes the existing values of the firm as a starting point for the analysis. It's often said that merger analysis is just another capital investment problem. In a sense that's absolutely true. But I personally don't like to say that because I think it gives the wrong impression. Merger analysis is different from standard capital budgeting in at least one very important way. The market gives you starting values for the pieces. And if you assume that the valuation of a merger target is simply another discounted cash flow calculation, you're effectively ignoring some very valuable information.

In fact, this point is so important that I'm going to digress even a little further on it. One of the problems with the MBAs that we send out into the world is their almost Pavlovian reliance on discounted cash flow. You tell them, "How much is this worth?" And they say, "Aha, value equals discounted cash flow. Let's project the cash flows. Tell me what the beta is, tell me what the discount rate is. Calculate NPV. Stop." There are lots of cases in which that's the worst thing you can do, lots of cases where you should try to restrict the application of discounted cash flows to only those parts of the problem where you really need it.

Let me give you a trivial example. Let's suppose that we were told that gold had been discovered (and only we knew this) under some piece of Weyerhaeuser timberland. And that we're sort of scribbling around in the back room of some investment banking house, trying to figure out what the value of Weyerhaeuser will be when news of that gold discovery comes out.

Now there's two different basic approaches you could take. One approach (and this is the one I have in mind when I think of the Pavlovian reliance on discounted cash flow) would be just to start from scratch and say, "Okay, the problem is to value Weyerhaeuser, which happens to have this gold deposit." So you start with an analysis of the lumber business and the paper business and everything else they do.

The inadequacy of DCF becomes especially apparent in cases offering "real" options.

You try to forecast capital expenditures, forecast everything under the sun, including how much it's going to take to develop the gold mine, how many ounces you're going to get out of it, etc. In so doing, you come up with some forecast of free cash flow for Weyerhaeuser. Finally you discount these cash flows using risk-adjusted estimates of cost of capital, and you come up with a number. Let's call that the "start from scratch" approach.

The second approach would be to start with what Weyerhaeuser is actually worth, which we can look up in the paper, and then just do an incremental analysis of the gold business. As a matter of fact, we might not even have to do a discounted cash flow analysis of how much that gold deposit is worth. We might be able get people who are really expert in the gold business to say, "With these chemical characteristics, that depth, and so on, we know that people in general are willing to pay so many dollars per ounce of recoverable gold," and thereby come up with a number in a process that doesn't ever use a discount rate. In any event, if we did use discounting and a discount rate, we'd apply it to the gold deposit separately and we'd add that to the observed market value of Weyerhaeuser. I call that the "incremental" approach.

Now which do you think would be likely to give you more accurate answers, the "incremental" approach or the "start from scratch" approach? Most of you, I hope, would vote for the incremental approach. It seems to me that there are really two separate issues. One, what is that gold deposit worth? We can think of the gold deposit as analogous to the value of synergy in the evaluation of an acquisition target. The second question would be: Is the market making a mistake about Weyerhaeuser?

The purpose of my approach is to separate those two questions. If the market is indeed making a mistake about Weyerhaeuser, and we're going to take it over, it would be appropriate to look at that when we're trying to figure out the cost of the takeover.

What I see happen more often than I'd like, however, is the situation where people just merge these two questions. Suppose we're going to take over Weyerhaeuser, and we make no attempt to separate these two issues. Essentially what you're doing is just to "start from scratch" in valuing the company. You throw in the analysis of the synergy together with the analysis of whether the market is right about Weyerhaeuser. Trouble is, you're going to make random errors in analyzing what Weyerhaeuser is worth as a separate business. Since that separate business is so much bigger than our gold deposit, or so much bigger than the synergy we might get out of a merger, your estimate of the incremental value of the gold deposit to Weyerhaeuser is going to be "swamped" by the errors in analyzing Weyerhaeuser as it exists.

To repeat, then, my suggested approach is designed to force people to focus on the synergies first, to focus on the incremental benefits, and then weigh those benefits against the incremental costs of the deal.

Valuing the Benefits of Merger

Let's now talk for a while about valuing the benefits. I'm not going to go down a list of the sources of possible merger benefits. Instead I'm just going to give you three possible motives to illustrate the threefold classification of cash flow benefits that I think can be useful in merger analysis.

Let's suppose that your motive for a merger is to make use of a tax-loss carryforward you couldn't use otherwise. A good example of this is one of my favorite companies, Penn Central, which is now a healthy, reorganized company. It is sitting with about a billion dollars of tax-loss carryforwards. To nobody's surprise, Penn Central has been out shopping for companies that are paying lots of taxes.

If that's the benefit you're seeking, tax savings, then you have a relatively simple problem in valuation. Tax savings generally turn out to be relatively safe, nominal flows. I don't mean to imply always, but when you think of something like the cash benefit of a depreciation tax shield you could not otherwise use, that is a relatively safe, nominal flow. I am calling such expected flows "debt equivalents," and such relatively safe, relatively certain nominal flows are fairly easy to value. If such flows are an important source of value in a prospective merger, they should be split off, put in a separate category.

The next category of merger benefits, operating cash flows, might come from, say, economies of scale. If there are economies of scale, the synergy benefits generated would be reflected in production cost savings. Those cost savings are real flows subject to business risks, and it's these kinds of uncertain or risky flows that we want to use our standard discounted cash flow technique to value.

A third motive might be growth opportunities provided by merger that you couldn't get otherwise: some intangible, some strategic advantage. Such op-

Managers don't always have a very good sense of what normal rates of return really are.

portunities do not promise a cash flow of the same kind that comes out of an established product or an established business. Instead, these growth opportunities are contingent on a lot of things and, in a rough way, have many of the qualities of options. The inadequacy of DCF becomes especially apparent in cases offering "real" options like these. My experience is that when people try to use discounted cash flow to value these kinds of intangible assets, these kinds of contingent flows, they generally don't get it right. They don't get it right for the same reason that you wouldn't get very far if you naively tried to value a call option using a discounted cash flow approach.

Valuing the Debt Equivalents

So what I propose to do now, in the next 10 or 15 minutes, is to go quickly through each category and just make a few comments. Let's take the "debt equivalent" flows first. If you really do have a flow that's safe and nominal (by "safe" we don't mean absolutely certain, but roughly as predictable as the payment of interest on a corporate bond), then you would simply discount that flow at the after-tax borrowing or lending rate. Whether you use the borrowing or lending rate depends upon exactly which question you ask, and I'll return to that shortly. The rationale is this: let's suppose that we have a safe, nominal inflow—cash coming in as a result, say, of being able to use a depreciation tax shield or investment tax credit that we would not otherwise be able to use. We could ask: How much could the firm borrow today if it used that inflow for debt service? The answer to that question can be obtained by discounting that inflow at the company's after-tax borrowing rate. It's as simple as that.

We could also ask the question in a slightly different way. How much would I have to spend to get this same inflow if I wanted to lend money to do it? In a way the logic is equivalent. You're simply changing the base point that you do your calculation from. In the first case, you're assuming you have the flow and are asking, "How much could I cash it in for?" In the second case you're thinking of the reproduction cost, in a sense, of that cash flow. If the cash flow was safe, nominal, but maybe a little bit risky, then this second one might be the more appropriate method. This way you could assume, "Well, I'll lend it with the same degree of risk as the cash flow itself." So, depending upon how you ask the question, you could use either the after-tax borrowing or the after-tax lending rate to value the expected inflows.

Now, suppose instead we wanted to value an outflow. Again you could ask the question in two ways. You could ask, "How much would I have to set aside today to cover the outflow?" In this case, it would be like having a liability and then setting up a sinking fund or an escrow account to—I believe the word is—"defease" the liability. In other words, just to cancel it out so you don't have to worry about it any more. In that instance, you'd end up calculating the present value of that outflow using the after-tax lending rate. On the other hand, you could ask, "How much could I borrow today if the outflow were available for debt service?" In that case you'd think about it in terms of a borrowing rate.

This last question, you may recognize, is exactly the logic that people use to analyze financial leases. If you're thinking about signing a lease contract, you want to calculate the value of the cash obligations, of that series of future outflows to which you're obligated if you sign. Then you say to yourself, "Suppose I don't sign the lease contract. How much could I borrow today if those flows were available for debt service?" In leasing terminology, that amount is called the "equivalent loan." Now the rule in leasing is that, with a given set of future cash obligations, if you could borrow more by an equivalent loan through regular channels than you could get with a financial lease, then you might as well borrow. On the other hand, if the lease is giving you more money up front than you could get through regular channels, given the same future outflows, then you take the lease.

Valuing Operating Flows

This sort of analysis breaks down when flows get risky, because we can't set up a clean, hypothetical transaction to either cash in the future value or to cover it in some way by borrowing or lending. This leads to my next topic: the evaluation of risky, operating cash flows. What do you do there? Well, that's the hard one. We know just enough about the problem to make it complicated. I'm not going to go into all the complications, but I thought I'd offer a few observations.

The first tip I'd have is that managers don't always have a very good sense of what normal rates of return really are. You hear the most outlandish numbers quoted as cost of capital estimates. So, if any of

**TABLE 1
Rates of Return on Corporate Government Securities 1926–1981**

Series	Arithmetic Means of Annual Returns	Standard Deviation of Annual Returns
Common Stocks	11.4	21.9
Small Stocks	18.1	37.3
Long-Term Government Bonds	3.1	5.7
Long-Term Corporate Bonds	3.6	5.6
US Treasury Bills	3.1	3.1
Consumer Price Index	3.0	3.1
Risk Premia on Common Stocks	8.3	22.0
Maturity Premia on Long-Term Gov't. Bonds	0.2	6.5
Default Premia on Long-Term Corp. Bonds	0.5	3.2
Real Interest Rates	0.1	4.5

Source: Roger G. Ibbotson and Rex A. Sinquefield, *Stocks, Bonds, Bills, and Inflation. The Past and the Future*, 1982 Edition, Financial Analysts Research Federation, Charlottesville, VA.

your companies are thinking about going on a program of buying other companies, one of the first things I think you ought to do is to educate yourself about what's a reasonable required rate of return on corporate investment.

Fortunately, we do have some useful historical information on corporate rates of return. I'm going to show you two sets of charts. The first one, which is probably familiar to a lot of people, comes from Roger Ibbotson and Rex Sinquefield's computations of rates of returns on corporate stocks, bonds, and government bonds and bills.

The only way you're going to get a reliable estimate of normal rates of return from historical evidence is to look at a very long time period. Ibbotson and Sinquefield's results are based on returns that go back to 1926 and run up through 1981. Over this period, the mean risk premium on common stocks (their average excess return over risk-free Treasury bills) has been 8.3 percent. If you calculate this premium over the post-war period alone—which many people are more comfortable with—you get virtually the same answer. If you do it for much shorter periods, you get answers all over the place. But these have no statistical significance.

To get an estimate of normal, *nominal* rates of return on common stocks at any given time, it's not at all a bad rule of thumb to take this historical risk premium and add it to some measure of the current risk-free rate of interest. For example, let's suppose we want to know what investors expect today to earn on a market portfolio of common stocks. Presumably we'd want to take advantage of our knowledge of what interest rates are today. The risk-free rate of interest today [March 23, 1983] is about 10 percent. That's above current Treasury bill yields, but because I'm assuming we'd be using this number to evaluate investments promising longer-lived cash flows, I'm using a medium-term government obligation instead.

So, you've got a 10 percent risk-free rate plus about 8 percent as a general market-wide risk premium. That gives you a normal or expected rate of return on common stocks of about 18 percent. And I don't think that's a bad number. The reason I'm giving you these numbers, again, is that people quote numbers like 30 percent without thinking about it. The Ibbotson-Sinquefield averages are a kind of antidote to people who throw crazy numbers around.

But there are a few intermediate steps before these data can be applied directly as a hurdle rate in merger analysis. The stock market returns reflected in Ibbotson and Sinquefield's numbers are computed using the Standard & Poor's composite index. Thus, the 8 percent risk premium I just showed you would apply only to assets with the same risk as the average company trading in the stock market. Also, we know that this number does not simply reflect operating or business risk. Because companies in the market on average have debt, that market risk premium of 8 percent also reflects some financial risk.

Now, when you're evaluating a merger candidate, and you want to establish the minimum required rate of return on your investment, you want to begin by looking at business risk alone. You want to look only at what's coming out of the *operations* of the company, and exclude the effects of financing. So as a first step we want to ask: how do you remove

**TABLE 2
Long Run After-Tax
Real Rates of Return
on Capital**

National Income Accounts	1926–1981	1946–1981
All Nonfinancial Corporations (NCFs).	6.5%	6.7%
All NFCs: Assets expanded to include land and net noninterest-berating monetary liabilities.	—	5.2%
All manufacturing corporations	—	7.7%
Capital Market Data		1947–1981
All NCFs	—	5.8%
All manufacturing	—	8.7%

Source: D.M. Holland and S.C. Myers, "Profitability and Capital Costs for Manufacturing Corporations and all Nonfinancial Corporations." *American Economic Review*, May 1980. Averages updated through 1981.

the effect of financial risk from the observed market risk premium? One way you can try to do that is by constructing a *portfolio* of all the securities of U.S. corporations, stocks and bonds, and then calculate the average rate of return earned on that portfolio over a long period of time. You take all the securities issued to finance corporate assets. The return on that portfolio has to be equal to the return on those assets from the point of view of the investors who hold those assets by holding corporate securities.

Dan Holland and I have constructed such a portfolio. Here are the numbers you get over the post-war period. From 1946–1981, the mean *real* rate of return on the securities of all non-financial corporations was 5.8 percent. This number, again, is a weighted average of rates of return on corporate bonds and corporate stocks, where the weightings are designed to get a portfolio which matches, as closely as possible, the underlying assets of the companies. If we split out the manufacturing corporations from the entire sample, you get a number that's 2 to 3 percent points higher, about 8.7 percent. (Incidentally, the reason why the manufacturing corporations appear to have a higher rate of return is that they're riskier. Their profits are much more sensitive to the business cycle than the profits of the larger aggregate, which includes not just manufacturing, but industries like utilities and retail trade, transportation, services, and so on.)

So, if you take 6 percent as a good estimate of the normal *real* rate of return on corporate assets in the aggregate, then to get the *nominal* rate of return today you'd have to add your own long-term forecast of inflation—say, 6 to 7 percent? If it's 6 to 7 percent, you are talking today about an expected nominal rate of return on assets of 12 to 13 percent for the average company—and, say, 15 percent for the average manufacturing firm.

In addition to our calculations, and Ibbotson and Sinquefield's data, we also have one other source of data on historical corporate rates of return available to us. This is the National Income Accounts, which are compiled by the Department of Commerce. Using all its elaborate machinery, the Department of Commerce has calculated after-tax *accounting* rates of return (on an inflation-adjusted basis) for all non-financial corporations going back to 1926.

Let me just mention some of these numbers. Over the period 1926–1981, the average real rate of return (after corporate taxes) on assets for all non-financial corporations has been about 6.5 percent. Over the post-war period, that number was 6.7 percent. These results are actually a little bit high because the published definition of capital does not include things like land and net trade credit—assets necessary to run a business, but which for some historical reason are not included in capital stock as the Department of Commerce measures it. To adjust for this problem, Dan Holland and I got some approximate estimates of the value of land, of net trade credit, and of non-interest-bearing monetary liabilities, and we added that extra capital to the denominator in the rate of return calculation. This addition to the capital base tends to knock the estimates down by about one-and-a-half percent.

While these estimates may be somewhat controversial, the important thing here is that we have two numbers (6.7 and 5.2 percent) which bracket, and thus reinforce, the 6 percent estimate we get from capital market data. If we do the same calculation for just manufacturing corporations, we get about 7.7 percent, which is close to the estimate of 8.7 percent we got from capital market data. (But that calculation does not include the land and non-interest bearing monetary liabilities, so that's undoubtedly an overstatement.) But, again, what I find

Anytime somebody leverages up an asset, but then doesn't also adjust its discount rate, the investment always looks better than it is.

very interesting is that if you compare these two completely independent sets of data, you get just about the same number. In other words, somebody who wanted to judge normal, inflation-adjusted corporate rates of return by measuring aggregate profitability as an accountant would measure it would come out somewhere around 6 percent for all corporations, and 7 to 8 percent for the smaller aggregate of manufacturing corporations. When you do the same calculation using returns on stocks and bonds, again you get roughly 6 to 8 percent real returns.

So, if somebody asked me, "Quick, what is the cost of capital?," I would say that, on the basis of historical evidence, the average, overall *real* cost of capital seems to be 6 to 8 percent, depending on the risk of the assets you're talking about. Obviously there are some assets in the economy which are safer than average and, therefore, would require less than 6 percent. Some no doubt are much riskier, and they should be required to return more than 8 percent.

But, having said this, let me just mention some of the other problems we run into in arriving at required rates of return for specific investments. Even if you have some sense about what normal rates of return are—whether from Ibbotson and Sinquefield, current interest rates, or the accounting rates of return I just showed you—you still have to worry about adjusting for risk. And there, of course, you can get very fancy. You can try to compute industry betas. You can try to look at the cyclicality or variance of the asset's return, and thus try to get proxies for the betas of the assets you're looking at. But, even if you do know how to measure and adjust for risk, you've got a variety of risk-return theories to choose among. You could use the standard capital asset pricing model (CAPM), or maybe some so-called empirical capital asset pricing model that adjusts for the fact that low beta stocks have done better, at least over the very long run, than the standard CAPM would have predicted. You could, I suppose, go to some arbitrage pricing theory, although I don't think that's much help at this point in this kind of calculation. And we could also end up arguing about "small firm" effects; that is, do small deserve a higher cost of capital? We can't answer any of these questions with complete assurance at this point.

Another thing I think is important in merger analysis is not to confuse return on equity with return on assets. One famous case where I understand this happened was Kennecott's takeover of Carborundum. According to some of the documents that later came out publicly, one of the things that Kennecott's analysts did was this: they had internal forecasts for Carborundum which showed cash flows, earnings, etc. over a 10-year period. But, before they actually did the present value calculation, they assumed that after Kennecott bought Carborundum, Carborundum would borrow (I believe it was) $100 million. Carborundum was then assumed to take the cash thus raised, and pay it back as a special dividend to Kennecott, the new parent. For purposes of calculating NPV, that dividend was assumed to reduce Kennecott's investment in Carborundum. They then applied a standard discount rate to get an NPV and they got what seemed to be a number justifying the price they paid.

But what they did in effect was to lever up the cash flow without raising the discount rate to reflect the increased leverage. Kennecott was really borrowing the money to buy the business. Thus, they were looking at a more leveraged asset than was there before. In so doing, they were jacking up the promised rate of return, but they forgot to jack up the discount rate. And therefore the investment looked good. It was a kind of "magic in leverage" argument. Anytime somebody leverages up an asset, but then doesn't also adjust its discount rate, the investment always looks better than it is. Simple things like that can turn out to be very important.

Valuing Real Options

I'm getting a little bit short on time, so let me skip back and make a comment or two on the third category of benefits: the evaluation of growth opportunities. This is the really tough one. The reason it's tough is that typically when a decision about a merger has to be made, after you've gone through and valued all the debt equivalents and operating flows, you're still likely to be faced with the following question: Do the intangibles or future opportunities that I can't put a number on justify the price I've got to pay?

So what are future opportunities worth? To my mind that's one of the greatest growth areas in the finance field. But it's an area, at the moment, where we can't go very far beyond saying they're like options, in principle, and therefore we ought to be able to value them with the same tools. I think in practice what people do when they are faced with this decision is one of two things. First, they may look at a

> *Obviously one of those markets was going to be wrong. But it wasn't clear to me why people leaped to the assumption that it had to be the stock market.*

sample of comparable companies to infer the value the market is placing on such opportunities. Often, however, the search for comparable projects or firms with publicly available market values is difficult, if not impossible. And in such cases, companies must resort finally to calling in their strategy people—or strategy consultants—to see whether the strategic case for the merger is sufficient to justify the price.

Undervaluation as a Motive for Merger

Now, I want to touch on one last issue, a most interesting one and a good one to end with. When is Firm A justified in buying firm B only because the target appears to be a bargain? I have four comments here. First, think back to our "start from scratch" analysis of Weyerhaeuser. I guarantee you that even the best discounted cash flow analysis of Weyerhaeuser or any other company is going to produce random errors. If I do an evaluation of a sample of companies in order to figure out which one is a bargain, and I do it right, then I know beforehand that half of them will appear to be bargains after I finish. In some cases I will be making a positive error and in other cases a negative error. And even if I take the one out of my sample which appears to be the greatest bargain, I still don't know whether that's a random error or not. That's trap number one.

Sometimes people say, "Well, it has to be a bargain because the company can be liquidated for more than its market price." Again I'm cautious for two reasons: one is that it isn't easy to liquidate a big company; and by the time you go through the process of getting it liquidated, you may not end up with as much cash as it looked at first glance you could get out of it.

Second, in cases like that, what you're often doing is just forcing yourself to make a choice between two market prices. At the time people were saying that all the oil companies were undervalued by the stock market, they were comparing prices of companies in the stock market with (estimates of) the price of oil in another market; namely, the price for oil deposits. Now, obviously one of those markets was going to be wrong. But it wasn't clear to me why people leaped to the assumption that it had to be the stock market. Right now it appears that the stock market was right. (But it's probably not fair to rely so much on hindsight here.)

One final point, and this is the one that, I think, clinches the argument. If you really thought there were no synergistic benefits to a merger but that you had found a bargain, you could get a lot more mileage out of that bargain by just buying the shares as a passive investor rather than paying a premium to take the firm over.

Concluding Comment

Finally, just by way of summing up: I suppose I tend to approach merger analysis from a very conservative point of view. I'm demanding to be shown that the merger generates some positive net benefits before I would give it my imprimatur. But I think this is really a very conservative approach, perhaps even too conservative. A company which comes to mind is Seagrams—not Seagrams when it finally made the offer for Conoco, but Seagrams over the two or three years prior to that. It had gotten the cash from selling off its previous oil properties, and announced that it was going to use that cash to buy another company. So it set out in a rational way to find the company that made the most economic sense.

The revealing thing was that I honestly think they tried hard to be rational and careful and conservative. They did not let themselves get carried away with these kinds of biases I've been inveighing against. But, it took them two or three years to make a major move, which was finally to go after Conoco. So, when you think about what I have been saying, if you were really going to adopt my approach and demand proof of positive benefits before you went ahead, you could see it would be hard to justify many mergers—particularly considering the price you have to pay in today's market.

QUESTION: Are you suggesting, then, that the price is irrelevant, and that the most important criterion for good acquisitions is, say, the strategic fit?

MYERS: I've never understood those words, "good fit." But maybe it refers to the strategic opportunities. They are very hard to value by discounted cash flow. If that's what "good fit" means, and if you truly have one, it may override the kinds of benefit calculations that you can put numbers on. But, the attempt to quantify the value of such opportunities should be made; and, as I suggested earlier, we are making some progress in learning how to value these strategic opportunities.

To return to the first part of your question, however, I don't think anybody would ever say—at least I hope they wouldn't—that the price is irrelevant.

PREDICTING TAKEOVER TARGETS

A Methodological and Empirical Analysis

Krishna G. PALEPU*

Harvard University, Boston, MA 02163, USA

Received January 1985, final version received August 1985

Several published studies claim that acquisition targets can be accurately predicted by models using public data. This paper points out a number of methodological flaws which bias the results of these studies. A fresh empirical study is carried out after correcting these methodological flaws. The results show that it is difficult to predict targets, indicating that the prediction accuracies reported by the earlier studies are overstated. The methodological issues addressed in this paper are also relevant to other research settings that involve binary state prediction models with skewed distribution of the two states of interest.

1. Introduction

A number of empirical studies have attempted to construct statistical models using publicly available financial information to predict acquisition targets. These include Simkowitz and Monroe (1971), Stevens (1973), Castagna and Matolcsy (1976), Belkoui (1978), and Dietrich and Sorensen (1984). The results reported by these studies indicate that such models have impressive ability to predict acquisition targets six to twelve months before the announcement of takeovers. For example, Simkowitz and Monroe report that their multiple discriminant model correctly predicts 83% of the targets and 72% of the non-targets in the sample used in estimating the model, and 64% of the targets and 61% of the non-targets in a holdout sample. The other studies report prediction accuracies ranging from 70% to 90%.

In contrast to the predictive ability claimed by the above studies, however, the stock market does not seem to predict acquisition targets with a high degree of accuracy even three months prior to the announcement of takeover bids. The pre-takeover stock price movement of target firms reported by Dodd

---

*I would like to thank Michael Jensen and Robert Kaplan for suggesting the idea for this paper and providing valuable comments on an earlier version. Parts of this paper are based on my doctoral dissertation research at MIT and I am indebted to my advisor Stewart Myers for his helpful guidance throughout that project. I also benefited from comments of Ken Gaver, Daniel McFadden, Morris McInnes, Jim Ohlson, Ram Ramkrishnan, Ross Watts, Jerold Zimmerman, and especially Richard Ruback. Partial funding for this research has been provided by the Division of Research, Harvard Business School.

0165-4101/86/$3.50©1986, Elsevier Science Publishers B.V. (North-Holland)

and Ruback (1977), Asquith (1983) and others indicates that the market receives most of the signals that a firm is a probable target during a very short period around the announcement of a takeover bid. In a recent review of this evidence, Jensen and Ruback (1983, p. 29) argue that 'it is difficult, if not impossible, for the market to predict future targets'.

In light of the above, the results reported by the earlier acquisition studies imply that the models developed by them are better able than the stock market to identify future takeover targets. Stated differently, if the claims of the earlier prediction studies are valid, it is possible to earn abnormal returns using the prediction models. To probe this further, this paper undertakes a methodological and empirical analysis of takeover prediction with two related objectives. The first objective is to analyze the methodological problems associated with the development of binary state prediction models when the distribution of the two states of interest is skewed and to illustrate ways to avoid these problems in an applied context. The second objective is to examine whether it is possible to predict targets with a high degree of accuracy after correcting the methodological flaws of the earlier studies.

A critical examination of the methodology used by the earlier acquisition studies shows that there are three principal methodological flaws which make their reported prediction accuracies unreliable. First, the use of non-random, equal-share samples in the model estimation, without appropriate modification to the estimators, leads to inconsistent and biased estimates of the model parameters and the acquisition probabilities. This results in overstating the model's ability to predict targets. Second, the use of equal-share samples in prediction tests leads to error rate estimates that fail to represent the model's predictive ability in the population. Third, the use of arbitrary cutoff probabilities in prediction tests without specifying a decision context, the relevant state-payoff matrix, and the prior state probabilities, makes the reported prediction accuracies difficult to interpret.

The empirical study described in this paper attempts to correct the above methodological problems. The estimation procedure explicitly considers the sampling scheme employed. The prediction tests are conducted on a group of firms that approximates the population over which the model would be used in a realistic forecasting application. The predictive usefulness of the model is tested in the context of a specific forecasting application, and the optimal cutoff probability used in the tests is derived by explicitly considering the relevant payoff function and prior probabilities. The study also improves upon the earlier ones by employing an acquisition probability model that is developed from the economics of the acquisition process and by specifying variables based on hypotheses suggested by the literature.

The empirical results reported in this study differ markedly from those of the earlier acquisition prediction studies. A group of 163 targets and 256 non-targets listed on the New York and American stock exchanges is used to estimate a logit probability model with nine independent variables. While the estimated model is found to be statistically significant, its explanatory power is small. The magnitudes of the estimated acquisition probabilities are in general very small. The predictive ability of the model is tested on a group of firms consisting of 30 targets and 1087 non-targets. The results indicate that, while the model correctly identifies a high percentage of actual targets, it erroneously predicts a large number of non-targets as targets. Hence, it is not possible to earn significant abnormal returns by investing in firms that are predicted by the model to be potential acquisition targets.

While the methodological issues raised in this paper are analyzed in the context of acquisition prediction, they are relevant to any research problem that involves the development of a binary state prediction model, especially when the two states of interest are present in the population with unequal frequencies. Prominent areas of accounting research where the issues addressed in this paper are relevant include the prediction of corporate bankruptcy and the explanation/prediction of accounting policy choices of firms. A number of bankruptcy prediction studies employ methodologies similar to those of the previous acquisition prediction studies and hence suffer from the methodological flaws discussed in this paper.[1,2] Similarly, the accounting policy choice studies that analyze policy alternatives which are chosen by firms in the population with vastly different frequencies face the sampling and prediction testing problems discussed in this paper.[3,4]

The rest of the paper is organized as follows. In section 2, the methodological issues in the acquisition prediction literature are analyzed. This includes the issues related to sampling and the optimal cutoff probability. Section 3 describes the data and methods used in the present study. The empirical results

---

[1] In a recent paper, Zmijewski (1984) provides a methodological critique of the bankruptcy prediction literature focusing specifically on three issues: the choice between various statistical specifications of the bankruptcy probability model, the problem of incomplete data availability for some members of the population, and the effects of using non-random state-based samples for model estimation. Zmijewski's analysis overlaps the analysis of this paper in examining the biases from using state-based samples for model estimation. His study, however, does not touch upon two other issues addressed by this paper, namely, the bias introduced by the use of state-based samples in prediction tests, and the problems of using an arbitrary cutoff probability in prediction tests. Also, in a more general critique of the use of discriminant analysis, Eisenbeis (1981) points to some of the problems discussed here.

[2] As pointed out later in this paper, the bankruptcy prediction studies by Ohlson (1980) and Altman, Haldeman and Narayanan (1977) avoid some of the problems pointed out in this study.

[3] See Holthausen and Leftwich (1983) for a recent review of this literature.

[4] Consider, for example, a study that investigates the determinants of depreciation accounting policy choice of firms. Since a very large proportion of firms in the population chooses straight-line depreciation policy, a non-random sample is usually employed to obtain adequate representation of other depreciation policy choices. As shown in this paper, in the absence of appropriate modification to the estimation procedure, this results in biased coefficient estimates and impairs the validity of hypotheses tests.

are presented in section 4. The paper ends with a summary and discussion of conclusions in section 5.

2. Methodological issues in acquisition prediction

Several methodological flaws in the acquisition prediction literature lead to erroneous conclusions on the predictive ability of the estimated models. These are discussed in this section and modifications to the methodology to avoid these problems are proposed.

2.1. Sampling

The typical procedure used in the acquisition studies is to draw a sample with an approximately equal number of targets and non-targets.[5] This type of sample, referred to as a state-based sample in this paper, is not a pure random sample because, unlike in random sampling, a firm's probability of being selected into a state-based sample is a function of its acquisition status, i.e., whether a firm is a target or not. The practice in the acquisition prediction literature has been to employ state-based samples in conjunction with inference procedures which assume random sampling. This leads to biased and incorrect inferences as shown below.

2.1.1. State-based sample for model estimation

Consider a population of N firms consisting of N_1 targets and N_2 non-targets. Suppose the desired sample size is n. In the case of random sampling, n firms are drawn randomly from the entire population. Under state-based sampling, n_1 firms are drawn randomly from the target subpopulation and n_2 firms are drawn from the non-target subpopulation, n_1 and n_2 totaling up to n. Typically, n_1 and n_2 are set to be approximately equal.

There is a valid econometric justification for preferring a state-based sample over a random sample in the estimation of an acquisition prediction model because the number of targets is very small compared to the number of non-targets in the population. If a random sample were to be drawn from such a population, the sample would be likely to consist of an overwhelming majority of non-targets and very few targets. The 'information content' of such a sample for model estimation is quite small, leading to relatively imprecise parameter estimates. The sample can be enriched informationally by making the sample proportions of targets and non-targets more evenly balanced. A state-based sample accomplishes just this.

---

[5] For example, Stevens (1973) uses a sample consisting of 40 targets and 40 non-targets for estimating the model, and another sample of 20 targets and 20 non-targets for testing the model's predictive ability. Similar samples are used by the other studies.

Manski and Lerman (1977) and Manski and McFadden (1981) show that in a population like the one described above, an appropriate state-based sample provides more efficient estimates compared to a random sample of the same size. Alternatively, for a given level of precision, state-based sampling reduces the required sample size. Based on an extensive simulation analysis, Cosslett (1981) reports that a state-based sample of equal proportions, like the type used by the acquisition prediction literature, is usually a close-to-optimum design.

While the use of a state-based sample is justified on the grounds of efficiency, realization of this efficiency gain is predicated on the use of a suitable estimation procedure that recognizes the nature of the state-based sampling process. Unfortunately, this is where the earlier studies fail; they employ estimators which assume random sampling. As Manski and Lerman (1977) show, this leads to inconsistent and asymptotically biased estimates of the model parameters and hence biased estimates of the acquisition probability. Cosslett (1981) reports possible biases of 30% or more, indicating the seriousness of this problem.

To see the nature of the bias, consider a firm i *in the population* with a probability p of being a target. Let p' be the probability that the firm i *in the sample* is a target. Using Bayes' formula for conditional probability,

$$p' = \text{probability}\,(i \text{ is a target}|i \text{ is sampled})$$

$$= \frac{\text{probability}\,(i \text{ is a target}) \times \text{probability}\,(i \text{ is sampled}|i \text{ is a target})}{[\text{probability}\,(i \text{ is a target}) \times \text{probability}\,(i \text{ is sampled}|i \text{ is a target}) + \text{probability}\,(i \text{ is a non-target}) \times \text{probability}\,(i \text{ is sampled}|i \text{ is a non-target})]}.$$

In the case of random sampling, the probability of firm i being sampled is the same whether it is a target or not. Hence the above expression simplifies to p. However, under state-based sampling, this is not so. If N_1 and N_2 are the number of targets and non-targets in the population and n_1 and n_2 are the corresponding numbers in the sample, then

$$p' = \frac{p(n_1/N_1)}{p(n_1/N_1) + (1-p)(n_2/N_2)} \neq p.$$

The practice in the acquisition prediction literature is to use the simple maximum likelihood (MLE) procedure to estimate the model parameters and hence the state probabilities. Note that the maximum likelihood procedure consists of maximizing the sample likelihood function. When a state-based sample is used, the sample likelihood is formed using p'. The maximization of the sample likelihood, thus, yields an unbiased estimate of p'. However, since p' does not equal p, the procedure does not yield an unbiased estimate of p, the population acquisition probability. Hence, the simple maximum likelihood estimation procedure, when used on state-based samples, does *not* lead to an unbiased estimate of the population acquisition probability. The resulting bias can be calculated as follows:

$$p' - p = \frac{(n_1/N_1 - n_2/N_2)\, p(1-p)}{(n_1/N_1)\, p + (n_2/N_2)(1-p)}.$$

Since usually N_1 is much smaller than N_2 and n_1 is equal to n_2,

$$(p' - p) > 0,$$

except for the uninteresting cases of p being equal to 0 or 1. In other words, the estimated acquisition probability always overstates the true value.

The magnitude of the bias varies across samples as a function of the sample design. The bias is directly proportional to the difference in the sampling ratios of the targets and non-targets. For a given sample design, the bias varies across firms as a function of the true acquisition probability.[6]

The bias in the estimated probabilities does not alter the relative ranking of firms in terms of their acquisition probabilities. It is simple to show that if the true acquisition probability of firm A is greater than that of firm B, the estimated probability of A would also be greater than that of B. Hence, if the purpose of the estimated model is only to *rank* probabilities, the above bias is unimportant. However, if the estimated parameters are to be used to test hypotheses, the bias and inconsistency become important. If the objective is to use the model to predict targets, which is the case with the earlier acquisition prediction studies, the bias leads to erroneous inferences.

When the biased estimates of the acquisition probabilities are used to predict targets and non-targets, the observed prediction accuracies do not reflect the true predictive ability of the model. It is simple to show that the observed error rates understate the model's true error rate in predicting targets and overstate the true error rate in predicting non-targets. To see this, consider the classification scheme where a firm is classified as a target if the acquisition

---

[6] To see the seriousness of the bias, let us consider the estimation sample used by Stevens (1973) which consists of 40 targets and 40 non-targets. Let us assume for the purpose of illustration that the total population consists of 1000 firms. Since Stevens samples all the targets, the sampling ratio for the non-targets is 40/960, or approximately 0.042. Now, let us consider a firm whose true acquisition probability is 0.1. Given the above sampling scheme, the acquisition probability of the firm estimated by the model will be approximately 0.73.

probability is greater than a pre-specified value $\bar{p}$. If a firm has a true acquisition probability p (or an unbiased estimate of the true probability), this classification would lead to one of the following four outcomes: (1) correct prediction of a target if p is greater than $\bar{p}$ and i is actually a target, (2) incorrect prediction of a non-target as a target (a Type II error) if p is greater than $\bar{p}$ and i is actually a non-target, (3) correct prediction of a non-target if p is less than $\bar{p}$ and i is actually a non-target, and (4) incorrect prediction of a target as a non-target (a Type I error) if p is less than $\bar{p}$ and i is actually a target.

Now, suppose p', a biased estimate from a state-based sample, is used instead of p. How would the outcome of the prediction change? Note that since p' is always at least as large as p, whenever p is greater than $\bar{p}$, so would p' be. Thus, the prediction does not change for cases (1) and (2) above. However, this is not true for cases (3) and (4) above. When p is smaller than $\bar{p}$, p' can either be smaller or larger than $\bar{p}$. If p' is also smaller than $\bar{p}$, the prediction would not change; if, on the other hand, p' is larger than $\bar{p}$, the prediction would shift from (3) to (2) or from (4) to (1). A shift from (3) to (2) would introduce an additional Type II error; a shift from (4) to (1) would eliminate a Type I error.

Using p' as the estimated acquisition probability, therefore, understates the error rate in predicting targets and overstates the error rate in predicting non-targets. The net effect on the overall error rate is uncertain and is determined by the cutoff probability employed and the 'true' acquisition probabilities of the firms in the sample.

The effect of state-based sampling on inferred prediction error rates has been examined above analytically. In a recent study, Zmijewski (1984) examines the same issue empirically. He estimates a single bankruptcy prediction model using several alternative samples with varying proportions of bankrupt and non-bankrupt firms. The results reported by him are consistent with the conclusions of the above analysis.

The biases pointed out above, which result from the use of state-based samples in model estimation, can be avoided. To do this, the estimators used have to be appropriately modified to recognize the nature of the sample. Manski and McFadden (1981) discuss two possibilities: the conditional maximum likelihood estimator (CMLE) and the weighted maximum likelihood estimator (WMLE).[7] Both these estimators are obtained from relatively simple modifications to the ordinary maximum likelihood estimators commonly em-

---

[7]Ohlson (1980) avoids the biases discussed in this section by using the entire population rather than a state-based sample to estimate his bankruptcy model. While this is a strategy which requires no modification to the ordinary likelihood estimator, there are two drawbacks associated with it: (1) significant increase in computational cost and (2) loss of a 'hold-out' sample to test the predictive usefulness of the model.

ployed.[8] In the empirical study in this paper, the CMLE approach is employed. The specific details of this procedure are discussed in section 3.

2.1.2. State-based sample as a prediction test sample

The previous subsection discusses the bias arising out of using a state-based sample in the estimation of a dichotomous state prediction model. State-based samples have also been employed to test the predictive ability of the model. This practice results in yet another source of error in assessing the true predictive ability of the model.[9]

In judging the forecasting usefulness of a model, the statistic of interest usually is the expected error rate when the model is used to forecast the firms in the population as targets and non-targets. Since a state-based sample is non-random by definition, the error rate inferences based on it are not directly generalizable to the population. The very unequal distribution of targets and non-targets in the population, which justifies the use of a state-based sample in model estimation, argues strongly against its use in prediction testing. Since only a small fraction of the firms are targets, predicting them is like searching for a needle in a haystack. The use of a contrived sample with a large proportion of targets tends to obscure this difficulty.

To understand the specific nature of the distortion, again consider a population of N_1 targets and N_2 non-targets. If an acquisition prediction model is used to classify a sample of n firms consisting of n_1 targets and n_2 non-targets, and if m_1 and m_2 are numbers of misclassified targets and non-targets, the sample forecast error rate is

$$e' = \frac{m_1 + m_2}{n_1 + n_2} = \frac{m_1 + m_2}{n}.$$

The expected prediction error rate in the population is

$$e = \frac{N_1(m_1/n_1) + N_2(m_2/n_2)}{N_1 + N_2}$$

$$= \frac{m_1(N_1/n_1) + m_2(N_2/n_2)}{n} \cdot \frac{n}{N_1 + N_2}.$$

---

[8] It is necessary to modify the estimator only if one is interested in obtaining unbiased and consistent estimates of the model parameters. If the objective is merely to use the estimated probabilities for prediction, an alternative to modifying the estimator is to adjust the cutoff probability appropriately to take into account the bias introduced by the state-based estimation sample.

[9] Eisenbeis (1977) also points out this problem.

Since for a state-based sample, by design,

$$\frac{n_1}{N_1} \neq \frac{n_2}{N_2} \neq \frac{n}{N_1 + N_2},$$

e is generally not equal to e'. Yet, the practice in the acquisition prediction literature is to use e' as the estimate of e. The bias from this can be calculated as

$$e' - e = \frac{(n_1 N_2 - n_2 N_1)}{n(N_1 + N_2)} (m_1/n_1 - m_2/n_2).$$

The sign of the right-hand part of the equation is determined by $(m_1/n_1 - m_2/n_2)$ since $(n_1 N_2 - n_2 N_1)$ is always positive. (Note that n_1 and n_2 are usually equal whereas N_1 is much smaller than N_2.) Since m_1/n_1 is the sample error rate for targets and m_2/n_2 is the sample error rates for non-targets, the bias is positive or negative depending on their relative magnitudes. The size of the bias is proportional to the difference in the two types of sample error rates as well as the difference in the ratios of population and sample shares of targets and non-targets.[10]

As pointed out already, unlike the case of model estimation, there is no econometric justification in employing state-based samples in prediction tests. Since actual use of a model involves the entire population, it is desirable to make the prediction test sample resemble the population as closely as possible. Once the parameters are estimated, the computation cost of state probabilities for prediction tests is relatively low. Hence, it is not unrealistic to suggest that a large sample, or even the entire population of firms at a given time, be employed in prediction tests to avoid the bias pointed out above. This, in fact, is the method employed in the empirical study described later in this paper.

2.2. Optimal cutoff probability

If a researcher is only concerned with testing whether a set of variables bears a significant statistical relationship to the acquisition probability of a firm, testing the predictive accuracy of a model is not necessary. Instead, the focus

---

[10] To see how serious the bias is, let us once again consider the study by Stevens (1973) which uses a sample of 40 targets and 40 non-targets and reports a prediction error rate of 15% for targets, 45% for non-targets, and an overall prediction error rate of 30%. He considers the population of firms listed on the COMPUSTAT tape. Let us assume that this consists of 1000 firms. Since Stevens samples all the available targets, the numbers of targets and non-targets in the population would be 40 and 960, respectively. The expected population error rate, based on the reported sample error rates would be 44%. Hence, the expected prediction accuracy in the population would be 56% and not 70% as reported by Stevens.

of interest in that case would be the significance of the overall explanatory power of the estimated model and, presumably, the significance of the estimated coefficients of the variables. Prediction testing becomes important only if the objective is to develop a statistical model to predict potential targets.

The prediction tests typically involve classifying a group of firms into targets and non-targets based on the estimated acquisition probability. To classify a firm, the estimated acquisition probability of the firm is compared with a predefined cutoff probability. If the estimated probability is less than the cutoff probability, the firm is classified as non-target.

The appropriate cutoff probability to be employed in the prediction tests is determined by the decision context in which the model's predictions are to be used. To derive the 'optimal cutoff probability', it is necessary to specify the decision context of interest, an appropriate payoff function, and the prior state probabilities. The standard decision theory methodology can then be applied to derive the optimal classification scheme.

The earlier acquisition prediction studies develop statistical models with a view to predicting takeover targets, and hence all of them conduct tests to examine the predictive ability of the estimated models. In performing the prediction tests, however, they do not derive an optimal cutoff probability as outlined above. Instead, they employ an arbitrary cutoff probability, usually 0.5. Since the decision context in which the estimated model's predictive ability is judged is not explicitly stated, the results of prediction tests in these studies are difficult to interpret.[11,12]

In order to rectify this problem, the empirical study in this paper uses the optimal cutoff probability derived below in a well-defined decision context. It is assumed that the purpose of the estimated acquisition model is to provide predictions which are to be used in a stock market investment strategy. As discussed earlier, the stock market does not seem to do well in predicting targets far in advance of the actual announcement of takeovers. The question examined in the prediction tests is whether the estimated acquisition model provides a superior mechanism not available to the market for predicting targets. Stated differently, we examine the hypothesis that it is possible to earn

---

[11] This is because, for a given set of estimated probabilities, the results of a prediction test are determined by the cutoff probability used. If the cutoff is derived within a decision context, the observed prediction accuracies indicate the extent to which the model's predictions are useful in that decision context. Otherwise, it is not clear what the observed prediction accuracies indicate. Further, if the results are statistically significant with one cutoff probability but not with another, it is not possible to choose between the two sets of results.

[12] The use of arbitrary cutoff probabilities in prediction tests has been pointed out as a problem by others. Eisenbeis (1977) points out that the use of arbitrary cutoff probabilities is one of the serious 'pitfalls' in using discriminant analysis. In the bankruptcy prediction literature, Ohlson (1980) discusses the problem and attempts to deal with it by presenting prediction error rates for a number of cutoffs rather than for a single cutoff probability. Altman, Haldeman and Narayanan (1977) address the issue by selecting bank loan classification as the decision context and by estimating from historical data the prior probability and misclassification costs.

abnormal returns by investing in firms that are predicted by the model to be potential targets.

To determine the classification scheme that maximizes the expected payoff, let us consider a firm i in the test sample. Let

q = the market's assessment of the probability that the firm becomes a target,
S_1 = the stock price if the firm becomes a target, and
S_2 = the stock price if the firm does not become a target.

The variables q, S_1 and S_2 are assumed to be common knowledge. Assuming market efficiency with respect to this information, the current stock price S would be such that

$$S = qS_1 + (1-q)S_2. \tag{1}$$

Denoting C_1 $(= S_1 - S)$ as the payoff if the firm becomes a target and C_2 $(= S_2 - S)$ as the payoff if it does not, the price S in eq. (1) would ensure that the *expected* payoff, based on market probability q, is zero. That is,

$$qC_1 + (1-q)C_2 = 0. \tag{2}$$

Now, suppose we develop a statistical model which predicts a probability of acquisition p for firm i. We hypothesize that the model's prediction is new information unavailable to the market and seek to exploit this 'private information' to earn abnormal returns. We agree with the market's assessment that S_1 would be the stock price if firm i becomes a target, and S_2 if not. Since the model prediction is hypothesized to be unknown to the market, the current stock price S, and hence the state payoffs C_1 and C_2, remain unchanged. The expected payoff from investing in firm i, however, changes (for us) in light of the new information from the model, p.

Given the market prior q and the model prediction p, the posterior probability q' can be computed using Bayes' formula:

$$q' = \frac{qf_1(p \mid i = \text{target})}{qf_1(p \mid i = \text{target}) + (1-q)f_2(p \mid i = \text{non-target})}, \tag{3}$$

where $f_1(p \mid i = \text{target})$ is the conditional probability density of observing p if i is in fact a target, and $f_2(p \mid i = \text{non-target})$ is the conditional probability density of observing p if i is a non-target.

The expected payoff from investing in firm i, given the posterior probability q' and the state payoffs C_1 and C_2, is $[q'C_1 + (1-q')C_2]$. Hence, firm i is expected to have a positive payoff if

$$q'C_1 + (1-q')C_2 \geq 0. \tag{4}$$

Using eq. (3), (4) can be rewritten as

$$\frac{f_1(p|i=\text{target})}{f_2(p|i=\text{non-target})} \geq \frac{-(1-q)C_2}{qC_1}. \tag{5}$$

Any firm with a predicted acquisition probability p which satisfies condition (5) has an expected positive payoff.

Assuming that there is no budget constraint, the scheme that maximizes expected payoff is to classify all firms that satisfy condition (5) as potential targets and invest in them. Firms that fail to satisfy condition (5) are to be classified as non-targets.[13] The relation between q, C_1 and C_2 implied by eq. (2) allows us to rewrite condition (5) as

$$\frac{f_1(p|i=\text{target})}{f_2(p|i=\text{non-target})} \geq 1. \tag{6}$$

The above condition implies that the optimal classification scheme is to classify a firm as a target if the predicted acquisition probability is such that the marginal probability of observing p *if* the firm is actually a target is greater than the corresponding marginal probability *if* the firm is a non-target. The optimal cutoff probability is the value where the two conditional marginal densities are equal.[14]

To use condition (6) to determine the optimal cutoff probability in an empirical context, we need to know the conditional probability density functions $f_1(\cdot)$ and $f_2(\cdot)$. Recall that $f_1(\cdot)$ is the distribution of the acquisition probability among targets; $f_2(\cdot)$ is the corresponding distribution for non-targets. By plotting the distribution of the estimated probabilities for the targets and non-targets in the same sample that is used to estimate the model parameters, we can obtain empirical approximations of $f_1(\cdot)$ and $f_2(\cdot)$. The cutoff probability is the value where the two plots intersect. This method is illustrated in section 3.

The empirical tests described in the next section use the above classification scheme and examine whether it is possible to earn abnormal stock returns by investing in the firms predicted by the model to be predicted targets. The tests thus assess whether the acquisition model provides predictions which are superior to the stock market's prediction. It is important to interpret the prediction test results in this context.

---

[13] The optimality of the classification scheme based on condition (5) is a well-known result from decision theory literature [see, for example, Press (1972, p. 371)].

[14] Note that eq. (2) implies that the *expected* costs of Type I and Type II errors are equal. The same assumption underlies an alternative procedure to determine the cutoff probability under which the probability which minimizes the overall sample error rate is chosen as the optimal cutoff. Thus, our procedure is equivalent to this alternative procedure.

2.3. Summary

Three methodological flaws have led to erroneous estimates of prediction error rates of extant acquisition prediction models. These are related to (1) sampling for model estimation, (2) sampling for prediction tests, and (3) specification of the cutoff probability. The nature of the biases introduced by each and ways to avoid them have been discussed above.

3. The empirical study

This section describes the data and methodology used in this paper to estimate and test an acquisition prediction model.[15] The discussion includes the specification of an econometric model, the selection of a set of potentially interesting variables, the sample selection, and the estimation methods employed.

3.1. Acquisition likelihood model

The following probability model is employed in this study to specify the exact functional relationship between the firm characteristics and its acquisition likelihood in a given period. Let $p(i, t)$ be the probability that the firm i will be acquired in period t, $x(i, t)$ a vector of measured attributes of the firm, and β a vector of unknown parameters to be estimated. Then,

$$p(i, t) = 1/[1 + e^{-\beta x(i, t)}].$$

In other words, $p(i, t)$ is a logit probability function of the measured attributes of the firm.

The intuition behind the above model is as follows. Whether or not a firm is acquired in a particular time period depends on the number and type of acquisition bids it receives in that period. This, in turn, depends on the firm's own characteristics as well as the motives and attributes of the bidders. In the above model, the relevant characteristics of the target which can be quantitatively measured are denoted by $x(i, t)$ and enter the model explicitly. The qualitative characteristics of the target which influence its attractiveness and the characteristics of the target–bidder combination are modeled as stochastic random variables. It is the probability distributions of these random variables, which are endogenous to the acquisition process, that determine the specific functional form of $p(i, t)$.

Under certain economic assumptions which include, among others, that there are a large number of active bidders in the market and that the shareholders of

---

[15] The acquisition model estimated in the study attempts to predict firms which are targets of successful takeover bids. This is consistent with the models developed by the earlier acquisition prediction studies.

a target accept the most profitable bid among those which offer a premium over the current market value of their stock, it is possible to show that the random variables in the above model follow the Type I extreme value distribution.[16] This, in turn, implies that $p(i,t)$ is a logit probability function of $x(i,t)$.[17]

3.2. Variables

The variables to be included in the acquisition likelihood model are specified on the basis of six hypotheses, frequently suggested in the academic and/or popular financial literature, on the types of firms that are likely to become acquisition targets.[18] The hypotheses and the variables implied by them are discussed below.

(1) *Inefficient management hypothesis*: Firms with inefficient managements are likely targets.

This hypothesis is based on the finance theory premise that acquisitions are a mechanism by which managers of a firm who fail to maximize its market value are replaced. The excess return on a firm's stock, averaged over an extended period of time is used as a proxy for management efficiency in this study. The excess stock return on a firm is calculated using a market model and daily stock return data and is averaged over a period of four years. As an alternative to the excess return measure, accounting profitability is also used as a proxy for management performance. The profitability is computed as the return on stockholders' equity averaged over a period of four years.[19] The

---

[16] The cumulative density function of the standard Type I extreme value distribution has the form: $1 - \exp(-\exp(x))$. The probability density function of a standard Type I extreme value distribution is very close to that of a log-normal distribution. The difference of two independent random variables, each with the same Type I distribution, has a logit distribution. For further discussion on this, see Johnson and Kotz (1970).

[17] The usual practice followed by the other acquisition prediction studies is to specify an *a priori* statistical model exogenously. Here, an attempt is made to take the economics of the acquisition process into consideration to arrive at an appropriate statistical model. A more formal development of this model is presented in Palepu (1982).

[18] Most of the earlier studies have not chosen the variables to be included in their model on the basis of a set of pre-specified hypotheses. Instead, the practice has been to start with a large number of popular financial ratios and then let the empirical analysis determine a subset of variables to be retained on the basis of their statistical significance in a step-wise procedure. For example, Simkowitz and Monroe (1979) start with a set of 24 ratios and finally retain 7 variables. This method of variable selection is arbitrary and leads to the statistical 'overfitting' of the model to the sample at hand. We attempt to avoid this problem by choosing variables based on a set of hypotheses from the literature.

[19] Accounting profitability measures only current performance. The excess return measure reflects, in addition to the current performance, the market's expectation of future performance. Hence, the excess return measure is probably a better proxy.

computation method for these variables, as well as for all the others, is described in the appendix.

(2) *Growth–resource mismatch hypothesis*: Firms with a mismatch between their growth and the financial resources at their disposal are likely targets.

This hypothesis implies that two types of firms are likely targets: low-growth, resource-rich firms and high-growth, resource-poor firms. The notion that low-growth, resource-rich firms are natural acquisition targets is commonly put forward in the popular financial press as well as in corporate finance textbooks. The hypothesis that high-growth, resource-poor firms may be attractive targets is suggested by the recent finance literature that analyzes the investing and financing decisions of firms under asymmetric information. [For example, see Myers and Majluf (1984).]

The growth–resource imbalance hypothesis indicates that growth and resource availability are important variables in determining a firm's acquisition likelihood. In this study, growth is measured as the average sales growth of a firm. Liquidity, measured as the ratio of net liquid assets to total assets, and leverage, measured as the debt to equity ratio are used to proxy the financial resource availability. A dummy variable, denoted as the growth–resource dummy (*GRDUMMY*) is employed to indicate the growth–resource mismatch. The *GRDUMMY* is assigned a value one for the combinations low growth–high liquidity–low leverage or high growth–low liquidity–high leverage. The dummy is set to zero for all other combinations. Each of the variables is defined as 'high' if its value for a firm is greater than the population average, and it is defined as 'low' otherwise.

The growth–resource dummy is included in the acquisition model to test the imbalance hypothesis. In another version of the model, in addition to the dummy, the three variables growth, liquidity, and leverage are also included. This is done to see if one of the two imbalances discussed earlier is predominant in our sample. No specific sign is hypothesized for the three variables since *a priori* it is not known which imbalance is predominant.

(3) *Industry disturbance hypothesis*: Firms that are in an industry subjected to 'economic disturbances' are likely acquisition targets.

The above hypothesis is suggested by the 'economic disturbance theory' proposed by Gort (1969) to explain observed variations in merger rates both across industries and over time. Gort argues that mergers are caused by valuation differentials among market participants which are triggered by economic shocks like changes in technology, industry structure, and regulatory environment.

The economic disturbance theory suggests that acquisitions cluster by industry. A factor that signals the acquisition likelihood of a firm is, therefore, the recent history of acquisitions in its industry. In this study, the variable industry dummy (*IDUMMY*) is used for this purpose. The industry dummy is assigned a value one if at least one acquisition occurred in a firm's four-digit SIC industry during the year prior to the year of observation.

(4) *Size hypothesis*: The likelihood of acquisition decreases with the size of the firm.

The above hypothesis is based on the premise that there are several size-related 'transaction costs' associated with acquiring a firm. These include the cost associated with the absorption of the target into the acquirer's organizational framework as well as the costs associated with fighting a prolonged battle that a target may wage to defend itself. These costs are likely to increase with the target size and hence the number of potential bidders for a firm is likely to decrease with size. To test this hypothesis, the size of a firm, measured by its net book assets, is included as a variable in the model.

(5) *Market-to-book hypothesis*: Firms whose market values are low compared to their book values are likely acquisition targets.

The proponents of the hypothesis assume that firms with low market-to-book value ratios are 'cheap' buys. Since the book value of a firm need not reflect the replacement value of its assets, the economic validity of this assumption is suspect. However, since this explanation of takeovers appears frequently in the popular press, it may be interesting to test it empirically. Hence the market-to-book ratio is included as a variable in this study. The market-to-book ratio is defined as the market value of the common equity divided by its book value.

(6) *Price–earnings hypothesis*: Firms with low P/E ratios are likely acquisition targets.

This is another popular explanation of acquisitions whose economic logic is questionable. According to the proponents of this hypothesis, bidders with high P/E ratios seek to acquire low P/E firms to realize an 'instantaneous capital gain' because of the belief that the stock market values the earnings of the combination at the higher P/E ratio of the acquirer. Once again, since P/E ratio is considered to be an important determinant of a firm's acquisition attractiveness, it is included as a variable in this study.

The above discussion leads to the identification of nine potential determinants of a firm's acquisition probability. The six hypotheses and the variables they imply are summarized in table 1. The hypothesized sign of each variable

Table 1

Acquisition likelihood hypotheses and independent variables.

Hypothesis	Variable(s)	Expected sign[c]
1. Inefficient management hypothesis[a]	Average excess return (AER) Accounting return on equity (ROE)	− −
2. Growth–resources imbalance hypothesis[b]	Growth–resources dummy ($GRDUMMY$)	+
3. Industry disturbance hypothesis	Industry dummy ($IDUMMY$)	+
4. Firm size hypothesis	$SIZE$	−
5. Asset undervaluation hypothesis	Market-to-book value (MTB)	−
6. Price–earnings magic hypothesis	Price–earnings ratio (P/E)	−

[a] Accounting return on equity is used as an alternative to the average excess return, a stock price based measure, in some versions of the model.

[b] The variables growth, liquidity and leverage are also included in some versions of model. These three variables are used in constructing the $GRDUMMY$. No definite signs are hypothesized for these three variables.

[c] A positive sign hypothesizes that the variable increases the likelihood of acquisition and a negative sign implies the opposite.

shows whether the acquisition likelihood is expected to go up (+) or down (−) with that variable.

3.3. Sample

A sample of 163 firms that were acquired during the period 1971–1979 and a random sample of 256 firms that were not acquired as of 1979 are used for the estimation of the acquisition model. Both the targets and non-targets (1) belong to the manufacturing or mining sectors, (2) are listed on either the New York or the American Stock Exchange, and (3) have data in the COMPUSTAT and CRSP files.

A list of targets from the period 1971–1979 was prepared from two sources: (1) The Statistical Report on Mergers and Acquisitions of the Federal Trade Commission, 1979 (published in July 1981) and (2) the delistments from the stock exchanges due to mergers and acquisitions, obtained from the CRSP files and confirmed by the Wall Street Journal Index. A total of 277 targets were

Table 2

Composition of the estimation sample.[a]

Year acquired	Number of firms
Targets	
1971	9
1972	5
1973	8
1974	12
1975	14
1976	20
1977	29
1978	35
1979	31
Total targets	163
Non-targets	
Firms not acquired during 1971-1979	256
Total sample	419

[a]All the firms in the sample (1) belong to the manufacturing or mining industries, (2) are listed on either the New York or the American stock exchange, and (3) are on the COMPUSTAT and CRSP data files.

initially identified. Of these, 163 were included in the estimation sample after screening for data requirements.

The population of 2054 firms, which were not taken over as of 1979 and satisfied the criteria for inclusion in the sample as non-targets, was first arranged in alphabetical order. Every sixth firm was selected from this list to generate a random group of 343 non-targets. Of these, 256 firms met the data requirements and were included in the sample. The composition of the estimation sample is summarized in table 2.

To test the predictive ability of the estimated model, a separate group of firms is used. This includes all the targets from the year 1980 and all the non-targets, other than those used in the estimation sample, listed on the COMPUSTAT tape in 1980. After screening for the criteria for inclusion in the study listed earlier, and the data requirements, this group consists of 30 targets and 1087 non-targets. Notice that the targets form only about 2.6% of this group. This is a more realistic group to test the true predictive ability of the model than the type of hold-out samples used by the earlier studies.

3.4. Model estimation

The parameters of the model are estimated by a maximum likelihood procedure using the statistical package QUAIL [Berkman et al. (1979)]. As pointed out earlier, since the estimation sample is a state-based sample, the population acquisition probability, $p(i, t)$, cannot be used to compute the sample likelihood function. Instead, we have to use the conditional probability that a firm is a target given that it is included in the sample. This probability, denoted as $p'(i, t)$, can be computed in the following manner.

In choosing the estimation sample, all the available targets in the population are selected. However, out of the 1384 non-targets which met the selection and data requirements, only 256 (or 18.5%) are included in the sample. Hence, the probability that a firm in the population is in the sample is one if it is a target and only 0.185 if it is a non-target. Under this sampling, suppressing the arguments i and t for convenience, we have

$$p' = \frac{(1)(p)}{(1)(p) + (0.185)(1-p)}.$$

Since

$$p = 1/(1 + e^{-\beta x}),$$

we have

$$p' = 1/(1 + 0.185 e^{-\beta x}) = 1/(1 + e^{\ln(0.185) - \beta x}).$$

Notice that the functional form of p' is also logistic. This is a convenient feature of the logistic probability model. The likelihood function to be maximized in the estimation uses the above expression for p'. Subsequent to the estimation, the parameters that determine the population probability p can easily be recovered since all the parameters other than the constant term are unaffected and the constant terms in the two models differs by a know value, $\ln(0.185)$ or -1.68.

In estimating the model, the dependent variable is assigned a value one for the targets and zero for the non-targets. Two versions of the logit model are estimated. In one version, the raw values of the independent variables are used. In the second version, each of the independent variables of an observation drawn from a given year is rescaled by its population average in that year, the population being defined as all the COMPUSTAT firms that met the criteria for inclusion in this study. Since the sample contains observations drawn from several different years, such a rescaling is likely to make these observations more homogeneous by eliminating the mean shift in the population characteristics that may have occurred from year to year during the period 1971–1979. The results of the two versions of the model are similar. The results presented in the next section correspond to the rescaled data.

Table 3

Estimates of logit acquisition likelihood models.[a]

Variables[b]	Expected sign	Estimates[c,d] Model 1	Model 2	Model 3	Model 4
Average excess return	−	−1.332 (−2.53)[g]	−1.338 (−2.50)[g]		
Return on equity	−			0.003 (0.086)	0.005 (0.11)
Growth–resource dummy	+	0.5467 (2.47)[g]	0.4432 (1.86)[h]	0.4616 (2.32)[g]	0.4024 (1.88)[h]
Growth			−0.0245 (−2.65)[g]		−0.0261 (−3.18)[g]
Liquidity			−0.005 (−0.49)		−0.008 (−0.85)
Leverage			−0.0035 (−2.07)[g]		−0.0034 (−2.17)[g]
Industry dummy	+	−0.7067 (−2.97)[g]	−0.6900 (−2.86)[g]	−0.5802 (−2.75)[g]	−0.5608 (−2.61)[g]
Size	−	−0.0005 (−2.61)[g]	−0.0005 (−2.62)[g]	−0.0004 (−2.52)[g]	−0.0004 (−2.63)[g]
Market-to-book ratio	−	−0.0044 (−0.17)	0.0117 (0.33)	−0.0051 (−0.2)	0.0126 (0.36)
Price–earnings ratio	−	0.0065 (0.78)	0.0099 (1.08)	0.0031 (0.51)	0.0041 (0.636)
Constant		−2.1048 (−2.49)[g]	−2.1096 (−2.45)[g]	−2.1533 (−3.35)[g]	−2.1898 (−3.47)[g]
Likelihood ratio index[e]		0.1010	0.1245	0.0695	0.0979
Likelihood ratio statistic[f]		58.65	72.32	47.78	67.29

[a] From a sample of 163 target firms that were acquired during the period 1971–1979 and 256 non-targets that were not taken over as of 1979. All the firms (1) belong to mining manufacturing industries, (2) were listed on the New York or the American stock exchange, and (3) have data on COMPUSTAT and CRSP tapes. For more details on the sample, see section 3.3.

[b] The independent variables are measured as of the end of the fiscal year prior to the year of takeover for targets and as of the end of the fiscal year prior to 1979 for non-targets. For a complete description of how these are computed, see the appendix.

[c] Four different versions of the model are estimated. Model 1 consists of six variables corresponding to the six hypotheses in table 1. Model 2 is a re-estimation of model 1 with the three additional variables growth, liquidity and leverage. Models 3 and 4 are re-estimations of models 1 and 2, respectively, with accounting return on equity replacing average excess return, a market performance measure. The constant term in all the four models is corrected for the sampling bias.

[d] The t-statistic, computed to test the null hypothesis that the estimated coefficient is equal to zero, is shown in parentheses for each coefficient estimate.

[e] The log likelihood ratio index is defined as (1 − log likelihood at convergence/log likelihood at zero). It is similar to the R^2 statistic in the case of a multiple regression model and provides an indication of the logit model's explanatory power.

[f] The likelihood ratio statistic is computed to test the hypothesis that all the parameters in the model are simultaneously equal to zero. Under this null hypothesis, the statistic has an asymptotic distribution which is a chi-square with the degrees of freedom equalling the number of parameters in the model. The statistic is significant at the 0.01 level for all the models.

[g] Significant at the 0.05 level, two-tailed test.

[h] Significant at the 0.10 level, two-tailed test.

characterized by low growth and low leverage; there is no significant difference between the targets and non-targets in terms of liquidity. In models 3 and 4, the coefficient of accounting return on equity, which is used as an accounting proxy for management efficiency, is insignificant; the coefficients of all the other variables are consistent with those in models 1 and 2, respectively.

The likelihood ratio index for the four models ranges between 6.95% and 12.45%. The associated likelihood ratio statistic, which is asymptotically chi-square distributed, is statistically significant for all four models. This implies that the models provide a statistically significant explanation of a firm's acquisition probability. However, the magnitude of this explanation is quite small since a maximum of only 12.45% of the variation in a firm's acquisition probability is explained by the models.

Of the four estimated versions of the acquisition model, model 2 has the largest explanatory power as measured by its likelihood ratio index of 12.45%. Further analysis of the predictive ability of the model, therefore, employs model 2. The coefficient estimates of model 2 from table 3 are used to compute estimated acquisition probabilities for the 163 targets and the 256 non-targets in the sample. The sample median probability for the targets is 0.144 and that for non-targets is 0.087. The values of the estimated probabilities are generally small, even for firms that subsequently become targets. Thus, while the model is statistically significant, it provides only a weak signal as to whether or not a firm will become a target in the future.[21]

4.2. Prediction tests

4.2.1. Estimation of cutoff probability

To test the predictive usefulness of the estimated model, the optimal cutoff probability to be used has to be estimated. As pointed out in section 2.2, the optimal cutoff probability is determined by the distributions of acquisition probability for targets and nontargets. Empirical approximations of these distributions are obtained below using the computed estimated acquisition probabilities for the 163 targets and 256 non-targets in the estimation sample.

The maximum estimated probability value in the estimation sample is 0.46, and all the probabilities except one are found to fall within the range 0 to 0.40. To obtain the sample distributions of the acquisition probability, the range 0 to 0.4 is divided into ten equal intervals. The number of (and the percentage of the total) targets that fall within each of these intervals is tabulated and shown

---

[21] If the bias arising from the state-based sample is ignored, the median takeover probability would have been 0.478 for the targets and 0.325 for the non-targets. Notice that the biased probabilities would lead us to conclude that the model provides a fairly strong signal regarding the takeover probability.

Table 4

Distribution of estimated acquisition probability for targets and non-targets in estimation sample.[a]

Estimated acquisition probability Range	Mid-value (p)	Target firms Number	Target firms Percent $f_1(p)$	Non-target firms Number	Non-target firms Percent $f_2(p)$	$f_1(p)/f_2(p)$
0.000–0.039	0.02	6	3.7%	37	14.4%	0.26
0.040–0.079	0.06	23	14.1	74	28.9	0.49
0.080–0.119	0.10	35	21.5	60	23.5	0.92
0.120–0.159	0.14	36	22.1	48	18.8	1.18
0.160–0.199	0.18	23	14.1	19	7.4	1.19
0.200–0.239	0.22	22	13.5	12	4.6	2.94
0.240–0.279	0.26	8	4.9	4	1.6	3.06
0.280–0.319	0.30	5	3.1	0	0	—
0.320–0.359	0.34	2	1.2	1	0.4	3.0
0.360–0.399	0.38	2	1.2	1	0.4	3.0
> 0.4	—	1	0.6	0	0	—
Total		163	100	256	100	

[a] The acquisition probabilities are computed for the 163 targets and 256 non-targets in the estimation sample using the coefficient estimates of model 2 in table 3. The maximum estimated probability value is 0.46 and all but one probability values are in the range 0 to 0.40. The range 0 to 0.4 is divided into ten equal intervals. The number of firms that fall within each of these intervals are tabulated separately for the targets and non-targets. The figures in the column under $f_1(p)$ are calculated by dividing the number of targets in each probability interval by 163 and expressing the result as a percentage. Similarly, the figures under $f_2(p)$ are calculated by dividing the number of non-targets in each interval by 256 and expressing the result as a percentage. In fig. 1, $f_1(p)$ and $f_2(p)$ are plotted against p.

in table 4. To obtain discrete approximation of the distribution of the acquisition probability for the targets, the percentage of targets in each probability interval, shown in table 4, is plotted against the mid-value of that interval. Similarly, the percentage of non-targets in each interval is plotted against its mid-value to get a discrete approximation of the density function for the acquisition probabilities of non-targets. These plots are shown in fig. 1.

The graphs show that while there is a considerable overlap between the two probability distributions, there is also a systematic difference. The two distributions intersect at a probability value 0.112. At probabilities below this, the distribution function for the non-targets is greater than that for the targets; at probabilities above this, the distribution function for the targets dominates. At 0.112, the values of the two distribution functions are equal.

It is shown in section 2.2 that the optimal cutoff probability, when the estimated probabilities are used for predicting targets with a view to investing in their stocks, is that value at which the distribution functions for the targets and non-targets are equal. Since this value is 0.112 in the present case, it is used as the cutoff probability in the prediction tests discussed next.

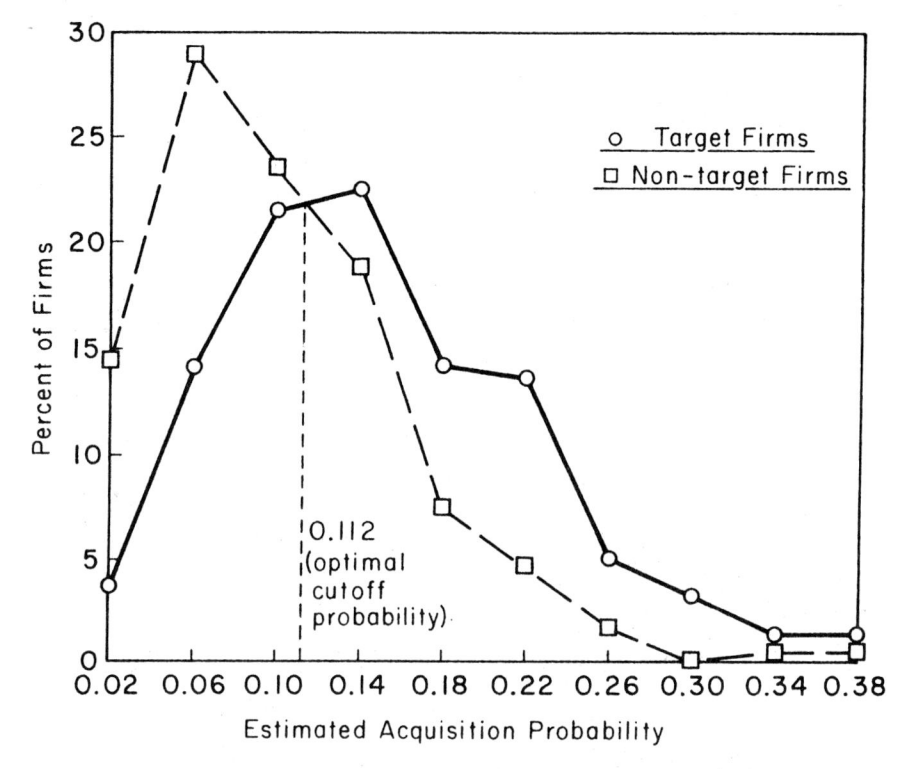

Fig. 1. Empirical probability density function of acquisition probability.

4.2.2. Predictions in a hold-out sample

To examine the ability of the model to predict targets in advance, the model has to be tested on a group of firms. Since the model parameters as well as the cutoff probability are obtained from the estimation sample, any test based on this sample is likely to be biased. Hence, the test described below uses a separate group of firms. This includes 30 firms which were actually taken over during 1980 and 1087 non-targets from the same year. These firms represent all those that are listed on the 1980 COMPUSTAT tape, meet the criteria for inclusion in this study, and have the required data. None of these firms were used in the estimation of the model parameters.

The values of the independent variables in the acquisition model are computed for each of the above 1117 firms following the methodology in the appendix.[22] The estimated parameters of model 2 from table 3 are then used to compute for each firm the probability that it will be a target in 1980. Using the

---

[22] The values of the independent variables are rescaled by their respective population averages to conform with the procedure used in the estimation sample.

estimated optimal cutoff acquisition probability, each firm is predicted to be a target if its acquisition probability is equal to or more than 0.112. Firms with an estimated acquisition probability less than 0.112 are predicted to be non-targets.

The above exercise results in classifying 625 firms to be targets and 492 to be non-targets. Of the 625 firms predicted to be targets, 24 are in fact targets in 1980. Of the 492 firms predicted to be non-targets, 486 are in fact non-targets. Stated differently, out of the 30 firms in the group that are actually targets, 24 (or 80%) are predicted by the model. However, in achieving this, the model misclassifies a large number of non-targets: of the 1087 non-targets, only 486 (45%) are correctly predicted.[23]

4.2.3. Excess returns from model predictions

The model predictions described above are used to examine the possibility of earning abnormal returns from investing in the stocks of predicted targets. The tests described in this section use daily excess returns drawn from the Center for Research in Security Prices (CRSP) excess return file. The CRSP excess returns are computed as

$$XR_{it} = R_{it} - E(\tilde{R}_{it}),$$

where

XR_{it} = excess return on asset i for day t,
R_{it} = return on asset i for day t,
$E(\tilde{R}_{it})$ = expected rate of return on asset i for day t.

$E(\tilde{R}_{it})$ is estimated by grouping annually all securities listed on the New York and the American stock exchanges into ten equal control portfolios ranked according to their betas. The observed return to the control portfolio which has approximately the same beta as security i is then used as the estimate of $E(\tilde{R}_{it})$.

The acquisition model identifies 625 firms as potential targets during 1980. The excess returns for these firms are examined over a holding period of 250 trading days beginning on January 2, 1980, which is the first trading day of the year. The excess returns of these firms on a given day are unlikely to be

---

[23] The overall accuracy rate, assuming for a moment that the two types of errors are additive, is 510/1117 or 45.6%. Notice that this is considerably worse than the accuracy rates reported by the earlier acquisition prediction studies. This is largely attributable to the fact that the prediction test here uses a very large number of non-targets. To see this, let us assume that the above test is conducted on 30 targets and 30 randomly drawn non-targets. With the prediction accuracy rates of 80% and 45% for the targets and non-targets, the overall accuracy rate would be 62.5%, which is closer to the rates reported by others.

independent. To take this contemporaneous cross-sectional correlation into account, the stocks of all the firms are formed into an equally weighted portfolio, and the tests are performed on the portfolio excess returns.

The average excess return for the portfolio on each relative day t is calculated as

$$AXR_t = \frac{1}{N} \sum_{i=1}^{N} XR_{it},$$

where N is the number of securities with excess returns during day t.[24] Average cumulative excess returns, CER, is the sum of the average excess returns over time,

$$CER = \sum_{t=1}^{k} AXR_t,$$

where CER is for days 1 to k.

To test the statistical significance of the excess returns, the daily portfolio excess returns are standardized by their standard deviation. The portfolio standard deviation is computed using the portfolio daily excess returns for 250 trading days preceding January 2, 1980 (relative days -250 to -1). Since the composition of the portfolio may vary over time, the portfolio standard deviation is recomputed for each day. The standardized portfolio daily excess return is computed as

$$SXR = \sum_{i=1}^{N} XR_{it} \bigg/ SD_t,$$

where SD_t is the standard deviation of portfolio on day t.

A t-statistic which tests whether the portfolio cumulative excess return is significantly different from zero is calculated as

$$t = \sum_{i=1}^{k} SXR_t \bigg/ \sqrt{k},$$

where k is the number of days over which the portfolio excess return is cumulated.

---

[24] Since some of the firms in the portfolio are taken over during the course of the holding period, the number of firms in the portfolio varies over time.

Table 5

Average daily cumulative excess returns over a holding period of 250 trading days beginning January 2, 1980 for 625 predicted target firms, 24 of which became targets during 1980, and for 492 predicted non-targets and 6 predicted non-targets which became targets during 1980.

Day	Predicted targets All firms (625) CER(%)	Predicted targets Actual targets (24) CER(%)	Predicted non-targets All firms (492) CER(%)	Predicted non-targets Actual targets (6) CER(%)
1	0.10	−0.61	−0.16	−0.59
10	0.63	−1.38	0.90	5.55
20	0.79	−3.01	0.82	4.57
30	0.79	−3.58	1.49	4.31
40	0.96	−1.68	1.50	4.61
50	0.50	−1.44	1.23	3.47
60	0.47	0.32	0.32	1.18
70	−0.79	−2.12	0.02	7.41
80	−1.62	−1.40	−0.56	11.03
90	−2.17	1.71	−1.39	16.80
100	−1.81	6.17	−1.22	14.35
110	−2.27	6.82	−1.08	15.15
120	−2.94	6.56	−1.74	13.79
130	−3.27	6.51	−1.53	14.63
140	−2.88	7.43	−1.40	14.98
150	−1.74	11.55	−1.44	16.23
160	−0.54	16.99	−1.18	14.27
170	0.16	17.03	−1.65	17.37
180	0.81	17.85	−1.64	22.30
190	0.51	18.77	−1.37	33.31
200	0.17	19.26	−1.40	31.98
210	0.05	19.52	−1.35	31.59
220	0.05	20.20	−1.12	31.64
230	−0.85	20.79	−0.26	32.96
240	−0.67	20.93	−1.53	35.16
250	−1.62[a]	20.98[b]	−1.51[a]	36.24[b]

[a] Not significant at the 5 percent level.
[b] Significant at the 5 percent level.

Table 5 reports the average daily cumulative excess return, CER, starting with the first trading day of 1980 in intervals of 10 trading days. In addition to the group of 625 firms which are predicted by the model to be potential targets, CERs are reported for three other portfolios: the 24 predicted targets which in fact became targets, the 492 firms which are predicted to be non-targets, and the 6 predicted non-targets which in fact became targets.

The results are not consistent with the hypothesis that it is possible to earn significant positive excess returns by investing in firms identified as potential targets by the model. The average cumulative excess return for the 625 predicted targets over the 250 days is −1.62% ($t = -0.77$). The average CER for the predicted targets is small and hovers around zero throughout the holding period. In contrast, the average *CER* for the subgroup of 24 predicted targets which became targets during the holding period is large and impressive. The 250-day *CER* for this group is 20.98% ($t = 2.28$). Thus, the reason for the insignificant returns for the predicted targets as a whole lies in the fact that this group consists of 601 firms which are incorrectly predicted by the model as potential targets. The large number of firms erroneously classified as targets significantly reduces the overall economic usefulness of the model's predictions.

For comparison, the *CER*s for the predicted non-targets are also presented in table 5. The *CER*s for the predicted non-targets mirror those of predicted targets. The 250-day *CER* for the 492 predicted non-targets is -1.51% ($t = -0.79$), and that for the 6 predicted non-targets which became targets during this period is 36.24% ($t = 2.46$). This indicates that, on average, excess returns for predicted targets are not very different from those of the predicted non-targets.

4.2.4. Discussion

The above prediction test results show that investing in the potential targets identified by the model does not yield significant excess returns. This implies that the model's ability to predict takeover targets is not superior to that of the stock market.

As in the previous acquisition prediction studies, the data used in the estimation and prediction in this study is on average six months old relative to the takeover announcements. As argued earlier, the pre-takeover stock price movement of target firms indicates that the stock market does not identify takeover targets very accurately six months prior to their takeover. Hence, the above results imply that the model, just like the stock market, does not predict targets with a high degree of accuracy long before the takeover announcements. This conclusion differs from that reported by the earlier acquisition prediction studies.

There are some limitations to the generalizability of our conclusion. First, the set of independent variables included in our model is not an exhaustive set of all possible variables. The conclusions, which are based on the limited set of variables considered, cannot therefore be interpreted to imply that targets are unpredictable from all public data. Two factors tend to mitigate this limitation. The variables in this study are selected based on a set of frequently stated acquisition hypotheses. Thus, the results at the minimum indicate that these six hypotheses do not enable the prediction of targets with a high degree of accuracy. Also, while no attempt has been made to try all the variables considered by the other studies, the set of variables in this study includes most of the variables found to be important by others. Hence, the difference in the conclusions of this study and the others can not be totally attributed to the variables considered.

A second limitation is that the data used in the model estimation and prediction are on average six months old relative to the takeover announcements. This reduces the ability of the model to identify potential targets accurately. In a realistic application, one would want to use the most recent data, which are likely to improve the predictive ability of the model. However, this is unlikely to alter the predictive ability of the model relative to the stock market.

5. Summary and conclusions

A number of studies develop statistical models to predict takeover targets. They claim the ability to identify targets with high accuracy rates ranging from 60% to 90%, using information which is publicly available six to twelve months prior to the takeover announcements. The pre-takeover stock price movement of target firms reported by Dodd and Ruback (1977) and others, however, indicates that the stock market does not identify potential targets with a high degree of accuracy even three months prior to the takeover announcements. Thus, the results reported by the earlier acquisition prediction studies imply that their models have a superior ability than the stock market in identifying takeover targets. To probe this issue further, this paper undertakes a methodological and empirical analysis.

An examination of the methodology used by the earlier acquisition prediction studies shows that there are three principal methodological flaws which make the reported prediction accuracies unreliable. First, the use of non-random samples in the model estimation stage, without appropriate modifications to the estimators, leads to inconsistent and biased estimates of the acquisition probabilities. This results in overstating the model's ability to predict targets. Second, the use of non-random samples in prediction tests leads to error rate estimates that fail to represent the model's performance in the population. Third, the use of arbitrary cutoff probabilities in prediction tests makes the computed error rates difficult to interpret.

This paper adopts methodological modifications to avoid the above problems. The empirical study described in the paper estimates a binomial logit model with the independent variables selected on the basis of a set of six frequently stated hypotheses on the determinants of a firm's acquisition probability. To obtain unbiased and consistent estimates from a state-based sample of 163 targets and 256 non-targets, the conditional maximum likelihood estimator proposed by Manski and McFadden (1981) is employed. The prediction ability of the model is tested on a large group of firms which resembles the population in a realistic use of the model. The cutoff probability is derived to test the possibility of earning excess returns by investing in potential targets identified by the model.

While the estimated model is found to be statistically significant, its explanatory power is quite small. The magnitudes of the acquisition probabilities are in general very small. When the model is tested on a group of 1117 firms, 24 of the 30 (80%) actual targets and 486 of the 1087 (45%) actual non-targets are correctly classified. The strategy of investing in the 625 firms identified by the model to be potential targets is found to result in statistically insignificant excess returns. Hence, the estimated model's ability to predict targets is not superior to that of the stock market. Since the market does not seem to identify targets very accurately long before the takeover announcements, it is concluded that the model also does not predict targets accurately.

The methodological issues addressed in this paper are relevant to other areas of research which involve the use of dichotomous state models with the population proportions of the two states skewed. Methodological critiques by others, including Eisenbeis (1977) and Zmijewski (1984), point out some of the same problems in the context of other applications. While the problems are well-known in the methodological literature, the applied research seems to lag behind in addressing them. This paper demonstrates that ignoring these problems can lead to serious biases in inferences. It is also shown that the problems can be avoided by using relatively simple modifications to the current methodology.

Appendix A

Definitions and computations of variables

(1) *Average excess return* (AER): The excess return on a firm's stock is defined as the difference between the firm's actual return and the expected return from a two-parameter market model. The data are drawn from the CRSP daily stock return file. The parameters of the market model are computed for each firm using one year's data, those of the fifth year prior to the observation year. The excess returns are computed over a period of four years prior to the observation year. (For example, consider a firm which was a target in the year 1975. Data from 1970 are used to estimate the market model, and the excess returns are computed over the period 1971–1974.) AER is computed as the average excess return per day over this four-year period. The unit of measurement of AER is percent per day.

(2) *Return on equity* (ROE): Return on equity is defined as the ratio of net income before extraordinary items and discontinued operations to the common and preferred equity of a firm. COMPUSTAT data items 10, 11 and 18 are used for net income, common equity and preferred equity, respectively.

The ratio is computed and averaged over a period of four years prior to the year from which an observation is drawn.

(3) *Growth (GROWTH)*: Growth of a firm is defined as the annual rate of change in the firm's net sales. COMPUSTAT data item 12 is used in the computations. The annual sales growth is computed and averaged over the three fiscal years prior to the observation year. (For example, consider a target firm from the year 1975 with a December 31 fiscal year. The sales data from the period January 1, 1972 to December 31, 1974 are used to compute the sales growth during the three fiscal years 1972, 1973 and 1974, and the average growth rate for these three years is used as the growth variable.) The unit of measurement of the growth variable is percent per year.

(4) *Liquidity (LIQUIDITY)*: Liquidity is defined as the ratio of the net liquid assets of a firm to its total assets. The net liquid assets are defined as the cash plus the marketable securities less the current liabilities. COMPUSTAT data items 1 and 2 are used to compute the net liquid assets and data item 6 is used for the total assets. The liquidity ratio is computed for the three fiscal years prior to the observation year, and the average is used as the liquidity variable. The unit of measurement for the liquidity variable is percentage per year.

(5) *Leverage (LEVERAGE)*: Leverage is defined as the ratio of the long-term debt of a firm to its equity. The equity is defined as the sum of the preferred and common equity. COMPUSTAT item 9 is used for the long-term debt, and the data items 10 and 11 are used to calculate the equity. The debt/equity ratio is computed for the three fiscal years prior to the observation year, and the average is used as the leverage variable. The unit of the leverage variable is percent per year.

(6) *Growth–resource dummy (GRDUMMY)*: The growth–resource dummy is a 0/1 variable defined on the basis of the three variables growth, liquidity and leverage defined above. The dummy variable is assigned a value one if the firm has a combination of either low growth–high liquidity–low leverage or high growth–low liquidity–high leverage. The dummy is set to zero for all the other combinations. Each of the three variables growth, liquidity and leverage is defined as 'high' if its value for a firm is larger than the average for all the COMPUSTAT firms, otherwise, it is defined as 'low'.

(7) *Industry dummy (IDUMMY)*: The industry dummy is a 0/1 variable. It is assigned a value one if at least one acquisition occurred in a firm's four-digit SIC industry during the year prior to the observation year; otherwise, it is given a value zero.

(8) *Firm size (SIZE):* The variable SIZE is defined as the total net book value of a firm's assets. COMPUSTAT data item 6 is used to measure the total book assets. The variable is measured as of the fiscal year end immediately prior to the observation year. The units are millions of dollars.

(9) *Market-to-book ratio (MTB):* MTB is defined as the ratio of the market value of the common equity of a firm to its book equity. COMPUSTAT data items 24, 25 and 60 are used in computing the ratio. Both the market value and the book value are measured at the end of the fiscal year preceding the observation year. The variable is expressed as a ratio.

(10) *Price–earnings ratio (P/E):* The price–earnings ratio is defined as the ratio of a firm's stock price per share to its earnings per share. COMPUSTAT data items 24 and 58 are employed in the computations. The P/E ratio is computed as of the fiscal year end preceding the observation year.

Note: The observation year is defined for a target firm as the year in which it was acquired; for the non-targets, it is defined as 1979, the year as of which they are observed to be not acquired.

References

Altman, E.I., R.G. Haldeman and P. Narayanan, 1977, ZETA analysis: A new model to identify bankruptcy risk of corporations, Journal of Banking and Finance 1, 29–54.

Asquith, P., 1983, Merger bids, uncertainty, and stockholder returns, Journal of Financial Economics 11, 51–83.

Belkoui, A., 1978, Financial ratios as predictors of Canadian takeovers, Journal of Business Finance and Accounting, Spring, 93–107.

Berkman, J., D. Brownstone and Associates 1979, Qualitative, intermittent, and limited dependent variable statistical program (Department of Economics, MIT, Cambridge, MA).

Castagna, A.D. and Z.P. Matolcsy, 1976, Financial ratios as predictors of company acquisitions, Journal of the Securities Institute of Australia, Dec., 6–10.

Cosslett, S.R., 1981, Efficient estimation of discrete-choice models, in: C.F. Manski and D. McFadden, eds., Structural analysis of discrete data with econometric applications (MIT Press, Cambridge, MA).

Dietrich, J. Kimball and E. Sorensen, 1984, An application of logit analysis to prediction of merger targets, Journal of Business Research 12, 393–402.

Dodd, P. and R. Ruback, 1977, Tender offers and stockholder returns: An empirical analysis, Journal of Financial Economics 5, 351–373.

Eisenbeis, R.A., 1977, Pitfalls in the application of discriminant analysis in business, finance, and economics, Journal of Finance 32, 875–900.

Gort, M., 1969, An economic disturbance theory of mergers, Quarterly Journal of Economics 83, 624–642.

Holthausen, R.W. and R.W. Leftwich, 1983, The economic consequences of accounting choice: Implications of costly contracting and monitoring, Journal of Accounting and Economics 5, 77–117.

Jensen, M.J. and R.S. Ruback, 1983, The market for corporate control: The scientific evidence, Journal of Financial Economics 11, 5–50.

Johnson, N.I. and S. Kotz, 1970, Distributions in statistics: Continuous univariate distributions – I (Houghton Mifflin, Boston, MA) 272–295.

Manski, C.F. and S.R. Lerman, 1977, The estimation of choice probabilities from choice based samples, Econometrica 45-8, 1977–1988.

Manski, C.F. and D. McFadden, 1981, Alternative estimators and sample designs for discrete choice analysis, in: C.F. Manski, and D. McFadden, eds., Structural analysis of discrete data with econometric applications (MIT Press, Cambridge, MA).

Ohlson, J., 1980, Financial ratios and the probabilistic prediction of bankruptcy, Journal of Accounting Research 18, 109–131.

Palepu, K.G., 1982, A probabilistic model of corporate acquisitions, Unpublished Ph.D. thesis (MIT, Cambridge, MA).

Press, S.J., 1972, Applied multivariate analysis (Holt, Rinehart and Winston, New York).

Simkowitz, M. and R.J. Monroe, 1971, A discriminant analysis function for conglomerate targets, Southern Journal of Business, Nov., 1–16.

Stevens, D.L., 1973, Financial characteristics of merged firms: A multivariate analysis, Journal of Financial and Quantitative Analysis 8, 149–165.

Zmijewski, M.E., 1984, Methodological issues related to the estimation of financial distress prediction models, Journal of Accounting Research 22, suppl., 59–82.

THE EFFECTS OF MANAGEMENT BUYOUTS ON
OPERATING PERFORMANCE AND VALUE

Steven KAPLAN*

University of Chicago, Chicago, IL 60637, USA

Received October 1988, final version received August 1989

This paper presents evidence on changes in operating results for a sample of 76 large management buyouts of public companies completed between 1980 and 1986. In the three years after the buyout, these companies experience increases in operating income (before depreciation), decreases in capital expenditures, and increases in net cash flow. Consistent with the operating changes, the mean and median increases in market value (adjusted for market returns) are 96% and 77% from two months before the buyout announcement to the post-buyout sale. The evidence suggests the operating changes are due to improved incentives rather than layoffs or managerial exploitation of shareholders through inside information.

1. Introduction

Management buyouts (MBOs) have increased in both size and number in recent years. Before 1980, MBOs were infrequent and usually involved smaller companies. According to the Joint Committee on Taxation (1989), MBOs and third-party leveraged buyouts accounted for approximately 20% of all takeover activity in the United States between 1985 and 1987. In the typical MBO, buyout investors, including some of the firm's current managers, pay prebuyout shareholders a premium of more than 40% above the prevailing market price to take the company private [see DeAngelo, DeAngelo, and Rice (1984), Marais, Schipper, and Smith (1989), and my results which follow]. Several sources of wealth increases to shareholders and buyout investors are frequently mentioned: reduced agency costs and new incentives, wealth transfers

---

*I wish to thank Paul Asquith, Alan Auerbach, George Baker, Richard Caves, Eugene Fama, Robert Glauber, Paul Healy, Richard Leftwich, Krishna Palepu, Andrei Shleifer, Robert Vishny, Karen Wruck, and seminar participants at the Harvard Business School, Sloan School, University of Rochester, University of Chicago, University of Michigan, University of Southern California, and New York University for comments on earlier versions of this paper. Harry DeAngelo (the referee) and Richard Ruback (the editor) were particularly helpful in improving the paper. I especially would like to thank my dissertation chairman, Michael Jensen, for his generous support throughout. Financial support was provided by the Graduate School of Business, University of Chicago and by the Division of Research, Harvard Business School.

from employees and public bondholders to the investor group, information held by managers that is not known by public shareholders, and tax advantages.[1] The first three of these nonmutually exclusive explanations for buyout gains predict that operating cash flows increase after the buyout.

Jensen (1986, 1988) argues that buyouts combine several powerful incentives that increase efficiency and value. Large debt-service payments force managers to find ways to generate cash and prevent them from wasting resources. Larger equity stakes give managers an incentive to find ways to pay off the debt while increasing value. Finally, the buyout specialist, who structures the transaction, monitors and controls the management team. According to this reduced-agency-cost or new-incentive hypothesis, the new incentives lead to increases in operating income and operating margins as well as reductions in wasteful capital expenditures.

Shleifer and Summers (1988) suggest that buyouts and takeovers transfer wealth to investors by laying off employees or reducing their wages. This employee-wealth-transfer hypothesis argues that operating income increases after the buyout at the expense of employee layoffs and wage reductions.

Lowenstein (1985) argues that managers have information about the company that is not available to other bidders. For example, at the time of the buyout announcement, managers may know that cash flows will be higher than the market expects. Because they have private information, managers can buy the company for less than a similarly informed bidder would be willing to pay, and informed shareholders would be willing to accept. This information-advantage or underpricing hypothesis also predicts that operating income is unusually high after the buyout.

This paper analyzes a sample of 76 management buyouts completed between 1980 and 1986 for evidence on whether the operating changes predicted by these hypotheses occur. The distinguishing feature of the analysis is the use of post-buyout information in addition to the pre-buyout information used in previous studies.

The 48 buyout companies with post-buyout financial data experience increases in operating income (before depreciation) and net cash flow as well as reductions in capital expenditures. Operating income, measured net of industry changes, is essentially unchanged in the first two post-buyout years and 24% higher in the third year. The change in operating income, however, does not control for post-buyout divestitures, which may lead the measured change in operating income to underestimate the true change. I measure operating income in relation to both assets and sales to control for post-buyout asset divestitures and acquisitions. The increases in both ratios are significantly greater than the industry changes, by approximately 20%.

---

[1] DeAngelo and DeAngelo (1987) and Shleifer and Vishny (1988) provide detailed descriptions of these sources of wealth gains.

The median net cash flow (the difference between operating income and capital expenditures), net of industry changes, in the first three post-buyout years is 22.0%, 43.1%, and 80.5% larger than in the last pre-buyout year. Similarly, buyout company increases in net cash flow to assets and to sales are significantly greater than the industry changes by approximately 50%.

The results for post-buyout operating changes are qualitatively similar to those in Smith (1989), who finds the buyout firms realize increases in (pre-tax) operating cash flow to operating assets as well as decreases in capital expenditures to sales.

The paper then considers whether the accounting changes represent valuable economic changes. To do so, I estimate market-adjusted returns to pre-buyout public shareholders and to post-buyout investors in those companies that can be valued after the buyout. Consistent with the results for operating changes, pre-buyout and post-buyout investors earn a median total market-adjusted return of 77.0% (mean = 96.0%). Pre-buyout public shareholders earn a median market-adjusted return of 37.2% (mean = 37.9%) and investors in post-buyout capital earn a median market-adjusted return of 28.0% (mean = 41.9%).

The results for post-buyout operating changes and for the total returns to management buyouts suggest that management buyouts are associated with valuable operating improvements. The remainder of the paper considers three hypotheses about the causes of the operating changes and value increases.

Employee-wealth-transfer hypothesis: Although some turnover may occur, the median change in employment for the buyout companies is 0.9%. This measure treats decreases in the labor force caused by divestitures as decreases in employment. For a subsample of buyouts that do not make large post-buyout divestitures, employment increases, by a median of 4.9%. The industry-adjusted change for this subsample is negative, but not significant. These results are not consistent with the notion that large numbers of employees are fired after buyouts. Because I do not have wage data, I cannot test for wage reductions.

Information-advantage or underpricing hypothesis: Although I cannot test this hypothesis explicitly, I examine several indirect pieces of evidence. First, I consider the pre-buyout shareholdings of informed parties (nonparticipating officers and directors as well as hostile third parties) who sell their shares into the buyout and do not invest in the equity of the post-buyout company. The informed nonparticipants hold a median $16.97 million or 10% of the equity of the pre-buyout company. If the buyout is underpriced, these nonparticipants irrationally sell their shares if they have the same information as the participating management team. Second, during the sample period, 46 proposed management buyouts were not completed. In 34 of these cases, the company was taken over by a different bidder. This suggests that managers and investors who propose a buyout must contend with an active market for corporate control. Third, I compare the pre-buyout financial projections managers give to shareholders with the actual post-buyout realizations. There is no evidence that the projections are low; in fact, they tend to be higher than future realizations. Finally, management turnover at the time of the buyouts is unusually high. None of these results supports underpricing.

Reduced-agency-cost or new-incentive hypothesis: As I do for the underpricing hypothesis, I examine indirect evidence concerning the new-incentive hypothesis. The equity holdings of the management team increase from a median of 5.88% to 22.63%. The increase is larger for managers other than the two top officers than the increase for the two top officers. These findings are consistent with new incentives having an important role in management buyouts.

In general, the results in this paper favor the reduced-agency-cost or new-incentive hypothesis over the employee-wealth-transfer and information-advantage hypotheses as explanations for post-buyout operating changes and wealth increases.

This paper complements previous work on sources of wealth gains in management buyouts. Kaplan (1989) and Schipper and Smith (1988) examine the value of tax benefits in management buyouts. Kaplan estimates tax benefits to have a lower bound of 21% and an upper bound of 143% of the premium paid to pre-buyout shareholders. Both Kaplan and Schipper and Smith argue that tax benefits are unlikely to be the entire source of value in management buyouts. In fact, Jensen, Kaplan, and Stiglin (1989) estimate that management buyouts increase net tax revenues under 1989 tax law. Marais, Schipper, and Smith (1989) examine wealth transfers from bondholders in a sample of MBOs announced between 1974 and 1985 and find minimal transfers on average.

The paper proceeds as follows. Section 2 describes the sample. Section 3 presents evidence on post-buyout operating changes. Section 4 measures returns to pre-buyout shareholders and post-buyout investors. Section 5 presents evidence on post-buyout changes in employment. Section 6 presents evidence on the information and reduced-agency-cost hypothesis. Section 7 concludes with a summary and discussion of the results.

2. Sample description

2.1. MBO companies

The sample of management buyouts is taken from companies delisted from the New York or American Stock Exchange during the period 1980–1985 and from companies listed as acquisitions (completed and pending) in W.T.

Grimm's Mergerstat Review from 1980 to 1985. The final sample satisfies the following criteria:

(1) The *Wall Street Journal* (*WSJ*) contains an announcement that the company proposes to go private.
(2) The newly private firm is an independent entity, not a subsidiary of another private company.[2]
(3) The proxy statement or *WSJ* confirms that at least one member of the incumbent management team obtains an equity interest in the new private firm.
(4) The total transaction value exceeds $50 million.[3]

Seventy-six companies, in buyouts completed between 1980 and 1986, meet these criteria. All 76 buyouts were announced in the period 1979–1985. Several buyouts listed as pending in 1985 were completed in 1986. Panel A of table 1 summarizes the distribution of these buyout announcements over time.

2.2. Pre-buyout data

For each successful MBO, information describing the transactions is taken from proxy, 10-K, 13-E, and 14-D statements and from the *WSJ*.[4] Stock prices two months before the buyout is announced and at delisting are obtained from Standard & Poor's *Daily Stock Price Record*. Other financial data are obtained from the COMPUSTAT Tapes.

2.3. Post-buyout data

Post-buyout information is available for 48 of the 76 MBOs in the *WSJ*, the list of SEC filing companies available from *Disclosure*, and *Going Public: The IPO Reporter*. Twenty-eight of these companies filed 10-Ks with the SEC because they had publicly held debt or preferred stock outstanding; nine companies issued publicly traded equity and filed offering prospectuses; two companies filed initial public offering prospectuses, but choose not to issue public equity; five companies were purchased by other publicly traded compa-

---

[2] Most of the sample companies filed a detailed proxy statement describing the proposed buyout. Proxy statements for leveraged buyouts with third-party buyers generally do not provide as much detail.

[3] The intent of this size criterion is to restrict the sample to larger, more fully disclosed transactions. This criterion also lowers the likelihood that the reduction of regulatory costs is a major source of value. Savings on the costs of preparing documents for public shareholders and the SEC are likely to be small in relation to value in these transactions.

[4] One company did not have any of these statements. The information used for this paper was obtained from the *Wall Street Journal* article.

Table 1

Distribution of 76 management buyouts completed in the period 1980–1986 by year, availability of post-buyout information, and information source.[a]

Panel A: Announcement dates of successful MBO proposals greater than $50 MM by year

	1979	1980	1981	1982	1983	1984	1985	Total
All firms	1	3	4	13	16	21	18	76
Firms with post-buyout data	0	1	3	7	9	15	13	48

Panel B: MBOs by original and latest source of post-buyout information[b]

	10-K report[c]	IPO filing[d]	Sale[e]	Releveraging filing[f]	Total
Original source of data	28	11	5	4	48
Latest source of data	14	13	14	7	48

[a] Firms included in the sample meet the following criteria: (1) The *Wall Street Journal* contains an announcement that the company proposed to go private; (2) the newly private firm is an independent entity; (3) the proxy statement or the *Wall Street Journal* confirms that at least one member of incumbent management will obtain an equity interest in the newly private firm; (4) the total transaction value exceeds $50 million. Companies were identified by (1) examining all companies delisted from the New York and American Stock Exchanges from 1980 to 1985 and (2) examining W.T. Grimm's Mergerstat Review from 1980 to 1985.

[b] Original source of data refers to the initial source of post-buyout information for a buyout company. Latest source of data refers to the most recent source of data or information for a buyout company.

[c] Company is in sample because it has publicly traded debt and files 10-K reports with the SEC.

[d] Company is in sample because it filed an initial public offering (IPO) prospectus after the buyout. After IPO, these companies file annual and 10-K reports.

[e] Company is in sample because it was purchased by a public company. The purchaser must file an 8-K report with the SEC describing its purchase.

[f] Company is in sample because it filed a prospectus to borrow money in the public bond markets after the buyout (usually to releverage the buyout company). After the debt issue, the company must file 10-K reports with the SEC.

nies; and four companies issued new publicly held debt to finance a releveraging. In addition to these 48 companies, one company made an initial public offering, but did not provide usable financial information; one company privately releveraged (twice); three companies were sold, but did not file usable public financial information; and one company filed for bankruptcy, but did not provide public financial information. Finally, 22 of 76 companies did not file a 10-K, had not gone public or bankrupt, and, apparently, had not been sold. Panel B of table 1 summarizes this information. The evidence presented in this paper reflects operating results through the end of fiscal year 1987.

2.4. Summary information and statistics

Table 2 provides summary information on the 76 sample buyout companies. The companies have a median equity market value of $253.8 million at the

Table 2

Summary statistics for size, premium, and leverage for 76 management buyouts[a] completed in the period 1980–1986 (dollars in millions).

Variable	Median	Mean	Std. dev.	N
Book value of total assets	$284.00	$525.8	$1081.0	76
Total equity value[b]	$253.8	$523.8	$ 889.1	76
Premium[c]	42.3%	45.9%	23.7%	76
Market-adjusted premium[d]	34.2%	32.3%	21.6%	76
Fees (% of market value of equity two months before proposal)	4.65%	5.26%	2.47%	70
Pre-buyout book value of total debt as percentage of value of total capital at time of buyout[e]	18.8%	20.7%	14.8%	76
Post-buyout book value of total debt as percentage of value of total capital at time of buyout[e]	87.8%	85.6%	14.3%	75
Post-buyout book value of new buyout debt as percentage of market value of equity two months before proposal	115.5%	122.1%	35.4%	75

[a] Financial and ownership data were obtained from proxy, 13-E, and 14-D statements describing the management buyouts. Stock price data were obtained from Standard and Poor's *Daily Stock Price Record*.
[b] Equity value is the value of all outstanding equity at the price paid to complete the buyout.
[c] Premium is calculated as the percentage difference between the final buyout price paid to pre-buyout shareholders and the value of the equity two months before the proposal.
[d] Market-adjusted premium equals $[(1 + \text{Premium})/(1 + \text{Market adjustment})] - 1$, where the market adjustment is the return to a portfolio with the same systematic risk over the same period.
[e] Value of total capital at the buyout is calculated as the sum of (1) the final buyout equity value, (2) the pre-buyout book value of debt, and (3) the pre-buyout book value of preferred stock.

time of the buyout. Pre-buyout shareholders of MBOs earn a median premium of 42.3%, where the premium equals the difference between the final purchase price of the equity in the MBO and the market price two months before the initial announcement.[5] [An analysis of excess returns suggests that the stock price begins to rise two months prior to the bid, either in anticipation of an MBO or because of hostile pressure.] In those cases where an MBO proposal followed a hostile takeover bid, the date of the hostile bid is considered the announcement date. The results also show that the buyouts experience very large increases in debt. The median ratio of (the book value of) pre-buyout debt to total capital at the buyout[6] equals 18.8%. The median ratio of post-buyout debt to total capital increases to 88.4%.

[5] Event-study methodology, which is not presented here, is consistent with these results. The median abnormal return from 40 trading days before through 60 days after the proposal is approximately 26%.

[6] Total capital equals the market value of equity (based on the buyout price) plus the pre-buyout book values of total debt and preferred stock.

3. Evidence on post-buyout operating cash flows

This section examines operating cash flows during the first three years after the buyout for the 48 companies in the sample with post-buyout financial information.

3.1. Methodology

The analyses focus on changes in three cash-flow variables:

(1) *Operating income (before depreciation)*, which equals net sales less cost of goods sold and selling, general, and administrative expenses before depreciation, depletion, and amortization are deducted. This is the definition for Compustat data item A13. Operating income measures the cash generated from buyout company operations before depreciation, interest, or taxes. My calculations as well as Compustat's do not include gains or losses from sales of divisions or assets. All three hypotheses described in the introduction suggest that buyout companies experience increases in operating income.

(2) *Capital expenditures* (including capitalized leases), which measures new investment by the buyout company. It does not include acquisitions or receipts from divestitures. This definition is the same as that for Compustat data item A128. The reduced-agency-cost hypothesis [presented as free-cash-flow theory in Jensen (1986, 1988)] argues that buyout companies previously were investing in negative net present value projects. According to this hypothesis, reductions in capital expenditures increase company profitability and value.

(3) *Net (operating) cash flow*, which equals operating income before depreciation minus capital expenditures. Net cash flow measures the net cash produced from a company's operations before depreciation, interest, and taxes.[7] Net cash flow would be the primary component of the numerator in a net present value analysis to value a buyout company. A permanent increase in net cash flow, therefore, should lead to an increase in value.

The three cash-flow variables are all measured before taxes. This is important because buyouts have large effects on the taxes paid by buyout companies [see Kaplan (1989)]. Managerial operating decisions, not taxes or financial decisions, affect the three cash-flow variables analyzed in this section.

The analyses measure the percentage differences or changes in the cash-flow variables in the first three full years after the buyout (years +1, +2, and +3) compared to the last fiscal year before the buyout (year −1).[8] Results for year 0, the fiscal year that includes both pre- and post-buyout operations, are not presented here because they are difficult to interpret as pre- or post-buyout

---

[7]This measure does not include changes in working capital. Working-capital changes are not available for several companies and are difficult to interpret in the presence of assets sales in other buyouts.

[8]This method is similar to that used by Healy and Palepu (1988) and DeAngelo (1988).

performance. [Furthermore, measured operating income in year 0 is biased downward because of buyout-related fees and inventory write-ups.] To control for economy-wide and industry effects, the analyses also present an industry-adjusted percentage change in the cash flows. The industry-adjusted change equals the percentage change in the cash-flow variable for the buyout company minus the median percentage change over the relevant period for all firms in the same industry.

The firms in the same industry as the buyout company are those that have (1) the same four-digit SIC code on *Standard and Poor's Compustat Industrial and Research* tapes (comparisons are made at the three-digit level and then at the two-digit level when fewer than three industry matches are found) and (2) a total capital value of at least $40 million at the end of the year before the buyout.[9]

I measure each cash-flow variable in three ways: (1) in levels, (2) as a fraction of end-of-period total assets, and (3) as a fraction of annual sales. Each of these measures is imperfect. If the post-buyout companies pursue the same growth, divestiture, and acquisition strategies as the control firms, the industry-adjusted change in levels would be the appropriate measure of abnormal performance. Post-buyout acquisition and divestiture activity, however, affects the measured changes in the levels. If the buyout companies divest more or grow more slowly than the control companies, changes in operating income and capital expenditures will be underestimated.

I partially control for divestitures by using restated financial information when post-buyout financial statements provide pre-buyout financial data restated for divestitures. Only 5 of 48 buyouts explicitly restate pre-buyout results to be comparable to post-buyout results, however. At the same time, at least 20 of the 48 buyouts divest operations valued at more than 5% of the value of the going-private transaction.[10] I use the caveat, at least, because it is not always possible to determine when and at what price a divestiture has occurred.

Dividing the annual cash-flow variables by year-end total assets (adjusted for buyout accounting changes) or by annual sales partially controls for divestitures and differences in growth. A year's cash-flow variables are based on the same continuing operations as year-end total assets and the year's sales. In a loose sense, these variables measure return on assets and return on sales. They can be interpreted as measuring the efficiency with which the buyout firms use a given amount of assets or sales.

---

[9]All of the buyout companies have a total capital value of at least $40 million at the end of year −1. This criterion places a similar size restriction on the control sample.

[10]The results that follow are similar for the subsample of buyouts that excludes the 20 firms with post-buyout divestitures valued at more than 5% of the value of the going-private transaction. They are not presented separately.

For most of the buyouts, buyout accounting leads to a change (usually an increase) in the book value of the assets, representing the difference between the market value of equity (the purchase price) and the book value. To make intertemporal comparisons meaningful, I adjust pre-buyout assets by the size of the buyout-induced accounting change in assets, which is usually provided in the proxy statement describing the buyout. When the change in book value of assets is not provided, it is estimated as the difference between the buyout purchase price of equity and the pre-buyout book value. It is not necessary to make any adjustment to pre-buyout sales.

Even measuring the variables as a fraction of total assets or annual sales, however, is subject to criticism. For example, if MBOs tend to sell unprofitable divisions, measured operating income and net cash flow divided by total assets or by sales may increase without any real change having taken place.

The results for medians (and Wilcoxon signed rank tests) are presented rather than for means (and Student t-tests) to control for outliers that dominate the means in some of the small samples analyzed. The results for means are similar, and usually larger in absolute value. All significance levels are based on two-tailed tests. This approach is conservative and implicitly assumes a null hypothesis that post-buyout cash flows equal pre-buyout cash flows. Obviously, the results would be more significant if one-tailed tests were applied.

3.2. Operating income

Table 3 summarizes the changes in operating income (before depreciation). Panel A shows that the median increases are 15.6%, 30.7%, and 42.0%, in years +1, +2, and +3 in comparison with year −1. Measured net of industry changes, operating income is essentially unchanged in the first two post-buyout years and 24.1% higher in the third year. However, as discussed above the change for many buyout companies will be downward biased because many observations are not restated to take account of post-buyout divestitures. Similarly, it is likely that the change in operating income for many control firms is upward biased because control company observations are not restated to take account of acquisitions. (This will be true if the operating income of control firm acquisitions exceeds that of control firm divestitures.) Consistent with this, I find (but do not present in the table) that the industry-adjusted percentage changes in sales of the buyout companies are −7.7%, −6.0%, and 2.7% in years +1, +2, and +3. The decreases in years +1 and +2 are significant at the 1% level. The buyout companies grow slower at first than the industry controls.

Changes in operating income as a percentage of assets and as a percentage of sales partially control for differences in divestitures and acquisitions for both the buyout and control companies. Panel B shows that industry-adjusted

Table 3

Effect of management buyouts on operating income.

Median percentage change and industry-adjusted change in operating income, in operating income as a percentage of assets, and in operating income as a percentage of sales for 48 management buyouts completed in 1980–1986. Operating income equals net sales less cost of goods sold and selling, general, and administrative expenses before deducting depreciation and amortization. Year -1 is the fiscal year ending prior to buyout completion. Year $+1$ is the first full fiscal year of post-buyout operations. Significance levels are based on two-tailed Wilcoxon signed rank tests.

Cash-flow measure	From year i to year j			
	-2 to -1	-1 to $+1$	-1 to $+2$	-1 to $+3$
A. Operating income[a]	$N = 48$	$N = 45$	$N = 37$	$N = 19$
Percentage change	11.4%[c]	15.6%[c]	30.7%[c]	42.0%[c]
Industry-adjusted percentage change[b]	-1.2	-2.70	0.7	24.1
B. Operating income/assets	$N = 46$	$N = 42$	$N = 34$	$N = 15$
Percentage change	5.9	13.7[c]	20.1[c]	14.6[d]
Industry-adjusted percentage change[b]	5.0	16.6[c]	36.1[c]	21.3[d]
Level (median) at year -1: 13.1%				
C. Operating income/sales	$N = 48$	$N = 45$	$N = 37$	$N = 19$
Percentage change	-1.7	7.1[c]	11.9[c]	19.3[c]
Industry-adjusted percentage change[b]	-1.9	12.4[c]	23.3[c]	34.8[c]
Level (median) at year -1: 10.9%				

[a] Data for year -1 are obtained from post-buyout financial statements when available and from proxy statements describing the buyouts otherwise. Panels B and C use data only from proxy statements.

[b] Industry-adjusted change for a given period equals the difference between the change for the buyout company and the median change for a sample of companies in the same industry during that period.

[c] Significant at 1% level.

[d] Significant at 5% level.

increases in operating income to assets are 16.6%, 36.1%, and 21.3% in years $+1$, $+2$, and $+3$ relative to year -1. Similarly, panel C shows that buyout company operating margins, the ratio of operating income to sales, increase after the buyout. The increases are significantly greater than those of their industry counterparts, by 12.4%, 23.3%, and 34.8% in the first three years after the buyout. The results in panels B and C suggest that the buyout companies have significantly better operating returns on assets and on sales than their industry counterparts.

In addition, the results in table 3 underestimate the true change in operating income in year $+1$ because most MBOs write up the book value of their inventories at the time of the buyout. This 'paper' inventory write-up is expensed in the partial and first full years after the buyout. As a result, cost of goods sold is artificially high and the measured change in operating income during these periods underestimates the true change.

For the 25 companies that report the inventory write-up, the median write-up equals 12.3% of inventory (at the end of the year before the buyout), which equals 10.9% of operating income in that year. Although not reported in a separate table, the buyout companies reduce their inventory to sales ratio by approximately 10% in the year after the buyout. The post-buyout reduction in inventory is consistent with both improved inventory management and the expensing of the 'paper' inventory write-up. This suggests that the actual change in operating income in year +1 is potentially greater than the measured change by up to 10.9% (the amount of the paper inventory write-up).

The results in table 3 are consistent with better post-buyout operating performance. The increases would also occur, however, if buyout company managers use accounting slack to reduce measured operating income before the buyout. According to this view, the managers can purchase the company for less than its true value, and benefit from a measured increase in operating income after the buyout. DeAngelo (1986) examines a sample of management buyouts and finds no evidence of unusually negative earnings in the year before the buyout. Similarly, table 3 shows that the buyout companies experience small and statistically insignificant changes in all three measures of industry-adjusted operating income from year −2 to year −1. This result is consistent with managerial reduction of measured operating income only if the buyout companies would have been above-average performers without accounting manipulations. With such manipulations, these companies are measured as average performers. Managerial manipulation is also consistent with the results if managers consciously begin to reduce operating income two years before the buyout. Section 6 presents evidence on changes in insider shareholdings at the buyout and on management turnover that is not consistent with this managerial manipulation view.

3.3. Capital expenditures

Table 4 reports changes in capital expenditures. Panel A finds that the buyout companies reduce their level of capital expenditures in years +1, +2, and +3 relative to year −1. None of these reductions, however, is significant. The industry-adjusted changes in capital expenditures, however, are very negative, equal to −35.9%, −32.6%, and −64.4% for years +1, +2, and +3 compared with year −1. These results are significant in years +1 and +2. As with operating income, the large decreases in capital expenditures may be caused by a failure to take divestitures and acquisitions fully into account.

The results in panels B and C for capital expenditures as a percentage of assets and sales are similar to those found in panel A although the industry-adjusted changes are smaller. Nevertheless, the percentage changes and the industry-adjusted changes in the two ratios are all negative.

Table 4

Effect of management buyouts on capital expenditures.

Median percentage change and industry-adjusted change in capital expenditures, in capital expenditures as a percentage of assets, and in capital expenditures as a percentage of sales for 48 management buyouts completed in 1980–1986. Year -1 is the fiscal year ending prior to buyout completion. Year $+1$ is the first full fiscal year of post-buyout operations. Significance levels are based on two-tailed Wilcoxon signed rank tests.

Cash-flow measure	From year i to year j			
	-2 to -1	-1 to $+1$	-1 to $+2$	-1 to $+3$
A. Capital expenditures[a]	$N = 48$	$N = 39$	$N = 32$	$N = 14$
Percentage change	-1.5%	-21.1%	-21.4%	-6.9%
Industry-adjusted percentage change[b]	-7.9[d]	-35.9[c]	-32.6[d]	-64.4
B. Capital expenditures/Assets	$N = 46$	$N = 40$	$N = 34$	$N = 13$
Percentage change	-8.5	-11.9[d]	-25.4[d]	-24.5
Industry-adjusted percentage change[b]	-3.5	-6.1	-5.7	-19.3
Level (median) at year -1: 4.1%				
C. Capital expenditures/Sales	$N = 48$	$N = 44$	$N = 37$	$N = 16$
Percentage change	-5.4	-23.2[d]	-31.6[e]	-28.1
Industry-adjusted percentage change[b]	-4.4[e]	-16.7[d]	-16.8[e]	-25.6
Level (median) at year -1: 3.0%				

[a] Data for year -1 are obtained from post-buyout financial statements when available and from proxy statements describing the buyouts otherwise. Panels B and C use data only from proxy statements.
[b] Industry-adjusted change for a given period equals the difference between the change for the buyout company and the median change for a sample of companies in the same industry during that period.
[c] Significant at 1% level.
[d] Significant at 5% level.
[e] Significant at 10% level.

Negative industry-adjusted capital expenditures are consistent with reduced agency costs and increased efficiency if the pre-buyout companies have large amounts of free cash flow and were investing in negative net present value projects.

Low capital expenditures are also consistent with the hypothesis that buyout companies are cash-constrained and underinvest after the buyout. Similarly, the measured increase in operating income might be a byproduct of postponed maintenance expenditures. Under this view, the buyout companies are so heavily burdened by debt that they fail to invest in positive net present value projects and activities. This would destroy rather than create value.

The accounting evidence presented here cannot determine whether reductions in capital expenditures are value-increasing or value-decreasing. Evidence presented in section 4 suggests, however, that value is created in these transactions.

Table 5

Effect of management buyouts on net cash flow.

Median percentage change and industry-adjusted change in net cash flow, in net cash flow as a percentage of assets, and in net cash flow as a percentage of sales for 48 management buyouts completed in 1980–1986. Net cash flow is the difference between operating income and capital expenditures. Observations are not included for one company with negative cash flow in year -1. Year -1 is the fiscal year ending prior to buyout completion. Year $+1$ is the first full fiscal year of post-buyout operations. Significance levels are based on two-tailed Wilcoxon signed rank tests.

	From year i to year j			
Cash-flow measure	-2 to -1	-1 to $+1$	-1 to $+2$	-1 to $+3$
A. Net cash flow[a]	$N = 47$	$N = 37$	$N = 30$	$N = 14$
Percentage change	11.2%	41.1%[c]	59.3%[c]	95.6%[c]
Industry-adjusted percentage change[b]	2.5	22.0[d]	43.1[c]	80.5[d]
B. Net cash flow/Assets	$N = 45$	$N = 39$	$N = 33$	$N = 13$
Percentage change	5.3	43.4[c]	66.3[c]	79.4[c]
Industry-adjusted percentage change[b]	4.3	50.5[c]	85.4[c]	64.3[c]
Level (median) at year -1: 7.8%				
C. Net cash flow/Sales	$N = 47$	$N = 43$	$N = 36$	$N = 16$
Percentage change	-1.3	29.2[c]	42.0[c]	43.2[c]
Industry-adjusted percentage change[b]	-8.4[e]	45.4[c]	72.5[c]	28.3[c]
Level (median) at year -1: 6.8%				

[a] Data for year -1 are obtained from post-buyout financial statements when available and from proxy statements describing the buyouts otherwise. Panels B and C use data only from proxy statements.
[b] Industry-adjusted change for a given period equals the difference between the change for the buyout company and the median change for a sample of companies in the same industry during that period.
[c] Significant at 1% level.
[d] Significant at 5% level.
[e] Significant at 10% level.

3.4. Net cash flow

The results for operating income and capital expenditures suggest that the buyout companies are successful in generating cash after the buyout. This section examines net cash flow, the difference between operating income and capital expenditures.

The industry-adjusted changes in net cash flow in panels A, B, and C of table 5 are all positive and significant. Panel A shows that the net cash flow of the buyout increases 22.0%, 43.1%, and 80.5% more than that of other companies in the same industry in years $+1$, $+2$, and $+3$ compared with year -1. Similarly, panel B shows that the increase in net cash flow to assets for the buyout companies in those three years are 50.5%, 85.4%, and 64.3%. Finally, panel C shows industry-adjusted increases of 45.4%, 72.5%, and 28.3% in net cash flow to sales in years $+1$, $+2$, and $+3$ for the buyout companies.

If the increases in net cash flow are permanent, then, in the absence of tax and financing effects, the value of the buyouts should rise by the same percentage. The large increases in net cash flow are consistent with large increases in values. In fact, the changes in net cash flow are of the same rough magnitude as the premiums or excess returns paid to pre-buyout shareholders to take the company private. Again, the accounting data cannot establish whether the large increases in net cash flows are permanent, but section 4 presents evidence bearing on their permanence by examining investor returns in the buyouts.

3.5. Potential selection bias

The sample analyzed here is subject to a selection bias if buyout specialists and managers in the more successful buyouts sell their shares in an initial public offering (IPO) or sell the company to another buyer. Such sales improve the reputation of the buyout specialists and reduce the non-diversifiable risk held by the managers. In less successful buyouts, the buyout investors may be unable or unwilling to sell their shares. If this bias is present, the sample includes atypically successful buyouts.

Alternatively, the most successful buyouts may not need to raise additional funds in the public capital markets and may remain private. Less successful buyouts may need to return to the public capital markets or obtain funds from corporate buyers. If this bias is present, the sample includes atypically unsuccessful buyouts.

Although I cannot examine those companies for which data are unavailable, I can divide the sample of companies with post-buyout data into those for which post-buyout filings are required and those for which such filings are voluntary, and, therefore, may be related to post-buyout performance.

The first group, the 10-K companies, consists of buyouts with publicly held debt outstanding immediately after the buyout. It includes companies that (a) do not retire previously issued debt, (b) issue new debt securities to the public to finance the buyout, or (c) pay pre-buyout public shareholders a combination of cash and debt securities for their pre-buyout common stock. As long as some of its debt is publicly and widely held, a buyout company must provide post-buyout data (in SEC 10-K filings) unconditional on post-buyout performance. The changes for the 10-K companies, therefore, should represent unbiased measures of post-buyout performance.

The second group, the IPO/sale companies, includes companies that subsequently (a) are sold, (b) are releveraged, or (c) file prospectuses describing an actual or anticipated initial public offering of equity. Because these companies do not have publicly traded debt outstanding at the time of the buyout, their subsequent release of post-buyout information is possibly conditional on

Table 6

Estimates of selection bias: Effect of management buyouts on operating income by post-buyout data source.

Median percentage change and industry-adjusted change in operating income, in operating income as a percentage of assets, and in operating income as a percentage of sales by post-buyout data source[a] for 48 management buyouts completed in 1980–1986. Operating income represents net sales less cost of goods sold and selling, general, and administrative expenses before deducting depreciation and amortization. Year −1 is the fiscal year ending prior to buyout completion. Year +1 is the first full fiscal year of post-buyout operations. Significance levels of differences in percentage changes and industry-adjusted percentage changes from 0 are based on two-tailed Wilcoxon signed rank tests. Significance levels of differences in industry-adjusted percentage changes of 10-K and IPO/sale companies are based on two-tailed Wilcoxon rank sum tests.

Cash-flow measure	From year i to year j			
	−2 to −1	−1 to +1	−1 to +2	−1 to +3
A. Operating income[b]				
A.1 10-K companies	$N = 28$	$N = 26$	$N = 18$	$N = 6$
Percentage change	11.0%	14.3%[c]	16.2%[e]	13.6%
Industry-adjusted percentage change[c]	−1.4	−10.1	−7.8	−40.8
A.2 IPO/Sale companies	$N = 20$	$N = 19$	$N = 19$	$N = 13$
Percentage change	9.3	25.3[d]	45.0[d]	65.6[d]
Industry-adjusted percentage change[c]	−2.0	15.6[e]	24.4	42.0[f]
Significance level of differences in industry-adjusted percentage changes of 10-K and IPO/sale companies	0.88	0.01	0.07	0.06
B. Operating income/Assets				
B.1 10-K companies	$N = 27$	$N = 26$	$N = 16$	$N = 5$
Percentage change	6.6	11.2	13.6	−2.6
Industry-adjusted percentage change[c]	6.0	12.7[e]	26.0[e]	8.9
Level (median) at year −1: 12.5%				
B.2. IPO/Sale companies	$N = 19$	$N = 16$	$N = 18$	$N = 10$
Percentage change	2.8	20.2[d]	38.7[d]	24.6[e]
Industry-adjusted percentage change[c]	4.0	37.4[d]	59.8[d]	32.2[e]
Level (median) at year −1: 14.6%				
Significance level of differences in industry-adjusted percentage changes of 10-K and IPO/sale companies	0.74	0.08	0.11	0.29

post-buyout performance. If there is a selection bias, the IPO/sale companies will perform differently than the 10-K companies.

Tables 6 and 7 present results for changes in operating income and in net cash flow for these two groups separately. Table 6 shows that the IPO/sale companies experience larger increases in operating income than the 10-K companies. In general, these differences are significant. The difference is particularly large for the change in levels. Here, the industry-adjusted decreases in operating income for the 10-K companies are associated with industry-adjusted decreases in sales.

Table 6 (continued)

Cash-flow measure	From year i to year j			
	-2 to -1	-1 to $+1$	-1 to $+2$	-1 to $+3$
C. Operating income/Sales				
C.1. 10-K companies	$N = 28$	$N = 26$	$N = 18$	$N = 6$
Percentage change	-1.0	1.7	-1.0	15.9
Industry-adjusted percentage change[c]	-1.7	5.8	17.5[f]	31.0
Level (median) at year -1: 11.9%				
C.2. IPO/Sale companies	$N = 20$	$N = 19$	$N = 19$	$N = 13$
Percentage change	-5.9	11.6[d]	21.2[d]	23.9[e]
Industry-adjusted percentage change[c]	-5.1	22.1[d]	34.1[d]	34.8[e]
Level (median) at year -1: 10.6%				
Significance level of differences in industry-adjusted percentage changes of 10-K and IPO/sale companies	0.84	0.01	0.06	0.50

[a] 10-K companies are those management buyouts that have publicly held debt outstanding after the buyout and therefore still file 10-K statements with the SEC. IPO/sale companies are those management buyouts that subsequently issue public equity, releverage using publicly held debt, or are sold to publicly held companies.

[b] Data for year -1 are obtained from post-buyout financial statements when available and from proxy statements describing the buyouts otherwise. Panels B and C use data only from proxy statements.

[c] Industry-adjusted change for a given period equals the difference between the change for the buyout company and the median change for a sample of companies in the same industry during that period.

[d] Significant at 1% level.
[e] Significant at 5% level.
[f] Significant at 10% level.

At the same time, however, the industry-adjusted changes in operating income to assets and to sales for the 10-K companies are all positive. Three of the six are significant at the 10% level or better. This is consistent with the hypothesis that the 10-K companies are using their assets more efficiently than the industry controls.

In table 7, the industry-adjusted changes in net cash flow for both groups are still large and, in most cases, still significant. The 10-K companies obtain industry-adjusted increases in net cash flow of 17.8%, 39.2%, and 99.5%, although only the result for year $+2$ is significant at the 5% level. The 10-K companies also obtain large and significant industry-adjusted increases in net cash flow to assets and to sales.

In all but one of nine cases, the industry-adjusted change for the IPO/sale companies is higher than the industry-adjusted change for the 10-K companies after the buyout. (In year $+3$, industry-adjusted change in net cash flow is 99.5% for the 10-K companies versus 80.5% for the IPO/sale companies.) None of these, however, is statistically significant.

Table 7

Estimates of selection bias: Effect of management buyouts on net cash flow by post-buyout data source.

Median percentage change and industry-adjusted change in net cash flow, in net cash flow as a percentage of assets, and in net cash flow as a percentage of sales by post-buyout data source[a] for 48 management buyouts completed in 1980–1986. Net cash flow is the difference between operating income and capital expenditures. Year -1 is the fiscal year ending prior to buyout completion. Year $+1$ is the first full fiscal year of post-buyout operations. Observations are not included for one company with negative net cash flow in year -1. Significance levels of difference in percentage changes and industry-adjusted percentage changes from 0 are based on two-tailed Wilcoxon signed rank tests. Significance levels of differences in industry-adjusted percentage changes of 10-K and IPO/sale companies are based on two-tailed Wilcoxon rank sum tests.

Cash-flow measure	From year i to year j			
	-2 to -1	-1 to $+1$	-1 to $+2$	-1 to $+3$
A. Net cash flow[b]				
A.1. 10-K companies	$N = 28$	$N = 25$	$N = 17$	$N = 4$
Percentage change	9.2%	41.1%[d]	57.1%[d]	54.2%
Industry-adjusted percentage change[c]	1.3	17.8	39.2[e]	99.5
A.2. IPO/Sale companies	$N = 19$	$N = 12$	$N = 13$	$N = 10$
Percentage change	17.0	49.1[f]	61.5[d]	112.5[d]
Industry-adjusted percentage change[c]	13.7	38.5[f]	57.5[d]	80.5[e]
Significance level of differences in industry-adjusted percentage changes of 10-K and IPO/sale companies	0.91	0.49	0.64	0.79
B. Net cash flow/Assets				
B.1. 10-K companies	$N = 27$	$N = 26$	$N = 16$	$N = 4$
Percentage change	5.3	40.4[d]	36.6[e]	30.6
Industry-adjusted percentage change[c]	4.3	43.8[d]	78.7[d]	52.1[f]
Level (median) at year -1: 7.5%				
B.2. IPO/Sale companies	$N = 18$	$N = 13$	$N = 17$	$N = 9$
Percentage change	6.8	52.5[e]	76.9[d]	98.6[e]
Industry-adjusted percentage change[c]	-14.0	79.1[e]	107.4[d]	69.2[e]
Level (median) at year -1: 8.2%				
Significance level of differences in industry-adjusted percentage changes of 10-K and IPO/sale companies	0.51	0.43	0.38	0.56

The results in tables 6 and 7 suggest that if a selection bias is present, it is small. The existence of any selection bias depends on whether changes in net cash flow or changes in operating income are the more appropriate determinants of value increases.

The results in this section support the existence of post-buyout operating changes in the first three years after the buyout. Over these years, buyouts experience industry-adjusted increases in operating income and net cash flow, and decreases in capital expenditures.

Table 7 (continued)

Cash-flow measure	−2 to −1	−1 to +1	−1 to +2	−1 to +3
C. Net cash flow/Sales				
C.1. 10-K companies	N = 28	N = 27	N = 18	N = 4
Percentage change	−1.2	26.0^d	23.1^e	23.2
Industry-adjusted percentage change^c	−6.7	41.6^d	51.6^d	28.2
Level (median) at year −1: 7.6%				
C.2. IPO/Sale companies	N = 19	N = 16	N = 18	N = 12
Percentage change	−1.4	45.1^e	59.9^d	50.8^d
Industry-adjusted percentage change^c	−15.7	55.6^d	82.1^d	34.3^d
Level (median) at year −1: 6.8%				
Significance level of differences in industry-adjusted percentage changes of 10-K and IPO/sale companies	0.57	0.24	0.37	0.73

[a] 10-K companies are those management buyouts that have publicly held debt outstanding after the buyout and therefore still file 10-K statements with the SEC. IPO/sale companies are those management buyouts that subsequently issue public equity, releverage using publicly held debt, or are sold to publicly held companies.

[b] Data for year −1 are obtained from post-buyout financial statements when available and from proxy statements describing the buyouts otherwise. Panels B and C use data only from proxy statements.

[c] Industry-adjusted change for a given period equals the difference between the change for the buyout company and the median change for a sample of companies in the same industry during that period.

[d] Significant at 1% level.
[e] Significant at 5% level.
[f] Significant at 10% level.

4. Wealth increases to investors in management buyouts

This section considers whether the accounting changes identified in section 3 represent real, that is, valuable, economic changes. To do so, I estimate the total market-adjusted returns earned by investors in a subsample of the management buyouts. Positive market-adjusted returns would be consistent with the existence of valuable operating changes.[11] Furthermore, if the changes in operating cash flows are real and valuable, they will be positively correlated with the market-adjusted returns.

4.1. Returns to investors

I was able to find a market value for the post-buyout equity of 25 buyout companies at some date after the buyout. I refer to the date that a market value is first available as the post-buyout valuation date. Eleven of the 25

---

[11] Operating changes are not the only explanation for large measured increases in value. Others include tax benefits and incorrect valuation by the market.

companies sold equity to the public through an IPO; six companies borrowed money in the public debt markets to purchase post-buyout equity and releverage themselves; and eight companies were sold to public companies or liquidated. The average time from the going-private date to the post-buyout valuation date was 2.68 years. For these 25 companies, I estimate the nominal and market-adjusted returns to pre-buyout shareholders, to post-buyout investors, and to the two groups combined.

The market-adjusted returns adjust the nominal returns obtained by pre-buyout shareholders and post-buyout investors by the return on investments with the same systematic risk over the same period. With the large and changing leverage in these buyouts and the extensive use of stock options, it is difficult to measure the systematic risk or β of the new buyout equity investments, and subsequently, market-adjusted returns to that equity. The systematic risk of total capital of the buyout companies (the asset β), however, should be relatively unaffected by the leverage. Accordingly, I calculate and present the nominal and market-adjusted returns to total capital (equity, debt, preferred stock, and capitalized leases) invested in the company at the time of the buyout. The appendix provides a detailed description of the method used to calculate the market-adjusted returns.

I use systematic risk as the measure of risk under the assumption that most pre-buyout public shareholders and post-buyout investors hold diversified investment portfolios. This may not be accurate for managerial holdings of post-buyout equity. Such holdings, however, account for only a small portion of the total capital invested in the buyout. The 25 companies with a post-buyout valuation have a median pre-buyout equity β, or systematic risk, of 0.73.[12] This suggests that the pre-buyout equity of the buyout companies has less systematic risk than that of the average company.

Panel A of table 8 presents the total returns to pre-buyout shareholders and post-buyout investors from two months before the buyout announcement until the post-buyout valuation date. The median total nominal return (*RET TOT*) is 220.3% (average = 235.0%). During the same period, the value-weighted index increases by a median of only 83.2% (average = 95.9%). Consistent with management buyouts generating large value increases, the median market-adjusted return to pre-buyout shareholders and post-buyout investors is 77.0% (average = 96.0%). This measure is positive in all but one case.

Table 8 also reports that the going-private or buyout equity price of these 25 companies is a median of 42.3% (average = 46.7%) higher than the price two months before the buyout announcement (*RET PRE*). The market-adjusted or excess return (*XRET PRE*) over this period is a median 37.3% (average = 37.9%). The median values of *RET PRE* and *XRET PRE* for the entire

---

[12] This is the Sholes and Williams (1977) beta estimate for the buyout company's common stock estimated from 600 to 100 trading days before the buyout announcement.

Table 8

Nominal and market-adjusted returns to investors in management buyouts.

Nominal and market-adjusted returns earned by pre-buyout shareholders and post-buyout investors for 25 management buyouts completed in 1980–1986 that have a post-buyout valuation. The market-adjusted return equals the nominal return adjusted for the return to a portfolio with the same systematic risk over the relevant period.

	Median[a]	Mean[a]	% > 0	N
A. Total returns to pre-buyout shareholders and post-buyout investors				
Total nominal return to buyout from two months before buyout announcement to post-buyout valuation date[b] $[RET\ TOT = (1 + RET\ PRE)*(1 + RET\ POST) + 1]$	220.3%	235.0%	100.0%	25
Total market-adjusted return[c] to buyout from two months before buyout announcement to post-buyout valuation date[b] $[XRET\ TOT = ((1 + XRET\ POST)*(1 + XRET\ PRE)) - 1]$	77.0	96.0	96.0	25
B. Returns to pre-buyout shareholders				
Percentage increase in stock price for (or nominal return to) pre-buyout shareholders from two months before buyout announcement to going-private date $[RET\ PRE]$	42.3	46.7	100.0	25
Market-adjusted return[c] to pre-buyout shareholders from two months before buyout announcement to going-private date $[XRET\ PRE]$	37.2	37.9	100.0	25

sample of 76 companies, 42.3% and 34.2%, are similar to the values for these 25 companies.

The nominal return on capital ($RET\ POST$) earned by the post-buyout investors from the going-private date until the valuation date for the buyouts is a median 111.3% (average = 127.9%). The median market-adjusted or excess return earned by post-buyout investors ($XRET\ POST$) is 28.0% (average = 41.9%). Post-buyout investors in 22 of the 25 companies earn positive market-adjusted returns during this period.

The finding that the market-adjusted return to post-buyout investors is positive contradicts the claim that similarly leveraged equity investments in the value-weighted market index would have earned more than equity investments (including stock options) in management buyouts. In fact, the returns imply that equity investors in the 25 buyout firms earn a median compound annual return of approximately 130% which exceeds the 74% compound annual return on a leveraged market-index investment calculated in a Goldman Sachs study.[13]

---

[13]See the letter from Louis Lowenstein in the *Harvard Business Review*, November–December 1989, p. 182, referencing a study by Leon Cooperman of Goldman Sachs. Furthermore, the quoted return of 74% is surely biased upward. It is based on a leveraged position in the S&P 400 (which is itself leveraged) purchased in mid-1982 (near the bottom of the market) and sold in mid-1987 (near the pre-crash market peak).

Table 8 (continued)

	Median[a]	Mean[a]	% > 0	N
C. Returns to post-buyout investors				
Nominal return to post-buyout total capital[d] from going-private date to post-buyout valuation date[b] [RET POST]	111.3	127.9	100.0	25
Market-adjusted return[c] to post-buyout capital from going-private date to post-buyout valuation date[b] [XRET POST]	28.0	41.9	88.0	25
Nominal return to investors in post-buyout equity[e] from going-private date to post-buyout valuation date[b] [EQRET POST]	785.6	4,274.6	100.0	25
Length of time from going-private date to post-buyout valuation date [TIME PRIVATE]	2.60 years	2.68 years		25

[a] All means and medians are significantly different from 0 at the 1% level.
[b] Market-adjusted return equals $[(1 + \text{Nominal return})/(1 + \text{Market adjustment})] - 1$, where the market adjustment is the return to a portfolio with the same systematic risk over the same period. The median systematic risk [Scholes and Williams (1977) beta] for pre-buyout equity is 0.73. Betas and market-adjusted returns are calculated using the return on the value-weighted NYSE–AMEX index. The median return on the value-weighted index is 83.2% (average = 95.9%) from two months before the buyout announcement to the post-buyout valuation date.
[c] Post-buyout total capital is valued as the sum of total common stock, preferred stock, debt, and capitalized leases (book value) at the going private date. The return to total capital is calculated as the sum of (1) the market value of common stock on the post-buyout valuation date; (2) the book value of preferred stock, debt, and capitalized leases on the post-buyout valuation date; and (3) the value of interest, dividend, and principal payments during the period between going private and the post-buyout valuation date.
[d] Post-buyout valuation date is the date of sale, IPO, or releveraging on which post-buyout equity can first be valued.
[e] Nominal return to investors in post-buyout equity equals the market value of post-buyout common equity (and options) at the post-buyout valuation date divided by the total investment in post-buyout common equity (and options) at the going-private date.

More detailed variable definitions are given in the appendix.

The market-adjusted returns calculated above probably underestimate the true returns for three reasons. First, the returns are net of the fees paid to investment bankers, bankers, and lawyers for help in taking the company private. The median fee in these transactions is 4.92% of the market value of equity two months prior to the buyout proposal. If these fees are included, the median total market-adjusted return increases from 77.0% to 88.5%, the average from 96.0% to 103.0%.

Second, the total return to post-buyout investors is calculated using the book value of debt at the post-buyout valuation date. Most of this debt is bank debt or privately held and therefore difficult to value. Using book value in this case probably underestimates the market value of the debt because total debt outstanding tends to be lower and operating income tends to be higher at the valuation date than at the going-private date. As a result, the outstanding debt will be less risky at the valuation date than at the going-private date. Holding the level of interest rates constant, the market value of debt will exceed the book value of debt at the valuation date. The market value of fixed-rate debt further exceeds its book value because interest rates tended to decline between 1980 and 1988.

Third, in at least two cases, post-buyout investors retain equity interests in divisions of the buyout companies that are spun off. Because the value of these spun off divisions is unknown, those values are not included in the return calculations. As long as the divisions have a positive value, the calculations underestimate the market-adjusted returns to buyout investors.

The evidence in table 8 that the buyouts earned large and significant market-adjusted returns is consistent with the evidence from the accounting data on changes in operating cash flows. As with the operating changes, these valuation results will be biased upward if the buyouts that can be valued are the better performers. The differences in post-buyout operating changes between the 25 buyouts that can be valued and the 23 that cannot are similar to those in tables 6 and 7. The industry-adjusted changes in net cash flow are similar for the two groups, and the industry-adjusted changes in operating income are larger for those companies that can be valued. The differences are not identical to those in tables 6 and 7 because some of the 10-K companies have a post-buyout valuation.

4.2. Comparison of returns and operating changes

This section tests whether changes in industry-adjusted operating income and net cash flow are related to the total market-adjusted return generated by the buyout. The analysis uses the last industry-adjusted change available at the time the buyout company can be valued. The buyout company value at the valuation date is likely to reflect the most recently available information. Because of the potential influence of outliers in a small sample and the noisy nature of the variables, this section focuses on nonparametric Spearman rank correlations.

The rank correlation of the industry-adjusted percentage change in net cash flow with the total market-adjusted returns is 0.56 (significant at the 2% level). The rank correlation of the industry-adjusted percentage change in operating income with the total market-adjusted return is 0.22 (significant at the 32% level). The respective parametric correlations are 0.37 and 0.36 (significant at the 12% and 9% levels).[14] These correlations suggest that the post-buyout operating changes have real valuation effects. The rank correlations suggest a

---

[14] The correlations are based on 19 and 22 observations, respectively.

stronger role for changes in net cash flow than for changes in operating income; the parametric correlations suggest the two measures have similar explanatory power.

The correlations of the industry-adjusted percentage changes measured in relation to assets and sales with total market-adjusted returns provide a different result. The rank correlation of the industry-adjusted percentage change in net cash flow to assets with the total market-adjusted returns is -0.15. The rank correlation of the industry-adjusted percentage change in operating income to assets with the total market-adjusted return is -0.06. The rank correlations, when the operating changes are measured in relation to sales, are -0.23 and -0.13. None of these is significant at greater than the 31% level. The results for parametric correlations are similar. These small correlations are less supportive of the hypothesis that post-buyout operating changes have real valuation effects (than the correlations using changes in levels).

The overall correlation results, therefore, give mixed support for the value of the operating changes. This is not surprising in view of the noise in the measures of operating change and market-adjusted returns.

Although they are not conclusive, the results in section 3 for post-buyout changes in operating income and net cash flow and those in section 4 for total returns to investors in management buyouts suggest that valuable operating improvements occur after the buyout. These results are consistent with three hypotheses or explanations. The remainder of this paper examines their relative merit.

5. Evidence on changes in employment

Shleifer and Summers (1988) argue that hostile takeovers and other control transactions can transfer value to shareholders from employees by breaking implicit contracts with those employees. Implicit contracts are broken by firing workers and/or reducing their wages. This section considers whether post-buyout decreases in employment accompany the operating changes.

Forty-two of the 48 buyout companies with post-buyout financial data also have post-buyout employment data. Table 9 presents the percentage change in employees at the end of the first full post-buyout year, year 1, in which employment numbers are reported in relation to the number of employees in the year before the buyout. In some cases, year 1 is the third or fourth year after the buyout. Table 9 then compares these changes in employment with the median industry change over the same period to obtain a measure of unexpected change in employees.

Panel A shows that the median change in employment for the buyout companies is 0.90%. Employment increases in 50% of the companies. At the same time, employment has grown 12.0% less in these buyout companies than

Table 9

Effect of management buyouts on employment.

Median percentage change and industry-adjusted change in employment following the buyout for 42 management buyouts completed in 1980–1986. Year −1 is the fiscal year ending prior to buyout completion. Year +1* is the first post-buyout year in which employment numbers are available. Significance levels are based on two-tailed Wilcoxon signed rank tests.

From year i to year j	N	Percentage change Median	% > 0	Industry-adjusted change[a] Median	% > 0
Panel A: Total sample					
−1 to 1*	42	0.9%	50.0%	−12.0[c]	30.9%[d]
Panel B: Sample excluding companies with significant divestitures and acquisitions[b]					
−1 to 1*	26	4.9	61.5	−6.2	38.5

[a] Industry-adjusted change for a given period equals the difference between the change for the buyout company and the median change for a sample of companies in the same industry during that period.
[b] The sample in panel B excludes companies that subsequently divested or acquired assets worth more than 10% of the capital value of the buyout company at the time of the buyout.
[c] Significant at 1% level.
[d] Significant at 5% level.

in other companies in the same industry (which is significant at the 1% level). This industry-adjusted result is consistent with the industry-adjusted decreases in sales experienced by the buyout companies.

The results in panel A do not control for post-buyout divestitures (or acquisitions). If a buyout company sells a division, its measured employment drops by the number of employees in the division. Unless the purchaser fires all of the division's employees, the measured change in employment in panel A overstates the true reduction in employment. Panel B controls for this overstatement by restricting the sample to the 26 companies whose post-buyout acquisition and divestiture activity does not exceed 10% of the buyout capital value. More than three-fifths (61.5%) of these companies increase employment, with a median increase of 4.9%. The industry-adjusted change is again negative (−6.2%), but is not significant.

In interpreting these results, the reader should note that the Shleifer and Summers (1987) argument pertains to actual employment changes rather than industry-adjusted changes. The results here do not support the view that buyout gains come from firing a large number of employees.

Although the data show that buyouts do not lead to large employment cuts, the results fail to address two important issues. First, I do not have data for buyout company wages. If the buyout companies succeed in negotiating wages downward, they will have an incentive to hire more workers. Second, it is not possible to estimate changes in the composition of employment; new employees may be hired after old employees are fired.

6. Evidence on information advantages and incentive changes

The information-advantage or underpricing hypothesis suggests that buyout investors and managers have information about potential operating changes or value increases that public shareholders do not have. Because of this information advantage, buyout investors can purchase the company for less than public shareholders would accept if all information were known. According to this view, operating changes would have occurred without the buyouts and public shareholders would have obtained the post-buyout returns earned by post-buyout investors. It is only because of their information advantage that buyout investors can obtain positive post-buyout returns.

In contrast to the underpricing hypothesis, the reduced-agency-cost or improved-incentive view argues that the debt burden, the equity incentives, and the monitoring associated with the buyout significantly reduce agency costs within the company. These improved incentives lead to value-increasing decisions and post-buyout operating improvements. Under this hypothesis, the buyout investors can obtain positive post-buyout returns even if public shareholders have the same information. The gains will not occur unless the buyout is completed or similar incentive changes occur in the public corporation. In this situation, public shareholders (and other potential bidders) bargain over the total gains from the buyout with the buyout investors. The likely outcome of such bargaining is a sharing of the gains in the buyout.[15]

The primary issue in distinguishing between the underpricing and reduced-agency-cost hypotheses is whether public shareholders (and other potential bidders) have the same information as buyout investors and managers. This section considers indirect evidence concerning this issue.

6.1. Evidence from the redistribution of equity in buyouts

6.1.1. Pre-buyout equity ownership

This section examines the shareholdings of managers and directors of the buyout company as well as other informed players who do not invest in post-buyout equity (referred to collectively as informed nonparticipants). According to the underpricing view, these informed nonparticipants know that the true value of the buyout company (even without the buyout) exceeds the buyout price. In this case, it would be irrational for them to approve the

---

[15]See DeAngelo, DeAngelo, and Rice (1984) for a discussion of the gain-sharing hypothesis.

buyout by selling their shares and thus forego participating in the MBO. The reduced-agency-cost hypothesis, on the other hand, has no such implications.

For each company in the sample, I distinguish those members of the board of directors and management who invest in post-buyout equity from those who do not. Those who invest in post-buyout equity are classified as management MBO participants. Those who sell their shares into the buyout transaction and do not invest in equity of the post-buyout company are classified as management nonparticipants.[16]

Similarly, I calculate the pre-buyout shareholdings of hostile parties that do not invest in post-buyout equity. Hostile parties are considered because they may have private information that leads them to invest in the pre-buyout equity of the buyout company. Hostile parties are classified as hostile nonparticipants. To be included as a hostile party, an investor group must have purchased more than 5% of the buyout company's stock in the two years before the buyout proposal and been opposed by incumbent management (as measured by public statements of opposition or targeted share repurchases). All stakes held at the time of the buyout proxy statement are included. Stakes are also included if they are held within three months of the buyout proposal, but sold before the date of the buyout proxy statement. The use of 5% shareholdings to measure hostile pressure understates the actual amount of hostile activity because hostile investors can exert pressure on companies without obtaining 5% stakes.

Table 10 presents the shareholdings of informed management participants in the MBO and informed nonparticipants. The results document the existence of significant informed nonparticipants. Panel A shows that management nonparticipants control a median 5.50% (average 9.66%) of the buyout company. In addition, hostile nonparticipants have stakes in 20 of 76 companies. The average stake of hostile parties in these 20 companies is 9.78%. The holdings of all informed nonparticipants equal a median of 10.00% (average 12.92%). These holdings are large, exceeding those of the management participants. In 5 of the 16 cases in which informed nonparticipants hold small stakes (less than 1%), the buyout company receives a hostile bid. In those five cases, however, the hostile bidder does not have an ownership stake. A significant nonparticipant exists, therefore, in all but 11 of the 76 buyouts in the sample.

This evidence is not supportive of the underpricing hypothesis. It is consistent with underpricing only if the informed nonparticipants receive large side-payments or are somehow coerced into accepting the buyout price. Pecuniary side-payments are not present in the buyouts in this sample – the

---

[16] In four MBOs, a father sold his shares in the company and retired, but his son succeeded him. In what follows, fathers are considered to be management nonparticipants. The results are not sensitive to this choice.

Table 10

Pre-buyout percentage and dollar shareholdings of informed parties in management buyouts.

Median and mean percentage and dollar shareholdings in buyout firm before management buyout by managers and directors participating in the buyout, managers and directors not participating in the buyout, and hostile investors not participating in the buyout in 75 management buyouts in 1980–1986.[a]

	Panel A: Percentage of total shares held in pre-buyout company			Panel B: Total value of shares held in pre-buyout company ($MM)		
	Median	Mean	N	Median	Mean	N
Management–MBO participants	4.67%	12.05%	74	$12.15	$39.80	74
All nonparticipants	10.00%	12.92%	75	$16.97	$32.56	75
Management nonparticipants	5.50%	9.66%	75	$ 8.30	$22.46	75
Hostile nonparticipants	0.00%	3.26%	75	$ 0.00	$10.11	75

[a] Shareholdings are calculated from information in proxy statements describing the buyout transactions. Shareholdings for management are calculated as of the time of the buyout. For hostile nonparticipants, shareholdings are calculated as of two months before the buyout proposal.

Management–MBO participants include those members of management and the board of directors of the buyout company who invest in equity of the post-buyout company. Management nonparticipants include those members of management and the board of directors of the buyout company who sell their shares into the buyout transaction and do not invest in equity of the post-buyout company. Hostile nonparticipants are outside investors who (1) hold at least 5% of the pre-buyout shares of the buyout company and (2) are opposed in some way by management, including statements of opposition or targeted share repurchases. All nonparticipants equals the sum of the shareholdings of management and hostile nonparticipants.

informed nonparticipants sever formal ties with the MBO company. Coercion also is unlikely because nonparticipating top managers and directors typically make up the special committee of directors that must approve the buyout proposal. If the buyout price is low, the informed nonparticipants can reject the buyout proposal. Underpricing is rational in this sample only if management nonparticipants receive nonpecuniary side-benefits, possibly from selling the company to their friends, the current managers.

6.1.2. Post-buyout equity ownership

Both underpricing and incentive considerations predict that the percentage of equity held by management increases after a MBO. If managers are risk-neutral, the expected value of the firm is maximized when managers own 100% of the equity [see, for example, Jensen and Meckling (1976) and Shavell (1979)]. Alternatively, if managers know the company is undervalued, they will rationally try to obtain as large an ownership interest as possible in the new buyout company. A risk-neutral manager would want to own 100% of the post-buyout equity if it were possible to purchase the company for less than its expected value.

If the principals who determine the equity stake of the agents in a buyout know the purchase price is low, the principals will want a larger amount of equity the larger the underpricing. They will compensate the agents with salary rather than with equity known to be undervalued. In contrast, if efficiency and incentive considerations are important, the principals will offer equity stakes to these agents.

As with pre-buyout equity ownership, I determine post-buyout equity ownership by examining the proxy statements for each company in the sample. Table 11 presents the distribution of pre- and post-buyout equity ownership held by buyout company managers, both as a percentage of total equity and in dollars. Panel A gives the pre-buyout ownership of the pre-buyout managers. Panels B and C present the pre- and post-buyout equity ownership of the post-buyout managers. And panel D presents the difference between these managers' pre- and post-buyout equity ownership.

As expected for both underpricing and incentive reasons, equity owned by managers as a percentage of total equity increases after the buyout. The pre-buyout management team owns a median of 5.88% of the pre-buyout equity (panel A), whereas the post-buyout management team owns a median of 22.63% of post-buyout equity (panel C). Panel D shows that the post-buyout managers increase their equity stakes by a median of 16.03%.

Similarly, before the buyout, directors and managers own a median of 19.30% of pre-buyout equity (in panel A). After the buyout, managers alone own a median of 22.63% of the post-buyout equity. Managers and directors control much more than 22.63%. In transactions involving a buyout specialist, at least one member of the buyout specialist sits on the board of directors. These specialists both own post-buyout equity and manage limited partnerships that buy post-buyout equity. In 62 transactions for which data are available, managers, directors, and buyout specialists together own or control a median 99.00% (average 83.10%) of post-buyout equity.

The distribution of the equity ownership between the two top managers and all other managers (summarized in table 11), however, favors an efficiency or incentive interpretation over one of underpricing. Panel D shows that the percentage of equity owned by the two top managers increases by a median of 4.41%, whereas the percentage owned by all other managers increases by 9.96%. In fact, the median total post-buyout percentage holdings of the two top managers are lower than those of the other managers. This is a puzzling result if the buyout participants know that the buyout price is low. On the other hand, the results suggest that new incentives for junior managers play an important role in buyouts.

The smaller increase in percentage equity for the two top managers could be caused by a liquidity constraint, but the changes in the dollar amount of

Table 11

Percentage and total dollar shareholdings in buyout firm before and after buyout by managers in 76 management buyouts in 1980–1986.[a]

	Percentage of total shares			Value of shares ($MM)		
	Median	Mean	N	Median	Mean	N
Panel A: Pre-buyout equity ownership of pre-buyout managers						
Chief executive officer	1.40	7.13	75	2.80	18.17	73
Two top managers	3.90	10.23	76	6.18	25.74	75
All other managers	1.19	1.97	76	2.54	5.59	75
All pre-buyout managers	5.88	12.20	75	12.80	31.33	74
All pre-buyout managers and directors	19.30	22.89	75	31.85	64.52	74
Panel B: Pre-buyout equity ownership of post-buyout managers						
Chief executive officer	1.09	6.42	74	2.55	17.17	73
Two top managers	1.48	7.59	76	3.95	21.06	75
All other managers	1.19	1.70	76	2.50	4.36	75
All post-buyout managers	3.50	9.30	76	7.87	25.42	75
Panel C: Post-buyout equity ownership of post-buyout managers						
Chief executive officer	6.40	14.75	67	1.03	12.24	65
Two top managers	7.54	18.39	68	1.54	13.41	67
All other managers	10.88	12.60	68	1.83	3.18	67
All post-buyout managers	22.63	30.99	68	4.13	16.58	67
Panel D: Difference between pre- and post-buyout equity ownership by post-buyout managers						
Chief executive officer	3.57	8.11	65	−1.55	−6.27	65
Two top managers	4.41	10.23	68	−1.55	−9.22	67
All other managers	9.96	10.79	68	−0.43	−1.50	67
All post-buyout managers	16.03	21.02	68	−3.69	−10.71	67

[a] Shareholdings are calculated from information in proxy statements describing the buyout transactions. Pre-buyout management is the management team of the buyout company at the time of the buyout proposal. Post-buyout management is the proposed management team for the post-buyout company. The top managers refer to those individuals who hold the title of chairman and president. Some companies will have only one top manager. All other managers refers to those managers who are not top managers. All post-buyout managers consist of the two top managers and all other managers.

equity holdings do not support this argument. Panel D of table 11 shows that the two top post-buyout managers reduce the dollar amount of their equity holdings by a median $1.55 million.

6.2. Hostile or competing bids

Section 6.1 does not consider MBOs that were proposed, but not completed. During the sample period, 46 companies made unsuccessful MBO proposals valued at $50 million or more. Of these, 22 were taken over by a publicly traded firm, 12 were taken over by a privately held firm, and only 12 did not experience a material change in control. Management lost control, therefore, in 34 of the 46 unsuccessful MBO bids. Overall, management lost control in 34 of 122 (46 + 76), or 27.9%, of the MBO bids proposed during the sample period. This measure understates the degree of competitive pressure on the buyout price because it does not include the unobservable cases in which potential bidders examined the buyout company and decided not to bid.

Lowenstein (1985) suggests that buyout investors pay public shareholders a low price unless a third party actually appears. He finds that the premium to pre-buyout shareholders is higher in nine management buyouts with at least three actual or potential bidders than in 19 management buyouts with fewer actual or potential bidders. I compare the market-adjusted returns earned by pre-buyout shareholders in buyouts with and without active third-party participation. Third-party participation is defined as buyouts in which hostile nonparticipants hold at least a 5% stake or in which a formal third party makes a competing bid. I find that the median market-adjusted returns are 33.1% and 37.1% for the two groups of firms. The 4.0% difference is not statistically significant ($p = 0.41$).

The evidence in this section suggests that managers and investors who propose a buyout face an active market for corporate control that limits the degree of underpricing that can occur.

6.3. Actual performance versus management projections

In the majority of MBOs, the buyout company includes the financial projections given to prospective lenders in the proxy statement describing the transaction. These typically include projections of operating income, but not of capital expenditures. If buyout company managers purposely mislead public shareholders by understating the projections, buyout company performance will systematically exceed the projections. Alternatively, performance that does not exceed the projections is consistent with the hypothesis that buyout investors, public shareholders, and other potential buyers have access to the same information. In a recent paper on management forecasts in 'normal', nontakeover circumstances, McNichols (forthcoming) finds that management forecasts of earnings are essentially unbiased. The median management forecast error (actual earnings less the management forecast) in her sample is −0.00001 times the company stock price.

Thirty-two of the buyout companies provide usable projections in the proxy statements that describe the buyout. To be usable, the projections must provide an estimate of earnings before interest and taxes ($EBIT$) or operating income before depreciation for year 1 after the buyout. To obtain projected operating income when only $EBIT$ is provided, I add the depreciation and

Table 12

Actual versus projected performance for management buyouts.[a]

Median difference between (1) actual and projected operating income and (2) actual and projected operating income to sales ratios of buyout companies in the two years following the buyout for 32 management buyouts completed in 1980–1986. Year −1 is the fiscal year ending prior to buyout completion. Operating income equals net sales less cost of goods sold and selling, general, and administrative expenses before deducting depreciation and amortization. Year +1 is the first full year of post-buyout operations. Significance levels are based on two-tailed Wilcoxon signed rank tests.

	(Actual−Projected) / Projected			
Performance measure	Year +1	% > 0	Year +2	% > 0
A. Total sample				
A.1. Operating income	N = 32		N = 25	
Percentage difference	−20.7%[c]	37.5%	−25.8%[c]	28.0[d]
A.2. Operating income/Sales	N = 29		N = 20	
Percentage difference	−6.4	37.9	−15.9[c]	20.0[c]
B. Limited acquisition and divestiture sample[b]				
B.1. Operating income	N = 20		N = 14	
Percentage difference	−19.4[c]	30.0	−20.7	35.7
B.2. Operating income/Sales	N = 19		N = 12	
Percentage difference	−7.1	36.8	−17.1[d]	25.0

[a] Projected operating income and projected sales are obtained from the proxy statements that describe the buyout transaction.
[b] The sample in panel B excludes companies that (1) subsequently divested or acquired assets worth more than 10% of the capital value of the buyout company at the time of the buyout.
[c] Significant at 1% level.
[d] Significant at 5% level.

amortization in the year before the buyout to projected *EBIT*. Because depreciation and amortization would have been expected to increase, this measure of projected operating income tends to understate actual projections.

Panel A.1 of table 12 shows that only 37.5% and 28.0% of the buyout companies meet the projections provided in the proxy statement in the first and second full years after the buyout. Actual operating income in those two years is 20.7% and 25.8% less than projected operating income. These shortfalls are significant at the 1% level. Panel A.2 presents a similar pattern for operating margins, with shortfalls of 6.4% and 15.9% in the first two post-buyout years. Restricting the sample to those buyouts with limited post-buyout divestiture and acquisition activity yields qualitatively similar results (panel B).

The finding that the MBOs underachieve their projections is not consistent with managers misleading public shareholders about company value by providing downward-biased estimates of operating income. The projection results suggest, but do not prove, that buyout investors and public shareholders have similar information sets. It is still possible that buyout investors have superior information, ex ante, about the distribution of future operating income. For example, buyout investors might know that the probability that operating income will fall below required debt service payments is much smaller than public shareholders believe.

6.4. Management turnover at the time of the buyout

The information-advantage hypothesis implies that the same managers run the company before and after the buyout. It would be irrational for a manager who knows the value of the company is higher than the buyout price to leave the company without investing in the new company. Alternatively, high management turnover would be consistent with the replacement of bad managers by good ones.

In 12 of 76 buyouts (15.8%), the CEO leaves the firm. In these 12 companies, the chairman also leaves the firm. (In most cases, the chairman and CEO are the same person.) In seven additional companies, the chairman, but not the CEO, leave. Therefore in 19 of 76 buyouts (25%), either the chairman, the CEO, or both do not join the new management team. In all of these cases, the departing executives approve the buyout either by tendering their shares or by voting for the buyout as members of the board of directors.

To put these numbers in perspective, Weisbach (1988) finds average annual CEO turnover to be 7.8% for a sample of 322 large firms. This turnover rate is not directly comparable to that for the buyout sample because it includes cases in which the CEO remains a manager of the company, usually as the chairman. The average annual frequency of a CEO leaving his company in Weisbach's sample is less than 7.8%. The 15.8% turnover rate of CEOs in the buyout sample exceeds Weisbach's average annual turnover of CEOs.

Warner, Watts, and Wruck (1988) find that the probability of a management change, defined as a change in the identity of the president, CEO, or chairman, in a given year is 18.3%. Again, this rate includes several cases in which the president, CEO, and chairman continue as managers of the company. Chairmen and CEOs leave the company in the Warner et al. sample less frequently on average. The 25% turnover for buyout-company chairmen or CEOs at the time of the buyout exceeds the average annual executive turnover in Warner et al. (1988). The unusually high top-executive turnover in buyout companies at the time of the buyout does not support a large role for superior managerial information.

If the findings on CEO turnover are combined with those on unsuccessful buyout proposals, the results are even more striking. In 34 of the 122 buyouts proposed, management loses control. In an additional 12, the CEO leaves the firm. Therefore, 46 of the 122 companies that propose buyouts, or 37.7%, effectively have new CEOs.

Overall, the results in section 6 on the distribution of pre-buyout and post-buyout equity, the number of unsuccessful bids, management projections, and management turnover do not support the hypothesis that superior managerial information is important in buyout transactions. Instead, the evidence supports the hypothesis that new buyout incentives play an important role in generating operating improvements and value increases.

7. Conclusion

This paper presents evidence on post-buyout operating changes in 48 large management buyouts completed between 1980 and 1986. These 48 companies experience increases in operating income (before depreciation) and net cash flow as well as reductions in capital expenditures. Operating income, measured net of industry changes, is essentially unchanged in the first two post-buyout years and 24% higher in the third year. The change in operating income, however, does not control for post-buyout divestitures, which may lead the measured change to underestimate the true change. Changes in the ratios of operating income to assets and to sales (which help control for divestitures and acquisitions) exceed the industry changes by approximately 20% in the first three post-buyout years.

The median net cash flow (the difference between operating income and capital expenditure), net of industry changes, in the first three post-buyout years is 22.0%, 43.1%, and 80.5% larger than in the last pre-buyout year. Similarly, buyout company increases in net cash flow to assets and to sales exceed the industry changes by approximately 50% during this period. The large magnitudes of the increases in net cash flow are driven both by increases in operating income and by decreases in capital expenditures.

Consistent with the evidence for operating changes, pre-buyout and post-buyout investors earn a combined median total market-adjusted return of 77.0% (mean = 96.0%). The changes in operating income and net cash flow are correlated (although not uniformly) with the market-adjusted returns.

I consider three explanations for the operating changes and value increases. First, I examine changes in employment after management buyouts. The median change for the buyout companies is 0.9%. For a subsample of buyouts that do not make large post-buyout divestitures, employment increases, by a median of 4.9%. The results do not support the view that investors benefit from large employment cuts.

I then present evidence that favors reduced agency costs rather than superior managerial information as an explanation for the operating changes. First, the holdings of informed parties who do not participate in the buyout (nonparticipating officers and directors as well as hostile third parties) are a median 10.0%, or $17 million. These nonparticipants irrationally sell their shares if the buyout is underpriced and they have the same information as the participating management team. Second, although the management team holds a much larger percentage of post-buyout equity than of pre-buyout equity, the increase is smaller for the two top managers than for all other managers. Third, post-buyout operating performance in the first two years after the buyout is below the projections provided by managers in the buyout proxy statement. Finally, management turnover at the time of the buyouts is unusually high.

Although not conclusive, the evidence presented here broadly supports the hypothesis that management buyouts experience post-buyout operating improvements and value increases. Moreover, the operating improvements and value increases appear to be generated by improved incentives rather than wealth transfers from employees or superior managerial information.

Appendix

Method for calculating excess returns to investors

This appendix describes the method used to calculate excess returns to pre-buyout shareholders and post-buyout investors.

In this analysis, time is measured as follows:

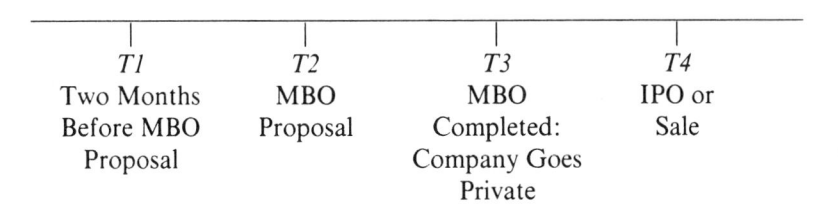

T1	T2	T3	T4
Two Months Before MBO Proposal	MBO Proposal	MBO Completed: Company Goes Private	IPO or Sale

The premium paid to pre-buyout shareholders ($RET\ PRE$) is calculated as the fractional difference between the buyout equity price (at $T3$) and the price of equity two months before the buyout proposal ($T1$):

$$RET\ PRE = [PRICE_{T3} - PRICE_{T1}] \div [PRICE_{T1}].$$

In general, the buyout price is the per-share cash payment received by pre-buyout shareholders. When the total payment includes a debt component, the buyout price is taken as the closing price per share on the day the buyout company stock is delisted. The excess or market-adjusted return to pre-buyout shareholders (*XRET PRE*) is obtained by adjusting *RET PRE* for the return to an investment with the same systematic risk over the same period:

$$XRET\ PRE = \left([1 + RET\ PRE] \div [1 + R_f + \beta^E * R_m \text{ over the same time period}]\right) - 1,$$

where R_f is the T-bill return, R_m is the Center for Research in Security Prices (CRSP) return on the value-weighted New York Stock Exchange–American Stock Exchange (NYSE–AMEX) index, and β^E is the Scholes and Williams (1977) β estimate for the firm's common stock estimated from 600 to 100 trading days prior to the buyout announcement. [The results for *XRET PRE* and *XRET POST* are qualitatively the same using an equal-weighted index and market-model estimates of β.] The total return to the investment of the same systematic risk is calculated by compounding monthly return data.

If the buyout company has issued equity (through an IPO), has borrowed debt from the public to repurchase private equity, or has been sold to a public company, the excess return earned by investors in the post-buyout company can be calculated. The calculations use the financial information provided in the initial public offering prospectuses, debt offering prospectuses, or 8-Ks describing the sales.

Because the buyouts are initially financed with a small amount of equity, it is difficult to estimate the beta that should be applied to that equity. Most equity betas would initially exceed five. Small percentage estimation errors could have large effects on measured expected returns. Instead, this paper measures post-buyout excess return as the excess return to total capital invested in the buyout company. With this method, it is not necessary to differentiate between debt and equity.

The total capital value of the buyout company at time T equals the sum of the values of equity, long-term debt, short-term debt, and capitalized leases when the buyout is completed:

$$TCAP_T = \text{Market value of equity}_T$$
$$+ \text{Book value of long-term and short-term debt}_T$$
$$+ \text{Book value of capitalized leases}_T.$$

At the time of the buyout ($T3$), the MBO is effectively a new company. The book value of new debt and new equity should equal their market values. Long-term debt issued by the company before the buyout, however, will typically have a book value different from its market value. Because such debt is typically a small part of total capital, $TCAP$ will be a good measure of total value. At the time of the sale or IPO, $TCAP$ will incorrectly estimate the true value of the company if the book value of the debt differs from its market value.

The total return to post-buyout investors is calculated as

$$RET\ POST = \frac{[TCAP_{T4} + \text{Interim payments to capital} - TCAP_{T3}]}{TCAP_{T3}}.$$

Interim payments to capital include the annual principal, interest, dividend and lease payments made between $T3$ and $T4$. It is assumed that the interim payments are invested in a portfolio with the same systematic risk as the company as a whole. This adjustment will tend to underestimate the terminal value because such payments are made throughout the year, rather than at year-end.

The excess return earned by investors in the MBO company ($XRET\ POST$) is estimated as the difference between the total MBO return and the return on an investment of the same systematic risk over the same period:

$$XRET\ POST = ([1 + RET\ POST]$$

$$/[1 + R_f + \beta^A * R_m \text{ over the same period}]) - 1,$$

where R_f is the T-bill return and R_m is the CRSP return on the value-weighted NYSE–AMEX index. β^A, the firm's asset β, is given by

$$\beta^A = \beta^E \div [1 + (1 - \tau) * D/E],$$

where β^E is the Scholes and Williams (1977) β estimate of the firm's common stock estimated from 600 to 100 trading days prior to the buyout announcement, τ is the marginal federal tax rate of 46% in effect during the estimation period, and D and E are, respectively, the book value of the firm's debt and the market value of the firm's equity at the end of the year before the buyout. This calculation (of the firm's asset β) assumes the firm's pre-buyout debt has a β equal to 0. Given the low level (and, therefore, risk) of pre-buyout debt, this assumption is reasonable. The calculation also assumes that the pre-buyout asset β equals the post-buyout asset β. This is conservative given the large increase in debt and accompanying interest deductions. The total return to the investment of the same systematic risk is calculated by compounding monthly return data.

References

DeAngelo, Harry and Linda DeAngelo, 1987, Management buyouts of publicly traded corporations, Financial Analysts Journal, May–June, 38–49.

DeAngelo, Harry, Linda DeAngelo, and Edward Rice, 1984, Going private: Minority freezeouts and stockholder wealth, Journal of Law and Economics 27, 367–401.

DeAngelo, Linda, 1986, Accounting numbers as market valuation substitutes: A study of management buyouts of public stockholders, The Accounting Review 61, 400–420.

DeAngelo, Linda, 1988, Managerial competition, information costs and corporate governance: The use of accounting performance measures in proxy contests, Journal of Accounting and Economics 10, 3–36.

Healy, Paul and Krishna Palepu, 1988, Earnings information conveyed by dividend initiations and omissions, Journal of Financial Economics 21, 149–176.

Jensen, Michael, 1986, Agency costs of free cash flow, corporate finance and takeovers, American Economic Review 76, 323–329.

Jensen, Michael, 1988, Takeovers: Their causes and consequences, Journal of Economic Perspectives 2, 21–48.

Jensen, Michael, Steven Kaplan, and Laura Stiglin, 1989, The effects of LBOs on tax revenues, Tax Notes 42, 727–733.

Jensen, Michael and William Meckling, 1976, Theory of the firm: Managerial behavior, agency costs and ownership structure, Journal of Financial Economics 3, 305–360.

Joint Committee on Taxation, 1989, Federal income tax aspects of corporate financial structures (U.S. Government Printing Office, Washington, DC).

Kaplan, Steven, 1988, Sources of value in management buyouts, Unpublished doctoral dissertation (Harvard University, Cambridge, MA).

Kaplan, Steven, 1989, Management buyouts: Evidence on taxes as a source of value, Journal of Finance 44, 611–632.

Lehn, Kenneth and Anette Poulsen, 1989, Free cash flow and stockholder gains in going private transactions, Journal of Finance 44, 771–788.

Lowenstein, Louis, 1985, Management buyouts, Columbia Law Review 85, 730–784.

Marais, Laurentius, Katherine Schipper, and Abbie Smith, 1989, Wealth effects of going private on senior securities, Journal of Financial Economics 23, 155–191.

McNichols, Maureen, forthcoming, Evidence on informational asymmetries from management earnings forecasts and stock returns, The Accounting Review.

Schipper, Katherine and Abbie Smith, 1988, Corporate income tax effects of management buyouts, Mimeo., June (University of Chicago, Chicago, IL).

Scholes, Myron and Joseph Williams, 1977, Estimating betas from nonsynchronous data, Journal of Financial Economics 5, 309–328.

Shavell, Steven, 1979, Risk sharing and incentives in the principal and agent relationship, Bell Journal of Economics 10, 55–73.

Shleifer, Andrei and Larry Summers, 1988, Breach of trust in hostile takeovers, in: Alan Auerbach, ed., Corporate takeovers: Causes and consequences (University of Chicago Press, Chicago, IL).

Shleifer, Andrei and Robert Vishny, 1988, Management buyouts as a response to market pressure, in: Alan Auerbach, ed., Mergers and acquisitions (University of Chicago Press, Chicago, IL).

Smith, Abbie, 1989, Corporate ownership structure and performance: The case of management buyouts, Mimeo., Jan. (University of Chicago, Chicago, IL).

Warner, Jerry, Ross Watts, and Karen Wruck, 1988, Stock prices, event prediction and event studies: An examination of top management restructurings, Journal of Financial Economics 20, 461–492.

Weisbach, Michael, 1988, Outside directors and CEO turnover, Journal of Financial Economics 20, 431–460.

CAMPEAU'S ACQUISITION OF FEDERATED
Value Destroyed or Value Added

Steven N. KAPLAN*

University of Chicago, Chicago, IL 60637, USA

Received April 1990, final version received July 1990

I analyze the acquisition of Federated Department Stores by Campeau Corporation and find that after the purchase the value of Federated assets increased by more than $1.8 billion. Federated and Campeau defaulted on the debt used to finance the acquisition because Campeau paid a premium of $3.4 billion for Federated, an overpayment of $1.6 billion, financed 97% of the purchase with debt, and did not have enough other assets to make up the shortfall. The Federated purchase illustrates that a highly leveraged transaction can increase value, but still not be able to make its debt payments.

1. Introduction

On January 15, 1990, Federated Department Stores, Inc. and Allied Stores Corporation, both controlled by Campeau Corporation, filed for protection from creditors under Chapter 11 of the Federal Bankruptcy Code. Campeau's inability to meet the required debt payments at the two companies has been attributed to its purchase of Federated Department stores in 1988.[1] Because of the bankruptcy, Campeau's acquisition of Federated has been widely criticized. *Business Week*, for example, ranked it among the ten worst deals of the 1980s. *Fortune* called it the 'biggest, looniest deal ever'.[2] If the transaction was as unsuccessful as the popular reaction suggests, it should have led to an overall loss in value. This paper compares the value of the Federated assets before and after Campeau's purchase and finds a substantial increase.

---

*I thank Harry and Linda DeAngelo, Douglas Diamond, Robert Gertner, Stuart Gilson, Monroe Greenstein, Daniel Raff, Richard Ruback (the referee), Andrei Shleifer, Jeremy Stein, Robert Vishny, and especially Michael Jensen for helpful comments.

[1] See, for example, 'Buy-out bomb: An extra $500 million paid for Federated got Campeau into trouble', *Wall Street Journal*, January 11, 1990, p. 1, and 'Campeau bankers are posing some $2 billion questions', *New York Times*, January 14, 1990, Business, p. 12.

[2] See 'The best and worst deals of the '80s', *Business Week*, January 15, 1990, p. 52, and Carol Loomis, 'The biggest, looniest deal ever', *Fortune*, June 18, 1990. Also see the two articles in footnote 1.

0304-405X/89/$3.50 © 1989, Elsevier Science Publishers B.V. (North-Holland)

At the end of 1987, one month before Campeau's initial bid, Federated assets, measured as the sum of equity and debt, had a market value of approximately $4.25 billion. At the end of 1989, before Campeau filed for bankruptcy protection, my 'most likely' estimate suggests that the Federated assets were worth $6.08 billion (market-adjusted to the end of 1987) – an increase of more than $1.8 billion. The $6.08 billion valuation represents the sum of the most likely estimates of (1) the proceeds from the sale of Federated divisions – $3.77 billion, (2) interim cash flows from the remaining Federated divisions – $0.22 billion, and (3) the value of the remaining Federated divisions in December 1989 – $2.09 billion. Under conservative assumptions for the interim cash flows and the remaining asset value, Federated appears to have been worth $5.28 billion – still $1 billion more than before the Campeau acquisition. Under optimistic, but plausible assumptions, the value of Federated assets reaches $6.88 billion – an increase of over $2.6 billion.

The estimated values under Campeau do not include direct bankruptcy costs or indirect costs of financial distress incurred since the Chapter 11 filing. These costs would lower the value of the remaining Federated divisions. Although estimating the bankruptcy costs at this date is not possible, they would have to reduce the terminal value of Federated assets in December 1989 to less than $0.26 billion (market-adjusted to December 1987) for the deal to result in a net destruction of value. (The market-adjusted $0.26 billion equals $0.37 billion in December 1989 dollars.) Recent prices paid for retailing assets and Federated's early post-bankruptcy operating performance suggest that the post-bankruptcy value of the remaining divisions exceeds that amount and may approach the most likely case estimates. It is too early to tell whether the assets will retain their value through the remainder of the bankruptcy proceedings.

If the value of Federated assets increased under Campeau's ownership, why has the transaction been so criticized? The $1.8 billion increase in value was less than the $3.4 billion premium paid to acquire Federated. At the end of 1987, Federated's stock traded below $33 per share. In January 1988, Campeau announced a hostile takeover bid at $47 per share. After a series of revisions, the bid was finally accepted in April at a price of $73.50 per share, a premium of 124%. At this price, the Federated assets (equity and total debt) cost Campeau $8.17 billion (or $7.67 billion market-adjusted to the end of 1987). The $7.67 billion market-adjusted purchase price is almost $1.6 billion greater than the $6.08 billion most likely estimate of Federated's post-acquisition asset value. Table 1 summarizes the different values (both actual and market-adjusted to December 31, 1987) placed on the Federated assets. Under all three valuations, Campeau overpaid for the Federated assets.

Table 1

Actual and market-adjusted value[a] of Federated Department Stores under pre-Campeau management, Federated assets under Campeau Corporation, and the purchase price paid by Campeau Corporation. Values of Federated under Campeau are the sum of asset sales, interim cash flows, and the value of remaining Federated assets. All values are in billions of dollars.

Federated market value December 31, 1987[b]	Three valuation estimates of Federated under Campeau as of December 31, 1989[c]	Price paid by Campeau (including fees)[d]
	(A) Actual value	
$4.25	Conservative: $6.20 Most likely: $7.35 Optimistic: $8.49	$8.17
	(B) Value market-adjusted to December 31, 1987	
$4.25	Conservative: $5.28 Most likely: $6.08 Optimistic: $6.88	$7.67

[a] Market-adjusted values equal the actual values discounted from the month in which they occur to December 31, 1987 by the actual return on the S&P 500. If invested in the S&P 500 on January 1, 1988, the market-adjusted value would equal the actual value in the month the cash flow occurs.

[b] Federated market value on December 31, 1987 equals the sum of the market value of equity and the estimated market value of Federated debt. Details are provided in the text.

[c] Value of Federated assets under Campeau equals the sum of asset sales, interim cash flows, and value of remaining assets for the most likely case, conservative case, and optimistic case valuations. Asset sales are the value of the divisions sold by Federated from May 1988 to February 1989. These values are detailed in table 2. Interim cash flows calculated in table 5 equal earnings before interest, taxes, depreciation, and amortization (*EBITDA*) less capital expenditures and the increase in net working capital. The values of the remaining assets in the three cases are described in table 6.

[d] Purchase price paid by Campeau is the sum of the market value paid for all equity and the fees paid in May 1988, and the book value of Federated debt outstanding on January 30, 1988.

Overpayment alone would not have been sufficient to force Federated and Campeau to seek protection under Chapter 11. Campeau effectively financed 97% of the Federated purchase with debt (including assumed Federated debt). In late 1989, the operating cash flow from the unsold Federated divisions was not sufficient to meet required debt service. In addition, Campeau did not have enough other, non-Federated assets to make up the shortfall. If Campeau had financed the purchase with at least $1.59 billion of equity – the difference between the $7.67 billion purchase price and the most likely valuation of $6.08 billion – the debt service payments presumably could have been structured in such a way that the asset sales and operating cash flow would have been sufficient to meet them. Campeau would have lost his equity investment, but Federated would not have landed in bankruptcy court.

The Federated purchase illustrates that a highly leveraged transaction can increase value, but still not be able to make its debt payments. The failure to make debt payments does not necessarily imply that value was destroyed. In Federated's case, the remaining divisions appeared to be healthy businesses before the bankruptcy filing, generating over $370 million in operating earnings in fiscal 1989. This is fundamentally different from the traditional notion of financial distress, in which a firm's inability to make debt payments follows a period of business decline and identifies the business as unhealthy. [See, for example, Baldwin and Mason (1983) on the Massey Ferguson case.]

Although I document the increase in Federated's value under Campeau's ownership, I cannot unambiguously determine its sources. Possible sources include asset sales to more efficient managers (both in related businesses and in management buyouts), tax benefits, and overpayment by the purchasers of the assets. As with any study relying on market values, one can always argue that the market undervalued the Federated assets at the end of 1987 and that the value increase came from correcting the undervaluation. More efficient management implies an increase in economic value, whereas tax benefits, overpayment, and undervaluation imply transfers of value.

The paper proceeds as follows. Section 2 describes Federated Department stores before the Campeau Corporation announced its acquisition attempt. Section 3 briefly describes the acquisition events, and section 4 compares the value of Federated under previous management with its value under Campeau. Section 5 discusses the possible sources of value in the transaction and section 6 concludes the paper.

2. Federated before the acquisition

On December 31, 1987, three weeks before Campeau launched its takeover attempt, Federated Department Stores' stock closed at $32.875 per share. With 88.9 million shares outstanding, Federated had a market value of equity of $2.93 billion. According to Federated's 10-K for the fiscal year ended January 30, 1988, Federated had short-term debt of $400 million and long-term debt of $957 million (both book values) on that date. Because financial statements are not available for December 1987, I assume that Federated had the same book value of debt, $1.36 billion, on December 31, 1987. The market value of the $755 million of publicly traded bonds equalled $725 million, $30 million less than book value.[3] Accordingly, I estimate the market value of Federated debt at $1.33 billion at the end of 1987. The estimated market value of Federated capital before Campeau's appearance was, therefore, $4.25 billion ($2.93 billion of equity and $1.33 billion of debt). The $4.25

---

[3] Bond prices were obtained from the 1987 year-end edition of *Moody's Bond Record*.

billion value of total capital reflects the market value of Federated's assets – the sum of its long-term assets and net working capital.

Federated operated ten department store divisions, three other store divisions, one supermarket division, and one mass merchandising division. These divisions operated 238 department stores, 76 mass merchandise stores, 129 supermarkets, and 232 other stores, while employing over 135,000 workers. In the fiscal year ended January 30, 1988, Federated had sales of $11.1 billion, earnings before interest, taxes, depreciation, and amortization (*EBITDA*) of $908 million, and capital expenditures of $487 million.

3. The acquisition events

On January 25, 1988, Campeau Corporation, advised by Bruce Wasserstein,[4] announced a hostile takeover offer for Federated at $47 per share. Federated opposed the bid and sought protection under Ohio's antitakeover laws. On February 3, Campeau raised its bid to $61 per share. On February 16, Campeau again raised its bid, this time to $66 per share contingent on a friendly deal, only to have it rejected by Federated's board. On February 29, R.H. Macy & Co. entered the bidding, offering $73.80 per share for 80% of Federated's shares. Campeau countered with an offer of $68 per share for all Federated shares. On March 22, Campeau raised its bid to $73 per share. Finally, on April 3, Campeau raised its bid to $73.50 per share for all Federated shares and Federated accepted the offer. On May 3, Campeau completed the tender offer by buying 87.2 million shares for $73.50 in cash per share. In four months, Federated's share price had increased from $32.875 to $73.50, an increase of 124%. On July 29, 1988, Campeau purchased the remaining 1.3 million shares at a cash price of $73.50 per share and Federated became an indirect subsidiary of Campeau through a formal merger. (Campeau purchased 0.4 million shares at an unknown cost before the January 25 bid.)

Campeau also paid $296 million in fees to complete the tender offer and an additional $133 million in fees as part of the merger. The subordinated debt offering prospectus of November 1988 does not fully describe either of these fees. The $296 million tender offer fees are described only as fees, expenses, prefunded tender offer facility interest, and certain other amounts in the 'Uses of Funds' section describing the tender offer financing. An undisclosed portion of the $429 million in total fees, therefore, represents interest expense, not a payment for the Federated assets. To simplify the

---

[4]Wasserstein has received publicity recently for his advisory role in several transactions that have turned out to be overpriced. See, for example, Deirdre Fanning, 'Bid-'em-up Bruce', in *Forbes*, August 7, 1989, p. 58, and George Anders and Francine Schwadel, 'Costly advice: Wall Streeters helped Interco defeat raiders, but at a heavy price', *WSJ*, July 11, 1990, p. 1.

discussion of Campeau's financing of Federated, I arbitrarily assume total noninterest fees equal the $296 million in tender offer fees.

Adding the price paid for the common shares ($73.50 for 88.5 million shares and an estimated $35 for 0.4 million shares), the $1.36 billion book value of assumed debt,[5] and total fees of $296 million implies that Campeau paid $8.17 billion for Federated.

The tender offer required $6.71 billion to pay for the stock and fees. Campeau used $3.22 billion in bank loans, $2.09 billion in bridge loans, and nominally $1.40 billion in equity to pay this amount. Campeau Corporation's $1.40 billion in equity, however, included $1.21 billion raised from loans to Campeau Corporation and its United States subsidiary Campeau Corporation (U.S.) Inc. These equity loans consisted of a $500 million bank loan to Campeau (U.S.) maturing in one year, a $480 million equity loan from the Edward J. DeBartolo Corporation to Campeau (U.S.) maturing in as little as three years, and $227 million in Campeau convertible debentures purchased by Olympia & York maturing in ten years. Campeau invested only $193 million in cash. The cash was obtained by selling Brooks Brothers, a division of Allied Stores that Campeau had acquired in 1986. In addition, Campeau did not use any equity to finance the purchase of the remaining 1.3 million Federated shares. Including the assumed debt and treating the equity loans as debt, Campeau financed at least $7.96 billion of the $8.17 billion Federated purchase – more than 97% – with debt.

The $980 million in equity loans to Campeau (U.S.) was secured by the holdings of Campeau (U.S.), which included the capital stock of Allied Stores, a 50% interest in five newly formed general partnerships with DeBartolo, and a $175 million note issued by a limited partnership that owned an office building in California, as well as the capital stock of Federated. The $227 million worth of convertible debentures were obligations of the parent company, Campeau Corporation. Campeau was already highly leveraged before the Federated acquisition. On January 31, 1988, the book value of Campeau's debt was $4.57 billion, while the book value of its equity stood at $0.09 billion (Canadian). The market value of Campeau Corporation's equity was higher, but still less than $0.70 billion. The Campeau (U.S.) subsidiary owned Campeau's U.S. properties (primarily Allied Stores), which were also highly leveraged. The highly leveraged structure of Campeau's assets before the Federated purchase suggests that it is reasonable to

---

[5]This calculation values the assumed debt at book value. This is the amount Campeau is liable for. The market value of the assumed debt was slightly lower than its book value. Using *Moody's Bond Record* to value Federated's long-term debt as of May 31, 1988, I estimate the market value of the assumed debt at $1.25 billion ($400 million short-term debt plus $846 million long-term debt).

consider the equity loans to Campeau (U.S.) and Campeau Corporation as Federated debt.

The Federated acquisition has often been confused with management or leveraged buyouts. The discussion of Campeau's organizational structure shows that Campeau's acquisition of Federated was a leveraged strategic acquisition, not a management buyout. Campeau had previously acquired Allied Stores – a company in businesses similar to Federated's. Campeau apparently hoped to take advantage of economies in managing the two similar companies. Unlike a typical management or leveraged buyout, Campeau did not give management an equity participation and Campeau was not under the control of a venture capital board. For a description of a typical leveraged buyout organization, see Jensen (1989).

4. The value of Federated under Campeau

This section estimates the three components of the value of Federated assets under Campeau: asset sales; interim cash flows from May 1, 1988 to December 31, 1989; and remaining Federated assets on December 31, 1989. Assumptions are required to generate both interim cash flows and the remaining asset value. For these two components, I present most likely, conservative, and optimistic case estimates. The components are calculated using the information in tables 2 to 5 and summarized in table 6.

The values of the asset sales, operating cash flows, and remaining Federated assets are nominal values at different times. To make it easier to compare them with the original capital value, I calculate market-adjusted values for each component. The market-adjustment procedure discounts each component to December 31, 1987, using the total return on the Standard and Poor's (S&P) 500. This compares the value of Federated assets under Campeau with the value that would have been obtained by investing the $4.25 billion pre-Campeau value of Federated assets in the S&P 500. The market adjustment can also be viewed as an assumption that the Federated assets would have performed no better or worse than the S&P 500 if Campeau had not appeared.

The market-adjustment calculation also assumes, somewhat conservatively, that the end-of-1987 Federated assets had an *asset* beta of one. In the year before the transaction, Federated had an *equity* beta of 0.95 (estimated using the market model and value-weighted index for 300 trading days before December 31, 1987). The Scholes–Williams beta during the same time period was 1.11. An asset beta using either equity beta estimate would be less than one. Because the S&P 500 increased by 40% from December 1987 to December 1989, the assumption of an asset beta of one understates the value of the Federated assets under Campeau.

Table 2

Division sold, month of sale, purchaser, sale price, and market-adjusted sale price for divisions of Federated Department Stores sold after Federated's acquisition by Campeau Corporation in May 1988.

Division sold	Month sold	Purchaser	Actual sale price ($ billion)	Market-adjusted sale price ($ billion)[a]
Bullock's	May 1988	R.H. Macy		
I. Magnin	May 1988	R.H. Macy	$1.10	$1.03
Filene's	May 1988	May Department Stores		
Foley's	May 1988	May Department Stores	$1.50	$1.41
Filene's Basement	July 1988	Management buyout	$0.13	$0.11
Ralph's Supermarkets	August 1988	Spin-off, buyout	$0.90	$0.85
Gold Circle	October 1988	Liquidated	$0.30	$0.27
Main Street	November 1988	Kohl's Department Stores	$0.09	$0.08
The Children's Place	February 1989	Management buyout	$0.03	$0.02
		Total proceeds	$4.04	$3.77

[a] Market-adjusted sale price is the sale price discounted from the month of sale to December 31, 1987 by the total return on the S&P 500. If invested in the S&P 500 on January 1, 1988, the market-adjusted sale price would equal the sale price at the month of sale.

4.1. Asset sales

Immediately after gaining control of Federated, Campeau began to sell Federated assets. Within nine months, Campeau sold 9 of the 15 operating divisions. Table 2 lists each division sold, the purchaser, the month of the sale, the actual sale price, and the market-adjusted sale price. Five divisions were sold to other department store owners. Two divisions were sold to investor groups that included management, and one was liquidated. Finally, one division, Ralph's Supermarkets, was spun off from Federated in a leveraged buyout, but remained a Campeau subsidiary. Ralph's paid Federated $900 million from the proceeds of $500 million borrowed from banks and $425 million borrowed from the public debt market.

Table 2 shows that Campeau realized $4.04 billion from the sale of the nine divisions. Discounted to December 31, 1987 (using the S&P 500), the value of these divisions is $3.77 billion. This value is assumed to be the same in the most likely, the conservative, and the optimistic cases presented in table 6. As noted in section 2, the value of all Federated assets on December 31, 1987 was $4.25 billion. Campeau, therefore, was able to sell the nine divisions for 89% of the previous value of all of Federated.

Table 3

Sales, operating profits, and capital expenditures for the fiscal year ended January 1988 of divisions sold and divisions retained by Federated Department Stores after its acquisition by Campeau Corporation. Results are in millions of dollars. Numbers in parentheses are percentages of total Federated results.

	Divisions retained[a]	Divisions sold	Total
Sales	4,522 (41.4%)	6,395 (58.6%)	10,918
Division earnings before taxes (*EBIT*)	357 (56.3%)	278 (43.9%)	635
Depreciation and amortization	120[b]	161	281
Earnings before interest, taxes, and depreciation (*EBITDA*)	477 (52.1%)	438 (47.9%)	915
Capital expenditures (*CAPX*)	241[b]	246	487
Operating cash flow (*EBITDA − CAPX*)	236 (55.0%)	193 (45.0%)	429

[a] Divisions retained are Abraham and Straus, Bloomingdale's, Burdine's, Lazarus, Rich's, and Goldsmith's.
[b] Includes amounts attributable to central office.

Table 2 compares the sales and profits of the divisions sold with those of the divisions retained and suggests that the assets retained by Federated and Campeau represented approximately one-half of Federated's value. The divisions sold provided $6.40 billion in sales in the year ending January 30, 1988. This represented 58.6% of Federated sales.[6] The divisions sold, however, were responsible for less than half of Federated's earnings before interest and taxes (*EBIT*) and earnings before interest, taxes, depreciation, and amortization – 43.9% and 47.9%, respectively. Similarly, these divisions were responsible for only 45.0% of Federated's operating cash flow (*EBITDA* less capital expenditures). This suggests that Campeau was a very able salesman of assets. He sold approximately 50% of Federated's original assets for 89% of the total assets' previous value ($3.77/$4.25).

Interestingly, the $3.77 billion realized in the divestitures is also approximately one-half of the $7.67 billion Campeau paid for all of Federated. If the prices of the divested units reflected the expected increase in value of all Federated assets, including the 50% Campeau did not sell, they suggest Campeau did not overpay for Federated, *ex ante*. There is some evidence, however, that the bond market was skeptical about the transaction almost

[6] See the Federated Department Stores prospectus dated November 4, 1988. The prospectus gives total Federated sales for fiscal 1987 as $10.92 billion rather than the $11.12 billion given in the Federated 10-K for fiscal 1987. The prospectus total excludes finance-charge revenues.

from the start. First Boston, Dillon Read, and Paine Webber were unable to refinance approximately $400 million of the $2 billion bridge loan used to finance the Federated acquisition.

4.2. Estimated value of remaining Federated divisions

As early as September 1989, Federated and Allied announced a cash shortfall, leading some trade creditors to recommend that vendors not ship them goods. A $250 million loan from Olympia & York helped avert a default at that time. Campeau apparently did not have enough other assets of its own to make up the shortfall. By December, however, it became clear that Federated and Allied would not be able to make their debt payments. On December 13, 1989, Campeau announced that those operations might have to file for bankruptcy protection. On December 23, Citibank notified Campeau that it had technically defaulted on $2.34 billion of debt. Uncertain of Campeau's ability to pay for shipments, suppliers and factors began to restrict shipments to Federated and Allied. Finally, on January 15, 1990, Federated and Allied filed for bankruptcy protection from creditors under Chapter 11 of the Federal Bankruptcy Code. At that time, Federated's debt stood at approximately $4.2 billion. In addition, the Debartolo equity loan and Olympia & York debentures remained outstanding. The filing indicated that Federated's operating cash flows were too small to meet required debt service payments, but did not imply that the operating cash flows (before interest) were negative or that the Federated assets were worthless.

4.2.1. Value before the Chapter 11 filing

In this section, I attempt to value the remaining Federated assets before the Chapter 11 filing and before any associated costs of bankruptcy were incurred. Because market values do not exist, such a valuation is necessarily subjective. The analysis begins with values estimated by Merrill Lynch and presented to Federated management and creditors on December 13, 1989.[7] These estimates relied on projections prepared in September 1989, about the same time Federated's financial difficulties began, but before suppliers severely restricted shipments. Merrill Lynch was hired as 'Campeau's financial advisor in connection with possible restructurings'. Because Merrill acted as Campeau's agent, I also present valuation estimates based on subsequent Federated results.

Merrill Lynch provided two sets of estimates, one based on an 'orderly sale process' and one on a 'distressed sale process'. For each process, Merrill Lynch presented a low and a high valuation, as well as estimates of pre-tax

---

[7] These are reported in the Federated Department Stores 8-K dated December 13, 1989.

and after-tax proceeds. (Sales at these prices apparently would trigger taxable gains; however, Merrill Lynch noted that some of the tax liability could be offset by operating losses.) The estimates were based on 'sales, profitability, *EBITDA* for each division, corporate overhead, central expenses, and multiples for transactions involving similar businesses'. Using projected operating results, Merrill Lynch estimated that Federated would have *EBITDA* of $501 million on sales of $4.92 billion in the fiscal year ending February 3, 1990 (fiscal 1989). Panel A of table 4 presents the Merrill Lynch pre-tax valuation estimates. Pre-tax proceeds range from 'low distressed proceeds' of $2.85 billion to 'high orderly proceeds' of $4.70 billion. The distressed proceeds estimates imply value to *EBITDA* multiples of 5.7 to 6.2; the orderly proceeds estimates, multiples of 8.3 to 9.4. Similarly, the distressed proceeds estimates imply value to sales multiples of 0.58 to 0.64; the orderly proceeds estimates, multiples of 0.85 to 0.96.

The valuation projections were made before suppliers restricted shipments to Federated. After the valuation, but before the Chapter 11 filing, Merrill lowered its projections of *EBITDA* for fiscal 1989, from $501 million to $483 million, as well as its projections of future operating income. Merrill noted that these revisions would lower the valuation ranges presented in its materials, particularly if the credit restrictions forced Federated to limit its operations. My alternative estimates are intended to measure the value of the remaining Federated assets just before the liquidity crisis and bankruptcy filing.

Merrill was hired by Campeau and may have had an incentive to overstate Federated's value. Merrill could have overstated value in two ways – by inflating the estimates of *EBITDA* and sales or by inflating the multiples applied to *EBITDA* and sales. Inflating a multiple is analogous to decreasing the rate used to discount a series of cash flows. The multiples used in the Merrill valuations are plausible, however, when compared with the multiples implied by the market values of Federated's competitors. The five companies noted as competitors in the Federated 8-K are Dillard's, May Department Stores, Mercantile Department Stores, Neiman–Marcus, and Nordstrom. At the beginning of 1990, the average value to *EBITDA* ratio for the five competitors was 9.97, with a median of 8.98 and a minimum of 5.83.[8] Similarly, the average value to sales ratio for these companies was 1.00, with a median of 1.08 and a minimum of 0.65. The minimum values are similar to those given in Merrill's distressed sale estimates.

Prices paid in the subsequent acquisitions of the retailers Marshall Field and Saks also suggest that the Merrill Lynch multiples are plausible. Marshall Field, with sales of $1.09 billion and *EBITDA* of $130 million in

---

[8] Value is calculated as the sum of market value of equity on January 2, 1990 and the book value of debt as of January 31, 1990.

Table 4

Estimated value of remaining Federated Department Stores assets before period of distress[a] by Merrill Lynch, by multiples of earnings before interest, taxes, depreciation, and amortization (*EBITDA*), and by multiples of sales.

	(A) Merrill Lynch value estimates[b]			
	Orderly process[c]		Distressed process[d]	
	Low	High	Low	High
1. Merrill Lynch estimates of pre-tax proceeds ($ billions)	$4.175	$4.700	$2.850	$3.125
2. Implied multiple of *EBITDA*	8.33	9.38	5.69	6.24
3. Implied multiple of sales	0.85	0.96	0.58	0.64

	(B) Values based on multiples of *EBITDA*[e]		
	4 × *EBITDA*	6 × *EBITDA* ($ billions)	8 × *EBITDA*
1. *EBITDA* of $483 million projected by Merrill Lynch	$1.932	$2.898	$3.864
2. *EBITDA* of $372 million for year ended February 3, 1990	$1.488	$2.232	$2.976

	(C) Values based on multiples of sales[f]		
	0.50 × Sales	0.75 × Sales ($ billions)	0.95 × Sales
1. Sales of $4.92 billion projected by Merrill Lynch	$2.460	$3.690	$4.674
2. Sales of $4.86 billion for year ended February 3, 1990	$2.430	$3.645	$4.617

[a] Values of the remaining Federated assets are estimated before the Chapter 11 filing and before any associated costs of bankruptcy or distress were incurred.

[b] The source of the Merrill Lynch estimates is the Federated Department Stores 8-K dated December 13, 1989. The Merrill Lynch estimates are based on September 1989 projections of $501 million in *EBITDA* and $4.92 billion in sales. Merrill Lynch later lowered the *EBITDA* projection to $483 million.

[c] Orderly process assumes divisions sold in 'orderly process', most likely to a 'strategic buyer'.

[d] Distressed process assumes divisions sold in 'distressed process' to either a 'strategic buyer' or 'financial buyer'.

[e] *EBITDA* equals earnings before interest, taxes, depreciation, and amortization. The value-to-*EBITDA* ratios of five Federated competitors noted in the Federated 8-K – Dillard's, May Department Stores, Mercantile Department Stores, Neiman–Marcus, and Nordstrom – average 9.97, with a median of 8.98 and a minimum of 5.83, on January 2, 1990.

[f] The value-to-sales ratios of the five Federated competitors average 1.00, with a median of 1.08 and a minimum of 0.65, on January 2, 1990.

fiscal 1989, accepted a winning bid of $1.04 billion.[9] The Field's transaction, therefore, was consummated at a multiple of value to sales of 0.95 and at a value to *EBITDA* multiple of 8.0. Saks, with sales of $1.3 billion in fiscal

[9] See the 8-K filed by Dayton–Hudson dated April 18, 1990.

1989, received a high bid of $1.5 billion, suggesting a value to sales multiple higher than that in the Field's transaction.

Panel B of table 4 presents estimates of Federated value based on multiples of *EBITDA*. The estimates use both the $483 million Merrill Lynch *EBITDA* estimate and the $372 million in *EBITDA* actually realized by Federated. This suggests that Merrill's *EBITDA* estimates may have been upward biased. However, the actual *EBITDA* is almost certainly lower than it would have been in the absence of Federated's liquidity problems before the bankruptcy filing. At the Field's multiple of value to *EBITDA* of 8, the value of Federated approaches $3.9 billion using the Merrill estimate and $3.0 billion using the actual value of *EBITDA*. I also present estimates using *EBITDA* multiples of 4 and 6. The multiple of 4 is 31% below the lowest multiple applying to Federated's five major competitors. If a multiple of 4 is applied to Federated's actual *EBITDA*, the remaining Federated assets are still worth $1.49 billion.

Analogously, panel C of table 4 presents estimates of Federated value based on multiples of sales, a metric commonly used in retailing. Merrill's sales estimates appear to have been accurate: actual sales of $4.86 billion were only slightly lower than projected sales of $4.92 billion. At the Field's multiple of value to sales of 0.95, the value of the remaining Federated assets exceeds $4.6 billion using both Merrill's sales estimate and actual sales. At smaller multiples of 50% and 75% of sales, Federated's value exceeds $2.43 billion and $3.64 billion. The 50% multiple is 23% below the lowest multiple applying to Federated's five major competitors.

The estimated values in table 4 for the remaining Federated assets represent a wide range. The assignment of values to the most likely, conservative, and optimistic cases in table 6 is necessarily subjective. In what follows, I assume a most likely estimate of $3.00 billion. This is approximately the midpoint of the distressed process proceeds estimated by Merrill. The $3.00 billion represents a value approximately 6.2 times Merrill's projected *EBITDA*, 8.1 times actual *EBITDA*, and less than 62% of both Merrill's projected sales and actual sales. In the conservative case, I assume a value of $2.00 billion. This is approximately 4.1 times Merrill's projected *EBITDA*, 5.4 times actual *EBITDA*, and less than 42% of Merrill's projected sales and actual sales. Finally, in the optimistic case, I assume a value of $4.00 billion. This is approximately 8.3 times Merrill's projected *EBITDA*, 10.8 times actual *EBITDA*, but less than 83% of Merrill's projected sales and actual sales. These three cases are chosen to represent a reasonable range of values.

4.2.2. Value after the Chapter 11 filing

Bankruptcy costs incurred since the Chapter 11 filing include direct court costs and indirect costs in the form of deterioration in Federated's going-concern value. Such costs will lower the value of the remaining Federated divisions and the combined value of the Federated assets under Campeau. Although it is not possible to estimate bankruptcy costs precisely, their potential magnitude can be gauged.

In the Section 341 meeting of Federated creditors on April 4, 1990, Federated projected a 3% sales drop in the first quarter, and flat sales in the second quarter of fiscal 1990. These projections compare existing store results for the post-bankruptcy periods with pre-bankruptcy, pre-distress periods. In the same meeting, Federated projected *EBITDA* of $29 million and $24 million for the first two quarters. Federated management also noted that '98% of our key vendors have resumed normal shipments... [and] inventory shortfalls have almost entirely been eliminated' (p. 43).

Financial statements filed in bankruptcy court show that Federated had sales of $1.01 billion and *EBITDA* of $58 million in the first quarter of fiscal 1990 (February 4 to May 5), with $61 million of *EBITDA* coming in April and May. (Retailers typically do worst in the first quarter.[10]) These short-term results do not suggest high indirect costs of financial distress. Rather, the post-bankruptcy operating results appear consistent with the values previously estimated for the remaining assets in the conservative and, potentially, the most likely case.

It is possible, although not yet observable, that reductions in capital expenditures in fiscal 1989 (and presumably continuing in fiscal 1990) will ultimately lower the value of the remaining Federated assets by reducing the future market share of the Federated stores. A strategy of lower capital expenditures and slower growth, however, can be value-increasing in mature or declining businesses like department stores.

Direct legal costs could also reduce Federated's value. Yet, Weiss (1990) finds that the direct costs of bankruptcy average only 3% of total assets (with a maximum of 7.0%) in 29 bankruptcies between 1980 and 1986. Applying these results to Federated's case, the implied costs are approximately $240 million, with a maximum of $560 million.

4.3. Interim cash flows

The interim cash flows generated and paid out to security holders have to be included in the valuation of Federated's under Campeau. This is equivalent to including dividend payments to measure the total return on a common stock. Interim cash flows are measured as *EBITDA* less capital expenditures, less the increase in net working capital. I estimate Federated's interim cash flows for the period from May 1, 1988 to February 3, 1990.[11]

[10] See the *Standard & Poor's* Retailing Industry Survey, April 20, 1989.

[11] There is a minor timing issue here because I include interim cash flows for one month after I calculate the value of the remaining assets. This is done for ease of exposition and has a trivial effect on the results.

For the nine months from May 1, 1988 to January 30, 1989, Federated Department Stores' *EBITDA* of $391 million less capital expenditures of $156 million[12] generated operating cash flow of $235 million. For the nine months ending January 31, 1988, under previous Federated management, these same divisions had *EBITDA* of $376 million, capital expenditures of $227 million, and operating cash flow of $149 million. This suggests a 58% increase in operating cash flow under Campeau management, from $149 million to $235 million, caused largely by a reduction in capital expenditures.

In contrast to the increase in operating cash flow, the small rise in *EBITDA* of $15 million, from $376 to $391 million, does not provide strong evidence of operating improvements. However, Federated's 10-K for fiscal year 1989 notes that it implemented a major cost-cutting program that reduced administrative employment by 20% and the sales force by 4%. Over 5,000 positions were eliminated. Federated also lowered ad spending, travel costs, and supply costs, and increased the use of incentive-based compensation. It is likely that some of the cost cuts were overhead costs of the sold divisions. A *Wall Street Journal* article quotes investment-banker estimates that these cost cuts totaled $240 million, but were $100 to $200 million short of expected.[13] At a value to *EBITDA* multiple of 8, annual cost cuts of $240 million would explain a premium of $1.9 billion, while a $200 million shortfall would explain $1.6 billion of overpayment.

For the fiscal year ending February 3, 1990, Federated had *EBITDA* of $372 million and made capital expenditures of $111 million for an operating cash flow of $261 million. (This includes the period of distress from September 1989 to January 1990 before Federated filed for protection under Chapter 11.) From May 1, 1988 to February 3, 1990, therefore, Federated generated $496 million ($235 + $261) in operating cash flow.

The final component of the interim cash flow is change in working capital. Unfortunately, the earliest financial statements showing working capital are as of July 30, 1988, not May 1. Accordingly, the estimates reported here measure the change in net working capital from July 30, 1988 to February 3, 1990. Net working capital – the sum of accounts receivable and inventory less the sum of accounts and income taxes payable – equals $1.17 billion on July 30, 1988. On February 3, 1990, net working capital equals $1.50 billion. However, the 1990 net working capital excludes $295 million in pre-Chapter 11 accounts payable, which are now liabilities subject to court proceedings. If the additional accounts payable are included, 1990 net working capital equals $1.21 billion. The increase in net working capital (which represents a negative

---

[12] Capital expenditures cited in this section equal gross purchases of property, plant, and equipment. These will be upward biased because they are not reduced by the proceeds from the disposition of property, plant, and equipment.

[13] See 'Buy-out bomb: An extra $500 million paid for Federated got Campeau into trouble', *WSJ*, January 11, 1990, p. 1.

Table 5

Interim cash flows for Federated Department Stores under Campeau Corporation from May 1, 1988 to February 3, 1990 in most likely, conservative, and optimistic cases. Interim cash flow equals earnings before interest, taxes, depreciation, and amortization (*EBITDA*) less capital expenditures and the increase in net working capital. Figures are in millions of dollars.

	Most likely	Conservative	Optimistic
1. Operating cash flow (*EBITDA* − capital expenditures)[a]	$496	$496	$496
2. Increase in net working capital[b]	$184	$332	$ 37
3. Interim cash flow[c]	$312	$164	$459

[a] Operating cash flow equals earnings before interest, taxes, depreciation, and amortization less purchases of property, plant, and equipment. Operating cash flow equals $235 million for the nine months ended January 31, 1989 and $261 million for the year ended February 3, 1990.

[b] Increase in net working capital is estimated as the change in net working capital from July 31, 1988 to February 3, 1990. Net working capital is calculated as the sum of accounts receivable and inventories less the sum of accounts and income taxes payable. The conservative case assumes the increase in working capital is $332 million; the optimistic case assumes the increase is $37 million; the most likely case assumes the increase is $184 million – one half of $332 plus $37 million. The difference depends on the treatment of pre-Chapter 11 accounts payable, which are now reorganization liabilities.

[c] Interim cash flow equals the difference between operating cash flow and the increase in net working capital.

cash flow) equals $332 million if the pre-Chapter 11 accounts payable are not included and $37 million if they are.

The $37 million figure appears more appropriate to a pre-bankruptcy valuation because it represents the going-concern increase in Federated's working capital. In the interest of conservatism, however, the conservative case assumes that the increase in working capital is $332 million and the optimistic case analysis assumes it is $37 million. The most likely case makes the intermediate assumption that net working capital increased by $184 million – one half of $332 plus $37 million.

Table 5 presents the assumptions for interim cash flow, the difference between operating cash flow and the increase in net working capital. The interim cash flows for the most likely, the conservative, and the optimistic cases are $312 million, $164 million, and $459 million. These cash flows are assumed to have occurred on December 31, 1989.

4.4. The total post-Campeau value of Federated

Table 6 combines the valuations obtained in the previous three sections to obtain total post-Campeau values – actual and market-adjusted – of Federated under the most likely, conservative, and optimistic case assumptions. These values are the sum of the value of the asset sales, the interim cash

Table 6

Components of combined actual value and market-adjusted value[a] of Federated Department Stores under Campeau Corporation. Values of Federated under Campeau are the sum of asset sales, interim cash flows, and the value of remaining Federated assets. All values are in billions of dollars.

Estimated values	Most likely Mkt-adj.	Most likely Actual	Conservative Mkt-adj.	Conservative Actual	Optimistic Mkt-adj.	Optimistic Actual	Breakeven[b] Mkt-adj.	Breakeven[b] Actual
Asset sales[c]	3.77	4.04	3.77	4.04	3.77	4.04	3.77	4.04
Interim cash flows[d]	0.22	0.31	0.12	0.16	0.33	0.46	0.22	0.31
Value remaining assets[e]	2.09	3.00	1.40	2.00	2.79	4.00	0.26	0.37
Combined value Federated assets[f]	6.08	7.35	5.28	6.20	6.88	8.49	4.25	4.72

[a] Market-adjusted values equal the actual values discounted from the month in which they occur to December 31, 1987 by the actual return on the S&P 500. If invested in the S&P 500 on January 1, 1988, the market-adjusted value would equal the actual value in the month the cash flow occurs.

[b] In the breakeven case, the combined (market-adjusted) value of Federated assets equals their pre-Campeau value of $4.25 billion. This case assumes most-likely-case interim cash flows and then calculates the value of the remaining assets needed to reach a market-adjusted value of $4.25 billion.

[c] Asset sales are the value of the divisions sold by Federated from May 1988 to February 1989. These values are detailed in table 2.

[d] Interim cash flow equals the difference between operating cash flow and the increase in net working capital. These values are detailed in table 5.

[e] The value of the remaining assets in the most likely case is approximately the midpoint of the distressed-process pre-tax values estimated by Merrill Lynch. In the conservative case, the value is less than 50% of sales and less than six times *EBITDA* for the year ended February 1990. In the optimistic case, the value is approximately 81% of sales and eight times *EBITDA* projected by Merrill Lynch.

[f] Combined value of Federated assets equals the sum of asset sales, interim cash flows, and value of remaining assets for the most likely case, conservative case, and optimistic case valuations.

flows, and the remaining assets. In all three cases, the post-Campeau market-adjusted values exceed the pre-Campeau values.

In the most likely case valuation, the market-adjusted value of Federated Department Stores under Campeau is $6.08 billion. This is over $1.8 billion more than Federated's $4.25 billion value on December 31, 1987. Under the optimistic (but plausible) case assumptions, Federated's post-Campeau value of $6.88 million exceeds the pre-Campeau value by more than $2.6 billion. Finally, under the conservative case assumptions, the market-adjusted value of Federated under Campeau of $5.28 billion still exceeds Federated's pre-Campeau value by more than $1 billion.

The breakeven case in table 6 shows that the combined value of Federated assets under Campeau's ownership exceeds their value under previous management as long as the remaining Federated divisions are worth more than $0.37 billion in December 1989 (or $0.26 market-adjusted to December

1987). This uses the most likely case assumptions for interim cash flows. Given the terminal value estimates in table 4, it seems unlikely that divisions generating over $370 million in *EBITDA* and $4.86 billion in sales in fiscal 1989 would have been worth so little. In fact, the minimal drop in post-bankruptcy sales combined with the recent multiples paid for retailers suggests that the value of the remaining Federated divisions may approach the most likely case valuation.

As reported earlier, table 1 shows that Campeau paid $8.17 billion for Federated in May 1988, or $7.67 billion market-adjusted to December 1987. Under all three of my scenarios – the most likely, conservative, and optimistic cases – the value of Federated assets is higher under Campeau than under previous management, but lower than the price Campeau paid. In the most likely case, the Federated assets are worth $1.59 billion less than Campeau paid. In December 1989 dollars, accrued at the same rate as the S&P 500, the $1.59 billion would equal $2.28 billion. The size of this overpayment helps explain why Federated's most junior subordinated debt (with a book value of approximately $800 million) traded at prices below 15% of par value at the time of the bankruptcy filing.[14]

5. Possible sources of value

The estimates in section 4 strongly suggest that the value of the Federated assets under Campeau's ownership exceeded their value under pre-Campeau management. This section discusses several potential explanations for the value increase.

First, approximately two-thirds of the divested assets were purchased by buyers in related businesses with reputations for managing retailing assets well. These buyers may be operating the Federated divisions more profitably than the previous Federated management team. In the year after acquiring Foley's and Filene's, May Department Stores eliminated approximately 1,000 jobs at Foley's, closed some unprofitable stores, and instituted tighter cost controls. Analyst reports in the summer of 1989 uniformly praised May's improvements.[15] Less information is available about the changes, if any, made by the purchasers of the other divisions. However, the buyers apparently left behind central office staff that Campeau later cut.

Second, the Campeau purchase was financed largely with debt and approximately one-third of the divested units (Ralph's and Filene's Basement) were sold in leveraged buyouts. Jensen (1986) argues that large debt service payments force managers to find ways to generate cash and prevent them

---

[14]See 'The big losers from Campeau', *The New York Times*, January 12, 1990.

[15]See the following analyst reports on May Department Stores: Value Line, June 2, 1989; Bear Stearns, July 7, 1989; Shearson Lehman, August 11, 1989; and A.G. Edwards, August 16, 1989.

from wasting resources. Kaplan (1989b) and Smith (1990) present evidence that highly leveraged management buyouts are associated with increases in operating profits and cash flows. In Campeau's case, there is evidence that Filene's Basement and Ralph's Grocery are performing well,[16] but the evidence of operating improvements for the remaining Federated assets is mixed. As mentioned, Campeau made substantial cuts in overhead and in capital expenditures. There is also anecdotal evidence that Campeau made several management mistakes, including carrying too much inventory.[17]

Third, the large increase in debt may have generated valuable interest tax shields. Kaplan (1989a) presents evidence that these benefits are significant for a sample of management buyouts. Although the Campeau purchase of Federated was financed almost entirely with debt, tax shields are available only if the debt is not retired immediately, and Campeau retired some Federated debt with the proceeds of the asset sales. Because a large portion of the asset sales were financed with debt, however, it is unlikely that these sales reduced the net amount of debt created by the Campeau purchase significantly.

Fourth, the purchasers of the sold divisions may have overpaid. The case for overpayment, however, receives weak support at best from the post-purchase performance of the buyers. May's stock-price performance was similar to that of the S&P 500 during the Federated takeover contest as well as after.[18] In addition to the favorable analyst reports described above, a recent *Wall Street Journal* article lauded May's performance over the last several years.[19] As mentioned, Filene's Basement and Ralph's Grocery are also apparently performing well. Although R.H. Macy took some criticism for its purchase of Bullock's and I. Magnin, the market value of Macy's publicly

---

[16] See 'Junk issued by Ralph's may be undervalued, even though the company is a Campeau unit', *WSJ*, January 22, 1990, p. C2.

[17] See Carol Loomis, 'The biggest, looniest deal ever', *Fortune*, June 18, 1990 and 'Can Allen Questrom get the up escalator moving?', *Business Week*, July 16, 1990, p. 66.

[18] Percentage changes are calculated relative to February 4, 1988, when May Department Stores stock closed at $34 per share, the S&P 500 at 252.21. The *Wall Street Journal* (*WSJ*) first named May as a potential bidder for Federated assets on February 8, 1988. May stock closed at 34\frac{1}{8}$ per share (+0.4%), the S&P 500 at 249.10 (−1.2%). On March 7, 1988, the *WSJ* reported that May had agreed to acquire Filene's and Foley's for $1.5 billion if Campeau acquired Federated. May stock closed at 36\frac{3}{8}$ per share (+7.0%), the S&P 500 at 267.38 (+6.0%). On April 4, the *WSJ* reported that Campeau had won the takeover battle and would sell Filene's and Foley's to May. May stock closed at 33\frac{7}{8}$ per share (−0.4%), the S&P 500 at 260.14 (+3.1%). None of the differences between May's stock return and the S&P 500 return are statistically significant.

On December 30, 1989, May stock closed at 47\frac{7}{8}$ per share (+40.8%), the S&P 500 at 353.40 (+40.1%). The difference between May's stock return and the S&P 500 return is not statistically significant.

[19] See 'As retailing's chic and indebted struggle, bland May Co. thrives', *Wall Street Journal*, January 19, 1990, p. 1.

traded debt increased by 1.5% during the acquisition period.[20] In addition, Macy has made its debt service payments through the end of 1989. Overpayment by Macy, however, cannot be ruled out given the concerns about its financial condition in May 1990.

However unlikely, it is possible to estimate the potential effect on the post-Campeau value of Federated of overpayment by the purchasers of the sold divisions. One plausible assumption is that these purchasers overpaid by the same amount as Campeau overpaid for all of Federated.[21] Using this assumption, the true value of the divisions can be obtained from the following (where all values are market-adjusted):

$$\frac{\text{Campeau Price Paid}}{\text{Most Likely Valuation}} = \frac{\text{Divisions' Sale Price}}{\text{True Division Value}}$$

or

$$\frac{\$7.67\text{ B}}{\$6.08\text{ B}} = \frac{\$3.77\text{ B}}{\text{True Division Value}}.$$

In this case, true division value equals $2.99 billion – $0.78 billion less than the $3.77 billion sale price. Although this adjustment would reduce the most likely case valuation of Federated's assets under Campeau to $5.30 billion ($6.08 billion – $0.78 billion), $5.30 billion is still more than $1 billion above Federated's pre-Campeau value.[22]

Finally, it is possible that the stock and bond markets valued Federated's assets incorrectly at the end of 1987 and that the value increase came from correction of the undervaluation. This view is arguably strengthened by the proximity of the pre-Campeau valuation date to the stock market crash of October 1987.

6. Conclusion

Overall, the estimates in section 4 strongly suggest that the value of the Federated assets under Campeau's ownership up to the time of the

---

[20]According to *Moody's Bond Record*, R.H. Macy's publicly traded bonds increased in price by a value-weighted average of 1.5% from December 31, 1987 to May 31, 1988. During the same period, interest rates were approximately constant.

[21]I thank Jeremy Stein for suggesting this.

[22]This calculation assumes Campeau overpaid relative to the value of Federated under Campeau – the most likely case. A more conservative assumption is that Campeau overpaid relative to the 'overpayment-adjusted value' of Federated assets – the most likely case valuation less the overpayment by the purchasers of the Federated divisions. This assumption would reduce the most likely case valuation to $4.54 billion. Given the lack of evidence for overpayment and the fact that most of the asset sales occurred when the tender offer was completed, this assumption seems implausible. However, even in this implausibly conservative case, the $4.54 value of Federated assets exceeds Federated's $4.25 billion pre-Campeau value.

bankruptcy filing exceeded their value under pre-Campeau management. In the most likely case, the value increased by more than $1.8 billion. The Federated transaction, therefore, illustrates how an overpriced, overleveraged acquisition can fail to meet its debt service requirements, yet succeed in increasing the private value of the underlying assets. Campeau's and Federated's difficulties have arisen because the value and cash flow increases were not large enough to meet the debt service payments required by Campeau's leverage. If Campeau had financed enough of the transaction with equity, the equity would have lost much of its value, but Federated would not have ended up in bankruptcy court.

I do not identify the sources of the increased value in the Federated transaction. Potential sources include cost cuts, the sale of underutilized assets to more efficient owners, tax benefits, overpayment by the purchasers of Federated divisions, and market undervaluation. The source of value is important because it determines the extent to which society benefits. More efficient management implies an increase in economic value, whereas tax benefits, overpayment, and undervaluation imply transfers of value. The paper presents evidence that at least one of the purchasers of the divisions (May Department Stores) implemented operating improvements and did not overpay. Even under the assumption that the purchasers did overpay, the overpayment is not large enough to account for all or even most of the value increase. It is more difficult to assess the importance of operating improvements in relation to tax benefits and undervaluation. Nevertheless, the evidence in the paper is consistent with the value of the Federated assets under Campeau increasing not only from a private perspective, but also from a social perspective.

The increase in Federated's value will be less than my estimates if the costs of financial distress are high. However, bankruptcy costs would have to reduce the value of Federated's remaining assets to less than $0.37 billion (in December 1989 dollars) to overturn the result that Federated assets increased in value under Campeau's ownership. Recent prices paid for retailing assets and Federated's early post-bankruptcy operating performance suggest that the post-bankruptcy value of the remaining divisions exceeds that level by a comfortable margin. It is too early to tell whether the assets will retain their value through the bankruptcy proceedings.

References

Baldwin, C. and S. Mason, 1983, The resolution of claims in financial distress: The case of Massey Ferguson, Journal of Finance 38, 505–516.

Jensen, Michael, 1986, Agency costs of free cash flow, corporate finance and takeovers, American Economic Review 76, 323–329.

Jensen, Michael, 1989, Active investors, LBOs, and the privatization of bankruptcy, Journal of Applied Corporate Finance 2, 35–44.

Kaplan, Steven, 1989a, Management buyouts: Evidence on taxes as a source of value, Journal of Finance 44, 611–632.
Kaplan, Steven, 1989b, The effects of management buyouts on operations and value, Journal of Financial Economics 24, 217–254.
Smith, Abbie, 1990, Corporate ownership structure and performance: The case of management buyouts, Working paper (University of Chicago, Chicago, IL).
Weiss, Lawrence, 1990, Priority claims and ex post re-contracting in bankruptcy, Working paper (Tulane University, New Orleans, LA).

Consequences of leveraged buyouts

Krishna G. Palepu*

Harvard Business School, Boston, MA 02163, USA

Received August 1990, final version received December 1990

Research suggests that leveraged buyouts create value through significant operating performance improvements. There is little evidence that buyouts lead to widespread employee layoffs, wage reductions, or wealth transfers from bondholders. LBOs continue to be controversial, however. Future research should focus on the effect of buyouts on firms' strategic investments, buyout firms' performance under difficult economic conditions, and the frequency and costs of financial distress associated with buyouts. Research can also focus on improving the performance of public corporations by examining the individual contributions of debt, management ownership, and corporate governance changes to post-buyout performance.

1. Introduction

A leveraged buyout (LBO) is a transaction in which a group of private investors uses debt financing to purchase a corporation or a corporate division. Although a significant increase in financial leverage is the most obvious characteristic of LBOs, several other important changes are associated with these transactions. Buyouts are structured so that management's ownership interest in the firm increases substantially. LBOs also bring about significant corporate governance changes – large-block equity investors join the firm's board of directors and actively monitor management's strategy and performance. Another important aspect of LBOs is that their investors lose access to public equity markets after the buyout. The high leverage, large management ownership, active corporate governance, and loss of investors'

---

*I wish to thank Michael Jensen and Richard Ruback (the editors), Karen Wruck, and the participants in the Conference on the Structure and Governance of Enterprise for helpful comments. The Division of Research, Harvard Business School, provided financial support for this research.

access to liquid public equity markets fundamentally distinguish an LBO from a typical public corporation.

As buyouts have increased in size and frequency during the last decade, their economic consequences have been hotly debated. Proponents of LBOs argue that the associated organizational changes improve managers' incentives to maximize value and therefore lead to better operating and investment decisions. An opposing view is that the increased financial leverage associated with LBOs makes firms short-term-oriented and vulnerable to financial distress, leading to a decline in their competitiveness. It is also suggested that buyouts often result in a redistribution of wealth from employees to investors. Several studies have attempted to address the LBO controversy by documenting the economic consequences of buyouts. This paper reviews the findings of these studies, and identifies issues yet to be resolved.

Pre-buyout equity investors reap substantial wealth gains from LBOs. Research suggests that the primary source of these gains is new value created through significant operating performance improvements. There is little evidence that buyouts lead to widespread wealth transfers from employees to equity holders through major layoffs or wage reductions. Although some of the pre-buyout bondholders suffer losses at the buyout, these losses account for a very small fraction of the total gains to pre-buyout shareholders.

Despite the lack of evidence that LBOs have significant negative consequences, these transactions continue to be controversial. Future research can address critics' concerns by examining in detail the effect of buyouts on firms' long-term investments, the performance of buyouts under difficult economic conditions, and the frequency and costs of financial distress associated with LBOs. Research can also help efforts to improve the performance of public corporations by examining the contributions of debt, management ownership, and corporate governance changes to the post-buyout performance.

2. Current evidence on the consequences of LBOs

Research shows that pre-buyout investors reap substantial wealth gains from LBOs. There is unambiguous evidence that pre-buyout equity holders earn large buyout premiums. Kaplan (1989a) reports that for 76 management buyouts completed in the period 1980–1986, pre-buyout equity holders earn a median premium of 42% over the equity value two months before the buyout. Similar findings are reported by DeAngelo, DeAngelo, and Rice (1984), Marais, Schipper, and Smith (1989), and Lehn and Poulsen (1989).

One of the major unresolved issues is the source of the spectacular wealth gains of pre-buyout investors from LBOs. Potential sources include: (1) improvements in operating performance, (2) transfers from employees, (3) transfers from taxpayers, (4) transfers from pre-buyout debtholders, and

(5) overpayment by post-buyout investors. Current research findings on the importance of each of these sources are reviewed below.

2.1. Performance improvements

2.1.1. Theory

Jensen (1989) suggests that the primary source of wealth gains from LBOs is organizational changes that lead to improvements in firms' operating and investment decisions. According to this view, when companies undergo a leveraged buyout, increased management ownership and high financial leverage associated with the buyout provide strong incentives for managers to generate higher cash flows through improved operating performance. The high financial leverage also limits managers' ability to undertake wasteful investments because free cash flow is committed to debt service. The substantial management equity ownership ensures that managers do not meet debt payments through short-term cash-flow improvement at the expense of long-term value. Further, active participation by equity investors in corporate governance leads to improved monitoring of top management's strategy and operating performance. Therefore, the operating performance and investment decisions after a buyout are likely to be superior to the performance of the firm as a public corporation. Leveraged buyouts are likely to be particularly valuable for companies with a strong cash-flow-generating capacity and few profitable growth opportunities. Kaplan (1989a), Smith (1990), Lichtenberg and Siegel (1990), and Baker and Wruck (1989) provide evidence supporting this proposition.

2.1.2. Evidence

Kaplan (1989a) analyzes the post-buyout operating performance of 48 management buyouts (MBOs) completed during the period 1980–1986. He defines operating income as net sales less cost of goods sold and selling, general, and administrative expenses before depreciation and amortization are deducted. His results indicate that, in comparison with the year before the buyout, operating income increases by 42% over a three-year period after the buyout. The ratio of operating income to assets increases by 15% and the ratio of operating income to sales by 19%. The sample average net cash flow, defined as the difference between operating income and capital expenditures, increases by 96% during the three-year period from one year before the buyout to two years afterward. The ratio of net cash flow to assets increases by 79% and the ratio of net cash flow to sales by 43% during these three years. These operating improvements persist even after the performance of MBO firms is adjusted for contemporaneous industrywide changes. The premiums earned by pre-buyout equity holders at the time of the LBOs are strongly correlated with the post-buyout operating gains, indicating that the increase in operating performance is an important source of the buyout premium.

Smith (1990) reinforces Kaplan's findings in an examination of 58 management buyouts (MBOs) between 1977 and 1986. She defines operating cash flows as profits before interest, taxes, and depreciation plus changes in working capital. Her results show that the operating cash flow per employee and the operating cash flow per dollar of book value of assets increase on average after an MBO, both in absolute terms and in relation to non-MBOs in the same industry. One source of improved cash flow appears to be better working capital management resulting in a reduction in the inventory-holding period and the accounts-receivable-collection period. Smith does not find any evidence that the post-buyout cash-flow improvements are driven by cutbacks in 'discretionary expenses' such as maintenance, advertising, or research and development. The improvements in operating cash flows are correlated with the buyout-induced changes in debt ratio and management ownership, consistent with the view that these organizational changes play an important role in the performance improvement.

Lichtenberg and Siegel also examine post-buyout changes in operating performance by investigating changes in total factor productivity. Unlike Kaplan and Smith, who analyze firm-level financial data, Lichtenberg and Siegel use plant-level physical data from the U.S. Census Bureau's Longitudinal Research Database on manufacturing establishments. Their total sample includes approximately 1,000 plants involved in LBOs during the period 1981–1986. The actual number of plants for which productivity changes are analyzed varies from year to year in relation to the buyout, and decreases to approximately 250 plants by three years after the LBO.

Lichtenberg and Siegel's main finding is that the productivity in the LBO plants in their sample, on average, is higher than that in non-LBO plants in the five years before (years -5 to -1) and three years after (years 1 to 3) an LBO. Further, there is a significant increase in productivity in the LBO plants in years 1 and 2 over the productivity in year -1. These results seem to be unstable over time, however, because Lichtenberg and Siegel find conflicting results when they divide their sample into early and late LBOs. The LBOs from 1981–1982, for which post-buyout data are available for five years, have no increases in post-buyout productivity. In contrast, the buyouts in the 1983–1986 period, for which post-buyout data are available for only three years or less, show a significant post-buyout productivity improvement. The study offers no explanation for the conflicting results for the two subsamples, making it difficult to interpret the study's findings.

2.1.3. Interpretation – Pre-buyout undervaluation or post-buyout organizational changes?

There are two possible interpretations for the post-buyout performance improvements documented by Kaplan (1989a), Smith (1990), and Lichtenberg and Siegel (1990). One view is that the performance improvements are specifically induced by the buyouts. According to this view, buyout investors pay a premium to pre-buyout equity holders because the buyout is expected to produce performance changes. An alternative view is that the performance improvements would have occurred with or without a buyout, and that the buyout premiums are merely a result of undervaluation of LBO firms by the stock market. Such undervaluation may arise when outside investors and managers have different information about the firm's future operating performance.[1] Baker and Wruck's (1989) detailed study of O.M. Scott & Sons after a management buyout (MBO) provides evidence that is useful in distinguishing between these two views.

Baker and Wruck conclude that increased leverage, greater emphasis on performance bonuses, active monitoring by the LBO partners, and increased management equity ownership are responsible for a significant post-MBO improvement in O.M. Scott's operating performance and investment policies. They report that, after the buyout, Scott's high financial leverage and greater emphasis on performance bonuses have directed managers' attention to improving the company's cash flow. The substantial management equity ownership has reduced managers' incentives to achieve short-term cash-flow improvements at the expense of long-term value, and the debt covenants restrict managers' ability to take short-term-oriented actions to improve cash flows. Further, the company's directors, who own or represent directly a substantial portion of the firm's equity, have taken an active interest in advising and monitoring top management, reducing the likelihood that managers will pursue value-decreasing strategies.

Baker and Wruck report that these organizational forces have led to a substantial improvement in Scott's working capital management and to a change in the company's product-market growth strategy. Scott's managers believe that post-buyout organizational changes have allowed them to take actions that were infeasible when the company was a division of a large public corporation (ITT). Baker and Wruck's description suggests that the post-MBO performance improvements are related to specific organizational

---

[1] Critics of management buyouts argue that MBOs allow managers to exploit their private information on firms' prospects at the expense of outside shareholders. This concern is mitigated by two factors, however. First, managers are required to share their projections of future firm performance with competing outside bidders. Second, competing buyout bids are evaluated by a committee of outside directors who do not participate in the buyout. Kaplan (1989a) reports that 34 of the 46 proposed management buyouts during his sample period have resulted in takeovers by nonmanagement bidders.

changes associated with LBOs, and that these organizational changes reduce the likelihood that the performance improvements are achieved at the expense of long-term value.

The undervaluation hypothesis predicts no relation between specific organizational changes accompanying a buyout and subsequent changes in performance. Baker and Wruck report, however, that the organizational changes associated with the buyout play an important role in the subsequent performance changes. Further, using a larger sample, Smith (1990) reports that the post-buyout operating improvements are correlated with buyout characteristics such as the change in debt level and change in management ownership. The evidence, therefore, indicates that post-buyout performance changes are attributable to the buyouts themselves, not merely to pre-buyout undervaluation.

2.1.4. Unresolved issues

The evidence supports the view that significant performance improvements follow a buyout. If we are to fully understand the performance consequences of LBOs, however, this evidence needs to be extended in three ways. First, studies to date have examined performance changes over a relatively short period following the buyouts; it is useful to gather evidence on post-buyout performance over a longer period. Second, more evidence is needed on the performance of LBOs under difficult economic conditions. The evidence discussed above is primarily drawn from a period of relative prosperity in the U.S., and some critics of LBOs argue that buyouts are likely to lead to severe financial distress in a recession. Third, the samples in the studies discussed above are primarily drawn from 1979–1986; it would be useful to examine whether there has been a change in the nature of LBO activity over time by analyzing the performance of the more recent and the early buyouts. These issues are discussed further in section 3.

2.2. Transfers from employees

Critics often argue that LBOs increase shareholders' wealth at the expense of employees.[2] Kaplan (1989a), Smith (1990), and Lichtenberg and Siegel (1990) investigate whether post-LBO operating-performance improvements are realized at the expense of workers by examining changes in number of employees and average wage per employee.

Kaplan reports that for the firms in his sample with post-buyout employment data, the median change in number of employees is 0.9% between the

---

[2] See Shleifer and Summers (1988) for a discussion of this concern.

year before and the year after the buyout. For the sample firms with no major divestitures, the median change is 4.9%, so there is no evidence that LBOs lead to a decrease in the number of employees.[3] Smith's results on employment levels are similar. Lichtenberg and Siegel also report no significant post-buyout reduction in the number of blue-collar employees. In addition, they examine the average wage rates of production workers, and report a significant increase in the average annual-compensation level from one year before the buyout to two years afterward.

The evidence shows that the investor wealth gains from LBOs cannot be attributed to significant employee layoffs or wage reductions. However, Kaplan reports that, on an industry-adjusted basis, the number of employees decreases by 12% for his total sample and by 6.2% for the sample with no major divestitures. Smith also reports declines in post-buyout employment levels on an industry-adjusted basis. One possible explanation for the lower growth rates of employment for the buyout firms is that their sales and assets grow more slowly. Another is that buyout firms use their labor more efficiently. Neither of these explanations is consistent with a simple wealth-transfer hypothesis.[4] Nonetheless, it would be useful to know why buyout firms offer lower growth in employment opportunities than other firms in their industries. It would also be useful to gather evidence on whether employment composition changes after a buyout.

2.3. Transfers from taxpayers

Although operating-performance improvements are an important source of buyout premiums, reductions in post-buyout corporate tax payments are also frequently suggested as a significant source of wealth gains to investors from LBOs. Some of the gains, therefore, potentially occur at the taxpayers' expense. Empirical research shows that although increased tax shields account for a part of the buyout premiums, LBOs are likely to increase, not decrease, the total tax revenues of the U.S. Treasury.

An LBO can potentially reduce a firm's tax liability in two ways. First, the debt used to finance the transaction creates interest tax shields. Second, an asset write-up following the buyout increases the depreciation deductions. Kaplan (1989b) estimates the value of tax benefits in 76 management buyouts completed between 1980 to 1986. Depending on the assumptions used, the median estimated value of interest deductions varies from 14% to 130% of

---

[3] When a division is divested, the number of employees of the parent company decreases. Many of the employees of the divested division are likely to retain their jobs, however. Therefore, it is useful to examine the change in employment after controlling for divestitures.

[4] Slower growth in employment as a result of more efficient investment or production policies cannot be viewed as a pure wealth transfer unless workers are assumed to be 'entitled' to gains from inefficiencies.

the premium paid to pre-buyout shareholders. For those companies that elect to step up the basis of their assets, the median value of the increased depreciation deductions is 30% of the premium paid in the LBO. The median value of the combined benefit from interest and depreciation deductions ranges from 21% to 143% of the premium paid to pre-buyout shareholders.

Kaplan's evidence shows that the median ratio of current federal taxes to operating income drops from 20% in the two years before the buyout to 1% in the first two years after the buyout. That is, the median firm in his sample pays no federal taxes in the two years immediately following the buyout. By the third year after the buyout, however, two thirds of the buyouts pay some federal income taxes.[5] Kaplan also reports a significant correlation between the buyout premiums and estimated tax benefits from the buyouts, as do Schipper and Smith (1988). The evidence, therefore, shows that tax benefits account for a significant fraction of the premium paid to pre-buyout shareholders.

Although firms undertaking LBOs pay lower taxes, at least for a time, for the U.S. Treasury the total tax consequences of buyouts are not necessarily negative. Jensen, Kaplan, and Stiglin (1989) show that LBO activity is likely to increase the total tax revenues of the U.S. Treasury. They point out that, although LBOs reduce tax revenues to the U.S. Treasury by giving firms greater interest and depreciation deductions, they also provide several sources of tax revenue increases: (1) taxes on capital gains realized by the pre-buyout shareholders, (2) taxes on operating cash-flow increases from buyouts, (3) taxes on interest income received by buyout lenders, and (4) taxes on capital gains from post-buyout asset sales.[6] Jensen, Kaplan, and Stiglin argue that the net effect of buyouts is to increase the present value of Treasury tax revenues by 61%. They estimate that at a total dollar volume of LBO transactions of $75 billion per year, the Treasury gains about $9 billion in the first year and about $16.5 billion per year in present value of future net tax receipts.

2.4. Transfers from pre-buyout debtholders

The leverage increases associated with buyouts can potentially impose considerable additional risk on the firms' current debtholders, leading to significant bondholder wealth losses. Asquith and Wizman (1990) examine

---

[5]Kaplan reports that the median ratio of taxes to operating income is 5% in year 3. Although this ratio is lower than the ratio in year −1, the amount of federal taxes paid in year 3 is likely to be closer to the pre-buyout level because there is a substantial increase in operating income between years −1 and 3.

[6]Taxes from increased cash flows after a buyout are attributable to the buyout only if the cash-flow increases are not expected to occur without the buyout.

whether pre-buyout shareholders' gains are attributable to pre-buyout bondholders' losses from an unexpected increase in financial leverage. Based on an analysis of 149 public bonds in 47 buyouts completed during the 1980–1988 period, they report a statistically significant abnormal loss of 2.1% to pre-buyout bondholders at the buyout. Their results suggest that the losses to bondholders constitute only about 3% of the 42% returns to pre-buyout equity holders, so equity gains from LBOs cannot be attributed primarily to wealth transfers from bondholders.

Asquith and Wizman also show that the pre-buyout bondholders do not always experience wealth losses. Their evidence indicates that wealth losses accrue only to bonds that do not have protective covenants against unexpected leverage increases. Presumably, these bonds are priced *ex ante* so as to compensate investors for the extra risk implied by the lack of protection. The losses at the buyout announcement therefore overstate the actual wealth consequences of buyouts to these bondholders. Bonds that have strong protective covenants against unexpected leverage increases actually experience a gain at the announcement of a buyout.[7]

2.5. Overpayment by post-buyout investors

Some of the wealth gains to pre-buyout investors could also be attributed to systematic overpayment by the post-buyout investors. Such overpayment is likely if there is a conflict of interest between investors and managers of buyout funds.

Kaplan (1989a) documents that post-buyout equity holders earn substantial risk-adjusted returns on their investments. He examines returns to 25 buyouts from the 1980–1986 period for which equity values were available in the post-buyout period, and reports that the equity investors earn a 42% mean excess return over a period of approximately three years. His analysis shows that the returns to equity investors in LBOs exceed returns on a similarly leveraged market equity index. Further, Kaplan and Stein (1990) show that the systematic risk of equity in leveraged buyouts is much smaller than what would normally be predicted given the amount of financial leverage in these transactions. They report that equity betas in twelve public recapitalizations (recaps) during the 1986–1988 period increase on average from 1.0 to 1.30. The observed 30% increase is surprisingly low in light of the leverage change: the standard unlevering and relevering of equity betas, assuming that asset

---

[7]Marais, Schipper, and Smith (1989), who also examine bondholder returns, report that the returns to pre-buyout bondholders are insignificant. Their sample is smaller than that of Asquith and Wizman, however, and they do not analyze separately bonds with and without protective covenants.

betas remain unchanged after a recap, would predict a 325% increase in the equity beta.[8]

The evidence of Kaplan (1989a) and Kaplan and Stein (1990) suggests that the LBO equity has lower systematic risk and a higher return than a similarly leveraged non-LBO equity. One explanation for the superior performance of LBO equity is that the organizational changes associated with LBOs result in changes in operating and investment decisions, leading to increased operating cash flows and reduced asset betas. Under this hypothesis, although LBOs increase financial risk, they reduce business risk.[9] Therefore, LBO investors bear substantially lower risks than implied by a simple financial analysis that ignores the consequences of organizational changes associated with LBOs. Assets sales might also explain some of the decline in the post-buyout asset betas if buyouts on average result on the sale of risky assets.

Although this research suggests that post-buyout equity earns superior risk-adjusted returns, evidence on risks and returns to LBO debt is inconclusive. Some recent studies show that, in general, lower-grade bonds have significant rates of default. Altman (1989) and Asquith, Mullins, and Wolff (1989) report an average annual default rate of 2.6% for lower grade bonds. As these studies point out, however, it is difficult to assess whether the default rates documented by them are 'too high' in relation to returns on these investments. Further, these studies examine lower-grade bonds in general and not LBO debt specifically.

Some observers argue that there has been a change in the nature of LBO activity over time, and that returns to investors in early LBOs may not be good indicators of returns from more recent buyouts. According to this view, the earlier LBOs were concentrated in mature, cash-rich industries which are suitable for high leverage, and the buyout premiums were justified by the expected performance improvements. The substantial returns earned by the investors in these early deals have enabled managers of LBO partnerships to raise a large amount of additional risk capital. The easy availability of capital and conflicts of interest between managers of LBO funds and investors may have led to unsound deals, with the buyout premiums and/or debt levels not justified by future cash flows. If this conjecture is valid, then the returns to debt and equity investors in LBOs that occurred in the late 1980s are likely to be substantially lower. It would be useful to gather more evidence on this issue by comparing the LBOs in the early and late 1980s.[10]

---

[8] These results should be extrapolated to LBOs with caution because there are important organizational differences between recaps and LBOs. This general issue is discussed later in the paper.

[9] Consistent with this hypothesis, Burkhardt, Jensen, and Barry (1990) document evidence of operating-risk reductions at Wisconsin Central Ltd. Railroad after a leveraged buyout.

[10] Fox (1990) compares the characteristics of LBOs that occurred in the early and late 1980s.

3. Future research on LBOs

The evidence to date suggests that operating performance improves markedly following an LBO. This improvement is a major source of value gains from LBOs. There is little evidence of widespread employee layoffs, wage reductions, or wealth transfers from bondholders. Although this evidence answers some key questions raised by the debate on LBOs, these transactions continue to be controversial. The following discussion focuses on issues future research can address to resolve the controversy.

3.1. What is the effect of LBOs on firms' long-term investments?

There are conflicting views on the effects of high leverage on firms' long-term investments. One hypothesis is that financial leverage compels firms to restructure operations and better allocate corporate resources. Since leverage requires managers to pay out cash generated from current operations, they have to rely on external markets to fund a larger proportion of capital investments. Subjecting investment proposals to market scrutiny reduces the likelihood that unprofitable investments will be made. An alternative hypothesis is that debt reduces firms' ability to respond to threats from competitors and forces them to cut valuable long-term investments in R&D and capital expenditures. Proponents of this view argue that it is often difficult for managers to communicate the benefits of strategic investments to outsiders, for example, because of proprietary information.[11] Therefore, if internally generated funds are not available for investment, managers may have to forego some profitable projects.

Research shows that LBO firms are typically not R&D-intensive, so LBOs have an insignificant effect on corporate R&D. There is, however, evidence that capital-expenditure levels decline after an LBO. Kaplan (1989a) reports that his sample buyouts reduce capital expenditures by 33% in relation to other firms in their industries in the two years following the buyout. The industry-adjusted capital expenditures to sales ratio decreases by 17% during the same period. Reductions in capital expenditures following a buyout are also reported by Smith (1990).

A reduction in the capital-expenditure level can come from a reduction in either wasteful investments or profitable investments. Evidence of large positive returns to investors in LBOs that subsequently go public supports the view that the reductions in capital expenditures following a buyout are not value-reducing activities [see Kaplan (1989a)]. This evidence comes from a limited sample, however, and there is room for further investigation of the

---

[11]This problem is likely to be more severe in a public corporation than in an LBO because investors serve on LBO firms' boards.

changes in capital-expenditure policies following buyouts and their long-term economic consequences.

3.2. How do LBOs perform under difficult economic conditions?

Much of the public concern about LBOs appears to stem from the fear that LBOs reduce firms' ability to survive and compete globally in difficult economic conditions. Critics argue that LBOs increase the probability of bankruptcy which can lead to job losses and destruction of going-concern value of corporations. Although current academic research documents impressive post-buyout performance improvements, critics point out that this evidence is inadequate to judge LBOs' performance in economic downturns, because the economy has been relatively strong in the period examined by the research.

The effect of high leverage on firms' ability to withstand economic downturns is not obvious. Although the large fixed payments resulting from leverage increase the probability of financial default in a recession, the organizational discipline imposed by leverage can make a firm more efficient, better preparing it to face economic downturns.[12] How LBOs perform in a downturn also depends on how liquid and dependable private sources of capital are under difficult economic conditions. If regulatory pressures on financial institutions supplying capital to LBOs increase in a downturn, for example because of the new banking regulations for highly leveraged transactions, buyouts may find it more difficult than public corporations to finance their activities in recessions.

It would be useful to gather evidence on the frequency of financial defaults by LBOs and the costs associated with the resulting reorganizations. The debate on LBOs can also be aided by an analysis of relative costs of financial distress for LBOs and public corporations with low leverage.

3.3. What can we learn from failed buyouts?

We will be able to understand better how LBOs affect performance if researchers study successful as well as unsuccessful buyouts. There are at least three reasons why a buyout might fail: (1) the structure of the buyout may be flawed (for example, the premium may be too high or there may be too much debt for the post-buyout cash flows to support), (2) post-buyout management performance may be poor, or (3) general economic conditions

---

[12] Jensen (1989) and Wruck (1990) also argue that the wealth losses from inefficient or poor strategic choices are likely to be lower for an LBO than for a public corporation with low leverage.

unrelated to the buyout may harm the firm. Future research can focus on the role these factors play in the success or failure of LBOs.[13]

3.4. Are all the changes associated with LBOs necessary to bring about performance improvements?

Four key organizational characteristics are associated with an LBO: going private, high financial leverage, significant management equity ownership, and monitoring of managers' strategies by active investors. An interesting question is whether it is possible to bring about performance improvements comparable to those associated with LBOs with only a subset of changes accompanying buyouts. Some of the changes associated with LBOs are inappropriate in certain business contexts. For example, high leverage is unsuitable for firms with high business risk, and eliminating investor access to public equity markets might be costly for certain firms.

The extent to which various organizational changes associated with LBOs contribute to performance changes can be analyzed by studying public leveraged recapitalizations and large-block investments in public corporations by equity partnerships. Public companies that undertake leveraged recapitalizations have high financial leverage and an increase in management ownership, but do not have an LBO-type corporate governance structure with active investors on the board of directors. Public corporations with large-block investors often have active monitoring of top management, but do not have high financial leverage or a large management ownership. An analysis of recaps and equity partnerships, therefore, will help us understand the role played by each of the changes associated with an LBO in bringing about performance changes.[14] Such evidence also might be useful to assess ways to improve the performance of corporations without necessarily increasing their financial risk or eliminating their access to public capital markets.

3.5. Why do LBOs go public again?

Some see the LBO as an organizational form superior to the public company because an LBO significantly reduces agency costs between owners and managers. The evidence on post-buyout performance improvements is consistent with the view that the LBO is a beneficial organizational form. There is also evidence, however, that firms voluntarily abandon the LBO structure to become public companies by issuing shares two or three years

---

[13]Kaplan (1989c) performs such an analysis of Campeau's acquisition of Federated.

[14]Klieman (1988) reports that there are significant shareholder gains at the announcement of public recaps. He does not, however, analyze the post-recap changes in firms' operating and investment decisions.

after the buyout.[15] This appears to be particularly true for large successful LBOs. For these reverse LBOs, the benefits of going public must exceed the benefits of continuing as an LBO. One benefit of going public is that the firm's investors, particularly managers who own large amounts of the firm's equity, gain access to public capital markets which offer liquidity and diversification.

The phenomenon of reverse LBOs raises some interesting questions. Why do some LBOs go public and others do not? Is an LBO a viable long-term organizational form, or it is merely a change agent? If the buyout is a change agent, are the performance improvements it induced sustainable even after the firm goes public? Why is it not possible to induce similar changes in public corporations?

3.6. How do LBO associations differ from conglomerate corporations?

There are several similarities between conglomerates and LBO associations. Both undertake investments in a wide range of businesses, both exercise financial control over these businesses, and both delegate day-to-day business decisions to operating managers. Given these similarities, is the current success of LBO associations similar to the short-lived success of conglomerates in the late 1960s and early 1970s? Or is there something fundamentally different in the way LBO associations are structured that avoids the problems of conglomerates? Jensen (1989) points out that one important difference between LBOs and conglomerates is that LBO headquarters cannot move cash from one LBO to another whereas conglomerates do not have such a restriction. He also reports that the LBO associations usually have significantly smaller staffs compared to the conglomerates. Are there any other systematic differences? How do LBO partnerships deal with the agency conflicts between the managers of LBO funds and investors in these funds?

4. Summary

As the last decade has seen a dramatic increase in the number and value of LBOs, the economic consequences of buyouts have been hotly debated by academics, practitioners, and policy makers. This debate has stimulated considerable academic research, which is reviewed in this paper. The principal findings of the research to date are:

(1) Stockholders of firms undergoing LBOs earn substantial returns from the transactions.

---

[15]Muscarella and Vetsuypens (1990) analyze reverse LBOs. They report that a relatively small fraction of the total buyouts appear to go public.

(2) Company productivity and operating performance improve substantially in the years immediately following a buyout. The improvements are a result of the changes in financial and management structure associated with the buyout. There is little evidence of a decline in employment levels or average wage rates of blue-collar workers after a buyout, suggesting that the post-buyout cash-flow improvements are not the result of widespread wealth transfers from workers.
(3) Although some pre-buyout bondholders suffer losses at the buyout, these losses account for a very small fraction of the total gains to pre-buyout shareholders.
(4) Buyouts give companies increased depreciation and interest tax shields which account for some of the equity gains from these transactions. Buyouts also increase tax revenues to the U.S. Treasury, in several ways however, and the net effect of LBOs on aggregate tax revenues is likely to be positive.
(5) LBOs appear to have two opposing effects on firm risk. Although the leverage increase associated with the buyouts increases financial risk, the changes in the organizational structure and strategy appear to reduce business risk. The net result is that LBO investors bear significantly lower risk than comparably levered investments in public corporations.

Although the evidence reviewed here implies there are substantial gains from LBOs, these transactions continue to be controversial. Future research can address critics' concerns by examining in detail the effect of buyouts on firms' long-term investments, the performance of buyouts under difficult economic conditions, and the frequency and costs of financial distress resulting from LBOs. Research can also help refine current theories about LBOs and public corporations by examining the contribution of debt, management ownership, and corporate governance changes to post-buyout performance.

References

Altman, Edward, 1989, Measuring corporate bond mortality and performance, Journal of Finance 44, 909–922.

Asquith, Paul, David Mullins, and Eric Wolff, 1989, Original issue high yield bonds: Aging analysis of defaults, exchanges and calls, Journal of Finance 44, 923–952.

Asquith, Paul and Thierry Wizman, 1990, Event risk, wealth redistribution, and the return to existing bondholders in corporate buyouts, Journal of Financial Economics, this volume.

Baker, George and Karen Wruck, 1989, Organizational changes and value creation in leveraged buyouts: The case of the O.M. Scott & Sons company, Journal of Financial Economics 25, 163–190.

Burkhardt, Willy, Michael Jensen, and Brian Barry, 1990, Wisconsin Central Ltd. Railroad and Berkshire Partners (A) and (B), Harvard Business School cases 9-190-062 and 9-190-070, (Harvard University, Cambridge, MA).

DeAngelo, Harry, Linda DeAngelo, and Edward Rice, 1984, Going private: Minority freezeouts and stockholder wealth, Journal of Law and Economics 27, 367–401.

Fox, Christopher J., 1990, Changes in the insolvency risk of LBO transactions: Evidence from the 1980s, Senior thesis (Harvard University, Cambridge, MA).

Jensen, Michael, 1989, Eclipse of the public corporation, Harvard Business Review, Sept.–Oct., 61–74.

Jensen, Michael, Steven Kaplan, and Laura Stiglin, 1989, Effects of LBOs on tax revenues of the U.S. Treasury, Tax Notes 42, 727–733.

Kaplan, Steven, 1989a, The effects of management buyouts on operations and value, Journal of Financial Economics 24, 217–254.

Kaplan, Steven, 1989b, Management buyouts: Evidence on taxes as a source of value, Journal of Finance 44, 611–632.

Kaplan, Steven, 1989c, Campeau's acquisition of Federated: Value destroyed or added?, Journal of Financial Economics 25, 191–212.

Kaplan, Steven and Jeremy Stein, 1990, How risky is the debt in highly leveraged transactions? Evidence from public recapitalizations, Journal of Financial Economics, this volume.

Klieman, R., 1988, The shareholder gains from leveraged cash-outs: Some preliminary evidence, Journal of Applied Corporate Finance 1, 46–53.

Lehn, Kenneth and Annette Poulsen, 1989, Free cash flow and stockholder gains in going private transactions. Journal of Finance 44, 771–788.

Lichtenberg, Frank and Donald Siegel, 1990, The effects of leveraged buyouts on productivity and related aspects of firm behavior, Journal of Financial Economics, this volume.

Marais, Laurentius, Katherine Schipper, and Abbie Smith, 1989, Wealth effects of going private on senior securities, Journal of Financial Economics 23, 155–191.

Muscarella, Chris and Michael R. Vetsuypens, 1990, Efficiency and organizational structure: A study of reverse LBO's, Journal of Finance 45, 1389–1413.

Schipper, Katherine and Abbie Smith, 1988, Corporate income tax effects of management buyouts, Working paper (University of Chicago, Chicago, IL).

Shleifer, Andrei and Larry Summers, 1988, Breach of trust in hostile takeovers, in: Alan Auerbach, ed., Corporate takeovers: Causes and consequences (University of Chicago Press, Chicago, IL).

Smith, Abbie, 1990, Corporate ownership structure and performance: The case of management buyouts, Journal of Financial Economics, this volume.

Wruck, Karen H., 1990, Financial distress, reorganization, and organizational efficiency, Journal of Financial Economics, this volume.

REFERENCES

Albrecht, W.S., L.L. Lookabill, and J. C. McKeown, "The Time-Series Properties of Annual Earnings," *Journal of Accounting Research* 15 (1977), pp. 226–244.

Altman, Edward I., "Financial Ratios, Discriminant Analysis, and the Prediction of Corporate Bankruptcy," *Journal of Finance* (1968) pp. 589–609.

Ball, Ray, "On the Development, Accomplishments and Limitations of the Theory of Stock Market Efficiency," forthcoming in *Managerial Finance* (1994).

Ball, Ray, and Philip R. Brown, "An Empirical Evaluation of Accounting Income Numbers," *Journal of Accounting Research* 6 (1968), pp. 159–178.

Ball, Ray, and Ross L. Watts "Some Additional Evidence on Survival Biases," *Journal of Finance* 34 (1979), pp. 197–206.

Ball, Ray, and Ross L. Watts, "Some Time Series Properties of Accounting Income," *Journal of Finance* (1972), pp. 663–682.

Beaver, William H., "Financial Ratios as Predictors of Failure," *Empirical Research in Accounting: Selected Studies 1966*, supplement to Vol. 4 of *Journal of Accounting Research* (1966), pp. 71–111.

Beaver, William H., Roger Clarke, and William F. Wright, "The Association between Unsystematic Security Returns and the Magnitude of Earnings Forecast Errors," *Journal of Accounting Research* 17 (1979), pp. 316–340.

Beaver, William H., Paul A. Griffin, and Wayne R. Landsman, "The Incremental Information Content of Replacement Cost Earnings," *Journal of Accounting and Economics* 4 (1983), pp. 15–39.

Beaver, William H., P. Kettler, and M. Scholes, "The Association between Market Determined and Accounting Determined Risk Measures," *Accounting Review* 45 (1970), pp. 654–682.

Beaver William H., and Wayne R. Landsman, "Note on the Behavior of Residual Security Returns for Winner and Loser Portfolios," *Journal of Accounting and Economics* 3 (1982), pp. 233–241.

Bernard, Victor L., and Jacob Thomas, "Post-Earnings-Announcement Drift: Delayed Price Response or Risk Premium," *Journal of Accounting Research* 27 (1989) (Supplement), pp. 1–36.

Black, Fischer, and Myron Scholes, "The Pricing of Options and Corporate Liabilities," *Journal of Political Economy* 81 (1973), pp. 637–654.

Brown, Larry D., and Michael S. Rozeff , "The Superiority of Analyst Forecasts as Measures of Expectations: Evidence from Earnings," *Journal of Finance* 33 (1978), pp. 1–16.

Brown, Larry D., Paul A. Griffin, Robert L. Hagerman, and Mark E. Zmijewski, "Security Analyst Superiority Relative to Univariate Time-Series Models in Forecasting Quarterly Earnings," *Journal of Accounting & Economics* 9 (1987), pp. 61–87.

Brown, Philip R., and Ray Ball, "Some Preliminary Findings on the Association between the Earnings of a Firm, Its Industry, and the Economy," *Journal of Accounting Research* 5 (1967) (Supplement), pp. 55–77.

Brown, Philip R., and J.W. Kennelly, "The Information Content of Quarterly Earnings: An Extension and Some Further Evidence," *Journal of Business* 45 (1972), pp. 403–415.

Chambers, A.E., and S.H. Penman, "Timeliness of Reporting and the Stock Price Reaction to Earnings Announcements," *Journal of Accounting Research* 22 (1984), pp. 21–47.

Chan, Louis K. C., and Josef Lakonishok, "Are the Reports of Beta's Death Premature?," working paper (1992), University of Illinois at Urbana-Champaign.

Dechow, Patricia M., "Accounting Accruals and Cash Flows as Measures of Firm Performance: The Role of Accounting Accruals," working paper (1993), University of Pennsylvania, Philadelphia.

Fama, Eugene F., "Stock Returns, Real Activity, Inflation, and Money, *American Economic Review* 71 (1981), pp. 545–565.

Fama, Eugene F., "Efficient Capital Markets: II," *Journal of Finance* 46 (1991), pp. 1575–1617.

Fama, Eugene F., and Kenneth R. French, "Common Risk Factors in the Return on Stocks and Bonds," *Journal of Financial Economics* 33 (1993), pp. 3–56.

Foster, George, "Quarterly Accounting Data: Time-Series Properties and Predictive-Ability Results," *The Accounting Review* 52 (1977), pp. 1–21.

Foster, George, "Intra-industry Information Transfers Associated with Earnings Releases," *Journal of Accounting and Economics* 3 (1981), pp. 201–232.

Galai, Dan, and Ronald W. Masulis, "The Option Pricing Model and the Risk Factor of Stock," *Journal of Financial Economics* 3 (1976), pp. 53–81.

Givoly, Dan, and Dan Palmon, "Timeliness of Annual Earnings Announcements: Some Empirical Evidence," *The Accounting Review* 57 (1982), pp. 486–508.

Jensen, Michael C., and Richard S. Ruback, "The Market for Corporate Control: The Scientific Evidence," *Journal of Financial Economics* 11 (1983), pp. 5–50.

Jensen, Michael C., "Agency Costs of Free Cash Flow, Corporate Finance, and Takeovers," *American Economic Review* 76 (1986), pp. 323–329.

Jensen, Michael C., "Eclipse of the Public Corporation," *Harvard Business Review* (September–October 1989), pp. 61–74.

Jones, Charles P., and Robert H. Litzenberger, "Quarterly Earnings Reports and Intermediate Stock Price Trends," *Journal of Finance* 25 (1970), pp. 143–148.

Little, I. M. D., "Higgledy, Piggledy Growth," *Bulletin of Oxford Institute of Statistics* 24 (1962), pp. 387–412.

Litzenberger, Robert H., and Cherukuri U. Rao, "Estimates of the Marginal Rate of Time Preference and Average Risk Aversion of Investors in Electric Utility Shares: 1960–66," *The Bell Journal of Economics and Management Science* 2 (1971), pp. 265–277.

Miller, Merton H., and Franco Modigliani, "Dividend Policy, Growth, and the Valuation of Shares," *Journal of Business* 34 (1961), pp. 411–433.

Patell, James M., and Mark A. Wolfson, "The Intraday Speed of Adjustment of Stock Prices to Earnings and Dividend Announcements," *Journal of Financial Economics* 13 (1984), pp. 223–252.

Rayner, A. C., and I. M. D. Little, *Higgledy Piggledy Growth Again,* Oxford: Basil Blackwell, 1966.

Rendleman, Richard J., Charles P. Jones, and H.A. Latané, "Further Insight into the Standardized Unexpected Earnings Anomaly: Size and Serial Correlation Effects," *Financial Review* 22 (1987), pp. 131–144.

Shliefer, Andrei, and Lawrence H. Summers, "Breach of Trust in Hostile Takeovers," in Alan Auerbach (ed.), *Corporate Takeovers: Causes and Consequences*, Chicago: University of Chicago Press, 1988.

Smith, Clifford W., and Jerold B. Warner, "On Financial Contracting: An Analysis of Bond Covenants," *Journal of Financial Economics* 7 (1979), pp. 117–161.

Verrecchia, Robert E., "Discretionary Disclosure," *Journal of Accounting and Economics* 5 (1983), pp. 179–194.

Wakeman, Lee M., "The Function of Bond Rating Agencies: Theory and Evidence," unpublished working paper (1981), Rochester, N.Y.: University of Rochester.

Wakeman, Lee M., and Ross L. Watts, "Introduction to Agency Costs," Chapter 6 in "Notes on Corporate Finance," unpublished manuscript (1978), Rochester, N.Y.: University of Rochester.

Watts, Ross L., and Richard W. Leftwich, "The Time Series of Annual Accounting Earnings," *Journal of Accounting Research* 15 (1977), pp. 127–150.

Weinstein, Mark, "The Effect of a Rating Change Announcement on Bond Price," *Journal of Financial Economics* 5 (1977), pp. 329–350.